P9-CIT-125

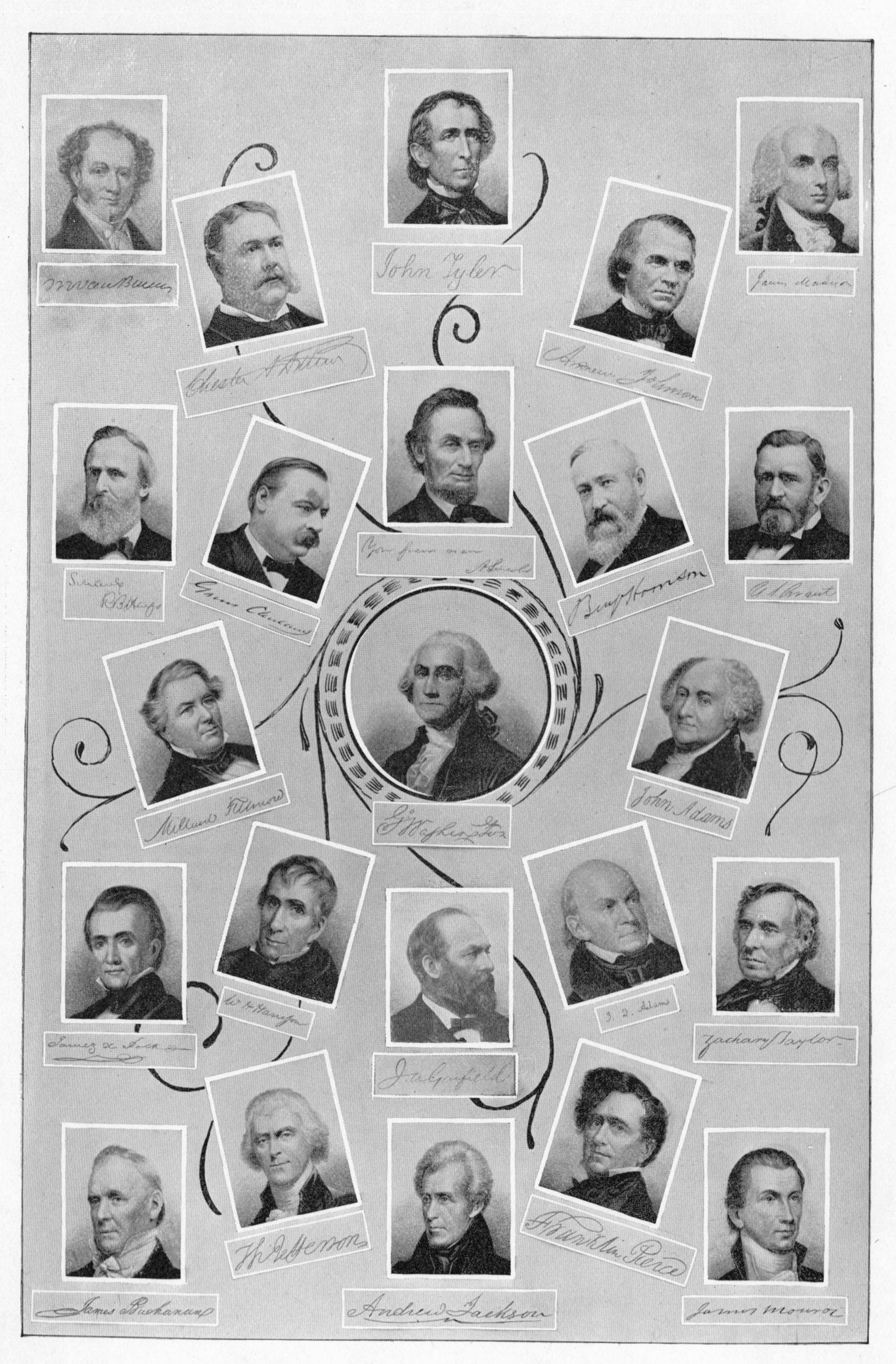

PRESIDENTS OF THE UNITED STATES.

College of the Pacific
Stockton, Calif.

DICTIONARY
OF
UNITED STATES HISTORY.

1492-1895.

Four Centuries of History.

WRITTEN CONCISELY AND ARRANGED ALPHABETICALLY
IN DICTIONARY FORM.

BY

J. Franklin Jameson, Ph.D.,

Professor of History in Brown University, formerly of Johns Hopkins University,
Editorial contributor to the Century Dictionary,
Author of a "History of Historical Writing in America."

ILLUSTRATED WITH NEARLY 300 PORTRAITS.

PURITAN PUBLISHING CO.,
BOSTON, MASS.

COPYRIGHT
1894.
JAMES DRUMMOND BALL.
4494

Ref
E
174
J31

PUBLISHERS' PREFACE.

4494
Ref 973.03 323

In offering this valuable book to the public, inasmuch as the subject is of vital and growing interest to every individual in this country, we feel that we are striking the popular chord and filling a long felt need. As to the comprehensiveness and accuracy of the work, we need only to refer you to the name of our author, whose life work is given to historical research and instruction, and whose name stands high as an authority in historical writing. This work will be of special value to teachers and pupils in all colleges and schools, as it enables them to refer in an instant to the facts and incidents of United States History, thereby saving much time and labor. It will be equally valuable to all other individuals who desire a comprehensive and accurate work of reference on the history of this country.

We have planned to furnish the reader a volume valuable from every point of view—authorship, subject, illustrations, readable type, quality of paper, beautiful and substantial bindings, and skilled workmanship, all of this combined with a low price putting the book within the reach of all those who desire it. A most attractive feature of this book is the large number of portraits of illustrious Americans. Many of these portraits are very rare and were secured only after a long and diligent search, and we desire to acknowledge our indebtedness to the friends of many of these eminent citizens for assistance rendered us in securing original portraits.

The people of America are a reading people, and we launch this book with great confidence, believing that it will be fully appreciated.

THE PUBLISHERS.

PREFACE.

THE preparation of this book was due to the belief that a DICTIONARY OF UNITED STATES HISTORY, in which the facts of our history should be concisely stated, in alphabetical form, for ready reference, would be useful to that large and increasing number of readers who are interested in the story of our nation's development. Usefulness, accordingly, has been the foremost consideration during the progress of the work. In order that such a book of reference should be useful, it is necessary that it should be, first, comprehensive, and secondly, accurate. Great pains have been taken to make it accurate, and it is hoped that the efforts thus made have not been without effect. In order to establish any claim to comprehensiveness, a few words of explanation are necessary, that the reader may know just what the book is intended to include. In the first place, it is confined to the history of the United States. The histories of other parts of America, or of the world, are included only in so far as they have some relation to United States history. Within the field thus defined, articles will, it is believed, be found upon nearly all important subjects. If any have been omitted, it has not been for want of care. The following classes of subjects included may be specified: political occurrences of various sorts; wars and insurrections; battles, and even important skirmishes, of all our wars, including sea-fights and sieges; colonies and settlements upon any part of our present territory; colonizing companies; the several States and Territories; those cities and towns which may fairly be called historic, or whose importance on other grounds makes their history interesting; famous old manors, houses and communities; political parties and factions; political terms which have played a prominent part in American history; departments of government, offices, courts and institutions, Federal, State, colonial or local; Indian tribes that have had a history; famous ships; noted legal cases of historic importance, such as constitutional cases decided by the Supreme Court or fugitive slave cases; historic laws, British and American; treaties with foreign countries and, under the name of each such country, the history of our diplomatic relations with its government; colleges, universities, libraries and other educational institutions; learned societies, especially those devoted to historical studies; famous historical publications; newspapers, especially those which were earliest published in the country, or in their respective States; coins; historic songs, etc.

One class, larger than any of those yet mentioned, deserves a more explicit reference; namely, the class of biographical subjects. Effort has been made to include a brief article on the life of every man or woman who has played a considerable part in the public life of the colonies or United States, either in the civil or the military and naval departments. Thus, in the earlier period have been mentioned such persons as the leading explorers and colonial governors, while in the later period the biographies embrace concise statements respecting the Presidents and Cabinet officers, and the leading Governors, Senators, Congressmen and judges, generals and naval officers. It has been thought that information respecting these characters in public life will especially be sought by those who use the book. Names eminent solely in literature and science, names of artists, divines and merchants, have naturally been less fully represented and more briefly treated. Historical writers have been more fully represented than others. Finally, beside Americans, many Britons and other foreigners—monarchs, ministers, generals and others—are included because they had much to do with the history of the United States.

Attention is called also to the tables and historical lists: that of the Cabinet officers, prepared from information supplied by the Department of State, and those of the Signers of the Declaration of Independence, of the members of the Convention of 1787 (see Convention), of the Presidents, of the Vice-Presidents, of the Speakers of the House of Representatives, of the Justices of the Supreme Court, of the Presidential elections (see Elections), of the sessions of Congress, and of the States and their populations.

Acknowledgments are due, for much valuable assistance rendered, to Mr. Edmund K. Alden, an assistant editor of the "Century Dictionary," and to Mr. George Carey, formerly of the "Review of Reviews." Further acknowledgments are due to the writer's father, John Jameson, Esq., A. M., to Mr. Seth H. Chace, of Brown University, to Messrs. J. Q. Dealey, J. F. Greene and S. S. Colvin, instructors in that university, to Mr. Henry K. Rowe, of Colby Academy, and to Mr. A. A. Freeman, teacher of history in Phillips Academy, Andover, who have rendered, in special departments, assistance highly appreciated.

J. FRANKLIN JAMESON.

BROWN UNIVERSITY,
Providence, R. I., May 28, 1894.

Dictionary of United States History.

A.

"A. B." Plot, a plot to destroy Crawford's popularity and political power by accusing him, in 1824, of malfeasance in the office of Secretary of the Treasury, which he then filled. A series of letters appeared in a Washington newspaper, signed "A. B.," reflecting upon Crawford's integrity, and demanding investigation. They were written by Ninian Edwards, who had just been appointed to the Mexican mission. In March, just previous to his departure for Mexico, Edwards acknowledged their authorship. He was brought to Washington and failed to sustain his charges, so Crawford was exonerated.

Abenakis, a tribe of Indians living in and near what is now Maine, with whom the New Englanders had occasional wars, as in 1702, 1722, 1724. See Rasle, Sébastien.

Abercrombie, James (1706–1781), a British major-general, commanding in America during part of the French and Indian War, 1758. He failed disastrously in an attack on Ticonderoga in July, 1758, losing 2000 men killed and wounded out of a force of 15,000, and was replaced by Sir Jeffrey Amherst.

Abingdon, Va., was captured on December 15, 1864, by Burbridge's division of Stoneman's (Federal) cavalry, which defeated Echols (Confederate).

Ableman vs. Booth, an important Supreme Court case from Wisconsin. In 1854, Booth was tried before a commissioner appointed by the U. S. District Court of Wisconsin for violation of the Fugitive Slave Law of 1850. He was commanded to appear before the District Court, and, failing to do so, was imprisoned by the U. S. Marshal Ableman. The Supreme Court of Wisconsin issued a writ of habeas corpus and Booth was released. Later the U. S. District Court found an indictment against him. He again appealed to the Supreme Court of the State and was released. The case came before the Supreme Court of the United States in 1858. That body reversed the decisions of the Supreme Court of Wisconsin. Booth had pleaded the unconstitutionality of the Fugitive Slave Law. The constitutionality of that law was now maintained by the court. It was also held that the marshal, in matters of habeas corpus, must obey the sovereignty of the United States rather than that of the State, the latter having no authority within the limits of the sovereignty assigned by the Constitution to the United States.

Abolitionists, a party or body of men bent on securing the immediate abolition of slavery in the United States. Throughout the eighteenth century there had been a sentiment, more or less widespread, in favor of the emancipation of slaves. At about the close of the Revolutionary War most of the

Northern States provided for emancipation, immediate or gradual. Before the end of the century several abolition societies had been formed. In 1816 interest in the matter revived, and the American Colonization Society was organized, its object being to promote emancipation and to colonize the freed negroes in Africa. But the movement took on a new character with the beginning of the work of William Lloyd Garrison in 1829, and with the formation of the American Anti-Slavery Society in 1833, and the term Abolitionist is generally applied rather to those who took part in this new agitation than to their less uncompromising predecessors. Garrison demanded the immediate and total abolition of slavery throughout the country, all laws and constitutions to the contrary notwithstanding. The Abolitionists soon divided, Garrison and his followers holding aloof from all connection with political action under the Constitution, and advocating disunion, while another wing of the agitators, under the name of the Liberty Party (see art.), put forward candidates and took part in the presidential elections of 1840 and 1844. In 1848 these joined the Free-soilers (see art.), and in 1855 and 1856 the Republican party. Throughout the years from 1833 to 1863 the Abolitionists continued their agitation. They did much to rouse Northern sentiment against slavery, to bring on the Civil War, and to secure, among its results, the emancipation of all slaves. The leaders of the radical Abolitionists were, beside Garrison himself, Wendell Phillips, John G. Whittier, Edmund Quincy, Samuel J. May, William Jay and others.

"Abominations, Tariff of," a name given to the tariff of 1828 because of the extremely high protective duties which it placed on all manner of both manufactured articles and raw materials.

Abraham, Plains of. On the evening of September 12, 1759, General Wolfe made a desperate attempt upon Quebec. While the fleet made a feigned attack below the town Wolfe and his men scaled the heights above the city, routed the sentries and took his position with 3500 troops. The French under Montcalm arrived early in the morning, made a somewhat disorderly attack and were beaten. Both generals fell. The loss of the English was 664, of the French 640.

Académie des États Unis, or the Academy of Arts and Sciences of the United States of America. This institution, after the model of the French Academy of Sciences, and whose plan was brought to America, in 1788, by the Chevalier Quesnay de Beaurepaire, was to have been located at Richmond, Va. A large sum was subscribed by the citizens of Richmond and by wealthy planters, and one professor, Dr. Jean Rouelle, was appointed, but the plan failed.

Academies, a name given in the United States to two classes of institutions: learned bodies, such as the National Academy of Sciences, and incorporated private institutions for secondary education. Of the former class, the American Academy of Arts and Sciences was founded at Boston in 1780, the Connecticut Academy of Arts and Sciences in 1799, the Pennsylvania Academy of Fine Arts in 1807. The National Academy of Sciences was founded in 1863, to "investigate, examine, experiment and report upon any subject of science or art," whenever called upon by any department of the national government. Of the latter class, a few dozen were in existence in 1789. Perhaps the most famous of these are Phillips Academy, Andover, Mass., and Phillips Academy, Exeter, N. H., founded in 1780 and 1781, respectively.

Acadia, or Acadie, the name given by the French to a province of their colonial empire in America, consisting of what is now Nova Scotia, New Brunswick and part of Maine, the important part being Nova Scotia. De Monts settled it in 1604. It was claimed by England. Argall conquered it in 1613. James I. gave it to Sir William Alexander, but he could not hold it. It was in English hands from 1654 to 1657. It was conquered by Sir William Phipps and New England troops in 1690, but retaken in 1691. Further attempts were made in 1704, 1707 and 1710. The last was successful, and in 1713 the treaty of Utrecht gave Acadia to England. Under British government the Acadians were accused of abusing their privileges as neutrals. In 1755 several thousand of them were transported, with much harsh treatment, to the British provinces southward. (Longfellow's "Evangeline.") Many made their way to Louisiana.

Acre Right, the share owned by any one in the common lands of New England towns. Their value varied in different towns, but was a fixed quantity in each town. In Billerica, for instance, a ten-acre lot or right was equivalent to 113 acres of upland and twelve acres of meadow, and so on in exact proportion.

"Active," case of sloop. (See Olmstead *v.* Rittenhouse.)

"Acts and Resolves," a publication issued by the government of Massachusetts, edited by Abner C. Goodell, Jr. It comprises all the acts and resolves of the Massachusetts Legislature from 1691 to 1780, including those obsolete and repealed. Publication began in 1869.

Acts of Trade. (See Navigation Acts.)

Adairsville, Ga., scene of an engagement in the Civil War, May 17, 1864, between Sherman's forces and those of Joseph Johnston—one episode in the continuous fighting which marked Johnston's retreat from Dalton to Atlanta.

"Adams and Liberty," a song written by Robert Treat Paine, Jr., which enjoyed great popularity during the time of John Adams' spirited resistance to French aggressions in 1798 and 1799. The air, formerly called "Anacreon in Heaven," is that now known as the "Star-Spangled Banner."

Adams, Abigail (1744–1818), wife of President John Adams, daughter of Rev. William Smith, of Weymouth, Mass. She was a woman of great spirit, good sense, strength of character and patriotism. Her letters to her husband, published 1848, are interesting and valuable historically.

Adams, Charles Francis (1807–1886), son of John Quincy Adams, was born in Boston, but was in Europe most of the time till 1817. Was graduated at Harvard College in 1825, studied law, and married a daughter of Peter C. Brooks. He was a Representative in the Massachusetts Legislature from 1831 to 1834, and a Senator from 1835 to 1837. He edited the Writings of John Adams, ten volumes, and was for three years the editor of a daily paper in Boston. Originally a Whig, he in 1848 became the candidate of the Free-soil party for the vice-presidency on the ticket with Van Buren. From 1859 to 1861 he was a member of Congress, and from 1861 to 1868 Minister of the United States in Great Britain. The relations of England to the United States during the Civil War made this post a very trying one, and Adams's tact, firmness and success were extraordinary. Few men performed services so valuable to the Union. Life by his son, C. F. Adams, Jr. a noted historical writer.

Adams, Hannah (1756–1832), of Massachusetts, famous as one of the earliest feminine writers in America; wrote a History of New England, 1799, and a History of the Jews, 1812.

Adams, Henry (Brooks), born 1838, third son of Charles Francis Adams, as assistant professor of history at Harvard College (1870–1877) stimulated historical instruction in American universities, and in 1889–1891 published a classic History of the United States under Jefferson and Madison.

Adams, John (1735–1826), second President of the United States, was born in Braintree (Quincy) Mass., October 19, 1735, the son of a small farmer. He was graduated at Harvard College in 1755, then taught school and studied law in Worcester. Taking up practice in Boston, he soon acquired prominence as a politician and writer, especially against the Stamp Act and other injurious acts of the British government. All his writings were spirited, terse, clear and pungent. In 1774 he was a delegate to the Continental Congress and was active in its work and that of the Provincial Congress of Massachusetts. In the Congress of 1775, he urged independence, and was made chairman of the Board of War. He was one of the committee of five which drew up the Declaration of Independence. After a brief mission to France in 1778, he was again sent out, in 1779, as one of the commissioners to negotiate a treaty of peace with Great Britain, which was signed in 1783. He also negotiated a loan with the Dutch. In 1785 he was appointed the first Minister of the United States to Great Britain, in which capacity he showed himself, as always, active, bold and patriotic, but could not negotiate a treaty of commerce. Returning in 1788, he was in 1789 chosen the first Vice-President of the United States, and soon became, in opposition to Jefferson, a leader of the Federalist party. In 1797, he became President, with Jefferson as Vice-President, Timothy Pickering Secretary of State (1800, John Marshall), Oliver Wolcott Secretary of the Treasury (1800, Samuel Dexter), James McHenry Secretary of War (1800, S. Dexter), and Charles Lee, Attorney-General (1798, Benjamin Stoddert, Secretary of the Navy). The administration had many difficulties, arising partly from the unfriendly course of the French Directory toward the ministers sent to them, (see Directory; Pinckney, C. C.; X. Y. Z. Mission), partly from the Cabinet, partly from the rivalry of Hamilton, and partly from the President's own warmth of temper, vanity and hasty indiscretion in speech and writing. Popular with the mass of his party by reason of his integrity and patriotism, he alienated the leaders by concluding an agreement with France and by reconstructing his Cabinet. These dissensions, and the unpopularity of the Alien and Sedition Acts (see arts.), gave the election of

1800 to Jefferson and the Democrats. Adams retired to private life in Quincy, Mass. In retirement he wrote much, vivaciously, often wittily, sometimes with impulsive bitterness, on public affairs, past and current. He became reconciled with Jefferson, and died on the same day with him, the fiftieth anniversary of the Declaration, July 4, 1826. Lives by J. T. Morse and C. F. Adams. Writings edited by C. F. A.

Adams, John Quincy (July 11, 1767–February 23, 1848), sixth President of the United States, was the eldest son of John Adams. A boy of precocious talents, he was early taken abroad by his father, studied at the University of Leyden, and at fourteen began his public career as secretary to Francis Dana, Minister to Russia. He was graduated at Harvard in 1788, admitted to the bar in 1791, and at once began to write on public affairs. From 1794 to 1797 he was Minister to Holland; from 1797 to 1801, Minister to Prussia. In 1803, the Federalists elected him to the U. S. Senate. Approving Jefferson's embargo, he became estranged from the Federalists, acted with the Republicans, and in 1808 resigned. In 1809, Madison appointed him Minister to Russia, and in 1814 he was one of the commissioners who negotiated the treaty of Ghent; he then became Minister to England. From 1817 to 1825, he was Secretary of State to President Monroe. In the election of 1824, though he received but eighty-four electoral votes to ninety-nine for Jackson, he was, by a coalition of his friends with those of Clay, chosen President by the House of Representatives. He appointed Clay Secretary of State; Richard Rush Secretary of the Treasury; James Barbour Secretary of War (1828, Peter B. Porter); Samuel L. Southard Secretary of the Navy and William Wirt Attorney-General. Calhoun was Vice-President. A cry of "bargain and corruption" with Clay was raised, though without foundation. Adams' administration was marked by intelligence and firmness, and by extreme integrity in all matters, especially that of appointments, but was made a stormy one by the bitter attacks of his enemies in Congress and by his own unbending and pugnacious character. He favored protection and internal improvements at Federal expense. (See also art. Panama, Congress of.) He failed of re-election in 1828. In 1831, still vigorous at sixty-four, he entered Congress as an independent member for the Quincy district in Massachusetts, which he continued to represent till his death. A model legislator, active and efficient in every valuable department of congressional business, his most memorable services were in behalf of the right of petition, threatened by the pro-slavery members, and in other assistance to the anti-slavery cause. (See also Broad Seal War.) He died at his post in the Capitol on February 23, 1848. Twelve volumes of his diary have been published, abounding in information and acute though censorious judgments on the events of his long public career, and in evidence of his high character and patriotism. Lives by W. H. Seward and J. T. Morse.

Adams, Samuel (1722–1803), orator, patriot and agitator, was born in Boston, a second cousin of John Adams, and studied for a time at Harvard College. Unsuccessful in business and in the office of tax-collector for the town of Boston, he soon began to take an active part in the Boston town-meetings. In 1764 he drew up Boston's early protest against Grenville's scheme of taxation. From 1765 to 1774 he was a member for Boston in the House of Representatives of Massachusetts, in which he was among the foremost in debate and as a writer of State papers. He was an adroit politician, prudent, yet zealous and inflexible in his love of liberty. He led in the protests against taxation without representation, and in 1770 secured from Hutchinson the removal of the troops from the city. He instituted the system of town committees of correspondence. From 1774 to 1781 he was a member of the Continental Congress; he signed the Declaration of Independence, and had an important part in making the Massachusetts Constitution of 1780. He was in 1781 a member of the Massachusetts Senate, and in 1788 of the State Convention which ratified the Constitution of the United States. Opposed to some of its provisions, he finally concluded to vote for it, which was of much influence upon others. In the party divisions which soon followed, he was of the Democratic-Republican party. From 1789 to 1794 he was Lieutenant-Governor of Massachusetts, from 1794 to 1797 Governor. Adams' public services, of the first importance in the earlier stages of the revolutionary struggle, became less valuable when the tasks of the hour were those of constructive statesmanship and administration, for which he had little talent; but perhaps no one did more to bring about the Revolution. Lives by S. A. Wells and J. K. Hosmer.

Addington, Isaac (1645–1715), secretary of the province of Massachusetts from 1690 to 1715, and also successively Judge of the Court of Common Pleas, Chief Justice of the Superior Court, and Judge of the Probate Court of Suffolk.

Adelbert College was founded in 1826 at Hudson, O., under the name of Western Reserve College. In 1882 it was transferred to Cleveland, taking the name of a chief benefactor's son. The Medical Department was established in 1842; the Case School of Applied Science in 1881. All are considered parts of Western Reserve University.

Adet, Pierre Auguste (1763–1832), chemist and politician, was Minister of the French Republic (the Directory) to the United States from 1795 to 1797. Resigned in protest against actions of the American government which he regarded as violations of neutrality in the war then pending.

Administrations. (See Cabinet.)

Admiral. This grade in the U. S. Navy (as distinguished from vice-admiral and rear-admiral) was first established by Act of Congress on July 25, 1866. There have been but two admirals; Farragut was commissioned in 1866, Porter on Farragut's death in 1870. On the death of Admiral Porter the grade became extinct, (1891.)

Admiralty Courts. In the colonial period the governor of each colony was vice-admiral in his colony, and as such had the right of deciding maritime cases, though often a judge was appointed by him for the purpose. The Constitution of the United States vests this jurisdiction in the Federal Courts. The District Courts judge such cases in the first instance. (See Prize Courts).

Adventists, or Second Adventists. About 1833 Wm. Miller began to lecture on the second coming of Christ, predicting that it would occur in 1842. Other dates were subsequently set; but at present the leaders of the sect content themselves with general prophecy of an early advent. In 1890 the sect numbered 60,000 members.

African Company, originating in an association formed at Exeter, England, in 1588, was chartered as a joint-stock company in 1618. Under successive charters it continued in existence till 1821, almost without interruption. In the period before the Revolution it was much engaged in the slave trade with the American colonies.

Agamenticus (now York), Me., one of the settlements which Sir Ferdinando Gorges made as lord proprietary of the province of Maine. It was settled in 1621. In 1642 it received a charter of incorporation, under the name of Gorgeana.

Agassiz, Louis J. R., (1807–1873), was born in Switzerland. In 1846 he came to the United States, and remained here as professor of geology and zoology. In both these sciences he did work of inestimable value, and exerted great influence upon their development in America by his enthusiasm, energy and organizing ability.

Agrarians, the name sometimes applied to the "loco-foco" or "equal rights" party formed in 1835, and which denounced special privileges. Later the Abolitionists and Republicans were branded as Agrarians by the pro-slavery party.

Agricultural Colleges. The first important institution of this sort in the United States was the Agricultural College of the State of Michigan, established in 1857, though that of Pennsylvania was established in 1854. The Morrill Act of 1862 gave each State 30,000 acres of government land or its equivalent, multiplied by the number of the State's senators and representatives, to found a college of the agricultural and mechanical arts. More than forty institutions of this sort have resulted. In 1890 the Federal subvention was increased.

Agricultural Experiment Stations. The first government station of this sort was established at Middletown, Conn., in 1875. Professor W. O. Atwater's success in conducting this station led to the establishment of others in different parts of the country. Nearly every State has one or more. In 1892 there were fifty-three fully equipped experimental stations, employing in all about 400 trained specialists in conducting scientific investigations.

Agricultural Societies. The first in the United States, the South Carolina Agricultural Society, was founded in 1784, the Philadelphia Agricultural Society in 1785, that of New York in 1791, that of Massachusetts in 1792. The first quasi-national society of this sort, the Columbian Agricultural Society, originated in a convention held in Washington in 1809.

Agriculture, Department of, an executive department of the Federal government, the head of which, the secretary of agriculture, is a member of the Cabinet. The department was founded by Act of May 15, 1862. It was given equality with the other chief executive departments by the Act of

February 11, 1889, and its head became in 1889 a member of the Cabinet. The weather bureau was transferred to it from the Department of War in 1891.

Aix-la-Chapelle, or Aachen, in Rhenish Prussia, is of importance in American history because of the Treaty of Aix-la-Chapelle, concluded in 1748, which ended the War of the Austrian Succession (King George's War). The treaty restored Louisbourg and Cape Breton to the French, which gave great offence to the New Englanders, who had conquered these possessions.

Akerman, Amos T., born in 1823, was District-Attorney for Georgia from 1866 to 1870. He was Attorney-General of the United States in Grant's Cabinet from 1870 to 1872.

Alabama, a Southern State; the ninth State admitted after the original thirteen. The region occupied by the State was originally a part of the territory of Georgia, though the southern portion was the subject of dispute with Spain, and indeed with the Federal government. In 1802 Georgia ceded all her western lands to the latter, and what is now Alabama became a part of the territory of Mississippi, organized in 1798 (1804). The portion south of lat. 31° and west of the river Perdido was acquired by seizure during the war of 1812. During 1813 and 1814 occurred the war with the Creeks (see art.), whose defeat by General Jackson at Horse Shoe Bend caused them to concede nearly all their territory. Rapid settlement followed. In 1817 Mississippi became a State, the eastern portion of the territory being erected into the territory of Alabama. The name is Indian, and is said to mean "Here we rest." The population of the new territory, from but 33,000 in 1817, grew to be 128,000 in 1820. On December 14, 1819, it was admitted as the State of Alabama. Of the population mentioned, 86,000 were whites and 42,000 slaves. Population, continuing to grow rapidly, reached nearly a million in 1860, and in 1890 was 1,513,000. On January 11, 1861, Alabama seceded from the Union. The act of secession was revoked in 1865. 1867–68 the State was under military rule. In 1868, under a new constitution, Alabama was declared by Congress to be restored to the Union.

"Alabama," Confederate cruiser, was built by an English firm at Liverpool expressly for the Confederacy, and, against the urgent remonstrances of the American Minister, was permitted by the British government to escape (July 29, 1862). At Terceira she received from other English vessels her armament and crew, and set out, under Captain Raphael Semmes, to destroy the commerce of the United States (August 29). By the end of October she had made twenty-seven prizes. After a long cruise in the waters of the West Indies, Brazil and the East Indies, the "Alabama" came to the harbor of Cherbourg, France. Off this harbor, after a memorable fight, she was sunk by the U. S. steamship "Kearsarge," June 19, 1864, after having destroyed sixty-five vessels and $10,000,000 worth of property.

"Alabama" Claims, claims of the United States Government against that of Great Britain, growing out of the depredations of the cruiser "Alabama" and other similar cruisers. May 13, 1861, the Queen had issued a proclamation of neutrality in the American Civil War, forbidding her subjects to take part with either combatant, and granting belligerent rights to both. Great Britain's Foreign Enlistment Act of 1819 also forbids the equipment of any land or naval forces within British dominions to operate against any friendly nation. Nevertheless, the "Florida," "Alabama," "Georgia," "Shenandoah," and other vessels built in Great Britain, were allowed to escape, and as Confederate cruisers inflicted enormous damage on American commerce, nearly driving it from the seas. C. F. Adams, Minister to Great Britain, protested vigorously. After the war the United States Government urgently pressed a claim for compensation. On January 12, 1866, it offered to submit the whole controversy to arbitration. Great Britain proposed limitations unacceptable to the United States. A treaty negotiated by Reverdy Johnson providing for arbitration was rejected by the Senate. Finally a Joint High Commission, meeting at Washington in 1871, agreed upon the Treaty of Washington, which provided for arbitration of the Alabama claims and several other disputed matters by a board of five arbitrators, appointed respectively by the President of the United States, the Queen of England, the King of Italy, the President of Switzerland, and the Emperor of Brazil. Those appointed were, in the above order, Mr. Charles Francis Adams, Sir Alexander Cockburn, Lord Chief Justice, Count Federigo Sclopis, M. Jacques Staempfli, and Viscount Itajuba; Count Sclopis presided. The tribunal met at Geneva on December 15, 1871. It rejected the American claims for indirect damages, but decided that the government of Great Britain had been culpable in not doing more to prevent the sailing and success of the cruisers, and awarded to the United States the sum of $15,500,000 as damages.

Alabama Historical Society. Founded in 1837 with its headquarters at Tuscaloosa, site of the State University. It has a large membership, but a poor library.

Alamance, or Great Alamance, a creek in North Carolina, tributary to the river Haw. Here, in 1771, Governor Tryon, with 1000 militia, defeated 3000 "regulators," or rebels against the royal government, killing some 200. Out of a large number taken prisoners six were executed for high treason, and the insurrection was suppressed.

Alamo, a fort at San Antonio, Tex., memorable for a siege and massacre in 1836, during the war of Texan independence from Mexico. Santa Anna, with from 1500 to 2000 Mexicans, besieged 140 Texans in the fort for two weeks. Finally, March 6, the fort, desperately defended, was taken by assault, only six of the defenders remaining alive. These six were at once butchered by order of Santa Anna, among them Colonel David Crockett.

Alaska, a territory of the United States, formerly constituting Russian America. In 1741 Vitus Bering, sailing for the Russians, discovered the range of Mt. St. Elias. In 1783 the Russians established a trading-post on the island of Kadiak. In 1799, by consolidation of existing companies, the Russian-American Fur Company was organized, and from this time to 1862 enjoyed a monopoly of trade in Alaska and the rule of the country. By treaty of March 30, 1867, the United States bought Alaska (area 580,000 square miles) from Russia, paying $7,200,000 In 1884 Alaska was organized as a district, with executive officers appointed by the President, but without representative institutions.

Albany, capital of New York. In 1614 a trading-post was established here by the Dutch, and called Fort Nassau, later Fort Orange, or New Orange. When the English took New Netherland, in 1664, they changed the name to Albany, in honor of James, Duke of York and Albany, the proprietor of the province. Albany was incorporated as a city in 1686, was the meeting place of the first colonial convention in 1754, and became the capital of the State in 1797.

Albany Convention, 1754. At the instance of the Lords of Trade, commissioners from the colonies of New Hampshire, Massachusetts, Rhode Island, Connecticut, New York, Pennsylvania and Maryland met at Albany on June 19, 1754, to arrange a treaty with the Six Nations. They also proceeded to consider a plan of colonial union proposed by Franklin, a member, and adopted it. It provided for a president-general of all the colonies, with veto power, and a grand council, to consist of from two to seven members from each colony, chosen by the assemblies to serve three years. These should have power to control Indian affairs, to raise and equip forces for colonial defence, and to lay taxes therefor. The crown rejected the plan because it gave too much power to the colonies, the colonies because it gave too much power to the crown; but it was among the beginnings of national union.

"Albany Regency," a name given to the group of politicians who, from 1820 to 1854, managed the concerns of the Democratic party in New York State. Its power was founded on the system of nominating conventions and on the system of appointment to office as a reward for partisan services. Its chief members were Martin Van Buren, William L. Marcy, Silas Wright, Edwin Croswell, Benjamin F. Butler and John A. Dix. Its position at the State Capital gave it its name.

Albemarle, the first permanent settlement in what is now North Carolina, was founded on the banks of the Chowan and the Roanoke by Roger Greene, in 1653, at the head of a small body of Dissenters from Virginia.

"Albemarle," a Confederate ironclad ram which, in April and May, 1864, destroyed or disabled several of the Federal gunboats at the mouth of the Roanoke River, and captured Plymouth, N. C., with 1600 Federal prisoners. On the night of October 27, Lieutenant Cushing, U. S. N., a youth of twenty-one, in command of a torpedo launch, getting within twenty yards of the "Albemarle" before he was discovered, blew her up with a torpedo and made a miraculous escape.

Albuquerque, New Mexico, an engagement in the Civil War, April 8, 1862, the Federal Colonel Canby attacking Albuquerque as a part of the operations by which he defeated General Sibley's attempt to conquer New Mexico for the Confederacy.

Alcalde, the principal official in the local government of the earlier towns of California. The office was borrowed from the Spanish settlements, and was first introduced in the mining camps, where the miners made laws and elected officers to enforce them.

Alcott, Amos Bronson (1799–1888), a transcendental philosopher, noted as an original, ingenious and sympathetic teacher, and as a lecturer and giver of formal conversations. Resided at Concord all his latter years. Was the father of Louisa M. Alcott.

Alden, John (1599–1687), the hero of Longfellow's "Courtship of Miles Standish," accompanied the Pilgrims from Southampton as a cooper. The youngest of the Pilgrims, he afterward became a magistrate of the colony, and was such for more than half a century.

Aldie, Va., scene of a fierce cavalry fight in the Civil War, June 17, 1863, Stuart's Confederate cavalry vainly assailing a part of Pleasonton's forces, during the great Confederate invasion of the North.

Aldrich, Nelson W., Senator, born 1841, a business man, representative from Rhode Island from 1879 to 1881, was Senator from that State from 1881 to the present time (1894). Senator Aldrich has had an important part in all recent financial legislation, and is an important authority on all matters of the tariff.

"Alert," Sloop. (See "Essex.")

Alexander VI., Pope from 1492 to 1503, (Rodrigo Borgia), by his bull of partition, May 4, 1493, divided the non-Christian world into two parts, Spain to have the western half and Portugal the eastern. The line of division was to be a meridian 100 leagues west of the Azores and Cape de Verde Islands. Afterward (1494) a meridian 370 leagues west of the Cape de Verde Islands was substituted.

Alexander, son of Massasoit, King of the Pokanokets, chief after his father's death in 1660, died in 1662 at Plymouth. King Philip was his brother.

Alexander, Archibald (1772–1851), eminent Presbyterian divine, born in Virginia, was president of Hampden-Sidney College from 1796 to 1801, and from 1812 to his death was professor of theology in the Theological Seminary at Princeton, and highly influential in relation to American theological thought.

Alexander, Sir William, called Lord Stirling (1726–1783), was born in New York City. In 1757 he laid claim before the House of Lords to the earldom of Stirling, but in vain. He became Surveyor-General of New York. In 1775 he became a colonel in the Revolutionary army, a brigadier-general in 1776, and a major-general in 1777. He distinguished himself at Trenton, Brandywine, Germantown and Monmouth.

Alexandria, Va., was founded in 1749. When the District of Columbia was formed, Virginia's cession included this town. In 1814 it was captured and plundered by the British. In 1846 it was retroceded to Virginia. It was entered by the Union troops in 1861 under Colonel Ellsworth, who was shot while hauling down the Confederate flag. It subsequently became the seat of government of the Virginian counties which adhered to the Union.

Alexandria Conference. On March 20, 1785, two commissioners from Virginia, George Mason and Alexander Henderson, met three from Maryland,

Daniel Jenifer, Thomas Stone and Samuel Chase, at Alexandria, commissioned to treat concerning the jurisdiction over the waters between the two. After four days they adjourned to Mount Vernon at Washington's request, and separated on the twenty-eighth. They discussed commercial regulations, etc., and their report to the Virginia Legislature caused the summons of the Annapolis Convention of 1786 and, indirectly, that of the Philadelphia Convention of 1787.

Alexandria Government. After the secession of Virginia, April 17, 1861, the Union members of her Legislature, mostly from the western part of the State, met at Wheeling and organized a State government, which was recognized by Congress as the government of Virginia. Francis H. Pierpont was Governor. After the admission of West Virginia this Virginia government was transferred to Alexandria. President Johnson recognized it as the lawful government of Virginia. It continued in operation until the installation of military government in 1867.

"**Algerine,**" in Rhode Island, in the times of the Dorr War, an opponent of Dorr; a member of the "Law and Order" party.

Algerine War. Following the example of other Christian powers, in their dealings with the piratical governments of Northern Africa, the United States Government had, in 1795, signed a treaty with the Dey of Algiers, paying him a million dollars for the ransom of American captives and promising an annual payment of tribute. In 1812 the Dey declared war against the United States. When the war of 1812 with England was ended, Congress declared war on Algiers, and Commodore Decatur, with ten vessels, sailed against her. Such successes were obtained over the Algerine Navy that by the time Decatur reached Algiers the Dey was ready to submit. He signed a treaty giving indemnity, renouncing all claim to tributes or presents, and promising not to reduce prisoners of war to slavery. Decatur then exacted similar submission from Tunis and Tripoli.

Algiers. The treaty of 1795 with Algiers secured commercial privileges to the United States on the payment of tribute. By the treaty of September 5, 1815, the United States secured from the Dey of Algiers exemption from tribute and release of captives from slavery, and indemnification for violation of the former treaty. This treaty was renewed a year later. All are obsolete by France's absorption of Algiers.

Algonquins, a family of Indian tribes, bearing a strong resemblance to each other in manners and customs and language, which at the time of the beginning of English colonization numbered about a quarter of a million, and occupied, beside part of Canada, most of the area now in the United States east of the Mississippi and north of latitude 37°. They were in the hunting-and-fishing stage, tilling little ground, and nomadic. The chief tribes in the family, beside the Canadian members, were the Abenakis, Massachusetts tribes, Pequods, Narragansetts, Mohegans, Delawares, Nanticokes, Powhatan tribes, Pampticoes, Shawnees, west of the Alleghanies the Chippewas, Pottawatomies, Miamis, Sacs, Foxes, Kickapoos and, west of the Mississippi, the Blackfeet and Cheyennes.

Alien and Sedition Acts, two acts of Congress, passed by the Federalists in 1798, under the excitement of hostile relations with France and bitter feeling against the influence of the French Revolution. The Alien Act authorized the President to order out of the country all such aliens as he might judge to be dangerous to the peace and safety of the United States or to be plotting against them. The Sedition Act provided heavy fines and imprisonment for any who should conspire to oppose the United States Government or laws, or who should print or publish any false, scandalous or malicious writings against the government, Congress or the President, intended to bring disrepute or hatred upon them or stir up sedition. These laws were regarded by the Republican Party as unconstitutional, and subversive of the liberty of the press and of speech, and were denounced in the Kentucky and Virginia Resolutions. They expired in 1800 and 1801 respectively.

Allatoona, Ga. During Sherman's march to the sea the Confederates on October 5, 1864, attacked Allatoona, where General Corse repulsed them after an heroic and desperate defence, losing one-third of his garrison.

Allen, Ethan (1737–1789), born in Connecticut, removed in early life to Vermont, and was for the remainder of his life its most conspicuous citizen. He had an active part in the resistance of the "Green Mountain Boys" to the New York government. May 10, 1775, with a small force he captured Ticonderoga from the British. Crown Point and Skenesborough were also taken. For three years ensuing Allen was a captive with the British.

Allen, Ira (1752–1814), brother of Ethan, served in the Revolution and was the first secretary of the State of Vermont, also its treasurer and surveyor-general. Wrote a history of Vermont (1798).

Allen, William Henry (1784–1813), was first lieutenant of the "United States" under Decatur when she captured the "Macedonian" in 1812. As commander of the "Argus" he distinguished himself by taking many prizes, but was killed in the fight with the "Pelican."

Allen's Farm, one of the actions in the "Seven Days," June 29, 1862. The Federal General Sumner, having bivouacked at Allen's Farm on his retreat from Fair Oaks, was attacked here for two hours by the Confederate General Magruder.

Allerton, Isaac (1583–1659), an important member of the company who came on the "Mayflower," and often business agent of the Pilgrims. Subsequently disagreeing with them, lived at New Amsterdam and New Haven.

Alliance. The only important alliance made by the United States was that with France, made by the treaty of February 6, 1778. Since 1776 France had privately aided the Revolution with arms and supplies. The two treaties of 1778 provided for a defensive alliance in case Great Britain should declare war on France, and declared that no peace should be made until the independence of the United States was recognized, and then only by mutual consent. Each party guaranteed the other's possessions in America, and the United States granted to France, when France was at war, more favorable treatment than should be accorded to the other belligerent. These concessions were subsequently troublesome to the United States in 1793. (See art. "France.")

"Alliance," United States vessel, took part in the cruise of John Paul Jones and the "Bonhomme Richard," and was one of the two ships remaining in the Continental service when the Revolutionary war ended.

Alliance, Holy, the name given to an alliance of the absolute sovereigns of the Continent, concluded in 1815 at the instance of Czar Alexander I. Its object was the government of Europe by mutual concert based on the profession of Christian brotherhood. It ultimately tended toward the repression of all liberal and revolutionary opposition to the existing political order. In 1823 the King of Spain invoked the aid of the other powers in suppressing the revolt of his South American colonies. President Monroe's enunciation of the "Monroe Doctrine," in his message of December, 1823, was a reply to this threatened movement.

Allison, William B., Senator, was born in Ohio in 1829. He was a delegate to the Chicago Convention of 1860, a Congressman from Iowa from 1862 to 1871, and a Senator from 1873 to the present time (1894). He has several times been a prominent candidate for the Republican nomination for President, and is a high authority on all matters of national finance.

Allston, Washington (1779–1843), one of the chief early American artists, studied and painted in Europe from 1801 to 1818, after which he resided in Boston and Cambridge. He chiefly painted Scriptural subjects, and was eminent as a colorist.

Almanacs. The first published in this country appeared at Cambridge, Mass., in 1639. It was compiled by William Pierce, mariner, and printed by Stephen Daye, and was called *An Almanac Calculated for New England.* It was the first book printed in the colonies. The first Boston almanac was published by John Foster in 1676. In Philadelphia the first appeared in 1686, edited by Daniel Leeds, and printed by William Bradford. In 1697, J. Clapp published an almanac in New York. Beginning with 1700, Samuel Clough published the *New England Almanac* at Boston for eight years. It bore the traditional woodcut, professing to show what parts of a man's body are governed by the moon, etc.; it foretold the weather, eclipses of the year, etc. *Nathaniel Ames' Astronomical Diary and Almanac* started at Boston in 1725, and continued half a century, with a circulation of 60,000. *Poor Richard's Almanac*, by Richard Saunders (Benjamin Franklin), continued by others as *Poor Richard Improved*, was issued from 1733 to 1786. It was filled with homely maxims and pithy proverbial counsels and was very popular. Other early almanacs were: *Father Abraham's Almanac*, Philadelphia, 1759–1799; Isaiah Thomas' *Massachusetts*, *Connecticut*, *Rhode Island*, *New Hampshire and Vermont Almanac*, Worcester and Boston, 1775–1822; Webster's Calendar, or the *Albany Almanac*, 1784, the oldest family almanac published extant in the United States; the *Virginia Almanac*, Williamsburg and Richmond, 1751–1829; *South Carolina and Georgia Almanac*, Charleston, 1760–1800; Gruber's *Town and Country Almanac*, Hagerstown, Md., 1822–1877. Political almanacs began with the *Whig Almanac*, issued by Horace Greeley 1838–1855, continued since as the *Tribune Almanac.*

The *World Almanac* began 1868, the *Herald Almanac* 1872. The *National Calendar* edited by Peter Force at Washington, 1820–1836, was an extensive publication of general information.

"Alta California," a weekly publication established at San Francisco, January 3, 1849, by Samuel Brannan. It was the first newspaper of any importance issued in California, and arose from a consolidation of the older journals, the *Star*, and the *Monterey Californian*. The daily publication of this paper was commenced in 1850. It is published at the present time under the original name.

Altamont, Tenn. On August 30, 1862, when Bragg was about invading Kentucky, the outposts of General McCook's division were attacked at Altamont by the Confederate General Wheeler. McCook retired.

Alton, Ill. In 1836 Elijah P. Lovejoy, an Abolitionist clergyman, began to publish an anti-slavery paper here. His press was twice destroyed by a pro-slavery mob. While defending his premises against a third attack in November, 1837, he was shot and mortally wounded.

Amana, a communistic society owning 25,000 acres of land seventy-four miles west of Davenport, Ia. The society was founded by some German emigrants, who settled near Buffalo in 1842. In 1855 they moved to their present home. The present society, numbering about 1500, is composed almost entirely of Germans, with a few Swiss and Pennsylvania Dutch. The base of its organization is religion; they are pietists and their religious head is supposed to receive inspiration directly from God, hence they call themselves "Inspirationists." The name Amana is taken from the Song of Solomon, iv. 8.

Ambassador. Though the term ambassador was used occasionally in respect to the first diplomatic appointments made by the Continental Congress, from that time on, in accordance with the usual practice of republics, the United States have appointed no diplomatic representative of higher rank than envoys. In 1893, however, the higher grade was authorized by act of Congress, and Thomas F. Bayard was made Ambassador to Great Britain. Ambassadors were also appointed to France, Germany, Italy and Russia.

Ambrister, a native of New Providence and an ex-lieutenant of British marines, who, together with Arbuthnot, a Scotch trader, was captured by Andrew Jackson, April 17, 1818, during his campaign against the Seminole Indians in Florida. These men were in league with the Indians in their raids against the States. They were both tried before an American court martial, Ambrister pleading guilty and begging mercy. Ambrister was shot and Arbuthnot hanged, though British citizens.

Amelia Island, Ga., was colonized by settlers under General Oglethorpe in 1736. In 1739 a party of Spaniards landed on the island and killed two unarmed Highlanders. This was the first blood shed in the Spanish war. After the prohibition of the slave trade in 1808 the island was a place of resort for pirates, smugglers and slave-traders, until in 1817 President Monroe suppressed them.

Amendments. It was one of the chief defects of the Articles of Confederation that they provided no means for their amendment save by unanimous consent of the thirteen States. Three proposals of amendment which would have usefully strengthened the articles, failed of obtaining this unanimous consent. The Convention of 1787, summoned to amend the articles, made a new constitution instead. This provided for amendment on proposal by two-thirds of both Houses of Congress or by a convention, if ratification were secured from three-fourths of the States, through legislatures or conventions. In fact, all have come from Congress and been ratified by State legislatures. In 1788 several States, beginning with Massachusetts, suggested amendments when ratifying the Constitution. Hence came, in the first Congress, the proposals which brought into existence the first ten amendments. Of many proposed, only fifteen amendments have been ratified since the adoption of the Constitution. The first ten were ratified December 15, 1791. They relate respectively to 1, freedom of religion, speech and the press; 2, the right to establish State militia; 3, the quartering of troops in private houses; 4, the security of persons against unwarrantable searches and seizures; 5, capital crime; 6, criminal prosecutions; 7, trial by jury in common-law cases; 8, bails, fines and punishments; 9, the relation of constitutional and natural rights; 10, powers reserved to the States. The series is thus of the nature of a bill of rights. The Eleventh Amendment was ratified January 8, 1798. Under its provisions no citizen or citizens of a State of the Union, or of a foreign State, can prosecute a suit against any other State of the Union in a Federal court. This relieves the dignity of the State, but weakens the power of justice toward a citizen, and facilitates repudiation by States. The Twelfth Amendment was ratified September 25, 1804, and settled a new method of electing the president and vice-president. Under its provisions, electors, chosen by the people, meet in their respective States and vote for the two highest officers by distinct ballots. If no candidate obtains a majority the House of Representatives elects a president by ballot from among the candidates. The Thirteenth Amendment was ratified by December 18, 1865. It provided that slavery should not exist within the United States and that Congress should make legislative appropriation for the enforcement of the article. This amendment was ratified by nineteen loyal States and eight of those engaged in the Rebellion. The Fourteenth Amendment was ratified July 21, 1868. It forbade the States to abridge the privileges of citizens of the Union, diminished representation in case the suffrage was thus restricted, closed offices to all persons who had engaged in insurrection or rebellion, and acknowledged the public debt. The Fifteenth Amendment was ratified March 30, 1870. It affirms that "the right of citizens of the United States to vote shall not be denied or abridged by the United States, or by any State, on account of race, color or previous condition of servitude."

America, so called after Amerigo Vespucci, who claimed to have first discovered and explored the coast of the mainland in 1497–98. The name probably originated from a little publication entitled *Cosmographiae Introductio*, edited and issued by two scholars, Ringmann and Waldseemüller, at the little college of St. Dié in the Vosges country. Ringmann is said to have been an ardent admirer of Vespucius, and to have inserted in his publication the four voyages of Vespucius. Tross, a bookseller of Paris, produced in 1881 a map dating as far back as 1517, on which the name "America" appears. It is also found on Schoner's globe of 1515, and seems to have been generally adopted from these.

American Antiquarian Society, founded by Isaiah Thomas at Worcester, Mass., in 1812 for the purpose of illustrating the antiquities of the New World as a separate department of history. It has published several volumes of collections and of proceedings, including the "Archæologia Americana."

American Archives, a valuable collection of documentary materials respecting the events leading up to the Revolution. This publication was begun by Peter Force at Washington in 1833–34, under instructions from the government. It contains letters, debates, notices of public affairs, and essays on constitutional government, the whole forming a complete documentary history of the colonies. The publication had included only nine volumes when appropriations ceased. Congress has never since continued this invaluable repertory.

American Association for the Advancement of Science, the most important among American scientific societies. Its organization was effected at Boston in 1847. Meetings have been held each year in some American city.

American Board of Commissioners for Foreign Missions, the oldest missionary society in the United States, organized June 29, 1810. It is an incorporated body with 250 members, and supports over 500 missionaries and many schools in Europe, America, Asia, Africa and the Pacific Islands.

American Historical Association, founded at Saratoga in 1884, was incorporated by Congress in 1889. It is now affiliated with the Smithsonian Institution, and its papers are published by Government. Its meetings have mostly been held in Washington. It now (1894) numbers about 700 members.

American Historical Society, founded in Washington in 1836. Its meetings were held in the House of Representatives at the Capitol, and the first president was John Quincy Adams. It published one volume of transactions.

American Institute, a New York institution founded in 1828 to promote domestic industry. A charter was granted by the State Legislature. Annual exhibitions showing the progress of industry, invention and manufacture have been held.

American Insurance Company vs. Canter, an important case in the U. S. Supreme Court, decided in 1828. An insured cargo of cotton, wrecked on the coast of Florida, was, by a decree of a territorial court, sold to satisfy the claim for salvage. The owners abandoned the cargo to the underwriters. Canter, having bought portions of the cargo, sold the same at auction in Charleston. The insurance company brought suit for recovery, alleging unconstitutionality and want of authority in the Territorial Court of Florida. The district judge pronounced the decree of the Florida court a nullity. The Circuit Court, however, confirmed the decree of the Territorial Court and maintained Canter's claims. This judgment was also confirmed by the

Supreme Court of the United States on the ground that the act of the Territorial Legislature of Florida, in erecting the Territorial Court, was not inconsistent with the laws of the United States, and was therefore valid. The opinion of the court is of importance because of Judge Marshall's decision respecting the basis of the government of territories.

American Party. Hostility to the political influence of foreigners showed itself in the formation of small and local nativist parties in New York and Philadelphia in 1835 and 1844. About 1852, when the old parties, Democratic and Whig, were obviously in a state of dissolution or re-formation, and when immigration had taken on large proportions, nativism revived. A secret, oath-bound fraternity, with numerous lodges, and with conventions which made nominations secretly, attained sudden importance. From the professions of ignorance with which its members met all questioning, they were called "Know-nothings." In 1854 the Know-nothings carried Massachusetts and Delaware; in 1855, most of New England, New York, Maryland, Kentucky and California, and polled a large vote in the South, mainly from former Whigs. Their platform demanded more severe naturalization laws and the selection of none but natives for office. In national convention at Philadelphia in February, 1856, they nominated ex-President Millard Fillmore for the Presidency, and A. J. Donelson, of Tennessee, for Vice-President. But the slavery issue thrust all others aside, and the ticket received but 874,534 votes in a total of over 4,000,000, and but eight electoral votes, those of Maryland. The party soon died out, though the Constitutional Union party of 1860 was in a way its successor. Recently the American Protective League and other similar organizations have revived the nativist programme.

American Philosophical Society, oldest among the American academies founded and conducted for the furtherance of science. It was established at Philadelphia in 1743 by Benjamin Franklin and his associates. Between the years 1771 and 1894 this society has published a series of its Transactions, numbering about twenty-five volumes, and about twenty volumes of Proceedings. These volumes contain valuable papers upon a great variety of subjects.

American Republican Party, formed in New York in 1842, as the successor of the Native American Party of 1835. They demanded that public offices should be filled only by native Americans, and that naturalization should not be allowed until after a sojourn of twenty-one years in the country. It was a precursor of the Know-Nothing Party.

"American Weekly Mercury," the third newspaper published in the United States. This journal was founded by Andrew Bradford, the first numbers appearing in Philadelphia in 1719. William Bradford was also an associate editor for a time, but he afterward removed to New York to continue his journalistic career. After Andrew Bradford's death in 1742, the publication of the *Mercury* was continued with considerable success by his widow. Its general object was the "encouragement of trade," little space being devoted to local news. Foreign news, commercial statistics and custom house entries

DISCOVERERS AND EXPLORERS.

Sir Henry Hudson.
Fernando de Soto.
Jacques Cartier.

Hernando Cortez.
Christopher Columbus.
Robert Cavelier de la Salle.

Amerigo Vespucci.
Sebastian Cabot.
Ponce de Leon.

constituted its chief matter, although there were occasional literary comments and extracts from English classics. Publication was suspended about 1746.

American Whigs, the first political party of America, came into existence in the struggles preceding the Revolution. They resisted the arbitrary measures of King George III, and declared their independence of him. They opposed the Tories, the supporters of the crown in America, and after the Revolution confiscated the property of banished Tories.

Americus Vespucius, Latinized from *Amerigo Vespucci* (1452–1512), was born at Florence. He engaged in trade in the employ of the house of Medici, and became known as an expert astronomer, calculator and map-maker. He made four voyages to America, two in the Spanish, and two in the Portuguese service, and acted as the sailing-master. The first voyage in 1497–98 was until recently confounded with the second voyage made in 1499–1500 along the northern coast of South America. In 1501–02 he visited the Brazilian coast, and in 1503–04 sailed in the same direction. He was pilot-major of Spain from 1508 till his death at Seville. To the region of his Brazilian discoveries he gave the name of *Mundus Novus*. This was considered to be a *Quarta Pars*, a "fourth part," added to the previously known world of the old maps; and a teacher of geography, Waldeesmüller, in the town of St. Dié, in Lorraine, proposed in 1507 the name America for the *Quarta Pars*. His little treatise, *Cosmographiae Introductio*, spread the suggestion, and the name *America* came gradually to be transferred from Brazil to the entire Continent.

Ames, Fisher (1758–1808), was born at Dedham, Mass. He was graduated at Harvard, and soon acquired a brilliant reputation as a lawyer and political writer. He served in the Massachusetts Legislature, and made his mark in the convention which met in 1788 to ratify the Federal Constitution. From 1789 to 1797 he was Congressman from Massachusetts, and achieved widespread fame as a Federalist leader and eloquent orator. Failing health compelled his retirement from public life, and he refused the presidency of Harvard College.

Ames, Oakes (1804–1873), of Massachusetts, manufacturer. His firm carried on an enormous business in the manufacture of shovels, especially in the early days of the gold-finding in California and Australia. They had a large interest in the building of the Union Pacific Railroad, which they transferred to the Crédit Mobilier. He was a member of Congress from 1862 to 1873. He was censured by the House for his connection with the Crédit Mobilier scandal.

Amherst, Jeffrey, Lord (1717–1797), soldier, was commissioned major-general by Pitt and sent to co-operate with Prideaux against the French in Canada. Took Ticonderoga in 1759. In 1760 he was appointed Governor-General of British America; in 1763 titular Governor of Virginia; and from 1793 to 1795, commander-in-chief of the British army.

Amherst College was founded by the Congregationalists in 1821. Its most famous presidents were Edward Hitchcock and Julius H. Seelye.

Amidas or Amadas, Philip (1550–1618), English navigator, in 1584 commanded one of the ships in Raleigh's exploring expedition to the coast of North Carolina.

Amistad Case, The. In 1839 the cargo of negro slaves on board this Spanish vessel bound for Puerto Principe from Havana, rose and killed the whites and took possession of the ship. The ship was seized by a U. S. war vessel off Long Island and carried to New London. The U. S. District Court of Connecticut decided that the slaves were "property rescued from pirates" and should be returned to their Spanish owners, under the treaty between the United States and Spain. The Supreme Court of the United States reversed this decision, declaring that the blacks, having been kidnapped from a foreign country, were free men and not bound by treaties with Spain.

Amnesty. In 1862 Congress authorized the President to offer full pardon to all persons, excepting the most prominent movers in the Rebellion, who would swear an oath of allegiance to the United States. President Lincoln issued the first proclamation of amnesty December 8, 1863. On March 26, 1864, a supplementary proclamation was issued. The next proclamation was issued by President Johnson May 29, 1865. A bill was passed in 1867 repealing the act of 1862, but President Johnson ignored it, adhering to his constitutional right to pardon. On September 7, 1867, President Johnson issued another proclamation extending pardon to all but a few classes. July 4, 1868, pardon was offered for treason to all, except those under indictment, and December 25, 1868, full amnesty to all. The Congressional Act of May 22, 1872, removed political disability from all but the most prominent Confederates.

Ampudia, Pedro de, Mexican soldier. As a general in the war with the United States, he unsuccessfully, but with great spirit, defended Monterey against General Taylor.

"Amy Warwick," a vessel belonging to persons living in Richmond, and captured July 10, 1861, by the U. S. cruisers as "enemy's property." The vessel was at the time of capture on the high seas from Rio Janeiro to Richmond, laden with tobacco and not attempting to run the blockade. This capture first distinctly raised the question of the right of the United States to exercise war powers in suppressing the Confederacy.

Anarchists. The Anarchists of the United States are almost entirely foreign born. Chief and best known among them is Johann Most, who edited the Anarchist paper *Freiheit.* Their greatest strength is in Chicago, where they incited a serious riot May 4, 1886. Several leaders were executed and others were imprisoned, but were pardoned in 1893 by Governor Altgeld, of Illinois. Popular reaction since 1886 has done much to decrease Anarchistic tendencies.

Anatomy Laws. Massachusetts in 1784 passed an act providing that the bodies of those killed in duels or executed for killing another in a duel should be given to the surgeons to be dissected. New York in 1789 passed a law punishing the disinterment of bodies for purposes of anatomy. Massachusetts in 1831 passed the first liberal law for the benefit of anatomy passed in any English-speaking country, giving to the surgeons the bodies of criminals and of State paupers who died without leaving relatives. But the New York law of 1789 had given judges the power to order the dissection of executed criminals as a part of their sentence. Most States have since 1831 passed acts more or less liberal to authorize dissection.

Anderson, Joseph (1757–1837), was a captain at the battle of Monmouth and the siege of Yorktown. Was U. S. Senator from Tennessee from 1797 to 1815.

Anderson, Martin B. (1815–1890), of New York, educator, was for some time a professor in Waterville College, and from 1853 was president of Rochester University.

Anderson, Mary, born in 1859, actress, first appeared on the stage as Juliet in 1875; was always a great favorite in the United States and has been well received in England.

Anderson, Rasmus Björn, born in 1846, of Wisconsin, author, was professor of Scandinavian languages from 1875 to 1884. He was appointed minister to Denmark in 1885, and served until 1889.

Anderson, Richard H. (1816–1879), soldier, a graduate of West Point, served in the Mexican War. Joined the Confederates in 1861; became lieutenant-general, and commanded a division at Gettysburg.

Anderson, Robert (1805–1871), of Kentucky, soldier, served in the Black Hawk, Florida and Mexican Wars. He was severely wounded at Molino del Rey. In November, 1860, he took command of the troops and forts in Charleston Harbor. In December he withdrew all his troops to Fort Sumter, which, after a bombardment of thirty-six hours by the Confederates, he was compelled to evacuate April 13, 1861.

Anderson, Fort, North Carolina, was garrisoned in 1865 by 6000 Confederates under Hoke. February 18 it was assaulted by fifteen Federal war vessels commanded by Admiral Porter and by a land force under Schofield and Terry. The attack from land and sea was simultaneous. The garrison fled almost immediately, leaving ten heavy guns and much ammunition. The national flag was raised the next day.

Anderson Case. A negro named Anderson was found by Seneca Diggs wandering about his plantation in Missouri without a pass, whereupon Mr. Diggs arrested him as a fugitive slave. Anderson plunged a knife into his captor's heart and escaped, making his way to Canada, where he remained until 1860, when the American government demanded that he be given up under the extradition treaty. Anderson was tried and discharged on a technical point. The eloquent speech of Mr. Gerrit Smith, the defendant's counsel, attracted widespread attention.

Anderson vs. Dunn (1821), an action of trespass, brought for assault and battery and false imprisonment against Dunn, sergeant-at-arms of the House of Representatives, by Anderson, a member of the House, who was arrested by order of the House for a breach of privilege. The Supreme

Court decided that the Constitution authorizes the House to punish its members for contempt, and judgment was affirmed for the defendant.

Andersonville, Sumter County, Georgia, site of a Confederate military prison for Federal soldiers during the Civil War. The mortality of this prison was very great, 12,926 soldiers dying there. Henry Wirtz, a Swiss adventurer, the superintendent of the prison, was tried, after the war, by a military commission and hung for excessive cruelty, November 10, 1865. As to the culpability of the Confederate government, opposite views have been maintained. Andersonville is now the site of a national cemetery for Union soldiers.

André, John (1751–1780), acting adjutant-general to Sir Henry Clinton, and the unfortunate victim of Arnold's treason. After varied experiences in the Revolutionary War he was sent by Clinton to arrange with Benedict Arnold the details of the latter's projected treachery. The two conferred in secret near Stony Point, on the Hudson, and André started back to New York. When near Tarrytown he was stopped by three Americans, searched and delivered to the military authorities. A military court condemned him to death as a spy, and he was hanged at Tappan, across the river, on October 2, 1780. He was buried in Westminster Abbey, and a monument was many years afterward erected in Tarrytown in memory of the affair. The three patriots, John Paulding, David Williams and Isaac Van Wart, were rewarded by Congress.

Andrew, John A. (1818–1867), the famous War Governor of Massachusetts, had become known as a lawyer and member of the Legislature, when in 1860 he was elected by the Republicans as Governor. His years of office, 1861 to 1866, coincide with the Civil War period, and he was the heart and soul of the patriotic sentiment in the State. His services in equipping and forwarding the militia, in co-operating with other executives, and his advocacy of radical measures in the latter half of the war, entitled him to a conspicuous place in the group of "War Governors."

Andrews, E. Benjamin, born in 1844, became president of Brown University in 1889. He was a U. S. Commissioner to the International Monetary Conference at Brussels in 1892. He wrote "Institutes of General History," "Institutes of Constitutional History," and "Institutes of Economics."

Andrews, Stephen Pearl (1812–1886), of New York, author, was an ardent Abolitionist, the founder of the present system of phonographic reporting and an accomplished linguist.

Andros, Sir Edmund (1637–1714), was born in London, and was early in life a soldier and bailiff of the Island of Guernsey. He began his American career as Governor of New York in 1674–81; to which in 1680 he added by seizure New Jersey. When his patron, the Duke of York, had become king as James II., he appointed Andros in 1686 Governor of the northern colonies, including New England and New York. Andros was arbitrary in his headquarters in Boston and elsewhere in New England, though the story of the "charter oak" of Connecticut is by some considered apocryphal. The overthrow of James II. led the people of Boston to depose Andros in April, 1689, and he was sent to England, but not tried. He was again Governor, 1692–98, this time of Virginia.

Angell, James B., born in Rhode Island in 1829, educator, was professor of modern languages and literature in Brown University from 1853 to 1860; editor of the "Providence Journal" from 1860 to 1866; president of the University of Vermont from 1866 to 1871, since which time he has been president of the University of Michigan, except during 1880 and 1881, when he was Minister of the United States in China.

Anian, Straits of, supposed by geographers and explorers of the sixteenth century to be the Northwest Passage to India. It was believed to have been discovered by Cortereal, a Spanish voyager, in 1500, and to have been named by him after three brothers, who accompanied him. It has been identified with both Behring Strait and Puget Sound. Many expeditions were sent in search of the strait during the sixteenth century.

"Ann," a small vessel, which arrived at Plymouth in August, 1623, accompanied by the "Little James," and brought reinforcements to the Pilgrims.

Annals of Congress. These annals were published by Gales and Seaton in 1834. They contain, in forty-two volumes, a complete record of the proceedings and debates from the first Congress down to May, 1824, besides valuable state papers, public documents and laws.

Annapolis, Md., was founded in 1649 by Puritan refugees from Virginia and became the capital of the colony in 1689. It was first called Providence, but was incorporated as a city in 1696, and received its present name (after Queen Anne) in 1708. The U. S. Naval Academy was established here in 1845.

Anne (1664–1714), Queen of Great Britain from 1702 to 1714. In 1704 a proclamation of Queen Anne regarding the Colonial currency, ordered a uniform scale of legalized depreciation in the Colonial coinage system. A proclamation of Queen Anne in 1713 forced the slave trade upon the colonies, England having been granted the monopoly of this trade under the provisions of the treaty of Utrecht. (See Queen Anne's War.)

Annexations. After the adoption of the Federal Constitution the different States ceded all the territories to the west of them and included in their original charters, to the Union. Many of these territories nominally extended to the Pacific coast, but in practice, only as far as the Mississippi River. Louisiana and the Floridas were then under Spanish dominion and thus the navigation of the Mississippi River was blocked, causing great inconvenience to settlers west of the Alleghanies. It had ever been the fixed policy of Spain to exclude all foreign commerce from this stream. She had refused to treat with Jay upon this point in 1780–82. In 1786 the United States withdrew its demand for a navigation treaty, but the clamorings of the western settlers caused their renewal, and, in 1795, Thomas Pinckney, Envoy Extraordinary, negotiated a treaty of friendship and boundaries, by which free navigation of the Mississippi was opened, as well as the port of New Orleans. In 1800 Spain retroceded Louisiana to France, to which country it had belonged until the peace of 1763. The treaty of 1795 was abrogated and the West was again in a ferment. It was proposed in the Senate that the President order out 50,000 militia and capture New Orleans. Instead James Monroe was sent to co-operate with Robert R. Livingston for the purchase of New Orleans in 1803. A prospective war with England induced France to sell all Louisiana, and the purchase was negotiated for $15,000,000 on April 30, 1803, the treaty being signed by Livingston and Monroe for the Union, and Barbé-Marbois for France. By this step Jefferson obtained for the United States 1,171,931 square miles of territory, comprising Alabama and Mississippi south of parallel 31°, all Louisiana, Arkansas, Missouri, Iowa, Nebraska, Dakota, Montana, Minnesota west of the Mississippi, most of Kansas, a large part of Colorado, and Wyoming. The Federalists angrily attacked this move of Jefferson as being utterly unconstitutional, and the President did not attempt to defend himself, but sought indemnity. Florida was next annexed. The United States claimed Florida, but Spain denied having ceded it to France with Louisiana. In 1810 the people of west Florida declared their independence. Governor Claiborne, of New Orleans, was sent by the President to take possession of Mobile and West Florida. In 1818 Spain was much annoyed by a war with the Seminoles, and accordingly a treaty was concluded February 22, 1819, by which Florida was ceded to the Union in consideration of the payment of $5,000,000 for Spain in private claims by citizens of the States. Texas had been claimed by both France and Spain, but after the revolt of Mexico was in reality under Mexican rule. In 1836 Texas seceded and declared herself free, defeating the Mexican General Santa Anna, but was not recognized by Mexico. The United States, England, France and Belgium recognized the new republic. Many politicians favored the annexation of Texas and in 1844 Calhoun, Secretary of State under Tyler, actually concluded a treaty to this effect, which was rejected by the Senate. After considerable manœuvring and political intrigue, a joint resolution was passed in the Senate February 27, 1845, and in the House February 28, and Texas was admitted to the Union. As a result of the Mexican War and by the payment of $15,000,000 and $3,250,000 in claims of private citizens against Mexico, California, New Mexico, Utah, Nevada, and part of Arizona and Colorado, were added to the Union in 1848 (545,783 square miles). By the Gadsen Treaty in 1853 the southern part of Arizona, 45,535 square miles, was purchased from Mexico. Alaska, 577,390 square miles, was ceded to the United States for $7,200,000 on June 30, 1867, by Russia.

Antarctic Expedition. In 1839 Captain Wilkes, of the U. S. Navy, conducted an exploring expedition toward the South Pole. He discovered in January, 1840, a portion of a large continent in latitude 61° 30′ S. and longitude 161° E. He traced the coast westward to longitude 101° E., but was prevented from landing by the ice.

Anthony, Henry Bowen (1815–1884), was born at Coventry, R. I., and died at Providence. He was graduated at Brown University in 1833, and became the editor of the Providence *Journal* and the most influential of New England journalists. He was elected Whig Governor of Rhode Island in 1849 and 1850. From 1859 to 1884 he was uninterruptedly Republican U. S. Senator from Rhode Island, and was several times chosen president *pro tempore* of the Senate. His career there is among the longest on record. His valuable collection, the Harris Library, was left to Brown University.

Anthony, Susan B., born in 1820, of New York, reformer, especially in matters connected with the civil status of women. In 1854 and 1855 she held conventions in every county of New York in favor of Woman Suffrage, and has done much to secure the passage of laws giving to women more control over their property than is permitted by the common law.

Antietam Creek, Md., one of the great battles of the war; a two days' fight between the Federals and Confederates under McClellan and Lee, September 16, 17, 1862. McClellan commanded 70,000 troops; Lee 40,000. The Confederates were stationed along the Antietam Creek, their flanks resting on the Potomac River, having placed strong guards at three of the four stone bridges which crossed the creek. Hooker's brigade was dispatched across the fourth and unguarded bridge to attack the Confederate flank, while the batteries of both sides kept up a continual fire. Scarcely more than a skirmish took place when darkness fell. At sunrise Hooker assaulted Jackson with some success, but reinforcements at that point forced him to give way. The hottest of the fighting continued on this flank throughout the morning, constant reinforcements being sent to Jackson, and Franklin and Sumner coming up to assist Hooker. Burnside had early been ordered to capture the bridge in his front and cross to attack Lee's centre, but this he delayed doing until he found it almost an impossibility. Finally, however, he succeeded, and crossing, he dislodged the Confederates, who were stationed upon the heights overlooking Sharpsburg. At this point Hill arrived with 2000 fresh Confederate troops, who, uniting with Lee, drove Burnside out and retook the heights. At night there was a mutual desistance, both sides having suffered severely. As Lee retreated, however, leaving 6000 prisoners and his unburied dead, McClellan is considered the victor.

Anti-Federalists, a political party which first came into existence in opposing the ratification of the Constitution. Its leaders were George Clinton, Patrick Henry and others. Failing in this they were for a time utterly demoralized. During the First Congress this party showed itself but little, but in the first session of the Second Congress there were symptoms of an Anti-Federalist revival. They opposed Hamilton and his followers and gradually became champions of the strict construction of the Constitution and opponents to what they termed "monarchical" Federalism. After the rise of the "Republican" party under Jefferson the Anti-Federalists lost their identity in the advocacy of its principles (1793).

Anti-Lecompton, the Congressional faction of the Democratic Party which opposed in 1858 the admission of Kansas to the Union under the provisions of the Lecompton slavery constitution. Crittenden and Douglas led this faction in the Senate, Montgomery in the House. A vote was taken in the House April 1, on the Crittenden-Montgomery resolution that the Lecompton constitution should have the honest test of popular vote in Kansas before she should become a State. The Anti-Lecomptons won by a vote of 120 to 112.

Anti-Masonry. The Freemasons had in 1820 many prominent politicians among their members. In 1826 William Morgan, of Batavia, N. Y., threatened to reveal the secrets of the society. He was arrested and a judgment was obtained against him for debt. He was then carried to Niagara in a closed carriage and never again heard of. Accordingly, in the next town and county elections candidates refusing to resign from the Freemasons found a strong Anti-Mason vote polled against them. From being local, anti-masonry became widespread through New York, and finally affected national politics. In 1828 the National Republican Party of New York nominated State candidates who were not Freemasons, and an Anti-Masonic State Convention nominated candidates pledged against freemasonry. This party soon displaced the National Republicans as opponents of the Democrats in New York. Anti-masonry spread to other States and, notably in Pennsylvania and Vermont, strongly affected the elections. In New York, William H. Seward, Thurlow Weed and Millard Fillmore were Anti-Masonic leaders. John Quincy Adams had by this time lost control of the National Republicans and Clay was becoming popular. In their National Convention at Baltimore in 1831 (the first of national nominating conventions) the Anti-Masons, hoping to force Clay, who was a Mason, out of the field, nominated Wirt and Ellmaker. But the National Republicans persisted in nominating Clay. Wirt and Ellmaker received the electoral vote of Vermont only. After this the Anti-Masons died out as a distinct national party, being absorbed by the Whigs. They continued to exercise some influence in a few States, however, for a time.

Anti-Monopoly Party was formed May 14, 1884, at Chicago, demanding economical government, equitable laws, including an Interstate Commerce law, laws establishing labor bureaus and providing industrial arbitration, direct vote for senators, graduated income tax, payment of the national debt as it matures, and "fostering care" for agriculture, and denouncing the tariff and the granting of land to corporations. It joined later with the Greenback Labor Party under the name of the "People's Party."

Anti-Nebraska Men, a name first given the Northern Whigs to distinguish them from the Southern Whigs in respect to the Kansas-Nebraska bill. Their ranks were reinforced by Anti-Slavery Democrats, and though not a distinct party they gained control of the House in the Thirty-fourth Congress. They soon became the Republican Party.

Antinomians, a sect originally founded by John Agricola, a disciple for a time of Martin Luther. He and his followers taught that the law was of no use or obligation under the dispensation of the Gospel. Antinomianism in the United States was preached by Mrs. Anne Hutchinson, an English woman, who came to Boston in September, 1634. She came for the sake of the spiritual comfort of the sermons of John Cotton and John Wheelwright. These men she pronounced to be "under a covenant of grace," all other ministers "under a covenant of works." Mrs. Hutchinson and her disciples believed that good works availed nothing toward salvation. Wheelwright, Vane, the young Governor of Massachusetts at the time, and others, upheld her. She was tried in 1637, and banished with Wheelwright and

Aspinwall. A number of her followers were fined or otherwise punished, and the rule of the Puritan hierarchy was firmly established at the expense of freedom of thought and speech.

Antioch College, Yellow Springs, O., was founded in 1852. Horace Mann was president of it.

Anti-Relief Party, a political party in Kentucky opposing the relief of delinquent debtors and consequently the so-called Relief Party. This party was defeated by the Relief Party in the Gubernatorial contest of 1824, but regained control two years later.

Anti-renters, a name given about 1840 to the tenants of the large estates in New York granted to patroons by the Dutch Company and James II. These tenants held deeds of the land, but paid rent annually, an arrangement which caused much dissatisfaction. In 1839, on the death of Stephen Van Rensselaer, one of the principal landholders, his tenants refused to pay rent to his successor. Open revolt followed, sometimes attended by riot and bloodshed. Attempts to collect rents by military aid led to the Helderberg War. In 1847 and 1848 the Anti-renters showed themselves as a political power in the State. The Court of Appeals in 1852 gave a decision in the main sustaining the tenants, and practically ended the anti-rent movement.

Apaches, a nation of roving Indians belonging to the Athabascan family. They were early the terror of the Spanish, and since the annexation of their territory to the United States the tribe has given great trouble. Mangos Colorado for fifty years led large hostile bands, until finally killed in 1863. Later, attempts were made to remove the Apaches to a reservation in New Mexico. The plan was opposed by the whites on the frontiers, and led to the massacre of over 100 Apaches at Camp Grant, Arizona, April 30, 1871.

Appeals, Court of. (See Court of Appeals in Cases of Capture.)

Appeals from Colonial Courts. (See Privy Council.)

Appointing Power. In the Colonial period the Crown appointed the governors and councils, and the governors appointed most other officers. The new constitutions made at the time of the Revolution, because of fear of tyranny, usually lessened the appointing power of governors. The Continental Congress appointed few officers. The Constitution of 1787 gives the President power to appoint all officers (subject to confirmation by the Senate), except such inferior officers as Congress may provide shall be appointed by the President alone, by the courts of law, or by the heads of departments. The participation by the Senate has led to much injurious collusion in appointments dictated by considerations of party politics, under the name of "the courtesy of the Senate." Presidents at first made appointments for fitness solely, and made no removals for political causes. But Jefferson first, and afterward, and more largely, Jackson, introduced that policy of partisan appointments and removals which is known as the "Spoils System." (See art. See also Tenure of Office, Removals, and Civil Service Reform.) History by Miss Salmon.

Appointment, Council of, a council of four members, instituted by the New York Constitution of 1777, whose function was to approve or disapprove of nominations to office made by the Governor. They strengthened their powers in 1801, became an instrument of great abuse in the way of partisan appointments, and were abolished in 1821.

Appomattox, Va., the final battle, between the Confederates 35,000 strong under Lee and the Federals numbering 100,000 under Grant, of the Richmond and Petersburg campaign of 1864–65. Lee's army was retreating as rapidly as its forlorn condition would permit, when, Crook and Sheridan having captured a Confederate provision train near Appomattox, Custer pushed on to that place and fought the wearied Confederates till dark. They were severely defeated and many prisoners were taken. This occurred April 8, 1865. The following day, as Sheridan was preparing for a charge, the Confederates waved a white flag and Lee, after interchange of communications, surrendered the army of Northern Virginia to Grant. The terms which Grant conceded were that both officers and men should be released on parole and should keep their horses, "because they would need them for the spring ploughing and farm work."

Apportionment, the distribution of representation in the Federal House of Representatives and in the houses of the different State legislatures. It is sometimes used in a fiscal sense as applied to the allotment of direct taxes on the basis of population. As far back as William Penn's plan of general government for the colonies objection was made against equal representation of colonies. The Albany Plan of Union provided that each colony should be represented in the Grand Council by from two to seven delegates, according to the amount of taxes paid by each. In the Continental Congress the rule of equal representation prevailed, each State having one vote. This rule was retained in the Articles of Confederation, for long contentions over the matter showed that no other plan could win acceptance. In the Convention of 1787 there was long and bitter dispute over questions of representation. Finally it was settled that the Federal legislature should consist of two branches, that the States should be equally represented in the upper, or Senate, and that in the lower, or House of Representatives, each should have a number of members proportioned to the number of its free inhabitants, plus three-fifths of the slaves. A provisional apportionment was inserted in the Constitution, and in 1790 a census was taken. Direct taxes were to be apportioned in the same manner as representation. The lower house should have no more than one representative for every 30,000 inhabitants. This constitutional rule governed apportionments during seventy years, though the ratio was changed from time to time. Much debate arose over the question of fractional representation. In the Thirty-first Congress Vinton, of Ohio, moved to divide the representative population of the entire country by 233 and that of each State by the quotient, assigning to each State representation for each full ratio and the remaining members necessary to make up 233 to the States having the largest fractions. This method has guided subsequent apportionments. Federal apportionments are made shortly after each decennial census, and the State apportionments are guided by the Federal. Methods of apportionment in different States vary, however. (See Gerrymander.)

Aquedneck, a settlement on Narragansett Bay, made in 1637, by a party of Antinomians under the leadership of William Coddington. It was made in anticipation of banishment from Massachusetts for upholding Mrs. Hutchinson, the leader of the Antinomians.

Arapahoes, a tribe of Indians residing at the headwaters of the Arkansas and Platte rivers. They have generally been friendly to the whites.

Arbor Day, a day set apart by most of the States and Territories for planting trees. Arbor Day was inaugurated by the Nebraska State Board of Agriculture in 1874, the second Wednesday in April being the day set.

Arbuthnot, Marriot (1711–1794), British admiral, was made vice-admiral and commander-in-chief on the American station in 1779 and co-operated with Clinton in the capture of Charleston in 1780.

Archæological Institute of America. This society was founded at Boston in 1879, and has devoted the larger part of its interest to classical archæology. Under the auspices of the institution, Mr. A. F. Bandelier was sent to New Mexico to study the Pueblos, and at the same time Aymé, American Consul at Mérida, was commissioned to explore Yucatan. In 1885 the *American Journal of Archæology* was started at Baltimore as the society's official organ.

Archbishop. There have been in America no archbishops except those of the Catholic church. The first of these was John Carroll, bishop of Baltimore, made archbishop in 1808.

Archdale, John, a Quaker, born in England, was, from 1694 for about two years, Governor of Carolina, into which he introduced the culture of rice.

Archer, William S. (1789–1855), of Virginia, was a member of Congress from 1820 to 1835, and U. S. Senator from 1841 to 1847.

Archive War. In 1842, after Texas had declared her independence of Mexico, the Texan seat of government was at Austin. During that year the Mexicans under Vasquez destroyed San Antonio and threatened Austin. The President fled to Houston and demanded that the government archives should be transferred to that city. This the citizens of Austin refused to allow. Vigilance and archive committees were appointed. In September the President sent Captain Smith and thirty-five men to take the archives by force. This was accomplished, but the citizens of Austin pursued the captors and recovered the archives, thus determining the permanence of the capital at Austin.

Arctic Discoveries. Dr. Kane conducted the first American expedition in Arctic regions, sailing from New York in the "Advance," May 30, 1853. He penetrated Smith Strait as far as Cape George Russell, and then returned to Van Rensselaer Harbor for the winter. Frequent excursions were made from this place, 125 miles of coast being traced to the North and East. Morton and another of Kane's company penetrated to Washington Land in latitude 82° 27′, discovering an open channel which they named Kennedy. Kane returned in 1855, having been further North than any other explorer. He had to abandon his ship and go overland to the Danish settlements in the South, where he was met by a relief party. During 1860 Dr. Isaac Hayes, one of Kane's party, advanced as far as 81° 35′ north latitude, but was obliged to return, without having made any important discovery. Dr. Charles F. Hall, of Connecticut, led an expedition the same year in search of Sir John Franklin. He lost his boat and was obliged to return. He made, however, some important discoveries of Frobisher's expedition 300 years before. Under Hall, the same year, another party found actual relics of Franklin's party, and learned from the natives that he had discovered a northwest passage before abandoning his ships. Hall spent five years among the Esquimaux. He then returned and organized a third party, which reached 82°, where Hall died. In 1881 Lieutenant Greely, of the U. S. Army, was sent to take charge of the American Signal Service Bureau at Lady Franklin Bay, it having been arranged that a relief expedition should be sent to him the following year. The first relief party, under Lieutenant Beebe, sailed in June, 1882, but could get no further than latitude 71° 20′. The second, under Lieutenant Garlington, 1883, was equally unsuccessful. In 1883 a third relief party was dispatched under Captain Winfield S. Schley, commanding the "Thetis" and the "Bear." The few survivors of the Greely party were found October 21, 1883, in an almost dying condition. Greely had reached in his explorations 83° 24′ north latitude, the highest ever reached. In 1891 Lieutenant Peary conducted an expedition to Greenland under the auspices of the Academy of Natural Sciences of Philadelphia. He reached latitude 82°, and showed the northern bounds of Greenland.

Argall, Sir Samuel (1572–1639), came to Virginia in 1609, where his first public exploit was the abduction of Pocahontas in 1612. In 1613 he commanded an expedition which destroyed Port Royal, Acadia. He was deputy-governor of Virginia from 1617 to 1619, so distinguishing himself by tyranny and rapacity that he was recalled to England in the latter year.

Argentina. The independence of Argentina was recognized by the United States in March, 1822, and by the Act of May 4, 1822, a mission to this government was established. By the treaty of July 10, 1853, the navigation of the rivers Paraná and Uruguay was secured to the United States under certain conditions. July 27, 1853, a favorable commercial treaty was concluded between the United States and Argentina.

"**Argus,**" an American war brig, Captain Allen. In cruising about the British Channel it destroyed twenty valuable merchantmen with cargoes valued at two million dollars. August 14, 1813, it was attacked by the "Pelican," eighteen guns. Captain Allen was mortally wounded. The American sailors, who were somewhat under the influence of captured wine, did not fight as well as usual, and after forty-five minutes' fighting, the vessel was surrendered. The "Argus" lost twenty-three men, the "Pelican" seven men.

Arista, Mariano (1802–1855), Mexican general. In the war with the United States he commanded at Palo Alto and Resaca de la Palma. He was elected president in 1850, but resigned in 1853.

Arizona was organized as a territory in 1863, partly from territory ceded by Mexico to the United States by the treaty of Guadalupe Hidalgo (1848) and partly from the Gadsden purchase (1853). It was first visited by the Spaniards, Nizan in 1539, and Coronado in 1540. Jesuit missions were early established among the Indians. The population of Arizona in 1890 was 59,620. (History by Bancroft.)

"**Ark**," a vessel of 250 tons burden, which Lord Baltimore provided in 1633 for his party of colonists for Maryland. The "Ark" sailed from Gravesend in October, 1633, accompanied by the "Dove," a small pinnace, and reached Point Comfort, Virginia, February 27, 1634.

Arkansas was first settled by the French in 1685. It formed a part of the Louisiana cession and was included in the territory called Louisiana until 1812 and then Missouri Territory until 1819, when it was organized as a separate territory, including the present Indian Territory. Arkansas became a State June 15, 1836, with its present boundaries. The State was steadily Democratic until the close of the Civil War. At first the opposition to secession in 1861 was very strong, but upon the call of President Lincoln for troops an ordinance of secession was passed May 6, 1861. The Federal troops captured Little Rock in 1863, and a loyal State government was organized. The State was re-admitted June 22, 1868. The Republicans controlled the State from this time until 1874. Two rival factions of that party caused an armed collision. Federal troops restored order and President Grant recognized Brooks, the Republican candidate, as Governor. A new Constitution was adopted in 1874, since which time the Democrats have controlled the State. The present Constitution dates from 1874. Arkansas had a population of 52,240 in 1836 and 1,128,179 in 1890.

"**Arkansas Gazette**," first newspaper published in Arkansas. The first edition, of less than one hundred copies, was issued at Arkansas Post, then the territorial capital, by William E. Woodruff, November 20, 1819. It is still continued.

Arkansas Post, Arkansas, occupied during Grant's and Sherman's campaign along the Mississippi River by Churchill and 5000 Confederates. On the night of January 10, 1863, Sherman ordered McClernand to advance against this post with his Federal column, while Admiral Porter's gunboats shelled the Confederate rifle pits. January 11, an intensely cold day, the assault was successfully made. The fort was captured and 5000 prisoners taken.

Arlington, Henry Bennet, Earl of (1618–1685). In 1673 Charles II granted to the Earl of Arlington and Thomas, Lord Culpepper, the entire territory of Virginia, for thirty-one years, at the yearly rent of thirty shillings. The patents entitled them to all rents and escheats and illegally authorized them to make conveyances in fee simple. Arlington was a member of the so-called "Cabal."

Arlington, in Alexandria County, Virginia, the home of Mrs. Washington's grandson, G. W. P. Custis, and the birthplace of Mary R. Custis, afterward the wife of General Robert E. Lee. Through the marriage Lee came into possession of this estate. During the Civil War Arlington was confiscated by the national government, and has been since the close of that struggle erected into a national cemetery for Union soldiers.

Armed Neutrality, an alliance formed in 1780–82, by nearly all the other maritime powers of Europe for protection against the continued British depredation on neutral commerce. The Armed Neutrality was suggested by the declarations of the Russian Empress in 1780, setting forth certain doctrines of international law, familiarly summarized as "free ships, free goods." The United States agreed to conform to these articles October 8, 1780.

Armistead, George (1780–1818), of Virginia, soldier, distinguished himself at the capture of Fort George, Canada, in 1813, and by his successful defence of Baltimore in 1814.

Armstrong, John (1758–1843), was born at Carlisle, Pa., and died at Red Hook, N. Y. He served in the Revolutionary War, and after its conclusion wrote the first "Newburgh letters." Entering civil life he was Secretary of State in Pennsylvania and member of the Continental Congress, and was a U. S. Senator in 1800–2 and 1803–4. He was Minister to France from 1804 to 1810. Appointed brigadier-general in 1812, in 1813 he entered the Cabinet as Secretary of War. His administration, despite some radical measures, was unsuccessful, and he was obliged to resign after the fall of Washington in 1814.

Armstrong, Robert (1790–1854), of Tennessee, soldier, was a captain of artillery under Jackson in the Creek War of 1813 and 1814, and distinguished himself at the battle of New Orleans.

Armstrong, Samuel C. (1839–1893), was brevetted brigadier-general during the Civil War. He was eminently successful in the education and improvement of the negro and Indian races, being for many years head of the Hampton (Va.) Institute.

Army. The army of the Revolution consisted of two elements, the Continental army, organized by Congress, and the militia organized by the States. Though upon the average of the years from 1775 to 1781 the total amounted to about 60,000, there were often not more than half that number present with the colors. In 1783 this army was disbanded, and the United States maintained but a few hundred soldiers. Temporarily increased by the Indian wars of 1792 and by the troubles with France in 1798, it numbered only from 3000 to 5000 until the War of 1812. During a portion of that war the number of regular troops rose above 30,000, while the number of militia enlisted was 470,000. During the next thirty years the army averaged but 9000 men. The regular troops enrolled during the Mexican War were about 27,000, the volunteers 74,000. Then the regular army dropped again to 10,000 men, later 12,000. During the first year of the Civil War the numbers of the regular army rose to 32,000. But the number of militia and volunteers was vastly greater. Lincoln's first call of April 15, 1861, was for 75,000 men for three months. Later enlistments were mostly for three years. At the beginning of 1862 the number of volunteers in the army was about 550,000. During 1863, 1864 and 1865 it was about 900,000. At the close of the war the entire Federal army numbered a million men. The total number furnished first and last was 2,850,000. The commander-in-chief of the army at the beginning of the war was General Scott; from November, 1861, to March, 1862, General McClellan; from July, 1862, to March, 1864, General Halleck; during the remainder of the war General Grant. The leading sub-divisions of the Union army were, in the East, the Army of the Potomac; in the West, those of the Mississippi, the Tennessee and the Ohio, all finally united under Sherman. The most important sub-divisions of the Confederate army were the Army of Northern Virginia and the Army of Tennessee. Conscription was employed in the filling up of both Union and Confederate armies. The Confederate forces at the beginning of 1862 numbered about 320,000; during 1863, 1864 and 1865 they averaged about 450,000 men. Early in 1865 General Lee was appointed commander-in-chief of all the Confederate forces. In 1867 the "peace establishment" of the regular army was fixed at 54,641 men. It was then reduced by successive enactments till, in 1875, it was brought down to 27,000 men, at which figure, approximately, it has ever since remained. The army expenditures of the government in time of peace were, down to the Mexican War, from one to five or six millions per annum. Recently they have been from $35,000,000 to $45,000,000.

Arnold, Benedict (1615–1678), of Rhode Island, was elected to its presidency upon the retirement of Roger Williams in 1657, and under the royal charter of 1663 was its first Governor. (See art. Mill at Newport.)

Arnold, Benedict (1741–1801), general and traitor, was born at Norwich, Conn. He was in business in early life, as a druggist, and in other lines. When the Revolutionary War broke out he was appointed colonel by the Massachusetts Congress. Served as a volunteer in the famous capture of Ticonderoga, and leaped into fame by his masterly conduct of the right wing in the attack on Canada in 1775. He led the columns amid extraordinary hardships and difficulties through the Maine woods, arrived in November and was wounded in the assault of Quebec on December 31. Having been made brigadier-general he was defeated by a British flotilla at Valcour Island in Lake Champlain in October, 1776, but effected a skillful retreat. His services were slighted by Congress, but he contributed to the repulse of Tryon in Connecticut. He was at last made a major-general and took a brilliant part in the Burgoyne campaign. He dispersed St. Leger's force at Fort Stanwix, and commanded the left wing at the first battle of Saratoga. Although Gates' jealousy caused him to be superseded, he fought gallantly without orders in the second battle and ended his military career in a blaze of glory. He next commanded in Philadelphia, was court-martialed on trivial charges and reprimanded by Washington. Obtaining the charge of West Point he intrigued with Clinton for the betrayal of that post to the British, but the capture of the negotiator, André, frustrated the scheme, and to Arnold there fell only a brigadier-generalship in the British army, a sum of money, predatory attacks on Virginia and New London, and eternal infamy. The remainder of his life was passed in England. (Life by I. N. Arnold.)

Arnold, Isaac N. (1815–1884), of Illinois, lawyer, was a Republican member of Congress from 1861 to 1865. He was intimate with Abraham Lincoln, of whom he published a biography, one of the best.

Arnold, Samuel G. (1821–1880), of Rhode Island, was Lieutenant-Governor of that State in 1852 and in 1861 and 1862, and U. S. Senator from December, 1862, to March, 1863. In 1860 he published what is still the standard history of Rhode Island.

Aroostook Disturbances. In 1838 a band of lawless men, chiefly from New Brunswick, trespassed upon that territory which is watered by the Aroostook, and which was then claimed by both Great Britain and the United States. The Governor of Maine drafted troops and drove off the intruders. The President sent General Winfield Scott to the Aroostook country. He arranged that it should be occupied as before, each government holding part, while the other denied its legal right. (See Ashburton Treaty.)

Arsenals. At the beginning of the Revolution no arsenals existed in the United States, but in 1776 powder was manufactured in Virginia, and brass cannon were cast in Philadelphia. An arsenal was established at Carlisle, Pa., the same year, and a foundry and laboratory at Springfield, Mass., on the recommendation of General Washington. This was the origin of the present national armory. The arsenal at Harper's Ferry was commenced in 1795, and continued in use until the Civil War. In 1838 the Ordnance Department was placed in charge of arsenals and armories. At the beginning of the Civil War there were twenty-three arsenals and armories, and their number has since been greatly increased.

Artaguette, of Louisiana, French soldier under Bienville, while leading an assault on the Chickasaw forts on the Mississippi River in June, 1736, was taken prisoner and burned at the stake.

Arthur, Chester Alan (October 5, 1830–November 18, 1886), twenty-first President of the United States, was born at Fairfield, Vt. He was graduated at Union College in 1848, and taught school for some years. He then studied law and practiced in New York City, obtaining local reputation as a champion of the rights of colored people in the city. He had been active in the State militia, and at the outbreak of the Civil War he joined Governor Morgan's staff. As engineer-in-chief, acting quartermaster-general and inspector-general, he performed notable services in the Rebellion. He was energetic in local politics, and was in 1871 appointed Collector of the Port of New York, from which position he was removed by President Hayes in 1878. After the bitter contest for the Republican nomination in 1880 had ended in the choice of Garfield, Mr. Arthur was selected for the second place on the ticket as a representative of the Stalwart faction. He became Vice-President in 1881, was suddenly called to the first position by the assassination of Garfield, and took the oath of office on September 20, 1881. The unfavorable apprehensions caused by his active interference in New York politics during his short term as Vice-President were happily allayed by his administration, which was on the whole dignified and conservative. Among his acts was the emphasis placed by him on the strengthening of naval defence, his veto of a Chinese immigration bill, and a veto of a portentously large river and harbor bill. He was in 1884 a candidate for the Republican nomination for President, but was defeated by Mr. Blaine. He retired from office in 1885, and died in New York City.

Artillery. In the United States the present field artillery of the army consists of ten mounted batteries, two to each regiment of artillery. The other ten batteries of each regiment are armed and equipped as infantry and serve mostly in forts and garrisons along the seaboard. During the War of 1812 field batteries were created by mounting foot batteries from the artillery regiments. In 1836 Captain Ringgold organized a field battery, for the artillery branch had been neglected since the War of 1812. The systems of field and siege artillery were chiefly derived from France. In 1820 there were four regiments of artillery. In the Civil War three field batteries were attached to each division of the Army of the Potomac. The introduction of the Parrott gun in 1861 greatly strengthened the artillery.

Asbury, Francis (1745–1816), missionary bishop of "the Methodist Episcopal Church in the United States," was consecrated in 1784, and became one of the most indefatigable and successful evangelists ever known.

Ashburton, Lord, Alexander Baring (1774–1848), English banker and diplomatist, became in 1810 the head of the banking house of Baring Brothers & Co., the financial agent of the United States during the War of 1812. In 1842 as special Minister to the United States he negotiated with Daniel Webster the "Ashburton Treaty," which settled the Northeastern boundary between the British provinces and the United States.

Ashburton Treaty, was a treaty negotiated between Great Britain and the United States by Lord Ashburton and Daniel Webster at Washington in 1842. It adjusted the boundary between the United States and the British possessions on the Northeast, the United States securing about seven-twelfths of the disputed territory. The mutual extradition of criminals and arrangements for the suppression of the slave trade were stipulated.

Ashe, John (1720–1781), of North Carolina, soldier, equipped a regiment at his own expense and joined Lincoln's army in 1778, was defeated at Brier Creek and captured at Wilmington in 1781.

Ashland, Ky., was noted for many years as the home of Henry Clay.

Ashmun, George (1804–1870), of Massachusetts, was a member of the General Court in 1833, 1835, 1836 and in 1841 was Speaker of the House, was U. S. Senator in 1838 and 1839 and a Representative from 1845 to 1851. In 1860 he was president of the convention which nominated Lincoln.

Asiento. Under one of the provisions of the treaty of Utrecht, 1713, the English South Sea Company had the contract (asiento) for the annual transportation to Spanish America of not less than 4800 negro slaves. This contract had formerly been accorded to a company of French merchants. Its possession by the English stimulated the English slave trade to the English colonies.

Aspinwall, William H. (1807–1875), of New York, merchant. In 1850 he secured the contract for building the Panama Railroad, which was completed in 1854, its eastern terminus being named Aspinwall.

Assemblies, Colonial. (See Legislatures.)

Assessments, a term used in a political sense to denote contributions levied upon office-holders and candidates of different political parties by Congressional, State and municipal committees to defray the expenses of canvasses and elections. The precise date of the introduction of this practice into politics is not known, but it is now a general custom, and is in some States, as New York, thoroughly systematized. The first specific instance of this sort of assessment was found in the Swartwout investigation before the House Committee of the Twenty-fifth Congress. A deputy collector of New York testified to having been called upon to contribute under pain of being reported to the general committee of Tammany Hall. It is now the custom for political committees to send circulars to all public officers requesting a certain percentage of their salaries for election expenses. The Republican campaign of 1880 was largely aided in this way. The main motive for payment seems to be fear of losing office. There has been no radical remedy for this system proposed by Congress, though in 1881 a bill was introduced "to prevent extortion from persons in the public service, and bribery and coercion by such persons."

Assiniboins, a tribe of Dakota Indians, in Montana and Manitoba. They separated from the Yankton Sioux after a bitter quarrel, about the beginning of the seventeenth century.

Associated Loyalists, a Tory society formed in New York in 1780 at the instance of the British government and independent of the orders of the British commander. It was called the "Honorable Board of Associated Loyalists," and was in reality a band of licensed outlaws. They continually raided the shores of New Jersey, Connecticut and Long Island in piratical expeditions, and were in league with the rebel freebooters, often exchanging prisoners with them. Dr. Franklin's son, the Tory Governor of New Jersey, was the leader of the society.

Associated Press, an association organized in 1848–49 by a number of New York newspapers, for the purpose of conveniently and inexpensively collecting and transmitting news. Its organization was suggested subsequently to the establishment of the first telegraph line between Washington and Wilmington, Del., and because of the delay in receiving dispatches, owing to the limited lines. The first members of the association were the New York *Sun*, the *Herald*, the *Tribune*, the *Journal of Commerce*, the *Courier and Inquirer* and the *Express*. Contracts for lower telegraph rates were arranged with the companies and other newspapers were admitted to the association. In 1880 355 newspapers were served by this association and a total number of 611,199,630 words were transmitted.

Association, American, an association formed among the American colonists in 1774 to enforce their claim of rights against the British government. Fourteen articles were agreed to, pledging the associators to an entire commercial non-intercourse with Great Britain, Ireland and the West Indies, denouncing the slave trade and appointing committees to detect and publish the names of violators of the articles. The association was formed against such acts as the Sugar, Stamp, Tea and Quartering Acts and the Boston Port Bill.

Assumption. In 1790 Alexander Hamilton, then Secretary of the Treasury, in his plans for restoring the national credit, proposed that the national government should assume the payment of the State debts contracted in the national cause during the Revolutionary War. Massachusetts, Connecticut and South Carolina enthusiastically favored the plan. The Middle States were divided, Pennsylvania holding off, New York and New Jersey favoring Hamilton. Virginia was the strongest opponent of the scheme, she having partially liquidated her debt by funding securities at a depreciated rate, and by selling Kentucky lands. Maryland, Georgia and New Hampshire also opposed it. The measure was near passage by Congress, when the North Carolina delegates took their seats and cast their votes against it. Later Hamilton secured its passage by effecting a combination with those who desired to have the Federal capital placed on the Potomac. August 4, 1790, an act passed by which State debts to the amount of $21,500,000 were assumed by the Federal government.

Astor, John Jacob (1763–1848), merchant, came from Germany to America in 1783. Founded the American fur trade in which he manifested far-reaching enterprise and acquired immense wealth.

Astor, William B. (1792–1875), of New York, capitalist, as a partner with his father (John J.) acquired great wealth, with which he richly endowed the Astor Library and other public institutions.

Astor Library, founded in New York City by John Jacob Astor, and opened in 1853. He bequeathed $400,000 to the library, and this has been increased by bequests of $200,000, and $450,000 by his son, William Black Astor, and his grandson, John Jacob Astor.

Astoria, Ore., was founded by the Pacific Fur Company in 1811, and was for a long time the chief fur-trading post of the West. In 1813 the British government took possession of the town and named it St. George. Astoria was restored to the United States after the conclusion of the War of 1812.

Atchison, David R. (1807–1886), of Missouri, U. S. Senator from 1843 to 1855, was a leader of the pro-slavery faction in the Kansas troubles of 1856 and 1857.

Atherton, Charles G. (1804–1853), of New Hampshire, a member of Congress from 1837 to 1843, in which he introduced the rule known as "the Atherton gag" (see "Gag rule"). Senator from 1843 to 1849 and from 1852 till his death.

Atherton Company, a land company formed in 1659 by Humphrey Atherton, of Massachusetts. The company purchased lands from the Indians along the west side of Narragansett Bay. When the boundary line between Connecticut and Rhode Island was decided in 1662, their territory was, at their request, placed under the government of Connecticut. In 1665 the Royal Commission forced the company to return its lands to the Indians on repayment of their price.

Atkinson, Edward, born in 1827, of Massachusetts, economist, is author of many pamphlets on banking, the currency, foods, the tariff, and the labor and other social questions.

Atlanta, capital of Georgia, was laid out in 1845 and incorporated in 1847. During the Civil War the city was the centre of important military operations. It was the scene of a sanguinary engagement July 22, 1864, between Sherman's army of the Tennessee numbering three corps and Hood's corps of Johnston's army, 45,000 strong, in which the Confederates were defeated and driven back to their intrenchments within the town. Atlanta was afterward besieged by Sherman and captured upon Hood's abandoning it, September 2, 1864. In the battle of July 22, Hood began the attack by falling upon Hardee on Sherman's left. McPherson gained a position upon a high hill, commanding the very heart of the town, and then the fight went on all along the line. Battery F, Second United States, was lost in a sharp skirmish on a country road and McPherson, riding to its assistance, was killed. The battle lasted over four hours. At four o'clock Hood plunged into the remnant of McPherson's line and drove it back 400 yards, carrying two important batteries in the face of a murderous fire. Schofield's batteries were hurried up to maintain this desirable position and aid the Fifteenth Corps to regain its lost ground at any cost. This move was successful. Hood retreated to his intrenchments having lost all his guns except the two advance ones. Sherman lost 3722 men and Hood many more. Atlanta became the capital of Georgia in 1878.

Atlantic Cable, was projected by Cyrus W. Field in 1854. In that year he obtained a charter from the Legislature of Newfoundland for a fifty years' exclusive right to the laying of a cable from Newfoundland to Great Britain and from the Continent of America to Newfoundland. The New York, Newfoundland and London Telegraph Company was occupied two years in completing the connection between America, at Cape Breton, and Newfoundland. In 1856 Field organized the Atlantic Telegraph Company. The first two attempts at connecting the two continents, in 1857 and the first time in 1858, failed. The third attempt, late in 1858, was successful but lasted only a few months. Then the Civil War suspended operations. In 1865 the "Great Eastern" laid 1200 miles, when the cable snapped. In 1866 two thousand miles were safely covered and the Atlantic Cable was established.

Attainder. During the Revolution bills of attainder were frequently passed by State Legislatures, and were productive of much evil. Accordingly, the Constitution provided that neither Congress nor the State Legislatures should thereafter pass any such acts.

Attorney-General. Colonies and States had their Attorneys-General before 1789. The Judiciary Act of that year, organizing the Federal judiciary under the new Constitution, provided for an Attorney-General of the United States, to act as government counsel, with a salary of $1500. At first he had little to do, and could practice for himself; but he was always a member of the Cabinet. In 1858 he was provided with an assistant. In 1861 he was given charge of U. S. district attorneys and marshals. In 1870 the office was organized as the Department of Justice. (For a list of the Attorneys-General see Cabinets.)

Attucks, Crispus, of Massachusetts, a mulatto, the first killed in the "Boston Massacre" of March 5, 1770. His funeral was conducted with great public ceremony.

Auditors of the Treasury. The auditor was, from 1782, the third officer of that department. The first auditor dates from September 2, 1789; the second auditor from March 3, 1817; the third auditor from March 3, 1817 (appointed in lieu of the Accountant of the War Department, created by Act of Congress, May 8, 1792); the fourth auditor and fifth auditor, March 3, 1817; the sixth auditor, July 2, 1836.

Audubon, John J. (1780–1851), an American naturalist, born in Louisiana, was devoted especially to ornithology. His magnificent work, the "Birds of America," brought him great fame and admission to membership in many learned societies.

Augur, Christopher C., born in 1821, soldier, served in the Mexican War as aid to General Caleb Cushing. In 1861 he was appointed major; as brigadier-general commanded a division at Cedar Mountain, where he was severely wounded. He was made major-general in 1862. Commanded the left wing of the army at Port Hudson. After the close of the war he was commandant of various military departments. Retired in 1884.

Augusta, Me., was founded as "Cushnoc" shortly after 1629. It was devastated in the second Indian War and was not again permanently settled until 1754. It was incorporated in 1787, and became the capital in 1832.

Augusta, Fort. In 1720 a certain Dr. Noyes erected at his own expense a strong fort on the Kennebec River, in Maine, which he called Augusta. In 1756–57 Colonel James Burd built a fort at Shamokin, in Georgia, and called it Augusta. It was for the protection of the colonists against the Indians, and was garrisoned by the king's troops. It was attacked by the Indians in 1764, but without success.

"Augusta Chronicle," the second newspaper established in Georgia. It was first issued by J. E. Smith, in 1785, at Augusta. It was afterward consolidated with the *Constitutionalist* and called the *Chronicle and Constitutionalist*, under which title it is still published daily, tri-weekly and weekly.

Aurora, a Dutch communistic settlement on the Oregon and California rivers, twenty-nine miles south of Portland, Ore. It is also called Dutchtown, and was founded in 1855 by Dr. Keil, a Prussian, who had also established the Bethel community in Missouri in 1844.

Austerfield, a small hamlet in the north of Yorkshire, England, whence came a number of the Pilgrims, the most notable among them from this town being William Bradford, who was born at Austerfield in 1590.

Austin, Benjamin (1752–1820), of Massachusetts, merchant, a political pamphleteer during the Revolution and writer of many fierce newspaper articles against the Federalist Party during the administration of John Adams.

Austin, Stephen F. (about 1790–1836), of Texas, pioneer. Obtaining from the Mexican government the confirmation of a grant to his father of land in Texas, he induced a large number of Americans to emigrate thither. In 1835 he became commander of the Texan Revolutionists and went to Washington to secure recognition from the Government of the United States. He died soon after his return.

Austin, Tex., was chosen as the capital of the Republic of Texas in 1839. For a brief period in 1842 this position was disputed with Houston, but Austin retained it, and since the annexation of Texas in 1845 has been capital of the State.

Austria-Hungary. A commercial treaty was concluded between the United States and Austria-Hungary in 1829. A convention relative to disposal of property was concluded in 1848, another relative to extradition in 1856, and a third concerning the rights, privileges and immunities of consuls, July 11, 1870. By a convention concluded September 20, 1870, the rights of naturalization were recognized of citizens of both countries after a residence of five years and legal naturalization. A convention relative to trade-marks was concluded November 25, 1871.

Avalon, the name of a colony established in Newfoundland in 1623 by George Calvert, first Lord Baltimore. He visited the colony himself in 1627, remaining there a few weeks. The colony was established under the royal charter and was so called after Avalon, in Somersetshire, England. Subsequently Calvert, becoming dissatisfied with this colony, obtained the grant which resulted in the founding of Maryland.

Averell, William W., born in 1832, of New York, cavalry officer, was ordered to frontier duty in 1857, where he saw much Indian fighting. In 1861 as colonel he commanded the cavalry in the defence of Washington. In March, 1863, he began the series of cavalry raids in Virginia and West Virginia that have made him famous. He attained the rank of brevet major-general.

Averysboro, N. C. Near this place on March 15, 1865, Slocum's division of Sherman's Federal army encountered 9000 Confederates under Hardee, who was marching to join Johnston. Hardee was posted in a swampy neck, and the Federals, after a severe conflict, succeeded in dislodging him. They, however, suffered most in killed and wounded. Hardee retreated in the night toward Smithfield.

Ayllon, Lucas Vasquez de (d. 1526), Spanish adventurer, was a member of the Superior Court of Santo Domingo. He sent an expedition to Florida in 1520 under Gordillo, who landed in latitude 33° 30′. In 1526 he sailed himself, landed at Santee, proceeded northward and founded a settlement on the later site of Jamestown, which was soon abandoned. He died there.

Ayres, Romeyn B. (1825–1888), of New York, soldier. In the Civil War he took part in the battles of Antietam, Fredericksburg, Chancellorsville, Gettysburg, and in the final movement against Richmond.

Azilia, Margraviate of, a grant secured by Sir Robert Montgomery in 1717 from the Lords Proprietors of Carolina. It included the districts between the Altamaha and Savannah rivers.

College of the Pacific
Stockton, Calif.

B.

Babcock, James F. (1809–1874), of Connecticut, journalist, was a prominent Whig till 1854, when he joined the Republicans, whose war policy he ably supported in the *Palladium*, but afterward joined the Democrats.

Babcock, Orville E. (1835–1884), officer of engineers, was at the siege of Vicksburg in 1863, and was an aide to General Grant from 1864 till 1869. He superintended the construction of many public works in Washington.

Bache, Alexander Dallas (1806–1867), of Philadelphia, scientist, is best known by his valuable work as superintendent of the Coast Survey, which office he held from 1843 till his death.

Bache, Sarah (1744–1808), of Philadelphia, only daughter of Benjamin Franklin, was active in aid of the suffering soldiers in 1780, having more than 2000 women sewing for the army under her direction.

Backus, Isaac (1724–1806), of Massachusetts, was pastor of a Baptist church in Middleborough from 1756, and for thirty-four years a trustee of Rhode Island College, now Brown University, and an influential delegate to the Massachusetts Convention of 1788. He wrote a history of the New England Baptists.

Bacon, Leonard (1802–1881), of Connecticut, was pastor of the First Congregational Church in New Haven fifty-seven years, and was one of the founders of the *New Englander* and *The Independent*.

Bacon, Nathaniel (about 1630–1677), was born in England, and became a planter in Virginia and member of the Governor's council. The disaffection with Governor Berkeley's measures found a natural leader in Bacon, who had conducted in an efficient manner a threatening Indian war. Bacon, proclaimed a rebel in May, 1676, was tried and acquitted, and was soon in command of an expedition against the Governor, in the course of which Jamestown was burned. The revolutionary party seemed to be in the ascendant, but the sudden death of Bacon was soon followed by its collapse.

Bacon's Rebellion. In July, 1676, Governor Berkeley, of Virginia, had become exceedingly unpopular because of his inefficiency in protecting the settlers from Indian ravages, his tendency to restrict the franchise and institute high tax rates. The people therefore, led by Nathaniel Bacon, a popular lawyer, took up arms, ostensibly against the Indians, but in reality in order to resist the Governor and bring him to terms. Berkeley was compelled to make concessions, dismantle the forts, dissolve the old assembly and issue writs for a new election. But he did not keep faith with the insurgents. Consequently a desultory war broke out in the course of which Jamestown, then the capital of the colony, was burned. Berkeley was forced to take refuge on some English vessels. Bacon died in 1677 and the Rebellion ended for want of a leader.

Badeau, Adam, born in 1831, soldier, was severely wounded at Port Hudson in 1863. He was military secretary to General Grant from 1864 to

1869, and consul-general at London from 1870 to 1881. He published a book on Grant's military career.

Baden. A convention for the extradition of criminals was concluded between the United States and Baden, January 30, 1857. By treaty in 1868 a naturalization agreement was reached between the two countries.

Badger, George E. (1795–1866), of North Carolina, was four years in the State Legislature and five years a Judge of one of its Superior Courts,—was Secretary of the Navy under President Harrison, 1841, and U. S. Senator from 1846 to 1855. He was a member of the Secession Convention of 1861, in which he spoke ably in defence of the Union.

Bailey, Gamaliel (1807–1859), of New Jersey, journalist, an active anti-slavery agitator. From 1836 to 1844 he, with James G. Birney, published the *Cincinnati Philanthropist*, whose publication office was three times sacked by a mob, and, from 1847 till his death, the *National Era* at Washington, in which "Uncle Tom's Cabin" originally appeared.

Bailey, Joseph (1827–1867), of Wisconsin, military engineer, as lieutenant-colonel accompanied the army under General Banks in the Red River Expedition, in which he distinguished himself by conceiving and executing in twelve days the celebrated dam by which he saved Admiral Porter's fleet and for which he received the thanks of Congress and the brevet rank of brigadier-general.

Bailey, Theodorus (1805–1877), naval officer, was active in the Mexican War on the Pacific Coast, and was second in command in Farragut's fleet which captured New Orleans in 1862.

Bainbridge, William (1774–1833), commodore, began life as a sailor at the age of fifteen, and had several impromptu encounters with British vessels before he was appointed to the navy in the war with France, 1798. In the Tripolitan War in 1803 he commanded the "Philadelphia," which in 1804 was wrecked. Bainbridge was held in captivity for over a year by the Tripolitans. His great exploit was in the War of 1812, when as commander of the famous "Constitution" he defeated and captured the British "Java," December 26, 1812. His later service was in the navy yards, in Mediterranean ports and as naval commissioner.

Baird, Henry M., born in 1832, of New Jersey, was graduated at the University of the City of New York in 1850. Afterward studied in Greece. In 1859 became professor of Greek in Princeton College; subsequently a professor in the University of the City of New York. He has written valued histories of the Huguenots.

Baird, Spencer F. (1823–1887), of Washington, D. C., naturalist, in 1878 he succeeded Professor Joseph Henry as secretary of the Smithsonian Institution, and from 1871 was U. S. Commissioner of Fish and Fisheries, for his work in connection with which he received several medals and decorations from foreign powers, and membership in many learned societies.

Baker, Edward Dickenson (1811–1861), attained distinction in Illinois as an eloquent orator, a lawyer, and Whig Congressman in 1843–49. He commanded a brigade in the Mexican War, and afterward settled in California. Removing to Oregon he was a Republican U. S. Senator in 1861. He was a colonel in the Civil War, and while commanding the Federal troops in the unfortunate battle of Ball's Bluff, October 21, 1861, he was killed in front of his men.

Baker, Lafayette C. (1826–1868), as Chief of the U. S. Secret Service during the Civil War, displayed great daring and energy, and frustrated many conspiracies against the government.

Baker, William M. (1825–1883), author and clergyman, was pastor from 1850 to 1865 in Galveston, where he wrote in secret "Inside: a Chronicle of Secession." Was a pastor in South Boston from 1874 till his death.

Baldwin, Abraham (1754–1807), of Georgia, was chaplain in General Greene's army from 1777 till the close of the war. As a member of the Legislature of Georgia he was the originator of the University of Georgia and was its first president. Was in Congress from 1785 to 1799, a member of the Federal Constitutional Convention of 1787, and U. S. Senator from 1799 till his death.

Baldwin, Henry (1780–1844), represented Pennsylvania in the U. S. Congress as a Federalist from 1817 to 1822. He was a Justice of the U. S. Supreme Court from 1830 to 1844.

Baldwin, Roger S. (1793–1863), of Connecticut, jurist, in 1839, jointly with John Quincy Adams, argued the "Amistad" case before the U. S. Supreme Court. He was Governor of Connecticut in 1844 and 1845.

Ball, Thomas, born in 1819, of Massachusetts, sculptor, has executed statues of almost all the public men of the United States, the noblest being that of Webster in Central Park, New York City.

Ballot. The first instance of the use of the ballot in American elections was in the choice of a pastor by the Salem Church on July 20, 1629. In 1634 it began to be used in elections of the Governor of Massachusetts. In 1639 a ballot with some restrictions was instituted in the fundamental orders of Connecticut. In 1629 the ballot was used in some municipal and ecclesiastical elections in the Netherlands, and seems not to have been used in England. It may, therefore, have been introduced by imitation of the Dutch, but this is not yet proved. Voting by ballot was made obligatory by the constitutions of Pennsylvania, New Jersey and North Carolina, adopted in 1776. Open voting long prevailed in some of the Southern States, but the ballot system has long been generally in vogue except in Kentucky, where the *viva voce* method prevailed till 1890 for local and State elections. Representatives in Congress are elected by ballot under the provisions of an Act of Congress of 1875. In Alabama, Florida, Indiana, Kansas, Kentucky, Louisiana, Nevada, North Carolina, Pennsylvania, Tennessee and Texas, there is a constitutional provision requiring the Legislature to vote *viva voce*. In 1888 the Australian ballot system was adopted at Louisville, Ky., and in Massachusetts. With more or less variation in the form a large majority (37) of the States have now (1894) followed this plan of voting, the exceptions being the Carolinas, Georgia, Florida, Louisiana, Texas and Idaho.

Ballou, Hosea (1771–1852), of Massachusetts, clergyman, prominent in the Universalist denomination, and pastor of one of its churches in Boston for more than thirty-five years.

Ball's Bluff, Va. Here, October 22, 1861, Colonels Baker and Devens, with 1900 Federal soldiers of McClellan's army, fell in with a Confederate ambush and were utterly routed. Devens had been sent to reconnoitre and capture, if possible, a supposed Confederate camp near Leesburg. The camp could not be found and Devens sent to Stone, his superior, for further orders. Baker was sent to join him, arriving in time to share the defeat. The Confederates fought from the shelter of the woods. The Federal troops were driven over the Bluff and many killed in a hand-to-hand fight, among them Colonel Baker, ex-Senator from Oregon.

Balmaceda, José M. (1840–1891), was President of Chili from 1886 to 1891. During the Chilian Revolution U. S. Minister Egan favored the government of Balmaceda, and incurred the displeasure of the provisional government, or congressional opposition.

Baltimore. (See Calvert.)

Baltimore, Md., was founded in 1729–30. At the outbreak of the Revolution it had 6000 inhabitants. In 1777 a mob assailed a Tory editor (Goddard). In 1812 there was a more serious outbreak against a Federal paper, Hanson's *Federal Republican*. In 1814 the British were repulsed from the city in the battle of North Point and the bombardment of Fort McHenry. On April 19, 1861, a body of Federal troops on their way to Washington were attacked in Baltimore by a mob and a number of citizens and soldiers were killed. On May 13 General Butler took military possession of the city. He was succeeded by General Banks and later by General Dix. Population in 1860, 212,418; in 1890, 434,151.

Bancroft, Edward (1744–1820), an American of literary and scientific tastes residing in England, during the Revolutionary War, through friendship with Deane and Franklin obtained information which he sold to the British government.

Bancroft, George (1800–1891), the most famous American historian, was born in Worcester, Mass., the son of a clergyman. He was graduated from Harvard College and studied extensively in Germany. Returning, he taught, and became active as a Democratic politician. In 1834 he published the first volume of a history of the United States, which speedily attained enormous popularity. The volumes appeared successively from this time to 1882. Under Polk Bancroft was Secretary of the Navy, 1845–46, established the Naval Academy at Annapolis, and caused the seizure of California. From 1846 to 1849 he was Minister to Great Britain; from 1867 to 1874 to Germany. His history is still the most important history of the United States by a single author. The last portion was separately published as a History of the Formation and Adoption of the Constitution. His narrative is learned, picturesque and ardently patriotic.

Bancroft, Hubert H., born in 1832, from youth a resident of California, has gathered an enormous library of material relating to the history of the

COLONIAL GOVERNORS.

James Oglethorpe. Peter Stuyvesant.
Sir Henry Vane. Josiah Winslow.
William Penn.
Lord Baltimore. John Winthrop.
Marquis de Montcalm. Sir Walter Raleigh. Capt. John Smith.

Pacific Coast, and published in thirty-nine volumes a comprehensive and valuable history of the same.

Bandelier, Adolph F. A., born in Switzerland in 1840, has distinguished himself as a student of American archæology, as an explorer for the Archæological Institute of America in New Mexico, Arizona, Mexico and Central America, and as a writer upon these subjects.

Bank of North America, chartered by Congress at Philadelphia, December 31, 1781, upon the suggestion of Robert Morris. It also received a charter from Pennsylvania in 1783. Morris believed this national bank would relieve the financial situation.

Bank of the United States vs. Halstead. This case came before the Supreme Court of the United States on a certificate of division from the Circuit Court of Kentucky in 1825. Certain property, including real estate, was exposed to sale for debt, but, less than three-fourths of its appraised value being bid, it was not sold. The Supreme Court decided that it had jurisdiction in a case to which the Bank of the United States was a party, and that a law which forbade sales of land under execution for less than three-fourths of its appraised value did not apply to writs of execution issued by Federal courts.

Bank of the United States vs. Planters' Bank of Georgia, an important Supreme Court case. This was a suit brought by the Bank of the United States for payment of a promissory note of which it was the endorsee for the Planters' Bank of Georgia. The State held stock in the latter bank. The case was tried in the Circuit Court where there was a division of opinion as to jurisdiction. The Supreme Court decided in 1824 that if a State became a party to a banking or commercial enterprise, the State could be sued in the course of the business; also that the Circuit Court had jurisdiction in such matters.

Bankruptcy. The Constitution of the United States gives Congress power to establish uniform laws on the subject of bankruptcy throughout the United States. This power has been exercised but three times. On April 4, 1800, a bankrupt act was passed by Congress, which remained in force until repealed in December, 1803. Another was passed on August 19, 1841, and repealed in 1843. The third, called the Lowell Act, was passed on March 2, 1867, and repealed in 1878. During the remainder of our history all matters relating to bankruptcy have been under the control of State laws.

Banks. Nearly all the colonies emitted paper money (bills of credit), and frequently these bills were issued under the forms of banking. The English government opposed these schemes. In 1781 the Continental Congress chartered the Bank of North America, but its power to do so was doubted, and the bank was chartered by Pennsylvania in 1783. Up to 1791 the only banks in the United States were this and two others, one in Boston and one in New York. In 1791, at the instance of Alexander Hamilton, Secretary of the Treasury, Congress, against considerable opposition, incorporated the Bank of the United States, with a capital of $10,000,000. The United States was to subscribe $2,000,000 of this. The charter was to run twenty years. The bills of the bank were to be receivable in payment of dues to the government, and it had the power to establish branch banks. The power of Congress to incorporate such a bank was denied by Jefferson and others. But Hamilton argued that such powers were implied in the very nature of a sovereign government, and were conferred by the clause in the Constitution giving Congress power to pass "all laws necessary and proper for carrying into execution" the enumerated powers. This view was upheld by the Supreme Court in the case of McCulloch *vs.* Maryland, which established the constitutionality of the Bank Act. The first bank of the United States led a prosperous and useful existence till 1811, when its charter expired, Congress refusing to recharter it. During the crisis of the War of 1812 only State banks, mostly ill-regulated, existed. In 1816 the second Bank of the United States was chartered, with a charter running twenty years and a capital of $35,000,000, four-fifths of it in government stocks. The government was to have the appointment of five of the twenty-five directors, and the bank was to have the custody of the public funds. In 1829 President Jackson, angered by the bank's refusing a political favor, began a series of attacks upon it. In 1832 Congress passed an act renewing its charter. Jackson vetoed it. In the election of 1832 Jackson was victorious over the Whigs and the bank, which he considered, and had indeed forced to be, dangerously implicated in politics. In September, 1833, by his orders, the Secretary of the Treasury caused the government deposits to be diverted from the bank, and lodged in State banks (called "pet banks"). (See art. Deposits.) The Senate's protests were unavailing. In 1836 the bank's charter expired. Tyler, in 1841, vetoed two bills to revive it, and in 1846 the Independent Treasury system, already tried in 1840–41, was permanently established. From 1836 to 1863 State banks alone existed. In the earlier part of this period they were often uncontrolled by the State governments and quite unsound, banks being established and bills issued by adventurers possessing no capital to sustain them. New York provided a system of State supervision, which was in part the germ of the national bank system of 1863. In that year, February 25, the National Bank Act was passed. It permits any five persons to establish a national bank and, on depositing United States bonds with the Comptroller of the Currency, to issue bank notes to an amount not exceeding ninety per cent. of the par value of those bonds. The notes so issued are guaranteed by the government, which inspects the banks from time to time, and are receivable in payment of taxes. On March 3, 1865, an act was passed imposing a tax of ten per cent. on the circulation of State banks. On September 30, 1892, there were 3773 national banks in the United States, and 3191 State banks.

Banks, Nathaniel P., born in 1816, originally a machinist, was Representative from Massachusetts from 1853 to 1857. In 1855 he was chosen Speaker, after a contest lasting more than two months, on the 133d ballot. He was Governor of Massachusetts in 1858, 1859 and 1860. As major-general in the Civil War he fought the indecisive battle of Cedar Mountain and took Port Hudson, but was unsuccessful in the Red River Expedition of 1864. Again a member of Congress from 1865 to 1873; from 1877 to 1879; and from 1889 to 1891.

Banks, Savings. The first incorporated in the United States was the Boston Provident Savings Institution, incorporated December 13, 1816. The Philadelphia Savings Fund Society went into operation the same year, and was incorporated in 1819. In 1818 savings banks were incorporated in Baltimore and Salem, Mass., and in 1819 in New York, Hartford, Conn., and Newport and Providence, R. I. There are now more than a thousand, with deposits amounting to more than $450,000,000.

Baptists. In most of the colonies the Baptists were persecuted. In Rhode Island they were especially numerous. They had much to do with that agitation for religious liberty which culminated in the passage of the first amendment to the Constitution of the United States. In 1762 there were fifty-six Baptist churches in the region now occupied by the United States; in 1792, 1000; in 1812, 2433; in 1832, 5322; in 1852, 9500; in 1872, 18,397. According to the census of 1890, there were in that year, of all varieties of Baptists, 41,629 church organizations, with 3,594,093 communicants. In 1845 the Baptists split into a northern and a southern body, because of differences arising out of the question of slavery.

Baranoff, Alexander Andrevitch (1746–1819), a Russian trader, founded a trading-post at Behring Strait in 1796, and was Governor of Russian America till his death.

Barataria, pirates of, a band of Louisiana outlaws, who, under their chief Lafitte, rendered General Jackson material assistance in his Louisiana and New Orleans campaign in 1815. They had refused offers from the British.

Barbary Powers. (See Algerine War, Tripoli, Tunis.)

Barbour, James (1775–1842), Governor of Virginia from 1812 to 1815; Senator from that State from 1815 to 1825; Secretary of War from 1825 to 1828; then for a year Minister to England.

Barbour, Philip P. (1783–1841), brother of the preceding, was a Representative from Virginia from 1814 to 1825, and from 1827 to 1830. He was Speaker of the House of Representatives from 1821 to 1823, and a Justice of the Supreme Court of the United States from 1836 to 1841.

Barlow, Arthur (1550–1620), was sent out by Raleigh in 1584, in command of an expedition of discovery preparatory to colonization. He explored Pamlico and Albemarle Sounds, in company with Philip Amidas, and brought home favorable reports.

Barlow, Francis C., general, born 1834, as colonel distinguished himself at Fair Oaks, as brigadier-general at Antietam, Chancellorsville and Gettysburg, and commanded a division with great success at Spottsylvania Court House. Since the war has been Secretary and Attorney-General of New York.

Barlow, Joel (1754–1812), born in Connecticut, was graduated at Yale College and, as one of the "Hartford Wits," distinguished himself in literature, especially by the publication of his epic poem, "The Vision of Columbus," in 1787. Going abroad as a land-agent in 1788, he engaged in

Republican politics in England and France, negotiated the treaty with Algiers in 1795, and devoted himself for several years to literary and mercantile pursuits, residing at Paris. Other poems of his were "Hasty Pudding" and "The Columbiad." In 1805 he returned to America. Appointed in 1811 minister to Napoleon, he died in Poland in 1812. Life by Todd.

Barnard, Frederick A. P. (1809–1889), an eminent educator, president of the University of Mississippi from 1856 to 1861 and of Columbia College from 1864 to 1889, held also many governmental appointments of an educational nature.

Barnard, Henry, born 1811, an eminent reformer of educational methods, was from 1867 to 1870 U. S. commissioner of education, having previously been school commissioner of Rhode Island and Connecticut. A prolific and influential writer on educational matters.

Barnburners, a faction of the Democratic Party in New York State, so called from an alleged eagerness for radical measures, in allusion to the story of the Dutchman who burned down his barn to clear it from rats. The election of Polk in 1844 resulted in a split of the party in New York into two factions, the "Barnburners," representing the Van Buren wing and opposing the extension of slavery in the territories, and the "Hunkers," representing the administration and its views. In 1848, in the Democratic National Convention there were contesting delegations from New York representing the two factions. Unable to secure complete recognition the Barnburners joined in the Free-Soil Convention, voted for Van Buren, and so helped to elect Taylor. The breach between Barnburners and Hunkers was healed in 1852, more or less perfectly.

Barnes, Joseph K. (1817–1883), surgeon-general U. S. A. from 1863 to 1882, founded the Army Medical Museum and the invaluable library of the surgeon-general's office.

Barney, Joshua (1759–1818), a naval officer in the Revolutionary War, distinguished himself by gallantry and by various adventures, and in 1782 commanded the "Hyder Ali" in its capture of the "General Monk." From 1794 to 1800 he was in the naval service of the French Republic. In 1814 he was appointed to the command of the flotilla which was to defend Chesapeake Bay, and was severely wounded at the battle of Bladensburg.

Barré, Isaac (1726–1802), a British colonel, member of Parliament from 1761 to 1790, obtained great popularity in America by his opposition to the Stamp Act and to the American policy of Lord North's administration.

Barren Hill, Pa., twelve miles from Philadelphia. In the Revolutionary War, the Americans, commanded by Lafayette, eluded an attempt of Howe to capture them at this point, May 20, 1778.

Barron, James (1769–1851), commodore in the U. S. Navy, commanded the "Chesapeake" when the "Leopard" attacked and captured her, in 1807. Barron was tried by court-martial, found guilty of negligence in preparation, and suspended for five years. In 1820 he killed Commodore Decatur in a duel arising out of this trial.

Barrowists, the followers of Henry Barrow, or Barrowe, a church reformer of the latter part of the sixteenth century. They advocated church government by elders, and freedom of religious thought within certain limits. Their creed resembled somewhat that of the modern Congregationalists, and the Pilgrim Fathers and the Congregational Church of New England sprang from them. (See Brownists.)

Barrundia, José M., Guatemalan revolutionist, sailed from Acapulco, Mexico, to San José, Guatemala, in an American merchant vessel (1890). At San José, the Guatemalan authorities, in an attempt to arrest him on board the steamer, killed him. U. S. Minister Mizner and Commander Reiter, U. S. Navy, refused to interfere, since international law conceded jurisdiction in such cases to the authorities of the country. The Navy Department censured Reiter.

Barry, John (1745–1803), born in Ireland, an active commander in the Revolutionary navy. In the "Lexington" he captured the "Edward," the first British war-vessel captured by a commissioned officer of the U. S. Navy. In 1781, in the "Alliance," he captured the "Atalanta" and the "Trepassy." On the revival of the navy in 1794 he was named senior officer, with the rank of commodore.

Barry, William T. (1785–1835), born in Virginia, attained distinction in Kentucky politics, and was Postmaster-General to Jackson from 1829 to 1835. He was the first Postmaster-General who was admitted as a member into the Cabinet.

Bartholdi, Frédéric, born 1834, French sculptor, executed, at the instance of the French-American Union, the colossal statue of "Liberty Enlightening the World," which has been placed on Bedloe's Island to adorn New York harbor.

Bartlett, Josiah (1729–1795), a physician of New Hampshire, was a member of the Continental Congress, and signed the Declaration of Independence. Afterward he was Chief Justice of his State, and from 1790 to 1794 was its President or Governor.

Bartlett, William Francis (1840–1876), a Massachusetts officer in the Civil War, especially conspicuous for gallantry in action, left his class at Harvard to enter the army as a private in 1861, and rose before the end of the war to be a brevet major-general. He was wounded at Yorktown and Port Hudson, and taken prisoner at Petersburg.

Barton, Clara, born in Massachusetts in 1830, bore an important part in caring for the wounded on the battle-fields of the Civil War, and again in the Franco-German War. In 1881 she became president of the American Red-Cross Society, and in 1884 represented the government at the red-cross conference at Geneva.

Basques. An ancient race dwelling in the Pyrenees. Basques are said to have visited the American coasts before Columbus, in the pursuit of whales or of the fish of the banks of Newfoundland. It is not improbable, but cannot be said to have been proved to general satisfaction.

Bassett, Richard (d. 1815), was a member of the Constitutional Convention of 1787, and a signer of the Constitution. From 1789 to 1793 he was a Senator from Delaware, and from 1798 to 1801 governor of that State.

Bates, Edward (1793–1869), born in Virginia, became a prominent lawyer in Missouri. Having warmly opposed the repeal of the Missouri Compromise, he was a somewhat prominent candidate for the Republican nomination to the presidency in the Chicago Convention of 1860. He was attorney-general under Lincoln from 1861 to 1863.

Bates, Joshua (1788–1864), born in Massachusetts, engaged in business in London and became senior member of the firm of Baring Brothers & Co. When the Boston Public Library was started he gave it about $100,000.

"Battle of the Kegs," a celebrated humorous poem of the Revolutionary War, written by Francis Hopkinson. Its theme was an unsuccessful attempt of the Americans, in January, 1778, to destroy the British shipping at Philadelphia by floating down combustibles from above.

Baton Rouge, La., capital of the State since 1849, was taken by a part of Farragut's fleet, in May, 1862, immediately after his capture of New Orleans. On August 5 General Williams was attacked there by the Confederate General Breckenridge, but the attack was repulsed, the ram "Arkansas" failing to support it. General Williams was killed.

Batture Cases. Some fifteen years before the cession of Louisiana to the United States, one Gravier had purchased a plantation along the Mississippi adjoining New Orleans. Portions of it had been cut up into lots and formed the village of St. Mary. Meantime an alluvial deposit or river beach had begun to form along the levee of the Gravier plantation and was used as a boat landing by the citizens of St. Mary, though the batture, under the law, still formed a part of the Gravier estate. This estate was purchased in 1808 by Edward Livingston, of New York, who immediately began improvements on the batture for his own private ends. The people raised a great outcry, but Livingston obtained a favorable verdict and proceeded with his improvements. Finally, however, the territorial court, in 1809, decided to appeal to President Jefferson, on the ground that the batture was public property under a French law which gave alluvions to the government. By Jefferson's orders, he having a private grudge against Livingston, the latter was dispossessed of the batture. Livingston immediately brought suit against Jefferson and the United States Marshal. The suit against the President was not allowed, but the Supreme Court decided that the batture be restored to Livingston.

Baum, Friedrich, lieutenant-colonel of the Brunswick dragoons, German mercenaries in Burgoyne's expedition, was attacked by Colonel Stark at Bennington, Vt., August 16, 1777, completely defeated and mortally wounded.

Bavaria. A convention for the abolition of the *droit d'aubaine* was concluded with Bavaria in 1845; a convention for the extradition of criminals in 1853, and a naturalization treaty in 1868.

Bay Psalm Book, the first book (except an almanac) printed in the English-speaking parts of America, was printed at Cambridge in 1640.

Bay State, a name given to Massachusetts, the early title of which was "The Province of Massachusetts Bay."

Bayard, James A. (1767–1815), born in Philadelphia, settled in Delaware as a lawyer. He represented Delaware in the House of Representatives from 1797 to 1803, and in the Senate from 1805 to 1813. He was one of the chief leaders of the Federalists in Congress, and in 1801 had a principal part in persuading the other Federalist Congressmen to vote for Jefferson rather than Burr when the election of a President fell to them. He was one of the five American negotiators who concluded in 1814 the treaty of Ghent. His sons and grandson represented Delaware in the Senate from 1836 to 1845, and from 1851 to 1885.

Bayard, Nicholas (1644–1707), born in Holland, but brought to New Amsterdam in infancy, became secretary of the province in 1672; Mayor of New York and a member of the Council in 1685. He was imprisoned by Leisler and later sentenced to death on accusation, but was finally released.

Bayard, Thomas F. (grandson of James A.), born in Delaware in 1828, practiced law in Philadelphia and Wilmington from 1851 to 1869. From 1869 to 1885 he was Senator from Delaware, and was one of the most able and prominent of the Democratic Senators. In 1877 he was a member of the Electoral Commission which decided the disputed Hayes-Tilden election. In 1881 he was president *pro tempore* of the Senate. In 1880 and again in 1884 he had many votes in convention as a candidate for the Presidency. In 1885 President Cleveland appointed him Secretary of State, in which office he served with credit till 1889, pursuing constantly a pacific policy toward foreign nations. In 1893, when the grade of ambassador was for the first time established in the American diplomatic service, he was appointed our representative in England with that title, and was the first to bear it.

Bayard vs. Singleton, North Carolina. This was a suit for the recovery of certain property, tried before the Court of Appeals of North Carolina in 1787. The property in question had been confiscated and sold to the defendant under an act of the legislature passed during the Revolution, authorizing the confiscation of property belonging to an alien. Counsel for the defendant moved the suit be dismissed in accordance with an act of the legislature of 1785 which "required the courts, in all cases where the defendant makes affidavit that he holds the disputed property under a sale from a commissioner of forfeited estates, to dismiss the case on motion." This the court refused emphatically and Judge Ashe boldly pronounced that act of legislature "unconstitutional and void." Judgment was, however, found for the defendant on the ground that aliens cannot hold land, and if they purchase, the land is forfeited to the sovereign. This is one of the earliest instances of a court's pronouncing upon the constitutionality of an act of the legislature. Ashe's decision is therefore important.

Bayonne Decree, a decree issued on April 17, 1808, by the Emperor Napoleon, in the course of his attempts to reduce England to terms by destroying the commerce of neutral powers like the United States. On pretext of falling in with the embargo policy of the American government, he ordered that all American vessels which should enter the ports of France,

Italy and the Hanse Towns should be seized, "because no vessels of the United States can now navigate the seas without violating the law of the said States."

Bayou Têche Expedition, an expedition sent up the Bayou Têche by General Banks in April, 1863. It completed the conquest of all Louisiana west of New Orleans and south of the Red River.

Bean's Station, Tenn. On December 14, 1863, after Longstreet had raised the siege of Knoxville, 4000 Union cavalry under Shackelford here fought Longstreet's cavalry under Gracie.

Bear Flag War, an insurrection against the Mexican government in California, raised in June, 1846, by a small body of settlers from the United States. The insurrection is supposed to have been fomented by Captain John C. Frémont, then in California with a small force of United States troops. A dozen Americans seized some government horses, and then, reinforced by others, seized Sonoma, and raised a flag bearing a figure of a bear. A republic was proclaimed. A force of the Californian government was defeated. Captain Frémont joined the revolutionary forces with his troops. In July, the Mexican War having begun, Sloat raised the American flag at Monterey, and the Bear Flag War became merged in the American operations for the conquest of California.

Beaufort, N. C., was captured by Burnside's troops on April 26, 1862.

Beaufort, S. C., was occupied by the Federal forces on December 6, 1861, having been abandoned by the Confederates after the naval fight at Hilton Head.

Beaumarchais, Pierre A. C. de (1732–1799), the brilliant author of the "Barbier de Séville" and the "Mariage de Figaro," rendered highly valuable services to the American cause in the Revolutionary War, persuading the French government to send the Americans large amounts of money, arms and ammunition, and extensively using his own credit in their behalf. The debt of the American government to him was never discharged.

Beauregard, P. Gustave T. (1818–1893), born in Louisiana, was graduated at West Point in 1838. He was employed in the engineer service of the United States until 1861, when he resigned, and entered that of the seceded States. Placed in command of the defences of Charleston, he opened fire on Fort Sumter on April 12, 1861. With General J. E. Johnston he won the victory of Bull Run on July 21. In the spring of 1862 he was ordered to Tennessee. When General A. S. Johnston was killed at Shiloh Beauregard succeeded him in the command, but was forced to retire, and subsequently to evacuate Corinth. From September, 1862, to April, 1864, he defended Charleston against General Gillmore and Admirals Dupont and Dahlgren. In May, 1864, he aided Lee at Petersburg; in the autumn he aided in the vain attempt of the Confederates to stop Sherman's march through Georgia. He surrendered with Johnston in April, 1865. He was afterward manager of the Louisiana State lottery.

Beaver Creek, Md., scene of a skirmish on July 10, 1863, when, on General Lee's retreat from Gettysburg, Sedgwick's corps came upon his rear-guard.

Beaver Dam, Upper Canada. At the end of Dearborn's campaign, Colonel Boerstler, with a force of 540, sent out from Niagara to Beaver Dam, was defeated and forced to surrender by a British and Indian force of 260, June 24, 1813.

Beaver Dam Creek, Va. In the "seven days'" fighting after Fair Oaks, General A. P. Hill's corps, while waiting for the arrival of Jackson, attacked McCall's division of McClellan's army in a strong position at Beaver Dam Creek, June 26, 1862, and were repulsed with heavy loss.

Bedford, Gunning, Jr. (1747–1812), a Delaware lawyer, represented Delaware in the Continental Congress from 1783 to 1786. He was a member of the Constitutional Convention of 1787, and signed the Constitution.

Beecher, Henry Ward (1813–1887), son of the eminent Rev. Dr. Lyman Beecher, and from 1847 to his death pastor of a great congregation in Brooklyn, had always an active part in public affairs. In 1863 he made many speeches in England, endeavoring to influence English public opinion in favor of the Northern cause in the Civil War.

Behaim, Martin (1459–1506), a Nuremberg cosmographer, resided in Lisbon and Fayal from 1480 to 1490, was a friend of Columbus, and shared his views as to the possibility of reaching land by sailing westward. A globe which he constructed after returning to Nuremberg is a famous and valuable record of geographical knowledge.

Behring. (See Bering.)

Behring Sea Question. Soon after the acquisition of Alaska by the United States the Pribylov Islands, which are the breeding-grounds of the fur seal, were leased to the Alaska Commercial Company, who were to have a monopoly of seal-killing, under stringent regulations designed to prevent the extermination of the seals. In spite of the vigilance of the government in guarding the islands, depredations increased, American and Canadian vessels pursuing the seals upon the open sea. In 1886 the American government set up the claim that Behring Sea was *mare clausum* and asserted its jurisdiction over the eastern half of it. Russia had purported to grant such rights of jurisdiction when ceding Alaska in 1867, yet in 1822 the United States had protested against Russia's claim to have rights of sovereignty over the sea, outside the usual three-mile limit of territorial jurisdiction. In consequence of the new doctrine, many seizures of Canadian and American sealers were made by a government vessel. Great Britain claimed damages. After much negotiation, mainly between Secretary Blaine and Sir Julian Pauncefote, it was agreed to submit to arbitration the questions of the rights of the United States in Behring Sea and of the regulations necessary for the protection of the seals if it were decided that the United States had not exclusive jurisdiction over the matter. Two arbitrators were to be appointed by the United States, two by Great Britain, and one each by the President of the French Republic, the King of Italy and the King of Sweden and Norway. The arbitrators appointed by these respectively were: Justice John M. Harlan of the Supreme Court, Senator John T. Morgan, Lord Hannen, Sir John S. D. Thompson, Baron de Courcel, the Marquis

Emilio Visconti-Venosta, and Gregers W. W. Gram. The tribunal began its sessions at Paris on March 23, 1893, and rendered its decision on August 15. It decided against the American claim to exclusive jurisdiction of any sort over the waters of Behring Sea outside the three-mile territorial limit, established a close season for seals in those waters from May 1 to July 31, and forbade pelagic sealing within sixty miles of the Pribylov Islands, sealing in steam vessels or with fire-arms. These regulations were to be carried out by the British and American governments concurrently.

Belcher, Jonathan (1681–1757), of Massachusetts, was Governor of Massachusetts from 1730 to 1741, when he was removed. In 1747 he was appointed Governor of New Jersey, which he ruled judiciously until his death.

Belgium. Commercial regulations were effected by the United States with Belgium by the treaty of 1845, the convention of 1858 and that of 1863, the treaty of July 20, 1863, the treaty of 1875, and the convention of 1884. Naturalization rights were recognized by the convention of November 16, 1868, and consular rights by the conventions of December 5, 1868, and of March 9, 1880. The extradition of criminals was regulated by the conventions of 1874 and 1882.

Belknap, Jeremy (1744–1798), of Massachusetts, clergyman and historian, was for twenty years pastor of a church in Dover, N. H., and, from 1787 till his death, of the Federal Street Church, Boston. He wrote an excellent history of New Hampshire in three volumes, and in 1791 founded the Massachusetts Historical Society.

Belknap, William W. (1829–1890), of Iowa, became major-general in the Civil War. From 1869 to 1876 he was Secretary of War in President Grant's Cabinet. He was impeached in 1876 for receiving bribes, but resigned a few hours before the resolution for impeachment passed the House. He then claimed not to be impeachable, and enough Senators took this view to prevent his conviction.

Bell, Alexander Graham, born in Scotland in 1847, physicist, came to the United States in 1872. Inventor of the telephone, which he first exhibited publicly at Philadelphia in 1876.

Bell, John (1797–1869), was born at Nashville, and graduated at the university of that city. He had been a lawyer and State Senator before he entered the House of Representatives as member from Tennessee in 1827. He served there until 1841, being Speaker in 1835–37. He was one of the founders of the Whig party. In 1841 he was Secretary of War, and in 1847–59 he was U. S. Senator from Tennessee. When the conservatives, under the name of the Constitutional Union party, decided to make a campaign for the Presidency in 1860, Bell was their candidate, and the Bell and Everett ticket received the electoral votes of three States.

Bellamy, Edward, born in 1850, of Massachusetts, for several years was assistant editor of the *Springfield Union*. Is a contributor to various magazines, and the author of "Looking Backward," which has made him famous.

Bellamy, Joseph (1719–1790), of Connecticut, theologian, was pastor of the Congregational Church in Bethlehem, Conn., from 1740 till his death, where he established a divinity school, in which he trained many of the most eminent ministers of New England.

"**Belleview Palladium**," the first newspaper issued in Nebraska. It was published at Belleview in 1854, and continues at the present time under that title.

Belligerent Rights were accorded to the Confederacy by a proclamation issued by the Queen of Great Britain recognizing the existence of war between the United States and the so-called Confederate States, and the right of each to the exercise of belligerent powers on the ocean, but not recognizing the national independence of the latter, and enjoining neutrality on her own subjects. Similar recognitions of belligerent rights were made by France and the other chief commercial powers of Europe, and by Brazil.

Bellingham, Richard (1592–1672), colonial Governor of Massachusetts, came to America in 1634. In 1635 was made deputy-governor, and Governor in 1641 by a majority of only six votes over Winthrop. In all he served thirteen years as deputy-governor and ten as Governor; was opposed to innovations in religion, and especially severe toward the Quakers.

Bellomont, Earl of (Richard Coote) (1636–1701), was an English politician, appointed by William III. Governor of New York and Massachusetts in 1695. He arrived in 1698, and addressed himself to the suppression of piracy and illegal trade, both rife in the colonies. The capture of the notorious pirate Captain Kidd fell during his administration.

Bellows, Henry W. (1814–1882), of New York, clergyman, became pastor of the First Congregational (Unitarian) Church of New York City in 1839. In the Civil War he was president of the U. S. Sanitary Commission.

Belmont, August (1816–1890), of New York, financier, came to the United States in 1837. Was appointed Minister to Holland in 1854. Was a liberal patron of the fine arts.

Belmont, Mo., a small town occupied by a detachment of Confederates from General Polk's army. It was destroyed, and the Confederates driven to the Mississippi River by General Grant, November 7, 1861.

Beltrami, Giacomo C. (1779–1855), explorer, was exiled from Italy, and came to the United States in 1821. He ascended the Mississippi River and discovered one of its principal sources.

Bemis Heights. (See Saratoga.)

Benjamin, Judah P. (1811–1884), was born at St. Croix, in the West Indies, of English Hebrew descent. He was educated at Yale, and as a lawyer became the head of the Louisiana bar. He was Whig U. S. Senator from that State, 1853–61. He sided with the Confederates, and entered President Davis' Cabinet, serving in turn as Attorney-General, Secretary of War, and Secretary of State. On the collapse of the Confederacy he made his escape to England, and was soon equally famous for his grasp of English law. He became a Queen's Counsel, and died in Paris.

Benjamin, Park (1809–1864), of New York, was editor or co-editor of the *New England Magazine*, the *American Monthly Magazine*, Horace Greeley's *New Yorker*, and other journals, and a contributor to many others.

Benjamin, Samuel G. W., born in Greece in 1837, author, was U. S. Minister to Persia from 1883 to 1885. His contributions to periodicals have been very numerous.

Bennet, or Bennett, Richard, was sent by the Commonwealth in 1651 as Commissioner to Virginia, of which he was soon after elected Governor, retiring in 1655.

Bennett, James Gordon (1795–1872), of New York, journalist, came to America in 1819; established the *Herald* in 1835. He first introduced the "Money Article," the employment of regular European correspondents, and the systematic sale by newsboys. During the Civil War he employed sixty-three war correspondents. The *Herald* sometimes yielded him an income of $100,000 a year.

Bennington, Battle of, August 16, 1777. As he marched southward from Canada, General Burgoyne sent 500 Germans under Colonel Baum to seize the American stores at Bennington. Not daring to take the offensive, Baum awaited attack on the bank of a stream. The Americans under Stark outnumbered the British two to one, but were inferior in drill and equipment. Half their force, whom Baum took to be Tories, got to a position in his rear. Being attacked both in front and in rear, the Germans were routed completely. Just at that moment 500 German reinforcements came, but this was offset by the appearance of 500 fresh men under Colonel Warner. Only sixty or seventy Germans reached camp. Out of their thousand 207 were killed and 700 captured. The American loss was fourteen killed and forty-two wounded.

Benton, Thomas Hart (1782–1858), was born in North Carolina, and settled early in Tennessee. He became a lawyer and a member of the Legislature and acquired the title of colonel in the War of 1812. Though an ardent supporter of Jackson in later times, he had a personal encounter with him in Nashville in 1813. He now became a journalist in Missouri, and served that State uninterruptedly as U. S. Senator from 1821 to 1851. During this long period he was second in prominence only to the famous trio, Clay, Calhoun and Webster. He played a distinguished part in securing favorable land laws, in opening the West and in furthering post-roads. His conservatism in finance earned for him the title of "Old Bullion." He championed Jackson during the latter's Presidency, and was active in procuring the passage of the *Expunging Resolutions* (which see). Later he was a vigorous opponent of Calhoun. He was in 1853–55 a member of the House of Representatives, but was defeated as candidate for Governor of Missouri in 1856. He published in 1854–56 his "Thirty Years' View," or historical memoirs; his "Abridgment of the Debates of Congress" was published in fifteen volumes. (Life by Roosevelt.)

Bentonville, N. C. Here, during his march from Savannah through the Carolinas, Sherman, at the head of 65,000 National troops, encountered

24,000 Confederates under Johnston. A battle took place March 18, 1865, Johnston having come up in great haste from Smithfield, intending to surprise Sherman. The latter, however, was ready for him and Johnston was thrown on the defensive near Mill Creek. Johnston was partially defeated and retreated in alarm to Smithfield.

Bering, or Behring, Vitus (1680–1741), Danish navigator in the Russian service. In 1728 Peter the Great sent him on an expedition in the course of which he discovered the strait which bears his name.

Berkeley, George (1684–1753), the celebrated philosopher, was dean of Derry in Ireland. In his advocacy of education in the Bermudas, he sailed thither, and reached Newport *en route* in 1729. His plans miscarried, but he remained in Newport until 1731, returning then to Great Britain, where he became bishop of Cloyne. His interest in American matters was evinced by his famous lines, "Westward the course of empire," etc., and more practically by the gift to Yale of his farm near Newport, as well as by gifts of books to Yale and Harvard.

Berkeley, Sir William (about 1610–1677), was an English courtier, who in 1642 was appointed Governor of Virginia. He continued in this office, with the exception of an intermission during the Cromwellian *régime*, until 1677. His gloating remark over the colony's backward condition in education and a free press is well known, and his oppression evoked a caustic comment even from Charles II. His inefficiency in conducting the relations with the Indians led to an armed uprising in 1676 under Nathaniel Bacon. This was suppressed after Bacon's death, but Berkeley was soon recalled.

Berlin Arbitration. (See San Juan question.)

Berlin Decree, The, was issued by Napoleon November 21, 1806, and declared the British Islands in a state of blockade. It forbade commerce with them and trade in their merchandise and declared all merchandise belonging to Englishmen or transported from England lawful prize. Its effect was to inflict great injury on the American carrying trade.

Bermuda Hundred, Va., a position selected by Butler, who, in 1864, commanded the army of the James, numbering about 25,000 Federals, where he might intrench himself and await Grant's arrival. In the vicinity of this position there was constant fighting between Butler's troops and those of the Confederate Beauregard, whose forces were 20,000 strong. The fighting continued from May 16 to 30. On the sixteenth Heckman's brigade was destroyed by the Confederates, who were then pushing on to Bermuda Hundred, when Ames and Gillmore came up and Beauregard's plans miscarried. On the nineteenth the Confederates assaulted the Federal rifle pits under Ames and Terry, but without success. Skirmishing continued until the thirtieth, when the Confederates desisted. Bermuda Hundred was a valuable position, since it was very near both Richmond and Petersburg.

Bernard, Sir Francis (1714–1779), royal Governor of Massachusetts, was appointed in 1760 and removed in 1769 because of his incessant conflicts with the assembly. In 1768 he caused British troops to be quartered in Boston.

Bernard, Simon (1779–1836), French soldier and chief engineer in the U. S. Army, came to the United States with Lafayette in 1824. His principal work was the planning and construction of Fortress Monroe.

Berrien, John McPherson (1781–1856), of Georgia, statesman, was Judge of the Eastern District of Georgia from 1810 to 1821, U. S. Senator from 1825 to 1829 and from 1840 to 1852. Was Attorney-General under Jackson from 1829 to 1831, when he resigned.

Berry, Nathaniel S., (1796–1894), was elected Governor of New Hampshire as a Republican in 1861 and held office till 1863. Was earnest in support of the war.

Bethel, a communistic settlement, composed chiefly of Germans, in Missouri. It was founded in 1844 by Dr. Keil, a Prussian, and a number of the settlers were seceders from Rapp's colony of Harmonists at Economy. These colonists purchased 4000 acres of land and immediately established communistic industries, manufactories, tanneries, distilleries, etc. Keil afterward went to Oregon, where he founded, in 1855, the Dutch communistic colony of Aurora, carrying with him about 400 of the 600 settlers at Bethel. The colony is governed by trustees who also plan the work of the community.

Bethlehem, Pa., was founded in 1741 by the Moravians. Lehigh University was founded in South Bethlehem in 1865.

Beverly, Robert (1675–1716), of Virginia, historian, was clerk of the council under Governor Sir Edmund Andros. Several editions of his "History of Virginia" have been published.

Beverly's Ford, Va., scene of a sharp cavalry fight during the Civil War, between Buford, Pleasonton and Gregg, commanding 9000 Federals, and Stuart leading 12,000 Confederates. Hooker had sent Pleasonton to find Stuart, who was said to be near Beverly's Ford. Pleasonton planned to surprise the Confederates, but his plans miscarried. Stuart was fully prepared for him. Pleasonton was badly beaten, though Stuart suffered severe losses also.

Bibb, George M. (1772–1859), of Kentucky, was three times chosen Chief Justice of the State. Was a member of the U. S. Senate from 1811 to 1814 and from 1829 to 1835. He was Secretary of the Treasury under President Tyler.

Bible Revision. On the invitation of the British committee for the revision of the Bible, a committee of United States scholars and divines was organized in 1871 and began active work in October, 1872. This committee was composed of twenty-seven members, who met each month in the Bible House, New York. Their intention was to adapt King James' version to the present state of the language. The revised New Testament was published in 1887. The revised Old Testament appeared in 1885.

Bible Societies. The first Bible Society of this country was founded at Philadelphia in 1808. It was quickly followed by others at Hartford,

Boston, New York and Princeton. May 11, 1816, the American Bible Society was organized at New York by a convention of representatives from thirty-five smaller societies, which felt the need of united and centralized effort. Nearly every denomination, except the Roman Catholic, was represented. Sectarian jealousy and party prejudice were laid aside in order to insure combined endeavors in promoting "a wider circulation of the Holy Scriptures without note or comment." The American Foreign Bible Society was established in 1836 by the Baptist denomination, which withdrew from the American Society because of some disagreement. The total issues of the American Bible Society from 1816 to 1892 have been 55,531,908.

Biddle, Clement (1740–1814), of Pennsylvania, "Quaker Soldier," was an officer in the Continental army from 1776 to 1780 and U. S. Marshal during the Whisky Rebellion.

Biddle, James (1783–1848), naval officer, in the War of 1812, in command of the "Hornet," captured the "Penguin." In 1817 he took possession of Oregon for the United States.

Biddle, Nicholas (1750–1778), of Philadelphia, naval officer, one of the first captains appointed by Congress in 1775. In 1778, while engaging the "Yarmouth," British, 64, his ship, the "Randolph," 32, blew up.

Biddle, Nicholas (1786–1844), after leaving Princeton entered the diplomatic service, and afterward edited the magazine, the *Portfolio*. He was a member of the Pennsylvania Legislature, and became a government director of the United States Bank and its president. In this latter position he was a central figure in the fierce struggle which Jackson waged with the bank. He resigned the presidency in 1839.

Bienville, Sieur de (Jean Baptiste le Moyne) (1680–1765), was a member of a noted French family of colonizers. He accompanied his brother Iberville to the Mississippi region, and in 1701 assumed the direction of the colony of Louisiana. In 1713 he was appointed Lieutenant-Governor of the colony, and in 1718 Governor, and in the same year he founded New Orleans. He was removed in 1720, but was re-appointed in 1733, returning to France in 1743.

Bierstadt, Albert, born in Germany in 1830, painter, was brought to the United States in 1831. Made extended tours in Colorado and California, obtaining there materials for his most celebrated pictures.

Big Bethel, Va. Here an unsuccessful attempt, directed by General Butler, was made by General Pierce, with four regiments, to dislodge outposts of Magruder's Confederate encampment at Yorktown, June 10, 1861. The Federal regiments, under Townsend and Bendix, *en route* for the Big Bethel camp, mistook each other for the enemy, and fired. This created great confusion. Pierce arrived and pushed on to the Confederate earthwork on Back River, destroying the camp at Little Bethel. The Federal troops crossed Back River and charged the earthwork, but were repulsed with considerable loss, Major Theodore Winthrop losing his life.

Big Black River, Miss. In this battle, which took place May 17, 1863, during Grant's pursuit of Pemberton toward Vicksburg, the Confederates were defeated, and lost heavily both in killed and captured. McClernand, swiftly following the retreating Confederates, came upon them drawn up on both sides of the Big Black River. McClernand led 10,000 Federals, Pemberton 8000 Confederates, his main command having gone on toward Vicksburg. McClernand began the fight. He was for a time unsuccessful, but Lawler, discovering a weak spot in the Confederate line, immediately took advantage of it and charged impetuously. The Confederates were routed.

Bigelow, John, born in 1817, of New York, in 1849 became, with William Cullen Bryant, joint owner of the *Evening Post*, and was managing editor till 1861, when he went to Paris as U. S. Consul, and was Minister to France from 1865 to 1867, when he became Secretary of State of New York. He is trustee under the will of Samuel J. Tilden and his literary executor. His chief literary work was the editing of the full text of Franklin's Autobiography.

"Biglow Papers," two series of extraordinarily brilliant political satires written by James Russell Lowell. The first, satirizing the Mexican War and contemporary politics, from the point of view of the New England Abolitionists, appeared (1846–1848) in the Boston *Courier* and the *National Anti-Slavery Standard.* The second, satirizing the South and contemporary politics during the period of Civil War and reconstruction, appeared (1861–1866) in the *Atlantic Monthly.* The papers are attributed to Hosea Biglow, a typical young Yankee farmer, Rev. Homer Wilbur, a typical old-school New England clergyman, and Birdofredum Sawin, a character intended to represent the non-Puritan element in the New England democracy.

Billeting Act, an act passed by Parliament in 1765 directing Colonial legislatures to make specific contributions toward the support of an army. Bernard, Governor of Massachusetts, caused it to be printed in the colony laws. It was resisted in New York and in South Carolina.

Bills of Credit. This was the term employed in the eighteenth century to indicate paper money issued by any government, and made a legal tender for debts. The Constitution of 1787 forbids any State to issue bills of credit, or to make anything but gold and silver a legal tender. This was done because of the discreditable and disastrous over-issues by the States during the twelve years preceding. A similar prohibition upon the Federal government was discussed but not incorporated in the Constitution. Hence, in 1862, the Federal government issued "greenbacks" which were to be a legal tender. (See "Legal Tender Cases.")

Bills of Rights. The first in America was the Declaration of Rights which accompanied the Virginia Constitution of 1776. It was the work of Colonel George Mason, and was largely based on the English Bill of Rights of 1688. Its phraseology was extensively followed in the constitutions of other States, most of which contained bills of rights, defining the rights of the individual citizen as over against his government. The Constitution of 1787 was strongly criticised for not including such a set of statements, and their absence made its ratification difficult. Accordingly the Federalists, in the First Congress, as they had promised, carried through amendments of this nature, and these now stand as the first ten amendments to the Constitution.

Biloxi, Miss, first settlement made in what is now Mississippi by white men, was founded in 1699 by Pierre Lemoyne d'Iberville.

Bingham, John A., born in 1815, of Ohio, lawyer, was a Republican member of Congress from 1855 to 1863 and from 1865 to 1873, and sat as judge-advocate at the trial of President Lincoln's assassins.

Binney, Horace (1780–1875), of Philadelphia, and an acknowledged leader of its bar. Such of his arguments as are in print are the admiration of the legal profession not only in this country, but in Great Britain, notably that in the case of Bidal *vs.* Girard's executors. He powerfully supported President Lincoln by his pamphlets on the right to suspend the writ of *habeas corpus.*

Birney, David B. (1825–1864), of Pennsylvania, soldier in the Civil War, became major-general and commanded the Third Corps at Gettysburg after General Sickles was wounded.

Birney, James Gillespie (1792–1857), was a graduate of Princeton, and a lawyer and politician in Kentucky. He became enthusiastically devoted to the Abolitionist cause, and was editor of the *Philanthropist.* He became secretary of the National Anti-Slavery Society, and when in 1840 and 1844 the Abolitionists, as the Liberty party, put a ticket in the field, he was their candidate for President.

Bishop Hill, in Henry County, Ill., a Swedish communistic settlement of seekers after religious freedom. The colonists left Sweden under the leadership of Eric Janson in 1846. Janson was murdered in 1850. The settlement did not prove a success and slowly decayed through financial mismanagement. It ceased to be a "community" in 1862.

Bishops. Few things more exasperated the colonists than the scheme of appointing and sending out a bishop from England. It is said that there was a project of making Dean Swift bishop of the American colonies. In 1771, at the instance of the clergy of New York and New Jersey, the plan was again urged. The clergy of Virginia generally assented. But throughout America the dissenters and the Episcopal laity opposed. After the Revolution the case was altered. The first Episcopal bishop, Samuel Seabury, of Connecticut, was consecrated by Scotch non-juring bishops in 1784. The Methodists began to use the term bishop in 1787. The first Catholic bishop, John Carroll, of Baltimore, was consecrated in 1790.

Bismarck, capital of North Dakota, dates its beginning from 1872.

Bissell, Wilson S., born in 1847, of New York, lawyer, in 1873 became a member of the law firm of Bass, Cleveland & Bissell in Buffalo, and was appointed Postmaster-General by President Cleveland in 1893.

Black, James (1823–1893), of Pennsylvania, reformer, was a leader in the organization of the Templars, was the first to propose a distinct Temperance party and in 1872 was its candidate for the Presidency.

Black, Jeremiah S. (1810–1883), of Pennsylvania, jurist, was one of the Judges of its Supreme Court from 1851 to 1857, became Attorney-General under Buchanan, serving as such till December, 1860, when he became his Secretary of State and exerted himself to save the government from falling into the hands of the secessionists. In 1861 and 1862 he was reporter of the U. S. Supreme Court.

Black Cockade, a badge worn first by the American soldiers during the Revolution, and later, during the hostility toward France occasioned by the X. Y. Z. dispatches, adopted by the Federalists as a patriotic emblem and as a rejoinder to the tri-colored cockade worn by the Republicans as a mark of affection toward France.

"**Black Friday,**" Friday, September 19, 1873, on which, with a great financial crash in Wall street, including the failure of Jay Cooke & Co., the leading American bankers, the panic of 1873 began. Also, Sept. 24, 1869.

Black Hawk (1767–1838), a noted Chief of the Sac and Fox Indians. He joined the British in the War of 1812. By the treaty of 1830 the tribes ceded all their lands east of the Mississippi, but their removal west was opposed by him and the so-called Black Hawk War ensued. On being completely defeated August, 1832, Black Hawk surrendered.

Black Hawk War. Under the provisions of the treaty with the chiefs of the Sac and Fox Indians at Prairie du Chien, July 15, 1830, their land east of the Mississippi was ceded to the whites. Black Hawk, a prominent chief, refused to submit to the treaty. In 1831 he made an attack upon some Illinois villages, but was driven off by a force of militia under General Gaines in June of that year. The next spring he returned with a strong force and began to massacre the whites. General Scott marched some United States troops against him. Black Hawk was defeated at the Wisconsin River July 21, 1832, by General Dodge and again, August 2, by General Atkinson at Bad Axe River. This ended the war.

Black Rock (near Niagara), was, in the War of 1812, bombarded by the British November 17, 1812. The barracks were fired, valuable property destroyed and a magazine exploded. No lives, however, were lost. Next year Lieutenant Colonel Bisshopp, with 400 men, crossed the Niagara July 11, 1813, to capture the stores and shipyard at this place. The attack at first was successful, but the Americans rallied and with the aid of friendly Indians drove the British back to their boats in confusion, with the loss of their commander. The total British loss was seventy; the Americans lost eight men and a large quantity of military stores. Later, General Riall, with 1000 British regulars and Indians, crossed the Niagara, December 30, 1813, and attacked the Americans, 2000 strong, at Black Rock and Buffalo. The American militia behaved in a cowardly manner and were forced back to Buffalo, which, however, was at once abandoned. The village was then plundered and burned, together with four war vessels. This ended the measures of retaliation for the burning of Newark.

"**Black Warrior,**" an American merchant vessel, seized and confiscated by Cuban customs officers in May, 1854. This seizure was used as an excuse for proposed filibustering expeditions against Cuba. Spain, however, made compensation for the seizure.

Blackburn, Joseph C. S., born in 1838, of Kentucky, served in the Confederate army through the war, and was a member of Congress from 1875 to 1885, since which he has been in the U. S. Senate.

Blackfeet Indians received their name after their separation from the Kena Indians and migration to the Missouri. Those in the United States are in Montana, and have been constantly at war.

Black's Reports, law reports of cases from the Supreme Court of the United States from 1861 to 1862, by Jeremiah S. Black. There are two volumes of these reports.

Blackstock Hill, Battle of, November 20, 1780. In the fall of 1780 the patriots of South Carolina became more active. At Blackstock Hill, General Sumter defeated Tarleton's cavalry, after a sharp encounter. The disgrace of Fishing Creek was thus wiped out.

Blackstone, William, died in 1675, a clergyman of the Church of England, and pioneer, was the first settler in Boston (1625). His land became the famous "Common;" he was afterward the first white settler of Rhode Island.

Bladensburg, Md., near Washington, laid out in 1742, is celebrated as the site, not only of the battle, but of the duelling-ground where many famous duels growing out of quarrels in Washington were fought, *e. g.*, that in which Barron killed Decatur in 1820. Toward the latter part of the War of 1812 General Ross and Admiral Cockburn with about 5000 men appeared in Chesapeake Bay to attack Washington. The American forces fell back to Bladensburg (four miles from Washington) and awaited the British. The Americans numbered about 7000 men, but were scattered and untrained. August 24, 1814, the British advanced to the attack. The American artillery held them in check for a time, but the troops rallied and pushed forward. The Americans fled in wild disorder; the confusion spread and soon General Winder, the American commander, gave orders for a general retreat. By this battle Washington was exposed to capture. The American loss was seventy-six men; the British more than 500 killed and wounded.

Blaine, James Gillespie (January 31, 1830–January 27, 1893), was born at West Brownsville, Pa. He was graduated at Washington College in Pennsylvania in 1847, and became a teacher. In 1854 he settled in Augusta, Me., and assumed the editorship of the *Kennebec Journal.* He was soon a power in State journalism and politics, was elected to the Legislature in 1858, and was chairman of the Republican State Committee. He entered Congress as a Representative from Maine in 1863, and acquired a brilliant reputation as an able and versatile debater and an aggressive party leader. These qualities with his knowledge of parliamentary law made him Speaker of the House for three terms, 1869–1875. In 1876–1881 he was United States Senator. This prominence and his "magnetic" character brought him to men's minds as a candidate for the Presidency. In 1876 he was one of the two leaders for the Republican prize; in 1880, while beaten himself by the persistency of the Grant advocates, he dictated the nomination of Garfield, and entered the latter's Cabinet in March, 1881, as Secretary of State. His interference in the Chilian-Peruvian imbroglio is a matter of history. He resigned office in December, 1881, soon after President Arthur's accession. In 1884 he was on the fourth ballot nominated to the Presidency, and between his advocates and those of Mr. Cleveland there ensued one of the most extraordinary and exciting personal campaigns on record. His reputation had been assailed before, particularly from his alleged connection with the Little Rock Railroad matter, and a formidable section of the Republican party bolted his candidacy. So much the more vigorous was the support of the many friends of the "Plumed Knight." The defection of the Mugwumps and the singular alliterative utterance of Mr. Burchard (see *Burchard*) are variously assigned as the cause of his loss of New York State by a small majority, and consequent loss of the election in the country at large. In 1889 he became Secretary of State in President Harrison's Cabinet. He will probably be best remembered in this office for his furtherance of the Pan-American conference and advocacy of reciprocity. He suddenly resigned in June, 1892, and was an unsuccessful candidate for the Republican nomination. He died at Washington. His political reminiscences and comments are given in his "Twenty Years in Congress" (published 1884–1886).

Blair, Francis Preston (1791–1876), was a prominent politician for half a century. As the editor of the *Washington Globe* he wielded a great influence in the Jacksonian wing of the Democratic party. After the political disintegration caused by slavery, he became one of the founders of the Republican party but avoided advocating a radical policy. Toward the close of his life he acted again with the Democrats.

Blair, Francis Preston (1821–1875), was the son of Francis P. Blair. He served in the Mexican War, after which he practised law and was a member of the Missouri Legislature. He was a Republican Congressman from Missouri in 1857–59 and 1861–63. He took an important part in saving Missouri for the Union at the opening of the war, and was afterward distinguished as a division and corps commander in the Vicksburg campaign and in Sherman's march through Georgia to the sea. Joining the Democratic party he was on its ticket with Seymour as unsuccessful candidate for Vice-President in 1868. His last important office was that of United States Senator from Missouri in 1871–73.

Blair, Henry W., born in 1834, of New Hampshire, Senator. In the Civil War he became lieutenant-colonel, and was twice severely wounded at Port Hudson. He was a Representative in Congress from 1875 to 1879 and U. S. Senator from 1879 to 1891. He introduced the so-called "Blair School Bill" which twice passed the Senate but failed in the House.

Blair, John (1732–1800), of Virginia, jurist, became a Judge of the Court of Appeals in 1777 and afterward Chief Justice; in 1780 Judge of the High Court of Chancery. He was a delegate to the Federal Constitutional Convention and a Justice of the Supreme Court of the United States from 1789 to 1796.

Blair, Montgomery (1813–1883), of Maryland, statesman, served in the Seminole War. Was Mayor of St. Louis in 1842 and Judge of the Court of

Common Pleas of Missouri from 1843 to 1849, but removed to Maryland in 1852. In 1861 he was appointed Postmaster-General by President Lincoln. His resignation was accepted in 1864, after which he acted with the Democratic party.

Blair Bill, a bill which passed the Senate in 1884 and 1886, for giving Federal money to States for purposes of education, in sums proportioned to their number of illiterates. It was introduced by Senator H. W. Blair, of New Hampshire. It failed in the House.

Blakeley, Johnston (1781–1814), of North Carolina, naval officer, was made master-commander in 1813 and appointed to the new sloop "Wasp," with which, in 1814, he captured the "Reindeer," after a severe action of nineteen minutes, for which Congress voted him a gold medal. After capturing several more vessels, the "Wasp" foundered at sea with all on board.

Bland, Richard (1710–1776), of Virginia, called the "Antiquary," was a member of the House of Burgesses from 1745 till the Revolution, and a very active patriot, and in 1774 a delegate to Congress.

Bland, Richard P., born in 1835, was a lawyer and business man and came into prominence as a Democratic Congressman from Missouri. Since 1873 he has been steadily a member of the Lower House, generally a leading member, and several times chairman of the important committee on coinage. He is one of the best-known advocates of the free and unlimited coinage of silver. He was a chief promoter of the Bland Act in 1875, and has championed the white metal persistently with or against the trend of his party or of the country.

"**Bland Dollar**," so called after Congressman Bland, of Missouri, author of the Bland Act of 1875, under the provisions of which the Secretary of the Treasury was to purchase each month sufficient bullion to coin 2,000,000 of silver dollars of 412½ grains each, to be considered a legal tender. Coinage began in 1878.

Blatchford, Samuel (1820–1893), of New York, jurist, was appointed Judge of the U. S. District Court for the Southern district of New York in 1867, and in 1882 an Associate Justice of the U. S. Supreme Court.

Blennerhassett, Harman (1764 or 1765–1831), was born in England. Becoming imbued with republican ideas, he disposed of his estates and came to the United States in 1797 and purchased an island in the Ohio River, upon which he erected a fine mansion. He became interested in the schemes of Aaron Burr, to which he contributed large sums and for complicity in which he was arrested on a charge of treason, but discharged. The proceedings ruined him.

"**Blessing of the Bay**," the first seaworthy vessel built in the United States. She was built at Mistick, Mass., for John Winthrop, and was launched July 4, 1631. She was used for a number of years in trade with the Connecticut colonies and the Dutch settlers of New York.

Block, or Blok, Adriaen, Dutch navigator, visited Manhattan (now New York) about 1613 and again in 1614 in the "Tiger," which being accidentally burned he built the "Unrest," a sixteen-ton yacht, in which he coasted as far north as Nahant, discovering the Housatonic and the Connecticut and the island which bears his name.

Blockade. At the outbreak of the Civil War the Federal government, in lieu of a competent navy, only twelve serviceable vessels being at home, fitted out a miscellaneous fleet of merchant craft for blockading the Confederate ports. The Confederate government had passed a law requiring every English vessel that entered its ports to bring arms and supplies as part of its cargo, and thus munitions were never lacking. Albemarle Sound and the ports of New Bern and Plymouth were the favorite entrances for blockade runners, many of whom were successful. The first naval expedition was against these places. West-bound blockade runners commonly went first to the British port of Nassau, in the Bahamas, and thence to Charleston or North Carolina ports. Charleston was blockaded in 1863, and blockade running became exceedingly hazardous thenceforth. United States cruisers exercised the right of stopping and searching neutral vessels in the manner usual in international war. Vessels captured because of attempts to break the blockade or to carry contraband goods, or as property of the enemy, were taken into port and submitted to the adjudication of the prize courts, as prizes of war. Congress passed no new laws establishing any new principles respecting condemnation; and the prize courts proceeded entirely upon the rules of international law. The capture of the brig "Amy Warwick" on the high seas, bound from Rio Janeiro to Richmond with a cargo of tobacco, first distinctly raised the question of the right of the United States to exercise war powers in suppressing the insurrection. The brig was captured as "enemy's property," since she belonged to persons at Richmond.

Blommaert, Samuel (about 1590–about 1670), Colonial patroon. In 1629 he, with Samuel Godyn, purchased of the natives most of what is now Delaware and planted a colony called Swaanendael which was soon utterly destroyed by the Indians.

Bloody Bill, sometimes called the Force Bill, passed by Congress March 2, 1833. Its aim was to enforce the tariff of 1832, which the Legislature of South Carolina had declared null and void.

Bloody Brook, Mass. (See Deerfield.)

Bloody Shirt. To wave the bloody shirt meant, in Congress or other places, to revive the memories of the Civil War by impassioned allusions. The term was mostly used in the times about 1880.

Blount, James H., born in 1837, of Georgia, was elected a Democratic Representative in Congress from 1873 to 1893. In March, 1893, he was appointed Special Commissioner to investigate affairs in Hawaii and the conduct of American officials there in connection with the then recent revolution in that government. In May he was appointed minister to the Hawaiian Islands, but returned in the autumn.

"Blue Laws." At the second stated meeting of the newly-formed General Court of New Haven, held in that town in April, 1644, it was ordered that "the judicial laws of God, as they were delivered by Moses," should be considered binding on all offenders and should be a rule to all the courts of the jurisdiction, "till they be branched out into particulars hereafter." These provisions have developed the current notions of New Haven's Criminal Code, and these notions have been greatly aided by the absurd code of "Blue Laws," published in a history of Connecticut by the Rev. Samuel Peters, an ingenious and highly unreliable writer. Here are specimens of the Blue Laws sometimes quoted:

"No one shall run on the Sabbath day, or walk in his garden, or elsewhere, except reverently to and from meeting."

"No woman shall kiss her child on the Sabbath or fasting day."

"No one shall read Common-prayer, keep Christmas or saints' days, make minced pies, dance, play cards, or play on any instrument of music except the drum, trumpet and jews-harp."

Blue Lights. During the second war with England, Decatur made several attempts on dark nights to escape from the blockaded port of New London (1813). He declared that his failure was due to signals of blue lights flashed from the shore to warn the British. This led to the opponents of the war being stigmatized as "Blue-light Federalists."

Blue Lodges, a secret pro-slavery order in Western Missouri, formed about 1854 to aid the Southern mission work of establishing slavery in Kansas. In March, 1855, they crossed the Missouri and forcibly deposited their ballots for the pro-slavery candidates.

Blunt, James G. (1826–1881), of Kansas, soldier, major-general in the Civil War, served in Arkansas and Missouri, which, after several engagements, he relieved of the Confederate invasion under Price.

Board of Admiralty, organized by the Continental Congress, October 28, 1779, from the earlier and more numerous Marine Committee. It consisted of two members of Congress and five others and had charge of all naval and marine affairs. It was abolished February 7, 1781, upon the creation of the Secretary of Marine.

Board of Trade and Plantations. Oliver Cromwell made some attempts to establish a board which should supervise and regulate the commerce of the colonies in America. No definite results were reached, however, until 1660, when Charles II. established two separate councils, one for trade and the other for foreign plantations. These were from 1672 to 1675 united. The "Board of Trade and Plantations" was established in 1695, and was the governing body having charge of the English colonies in America from that time to 1768, when the "Secretary of State for America" was called into existence. In 1782 the board was abolished.

Board of War. On June 12, 1776, the Continental Congress, urged by an appeal from Washington, established a Board of War and Ordnance, based upon the contemporary English Ordnance Department. It consisted of five members of the Congress, and John Adams was made chairman. October 17, 1777, it was resolved to create a Board of War, to consist of three members (later five), not delegates. The board had charge of all matters pertaining to war, including records, supplies, the raising of troops and money.

The original Board of War and Ordnance, however, continued to exist. In 1781 a Secretary of War was instituted, who in 1782 took the place of the board.

Body of Liberties, a code of 100 fundamental laws established by the General Court of Massachusetts in December, 1641. Hitherto there had been no written law in the colony, justice having been administered wholly upon principles of equity. The Body of Liberties was drafted by Nathaniel Ward, pastor of the church at Ipswich. It laid down the fundamental principles of the sacredness of life, liberty, property and reputation, and prescribed general rules for judicial proceedings.

Bohemia Manor, a grant of 5000 acres of land along the Elk River made by Lord Baltimore, in 1666, to Augustine Herman, a Bohemian surveyor, who promised therefor to make a map of Maryland. Herman obtained papers of denization and was naturalized with his family under the first act of that kind passed in the province.

Boisé City, Idaho, was first settled as a trading post of the Hudson Bay Company. The town was laid out in 1863 and became the capital of the State (then territory) in 1864.

Boker, George H. (1823–1890), of Philadelphia, author, wrote several successful plays and many patriotic lyrics. He was U. S. Minister to Turkey from 1871 to 1875 and to Russia from 1875 to 1879.

Bolivar, Simon (1783–1830), liberator, was the most prominent figure in the struggle of the Spanish South American provinces for independence, being at times absolute dictator. He had the warm sympathy of American public men.

Bolivia. A treaty of peace, friendship, commerce and navigation was concluded between the United States and Bolivia May 13, 1858. The rights of neutrals in this treaty were carefully explained.

Bollman's Case. Bollman was brought before the Supreme Court of the United States in 1807 on a writ of *habeas corpus ad subjiciendum*, charged with being implicated in a treasonable attempt to levy war upon the United States. (See Burr, Aaron.) The argument of the counsel for the defendant turned upon the authority of the Supreme Court to issue writs of *habeas corpus ad subjiciendum*, also upon the nature of a treasonable act. It was decided that the court could issue writs of *habeas corpus ad subjiciendum*, but judgment was found for the plaintiff for lack of precision in evidence, to prove the place of commission of the treasonable act. Also it was decided that a mere conspiracy to subvert the government by force is not treason; an actual levying of war is necessary.

Bonaparte, Charles J., born in Baltimore in 1851, lawyer, the only surviving grandson of Madame (Patterson) Bonaparte, has been prominent in the movement for civil service reform.

Bonaparte, Charles Lucien Jules Laurent (1803–1857), ornithologist, eldest son of Lucien Bonaparte, Napoleon's brother, came to Philadelphia and published several valuable works on his favorite science. In 1848 was a republican leader in Rome and vice-president of the constituent assembly.

Bonaparte, Elizabeth (Patterson) (1785–1879), wife of Jerome Bonaparte (youngest brother of Napoleon), to whom she was married in 1803 by Archbishop Carroll with all requisite legal formalities. She sailed for Europe in 1805, but the opposition of Napoleon prevented her landing and she was obliged to take refuge in England. The marriage was annulled by a decree of the Council of State, and she returned to America. Jerome married the Princess Caroline of Würtemberg.

Bonaparte, Jerome (1784–1860), King of Westphalia, youngest brother of Napoleon. His marriage with Miss Patterson, of Baltimore, in 1803 was declared null by Napoleon, who made him, in 1807, King of Westphalia. He commanded a division at Waterloo. From his exile at Trieste he returned to France and was made Field Marshal in 1850.

Bonaparte, Joseph (1768–1844), King of Spain, elder brother of Napoleon, was made King of Spain by Napoleon in 1808, but left it after his defeat by Wellington at Vittoria. He came to the United States after Waterloo and, except for a brief period, lived till 1841 in Bordentown, N. J., where he was very popular.

Bonaparte, Louis Napoleon. (See Napoleon III.)

Bonaparte, Napoleon. (See Napoleon I.)

"Bonhomme Richard," an old East Indiaman fitted up as a man-of-war by the French at L'Orient in 1779, and commanded by Paul Jones. She sailed from L'Orient under American colors, but with French instructions and accompanied by two French vessels, the "Alliance" and the "Pallas." Jones attempted to enter the harbor of Leith, Scotland, but was prevented by storms. On September 23 the vessels encountered a British merchant fleet, guarded by two British warships, the "Serapis" and the "Countess of Scarborough." The "Pallas" quickly captured the "Scarborough," a small twenty-gun vessel. Jones unhesitatingly attacked the "Serapis," though his vessel was far inferior at every point. He lashed the "Serapis'" bowsprit to the "Richard's" mizzenmast and raked the former's deck with musketry. The "Serapis" poured broadside after broadside into the "Richard." Finally a bucket of hand grenades, thrown down the "Serapis'" hatchways, compelled her commander to surrender. Jones transferred his crew to the "Serapis," and the "Richard" sank in a few hours.

Bonus Bill, a bill submitted by Calhoun, December 23, 1816, appropriating $1,500,000 "for constructing roads and canals and improving the navigation of watercourses." The bill was passed, being strongly supported by New York and the South. It was supposed the money would immediately be applied to the construction of a canal between Albany and the lakes. President Madison vetoed the bill during the last days of his administration, insisting that internal improvement measures needed a constitutional amendment. Accordingly New York State undertook the construction of the Erie Canal.

Bonvouloir, M. de, French diplomatist. His reports to Vergennes of his conferences with Franklin at Philadelphia in 1775 did much to bring about the French alliance.

Boone, Daniel (1735–1820), was born in Pennsylvania and died in Missouri. He was a daring and skillful hunter in North Carolina and in 1769 started for the region which is now Kentucky, thus becoming the pioneer in the settlement of that State. He founded Boonesborough on the Kentucky River and was for many years the chief hero among the many rude and picturesque figures of the frontier. He excelled especially in Indian warfare, the most striking episode of which was perhaps the battle of the Blue Licks in 1782. Countless stories are related of his adventures and hair-breadth escapes. His last years were passed in poverty, though a grant of lands was finally bestowed upon him by Congress.

Boonville, or **Booneville, Mo.** Here, June 17, 1861, Captain Nathaniel Lyon, commanding about 2000 Federal troops, defeated Price, the Confederate general, whose army numbered several thousand poorly armed and unorganized volunteers. This battle was the outcome of numerous secessionist plots fomented by Governor Jackson, of Missouri, and General Price. Lyon captured twenty prisoners, two six-pounder guns and the supplies of the Confederate camp.

Booth, Edwin (1833–1893), actor, first appeared as such at the Boston Museum in 1849. He was brilliantly successful, not only in the United States, but in England and Germany, in Macbeth, King Lear, Othello, Iago, Richard III., Shylock and other parts, and especially in Hamlet, with which his name is inseparably connected.

Booth, John Wilkes (1839–1865), actor, during the Civil War was a violent secessionist. On the night of April 14, 1865, he shot President Lincoln at Ford's Theatre, Washington. He was concealed for a time by friends in Maryland, but fled to Virginia, where he was shot in a barn by his pursuers, April 26.

Booth, Junius Brutus (1796–1852), actor, after establishing his reputation in England came to the United States in 1821, where, and in occasional visits to England, he greatly extended his fame.

Border Ruffians, a name applied to the pro-slavery men of Missouri who, in 1855 and after, during the struggle in Kansas, were accustomed to cross over into that State to carry elections and harass the anti-slavery settlers. The name was sometimes used by these men themselves and not always regarded as a term of reproach.

Border States, a name applied to the Slave States of Delaware, Maryland, Virginia, Kentucky and Missouri, as lying next to the Free States, and sometimes including North Carolina, Tennessee and Arkansas. These States were particularly anxious both before and during the Civil War for an amicable settlement of all difficulties. They originated the Peace Conference of 1861. Of the Border States only Virginia, North Carolina, Tennessee and Arkansas seceded.

Borie, Adolph E. (1809–1890), of Philadelphia, merchant, acquired a large fortune and gave large sums to aid soldiers in the Civil War. From March to June, 1869, he was Secretary of the Navy.

Borneo. A commercial treaty was concluded between the United States and Borneo in 1850.

Boroughs. William Penn's charter of the territory west of the Delaware River authorized him, in 1681, to erect the country, among other divisions, into boroughs similar to those of England. This system of boroughs continues in Pennsylvania to the present time, and exists also in New Jersey, Minnesota and Connecticut. In New Jersey boroughs were established in the early part of the last century; in Connecticut in the early part of the present century. Their growth was gradual. Beginning with 1619 Virginia had eleven boroughs. These were later reduced to two. Lord Baltimore's charter entitled him to create boroughs in Maryland. Gorges also established boroughs in Maine under his charter of 1639.

Boscawen, Edward (1711–1761), British admiral, distinguished himself at Porto Bello and Carthagena and in 1758 in conjunction with Lord Amherst reduced Louisbourg and Cape Breton.

Boston, capital of Massachusetts, was founded by John Winthrop and his company in 1630. The settlement grew in prosperity until the French and Indian War, when it suffered heavy exactions. Opposition to the measures of the British ministry began here. The Stamp Act and Tea Act aroused indignation. Troops were quartered in the town. On December 16, 1773, a party disguised as Mohawk Indians emptied three cargoes of tea into the harbor. The port was closed by the British Parliament June 1, 1774. The British army, besieged in Boston by the Americans from June, 1775, evacuated the town in March, 1776. The Constitution of the State was here adopted in 1780. In 1822 Boston became a city. From 1830 to 1860 it was regarded as the headquarters of the anti-slavery and other reform movements. The city was visited by a disastrous fire in 1872, which burned on two days, November 9 and 10, involving a loss of over $80,000,000. The population of Boston in 1708 was 12,000; 1719, 18,000; 1780, 23,000; 1800, 25,000; 1850, 139,000; 1875, 360,000; 1890, 448,477.

Boston Athenæum, a library supported by subscription and founded, with a governing board of trustees, April 7, 1807. When John Quincy Adams went as Minister to Russia he deposited his library in the Athenæum, nearly doubling its collection. A valuable collection of coins, antiques and curiosities is also contained in the Athenæum. It now possesses over 105,000 volumes.

"Boston" Case (1837). A Georgia fugitive slave escaped on the ship "Boston" bound for Maine and reached Canada. The Governor of Georgia charged the captain with slave-stealing and demanded his return as a fugitive from justice. The Governor of Maine refused, whereupon the Legislature of Georgia called upon Congress to so amend the laws as to compel the Maine Governor to comply. No action was taken.

"Boston Gazette," the second newspaper issued in the American colonies. It was begun December 14, 1719, by William Brooker, who succeeded John

Campbell as the postmaster of Boston. Campbell had founded the *Boston News Letter*, which now encountered its first opposition in the rival *Boston Gazette*. The latter journal was owned and conducted by five successive postmasters until 1739, when it was merged with the *New England Weekly Journal*, a paper started in 1727. This paper proved a sore trial to Campbell, the owner of the *Boston News Letter*, which had had a clear field for fifteen years.

Boston Massacre. During 1769 and the early months of 1770 continual quarrels and misunderstandings occurred between the Boston populace and the British soldiers stationed in the town, over the persistent non-observance of the navigation acts. In February, 1770, a press gang from the British frigate "Rose" boarded a ship belonging to Hooper, of Marblehead, and a riot followed. On the night of March 5, the ringing of fire bells brought together a large crowd and the usual collision with the soldiers took place. The soldiers fired. Three persons were killed and several others severely wounded. The news of the Boston Massacre spread rapidly, strengthening the revolutionary spirit. The soldiers were acquitted.

"Boston News Letter," the first genuine newspaper published in the United States. The first issue appeared at Boston April 24, 1704. The paper was a weekly, was edited and published by John Campbell, then postmaster at Boston, and was printed by Bartholomew Green. It was issued every Monday and appears to have been the outgrowth of a series of news letters from London, which Campbell, as controlling the news centre, in his capacity of postmaster, received from time to time and sent to the Governors of the several New England colonies. These letters were a digest of the happenings, political and social, in England and on the Continent, with here and there a suggestion as to the politics and government of the American colonies. The *Boston News Letter* consisted at first of two pages, eight by twelve inches. Its publication was suspended in 1776.

Boston Port Act, an act proposed in Parliament by Lord North and passed March 31, 1774, in retaliation for the destruction of cargoes of tea in Boston harbor. The act provided for the discontinuation of "landing and discharging, lading or shipping of goods, wares and merchandise at the town and within the harbor of Boston." Commerce was transferred to Salem and Marblehead. General Gage arrived to enforce this measure on June 1. Much indignation and sympathy were felt for the Bostonians throughout the colonies, and material aid in gifts was rendered them. Broadsides were forthwith issued in Boston and Worcester against the use of British goods.

Boston Public Library, authorized by an act of the Massachusetts State Legislature April 3, 1848, and formally opened in Mason street near its present site March 20, 1854. The second building was begun September 17, 1855, and was completed in 1858. Gifts of books and money have been made by a number of prominent New Englanders. The Library with eleven branches contains nearly 600,000 volumes. The new building is now (1894) nearly completed.

Boston, Siege of. Immediately after Lexington and Concord, Boston was invested by 16,000 Americans under General Ward. The first attempt to narrow the lines resulted in the defeat of the Americans at Bunker Hill (q. v.). On July 3 Washington succeeded Ward. Through the fall and winter he drilled his men and drew his siege lines closer. He waited only for ammunition and siege guns to begin more active operations. Having secured these in the early spring of 1776 from Ticonderoga (q. v.), he seized Dorchester Heights on the night of March 4, 1776. Here he commanded the city and the fleet, and on March 17 Howe, who had succeeded Gage, was obliged to evacuate Boston.

Boston University was chartered by the Methodists in 1869. Its school of Theology was founded in 1847, its Law School in 1872, its Medical School in 1873.

"Boston Weekly Post," an older paper under a new name. In 1735 Thomas Fleet became possessed of the *Boston Weekly Rehearsal*, which he continued under the name of the *Boston Weekly Post*. He declared himself of no party and invited contribution from all parties and upon all subjects. This paper was issued with considerable success until 1775, when it was suspended.

"Boston Weekly Post-boy," a newspaper founded at Boston in 1734 by Ellis Hushe, appointed postmaster that year. It was published in opposition to the *Boston Gazette* and continued until 1755, when it was suspended.

Botetourt, Norborne Berkeley, Baron (1717–1770), became colonial Governor of Virginia in 1768, and as such exerted himself to effect reconciliation between the colonists and the mother country. He was highly popular.

Botts, John Minor (1802–1869), of Virginia, statesman, was first elected to Congress in 1839. When President Tyler seceded from the Whig party Mr. Botts violently denounced him and thereafter supported Mr. Clay. During the Civil War he was a strong Unionist.

Boudinot, Elias (1740–1821), of New Jersey, was Delegate to Congress most of the time from 1777 to 1784, was its president in 1782 and as such signed the Treaty of Peace with England. He was a member of Congress from 1789 to 1795, Director of the Mint from 1795 to 1805, and was much interested in the education of the Indians and in missionary enterprises.

Boundaries. Colonial boundaries were often disputed, grants having been made by kings ignorant or careless of American geography. For these the tribunal was most commonly the Privy Council of the King of Great Britain. After the Revolution Congress took jurisdiction over them. The Articles of Confederation in 1781 provided an elaborate mode, modelled on English procedure under the Grenville Act of 1770, for selecting a court which should try such disputes between States. Since 1789 such cases have been within the jurisdiction of the Supreme Court, like other cases between States. (For the boundaries of the United States and their history, see Versailles, Treaty of, Annexations, Northeast Boundary and Northwest Boundary.)

Bounty Lands. On September 16, 1776, Congress passed a resolution, promising both commissioned and non-commissioned officers who would enlist in the cause of the Revolution certain "bounty lands," to be taken from the "Crown lands," or Northwest Territory, which was then claimed in portions by several States. Maryland protested vigorously against this resolution on the ground that she had no extra lands, and would therefore be unfairly taxed.

Boutwell, George S., born in 1818, cabinet officer, was a lawyer and Democratic member of the Massachusetts Legislature. By a coalition of the Free-soilers and Democrats he was elected Governor of Massachusetts in 1851 and 1852. He was a delegate to the Peace Conference, and was in 1862–1863 the first commissioner of internal revenue. He next served as Republican Congressman 1863–1869, and was one of the managers of the impeachment of President Johnson. In Grant's first administration Boutwell was Secretary of the Treasury 1869–73, and then became U. S. Senator, serving until 1877.

Bowditch, Nathaniel (1773–1838), of Massachusetts, mathematician. His greatest work was a translation of Laplace's "Mécanique Céleste," but his best known is the "American Navigator."

Bowdoin, James (1727–1790), of Massachusetts, statesman. In 1756 he became an executive councillor, in which capacity he opposed the encroachments of the governors. In 1775 he was president of the council; in 1779 presided over the State Constitutional Convention. In 1785 and 1786 he was chosen Governor, in which position he put down Shays' Rebellion.

Bowdoin College, (Congregational), was chartered in 1794 and opened in 1802 at Brunswick, Me. It was named in honor of Governor James Bowdoin, of Massachusetts. The Medical School of Maine, founded in 1820, is connected with this college.

Bowie, James (1790–1836), of Texas, soldier. A weapon which he used in a mêlée was the model of the celebrated "Bowie knife." He went to Texas about 1830 and was killed at the Alamo.

Bowles, Samuel (1826–1878), entered the office of the *Springfield Republican* at an early age, and in 1851 succeeded his father in the management of the journal. He made his paper one of the foremost organs of public opinion in New England, and acquired a national reputation as a journalist. He visited Europe and the Pacific slope on several occasions, and wrote accounts of his travels, including the work "Our Great West." He was a Republican in politics down to his support of Greeley's candidacy in 1872.

Bowyer, Fort (Mobile Bay), attacked September 14, 1814, by a combined land and naval force of British and Indians. They were repulsed with the loss of one vessel and 232 men. The Americans lost eight men.

"**Boxer,**" brig. (See "Enterprise.")

Boyd, Linn (1800–1859), of Kentucky, was first elected to Congress in 1835, was re-elected from 1839 to 1855, and was Speaker of the House from 1851 to 1855. He was afterward Lieutenant-Governor for one year.

Boydton Road, Va., a charge upon the Confederates by Ord's two divisions of Grant's army, then operating about Richmond and Petersburg, April 1, 1865. This was one of the closing battles of that famous campaign. The charge took place at dawn and was directed along the Boydton Road toward Hatcher's Run against the rear of the Confederate intrenchments. The lines were forced and several thousand prisoners captured.

Braddock, Edward (about 1695–1755), was an English general of the old school, who was sent by the government as generalissimo in America soon after the opening of the French and Indian War. He confidently expected to reduce the French posts, and marched from Virginia on Fort Duquesne, taking few precautions, and disregarding the advice of Washington and others. On July 9, 1755, his army was entrapped on the banks of the Monongahela near the fort by an inferior Franco-Indian force. Braddock had five horses shot under him and was mortally wounded in a contest in which he showed little generalship, but much bravery. He died four days later.

Braddock's Field (July 9, 1755). On May 10, 1755, General Braddock took command of 2200 men at Fort Cumberland to advance upon Fort Duquesne. The army moved slowly, clearing a way, and on July 7 was about eight miles from the fort. The fort was strongly situated and well garrisoned; but the commandant determined to strike a blow on the advancing English. On the morning of the ninth an ambuscading party of 900 left the fort. The British had passed the ford of the Monongahela, and were advancing through thick woods when they were assailed from all sides. They stood bravely, but could see no foe. Being huddled together they were fairly mowed down. Their courage at length forsook them—they broke and fled. The mortality was terrible. Of eighty-six officers sixty-three were killed and disabled. Of 1373 troops only 459 came off unharmed. The French loss was trifling. Colonel Washington distinguished himself by his bravery. Braddock was mortally wounded. Dunbar, next in command, insisted on retreat, and left the frontier unguarded.

Bradford, William (1588–1657), was born at Austerfield, in England, and was prominent in the company of Separatists, who, in 1607–08, left England for Holland. He was among the leaders of the *Mayflower* Pilgrims, and on the death of Carver, in April, 1621, was chosen Governor of the struggling Plymouth Colony. This post he retained, with a few intermissions, until his death. Governor Bradford was the author of a very valuable "History of the Plymouth Plantation" down to the year 1647. This volume, which had remained in manuscript, and had been frequently quoted, disappeared from Boston during the confusion of the Revolution, and was singularly discovered in England in the Fulham library in 1855, and printed the next year.

Bradford, William (1755–1795), of Philadelphia, jurist, in 1780 was appointed Attorney-General of Pennsylvania, in 1791 a judge of its Supreme Court, and from 1794 until his death, was Attorney-General of the United States.

Bradley, Joseph P. (1813–1892), jurist, was appointed an Associate Justice of the Supreme Court of the United States by President Grant in 1870, which office he held until his death. He was a member of the celebrated "Electoral Commission" of 1877, and is generally regarded as having given the casting votes which decided the contest in favor of Hayes.

Bradstreet, Anne (1612–1672), of Massachusetts, poetess, married Governor Bradstreet in 1628. Some of her poems were published, and received great praise from her contemporaries. They are interesting as the work of the first poetess of New England.

Bradstreet, John (1711–1774), soldier, served in Pepperell's regiment in the expedition against Louisbourg in 1745. In 1758 he captured Fort Frontenac, served with Amherst against Ticonderoga in 1759, and negotiated a treaty of peace with Pontiac in 1764. He was made major-general in 1772.

Bradstreet, Simon (1603–1697), colonial Governor of Massachusetts, to to which he came in 1630, in 1660 was sent to England to congratulate Charles II. on his accession, was Governor from 1679 to 1686, and again after Andros' recall till 1692. He was in the service of Massachusetts sixty-two years. He opposed the witchcraft delusion.

Bragg, Braxton (1817–1876), was graduated at West Point in 1837. In the Mexican War he was distinguished at the battle of Buena Vista. He resigned from the army, and on the outbreak of the Civil War joined the Confederates. He served at Shiloh and succeeded Beauregard in command in the West. In the summer of 1862 he invaded Kentucky, and was defeated at Perryville. He was defeated again at Murfreesboro', but in 1863 won the battle of Chickamauga. Grant defeated his army at the battles around Chattanooga, and General Bragg was removed from command. He served against Sherman toward the close of the war.

Bragg, Edward S., born in 1827, of Wisconsin, soldier. In the Civil War he rose to the rank of brigadier-general and was a prominent member of the Forty-fifth, Forty-sixth, Forty-seventh and Forty-ninth Congresses.

Branch, John (1782–1863), was Governor of North Carolina from 1817 to 1820. He was a Democratic U. S. Senator from 1823 to 1829, and was Secretary of the Navy in Jackson's Cabinet from 1829 to 1831.

Brandon or Brendon, Saint (fifth century), is related to have visited a Western land in which he traveled as far as a great river. In the early maps his country is represented west of the Cape Verde Islands and south of the Island of Antilia.

Brandywine, Battle of, September 11, 1777. On Howe's advance upon Philadelphia from the head of Chesapeake Bay, Washington took up a strong position at Brandywine Creek, though he had but 11,000 to oppose to Howe's 18,000. While Knyphausen engaged the centre, Cornwallis attempted a flank movement upon the American right. He met with obstinate resistance from Sullivan's division, which had formed a new front, but he forced it to retire. The American centre was now obliged to fall back; this movement was directed in a masterly way by General Greene. The right, attacked by Knyphausen in front and Cornwallis on the flank, also accomplished its retreat in good order. The British were thus masters of the field. It was a battle in which the flank movement was warranted, but it was met with a promptness and sagacity which saved the Americans from defeat. About 1000 Americans fell. The British losses slightly exceeded that number.

Brant, Joseph (1742–1807), chief of the Mohawk Indians, served in the British army during the Revolutionary War. He was active in the massacre at Cherry Valley and at Minisink in 1779. He led a tribe in St. Leger's expedition against Fort Stanwix in 1779. After the war he aided the U. S. Government in negotiating Indian treaties.

Brashear City, La., a battle of the Civil War, occurring during Banks' command of the Federal army in Louisiana, June 23, 1863. Banks had several times engaged Dick Taylor during this campaign and his outposts were stationed in Brashear, while Banks himself was in pursuit of the Confederates. Taylor, aware of the weakness of the Federal force, 2000 in all, eluded Banks, and joining Green and Mouton, together they hurried down to the town with 15,000 men. The Federals were easily defeated and the town captured, together with 1000 prisoners and large quantities of valuable stores. Five thousand refugee negroes were seized and returned to slavery.

Brattleboro, Vt., was first settled as a military post (Fort Dummer) in 1724.

Braxton, Carter (1736–1797), was a member of the Virginia Legislature from 1761 to 1771. He was one of the Virginia Committee of Safety, a delegate to the Continental Congress from 1775 to 1776, and signed the Declaration of Independence. He was a member of the Executive Council of Virginia from 1786 to 1791, and from 1793 to 1797.

Brazil. A commercial treaty was concluded between the United States and Brazil December 12, 1828. By the convention of January 27, 1849, Brazil agreed to pay 500,000 milreis to settle claims of American citizens. An agreement regarding trade-marks was made in 1878. A reciprocity treaty was concluded January 31, 1891.

Bread Riots. In 1837, during the period of general financial panic, prices rose enormously. Rents were exorbitant and flour was twelve dollars per barrel. During February and March the poor of New York held frequent riotous meetings, which culminated in violent assaults upon flour warehouses. In several instances storehouses were broken open and the mob helped themselves. The militia was called out to quell the disturbance.

Brearley, David (1745–1790), was an ardent patriot during the pre-Revolutionary movements. He served in the Continental army from 1775 to 1779. He was Chief Justice of New Jersey from 1779 to 1789 (see Holmes *vs.* Walton), when he became a U. S. District Judge. When a member of the Federal Convention of 1787, he zealously opposed the unequal representation of States. He signed the Constitution.

Breckenridge, John (1760–1806), was a member of the Kentucky Legislature from 1797 to 1800. In 1798, with Jefferson and Nicholas, he draughted the famous "Kentucky Resolutions" and introduced them in the Legislature. He was a Democratic leader in the U. S. Senate from 1801 to 1805, and was prominent in the legislation concerning the annexation of Louisiana. He was Attorney-General in Jefferson's Cabinet from 1805 to 1806.

Breckenridge, John Cabell (1821–1875), Vice-President of the United States, was a grandson of John Breckenridge. He fought in the Mexican War, and was a Democratic Congressman from Kentucky, 1851–55. He was elected Vice-President in 1856 on the ticket with Buchanan, and served from 1857 to 1861, and was the youngest man ever elected to the office. In 1860 he was the unsuccessful candidate for President of the ultra slavery wing of the Democratic party, and received seventy-two electoral votes. He was U. S. Senator in 1861, but joined the Confederates and was expelled from the Senate. He was at the battle of Shiloh in 1862, and commanded at the defence of Baton Rouge the same year. He led the right wing at Murfreesboro', was at Chickamauga and Chattanooga, gained the battle of Newmarket in 1864, and served at Cold Harbor, in the Shenandoah Valley, in Eastern Tennessee, and at Nashville. For a short time before the end of the Rebellion he was Confederate Secretary of War.

Breckenridge, William C. P., born in 1837, attained the rank of brigadier-general of cavalry in the Confederate service. He has represented Kentucky in the U. S. Congress as a Democrat since 1884. His present term expires in 1895.

Breda, Treaty of, was a treaty concluded between England, France, Holland and Denmark at Breda in 1667. Among its provisions, those relating to America were the restoration of Acadia (Nova Scotia) to France by England, while England secured her claims in the West Indies and retained New Netherlands (New York) from Holland.

Bremen. An extradition convention was concluded in 1853 between the United States and Bremen.

Brentwood, Tenn., a minor battle of the Civil War, occurring March 25, 1863, in which Wheeler, Forrest and Wharton, commanding 5000 Confederates, defeated 800 Federals under Bloodgood and G. C. Smith.

Brevard, Ephraim (1750–1783), was a prominent and influential patriot of North Carolina. He was secretary of the Mecklenburg Convention of 1775, and is said to have been the author of the famous (alleged) declaration which anticipated by over a year the Declaration of Independence of Congress. He served in the Continental army, and was taken prisoner at Charleston in 1780.

Brewster, Benjamin H. (1816–1888), was Attorney-General of Pennsylvania from 1867 to 1869. He was Attorney-General in Arthur's Cabinet from 1881 to 1885. He distinguished himself in the prosecution of the Star Route trials.

Brewster, William, "Elder" (1560–1644), led a band of "Separatists" from England to Holland in 1608. He obtained a grant of land in North America from the Virginia Company and brought over the first company of Pilgrims to what is now Plymouth, Mass., in 1620. He was pastor of the Plymouth colony till 1629.

Brier's Creek, Battle of, March 3, 1779. General Lincoln detailed Ashe with 1500 men to narrow the lines about the British in Savannah. The British turned his position at Brier's Creek, and of Ashe's force only 500 again reached the American camp.

Briggs, George N. (1796–1861), represented Massachusetts in the U. S. Congress as a Whig from 1831 to 1843, and was prominent as an eloquent debater. He was Governor of Massachusetts from 1843 to 1851. He was a Judge of the Massachusetts Court of Common Pleas from 1851 to 1856, and a member of the State Constitutional Convention of 1853.

Briggs Case. In his address on the occasion of his installation into the Edward Robinson professorship of Biblical Theology in the Union Theological Seminary, of New York, January 20, 1891, Professor Charles A. Briggs asserted that reason is a fountain of divine authority no less savingly enlightening than the Bible and the church. His views were deemed not in accordance with the Presbyterian Confession of Faith. Charges were brought against Dr. Briggs before the Presbyterian General Assembly. He was supported by his colleagues in the seminary. In 1892 Briggs was tried and acquitted by the New York Synod, the several charges not having been sustained.

Bright, Jesse D. (1812–1875), was Lieutenant-Governor of Indiana in 1841. He represented Indiana in the U. S. Senate as a Democrat from 1845 to 1862, when he was expelled for having, in a letter to Jefferson Davis, recognized him as president of the Confederate States. He was a member of the Kentucky Legislature in 1866.

Brinton, Daniel G., born in 1837, has made valuable contributions to the study of American archæology, ethnology and linguistics. He wrote "American Hero-Myths," "The American Race," and edited a "Library of Aboriginal American Literature."

Briscoe vs. Bank of Kentucky. The Bank of Kentucky brought suit against Briscoe and others as holders of a promissory note for which the notes of the bank had been given, as a loan, to the drawers of the note. The defendants claimed that their note was void since those given in return by the bank were nothing else than "bills of credit" and repugnant to the clause of the Constitution which prohibited States from issuing such bills. The Circuit Court and the Court of Appeals of Kentucky gave judgment for the bank on the ground that the act incorporating the Bank of Kentucky was constitutional and that the notes issued were not "bills of credit" within the meaning of the National Constitution. In 1834 the Supreme Court came near deciding adversely; but in 1837, when the case was finally decided, it was decided in favor of the bank, the bills not being deemed "bills of credit" in spite of the close relations of bank and State.

Bristoe, or Bristow Station, Va. Here, August 27, 1862, while Jackson was awaiting Lee's arrival with reinforcements from Longstreet's division, 40,000 troops under McDowell were sent against him by General Pope. A brief engagement ensued, Jackson retiring slowly toward Manassas Junction with the main body and leaving his rear-guard to cope with McDowell. October 14, 1863, during Lee's operations in Northern Virginia, Warren, commanding a large force of Meade's Union Army, encountered here and defeated A. P. Hill, leading a strong body of Confederates. Warren lost 200 killed and wounded. The Confederate loss was greater.

Bristol, R. I., was not settled by white people until the termination of King Philip's War in 1679. Until 1747 it was a part of Massachusetts. It was the ancient residence of King Philip who was killed here in 1676. During the Revolutionary War it was bombarded by the British, and much of the town destroyed by fire. In the French and Revolutionary wars and the War of 1812 it was noted for its privateers.

Bristow, Benjamin, born in 1832, attained distinction as a lawyer, served in the Civil War and afterward in the Kentucky State Senate and as District Attorney. In 1870–72 he filled the office of Solicitor-General. His national importance rests on his conduct of the treasury department under Grant in 1873–76. His reputation for reform led to his candidacy for the Republican nomination for President in 1876. In this contest, however, Blaine and Bristow, the two leading candidates, were set aside, and Hayes received the nomination.

Broad River, Battle of, November 12, 1780. Cornwallis, having learned the size and position of Sumter's force above Camden, sent Major Wemyss against him with mounted infantry. He charged the picket but his force was repelled and himself wounded and taken prisoner.

Broad Seal War, a controversy arising from disputed election returns in Middlesex County, N. J. In the congressional elections of 1838 the clerk of this county had thrown out the vote of South Amboy for the Democratic nominees on the ground of defects in the returns. The Democrats protested, but the Whig representatives were declared elected and given certificates under the broad seal of the State. When Congress met, December 2, 1839, the House contained 119 Democrats and 118 Whigs outside of New Jersey. The clerk refused to recognize the five New Jersey Whigs and the greatest confusion followed until on December 5, John Quincy Adams was elected speaker *pro tempore*. On December 17 the House after much wrangling chose R. M. T. Hunter, of Virginia, permanent speaker. The Democratic contestants were finally seated.

Brock, Sir Isaac (1769–1812), came to Canada from England in 1802 in the British army. In 1810 he took command of the troops in upper Canada and prepared the country for defence. In 1812 he received the surrender of General Hull's army at Detroit with all the stores, arms and cannon. He was killed at the battle of Queenstown.

Brodhead, John Romeyn (1814–1873), was Secretary of Legation in Holland from 1841 to 1844 and in England from 1846 to 1849. He collected the valuable records and documents relating to the history of New York, published as "N. Y. Colonial Documents," and wrote a valuable colonial "History of New York."

Broke, Sir Philip B. V. (1776–1841), commanded the British ship "Shannon," which in 1813 captured the American ship "Chesapeake," Captain Lawrence, off Boston harbor after an engagement of fifteen minutes.

Brook Farm, a communistic industrial and literary establishment founded in Massachusetts, in 1841, by George Ripley and other persons of socialistic tendencies. It was suggested by the schemes of Robert Owen and the writings of Fourier. The farm was bought and stock assigned on a communistic basis, and labor, manual or mental, received compensation on a time basis. The establishment failed in 1846, one of the largest buildings being destroyed that year by fire. Nathaniel Hawthorne and Horace Greeley were among those interested in the scheme.

Brooke, Robert Greville, Lord (1608–1643), a Puritan lord, became one of the patentees of the Connecticut colony with Lord Say and Sele and others in 1632. Saybrook, Conn., was named for Lord Say and Lord Brooke.

Brooklyn, N. Y., was settled in 1636 by a few Walloon colonists. English and Dutch settlers followed and in 1667 a charter was granted the town. In 1776 the site of the present town was the scene of the battle of Long Island. In 1834 Brooklyn became a chartered city. The population of Brooklyn was in 1800, 3298; 1830, 15,292; 1850, 96,850; 1860, 266,661; 1876, 500,000; 1890, 806,343.

Brooklyn Heights. (See Long Island, Battle of.)

Brooks, James (1810–1873), established the *New York Express* in 1836. He represented New York in the U. S. Congress as a Whig from 1849 to 1853 and as a Democrat from 1865 to 1873. He was associated with the "Credit Mobilier," and was censured by the House.

Brooks, John (1752–1825), commanded a regiment at Saratoga and was adjutant-general at Monmouth. He was Governor of Massachusetts from 1816 to 1823.

Brooks, Phillips (1835–1893), was rector of Trinity Church, Boston, from 1869 to 1891. He was Protestant Episcopal Bishop of Massachusetts from 1891 to 1893. He was regarded in England and the United States as the greatest preacher of his church.

Brooks, Preston S. (1819–1857), served during the Mexican War. He represented South Carolina in the U. S. Congress as a States-rights Democrat from 1853 to 1859. In 1856 he savagely assaulted Senator Sumner with a cane in the Senate chamber for certain expressions in a speech "on the crime against Kansas." The resolution for his expulsion from the House was not carried.

Brough, John (1811–1865), was prominent in Western journalism. He was a member of the Ohio Senate from 1835 to 1838, and was active in politics. He was Governor of Ohio from 1864 to 1865.

Brown, Aaron V. (1795–1859), represented Tennessee in the U. S. Congress as a Democrat from 1839 to 1845. He was Governor of Tennessee from 1845 to 1847, and Postmaster-General in Buchanan's Cabinet from 1857 to 1859.

Brown, Benjamin Gratz (1826–1885), was a member of the Missouri Legislature from 1852 to 1858. He edited the *Missouri Democrat* from 1854 to 1859. He commanded a brigade during the Civil War. He represented Missouri in the U. S. Senate as a Republican from 1863 to 1867, was Governor of Missouri in 1871, and having an important part in the Liberal Republican movement, was the Liberal Republican and Democratic candidate for Vice-President on the ticket with Horace Greeley in 1872.

Brown, Charles Brockden (1771–1810), was the first American to adopt literature as a profession. He wrote upon topics of the times, and published six successful novels which were unsurpassed in America until the appearance of Cooper's works.

Brown, Fort, scene of the two opening engagements of the Mexican War. Captain Thornton, of General Taylor's dragoons, was captured after some fighting on April 25, 1846, by Torrejon, the Mexican general. On May 3 of the same year Arista, commander-in-chief of the Mexican forces, opened fire upon the fort with the batteries of Matamoras. The fort is now so called because commanded by Major Brown, who withstood a bombardment of 168 hours, and died on May 8. It was originally Fort Texas.

Brown, Henry B., born in 1836, of Michigan, jurist, was appointed Judge of the U. S. District Court for the eastern district of Michigan in 1875, and Associate Justice of the Supreme Court of the United States in 1890.

Brown, Jacob (1775–1828), had been a militia general in New York when the War of 1812 called out his abilities. He gained a victory at Sackett's Harbor in 1813, was made a major-general in the regular army, and in 1814 won the victories of Chippewa and Lundy's Lane. In 1821 he succeeded to the command of the army as general-in-chief.

Brown, John (1736–1803), of Providence, R. I., a rich merchant, led the party which destroyed the "Gaspee" in 1772. He was a delegate from Rhode Island to Congress from 1799 to 1801.

Brown, John (1744–1780), of Massachusetts, aided in the capture of Ticonderoga and took Fort Chambly in 1775. He served under Montgomery at Quebec. In 1777 he captured Ticonderoga together with large supplies.

Brown, John [of Ossawatomie] (1800–1859), was born at Torrington, Conn., and early removed his home to Ohio. He was engaged in the wool business and farming, and developed into an ardent and uncompromising abolitionist. On the outbreak of the Kansas troubles he settled near Ossawatomie in 1855, and took an active part in the desultory warfare in that region, including the "Pottawatomie Massacre" of 1856. He had many sympathizers in the Northern States, and by 1859 his plans to liberate the slaves were matured. Having collected a small force, well armed, he suddenly on October 16, 1859, seized the arsenal at Harper's Ferry in Virginia. He was immediately blockaded, captured after a desperate resistance, tried by a Virginia court, and executed at Charlestown, Va., December 2, 1859. The effect of this abortive undertaking was immeasurable. It helped to "clear the air" both in the North and South and was an important link in the chain of events leading up to the war. Brown became a hero in the songs of the Northern armies. His life is written by F. B. Sanborn.

Brown, Joseph Emerson, born in 1821, had risen to prominence as a lawyer when he became Governor of Georgia. His service in this position lasted from 1857 to 1865, including the Civil War period. In this struggle he took an active part, seizing Forts Pulaski and Jackson at the beginning of 1861, and advocating earnest resistance, though he was several times opposed to President Davis. He was Chief Justice of the State Supreme Court and U. S. Senator 1881–91.

Brown, Nicholas (1769–1841), of Providence, R. I., a successful merchant, was a liberal benefactor of Rhode Island College, which in 1804 changed its name to Brown University in his honor.

Brown University was founded in 1764, by a union of Baptists with other sects, at Warren, R. I. In 1770 it was removed to Providence. It received its present name in 1804. Francis Wayland was its president from 1827 to 1855. From 1811 to 1828 it had a medical school.

Browning, Orville H. (1810–1881), represented Illinois in the U. S. Senate as a Republican from 1861 to 1863. He advocated the abolition of slavery. He was Secretary of the Interior in Johnson's Cabinet from 1866 to 1869.

Brownists, the nickname applied to the religious Separatists of England during the latter part of the sixteenth century. Robert Brown, who introduced the Separatist doctrines, was a Church of England clergyman of Norwich until 1580, when he began declaiming against the discipline and ceremony of the church. The Puritans were largely influenced by the Separatist doctrines. The Pilgrim Fathers were Brownists.

Brownlow, William Gannaway (1805–1877), was in early life a Methodist preacher, and for many years edited the *Knoxville Whig*. He strongly opposed secession and became known as the "Fighting Parson." During the war he was a centre of the Unionist feeling in Eastern Tennessee, and was at one time imprisoned. He was Governor of the State in 1865–69, and U. S. Senator 1869–75.

Brown's Ferry, Tenn., a skirmish of the Civil War during the manœuvres around Chattanooga. At this place, October 27, 28, 1863, portions of Longstreet's Confederate troops were surprised and routed by the Federals under Hooker and Smith. The latter general secured an advantageous position upon a height overlooking the ferry. Howard with a small force cut off the pickets on one side while Geary did the same on the other. The Confederate pickets had therefore to surrender.

Brownson, Orestes A. (1803–1876), a versatile writer and theologian, was prominent in social and political reforms. He was active in the formation of the Workingmen's and Loco-foco parties in New York.

Brownstown, Mich. Major Van Horne with 200 men was here defeated August 5, 1812, by a body of Indians in ambush; seventeen men were killed and mail containing important information as to the needs at Detroit was captured.

Brownsville, Texas, captured November 5, 1863, during Banks' expedition to the Rio Grande, by Dana with a small party of Federal soldiers. Bee, the Confederate general, was encamped at this place with a small force. He was easily defeated and driven out.

Bruce, Blanche K., born in 1841, was a slave in early life. He represented Mississippi in the U. S. Senate as a Republican from 1875 to 1881. He became Register of the Treasury in 1881.

Brunswick. Brunswick concluded with the United States in 1854 a convention respecting property.

Brussels Conference, an international monetary conference, held at Brussels in the autumn of 1892 at the suggestion of the United States Government. The debate was chiefly upon the initial thesis of the American programme suggested in the invitation to the convention, *i. e.*, that it was desirable to find some means of increasing the use of silver in the currency systems of the nations. No definite step was taken at this conference, though it was pretty clearly shown that some agreement regarding an international free mintage of silver might be arrived at, if Great Britain could be induced to give her consent.

Bryant, William Cullen (1794–1878), poet, first won distinction by his poem "The Embargo" in 1807. He was editor-in-chief of the *New York Evening Post* from 1828 to 1878. The paper was noted for its democratic spirit and strongly supported the Government during the Civil War. He aided in forming the Republican party and entered zealously into all public questions. His most famous poem was "Thanatopsis."

Bryn Mawr College, near Philadelphia, was founded in 1884 by Jas. W. Taylor, M. D.

Buchanan, James (April 23, 1791–June 1, 1868), the fifteenth President of the United States, was born near Mercersburg, Pa. He graduated at Dickinson College in 1809, studied law, and soon entered the Pennsylvania Legislature. In 1821–31 he was Congressman and served as chairman of the Judiciary Committee. President Jackson sent him as Minister to Russia in 1832; he returned the next year and in 1834 entered the U. S. Senate. In that body he continued until 1845 when he entered President Polk's Cabinet as Secretary of State. While secretary he was called on to conduct the delicate questions arising from the Oregon dispute, the acquisition of Texas, and the Mexican War. He had been in 1844 mentioned for the Presidency and was a candidate in 1852. During 1853–56 he was U. S. Minister to England. As the Democratic candidate for President in 1856 he was elected over Frémont the Republican and Fillmore the Know-Nothing, and served for the term 1857–61. His foreign policy was generally successful. As his term went on, the absorbing slavery question overshadowed all other issues. After the election of Lincoln and the beginning of secession it was President Buchanan's misfortune to have the conduct of affairs for three or four months of extreme excitement. His so-called "temporizing policy" during this period met with severe criticisms. After the close of his term he lived in retirement, and died at Lancaster, Pa. His life has been written by G. T. Curtis.

Buckingham, Joseph T. (1779–1861), published the *New England Galaxy* from 1817 to 1828, and the Boston *Courier* from 1824 to 1848. He was a member of the Massachusetts Senate from 1847 to 1850.

Buckingham, William A. (1804–1875), one of the "War Governors," was Governor of Connecticut from 1858 to 1866. He actively supported the Civil War. He represented Connecticut in the U. S. Senate as a Republican from 1869 to 1875.

Buckner, Simon B., born in 1823, fought with distinction at Contreras, Churubusco and Molino del Rey. He fought at Fort Henry, and commanded a brigade at Fort Donelson, which he surrendered to General Grant when left in command. He led a brigade in General Bragg's army in Tennessee, and commanded a division at Murfreesboro and Chickamauga. He was Governor of Kentucky from 1887 to 1891.

Buckshot War. The control of the Pennsylvania House of Representatives in 1838, on which depended the choice of a United States Senator, turned upon the election in Philadelphia (October 9) where the Democratic candidates for the Legislature were elected by small majorities; but their Congressional candidate was defeated. Thereupon the Democratic return judges cast out 5000 Whig votes, claiming fraud. The Whig judges then issued certificates of election to both their Congressional and Legislative candidates, and these returns were accepted by the Whig Secretary of State. At the opening of the Legislature, at Harrisburg, December 4, 1838, armed partisans were present. The Whig Senate adjourned because of the mob, and in the House two warring bodies assembled. The Whig Governor called on the militia, and tried, without effect, to obtain Federal aid. The Democratic House was finally recognized December 25.

Bucktails, a name first given to the Tammany Society of New York City, from the circumstance of the members of the organization wearing a buck's tail in the hat as a badge. The Bucktails, from 1812 to 1828, were anti-Clintonian New York Democrats. They were the most vigorous opponents of the Clinton canal policy from its inception (1817), and the name was finally applied to all who protested against this policy throughout the State. Under Martin Van Buren the Bucktails obtained control of the State temporarily. After Governor Clinton's death, in 1828, they became the Democratic party of the State.

Buell, Don Carlos, born in 1818, graduated at West Point in 1841, and served in the Mexican War. In the Civil War he was appointed in 1861 to the Department of the Cumberland, and occupied the strategic point of Bowling Green. Part of his army arrived on the battle-field of Shiloh in time to render important aid in retrieving the fortunes of that contest. In the same year, 1862, he skillfully manœuvred against Bragg's army of invasion, and defeated it at Perryville October 8. He was soon after superseded by General Rosecrans.

Buena Vista, Mexico, a celebrated battle between the American army under General Taylor, and the Mexicans under General Santa Anna. It is sometimes called Angostura after the plateau upon which Taylor drew up his army. This battle lasted two days, September 22, 23, 1847, was hard fought, attended with considerable loss on both sides, and remained undecided until late in the second day, when Taylor, by concentrating his batteries against the enemy's centre, and ordering his riflemen to cover his right flank, gained a complete victory. The first day's fighting had been confined to unsuccessful attempts by the Mexicans to drive Taylor from his position on Angostura heights. Hostilities were suspended during the night, the two armies suffering from the intense cold. The battle was nearly lost to the Americans at one time. Lane and O'Brien in charge of three guns and the second Indiana volunteers were driven from their position along the southern ridge of the heights, and were obliged to retreat to Buena Vista. Taylor arrived in time to cover their retreat with the second dragoons and the Mississippi riflemen. Santa Anna's poor generalship alone prevented defeat. Number engaged, Americans 4769, Mexicans 17,000.

Buenos Ayres. (See Argentina.)

Buffalo, N. Y., was founded in 1801, and became a military post in 1813, when it was burned by the British. It was rebuilt after the war and in 1832 attained the rank of a city. After the opening of the Erie Canal in 1825 its growth was rapid.

Bull Run, Va., the scene of two important battles of the Civil War. The first, the first great battle of the war, took place July 21, 1861, between McDowell commanding 28,000 Union soldiers, and Johnston and Beauregard leading 31,000 Confederates. Six Confederate brigades lay posted along the stream, and upon these McDowell resolved to begin his attack. Tyler was sent across the stone bridge to threaten the Confederate front. Hunter and Heintzelman were dispatched to make a detour and attack the enemy's flank and rear. But Johnston had also decided to hasten the attack in order to anticipate Patterson's arrival with reinforcements for McDowell. However, the latter moved first, so Johnston acted on the defensive. Tyler and Hunter were slow in their movements; still by midday McDowell had turned the Confederate left and uncovered the stone bridge. But now, instead of following his advantage and taking up his position at Manassas depot, he pursued the fleeing Confederates to the forest and was there repulsed by Jackson, who here gained his sobriquet of "Stonewall." Johnston rallied the right, Beauregard the left, and the tide of battle began to turn in the Confederates' favor. Suddenly 17,000 fresh Confederate troops rushed across the field from Manassas, and Kirby Smith, having escaped Patterson in the valley, charged the already weakening Unionists. McDowell was instantly driven from the plateau which he occupied and a complete rout followed. McDowell in vain tried to cover his retreat with 800 regulars. There was a panic which spread almost to Washington.—Bull Run the second, or the battle of Manassas, occurred August 29, 30, 1862. General Pope, commanding a Union army of 40,000 men, advanced to attack Jackson, who was awaiting reinforcements from Lee at Bristoe station. McDowell had been dispatched to intercept Lee's conjunction with Jackson, but he was immediately recalled and ordered to join Pope at Manassas Junction. Jackson, finding the way open, immediately retired toward Manassas Junction and took a strong position near Gainsville behind an old railroad grading. Pope ordered Sigel to attack him at daylight August 29. All the morning a duel of batteries continued and Pope, arriving about noon from Centreville, found both armies badly cut up. Pope expected McDowell and Porter to join him. The former arrived in the afternoon, but the latter never came. The battle continued until sunset, Jackson seeming several times on the point of retreating before such heavy odds. But Longstreet came up and the fighting ceased for the night. It began again the next day, but Pope's troops were so wearied out that he was early compelled to retire.

Bulloch, Archibald (1730?–1777), was president of the Georgia provincial congress in 1775 and 1776. He was a delegate to the Continental Congress in 1776, and president of Georgia from 1776 to 1777.

Bullock, Rufus B., born in 1834, was Governor of Georgia from 1869 to 1870, when he resigned because of the opposition to negro representatives in the Legislature, whose rights he supported.

Bulwer, Sir William Henry L. E. (1801–1872), was British Minister to the United States from 1849 to 1852. He negotiated with Senator John M. Clayton the Clayton-Bulwer treaty which related to the establishment of a communication between the Atlantic and Pacific oceans by canal at the Isthmus of Panama, each party guaranteeing neutrality of communication.

Buncombe, effusive rhetoric irrelevant to the business in hand. It is said that, many years ago, a member of Congress from Buncombe County, N. C., replied, on being taxed with the irrelevancy of his speech, "I am speaking not for you, but for Buncombe."

Bunker Hill, Battle of (June 17, 1775). After the investment of Boston by the Continental troops it became evident that Boston was untenable unless the surrounding heights were secured. This General Gage intended to do. The committee of safety anticipated him and sent 1200 men under Colonel Prescott to seize and fortify Bunker Hill, on the night of the sixteenth. Breed's Hill, a more advanced though less protected position, was fortified instead. Dawn disclosed the American works to the British and a lively cannonade was directed upon the works. About three p. m., 3000 British veterans under Howe and Pigott charged up the hill, but a deadly volley awaited both. They gave way and retreated. In the meantime the village of Charlestown had been fired by shells from the fleet. Again the British charged. The Americans reserved fire until they were within thirty yards. Again the British ranks gave way before the fatal fire. Owing to confusion at headquarters neither reinforcements nor ammunition were promptly despatched to the American troops. About five o'clock the British charged again. They were at first shaken by the American fire, but the latter's cartridges were soon spent and after a stubborn hand-to-hand fight they left the field. The most lamented among the slain was the gallant General Warren, who had fought as a volunteer in the ranks. 1054 of the British or over one-third of their whole number perished, of the Americans about a quarter or 449. Bunker Hill is thus one of the bloodiest battles of modern times. The immediate result was the possession of a strategic point by the English; upon the Americans its moral effect was to encourage their spirits and to inspire general respect for their soldierly ability.

Bunker Hill Monument. The corner-stone was laid June 17, 1825, by Lafayette, before an enormous and enthusiastic crowd, among them many aged survivors of the battle fought fifty years before, who had gathered from far and near. After the singing of "Old Hundred," Daniel Webster delivered his famous address. The monument was completed June 17, 1843, and again Webster delivered the address before a tumultuously appreciative audience, among them President Tyler and some of his Cabinet.

Burchard, Samuel D. (1812–1891), lecturer and preacher in New York. During the political campaign of 1884 he made a speech at a "ministers' meeting" called by the Republican party managers, during which he stigmatized the Democrats by the words "Rum, Romanism and Rebellion." This helped to lose the Republicans the election, by alienating the Roman Catholic vote.

Bureau of American Republics. A bureau established under the recommendation of the Pan-American Conference of October, 1889, for the prompt collection and distribution of commercial information concerning the American Republics.

Bureaus of Labor Statistics. The first such government office established was that of Massachusetts, created by Act of June 23, 1869. Pennsylvania established one in 1872. Connecticut had one from 1873 to 1875, and re-established it in 1885. That of Ohio was established in 1877, that of New Jersey in 1878, those of Indiana, Missouri and Illinois in 1879, those of California, Wisconsin, New York and Michigan in 1883, those of Maryland and Iowa in 1884. The U. S. Bureau of Labor was established by Act of June 27, 1884; an Act of June 13, 1888, substituted the Department of Labor. Since then thirteen other States have organized such bureaus.

Burgesses, House of, the lower branch of the Colonial Legislature of Virginia. The first House of Burgesses was summoned in 1619. The House met at Jamestown in the seventeenth century, at Williamsburg in the eighteenth. It consisted of two burgesses from each county, and one from each of three towns and William and Mary College. The printed journals begin with the year 1732. The forms of procedure were those of the House of Commons. The last session of the burgesses occurred in 1774.

Burgoyne, John (1723–1792), one of the chief British commanders in the Revolutionary War, was a member of the House of Commons, and an army officer; he reached the grade of lieutenant-general, served in Canada in the early stages of the war, and was in 1777 intrusted with the command of a large force which was to pierce the American centre. He ascended Lake Champlain and captured the forts without great difficulty. But his march from the head of the lake to Fort Edward was delayed by Schuyler's obstructions, while the auxiliary force under St. Leger came to grief, and Baum's diversion into Vermont was defeated at Bennington. He fought the first indecisive battle of Stillwater with Gates' army September 19, 1777; in the second battle on October 7 he was defeated, and was obliged to surrender with nearly 6000 men at Saratoga October 17. He returned to England the next year and published in 1780 his "State of the Expedition." He was an author of some note, composing a number of poems and comedies.

Burke, Edmund (1729–1797), the English orator and statesman, was born in Ireland, educated in Trinity College, Dublin, and gained attention in literature, especially as the author of a treatise on "The Sublime and Beautiful." After some years spent as private secretary he was returned to the House of Commons in 1766. In the exciting debates attendant on the American Revolution he took a leading part. He favored constitutional order, freedom, championed the colonies, and held the first rank as an orator and political thinker. In 1774 he delivered a great speech on American taxation, and the next year favored strongly a policy of conciliation. In 1782, and again in 1783, he held the office of paymaster of the forces, and draughted Fox's East India Bill. Burke led the attack on Warren Hastings in the House of Commons in 1786–87, and in 1788 was one of the managers in that statesman's impeachment, and made a celebrated speech. Soon after the outbreak of the French Revolution Burke, as a lover of order and conservatism, broke with his friend Fox, denounced the Revolution, and published his "Reflections" on that event. The best biographies are by Prior and Morley.

Burkesville, Va. Here Sheridan, pursuing the Confederates, defeated and fleeing from the battlefield of Five Forks, overtook, April 3, 1865, a body of their cavalry. They endeavored to make a stand and receive the Federal assault, but in vain. Sheridan easily dispersed them, taking many prisoners. This battle is to be remembered in connection with the close of the campaign around Richmond and Petersburg.

Burlingame, Anson (1820–1870), rose to prominence in Massachusetts as a lawyer and politician. In 1855–61 he was Republican Congressman, and in 1861 he was sent as U. S. Minister to China. His diplomatic services there were so important that in 1868 he was appointed by the Chinese Government a special envoy to the United States and Europe. He negotiated at Washington in 1868 the Burlingame Treaty with China, and effected treaties with England, Prussia, Holland and other European countries.

Burlington, N. J., was founded in 1677 by Friends.

Burnet, David G. (1789–1870), was active in securing the independence of Texas. He was chosen provisional president of the republic in 1836 and afterward served as vice-president.

Burnett, Frances Hodgson, born in 1849, came to America from England in 1865. She wrote "Through One Administration," "Little Lord Fauntleroy," "That Lass o' Lowrie's," and other popular works of fiction.

Burns Case (1854), the last great fugitive slave case in Boston. Burns was an escaped slave of a Virginia planter and was arrested in Boston on the charge of theft. He was then claimed as a fugitive. This aroused the people to fever-excitement and large meetings, addressed by Wendell Phillips and Theodore Parker, were held in Faneuil and Meionaon Halls on the evening of May 26. The audience, refusing to wait until morning, armed themselves with clubs and axes and broke into the jail, but were driven away by a pistol shot. Burns was tried and the order for his rendition issued. He was conveyed to the cutter "Morris," surrounded by a large military force. The streets were thronged and many of the houses were draped in black. Indictments for riot brought against Phillips, Parker and others were quashed on technical grounds.

Burns, John (1793–1872), soldier, fought at Plattsburg, Queenstown and Lundy's Lane. He distinguished himself by his patriotic zeal during the Civil War, particularly at the battle of Gettysburg.

Burnside, Ambrose Everett (1824–1881), commander of the Army of the Potomac, graduated at West Point in 1847. He invented a breech-loading rifle, retired from the army and engaged in business. In the Civil War he led a brigade at the first battle of Bull Run and was in 1862 placed in command of an expedition to North Carolina; this force captured Roanoke Island on February 8, and Newbern March 14. He was now made a corps commander in the Army of the Potomac, and rendered important services at the battle of South Mountain and at Antietam where he held the stone bridge against repeated attacks. In November, 1862, he succeeded McClellan in command of the army. On December 13 was fought the fatal and ill-advised battle of Fredericksburg, and in January, 1863, General Burnside was superseded by Hooker. Having been appointed to the command of the Department of the Ohio he kept down treason, and was later in 1863 besieged in Knoxville by Longstreet. He acted as corps commander in the Army of the Potomac at the Wilderness, Cold Harbor, Petersburg, etc. In 1866–68 he was Republican Governor of Rhode Island, and in 1875–81 U. S. Senator from the same State.

Burr, Aaron (February 6, 1756–September 14, 1836), was born at Newark, N. J., and was the grandson of Jonathan Edwards. He graduated at Princeton in 1772, and joined the army at the outbreak of the Revolution. He served in Arnold's famous expedition through Maine to Canada, and afterward rose to the rank of colonel. Studying law, he rose soon to a position among the leaders of the New York bar, and was a member of the Legislature, and Attorney-General of the State. Of fascinating manners and unscrupulous principles he rapidly became a political power in the State and the nation. He was Republican U. S. Senator from New York in 1791–97, and later was a member of the New York Assembly. His prominence and power in the Republican party caused him to be a formidable aspirant for the Presidency. In the exciting contest of 1800–01 Colonel Burr and Jefferson each received seventy-three electoral votes for President, and the matter was left to the House of Representatives, which finally chose Jefferson for the first and Burr for the second place. Burr was accordingly Vice-President in 1801–05. A bitter personal and political rivalry with Hamilton led to a duel between the two at Weehawken, July 11, 1804, in which Hamilton was mortally wounded. On his retirement from the Vice-Presidency Burr engaged in mysterious and wide-reaching schemes, the purpose of which was apparently the formation of an independent State in the Southwest. These schemes were arrested by a proclamation of President Jefferson in October, 1806, and in the following year Burr was tried for treason at Richmond, but was acquitted. After some years of wandering in Europe he returned to New York to the practice of law, but died in obscurity and poverty at Staten Island. There are lives by Parton, Davis, etc.

Burrites, in New York politics, the followers of Aaron Burr, a faction, chiefly of Democrats, organized by him through his connection with the Tammany Society. In 1807 they coalesced with the Lewisites, adherents of Morgan Lewis, to form the body called "Martling men," later Bucktails.

Burritt, Elihu (1810–1879), while pursuing the trade of a blacksmith, acquired proficiency in many languages. He established the *Christian Citizen* in 1842 in the interests of international peace, and the abolition of slavery. He was an ardent advocate of the compensated emancipation of slaves. He was U. S. Consul at Birmingham from 1865 to 1870. He wrote "Handbook of the Nations" and "Walks in the Black Country."

Burrows, Julius C., born in 1837, has represented Michigan in the U. S. Congress as a Republican since 1885. He was twice elected Speaker *pro tempore* during the Fifty-first Congress. His present term expires in 1895.

Burrows, William (1785–1813), was acting lieutenant in Preble's squadron during the Tripolitan War. He commanded the "Enterprise," which captured the "Boxer" in 1813, but was killed during the engagement.

Bushnell, Horace (1802–1876), Congregational pastor in Hartford, Connecticut, from 1833 to 1859, was prominent for the originality and boldness of his thought on religious topics.

Bussey, Cyrus, born in 1833, commanded a brigade at Pea Ridge. He was chief of cavalry at Vicksburg, and defeated General Jackson at Canton in 1863. In 1864 he commanded and organized the Department of Kansas.

Butler, Benjamin F. (1795–1858), was a New York district attorney from 1821 to 1825. He was appointed one of the three commissioners to revise the statutes of New York in 1825. He was Attorney-General of the United States in the Cabinets of Jackson and Van Buren from 1833 to 1838. He was also acting Secretary of War from 1836 to 1837, and was a prominent member of the "Albany Regency."

Butler, Benjamin Franklin (November 5, 1818–January 11, 1893), was graduated at Waterville College in Maine in 1838. He became a successful lawyer at Lowell and was elected to the Massachusetts House of Representatives and Senate. In 1860 he was delegate to the Democratic National Convention at Charleston and withdrew from the adjourned convention which met at Baltimore. At the outbreak of the Civil War he was made a brigadier-general and took possession of Baltimore. Becoming a major-general, he commanded in Eastern Virginia, where he lost the battle of Big Bethel in June, 1861, and issued the famous order referring to the negroes as contraband of war. Later in the year he captured Forts Hatteras and Clark. In April, 1862, he co-operated with Farragut in the capture of New Orleans and was appointed commandant in that city. It was here that he attracted wide attention by his stern measures for the preservation of order, and roused considerable criticism as well as earned the undying hatred of many of the Southerners. In 1864, as commander of the Army of the James, he co-operated with Grant in the advance on Richmond. His military career closed with an unsuccessful attack upon Fort Fisher in December, 1864. He was a Republican Congressman from Massachusetts, 1867–75 and 1877–79. He failed in his attempts to secure the Republican nomination for Governor of Massachusetts in 1871 and 1872, and in 1878 and 1879 he was defeated as the Greenback candidate. He was, however, elected in 1882 by the Democrats as one of the "tidal wave" Governors and aroused considerable excitement in 1883 by his administration. He failed of a re-election and in 1884 ran for President as the Greenback and Anti-Monopoly candidate. Besides his reputation as politician and general he was widely known as a skillful lawyer. He wrote an autobiography entitled "Butler's Book."

Butler, John, died in 1794. He commanded the Indians in Sir William Johnson's Niagara campaign in 1759 and in the Montreal expedition of 1760. He joined the British at the outbreak of the Revolution and conducted predatory warfare in New York. He conducted the famous "Wyoming massacre" in 1778. He engaged in Johnson's raid on the Schoharie and Mohawk regions in 1780.

Butler, Matthew C., born in 1836, became a major-general in the Confederate service. He has represented South Carolina in the U. S. Senate as a Democrat since 1877. His present term expires in 1895.

Butler, Pierce (1744–1822), came to America from Ireland as a British soldier. He was a delegate from South Carolina to the Old Congress in 1787, was a member of the convention that framed the Federal Constitution, and signed the Constitution. He represented South Carolina in the U. S. Senate from 1789 to 1796 and from 1802 to 1804.

Butler, William Orlando (1791–1880), was an officer in the War of 1812. In 1839–43 he was a Democratic Congressman from Kentucky, and ran unsuccessfully in 1844 for Governor of that State. He was a major-general in the Mexican War, and was distinguished at the taking of Monterey in 1846. He was in 1848 the unsuccessful Democratic candidate for Vice-President on the ticket with General Cass.

Butler, Zebulon (1731–1795), served in New Jersey from 1777 to 1778, He was commander at Wyoming, Pennsylvania, at the time of the massacre. He served with distinction in General Sullivan's Indian expedition of 1779.

Butterfield, Daniel, born in 1831, led a brigade at Hanover Court House and Gaines' Mills. He commanded a corps at Fredericksburg and was chief of staff at Chancellorsville, Gettysburg, Lookout Mountain and Missionary

Ridge. He commanded a division at Resaca, Dallas and Kenesaw. He resigned in 1869 and was for some time Sub-Treasurer of the United States in New York.

Butterworth, Benjamin, born in 1822, represented Ohio in the U. S. Senate as a Republican from 1878 to 1882. He was Commissioner of Patents in 1883, and a U. S. Congressman from 1884 to 1886.

Butts, Isaac (1816–1874), edited the *Rochester Advertiser* from 1845 to 1849. He originated and promulgated the doctrine known as "Squatter Sovereignty" or "Popular Sovereignty," that the people of each territory should decide the question of slavery for themselves. He edited the *Rochester Union* from 1857 to 1864. He was an original writer upon economic and political subjects.

C.

Cabeza de Vaca, Alvar Nuñez (1507–1559), Spanish explorer, went with Narvaez to Florida in 1527, and accompanied him on his westward march and voyage. He was wrecked near Matagorda Bay in Texas, and captured by the Indians, among whom he became a medicine-man. Finally escaping he reached Mexico after many wanderings, during which he discovered the Rio Grande. He was afterward the first explorer of Paraguay.

Cabinet. The Constitution, without providing distinctly for a cabinet, authorizes the President to consult the heads of the departments. Washington thus consulted his Secretary of State, Secretary of the Treasury, Secretary of War and Attorney-General. The secretaryship of the navy was instituted in 1798, and its incumbent was at once treated as a member of the cabinet. The Postmasters-General before 1829 were not. The Secretary of the Interior became such at once upon his institution in 1849, the Secretary of Agriculture similarly in 1889. Lists of the holders of cabinet office follow.

Cabinet Officers. The figures at the left indicate the administrative periods of four years, corresponding to the following Presidents: 1, 2, Washington; 3, John Adams; 4, 5, Jefferson; 6, 7, Madison; 8, 9, Monroe; 10, J. Q. Adams; 11, 12, Jackson; 13, Van Buren; 14, W. H. Harrison; 14*a*, Tyler; 15, Polk; 16, Taylor; 16*a*, Fillmore; 17, Pierce; 18, Buchanan; 19, 20, Lincoln; 20*a*, Johnson; 21, 22, Grant; 23, Hayes; 24, Garfield; 24*a*, Arthur; 25, Cleveland; 26, B. Harrison; 27, Cleveland.

Secretaries of State.

			Date of Commission.
1.	Thomas Jefferson,	Virginia,	September 26, 1789
2.	Thomas Jefferson,	Virginia.	
	Edmund Randolph,	Virginia,	January 2, 1794
	Timothy Pickering,	Pennsylvania,	December 10, 1795
3.	Timothy Pickering,	Pennsylvania.	
	John Marshall,	Virginia,	May 13, 1800
4.	James Madison,	Virginia,	March 5, 1801

	Name	State	Date of Commission.	
5.	James Madison,	Virginia.		
6.	Robert Smith,	Maryland,	March	6, 1809
	James Monroe,	Virginia,	April	2, 1811
7.	James Monroe,	Virginia,	February	28, 1815
8.	John Quincy Adams,	Massachusetts,	March	5, 1817
9.	John Quincy Adams,	Massachusetts.		
10.	Henry Clay,	Kentucky,	March	7, 1825
11.	Martin Van Buren,	New York,	March	6, 1829
	Edward Livingston,	Louisiana,	May	24, 1831
12.	Louis McLane,	Delaware,	May	29, 1833
	John Forsyth,	Georgia,	June	27, 1834
13.	John Forsyth,	Georgia.		
14.	Daniel Webster,	Massachusetts,	March	5, 1841
14*a*.	Hugh S. Legaré,	South Carolina,	May	9, 1843
	Abel P. Upshur,	Virginia,	July	24, 1843
	John Nelson (*acting*),	Maryland,	February	29, 1844
	John C. Calhoun,	South Carolina,	March	6, 1844
15.	James Buchanan,	Pennsylvania,	March	6, 1845
16.	John M. Clayton,	Delaware,	March	7, 1849
16*a*.	Daniel Webster,	Massachusetts,	July	22, 1850
	Edward Everett,	Massachusetts,	November	6, 1852
17.	William L. Marcy,	New York,	March	7, 1853
18.	Lewis Cass,	Michigan,	March	6, 1857
	Jeremiah S. Black,	Pennsylvania,	December	17, 1860
19.	William H. Seward,	New York,	March	5, 1861
20.	William H. Seward,	New York.		
20*a*.	William H. Seward,	New York.		
21.	Elihu B. Washburne,	Illinois,	March	5, 1869
	Hamilton Fish,	New York,	March	11, 1869
22.	Hamilton Fish,	New York,	March	17, 1873
23.	William M. Evarts,	New York,	March	12, 1877
24.	James G. Blaine,	Maine,	March	5, 1881
24*a*.	Frederick T. Frelinghuysen,	New Jersey.	December	12, 1881
25.	Thomas F. Bayard,	Delaware.	March	6, 1885
26.	James G. Blaine,	Maine,	March	5, 1889
	John W. Foster,	Indiana,	June	29, 1892
27.	Walter Q. Gresham,	Indiana,	March	6, 1893

Secretaries of the Treasury.

	Name	State	Date of Commission.	
1.	Alexander Hamilton,	New York,	September	11, 1789
2.	Alexander Hamilton,	New York.		
	Oliver Wolcott, Jr.,	Connecticut,	February	2, 1795
3.	Oliver Wolcott, Jr.,	Connecticut.		
	Samuel Dexter,	Massachusetts,	January	1, 1801
4.	Samuel Dexter,	Massachusetts.		
	Albert Gallatin,	Pennsylvania,	May	14, 1801
5.	Albert Gallatin,	Pennsylvania.		

			Date of Commission.
6.	Albert Gallatin,	Pennsylvania.	
	George W. Campbell,	Tennessee,	February 9, 1814
7.	Alexander J. Dallas,	Pennsylvania,	October 6, 1814
	William H. Crawford,	Georgia,	October 22, 1816
8.	William H. Crawford,	Georgia.	
9.	William H. Crawford,	Georgia.	
10.	Richard Rush,	Pennsylvania,	March 7, 1825
11.	Samuel D. Ingham,	Pennsylvania,	March 6, 1829
	Louis McLane,	Delaware,	August 8, 1831
12.	William J. Duane,	Pennsylvania,	May 29, 1833
	Roger B. Taney,	Maryland,	September 23, 1833
	Levi Woodbury,	New Hampshire,	June 27, 1834
13.	Levi Woodbury,	New Hampshire.	
14.	Thomas Ewing,	Ohio,	March 5, 1841
14*a*.	Walter Forward,	Pennsylvania,	September 13, 1841
	John C. Spencer,	New York,	March 3, 1843
	George M. Bibb,	Kentucky,	June 15, 1844
15.	Robert J. Walker,	Mississippi,	March 6, 1845
16.	William M. Meredith,	Pennsylvania,	March 8, 1849
16*a*.	Thomas Corwin,	Ohio,	July 23, 1850
17.	James Guthrie,	Kentucky,	March 7, 1853
18.	Howell Cobb,	Georgia,	March 6, 1857
	Philip F. Thomas	Maryland,	December 12, 1860
	John A. Dix,	New York,	January 11, 1861
19.	Salmon P. Chase,	Ohio,	March 5, 1861
	William P. Fessenden,	Maine,	July 1, 1864
20.	Hugh McCulloch,	Indiana,	March 7, 1865
20*a*.	Hugh McCulloch,	Indiana.	
21.	George S. Boutwell,	Massachusetts,	March 11, 1869
22.	William A. Richardson,	Massachusetts,	March 17, 1873
	Benjamin H. Bristow,	Kentucky,	June 2, 1874
	Lot M. Morrill,	Maine,	June 21, 1876
23.	John Sherman,	Ohio,	March 8, 1877
24.	William Windom,	Minnesota,	March 5, 1881
24*a*.	Charles J. Folger,	New York,	October 27, 1881
	Walter Q. Gresham	Indiana,	September 24, 1884
	Hugh McCulloch,	Indiana,	October 28, 1884
25.	Daniel Manning,	New York,	March 6, 1885
	Charles S. Fairchild,	New York,	April 1, 1887
26.	William Windom,	Minnesota,	March 5, 1889
	Charles Foster,	Ohio,	February 24, 1891
27.	John G. Carlisle,	Kentucky,	March 6, 1893

Secretaries of War.

1.	Henry Knox,	Massachusetts,	September 12, 1789
2.	Henry Knox,	Massachusetts.	
	Timothy Pickering,	Pennsylvania,	January 2, 1795

			Date of Commission.	
	James McHenry,	Maryland,	January	27, 1796
3.	James McHenry,	Maryland.		
	Samuel Dexter,	Massachusetts,	May	13, 1800
	Roger Griswold,	Connecticut,	February	3, 1801
4.	Henry Dearborn,	Massachusetts,	March	5, 1801
5.	Henry Dearborn,	Massachusetts.		
6.	William Eustis,	Massachusetts,	March	7, 1809
	John Armstrong,	New York,	January	13, 1813
7.	James Monroe,	Virginia,	September	27, 1814
	Alexander J. Dallas (*acting*),	Pennsylvania,	March	14, 1815
	William H. Crawford,	Georgia,	August	1, 1815
8.	George Graham,	Virginia,	April	7, 1817
	John C. Calhoun,	South Carolina,	October	8, 1817
9.	John C. Calhoun,	South Carolina.		
10.	James Barbour,	Virginia,	March	7, 1825
	Peter B. Porter,	New York,	May	26, 1828
11.	John H. Eaton,	Tennessee,	March	9, 1829
	Lewis Cass,	Ohio,	August	1, 1831
12.	Lewis Cass,	Ohio.		
	Benjamin F. Butler (*acting*),	New York,	March	3, 1837
13.	Joel R. Poinsett,	South Carolina,	March	7, 1837
14.	John Bell,	Tennessee,	March	5, 1841
14*a*.	John McLean,	Ohio,	September	13, 1841
	John C. Spencer,	New York,	October	12, 1841
	James M. Porter,	Pennsylvania,	March	8, 1843
	William Wilkins,	Pennsylvania,	February	15, 1844
15.	William L. Marcy,	New York,	March	6, 1845
16.	Reverdy Johnson (*acting*),	Maryland,	March	8, 1849
	George W. Crawford,	Georgia,	March	8, 1849
16*a*.	Winfield Scott (*ad interim*),	Virginia,	July	23, 1850
	Charles M. Conrad,	Louisiana,	August	15, 1850
17.	Jefferson Davis,	Mississippi,	March	7, 1853
18.	John B. Floyd,	Virginia,	March	6, 1857
	Joseph Holt,	Kentucky,	January	18, 1861
19.	Simon Cameron,	Pennsylvania,	March	5, 1861
	Edwin M. Stanton,	Pennsylvania,	January	15, 1862
20.	Edwin M. Stanton,	Pennsylvania.		
20*a*.	Edwin M. Stanton.	(*Suspended August 12, 1867.*)		
	Ulysses S. Grant (*ad interim*),		August	12, 1867
	Edwin M. Stanton (*reinstated*),	Pennsylvania,	January	14, 1868
	John M. Schofield,		May	28, 1868
21.	John A. Rawlins,	Illinois,	March	11, 1869
	William T. Sherman (*ad interim*),		September	9, 1869
	William W. Belknap,	Iowa,	October	25, 1869
22.	William W. Belknap,	Iowa.		
	George M. Robeson (*acting*),	New Jersey,	March	2, 1876
	Alphonso Taft,	Ohio,	March	8, 1876
	J. Donald Cameron,	Pennsylvania,	May	22, 1876

			Date of Commission.
23.	George W. McCrary,	Iowa,	March 12, 1877
	Alexander Ramsey,	Minnesota,	December 10, 1879
24.	Robert T. Lincoln,	Illinois,	March 5, 1881
24*a*.	Robert T. Lincoln,	Illinois.	
25.	William C. Endicot	Massachusetts,	March 6, 1885
26.	Redfield Proctor,	Vermont,	March 5, 1889
	Stephen B. Elkins,	West Virginia,	December 22, 1891
27.	Daniel S. Lamont,	New York,	March 6, 1893

Secretaries of the Navy.

3.	George Cabot (*declined*),	Massachusetts,	May 3, 1798
	Benjamin Stoddert,	Maryland,	May 21, 1798
4.	Benjamin Stoddert,	Maryland.	
	Robert Smith,	Maryland,	July 15, 1801
5.	Jacob Crowninshield,	Massachusetts,	May 3, 1805
	(Robert Smith,	Maryland,	May, 1805)
6.	Paul Hamilton,	South Carolina,	March 7, 1809
	William Jones,	Pennsylvania,	January 12, 1813
7.	Benjamin W. Crowninshield,	Massachusetts,	December 19, 1814
8.	Benjamin W. Crowninshield,	Massachusetts.	
	Smith Thompson,	New York,	November 9, 1818
9.	Smith Thompson,	New York.	
	John Rodgers (*acting*),	Maryland,	September 1, 1823
	Samuel L. Southard,	New Jersey,	September 16, 1823
10.	Samuel L. Southard,	New Jersey.	
11.	John Branch,	North Carolina,	March 9, 1829
	Levi Woodbury,	New Hampshire,	May 23, 1831
12.	Mahlon Dickerson,	New Jersey,	June 30, 1834
13.	Mahlon Dickerson,	New Jersey.	
	James K. Paulding,	New York,	June 25, 1838
14.	George E. Badger,	North Carolina,	March 5, 1841
14*a*.	Abel P. Upshur,	Virginia,	September 13, 1841
	David Henshaw,	Massachusetts,	July 24, 1843
	Thomas W. Gilmer	Virginia,	February 15, 1844
	John Y. Mason,	Virginia,	March 14, 1844
15.	George Bancroft,	Massachusetts,	March 10, 1845
	John Y. Mason,	Virginia,	September 9, 1846
16.	William B. Preston,	Virginia,	March 8, 1849
16*a*.	William A. Graham	North Carolina,	July 22, 1850
	John P. Kennedy,	Maryland,	July 22, 1852
17.	James C. Dobbi	North Carolina,	March 7, 1853
18.	Isaac Toucey,	Connecticut,	March 6, 1857
19.	Gideon Wells,	Connecticut,	March 5, 1861
20.	Gideon Wells,	Connecticut.	
20*a*.	Gideon Wells,	Connecticut.	
21.	Adolph E. Borie,	Pennsylvania,	March 5, 1869
	George M. Robeson,	New Jersey,	June 25, 1869
22.	George M. Robeson,	New Jersey.	

			Date of Commission.
23.	Richard W. Thompson,	Indiana,	March 12, 1877
	Nathan Goff, Jr.,	West Virginia,	January 6, 1881
24.	William H. Hunt,	Louisiana,	March 5, 1881
24*a*.	William E. Chandler,	New Hampshire,	April 12, 1882
25.	William C. Whitney,	New York,	March 6, 1885
26.	Benjamin F. Tracy,	New York,	March 5, 1889
27.	Hilary A. Herbert,	Alabama,	March 6, 1893

Postmasters-General.

(Not in the Cabinet until 1829.)

1.	Samuel Osgood,	Massachusetts,	September 26, 1789
	Timothy Pickering,	Pennsylvania,	August 12, 1791
2.	Timothy Pickering,	Pennsylvania.	
	Joseph Habersham,	Georgia,	February 25, 1795
3.	Joseph Habersham,	Georgia.	
4.	Joseph Habersham,	Georgia.	
	Gideon Granger,	Connecticut,	November 28, 1801
5.	Gideon Granger,	Connecticut.	
6.	Gideon Granger,	Connecticut.	
7.	Gideon Granger,	Connecticut.	
	Return J. Meigs,	Ohio,	March 17, 1814
8.	Return J. Meigs,	Ohio.	
9.	John McLean,	Ohio,	June 26, 1823
10.	John McLean,	Ohio.	
11.	William T. Barry,	Kentucky,	March 9, 1829
12.	Amos Kendall,	Kentucky,	May 1, 1835
13.	Amos Kendall,	Kentucky.	
	John M. Niles,	Connecticut,	May 19, 1840
14.	Francis Granger,	New York,	March 6, 1841
14*a*.	Charles A. Wickliffe,	Kentucky,	September 13, 1841
15.	Cave Johnson,	Tennessee,	March 6, 1845
16.	Jacob Collamer,	Vermont,	March 8, 1849
16*a*.	Nathan K. Hall,	New York,	July 23, 1850
	Samuel D. Hubbard,	Connecticut,	August 31, 1852
17.	James Campbell,	Pennsylvania,	March 7, 1853
18.	Aaron V. Brown,	Tennessee,	March 6, 1857
	Joseph Holt,	Kentucky,	March 14, 1859
	Horatio King,	Maine,	February 12, 1861
19.	Montgomery Blair,	District Columbia,	March 5, 1861
	William Dennison,	Ohio,	September 24, 1864
20.	William Dennison,	Ohio.	
20*a*.	William Dennison,	Ohio.	
	Alexander W. Randall,	Wisconsin,	July 25, 1866
21.	John A. J. Creswell,	Maryland,	March 5, 1869
22.	John A. J. Creswell,	Maryland,	
	J. W. Marshall,	Virginia,	July 3, 1874
	Marshall Jewell,	Connecticut,	August 24, 1874

			Date of Commission.	
	James M. Tyner,	Indiana,	July	12, 1876
23.	David M. Key,	Tennessee,	March	12, 1877
	Horace Maynard,	Tennessee,	June	2, 1880
24.	Thomas L. James,	New York,	March	5, 1881
24*a*.	Thomas L. James,	New York.		
	Timothy O. Howe,	Wisconsin,	December	20, 1881
	Walter Q. Gresham,	Indiana,	April	3, 1883
	Frank Hatton,	Iowa,	October	14, 1884
25.	William F. Vilas,	Wisconsin,	March	6, 1885
	Don M. Dickinson,	Michigan,	January	16, 1888
26.	John Wanamaker,	Pennsylvania,	March	5, 1889
27.	Wilson S. Bissell.	New York,	March	6, 1893

Attorneys-General.

1.	Edmund Randolph,	Virginia,	September	26, 1789
2.	Edmund Randolph,	Virginia.		
	William Bradford,	Pennsylvania,	January	27, 1794
	Charles Lee,	Virginia,	December	10, 1795
3.	Charles Lee,	Virginia.		
4.	Levi Lincoln,	Massachusetts,	March	5, 1801
	Robert Smith,	Maryland,	March	3, 1805
5.	John Breckinridge,	Kentucky,	August	7, 1805
	Cæsar A. Rodney,	Pennsylvania,	January	20, 1807
6.	Cæsar A. Rodney,	Pennsylvania.		
	William Pinkney,	Maryland,	December	11, 1811
7.	William Pinkney,	Maryland.		
	Richard Rush,	Pennsylvania,	February	10, 1814
8.	William Wirt,	Virginia,	November	13, 1817
9.	William Wirt,	Virginia.		
10.	William Wirt,	Virginia.		
11.	John M. Berrien,	Georgia,	March	9, 1829
	Roger B. Taney,	Maryland,	July	20, 1831
12.	Benjamin F. Butler,	New York,	November	15, 1833
13.	Benjamin F. Butler,	New York.		
	Felix Grundy,	Tennessee,	July	5, 1838
	Henry D. Gilpin,	Pennsylvania,	January	11, 1840
14.	John J. Crittenden,	Kentucky,	March	5, 1841
14*a*.	Hugh S. Legaré,	South Carolina,	September	13, 1841
	John Nelson,	Maryland,	July	1, 1843
15.	John Y. Mason,	Virginia,	March	6, 1845
	Nathan Clifford,	Maine,	October	17, 1846
	Isaac Toucey,	Connecticut.	June	21, 1848
16.	Reverdy Johnson,	Maryland,	March	8, 1849
16*a*.	John J. Crittenden,	Kentucky,	July	22, 1850
17.	Caleb Cushing,	Massachusetts,	March	7, 1853
18.	Jeremiah S. Black,	Pennsylvania,	March	6, 1857
	Edwin M. Stanton,	Pennsylvania,	December	20, 1860

			Date of Commission.
19.	Edward Bates,	Missouri,	March 5, 1861
	James Speed,	Kentucky,	December 2, 1864
20.	James Speed,	Kentucky.	
20a.	James Speed,	Kentucky.	
	Henry Stanberry,	Ohio,	July 23, 1866
	William M. Evarts,	New York,	July 15, 1868
21.	E. Rockwood Hoar,	Massachusetts,	March 5, 1869
	Amos T. Akerman,	Georgia,	June 23, 1870
	George H. Williams,	Oregon,	December 14, 1871
22.	George H. Williams,	Oregon.	
	Edwards Pierrepont,	New York,	April 26, 1875
	Alphonso Taft,	Ohio,	May 22, 1876
23.	Charles Devens,	Massachusetts,	March 12, 1877
24.	Wayne MacVeagh,	Pennsylvania,	March 5, 1881
24a.	Benjamin H. Brewster,	Pennsylvania,	December 19, 1881
25.	Augustus H. Garland,	Arkansas,	March 6, 1885
26.	William H. H. Miller,	Indiana,	March 5, 1889
27.	Richard Olney	Massachusetts,	March 6, 1893

Secretaries of the Interior.

16.	Thomas Ewing,	Ohio,	March 8, 1849
16a.	Alexander H. H. Stuart,	Virginia,	September 12, 1850
17.	Robert McClelland,	Michigan,	March 7, 1853
18.	Jacob Thompson,	Mississippi,	March 6, 1857
19.	Caleb B. Smith,	Indiana,	March 5, 1861
	John P. Usher,	Indiana,	January 8, 1863
20.	John P. Usher,	Indiana.	
20a.	John P. Usher,	Indiana.	
	James Harlan,	Iowa,	May 15, 1865
	O. H. Browning,	Illinois,	July 27, 1866
21.	Jacob D. Cox,	Ohio,	March 5, 1869
	Columbus Delano,	Ohio,	November 1, 1870
22.	Columbus Delano,	Ohio.	
	Zachariah Chandler,	Michigan,	October 19, 1875
23.	Carl Schurz,	Missouri,	March 12, 1877
24.	Samuel J. Kirkwood,	Iowa,	March 5, 1881
24a.	Henry M. Teller,	Colorado,	April 6, 1882
25.	Lucius Q. C. Lamar,	Mississippi,	March 6, 1885
	William F. Vilas,	Wisconsin,	January 16, 1888
26.	John W. Noble,	Missouri,	March 5, 1889
27.	Hoke Smith,	Georgia,	March 6, 1893

Secretaries of Agriculture.

25.	Norman J. Colman,	Missouri.	
26.	Jeremiah M. Rusk,	Wisconsin,	March 5, 1889
27.	J. Sterling Morton,	Nebraska,	March 6, 1893

Cable, George W., author, born in New Orleans in 1844. In his writings (mostly novels) he has vividly depicted the life and accurately rendered the dialect of the creoles and negroes of southern Louisiana, thus opening a new field in literature.

Cabot, George (1751–1823), statesman, entered Harvard, but left to go to sea, and became master mariner before he was of age. At twenty-five he was chosen to the Massachusetts Provincial Congress. In 1788 he was a member of the State convention that adopted the Federal Constitution. He was U. S. Senator from Massachusetts, 1791–96, and was President Adams' first choice for Secretary of the Navy when that department was organized in 1798. He was a leading Federalist, an able coadjutor of Hamilton, and a high authority in political economy. He was chosen president of the celebrated Hartford Convention in 1814. Life by Lodge.

Cabot, John, the founder of the English claim to North America, was born at Genoa, settled in Venice as a merchant and mariner, and removed to Bristol in England about 1490. In May, 1497, he sailed from Bristol on a voyage of discovery, under the authority of letters patent from the king, Henry VII. He discovered a region which was supposed to be the coast of China, returned to England with the news, and received from the frugal king the sum of ten pounds. The next year he sailed again and explored the coast of North America. The exact extent of his voyages is uncertain, but he probably visited Labrador, the Gulf of St. Lawrence and the coast of New England, southward perhaps to Cape Cod. After the second voyage he disappears from history. The best account of the Cabots is by Harrisse.

Cabot, Sebastian, the son of John, was born in Bristol or Venice about 1474, and died in London about 1557. He probably accompanied his father on the latter's first voyage to America, and may have succeeded him as commander in the second expedition. He was subsequently in the service of Spain, and returned late in life to England. The voyages of the two Cabots in 1497 and 1498 laid the foundation of England's claim to North America.

Cadillac, Antoine de la Mothe, born 1660 of noble French family. In 1694 Frontenac appointed him commander of Michilimackinac. July 24, 1701, with fifty settlers and fifty soldiers he founded Detroit. In 1707 he reduced the Miamis to subjection. In 1711 he was made Governor of Louisiana. In 1714 he established a post in the Natchez country. In 1717 he returned to France. He died after 1717.

Cadwalader, John (1742–1786), was a member of the Philadelphia Committee of Safety. He was a brigadier-general at Trenton and a volunteer at Brandywine and Germantown. He wounded General Conway, the noted conspirator against Washington, in a duel.

Cahokia, Ill., was settled by the French in 1683, and received its name from an Indian tribe.

Calef, or Calfe, Robert, author, died about 1723. In 1700 he attacked the witchcraft delusion in a book called "More Wonders of the Invisible World," whose common-sense arguments greatly affected public opinion.

Calhoun, John Caldwell (March 18, 1782–March 31, 1850), Vice-President of the United States, was born near Abbeville in South Carolina. He graduated at Yale, studied law, and developed qualities of statesmanship at an early period. In 1811 he entered the House of Representatives as member from South Carolina, and became prominent at once as a leader of the younger element of the Democratic party; he advocated the war against Great Britain, and was foremost in the controversy over the United States Bank. He left the House for the War Department in 1817, and served throughout Monroe's administration. In 1824 he was elected Vice-President, and served from 1825 with Adams. Again elected in 1828, he continued in office, this time with Jackson, and between these two great Democratic leaders a bitter feeling of opposition soon arose. In the Nullification trouble which was now developing, Calhoun's abilities and views made him the leader on the side of his native State. He resigned his office in 1832, and immediately entered the U. S. Senate, where he was the champion of the "States Rights" men. His career in the Senate was interrupted for a short period, when in 1844–45 he was Secretary of State in Tyler's administration. During this time he concluded a treaty of annexation with Texas. Retiring from the Cabinet in 1845 he re-entered the Senate, resuming the leadership of the Southern Democrats. It was during this last term that his severe controversy with Benton occurred. Calhoun died at Washington while the compromise measures of 1850 were pending. In gifts of logic he is commonly said to have surpassed Clay and Webster, the two Senators with whose names his own is inseparably connected. His works were edited by Crallé, and there is a scholarly biography by Professor von Holst in the *American Statesmen Series.*

California was formed from the Mexican cession of 1848. The name originated from a Spanish romance of 1521. The coast of California was explored by the Spaniards Cabrillo (1542) and Ferrelo (1543), and by the Englishman Drake (1579), who named the country New Albion. Two hundred years later (1769) Franciscan monks founded a mission at San Diego and discovered the Bay of San Francisco. The missions in 1823 numbered twenty-one and were very wealthy. The priests opposed the government of the towns which was established by the Mexican Government and the Mexican Revolution of 1822, and in 1834 the mission lands were divided. In 1826 the first American emigrant wagon-train reached California. Before the Mexican War the United States Government feared that England intended to seize California, and accordingly encouraged the inhabitants to revolt from Mexico. June 14, 1846, the American settlers, upon the advice of Frémont, proclaimed a republic, and Sloat, in command of an American fleet, occupied Monterey July 7. By the treaty of Guadalupe Hidalgo, signed February 2, 1848, California was ceded by Mexico to the United States. On the nineteenth of the preceding month gold had been discovered near Coloma. By the close of 1849 the population was about 100,000. A State Constitution was ratified November 13, 1849, which prohibited slavery. The admission of California as a free State formed part of Clay's famous "Omnibus Bill" of 1850 (September 9). For ten years the State was steadily Democratic until the division in that party in 1860 gave the electoral vote to the Republicans, who controlled the State in national politics until 1876. From 1851 to 1856 San Francisco was governed by a "Vigilance Committee" who put down the lawlessness in the city. In 1880 the Democratic presidential electors were elected with one exception. In 1892 the electors were again Democratic. In State politics the State has always been very doubtful. Opposition to Chinese immigration, monopoly in land, and the influence of corporations in politics have complicated the political history of the State. The population in 1850 was 92,597; in 1890, 1,208,130. History by Bancroft.

California, University of, Berkeley, Cal., was established in 1868 as the State University; formerly known as the College of California, it was chartered in 1855.

Call, Richard K. (1791–1862), soldier, was appointed first lieutenant in 1814, brigadier-general of West Florida Militia, 1823, was delegate to Congress 1823–1825, Governor of Florida, 1835–1840 and 1841–1844.

Callava, the Spanish ex-Governor of Florida, whom Andrew Jackson arrested in September, 1821, because he refused to deliver certain papers, Florida having been ceded to the United States in 1819. The papers were seized forcibly and Callava was then released. He claimed the privileges of a Spanish Commissioner, but could get no hearing from Jackson.

Calvert, Cecilius (or Cecil), second Lord Baltimore (1605–1675). In 1632 the charter intended for his father was issued to him. It granted to him many feudal rights, but with popular government.

Calvert, Sir George, first Lord Baltimore (1582–1632), was knighted by James I. in 1617, became a Roman Catholic in 1624; was much interested in the colonization of the New World; and in 1632 obtained from Charles I. a patent for what are now Delaware and Maryland. He died before it had passed the Great Seal, and it was issued to his son Cecil, q. v.

Calvert, Leonard (1606?–1647), Governor of Maryland, was sent by his brother Cecil, Lord Baltimore, to found the Maryland Colony, which he did at St. Mary's, May 27, 1634. His authority was disputed by William Claiborne, who at once began hostilities against him, and it was not till 1647 that his possession was fully established.

Cambridge, Mass., was settled by colonists under Governor Winthrop in 1630, and first called Newtown. The American army occupied Cambridge during the period while the British held Boston. The city was incorporated in 1846. Harvard College was founded here in 1636.

Cambridge Platform, a system of church government drawn up by a synod at Cambridge, in the colony of Massachusetts Bay, in 1648. The Congregational churches differed somewhat at that time, some inclining to Presbyterianism, some to Independency. The synod reaffirmed the Westminster Confession, but recommended a form of church discipline which prevails now in the Congregational churches.

Camden, Charles Pratt, Earl of (1713–1794), constantly opposed the American policy of the Rockingham ministry. His sympathy with the colonies continued during his term as Lord Chancellor from 1766 to 1770. He opposed the oppressive colonial policy pursued by Lord North, and, on account of his liberal policy during the Revolution, he was very popular in America.

Camden, Battle of, August 16, 1780. On his appointment to command in the South, Gates determined to seize Camden, S. C. He made an unwise choice of roads so that his army was exhausted when it came to face the enemy. When within ten miles of Camden he delayed two days. Meanwhile Cornwallis had come up from Charleston to assist Rawdon. Gates also made the fatal mistake of sending out 400 of his best troops on a foray. With 3052 troops, only 1400 of whom were regulars, he faced 2000 British veterans. Both parties attempted a night march, but as the surprise failed they waited for daylight. The American left of raw militia was routed. The right composed of Maryland regulars held its ground bravely until it was attacked upon its exposed flank and forced to retire. This it did in good order. Of the Americans 1000 were killed or wounded, and 1000 captured. The loss of the British was 324. It was a clear piece of bad generalship on the part of Gates, who fled precipitately to the North.

Cameron, James Donald, son of Simon, born 1833; as president of the Northern Central Railway Company of Pennsylvania, did good service during the Civil War. He has been U. S. Senator from 1877 to the present time (1894).

Cameron, Simon (1799–1889), politician, worked at the printer's trade in his boyhood and youth. In 1822 he edited a newspaper in Harrisburg. He soon became interested and acquired wealth in banking and railroad construction—was for a time Adjutant-General of Pennsylvania. He was U. S. Senator from Pennsylvania 1845–1849, acting with the Democrats. Upon the repeal of the Missouri Compromise in 1854 he broke with that party and joined the Republican party upon its organization, by which he was elected to the U. S. Senate in 1857. He was appointed by President Lincoln his first Secretary of War, resigned in 1862 and was appointed Minister to Russia. He was again U. S. Senator 1867–1877.

"Camillus," a literary pseudonym of Alexander Hamilton. In 1795 there were published at New York a series of papers called a "Defense of the Treaty," Jay's treaty of the previous year with Great Britain. These papers were nearly all signed "Camillus," but were written by Hamilton.

Campbell, Alexander (1788–1866), theologian, a native of Ireland, came to the United States in 1809. He was the founder of the sect called Disciples of Christ or Campbellites, and of Bethany College in West Virginia.

Campbell, Sir Archibald (1739–1791), British soldier, came to Boston as lieutentant-colonel in 1775, led an expedition in 1778 against Savannah, which he took; and took Augusta, Ga., in January, 1779. He was afterward Governor of Jamaica.

Campbell, Donald (1735–1763), British soldier, while stationed at Detroit met Pontiac (then besieging it) in conference. He was not permitted to return, and was put to death with torture.

Campbell, George W. (1768–1848), of Tennessee, statesman, was graduated at Princeton in 1794, was Representative in Congress 1803–1809, and was chairman of Ways and Means in his last term. He was U. S. Senator from 1811 to 1814, when he became Secretary of the Treasury; was again elected to the Senate in 1815. In 1818 he was appointed Minister to Russia. He returned in 1820.

Campbell, James (1813–1893), was Attorney-General for Pennsylvania in 1852. He was Postmaster-General in Pierce's Cabinet from 1853 to 1857.

Campbell, John A. (1811–1889), jurist, was graduated at the University of Georgia in 1826, studied law and was admitted to the bar in 1829. He was several times a member of the Assembly of Alabama. He was appointed a Justice of the U. S. Supreme Court in 1853, resigned in 1861. He was opposed to secession although he believed in the right. He was Assistant Secretary of War of the Confederate States and was one of the peace commissioners who met President Lincoln at Fort Monroe in February, 1865.

Campbell, William (1745–1781), soldier, of Virginia, led a corps of riflemen at King's Mountain, Guilford Court House and Eutaw Springs. In 1778 he was a commissioner to run the boundary-line between Virginia and the Cherokee country.

Campbell's Station, Tenn. Here, November 16, 1863, occurred a sanguinary conflict between Longstreet leading about 35,000 Confederates, and Burnside at the head of a slightly smaller number of Union soldiers. Bragg, under orders from Richmond, had ordered Longstreet to proceed against Burnside. This Longstreet found some difficulty in doing, for his troops were in a deplorable condition for want of clothing and provisions. Nevertheless he started in pursuit of the Federal leader, who slowly retreated toward Knoxville. At Campbell's Station Longstreet came up with him and Burnside turned upon them, firing at long range as the Confederates advanced over the undulating ground. Unheeding the bullets the Confederates pressed forward until at close range. Then they opened fire, raking the Federal lines. Burnside was forced after a brief fight to retire to Knoxville, where Longstreet followed him and beleaguered the town.

Campbellites. (See Disciples.)

Camp Alleghany, Va. In this battle, December 13, 1861, the Federals numbering 3000 troops and commanded by Milroy were defeated, but retired in good order, before 2000 Confederates led by Edward Johnston. The latter had been left by Jackson in charge of a strong position on a high bluff. Milroy dispatched Moody to attack his flank, while Jones assaulted his front. Both attempts were unsuccessful, so Milroy retired. The losses were about equal on both sides.

Camp Cole, Mo. Here, June 18, 1861, a half-organized Unionist regiment under Captain Cook was surprised, while asleep in a barn, by a Confederate force under Colonel O'Kane, and completely routed.

Camp Defiance, Ala. Here General Floyd, in the Creek War, was attacked January 27, 1814, by the Indians. The attack was repulsed, but at so heavy a loss that Floyd had to fall back. The American loss was twenty-two killed and 147 wounded.

Canada. For the history of the relations of the English colonies with Canada before the Revolution, see New France and Quebec Act. The Continental Congress attempted, but without avail, to induce Canada to take part in the Revolution. In 1775 Montgomery and Arnold conducted an expedition into Canada, which ultimately failed. From Canada Burgoyne invaded New York in 1777. The land operations of the War of 1812 were mainly efforts for the conquest of Canada. Since then our relations with Canada have been mostly in the way of trade, though the sympathy of Americans with Canadian insurgents in 1837, the Caroline affair, the Aroostook disturbances and the Fenian invasion of 1866 have at times interrupted friendliness. The treaty of 1871 provided for the free transit of certain goods into Canada through the United States and into the United States through Canada. There has been of late years a strong movement for the annexation of Canada to the United States.

Canada Company, a company formed by Sir William Alexander in 1621. On September 21, James I. granted to this company an enormous territory in America, covering a large part of the United States and the whole of Canada. Alexander, with whom was associated David Kirke, endeavored to sell his lands as baronetcies. This scheme failed and the company was dissolved.

Canals. The oldest completed canals in the United States are the South Hadley and Montague Canals of Massachusetts, both undertaken by a company chartered in 1792. They are two and three miles long respectively, passing through the rapids at South Hadley and the Montague Falls on the Connecticut River. The Middlesex Canal, connecting Boston harbor with the Merrimac, was completed in 1808. The Erie Canal, largest and most important in this country, connecting the Hudson River at Albany and Troy with Lake Erie at Buffalo, was projected by DeWitt Clinton, and begun in 1817. It was completed in 1825. The Chesapeake and Ohio Canal, the outcome of a project for improving navigation on the Potomac River by General Washington, was begun by the Board of Public Works of Virginia in 1820 and completed in 1850. It extends from Georgetown to Cumberland, 184 miles. The Delaware and Hudson Canal, constructed by a company for the transportation of coal, was completed in 1829. It extends from Rondout to Port Jervis, 108 miles. The Schuylkill Coal and Navigation Canal, extending from Mill Creek to Philadelphia, 108 miles, was begun in 1816 and completed in 1825. The Lehigh Coal and Navigation Canal, from Easton to Coalport, was begun in 1821 and completed in 1829. The chief period of canal construction was from about 1820 to about 1840, when railroads began to supplant them. In 1880 there were about 2500 miles of canals in operation, while about 2000 miles had been abandoned. For interoceanic canals, see arts. Panama Canal and Nicaragua Canal.

Canby, Edward R. S. (1819–1873), of Kentucky, soldier, served in the Florida War 1839–1842, and received a brevet of lieutenant-colonel for services in Mexican War. In 1858 he served in the so-called Mormon War.

In 1863 he commanded the United States troops in the New York draft riots; assisted by Farragut's fleet he captured Mobile in 1865. In 1873 he was treacherously murdered by Modocs while negotiating a treaty of peace.

Cane Ridge Revival, a religious revival in 1799 and 1800, the first famous one in the United States after the "Great Awakening," along the western frontier, particularly in Kentucky. It was begun by the inspired preaching of two brothers from Ohio, who addressed a camp meeting on the Red River, and made numerous enthusiastic converts. At the Cane Ridge camp meeting of 1800, the religious enthusiasm was intense. Converts were made by hundreds.

Cane River, La., a battle in the course of Banks' expedition through the Southwest, occurring April 23, 1864. The Confederate General Bee was stationed along Cane River with 8000 troops, when Emory, Birge and Fessenden of Banks' army suddenly flanked his position and fell heavily upon his right. The movement was a complete success. The Confederates abandoned their position and retreated in disorder.

Canning, George (1770–1827), was British Secretary for Foreign Affairs from 1807 to 1809, during the controversies with America concerning the Chesapeake affair and the difficulties which led to the War of 1812. He approved the British orders in council in 1807, which destroyed American neutral commerce. He supported the War of 1812. While Secretary of Foreign Affairs from 1822 to 1827, he assented to the policy expressed in the Monroe doctrine.

Canning, Stratford, Viscount Stratford de Redcliffe (1786–1880), succeeded Mr. Bago as British Minister to the United States in 1820. He returned to England in 1823 and arranged a treaty which was signed by the British and American Commissioners, but was rejected by the U. S. Senate. In 1830 he framed the British claims in the American boundary question which was submitted to the arbitration of the King of the Netherlands. He was afterward famous as Ambassador to Turkey at the time of the Crimean War.

Cannon, Joseph G., born in North Carolina in 1836, was State's attorney in Illinois from 1861 to 1868. He has been a Republican member of Congress from Illinois from 1873 to the present time (1894), and is one of the most prominent members.

Canonicus (1565?–1647), an Indian chief, king of the Narragansetts. He cordially received Roger Williams to his country and was ever friendly to the whites, but often at war with the Pequots.

Cape Ann, Settlement at. In 1625 the Dorchester Company attempted to plant a colony near the site of the present town of Gloucester. Roger Conant, of Plymouth, and a number of other persons were invited to settle there. But the attempt failed in a short time, and this resulted in the dissolving of the Dorchester Company. The Naumkeag settlement resulted.

Cape Girardeau, Mo., a National storehouse during the Civil war. It was assailed by the Confederate Marmaduke, April 26, 1863, who although he commanded 8000 men was obliged to retreat before McNeil's garrison of 2000.

Capital, The. From the beginning of the Revolution until the adoption of the Constitution the Congress of the United States had no fixed place of holding its sessions, but met on various occasions at Philadelphia, Baltimore, Lancaster, York, Princeton, Annapolis, Trenton and New York. In 1783 after a long debate Congress selected a site near the falls of the Delaware, and in 1784 resolved to meet at New York until the new town was completed. The plans for the capital were not carried out and nothing further was done until after the adoption of the Constitution. During the session of the first Congress the matter was again called up, and after a lengthy discussion in which sectional jealousy ran high an act was passed June 28, 1790, selecting a site upon the Potomac. Maryland and Virginia ceded land for this purpose. By this act Congress met at Philadelphia until November, 1800, when the Government removed to its permanent capital (Washington).

Capitol. The corner-stone of the Capitol building at Washington was laid by President Washington, September 18, 1793. The north wing was completed November 17, 1800. The south wing was completed in 1808, and the interior of both was burned by the British, August 24, 1814. Reconstruction was begun in 1815. The foundation of the main building was laid March 24, 1818, and the whole was completed in 1827. The act of September 30, 1850, provided for an extension. President Fillmore laid the corner-stone of the extension July 4, 1851, and Daniel Webster delivered the address. It was finished in 1867.

Cardinal. The first American cardinal was John McCloskey, archbishop of New York, who was made a cardinal in 1875. Upon his death in 1885 Archbishop Gibbons, of Baltimore, was made a cardinal (1886).

Carey, Henry C. (1793–1879), political economist, son of Mathew. In 1821 he established the firm of Carey & Lea, which became the leading publishing house in the country. He withdrew in 1835 and devoted himself to political economy, on which subject the most important of his writings have been translated into other languages. He viewed free trade as the ideal, and protection as the means of attaining it.

Carey, Mathew (1760–1839), publisher, came to Philadelphia from Ireland in 1784. In 1796 was a founder of the first Sunday-school Society. In 1822 he published "Essays on Political Economy," followed by numerous tracts in the interest of protection. His "Olive Branch" was an important and influential pamphlet.

Carleton, Sir Guy (1724–1808), British soldier, distinguished himself at the sieges of Louisbourg and Quebec. He was Governor of the latter from 1766 to 1770 and from 1775 to 1778, and defended it against the Americans under Montgomery in 1775. He commanded the army that invaded New York in 1776, and fought a severe battle with Arnold on Lake Champlain. In 1782 he superseded Sir Henry Clinton as commander-in-chief. From 1786 to 1796, as Lord Dorchester, he was Governor of Canada. He became a lieutenant-general in 1777.

Carlisle, Frederick Howard, fifth earl of (1748–1825), British statesman. In the House of Lords he advocated reconciliation with America, and was one of the commissioners sent over in 1778 to endeavor to effect it.

Carlisle, John Griffin, born in 1835 in Kentucky, served in the Legislature of the State, and was its Lieutenant-Governor in 1871–75. He entered the National House of Representatives in 1877 as Democratic member from Kentucky, and became widely known as leader of the tariff-reforming wing of the party. He was Speaker of the House for three terms, 1883–89, and achieved a high reputation as an able parliamentarian and impartial presiding officer. In 1890 he was elected to the U. S. Senate, whence, in 1893, he was called to enter President Cleveland's Cabinet as Secretary of the Treasury.

Carnegie, Andrew, born in Scotland in 1835, came to the United States in 1845. He is the largest proprietor of iron and steel making works in the world. He has given liberally to educational appliances and institutions.

Carnifex Ferry, W. Va. Here, August 10, 1861, General Floyd, formerly Buchanan's Secretary of War, was attacked and compelled to retreat by General Rosecrans of McClellan's army. Floyd had superseded Wise in the command of the Confederate forces. The latter failing to obey orders and come to his relief, he was obliged to retire to Big Sewell Mountain. The numbers engaged on either side were small.

"Caroline." In 1836–37 there was a strong republican spirit rife in parts of lower Canada, which culminated, in December, 1837, in an insurrection in Toronto. The leaders fled to the United States, and one, Mackenzie, with twenty-five men, among them some citizens of Buffalo, whom he had persuaded to join him, seized, December 12, 1837, the Canadian Navy Island in the Niagara River, set up a provisional government, and issued paper money. December 26, a party of Canadians crossed the Niagara and seized, at Schlosser, on the American side, the "Caroline," a steamer in the service of the rebels. Several men were killed, and the vessel was burned. This invasion of the American lines caused great indignation. President Van Buren issued a proclamation declaring that the neutrality laws should be observed. The New York militia was called out and placed under the command of General Scott. The rebels finally abandoned Navy Island January 13, 1838.

Carpenter, Matthew Hale (1824–1881), Senator, settled in Wisconsin in 1848, and soon acquired an extensive law practice. He successfully argued the reconstruction act of 1867 before the U. S. Supreme Court. He was U. S. Senator from 1869 to 1875 and from 1879 till his death.

Carpenters' Hall, Phila., was the hall of the company or organization of the carpenters of the city, analogous to the guild halls of London. When the first Continental Congress met in Philadelphia in September, 1774, the State House was offered them, but the offer of the carpenters was accepted by the members, to show their respect for the mechanics. The second Continental Congress also began its sessions there.

Carpet Baggers, a name given first to Northern politicians who sought temporary homes in the Southern States to obtain qualifications for admission to Congress from these States. After 1865 the name was given to Northern Republicans who settled in the South and later to all whites who endeavored to control the colored vote.

Carpet-bag Governments. During the period between 1865 and 1870 the government of a majority of the Southern States was controlled by unscrupulous adventurers, who excluded the better class of whites from voting and controlled elections by negro majorities. Fraudulent taxes were levied and enormous State debts were rolled up. These governments were known as "Carpet-bag Governments."

Carr, Sir Robert, died in England in 1667. He was one of the commissioners sent over by Charles II. in 1664. New Amsterdam and the settlements on the Delaware capitulated to their fleet, but Massachusetts refused to recognize their commission.

Carrick's Ford, W. Va., a running fight between the rear ranks of Garnet's retreating Confederate forces and McClellan's vanguard under Steedman. Garnet was slain and a number of captures were made, July 13, 1861.

Carroll, Charles, of Carrollton (1737–1832), last surviving signer of the Declaration of Independence, was educated by Jesuits in France. He returned to Maryland in 1765. In 1775 he was one of the council of safety. July 4, 1776, he was appointed deputy to Congress, and on August 2, signed the Declaration.

Carroll, John (1735–1817), cousin of Charles Carroll of Carrollton, was educated as a priest at St. Omer's. In 1774 he returned to Maryland and enthusiastically espoused the patriot cause. At the suggestion of Dr. Franklin he was appointed superior of the clergy of the United States in 1784. He became bishop in 1790. By unanimous request of Congress he pronounced a panegyric on Washington, February 22, 1800. He was consecrated archbishop in 1808, and was the first Catholic bishop and archbishop in the United States.

Carson City, capital of Nevada, was founded as a ranch in 1848, but its real history dates from the discovery of gold in Nevada in 1849.

Carson, Christopher (Kit) (1809–1868), explorer, was for eight years a trapper on the plains. He afterward accompanied Frémont on two of his expeditions, to the success of which he greatly contributed.

Carter, Robert (1819–1879), editor and author, was one of the founders of the Free-Soil and Republican parties, to whose success he largely contributed by his brilliant writings in the periodicals of his time.

Carter Brown Library, the most famous and valuable of private collections of Americana, made by the late John Carter Brown, of Providence, R. I.

Carthage, Mo., a brief but severe engagement, July 5, 1861, between 12,000 Union troops under General Franz Sigel and 5000 Confederates, chiefly volunteers from Missouri, Texas and Arkansas, led by Generals Price,

SIGNERS OF THE DECLARATION OF INDEPENDENCE.

McCulloch and Pillow. General Sigel was compelled to retreat, although victorious.

Carthagena, in Spanish America, attacked in 1741 by a powerful fleet and a strong body of soldiers, both English and colonial, under Admiral Vernon. When England was preparing to send a force against the Spanish West Indies, the colonies north of Carolina were summoned to contribute four battalions to the armament. The requisition was generously complied with. But the expedition against Carthagena was anything but successful, though it was composed of twenty-nine ships and 12,000 land troops. The sailors and soldiers quickly fell ill with the fever. Only the outer fortifications were demolished; then the English were obliged to retire.

Carver, John (1590?–1621), first Governor of Plymouth colony. He was probably elected Governor on board the "Mayflower" in Provincetown harbor in November, 1620; was re-elected March, 1621, but died the next month.

Carver, Jonathan (1732–1780), traveler, in 1766 explored the country between Michilimackinac and the Falls of St. Anthony, and in 1767 the borders of Lake Superior. He died in England in great destitution.

Cary Rebellion. In 1705, Thomas Cary, then Deputy Governor of North Carolina, was deposed at the solicitation of the Quakers for disfranchising them through the requirements of the Test Act. He endeavored to usurp the government during several years. Finally, in 1711 he endeavored to capture Governor Hyde by force. Governor Spotswood, of Virginia, sent a troop to Hyde's assistance. Cary was forced into submission.

Cary, Samuel F., born in 1814, Congressman, of Ohio, served in Congress one term, 1867–1869, and was the only Republican member of the House who voted against the impeachment of President Johnson.

Cass, Lewis (1782–1866), was born at Exeter, N. H. His early life was passed as a lawyer and politician in Ohio, broken by service in the War of 1812, during which he became brigadier-general, and fought at the battle of the Thames. In the years 1813–31 he was Governor of Michigan Territory; during this period his management of Indian relations was highly regarded, and an expedition in 1820 into the heart of the Indian country yielded important results. General Cass published in 1823 "Inquiries Concerning the Indians." His reputation was increased as Secretary of War 1831–36, U. S. Minister to France 1836–42, U. S. Senator from Michigan 1845–48 and 1849–57, and Secretary of State 1857–60. He was an unsuccessful candidate for the Democratic nomination for the Presidency in 1844 and 1852. In 1848 he gained the nomination, but was defeated in a close contest by General Taylor.

Cassidy, William (1815–1873), journalist and politician, of New York,—was editor of the *Albany Atlas* and afterward of the *Albany Argus*, and one of the principal members of the "Albany Regency."

Castine, Me., was settled by the French under Baron de Castine in 1667. It was subsequently abandoned on account of wars with the Indians and English colonists. In 1760 it was settled by the English.

Castro, Manuel (1801–1891), of California, as Mexican prefect of Monterey opposed by military force the entrance of the Americans under Frémont into California.

Catholic Church in America. Most of the early explorers of this country were fervent Catholics, and very soon Catholic colonial empires had been formed in Mexico and Central and South America. In 1528 the first Catholic missionaries landed in the United States, at Florida, and in 1565 the first settlement was made at St. Augustine. From this were sent out missionaries to the neighboring tribes and colonies, till Florida was ceded to the English in 1763, which proved a fatal check to missionary efforts. Other missions were established along the great lakes, the Mississippi, in the Far West and in the English colonies, with more or less success, but the real history of the Church in the United States begins with the Catholic colony of Lord Baltimore in Maryland. The Church, however, prospered little, and at the outbreak of the Revolution there were only about twenty-five thousand members, of whom two-thirds were in Maryland. After the war, immigration from Catholic countries and natural development had increased the number in the States to 150,000 by the year 1807. From that time on, its growth has been very rapid. The work of the religious orders, including the Jesuits, the development of educational facilities, and the large influx of Catholics from immigration have all so built up the Church that it now practically claims about one-sixth of the entire population of the United States, and a large majority of the population of the countries to the south. The first Catholic bishop was consecrated in 1790.

Catlin, George (1796–1872), painter and traveler. He spent eight years in travel among the Indians, of whom he painted 470 full-length portraits. He also traveled in South America.

Catron, John (1778–1865), was Chief Justice of the Supreme Court of Tennessee from 1830 to 1836. He was a Justice of the U. S. Supreme Court from 1837 to 1865.

Caucus. The caucus originated in Boston in the earlier part of the eighteenth century. It is said to have derived its name from having been a meeting of the caulkers connected with the shipping business in the North End. From these private and local meetings the term was extended, after the installation of the Federal Government, to the Congressional meetings which nominated candidates for the Presidency of the United States. Members of Congress early began to hold caucuses to nominate candidates, between whom it was an understood thing that the constitutional electors should choose, despite the provision of the Constitution that "no Senator or Representative, or person holding an office of trust or profit under the United States, shall be appointed an elector." There were seven Congressional caucuses held between 1800 and 1824. In 1800 the Federalist leaders, disliking Adams, met in caucus and nominated the latter and Pinckney, hoping the latter might be elected. The Republicans nominated Jefferson and Burr in the same way. In 1804 the first open Republican caucus nominated Jefferson and Clinton. There was no Federalist caucus that year. In 1808, Jefferson having refused a third nomination, the Republican caucus nominated Madison and Clinton. No Federalist caucus was held that year. In 1812 the Republican became a war party, and the Congressional caucus renominated Madison unanimously with John Langdon for Vice-President. The Federalists in a secret caucus agreed to support Clinton and Ingersoll. Monroe was nominated by the Republicans in caucus in 1816, the Federalists making no nominations, but their electors voting for Rufus King. The caucus of 1820, called by Samuel Smith of Maryland, separated without action. The last caucus for nominating a President was held by the Republicans in 1824 and Crawford was nominated, with Gallatin as Vice-President. In 1828 nominations were made by the State Legislatures, and in 1831 the existing nominating system began to be introduced. Similarly, State nominations were made in legislative caucuses, until, somewhat earlier than in the federal party-system, nominating conventions took their place.

Cayuga Indians, one of the Six Nations, originally inhabited a district on Cayuga Lake. Though visited by French missionaries, they allied themselves with the English. During the Revolution the Cayugas joined the British, being already in arms against the colonists at Point Pleasant. They annoyed General Clinton on his march to join Sullivan in 1779. Their villages were then destroyed. After the war they ceded nearly all their lands to the State of New York. They later became scattered and almost totally disappeared.

Cedar Creek, Va., the final battle of Sheridan's campaign against the Confederate Early in the Shenandoah Valley, occurring October 19, 1864. Each general led about 30,000 men. During the early part of the fight Sheridan himself was absent, the battle of Winchester, or Opequan, being still in progress. Wright therefore commanded the Federals. His forces, under the immediate command of Emory and Crook, were drawn up along Cedar Creek and were there attacked at daybreak by the Confederates, who fell upon the Eighth Corps and routed it utterly. Wright immediately reformed his line, making a change of front and a retrograde movement, but losing heavily during the formation. At this point Sheridan came up, assumed command and fell upon the Confederates, putting them to flight with great slaughter. This was the last attempt of the Confederates toward the North by the Shenandoah Valley.

Cedar Mountain, Va., July 9, 1862. General Pope, commanding the Union troops, having come into contact with a portion of Jackson's army, Banks was detailed with a force of 8000 to engage him, although Jackson's army numbered more than 16,000. Banks charged Jackson's rear as he retreated toward Culpeper. The Confederates were for a time in great confusion, but Jackson succeeded in rallying them and in repelling Banks' assault. Banks fell back to a strong position and Jackson, unwilling to attack him, retreated to Gordonsville. The Union loss was 1800, that of the Confederates 1300.

Céloron de Bienville, born about 1715, French explorer. In 1749 he was sent by the Governor of Canada to take possession for France of the Ohio Valley in accordance with the terms of the then recent treaty.

Censors. The Constitution of Pennsylvania, framed in 1776, provided that every seven years the people should choose a Council of Censors, two for each city or county, who should investigate the doings of departments of government, inquire whether the Constitution had been violated, etc. This institution was not continued by the Constitution of 1790. The Vermont Constitution of 1777, modeled on that of Pennsylvania, made similar provision for a Council of Censors, to convene every seven years, and this provision, continued by the Constitutions of 1786 and 1793, was not abrogated until 1870.

Censure, Resolutions of. In case of a violation of law by the President, the constitutional process of punishment is impeachment by the House, conviction by the Senate and removal from office. On March 28, 1834, after a three months' debate, Congress resolved "that the President (Andrew Jackson) in the late executive proceedings in relation to the public revenue, has assumed upon himself authority and power not conferred by the Constitution and laws, but in derogation of both." Jackson protested against this as accusing him of perjury. The resolution was expunged in 1837, after a long struggle on the part of Jackson's friends.

Census. Occasional censuses were taken in individual colonies. The Constitution of 1787 requiring that the representation of each State in Congress should be in proportion to its population, it became necessary also to provide for enumerations. The Constitution provided that they should be made decennially. The first was made in 1790 (the first of Great Britain was taken in 1801), and consisted simply of an enumeration of the population, taken by the U. S. marshals. Since then the censuses have been made increasingly elaborate. The office of Superintendent of the Census, in the Interior Department, once decennial, is now virtually perpetual, since it takes ten years to publish the results of a census. For the figures, see art. Population.

Cent, a copper coin stamped with various designs and issued first by the States, later by the Federal Government. Vermont was the first State to issue copper cents, having permitted, June, 1785, Reuben Harmon, Jr., to make money for the State for two years. He started a mint at Rupert, Bennington County, coining the Vermont cent of 1785. Obverse, wooded mountains and rising sun with a plough, Vermontis. Res. Publica. Exergue 1785. Reverse, a ring surrounded by thirteen stars with rays springing from the circle; legend, Stella. Quarta. Decima. Connecticut, in October, 1785, granted to Bishop, Hopkins, Hillhouse and Goodrich the right to coin £10,000 of copper cents, known as the Connecticut cent of 1785. Obverse, a mailed bust, head laureated; legend, Auctori. Connec. Reverse, Goddess of Liberty grasping olive branch in right hand and liberty staff in left, which is surmounted by a liberty cap; legend, Inde. Et Lib. Exergue 1785. Massachusetts established a mint in 1786, and coined $60,000 in cents and half cents. Obverse of cent: a clothed Indian, in his right hand a bow, in his left an arrow; legend, Common * Wealth. Reverse, a spread eagle, a shield on his breast bearing the word cent, his talons grasping an olive branch and a bundle of arrows; legend, Massachusetts, Exergue 1787, beneath a horizontal bar. New Jersey granted to Goadsby and Cox, in 1786, the right to coin £10,000 at fifteen coppers to the shilling, known as New Jersey copper coin of 1786. Obverse, horse's head, heraldic wreath and plough; legend, Nova. Cæsarea. Exergue 1786. Reverse, a shield; legend, E Pluribus Unum. In 1781 the Continental Congress directed Robert Morris to look into the matter of Governmental Coinage. Morris proposed a money unit equal to one-fourth of a grain of fine silver, an equivalent of one-fourteen-hundred-and-fortieth of a Spanish dollar. The coin equal to one hundred of these units was to be called a cent [Latin *centum*, one hundred], 500 units a quint, 10,000 units a mark. These were not accepted, but in 1784 Jefferson proposed in his coinage report to Congress that the "smallest coin be of copper, of which two hundred shall pass for one dollar." In 1786 the hundredth was substituted. Copper cents began to be coined in 1793. In 1796 their weight was reduced. In 1857 the small nickel cent was substituted, in 1864 the small bronze.

Centennial Exhibition, an international exhibition of arts, manufactures and products of the soil and mines held at Fairmount Park, Philadelphia, during the summer of 1876. It was the first international exhibition held in this country, and was also an anniversary exhibition of the world's progress in the hundredth year of the existence of the United States. The exhibition was proposed by the citizens of Philadelphia in 1870. In 1872 Congress permitted the appointment of a Board of Finance. This board raised a capital stock of $10,000,000 from among the citizens of Philadelphia. Congress afterward appropriated $2,000,000 as a loan; the State of Pennsylvania $1,000,000, and Philadelphia $1,500,000. Many European and other foreign countries sent exhibits, which were admitted free of duty under bond. The exhibition was open from May 10 to November 10. The paid admissions numbered 8,000,000.

"Centinel, Massachusetts or Columbian." The *Massachusetts Centinel*, or *Columbian Centinel*, as it was afterward called, was founded by Benjamin Russell at Boston, March 24, 1784. It is considered the best type of the early political newspaper of the United States. The most eminent Federalist statesmen and writers contributed to this journal, which wielded no little influence in the early history of New England. It was united with the *New England Palladium* in 1830 and with the *Boston Gazette* in 1836. In 1840 it became merged in the *Boston Daily Advertiser*, under which title it is still published daily, tri-weekly and weekly. It was at first semi-weekly.

Central America. The United States concluded a commercial treaty with the federation of Central America in 1825. See the several States.

Century Magazine; its publication was begun as a continuation of the *Scribner's Monthly*, by a company organized by Roswell B. Smith, which bought out the *Scribner's Monthly* in 1881 and styled itself the Century Publishing Company.

Cerro Gordo, a mountain pass commanding General Taylor's line of march from Vera Cruz toward the city of Mexico. It was occupied and fortified by the Mexican leader, Santa Anna, and a battle took place there April 17–18, 1847. Taylor first succeeded in occupying the Ataloga heights which overlooked Santa Anna's position and which he had, contrary to the advice of his generals, left unguarded, as impossible of access to the Americans. This step of Taylor's practically won the day. Actual fighting began early April 18. The guns on the Ataloga heights opened fire upon Santa Anna's fortifications on Cerro Gordo, while General Twiggs and Colonel Baker attacked the Mexicans' unprotected rear. This resulted in defeat for the Mexicans. Santa Anna fled. Number engaged: Americans, 8500; Mexicans, 12,000.

Chadbourne, Paul Ansel (1823–1883), of Massachusetts, president of Williams College, of the Massachusetts Agricultural College, and of Wisconsin University, was two years State Senator and a Presidential elector in 1880.

Chaffee, Jerome B. (1825–1886), of Colorado, Senator, was one of the first settlers of Denver. Was delegate in Congress from Colorado till its organization as a State when he was elected to the U. S. Senate.

Chalmette's (near New Orleans), one of the fights preceding the battle of New Orleans. General Jackson, here entrenched, was attacked December 28, 1814, by the British under General Pakenham. After severe fighting the British were driven back with the loss of 150 men.

Chamberlain, Daniel H., born in Massachusetts in 1835, was Governor of South Carolina in 1874–75, and was declared re-elected in 1876. The Democrats claimed the election of Wade Hampton, and Governor Chamberlain retired from the contest.

Chamberlain, Joshua L., born in 1828, soldier, of Maine, was promoted brigadier-general on the field by Grant in 1864, was Governor of Maine from 1867 to 1871, was president of Bowdoin College from 1871 to 1883.

Chambersburg, Pa., burned by M'Causland and Johnson of Early's Confederate army July 30, 1864. These generals were at the time engaged in raiding toward the Susquehanna with a cavalry troop of 3000 men. They demanded of the citizens of Chambersburg, largely Union sympathizers, $200,000 in gold, or $500,000 in greenbacks. This being refused, the town was fired. This is said to have been done in retaliation for Hunter's burning of Governor Letcher's house at Lexington, Va.

Champ d'Asile (field of refuge), a colony of French soldiers of the Empire, founded by General Lallemand and others in Texas in 1818. It proved a failure.

Champion Hills, Miss. At this place during Grant's pursuit in 1863 of Pemberton toward Vicksburg, Pemberton having 25,000 Confederates, there occurred, on May 16, a severe battle in which the Confederates were badly beaten. The Confederates held a position along a narrow ridge, their left resting on a height overlooking the Vicksburg road. Hovey's division of Grant's army was engaged in building a bridge at this point, and that leader began the battle. He was quickly reinforced by McClernand and McPherson. Logan's brigade had meantime reached the Confederate flank by a detour, so they were compelled to retreat hurriedly to escape being captured. As it was, many of their batteries fell into the hands of the Federals.

Champlain, Samuel de (1567–1635), French navigator. In 1599 he sailed in the "St. Julien" for the West Indies, and returned by way of the

Isthmus of Panama, across which he conceived the plan of a ship-canal. In 1603–04 he in two voyages explored the St. Lawrence River. In 1604–06 he explored and mapped the coast as far as Cape Cod. On his next voyage he founded Quebec in 1608. In 1609 he joined the Montagnais against the Iroquois. They ascended the Sorel River and entered the lake to which he gave his own name.

Chancellorsville, Va., a famous battle of the Civil War, occurring May 1–4, 1863, during Hooker's command of the Army of the Potomac. The Federals numbered 100,000 troops; the Confederates under Lee, who lay on the west side of the Rappahannock River, were about 90,000 strong. Lee had, during the winter, constructed an impregnable line from Bank's Ford to Port Royal. Hooker dispatched Sedgwick across the river to menace Fredericksburg, and Stoneman's cavalry to attack Lee's rear, while he, with the main column, intended crossing lower down the stream and assaulting the Confederate flank. Before Lee was aware he had moved, he was established at Chancellorsville with 46,000 troops. Lee at once decided to begin the attack. May 1 several short attacks were made upon the Federals to ascertain their position and strength. May 2 Jackson, with 26,000 Confederates, making a long detour swept down upon Hooker's left under Howard, and completely demolished it. The counter charge of Keenan's Pennsylvania troops alone saved the left from utter destruction. Late in the afternoon Stonewall Jackson was fired upon by mistake by his own men and mortally wounded. May 3 the fight was renewed with terrible vigor. Lee and J. E. B. Stuart combined forces and attacked Hooker's centre. Hooker himself was wounded, and the National line became completely demoralized. The Federals were rapidly forced back to some strong intrenchments that had been constructed the previous night. Just then Lee heard that Sedgwick had captured Fredericksburg heights, and was advancing upon his rear. His attention was turned to defeating Sedgwick. Hooker retreated, beaten and in confusion.

Chandler, William E., born in 1835, of New Hampshire, politician and Senator, was several times member of the Legislature of his State and twice Speaker of its House of Representatives. From the time of his coming of age he has been an active Republican politician and secretary of its national committee from 1868 to 1876, was Secretary of the Navy from 1882 to 1885 and was elected U. S. Senator in 1889 for a term to expire in 1895.

Chandler, Zachariah (1813–1879), of Michigan, Senator, removed from New Hampshire to Detroit in 1833 and engaged in the dry-goods business, in which he was successful. He became a prominent Whig and a director of the "underground railroad." Was elected to the U. S. Senate to succeed General Cass in 1857, and remained in that post till 1874, when he was appointed Secretary of the Interior by Grant. He was again elected to the Senate in 1879.

Channing, William Ellery (1780–1842), of Massachusetts, preacher and writer. He was graduated at Harvard in 1798, for the next two years was a private instructor in Richmond, studied theology at Cambridge and was settled over the Federal Street Church in Boston in 1803, where he became the leader of the Unitarian movement then stirring New England, and active in all the philanthropic enterprises of his time.

Chantilly, Va., a fierce fight during a violent thunderstorm, September 1, 1862, between Jackson's division of Lee's army and portions of Hooker's, Reno's, McDowell's and Kearny's divisions of Pope's army. Pope had retreated from Manassas to Fairfax Court House and Jackson was dispatched by Lee to cut off his communications with Washington. Jackson fell heavily upon Pope's flank, which resisted him stoutly and finally repulsed his attack. Many lives were lost on both sides, however, and among the dead was General Kearny, an old and experienced Union commander.

Chapin Farm, Va., a brief engagement, September 28, 1864, between small detachments of Federals and Confederates. The former were worsted. This occurred during the campaign in the vicinities of Richmond and Petersburg.

Chapultepec, Mexico, a famous battle of the Mexican War, September 12–14, 1847, Scott commanding the Americans, Santa Anna the Mexicans. Pillow and Quitman were ordered to attack the castle, supported by Worth, Twiggs checking reinforcements from the city. An entrance into the castle groves and the castle itself was quickly effected and the fighting raged along the streets of the city. The castle flag was shot away and General Bravo, four other generals, 100 officers and 800 men surrendered. Worth had meanwhile established his headquarters within the city gates. September 14, Worth captured the citadel and hoisted over the palace the Stars and Stripes. Santa Anna sent to Scott demanding guarantees of life and property. Scott refused to be bound by terms other than those imposed by honor and usage. Scott was obliged to sweep the streets with canister and grape because of attacks from the houses. Numbers engaged: Americans, 7200; Mexicans, 25,000.

Charles I. (1600–1649), King of Great Britain from 1625 to 1649, in 1628 granted a charter to the Governor and company of Massachusetts Bay Colony. His arbitrary rule and his persecutions of religious sects through Archbishop Laud caused a great emigration to New England. He was always hostile to the government set up there. In 1629 he gave the "Province of Carolana" to Sir Robert Heath, his attorney-general. In 1632 he gave to Cecilius Calvert, second Lord Baltimore, a proprietary grant of Maryland.

Charles II. (1630–1685), King of Great Britain from 1660 to 1685, was displeased with the independent spirit of New England, and in 1664 sent four royal commissioners, Nicolls, Carr, Cartwright and Maverick, who should correct abuses in those colonies. He was especially displeased with the treatment of the Quakers by Massachusetts. He granted liberal charters to Connecticut and Rhode Island, 1662–63. In 1664 he claimed and took possession of New Netherland. In 1670 he chartered the Hudson Bay Company. In 1673 he reaffirmed Carteret's New Jersey charter. In 1681 he granted Pennsylvania to William Penn, giving him a proprietary grant of 40,000 square miles. In 1684 he revoked the charter of Massachusetts.

Charles, Cape, Va., so named in April, 1607, by Admiral Newport, in honor of the baby Charles, son of James I., who was afterward Charles I. of England.

Charles City Cross Roads. (See Glendale.)

Charles River Bridge Case, an important Supreme Court case. In 1785 the Legislature of Massachusetts incorporated a company to build a bridge over the Charles River from Charlestown to Boston, granting tolls. In 1828 the Legislature granted the incorporation of another company to build what is known as the Warren Bridge, which was eventually to be free. The first company brought suit in the Supreme Court of Massachusetts for an injunction to prevent the erection of the Warren Bridge, stating that the act of the Legislature incorporating the second company impaired the obligations of a contract made with the first company and was therefore repugnant to the National Constitution. The Supreme Court of Massachusetts found judgment for the defendant, and this decision was confirmed by the Supreme Court of the United States in 1837, on the ground that a State law may be retrospective and may divest vested rights, without impairing contract. This was a limitation of the decision given in the Dartmouth College case.

Charleston, S. C., was founded 1670 (in its present situation 1672), by English colonists under William Sayle. The city joined with the colonists against Great Britain at an early period. It was thrice attacked during the Revolution, first by Sir Peter Parker and Sir Henry Clinton in 1776, again by General Prevost in 1779. In May, 1779, Prevost summoned Charleston to surrender, but was forced to retire by the sudden appearance of American reinforcements. Again early in 1780, Clinton advanced upon Charleston with 16,000 men. Lincoln undertook the defense with only 7000 men. The British army encompassed the city, and the fleet ran past the forts. Lincoln was surrounded and forced to surrender his stores and army. Thus a whole army was lost to the Americans. After the capture of Fort Washington this was the greatest disaster that befell their cause during the war. For events at the opening of the Civil War, see Secession and Sumter, Fort, also Charleston Harbor. The city was occupied February 18, 1865, by Sherman's Federal troops, about 75,000 strong, Hardee having evacuated it with his 35,000 Confederates. This occupation of Charleston took place without bloodshed, but Hardee, before leaving the city, set fire to nearly all the warehouses and cotton wharves, for he was determined not to leave anything for the Federals. An accidental explosion of powder destroyed about 200 persons. The National flag was once more raised on Fort Sumter by the officer commanding the Federal garrison at Fort Morris. The Federals captured 450 guns, which Hardee had left. Charleston was visited by an earthquake August 31, 1886, which destroyed a large part of the city and many lives.

Charleston, W. Va., became the capital of that State in 1872. John Brown was tried and executed here on December 2, 1859.

Charleston, College of (S. C.). In October, 1775, the General Assembly passed an act for the establishment of a college at Charleston. Owing, however, to the Revolution its first class was not graduated till 1794. In 1886 the college was almost destroyed by an earthquake, but was very soon rebuilt. Its law school was opened in 1864.

Charleston Harbor, a battle of the Civil War occurring April 7, 1863, in which monitors were first tried, and without success, against land fortifications. The Federal Admiral Dupont proposed to capture Charleston from the Confederates by destroying Fort Sumter with iron-clads and rams. He entered the harbor with seven Ericsson monitors, the frigate "Ironsides" and the "Keokuk," both partially iron-clad. The monitor "Weehawken" led the way. An advance was immediately made upon Fort Sumter, Forts Morris and Moultrie being disregarded. The Confederates opened fire upon the fleet from all three forts, including 300 guns. The fleet was quickly disabled and thrown into the utmost confusion. The "Ironsides" became entangled with the monitors; the "Keokuk" was struck ninety-nine times, the "Passaic" twenty-seven times. Dupont was compelled to leave the harbor after a few hours' firing, acknowledging the impossibility of taking the city with his fleet.

Charlestown, Mass., was founded in 1629. During the battle of Bunker Hill, Charlestown was completely destroyed by shells and fire (June 17, 1775). Charlestown was incorporated with Boston in 1874.

Charnay, Désiré, born in France in 1828, explorer. In 1880 was sent by the French Government to explore Central America, in which he was aided by Pierre Lorillard, of New York.

Charter Oak, a tree near Hartford, Conn., in the hollow of which Captain Wadsworth hid the charter of the colony to prevent its being taken by Sir Edmund Andros in 1687. The tree was prostrated by a gale August 20, 1856. The story has been doubted.

Charters. The kings of England made grants by letters patent to individuals, giving them land and jurisdiction in America. The name charter is commonly restricted to the grants made to companies or large bodies of men. Of these the chief were those of the Virginia Company in 1606, 1609 and 1612, of the Council for New England (1620), of the Massachusetts Bay Company (1629), of Providence Plantations (1644), of Connecticut (1662), of Rhode Island and Providence Plantations (1663), of Massachusetts (1691), and of Georgia (1732). Of a similar sort were the charters which were given to the Dutch West India Company by the States General of the United Netherlands in 1621, and to the Swedish Company by Gustavus Adolphus in 1624. The attempt has been made to derive the constitutions or forms of government of our colonies from the forms of internal government prescribed, in these charters, for the colonizing companies. But it is much more probable that the colonial institutions are modeled on the governmental institutions of England itself. The theory that a charter constituted a contract between the granting government and the grantee was apparently first advanced by Jeremiah Dummer, in his "Defence of the Charters." See Dartmouth College case.

Chase, Samuel (1741–1811), of Maryland, signer of the Declaration of Independence, was an ardent patriot, was a delegate to the Continental Congress 1774–78, became Chief Justice of the General Court of Maryland in 1791, and was appointed a Justice of the Supreme Court of the United States in 1796. In 1804 he was impeached by the House of Representatives, on the ground of Federalist partisanship, but the Senate failed to sustain the charges.

Chase, Salmon Portland (1808–1873), Chief Justice of the Supreme Court, was born at Cornish, N. H. He graduated at Dartmouth College in 1826, and became a school teacher and finally a lawyer in Cincinnati. From an early period he was profoundly interested in the anti-slavery movement, and was one of the leaders of the Liberty party and of the later Free-Soil party. In 1849 he entered the U. S. Senate from Ohio, having been elected by a coalition of Democrats and Free-Soilers. He distinguished himself as an opponent of the Kansas-Nebraska Bill and in 1856–60 was Republican Governor of Ohio. When the Republican convention of 1860 met, Mr. Chase was a leading candidate, and was naturally a member of President Lincoln's Cabinet. His services in 1861–64 in supervising the finances of the nation during a critical and difficult period have been rated at a very high value. Shortly after leaving the Treasury Department he was appointed in 1864 Chief Justice of the Supreme Court, and held that office till his death. His name had been mentioned for the Presidency in 1864, and in 1868 it was before the Democratic National Convention; but his position respecting negro suffrage led to the rejection of his candidacy. Life by Schucker.

Chastellux, François Jean, Marquis de (1734–1788), French author, was major-general in America under Rochambeau. In his "Voyage dans l'Amérique septentrionale," etc., he notes his observations of men and events in America in a lively manner.

Chateaubriand, François Auguste, Vicomte de (1768–1848), French statesman. In 1791 he came to the United States and traveled extensively among the Indians. He returned to France, where he attained high political honors and wide fame in literature.

Chateaugay (N. Y.), action of October 25, 1813. On the banks of this stream guarding a ford was Lieutenant-Colonel Salaberry with 1000 British. General Hampton with 4000 men attacked in two divisions. A series of blunders, disgraceful to the American arms, resulted in the inglorious retreat of the Americans. Their loss was thirty-eight men, the British twenty-five.

Chatham, Earl of (William Pitt), (November 15, 1708–May 11, 1788), the great English statesman, was a cornet of horse in the army before he entered the House of Commons in 1735. He had been paymaster of the forces, but his great period is from 1756 to 1761, when he was Secretary of State and practically Prime Minister in the administrations of the Duke of Devonshire and the Duke of Newcastle. During this epoch he was the life and soul of the great struggle against France. He supported Frederick the Great on the Continent, and retrieved the British reverses in America. He was the idol of the nation, the "Great Commoner," and on the English side the central figure of the Seven Years' War. He resigned in 1761, sided with the Americans in the Revolutionary struggle, and held office as Privy Seal in the Grafton ministry 1766–68, having been created Earl of Chatham. He continued to champion the cause of the Americans, and of his speeches in their behalf that of 1777 is especially celebrated.

Chatham, Canada, War of 1812. General Procter and Tecumtha, when pursued by General Harrison, here made a stand October 4, 1813, but were again driven in flight with the loss of several men and military supplies.

Chattanooga, Tenn., a famous battle of the Civil War in which Bragg with an army of 53,000 Confederates was utterly routed by Grant and his 80,000 Federals. Bragg, after defeating Rosecrans at Chickamauga, advanced upon Chattanooga and Grant hastened to meet him. Bragg's army extended about twelve miles, lying along Lookout Mountain and Missionary Ridge with its centre stretching across Chattanooga valley. The battle took place November 23–25, 1863. Grant placed Sherman on his left facing Missionary Ridge, Thomas in the centre across the valley and Hooker on his right opposite Lookout Mountain. Laying two bridges across the Tennessee River on the night of the 23d, Sherman crossed and attempted to attack Missionary Ridge. Hooker, on the 24th, made a detour of Lookout Mountain, climbed its heights and dispersed the Confederates stationed there. This was called the "battle of the clouds." On the 25th, Grant, perceiving that Bragg was massing his forces against Sherman, ordered Thomas to advance against the Confederate centre. Thomas broke the centre and followed Sherman to Missionary Ridge. The Confederates were routed, their guns being captured and turned against them. The defeat of the entire Confederate army followed and Bragg joined the flight.

Chauncy, Charles (1592–1672), educator. He fled to New England in 1638; was settled as minister at Scituate, Massachusetts, in 1641; was president of Harvard College from 1654 till his death.

Chauncy, Isaac (1772–1840), naval officer, distinguished himself in naval actions off Tripoli. In 1812–1814 he commanded the fleet on Lake Ontario, displaying great skill and energy, and gained important advantages over the British.

Chautauqua, an educational institution with headquarters at Lake Chautauqua, New York, organized in 1874 by Lewis Miller, of Akron, O., and the Rev. John H. Vincent. The first assembly was called for the discussion of religious and secular topics, and opened on the first Tuesday in August, 1874. Since then the assembly has been held regularly every year, and a vast system of education by reading at home has been organized.

Cheat Mountain Pass, W. Va., a strong position occupied by General Reynolds of McClellan's army with a small force. Skirmishing occurred September 12, 13 and 14, Lee endeavoring to drive Reynolds from the pass. Reynolds' troops numbered less than half of Lee's, but so impregnable was his position that Lee found it impossible to dislodge him. October 3, 1861, Lee having departed for the South, the pass was occupied by General H. R.

Jackson, of Georgia, whom Reynolds in his turn in vain endeavored to dislodge.

Chemung, Battle of, August 29, 1779, an engagement between Sullivan's troops and the Indian and Tory force of Western New York, during Sullivan's march on Fort Niagara. The savages commanded by Brant and Johnson fought bravely, but were at length routed by bringing artillery into action.

Cherokee Indians down to 1830 occupied the upper valley of the Tennessee River. They supported the English against the French. In 1755 they ceded lands to Governor Glen and permitted the construction of English forts within their territory. In 1757 difficulties arose which led to hostilities with the English, finally terminated by the Cherokees' defeat in 1761. In 1773 they ceded to Georgia a large tract of land. At the commencement of the Revolution they joined the English, and in 1780 served at Augusta. They were finally reduced by General Pickens and acknowledged the sovereignty of the United States (November 28, 1785). They ceded other portions of their territory, and in 1790 a part of the tribe migrated to Louisiana. The Cherokees rendered important services in Jackson's army in 1812, but the Georgians desired to get rid of them. In 1817 they ceded lands to the United States, who in turn provided lands on the Arkansas and White. Here 3000 emigrated in 1818, and finally in 1835 the remainder found homes in Indian Territory, west of the lands given the first immigrants. During the Civil War they first joined the Confederates, taking part in the battle at Pea Ridge, but afterward were separated into two parties. (See next art.)

Cherokee Nation vs. Georgia, an important case before the U. S. Supreme Court, decided in 1831. By the Hopewell treaty of 1785 the United States recognized the Cherokees as a nation capable of making peace and war, of governing its citizens and of owning and governing its lands. About 1826 the Georgia Legislature through Governor Troup declared these treaties not binding upon the State, on the ground that Georgia and the Federal Government were equal and independent powers, and that disputes between them could not be decided by the Supreme Court, but by negotiation. In 1830 an act was passed by the Georgia Legislature authorizing a survey and apportionment of the Cherokee lands within the State, their gold mines were seized and they were considered under the State's dominion, thus ousting the Cherokees from the lands solemnly guaranteed by the United States. The Cherokees applied to President Jackson without success. Then they tried the Supreme Court. This court decided them not a foreign State, capable of maintaining an action in the court, but a domestic, dependent nation. The injunction was refused and the Cherokees relegated to the mercy of Georgia. Later, in the case of Worcester *vs.* Georgia, State authority in such matters was denied by the Supreme Court, Federal treaties being declared to have precedence. (See Worcester *vs.* Georgia.)

Cherry Valley, Massacre of. On December 10, 1778, the village of Cherry Valley in Central New York was destroyed by 700 Tories and Indians. About fifty inhabitants were murdered without regard to age or sex. Many persons of refinement were among the victims. Such atrocities as this and that of the Wyoming thoroughly incensed the colonists against Tory methods of warfare.

"Cherub," sloop. (See "Essex.")

Chesapeake and Delaware Canal. This canal was begun in 1825, and Congress, by Act of March 3, 1825, appropriated $300,000 to be subscribed to its stock. This was among the first acts relating to internal improvement.

"Chesapeake" and "Leopard" affair. In 1807 three negro sailors deserted from the British man-of-war "Melampus" and enlisted on the United States ship "Chesapeake." The British squadron was then just within the Virginia capes. The British admiral demanded a surrender of the sailors. This was refused by our Government. Accordingly, June 22, as the "Chesapeake," in a half-prepared condition, was sailing out from Hampton Roads, a lieutenant from the British ship "Leopard" boarded her and again demanded the deserters. Upon being refused, Captain Humphrey immediately opened fire upon the "Chesapeake," which Commodore Barron, who was wholly unprepared, was compelled to surrender without firing a gun. President Jefferson at once issued a proclamation demanding a disavowal of the act, the restoration of the captured sailors and the recall of Admiral Berkeley. Though some tardy reparation was made, the affair greatly exasperated American opinion against the British, and contributed to bring on the War of 1812.

"Chesapeake" and "Shannon." The "Chesapeake," thirty-eight guns, Captain Lawrence, was challenged by the "Shannon," a British thirty-eight gun vessel, but then carrying fifty-two guns. June 1, 1813, was the day set for the duel, which took place near Boston. After twelve minutes the "Chesapeake" became unmanageable through its injuries. Its decks were now swept by the guns of the "Shannon." Lawrence was mortally wounded and was carried below with the exhortation, "Don't give up the ship." The boarders from the "Shannon" now swarmed over the sides and after a severe struggle were victorious. The American loss was 146 men, the British eighty-four. The "Shannon" sailed at once to Halifax with its prize, which was afterward sold to the Government and used as a war vessel. In 1820 it was sold as old timber and used as building material.

Chester, Pa., oldest town in the State, was settled by Swedes in 1643, and originally called Upland. The provisional assembly of William Penn's government was held here in 1682.

Chestertown, Md., was laid out in 1706, and was in colonial times a noted seat of social life.

Chestnut Hill, Pa., scene of a sharp skirmish, December 4, 1777, between the British troops under Howe, and the Pennsylvania militia led by General James Irvine. The militia fled and Irvine was left wounded in the hands of the enemy.

Cheves, Langdon (1776–1857), of South Carolina, statesman, was elected to Congress in 1810; was chairman of the Naval Committee in 1812 and of that of Ways and Means in 1813. In 1814 he succeeded Henry Clay as Speaker, serving during Clay's absence in Europe, one year. He was president of the United States bank 1819–1822. In 1832 he condemned nullification as not sufficiently thorough-going.

Cheyenne, capital of Wyoming, was settled in 1867, when the Union Pacific road first reached that point.

Cheyennes, an Indian tribe of the Algonquin family, settled near the Black Hills before the beginning of the present century. In 1825 the first treaty of friendship was made with them by General Atkinson. The tribe separated later, and one part moved South. A number of treaties between both divisions of the tribe and the United States were executed. The failure to fulfill the one of 1861 led to war. Negotiations for peace were being made, when, on November 29, 1864, Colonel Chevington attacked the Sandy Creek village, and massacred 100 Cheyennes. A disastrous war followed. In 1865 the southern division agreed to go on a reservation, except the Dog Soldiers whose village was burned by General Hancock in 1867. This led to another disastrous war, in which General Custer defeated them at Washita. The northern band continued peaceable.

Chicago, Ill., was organized as a town in 1833, and became a city in 1837. In the latter part of the seventeenth century, the French built a fort on the site of the present city, and later the United States Government erected a fort (Fort Dearborn) which was not abandoned until 1837. In October, 1871, Chicago was visited by the most disastrous fire of modern times. Chicago University was opened here in 1892, and here in 1893 the Columbian Exposition was held. The population of Chicago was in 1840, 4479; 1850, 29,963; 1860, 109,206; 1870, 306,605; 1880, 503,185; 1890, 1,099,880.

Chicago, Historical Society of, began in 1851 and is still in flourishing condition, though 17,000 volumes of its books and its collections were destroyed in the Chicago fire in 1871.

Chicago, University of, was first founded 1857, but closed 1886 through financial troubles. In 1890 it was entirely reorganized, largely through the gifts of John D. Rockefeller, and now has an endowment of over seven millions. Its work is largely graduate.

Chickamauga, Ga., a bloody battle of the Civil War between Rosecrans and Bragg, commanding 55,000 Federals and 70,000 Confederates respectively. It occurred September 19–20, 1863. The Federals were badly defeated. They lost 16,000 men and the Confederates 18,000. Rosecrans was marching on Chattanooga, Bragg slowly retreating and expecting reinforcements before he should decide to give battle. These reinforcements came suddenly and unknown to Rosecrans. Bragg suddenly halted at Chickamauga, and deployed his troops for battle. Rosecrans placed his troops with Thomas on the left, Crittenden in the centre and McCook on the right, along the Chickamauga Creek. September 19 the Confederates crossed the creek, and Polk struck Thomas' line. That general speedily returned the assault, thereby confusing Bragg's plan. September 20 Thomas was again attacked. He had frequently to call for reinforcements, though he held his position stoutly. Finally General Wood, misinterpreting an order, made a false move, which precipitated the Confederate attack upon a weak point in the Federal line, and the day was lost. Rosecrans fled to Chattanooga, but Thomas kept fighting until Garfield was sent to summon him. Here he acquired his sobriquet of "The Rock of Chickamauga."

Chickasaw Case. In 1836 a writ of habeas corpus was served against Captain Eldridge of the brig "Chickasaw," for holding two colored women with the intent of carrying them South. The women were ordered discharged on their presenting free papers. This action against Eldridge resulted from the efforts of Northern people in organizing vigilance committees against kidnapping.

Chickasaw Indians, first known to the whites as residing east of the Mississippi. They early joined the English against the French and in 1739 entered into friendly relations with General Oglethorpe. In 1765 their head men with those of the Choctaws met Governor George Johnson in a congress at Mobile and established friendly trade relations. By the treaty of 1786 their territory was fixed with a boundary at the Ohio on the north and extended down into what is now Mississippi. They continued friendly with the whites during Indian hostilities and aided them against the Creeks in 1793. By treaties in 1805, 1816 and 1818 they ceded all their lands east of the Mississippi, some of the tribe having previously, about the year 1800, migrated to the Arkansas. In 1832 and 1834 the Chickasaws ceded the remainder of their lands and migrated to the territory of the Choctaws, with whom they lived under one government until 1855, when they were granted a political separation. Early in the Civil War they took sides with the South.

Chihuahua, Mexico, occupied by an American army under Doniphan, February 28, 1847. Doniphan had been sent by General Kearny to relieve General Wool, who had been dispatched on an expedition against Chihuahua in October, 1846. Wool had, however, failed of his destination. Doniphan took possession of Chihuahua without difficulty, experiencing no opposition. He retained possession of the city and then abandoned it, finding that Wool did not seem likely to join him. His troops were led to New Orleans and there disbanded.

Child, Lydia Maria (1802–1880), of Massachusetts, author. Her voluminous writings were mainly in the interest of the anti-slavery cause, and were widely circulated and very influential.

Childs, George William (1829–1894), of Philadelphia, publisher. In 1864 he became proprietor of the *Public Ledger*, the wealth derived from which he liberally used for public purposes.

Chili. The independence of Chili was recognized by the United States in March, 1822. A general commercial convention between the United States and Chili was concluded in 1832 and augmented in 1833. By the convention of 1858 the "Macedonian" claims of United States citizens against Chili were left to the arbitration of the King of Belgium, who decided in favor of the United States. The attack on the sailors of the U. S. Steamship "Baltimore," October 16, 1891, by a Chilian mob, has necessitated the payment of an indemnity of $75,000 from Chili. The Chilian Congress of 1891, victorious in its revolution against Balmaceda, established a provisional government June 4, which was promptly recognized by the United States.

Chillicothe, O., was founded by emigrants from Virginia in 1796. It was the State capital from 1800 to 1810.

China. By the treaty with China of 1844, all citizens of the United States enjoy complete rights of extra-territoriality. These rights, together with commercial regulations, were still more firmly secured by the treaty of 1858. In November of the same year a convention for the regulation of the tariff was concluded, and a convention for the settlement of claims against China. A treaty embodying additional regulations to that of 1858 was concluded July 28, 1868. These regulations granted chiefly the right to exchange consuls, the right of religious liberty, the right of voluntary emigration. The two treaties of November 17, 1880, regulated Chinese immigration into the United States, prohibited the importation of opium, and further regulated judicial procedure. (See art. Chinese Immigration.)

Chinese Immigration. The relations of the United States with China date back to 1844, when Caleb Cushing negotiated the first treaty, by which five Chinese ports were opened for trade purposes, and the protection of American life and property in China and extra-territorial consular jurisdiction granted the United States. The Reed treaty of 1858 gained still greater advantages. Under the Burlingame treaty of 1868 the right of migration was acknowledged inalienable, and the express promise was made that "the subjects of China shall enjoy the same privileges, immunities and exemptions in respect to travel and residence as may be enjoyed by the citizens and subjects of the most favored nation." The census of 1880 showed 105,000 resident Chinese. They had become obnoxious to the Californians. They were persecuted, and every effort made to have the treaty of 1868 abrogated. It was said that they could not be assimilated and that their habits were vicious. In 1876 the report of the Chinese Committee was violently denunciatory of the Chinese. In 1879 a bill for the restriction of Chinese immigration passed both Houses, but was vetoed by President Hayes. In 1880 a commission sent to China negotiated an agreement under which immigration could be partially prohibited. Chinamen leaving this country could not return unless possessed of a certificate issued by the United States Government, proving their former residence. In 1885, twenty-eight Chinamen were murdered by miners in Wyoming for refusing to join a strike and $147,000 of property was destroyed. In 1888 a bill was passed and signed by the President, excluding Chinese immigration and rendering certificates of returning Chinamen valueless. This was because of China's tardiness in ratifying a new treaty. In 1892 Congress passed the "Geary Act," in accordance with which any Chinaman adjudged to be not lawfully entitled to remain in the United States should be removed to China; all Chinese laborers should be obliged to procure certificates of residence from the collectors of internal revenue, and any who did not do so within a year should be sent back to China. Means of executing the act failing, it was partially rescinded in 1893.

Chippewa (Canada, opposite Niagara), scene of a battle in the War of 1812. After the capture of Fort Erie, General Brown advanced to attack the British at Chippewa, July 5, 1814; the armies were only two miles apart. The British advance corps fled back upon the advancing main body. The British charge was successful at first, but repeated rallies, reinforcements and finally a flank movement changed the day. The fugitives destroyed the bridge over the Chippewa, and stopped the pursuit. The American loss was 355 in all, the British 604, of whom 236 were killed.

Chippewas. (See Ojibways.)

Chisholm vs. Georgia, an important case in the U. S. Supreme Court. In 1792 Alexander Chisholm, of South Carolina, brought suit against the State of Georgia for the payment of a private claim. Counsel for the plaintiff argued that this court was vested by the Constitution with jurisdiction in cases of this sort, and that the plaintiff could legally recover. The court found judgment for the plaintiff upon this ground, and a writ of inquiry was issued, but never executed, since the Legislature of Georgia passed an act making the execution of such a writ punishable by death. The Eleventh Amendment was at once resolved upon. In 1798 the Supreme Court declared the Eleventh Amendment to have been constitutionally adopted, and renounced its jurisdiction in such cases.

Chisholm, William W. (1830–1877), of Mississippi, was a Unionist during the Civil War, notwithstanding which he was repeatedly elected probate judge. He was murdered by a Ku-Klux mob.

Choate, Rufus (1799–1859), of Massachusetts, lawyer. He was graduated as valedictorian, at Dartmouth, in 1819, when he was already remarkable for scholarship. In 1821 he studied law with William Wirt in Baltimore, and was admitted to the Massachusetts Bar in 1823, at which he soon took the foremost place as an advocate. He was a member of Congress 1831–35, and of the U. S. Senate 1841–45, in which he made many brilliant speeches, notably one against the annexation of Texas.

Choctaw Indians, originally occupying lands along the Gulf of Mexico, early took sides with the French; but later a part became friendly to the English. They acknowledged the sovereignty of the United States in 1786. At the beginning of the present century a migratory movement to the West was begun. They served in the war with England and in the Creek War. In 1820 they ceded a part of their territory to the Government for lands west of Arkansas. Georgia assumed control over their lands in the East, giving the Indians the rights of citizenship. In 1830 they ceded the remainder of their lands and moved West with the Chickasaws. By joining the Confederate cause they lost their civil rights. New treaties were made in 1866.

Christian Endeavor, Young People's Society of, was first established by Rev. F. E. Clark at Portland, Me., February 2, 1881. There are now more than 22,000 societies in all parts of the world, with 1,500,000 members.

Christiana Case (1851) grew out of an attempt of Edward Gorsuch and a Maryland party to seize a fugitive slave in Christiana, Pa. A riot followed and Gorsuch was killed. Castner Hanway, a Quaker in feeble health, was ordered by Marshal Kline to assist in quelling the disturbance. The Quaker refused, though he tried to prevent bloodshed. He was subsequently charged with treason, and later with riot and bloodshed, together with Elijah Lewis, another Quaker. No indictments were found, but the case became notorious.

Chrystler's Field (St. Lawrence River), War of 1812. General Wilkinson with the main body of the American army here fought a slightly superior force of British. The battle lasted five hours, victory alternately favoring one and then the other. Night ended the conflict, with the British in possession of the field. The American loss was especially severe; many of the bravest officers were killed or wounded. The total American loss was 339; the British, 187 killed, wounded and missing.

Church, Benjamin (1639–1718), of Massachusetts, soldier, was active in King Philip's War, was in the Great Swamp Fight in the Narragansett country and finally compassed Philip's death on August 12, 1676.

Church, Frederic E., born in 1826, of New York, painter, has traveled extensively for the purposes of his art. His best known pictures are "Icebergs," "The Great Fall at Niagara" and "The Heart of the Andes."

Church, Sanford E. (1815–1880), of New York, jurist, was Lieutenant-Governor 1851–1855; Comptroller 1858–1869; and Chief Justice of the Court of Appeals from 1870 till his death.

Church and State in America. The relationship of Church and State in the United States differs from all previous relationships in Europe and in the colonies. In the colonies of Massachusetts and Connecticut, the Congregational Church was established; in most of the others the Church of England. Rhode Island, Maryland and Pennsylvania early provided for religious freedom. The Revolution brought disestablishment and religious freedom in several States. There are two provisions in the Constitution of 1787 bearing on the question of religion, which secure its freedom and independence. In Article VI. it is declared that "no religious test shall ever be required as a qualification to any office or public trust under the United States." But this was not deemed a sufficient guarantee for absolute religious freedom, so the first amendment was to the effect that "Congress shall make no law respecting an establishment of religion, or prohibiting the free exercise thereof." In the Legislatures of some of the States a fear was early expressed that government might pass into the hands of Roman Catholics, Jews or infidels, but the spirit of freedom everywhere proved too strong to admit of religious tests in matters of government. State conventions held to ratify the Constitution all proposed amendments guaranteeing religious freedom. Hence followed the first amendment. There are of course certain limitations to religious liberty, which have been set by law. In 1882 in the case of the Mormons, Congress prohibited polygamy and was sustained by the Supreme Court.

Church Members' Suffrage. In 1631 a law was enacted by the Massachusetts Assembly, providing that no man should be a freeman of the colony unless he became a member of some church. This requirement was abolished under the charter of 1691. A similar rule prevailed in the New Haven colony, 1639–1662.

Churubusco, Mexico, a small village near the city of Mexico, where, on August 20, 1847, the advance divisions of Taylor's forces, pursuing the fugitives of Padierna, encountered Santa Anna's soldiers. The convent of San Pablo was the strong point, and against this Twiggs was sent, Worth advancing toward the south and Quitman and Pillow co-operating against Santa Anna's rear. The hottest fighting took place along the Rio Churubusco, where for some hours the Americans seemed threatened with defeat, but rallying they drove the Mexicans before them and carried the river dikes with their *tête de pont*, the key to Santa Anna's position. The attack was then concentrated upon the convent of San Pablo, Worth, Smith and Clarke joining with Twiggs. Worth's guns were directed from an utterly unsuspected and unguarded quarter, throwing the garrison into confusion. The white flag was immediately raised and the stronghold surrendered. Numbers engaged: Americans, 8000; Mexicans, 25,000.

Cibola, a legendary country containing seven wonderful Indian cities, supposed by explorers of the sixteenth century to be located either in Florida or Northern Mexico. The legend originated from the story of the flight of a Portuguese archbishop, who during the conquest of Spain by the Arabs escaped to the Cape de Verde Islands, and founded seven cities. Numerous, and in nearly every instance fatal, expeditions were sent in search of these mythical cities. That of Pamfilo de Narvaez, of 1527 to Florida was especially disastrous.

Cider, Hard. (See Log Cabin.)

Cilley, Jonathan (1802–1838), of Maine, was Speaker of the Maine House of Representatives in 1836, was elected to Congress in 1837 as a Democrat and served till his death, which was the result of a duel with Congressman Graves, of Kentucky.

Cincinnati, O., was settled in 1788 by persons from New Jersey. The village was laid out in 1789 under the name of Losantiville (which see), and received its present name in 1790. It was incorporated as a city in 1814. The introduction of steamboats on the Ohio had a great influence in extending the trade of the city. In September, 1862, martial law was for a brief time declared, when an attack by the Confederate troops was expected on the city.

Cincinnati, Society of the, an organization founded in 1783 by Revolutionary officers. Membership was first extended mainly to the officers and their eldest sons, though a number of French officers were included. The principle of hereditary membership aroused popular jealousy. A pamphlet was published against it, the Governor of South Carolina denounced it, and the Legislatures of Massachusetts, Rhode Island and Pennsylvania censured it. In 1784 Washington persuaded the order to abandon the hereditary feature. The society still exists.

Cipher Dispatches, certain telegraphic communications regarding the Presidential election of 1876, which were delivered by the Western Union Telegraph Company to the Senate Committee on Privileges and Elections, to aid in the investigations of the election frauds. While in the possession of this committee in 1878, some 700 of these dispatches were taken and made public, chiefly through the *New York Tribune*. They were sent by friends of Tilden, the Democratic candidate, and purported to arrange for the payment of certain moneys to ensure the carrying of South Carolina and Florida for Tilden. The latter in an open letter denied all knowledge of the dispatches.

Circuit Courts. The Judiciary Act of 1789 provided for two classes of United States courts inferior to the Supreme Court—circuit courts and district courts, but not for circuit judges. The circuit courts, from that time to 1869, were held by Justices of the Supreme Court or by district judges. In February, 1801, the Federalists, trying to extend the scope of the Federal judiciary, provided for sixteen circuit judges; but the Republicans promptly repealed this in 1802. Beginning with three, the circuits have increased to nine. In 1869 provision was made for special judges for the circuit courts, and the New York circuit has since been given an additional one. (See also art. Circuit Court of Appeals.)

Circuit Court of Appeals. By increase of business the U. S. Supreme Court had fallen much in arrears with its cases. After many projects had been discussed, Congress, in 1891, provided for an additional circuit judge in each circuit, and established in each a circuit court of appeals, to consist of its circuit and district judges and a Justice of the Supreme Court, the new court to have final jurisdiction over appeals from the district and circuit courts, except in constitutional, prize and capital cases, and in questions of the jurisdiction of these courts.

Cities. The census of 1790 showed only thirteen cities with more than 5000 inhabitants and none with more than 45,000. In 1880 there were 494 exceeding 5000, forty exceeding 40,000 and twenty (in 1890, twenty-eight) exceeding 100,000. The percentage of inhabitants of the United States living in cities of more than 8000 inhabitants was, in 1790, 3.3; in 1880, 22.5. Of the ten chief cities of 1890 only four had municipal corporations in 1820: New York, Philadelphia, Baltimore and New Orleans.

Citronella, Ala. Here, April 8, 1865, the Federals under Canby defeated Dick Taylor, who commanded a strong force of Confederates. This occurred after the evacuation of Mobile by Maury, May 8, on the news of Johnston's capitulation. Taylor surrendered all the Confederate forces east of the Mississippi to Canby at Citronella.

Civil Rights Act, an act passed by Congress over President Johnson's veto April 9, 1866, aiming to place the negro on the same civil footing as the whites. Its principal section provided that all persons born in the United States, and not subjected to any foreign power, excluding Indians not taxed, were to be recognized as citizens of the United States. The violation of this act was made a misdemeanor to be considered by the Federal courts alone. The President was given power to enforce the act by special or military force. The controversy over the constitutionality of the act led to the framing of the Fourteenth Amendment, passed June 13, 1866. After this, a more stringent act to secure the civil rights of the negro was passed in 1875. But the Supreme Court in 1883 declared its most important sections unconstitutional.

Civil Rights Cases, being those of United States *vs.* Stanley, United States *vs.* Ryan, United States *vs.* Nichols, United States *vs.* Singleton and Robinson and Wife *vs.* Memphis and Charleston Railroad Company. They were brought before the Supreme Court of the United States, 1883, on certificates of division from the circuit courts respectively of Kansas, California, Missouri, New York and Tennessee. The cases against Stanley and Nichols were on indictments for denying to certain persons the privileges of a hotel, against Ryan and Singleton for denying the privileges of a theatre. Robinson sued the railroad company for refusing his wife, a colored woman, the privileges of the ladies' car. In this latter case and that of Ryan, in which a colored person was plaintiff, judgment was confirmed for the plaintiff, in consideration of the violation of sections one and two of the Fourteenth Amendment to the Constitution. In the other case judgment was found for the defendants, certain sections of the Civil Rights Act of 1875 being deemed unconstitutional and void.

Civil Service Commission, a commission created under the civil service law prepared by Senator Pendleton, of Ohio, and approved January 16, 1883. The commission was to consist of three persons, at an annual salary of $3500, appointed by the President, to regulate and supervise the examination of candidates for civil service offices, and to report on all matters touching the civil service system. An earlier commission had existed from 1871 to 1873.

Civil Service Reform. The evils of the "spoils system" had long been felt, when in 1865, Mr. Thomas A. Jenckes, of Rhode Island, introduced into the House his first bill to reform the civil service. It was defeated several times. In 1871 an act was passed giving the President authority to prescribe rules for admission into the civil service. A civil service commission was appointed, with George William Curtis at its head, and began the work of introducing tests of fitness in the place of political influence. But in 1873 Congress discontinued its appropriation for the commission, and in 1874 President Grant abandoned the system. In 1883 the Pendleton Act, so called from Senator Pendleton, of Ohio, was passed. It provided for a civil service commission of three, representing both parties, which should provide competitive examinations for entrance into such classes of the civil service as the President should designate. The President (Arthur) applied the system at once to the departments at Washington, and to all custom-houses and post-offices where more than fifty clerks were employed. It has since been extended to the railway mail service and to the Indian service, etc., and now includes some thirty or more thousand employes in its scope.

Civil War. Sectional differences had prevailed from the beginning of the existence of the Union. After the time of the Missouri Compromise of 1820, their main basis was the economic and social divergence between North and South caused by the existence of slavery. This caused frequent tendencies to disruption, which increased after 1850. Disunion sentiment was brought to a head by the election of Lincoln in 1860. Secessions of the Southern States immediately followed. In February, 1861, the seceding States, in provisional Congress at Montgomery, formed the Confederate States of America. Most persons, North and South, at first expected peaceable separation. Buchanan temporized. Lincoln could not be clear of his course at first. But the firing on Fort Sumter precipitated conflict. President Lincoln called for troops to enforce the authority of the Union, and the border States seceded. The eleven seceding States had a population of 9,000,000, of whom 3,500,000 were slaves; the remaining States had a population of 22,000,000. The North was rich and of varied industrial life, the South poor and almost entirely agricultural. The North was less united than the South, and of a less military spirit. Unscientific as was the financial management on both sides, that of the National Government was, from the nature of the case, more successful. Extraordinary taxes were levied and enormous loans raised. Supplies of men were obtained for both armies by conscription. Toward the close of the war the North had a million men in her military and naval service, the South 450,000. Though Confederate cruisers did great damage to American commerce, the naval operations of the war were mostly not oceanic, but confined to the assistance of land forces by expeditions on the Atlantic coast, in the Gulf and on the rivers, and to the maintenance of the blockade of Southern ports. In the first year of the war the leading land operations of the war were those in attack and defense of Washington, the chief battle being that of Bull Run. In 1862, in the West, Buell, Pope and Grant cleared the upper Mississippi, the lower Cumberland and Tennessee, with battles at Shiloh and Corinth, while Farragut took New Orleans. In the East, Lee defeated McClellan in the Peninsular campaign, and Pope and McClellan at Manassas, fought McClellan at Antietam, and defeated Burnside at Fredericksburg. In 1863 Lee, having defeated Hooker at Chancellorsville, invaded Pennsylvania, where he was defeated at Gettysburg, the most important decisive battle of the war. Meantime Grant had taken Vicksburg and opened the Mississippi, and the western armies were concentrated upon the struggle for the possession of the central highlands which commanded the heart of the Confederate territory. Here Rosecrans had defeated Bragg at Murfreesboro', but had been defeated at Chickamauga. Grant took his place. Grant and Sherman were henceforth the leading figures of the war, on the Federal side. In 1864 Grant, in a series of severe battles, forced Lee back upon Richmond and began the siege of Petersburg, while Sherman, starting from the central highlands, forced back Johnston and Hood and effected his famous and destructive "march to the sea" through Georgia. Sherman then marched northward toward Grant, who had finally succeeded in reducing Lee to extremities. April 9, 1865, Lee surrendered to Grant at Appomattox. Johnston surrendered, and the war ended, having cost the nation the lives of probably 300,000 men, and money losses of perhaps $8,000,000,000. The great results, which justified all these efforts, were the destruction of slavery and of that extreme States-rights view of the Constitution which permitted secession. In many respects the most gigantic conflict of modern times, the war had ended in the triumph of the national idea and the consolidation of the Union. That the great armies returned to civil life so quietly and with so little difficulty was not the least of its marvels. Histories by Draper and the Count of Paris, and the Century Company's "Battles and Leaders of the Civil War;" Greeley, Pollard and Stephens.

Claflin, Horace B. (1811–1885), of New York, merchant. From 1865 to the time of his death the sales of his firm (H. B. Claflin & Co.) exceeded those of any other in the world.

Claiborne, Ferdinand L. (1772–1815), of Mississippi, soldier, as brigadier-general of United States volunteers, commanded in the engagement with the Creeks, at the Holy Ground, in 1813. In 1815 he became a legislative councillor of Mississippi.

Claiborne or Clayborne, William (1589–1676), of Virginia and Maryland, colonizer. In 1631, under a license from Charles I., he established a trading post on Kent Island in Chesapeake Bay. His claim to this involved Virginia and Maryland, as well as himself, in fierce disputes. Lord Baltimore expelled him in 1635, but in 1645 he, in co-operation with Captain Richard Ingle, overthrew the Roman Catholic government. In the following year Calvert was reinstated, but in 1651 Claiborne, as a commissioner of Parliament, reduced Virginia and Maryland to submission.

Clarendon, Edward Hyde, Earl of (1609–1674), Lord Chancellor of England, was one of the proprietors of Carolina. He was one of a special committee to settle the government of New England in 1660. He sought to weaken Massachusetts and prevent the united action of New England.

Clarendon, Colony of, a colony established in what is now North Carolina by a party of adventurers from Barbadoes in 1664. They purchased lands from the Indians, and in 1665 obtained grants from the lords proprietors. John Yeamans, of Barbadoes, was knighted and made governor over territory extending as far south as Florida.

Clark, Abraham (1726–1794), of New Jersey, signer of the Declaration of Independence, at the beginning of the Revolution was an active member of the New Jersey Committee of Safety, was a member of the Continental Congress from June, 1776, to 1783, except in 1779, and also in 1787 and 1788; was a member of the New Jersey Legislature from 1782 to 1787 and of the U. S. Congress from 1791 till his death. He was chosen to the Constitutional Convention of 1787, but did not attend.

Clark, Alvan G., born in 1832, of Massachusetts, astronomer and optician, made the 36-inch refractor, the largest in the world, for the Lick Observatory, and discovered the companion to Sirius. His firm has attained great fame in the manufacture of lenses for telescopes.

Clark, George Rogers (1752–1818), soldier, went from Virginia to Kentucky in 1775, where he became the leader against the hostile Indians and British, and did more than any other to secure the Northwest to the Republic. Among his more important enterprises were the defence of Harrodsburg, the capture of Kaskaskia and Vincennes by a famous expedition in 1778, the relief of Cahokia, the invasion of the Shawnee country and the defeat of the Miamis.

Clark, William (1770–1838), of Missouri, soldier. In 1804, by appointment of Jefferson, he joined Captain Meriwether Lewis in the famous expedition to the mouth of the Columbia River; was Governor of Missouri Territory from 1813 to 1821 and, from 1822 till his death, superintendent of Indian affairs at St. Louis.

Clarke, James Freeman (1810–1888), of Massachusetts, clergyman and author. In 1841 he founded in Boston the (Unitarian) Church of the Disciples, of which he was pastor for forty-five years. He was prominent in the anti-slavery cause.

Clarke, John (1609–1676), a physician, came to Rhode Island and settled Aquidneck in 1638. In 1663 he obtained from Charles II. a charter guaranteeing religious liberty to the colonists. He was Deputy Governor in 1669 and 1671.

Clay, Cassius M., born in 1810, of Kentucky, politician. In 1832 he became an earnest Abolitionist. In 1845 he established the *True American*, an anti-slavery paper, at Lexington, Ky., and was obliged to fortify the publication office against violence. He was a captain in the Mexican War. He supported General Taylor for the Presidency in 1848, Frémont in 1856, and Lincoln in 1860. He was sent as Minister to Russia in 1861, and again in 1863.

Clay, Clement C. (1819–1882), of Alabama, was U. S. Senator from 1853 till his State seceded in February, 1861. He was a strong supporter of the doctrines of Calhoun.

Clay, Henry (April 12, 1777–June 29, 1852), statesman, orator and political leader, was born in the "Slashes," Va. He studied law, and at the age of twenty removed to Kentucky. Having served in the Legislature, he was at a very early age elected to the U. S. Senate, and represented Kentucky at Washington from 1806 to 1807. He was soon attached to the cause of internal improvements, with which his name became identified. In rapid succession came his term as Speaker of the Kentucky Assembly, as U. S. Senator again 1809–11 and as member of the House, which he entered in 1811. Although a newcomer, he was immediately chosen Speaker, and served until his resignation in 1814. He was a leader of the war party which forced Madison into the contest with Great Britain. His life in Congress was interrupted in 1814, as he had been chosen one of the envoys to treat for the peace finally negotiated at Ghent in December, 1814. In 1815 he was again in the House and served continuously as its Speaker until 1821. During this period he was a powerful advocate of the Spanish-American States in insurrection, and was instrumental in effecting the Missouri Compromise (which see). After a brief absence from Congress he was again Speaker of the House in 1823–25. He was in 1824 a candidate for the Presidency, and received thirty-seven electoral votes. In the exciting contest in the House of Representatives Adams was finally chosen President, and his appointment of Clay as Secretary of State caused not unnaturally the groundless charge of a "bargain" between the two. (See Adams, J. Q.) Clay had ardently supported the tariff of 1824, and denominated the protective the "American

System." While he was Secretary the principal diplomatic matter which arose was the Panama Congress. He retired from office in 1829, but in 1831 he entered the Senate from Kentucky. For twenty years he was the natural leader of the great party known first as the National Republican, but soon as the Whig. He was nominated as its candidate for President in December, 1831, but was overwhelmingly defeated by Jackson. He was active in the bank controversy and other questions of the time, and brought about the tariff compromise of 1833, and the settlement with France in 1835. In 1840 he failed to receive the Whig nomination, and in 1843 he retired from the Senate. The Whig National Convention of 1844 nominated him by acclamation, but Clay's trimming "Alabama Letter" turned the scale in favor of Polk. He re-entered the Senate in 1849, and took the foremost part in the great compromise bill of 1850. Although by far the most popular man in the party, he never again received the nomination for President. In comparison with his great colleagues he shone chiefly as a brilliant debater, "magnetic" platform orator and contriver of compromise measures, intended to preserve the Union. There is an excellent biography by Carl Schurz (two volumes).

Clayton, John M. (1796–1856), of Delaware, of which he was Chief Justice from 1837 to 1840, was U. S. Senator from 1829 to 1835, from 1845 to 1849, and from 1851 till his death. In 1849 he became Secretary of State under President Taylor, in which office he was continued by President Fillmore till July, 1850. As such he negotiated the celebrated Clayton-Bulwer treaty with Great Britain.

Clayton, Powell, was born in Pennsylvania in 1833. In 1861 he entered the Union army and became brigadier-general in 1864. After the war he became Governor of Arkansas, and represented it in the U. S. Senate from 1871 to 1877.

Clayton-Bulwer Treaty, a treaty concluded between Great Britain and the United States in 1850, the negotiators being Secretary John M. Clayton and Sir Henry Bulwer. It related to establishing communication between the Atlantic and Pacific Oceans by means of a ship canal across Nicaragua. It forbade the exclusive control of communication by either party. Contradictory constructions have since been placed upon this treaty, and the claims are as yet unadjusted.

Clearing House. The system was first introduced into the United States by the banks of the city of New York in 1853. During the Civil War the clearing houses proved of the greatest value to the Government in establishing credit and securing loans. The panics of 1873 and of May, 1884, were checked only through the same instrumentality, which similarly operated in 1893.

Cleaveland, Moses (1754–1806), of Connecticut, pioneer, was a promoter of the purchase from Connecticut of the so-called Western Reserve, and was the founder of the city of Cleveland.

Cleburne, Patrick R. (1828–1864), a descendant of William Claiborne (q. v.); came to the United States and joined the Confederates in the Civil War. He commanded a corps at Franklin when he was killed.

Cleveland, Frances (Folsom), was born in Buffalo, N. Y., in 1864, and was married to President Cleveland June 2, 1886. Except Mrs. Madison she is the youngest person who has been mistress of the White House. She has performed the duties and dispensed the courtesies and hospitalities of her high position with rare tact, sweetness and grace.

Cleveland, Grover, the twenty-second President of the United States, was born at Caldwell, N. J., in 1837. He received a fair education, studied law, and entered upon its practice at Buffalo. He served as sheriff, but his great opportunity did not come until 1881, when a reform movement made him the mayor of Buffalo. His efficient administration attracted favorable notice, and in the summer of 1882 he received the Democratic nomination for Governor of New York. Republican demoralization contributed to his election by the enormous majority of 192,000. The prestige of this achievement was followed by such a conduct of State affairs that he received in 1884 the Democratic nomination for President. The election turned on the result in the State of New York, where Cleveland received about 1000 majority over Blaine. The new President became known as a supporter of civil service reform, hard money, and especially of tariff reform, which he advocated in his celebrated message to Congress in December, 1887. He was again the party candidate in 1888, but was defeated by the Republican, Harrison, in a campaign which had the tariff as its leading feature. After retiring from office in 1889 he resumed the practice of law, and settled in New York City. As the new election approached, his candidacy was again suggested, and he received in 1892 for the third time the party nomination. His former competitor was again in the field, and was this time decisively beaten. President Cleveland commenced his second term in March, 1893, and the chief features of his administration so far have been the repeal of the Silver Purchase Act, or Sherman Act, the introduction of a bill for the reduction of the tariff, and the Hawaiian imbroglio.

Cleveland, Rose E., was born in Fayetteville, N. Y., in 1846, youngest sister of President Cleveland, teacher and author. She was mistress of the White House in 1885 and 1886.

Cleveland, O., was founded in 1796. It was an important point in the War of 1812, and was incorporated as a city in 1836.

Clifford, Nathan (1803–1881), of Maine, jurist, was Speaker of the Maine House of Representatives in 1833 and 1834; Attorney-General of Maine from 1834 to 1838, and member of Congress from 1839 to 1843. From 1846 to 1848 he was Attorney-General in President Polk's Cabinet. In 1858 he was appointed by President Buchanan a Justice of the U. S. Supreme Court. In 1877 he was president of the Electoral Commission.

Clinton, De Witt (1769–1828), was a nephew of George Clinton, and after graduating at Columbia he acted as secretary to his uncle. He was a Republican member of the New York Legislature and entered the U. S. Senate in 1802, but left that body soon to become mayor of New York City. In this office he served until 1807, and again in 1809–10 and 1811–15. He was also State Senator, Lieutenant-Governor and a member of the council of appointment. In 1812, he was the candidate of the Federalists and of the New York Democrats for President, receiving eighty-nine electoral votes. Clinton was ardently devoted to the policy of internal improvements, and especially to the development of the Erie and Champlain canals. In 1817–23 and 1825–28 he was Governor of New York.

Clinton, George (1739–1812), Vice-President of the United States, was a soldier in the French and Indian War and a member of the New York Assembly; in the first part of the Revolution he was for a short time member of the Continental Congress, and then served in the field. As a brigadier-general he defended unsuccessfully the Highland forts against the British in 1777. For the long period of 1777–95 he was Governor of the State, and threw his great influence against the ratification of the Federal Constitution. Thereafter he was an Anti-Federalist and Republican leader. He received a few votes for Vice-President in 1789, fifty votes for Vice-President in 1792 and several in 1796. He was again Governor in 1801–04, and was elected Vice-President in 1804, serving as such, under Jefferson and Madison, until his death. In 1811 he gave the casting vote against the U. S. Bank.

Clinton, Sir Henry (1738–1795), British soldier, came to Boston as major-general in 1775 with Howe and Burgoyne. In 1778 he was appointed commander-in-chief of the British forces. He evacuated Philadelphia in June and on his retreat thence to New York fought with Washington the indecisive battle of Monmouth. In May, 1778, he captured Charleston and the whole army under Lincoln. During the following summer he planned with Arnold the treasonable surrender of West Point. He failed to relieve Cornwallis in October, 1781, and returned to England in 1782.

Clinton, James (1736–1812), of New York, soldier, during the French and Indian War captured a French sloop-of-war on Lake Ontario. As colonel of a New York regiment he was with Montgomery at Quebec in 1775. As brigadier-general he commanded at Fort Clinton when it was taken by the British in 1777, and was present at Yorktown. He was a member of the New York convention that adopted the Federal Constitution.

Clinton Bridge Case, an important litigation in the United States Supreme Court, 1870, which established the doctrine by which railroad bridges may be said to have gained clear recognition of their rights of way in preference to the navigable waters crossed by them, through the power of Congress to regulate interstate commerce.

Clymer, George (1739–1813), of Pennsylvania, signer of the Declaration (although not present at its adoption). In 1775 he became continental treasurer, and was a member of Congress in 1776, 1777 and 1780. In 1778 he, with John Nixon, organized the Bank of North America. He was a member of the convention that framed the Federal Constitution, and elected to the first Congress held under its provisions.

Coal. The first organized effort to mine anthracite coal was in 1793 on the Mammoth bed at Summit Hill, near Mauch Chunk, Pennsylvania, but regular shipments did not begin until 1820. It was not until 1825 that it was in general use for the generation of steam, and not until 1839 that it was employed as an exclusive fuel in the manufacture of pig iron. The industry in bituminous coal and coke was begun in Connellsville, Pa., in 1841, by McCormick and Campbell. Regular manufacture commenced in that district in 1861. The coal-mining industry is now more or less prosperous in a very large number of the States and Territories, though Pennsylvania still holds the lead. The most recent extensive developments have been made in West Virginia. The total output of anthracite for 1889 exceeded 33,000,000 tons; the annual output of coke is also enormous.

Coast and Geodetic Survey. The establishment of this important bureau was first contemplated in 1807. President Jefferson suggested it in his message to Congress of that year. Congress appropriated $50,000 for the survey. Nothing practical was accomplished until 1811. Then F. R. Hassler, an Englishman, was made chief of the survey and commenced operations near New York. Since then its work has progressed constantly, under Alexander Dallas Bache and other eminent engineers and organizers. It has been a bureau of the Treasury Department.

Cobb, Howell (1815–1868), of Georgia, statesman, entered Congress as a Democrat in 1843, and served till 1853 and again 1855; was elected Speaker in 1849; was a warm defender of the Union, but also a strong advocate of State rights and of the compromise measures of 1850; was elected Governor of Georgia by the Union party in 1851. In 1857 he became President Buchanan's Secretary of the Treasury. In 1860 he urged forward the secession movement, and was a delegate to the provisional Congress which adopted the Confederate Constitution.

Cobbett, William (1762–1835), British journalist and pamphleteer, came to Philadelphia in 1792, wrote in aid of the Federalists a series of powerful pamphlets under the name of "Peter Porcupine," and returned to London in 1800.

Cochrane, Sir Alexander F. I. (1758–1832), British admiral, commanded the British North American fleet in 1812, assisted in the capture of Washington in 1814, and in the attack on New Orleans.

Cockburn, Sir George (1772–1853), British admiral. In 1813 expeditions from his squadron ravaged the coasts of the United States from Delaware to Georgia. In 1814 under Admiral Cochrane and in conjunction with General Ross he captured Washington, burning the Capitol and other public buildings, and unsuccessfully attempted to take Baltimore. In 1815 he conveyed Napoleon to St. Helena.

Cockrell, Francis M., born in 1834, of Missouri, Senator, entered the Confederate army, in which he rose to the rank of brigadier-general. He became U. S. Senator in 1875, in which position he still (1894) continues.

Cod, Cape, discovered and named May 15, 1602, by Bartholomew Gosnold.

Coddington, William (1601–1678), came to Salem, Mass., in 1630. In 1638 with John Clarke he founded the colony of Rhode Island at Aquidneck and was its first Governor.

Cody, William F., born in 1845, of Kansas, served with distinction as a scout through the Civil War and afterward in several expeditions; widely known as "Buffalo Bill."

Cœur d'Alene, an Indian tribe in Idaho and Washington territories. In 1858 a part of the tribe joined in an attack on Colonel Steptoe. They were subsequently defeated by Colonel Wright and became peaceful. In 1867 a reservation was set apart for those in Idaho, and in 1872 a band in Paradise Valley was removed to land between the Okinokane and Columbia rivers.

Coffee, John (1772–1834), of Tennessee, soldier. In the War of 1812 he became brigadier-general, fought and won the battle of Tallushatchie and commanded Jackson's left wing at New Orleans.

Coffin, Charles Carleton, born in 1823, of Massachusetts, under the name of "Carleton" was war correspondent of the *Boston Journal* during the whole of the Civil War and the Prusso-Austrian War of 1866.

Cogswell, Joseph G. (1786–1871), of Massachusetts, was appointed librarian of Harvard College in 1820. In 1823, in conjunction with George Bancroft, he founded the Round Hill School at Northampton. Afterward he was for many years (till 1860) librarian of the Astor Library.

Cohens vs. Virginia, an important case before the U. S. Supreme Court, decided in 1821. In 1820, P. J. and M. J. Cohen were presented before the Quarter Sessions Court at Norfolk for selling lottery tickets in defiance of the statute of the State prohibiting such sales. The Cohens appealed to the Supreme Court of the United States against the fine imposed by the Virginia court, pleading the legality of their sale under the "Act to amend the charter of the city of Washington," passed by Congress 1812, which permitted the drawing of lotteries. The attorney for Virginia denied the jurisdiction of the court, because a State was defendant (see Eleventh Amendment) and because in cases in which States were parties its jurisdiction was original and not appellate. But the court decided that the Eleventh Amendment did not apply, and that in constitutional cases it had always appellate jurisdiction.

Coinage Laws. By the law of April 2, 1792, any person could have gold or silver coined at the mint into lawful money, receiving therefor coins of the same species of bullion, weight for weight of the pure metal contained therein. The standard for gold was eleven parts pure to one alloy; for silver, 1485 parts pure to 179 alloy. The ratio of gold to silver was fifteen to one, and both coins were legal tender. By the law of March 3, 1795, the Treasurer retained twenty-four cents per ounce for silver below the standard, four cents for gold. By the law of April 21, 1800, there was retained for deposits of gold and silver below the standard a sum sufficient for the expense of refinement. By the law of May 8, 1828, a sum was retained from silver bullion requiring the test, for materials and wastage. By the law of June 28, 1834, a deduction of one-half per cent was to be made from all standard gold and silver deposited for coinage, if paid for in coin within five days from deposit. By the law of January 18, 1837, the standard gold and silver coin was made nine-tenths pure, one-tenth alloy and legal tender for any sum. By the law of February 21, 1853, the weight of the half dollar was reduced from 206¼ to 192 grains and lesser silver coins in the same proportion; legal tender to five dollars. No private deposits for coinage in these coins were received and charges of one-half per cent were made for refining. By the law of February 12, 1873, the weight of the trade dollar was to be 420 grains, of the half dollar 193 grains; legal tender to five dollars. Silver bullion could be deposited for coinage into trade dollars only; gold for coinage for the benefit of the depositor. The directors of the mint were to buy silver for coins less than one dollar. One-fifth of one per cent was charged for converting standard gold bullion into coin, and silver into trade dollars. Silver coins, except trade dollars, were to be exchanged at par for gold coins in sums not exceeding $100. The charges on gold were removed in 1875. By the law of July 22, 1877, the trade dollar ceased to be a legal tender. By the law of February 28, 1878, silver dollars of 412½ grains were made legal tender for all debt, and the Secretary of the Treasury was authorized to purchase at market value, and coin not less than $2,000,000 worth of silver bullion per month and not more than $4,000,000 worth per month. By the law of June 9, 1879, silver coins less than one dollar were made legal tender to ten dollars. By the law of July 14, 1890, that of 1878 was repealed and the Secretary of the Treasury was authorized to purchase 4,500,000 ounces of silver bullion per month, issuing in payment United States notes, to be a legal tender; and to make a sufficient monthly coinage for the redemption of these notes. In 1893 the silver-purchase clauses of this act were repealed.

Cold Harbor, Va., battles between the Federals and Confederates under Grant and Lee, fought irregularly during twelve days, June 1–12, 1864, while Grant was attempting his famous campaign against Richmond. Lee held the vicinity of Cold Harbor with about 100,000 men, having thrown up hasty fortifications. Grant had 120,000 troops. Sheridan advanced to Cold Harbor on the thirty-first of May. June 1 the Sixth Corps and Smith's troops began the attack by endeavoring to take the Confederate fortifications. The assault was ineffectual, the Federals being repulsed with heavy loss. June 2 rain prevented battle, so the day was passed on both sides in arranging the lines. June 3 Lee's position had been immensely strengthened by slashes and rifle trenches. Sheridan's cavalry guarded the crossing of the Chickahominy, and Wilson watched the Confederates' right. Early in the morning the Federals advanced upon the Confederate intrenchments. Hancock's corps forced the enemy from their front, and with Wright, Smith and Warren made vigorous assaults upon the impregnable earthworks. Burnside failed to come to their aid. Several regiments, however, mounted the parapets and placed their banners upon them. Many of the bravest Federal officers lost their lives. The last assault lasted half an hour, and then the Federals retired. For ten days the armies lay idle, their sharpshooters picking off many men. Federal loss, 10,000; Confederate, 8000.

Colden, Cadwallader (1688–1776), of New York, was the first surveyor-general of New York, was an ardent royalist, was president of the council in 1760 and Lieutenant-Governor in 1761, took an active part in founding the American Philosophical Society, and was a correspondent of the prominent scientific men of his time, including Linnæus and Franklin.

Cole, Thomas (1801–1848), of New York, landscape painter. Among his most popular works are the "Voyage of Life," "The Course of Empire," "The White Mountains," and the "Dream of Arcadia."

Coleman, William T. (1824–1893), of California, pioneer, was an active member of the "Vigilance Committee" of 1851, and chairman of the executive department of that of 1856.

Colfax, Schuyler (1823–1885), of Indiana, Vice-President. In 1844 he made campaign speeches for Clay. In 1845 he established the *St. Joseph Valley Register*, which became a very influential Whig journal. He was secretary of the national Whig conventions of 1848 and 1852, and was in Congress as a Republican from 1855 to 1869. He was Speaker of the House from 1863 to 1869, and Vice-President from 1869 to 1873, but failed to obtain a renomination for the next term. He was charged, probably unjustly, with complicity in the "Crédit Mobilier" scandal of 1873.

Colgate University (formerly Madison University), Hamilton, N. Y., was founded in 1820 and chartered 1846 by Baptists. Its theological school was founded in 1819. In 1889 its name was changed to Colgate, in honor of a benefactor.

Collamer, Jacob (1791–1865), of Vermont, was a Representative in the Vermont Assembly in 1821 and 1827. From 1833 to 1842 and from 1850 to 1854 he was a Justice of the Supreme Court of Vermont, a member of Congress from 1843 to 1849, and Postmaster-General from 1849 to 1850. From 1854 until his death he was a U. S. Senator.

Colleges. In spite of the vote of the Virginia Company in 1619 to establish a college there, the first college established in the United States was Harvard (1636). The second was the College of William and Mary (1693), the third Yale (1701). Other colleges established before 1789 were the following: the College of New Jersey (Princeton), opened in 1746, the University of Pennsylvania in 1753, King's College (now Columbia) in 1754, Rhode Island College (now Brown University) in 1765, Dartmouth in 1770, Rutgers in 1770, Dickinson in 1783, the College of Charleston in 1785. The colleges will be found treated under their several names.

Colleton, James, of Barbadoes, was appointed Governor of South Carolina in 1686. His authority was resisted by the Legislature which, after the English revolution, impeached, disfranchised and banished him (1690).

Collyer, Robert, born in 1823, clergyman, came to the United States in 1850. In 1859 he became a Unitarian, and in 1879 pastor of the Church of the Messiah in New York City.

Colombia. The independence of Colombia was recognized by the United States in March, 1822. A commercial treaty was concluded between the United States and the undivided republic of Colombia October 3, 1824. In 1831 the republic was divided into New Granada, Venezuela and Ecuador. New Granada concluded a commercial treaty with the United States in 1846.

SIGNING THE DECLARATION OF INDEPENDENCE.

By this treaty the United States guaranteed the neutrality of the Isthmus of Panama in compensation for specified commercial advantages, and on these grounds the United States has claimed the right to be heard in Panama Canal affairs. A consular convention was concluded in 1850, and claims conventions favorable to the United States in 1857 and 1861.

Colonial System. Until the close of the last century, it was the invariable practice of European States to manage their colonies with a view almost solely to the benefit of the mother country. Spain, Portugal, France, the Netherlands and England, though they differed otherwise in their colonial systems, agreed in this. Yet on the whole the disregard of colonial interests which the English Government manifested was less extreme than that of other governments. Adam Smith, by his "Wealth of Nations," published in 1776, taught governments the expediency of a more liberal system.

Colonization Society, The National. An organization formed in 1816, at Princeton, N. J., and immediately reorganized at Washington, its principal object being to encourage the emancipation of slaves by obtaining for them a place without the United States to which they might emigrate. The scheme was also intended to relieve the South of the free black population with which it was burdened. Branches of the society were soon established in almost every State. Free negroes were first sent to Sierra Leone, later for a short time to Sherbrooke Island, and finally in 1821 a permanent location was purchased at Cape Mesurado. In 1847 this colony declared itself an independent republic under the name of Liberia. The society engaged the attention of many anti-slavery advocates until the rise of the Abolition party in 1831.

Colorado, a State of the Union, was named from the river of that name. It was formed in part from the Louisiana purchase, and in part from the Mexican cession. The early Spanish gold-hunters visited Colorado, and in 1806 Major Pike led a Government expedition into the region. In 1843 Frémont explored the northern part. The discovery of gold in 1858 attracted immigration. Two acts for the admission of Colorado as a State were vetoed by President Johnson in 1866 and 1867. August 1, 1876, the President announced the admission of Colorado. Down to 1892 the State was Republican. In that year the electoral votes were cast for Weaver, the Fusion candidate. The population of the State in 1880 was 199,327; in 1890 it was 412,198.

Colquitt, Alfred H. (1824–1894), of Georgia, Senator, served as major-general in the Confederate army. He was Governor from 1877 to 1883, after which he was U. S. Senator until his death.

Colt, Samuel (1814–1862), of Connecticut, inventor. In 1829, while a runaway sailor-boy, he made a model in wood of his celebrated revolver. In 1852 he built immense armories at Hartford for their manufacture.

Columbia, S. C., became the capital of the State in 1790 under an act of the Legislature which provided for the founding of the city. It was taken by the Federal forces under General Sherman, February 17, 1865. On the evacuation of the city by General Wade a large quantity of cotton was fired either by accident or design, and caused immense damage.

Columbia, District of. (See District of Columbia.)

Columbia College, New York City. Originally called King's College and chartered 1754. During the Revolution studies were suspended and its building made into a military hospital. In 1784 the college was reorganized and resumed work under the new name. In 1891 the College of Physicians and Surgeons became a part of the college. In 1858 a law department was established and in 1864 a school of mines with eight distinct courses of study. In 1880 and 1890 the facilities in graduate work were largely increased.

Columbia River was discovered by the Spaniard Heceta in 1775 and called St. Roque. Afterward, in 1792, Captain Gray, of Boston, explored the stream and changed the name to Columbia. In 1805–06 Lewis and Clarke, under orders from President Jefferson, explored the Columbia River and opened up the northwest region. Questions concerning the discovery of the region had an important part in the discussion of the Oregon question.

Columbian Institute, founded at Washington in 1819, by Joel Barlow, sometime American Minister at Paris. Barlow was aided by Josiah Meigs, Thomas Law, Edward Cutbush, Judge Cranch and others, citizens of Washington. Its purpose was the advancement of knowledge by associations of scientific men, and the dissemination of its rudiments by the instruction of youth.

Columbian Order. (See Tammany Society.)

Columbus, Christopher (about 1436–1506), the discoverer of America, was born probably at Genoa in Italy, about 1436. His early life was passed at sea, interspersed with work as a maker of maps and charts. About 1470 he went to Lisbon, and engaged in voyages to Guinea and probably visited Iceland. He became acquainted with the map of Toscanelli and the results of geographical investigation, and planned the discovery of a short route to China, Japan and the Indies. As his project was rejected by the King of Portugal, he followed the court of Ferdinand and Isabella, setting forth his schemes at Cordova, Salamanca, Malaga and elsewhere, but he failed to enlist support until after the fall of Granada in 1492. Having obtained authority from the sovereigns and financial aid, he sailed with his fleet of three caravels, the "Santa Maria," "Pinta" and "Niña," from Palos on August 3, 1492. He held a westerly course, quelled insubordination, and reached land in the Bahama group October 12, 1492; the island of the landfall may have been Watling's or Samana Island. He further discovered Cuba and Hayti, and arrived home after severe vicissitudes in March, 1493. In the following autumn he sailed with a larger expedition, and remained in the West Indies until 1496. On his third voyage in 1498, he reached the mainland at the mouth of the Orinoco, rightly surmising that he had found a continent, though still fancying himself on the eastern coast of Asia. Proceeding to the West Indies he was imprisoned by enemies and sent in chains to Spain, but was soon released. In his fourth voyage, 1502 to 1504, he explored the coast of Central America. He survived his patron Isabella a short time, dying at Valladolid in Spain, May 20, 1506. There is a well-known biography by Irving, and recent lives by Harrisse and Winsor, the last being distinctly unfavorable.

Columbus, O., settled in 1812, became the capital of the State in 1816. It became a city in 1834.

Comanche Indians, originally a roving tribe, early engaged in disastrous wars with the Spanish. They have always been dangerous and troublesome. They were at one time on a Texas reservation, but on being expelled became bitter enemies of the State. The Government later collected a portion on lands in the western part of Indian Territory. A part of these, the Quanhado, refused to settle down until defeated by Colonel McKenzie at McClellan's Creek in 1872.

Commerce. From their first foundation, the colonies of New Netherland and New England were engaged to an important extent in commerce, while the chartered colonizing companies, like the Virginia Company, were largely intended for that pursuit. The Navigation Acts of 1646, 1651, 1660 and 1663 aimed to restrict colonial commerce for the benefit of the mother country; and similar restrictions were, beginning in 1673, laid on intercolonial commerce. But all these acts were constantly evaded. The efforts finally made to enforce them more strictly were among the chief causes of the Revolution. By 1789 the tonnage of American vessels engaged in foreign trade was about 325,000 tons, of that engaged in the coasting trade 125,000 more, while that of foreign vessels trading with the United States was about 250,000, chiefly British. At that time two-thirds of the imports were from England, and half the exports went to that country. Trade with the East Indies was then just beginning. New England and New York were the chief commercial regions at that time. From that date American commerce has been too various to summarize. (See Imports, Exports.)

Commissary. The English church in the colonies was under the nominal supervision of the Bishop of London, of whose diocese the colonies formed a part. To remedy disorders caused by want of real supervision, commissaries were appointed by him in Virginia and Maryland, with limited powers of control and supervision over the clergy of their respective provinces.

Commissioner of the Revenue. An office created by Act of Congress May 8, 1792, for the management of national finances, abolished April 6, 1802; re-established July 24, 1813, and again abolished December 23, 1817. The duties of the commissioner were similar to those of the Assistant Secretary of the Treasury.

Committees. It is the universal custom of American legislative bodies to transact their business through standing committees, each of which is charged with a special branch of the business of the body. This is not the present English custom, but is nevertheless not an American invention. The House of Commons developed the rudiments of such a system in Queen Elizabeth's time, and it was in full operation during the Commonwealth. During the latter part of the seventeenth and the beginning of the eighteenth centuries Virginia, Maryland, Pennsylvania, New York and North Carolina adopted this system from England, with nearly the same names of committees as those of the House of Commons (in which this system has since become obsolete because of cabinet government). Therefore it was readily adopted as the mode of transacting business by the Continental Congress, though it was not used in the Legislatures of the New England colonies. In the Congresses under the Constitution, beginning in 1789, but few committees were at first used, but the number gradually increased. By Speaker Clay's time the system of standing committees had reached full development. The Senate had followed, a little more slowly. Committees of the Senate have always been appointed by the Senate. In the House a similar practice was occasionally followed at first, but soon their appointment was given to the Speaker, which is the foundation of his power in the U. S. Government.

Committees of Correspondence. Committees of this name had existed in some of the colonial Legislatures much before the Revolution, *e. g.*, in Pennsylvania from 1744 on. Their object was to keep up correspondence with the agents of the colonies in England. But this gave only a name to the famous Revolutionary committees. In a Boston town meeting of November, 1772, Samuel Adams moved that a "Committee of correspondence" be appointed to state the rights of the colonists, and correspond with the other provinces and towns of New England. Their proceedings were to be secret. The system resulted in a union of the colonies, and fostered the germs of revolution. About eighty towns in Massachusetts responded promptly, and the plan worked admirably. In the Virginia Legislature similar committees, but intercolonial, were proposed in March, 1773, by Dabney Carr, and were eloquently advocated by Patrick Henry and Richard Henry Lee. The resolutions finally adopted were more comprehensive. and calculated to form the Confederacy, than those of Massachusetts.

Committees of Safety. A committee of eleven men was appointed by the second provincial Congress of Massachusetts in February, 1775, to resist every attempt at executing the acts of Parliament. They were empowered to muster the militia and take possession of warlike stores. In April of the same year the committee wrote to the various Massachusetts towns, and to New Hampshire and Connecticut, begging for aid against the tyranny of Parliament. Upon this ensued, as the Revolution advanced, the formation of such committees in each province. In each the Committee of Safety, appointed by the popular conventions, took the place of the royal Governor as the executive of the province or State, and remained such until the framing of the new State Constitutions. The name first appears as the name of a committee organized in England during the Civil War of 1642–44.

Commodore. Until 1862 the grade of captain was the highest naval office recognized by law. A captain who commanded two or more ships was called a commodore by custom, and the title, having been once applied, usually continued. In 1862 the grade of commodore, along with that of rear-admiral, was created.

Common Law. The fundamental documents of all the colonies declared the colonists entitled to the benefits of the common law of England. But it was left to the colonial courts to decide what the common law was, and the colonial Legislatures variously modified the law. Under the Constitution the strict-constructionist school maintained that there was no common law in respect to the jurisprudence of the Federal Government, the national school maintaining the opposite.

Commons, the lands cultivated in common by the townspeople under the early land system of New England. Common cultivation was at first upon a considerable scale, though varying for different towns. The commons sometimes included nearly all the improved lands of the town, being laid out by a committee of the general court. In other instances they included smaller portions, in which, nevertheless, all the people were interested. Occasionally authority over such lands was given to the selectmen, or to the major body of the freemen. These commons were formed for the sake of convenience generally, but sometimes from lack of facility in fencing separately. The bounds of such lands were marked by their particular proprietors and scrupulously kept up. Generally the "proprietors" were a distinct body from the town, and kept separate records. The system was adopted from English villages.

Commons, House of, the name borne by the lower House of the Legislature of North Carolina from 1776 to 1868.

Commonwealth vs. Caton, Virginia. John Caton and others, having been convicted of treason by the general court of Virginia and sentenced to death, were pardoned in 1782 by the House of Delegates of the State, the Senate not concurring. The pardon was not executed, and the attorney-general denying its validity, the case was brought before the Court of Appeals of Virginia in 1782. There it was decided that this court had jurisdiction in such matters, but it was declared that the pardon was not valid without the concurrence of the Senate, and that this act of the Legislature was unconstitutional. This is the second instance in which a court assumed authority to pronounce upon the constitutionality of an act of the Legislature.

Compagnie de l'Occident, or Mississippi Company. A company chartered September 6, 1717, which succeeded to the rights granted by Louis XIV. in 1712, to Anthony Crozat, to trade in all French possessions in America which were bounded by New Mexico and by the lands of the English in Carolina. In 1719 it was absorbed by the Compagnie des Indes.

Compagnie des Indes (Company of the Indies), a corporation organized in Paris by John Law in 1719, by combination of the Guinea Company, the Company of the West, the East India Company and the China Company. It was the basis of his great credit operations, in connection with his bank, and of the Mississippi Bubble, but is of importance in American history because it for several years owned Louisiana.

Compromise, Crittenden. (See Crittenden Compromise.)

Compromise, Missouri. (See Missouri Compromise.)

Compromise of 1833, a tariff measure passed by Congress March 1, 1833, as a compromise for the high tariff act of 1828, which had caused intense dissatisfaction through the South, and had brought about nullification by South Carolina and a threat of secession in the event of its being too strictly enforced. The compromise was proposed and passed in the House while Clay himself was endeavoring to get a compromise measure through the Senate. The bill as passed was in effect practically the same as that proposed by Clay in the Senate. It was designed to scale down periodically the high duties then existing, until after ten years a free-trade basis should be reached. The Verplanck low tariff measure, then under debate in the House, was thus thrown out.

Compromise of 1850. As this compromise between the anti-slavery and pro-slavery parties was finally passed, it took the form of several separate bills, which had been practically comprehended in Clay's "Omnibus Bill," proposed and defeated a short time before. Under the compromise, Texas was allowed $10,000,000 for New Mexico, and the boundary of that territory was cut down considerably. August 13, California was admitted to the Union with her free Constitution. August 15, bills for establishing territorial governments in New Mexico and Utah were passed, containing a slavery option clause proposed by Senator Soulé. August 26, the fugitive slave bill, denying arrested negroes a trial by jury, and prohibiting redress to free colored seamen imprisoned in Southern ports, was passed.

Compromises of the Constitution. The Convention of 1787 was mainly divided as to whether, in the new government, one State's influence should be equal to that of any other State, or should be based on population. The plans for a Constitution submitted by Edmund Randolph, of Virginia, and William Paterson, of New Jersey, were diametrically opposed in this respect. The former favored representation according to population in both Houses; the latter an equal vote for each State and only one House. Johnson, of Connecticut, proposed as a compromise, two Houses, an equal representation in the Senate and a proportionate one in the House. Ellsworth formally moved that this be adopted, and thus the first compromise was effected after considerable debate. The second was in regard to the regulation of commerce by Congress. It was proposed to tax both exports and imports at the discretion of Congress. C. C. Pinckney declared that South Carolina would not enter the Union if exports were to be taxed, since nearly the whole of her wealth lay in one article of export, rice. Hence it was decided, August 6, that "no tax or duty shall be laid by the Legislature on articles exported from any State," and on these terms the Federal control over commerce was conceded. Georgia, South Carolina and North Carolina refused to enter the Union if the slave traffic was to be prohibited, so the third compromise effected that Congress should not prohibit the slave trade until 1808, and that a fugitive slave law should be provided.

Concord, capital of New Hampshire, settled in 1725. It was known as Rumford until 1765, when it received its present name. It became capital of the State in 1807, and a city in 1853.

Concord. (See Lexington.)

Confederate Constitution. The Constitution framed by the Montgomery Convention of 1862 was based upon that of the Union with a few important changes. It recognized the "sovereign and independent character" of the

States and the protection of slavery in all new Territories. It prohibited protective tariffs and general internal improvements at Federal expense. The admission of a new State was to be accorded by a vote taken by the poll of the States. State Legislatures could impeach Confederate officers acting within their individual jurisdictions. The Presidential term was lengthened to six years, and the President was made ineligible for re-election. Heads of the executive departments were granted the right of debate in Congress, and the latter's appropriating power was restricted.

Confederate States, a government formed in 1861 by seceding States. The second State to secede, Mississippi, at the time of secession, January 9, 1861, proposed a convention to form a Southern Confederacy. This provisional Congress met at Montgomery, Alabama, on February 4, with delegates present from six of the seven States which had then seceded. It voted by States. On February 8, it adopted a provisional Constitution, and the next day chose Jefferson Davis, of Mississippi, provisional President and Alexander H. Stephens, of Georgia, Vice-President. The permanent Constitution was adopted on March 11. It set forth the doctrines of State sovereignty and recognized slavery, though it forbade the slave trade. It forbade protective tariffs and Federal expenditures for internal improvements. Congress was forbidden to emit bills of credit. It could permit members of the Cabinet to speak before it. The President was empowered to veto single items in appropriation bills. His term was to be six years, and he was not to be re-elected. All the seceding States ratified the Constitution through conventions. Virginia, North Carolina, Tennessee and Arkansas seceded, and were admitted into the Confederacy. The seat of government was removed to Richmond, and Davis and Stephens were chosen again under the permanent Constitution. They were inaugurated as such on February 22, 1862. During most of the existence of the Confederate Government, Judah P. Benjamin was Secretary of State, Charles G. Memminger Secretary of the Treasury, James A. Seddon Secretary of War, Stephen R. Mallory of the Navy and John H. Reagan Postmaster-General. In this government Congress (see art. Congress, Confederate) was of little account. Everything was subordinated to the energetic prosecution of the war, for which the President assumed almost dictatorial powers. Extraordinary efforts were made. Money was obtained by means of the issue of Treasury notes, by cotton loans and by requisitions. Supplies were obtained by any means possible. Troops were obtained, finally, by conscription. The Government, though given belligerent rights by most maritime nations, could not secure any recognition of its independence. As the armies began to be more and more completely destroyed, dissensions broke out. Violent criticism of Davis prevailed. Finally, the surrender of Lee brought the Confederate Government to an end. The Federal Government never recognized its existence.

Confederation, Articles of, the first Constitution of the United States. On the same day on which the Continental Congress appointed a committee to frame a declaration of independence, it appointed another to prepare articles of confederation. The committee soon reported a scheme. But it was not till November 15, 1777, that Congress adopted the "Articles of Confederation and Perpetual Union." The articles provided for a single-chambered

Congress, with limited powers over war, peace, foreign affairs, coin, weights and measures, Indians and postal arrangements; it could raise money only by requisitions upon the States. In it each State had but one vote. Nine votes were necessary for the most important acts. Ratification by every State was necessary, and was not secured till March 1, 1781. The articles then went into operation. Their leading defects were, that they left too much power to the States, and left Congress entirely dependent upon them for money and the enforcement of its decrees; that they did not operate on individuals, nor prevent the violation of treaty obligations, nor command respect abroad, nor ensure tranquillity at home; and that they could not be amended save by consent of every State. After vain efforts to secure such consent to amendments which would at least have enabled the Government to pay its debts, it became obvious that more drastic alterations were necessary. Accordingly the Annapolis Convention of 1786 called the Philadelphia Convention of 1787, and the articles were superseded by a better Constitution.

Confiscation. In 1861 Congress passed an act directing a blockade of Southern ports and the confiscation of all property used against the National Government. This was necessary in order to strengthen the depleted treasury. This policy was unflinchingly enforced in 1862 and later.

Congo. A declaration of the intention of the International Association of the Congo and recognition of its flag by the United States took place April 22, 1884.

Congregationalists. This denomination came first to this country with the "Pilgrim Fathers" at Plymouth, Mass. The Puritans and other settlers of New England gradually were led to separate from the Church of England and to form themselves into Congregational churches. At first these were closely connected with the colonial government. Expenses of church and pastor were met by public taxes and even the rights of citizenship depended upon church fellowhip. These features, however, were gradually eliminated (in Connecticut in 1818, in Massachusetts in 1833). The first colonial synod was held 1637 at Cambridge, Mass.; the second, 1646, approved the Westminster Assembly's Confession of Faith and set forth a statement of church polity known as the "Cambridge Platform." The fourth, held in Boston, 1865, revised the platform of church polity and issued a declaration of faith. This denomination still has its main strength in New England, but has been carried westward by settlers in the newer States. Number of members in 1890, 513,000.

Congrés des Americanistes, a gathering of European students of American history, more especially of the aboriginal antiquities and voyages of exploration, which has met periodically at various places in Europe since 1875.

Congress (see arts. Senate, House of Representatives). (For the Congresses existent before 1789, see Stamp-Act Congress and Congress, Continental.) The Convention of 1787 planned a Congress of two Houses, and reconciled the contest between the large and the small States by providing an upper

House in which States were represented equally and a lower House in which they were represented proportionally to population. The old Congress summoned the new Congress to meet on March 4, 1789, but the House did not have a quorum till April 1, nor the Senate till April 6. Each Congress has been in existence two years, from March 4 to March 4. (See art. Sessions.) The relations of Congress with the President have mostly depended on whether they were or were not of the same party. The warmest struggles have been in the times of Presidents J. Q. Adams, Jackson, Tyler, Buchanan and Johnson. The latter was impeached by the House.

Congress, Confederate. The Confederate Congress was practically controlled by the executive. It never met the executive face to face, but was obliged to provide for every executive need. Its make-up was fictitious and carried little weight, the need for force and executive ability being far more urgent in the field than in counsel. In both the first and second Congresses Representatives were present from Kentucky and Missouri, though those States did not succeed in seceding. The provisional Congress held four sessions, the first beginning February 4, 1861, the fourth ending February 17, 1862. Under the Constitution there were two Congresses; the first (February 18, 1862–February 18, 1865) had four sessions, the second (May 2, 1864–March 18, 1865) two. They included about twenty-four Senators and a hundred Representatives.

Congress, Continental, was first suggested by a letter of Benjamin Franklin to the Assembly of Massachusetts in 1773. Franklin was then agent for that colony at London. The first step was taken by the Virginia Assembly in 1774, upon the news of the passage of the Boston Port Bill. Its committee advised a Congress of all the colonies. The first Continental Congress, therefore, assembled at Philadelphia September 5, 1774, Georgia alone being unrepresented. Action was confined to a declaration of the rights and wrongs of the colonies, a recommendation of an agreement not to import British goods after December 1, 1774, and not to export goods to England after September 10, 1775, unless their wrongs were righted; and a resolution commending the people of Massachusetts for their temperate resistance to the objectionable measures of Parliament, and a declaration that if these acts "shall be attempted to be carried into execution by force, all America ought to support them in their opposition." The second Continental Congress assembled May 10, 1775, at Philadelphia, was a revolutionary body, plenipotentiary in its nature, and was theoretically in perpetual session till March, 1781. Each State had but one vote. The appointment of delegates was generally by the State Legislatures. The Congress declared independence, carried on the war, and in many respects governed the country. The Articles of Confederation, adopted in 1781, weakened the Congress by requiring the assent of nine States to make valid its most important acts, and forbidding any man to be a member more than three years in succession. Under its provisions each State should have from two to seven delegates, but only one vote. This Congress sat at Philadelphia until December, 1776, then at Baltimore until March, 1777, then at Philadelphia again, at Lancaster, Pa., in September, 1777, at York until the ensuing June, at Philadelphia again from

July, 1778, to June, 1783, then at Princeton until November, then at Annapolis until June, 1784. In November and December, 1784, it sat at Trenton. From January, 1785, until its last recorded session (October 21, 1788), it sat in New York. Peyton Randolph and Henry Middleton were presidents of the first Congress; of the rest, successively, Peyton Randolph, John Hancock (1775–1777), Henry Laurens (1778), John Jay (1779), Samuel Huntington (1779–1781), Thomas McKean (1781), John Hanson (1782), Elias Boudinot (1783), Thomas Mifflin (1784), R. H. Lee (1785), John Hancock (1786), Nathaniel Gorham (1786), Arthur St. Clair (1787), Cyrus Griffin (1788). Charles Thomson was secretary from 1774 to 1788.

Conkling, Roscoe (1829–1888), of New York, Senator, was elected to Congress as a Republican in 1858, 1860 and 1868, was chosen U. S. Senator in 1867 and re-elected in 1873 and 1879. In the Senate he was from the first a member of the Judiciary Committee, was a zealous supporter of the administration of President Grant, and advocated his election for a third term. In 1881 he broke with President Garfield on a question of patronage and resigned his seat in the Senate, and was not re-elected.

Connecticut is named from the river of that name, which is an Indian word meaning "long river." Two colonies were established in Connecticut. Certain people, who were dissatisfied with the close connection of church and State in Massachusetts Bay colony, left that province for the valley of the Connecticut under Thomas Hooker, where they settled Hartford, Windsor and Wethersfield. In 1639 they adopted a Constitution which made no reference to the King of England, and provided for the election of all officers annually by the people, with no religious qualification. In 1635 John Winthrop founded Saybrook. Two years later New Haven was founded by a company from England, who came over under Theophilus Eaton and John Davenport, to establish a strict theocracy. They adopted the Bible as their Constitution, and refused to institute trial by jury, because it was not recognized by the Bible. In 1643 Hartford and New Haven both joined the New England Confederation for protection against the Dutch, who claimed the valley of the Connecticut. New Haven was incorporated with Hartford in 1662, under a charter from Charles II., which named the South Sea as the western boundary. This charter was adopted as a Constitution in 1776, and continued in force until 1818. In 1687 Andros had demanded this charter, but it was concealed in the "charter oak." In 1700 Yale College was founded. The claims of Connecticut to western lands were surrendered to the General Government. Her claim to Westmoreland County in Northern Pennsylvania was set aside in 1782. Connecticut ratified the national Constitution January 9, 1788, by a vote of 128 to 40. Connecticut was strongly Federalist until 1820, was opposed to the War of 1812, and sent delegates to the Hartford Convention of 1814. The State cast its electoral votes for the Democratic candidates in the years 1836, 1852, 1876, 1884, 1888 and 1892. The State has been doubtful in State politics. In 1891 there was a dispute over the election of Governor, which caused Governor Bulkley to hold over after the expiration of his term. The population of the State in 1790 was 237,496; in 1890 it had increased to 746,258. History by Hollister.

Conquistadores, Spanish for conquerors, the name given to those Spanish adventurers who conducted expeditions of conquest in the New World.

Conrad, Charles M. (1804–1878), represented Louisiana in the U. S. Senate as a Whig from 1842 to 1843, and in Congress from 1848 to 1850. He was Secretary of War in Fillmore's Cabinet from 1850 to 1853.

"**Conscience Whigs,**" in the decade preceding the disruption of the Whig party, those Whigs who were conscientiously opposed to the extension of slavery. These mostly became Free-Soilers, or later, Republicans. when that party was formed.

Conscription. (See Draft.)

Conservative, a name given to those Democrats who during the years from 1837 to 1840 voted with the Whigs against the sub-treasury bill, which was then supported by the Democrats at large. On other questions the Conservatives generally adhered to the principles of their party.

Constable. In colonial times the duties of the constable were both varied and extensive. In New England he was usually appointed by the selectmen of the town; in Virginia and Maryland by the Hundred; in some States he was appointed for the parish. The constable gave notice of town meetings, collected and disbursed taxes, was often overseer of the roads, made arrests and preserved the peace, and filled some judicial functions. His scope of office varied for different States and even for different towns, but was in earlier times of more importance and dignity than now.

"**Constellation,**" the United States man-of-war commanded by Truxton, which, February 9, 1800, during the troubles with France of that period, defeated and captured the French frigate "L'Insurgente" in the West Indies. Truxton was presented by Congress with a gold medal for his bravery.

Constitution. The first written Constitution of modern times seems to have been the Union of Utrecht, or Constitution of the United Netherlands, framed in 1579. The first suggestion of a written Constitution for England was made in the "Agreement of the People," drawn up in 1647. During the Commonwealth England had two written Constitutions, the Instrument of Government, 1653, and the Humble Petition and Advice, 1657. Vane's "Healing Question" (1656) first suggested the separate constitutional convention. The first written Constitution which any American community framed for itself was the Fundamental Orders of Connecticut, 1639. At the time of the Revolution, the desire to have governments of limited powers made it inevitable that the Constitutions should be set down in writing. The existence of colonial charters helped to familiarize the idea. (See Convention, Constitutional.)

"**Constitution,**" the most famous of American frigates, a vessel of forty-four guns, was finished in 1798. Under Barry it had some service against the French in 1799. On July 5, 1812, under Captain Hull, it started from Annapolis and ran into a British fleet of five frigates. For three days it avoided an attack by masterly seamanship and at last escaped without damage. On August 19 it encountered the "Guerriere," Captain Dacres, not far from Cape Race. The "Constitution" was the stronger ship in the proportion of ten to seven, but Captain Dacres of the "Guerriere" believed the Americans could not fight. Within thirty minutes after the battle began his vessel was a wreck and seventy-nine of his men killed or wounded. This victory greatly strengthened the Americans in self-confidence and prestige. On December 29, 1812, in the West Indies, the "Constitution" encountered the "Java," thirty-eight guns, Captain Lambert. After two hours' battle and an hour spent in repairing damages, Captain Bainbridge (now commander of the "Constitution") was about to renew the attack, when the "Java" surrendered. The British lost about 100 killed and 200 wounded. The Americans lost thirty-four in all. The "Constitution" in this battle earned the name of "Old Ironsides." Both the "Guerriere" and the "Java," on capture, were so disabled that they were blown up. December 30, 1813, the "Constitution," Captain Stewart, sailed toward the West Indies. February 14, 1814, it captured the "Picton," sixteen guns, and a convoy. Next year, February 15, 1815, it attacked and captured two vessels, the "Cyane," thirty-six guns, and the "Levant," eighteen guns. The latter was afterward recaptured, the "Constitution" itself narrowly escaping capture at the same time from three British frigates.

Constitution of the United States. The first Constitution of the United States was the Articles of Confederation (see art.). Its defects and failure caused many to consider the desirability of drastic amendment. The Alexandria Conference of Maryland and Virginia led to the Annapolis Convention of 1786, this to the Convention of 1787 at Philadelphia. That convention forthwith proceeded, not to amend the Confederation, but to make a new Constitution. (See art. Convention of 1787.) This Constitution differed from its predecessor in that it dealt directly with individuals, that it invested the Federal Government with coercive powers, that it provided an efficient executive, and that it was susceptible of amendment by easier means than unanimous consent. Since it went into operation in 1789 it has been developed by amendment (see art. Amendments), by interpretation and by custom. Courts, especially the Supreme Court, have developed it by interpretation. Under Chief Justice Marshall the court much enlarged the powers of the Federal Government in this way. Expansions of this sort have come mostly from the clauses giving Congress the taxing power and the power to regulate commerce, and from the war powers of the President and Congress. Usage has added such features as the committee system, the Speaker's power, the spoils system, the gerrymander and so forth. In fact we have a written Constitution plus an unwritten Constitution.

Constitutional Union Party, a name assumed by the remnants of the Whig party in the South in the election of 1860. The party held a convention at Baltimore May 9, 1860, in which delegates from twenty States were present. John Bell, of Tennessee, was nominated for President and Edward Everett, of Massachusetts, for Vice-President. The platform of the party was of the most general character, recognizing "no political principle but the Constitution of the country, the union of the States and the enforcement of laws." In the election it carried Kentucky, Tennessee and Virginia, but failed utterly in the North. The Civil War blotted it out immediately.

Constitutionalists, in Pennsylvania, under the Constitution of 1776–1790, the party who favored the maintenance of that democratic Constitution, as opposed to the party called Republicans, who desired to see a stronger government substituted. They formed the germ of the Pennsylvania Anti-Federalists and Democrats of a later time. From 1804 to 1808 the name Constitutionalists was assumed by those moderate Democrats who desired to maintain the then existing Constitution, as opposed to the Conventionalists or "friends of the people," who desired to see it made more popular.

Constitutionality. The power of American courts to "set aside" (neglect) a statute of the State or the Federal Congress for want of conformity to the Constitution is treated under Unconstitutionality.

Constitutions, First State. Upon the establishment of independence in 1776, the thirteen colonies necessarily passed from the crown. Not one of the thirteen was a State prior to that event, though a few had established temporary governments at the suggestion of Congress. Massachusetts remained under the form of government fixed by her colonial charter until 1780, Connecticut until 1818 and Rhode Island until 1842. New Hampshire was the first to modify and establish a local government. She did so in January, 1776. South Carolina, Virginia and New Jersey followed in March, June and July of the same year, Delaware and Pennsylvania in September, Maryland in November, North Carolina in December, Georgia and New York in 1777. By 1780 all had formed local governments except Connecticut and Rhode Island.

Consul. Consuls have been appointed from the beginning of the Government. By acts of 1848 and 1860 they are empowered to hear and determine judicial cases in uncivilized countries.

Consul-General. The title Consul-General was first introduced in the American service in 1855.

Continental Money. The second Continental Congress, in its straits for money, began in June, 1775, to issue paper money. Altogether, about $242,-000,000 were issued up to the end of 1779, when further issues were stopped. For the first year these issues continued equal in value to gold; then they began to depreciate. In two years they had become reduced till they stood at two to one. In three years they stood at four to one; in September, 1779, at twenty to one; in the ensuing March at forty to one. Congress now required the notes to be brought in, to be redeemed at their market value, or, to a certain extent, replaced by "new tenor" notes at twenty to one, the new issues to bear interest at five per cent. The old notes sank to one thousand to one, and finally ceased to circulate.

Continentals, the regular troops of the American army during the Revolution, enlisted and paid by the Continental Government and commanded by Washington. They are to be distinguished from the militia and guerrilla companies. The name was first applied in June, 1775, when Congress appropriated £6000 for the support of a "Continental army," and appointed Washington commander-in-chief. Washington at once took command of the forces then beleaguering Boston, and ten companies of expert riflemen were enlisted in Pennsylvania and Virginia.

Contraband. Under the laws of war, goods (such as arms) which may aid an enemy to prolong the war are called contraband and held liable to seizure and condemnation, if a neutral tries to introduce them into the country of the other belligerent. In 1861 General B. F. Butler attempted to apply this distinction and regulation to the slaves of Southerners, when they fell into his hands.

Contrecœur, born about 1730; French soldier. In 1754 he conducted a French force down the Allegheny River and constructed Fort Duquesne, in attempting to capture which Braddock was defeated the next year.

Contreras, Mexico, a short battle between Pillow's and Twiggs' divisions of General Scott's army and Valencia, an officer of General Santa Anna, on August 19–20. Pillow and Twiggs had been left by Scott upon the construction of a road during his approach to the city of Mexico. August 19 Valencia made an attack, but was repulsed and ordered by Santa Anna to retreat. This he refused to do and the next day his camp was attacked and his forces routed. Americans 4000, Mexicans 6000.

Convention, Constitutional. In almost all the States, the new Constitutions framed at the beginning of the Revolutionary period were made by the Revolutionary Conventions which were managing all the affairs of the State, in the absence of any constitutional government .But soon the feeling grew that Constitutions should be made by conventions which the people chose especially for that purpose. The Massachusetts Constitution of 1780 was so made, and was submitted to the people afterward. Since then this has been the regular practice, both in the case of old States making new Constitutions, and in that of new States formed out of territories and old States; and also in that of reconstructed Southern States. For the convention which framed the Constitution of the United States, see Convention of 1787. A convention held at Montgomery, Ala., identical with the Confederate provisional Congress, framed the Constitution of the Confederate States, March, 1861.

Convention, Nominating. In the first stages of American political life, candidates for offices within the gift of the people either themselves made public announcement of their candidacy or were nominated by more or less private or informal caucuses of party leaders. Next came the legislative caucus (which see), the candidate of a party being chosen by a caucus of the members of the Legislature belonging to that party. Though a sporadic case of a nominating convention (at Harrisburg) as early as 1788 is mentioned, yet in general the legislative caucus was the ordinary practice at that time. But this gave, in the case of a given party, no representation of those districts whose legislative delegates were not of that party. Hence arose a modification of the caucus; the legislative caucus being supplemented by the addition of delegates specially sent up from those unrepresented districts. This was the half-way stage to the nominating convention pure and simple, which consisted of delegates from all parts of the State, chosen especially and solely for the purpose of making nominations. This institution, which has prevailed universally ever since, arose soon, as improved means of communication between different parts of a State made it easy for such bodies to be convened. In Pennsylvania the fully developed nominating convention of the modern type appears in (1792) 1817, in New Jersey in 1812, in Rhode Island and New York in 1825. After becoming fully developed in the States, the system was applied to Federal elections. The Presidential nominations of 1824 (except Crawford's caucus nomination) had been made on no well-defined plan, those of 1828 mostly by State Legislatures. The first national nominating convention was that held by the Anti-Masons at Baltimore in September, 1831, by which Wirt and Ellmaker were nominated. The National Republican Convention at Baltimore, December, 1831, followed. In May, 1832, a Democratic Convention nominated Van Buren for Vice-President. In 1835 the Democrats at Baltimore nominated Van Buren and Johnson in National Convention; the Whigs held none. In 1840 both parties adopted this practice, which has since been followed without exception. Beginning with that year, the principal conventions have been the following: 1839, Whig, at Harrisburg, nominating Harrison and Tyler; 1840, Democratic, at Baltimore, nominating Van Buren but no Vice-President; Liberty party at Albany, nominating Birney and Earle; 1844, Whig at Baltimore, Clay and Frelinghuysen; Democratic at Baltimore, Polk and Dallas; Liberty party at Buffalo (1843), Birney and Morris; 1848, Democratic at Baltimore, Cass and Butler; Whig at Philadelphia, Taylor and Fillmore; Free-Soil at Buffalo, Van Buren and Adams; 1852, Democratic at Baltimore, Pierce and King; Whig at Baltimore, Scott and Graham; Free-Soil at Pittsburgh, Hale and Julian; 1856, American ("Know-Nothing") at Philadelphia, Fillmore and Donelson; Democratic at Cincinnati, Buchanan and Breckinridge; Republican at Philadelphia, Frémont and Dayton; Whig at Baltimore, ratified the American nominations; 1860, Democratic (Moderate) at Charleston and Baltimore, Douglas and Johnson; Democratic (Extreme) at Charleston, Richmond and Baltimore, Breckinridge and Lane; Constitutional Union at Baltimore, Bell and Everett; Republican at Chicago, Lincoln and Hamlin; 1864, Republican (Radical) at Cleveland, Frémont and Cochrane; Republican (Regular) at Baltimore, Lincoln and Johnson; Democratic at Chicago, McClellan and Pendleton; 1868, Republican at Chicago, Grant and Colfax; Democratic at New York, Seymour and Blair; 1872, Liberal Republican at Cincinnati, Greeley and Brown; Republican at Philadelphia, Grant and Wilson; Democratic at Baltimore, ratified the Liberal Republican nominations; 1876, Greenback at Indianapolis, Cooper and Carey; Republican at Cincinnati, Hayes and Wheeler; Democratic at St. Louis, Tilden and Hendricks; 1880, Republican at Chicago, Garfield and Arthur; Greenback at Chicago, Weaver and Chambers; Democratic at Cincinnati, Hancock and English; 1884, Republican at Chicago, Blaine and Logan; Democratic at Chicago, Cleveland and Hendricks; Prohibitionist at Pittsburgh, St. John and Daniel; Greenback Labor party, Butler and West; 1888, Prohibitionist at Indianapolis, Fiske and Brooks; Democratic at St. Louis, Cleveland and Thurman; Republican at Chicago, Harrison and Morton; 1892, Republican at Minneapolis, Harrison and Reid; Democratic at Chicago, Cleveland and Stevenson; Prohibitionist at Cincinnati, Bidwell and Cranfell; People's party at Omaha, Weaver and Field. (See Elections.)

Convention of 1787, the body which framed the Constitution of the United States, was first suggested by a private letter of Alexander Hamilton in 1780. The State Legislatures were slow in considering the matter. The convention was really brought about by the recommendation of a previous convention of delegates from several States, who had assembled at Annapolis in September, 1786, to consider the regulation of trade. Virginia taking the lead, delegates were chosen to a convention to amend the faulty Articles of Confederation. By June 2, 1787, delegates from New York, Pennsylvania, New Jersey, Delaware, Virginia, North Carolina, South Carolina, Massachusetts, Connecticut, Georgia and Maryland, had assembled at Philadelphia, those from the first seven States having arrived May 25. On May 29 Edmund Randolph, of Virginia, presented a plan for "a more energetic government," and inclining to reduce the "idea of States" to a minimum. He proposed a correction of the Articles of Confederation; representation by population; two branches of Congress, the first chosen by the people, the second by the first on nomination by the State Legislatures; that Congress should legislate concerning commerce and taxes and should have a veto power over State laws; that Congress should choose the executive, who should have veto power, and a number of other clauses. Charles Pinckney, of South Carolina, submitted another draft of a Constitution. These were considered and reported favorably. After much debate it was decided that a national government ought to be established. June 15, William Paterson, of New Jersey, submitted a draft which was in nearly every respect incompatible with Randolph's, leaving far more to the States, that the small States might be protected. On the motion of Ellsworth a compromise was effected by giving the States an equal representation in the Senate and a representation proportionate to population in the House. A compromise was also effected regarding the regulation of commerce and the taxation of exports. The third compromise forbade Congress to prohibit the slave trade, and established a fugitive slave law. July 24 a committee of detail was appointed. August 6 this committee of detail reported a draft strongly resembling the Constitution. A month was spent in debate, and on September 12, this draft, amended by the third great compromise, was given to a committee of style, consisting of Gouverneur Morris, Johnson, Madison, Hamilton and King. September 13 the Constitution was reported to the convention very nearly in its present form. In the debates the leaders of the nationalizing party were, Hamilton, Madison, King, Wilson and Morris; of the States' rights, Lansing, Yates, Paterson, Martin. On September 17, 1787, the convention adjourned, after sending the Constitution to Congress for transmission to the States. Its proceedings were marked by great moderation and wisdom. It consisted mostly of somewhat conservative men. A movement toward a second general convention in 1788, started by George Clinton, Patrick Henry and other Anti-Federalists, proved abortive.

Convention of 1787, Members of. In the following list of members elected, those who signed the Constitution are designated by numbers; those whose names are written in italics did not attend; the rest attended, but did not sign:

New Hampshire.

1. John Langdon,
John Pickering,
2. Nicholas Gilman,
Benjamin West.

Massachusetts.

Francis Dana,
Elbridge Gerry,
3. Nathaniel Gorham,
4. Rufus King,
Caleb Strong.

Connecticut.

5. William Samuel Johnson,
6. Roger Sherman,
Oliver Ellsworth.

New York.

Robert Yates,
7. Alexander Hamilton,
John Lansing.

New Jersey.

8. David Brearley,
William Churchill Houston,
9. William Paterson,
John Neilson,
10. William Livingston,
Abraham Clark,
11. Jonathan Dayton.

Pennsylvania.

12. Thomas Mifflin,
13. Robert Morris,
14. George Clymer,
15. Jared Ingersoll,
16. Thomas Fitzsimons,
17. James Wilson,
18. Gouverneur Morris,
19. Benjamin Franklin.

Delaware.

20. George Read,
21. Gunning Bedford,
22. John Dickinson,
23. Richard Bassett,
24. Jacob Broom.

Maryland.

Robert Hanson Harrison,
Charles Carroll, of Carrollton,
Thomas Stone,
25. James McHenry,
Thomas Sim Lee,
Gabriel Duvall,
26. Daniel Jenifer, of St. Thomas,
27. Daniel Carroll,
James Francis Mercer,
Luther Martin.

Virginia.

28. George Washington,
Patrick Henry,
Edmund Randolph,
29. John Blair,
30. James Madison,
George Mason,
George Wythe,
Richard Henry Lee,
Thomas Nelson,
James McClurg.

North Carolina.

Richard Caswell,
Alexander Martin,
William Richardson Davie,
31. Richard Dobbs Spaight,
Willie Jones,
32. William Blount,
33. Hugh Williamson.

South Carolina.

34. John Rutledge,
35. Charles Cotesworth Pinckney,
36. Charles Pinckney,
37. Pierce Butler,
Henry Laurens.

Georgia.

38. William Few,
39. Abraham Baldwin,
William Pierce,
George Walton,
William Houston,
Nathaniel Pendleton.

Convention, Revolutionary. In English history, conventions, resembling Parliaments in everything but in not being summoned by the crown, were held in 1660 and in 1689. Thence the name came to America and was similarly applied, as in Massachusetts in 1689 and in South Carolina in 1718, to irregular meetings of the popular branch of the Legislature, summoned in the absence of executive authority. In the troubles that led to the Revolution, when royal governors dissolved assemblies, they often met again at once in "conventions." These representative bodies soon came to have all authority, to the exclusion of the royal government. In the provisional governments which managed the Revolution in each State, the controlling body, up to the time when the first Constitution was made for the State, was the convention. These revolutionary conventions were sovereign bodies, and most commonly they made the State's first Constitution, though soon the feeling grew that this should be done by a special convention elected by the people for that express purpose. Conventions, supposed to represent the sovereignty of the State in a more complete degree than Legislatures could, controlled the nullification proceedings in South Carolina in 1832, and passed the ordinances of secession on behalf of the Southern States in 1860 and 1861.

Convention Troops. On October 14, 1777, the British General Burgoyne, finding himself surrounded at Saratoga, proposed to surrender to General Gates. Accordingly, October 16, a convention was signed fixing the terms of capitulation. It was decided that Burgoyne, his officers and troops should march out of camp with the honors of war, and should be accorded passports to England upon promising to abstain from war against the States. In obedience to these terms the troops were marched to Boston, there to await transports from Howe. During the winter the troops remained quartered on Prospect Hill and Winter Hill, the officers being placed at Cambridge. Numerous delays followed. Congress disliked the terms; an expression of Burgoyne's was construed as a repudiation of them. Finally General Heath was instructed by Congress to suspend the embarkation indefinitely. Burgoyne and his staff returned to England on parole. The troops were transferred to Rutland, Vt., and afterward to Charlottesville, Va., where they remained till the close of the war.

Conventionalists, in the Pennsylvania politics of 1804–1808, the name assumed by those extreme Democrats who desired to see a new convention called, to modify the Constitution of the State in a radically democratic sense, as opposed to the so-called "Constitutionalists." Their leaders were Leib and Duane.

Convicts. In 1619, by order of King James I., one hundred convicts were sent from England to be sold as servants. For more than a century this practice was from time to time followed in the case of the royal colonies, in spite of colonial protests.

Conway, Thomas (1733–1800 ?), soldier, came to the United States in 1777 and was made brigadier-general, and was present at Brandywine and Germantown. He was leader of the conspiracy against Washington, known as the "Conway Cabal," on account of which he was wounded in a duel with

General John Cadwalader. Soon after he returned to France, and was made Governor of Pondicherry.

Conway Cabal. An intrigue by Gates, Lee, Mifflin, Wilkinson and others of Washington's officers, in 1777, for the promotion of Brigadier-General Conway, contrary to Washington's judgment. Washington was accused of incompetence and partiality, and finally Congress was prevailed upon to promote Conway to major-general and inspector-general. In 1778 Conway was wounded in a duel and apologized to Washington, confessing his wrong.

Coodies, a name given to small bodies of Federalists who became prominent in New York City in 1812, under the leadership of G. C. Verplanck ("Abimalech Coody"). They opposed DeWitt Clinton and favored war with England.

Cook, F. Joseph, born in 1838, of New York, author and lecturer; has traveled extensively, but is best known as a lecturer on theological subjects, and especially by his "Boston Monday Lectures."

Cook, James (1728–1779), naval captain, commanded a frigate at the capture of Quebec in 1759. In 1768 he made an expedition, during which he sought for the great continent supposed to exist near the South Pole. From 1772 to 1775 a more thorough exploration was made. In 1776 he conducted an expedition to discover a northwest passage by way of Behring Strait. He discovered the Sandwich Islands, where he was killed by the natives of Hawaii.

Cooke, Jay, born in 1821, established the banking firm of Jay Cooke & Co., at Philadelphia, in 1861, which was the agent of the United States for the war loans during the Civil War. Its failure on September 19, 1873 ("Black Friday"), began the panic of that year.

Cooke, John Esten (1830–1886), of Virginia, author, entered the Confederate army, his experiences in which furnish the materials for some of his writings. He also wrote on Virginian history.

Cooley, Thomas M., born in 1824, of Michigan, jurist, was appointed to compile the statutes of Michigan in 1857, and was reporter of the Supreme Court in 1858. He was a Justice of the Supreme Court of Michigan from 1864 to 1885 and Chief Justice in 1868–69. He was chairman of the Interstate Commerce Commission from its beginning in 1887 till 1891. He now holds the chair of American History in the University of Michigan and is lecturer on constitutional law and political science. He has published a "Digest of Michigan Reports" and has edited an edition of Blackstone's "Commentaries," with copious notes.

Coons, a nickname given to the members of the Whig party, who had adopted the raccoon as an emblem.

Cooper, Edward, an active business man, son of Peter Cooper, was born in 1824. He was mayor of New York from 1879 to 1881 and 1883, and was active in the overthrow of the Tweed ring.

Cooper, James Fenimore (1789–1851), was born in Burlington, N. J. He entered the navy in 1801, but resigned in 1811. In 1821 he published "The Spy," the first of his historical novels and one of the first of American historical novels. This was followed by "The Pioneers," "The Last of the Mohicans," and a long series of romantic novels dealing with the Revolution, frontier life, sea life and the American Indian. He also wrote a history of the American navy.

Cooper, Myles (1735–1785), an English clergyman, was president of King's College, New York, from 1763 to 1775, in which year, being a Tory, he returned to England. His sermon at Oxford, "On the Causes of the Present Rebellion in America," aroused much controversy.

Cooper, Peter (1791–1883), philanthropist, was born in New York City. He greatly promoted the progress of industrial improvement in the United States, and in 1854–59 erected the "Cooper Union for the advancement of Science and Art," where the working classes may receive free instruction. He was a careful thinker on questions of government and finance. In 1876 he was the Presidential candidate of the National Independent party.

Cooper, Samuel (1798–1876), from 1815 an officer in the U. S. army, was adjutant-general from 1852 to 1861. Resigning then, he became adjutant-general and inspector-general of the Confederate army.

Cooper, Thomas (1759–1840), scientist. An English democrat, he emigrated to the United States in 1795. He was one of those tried under the Sedition Act, was president of the College of South Carolina, and was one of the founders of political economy in America.

Cope, Edward Drinker, naturalist and comparative anatomist, was born in Philadelphia in 1840. He has contributed extensively to the development of palæontology, and has been honored by scientific societies at home and abroad.

Copley, John Singleton (1737–1815), an eminent portrait painter, was born in Boston. In 1775, after a year spent in study in Italy, he established himself in London, and was shortly afterward chosen a member of the Royal Academy. His painting, "The Death of Lord Chatham," is the most famous of his numerous productions. Lord Lyndhurst, Lord Chancellor of England, was his son.

Copper. The mining of copper was carried on to a limited extent in Connecticut, New Jersey and Pennsylvania, in colonial times, and its existence was known of as early as 1660 by Jesuit missionaries about Lake Superior in Michigan. The first systematic mining for copper was begun in Michigan in 1844. From 1867 to 1881 about ninety per cent of the copper product of the United States came from Lake Superior. Immense copper fields have since been opened in Montana and Arizona.

Copperhead, the name applied to Northerners who sympathized with the South in the Civil War.

Copyright. Clause 8 of the Constitution authorized Congress to issue copyrights to authors and artists and patents to inventors. Prior to the adoption of the Constitution the States issued copyrights, and the first act of Congress recognized the rights thus granted. The first law was enacted in 1790, giving to authors exclusive right to their works for fourteen years, with the liberty of renewal for the same number of years. In 1831 the term was made twenty-eight years, with the right of renewal for fourteen years. A copy of the title of the book or a description of the article must be sent to the Librarian of Congress, and not later than the day of publication two copies of the book must be sent to the librarian. Copyrights were formerly issued by the Clerks of the District Courts of the United States. In 1891 Congress passed an act granting the privileges of copyright to foreigners of nations whose governments give American citizens similar privileges. This reciprocity was to be determined by proclamation of the President. It was at once extended to Great Britain, France, Belgium and Switzerland, and subsequently to Germany and Italy.

Corcoran, William W. (1798–1888), a banker and successful financier during the Mexican War, was noted as founder of the Louise Home and the Corcoran Art Gallery at Washington, D. C., and for liberality toward charitable institutions.

Corea. The United States concluded a commercial treaty with Corea in 1882.

Corinth, Miss., fortified and occupied by General Beauregard, commanding 53,000 effective Confederate troops, and captured May 30, 1862, by Generals Halleck and Pope, leading an army of over 100,000 Federals, after some twelve days spent in skirmish, siege and bombardment. Beauregard's lieutenants were Van Dorn and Price. Corinth was but weakly fortified, but this fact was unknown to the Federal generals, strong outposts of Confederate troops being constantly opposed to their advancing columns. Pope sent Elliot, Hatch and Sheridan with strong detachments to make a circuit of forty miles around the town and strike the railroad. Stanley's division pushed forward, and, after a sharp skirmish with the Confederate outposts, secured and fortified a position directly opposite the Confederate works. Paine, Crittenden and Nelson joined him there. Sherman had meantime captured a loop-holed log house, manned by Confederates and situated south of Corinth. Sharp-shooters annoyed him from this place. The house was destroyed and Sherman advanced close to Beauregard's earthworks. Beauregard, seeing himself nearly hemmed in, began to evacuate on the night of the twenty-ninth, destroying as much as he could, but leaving many valuable stores, nevertheless. His evacuation was concealed by the shouting of his men and the blowing of whistles, which the Federals mistook for reinforcements. Later, the place, when in Federal possession, was assaulted, but without success, by a large Confederate force commanded by Price and Van Dorn, October 3–4, 1862. Rosecrans held the place with 20,000 Federal troops posted behind three rows of earthworks. Hamilton held the right, Davies the centre and McKean the left. Price advanced from the left and Van Dorn from the right. The assault was begun by an impetuous charge by the latter general. Little was done, however, the first day. Early October 4, Price's column advanced, drawn up like a wedge. The charge was a daring one, but the Confederates were driven back and literally cut to pieces. The Texan and Mississippi troops under Rogers fared as badly, their charge ending the assault. They fled in great disorder and were pursued for some distance by an Ohio regiment.

Cornbury, Edward Hyde, Lord (1661–1724) cousin of Queen Mary and Queen Anne, was made Governor of New York by William III. In 1708, after six years of severe rule, he was removed, but for a long time was imprisoned for debt.

Cornell, Alonzo B., was born in Ithaca, N. Y., in 1832. In 1866–67 he was a member of the Republican State Committee, and in 1868 was nominated for Lieutenant-Governor. He was elected to the State Assembly in 1872 and made Speaker in 1873. He received important appointments from President Grant, and was Governor of New York from 1880 to 1883.

Cornell, Ezra (1807–1874), founder of Cornell University, was a member of the first Republican National Convention, was elected to the New York Assembly in 1862–63, and served in the State Senate from 1864 to 1867.

Cornell University was chartered in 1865 and organized in 1868.

Cornstalk, an Indian chief who led a clever and spirited attack upon General Lewis at Point Pleasant, near the mouth of the Great Kanawha (1774). Each side lost about seventy-five killed and one hundred and forty wounded.

Cornwallis, Charles, Earl and later **Marquis Cornwallis** (1737–1805), served in the Seven Years' War. He took his seat in Parliament and favored the Americans during the preliminary troubles. Having been made lieutenant-general he was sent to America in 1776, fought in the battle of Long Island, and pursued Washington's army through New Jersey. He was defeated at Princeton, decided the victory of Brandywine in 1777, and served at Germantown and Monmouth. Having been appointed to the command of the Southern army he overwhelmed Gates at Camden in 1780, but in his contest with Greene he was worsted, although he won a technical victory at Guilford Court House in 1781. Then followed his campaign in Virginia against Lafayette, the siege of his army in Yorktown, and its surrender to the Franco-American troops on October 17, 1781. He was the ablest of the British commanders in the war. As Governor-General of India, 1786–93 and 1805, he rendered valuable military and administrative services. He was also lord-lieutenant of Ireland, 1798–1801, at the epoch of the Union.

Coronado, Francisco Vasquez de (1510–1542), a Spanish explorer, sent out expeditions in 1539 and 1540, which explored the regions of the Gila, the Little Colorado and the Rio Grande.

Corporal's Guard, the term applied to the small party or group which supported Tyler's administration (1841–45).

Corps, in the Civil War. First Corps organized March 13, 1862, and commanded by McDowell; afterward reorganized and merged in the Army of the Potomac and commanded by Wadsworth, Newton and Hancock in succession; disbanded in 1865. Second Corps organized August 12, 1862, and at first commanded by Banks; afterward by a number of other generals; disbanded in 1865. Third Corps organized August 12, 1862, and commanded by Heintzelman; disbanded in 1864. Fourth Corps organized August 1, 1863, and commanded by Keyes; afterward consolidated with the Twentieth and Twenty-first Corps; disbanded in 1865. Fifth Corps organized July 2, 1862, and commanded by Banks; afterward by Porter in the Army of the Potomac; disbanded in 1865; many successive commanders. Sixth Corps organized July 22, 1862, with Franklin in command; disbanded in 1865. Seventh Corps organized July 22, 1862, with Naglee in command; merged with Eighteenth Corps in 1863. Eighth Corps organized July 22, 1862, and commanded by Schenck and Lockwood; afterward by Lew Wallace; disbanded in 1865. Ninth Corps organized July 22, 1862, and commanded by Burnside and others in succession; disbanded in 1865. Tenth Corps organized September 3, 1862, with Mitchell in command; discontinued in 1864, but reorganized in 1865 and continued till the close of the war under various generals. Eleventh Corps originally organized as the Second Corps; organized as the Eleventh September 12, 1862, and commanded by Banks; consolidated with the Twelfth in 1864, and constituted the Twentieth; disbanded in 1865. Twelfth Corps first organized as the Third Corps; as Twelfth September 12, 1862; afterward merged with the Eleventh to form the Twentieth, with Banks in command; disbanded in 1865. Thirteenth Corps organized October 24, 1862, with McClernand in command; reorganized in 1865 and commanded by Granger. Fourteenth Corps organized October 24, 1862, and commanded by Rosecrans; disbanded in 1865. Fifteenth Corps organized December 18, 1862, and commanded by Sherman; disbanded in 1865. Sixteenth Corps organized December 18, 1862, and commanded by Hurlbut; disbanded in 1865. Seventeenth Corps organized December 18, 1862, with McPherson in command; disbanded in 1865. Eighteenth Corps organized December 24, 1862, and commanded by Foster; reorganized in 1864, and commanded by W. F. Smith; disbanded in 1865. Nineteenth Corps organized January 5, 1863, with Banks in command; organization abolished in 1864, and entirely disbanded in 1865. Twentieth Corps organized January 3, 1863, and commanded by McCook; afterward reformed from Eleventh and Twelfth in 1863; disbanded in 1865. Twenty-first Corps organized January 9, 1863, and commanded by Crittenden; consolidated with the original Twentieth in 1863 to form the Fourth. Twenty-second Corps organized February 2, 1863, with Heintzelman in command; disbanded in a few months. Twenty-third Corps organized April 27, 1863, with Hartsuff in command; disbanded in 1865. Twenty-fourth Corps organized December 3, 1864, and commanded by Ord; disbanded in 1865. Twenty-fifth Corps organized December 3, 1864, of colored troops, and commanded by Weitzel and Heckman; disbanded in 1866. Potomac Cavalry Corps organized April 15, 1863, and commanded by Stoneman and afterward by Sheridan. Wilson's Cavalry Corps not organized under Act of Congress, as the others were. Engineer and Signal Service Corps organized in 1864.

Corrigan, Michael Augustine, Roman Catholic prelate, born in Newark, N. J., in 1839, was Bishop of Newark 1873–1880; coadjutor to Cardinal McCloskey 1880–1885, and Archbishop of New York from 1885 to the present time (1894).

Cortereal, Gaspar, born in Lisbon, died in 1501. He received a license from the King of Portugal to make a voyage of discovery in 1500. He is reported to have visited a country far to the North, which was probably Greenland. He made a second voyage with three ships in 1501, during which he sailed for six or seven hundred miles along the coast of America. His vessel was never heard from.

Corwin, Thomas (1794–1865), statesman, was a member of the Ohio Legislature 1822–1829, and of the U. S. House of Representatives in 1831, where he represented the Whig party until 1840, when he was elected Governor of Ohio. He was elected to the U. S. Senate 1844–1850 and to Congress in 1858 and 1860. He was appointed Minister to Mexico by President Lincoln, serving from 1861 to 1864.

Costa Rica. The United States concluded a commercial treaty with Costa Rica in 1851. A convention relative to claims of United States citizens was concluded in 1860.

Cotton, John (1585–1652), clergyman, fled to America in 1633 to escape a charge of nonconformity in church service, and was established in the first church in Boston, where he remained until his death. In controversies with Roger Williams he defended the interference of the civil power in religious matters. He was a scholar of profound learning and a voluminous writer.

Cotton. The cotton plant began to be cultivated in Virginia in the times of the earliest colonists. Small patches were grown, and the lint, picked from the seed by hand, was woven into cloth for domestic use. The development of cotton manufacture was gradual, and it was not until 1750, when the fly shuttle was invented, that the industry became extensive through the Southern States of the Union. The spinning jenny was invented in England in 1767 and immediately brought into use in this country. In 1769 Arkwright patented a spinning frame, or "throstle," in which was a useful device for spinning with rollers. Arkwright adapted to this machine the principle now known as the "flyer." Samuel Crompton combined the principles of the fly shuttle and the "throstle" in 1779, and Cartwright invented the power loom in 1785. The first steam engine used in a power mill was set up in 1785, thus supplying the mechanical power so long needed. Eli Whitney's cotton gin, invented in 1792, brought about an enormous increase in the cotton industry. The first successful cotton factory in the United States was that of Samuel Slater, of Pawtucket, R. I., established in 1790. In 1810 the whole consumption of cotton in this country was 10,000 bales; in 1815 it had reached 90,000. The total product in 1890 was 14,188,103 bales, with a capital of $354,000,000 employed in the industry.

Cotton Gin, invented by Eli Whitney, of Massachusetts, in 1792. With this machine the preparation of cotton for market was enormously facilitated and the cotton industry increased proportionately. The price of slaves immediately rose and the faint glimmerings of emancipation sentiment in the South were quickly extinguished, slave labor being invaluable in the cultivation of cotton.

Cotton Loans, loans negotiated by the Confederate Government. It induced the planters to promise that, when their cotton was sold, certain sums or a certain proportion of the crop should be paid to the government for the management of the war. In return, and on this basis, the government issued eight per cent bonds. The loan proved worthless to subscribers.

"Cotton Whigs," a name given in the decade preceding the Civil War to those Whigs in the North who were willing, for the sake of conciliating the Southern Whigs, to make as little opposition as possible to the extension of slavery.

Couch, Darius N., general, born in South East, N. Y., in 1822. He was graduated at the U. S. Military Academy, and served against the Seminoles in 1849–50. During the Civil War he served as colonel and brigadier-general, and commanded the Second Army Corps at Fredericksburg and Chancellorsville. He was quartermaster-general of Connecticut in 1877–78, and adjutant-general in 1883–84.

Council. Under the colonial governments, the council, legislative council, or executive council, was a body partaking of the nature and functions of an upper House of the Legislature, and of a privy council. The name was retained for the upper House of the Legislature by Delaware until 1792, by Georgia until 1798, by South Carolina until 1790 and by Vermont until 1836. In later days this name has also been applied to the upper House of the Territorial Legislatures. In a few States the Governor has an executive council.

Count of Presidential Votes. The two Houses meet in the House of Representatives. The votes are opened by the president of the Senate and handed to tellers, who count the votes and announce the results. In 1876 double returns were received from certain States. In 1877 an act was passed applicable to that election only, that no vote should be rejected except by concurrent vote of both Houses, and that disputes should be decided by a special Electoral Commission. In 1887 an act was passed providing that the determination by the States, under State laws, of all contests as to the appointment of electors, shall be final, so far as is possible.

County. In England the county was the primary subdivision of the kingdom. In the sparsely settled Southern colonies it was natural that the county institutions of England should be kept in existence rather than those of the smaller areas. Here, therefore, county government prevailed. In 1634 eight shires were erected in Virginia, called counties in 1639; in 1680 there were twenty. In Maryland the term county first appears in 1638. In South Carolina the original subdivision of the colony was the parish, to which afterward was added the district. Except for the years 1786–1790, the county did not come into existence until 1868. These Southern counties had institutions and officers resembling those of English counties—lieutenants, sheriffs, justices and quarter sessions. In Massachusetts counties were first incorporated in 1643; but the life of local government was mainly in the towns. In Rhode Island no counties were erected until 1703. In the Middle colonies the county came into existence with the beginnings of English rule or soon after.

County Democracy, a faction of the Democratic party in New York City, which opposed Tammany Hall, especially before 1886, since which time it has been of little importance.

"Courant, Connecticut," chief among the earlier newspapers of the State. Its publication was begun at Hartford by Thomas Green in December, 1764, and it is still issued as a daily and weekly.

Court, General, the proper title of the Legislature of Massachusetts. Its origin is from the Massachusetts Company. In the seventeenth century, the general stockholders' meeting of a corporation was called its general court. Hence the primary assembly of the freemen of the Massachusetts Company was from the first called the general court, and the name remained when the assembly became representative.

Court Leet. In old English manors this court, consisting of the tenants of the manor, presided over by the lord's steward, judged petty criminal cases, and had also some administrative duties. In Maryland courts leet were held in the seventeenth century, and their records have been preserved.

Court of Appeals in Cases of Capture, a tribunal which constituted the main portion of the Federal judiciary before 1789. General Washington made the first suggestion of a Federal prize court, to hear appeals from State courts in cases of capture of prizes. From 1776 to 1780 Congress heard appeals by means of committees. The complications arising out of the case of the sloop "Active," which embroiled the Federal Government with Pennsylvania and showed the weakness of the former, led to the establishment of a permanent Court of Appeals in Cases of Capture, in 1780. The court held sittings from that time to 1787, and consisted of three judges. The court and the committees which preceded it took cognizance of 118 cases. It was a precursor of the U. S. Supreme Court.

Court of Claims. This court, founded in 1855, hears claims against the Government on any regulation of an executive department or on any contract, express or implied, with the Government of the United States. Before the establishment of this court, those having just claims against the Government had no remedy but to petition Congress. The court at first reported its proceedings to Congress, and that body acted upon the reports. Since 1863 report to Congress has not been required.

Courts. (See Judiciary.)

Covode, John (1808–1871), of Dutch descent, was elected to Congress in 1854 as an Anti-Masonic Whig from Pennsylvania, and served from 1855 to 1863 as a Republican. He was chairman of the committee to investigate charges against President Buchanan in 1860.

Covode Investigation, an action taken by the Thirty-sixth Congress during President Buchanan's administration in inquiring into certain charges made by two Anti-Lecompton Democrats of the House, who alleged that the administration had endeavored to influence them corruptly to vote for the Lecompton Bill. A committee of five investigated the charges, the Republican majority sustaining them, and the Democratic minority exonerating the President. No action was taken.

Cowboys, the name given to British camp-followers and marauders who infested the neutral ground between the two armies in New York State during the Revolution. They were constantly skirmishing with the "Skinners," the Continental marauders.

Cowpens, Battle of the, January 17, 1781. When Cornwallis marched into North Carolina he sent Tarleton with 1100 men against Morgan. On Tarleton's approach Morgan took his position at the Cowpens upon the slope of a hill. His militia was in front, his regulars on higher ground and at the top of the slope Colonel Washington with the cavalry. As the British advanced Pickens' militia delivered a number of deadly volleys and retired behind the lines. The regulars then met the enemy with a murderous fire followed by a bayonet charge. At the same time the American cavalry struck their right flank and the militia formed again behind the lines on the left. The rout was complete. The British loss was 230 killed and wounded and 600 taken prisoners, a number equal to the whole American force engaged. In point of tactics this was one of the most brilliant battles of the war.

Cox, Jacob D., born in 1828, during the Civil War was promoted to be major-general and commanded at the battle of Kingston, N. C. He was Secretary of the Interior 1869–70, and Representative in Congress 1877–79.

Cox, Samuel S., (1824–1889), was editor of the Columbus, Ohio, *Statesman*, in which he published the gorgeous article which gave him the sobriquet of "Sunset" Cox. In 1855 he was Secretary of Legation to Peru, and in 1885–86, Minister to Turkey. He spent twenty years in Congress, beginning in 1857, and was an effective speaker, lecturer and writer.

Coxe, Tench (1756–1824), successively a Royalist, Whig, Federalist and Republican, was a commissioner to the Annapolis Convention in 1786, member of the Continental Congress in 1788 and Assistant Secretary of the Treasury from 1789 to 1792.

Craft Case, an important fugitive slave case. In 1848 William Craft and his wife Ellen, who was nearly white, fled from Macon, Ga. Ellen impersonated a Southern lady, carried her right arm in a sling that she might not be expected to write, bandaged her face and wore green goggles. William accompanied her as her servant. The couple at length reached Boston, and here engaged the attention of Theodore Parker. After the passage of the Fugitive Slave Law of 1850 their identity was discovered and they were finally obliged to leave the city. They reached England, where the remainder of their days was spent in peace.

Cranch's Reports, law reports by William Cranch of cases in the Supreme Court, covering the period from 1801 to 1815, in nine volumes.

Craney Island (Chesapeake Bay) commanded the approach to Norfolk. 1500 troops were sent on June 3, 1813, from the British fleet under Admiral Warren to capture the island, which was defended by 737 men directed by General Robert B. Taylor. The American artillery opened upon them with terrible effect. Five of the transport barges were sunk and the rest retreated. The British loss was eighty-one, the Americans lost none. This defeat frustrated all hope of capturing Norfolk.

Crawford, Francis Marion, son of Thomas, was born in Italy in 1845 and lived mostly abroad, but made short visits to the United States. He has been very successful as a voluminous writer of novels.

Crawford, George W., born in 1798, was Attorney-General of Georgia from 1827 to 1831. He was a Whig member of Congress in 1843. He was Governor of Georgia from 1843 to 1845. He was Secretary of War in Taylor's Cabinet from 1849 to 1850.

Crawford, Thomas (1814–1857), an American sculptor, worked mostly in Rome, visiting the United States in 1844–49 and 1856. He was famous chiefly for his historical and allegorical works of art.

Crawford, William (1732–1782), participated in Braddock's expedition against Fort Duquesne, fought at Long Island, Trenton and Princeton during the Revolutionary War, and was captured and put to death in an expedition against the Wyandot and Delaware Indians.

Crawford, William Harris (1772–1834), served in the Georgia Legislature and obtained distinction as a lawyer. He was a member of the U. S. Senate in 1807–13, being president *pro tem.* for a part of the time. His career in this office, followed by his Ministry to France in 1813–15, and his long service as Secretary of War, 1815–16, and of the Treasury, 1816–25, brought him prominently forward as a candidate for Monroe's successor in the Presidency. He was one of the four candidates voted for in the famous election of 1824, receiving forty-one electoral votes, and with Adams and Jackson he was, after that indecisive contest, brought before the House of Representatives, and like Jackson he went down before the Adams and Clay forces. He left the reputation less of a statesman than of a political manipulator.

Crazy Horse, an Indian chief of the Sioux nation, brother-in-law of Red Cloud. With Sitting Bull he destroyed General Custer's command on the Little Big Horn in 1876, but surrendered to General Crook in 1877.

Crédit Mobilier, a corporation chartered by the Pennsylvania Legislature as the "Pennsylvania Fiscal Agency," which in 1864 became a company to construct the Union Pacific Railroad. In the Presidential campaign of 1872 the Democratic leaders charged the Vice-President, the Vice-President elect, the Secretary of the Treasury, Speaker of the House and other prominent men with accepting Crédit Mobilier stocks in return for political influence. An investigation which followed resulted in the censure of Representatives Oakes Ames and James Brooks.

Creek Indians originally lived on the Flint, Chattahoochee, Coosa and Alabama Rivers, and in the peninsula of Florida. It was not until the overthrow of the French power that they came completely under English influence. During the Revolution the Creeks joined the British, assisting in an attack on Wayne's army in 1782. In 1790 they made a friendly treaty, but renewed hostilities in 1792. Another treaty was made in 1796, and in 1802 and 1805 they began to cede lands. Joining the English in the War of 1812, they attacked Fort Mimms, August 30, 1813, and massacred 400 people. They suffered repeated defeats, and were completely overthrown by General Jackson at Horseshoe Bend, March 27, 1814. A treaty of peace followed in which they surrendered large tracts of land. Early in the century a part removed to Louisiana and later to Texas. A treaty was made in 1825 ceding more lands, but was repudiated. The nation then divided, one party favoring emigration, the other opposing it. In 1836 a part aided the Government against the Seminoles, but the remainder attacked the frontier towns of Georgia and Alabama. General Scott reduced them, and the tribe was removed to a reservation between the Arkansas and the Canadian. The Civil War divided the tribe, those adhering to the Union being finally defeated by the Confederates. In 1866 the Creeks ceded a large tract to the Government.

"Creole" Case. On November 7, 1841, seventeen negroes rose against the officers of the brig "Creole," bound from Hampton Roads to New Orleans with a cargo of slaves. One of the vessel's owners was killed, and the vessel was captured and run into Nassau. Here all were set at liberty except those charged with murder. The demand for their surrender, made by the administration, was refused by Great Britain, but the matter was finally adjusted by the treaty of August 9, 1842. During the progress of negotiations J. R. Giddings, of Ohio, offered a series of resolutions which laid down the fundamental positions of the anti-slavery party.

Creswell, John A. J. (1828–1891), was a member of Congress from 1863 to 1865. He was Postmaster-General of the United States from 1869 to 1874.

Crévecœur, Hector St. John de (1731–1813), an Englishman emigrating to America in 1754, who, during the Revolutionary War, was made prisoner and exchanged in England. In 1783 he was appointed French Consul at New York, and wrote extensively concerning America.

Crisp, Charles Frederick, of Americus, Ga., was born in Sheffield, England, in 1845. He served in the Confederate army from 1861 to 1864. In 1866 he was admitted to the bar, and from 1872 to 1877 was Solicitor-General of Georgia. He served as Judge of the Supreme Court of Georgia from 1877 to 1882, when he resigned and accepted a nomination to Congress, of which he was chosen Speaker in 1891 and again in 1893.

Crittenden, George B. (1812–1880), son of J. J., a major and lieutenant-colonel in the Texan Revolution, joined the Confederates as brigadier-general, and as major-general was defeated in a rash attack upon General Thomas at Fishing Creek.

Crittenden, John Jordan (1787–1863), was in early life a lawyer, Attorney-General of Illinois Territory, and a soldier in the War of 1812. Few Americans have been U. S. Senators at such different periods. Crittenden was in the Senate from Kentucky in 1817–19, and again in 1835–41, 1842–49, and 1855–61. In the intervals he was a U. S. District Attorney, was Attorney-General under Harrison in 1841, and again under Fillmore in 1850–53. He was a prominent Whig. He supported Bell and Everett in 1860, and after the election he came forward with the "Crittenden Compromise" in the vain attempt to avert the impending war. He sided with the North, and in 1861–63 was a member of the House of Representatives from Kentucky.

Crittenden, Thomas L., son of J. J., born in 1815, a lieutenant and aide to General Taylor in the Mexican War, was Consul to Liverpool 1849–53 and served with distinction in the Civil War, commanding a division at Shiloh and a corps at Chickamauga.

Crittenden Compromise. In 1860 Senator John J. Crittenden introduced a proposition for a constitutional amendment which would permanently divide the Union into a free-state and a slave-state portion, the boundary being the line of 36° 30′. The United States was to pay the owner for any fugitive slave rescued. The proposition met with no success in Congress.

Crockett, David (1786–1836), a famous frontiersman, with General Jackson in the Creek War, was a member of Congress from 1827 to 1831 and from 1833 to 1835. He was one of the six survivors at Fort Alamo who were massacred by Santa Anna.

Croghan, George (1791–1849), serving as aide, colonel and lieutenant-colonel in the War of 1812, distinguished himself at Fort Meigs and at Fort Stephenson. In 1825 he was made inspector-general of the U. S. army.

Crompton, William, born in 1806, devised a loom for the manufacture of fancy cotton goods in 1837, which, since its adaptation to woolens in 1840, has been employed almost exclusively.

Cromwell, Oliver (1599–1658), Lord Protector of England from 1653 to 1658, was appointed in 1643 one of a board of commissioners for the general management of all the English colonies in America. After his elevation he proposed to the colonists of Massachusetts that they move to Jamaica, then recently conquered (1656). During the war between England and Holland he sent at the solicitation of Connecticut a fleet with a land force on board for protection against the Dutch settlers, and to take summary possession of New Netherland; but the war soon ended.

Crook, George (1828–1890), commanded the Pitt River expedition in 1857, and during service in the Civil War was brevetted lieutenant-colonel and commanded the second cavalry division at Chickamauga. He had charge of the cavalry of the Army of the Potomac from March 26, 1865, till the surrender at Appomattox, and from 1866 on was chiefly occupied in quelling Indian disturbances. In 1888 he was appointed a major-general of the U. S. army.

Cross Keys, Va., an indecisive action, June 8, 1862, between 20,000 Federals under Frémont and Ewell's column of Jackson's army of 17,000 Confederates. Ewell was reinforced by Taylor and Patton leading a Louisiana and a Virginia brigade. Frémont's line of battle, a mile and a half long, was advantageously arranged. The Federals began the battle, advancing steadily under a heavy fire, Stahl's Pennsylvania troops faring the worst. He was, however, supported by Bohlen, Schenk and Milroy, and thus was not compelled to retreat. Taking a strong position on a hill he was repeatedly cannonaded by the Confederates, but they were easily driven off by his superior batteries.

Croswell, Edwin (1797–1871), from 1824 to 1854 was editor of the *Albany Argus*, which became the official organ of the Democratic party, and by which the Albany Regency advanced its interests.

Crown Lands. After the treaty of Paris, in 1763, a royal proclamation from Great Britain set aside all lands west of the colonies as "crown lands," exclusively under the jurisdiction of the home government, and as reserved for the use of the Indians. The colonies were forbidden to make purchase of, or settlement in, any of this reserved territory without the royal permission. After the Revolution this reserve was claimed by various States.

Crown Point, was fortified by the French in 1731, and, in spite of expeditions against it in 1755 and 1756, was held by them until 1759. It was then abandoned by reason of the fall of Ticonderoga. In 1775, at the beginning of the Revolutionary War, as a part of the scheme to seize the route to Canada, and capture the British stores at Ticonderoga (q. v.) and Crown Point, Seth Warner was despatched against the latter place. On the morning of May 10, while Arnold and Allen were busy at Ticonderoga, Warner seized Crown Point, thus gaining possession of more than 200 cannon, and a great supply of powder and ball.

Crowninshield, Benjamin W. (1772–1851), of Massachusetts, was Secretary of the Navy from 1814, in Madison's, until 1818 in Monroe's Cabinet, was a Presidential elector in 1820, and a Democratic member of Congress from 1823 to 1831.

Cuba. In 1849–52 three filibustering expeditions were made against Cuba from this country. They were incited by Narcisso Lopez, a South American military adventurer, who persuaded Governor Quitman and other Southern expansionists that the island was ripe for revolt from Spain and annexation to the United States. These expeditions failed, and Lopez was executed by the Cuban authorities. Again, in 1854, Southern annexationists attempted to fit out an expedition for the capture of Cuba, but were prevented by a timely warning from the President. In that year an American steamer, the "Black Warrior," was seized by the Cuban authorities. Indemnity was demanded from Spain, which was accorded finally, but not before the Ostend Manifesto had been issued by a conference of our ministers to the English, French and Spanish courts, demanding the sale of Cuba by Spain. Subsequent attempts to revolutionize Cuba have met with assistance from citizens of the United States. In 1873 occurred the "Virginius" affair, which see. In 1891 the United States made a reciprocity treaty with Spain respecting trade with Cuba and Porto Rico.

Cullom, Shelby M., born in 1829, chosen Speaker in the Illinois Legislature in 1860, was a member of the war commission at Cairo in 1862 and a member of Congress from 1865 to 1871. As chairman of the Illinois delegation at the Republican convention he placed General Grant in nomination in 1872 and General Logan in 1884; and from 1883 to 1894 was U. S. Senator.

Cullum, George W., born in 1809, a graduate, instructor and (1864–66) superintendent of the U. S. Military Academy; was from 1838 to 1874 engaged largely in Government engineering and during the Civil War was brevetted major-general.

Culpeper, John, leader of an insurrection in the Northern colony of the Carolinas in favor of popular liberty in 1678. While in England negotiating for the new government he was indicted for high treason, but was acquitted.

Culpeper, Thomas, Lord, in 1673 received an exclusive grant from Charles II. for thirty-one years of the territory of Virginia and in 1675 was proclaimed Governor for life, coming to this country in 1680. He forfeited his commission in 1683 by returning to England without royal permission and by political corruption. Lord Fairfax, patron of Washington, was his heir.

Cumberland, Fort. This fort was erected in Maryland at the instance of General Braddock in 1755 during his fatal expedition against the French Fort Duquesne. Colonel James Innes was left in command with a small force and thither Braddock's forces fled after their defeat by the French and Indians. Colonel Washington afterward commanded the fort, to protect the settlers from Indian raids.—In 1755, Fort Beauséjour on the Maine frontier, which had been built by the French in 1754, was captured by English troops and the name changed to Fort Cumberland.

Cumberland Gap, Tenn., captured by the Nationals under Morgan during the battle of Chattanooga and afterward abandoned. It was occupied by the Confederates in 1863, and from it General Frazier commanding 2000 men was dislodged by 8000 Federals under Burnside. Frazier held out for four days, but his provisions gave out and Burnside was reinforced by Shackleford's brigade. Frazier surrendered September 9.

Cumberland Presbyterian Church. This denomination was a development of the "Great Western Revival of 1800." The Presbytery in Kentucky appointed lay preachers, who were said to be illiterate and unsound in doctrine. The suspension of these by the synod resulted in a schism in 1811 and the formation of the above named sect. In the main it is an attempt to steer between the Calvinism of the Presbyterians and the Arminianism of the Methodists. They now number over 165,000 members, largely confined to the South.

Cumberland Road. (See National Road.)

Curry, George L. (1820–1878), in 1846 established the *Oregon Spectator*, the first paper published on the Pacific coast, and in 1848 founded the *Oregon Free Press*. He was Governor of Oregon from 1854 to 1859.

Curtin, Andrew G., born in Pennsylvania in 1815, a Presidential elector in 1848, and Governor of Pennsylvania from 1861 to 1865. He was one of the "war governors" who supported the National Government, and furnished 25,000 men known as the "Pennsylvania Reserve." He was appointed Minister to Russia in 1869 and was elected to Congress by the Democratic party, serving from 1881 to 1887. Died 1894.

Curtin, Jeremiah, linguist, born in Wisconsin in 1835; was appointed Secretary of the U. S. Legation to Russia in 1864. Since 1888 he has rendered valuable assistance to the Bureau of Ethnology of the United States. He is noted as a translator of Polish historical novels.

Curtis, Benjamin R. (1809–1874), appointed to the U. S. Supreme Court in 1851 by President Fillmore, dissented in the Dred Scott case and resigned in 1857. He was one of the counsel for President Johnson in the impeachment trial of 1868.

Curtis, George Ticknor (1812–1894), a Boston lawyer from 1836 to 1862, when he removed to New York, was largely engaged in professional and historical investigations, and published many valuable works, among them being "Commentaries on the Jurisprudence, Practice and Peculiar Jurisdiction of the Courts of the United States" and a "History of the Origin, Formation and Adoption of the Constitution of the United States," and the first volume of a "Constitutional History of the United States."

Curtis, George William (1824–1892), was in early life a member of the famous Brook Farm community, a European traveling correspondent of the *New York Tribune*, and an editor of *Putnam's Monthly*. His later reputation rests on four forms of achievement: as an eloquent and cultured lyceum lecturer and platform orator; as the author of several books, including "Nile Notes," "Lotus Eating," "Prue and I," "Trumps," "Potiphar Papers," etc.; as an editor of *Harper's Weekly* and the writer of "Easy Chair" of *Harper's Magazine*, and as a politician. He was a noted delegate in the Republican National Conventions of 1860, 1880 and 1884. He was identified with civil service reform from the start, and was by President Grant appointed in 1871 a commissioner for the purpose of drawing up rules. The National Civil Service Reform League was largely his work.

Curtis, Samuel R. (1807–1866), an Ohio lawyer from 1841 to 1846, became adjutant-general of militia in 1846, and in the Mexican War commanded at Camarago against General Urrea. He was a Congressman from Iowa from 1857 to 1861, when he was commissioned brigadier-general and gained a great victory at Pea Ridge, Ark. He commanded Fort Leavenworth during the Price raid in 1864, and was U. S. Commissioner to negotiate Indian treaties.

Cushing, Caleb (1800–1879), graduated at Harvard and rose to eminence at the Massachusetts bar. He was a Representative from Massachusetts in Congress in 1835–43, having been a Whig and, from Tyler's time, a Democrat. He was a U. S. Commissioner to China, a brigadier-general in the Mexican War, and an unsuccessful candidate for Governor of Massachusetts. In 1853–57 he was a member of Pierce's Cabinet as Attorney-General. In

1860 he presided over the Democratic National Convention which met at Charleston. His high reputation as a lawyer led to his appointment as U. S. counsel before the Geneva Tribunal of 1872, and to his nomination by Grant as Chief Justice of the Supreme Court. He failed of confirmation to the latter office, and was sent as U. S. Minister to Spain in 1874, where he remained until 1877.

Cushing, Frank H., born in 1857, was chosen curator of the Ethnological Department of the National Museum in 1876, and from 1879 to 1884 lived among the Zuñi Indians, studying their language, habits and history, the results of which he has published.

Cushing, Luther S. (1803–1856), from 1832 to 1846 clerk of the Massachusetts House of Representatives, was reporter of the Massachusetts Supreme Court decisions from 1850 to 1856. He was author of "Cushing's Manual of Parliamentary Practice."

Cushing, Thomas (1725–1788) from 1766 to 1774 Speaker of the Massachusetts Assembly, was elected to the first and second Continental Congresses, and was a member of the convention that ratified the Federal Constitution in 1788. From 1783 to 1788 he was Lieutenant-Governor of Massachusetts.

Cushing, William (1732–1810), Judge of the Massachusetts Superior Court in 1772, Chief Justice in 1777 and the first Chief Justice under the State Constitution in 1780, was Associate Justice of the U. S. Supreme Court from 1789 to 1810.

Cushing, William B. (1842–1874), in 1861 captured the first prize of the war, and in 1864 by extraordinary boldness destroyed the Confederate iron-clad "Albemarle." He was promoted lieutenant-colonel and distinguished himself at Fort Fisher.

Cushman, Charlotte S. (1816–1876), a noted American actress, was born in Boston. She was a very successful actress in historical plays and from 1870 developed marked abilities as a dramatic reader.

Cushman, Robert (1580–1625), was active in preparing for the departure of the Pilgrims and acted as their English agent till 1621, when he came to America and preached the first sermon in America which was ever published.

Custer, George Armstrong (1839–1876), born in Ohio, served throughout the Civil War and distinguished himself at Gettysburg as commander of the Michigan brigade, also winning fame at Winchester, Fisher's Hill, Cedar Creek, Waynesboro, Five Forks and Dinwiddie Court House. In 1876, being then a general in the regular army, he was overpowered by the Sioux Indians at the Little Big Horn River, and his entire command was slain.

Custis, George W. P. (1781–1857), grandson of Mrs. Washington, until 1802 a member of Washington's family, erected the Arlington House. It is now national property, and his estate is the site of a soldiers' cemetery.

Customs Revenue. For the laws relating to the customs, see art. Tariff. The Continental Congress desired to have a revenue from customs, but the

States would not all agree to this. From 1789 on, a great part of the revenue of the Government has been derived from this source, about five-sixths from 1789 to 1830, except in war-time, sometimes more than nine-tenths in the period from 1837 to 1861, and from one-half to three-fifths in the period since 1868. At first amounting to about $3,000,000 per annum, customs have of recent years averaged about $200,000,000.

Cutler, Manasseh (1742–1823), a clergyman, was born in Connecticut. During the Revolutionary War he served as chaplain, and in 1786 was agent for the Ohio company which founded Marietta. He drafted for Nathan Dane the Ordinance of 1787 which excluded slavery from the Northwest Territory, and was a Massachusetts Federal Congressman from 1801 to 1805.

Cuttyhunk, Mass., discovered May 25, 1602, by Bartholomew Gosnold, who made a settlement there and erected a house and palisades.

"**Cyane**," ship. (See "Constitution.")

Cynthiana, Ky., burned during the Civil War by the Confederate guerrilla Morgan, June 10, 1864. Morgan also, with 2000 Confederates, defeated 600 Federals under Burbridge and Hobson, but was, June 12, defeated in return by them at Cynthiana.

D.

Dabney's Mills, Va. Here, during Grant's and Lee's campaigns about Richmond and Petersburg, in 1865, there occurred, February 6 and 7, some severe skirmishing between Crawford's division of Warren's Federal corps and a Confederate force under Pegram. The Federal leaders were endeavoring to lengthen their line toward Hatcher's Run when Pegram fell upon them. The Confederates were defeated and Pegram was killed.

Dacres, James R. (1788–1853), British naval officer, commanded the "Guerriere" when it was beaten by the "Constitution," August 19, 1812. Later, commanding the "Tiber," he captured the "Leo" in March, 1815.

Dade, Francis L., born in Virginia, a lieutenant, captain and, in 1828, a brevet-major in the U. S. army, was killed in a treacherous attack of the Seminole Indians, in 1835, near Fort King, Florida.

Dahlgren, John Adolph (1809–1870), entered the U. S. navy at an early age. He became noted as the designer of the improved Dahlgren cannon. At the outbreak of the Civil War he was assigned to the command of the Navy Yard at Washington. He was naturally made chief of the ordnance bureau, was promoted to be rear-admiral, and commanded in the attack on the Charleston defences in 1863. His last important service was in co-operation with General Sherman, in the taking of Savannah, in 1864.

Dale, Richard (1756–1826), was first lieutenant on the "Bon Homme Richard," and served with Paul Jones on the "Alliance" and the "Ariel." He commanded the Mediterranean Squadron during the troubles with Tripoli.

Dale, Samuel (1772–1841), a U. S. army scout in 1793, commanded a battalion against the Creeks in 1814. He was appointed with Colonel George

S. Gaines to remove the Choctaw Indians to their reservation on the Arkansas and Red Rivers.

Dale, Sir Thomas, died in 1620. He was sent as Governor to Virginia, and established there a military government. He was succeeded by Sir Thomas Gates, from 1611 to 1614, when he resumed the government, and held it till 1616.

Dallas, Alexander James (1759–1817) born in Jamaica, took the oath of allegiance to Pennsylvania in 1783, and was U. S. District Attorney from 1801 to 1814, when he became Secretary of the Treasury in Madison's Cabinet. On his suggestion the Second National Bank was incorporated in 1816, and to his efforts is largely due the financial success of the U. S. Government from 1814 to 1817.

Dallas, George Mifflin (1792–1864), Vice-President of the United States, had a training in diplomacy and law, was mayor of Philadelphia, and district attorney. From 1831 to 1833 he was U. S. Senator from Pennsylvania, and was Attorney-General of the State in the two succeeding years. In 1837–39 he was U. S. Minister to Russia. When Polk was nominated by the Democrats in 1844, Dallas received the second honor, as a kind of protectionist gift to hold Pennsylvania. They were elected, and Dallas served as Vice-President 1845–49. In spite of his supposed protectionist leanings Dallas gave the casting vote in the Senate in favor of the Walker Tariff of 1846. His last public office was that of Minister to England in 1856–61.

Dallas-Clarendon Treaty. A treaty arranged in England in 1856, to adjust difficulties between Great Britain and the United States respecting Central America, arising under the Clayton-Bulwer Treaty. It was not ratified by the Senate.

Dallas' Reports. Law reports by A. J. Dallas of cases from all inferior State Courts and all United States Courts sitting in Philadelphia and from the Supreme Court of Pennsylvania; in four volumes, covering the period from 1754 to 1806 (Supreme Court, 1790–1800). Also cases in Federal Court of Appeals 1781–87. The series of reports of the U. S. Supreme Court begins with 2 Dallas.

Dallas (Vicinity), Ga., a four days' fight between Johnston's and Sherman's armies, during the latter's advance upon Atlanta in 1864. The fighting took place May 25 to 29. The Confederates, about 40,000 strong, were under the immediate command of Hardee, and lay entrenched about Dallas. McPherson attacked them with 20,000 Federals. Schofield was ordered to flank the Confederate right, but as he made this attempt Johnston himself struck heavily upon McPherson's main command. However, the Federals moved to the left along the Confederate front and gained the Allatoona Pass. Johnston was thus forced to leave his intrenchments and retire, May 29.

Dana, Charles A., born in 1819, from 1848 to 1862 managing editor of the *New York Tribune*, edited by Horace Greeley; was appointed Assistant Secretary of War in 1863, and in 1867–1868 organized and became editor of the *New York Sun*.

Dana, Francis (1743–1811), a Massachusetts delegate to the Continental Congress in 1776, was Congressman in 1778 and secretary to the embassy of John Adams in 1779. He was Minister to Russia from 1780 to 1783. In 1785 he was made Justice of the Supreme Court of Massachusetts, and was a delegate to the Annapolis Convention in 1786, and Chief Justice of Massachusetts from 1791 to 1806.

Dana, James Dwight, professor in Yale University, born in 1813, made extensive reports, geological and other, upon material collected in a United States expedition to the Southern and Pacific Oceans, and in 1850 became associate editor of the *American Journal of Science and Art*, of which he is now editor.

Dana, Richard H. (1787–1879), admitted to the Massachusetts bar in 1811, was one of the projectors of the *North American Review* in 1815, and associate editor till 1821; he wrote poems, of which "The Buccaneer" is the most noted.

Dana, Richard H., 2d (1815–1882), contributed largely to legal publications. He was author of "Two Years Before the Mast," a popular book, and revised "Wheaton's International Law," bringing it up to 1866.

Dane, Nathan (1752–1835), a delegate to the Continental Congresses from 1785 to 1788, was the framer of the celebrated Ordinance of 1787 for the government of the Northwest Territory. In 1811 he was appointed to revise and publish the charters of Massachusetts, and in 1812 to publish the statutes. He was a delegate to the Hartford Convention in 1814.

Daniel, John W., Senator and orator, born in Virginia in 1842, a Confederate adjutant-general, was Representative from Virginia from 1885 to 1887, and Senator from 1887 to the present time (1894).

Daniel, Peter V. (1784–1860), was a member of the Virginia Privy Council from 1812 to 1835. He was a Justice of the U. S. Supreme Court from 1841 to 1860.

Daniel, William, of Maryland, was born in 1826. He was prominent in Maryland prohibition movements, a delegate to the State convention for the emancipation of slaves in 1864, and a candidate for Vice-President on the Prohibition ticket in 1884.

Darbytown Road, Va. Along this highway there occurred, during the campaign around Richmond and Petersburg, three brief fights between the Federals and Confederates. In the first, July 29, 1864, Hancock's corps of Grant's army, having been sent to co-operate in the mine explosion of Petersburg, met and defeated a large force of Confederates, Gregg's and Kautz's cavalry bearing the brunt of the fight. Again, October 7, Kautz's cavalry was defeated with heavy loss along the Darbytown road; many Federals were killed and wounded and nine pieces of artillery were lost. October 13 Butler endeavored to drive the Confederates from some new works he was constructing along this road. The Tenth Corps took the chief part in this engagement and were badly defeated, so Butler desisted from the work.

Dare, Virginia, born in 1587 at Roanoke, Va., (N. C.), was the first English child born in the New World. She was the granddaughter of John White, Governor of the colony sent out by Sir Walter Raleigh in 1587.

Darling, Fort. (See Drewry's Bluff.)

Dartmoor Massacre, a massacre of a number of American sailors captured during the Revolution and confined in Dartmoor Prison, in Devonshire, England. It occurred April 6, 1815. In the prison were 6000 Americans and 10,000 Frenchmen. The former becoming impatient for their liberty, since the war was then long ended, attempted to escape. They were set upon by the guards and a number of them were killed. An investigation of the matter was made and the British Government offered ample satisfaction.

Dartmouth College, Hanover, N. H., was founded by Congregationalists, and chartered in 1769. It is famous in constitutional history for having supplied the test case as to whether the State Legislature had the power to dissolve private trusts. It originated out of a school for Indians established at Lebanon, Conn., by Rev. Eleazar Wheelock. His son, John Wheelock, succeeded him in the presidency. Daniel Webster was graduated here in 1802. The Medical School was founded in 1797, the Chandler Scientific School in 1852, the New Hampshire College of Agriculture in 1868.

Dartmouth College vs. Woodward, a celebrated case brought to the Supreme Court of the United States upon writ of error from the Superior Court of the State of New Hampshire, and decided in 1819. William Woodward had been appointed secretary and treasurer of the corporation of Dartmouth College by the trustees of the college, twelve in number, as designated by the ancient charter granted by George III. in 1769 to Governor Wentworth, Eleazar Wheelock and ten others. Woodward was removed from office by the trustees August 27, 1816, and refused to give up certain goods, chattels and property then in his keeping, but belonging to Dartmouth College. On June 27, 1816, the New Hampshire Legislature, under the influence of the Democrats, had passed an act amending the charter and enlarging and altering the (Federalist) corporation of Dartmouth College; that is, the number of trustees was increased to twenty-one, there were twenty-five special overseers appointed, and the State was to have a general supervision of the affairs of the college. This act, and a similar one, passed December 26, 1816, to enforce the first, were wholly repugnant to the trustees, who refused to obey them. William Woodward had been appointed secretary and treasurer of the new board of twenty-one trustees selected by the State. Suit was brought against him by the old trustees to recover the property of the college then in his keeping. The Superior Court of New Hampshire gave a verdict for the defendant. The U. S. Supreme Court reversed and annulled this decision, allowing the plaintiffs $20,000 damages. It was decided by the court that the "charter of Dartmouth College is a contract within the meaning of that clause of the Constitution which prohibits the States from passing any law impairing the obligation of contracts." Hence the New Hampshire law was declared unconstitutional. Daniel Webster was chief counsel for the plaintiff.

Daughters of Liberty, a society of women formed in Boston in 1769–70, who pledged themselves not to buy goods from British importers and shopkeepers, and to help on the cause of liberty.

Daughters of the American Revolution, a society of the female descendants of distinguished soldiers, sailors and patriots of the Revolution, organized at Washington October 11, 1890. There are now twenty-odd State branches.

Davenport, John (1597–1670), an English clergyman, who emigrated to Boston in 1637. In 1638 he founded New Haven, of which colony for thirty years he was minister, and a chief member of the government. Since none except members of the church were burgesses, he had great power and influence.

Davie, William R. (1756–1820), born in England, arrived in America in 1763. He commanded at Stono Ferry in 1779, and in 1781 was appointed commissary-general of the Southern army. He was a member of the Constitutional Convention of 1787 from North Carolina, and of the special embassy to France in 1799. He was prominent among the North Carolina Federalists.

Daviess, Joseph H. (1774–1811), was killed at Tippecanoe. While U. S. Attorney for Kentucky he advocated the trial of Aaron Burr in 1806 on a charge of unauthorized warfare which could not be sustained and brought him into disfavor.

Davis, Charles H. (1807–1877), founder of the *American Nautical Almanac*, was connected with the U. S. navy from 1823 to 1867. In 1862 he was chief of the board of navigation, and commanded the Mississippi flotilla, and was superintendent of the naval observatory from 1865 to 1867 and from 1870 to 1877.

Davis, David (1815–1886), jurist, graduated at Kenyon College in Ohio, and settled to the practice of law at Bloomington, Ill. He was a member of the Illinois Legislature, a State judge, and an intimate friend of Abraham Lincoln. He was a delegate to the Republican National Convention at Chicago in 1860. President Lincoln appointed him an Associate Justice of the Supreme Court, where he remained from 1862 to 1877, being in the latter year a member of the Electoral Commission. His reform tendencies had, meanwhile, made him the candidate for President, in 1872, of the Labor Reform party, and brought him some votes at the Liberal Republican Convention in the same year. In 1877–1883 he was U. S. Senator from Illinois, and at one time president of the Senate. While in that body he was classed as an Independent, though he acted frequently with the Democrats.

Davis, Edwin H. (1811–1888), physician from 1838 to 1850, has made extensive exploration of ancient mounds, the report of which was the first scientific publication of the Smithsonian Institute.

Davis, Henry Winter (1817–1865), was born in Maryland. He attained considerable celebrity as a lawyer, and was elected to the Congress of the United States as a Democrat, serving from 1855 to 1861, and decided a tie vote for Speaker, in 1859, by voting for Mr. Pennington, the Republican candidate. He was again a member of Congress from 1863 to 1865, and served as chairman of the Committee on Foreign Affairs. Though representing a slave State, he was an ardent advocate of emancipation and negro suffrage, but opposed the assumption of extraordinary powers by the executive.

Davis, Jefferson (June 3, 1808–December 6, 1889), President of the Southern Confederacy, was born in Kentucky, and graduated at West Point in 1828. He saw some service in the Black Hawk War, but resigned from the army and became a cotton planter in Mississippi. He represented that State in Congress in 1845–46, but left Congress to take part as colonel in the Mexican War. In the storm of Monterey and the battle of Buena Vista he distinguished himself and was straightway chosen to the U. S. Senate, where he served 1847–51 and 1857–61. In 1851 he ran unsuccessfully as the States-rights candidate for Governor of Mississippi. In President Pierce's administration Mr. Davis was the Secretary of War 1853–57. He had become one of the Southern leaders, received some votes for the Democratic nomination for President in 1860, and in January, 1861, he left the U. S. Senate. He was thereupon elected provisional President of the Confederacy February 9, 1861, and was inaugurated February 18. In November of the same year he was elected President and was inaugurated February 22, 1862. From the second year of the war till the close many of his acts were severely criticised in the South itself. Many Southerners admit that President Davis' actions, especially his interference in military matters, impaired the prospects of success. An instance in point was his removal of General J. E. Johnston from command in 1864. Early in 1865 he conducted unsuccessful negotiations for peace. On the second of April the successes of Grant's army obliged President Davis to leave Richmond; he took the train for Danville, and after consultation proceeded southward and was captured by the Federals near Irwinsville, Ga., May 10, 1865. Until 1867 he was confined as a prisoner in Fort Monroe. He was in 1866 indicted for treason, released on bail the following year, and the trial was dropped. He passed the remainder of his life at Memphis and later in Mississippi, dying in New Orleans. He is the author of "Rise and Fall of the Confederate Government," two volumes. There are lives by Pollard and Alfriend.

Davis, Jefferson C. (1828–1879), Federal general, after serving during the Mexican War, was in Fort Sumter at the time of the bombardment in 1861, served with distinction at Pea Ridge and Stone River, and commanded a corps in Sherman's march through Georgia.

Davis, John (1550–1605), an English navigator, in 1585, 1586 and 1587 made attempts to discover a northwest passage, penetrating as far as the strait which bears his name.

Davis, John (1787–1854), was a National Republican Congressman from 1825 to 1834, when he became Governor of Massachusetts. From 1835 to 1840 he was a U. S. Senator, and opposed the administrations of Jackson and Van Buren. After again serving as Governor from 1840 to 1841, he was returned to the Senate from 1845 to 1853. He opposed the Mexican

War and the introduction and extension of slavery, and received the appellation of "Honest John Davis."

Davis, John C. Bancroft, jurist, was born in Massachusetts in 1822. From 1869 to 1871, from 1873 to 1875, and in 1881 he was Assistant Secretary of State of the United States. In 1871 he represented the U. S. Government in the arbitration of the "Alabama" claims at Geneva, having been secretary of the commission concluding the Treaty of Washington. From 1877 to 1881 he was a Judge of the U. S. Court of Claims, and in 1883 became reporter of the U. S. Supreme Court.

Davis, John W. (1799–1859), was Speaker of the Indiana Legislature in 1832 and a Democratic U. S. Congressman from 1835 to 1837, 1839 to 1841 and from 1843 to 1847. He was Speaker of the House from 1845 to 1847, and U. S. Commissioner to China from 1848 to 1850.

Davis, Noah, born in 1818, was a Judge of the Supreme Court for the Eighth Judicial District from 1857 to 1868 and a U. S. Representative from 1869 to 1870, when he became U. S. Attorney for Southern New York. From 1872 to 1887 he was a Justice of the New York Supreme Court, becoming Presiding Justice in 1874.

Dawes, Henry L., born in 1816, was a member of the Massachusetts Constitutional Convention in 1853. He was a Representative from Massachusetts from 1857 to 1873, and succeeded Charles Sumner in the Senate in 1875 and served till 1893. He was for a time chairman of the Ways and Means Committee in the House, and has been prominent in legislation for the tariff and for Indian education.

Dawson, Henry B., born in England in 1821, arrived in America in 1834 and from 1840 was editor and publisher of many historical writings and much engaged in newspaper work. In 1863 he published his edition of the *Federalist*. For many years he edited the *Historical Magazine*.

Day, Jeremiah (1773–1867), clergyman, was a professor at Yale from 1803 to 1817, when he was made president, serving till 1846. He was the author of many educational works.

Dayton, Jonathan (1760–1824), was born in New Jersey. In 1776 he entered the Continental army, in which he held numerous commissions, and under Lafayette commanded at Yorktown. In 1783 he was elected to the Legislature, and was made Speaker in 1790. In 1787 he was a delegate to the convention which framed the Federal Constitution. He was elected U. S. Congressman from New Jersey, serving from 1791 to 1799, being chosen Speaker of the House from 1795 to 1799, and was a U. S. Senator from 1799 to 1805. A friend of Burr, he had a part in Burr's conspiracy of 1807.

Dayton, William L. (1807–1864), a U. S. Senator from New Jersey from 1842 to 1851, was candidate for Vice-President in 1856 on the Republican ticket, and was Attorney-General for New Jersey from 1857 to 1861, when he was appointed Minister to France, where he served during the Civil War, till his death.

Deane, Charles (1813–1889), born in Maine, the author of many historical writings and owner of a very valuable library on early New England history, was eminent for his learning and sagacity in that field.

Deane, Silas (1737–1789), born in Groton, Conn., died in Deal, England. He was a member of the Connecticut Committee of Correspondence, and afterward a Representative in the Continental Congress. In 1776 he was sent to France to purchase supplies for the Confederacy. Vergennes, the French Minister of Foreign Affairs, referred him to Beaumarchais, a secret agent of the French Government, and with him Deane negotiated. He was accused of extravagance and dishonesty, chiefly by his colleague, Arthur Lee. Deane, Lee and Franklin negotiated treaties of amity and commerce with France, which were signed February 6, 1778. Deane was recalled the same year at the instigation of Lee. Congress refused him a hearing for some time and finally required a full statement. Returning to France for the necessary papers, he found himself unpopular there, and had to retire to Holland. He died just as he was re-embarking from England for America in 1789.

Dearborn, Henry (1751–1829), a captain at Bunker Hill, distinguished himself at the battles of Stillwater, Saratoga and Monmouth. He became major-general in 1795. He was a U. S. Congressman from 1793 to 1797, and Secretary of War in Jefferson's Cabinet from 1801 to 1809. From 1822 to 1824 he was Minister to Portugal.

Dearborn, Fort (Chicago), was evacuated August 15, 1812, by orders of General Hull; burned next day. The Americans while retreating were attacked by hostile Indians, and two-thirds of their number massacred, including twelve children. The survivors surrendered on promise of safety, were taken to Fort Mackinaw, and finally were sent back to their homes.

Deatonsville, Va. Near this place the Confederate army under Lee, while in full retreat from Petersburg, at the close of the last campaign about that city and Richmond, was struck April 6, 1864, by Crook, commanding the left of Sheridan's pursuing forces. Crook's forces were repulsed by superior numbers, but his assault enabled Custer to join him and attack Lee a little further on at Sailor's Creek. Ewell's forces were cut off and compelled to surrender.

De Bow, James D. B. (1820–1867), of South Carolina, statistician, a voluminous writer of magazine articles upon economics and finance, was appointed Superintendent of the Census from 1853 to 1855.

Debt. At the installation of the new Government in 1789, the foreign debt amounted to $13,000,000, the domestic debt to $42,000,000, and Hamilton also persuaded the Congress to assume State debts contracted in the Revolution to the amount of $21,500,000 more. It was then funded. In 1796 it amounted in the total to $83,800,000. It then began to be reduced and, though raised by the expenditures for the Louisiana purchase, was brought down to $45,200,000 in 1812 by the skillful management of Hamilton and Gallatin successively. The War of 1812 brought it up to $127,000,000 in 1816, but the abounding prosperity of the country enabled the

Government to pay it all off, virtually, by 1835. It then grew again. The Mexican War brought it up from $15,600,000 to $68,300,000, whence it again declined to $28,700,000 in 1857. The Civil War required not only heavy and almost indiscriminate taxation but enormous loans, so that the debt on the thirty-first of August, 1865, amounted to $2,845,000,000. Successful efforts to refund at lower rates of interest, together with the prosperity of the country and the great revenue from customs, enabled the debt to be reduced to $2,000,000,000 in 1878, if cash in the Treasury be subtracted, to $1,500,000,000 in 1883, and to $1,000,000,000 in 1889. On November 1, 1893, the total debt, less cash in the Treasury, amounted to $820,109,339.

Debts, British. At the outbreak of the Revolution, many Americans owed money to British citizens, merchants and others. The Treaty of 1783 provided for their payment. But many obstacles were thrown in the way, State governments having provided, or even providing after the ratification of the treaty, that they might be paid into the treasury of the State, which would then refuse to entertain suits on the part of the creditors. The apprehension that a Federal judiciary would compel these debts to be paid was one cause of opposition to the Constitution of 1787. In 1796, in the case of Ware *vs.* Hylton, the Supreme Court decided that such debts must be paid.

Decatur, Stephen (1779–1820), was born in Maryland. He began service in the U. S. navy on the "United States" in 1798, and in 1803 commanded the "Argus," and later the "Enterprise." In 1804 he distinguished himself by successfully destroying the "Philadelphia," which had fallen into the possession of Tripoli. In 1812, on the "United States," while commanding an Atlantic squadron, he captured the British ship "Macedonian," and in 1814, after a stubborn battle, was compelled to surrender the unseaworthy ship "President." In 1815, with ten vessels, he humbled the Barbary powers, and concluded a treaty by which tribute was abolished and prisoners and property were restored. He was one of the navy commissioners from 1816 to 1820, when he was killed by Commodore Barron in a duel.

Declaration of Independence. Absolute separation from Great Britain was not at first contemplated by the colonies. New England favored it, but the Southern States were opposed. The transfer of the war to the southward in May and June, 1776, brought them to this view. The North Carolina Convention took the first step toward independence by a resolution "to concur with those in the other colonies in declaring independence," April 22, 1776. Virginia, May 17, 1776, prepared the title of the document by directing her Representatives to propose in Congress a "Declaration of Independence." Such a resolution was offered by Richard Henry Lee, June 7, 1776. This resolution was adopted July 2. Thomas Jefferson, John Adams, Benjamin Franklin, Roger Sherman and Robert R. Livingston were the committee appointed to draft the Declaration. The draft was formulated almost entirely by Jefferson. Before July 1, Pennsylvania, Maryland and New Jersey had instructed their delegates to vote against the Declaration. This instruction was rescinded, South Carolina came over to the majority, and Delaware's vote, at first divided, was in the affirmative. The Declaration was, therefore, adopted by the unanimous vote of twelve States, New York alone not voting, July 4, 1776. The New York Convention afterward ratified the Declaration. The engrossed copy was signed on August 2. The Declaration sets forth the rights of man and of the colonists, enumerates their grievances against the British Government, and declares "that these united colonies are, and of right ought to be, free and independent States."

Declaration of Independence, Signers of.

New Hampshire.

Josiah Bartlett,
William Whipple,
Matthew Thornton.

Massachusetts.

John Hancock,
Samuel Adams,
John Adams,
Robert Treat Paine,
Elbridge Gerry.

Rhode Island.

Stephen Hopkins,
William Ellery.

Connecticut.

Roger Sherman,
Samuel Huntingdon,
William Williams,
Oliver Wolcott.

New York.

William Floyd,
Philip Livingston,
Francis Lewis,
Lewis Morris.

New Jersey.

Richard Stockton,
John Witherspoon,
Francis Hopkinson,
John Hart,
Abraham Clark.

Pennsylvania.

Robert Morris,
Benjamin Rush,
Benjamin Franklin,
John Morton,
George Clymer,
James Smith,
George Taylor,
James Wilson,
George Ross.

Delaware.

Cæsar Rodney,
George Read,
Thomas M'Kean.

Maryland.

Samuel Chase,
William Paca,
Thomas Stone,
Charles Carroll, of Carrollton.

Virginia.

George Wythe,
Richard Henry Lee,
Thomas Jefferson,
Benjamin Harrison,
Thomas Nelson, Jr.,
Francis Lightfoot Lee,
Carter Braxton.

North Carolina.

William Hooper,
Joseph Hewes,
John Penn.

South Carolina.

Edward Rutledge,
Thomas Heyward, Jr.,
Thomas Lynch, Jr.,
Arthur Middleton.

Georgia.

Button Gwinnett,
Lyman Hall,
George Walton.

Fac-similes of the Signatures to the Declaration of Independence July 4 1776

John Penn John Hancock John Hart
Wm Floyd Wm Paca
Geo: Read Wm Hooper Saml Adams
Step. Hopkins Thos Nelson jr. Geo Clymer
Charles Carroll of Carrollton Elbridge Gerry
Tho M:Kean Roger Sherman Saml Huntington
Wm Whipple Thomas Lynch Junr.
Geo Taylor Josiah Bartlett Benja Franklin
Wm Williams Richd Stockton
John Morton
Oliver Wolcott Jno Witherspoon Geo. Ross
Thos Stone Samuel Chase Robt Treat Paine
George Wythe Matthew Thornton
Fran.s Lewis Th Jefferson Benja Harrison
Lewis Morris Abra Clark Phil. Livingston
Caesar Rodney
Arthur Middleton Fras Hopkinson
Geo Walton Carter Braxton James Wilson
Richard Henry Lee Thos Heyward Junr.
Benjamin Rush John Adams Robt Morris
Lyman Hall Joseph Hewes Button Gwinnett
Francis Lightfoot Lee
William Ellery Edward Rutledge Jas Smith

"Department of State 19th April 1819. I Certify that this is a CORRECT Copy of the original Declaration of Independence deposited at this Department, and that I have compared all the signatures with those of the original, and have found them EXACT IMITATIONS." John Quincy Adams

Declaration of Rights. In 1765, the Stamp Act Congress published a "Declaration of Rights and Grievances of the Colonists of America," in which they protested against the Stamp Act and all efforts to tax them in a Parliament in which they could not be represented, and claimed for themselves all the rights of British subjects. A similar declaration of rights was issued by the Continental Congress of 1774, adapted to meet also the aggressive acts which had more recently been passed by Parliament. Another such was included in the Declaration of Independence. For the statements of the rights of the individual as over against his government which accompanied most of the new Constitutions of this period, see Bills of Rights.

Declaratory Act, an act passed by Parliament, March 7, 1766, vindicating the previous enactments affecting the colonies, and declaring that the king, with the advice of Parliament, had full power to make laws binding America in any cases whatsoever. This law accompanied the repeal of the Stamp Act.

Decoration Day, known as "Memorial Day" in the Southern States. The custom that led up to it originated in the South before the close of the Civil War. Early in the spring of each year the Southern women were in the habit of decorating the graves of their dead soldiers with flowers, and thus an unwritten law fixed May 30 as the day of observance. Similar observances had been inaugurated in the North with no especial unanimity. May 5, 1868, General John A. Logan, then commander-in-chief of the Grand Army of the Republic, issued an order fixing May 30 of that year for strewing with flowers the graves of dead soldiers. There has been no Federal legislation regarding Decoration Day, but many States have made it a legal holiday.

Deep Bottom, Va., selected by Butler during the campaigning around Richmond and Petersburg in 1864 as a position from which to threaten Lee. A lodgment was effected there June 21, and Foster was there posted with a strong force. Lee, fearing this position, made several ineffectual attempts to secure it, and at last Grant ordered a counter attack on July 26 and 27. Hancock turned the Confederates' advance position while Foster feinted an attack upon his front. The plan worked so successfully that Miles' brigade outflanked the Confederates' outpost and carried away four guns. Lee fell back to Bailey's Creek, but continued to hold his strong defensive work at Chapin's Bluff.

Deerfield, Mass., was first settled in 1670. During King Philip's War a company under Captain Lothrop was attacked at Bloody Brook, in Deerfield, by savages in ambush and almost totally destroyed. Deerfield was sacked by French and Indians in 1704 and many of the inhabitants killed.

Delancey, James (1703–1760), of New York, member of the council of the province from 1729, Chief Justice from 1733, Lieutenant-Governor from 1753, acted as Governor from 1753 to 1755 and from 1757 to 1760. He presided over the Albany Convention of 1754.

Delancey, James (1732–1800), son of the preceding, served in the French and Indian War, and took a prominent part in Athe ssembly before the Revolution, but on its outbreak retired to England, and died there. His estates were confiscated.

Delancey, James (1750–1809), cousin of the preceding, was during the Revolutionary War noted as a bold and successful commander of the Tory light-horse, known as "Cowboys." After the war, his estates having been confiscated, he retired to Nova Scotia.

Delancey, Oliver (1708–1785), brother of Governor James Delancey, commanded the New York troops in Abercrombie's campaign in the French and Indian War, and during the Revolutionary War was commander of a brigade of Tories. At the close of the war he retired to England.

Delancey, Oliver (1752–1822), son of the preceding, an officer in the British army, served with distinction throughout the American war, and finally became full general in the British service.

Delano, Columbus, born 1809, member of Congress from Ohio, was Secretary of the Interior in Grant's Cabinet from 1870 to 1875.

Delaware. In 1631 the Dutch from New Netherland founded a settlement in what is now Delaware, but it proved temporary. In 1638 the Swedish West India Company settled a colony on the site of Wilmington. The colony of New Sweden, lying along the shores of Delaware River and Bay, became involved in quarrels with the neighboring settlements of the Dutch, who claimed the region. In 1655 Governor Stuyvesant conquered the region for the Dutch. In 1664 it fell, with all New Netherland, into the hands of the English. William Penn in 1682 obtained possession of what is now Delaware, and for twenty years it was governed as a part of Pennsylvania, except from 1691 to 1693. In 1703 the "territories" or "three lower counties on the Delaware" obtained recognition as a separate colony, with an assembly of its own, though the proprietary always appointed the same man Governor of both Pennsylvania and Delaware. Delaware framed its first Constitution as a State in 1776. On December 7, 1787, Delaware ratified the Constitution of the United States, and was the first State to do so. The vote in convention was unanimous. In 1792 a second State Constitution was established. That of 1831, the last made, differs little from this. Up to 1850 the State was usually Federalist and Whig, since then it has usually been Democratic. Though a slave State it took no part in secession. The population, which in 1790 was 59,096, in 1890 was 168,493.

Delaware, Crossing of the. On Christmas night, 1776, after a period of discouragement, Washington made his way across the river Delaware through the floating ice, and on the next day, at the head of 2400 men, surprised, attacked and captured a force of 1000 British troops (Hessian mercenaries) under Rahl.

Delawares, an Indian tribe, a branch of the Algonquin family, who, when the whites first came to the Delaware River, were found dwelling near it. Penn bought much land of them. At first a peaceable tribe, they were largely under the control of the Five Nations. Later, they became warlike, and had a part in the war with Pontiac. In 1774 they received a signal defeat. After 1768 there were none east of the Alleghanies. The Christian Delawares, converts of the Moravians, were largely massacred by the Americans at Gnadenhütten, near the close of the Revolutionary War. From

Ohio the tribe emigrated to Missouri in 1818, in 1829 into Kansas, and in 1868 into the Indian Territory, having now become almost completely civilized.

Delawarr, Thomas West, Lord, a man of noble and philanthropic character, was appointed Governor of Virginia in 1609, and administered the colony with success until 1611. In that year he entered the river that bears his name. He died in 1618.

Delfthaven, a small town in South Holland, port of Delft, is famous in American history as the place at which the Pilgrim Fathers embarked on board the "Speedwell" for Southampton, July 22, 1620.

De Long, George W. (1844–1881), a lieutenant-commander in the U. S. navy, commanded the "Jeannette" in her Arctic voyage via Behring Strait. His vessel being crushed in the ice, he made a long and adventurous journey to the Siberian mainland and up the Lena delta, but died of exposure and starvation when within reach of help.

Democracy. Democracy, though one of the foremost elements in American constitutional life, has grown up entirely outside the Constitution. The Constitution leaves the suffrage to be prescribed entirely by the States. For its stages of advance, see art. Suffrage. An important landmark in its history, in the Federal Government, is the inauguration of Jackson in 1829. He was felt to be the people's candidate, and his election was felt to be their triumph. From this time on American Democracy was recognized as the permanent and characteristic system of politics in the United States. With this has gone a liberal policy in regard to naturalization and immigration.

Democratic Party, historically the most important of American political parties, having been in continuous existence for a hundred years. The rise of such a party, as soon as national politics began under the new Constitution, was natural. The love of individual liberty rather than strong government, was native in the minds of most Americans. Those who felt this most strongly would be likely to look with apprehension upon the Federal Government, and the possibility of its encroaching upon the States under cover of the new Federal Constitution. They were therefore likely to be advocates of strict construction of the Constitution and of States' rights. To these elements of party feeling, which had drawn the Anti-Federalists together in 1788, was added a few years later the strong sympathy of many Americans with the French Revolution, and the desire that Government should aid France in her contest with England. Thomas Jefferson put himself at the head of the party drawn together by agreement in these sentiments, and led them in opposition to the Federalists. The party took the name of Democratic-Republican, still its official title. Before Monroe's administration its members were more commonly called Republicans, since then most commonly Democrats. From the first the party was strongest in the Southern States. From its origin in 1792 to 1801, it was in opposition. In 1798 and 1799, upon the passage of the Alien and Sedition laws, it took strong ground for States' rights in the Kentucky and Virginia Resolutions. The election of Jefferson in 1801 brought it into power. The chief tenets of the party were, belief in freedom of religion, of politics, of speech and of the press, in popular rule, in peace, in economical government, in the utmost possible restriction of the sphere of government, in hospitality to immigrants, and in the avoidance of foreign complications. Placed in control of the government, the majority of the party drifted away from its strict-constructionist ground, and supported measures of a nationalizing character. After the War of 1812, the Federalist party went out of existence, and the Democratic party had complete possession of the field. In 1820, Monroe was re-elected without opposition. But opposing tendencies in the nation and in the party were already showing themselves, and preparing the way for a new party division, between the Whigs, advocates of protection and other nationalizing measures, and those Democrats who held to the old programme of States' rights and free trade and restricted government. With the accession of Jackson in 1829, new social strata came into power in the Democratic party, the widening of the suffrage giving it a more popular character. Managed by skillful politicians, not without the aid of the "spoils system," the party won every Presidential election but two (1840, 1848) from this time to 1860, destroyed the U. S. bank, annexed Texas, and carried the country through the war with Mexico. But meanwhile the slavery question, coming into increasing prominence, was gradually forcing a division between the Democrats of the South and the great body of those in the North, who were unwilling to go so far in the protection of slavery by national authority as was desired by their Southern allies. The final split came in the nominating convention of 1860. Two candidates were nominated, Lincoln and the Republicans won the election, and the Civil War broke out. Though many "War Democrats" aided the administration in preserving the Union, the party was discredited in the eyes of many by its previous connection with the Southern leaders and the proslavery cause, and won no Presidential election till that of 1884, when in the minds of many the war issues were extinct and economic questions had taken their place. Defeated in 1888, it was again successful in 1892. At present the party is hardly more strict-constructionist than the Republican, nor more marked by devotion to States' rights. Still holding with these exceptions the general views with which it started, the party is at present mostly noted as the opponent of a high tariff.

Democratic Societies, clubs formed in many American towns in 1793, in imitation of the Jacobin and other political clubs of France, to express sympathy with that country and the principles of the French Revolution, and to propagate extreme Democratic views on American politics. They opposed the strongest measures of Washington's administration, especially those employed in the suppression of the Whisky Insurrection of 1794, and were vigorously denounced by him. Soon after this they declined and went out of existence.

De Monts, Pierre de Guast, Sieur, a Calvinist gentleman of France, was in 1603 given by Henry IV., the vice-royalty of Acadia, from latitude 40 to latitude 60, and the monopoly of its fur-trade. In 1604 he settled a colony in Acadia, near the present borders of Maine and New Brunswick, which he removed in 1605 to Port Royal, now Annapolis, Nova Scotia. In 1607 the colony was abandoned.

Denio, Hiram (1799–1871), an eminent jurist of New York, was a Judge of the Court of Appeals from 1853 to 1866.

Denmark. A commercial treaty was concluded between the United States and Denmark in 1826. By treaty in 1857 the United States paid Denmark $393,000 in commutation of the Sound dues. October 25, 1867, a treaty was concluded with Denmark, providing for the cession of the islands of St. Thomas and St. John for $7,500,000. Denmark ratified it, but the U. S. Senate, at the instance of Senator Sumner, refused to do so. A convention relative to naturalization was concluded in 1872.

Dennie, Joseph (1768–1812), a journalist, was one of the first Americans to obtain fame in light literature. Removing from New England to Philadelphia, he was editor, from 1801 on, of the *Portfolio*, a literary magazine which maintained a higher standard than any of its predecessors. He had also a reputation as a graceful and humorous essayist.

Dennison, William (1815–1882), "War Governor" of Ohio, was elected Governor in 1860. An ardent Republican and anti-slavery man, he with great energy and ability prepared the State for the Civil War and organized and supplied its forces. He was chairman of the Republican National Nominating Convention in 1864, and from that year to 1866 was Postmaster-General, in the cabinets of Lincoln and Johnson.

Denonville, Marquis de, French Governor of Canada from 1685 to 1689, worked zealously against the British settlements and Governor Dongan, but alienated the Indians by cruelty.

Denver, capital of Colorado, was settled in 1858.

Departments, Executive. Executive departments of the U. S. Government existed before 1789. The Continental Congress at first transacted all executive business through committees; then through commissions composed partly of its own members, partly of others. In 1776 the Treasury Office of Accounts was established, and a comptroller, auditor and treasurer were added two years later. In 1781 four executive departments were organized, under a Superintendent of Finance and Secretaries of War, Marine and Foreign Affairs, respectively. A Postmaster-General had been provided in 1775. In 1784 the Treasury Department was put in the charge of a board of three, but otherwise the system continued until the inauguration of the new government in 1789. In that year Congress provided for Departments of State, the Treasury and War, and instituted the office of Attorney-General. The first plan contemplated separate departments of foreign affairs and home affairs, but finally these were united in the Department of State. The Navy Department was established in 1798, the Interior Department in 1849, the Department of Justice in 1870, the Department of Agriculture in 1889. For details of their history, see articles under their individual names.

Dependency Act. (See Declaratory Act, of March 17, 1766.)

Depew, Chauncey M., president of the New York Central Railroad and eminent as a public speaker, was born in Peekskill, N. Y., in 1834. Since 1860 he has had an active part in politics. He was Secretary of the State of New York from 1863 to 1866 and has had an important influence in Presidential nominations.

Deposits, Removal of the. President Jackson, on being successful in the election of 1832, believed himself authorized by the popular voice to pursue to extremities his war upon the Bank of the United States (see Bank). By the Act of 1816 creating the bank, the funds of the Federal Government were to be deposited in it, subject to removal by the Secretary of the Treasury, who should state to Congress the reasons for so doing. Jackson, believing that the bank was unsound, and that its influence was used to corrupt politics, determined that the deposits should be removed. McLane, Secretary of the Treasury, not favoring this course, was transferred to the State Department. The new Secretary, Duane, refused to give the necessary order, and was dismissed by Jackson. Roger B. Taney was then appointed, and ordered the removal, more strictly cessation, of deposits, September 26, 1833. Jackson set forth his reasons to Congress, on its assembling. The Senate replied by a vote of censure. Jackson sent in a protest, declaring that the matter rested entirely within his competence as head of the Executive Department. In 1837 his friends succeeded in inducing the Senate to expunge its resolution of censure.

Derne Expedition. General William Eaton, U. S. Consul at Tunis, persuading his Government to lend the co-operation of its naval forces in the Mediterranean, marched from Egypt across the desert with Hamet, rightful bashaw of Tripoli, in an attack upon his usurping brother Joseph. On April 27, 1805, he took Derne. Upon this success a highly favorable treaty was extorted from the bashaw, Hamet being induced to retire.

De Russy, Fort, La., wrested from Dick Taylor, commanding about 12,000 Confederates, by A. J. Smith, leading an army of some 10,000 Federals. This battle is to be remembered in connection with Banks' Red River expedition. It occurred March 14, 1864. Smith had been ordered to join Banks. Hearing that Taylor was at Shreveport he followed him to Fort de Russy. After a cannonade of two hours Smith ordered a charge, when suddenly the garrison surrendered.

De Saussure, Henry William (1763–1839), of South Carolina, was director of the U. S. Mint, 1794–95, and coined the first gold pieces issued from that mint. From 1809 to 1837 he was a chancellor of South Carolina, and was eminent as a jurist.

Deseret, said to mean "the land of the honey-bee," the name given by the Mormons to their settlement ("State") in Utah at the time of its settlement in 1848.

Desert Land Act, an Act of Congress, March 3, 1877, allowing, on credit for three years, a entry of 640 acres of desert land for purposes of irrigation and improvement.

Des Moines, Ia., laid out in 1846 and incorporated as Fort Des Moines in 1851. In 1857 it became a city and the capital of the State.

De Smet, Peter John (1801–1872), a Belgian Jesuit, was a professor in the University of St. Louis from 1828 to 1838. From 1838 he was a missionary among the Pottawatomies; from 1840 on, a missionary of remarkable zeal and success among the Flatheads and other tribes of the Northwest. In the first fifteen years of his mission he estimated that he had traveled 120,-000 miles. His influence over the Indian tribes was immense.

De Soto, Fernando (?1496–1512), a Spanish noble, came to America in 1519 in the service of Pedrarias Davila, and accompanied Pizarro in the conquest of Peru. In April, 1538, he set out from Spain with 600 men, commissioned to undertake the conquest of Florida, reputed to be a land of great wealth. His well-appointed expedition landed in Tampa Bay in May, 1539. During the next three years he wandered over large parts of what are now Alabama and Mississippi. In the spring of 1541 he discovered the Mississippi River. Crossing it, he penetrated as far westward as to the highlands of the White River. Returning, he died on the banks of the Mississippi in the spring of 1542. Some of his followers escaped to Mexico.

Detroit, Mich. The site was visited by the French in 1669. Detroit was settled in 1701 by a party under Antoine de la Mothe Cadillac. It fell to the British in 1763, and was besieged by Pontiac; to the United States in 1783. On August 16, 1812, General Hull, with 2000 men, made an inglorious surrender of Detroit to the British and Indians under General Brock and Tecumseh. Hull was cashiered. Harrison retook the town in October, 1813, after Perry's victory on Lake Erie. From 1805 to 1847 Detroit was the capital of Michigan Territory and State.

Devens, Charles (1820–1891), an eminent lawyer in Massachusetts at the time of the outbreak of the Civil War, entered the army as a major and, after a brilliant military service, became a brevet major-general. From 1873 to 1877, and again from 1881 to his death, he was a Judge of the Supreme Court of Massachusetts. From 1877 to 1881 he was Attorney-General in the Cabinet of President Hayes.

De Vries, David Pieterssen, an important member of the Dutch West India Company, was one of the group who sent out the first colony at Zwaanendael on the Delaware River, and himself took out the second colony in 1632.

Dexter, Henry M. (1821–1890), Congregationalist clergyman and editor, of Massachusetts, was the author of many learned writings on the early history of Congregationalism and of the Pilgrim Fathers.

Dexter, Samuel (1761–1816), a noted lawyer of Massachusetts, was successively, for short periods in 1800 and 1801, Secretary of War and of the Treasury in the Cabinet of President John Adams.

Dickerson, Mahlon (1770–1853), a New Jersey and Pennsylvania lawyer, was Governor of New Jersey from 1815 to 1817, and a Senator from that State from that time to 1833. From 1834 to 1838 he was Secretary of the Navy, serving under Jackson and Van Buren.

Dickinson, Daniel S. (1800–1866), was Lieutenant-Governor of New York from 1842 to 1844, and Senator from New York from 1844 to 1851. He was noted as an orator, and was a "War Democrat."

Dickinson, Don M., born in 1846, was Postmaster-General in Cleveland's Cabinet from 1888 to 1889.

Dickinson, John (1732–1808), a Philadelphia lawyer, was in 1765 elected to the Colonial Congress, and in 1768 distinguished himself by writing "Letters from a Pennsylvania Farmer" in defence of the liberties of America. Elected to the Continental Congress in 1774, he wrote its "Address to the Inhabitants of Quebec," its "Declaration to the Armies," its "Address to the States," and its two petitions to the king. He opposed the Declaration of Independence as premature, but served loyally in the army. Again a member of Congress, he was chosen president of Delaware in 1781, and was president of Pennsylvania from 1782 to 1785. He was a member of the Federal Convention of 1787, and advocated the adoption of the Constitution. He was a man of high character and cultivation. Life by Stillé.

Dickinson College, one of the older American colleges, was founded at Carlisle, Pa., in 1783, and named in honor of John Dickinson, then president of the State, who gave it valuable gifts. A Presbyterian institution from its foundation to 1833, it was then transferred to the Methodists. President Buchanan and Chief Justice Taney were among its alumni.

Dieskau, Ludwig August von (1701–1767), a soldier of Saxon birth, who had served under Marshal Saxe in the French service, was sent to Canada as major-general in 1755, and commanded an expedition against the English colonies by way of Lake Champlain. At first victorious in the fight near Fort Edward, he was finally defeated, severely wounded and taken prisoner.

Dighton Rock, a rock lying in the tide on the side of Taunton River, in Berkeley, Mass., formerly in Dighton, and marked with a curious inscription, attracted early attention on the part of antiquaries. Rafn, 1837, declared that its markings were a runic inscription of the Northmen, relating to the expedition of Thorfinn Karlsefne, but this view has now been generally abandoned, though the central portion may be Norse.

Dime, from the French word *dixième*, a tenth, expressive of a tenth part of the standard silver dollar. It was at first spelled "disme," and thus appeared on some trial pieces struck by the United States Mint in 1792. The coin is of silver, having been authorized in 1792 (with a weight of 41.6 grains). Coinage was begun in 1796. Its weight was in 1853 reduced to 38.4 grains. There were no issues of dimes during the years 1799, 1806, 1808, 1812, 1813, 1815 to 1819 inclusive, 1824 and 1826.

Dinwiddie, Robert (?1690–1770), a Scotchman, was Governor of Virginia from 1752 to 1758. His chief merit was his perception of the military abilities of Washington, whom he sent upon the mission to the French commander on the Ohio, and then upon the military expedition which opened the French and Indian War. In the conduct of the war, he quarreled with the Virginian Assembly, and suggested taxation of the colonies. He was unpopular and incapable.

Direct Taxes. Congress has levied direct taxes on but five occasions. In 1798, 1813, 1815 and 1816, a direct tax was levied by Federal authority on lands, houses and slaves. In August, 1861, to meet expenses of the Civil War, a direct tax of $20,000,000 was levied on all lots of ground with their improvements and dwelling-houses. The operation of the act was suspended on July 1, 1862. By Act of March 2, 1891, $15,000,000, collected under this act, were refunded to the States.

Directories. The first city directory issued in the United States was published in New York as early as 1786. It was a small volume of eighty-two pages and contained only some nine hundred names. Since that time annual directories have appeared in New York. Nearly every town of importance in the Union now has its directory. In several States there have also been published State directories.

Directory. The French Directory of five members was established as the Executive Government of France in 1795, and was suppressed by Bonaparte in 1799 (November 9). It came into collision with the Government of the United States because of the action of France in seizing American provision-ships and permitting illegal captures of American vessels by her privateers. Our Government recalling Monroe in 1796, the Directory refused to recognize his successor, C. C. Pinckney, and complained of the failure of the United States to stand by the treaty of alliance of 1778. New envoys were sent out by President Adams,—Pinckney, Marshall and Gerry,—but were dismissed without satisfaction, after attempts made to bribe the U. S. Government (see X. Y. Z. Mission). A virtual state of war ensued (1798), but in 1799 Adams, on a more favorable turn of affairs, sent a new embassy, Murray, Ellsworth and Davie. When they arrived Bonaparte had already overthrown the Directory. With his government the treaty of Morfontaine (September 30, 1800) was concluded.

Disciples, Church of the, also called "Christians" and "Campbellites," a religious body founded in 1809 by Thomas and Alexander Campbell. Taking the express teachings of the Bible as the only authoritative guide in religious matters, their purpose was to bring about Christian unity. Their first stage consisted in the uniting in one body of various Protestants of Western Pennsylvania, chiefly Presbyterians and Baptists. Thence they spread westward. In 1831 they were joined by another body which had grown up upon similar principles in Kentucky and neighboring States. In 1867 the number of Disciples in the United States was estimated at 425,000. The census of 1890 ascribed to them 7246 organizations and 641,000 members.

"**Discovery,**" a vessel dispatched on a voyage of discovery toward Greenland in 1602 by the East India Company, and in 1606 to Virginia by the Virginia Company, accompanied by the "God-Speed" and the "Susan Constant."

District. The name District has been given in American history to divisions of the country resembling territories in organization, but without representative or elective institutions. Existing instances are the District of Columbia and that of Alaska. An early instance was the District of

Louisiana, which from 1804 to 1812 comprised all that portion of the Louisiana Purchase which lay north of the northern boundary of the present State of Louisiana. In South Carolina the counties were at one time called districts.

District Courts. The Judiciary Act of 1789 provided for two classes of U. S. Courts inferior to the Supreme Court,—Circuit Courts and District Courts. Each district consisted of one State, and had its district judge. Since then, some States have been divided, and these Federal courts of the lowest grade now number more than sixty. In 1891 an act was passed fixing the judges' salaries at $5000.

District of Columbia. The Constitution of 1787 gave Congress power "to exercise exclusive legislation in all cases whatsoever over such district (not exceeding ten miles square) as may, by cession of particular States and the acceptance of Congress, become the seat of government of the United States." In 1790, after warm discussions, the present site was selected. A ten-mile square was laid out on the Potomac. Maryland ceded sixty-four square miles on the north bank of the river, Virginia thirty-six square miles on the south. In 1791 this area received the official name of the Territory of Columbia. The seat of government was removed thither in 1800. In 1846 the portion south of the Potomac was retroceded to Virginia. The laws of Maryland and Virginia were in force in the district, unless repealed by Congress; *e.g.*, their slave laws. From 1871 to 1874 the district had a Territorial government, with elective institutions. This proved extravagant, and government by commissioners under the authority of Congress was substituted.

Dix, John A. (1798–1879), born in New Hampshire, was in the army from 1812 to 1828. From 1833 to 1840 he was Secretary of the State of New York, and became a member of the "Albany Regency." From 1845 to 1849 he was a Democratic Senator. In the last months of Buchanan's administration he was Secretary of the Treasury, and aided to restore confidence in the Federal Government. An ardent "War Democrat," he served through the war as a major-general of volunteers. From 1872 to 1874 he was Governor of New York.

"Dixie." This favorite song of the Confederate armies was originally a negro melody, and is said to have originated in New York.

Dixon, Jeremiah, English mathematician, with Charles Mason, ran "Mason and Dixon's Line," beginning in 1766.

Dobbin, James C. (1814–1857), represented North Carolina in the U. S. Congress as a Democrat from 1845 to 1847. He was Secretary of the Navy in Pierce's Cabinet from 1853 to 1857.

Dollar. The Spanish milled dollar was the type of the American silver dollar. By Act of 1792, 371¼ grains of pure silver and 24¾ grains of pure gold were declared to be equivalent to each other and to the dollar of account. The silver dollar was first coined in 1794, weighing 416 grains (371¼ plus alloy). In 1837 the weight of alloy was so reduced that the weight of the coin should be 412½ grains. The gold dollar was first coined in 1849. In

1873 provision was made for a trade dollar of 420 grains, for use in the trade with China and Japan. From 1873 to 1878 the issue of the old silver dollar was suspended. The gold half-dollar and quarter-dollar were never coined by the U. S. Government. The silver half-dollar has been coined since 1794. Its weight, at first 208 grains, was subsequently reduced to 206.25 in 1837, to 192 in 1853, and raised to 192.9 in 1873. The quarter-dollar, coinage of which began in 1796, has undergone corresponding changes of weight.

Dominican Republic. The United States concluded with the Dominican Republic a convention relative to commerce and extradition in 1867. In 1871 a movement was made to annex the Dominican Republic to the United States. (See San Domingo Question.)

Donaldson, Edward (1816–1889), rear-admiral, served in the U. S. navy from 1835 to 1876. In the Civil War he took part in the capture of New Orleans and in the passage of Vicksburg, and at the battle of Mobile Bay commanded the "Seminole."

Donaldsonville, La., occupied in 1863 by a band of Confederate guerrillas and bombarded, June 28, by Admiral Farragut during his operations along the Mississippi River in command of the Union fleet.

Donation Lands. August 4, 1842, Congress passed a donation act for the Territory of East Florida. Persons who could bear arms were allowed one quarter section of land upon which to settle. September 27, 1850, a donation act was passed for Oregon, granting settlers from 160 to 640 acres.

Donelson, Andrew Jackson (1800–1871), nephew of General Jackson, was private secretary to his uncle during the latter's Presidency, Minister to Prussia and the German Confederation from 1846 to 1849, and in 1856 was nominated for the Vice-Presidency by the American party on the ticket with Fillmore.

Donelson, Fort, Tenn., an important Confederate fortification on the Cumberland. After the capture of Fort Henry, on the Tennessee, February 6, 1862, General Grant moved his forces over to the Cumberland and attacked Fort Donelson. The Federal gunboats were driven off at first, but Grant's land forces attacked the fort in such numbers and with such vigor that surrender became necessary. Grant, in a memorable letter, demanded its unconditional surrender of General Buckner, who commanded it after the flight of Floyd and Pillow. 15,000 Confederates were made prisoners by this victory, and the fall of Nashville and Columbus became inevitable. An attempt to recapture this place from the Federals was made February 15, 1863, by Wheeler, leading 4500 of Bragg's Confederate army. The garrison of the fort was 600 Federals under Harding. Wheeler demanded a surrender, but Harding replied by sending out skirmishers to delay an attack while he sent for aid to Fort Henry. In the evening the gunboat "Fair Play," Lieutenant Fitch, came up the river, and the Confederates withdrew.

Doniphan, Alexander W. (1808–1887), colonel in the Mexican War, accomplished amid many hardships a difficult march from New Mexico to

Chihuahua, and near the latter place defeated a Mexican force more than four times as numerous as his own.

Donop, Count (1740–1777), commander of Hessians in the Revolutionary War, was mortally wounded in an attempt to take by assault Fort Mercer, near Red Bank, N. J., October 22, 1777.

Doolittle, James R., born in New York in 1815, from 1853 to 1856 was Judge of the Wisconsin Supreme Court, was U. S. Senator from 1857 to 1869, and a delegate to the Peace Convention of 1861.

Dorchester Company. In 1623, under the lead of Rev. John White, certain English Puritans, wearied of King Charles' persecutions, formed the Dorchester Company, for trading and fishing, and established a settlement at Cape Ann. The company was dissolved in 1626, but was revived in 1628 by a number of wealthy Englishmen, and John Endicott assumed the government at Naumkeag, now Salem, whither the first settlers had removed. In 1629 the company was enlarged and, obtaining a royal charter, formed the Massachusetts Bay colony.

Dorchester Heights were, at Washington's command, occupied and fortified by General Thomas with 2500 of Washington's troops March 4 and 5, 1776. This proved so dangerous to Howe that he was obliged to evacuate Boston with all speed.

Dorchester, Lord. (See Carleton, Sir Guy.)

Dorr, Thomas W. (1805–1854), was born in Providence. He was graduated at Harvard in 1823, studied in New York and was admitted to the bar. He was a member of the Rhode Island Assembly from 1833 to 1837, when he agitated governmental reform. See "Dorr War." He died in 1854.

Dorr Rebellion, an effort made in 1840–42 to overturn the State government of Rhode Island by revolutionary means. After the Declaration of Independence, Rhode Island retained her charter government. Many of the citizens, headed by Thomas W. Dorr, of Providence, became discontented with the existing government and its limited suffrage. Mass meetings were held, and in October, 1841, a convention of delegates prepared a Constitution, which was submitted to a popular vote, and was claimed to have received a majority of the votes of the State. The legitimate government treated these proceedings as nugatory, and, in a measure, criminal. May 3, 1842, the "suffrage legislature" assembled at Newport, with Dorr as Governor. King, the legitimate Governor, proclaimed martial law. The suffrage party appealed to arms. Their troops were dispersed and Dorr fled. He was afterward captured and convicted of treason, but was pardoned in 1852.

Dorsey, Stephen W., was born in Vermont in 1842. He served in the Civil War, was a member of the Arkansas Republican State Committee, a U. S. Senator from 1873 to 1879, and in 1880 Secretary of the Republican National Committee. He was connected with the "Star route" frauds exposed in 1881.

Double Eagle, or twenty-dollar gold piece, coinage authorized by Congress March, 1849, coinage begun in 1850. Legal tender to an unlimited amount. So called from the figure of the national bird stamped on reverse.

Doubleday, Abner (1819–1893), general, born in New York, aimed the first gun in the defense of Fort Sumter, and served with distinction at Antietam, Fredericksburg, Chancellorsville and Gettysburg. He retired from the army in 1873.

Doughface, a Northern politician over-anxious to please the South. The term is said to have been invented by John Randolph, of Roanoke, and was much used during the heat of the slavery conflict.

Douglas, Stephen Arnold (April 23, 1813–June 3, 1861), was born at Brandon, Vt. He worked on a farm, taught school, and at the age of twenty-one began the practice of law in Illinois. Soon afterward he was Attorney-General of the State, member of the Legislature, and an unsuccessful Democratic candidate for Congress. In 1840 he became Secretary of State of Illinois, and in 1841, Judge of the Supreme Court of the State. Judge Douglas was in the House of Representatives from 1843 to 1847, and in the Senate from 1847 to 1861. During this period, when the slavery issue came to overshadow all other questions, the "Little Giant," as Douglas was affectionately styled, became one of the leaders of his party. In Congress he favored the acquisition of the whole of Oregon, and was chairman of the important Committee on Territories. He advocated the compromise of 1850, and formulated the doctrine of Popular Sovereignty (which see). In accordance with the latter idea he reported in December, 1853, the famous Kansas-Nebraska Bill (which see). His name was presented to the Democratic National Conventions in 1852 and 1856. While running for re-election to the Senate in 1858, he carried on a joint debate with Lincoln, which brought the latter into national prominence. Douglas was nominated for President by the Northern wing of the Democratic party in 1860, but received only twelve electoral votes although a large popular vote was thrown for him. He survived the outbreak of the Civil War but a few months, supporting to the end the cause of the Union. Life by Sheahan.

Douglass, Frederick, the most eminent of American negroes, was born in Maryland in 1817. He escaped from slavery in 1838, and was educated by William Lloyd Garrison. He lectured for the Massachusetts Anti-Slavery Society from 1841 to 1845, and then labored in Europe till 1847. In 1871 he was commissioner for the District of Columbia, and in 1872 was Presidential elector-at-large for New York. He was U. S. Marshal for the District of Columbia from 1876 to 1881, and Recorder of Deeds from 1881 till 1886. From 1889 to 1891 he was U. S. Minister to Hayti.

"Dove," a small vessel, which accompanied the "Ark" in 1633 on Lord Baltimore's colonizing expedition to Maryland.

Dover, Del., was settled in 1687 and incorporated in 1720. Dover was made the capital of the State at the opening of the Revolution.

Dover, N. H., one of the oldest towns in the State, was settled in 1623. On the night of June 27, 1689, the town was attacked by Indians, and twenty-three of the inhabitants were killed. Dover became a city in 1855.

Dow, Neal, temperance reformer, was born in Maine in 1804. He secured the passage of the Maine liquor law in 1851, and was a member of the Legislature from 1858 to 1859. He served during the Civil War, lectured in England in 1857, 1866 and 1874, and in 1880 was the Presidential candidate of the Prohibition party.

Downes, John (1786–1855), entered the navy in 1802, commanded the "Essex" and captured the "Georgiana," which, named "Essex Junior," he afterward commanded till 1814, and from 1819–1821 commanded the "Macedonia," from 1828 to 1829 the "Java," and from 1832 to 1834 the Pacific squadron.

Downie, George, born in Ireland, died in 1814. He was a British naval officer, who in 1812 commanded the Canadian squadron, and was killed in the battle of Plattsburg, fighting against Commodore Macdonough.

Downing, Sir George (1623?–1684), of the class of 1642 of Harvard College, went to England in 1645, and was envoy of Cromwell and of Charles II. to the Netherlands, 1657–1663 and in 1671. He is said to have instigated the conquest of New Netherland.

Drafts, methods employed twice by the United States Government and twice by the Confederacy for raising and increasing the armies. The first measure, introduced into Congress in 1814, during the war with Great Britain, was due to a proposal by New York and Virginia of a Federal classification and draft from the State militia. This bill was prepared largely by James Monroe, but was highly unacceptable to the Federalists and proved a failure, though the army was much in need of men. In 1863 a somewhat similar plan was introduced in Congress, but was objected to by the Democrats on the grounds of unconstitutionality and failed. Accordingly May 3, 1863, another bill passed both Houses, which had no reference to the militia, but called every able-bodied citizen of military age into the Federal service. A commutation of $300 for exemption was permitted, and persons refusing obedience were treated as deserters. April 16, 1862, and July 18, 1863, the Confederate Congress passed conscription laws levying on all persons between the ages of eighteen and forty-five years. The unpopularity of the conscription caused the "draft riots" in New York City July 13–16, 1863, when the city was for four days in the possession of the mob.

Drake, Sir Francis (1546–1596), an Elizabethan navigator, made an expedition to Mexico in 1567, and to South America in 1572. He explored the Pacific coast from 1577 to 1579, landed on the coast of California and returned to England by the Pacific and Indian Oceans, making a successful circumnavigation of the globe.

Drake, Joseph Rodman (1795–1820), poet, was born in New York City, was author of the "Culprit Fay," written in 1816, and a life-long friend of Fitz-Greene Halleck, with whom he wrote the "Croakers."

Dranesville, or Drainsville, Va. Here December 20, 1861, J. E. B. Stuart, commanding 2500 Confederates, attacked 4500 Federals under Ord, who was engaged in loading his forage wagons. The fight was short, but severe. The Confederates were greatly outnumbered and were defeated.

Draper, John W. (1811–1882), born in England, came to America in 1832. He made extensive contributions to science, particularly in the line of chemistry and the action of light. During the Civil War he was inspector of hospitals. He wrote an excellent "History of the Civil War," 3 vols., 1870, and a "History of the Intellectual Development of Europe," 1863, after the manner and theories of Buckle.

Draper, Lyman C. (1815–1891), made thorough and valuable investigations regarding Western history and biography. He published "Collections of the Wisconsin Historical Society" from 1853 to 1887, and "King's Mountain," and nearly completed his "Mecklenburg Declaration of Independence" and "Border Forays and Adventures."

Drayton, William H. (1742–1779), born in South Carolina, went to England, and in 1771 was appointed a privy councillor of South Carolina. He was deprived of his crown offices on account of sympathy with the colonies, and was made president of the Provincial Congress in 1775. In 1776 he became Chief Justice of South Carolina and in 1777 president, and in 1778 was a member of the Continental Congress.

Drayton and Sayres' Case (1848), a fugitive slave case which resulted from Captain Drayton, of the schooner "Pearl," carrying seventy-five escaped negroes up the Potomac on his vessel. An armed steamer captured the vessel and brought those on board back. The captain and another of the vessel's officers were put in prison, where they remained till 1852, when they were released through the instrumentality of Charles Sumner.

Dred Scott vs. Sanford. In 1834 Dred Scott, a negro slave of Missouri, was taken by his master, who was a surgeon in the regular army, first into Illinois and then into Minnesota, a region from which slavery was expressly excluded by the celebrated Missouri Compromise of 1820. While in Minnesota Scott was married with his master's consent, but on being brought back to Missouri in 1838, he and his wife and children were sold to another master. Scott brought action for trespass in a St. Louis court, and a decision was made in his favor on the ground that, under the provisions of the Missouri Compromise, the negro was free. The Supreme Court of Missouri reversed this decision, and the case came before the Federal Circuit Court in 1854. The defendant slave-holder pleaded that Scott was not a citizen entitled to sue and be sued in the U. S. Courts. The court held the contrary, but the jury's verdict decided the plaintiff still a slave. The case came before the Supreme Court of the United States in 1857. Here the judgment of the Circuit Court was reversed, and the case dismissed on the ground that no negro, bond or free, could plead in the U. S. Courts as a "citizen." The court then, though denying its jurisdiction over the dispute, discussed the constitutional points. Scott's status in Illinois was declared determined by his Missouri domicile. As regarded the Minnesota Territory the court declared the Missouri Compromise unconstitutional and void, it being held that States alone could prohibit slavery from their boundaries. Chief Justice

Taney read the opinion of a majority of the court, all slave-holders, declaring "negroes so inferior that they had no rights which the white man was bound to respect." Justices Curtis and McLean dissented. Scott was afterward freed by his master. The decision aroused great excitement in the North.

Drewry's Bluff, or Fort Darling, on James River, Va., attacked May 15, 1862, by five Federal war-ships, including the "Monitor." Captain Farrand held the fort with 20,000 Confederates. The Federal fleet was badly disabled and had to retire. Again, May 13–16, 1864, during Butler's operations with the Army of the James around Bermuda Hundred, Fort Darling, or Drewry's Bluff, was the scene of some sharp fighting. It was held at that time by Beauregard, who had about 20,000 men. Butler made an attack the morning of the fourteenth and succeeded in carrying some of the Confederate lines. Beauregard hastened to strengthen his position with reinforcements, which opportunely arrived. On the sixteenth Beauregard made a return attack with a strong force and compelled Butler to retire. Butler's army was also about 20,000 strong.

Drummond, Sir George Gordon (1771–1854), a British soldier, served in Canada from 1808 to 1811 and from 1813 to 1816. He stormed Niagara, captured Oswego, commanded at Lundy's Lane, and from 1814 to 1816 administered the government of Canada.

Drummond, William, died in 1677. He was appointed Governor of Albemarle (*i. e.*, North Carolina) by Governor Berkeley, of Virginia (1663–67). Afterward he was prominent as a leader in the Bacon Rebellion of 1676, and was executed by Berkeley.

Duane, James (1733–1797), first prominent as a New York advocate for the New Hampshire land grants, was a member of the first Continental Congress, where he championed the British navigation acts and a colonial union subordinate to Parliament. In 1776 he opposed the Declaration of Independence as hasty. He was a member of the New York Provincial Congress from 1775 to 1777 and one of the committee to draft the State Constitution. He was a member of the convention that adopted the Federal Constitution in 1788, and from 1789 to 1794 was District Judge for New York.

Duane, William (1760–1835), born in New York, was abroad from 1771 to 1795, when he returned to Philadelphia, and till 1822 edited the *Aurora*, the leading Democratic paper. He served as adjutant-general from 1813 to 1815, and was an important figure in anti-Jeffersonian Democratic politics in Pennsylvania.

Duane, William J. (1780–1865), a distinguished lawyer, became Secretary of the U. S. Treasury in 1833, and was removed by President Jackson for refusing to withdraw the deposits from the U. S. bank.

"Dubuque Visitor," established at Dubuque Lead Mines, Wisconsin Territory (now Dubuque, Iowa), May, 1836, by John King. It was the first of the early news publications in Iowa. It is now published as the *Dubuque Herald*.

Duché, Jacob (1737–1798), Episcopal clergyman in Philadelphia, espoused the patriot cause at the beginning of the Revolution. He was the first chaplain of the Congress in 1774. He despaired of success for the colonies, and in 1777 advised Washington by letter to abandon the attempt. This made him so unpopular that he went to England.

Dudley, Joseph (1647–1720), of Massachusetts, was one of the Commissioners for New England from 1677 to 1681, and in 1682 went to England on behalf of the Massachusetts colony. He was appointed president of New England by James II. in 1685, and Chief Justice of the Supreme Court in 1687. From 1690 to 1693 he was Chief Justice of New York, and from 1702 to 1715 was Governor of Massachusetts. He was always friendly to the royal interests.

Dudley, Thomas (1576–1652), born in England, came to Massachusetts in 1630 as Deputy-Governor. He was Governor from 1634 to 1635, from 1640 to 1641, from 1645 to 1646, and from 1650 to 1651. During most other years from 1630 to 1652, he was Deputy-Governor. He was at times an opponent of Winthrop.

Duer, William (1747–1799), arrived in New York from England in 1768. He was a member of the committee that drafted the first Constitution of New York in 1777, was a delegate to the Continental Congress in 1777 and 1778, and Secretary of the Treasury Board in 1789.

Duer, William A. (1780–1858), prominent in the New York Assembly in 1814, was Judge of the New York Supreme Court from 1822 to 1829, when he became president of Columbia College, resigning in 1842, and published some historical works.

Dug Spring, Mo., a sharp skirmish, August 1, 1861, between General Nathaniel Lyon's Federal force of 5500 and McCulloch's Confederate volunteers numbering 12,000. McCulloch was worsted.

"Duke's Laws." A code of laws drawn up in 1664 by Colonel Nicolls, then governing the colonies of the Duke of York's patent. They were first arranged for the government of the Dutch settlers of Long Island. They prohibited the election of magistrates, but provided for trial by jury, equal taxation, tenure of lands from the Duke of York, freedom of religion, liability to military duty, and recognition of negro slavery under certain restrictions.

Du Lhut, Daniel G., died in 1709, was engaged as fur-trader and explorer on the frontier, and was of much service to the French colonists in aiding them against Indian attacks. Duluth is named for him.

Dummer, Jeremiah (1680?–1739), was London agent of the Massachusetts colony from 1710 to 1721. He wrote "Defence of the New England Charters," declaring that the charters were compacts, and that the land-titles were not derived from the crown.

Dummer's War, a war during 1724–25 between the border settlers of Vermont and Maine, and the Indian tribes incited by the French of Canada. William Dummer was then acting Governor of Massachusetts, and it was through his efforts that the trouble was terminated by a treaty with the

Indians in 1725. Fort Dummer was erected at the present site of Brattleboro' in 1724. May 9, 1725, Captain John Lovewell defeated the Indians in a bloody battle at Fryeburg, Maine. Four sagamores signed the treaty with Dummer at Boston in November of the same year.

Dunbar, Thomas, died in 1767. He was a British colonel who was left at Little Meadows in Braddock's expedition against Fort Duquesne, and after Braddock's defeat, destroyed the munitions of war and retreated.

Dunkers (Dunkards or Brethren), a denomination of American Baptists who originated in Germany in 1708, but were driven by persecution to this country between 1719 and 1729. They are now most numerous in Ohio. In 1790 a number who held Universalist views seceded and still remain apart. They strive to reproduce the exact order of the apostolic church, dress plainly, refuse to go to law or to engage in war, take no interest on money lent to the brethren, and take especial care of the poor. Their membership is estimated at about 10,000, but they themselves keep no statistics.

Dunmore, John Murray, Earl of (1732–1809), a descendant of the Stuarts, succeeded to the peerage in 1766 and became Governor of New York in 1770 and of Virginia in 1771. In 1774 the Virginians under Patrick Henry took up arms against his government. He fled in 1775 and during the first year of the Revolution conducted petty warfare and led plundering expeditions on the coast, burning Norfolk, but was dislodged in 1776.

Du Pont, de Nemours, Pierre S. (1739–1817), celebrated French economist, twice president of the National Assembly, resided in America from 1798 to 1802 and in 1815 settled in Delaware.

Dupont, or Du Pont, Samuel Francis (1803–1865), entered the navy in his youth, but had no opportunities for distinction until the Mexican War, when he took San Diego. His great naval feat was in the first year of the Civil War; he captured the fortifications of Port Royal harbor on November 7, 1861, and followed up this success by seizing Tybee and reducing many points on the coast of Georgia and Florida. For these successes he was made rear-admiral. The unsuccessful attacks on the defences of Charleston, under his lead, in 1863, were made against his better judgment.

Duquesne de Menneville, Marquis, was born in France early in the eighteenth century. He was Governor of New France from 1752 to 1755, and was active in extending the interests of France and resisting the encroachments of the English colonies. Fort Duquesne was named for him.

Duquesne, Fort, erected at the junction of the Allegheny and Monongahela rivers in Pennsylvania by the French under Captain Contrecœur in 1754. It became at once the centre of French military operations in that section. In 1755 Braddock was sent to capture it. He was defeated July 9 by the French and Indians. Major Grant and 800 men were defeated and cut to pieces in a second expedition against the fort October 15, 1757. In the summer of 1758 General Forbes with 6000 men moved against it. His march was slow. The rains ruined roads as soon as constructed. A reconnoitring party under Grant was cut off. At length the whole force advanced. On the evening of September 24 the fort was evacuated and blown up. By Forbes' slow advance the patience of the Indians in alliance with the French had been exhausted and the garrison reduced to less than 1000. The place was named Fort Pitt (Pittsburg) in honor of the English Minister, and a strong fort erected there the next year.

Durell, Edward H. (1810–1887), drafted the bureau system of government for New Orleans in 1862, was a U. S. Judge in Louisiana from 1863 to 1874, and from 1875 to 1887 published a considerable amount of historical literature.

Dustin, Hannah, of Massachusetts, born about 1660, was taken prisoner by the Indians in 1697 and, aided by a boy, Samuel Leonard, killed ten of her captors in camp and escaped to her home in Haverhill, after notable adventures.

Dutch. The chief settlements of the Dutch in the American colonies were in New Netherland, now New York and the adjoining part of New Jersey. They were successful in commerce and industrious in agriculture, but indifferent to politics. Probably at the time of the Revolution more than half of the population of the State were of Dutch descent, and Dutch was still spoken in the villages along the Hudson in the earlier years of this century. Of late, efforts have been made to prove that the chief influence in the formation of American institutions was Dutch rather than English, that for instance the ideas of a written constitution, the ballot, freedom of religion, democracy, equal partition of the goods of an intestate, the recording of deeds by the State, and free schools, were derived from Dutch example. In the case of most of these claims, it must be said that they are still quite unproved. It is true that the Netherland Republic was in 1620 far in advance of England in respect to freedom, institutional development and general civilization, and that it was then in close association with England, and that the Pilgrim Fathers and some other colonists were well acquainted with the life of the Dutch. In the case of free schools, registration of deeds and the laws of succession, and a few other particulars, a probability of Dutch influence has been shown. But in the case of the fundamentals of American constitutional life, the new theory not only has not been proved, but is in most respects highly improbable.

Duval, Gabriel (1752–1844), represented Maryland in the U. S. Congress as a Democrat from 1794 to 1796. He was a Justice of the U. S. Supreme Court from 1811 to 1836.

Duxbury, Mass., was founded by Miles Standish about 1630, and incorporated as a town in 1637.

Duyckinck, Evert A. (1816–1878), admitted to the New York bar in 1837, was editor of the *Literary World* from 1847 to 1853, and wrote extensively upon American biography, history and literature. His chief work was a "Cyclopædia of American Literature," 1856.

Duzine, the twelve patentees of the settlement of New Paltz, made some miles west of what is now Kingston on the Hudson, in 1677, by Louis Dubois and others. The "Duzine" were elected as the legislative and judicial body of the colony, and they and later Duzines maintained control during 100 years.

Dwight, Theodore (1764–1846), edited the *Connecticut Mirror*, the official organ of the Federalists, was secretary of the Hartford Convention, and founded the *New York Daily Advertiser*, editing it from 1817 to 1836.

Dwight, Theodore W. (1822–1892), from 1858 to 1891 professor of law in Columbia College, was a member of the New York Constitutional Convention of 1867, and from 1874 to 1875 a member of the Commission of Appeals. He was one of the most famous of American teachers of law.

Dwight, Timothy (1752–1817), of Connecticut, divine, poet and teacher, while chaplain in the Continental army composed his poem "Columbia." From 1795 to 1817, he was president of Yale College and did much to broaden and advance higher education. His "Travels in New England and New York" are noteworthy.

Dwight, Timothy, born in 1828, an editor of the *New Englander* from 1856, was a member of the committee to revise the English version of the Bible, from 1878 to 1885, and in 1886 was chosen president of Yale University.

Dyer, Eliphalet (1721–1807), was Connecticut Commissioner to the Stamp-Act Congress in 1765, Judge of the Superior Court from 1766 to 1793, a delegate to the Continental Congresses of 1774, 1775 and 1778, and a member of the Connecticut Committee of Safety in 1775.

E.

E Pluribus Unum. First suggested as the motto of the United States by Franklin, John Adams and Jefferson, August 10, 1776, they having been appointed the committee to choose a design for the Great Seal. It was probably suggested by the similar motto of the *Gentleman's Magazine*, which had a popular circulation in the colonies at that time. It occurs in a Latin poem ascribed to Virgil and called "Moretum." It first appeared on coin in New Jersey in 1786, when copper coins were issued in that State.

Eads, James B. (1820–1887), was noted for his achievements in engineering, among them being the construction of the St. Louis bridge, with a central span of 520 feet, and the jetties of the Mississippi River.

Eagle, a gold coin of the value of ten dollars. So called because of the figure of the national bird, which is stamped on the reverse. It was authorized in 1792 and coinage was begun in 1794. It has always been legal tender to an unlimited amount. The first delivery of eagles was made September 22, 1795, 400 in number. It was not coined from 1805 to 1837. By Act of 1834 its weight was slightly reduced.

Earle, Thomas (1796–1849), was active in calling the Pennsylvania Constitutional Convention of 1837, and is supposed to have drafted the new

STATESMEN OF THE REVOLUTION.

Patrick Henry.
John Hancock.
Benjamin Franklin
Robert Morris.
John Dickinson.
Richard Henry Lee.
Robert R. Livingston.
James Otis.
Roger Sherman.
Samuel Adams.

Constitution. In 1840 he was the candidate of the Liberty party for Vice-President.

Early, Jubal Anderson (1815–1894), Confederate general, was attorney for Virginia from 1842 to 1844 and from 1848 to 1852, and served as major in the Mexican War from 1847 to 1848. In 1861 he became a colonel in the Confederate army and fought at Bull Run and Williamsburg. Promoted to brigadier-general in 1863 he was a commander at Fredericksburg and Gettysburg. Successful at first in his Shenandoah campaign he was defeated by Sheridan on the Opequan, at Fisher's Hill and at Cedar Creek, and by General Custer at Waynesboro. For these defeats he was retired. He was president of the Southern Historical Society.

East India Company, the Dutch trading company under whose auspices Henry Hudson in his vessel, the "Half Moon," sailed up the Hudson River and established three trading posts. The object of the company was not colonization, but a monopoly of the fur trade. In 1621 a similar monopoly was granted by the States General to the newly formed West India Company.

East Jersey. (See New Jersey.)

Eaton, Dorman B., was born in Vermont in 1823. Prominent in promoting civil service reform, he was appointed a member of the Civil Service Commission by President Grant in 1873 and in 1883 by President Arthur, serving till 1886. He drafted the national civil service act of 1883, and has written extensively upon the subject.

Eaton, John, born in New Hampshire in 1829, served during the Civil War, and was appointed U. S. Commissioner of Education, serving from 1870 to 1886. He was president of the international congress of education at New Orleans, and vice-president of the congress at Havre, France.

Eaton, John H. (1790–1856) was a U. S. Senator from Tennessee from 1818 to 1829, was Secretary of War in Jackson's Cabinet from 1829 to 1831, and Minister to Spain from 1836 to 1840. He was one of Jackson's closest friends and political advisers.

Eaton, Margaret L. (1796–1879) ("Peggy O'Neill"), a woman of great beauty and of fascinating manner, but of low social position, married John H. Eaton in 1828. When he became Secretary of War she was refused recognition by the families of the Cabinet members. Her cause was supported by President Jackson, who attempted to enforce her recognition, which led to the disruption of the Cabinet in 1831.

Eaton, Theophilus (1591–1658), a prosperous English merchant, came to Massachusetts in 1637, explored the Connecticut coast, and in 1638 planted a colony at New Haven, of which he became one of the "Seven Pillars" who formed the government, and was made the first Governor. He was one of the commissioners who formed the "United Colonies of New England" in 1643.

Eaton, William (1764–1811), born in Connecticut, served in the Revolutionary War from 1780 to 1783, and was Clerk of the Connecticut House of Representatives from 1791 to 1797. He was Consul at Tunis, where he conducted important negotiations from 1799 to 1803, and was U. S. Naval Agent to the Barbary States from 1804 to 1805. In 1805 he conducted the celebrated Derne expedition. (See Derne.)

Ebenezer, the chief settlement of the Salzburger colonists of Georgia. It was founded near the confluence of the Savannah River and Ebenezer Creek in 1734. Its Salzburger inhabitants were mainly farmers and Indian traders.

Economy. (See Harmonists.)

Ecuador. In 1839 a commercial treaty was concluded between the United States and Ecuador. Conventions were concluded in 1862 for the settlement of claims, and in 1872 relative to naturalization and extradition.

Eden, Sir Robert, born in England, died in 1786. He was made Governor of Maryland in 1768, and ruled with moderation, causing the Maryland colonists to hope for reconciliation with Great Britain at the outbreak of the Revolution. In 1776 he was obliged to depart.

Edenton, N. C., was founded in 1715, named for Governor Charles Eden, and for a time was the place of meeting of the Legislature of the colony.

Edes, Benjamin (1732–1803), from 1755 to 1798 was editor of the *Boston Gazette and Country Journal*, which became very influential during the Revolutionary period. He materially aided the members of the "Boston Tea Party" in 1773.

Edison, Thomas A., was born in Ohio in 1847. One of the most successful of inventors, he accomplishes his great achievements empirically by almost incessant labor. Among his inventions are the carbon telephone, the phonograph, the microtasimeter, by which has been measured the heat of the sun's corona, and a quadruplex system of telegraphy.

Edmunds, George Franklin, Senator, was born in Vermont in 1828. He was a Representative in the Vermont Legislature from 1854 to 1859 (except one year), serving as Speaker for three years, and was president *pro tempore* of the State Senate from 1861 to 1862. He drew up the resolutions adopted at the convention for uniting the Republicans and the War Democrats. In 1866 he was appointed to succeed Solomon Foote, deceased, in the U. S. Senate, and held office till his resignation in 1891. In 1877 he was a member of the Electoral Commission. While in the Senate he served as chairman of the Judiciary Committee, and had the drafting of many important bills. His services in the Senate were marked by uprightness of character, ability to detect imperfections in pending legislation, and hostility to irregular procedure.

Edmunds Act, a bill submitted by Senator Edmunds, of Vermont, and passed by Congress March 22, 1882, to regulate and restrict the polygamous institutions of the Mormons in Utah. Under its provisions Mormons were in a great measure excluded from local offices, which they had hitherto wholly controlled. Many persons were indicted and punished for polygamy also.

Education. (See Schools, Academies, Colleges, Universities.)

Education, Bureau of. This office was established in 1867 for the purpose of collecting statistics showing the condition and progress of education in the States and Territories, and of diffusing such information as might promote the cause of education throughout the country. At first an independent office, it was in 1868 made a bureau of the Department of the Interior.

Educational Land-grants. In the disposal of the lands of the Northwest Territory large tracts were, in some instances, granted to the States formed therefrom, to be sold by the State Legislatures for an educational endowment; or else the lands were sold by the Federal Government, and a percentage of the proceeds bestowed upon the State for the erection of schools and colleges. When Illinois became a State three per cent of the proceeds of the sales of public lands was granted for this purpose, to be paid as fast as the sales were made. In 1829 the Legislature borrowed the school fund for State purposes, and failed to pay interest thereon, hence the Federal grant was withheld for some years. The total amount received was $712,-745.24. In Michigan, the charge of the public lands was intrusted first to the Territorial, and then, in 1835, to the State Legislature. In general, these grants were mismanaged by the States. History by Knight.

Edward, Fort, erected on the Hudson River in 1755, and at first called Fort Lyman after the builder; an important post during the French and Indian War. It was garrisoned, in 1755, by the Earl of Loudoun and 2500 men, and afterward by General Webb. From this fort there were frequent expeditions against the French along the Canadian border. After the massacre at Fort William Henry, in 1757, the remnant of the latter's garrison took refuge in Fort Edward. The French General Montcalm proposed to attack Fort Edward, but failed to do so. During the winter of 1757 the troops under General Webb, tired of inaction, mutinied and caused serious trouble. Captain Haviland then assumed command, and despatched a scouting expedition under Rogers against the French border in 1758. This party was defeated near Lake George.

Edwards, Jonathan (1703–1758), born in Connecticut, was the most eminent metaphysician America has ever produced. In 1727 he was ordained pastor at Northampton, Mass., where he remained until 1750. From 1751 to 1758 he preached to the Indians at Stockbridge. He was a most prolific writer upon religion and metaphysics, and in 1754 published his famous "Inquiry into the Freedom of the Will."

Edwards, Ninian (1775–1833), a prominent lawyer, was Governor of the Territory of Illinois from 1809 to 1818, was U. S. Senator from 1818 to 1824 and was, by election, Governor from 1826 to 1830.

Eggleston, Edward, was born in 1837. He is a popular novelist and the author of a series of biographies of American Indians and a history of social life in the colonies.

Egypt. A commercial agreement was made in 1884 between the United States and Egypt.

Eight-Hour Law. The Act of August 1, 1892, restricts to eight hours the working day of all laborers and mechanics employed by the United States Government, by the District of Columbia, or by any contractor upon any of the public works. Violation of this law is punishable by fine and imprisonment.

El Bracito, N. M., a short, but hotly contested battle between Colonel Doniphan's army of 900 men and a force of 1100 Mexicans, under an officer named Ponce de Leon, December 24, 1846. These troops charged upon the Americans, but were easily repulsed by a volley from rifles. This occurred during Doniphan's celebrated expedition against Chihuahua to join and relieve General Wool.

El Dorado, meaning "The Gilded Man." Among the Muysca Indians of Bogotá it was customary, at the time of the Spanish explorations of the sixteenth century, for each new chief, with his naked body anointed with resinous gums and covered with gold dust, to head a solemn procession to the Lake of Govita, and to wash himself therein after much impressive ceremony. At the same time the assembled savages cast into the lake gold trinkets and precious stones, as offerings to the goddess of the lake, the drowned wife of a former chieftain. Hence the term *el dorado* came to be applied to any place where gold was reported to exist. Many expeditions were undertaken in search of the mythical *el dorado* by the Spaniards. South America, Mexico and Florida were all, at different times, supposed to be the country of the long sought *el dorado.*

Election Laws. Each colony and State has had its own laws for local elections. The Constitution gives the Congress power to regulate Federal elections. Elections to the Senate were first put upon a uniform plan by Federal legislation in 1866, and elections to the House by Act of 1875. For the recent attempt to carry still further the policy of Federal control of Federal elections, see art. "Force Bill." History of colonial elections by Bishop.

Elections. In the colonial period only Massachusetts (till 1691), Connecticut and Rhode Island elected their Governors. But in all the people elected their Representatives in the Assembly, and this was done either by ballot or, as in Virginia, after the English manner, *viva voce.* Election disturbances were common in the Southern colonies, though laws against violence and treating prevailed. Under the Constitution of 1787 the Federal Congress did not pass laws controlling the election of Senators until 1866, when the present system was introduced, nor of Representatives, completely, until 1875. The first Presidential election was held in January and February of 1789. The times of election formerly varied much in different States, but now nearly all elect their Congressmen in November.

Elections, Presidential. The following table gives the electoral and popular votes for President and Vice-President at each election. It is to be remembered that in the elections preceding that of 1804 the electors did not vote for President and Vice-President separately; he who had most votes was made President, he who stood second Vice-President. Up to 1824 electors were largely chosen by State Legislatures without popular voting:

Year.	No. of Electors.	Party.	President. Candidate.	Popular Vote.	Electors.	Vice-President. Candidate.	Electors.
1789	73		George Washington		69		
			John Adams				34
			John Jay				9
			R. H. Harrison				6
			John Rutledge				6
			John Hancock				4
			George Clinton				3
			Samuel Huntington				2
			John Milton				2
			James Armstrong				1
			Benjamin Lincoln				1
			Edward Telfair				1
			Vacancies		4		4
1792	135	Federalist	George Washington		132		
		Federalist	John Adams				77
		Republican	George Clinton				50
		Republican	Thomas Jefferson				4
			Aaron Burr				1
			Vacancies				3
1796	138	Federalist	John Adams		71		
		Republican	Thomas Jefferson				68
		Federalist	Thomas Pinckney				59
		Republican	Aaron Burr				30
			Samuel Adams				15
			Oliver Ellsworth				11
			George Clinton				7
			John Jay				5
			James Iredell				3
			George Washington				2
			John Henry				2
			Samuel Johnston				2
			Charles C. Pinckney				1
1800	138	Republican	Thomas Jefferson*		73		
		Republican	Aaron Burr				73
		Federalist	John Adams				65
		Federalist	Charles C. Pinckney				64
			John Jay				1
1804	176	Republican	Thomas Jefferson		162	George Clinton	162
		Federalist	Charles C. Pinckney		14	Rufus King	14
1808	176	Republican	James Madison		122	George Clinton	113
		Federalist	Charles C. Pinckney		47	Rufus King	47
			George Clinton		6	John Langdon	9
						James Madison	3
						James Monroe	3
			Vacancy		1		1
1812	218	Republican	James Madison		128	Elbridge Gerry	131
		Federalist	De Witt Clinton		89	Jared Ingersoll	86
			Vacancy		1		1
1816	221	Republican	James Monroe		183	D. D. Tompkins	183
		Federalist	Rufus King		34	John E. Howard	22
						James Ross	5
						John Marshall	4
						Robert G. Harper	3
			Vacancies		4		4

*Jefferson was chosen President by the House of Representatives.

Year.	No. of Electors.	Party.	PRESIDENT. Candidate.	Popular Vote.	Electors.	VICE-PRESIDENT. Candidate.	Electors.
1820	235	Republican	James Monroe		231	D. D. Tompkins	218
		Republican	John Q. Adams		1	Richard Stockton	8
						Daniel Rodney	4
						Robert G. Harper	1
						Richard Rush	1
			Vacancies		3		3
1824	261	Republican	Andrew Jackson	153,544	99	John C. Calhoun	182
		Republican	John Q. Adams*	108,740	84	Nathan Sanford	30
		Republican	William H. Crawford	46,618	41	Nathaniel Macon	24
		Republican	Henry Clay	47,136	37	Andrew Jackson	13
						Martin Van Buren	9
						Henry Clay	2
			Vacancy				1
1828	261	Democratic	Andrew Jackson	647,276	178	John C. Calhoun	171
		Nat. Repub.	John Q. Adams	508,064	83	Richard Rush	83
						William Smith (S. C.)	7
1832	288	Democratic	Andrew Jackson	687,502	219	Martin Van Buren	189
		Nat. Repub.	Henry Clay	530,189	49	John Sergeant	49
			John Floyd		11	Henry Lee	11
		Anti-Mason	William Wirt	33,108	7	Amos Ellmaker	7
						William Wilkins	30
			Vacancies		2		2
1836	294	Democratic	Martin Van Buren	762,678	170	R. M. Johnson†	147
		Whig	Wm. H. Harrison		73	Francis Granger	77
		Whig	Hugh L. White	735,651	26	John Tyler	47
		Whig	Daniel Webster		14	William Smith (Ala.)	23
		Whig	W. P. Mangum		11		
1840	294	Whig	William H. Harrison	1,275,017	234	John Tyler	234
		Democratic	Martin Van Buren	1,128,102	60	R. M. Johnson	48
		Liberty	James G. Birney	7,069	...	Francis J. Lemoyne.	
						L. W. Tazewell	11
						James K. Polk	1
1844	275	Democratic	James K. Polk	1,337,243	170	George M. Dallas	170
		Whig	Henry Clay	1,299,062	105	T. Frelinghuysen	105
		Liberty	James G. Birney	62,300	...	Thomas Morris.	
1848	290	Whig	Zachary Taylor	1,360,101	163	Millard Fillmore	163
		Democratic	Lewis Cass	1,220,544	127	William O. Butler	127
		Free-Soil	Martin Van Buren	291,263	...	Charles F. Adams.	
1852	296	Democratic	Franklin Pierce	1,601,274	254	William R. King	254
		Whig	Winfield Scott	1,386,578	42	William A. Graham	42
		Free Dem.	John P. Hale	156,825	...	George W. Julian.	
1856	296	Democratic	James Buchanan	1,838,169	174	J. C. Breckinridge	174
		Republican	John C. Frémont	1,341,264	114	William L. Dayton	114
		American	Millard Fillmore	874,534	8	A. J. Donelson	8
1860	303	Republican	Abraham Lincoln	1,866,452	180	Hannibal Hamlin	180
		Democratic	J. C. Breckinridge	845,953	72	Joseph Lane	72
		Cons. Union	John Bell	590,631	39	Edward Everett	39
		Ind. Dem.	S. A. Douglas	1,375,157	12	H. V. Johnson	12
1864	314	Republican	Abraham Lincoln	2,213,667	212	Andrew Johnson	212
		Democratic	Geo. B. McClellan	1,802,237	21	G. H. Pendleton	21
			States not voting		81		81
1868	317	Republican	Ulysses S. Grant	3,012,833	214	Schuyler Colfax	214
		Democratic	Horatio Seymour	2,703,249	80	F. P. Blair, Jr.	80
			States not voting		23		23

* Adams was elected President by the House of Representatives.

† Johnson was chosen Vice-President by the Senate.

Year.	No. of Electors.	Party.	PRESIDENT.			VICE-PRESIDENT.	
			Candidate.	Popular Vote.	Electors.	Candidate.	Electors.
1872	366	Republican	Ulysses S. Grant	3,597,070	286	Henry Wilson	286
		Dem. & Lib.	Horace Greeley	2,834,079	...	B. Gratz Brown	47
		Democratic	Charles O'Conor	29,489	...	George W. Julian	5
		Temperance	James Black	5,608	...	A. H. Colquitt	5
			Thos. A. Hendricks	...	42	John M. Palmer	3
			B. Gratz Brown	...	18	T. E. Bramlette	3
			Charles J. Jenkins	...	2	W. S. Groesbeck	1
			David Davis	...	1	Willis B. Machen	1
						N. P. Banks	1
			Not counted	...	17	...	14
1876	369	Republican	Rutherford B. Hayes	4,033,950	185	William A. Wheeler	185
		Democratic	Samuel J. Tilden	4,300,590	184	T. A. Hendricks	184
		Greenback	Peter Cooper	81,740	...	Samuel Cary.	
		Prohibition	Green Clay Smith	9,522	...	G. T. Stewart.	
			Scattering	2,636			
1880	369	Republican	James A. Garfield	4,454,416	214	Chester A. Arthur	214
		Democratic	Winfield S. Hancock	4,444,952	155	William H. English.	155
		Greenback	James B. Weaver	308,578	...	B. J. Chambers.	
		Prohibition	Neal Dow	10,305	...	H. A. Thompson.	
		American	John W. Phelps	707	...	Samuel C. Pomeroy.	
			Scattering	989			
1884	401	Democratic	Grover Cleveland	4,874,986	219	T. A. Hendricks	219
		Republican	James G. Blaine	4,851,981	182	John A. Logan	182
		Prohibition	John P. St. John	150,369	...	William Daniel.	
		Greenback	Benjamin F. Butler	175,370	...	A. M. West.	
			Scattering	11,362			
1888	401	Republican	Benjamin Harrison	5,440,551	233	Levi P. Morton	233
		Democratic	Grover Cleveland	5,538,434	168	A. G. Thurman	168
		Prohibition	Clinton B. Fisk	250,290	...	John A. Brooks.	
		Union Lab.	Alonzo J. Streeter	147,045	...	C. E. Cunningham.	
			Scattering	10,312			
1892	444	Democratic	Grover Cleveland	5,553,142	276	Adlai E. Stevenson	276
		Republican	Benjamin Harrison	5,186,931	145	Whitelaw Reid	145
		People's	James B. Weaver	1,030,128	23	James G. Field	23
		Prohibition	John Bidwell	268,361	...	J. B. Cranfell.	

Electoral Commission, a commission appointed by an Act of Congress, January 29, 1877, to investigate certain charges of fraudulent return of electoral votes from Florida, Louisiana, Oregon and South Carolina, during the Presidential election of 1876. Hayes and Tilden were the respective Republican and Democratic candidates for that term. The commission numbered fifteen: three Republican Senators, two Democratic Senators, three Democratic Representatives, two Republican Representatives, and five Associate Justices of the Supreme Court. Bradley, the fifth Justice selected, had the casting vote. February 9, the commission sustained the validity of the Hayes electoral ticket in Florida, and later gave similar decisions regarding the other States. The appointment of a commission of this sort was hitherto an unheard-of step and has by some been deemed unconstitutional.

Electors. The Constitution provides that a number of electors for choosing the President and Vice-President shall be appointed by each State, equal to the number of Senators and Representatives from that State, no one of them holding a public national office. Electors have been chosen in four different ways: by joint ballot of the State Legislatures, by a concurrent vote of the two branches of the Legislature, by a general vote and by a district vote. By 1872, the general ticket method was adopted in every State. An elector is chosen from each Congressional district. Originally the electors voted for two persons without designating either as President or Vice-President. The one receiving the greatest number of votes was President. If no one had a majority the House was to choose from the five highest. Under the Twelfth Amendment the electors vote for President and Vice-President as such, and if the election goes to the House of Representatives the choice is from the three highest instead of from the five highest, as originally provided.

Elevator Cases. (See art. Munn *vs.* Illinois.)

Eliot, Charles W., was born in Massachusetts in 1834. He was elected president of Harvard College in 1869. His administration has been marked by great advancement. He has written various works upon chemical and educational topics.

Eliot, John (1604–1690), "the Apostle of the Indians," emigrated to Boston from England in 1631. Soon after his arrival he began studying the Indian language and translated portions of the Gospel, and in 1646 began to preach to the Indians without the aid of an interpreter. In 1660 he founded an Indian church at Natick, and in 1663 a catechism was published, the first publication ever made in the Indian language. The same year he completed a translation of both the Old and New Testaments. Eliot's Indian Bible is now a very rare book, commanding a very high price.

Elizabeth (1533–1603), Queen of England from 1558 to 1603, granted in 1578 to Sir Humphrey Gilbert letters patent to conquer and possess any heathen lands not already in the hands of Christians. Gilbert's expedition failed. In 1584 Elizabeth granted a similar charter to Raleigh. In 1585, with the Queen's assistance, Raleigh sent seven vessels and 100 colonists to settle in Virginia, which had been taken in the Queen's name under the charter of 1584 and named by Elizabeth. In 1602 Gosnold named (one of) the Elizabeth Islands for her.

Elizabethtown (Brockville, near the Thousand Islands). Here, in the War of 1812, were confined some American prisoners. February 7, 1813, Major Forsyth crossed the river, released the captives, seized some military stores and a number of British, and returned without the loss of a man.

Elk Creek, Ind. Terr. Here General Blunt, leading 2400 National soldiers toward Fort Blunt, encountered the Confederate General Cooper at the head of 5000 men. A brief fight took place in which Cooper was worsted.

Elkins, Stephen B., born in 1841, was a delegate in Congress from New Mexico from 1873 to 1877, was one of the defendants in the "Star route" trials, and was Secretary of War from 1891 to 1893, in the Cabinet of President B. Harrison.

Ellery, William (1727–1820), born in Rhode Island, was chosen a delegate to the Continental Congress in 1776, and served on the board of admiralty, and the treasury and marine committees. He was one of the signers of the Declaration of Independence, and continued, except in 1780 and 1782, a member of the Congress till 1786.

Ellicott, Andrew (1754–1820), of Pennsylvania, surveyed and laid out the city of Washington in 1790, and was surveyor-general of the United States in 1792. In 1796 he was appointed a commissioner to determine the boundary between the United States and the Spanish possessions on the south.

Elliot, Jonathan (1784–1846), came to New York from England about 1802, served in the navy in 1812; was editor of the collection called "Elliot's Debates on the Constitution," and author of numerous political works concerning the United States.

Elliott, Jesse D. (1782–1845), entered the navy in 1804, captured the "Detroit" and "Caledonia" from the British at Fort Erie in 1812, commanded the "Madison" at the capture of York, and served with distinction in the battle of Lake Erie.

Ellis, George E., clergyman, born in Massachusetts in 1814. Since 1887 he has been president of the Massachusetts Historical Society. He has written extensively upon historical and biographical subjects, *e. g.*, "The Puritan Age in Massachusetts."

Ellmaker, Amos (1787–1851), served in the Pennsylvania Legislature from 1812 to 1814, was State Attorney-General from 1816 to 1819 and in 1832 was the Anti-Masonic candidate for Vice-President of the United States.

Ellskwatawa, born about 1770, a Shawnee Indian prophet, brother of Tecumseh, ordered the attack at Tippecanoe in 1811.

Ellsworth, E. E. (1837–1861), in 1861 was appointed colonel of a regiment of Zouaves, and was shot by the proprietor of a hotel in Alexandria, Va., while tearing down a Confederate flag from the hotel.

Ellsworth, Oliver (1745–1807), was admitted to the Connecticut bar in 1771, and became State's Attorney in 1775. He was a delegate to the Continental Congress from 1778 to 1783, and from 1780 to 1784 was a member of the Governor's Council. He was Judge of the Connecticut Supreme Court from 1784 to 1787, when he became a member of the Federal Convention at Philadelphia, and was of influence in securing the compromise in the Constitution which reconciled the interests of the small States and the large States. He was a U. S. Senator from 1789 to 1796, when he resigned; was Chief Justice of the U. S. Supreme Court from 1796 to 1800, and Envoy Extraordinary to France in 1799.

Emancipation Proclamation. During the first eighteen months of the Civil War President Lincoln listened unmoved to the clamorings of abolitionists for an emancipation proclamation. He declared he would preserve the Union without freeing the slaves, if such a thing were possible. September 22, 1862, he issued a preliminary proclamation that, unless the inhabitants of the revolted States returned to their allegiance by January 1, the slaves should be declared free. This had no effect. January 1, 1863, the proclamation was issued declaring the freedom of slaves in all the States which had seceded except forty-eight counties of West Virginia, seven counties in Virginia, including the cities of Norfolk and Portsmouth, and thirteen parishes of Louisiana, including New Orleans. These districts were practically under the control of the Union army. Lincoln expected the proclamation to take effect gradually. Its legal effect has been disputed; its practical effect was enormous.

Embargo, a prohibition of commerce by national authority, laid in various forms and at various times from 1794 until 1815. Upon the declaration of war between France and Great Britain in 1793, each Government ordered the seizure of neutral vessels bound for the ports of the other. This caused great excitement in the United States, and the first embargo was laid March 26, 1794, to continue for thirty days and afterward prolonged to sixty. In consequence of the depredations of England and France upon the neutral commerce of the United States, the non-importation act was passed April 18, 1806, prohibiting trade with Great Britain and her colonies, but it did not go into effect until December 4. On December 22, 1807, Congress, at the instance of Mr. Jefferson, passed an embargo act, prohibiting the sailing of any merchant vessel from any American port, save coasters. The act was extensively evaded. The embargo failed to bring either England or France to terms, and meanwhile it inflicted great injury on the shipping interest and the export trade of the United States. On February 28, 1809, an act was passed repealing the embargo, and replacing it by a non-intercourse law which forbade British or French vessels to enter American ports. Another embargo act was passed in 1813, during the war.

Emerson, Ralph Waldo (1803–1882), an eminent American poet and philosopher, was born in Boston. He was ordained a preacher of the Gospel in 1829, but resigned his pastorate in 1832, because he could not sympathize with the formalities practiced in the church. He then began his career as an eminent lecturer, giving courses of lectures for the most part upon biographical and philosophical subjects. He contributed largely to periodicals and published numerous works in literature and philosophy. His influence upon the more thoughtful portion of the American public has never been surpassed. He resided in Concord, Mass., during all the latter part of his life.

Emigrant Aid Company, Massachusetts, the first organization formed for the purpose of settling Kansas with free-State emigrants. It was planned by Eli Thayer, and chartered by the Legislature of Massachusetts in April, 1854. But before the actual work of settlement began, the "New England Emigrant Aid Society" took its place, with a less ambitious design.

Emory, William K., born in 1811, was one of the Mexico and U. S. boundary commissioners, and served with distinction during the Civil War, at Yorktown, Sabine Cross-Roads, Fisher's Hill and Cedar Creek, attaining the rank of major-general.

Endicott, John (1588?–1665), arrived from England in 1628 to assume the government of the colony at Salem, where he continued Governor till

1630, at which time the government of the Massachusetts Company and colony was transferred to New England. From 1641 to 1644 and in 1650 he was Deputy Governor, and was made Governor in 1644, 1649, and from 1651 to 1665 except 1654, when he was again Deputy Governor. In 1645 he was appointed to the highest command in the colonial army, and in 1658 was made president of the colonial commissioners. He was a man of firm convictions and choleric disposition, who tolerated no divergence from the strictly orthodox in religion, and meted out a severe type of justice to all who disobeyed the laws of the colony.

Endicott, William C., born in 1827, was a Judge in the Massachusetts Supreme Court from 1873 to 1882, and from 1885 to 1889 was Secretary of War in Cleveland's Cabinet.

Endicott Rock. The so-called Endicott Rock, with its inscription dated 1652, fixed the northern limit of New Hampshire at the head waters of the Merrimac River, and as a part of Massachusetts.

England, John (1786–1842), born in Ireland, was made Bishop of North and South Carolina and Georgia in 1850, and was the first Catholic clergyman invited to preach in the Hall of Representatives at Washington.

English, William H., born in 1822, was secretary of the Indiana Constitutional Convention in 1850, Speaker of the State Legislature in 1851, U. S. Congressman from 1853 to 1861, and the Democratic candidate for Vice-President in 1880.

Entails were unknown in New England. South Carolina abolished them in 1733, Virginia in 1776, Georgia in 1777, Maryland in 1782, North Carolina in 1784.

"**Enterprise**," an American brig of fourteen guns, Captain Burrows. September 5, 1813, the brig, while sailing off the Maine coast, met the British brig "Boxer," also of fourteen guns. Both vessels opened fire at the same time. The wind was light and the cannonading very destructive. The "Enterprise," crossing the bows of the "Boxer," gave such a raking fire that the latter surrendered. The battle lasted forty minutes. Both commanders were killed. Two days later the prize was taken into Portland harbor.

Entomological Commission, a commission created by Act of Congress, March 3, 1877, and placed under the supervision of the Interior Department.

"**Épervier**," brig. (See "Peacock.")

Episcopal Church. (See Protestant Episcopal.)

Epworth League, an organization of young people of the Methodist Episcopal Church formed in 1889. There are now (1893) 10,972 local leagues and over 650,000 members.

Equal Rights Party, 1884, the title assumed by a party headed by Belva Lockwood in 1884. Belva Lockwood was its self-nominated Presidential candidate, her platform advocating woman suffrage. (For the earlier Equal Rights party, see Loco-focos.)

Era of Good Feeling, a name applied to the period between 1817 and 1823, during Monroe's administration, when national political contests were suspended, the Democrats having a triumphant majority and the Federalist party being almost extinct. The War of 1812 was ended and the new issues of tariff and internal improvement had not arisen. Monroe's inaugural address soothed the few Federalists and the leaders of both parties joined in receiving the President and announcing the "era of good feeling."

Eric the Red, a Norwegian who is reported to have been banished from Iceland and to have gone on a voyage of discovery about 981, in which he landed at a place previously discovered by Gunniborn. On his return three years later he called it Greenland. Thither about 985 he led an expedition and planted a colony. About 986 a vessel on its way to the settlement wandered from its course and landed on a coast nine days' sail south of Greenland, and in 1000 A. D., a son of Eric the Red made a voyage of discovery to this region and named it Vinland, which is supposed to have been somewhere on the New England coast. Authorities differ as to the authenticity of this account, but the general opinion prevails that some such discoveries were made, though the details are not reliable.

Ericsson, John (1803–1889), born in Sweden, early in life gave promise of great achievements in invention. He came to the United States in 1839, and in 1841 produced the war steamer "Princeton," which revolutionized the navies of the world. During the Civil War he was employed in building monitors; the first of which, the "Monitor," destroyed the Confederate iron-clad "Merrimac," in 1862. He is the author of a great number of valuable inventions, the most important of which are connected with engines and naval equipments.

Erie Canal, the most important artificial water-course in the United States. Its construction was conceived by De Witt Clinton in 1812, and begun as a State work in 1817, being completed in 1825. It extends 363 miles through New York State, through what was, at the time of its commencement, a wilderness, from the Hudson River at Albany and Troy to Lake Erie at Buffalo. Clinton had at first intended it should be a national enterprise, and from the interest he displayed, he was deputed with others to lay the plan before the General Government, but without success. It was executed instead as a State work, chiefly during his Governorship of New York. It contributed enormously to the development of the West and of the trade prosperity of New York City and State. Property along the canal has increased enormously and the tolls have been a valuable addition to the State revenue.

Erie, Fort, Can., during the War of 1812, was abandoned and fired with all its stores, May 28, 1813, by orders of General Vincent. The same day the Americans crossed the Niagara and took possession of the ruins. After the Americans had withdrawn from the Canadian shore, the British rebuilt the fort and stationed there 170 men under command of Major Buck. July 3, 1813, General Jacob Brown, preparatory to an invasion of Canada, invested the fort, and on demand it surrendered. The fort was now strengthened, and made capable of enduring a siege. After the battle of Niagara, the British advanced against the American position. From

August 7 to 14 the bombardment was almost incessant. At two o'clock on the morning of the fifteenth, the British, 1500 strong, tried to surprise the Americans. Attacks were made upon three points, but one only was successful. The main bastion of the fort was captured and held against all attack. Suddenly its magazine blew up with tremendous force, the attack was renewed and the British retreated, leaving 221 dead, 174 wounded and 186 prisoners. The Americans lost, all told, 137 men. The siege still continued, the attacking works were continually pushed nearer; but on September 17 General Brown, in charge at the fort, planned a sortie to destroy the British works. An attack in three divisions was arranged and executed under cover of a fog. It was completely successful. The works were captured and destroyed, the British broke camp and gave up the siege, leaving behind over 800 men killed, captured or wounded. When the Americans finally abandoned Canada, Fort Erie was blown up November 5, 1814, and never rebuilt.

Erie Purchase, a purchase of land, in 1788, made by the State of Pennsylvania. The tract is now included in Erie County, and is still known as the "Erie Purchase."

Erskine, David Montagu, Baron (1776–1855), was British Minister to the United States from 1806 to 1809 (being then simply Mr. Erskine). In 1809 he officially announced that atonement would be made for the "Chesapeake" outrage, and that the British orders in council would be withdrawn, provided the American embargo and non-intercourse acts ceased as to Great Britain. In consequence of this, President Madison proclaimed that, on June 10, 1809, all interdicts against Great Britain would cease. The British Ministry repudiated the Erskine arrangements and declared them unauthorized. President Madison was, therefore, compelled to restore the suspension of intercourse on August 9.

"Essaie du Michigan," the earliest newspaper issued in Michigan. It was published by Father Gabriel Richard in English and French, the first edition appearing at Detroit August 31. 1809. Only eight or nine numbers appeared.

"Essex," U. S. frigate of thirty-two guns, Captain Porter, was attacked on August 13, 1812, by the "Alert," a twenty-gun sloop-of-war. One broadside from the "Essex" nearly sunk the "Alert," and caused its surrender. Late in the year the "Essex" started on an independent cruise in the Pacific. Here it did noble service. It captured nearly every British whaling vessel off the west coast of South America, and deprived the enemy of $2,500,000 worth of property and 360 seamen. In February, 1814, it was surprised while in the port of Valparaiso by the appearance of two British men-of-war, the "Phœbe," thirty-six guns, and the "Cherub," twenty-two guns. On March 28, 1814, the "Essex" set sail for the open sea, and was at once attacked by the enemy. It was a desperate and bloody battle. After two-thirds of its men had been killed or disabled, including every officer but one, and with his vessel a helpless wreck, Captain Porter surrendered.

Essex Junto, the name applied first by John Hancock in 1781 to a group of leaders of Essex County, Massachusetts, and their adherents. They were upholders of the commercial interests of the country, and desired a stronger Federal Government. Upon the development of the Federal party they at once fell in line and were extreme members of that party. President Adams accused them of trying to force a war with France in 1798–99, and thus they acquired a national reputation. During the embargo period the name became a synonym for New England Federalism. Among its number were Fisher Ames, Cabot, the Lowells, Pickering, Theophilus Parsons, Higginson and Goodhue.

Estaing, Charles H. T., Count d' (1729–1794), a French naval officer, commanded the fleet sent in 1778 to aid the colonies against Great Britain, and brought Gérard, the first French Envoy to the United States. He planned an attack upon the British fleet in Newport harbor, but the campaign was not successful, and in 1779 with General Lincoln he attempted to take the city of Savannah by assault. He captured a number of British vessels and on his return to France he prevailed upon the Ministry to send 6000 men to America under Count de Rochambeau.

Eustis, William (1753–1825), represented Massachusetts in Congress from 1801 to 1805, and from 1820 to 1823. From 1809 to 1813 he was Secretary of War in Madison's Cabinet. From 1814 to 1818 he was Minister to Holland, and from 1823 to 1825 was Governor of Massachusetts.

Eutaw Springs, Battle of, September 8, 1781. Shortly after the capture of Ninety-Six, Greene moved upon the British so secretly they were not aware of his presence. At Eutaw Springs he came upon them. At 4 a. m. on September 8, Greene attacked the British in his usual order. The militia in the first line under Marion and Pickens did gallant service and were supported by the regulars in the second line. A bayonet charge followed, the British were routed and many fell or were made prisoners. A little later the retreating British took shelter in a brick house. Greene's artillery was brought to bear upon it in vain. The gunners were shot and the pieces captured. A cavalry charge by Colonel Washington was repulsed and that officer was taken prisoner. Thus there were two engagements. In the first Greene won a brilliant victory, in the second he lost many of his best men. The total American loss was 554, that of the British 1000. Again a tactical defeat proved to the Americans a strategic victory. In the course of the night the British retreated to Charleston in such haste as to leave their wounded.

Evans, George (1797–1867), was born in Portland, Me. He was a member of the State Legislature from 1825 to 1828. He represented Maine in the House of Representatives from 1829 to 1841, and was elected to the Senate, serving from 1841 to 1847. He was chairman of the Committee on Finance, and was an authority on questions of the tariff and finance.

Evans, Sir George de Lacy (1787–1870), led the British soldiers who destroyed the public buildings in Washington in 1814, and served at Bladensburg, Baltimore and New Orleans.

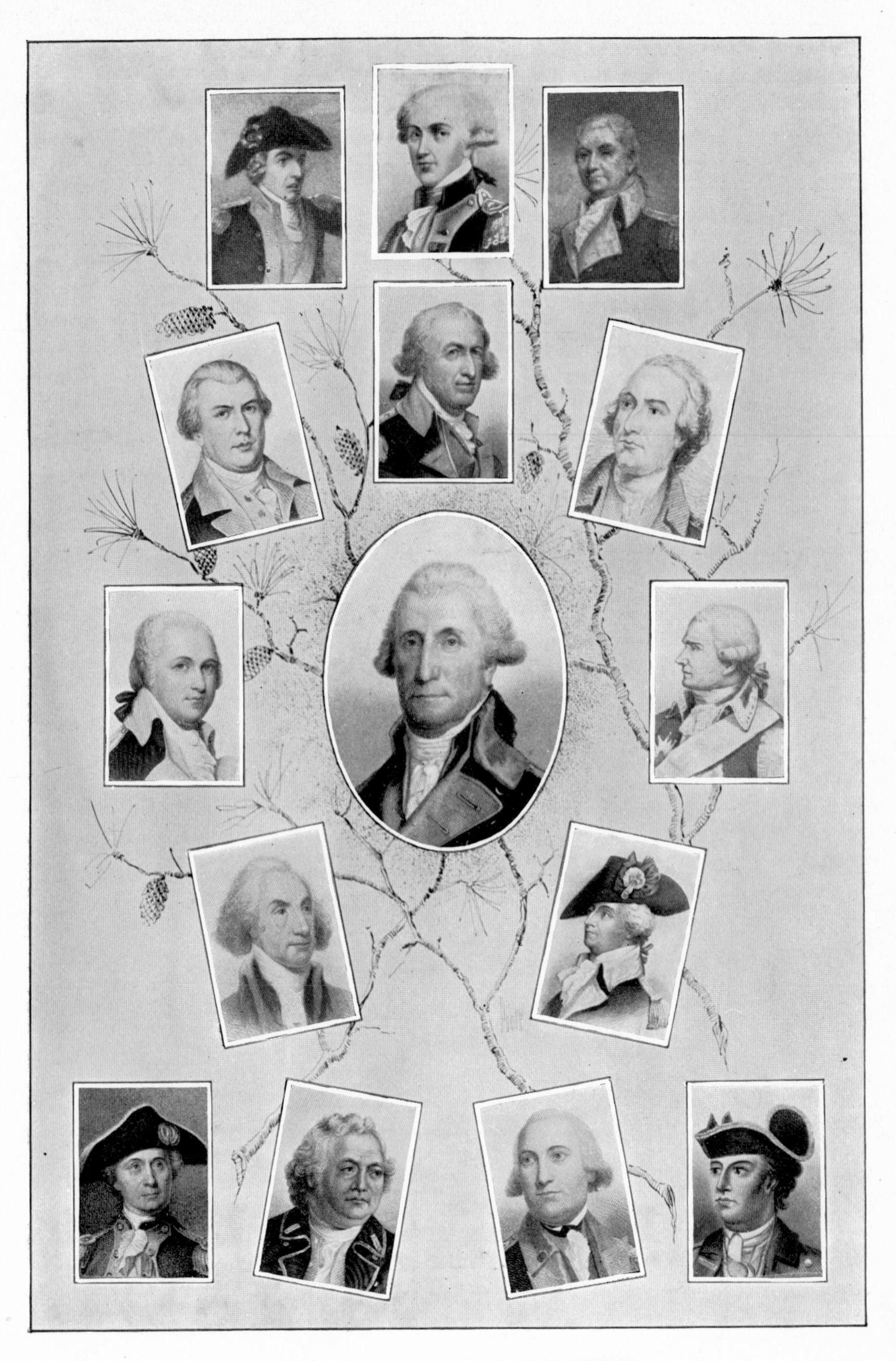

GENERALS OF THE REVOLUTION.

Francis Marion. Lafayette. Henry Knox.
Nathaniel Greene. Horatio Gates. Charles Lee.
Henry Lee. George Washington. Rochambeau.
Philip Schuyler. Anthony Wayne.
John Paul Jones. Israel Putnam. Baron Steuben. John Sullivan.

Evarts, William Maxwell, lawyer and Senator, was born in Boston in 1818. In 1860 he was chairman of the New York delegation to the Republican convention. In 1865 and 1866 he established the unconstitutionality of State taxation of U. S. bonds or National Bank stock, and in 1868 was counsel for President Johnson in the impeachment trial. From 1868 to 1869 he was Attorney-General of the United States, and in 1872 was U. S. counsel on the "Alabama" claims at Geneva. In 1877 he was the Republican counsel before the Electoral Commission, and was Secretary of State from 1877 to 1881, in the Cabinet of President Hayes. He was a delegate to the International Monetary Conference in 1881, and from 1885 to 1891 was a U. S. Senator from New York.

Everett, Alexander H. (1792–1847), of Boston, chargé d'affaires to the Netherlands from 1818 to 1824, was Minister to Spain from 1825 to 1829, and was a prolific writer upon political, economic and literary subjects.

Everett, Edward (1794–1865), an eminent American statesman, orator and scholar, was born in Massachusetts. He was graduated from Harvard at the age of seventeen, and in 1813 was ordained pastor of a church in Boston, but resigned in 1814. In 1819 he accepted a position as professor of Greek at Harvard College and held it until 1829, when he became editor of the *North American Review*. From 1836 to 1840 he was Governor of Massachusetts, chosen by the Whigs. He was appointed Minister Plenipotentiary to Great Britain, and served from 1841 to 1845, when he became president of Harvard, resigning in 1849. He was Secretary of State for four months in 1852 at the close of President Fillmore's administration, and from 1853 to 1854 was a member of the U. S. Senate. In 1860 the "Constitutional Union party" made him its candidate for the Vice-Presidency.

Everett, William, son of Edward Everett, was born in 1839. He was assistant professor of Latin at Harvard from 1863 to 1881, and became principal of the Adams School in 1882. In 1893 he was elected to Congress from Massachusetts as an Independent Democrat.

Evertsen, Cornelis, a Dutch naval officer, born in Zealand. In command of a squadron he secured the surrender of New York by the British in 1673, changed its name to New Orange, and re-established the old form of government, with Colve as Governor.

Ewell, Richard S. (1817–1872), general, was graduated at the U. S. Military Academy in 1840, and served in the Mexican War from 1846 to 1848. He entered the Confederate army as a brigadier-general, fought at Blackburn's Ford and at Bull Run, and was promoted major-general in the Shenandoah campaign. He served with distinction at Malvern Hill and at Cedar Mountain. In 1863 he commanded Jackson's troops, and fought at Gettysburg, the Wilderness and Spottsylvania Court House. He surrendered to Sheridan in 1865 at Sailor's Creek with his entire force of 6000 men.

Ewing, Thomas (1789–1871), statesman, born in Ohio, was admitted to the bar in 1816. From 1831 to 1837 he represented Ohio in the U. S. Senate, where he supported Clay's tariff system, advocated the recharter of the U. S. Bank, and also the "Force Bill," and opposed the removal of the deposits from the U. S. Bank. In 1841 he was appointed Secretary of the Treasury in Harrison's Cabinet, and was the first Secretary of the Interior, serving in Taylor's Cabinet from 1849 to 1850. From 1850 to 1851 he was in the U. S. Senate, succeeding Thomas Corwin.

Excise Law. The first excise law was passed after an excited debate in 1790, Secretary Hamilton insisting upon the necessity of such an enactment. It levied a tax varying from nine to twenty-five cents upon every gallon of liquors distilled in the United States and a higher rate for imported liquors. Lower rates were established in 1792. The opposition was strong throughout the country, culminating in the Whisky Insurrection in Pennsylvania in 1794. During Jefferson's administration the excise was abolished, but was revived in 1813 during the War of 1812, imposing a tax on liquor, sugar, salt, carriages, and instruments of exchange, and a stamp duty. In 1817 these duties were repealed and no excise duty was levied until 1862, during the Civil War. This system embraced taxation upon occupations and trades, sales, gross receipts and dividends, incomes of individuals, firms and corporations, manufactures, legacies, liquors, tobacco, distributive shares and successions. (See Internal Revenue.)

Executive. The executives of the colonies were their Governors, appointed by the crown in most colonies, elected by the people in Rhode Island and Connecticut and in early Massachusetts. At the outbreak of the Revolution, after the royal Governors had ceased to control and before the new Constitutions were set up, the executive was the committee or council of safety. The States, in making their Constitutions, mostly instituted Governors, though some created an executive council, forming an executive like that of Switzerland. From 1775 to 1789 the U. S. Government had no other executive than Congress. The Constitution of 1787 gave executive powers to the President, the Senate sharing in the executive powers of appointment and treaty making. There was talk in the convention of a plural executive, but a single head was finally resolved on. Executive departments had already come into existence. The Continental Congress at first managed all executive business through committees. Later, commissions were formed, partly of its own members, partly of others. Early in 1781 Congress organized departments under single heads—the Secretary for Foreign Affairs, the Superintendent of Finance, the Secretary of War and the Secretary of Marine. The history of these offices and of the departments which followed them in 1789, may be seen under their names individually.

Exeter, N. H., was founded about 1638. During the latter part of the seventeenth and early part of the eighteenth century the town suffered severely from attacks by Indians, especially in 1690 and 1709. Phillips Exeter Academy was established here in 1781.

Exhibitions. The first exhibition of national importance held in the United States was one held in New York in 1853, the next the Centennial of 1876, held at Philadelphia, both as an international exposition of this country's progress in its hundredth year of existence and an anniversary. The Centennial was under the management of the city of Philadelphia, and was open from May 10 to November 10. Many foreign nations were represented. The exhibition cost over $15,000,000. The International Cotton Exposition was held at Atlanta, Ga., from October 5 to December 31, 1881. It was suggested by Mr. Edward Atkinson, of Boston, and was designed to show the progress in the manipulation of cotton. The Southern Exposition opened at Louisville, Ky., August 1, 1883, and continued 100 days. The World's Columbian Exposition was created by Act of Congress April 25, 1890. The dedication ceremonies took place October 21, 1892, and the opening May 1, 1893. The exposition terminated October 30. The total cost was about $25,000,000. The exposition was held at Jackson Park, Chicago, nearly every nation being represented. The Midwinter Exhibition in California, 1893–94, is also to be noted.

Expatriation. There is no law in the United States permitting the voluntary expatriation of a citizen. Expatriation has been pleaded before the Supreme Court frequently, but has been allowed in no case. It has been claimed that freedom of emigration involved the right of voluntary expatriation and many learned authorities have argued that such is the fact, and that expatriation is a natural right. So far as custom and usage sanctions the right has been accorded, the United States Government having in a number of instances refused protection to both native-born and naturalized citizens on the grounds that they have expatriated themselves.

Expenditures. In 1794 the total expenditures of the Federal Government amounted to $6,300,000, in 1814 they temporarily ran up to $34,700,000. In 1834 they were $18,600,000; in 1854, $55,000,000. During the war they ran up to $1,295,000,000 in 1865. Then they declined to $237,000,000 in 1878. During the ensuing decade they averaged $260,000,000 per annum. In the fiscal year ending June 30, 1893, they were $459,400,000. Of the annual expenditures, interest charges have sometimes been a large amount. (See Debt.) In times of peace, expenditures for the army have usually been about two-thirds those for the civil departments of Government work, those for the navy about two-thirds those of the army. Since 1888 pensions have been the largest item.

Exports. The specie value of American exports in 1790 was $20,200,000. Except in years of war and embargo exports steadily rose until in 1836 they amounted to $129,000,000. In 1860 they amounted to $400,000,000; in 1870 to $451,000,000; in 1880 to $871,000,000; in 1892 to $1,113,000,000.

Express. This system of transportation was begun March 4, 1839, by William F. Harnden, who established express communication between New York and Boston. Alvan Adams and P. B. Burke started the Adams Express Company in 1840. The Wells Fargo Company was started in 1845, the United States Express Company in 1853.

Expunging Resolution. In 1834 a resolution of censure had been adopted by Congress against President Jackson for removing certain money deposits from the Bank of the United States. This resolution was expunged by the "Expunging Resolution" of January 16, 1837, Senator Benton being the prime mover toward its adoption. Clay, Webster and Calhoun opposed it with vehemence. A black line was drawn in the Journal around the resolution of censure, and the words "Expunged by order of the Senate this sixteenth day of January, 1837," inserted.

Extra Sessions. (See Sessions.)

Extradition, International. The first treaty of the United States which made any provision for extradition was the Jay Treaty of 1794, and Congress made no law to carry this into effect. After this, the first extradition treaty concluded by the United States was the Treaty of 1842 with Great Britain. In 1875, in the case of a criminal who had committed an offense not mentioned in the treaty, the United States procured his extradition on another charge, then tried him on the first. Great Britain protested against this. In many ways the Treaty of 1842 had become inapplicable to modern conditions. In 1886, the Phelps-Rosebery Convention, which aimed to substitute a more satisfactory system, was rejected by the Senate. But in 1889 the Senate ratified the Blaine-Pauncefote Convention, which accomplished the desired results. Extradition treaties have been concluded with all the leading countries of the world, and most of the minor countries: France, 1843; Hawaii, 1849; Switzerland, 1850; Prussia, 1852, etc.

Extradition, Interstate. The New England Confederation of 1643 provided for the mutual extradition of criminals, and so did the Articles of Confederation. The Constitution provides that a person charged with crime in any State, who flees to another State, shall, on demand of the Governor of the State from which he fled, be given up. An act of 1793 provided the process.

Ezra Chapel, Ga. Here, July 28, 1864, Hood, leading about 30,000 Confederates from his intrenchments in Atlanta, which was then invested by Sherman's Army of the Tennessee, advanced against the Federal troops, consisting of three corps under Sherman and Logan. The Federals were engaged in throwing up earthworks, but stopped hastily and received Hood's charge staunchly. Hood was defeated with great loss and forced back to his fortifications within the town.

F.

Fair Oaks, or Seven Pines, Va., a two days' engagement in the Peninsular campaign, May 31, June 1, 1862, between the Confederates, numbering about 35,000 men under Johnston, and a detachment of some 11,000 troops of McClellan's army under Casey. That leader had been sent across the Chickahominy River, and was accordingly isolated from the main army. Johnston decided to attack him. He therefore sent Hill and Longstreet against Casey's left flank and Gustavus Smith against his right. Casey was overwhelmed, and retreated to Couch's position at Seven Pines, where the latter was fiercely defending himself and waiting for reinforcements from Heintzelman. The Confederates were forcing their way down along the Chickahominy to Bottom's Bridge, when they were intercepted by Sumner's batteries and routed with great slaughter.

Fairchild, Charles S., born in 1842, was Attorney-General of New York from 1876 to 1878. He was Assistant Secretary of the Treasury in Cleveland's Cabinet from 1887 to 1889.

Fairchild, Lucius, born in 1831, was Governor of Wisconsin from 1865 to 1871. He was U. S. Consul at Liverpool from 1872 to 1878, Consul-General in Paris from 1878 to 1880, and U. S. Minister to Spain from 1880 to 1882.

Fairfax, Thomas, sixth **Baron** (1691–1782), came from England to an inherited estate of over five million acres in Virginia, where he lived from 1745 to 1782. He was a patron and intimate friend of Washington.

Falling Waters, W. Va., a smart skirmish between Federal and Confederate troops under Generals Patterson and Johnston respectively. This occurred early in July, 1861, during Patterson's campaign in West Virginia.

Falmouth, Mass. (See Portland, Me.)

"Falmouth Gazette and Weekly Advertiser." This newspaper, the first printed in Maine, was established at Portland, Me., by Titcomb and White, in 1785. In 1786 it was changed to the *Cumberland Gazette*, and in 1792 to the *Eastern Herald*. In 1796 it was consolidated with the *Gazette of Maine*, and was published as the *Eastern Herald and Gazette of Maine*. Again in 1804 it was united with the *Portland Gazette*. In 1831 it was established as a daily under the title of the *Advertiser*, but was suspended for two years, beginning with 1866. In 1868 its publication was once more resumed, and continues at the present time, in connection with the weekly edition, under the name of the *Advertiser*.

Faneuil, Peter (1700–1743), a rich merchant of Boston, was born in New York, of French blood. He is honored as the giver of Faneuil Hall to the city of Boston in 1742.

Faneuil Hall, the gift to Boston of Peter Faneuil, a merchant. The hall was begun in 1740. It was designed to be both a market-house and a place of public meeting. In 1761 it was destroyed by fire. It was restored in 1763, and was used as a theatre during the British occupation of Boston, in 1775. In 1805 it was enlarged by the addition of a third story and an increase in width. During the Revolution it was the usual meeting place of patriots, and was the scene of many stirring debates and important resolutions. It has been called the "Cradle of American Liberty."

Fannin, James W. (1800–1836), of Texas, commanded a force in 1836 at Coleta River against General Urrea. After his surrender 357 of their number, including Fannin, were shot by the Mexicans.

Fanning, Edmund (1737–1818), at first a clerk of the North Carolina Supreme Court and a legislator. In 1777 he commanded a corps of loyalists, and fled to Nova Scotia at the close of the war, having been notorious for his barbarity as a leader in partisan warfare.

Farewell Address. Upon Washington's retirement in 1796 he adopted the suggestion made him by Madison, and delivered a farewell address to the American people, partly from Madison's draft of 1792 and partly from a draft made by Hamilton and himself. Its most important paragraph was a recommendation of abstention from interference in European affairs. Andrew Jackson also delivered a farewell address in 1837.

Faribault, John B. (1769?–1860), a pioneer of great influence over the Indians among whom he traded; was the first to cultivate land west of the Mississippi and north of the Des Moines.

Farmers' Alliance, an anti-secret, national organization of agriculturists for mutual improvement and furtherance of political ends. It was founded in New York in 1873 and spread rapidly westward. Alliances were at first State organizations. The national organization was completed in 1889 with the "Agricultural Wheel" under the name of "National Farmers' Alliance and Industrial Union." Annual conventions have been held at different places, the most noted at Ocala in 1890. The Alliance is opposed to national banks, the alien ownership of land, special privileges and Federal election laws.

Farmington, Miss., occupied by General Pope's brigade of Halleck's Federal army, May 20, 1862. Halleck was engaged in concentrating his forces about Corinth, and Pope was ordered to push on and occupy Farmington. Buell was to join Pope at this place, but was delayed, and Pope's advance was therefore slow. Two brief, but severe engagements took place May 3 and 9, before Pope finally joined Buell. The Confederates were defeated.

Farmington, Tenn., a battle of the Civil War during Wheeler's raid through Tennessee. At Farmington Wheeler fell in with Crook, leading a strong National force, who effectually stopped his ravaging in that neighborhood, by defeating him.

Farragut, David Glasgow (1801–1870), the most famous naval hero of modern times, entered the U. S. navy at the age of nine. In the War of 1812, while a mere boy, he was intrusted with important missions; but in the long period of peace he found little opportunity for distinction. A Southerner by birth, he threw in his lot with the Union, and toward the end of the first year's fighting in the war he was assigned to important command. He had charge of the flotilla in the approach to New Orleans in April, 1862; his fame was founded on the passage of the river past the forts on April 24, which caused the fall of the city and its delivery into the hands of the Federals under Butler. On June 28 he ran the batteries of Vicksburg, and the following year, having meanwhile received the rank of rear-admiral, he contributed to the fall of Port Hudson and the final opening of the river. The greatest event in Farragut's life, and one of the greatest naval battles in modern times, was the battle of Mobile Bay on August 5, 1864. Farragut's oversight of the contest while lashed to the mast of his flag-ship, the "Hartford," has become one of the most familiar episodes of the war. The office of vice-admiral was specially created for him in December, 1864, and that of admiral in 1866.

Fast Days. The following days have, by Presidential proclamation, chiefly in time of war, been appointed as days of national fasting, humiliation and prayer: May 9, 1798, January 12, 1815, September 26, 1861, April 30, 1863, August 4, 1864, June 1, 1865, September 26, 1881, the last on account of the death of Garfield.

Faulkner, Charles J. (1806–1884), author of the Fugitive Slave Law of 1850, was a U. S. Congressman from Virginia from 1851 to 1859, Minister to France from 1859 to 1861, when he was recalled as disloyal. He was a U. S. Representative from 1875 to 1877.

Fauquier, Francis (1720?–1768), was an able and popular Governor of Virginia from 1756 to 1768, was opposed to all disloyalty, and was the author of several minor works on finance.

Federal Hall, in New York, the building upon the balcony of which George Washington received the oath and made his first inaugural address, April 30, 1789. The Hall had been fitted up for the use of the first Congress.

"**Federalist,**" a collection of papers first published in the *Independent Journal*, of New York City, by Hamilton, Madison and Jay, from October, 1787, until March, 1788. They were eighty-five in number and appeared under a joint signature, "A Citizen of New York" at first, afterward "Publius." The first of these essays appeared immediately after the adoption of the Constitution. They were in explanation and defense of the new system of government. Gouverneur Morris was also invited to take part, but was prevented by private business. Jay wrote five, Hamilton fifty-one, Madison twenty-six and their joint effort contributed three, by the most probable conclusions. These papers did much toward securing the ratification of the Constitution, and form one of the most important commentaries on the Constitution.

Federalists, Federal Party, the first political party which had control of the Federal Government. When the Constitution of 1787 was before the people for ratification, those who favored its adoption took the name of Federalists, giving to its opponents that of Anti-Federalists. In the First Congress, definite party divisions were not found. Before the second had ended, there was a definite division between Federalists and those whc called themselves Republicans or Democrats. Hamilton was the leader of the former, Jefferson of the latter. Hamilton's financial measures had been acceptable to those who desired strong government, the commercial classes, those who wished to see the Union drawn still more closely together, still further in the direction of centralization and national consolidation. Their opponents stigmatized them as monarchists. Beside Hamilton and Vice-President John Adams, the party's chief leaders were Fisher Ames, Cabot, Sedgwick, Strong, Pickering and Quincy, of Massachusetts; Ellsworth, Tracy, Griswold and Hillhouse, of Connecticut; Rufus King, Jay and Gouverneur Morris, of New York; Dayton, of New Jersey; Bayard, of Delaware; Marshall, Henry Lee, of Virginia, and C. C. Pinckney, of South Carolina. Washington was more inclined to this party than to the other. Its strength was always greatest in New England. When war broke out between England and France in 1793, the Federalists, conservative and averse to the French Revolution, favored Great Britain. In 1796 they elected John Adams President, but failed to elect Thomas Pinckney Vice-President. In 1797 they tried to bring the country into war with France, but Adams, never so extreme as the bulk of the party, prevented this; the result was a schism in the party. In 1798 the party passed the Alien and Sedition laws, which forever destroyed their popularity. In the election of 1800 Adams and Pinckney were decisively defeated by Jefferson and Burr; the causes were, the acts mentioned, internal dissensions, and the indifference of intellectual and acute leaders to popular feelings. During the administrations of Jefferson and Madison the party dwindled. As an opposition party, it took strict-constructionist ground. Some of its leaders engaged in projects for a disruption of the Union. Finally, its unpatriotic course in the War of 1812 and the odium excited by the Hartford Convention destroyed it utterly. Holding the Government during the critical years 1789–1801, it had given it strength, but it distrusted the people too much for permanent success in America.

Felton, Cornelius C. (1807–1862), appointed Greek professor at Harvard in 1834, was president of Harvard from 1860 to 1862, and was the author of many classical works.

Fenceviewers, town officers appointed in the early days of the New England colonies to look after fences. They had to take care that the fences were four feet high, of reasonable strength and in a good state of repair, and they had considerable authority to carry out these orders.

Fenians, an organization of Irish-American revolutionists, established in 1861, which advocated the forcible separation of Ireland from England. By 1863 they had a large following in this country, John O'Mahoney being the moving spirit. Emissaries visited all parts of the country. The British Government watched them closely and spoiled their nearly matured plans for revolution by seizing, September 15, 1865, their organ, the *Irish People*, in Ireland and arresting a number of their leaders, Luby, O'Leary and O'Donovan Rossa. O'Mahoney proposed to establish an independent government in America, and a convention was held at New York in 1865 for that purpose, O'Mahoney being elected president. The Fenians made several attacks along the Canadian frontier in 1866, and rebellion broke out in Ireland in 1867. It was quickly suppressed and the Fenians rendered harmless.

Fenton, Reuben E. (1819–1885), was born in New York. He was a Representative to Congress from New York from 1857 to 1864, when he was elected Governor and served until 1868. He succeeded E. D. Morgan in the U. S. Senate and served from 1869 to 1875, and was chairman of the U. S. Commission at the Paris International Monetary Conference in 1878. He was a prominent Republican leader.

Ferguson, Patrick, died in 1780. He was a British soldier who came to America in 1777, fought at Brandywine, was active along the Hudson in 1779, and was promoted major for services at the siege of Charleston. He enlisted many loyalists in South Carolina, but was defeated at the battle of King's Mountain.

Ferry, Orris S. (1823–1875), was born in Connecticut. He was Judge of Probate in 1849, a member of the Connecticut Legislature from 1855 to 1857, and a U. S. Representative from 1859 to 1861. He served during the Civil War, being promoted to brigadier-general in 1862. He was a U. S. Senator from 1867 to 1875.

Ferry, Thomas W., born in 1827, was a member of the Michigan House of Representatives in 1850, and Senator in 1856, and was a member for Michigan in the Chicago Republican Convention of 1860. He was a Representative in the U. S. Congress from 1865 to 1871, and a U. S. Senator from 1871 to 1883. He acted as president of the Senate from 1875 to 1877, during which time he presided over the impeachment trial of Secretary Belknap, and over the joint meetings during the electoral count of 1877.

Fessenden, William Pitt (1806–1869), was born in New Hampshire. He was admitted to the bar in 1827, and soon began practice in Portland, Me. He served in the Maine House of Representatives from 1832 to 1840, 1845 to 1846, and 1853 to 1854. He was a member of the Whig National Conventions of 1840, 1848 and 1852, and became one of the founders of the Republican party. He was elected to the U. S. Congress from 1841 to 1843, and served in the U. S. Senate from 1854 to 1864, when he was appointed Secretary of the Treasury by President Lincoln, and served till 1865. He was again a U. S. Senator from 1865 to 1869. While in the Senate he made a famous speech against the Kansas-Nebraska bill, and in 1861 was appointed chairman of the Finance Committee, where he very ably sustained the national credit. He was one of the seven Republican Senators who voted for the acquittal of President Johnson in the impeachment trial of 1867.

F. F. V's, an abbreviation of "First Families of Virginia," applied generally to the Southern aristocracy. The term was of Northern origin.

Field, Cyrus West (1819–1892), born in Massachusetts, was engaged in business in New York till 1853. He conceived the idea of a submarine telegraph across the Atlantic, and formed the New York, Newfoundland and London Telegraph Company, consisting of Peter Cooper, Moses Taylor, Marshall Roberts and Chandler White. The necessary rights for fifty years were obtained, and communication was secured in 1858, but the cable proved worthless after a few weeks. The Atlantic Telegraph Company was formed and attempts were made with the "Great Eastern" in 1865 and 1866, the last of which was completely successful. For this great achievement he was honored both at home and abroad. After this success he was active in improving the rapid transit system of New York.

Field, David Dudley (1805–1894), was prominent in law reform movements. From 1847 to 1850 he was a commissioner to prepare "Codes of Civil and Criminal Procedure," now in several instances adopted; and from 1857 to 1865 was chairman of a New York commission to prepare political, penal and civil codes. In 1873 he published "Outlines of an International Code," which has attracted wide attention.

Field, Stephen J., brother of Cyrus W. and David D., born in Connecticut in 1816, practised law with his brother, David Dudley, and went to

California in 1849, being one of the founders of Marysville. In the first State Legislature he served on the Judiciary Committee, where he was active in improving the judiciary system. From 1857 to 1864 he was Judge of the California Supreme Court, and Chief Justice from 1859 to 1863, when he was appointed to the U. S. Supreme Court by President Lincoln. He was a Democratic member of the Electoral Commission in 1877. He still serves upon the supreme bench (1894).

Fifty-four forty or fight. Under the treaty with Spain of 1819, parallel 42° was fixed as the northern limit of that country's possessions in America. Between 42° and 54° 40′ lay the special "Oregon country," claimed by both England and the United States. English fur-traders had passed to the south of parallel 49°, below which surveys had been made by the United States, and where settlements were being slowly made. In 1844 the hot-headed among the Democrats started the cry, "Fifty-four forty or fight," referring to 54° 40′, for which limit they wished to resort to war. For a time war seemed inevitable, but in 1846 a treaty was concluded fixing the boundary between the British and United States possessions at 49° north latitude.

Filibusters, a name borrowed from the West Indian freebooters of the sixteenth and seventeenth centuries and applied to associations originating in the United States for the ostensible purpose of freeing Cuba and other West Indian islands or Central American districts from European control. The acquisition of Texas was a successful filibustering expedition. In 1850 Lopez, a Cuban, Governor Quitman, of Mississippi, and others, were arrested for violating the neutrality law of 1818, by a proposed filibustering expedition against Cuba. They were afterward released. In 1855 General William Walker, with a California company, sailed on a filibustering expedition against Nicaragua. He took possession of the country, was elected President and was recognized by the American Minister. He surrendered to the United States, but organized another expedition in 1860. He was captured and shot by the President of Honduras. This ended filibustering. The term "filibuster" as used in respect to parliamentary proceedings, in the sense of engaging in dilatory tactics, is no doubt derived from this, in the meaning of carrying on irregular warfare.

Fillmore, Millard (1800–1874), was born in New York. He was admitted to the bar in 1823 and began practice in Aurora, N. Y. He was elected by the Anti-Masons a member of the New York House of Representatives from 1829 to 1831, and drafted the bill abolishing imprisonment for debt. He represented New York as a Whig in the Congress of the United States from 1833 to 1835, and again from 1837 to 1843, when he served as chairman of the Ways and Means Committee and drafted the tariff bill of 1842. From 1847 to 1849 he was State Comptroller. In 1848 he was elected Vice-President of the United States on the Whig ticket with Zachary Taylor for President. After the death of Taylor on July 9, 1850, he became President and served until March 3, 1853. During his administration the Compromise Acts of 1850 were passed and the Japanese expedition of 1852 was arranged. In 1856 he was defeated as the National American candidate for President of the United States. He commanded a corps during the Civil War, and was president of the Buffalo Historical Society.

Filson, John (1747–1788), was an early explorer on the Western frontiers of the United States, who collected and published much information in regard to the history of Kentucky.

Finance. (See Revenue, Expenditure, Debt, Banks, Tariff, Silver, Treasury, Greenbacks, Treasury Notes, Internal Revenue, Customs, etc.)

Findlay, William (1768–1846), was a member of the Pennsylvania Legislature in 1797 and 1803, State Treasurer from 1807 to 1817, Governor from 1817 to 1820 and a U. S. Senator from 1821 to 1827.

Finney, Charles G. (1792–1875), clergyman, met with great success as an evangelist. In 1834 the Broadway Tabernacle, in New York, was constructed for him. From 1851 to 1866 he was president of Oberlin College.

Fire-eaters, a name given, especially in the fifties, to those Southern politicians who were most extreme in their advocacy of Southern claims and in their hostility to the North and to anti-slavery agitation.

Fiscal Bank of the United States. In 1841, Tyler having just taken Harrison's place as President, the Sub-Treasury Act was repealed, and the Whigs passed an act chartering the Fiscal Bank of the United States. Tyler vetoed the bill, to every one's surprise. Another bill, framed with Tyler's approval, was then passed, but its opponents had filled the President's mind with jealousies and suspicions, so he vetoed this bill also, and the Whigs could not override the veto.

Fish, Hamilton (1808–1893), born in New York City, was admitted to the bar in 1830. He was elected to the U. S. House of Representatives from New York, serving from 1843 to 1845, and was a State Senator in 1847. He was Governor of New York from 1848 to 1850, and was a U. S. Senator from 1851 to 1857. He was Secretary of State in Grant's Cabinet, serving from 1869 to 1877. He negotiated the Treaty of Washington in 1871, and the St. Domingo treaties.

Fish Commission, created by Act of Congress in 1870. The head of this department is the Commissioner of Fish and Fisheries. There is also an Assistant Commissioner. These officers collect statistics of fish and fisheries of the whole country, experiment concerning the best methods of capture, and investigate the food and habits of fish.

Fisher, Fort, N. C., twice assaulted by the Federals during the Civil War. The fort protected the harbor of Wilmington. The first attack was made December 23 and 25, 1864, by Porter's fleet and a land force of 6500 men under Butler and Weitzel. The fleet contained 500 guns. Butler attempted to blow up the fort with a powder boat, but failed. This attempt to take Fort Fisher failed, so Grant sent 1500 more men under Terry, and on January 13 and 15, 1865, a combined attack was made by land and sea. The fort was garrisoned by Whiting with 2300 Confederates. Throughout the thirteenth the fleet kept up a continuous fire, but the garrison held out bravely. On the fifteenth the land force made an attack, and a hand-to-hand fight of five hours took place. Then the fort surrendered, the entire garrison being captured. Next day the powder magazine blew up, killing 200 men.

Fisheries Question. Previous to the Revolution fishermen of the American colonies had free access to the fishing grounds of Labrador, Newfoundland and the Gulf of St. Lawrence. Subsequently to the war this privilege was protested against by the inhabitants of the Canadas. The question was long debated. Finally a compromise was effected in the Treaty of Paris, September 3, 1783. United States fishermen were allowed access to the fishing grounds of Nova Scotia, Newfoundland, Labrador, the St. Lawrence and the Magdalen Islands, on an equal footing with British fishermen, in such parts as were unsettled or where permission could be obtained from the settlers. The War of 1812 did away with this treaty, the fishery right was denied the United States and Canadian Governors were instructed to exclude our fishermen. A commission of the two countries decided in 1818 that the United States should forever have the right to fish on the western and northern coast of Newfoundland and the Magdalens only. Reciprocal trade being established between the United States and Canada by the Treaty of 1847, fishing was allowed the former in all British colonies except Newfoundland, which refused consent. This treaty was terminated in 1866 by the United States and the conditions of 1818 were revived. By the Treaty of Washington in 1871, the United States fishermen were allowed to take fish of any description, except shell-fish, in all Canadian waters, the British fishermen to have the same privileges in United States waters north of latitude 39° north.

Fisher's Hill, Va., a battle of the Civil War between Sheridan's army of the Shenandoah Valley, about 20,000 strong, and Early, commanding a large Confederate force. After the battle of Opequan, when Early was defeated, the latter retreated to Fisher's Hill and was there overtaken, October 21, 1864, by Sheridan. Early held an unusually strong position. The Eighth Corps gained a wooded approach in the Confederate rear, attacking the Confederates thence while they were busy with Sheridan's main command on their front. The success of this plan was instantaneous. The Confederates fled in all directions, and were pursued by Sheridan to the Blue Ridge.

Fishing Creek, Battle of, August 18, 1780. At this place General Sumter had taken his position with considerable stores and 100 prisoners captured from the British. Here Tarleton attacked him and routed his forces, freed the captives, recovered the booty, and besides took 300 prisoners.

Fishing Creek. (See Mill Springs.)

Fisk, Clinton B. (1828–1890), entered the Civil War as colonel and became major-general. He was president of the Indian Commission under President Grant, and was the Prohibitionist candidate for President in 1888.

Fiske, John, born in 1842, first came to public prominence as an expounder of the theory of evolution, making extensive and valuable contributions. Since 1869, residing in Cambridge, he has lectured on American history throughout the United States and in England. Among his works relating to the history of the United States are, "The Critical Period of American History," "The Beginnings of New England," "Civil Government in the United States," "The Discovery and Spanish Conquest of America," and "The American Revolution."

Fitch, John (1743–1798), was born in Connecticut. He was a watchmaker, and at the outbreak of the Revolution, engaged in gun-making for the American forces. He spent the winter with the troops at Valley Forge, and in 1780 was appointed deputy-surveyor of Virginia. In 1785 he constructed a boat propelled by steam power, and in 1790 one of his improved passenger boats plied regularly between Philadelphia and Burlington. Robert Fulton is said to have had access to his drawings and papers, and it was proved by the courts in 1817, that his inventions and those of Fitch were in substance the same.

Fitzpatrick, Benjamin (1802–1869), Governor of Alabama from 1845 to 1855, was a U. S. Senator in 1848 and 1849, and from 1853 to 1861. He earnestly supported the Confederacy.

Five-Cent Piece, or Half Dime, originally a silver coin authorized in 1792, and coined the same year (original weight, 20.8 grains). In 1853 it was reduced to 19.2 grains. In 1873 it was discontinued. In 1866 the coinage of nickel five-cent pieces was authorized, the value remaining, as at first, one-twentieth of the standard dollar. The legal-tender value was, however, reduced from five dollars to thirty cents. There were no issues of half dimes during the years 1798, 1799, 1804, 1806 to 1828 inclusive. Some silver half dimes were the first coins struck by the U. S. Mint in 1792.

Five Forks, Va., a battle of the Civil War which practically sealed the fate of Richmond and Petersburg. It occurred April 1, 1865, during that last celebrated campaign. Here Sheridan cut to pieces Pickett's Confederate troops after many hours of the most desperate and sanguinary fighting of the whole war. The Confederates lost over 5000 in killed and prisoners. This victory for the Federals precipitated a general attack upon the Confederate lines on April 2.

Five Nations. (See Iroquois.)

Five-twenties. Bonds bearing six per cent interest payable in gold, and redeemable at any time after five years from the date of issue, and payable in full at the end of twenty years, issued by the U. S. Government in 1862, 1864 and 1865.

Flag. The Stars and Stripes gradually grew; it was a creature of circumstance; there is no record of its birth. Among the colonies the British was, of course, the recognized standard. Here and there were minor modifications, but the retention of the "union" with its two crosses of St. Andrew and St. George marked all as essentially British. Even after the beginning of the Revolution the union was retained to show that the war did not mean separation. Congress made at first no effort to fix a national standard. There were two classes of flags in vogue in the early years of the Revolution, the "pine tree" flags of New England origin, and the "rattlesnake" flag, more national in its make-up. The latter was white with a rattlesnake cut into thirteen pieces, each marked with the initial of a colony, and the legend *Join, or die.* The need of a national flag became evident in 1775. The stripes were first used by a Philadelphia light-horse troop, and Congress adopted them in 1775 on the recommendation of a committee consisting of

Franklin, Lynch and Harrison, still retaining the British "union." This flag was raised over the American headquarters at Cambridge, Mass., January 1 or 2, 1776. After the Declaration of Independence, Congress, June 14, 1777, ordered the "union" to be displaced by thirteen stars. It was first displayed at the battle of Brandywine, September 11, 1777. On the admission of Vermont and Kentucky, 1794, two new stripes were added, but by the Act of April 4, 1818, the number of stripes was limited to thirteen, the number of stars increasing with the number of the States. (See also Revenue Flag and Stars and Bars.)

Flagg, Azariah C. (1790–1873), an influential New York politician, was appointed Secretary of State in 1826 by Governor Clinton, and served till 1833, was Comptroller of New York from 1834 to 1839 and 1842 to 1846, and was a member of the "Albany Regency" and one of the founders of the Barnburner faction.

Flanaghan, Webster, born in 1832, was a brigadier-general in the Confederate army. He was a member of the Texas Constitutional Conventions of 1869 and 1875; was Lieutenant-Governor in 1871 and served in the Republican National Conventions of 1872, 1880 and 1884.

Flatheads, a term incorrectly applied to the Selish Indians. They have always been friendly to the whites and originally resided on the Bitter Root or St. Mary's River. In a treaty approved in 1859 they ceded all their lands to the United States, and in 1871 were removed to a reservation in northwest Montana.

Fletcher, Benjamin, was appointed Governor of New York by William and Mary. He arrived in 1692 and received a commission to assume also the government of Pennsylvania, which he did in 1693. He was zealous in the extension of the English Church. In 1698 he was deposed on account of suspicions of complicity with pirates.

Fletcher vs. Peck, a breach of covenant case before the Supreme Court in 1809–10, by writ of error from the Circuit Court of Massachusetts. Peck had sold to Fletcher certain lands in the State of Georgia, which had been purchased from the State. The breach assigned was that the Legislature of Georgia had no authority to dispose of the lands. Peck had averred that the title was good and that by the Act of the Georgia Legislature of January 7, 1795, the State was empowered to dispose of unappropriated lands. But in 1796 this act was repealed (see art. Yazoo Frauds). The Supreme Court decided that the grant of land by the State was a contract, and that the Act of 1796, impairing the obligation of this contract of 1795, was therefore unconstitutional and void.

Flogging. Until 1850 this was one of the punishments inflicted in the navy. It was abolished in that year in the navy and on merchant vessels. It was finally prohibited in the army in 1861.

Florida was acquired by the treaty with Spain of February 22, 1819, which was not finally ratified by Spain until 1821. It was first discovered by Ponce de Leon, a Spaniard, in 1513, on Easter day, whence its name. It was explored by Narvaez in 1528, and by De Soto in 1539. In 1564 a settlement was made near Florida by French Huguenots under Laudonnière, but in the following year Melendez sailed from Spain to exterminate the heretics; and having founded St. Augustine, 1565, massacred the entire French colony. The Spaniards held Florida until 1763, when they exchanged it with England for Cuba. In 1783 England gave Florida back to Spain in exchange for the Bahama Islands. In 1795 the territory west of the Perdido was ceded to France, and passed into the possession of the United States with the Louisiana Purchase of 1803. During the War of 1812 the government of Florida was weak, and the State became a refuge for fugitive slaves and Indians. The Governor of Georgia sent a force against them, which increased the disorder. In 1818 General Jackson invaded Florida, attacked the Seminoles and captured Pensacola, which was restored to Spain. Ceded by Treaty of 1819, in 1822 Florida became a territory of the United States, and in 1845 it was admitted as a State. In 1835–44 a war with the Seminoles resulted in their removal to the Indian Territory. From 1845 to 1852 the State was controlled by the Whigs, when it became Democratic. An ordinance of secession was passed by a State Convention, January 10, 1861. It was restored to its full standing as a State on June 25, 1868. From this time until 1876 the Republicans controlled the State. In that year the dispute over the electoral vote was decided by the Electoral Commission at Washington in favor of the Republicans. Since 1876 the State has been Democratic. In 1869 Alabama offered $1,000,000 for West Florida, and a popular vote in that part of the State voted in favor of the annexation to Alabama, but it was not accomplished. The present Constitution was made in 1868. The population of the State in 1845 was 54,477; in 1890 it was 391,422.

"**Florida,**" a Confederate cruiser fitted out in England in 1862, and sailing at first under the name of the "Oreto." She proceeded immediately to Nassau, in the Bahama Islands, and was twice seized, but eventually escaped. Her name was then changed to the "Florida." For two years she did great damage to the Union cause all along the coast and among the West Indies. She was captured and sunk October 7, 1864, in the Brazilian harbor of Bahia, by the Union vessel "Wachusett," Captain Collins, who surprised her when unprepared for battle.

Flower, Roswell P., born in New York in 1835, represented New York in Congress from 1881 to 1883 as a Democrat, and was elected Governor of New York in 1892.

Floyd, John (1770–1837), a States-rights Democrat from Virginia, in Congress from 1817 to 1829, was Governor of Virginia from 1830 to 1834, and was a personal friend of Jefferson, Madison, Crawford and Jackson. In 1832 South Carolina cast her electoral votes for him as President.

Floyd, John B. (1807–1863), was born in New York. He served in the Virginia Legislature in 1847–1849 and 1853, and was Governor from 1850 to 1853. He was appointed Secretary of War by President Buchanan, and served from 1857 to 1860, when he resigned. He was accused of conspiracy in aiding the Secessionists while Secretary of War, especially in removing war materials to Southern arsenals. He joined the Confederate army as a brigadier-general and fought at Fort Donelson, but was soon after relieved of command by Mr. Davis.

Floyd, William (1734–1821), was a delegate from New York to the Continental Congresses from 1774 to 1783, and signed the Declaration of Independence. He was a State Senator from 1777 to 1778, and a member of the first U. S. Congress from 1789 to 1791. He was a Presidential elector in 1800, 1804 and 1820, and again State Senator in 1808.

Folger, Charles J. (1818–1884), was chairman of the Judiciary Committee of the New York Senate from 1861 to 1869, and was appointed by President Grant assistant treasurer in New York City, 1869 to 1870. He was made Associate Judge of the State Court of Appeals in 1871, Chief Justice in 1880, and Secretary of the Treasury in Arthur's Cabinet from 1881 to 1884. In 1882, as Republican candidate for Governor of New York, he received a remarkable defeat at the hands of Mr. Cleveland.

Follen, Charles T. C. (1796–1840), born in Germany, came to America in 1824, and from 1825 to 1834 was professor of German at Harvard College. He was an ardent anti-slavery advocate.

Foot, Solomon (1802–1866), was a member of the Vermont Legislature in 1833 and 1836, and Speaker in 1837, 1838 and 1847. He was a Whig Congressman from 1843 to 1847, and Senator from 1857 to 1866.

Foote, Andrew H. (1806–1863), entered the navy in 1822, and from 1849 to 1852 was active in suppressing the African slave trade. At the beginning of the Civil War he was placed in command of the western flotilla. In 1862, in connection with the army of General Grant, he compelled Fort Henry to surrender and aided in a combined attack upon Fort Donelson. He succeeded in capturing Island No. 10 from the Confederates, and in 1863 was promoted rear-admiral. He was one of the most noble and courageous officers of the U. S. navy.

Foote, Henry S. (1800–1880), was elected a U. S. Senator from Mississippi in 1847, and served till 1852, when he became Governor of the State and served till 1854. He was a zealous opponent of secession in the Southern convention at Knoxville in 1859, but served in the first two Confederate Congresses. He published "Texas and the Texans" and "The War of the Rebellion."

Foote, Samuel A. (1780–1846), was a Representative from Connecticut in the U. S. Congress from 1819 to 1821 and 1823 to 1825; was Speaker of the State Legislature from 1825 to 1826, and a U. S. Senator from 1827 to 1833. In the Senate he offered the resolution which caused the famous debate between Webster and Hayne. He was Governor of Connecticut in 1834.

Foraker, Joseph B., was born in 1846. He served in the Army of the Cumberland during the war; was Judge of the Cincinnati Superior Court from 1879 to 1882, and Republican Governor of Ohio from 1886 to 1890.

Forbes, John (1710–1759), British soldier, was appointed brigadier-general in America in 1757, and was adjutant-general in the expedition against

Louisbourg. He commanded the expedition against Fort Duquesne, accompanied by Washington with 2000 Virginians; and after taking possession named it Fort Pitt (now Pittsburg), in honor of William Pitt.

Force, Peter (1790–1868), an enthusiastic collector of materials for American history, from 1823 to 1830 published the *National Journal*, the first to be called an "official organ." From 1833 to 1867 he was occupied in preparing a documentary history of the Revolution. Nine volumes, entitled "American Archives," were published. The remainder still waits for publication. Colonel Force collected 22,000 books and 40,000 pamphlets relating to colonial history, probably the most valuable collection then in existence.

Force Bill. After the passage of the Act of 1828, authorizing a higher protective tariff system, great discontent prevailed through many of the Southern States. In 1832–33 South Carolina claimed that State power to nullify objectionable Federal enactments was an integral feature of American constitutional law. A bill, nullifying the protective tariff law, prepared according to John C. Calhoun's theory, was passed by the State Legislature. A bill to enforce the tariff law was therefore at once introduced into Congress and became law March 2, 1833. It was called the "force bill," or the "bloody bill." Compromise adjusted the trouble.—During the reconstruction period, at the first indication of an attack on the reconstructed governments, Congress at once took steps to defeat the attempt. A bill for the enforcement of the Fourteenth and Fifteenth Amendments, commonly called the "force bill," was passed in Congress by a strict party vote and became law May 31, 1870. It made punishable by fine or imprisonment all attempts at intimidation, bribery or hindrance in the matters of registration and qualifying for voting. April 20, 1871, a much more stringent law was enacted to put down the conspiracies against civil rights by the Ku-Klux Klan and similar organizations. —The name has recently been applied to the Lodge Election Bill. July 2, 1890, a bill "to amend and supplement the election laws of the United States, and to provide for a more efficient enforcement of such laws," passed the House, having been submitted by Lodge, of Massachusetts, but was forced out of the way in the Senate by a combination of Democratic and Republican Senators anxious for the adoption of free coinage legislation.

Forefathers' Day. The celebration of the landing of the Pilgrims began in 1769. At that time December 11, old style, was taken to be December 22 of new style, instead of December 21, as it should be. Hence an error and confusion regarding the day was perpetuated.

Foreign Affairs, Secretary of. This office was created by the Continental Congress, January 10, 1781, upon the urgent appeal of the representatives in foreign countries. Robert R. Livingston, of New York, was the first to fill the office. The secretary had charge of all matters concerning foreign governments and interstate affairs as well. His scope was much restricted at first, but was enlarged by reorganization in 1782. Later (1784–1789) the office was held by John Jay.

Forney, John W. (1817–1881), between 1837 and 1855 edited the Democratic *Intelligencer*, *Journal* and *Pennsylvanian*. From 1851 to 1855 he was clerk of the U. S. House of Representatives, and also edited the *Union*. He edited the *Press*, of Philadelphia, from 1857 to 1859, when he again became clerk of the House, and edited the *Chronicle* till 1870. From 1861 to 1867 he was clerk of the U. S. Senate. and in 1879 established the *Progress*, of Philadelphia.

Forrest, Edwin (1806–1872), born in Philadelphia, made his first appearance on the stage in 1820. After his appearance as "Othello," at the Park Theatre in New York, in 1826, his success was almost uninterrupted. He was most successful in melodramatic plays, and was exceedingly popular as Othello, Richard III., Coriolanus, Lear, Spartacus and Damon. At Philadelphia he collected the largest dramatic library in the United States.

Forrest, Nathan B. (1821–1877) born in Tennessee, enlisted in the Confederate service, and commanded a regiment of cavalry at Fort Donelson. He took part in the battle of Shiloh, and made a successful attack upon Murfreesboro. He served at Chickamauga in 1863, captured Fort Pillow in 1864, and surrendered to General Wilson, at Gainesville, in 1865.

Forsyth, John (1780–1841), born in Virginia, was made Attorney-General of Georgia in 1808. He was a Democratic Congressman from 1813 to 1818 and a U. S. Senator from 1818 to 1819, when he was appointed Minister to Spain, serving till 1823 and securing the cession of Florida to the United States. He was again a U. S. Congressman from 1823 to 1827, when he was elected Governor of Georgia. From 1829 to 1834 he was a U. S. Senator, and from 1834 to 1841 was Secretary of State in the Cabinets of Jackson and Van Buren.

"**Fortune,**" a vessel which arrived at Plymouth November 11, 1621, bringing thirty-five colonists to strengthen the feeble number of the Pilgrims and a patent from the president and council of New England empowering the grantees to make laws and set up a government.

Fortune Bay. Under the fisheries treaty of 1871 between the United States and Great Britain, our fishermen were granted a participation in the Newfoundland fishing grounds. In January, 1878, in violation of these provisions, several Gloucester vessels were attacked by the natives at Fortune Bay, and driven away. Great Britain awarded damages of £15,000.

Forward, Walter (1786–1852), was a Congressman from Pennsylvania from 1822 to 1825, and was active in the State Constitutional Convention in 1837. He was appointed First Comptroller of the Treasury in 1841, was Secretary of the Treasury in Tyler's Cabinet from 1841 to 1843, and Chargé d'affaires to Denmark from 1849 to 1851.

Foster, Sir Augustus J. (1780–1848), was appointed British Minister Plenipotentiary to the United States in 1811. His manners were not conciliatory, and the difficulties which led to the War of 1812 were not settled. He returned in 1812.

Foster, Charles, born in Ohio in 1828, was a member of Congress from 1870 to 1876, and served on the Committee of Ways and Means. He was Governor of Ohio from 1879 to 1884. From 1891 to 1893 he was Secretary of the Treasury in Harrison's Cabinet.

Foster, John W., born in Indiana in 1836, served in the Civil War, commanding in East Tennessee; and was Minister to Mexico from 1873 to 1880; to Russia from 1880 to 1881, and to Spain from 1883 to 1885. From 1892 to 1893 he was Secretary of State in the Cabinet of President Harrison.

Foster, Lafayette S. (1806–1880), was born in Connecticut, a descendant of Miles Standish. He was admitted to the bar in 1831, was elected to the State Legislature in 1839, 1840 and 1846, and was Speaker in 1847, 1848 and 1854. He was a U. S. Senator from 1855 to 1867, and served on the committees on land claims, public lands, pensions, the judiciary and foreign relations, and was president of the Senate from 1865 to 1867. He was Speaker of the Connecticut Assembly in 1870, and was a judge of the State Supreme Court from 1870 to 1876.

Foster, Stephen S. (1809–1881), anti-slavery agitator, studied for the ministry, but zealously opposed the pulpit for upholding slavery, and published "The Brotherhood of Thieves: a True Picture of the American Church and Clergy," and many articles on the abolition of slavery.

Four Years' Law, a law passed by Congress in May, 1820, limiting the term of office of all persons employed in collecting the revenue to four years. The bill was hurried through with little debate and signed by President Monroe after a brief consideration. Its purpose was avowedly to bring revenue accounts for inspection each year and withhold reappointment for remissness. Its framers have been suspected of passing it in order to strengthen Crawford's chances for the Presidency. At all events, its passage much facilitated the growth of the spoils system. It included all postmasters.

Fox, George (1624–1691), founder of the Society of Friends, came to America and visited the colonies of Maryland, New Jersey, New York and Rhode Island (1671–73).

Fox, Gustavus V. (1821–1883), enlisted in the navy in 1838, and served most efficiently as Assistant Secretary of the Navy from 1861 to 1865, when he was sent to Russia on a special commission and secured Alaska for the United States.

Foxes, a tribe of Algonquin Indians and kinsmen of the Sacs. They were early driven from place to place, and finally settled on the Wisconsin. In the Revolution they joined the British under De Langlade. They made a treaty in 1804 and ceded lands, but with the English attacked Sandusky in the War of 1812. In 1824 and 1830 they ceded large tracts of land. Though involved in the Black Hawk War they gave up more of their territory in a treaty with General Scott at its close. Later they centred on the Des Moines, and in 1842 were removed, settling on the Osage.

France. The first treaty which the independent States of North America made was with France, February 6, 1778. An offensive and defensive alliance was thus effected between the two countries against Great Britain, and the "essential and direct end" was to maintain the sovereignty and independence of the United States. The United States, as an equivalent, guaranteed to the crown of France all its then possessions in the West India

Islands; exclusive mutual privileges were granted as to ships of war and privateers bringing prizes into port. France powerfully aided in securing American independence, by troops under Rochambeau and fleets under D'Estaing and De Grasse. The attempt of the United States to escape the responsibilities of its guarantees gave rise to strained relations during the French Revolution, but the treaty of 1800 (to remain in force eight years) restored good feeling between the two countries, and in the amendments on each side the old treaties entirely disappeared. On April 30, 1803, France ceded to the United States the province of Louisiana, as it had been retroceded from Spain to France in 1800, for the payment of 60,000,000 francs, independent of the assumption of spoliation claims against France, which amounted to 20,000,000 francs more. In 1831 a mutual settlement of all claims was agreed upon between the two countries, the United States agreeing to pay 1,500,000 francs, and France 25,000,000. Difficulties arising from this treaty postponed the fulfillment of its provisions, and it was not until 1836 that the whole matter was settled. Conventions for the extradition of criminals were concluded in 1843, 1845, 1858 and 1893. A consular convention was concluded in 1853. French difficulties in Mexico, the Civil War of the United States and the war of 1870–71 between France and Germany gave rise to claims on the part of citizens of each country against the other. Accordingly the convention of 1880 was concluded by which commissioners were appointed for the settlement of these claims. The commissioners finally allowed claims of $2,636.21 against France, and claims of $625,566.35 against the United States. A reciprocity treaty was concluded March 15, 1892. (See also French Revolution, and Directory.)

Frank, Manor of, a territory with privilege of local self-government granted to certain Welsh colonists, known as the "Free Society of Traders," by William Penn, March 20, 1682. The grant empowered them to hold courts of sessions and jail deliveries, and to appoint certain civil officers. The company purchased 20,000 acres of Penn.

Frankfort, Ky., was laid out in 1787, and was made the capital of the State in 1792. It was held by the Southern forces for a month in 1862.

Frankfort Land Company, a company formed in 1686 of wealthy and distinguished persons of Germany and Holland. The members were chiefly Pietists, and they had intended coming to Pennsylvania themselves, but gave up the idea, so the colonists were led by Francis Daniel Pastorius, a lawyer and scholar. They came out in 1683, and began the foundation of Germantown the same year. Later the company was organized, and 25,000 acres were purchased from William Penn.

Franking Privilege, a privilege formerly enjoyed by the President, Vice-President, the Cabinet officers, the members of Congress, the delegates from the Territories and a few others, of sending mail matter free. To each of the first four Presidents this privilege was voted for the remainder of his life, and it has also been voted to the widows of ex-Presidents. The privilege as regards individuals was abolished in February, 1873, but there is still a provision permitting packages and business letters to be sent free from the departments.

Frankland, Sir Charles Henry (1716–1768), collector of the port of Boston from 1741 to 1757, is noted on account of his romantic connection with Agnes Surriage, a maid at a Massachusetts tavern, who afterward became Lady Frankland. He was a man of great wealth, and lived in a state of luxury unusual in colonial times.

Frankland or Franklin, the name given to a State assumed to be organized by the inhabitants of what is now Tennessee, in 1784, in revolt from the control of North Carolina. A Constitution was framed and ratified by popular vote, a Legislature and a Governor, John Sevier, were elected, and civil war with the older parts of North Carolina seemed imminent. But the party favorable to the old government suppressed the State government of Frankland in 1788, and the cession of the lands to the United States, in 1790, quieted the disturbance.

Franklin, Benjamin (January 17, 1706–April 17, 1790), one of the most eminent American statesmen, philosophers and writers, was born in Boston, the son of a tallow-chandler and soap-boiler. He was apprenticed to his elder brother, a printer, and developed an eager fondness for books and writing. At seventeen he ran away to Philadelphia, where, in 1729, he established a newspaper. His public spirit, his talents as a writer and the fame of his scientific discoveries advanced him in prominence. In 1753 he was appointed deputy postmaster-general of the British colonies. In 1754, being a member of the Albany Convention, he proposed an important plan for colonial union. From 1757 to 1762, and again from 1764 to the Revolution, he was agent of Pennsylvania in England; part of the time, also, for Massachusetts, New Jersey and Georgia. In 1773, acting as agent for the political leaders in Massachusetts, he sent over to them the correspondence of Hutchinson, Oliver and other Massachusetts loyalists with a confidant of the British Ministry. The publication of the letters aroused great excitement in the colonies, and brought down upon Franklin violent abuse on the part of the ministerialists, and dismissal from his office of postmaster-general. In 1775, seeing that reconciliation was impossible, he returned to Pennsylvania, and was at once chosen a delegate to the Continental Congress. In 1776 he was one of the committee of five who drew up the Declaration of Independence, and in the autumn was sent to join Arthur Lee and Silas Deane in the mission to France. In Paris he was received with great enthusiasm. He succeeded in obtaining from the French Government not only the treaty of 1778, but also large sums of money supplied in secret before that government declared war on England and openly afterward. Franklin had a leading part in the beginnings of negotiation with Great Britain for peace and independence. In respect to the actual manner in which the treaty was concluded, he was overruled by Adams and Jay, who deemed it best, contrary to the instructions of Congress, to negotiate apart from France and make separate terms. Franklin played an important part in the arrangements of the treaty, especially those respecting the loyalists. After the Treaty of Versailles had thus been signed (September 3, 1783), Franklin negotiated a favorable treaty with Prussia. In 1785 Franklin returned to America, and was chosen president of Pennsylvania, and again in 1786 and 1787. He was an influential member of the Convention of 1787, and died at Philadelphia a few years later. Beside his eminence as a statesman and as a philosopher and scientific discoverer, Franklin was noted as a shrewd and practical philanthropist, and was one of the best of English writers. Writings edited by Sparks (1850) and by Ford (1887); autobiography; lives by Parton and Hale.

Franklin, William (1729–1813), last royal Governor of New Jersey, was an illegitimate son of Benjamin Franklin. During a residence in Great Britain he was appointed Governor of New Jersey, and held the office from 1762 to 1776. In that year he was arrested as a Tory by the provincial Congress of New Jersey. In 1778 he was exchanged, lived in New York till the close of the Revolutionary War, and then retired to England, where he died.

Franklin, William B., general, born in Pennsylvania in 1823, was graduated at West Point in 1843, and served with distinction in the Mexican War, during which he was attached to the staff of General Taylor. From this time to 1861, he was engaged in engineering work for the Government. He entered the Civil War as a colonel of the regular army, and took part in most of the battles of the Peninsular campaign, commanding the Sixth Army Corps throughout the year 1862. At Fredericksburg he commanded the left wing, and was removed by General Burnside after the battle. The order of removal was not approved by President Lincoln, and Burnside resigned his command. In 1863–64 Franklin commanded the Nineteenth Corps and took part in the Red River expedition.

Franklin, Tenn., scene of an important battle of the Civil War, November 30, 1864. General Hood, Confederate, attempted to draw Sherman back from his march through Georgia by moving northward into Tennessee and attacking Thomas. At Franklin Hood brought to a stand a portion of Thomas' army under Schofield, and, after several desperate attacks, compelled him to withdraw. But the Confederate loss was 5500, while that of Schofield was 2300. Soon followed Thomas' great victory over Hood at Nashville.

Franklin and Marshall College, Lancaster, Pa., under the control of the Reformed (German) Church, was founded in 1853 by the consolidation of Franklin College (founded 1787) and Marshall College (founded 1836). Its theological seminary was founded in 1825.

Fraser, Simon (1729–1777), British brigadier-general, who in 1776 had commanded at Three Rivers, had command of Burgoyne's right wing in his advance upon New York. He won the victory of Hubbardton on July 7, 1777, but was mortally wounded in the battle of Saratoga, October 7.

Frayser's (or Fraser's) Farm, Va., also called Glendale, an action in the Seven Days' fighting in the Peninsular campaign, on the fifth day, June 30, 1862. McClellan was retreating to the James, pursued by Jackson. Longstreet and A. P. Hill attacked him at Frayser's Farm, intending to pierce his line. The Confederates attacked McCall's division with reckless impetuosity, but failed to break the line. They lost 7000 men killed, wounded and missing, the Federals 4000.

Frederic II. (1712–1786), King of Prussia from 1740 to 1786, in 1783 instructed his ambassador in Paris to make friendly overtures to the Ministers of the United States there. Offers of a treaty of commerce and navigation were made in 1784, and in 1785 such a treaty was signed. Frederic sent General Washington a sword. "from the oldest general in the world to the greatest."

Frederica, Ga., on St. Simon's Island, was founded by General Oglethorpe in 1736, an armed colony being settled there to guard the frontier against the Spaniards. In 1742, during the war between England and Spain, Frederica was attacked by a large force of Spaniards by land and sea, but Oglethorpe succeeded in holding it until the arrival of English ships drove the besiegers away.

Fredericksburg, Va., scene of one of the most important battles of the Civil War, December 13, 1862. Burnside had been appointed to the command of the Army of the Potomac on November 7. He resolved to make a direct march on Richmond, and moved his troops to the heights opposite Fredericksburg, on the north side of the Rappahannock. His force numbered about 125,000. The right was commanded by Sumner, the centre by Hooker, the left wing by Franklin. The army of Lee, 80,000 in number, was strongly intrenched on the heights behind Fredericksburg, the right being commanded by Jackson, the left by Longstreet. A road connected these wings. A stone wall ran along the foot of the heights between the left wing and the town. The Federal forces crossed the river by three pontoon bridges during the two days preceding the battle. Burnside's plan was that Franklin should make the chief attack and seize the road, and that Sumner and Hooker should then carry the stone wall and the heights behind it. Franklin did not employ enough troops to effect the object assigned him. Sumner's troops attacked the fortifications on Marye's Heights with great bravery and persistency, but were finally repulsed with great slaughter at the stone wall. The assault made by Hooker's forces at another portion of the wall was also repulsed with terrible slaughter, lacking support from Franklin. The Federal loss in the battle was 12,800, the Confederate 4300. Two days later Burnside withdrew from Fredericksburg. On the thirtieth he and Franklin were relieved of their commands.

Free Banking System. In 1838 the New York State Government established a "free banking" system, which set the fashion of reform elsewhere and was followed as a basis of the national banking system of 1863. Under this system the practice of granting special charters was abandoned. Any persons could form a bank who should deposit securities with the State to the full amount of its circulating notes. Many of the other States quickly followed New York's example, for the unregulated banking methods were beginning to affect seriously the State finances.

Free Masons. An attempt to introduce freemasonry into the colonies was made in 1730 by the appointment of a provincial grand master of New Jersey, but so far as is known the first lodge was established in 1733 at Boston. Others speedily followed. After the securing of independence the lodges established grand lodges in the separate States. For the history of the opposition to freemasonry in the United States, see Anti-Masonic party.

Free Negroes. According to the census of 1790, there were 59,481 free colored persons in the United States. Of these 28,558 were in the Southern States, as against about 647,000 slaves, 17,852 in the Middle States, as against about 45,000 slaves, and 13,071 in New England, as against about 3800 slaves. As aversion to slavery decreased in the South, emancipation was made less easy, and free negroes were put under certain disabilities. The view that they were a dangerous element in the population strengthened the movement for colonization of them in Africa (see arts. Colonization Society, Liberia). In 1857 the Supreme Court declared that free negroes were not citizens of the United States (see Dred Scott). The Thirteenth Amendment made all negroes free.

"Free Ships, Free Goods." A popular summary of the doctrine that, in time of war, all goods, whether belonging to neutrals or to members of the belligerent states, are, if carried in neutral vessels, thereby exempted from capture, unless they are by nature contraband of war. This doctrine was generally held by neutrals. It was maintained by the United States during the wars between England and France, 1793–1815. England, on the other hand, had always maintained that the determining characteristic was the ownership of the property, whatever the ownership of the vessel. This was one of the differences from which arose the War of 1812. The Treaty of Ghent did not settle the question. By the Declaration of Paris (1856) it was agreed by the signatory powers that free ships should make free goods, and indeed that both enemy's goods in neutral ships and neutral goods in enemy's ships should be exempt from capture. While the United States did not accede to the Declaration as a whole, they naturally welcomed this part of it.

Free Society of Traders, a Welsh colonization company formed in 1682 to establish colonies in Pennsylvania. March 20 of that year, William Penn granted them the "Manor of Frank," with privileges of local self-government, and later they bought from Penn 20,000 acres of land.

Free-Soil Party, a short-lived party of anti-slavery men, which sprang into existence in 1848. Immediately after Taylor's nomination a plan was laid for a great anti-slavery meeting at Buffalo in August. Thousands attended the meeting, chiefly of two elements: the members of the Liberty party, though in October, 1847, they had nominated John P. Hale as candidate for President; and the "Barnburners," or dissatisfied anti-administration Democrats of New York, followers of Van Buren, desirous of avenging him for the nomination of Polk in 1844. These last had in June nominated Van Buren by convention held at Utica. The Buffalo Convention, composed of these two partly incongruous elements, nominated Van Buren and C. F. Adams. Its resolutions declared that Congress had no more power to make a slave than to make a king, and ought to keep slavery out of the Territories. The "Free-Soilers" polled 291,263 votes in 1848. They were strongest in New York, Massachusetts and Ohio. They also won fourteen Congressmen, and in the next House had seventeen. In 1852 the Van Buren faction was reunited with the regular Democracy. The Free-Soilers met in convention at Pittsburgh in August, and nominated John P. Hale and George W. Julian, but polled only 155,825 votes. The Kansas-Nebraska Bill called into existence the Republican party, and the Free-Soil party was absorbed in it.

Freedmen's Bureau, a bureau of the War Department of the United States Government, established by Act of March 3, 1865, to have general charge of the interests of the enfranchised negroes of the Southern States. Its title was "bureau of refugees, freedmen and abandoned lands," and it was authorized to assign to the freedmen allotments of confiscated or abandoned lands given over to it by the President for such purposes. It was to continue one year. A bill continuing it for two years more was vetoed by President Johnson in 1866, but was passed over the veto. Its general work continued till 1869, its educational work till 1870. It expended in its work over $15,000,000.

Freeman's Farm, N. Y., an indecisive battle, September 19, 1777, between the British army under Burgoyne, and Gates commanding the Continental troops. The latter was worsted at first, but Benedict Arnold attacked Burgoyne's centre and saved the Americans.

Freewill Baptists. This denomination originated in 1780, in a church founded at New Durham, N. H., by Benjamin Randall, and professing the doctrines of free salvation and open communion. Their general conference originated in 1827. In 1890 they numbered 1586 churches and about 88,000 members.

Frelinghuysen, Frederick T. (1817–1885), nephew of Theodore, was Senator from New Jersey from 1866 to 1869, and from 1871 to 1877, and a member of the Electoral Commission of 1877. From 1881 to 1885 he was Secretary of State in General Arthur's Cabinet.

Frelinghuysen, Theodore (1787–1861), Senator from New Jersey from 1829 to 1835, was nominated for Vice-President by the Whigs in 1844 on the ticket with Clay, but defeated. From 1839 to 1850 he was chancellor of the University of New York, and from 1850 to his death president of Rutgers College.

Frémont, John Charles (1813–1890), was born in Norfolk, Va., and educated at Charleston, S. C. After a brief service in the navy he joined the U. S. corps of topographical engineers, and married the daughter of Senator Benton. In 1842 he explored a portion of the Rocky Mountains. In 1843 and 1844, with remarkable skill and energy, he conducted an exploration of the regions of Utah, the basin of the Columbia, and the passes of the Sierra Nevada. In 1846, while in conduct of another exploration in California, he assisted in the Bear Flag War, alleging instructions from Washington, co-operated with Commodore Stockton in the conquest of California, but was court-martialed for disobedience to General Kearny. In 1848 he explored, amid great hardships, the paths from Sante Fé to Sacramento, and made a similar expedition in 1853 and 1854. These explorations made him famous as the "Pathfinder," and in 1856 the new Republican party made him its candidate for the Presidency, but was defeated. In 1861 he commanded in Missouri, but, prematurely ordering emancipation, was removed.

In 1862 he commanded against Jackson in the Valley. In 1864 he was nominated for the Presidency by a convention of radical Republicans dissatisfied with Mr. Lincoln. but finally withdrew. A partial autobiography has been published.

French and Indian War (1754–1763), the American phase of the Seven Years' War, and the culminating portion of the struggle between France and England for the possession of North America. In 1754 France claimed the whole region west of the Alleghanies as a part of the basins of the St. Lawrence and the Mississippi. England laid claim to all the country west of its Atlantic settlements. The French colonists numbered only about 80,000 whites, the English more than 1,100,000. But the latter were divided under thirteen discordant governments and were industrial, while the French rule was unified and military, and had help from the Indians. The war began with a struggle for Pittsburgh (Fort Duquesne), Washington attacking the French at Great Meadows and being forced to surrender at Fort Necessity (1754). In 1755 the English planned four attacks: Braddock's expedition against Fort Duquesne, and others by way of Lake Champlain, by way of Oswego and Niagara, and against the French posts near Nova Scotia. The first was disastrous, the second and third accomplished nothing substantial, but the fourth was successful. From 1756 on, the French and Indians being under the command of the able Marquis of Montcalm, the English made no progress until the advent of William Pitt to the head of the ministry in England in 1757. He formed a general scheme of conquest in America. In 1758 Amherst and Wolfe took Louisbourg, Bradstreet captured Fort Frontenac and Forbes took Fort Duquesne. Encouraged by these successes, Pitt undertook the conquest of Canada. In 1759 Amherst took Ticonderoga and Crown Point, while Prideaux took Niagara. But the chief operation of the year was a direct attack upon Quebec, entrusted to General Wolfe, who captured that town, considered impregnable, by means of the battle upon the Plains of Abraham. The French were unable to retake Quebec. Montreal was taken in 1760, and the conquest of Canada was completed. The French empire in North America came to an end. By the peace of Paris (1763) France resigned to England all her possessions east of the Mississippi, and to Spain New Orleans and all her possessions west of that river. To the colonists the war was important as relieving them from the pressure of hostile neighbors, as giving them military experience and as enforcing the necessity of union.

French Creek (near Clayton, N. Y.). General Brown, here entrenched with his division, was attacked November 1, 1813, by a small British fleet. A battery, skillfully handled, drove them back in two engagements. The British loss was severe, the American slight.

French Revolution. The French Revolution began with the meeting of the States General in May, 1789, and continued through the period of the National Assembly and Legislative Assembly and Convention to 1795, or, if the Directory be included, to 1799. It not only started movements of enormous and permanent effect in Europe, but exerted a great influence in America. At first Americans were favorable to it, as to a natural consequence of the American Revolution and a movement in favor of human liberty and progress. But the execution of the king in January, 1793, and the ensuing Reign of Terror increased the conservative feeling against it. It was one of the main matters upon which our first parties were divided, the Federalists opposing it, the Republicans favoring it; with the result that the former seemed to be especially the friends of England, the latter of France, attacking Washington's administration with great vigor on account of his neutrality.

French Spoliation Claims. During the difficulties with France in 1798, which nearly amounted to a state of war, French war-vessels and privateers committed many depredations upon American commerce, and many similar acts had been committed before, in the course of the war between France and Great Britain. The American negotiators in 1798, 1799 and 1800 attempted to obtain redress for these. But in the convention finally negotiated with the First Consul Bonaparte in 1800, it was found necessary to drop the claim. The claims were then made against the U. S. Government by its injured citizens. Bills for their relief were vetoed by Polk in 1846 and Pierce in 1855. In 1885 they were referred to the Court of Claims, before which several thousand such cases have now come.

Frenchtown, now Monroe, in Southeast Michigan, scene of a battle in the War of 1812, on January 22, 1813. The British were driven out of the town on the twentieth by Winchester, commanding the advance of Harrison's forces intended for the reduction of Detroit. On the twenty-second the British, under Colonel Proctor, fell upon Winchester, and compelled him to surrender. Many of the prisoners were massacred by the Indian allies of the British. Hence the affair is sometimes called the Massacre of the River Raisin.

Freneau, Philip (1752–1832), poet, was graduated at Princeton in 1771. He wrote several popular poems during the Revolutionary War, and edited various periodicals. In 1790 he became editor of the *New York Daily Advertiser*. He was soon appointed by Jefferson translator for the State Department, and became editor of the *National Gazette*, in which he abused the Federalists so violently that his official connection with Jefferson led to embarrassing criticisms upon the latter.

Friends, or Quakers. In 1656 Quakers began to come to Massachusetts, where they were imprisoned, banished, and in four cases in which they returned, hanged. Charles II. put a stop to the persecution. George Fox, their founder, visited America in 1671–73. Friends settled largely in Rhode Island, and especially in Pennsylvania, which, founded by a Quaker (Penn), was largely a Quaker colony. New Jersey also was largely settled by Quakers. Everywhere they were thrifty and excellent citizens, though their aversion to war hampered Pennsylvania in making successful defence against the French. They were constantly forward in movements of philanthropy and reform, and had a most important part in the abolition movement. In 1827 occurred a rupture between the "Orthodox" Friends and the Hicksites, or followers of Elias Hicks, the dispute being with regard to the atonement. In 1890 the Friends numbered 107,000.

Fries, John (?1764–?1825), leader of a small insurrection against the U. S. Government in Northampton, Bucks and Montgomery counties, Pa., in the spring of 1799, raised several hundred men in opposition to the direct tax on houses ("window tax"), and at Bethlehem resisted a U. S. Marshal. Convicted of treason in 1799 and again upon a new trial in 1800, he was sentenced to death, but was pardoned by President Adams.

Frobisher, Sir Martin (?1535–1594), an English navigator, in 1576 sailed to find the northwest passage, and discovered Frobisher's Strait. Later he made other voyages toward the northwest and took part in the destruction of the Spanish Armada.

"**Frolic**," brig. (See "Wasp.")

Fromentin, Judge of the western district of Florida in 1821. Callava, the Spanish ex-Governor, applied to him for a writ of *habeas corpus* when he, Callava, was arrested at Andrew Jackson's orders. Fromentin granted the writ. Jackson deemed this contempt and a quarrel followed. Each appealed to the President.

Front Royal, Va., an action in Jackson's Valley campaign, May 23, 1862. Banks lay at Strasburg, with a large detachment at Front Royal under Colonel Kenly. After forced marches Jackson surprised and routed Kenly.

Frontenac, Louis de Buade, Count (1620–1698), Governor of New France, a man of high military reputation, was appointed to that post in 1672. Being a man of violent passions and great self-will he quarreled with the intendant Duchesneau, the priests and the Jesuits, and was recalled in 1682. But in 1689, the colony having fallen into grave difficulties, he was reappointed. He organized the war against the English with great spirit and skill, and sent out in 1690 the expeditions which destroyed Schenectady, N. Y., Salmon Falls, N. H., and Casco, Maine. In the same year he repulsed the attack of Sir William Phips upon Quebec. In 1696 he invaded in person the country of the Iroquois and inflicted upon them a crushing defeat.

Frontenac, Fort, a fort established by Count Frontenac in 1672, on the present site of Kingston, Ontario. Abandoned in 1689, it was reoccupied in 1696. In 1758 it was captured and destroved by Bradstreet, with 3000 men, mostly provincials.

Frontier Posts. The treaty of peace with Great Britain (1783) provided that the boundary of the United States should be Lakes Ontario, Erie, St. Clair, Huron and Superior, and that the British should at once evacuate all posts within the United States. But Great Britain continued to hold the posts on the great lakes, Oswegatchie (now Ogdensburg), Oswego, Niagara, Presque Isle (now Erie), Sandusky, Detroit, Mackinaw, and some others of less importance, on the ground that the American States had not complied with the requirement that debts due to British citizens should be paid. Again their surrender was stipulated in the Jay Treaty, and they were finally given up in June, 1796.

Frothingham, Richard (1812–1880), editor, of Charlestown, Mass., wrote a history of the siege of Boston, published in 1849, and in 1871 published the "Rise of the Republic of the United States."

Fry, James B., born 1827, an officer of the U. S. army, was chief of staff to McDowell and Buell from 1861 to 1863, and from 1863 to 1866 occupied the responsible and difficult post of provost-marshal-general of the army.

Frye, William P., born in 1831, Senator, was Representative from Maine from 1871 to 1881, and was then elected a Senator, which office he has held, as a Republican, to the present time (1894).

Fryeburg, Me., scene of an Indian fight in April, 1725. John Lovewell, after two successful expeditions against the Indians, undertaking a third, was surprised and slain at this place.

Fuca, Juan de, a Greek of Cephalonia, asserted that in 1592, sailing in the Spanish service on the northwest coast of America, he had sailed into a strait in latitude 47° or 48°, which led into the Atlantic Ocean. It has been thought that this was the strait now called by his name, but his narrative is disbelieved by good judges.

Fuca Strait. (See San Juan Arbitration.)

Fugio, also known as Franklin and sun-dial cents, were the earliest copper coins struck off by order of the U. S. Government, from the dies of Abel Buel, in 1787. The first was struck off in New York. Obverse: Thirteen linked rings, making an endless chain. Legend: United States, inscribed around a small central field inclosing inscription, We are one. Reverse: An erect sun-dial, sun appearing above. Legend: Fugio, 1787. Exergue: Mind your business.

Fugitive Slaves, Fugitive Slave Laws. In all the colonies provision was made by law for the arrest and return of fugitive slaves. The articles of confederation between the New England colonies in 1643 provided for mutual restoration between those colonies. Somersett's case prevented extradition from England. The Ordinance for the Northwest Territory provided for return of fugitives thence. The Constitution of 1787 provided that no fugitive slave, fleeing into a free State, should therefore be free, but that he should be delivered up on claim by his owner. In 1793 Congress passed the first Fugitive Slave Act, providing that, on the owner's giving proof of ownership before a magistrate of the locality where the slave was found, the magistrate should order the slave delivered up to him, without trial by jury. Hindering arrest or harboring a runaway slave was punishable by fine of five hundred dollars. The law was open to much abuse. Many free negroes in Northern States were kidnapped. Interference with captures and rescue of arrested negroes became more frequent as anti-slavery feeling increased in the North. In Prigg *vs.* Pennsylvania the Supreme Court held that the law must be carried out by Federal authorities alone; States or State authorities could not be forced to act (1842). Several States then forbade them to do so. The escape of slaves to Canada was extensive, and systematically aided by the Underground Railway. (See art.) In 1850, as a part of the compromise measures of that year, a law was passed providing for a stricter practice in the matter, through U. S. commissioners appointed by the U. S. courts. Proof of identity and two witnesses to the fact of escape were all that was required as evidence. The negro could not testify, nor have jury-trial. Upon this many Northern States passed "Personal Liberty Laws" for the protection of negroes. Some of these conflicted with the Act of 1850 and even with the Constitution. The Act of 1850 aroused great feeling in the North, the "Personal Liberty Laws" in the South. The question of fugitive slaves did much to bring on the Civil War. The war and emancipation ended the whole matter. The acts were repealed in 1864.

Fuller, Margaret, Marchioness of Ossoli (1810–1850), of Cambridge, Mass., a woman of great learning, intellectual gifts and social charm and influence, and a prominent leader among the Transcendentalists, was editor of the *Dial*, their organ, from 1840 to 1842. She took an interesting part in aiding the Italian cause in 1848, and was shipwrecked and drowned off Long Island on her return.

Fuller, Melville W., born in Maine in 1833, was graduated at Bowdoin College in 1853, and was a lawyer in Chicago from 1856 to 1888. In 1862 he was a member of the Illinois Constitutional Convention. In 1888 he was appointed by President Cleveland Chief Justice of the Supreme Court of the United States.

Fulton, Robert (1765–1815), practically the inventor of the steamboat, was born in Pennsylvania. At first a portrait-painter, he went to England in 1786. After a few years he began to occupy himself with engineering and inventions. The subject of steam navigation already interested him. From 1797 to 1804 he resided in France, where, inventing the torpedo, he attempted to induce Napoleon to adopt it, but in vain. In England (1804–06) he had similar want of success with the British Ministry, and in 1806 returned to America. At New York, in 1807, he successfully realized his project of a vessel propelled by steam power, his steamboat, the "Clermont," successfully steaming from New York to Albany. His invention was of the first importance in developing the interior parts of the United States. (See also, for prior inventions, Fitch and Rumsey.)

Fundamental Constitutions of Carolina, an elaborate constitution for that colony, drawn up in 1667 for the proprietors by John Locke, the philosopher. It provided for a territorial aristocracy, the proprietors at the head and two orders of nobility, called landgraves and caciques, below them. These were to have entailed estates called seigniories and baronies. The proprietors were to be respectively palatine, chancellor, chief justice, constable, admiral, treasurer, high steward and chamberlain. There was to be a palatine's court, a grand council and a parliament. Property qualifications prevailed. Some religious liberty was granted. The whole scheme was unsuited to the needs of a pioneer colony, and never went into practical operation.

Fundamental Orders of Connecticut, "the oldest truly political constitution in America" (Bryce), were framed in January, 1639, by the towns of Windsor, Hartford and Wethersfield, uniting to form "one publike State or commonwealth." The orders provided for two general representative assemblies each year, composed of delegates from each town, one for the election of Governor and magistrates, the other for the making of laws.

Funding, the converting of floating debt into debt having a definite time to run before maturity, usually into interest-bearing bonds. The most famous such operation in United States history was that accomplished by the Act of August 4, 1790, suggested by Hamilton, as Secretary of the Treasury. It provided for paying in full not only the foreign and domestic debt of the United States, but also those debts which the States had incurred in the prosecution of the Revolutionary War, by means of six per cent bonds, of which, in the case of the domestic debt, one-third were to be deferred stock, interest beginning to be paid in 1800. (See art. Assumption.)

Fur-trade. This trade, especially that in beaver, was an important element in the economic life of all the colonies in the seventeenth century, and in the struggle between England and France for the possession of North America, also in all negotiations respecting the northwest boundary of the United States. As the trade receded farther and farther to the northwest, the Hudson Bay Company and the Northwest Company, established in 1783 by England, tried to monopolize it. In 1809 John Jacob Astor secured the incorporation of the American Fur Company. He founded Astoria in Oregon, and attempted to connect it with Mackinaw by a line of posts and consolidate the whole northwestern fur-trade. After the War of 1812 he renewed his attempt. In 1816 Congress passed an act excluding foreign fur-traders.

Fuss and Feathers, the army nickname for General Winfield Scott, also used politically when he ran for the Presidency in 1852; due to his punctiliousness as to dress.

G.

Gabriel's Insurrection, an insurrection incited among the negro slaves of the vicinity of Richmond, Va., in 1800, by a slave of Thomas Prosser, called "General Gabriel," and "Jack Bowler." They intended to attack Richmond by night with a thousand negroes and murder the inhabitants. An escaped negro revealed the plot. Governor James Monroe ordered out the militia and attacked the insurgents. The ringleaders were captured and punished.

Gadsden, James (1788–1858), served in the War of 1812, was aide-de-camp to General Jackson in the subjugation of the Seminole Indians, and constructed works for the defense of the Gulf. He was appointed Minister to Mexico in 1853 by President Pierce, and negotiated the Gadsden Treaty, which secured the purchase of the southern portion of Arizona and New Mexico.

Gadsden Treaty was a treaty negotiated with Mexico in 1853 by James Gadsden. By this treaty the United States secured 45,000 square miles of land in what is now Arizona and New Mexico. The United States paid Mexico $10,000,000, but received a considerably larger amount from Mexico for Indian depredation claims.

Gage, Thomas (1721–1787), came to America in 1754 in command of a regiment accompanying Braddock's expedition. He was appointed Governor of Montreal in 1760, and from 1763 to 1772 was commander-in-chief in America. In 1774 he was appointed Governor of Massachusetts, and attempted to subdue the antagonism of the colonists to English rule. In 1775 he sent troops to destroy stores collected at Concord, and this led to the battle of Lexington. The colonists refused to recognize Gage as Governor, and soon after the battle of Bunker Hill he resigned his commission.

Gag-rule. A rule adopted by Congress in January, 1836, on motion of John C. Calhoun. Congress had long been besieged by petitions from abolitionists all over the country. Calhoun proposed that henceforth all anti-slavery petitions be laid on the table unnoticed. This infringement upon the right of petition only increased the petition spirit in the North, and the "gag-rule" was, after a long struggle, abolished December 3, 1844. John Quincy Adams was its bitterest opponent and an ardent upholder of anti-slavery principles in Congress during ten years.

Gaillard, John (1765–1826), born in South Carolina, served in the U. S. Senate from 1805 to 1826, and was president *pro tempore* in every Congress from the eleventh to the eighteenth inclusive.

Gaines, Edmund P. (1777–1849), served during the War of 1812, and was promoted major-general for services in defense of Fort Erie in 1814. He was commissioner to the Seminole Indians in 1816, and took command against them in 1817.

Gaines, Myra Clark (1805–1885), wife of Edmund P. Gaines, was for many years plaintiff in an extraordinary lawsuit to recover the estate of her father, Daniel Clark. Her claim included much valuable property in New Orleans, estimated at $35,000,000.

Gaines' Mills, or Chickahominy, Va., June 27, 1862. In this engagement of the Civil War, Porter, commanding 20,000 troops of McClellan's army, was defeated by Lee with a Confederate force of 35,000. On the morning of June 27, Porter fell back to a range of low hills, and there repelled the Confederate attack until 5000 more men were sent him by McClellan. Meantime Jackson had joined Lee with 25,000 fresh troops. A. P. Hill first attacked Porter's position, and was driven back with great loss after a two hours' struggle. Then Jackson came up and joined the attack. Porter, having no intrenchments, was forced to give way before the superior numbers. He crossed the Chickahominy in rapid retreat, and burned the bridges behind him.

Gales, Joseph (1786–1860), an editor of the *Nationa Intelligencer* from 1807 to 1860 in partnership with W. W. Seaton, published valuable reports of proceedings in Congress, which would otherwise be unavailable—the "Annals of Congress," in forty-two volumes.

Gallatin, Albert (January 29, 1761–August 12, 1849), was born at Geneva, Switzerland, and is one of the most illustrious American statesmen of foreign birth. He was educated at the university of his native city, and emigrated to America in 1780. After varied experiences he settled as a manufacturer

STATESMEN OF THE EARLY REPUBLIC.

DeWitt Clinton. Timothy Pickering. Albert Galatin. Josiah Quincy. Alexander Hamilton.
Rufus King. Gouverneur Morris. Charles C. Pinckney. John Randolph.

in Pennsylvania in 1784. By 1790 he was in the Legislature. His rise to State and national prominence as a leader in the Democratic-Republican party was rapid. He was elected U. S. Senator in 1793, but was not admitted to his seat. The following year he helped by his influence to suppress the Whiskey Insurrection. From 1795 to 1801 he was a member from Pennsylvania of the National House of Representatives, and took a leading part almost from the start, especially on financial topics. When his party came into power with Jefferson, Gallatin was invited to take the Treasury portfolio. He filled this position from 1801 to 1813, and has passed into history as one of the ablest of American financiers. In 1813–14 he was peace commissioner in Europe, where his services in negotiating the Treaty of Ghent were conspicuous. He was U. S. Minister to France 1816–1823, and in 1826 he was sent as Envoy Extraordinary to Great Britain. He was later a bank president in New York City, and died at Astoria on Long Island. Gallatin published various pamphlets on finance, on the Oregon question, on the war with Mexico, "Considerations on the Currency and Banking System of the United States" (1831); he was moreover an ethnologist, and published "Synopsis of the Indian Tribes" (1836) and other works. Biography by Henry Adams, who has also edited his writings.

Gallaudet, Thomas H. (1787–1851), was the first to undertake in America the instruction of deaf mutes (1817), and founded at Hartford an institution for that purpose.

Gallipolis, O., was settled by French refugees in 1789. It was a depot of supplies during the Civil War.

Galloway, Joseph (1729–1803), was Speaker of the Pennsylvania Assembly from 1766 to 1774, proposed a form of government favorable to the crown at the Provincial Congress in 1774, and joined the British forces in 1776.

Galveston, Tex., was first settled in 1816, but first permanently settled in 1838. From 1817 to 1821 it was the haunt of the famous pirate Lafitte.

Galvez, Bernardo de (1755–1786), count, was born in Spain, became colonel in Louisiana in 1776 and was Governor from 1777 to 1783. He aided the colonies against the British in the Revolutionary War and was made Viceroy of Mexico in 1785.

Gamble, Hamilton R. (1798–1864), was Secretary of State in Missouri in 1824, a Judge of the Supreme Court from 1851 to 1855, was appointed Governor of the State in 1861 by the Constitutional Convention and served until 1864.

Gananoqui (near Thousand Islands, Can.). Here Captain Forsyth, with slight loss, captured, on September 20, 1812, a large supply of ammunition and provisions from the British, whose loss was ten killed and twelve taken prisoners.

Gansevoort, Peter (1749–1812), born in New York, accompanied Montgomery to Canada in 1775; withstood the British and Indians at Fort Schuyler in 1777; was appointed Indian Commissioner and promoted brigadier-general in 1809.

Gardoqui, Don Diego de, was Minister of Spain to the United States from 1785 to 1789, and negotiated concerning the Mississippi with Secretary Jay.

Garfield, James Abram (November 19, 1831–September 19, 1881), twentieth President of the United States, was born at Orange, Cuyahoga County, O., and after miscellaneous experiences, including work on a canal tow-path, he entered Hiram College in Ohio. From there he went to Williams College, and graduated in 1856. For a short time he taught the classics in Hiram College, and in 1857 became the president of that institution. Two years later he entered the State Senate. In the opening year of the war he was appointed lieutenant-colonel of volunteers; having been entrusted with a small independent command he routed the Confederates at Middle Creek, Ky., January 10, 1862. He was made a brigadier-general, served at Shiloh, etc., and became chief of staff in Rosecrans' Army of the Cumberland. In this capacity he rendered important services, and was made major-general after Chickamauga. He had been already elected to Congress, and took his seat in December, 1863. From this time he served continuously and was one of the leading debaters and orators on the Republican side. He was member of important committees, like Military Affairs and Ways and Means, and was chairman of the Committee on Banking and Currency and on Appropriations. General Garfield served on the Electoral Commission of 1877 and was elected U. S. Senator from Ohio in 1880. The same year he attended the National Convention, and on the thirty-sixth ballot received the nomination, through the influence of Blaine. Entering office March 4, 1881, he chose Blaine for the State Department, Windom for the Treasury, and R. T. Lincoln for War. He became almost immediately involved in the Republican factional quarrels of New York. His appointment of the "Half-Breed" Robertson to the collectorship of New York caused the "Stalwart" Senators, Conkling and Platt, to resign and demand a "vindication." In the midst of these proceedings President Garfield was shot at Washington, July 2, by a fanatic, Guiteau. He lingered through the summer, was removed in September to Elberon, New Jersey, and there passed away. Life by J. R. Gilmore.

Garfield, Lucretia R., born in Hiram, O., in 1832, became the wife of James A. Garfield in 1858. Her name became famous by reason of her husband's Presidency, and of her care over him during his long period of suffering from his mortal wound.

Garland, Augustus H., was born in Tennessee in 1832. He opposed secession in the State Convention in 1861, but served in the Confederate Congress till the close of the war. He won the famous test-oath case in 1866, and in 1874 was chosen Governor of Arkansas. He served in the U. S. Senate from 1876 to 1885, and was Attorney-General in Cleveland's Cabinet from 1885 to 1889.

Garland, Hugh A. (1805–1854), a Virginia Assemblyman for five years, was clerk of the U. S. House of Representatives from 1838 to 1841. He secured a Democratic majority at the opening session, in 1839, by omitting the names of the contested New Jersey delegates. (See Broad Seal War.)

Garland's Case, an important case decided by the U. S. Supreme Court in 1866. In 1860 A. H. Garland, of Arkansas, was admitted to the Supreme Court of the United States as attorney and counselor, taking the oath then required. In 1862 Congress passed an act requiring all candidates for office to take oath that they had never in any way engaged in hostility against the Union. In 1865 all persons admitted to the bar of the U. S. Courts were required to take this oath. Garland participated in the war against the Union, but was freely pardoned. He entered a plea before the Supreme Court in 1866 against his taking the prescribed oath of 1865, saying it was unconstitutional and void as affecting his status in court, and that his pardon released him from compliance with it, even if it were constitutional. His plea was granted by the court, on the ground that the act was *ex post facto.*

Garner Case (1856), the saddest of many noted fugitive slave cases. Simeon Garner, his son and their families escaped from Kentucky to Cincinnati. They were pursued and after a desperate struggle captured. Margaret Garner, in order to save her children from slavery, had attempted to kill them during the struggle, and one was found dead when the fugitives were captured. The courts decided upon returning the slaves. On their way back to Kentucky Margaret made an unsuccessful attempt to drown herself and child.

Garnett, Robert S. (1819–1861), born in Virginia, was a Democratic Representative from Virginia from 1817 to 1827. He voted alone against the recognition of the South American Republics. Commanding Confederate forces in West Virginia, he was defeated and killed at Carrick's Ford in 1861.

Garrison, William Lloyd (1805–1879), was born in Massachusetts. He began his career in the employ of the *Newburyport Herald* in 1818, making anonymous contributions reproving the general apathy on the subject of slavery. Between 1826 and 1831 he edited various emancipation papers, among them the *Herald*, *Free Press*, *National Philanthropist*, *Journal of the Times* and the *Genius of Universal Emancipation.* He also delivered series of lectures in the interest of emancipation. From 1831 to 1860 he edited the *Liberator*, which exerted an immense influence against slavery. In 1832 the American Anti-Slavery Society was formed and organized by him, and soon afterward he became its president. His efforts for the abolition of slavery were unceasing until the emancipation proclamation of President Lincoln had gone into effect. His influence in the anti-slavery cause was greater than that of any other man. Life by his sons, four volumes.

Gas-light was first successfully introduced into Boston in 1822, into New York in 1823, into Philadelphia in 1835.

"Gaspee." During the spring of 1772 the British armed schooner "Gaspee" remained in Narragansett Bay and annoyed the inhabitants along the coast by excessive zeal in the suppression of smuggling. Chief Justice Hopkins, of Rhode Island, sent a sheriff on board to know by what authority Dudingston, her commander, acted, and found he was upheld by the British admiral. June 9, the "Gaspee" gave chase to the "Providence," a small packet, and ran aground near Pawtuxet. That night a party of citizens attacked her, wounded and captured Dudingston and the crew, and burned the "Gaspee." Efforts to bring the perpetrators to justice failed.

Gates, Horatio (1728–1806), general, born in England, came to America in 1755, and was a captain in Braddock's expedition. At the outbreak of the Revolution he was appointed adjutant-general in the colonial army, and in 1777 commanded the Northern forces and gained a decisive victory over the British at Saratoga. Highly honored for this success he overestimated his abilities and conspired to gain chief command of the colonial army, but his schemes were disclosed. In 1780 he was placed in command of the Southern army, and met with a severe defeat at Camden. He was retired from command, and was not acquitted by court-martial from blame for this defeat until 1782.

Gates, Sir Thomas, was appointed lieutenant-general under the Virginia Company, and came to Virginia in 1609 with seven ships. The colony did not prosper, and Gates was sent to England in 1610, returning with men and provisions in 1611. He assumed the government, and the colony became more prosperous under his rule. which continued till 1614, when he returned to England.

Gatling, Richard J., was born in North Carolina in 1818. He has invented various labor-saving devices, but is best known as inventor of the revolving battery-gun bearing his name, which is capable of firing 1200 shots per minute.

Gay, Sydney Howard (1814–1888), born in Massachusetts, edited the *Anti-Slavery Standard* from 1844 to 1857, when he became an editor of the *Tribune*, serving as such until 1866. He is the author of an illustrated history of the United States.

Gayarré, Charles E. A., born in 1805, served in the Louisiana Legislature, was Secretary of State for seven years, and is the author of numerous historical works, chiefly histories of Louisiana in various periods.

Geary, John W. (1819–1873), commanded at Chapultepec in 1846, was prominent in California politics from 1849 to 1852, was Governor of Kansas 1856–57, and during the Rebellion won distinction at Bolivar Heights, Cedar Mountain and Lookout Mountain, being promoted major-general. He was Governor of Pennsylvania from 1866 to 1873.

General. This grade was first created by Act of Congress March 3, 1799, and General Washington was appointed to fill it. The office was abolished in 1802. It was not revived again until 1866, when General Grant was appointed. On the election of Grant to the Presidency, William T. Sherman succeeded him in the grade of general. On the retirement of General Sherman, November 1, 1883, the office again became extinct. It was revived for a brief time (June to August, 1888), for Lieutenant-General Philip H. Sheridan. Since his death in 1888 the office has ceased to exist, as has that of lieutenant-general.

Genêt, Edmond C. (1765–1834), was born in France. He was appointed Minister to the United States in 1792, and arrived in Charleston, S. C., in 1793. He immediately took steps to induce the United States to aid France in her troubles with Great Britain, and unlawfully commissioned privateers from American ports. The executive had determined upon neutrality. Genêt succeeded for a time in arousing enthusiasm among the people of the United States, and acted so imprudently that Washington's administration requested his recall in 1794. He was afterward naturalized and became a citizen of the United States.

Geneva Arbitration. A tribunal of arbitration assembled at Geneva in Switzerland, December 15, 1871, to arbitrate upon the "Alabama" claims. (See art.) The tribunal consisted of Count Federigo Sclopis, of Italy; Viscount Itajuba, of Brazil; Mr. Jacques Staempfli, of Switzerland; Charles Francis Adams, of the United States, and Sir Alexander Cockburn, of England. The tribunal decided that an award of compensation for the "indirect claims" advanced by America was not in keeping with the principles of international law. This preliminary decision was accepted. The tribune also decided that Great Britain had not exercised due diligence in preventing the construction, equipment and provisioning of such ships as the "Alabama;" that $15,500,000 should be awarded in a gross sum to the United States, but no compensation should be made for the pursuit of cruisers or for prospective earnings.

Geneva Convention. A convention was concluded in 1864 for the amelioration of the condition of the wounded in armies in the field, between Switzerland, Baden, Belgium, Denmark, Spain, France, Hesse, Italy, Netherlands, Portugal, Prussia and Württemberg, and acceded to by most civilized nations, including the United States. Additional articles in 1868 extended to naval forces the advantages of the previous convention.

Gentry, Meredith P. (1809–1866), served in the North Carolina Legislature from 1835 to 1839, was a U. S. Congressman from 1839 to 1843 and from 1845 to 1853, and served in the Confederate Congress in 1862 and 1863.

Geographer of the United States, an office created by the Act of May 20, 1785. The geographer's duties consisted in the supervision of surveys and in the transmission to the Board of Treasury of the series of plats whenever the seven ranges of townships had been surveyed.

Geological Survey. The U. S. Geological Survey was established by Congress in March, 1879, as a bureau of the Department of the Interior. The interior surveys, topographical and geological, heretofore carried on by other Government agencies, were confided to it.

George I. (1660–1727), King of Great Britain and Elector of Brunswick, ascended the English throne in 1715, and ruled uneventfully over England and the colonies for twelve years.

George II. (1683–1760), King of Great Britain from 1727 to 1760, granted in 1732 a tract of country from the reserved Carolina tract to James Oglethorpe and a company formed by him. The government of the colony was to be conducted by the proprietors during twenty years, and after that time the form of government was to be decided by the king. In 1749 George II. granted to the Ohio Company, formed by certain wealthy Virginians, 500,000 acres of land, on which they were to plant 100 families, and were to build and maintain a fort. (See King George's War, Seven Years' War, French and Indian War.) His reign is chiefly memorable in American history for the conquest of Canada.

George III. (1738–1820), son of Frederick, Prince of Wales, succeeded to the throne of England in 1760. His obstinate determination to increase the royal authority had much to do with the provoking of American resistance. At the outbreak of the Revolution he insisted merely upon maintaining the right to tax the colonies, but when they showed persistent determination he became exasperated and wrote, "Every means of distressing America must meet with my concurrence." Under his direction the war was prosecuted with vigor and he reluctantly consented to peace in 1782. He was kind-hearted, upright and truthful, with a very forcible character, but was narrow-minded and obstinate.

George, Henry, born in Philadelphia in 1839, is well known as a writer upon economics. He published various newspapers in California from 1858 to 1879. He first became prominent through his work, "Progress and Poverty," which advocates a common ownership of land to be brought about by taxing land to the full amount of the rent. He is the author of "Social Problems," "Protection or Free Trade," etc.

George, James Z., born in 1826, signed the Mississippi ordinance of secession in 1861 and was a U. S. Senator from Mississippi from 1881 to the present time (1894).

George, Fort (Niagara River). In the War of 1812, after the capture of York by the Americans, they moved against Fort George. On May 27, 1813, the troops were landed under cover of the guns of the fleet. The attack, led by Colonel Winfield Scott and Commodore Perry, was successful. The British, after spiking the guns and destroying the ammunition, abandoned the fort. Soon after, Forts Erie and Chippewa were likewise abandoned, and the whole Niagara frontier passed into the hands of the Americans.

George, Fort, the name given by the French to Fort William Henry. (See William Henry, Fort.)

Georgetown College, D. C., was founded as a college by the Jesuits in 1789 and chartered as a university in 1815.

Georgia, one of the original thirteen States, was founded by Oglethorpe in 1733 as a refuge for debtors. The territory was originally claimed by the Spanish Government, who explored it. In 1663 it constituted a part of the Carolinas, but in 1732 it was set apart and given to James Oglethorpe and others, to be held in trust for twenty-one years. The territory was styled Georgia in honor of George II., and included the land between the Savannah and the Altamaha and the South Sea. The colony was expected to serve as a protection to the Carolinas against the Spaniards of Florida. In 1752 Georgia became a royal colony. In 1763 the southern boundary was extended to St. Mary's River and the western boundary to the Mississippi. The State suffered greatly from war and disorder during the Revolution. The first Constitution was made in 1777; the present in 1868. January 2, 1788, Georgia unanimously ratified the National Constitution. In 1798 the western territory of the State was organized into the Mississippi Territory by the U. S. Government. Georgia's claims were satisfied in 1802 by the payment on the part of the United States of $1,250,000, and the promise to purchase for Georgia the claims of the Indians to lands within the State. In 1795 occurred the "Yazoo fraud," by which the western territory was sold to land companies. The sale was afterward repealed, and the landholders were compensated by the National Government. The State authorities demanded the fulfillment of the promise of 1802 relative to the Indian removal, but not until 1826 did the General Government succeed in obtaining the Georgian lands of the Creeks. The Creeks, however, refused to move, and were protected by the decision of the U. S. Supreme Court. The Indians were eventually driven out by the authorities of Georgia, as President Jackson refused to support the decision of the court. Georgia seceded January 19, 1861. During the war Confederate prisons were established at Andersonville and Millen. General Sherman, marching through Georgia, captured Atlanta, September 2, 1864, and Savannah, December 21. The reconstruction of the State was delayed until July, 1870, because of the refusal to extend the suffrage to the blacks. Since reconstruction the State has been uniformly Democratic. The population of the State in 1790 was 82,548; in 1890 it was 1,837,353. Histories by Jones and by Stevens.

"Georgia," an iron steamboat built at Glasgow in 1863 and used as a Confederate cruiser. She sailed from Glasgow in April, 1863, under the name of the "Japan." She destroyed a large number of Union merchant ships along the French coast, and then sailed for England, where it was given out she was to be chartered by the Portuguese Government. She was nevertheless seized, August 15, 1863, by Captain Craven, commanding the United States ship "Niagara," and returned to England.

"Georgia Gazette," first newspaper printed in Georgia. It was established at Savannah by James Johnston, April 17, 1763, and continued until 1802, when its publication was suspended.

Georgia Historical Society, founded at Savannah in 1839. It has published four volumes of papers and part of a fifth. At the instance of the society Bishop Stevens undertook his "History of Georgia." It possesses many valuable manuscripts.

Gerard, Conrad A., died in 1790. He was the first French Minister to the United States. Having negotiated the treaty between France and the United States, he came to America in 1778, returned in 1779, and was active in the negotiations with Great Britain in 1782.

Germaine, Lord George (1716–1785), was appointed colonial secretary by George III. of England in 1775, and superintended the conduct of the British forces during the Revolutionary War. He advocated vigorous measures against the colonies, enlisted the services of the Six Nations, and was influential in the bribery of Benedict Arnold. Resigned in 1782.

German Empire. One treaty of importance has been concluded between the United States and the new German Empire, that to define the rights, privileges and duties of consular agents, and to establish an agreement upon trade-marks (1871). A reciprocity treaty was concluded in 1892.

Germans. There were more Germans in Pennsylvania than in any other of the colonies. Penn encouraged their immigration. They were largely of sects persecuted in Germany. They were averse to war and indifferent to politics, but had important influence on the development of manufactures. Palatine, Moravian and other Germans were also settled in large numbers in Maryland, New York, Virginia and the Carolinas, and Salzburgers in Georgia. They were sober and industrious. In the Revolution they were in general not active. Of immigrants into the United States since 1820, more than one-third have been Germans. The revolutionary movements of 1848 caused the emigration of large numbers to the United States.

Germantown, Battle of, October 4, 1777. Howe after occupying Philadelphia sent a considerable detachment down the river to seize Forts Mercer and Mifflin. When Washington learned of this he determined to crush the British at Germantown. In the early morning of October 4 his army in two columns, the centre under Sullivan, the left under Greene, advanced upon the village. The central column drove in the British outposts and was forcing back the British line opposite. Greene also was driving the right back when an accident happened to destroy the whole plan. Stephen, who was upon the right of Greene's division, came on through the heavy fog, and mistaking the American left-centre for the enemy, charged upon them. This at once caused a panic and the battle was lost. However, the troops retreated in good order before Cornwallis, who had hurried from Philadelphia with two battalions. The Americans lost 673, the British 575.

Geronimo, a chief of the Chiricahuas of the Apache tribe of Indians. He was captured by General Miles in 1886 for making depredations, and was placed under surveillance at Fort Perkins, Florida.

Gerry, Elbridge (1744–1814), Vice-President, born in Massachusetts, was a member of the Massachusetts colonial House of Representatives from 1772 to 1775 and a delegate to the Continental Congress from 1776 to 1780 and from 1783 to 1785. He signed the Declaration of Independence and aided in framing the Constitution, but refused to sign it, believing that too great powers were delegated to the National Government. He was elected a Representative from Massachusetts to the first U. S. Congress in 1789 and served till 1793. He was a special commissioner to France in 1797 with Pinckney and Marshall, and was elected Governor of Massachusetts in 1810 and 1811. He was elected Vice-President of the United States in 1812 as a Democrat and served until his death (1813–1814). Life by Austin.

Gerrymander, an arrangement of the boundaries of election districts so contrived as to secure an unfair advantage to the dominant party. In colonial times elections were by counties or by towns, and the gerrymander was not developed. The first gerrymander has been said to be an arrangement of Patrick Henry's, whereby Madison should not be elected to the First

Congress. But in reality the districting of Virginia at that time was not clearly unfair. The name arose from a redistricting scheme carried out by the Republicans of Massachusetts in 1811, in accordance with which the Essex District bore a fanciful resemblance to a salamander. Hence the name "gerrymander" was given to it from Governor Elbridge Gerry, under whom the act was passed. The practice has since become well-nigh universal in American politics, with most injurious effects upon public morality.

Getty, George W., born in 1819, was promoted major-general for gallantry during the Civil War, serving in the Virginia campaign and having a command at Yorktown, Antietam, Fredericksburg and the Wilderness. He defended Washington, and served in the Shenandoah campaign. He retired in 1883.

Gettysburg, Pa., a memorable battle of the Civil War, considered the turning point of the struggle between the Confederates and Federals. The Confederates numbering 80,000, under Lee, were defeated by about an equal number of National soldiers, led by Meade. The battle occurred July 1–3, 1863. Lee, having pushed thus far in his great invasion of the North, lay at Chambersburg awaiting the results of disturbances among the "Copperhead" faction in the Northern cities. Ewell was posted between York and Carlisle with a strong Confederate force. Longstreet's columns and Stuart's cavalry were also separated from the main Confederate command. Meade had just taken command of the National troops, vice Hooker, resigned, had ordered the evacuation of Harper's Ferry, and contemplated a concentration of his forces at Pipe Creek, fifteen miles from Gettysburg, hoping to offer battle to Lee at that place. The absence of Stuart's cavalry prevented Lee from ascertaining the strength of the Nationals. Meade's plans of battle at Pipe Creek were frustrated, July 1, by an attack by the Confederates upon Reynolds' division at Gettysburg. Reynolds, though supported by Buford's cavalry, was routed and killed. The fighting became general. Ewell's and Longstreet's columns had arrived, and Meade sent Howard to assume command of the National field. Howard placed his forces upon the right, extending his line beyond the town to the north. This line was broken in the centre by Lee's repeated charges, but not without severe losses to the Confederates. Hancock arrived and rallied the Federals, placing his line along Round Top and Little Round Top, two strong positions. The National line now was, beginning with the right: Slocum's, Howard's, Hancock's and Sykes', with Sedgwick in reserve. The bloodiest fighting of the day, July 2, was between Vincent's and Hood's men on Little Round Top. The battles of the first two days were indecisive. Meade began the attack, July 3, by driving Ewell from his position on Rock Creek. Then followed Pickett's disastrous charge upon Cemetery Ridge, in which nearly 14,000 Confederates were killed. Lee was obliged to retreat. The Nationals lost 23,190, the Confederates nearly 30,000 and 7000 Confederates were left unburied. Many generals were killed on both sides.

Ghent, Treaty of, a treaty of peace concluded between British and American commissioners, assembled at Ghent in 1814. Clay, Adams, Gallatin, Bayard and Russell represented the United States. The treaty was concluded December 24, 1814, and was ratified early in 1815. It provided for universal peace between the belligerents; the mutual restoration of territory, property and archives; a cessation of hostilities immediately upon ratification; a restoration of prisoners of war; an establishment of the disputed northeastern boundary by construction of the treaty of 1783, with possible final reference to some friendly power; other boundary questions to be disposed of in a similar manner; and a mutual promotion of the abolition of the slave trade. Nothing was said of the impressment of seamen, the search of American vessels, and the oppressive decrees respecting neutral commerce the three grievances which mainly caused the war.

Gherardi, Bancroft, born in 1832, nephew of George Bancroft, entered the navy in 1846, was made lieutenant-commander in 1862, and in command of the "Port Royal" distinguished himself at Mobile Bay. He became a commodore in 1884, and a rear-admiral in 1886.

Gibbon, John, born in 1827, served during the Mexican War, and in the Civil War, on the Federal side, taking part in the battles of South Mountain, Antietam, Fredericksburg, Chancellorsville, Gettysburg and the Wilderness. He is author of an essay on "Our Indian Question."

Gibbons, James, Roman Catholic prelate, born in Maryland in 1834, ordained a priest in 1861, became Archbishop of Baltimore in 1877, and was confirmed cardinal in 1886.

Gibbons vs. Ogden, an important case in the U. S. Supreme Court. Aaron Ogden, having obtained by assignment the exclusive right of navigation of all waters within the jurisdiction of the State of New York, granted by that State to Livingston and Fulton for thirty years, beginning 1808, filed a bill in the Court of Chancery of New York for an injunction against one Gibbons, of New Jersey, who possessed two steamboats running between New York and Elizabethtown, N. J. The injunction was granted. Gibbons appealed to the Supreme Court in 1824. The court gave judgment for the appellant, it being deemed that the granting of exclusive navigation of waters within the State of New York by that State's Legislature, extending to coastwise traffic with another State, was repugnant to the clause of the Constitution of the United States authorizing Congress to regulate commerce.

Gibson, Randall L. (1832–1892), Senator, entered the Confederate army as a private, and rose to various commands at Shiloh, Murfreesboro and Chickamauga. He represented Louisiana in the U. S. Congress from 1875 to 1883, and in the Senate from 1883 to 1892.

Giddings, Joshua R. (1795–1864), was born in Pennsylvania. He served in the Ohio militia during the War of 1812, after which he studied law and was admitted to the bar in 1820. He was elected to the State Legislature in 1826, and was a Representative from Ohio in the U. S. Congress from 1838 to 1859, during which time he was prominent as an advocate of the right of petition and one of the foremost opponents of slavery. In 1842 he was censured by the House of Representatives for his advocacy of anti-slavery measures. He at once resigned, and was triumphantly re-elected.

In 1861 he was appointed Consul-General in Canada, and in 1864 published a history of the Rebellion.

Gilbert, Sir Humphrey (1539–1584), English navigator, half brother of Sir Walter Raleigh, sought to discover a northwest passage to India, and wrote a treatise on the subject. In 1578 he made an expedition which met with no success. In 1583 he planted a colony at Newfoundland which did not prosper. On his return he was lost at sea.

Giles, William B. (1762–1830), represented Virginia in the U. S. Congress from 1790 to 1799, 1801 to 1803, and in the Senate from 1804 to 1815. In 1826 he was a member of the Virginia Legislature, and was Governor of the State from 1826 to 1829. He was a skillful parliamentary leader.

Gillmore, Quincy A. (1825–1888), was born in Ohio. He was graduated at the U. S. Military Academy in 1849, was chief of engineers in the Port Royal expedition in 1861, superintended the attack on Fort Pulaski, defeated the Confederates at Somerset in 1862, commanded at Fort Sumter, Fort Wagner and Morris Island, and was promoted major-general for services at Charleston. He was an authority in engineering subjects.

Gilman, Arthur, born in Illinois in 1837, in 1876 established the "Harvard Annex," of which he has since been executive officer. He has contributed largely to historical study.

Gilman, Daniel C., born in 1831, one of the foremost of American educators, was associated with Yale College from 1856 to 1872, and was president of the University of California from 1872 to 1875, since which time he has been president of the Johns Hopkins University.

Gilman, Nicholas (1755–1814), promoted adjutant-general during the Revolution, was a New Hampshire delegate to the Continental Congress from 1786 to 1788, a U. S. Representative from 1789 to 1797, and a Senator from 1805 to 1814.

Gilmer, Thomas W., died in 1844, was Governor of Virginia from 1840 to 1841. He was a U. S. Democratic Congressman from 1841 to 1844. He was Secretary of the Navy in Tyler's Cabinet in 1844, and was killed in the "Princeton" disaster.

Gilmore, James R., born in Massachusetts in 1823, at the beginning of the Civil War published influential novels portraying Southern life.

Gilpin, Henry D. (1801–1860), was U. S. attorney for Pennsylvania in 1832, solicitor of the U. S. Treasury in 1837, and Attorney-General for the United States from 1840 to 1841, and was deeply interested in historical work. He edited the papers of James Madison, 1840.

Girard, Stephen (1750–1831), was born in France, but came to Philadelphia about 1776. He amassed an immense fortune by commercial enterprises and speculation during financial crises. During the War of 1812 he greatly aided the Government by a loan of $5,000,000. He was rigidly frugal and inhospitable in private life, but very generous in public affairs, giving large sums for public and charitable purposes. He founded Girard College for orphans at Philadelphia.

Girty, Simon (1750?–1815), a Kentucky loyalist who led the Indians in their depredations during the Revolutionary War and in the War of 1812, committing many atrocious deeds.

Gist, Mordecai (1743–1792), was elected captain of the first Maryland company in the Revolutionary War, fought at Camden in 1780, and gained a victory over the British at Combahee in 1782.

Glass. The first mention of the manufacture of glass in the United States is in Captain John Smith's "History of Virginia," in which he speaks of a glass factory having been founded at Jamestown in 1615, and a second in 1622. The work was coarse, being chiefly confined to bottles. In 1754, a successful factory was established in Brooklyn by Bamper, a Dutchman. In 1779, factories were founded at Temple, N. H., and in 1795 the industry was begun at Pittsburgh. By 1813 there were five glass factories, valued at $160,000, at Pittsburgh. In 1840 there were eighty-one factories in the States, having a capital of $2,014,100. By 1870, 201 factories flourished in different places, having a total capital of $14,111,642. Since then the industry has rapidly increased.

Glazier, Willard, born in 1841, a lieutenant in the Civil War, was confined in Southern prisons from 1863 to 1864, and wrote "Capture, Prison-Pen and Escape," a popular account of his experiences.

Glendale, or Frayser's Farm, Va., a battle in the Peninsular campaign of the Civil War, occurring June 30, 1863. McClellan's army had just emerged from White Oak Swamp, where had also been a fierce battle with Jackson's troops. Hill and Longstreet fell upon the Federal rear and there was terrific fighting all the afternoon. McCall's division of the Federals fared worst and that leader was captured. Darkness ended this indecisive battle. This fight is also called Nelson's Farm and Charles City Cross-Roads.

"Globe," a newspaper established at Washington by Francis P. Blair in 1830, and succeeding the *U. S. Telegraph* as the official organ of Jackson's administration. Later as the *Congressional Globe* it became the publisher of official debates, and is now continued as the *Congressional Record*, published by Congress.

Globe, Congressional. A continuation of the "Register of Debates," containing in 108 volumes a verbatim report of Congressional proceedings, debates and laws from 1837 to 1872. Its place was then taken by the *Congressional Record.*

Gnadenhütten, a settlement of Indians, christianized by the Moravians, made in 1783. It was situated on the Muskingum River. For many years this village and the sister settlements of Salem and Schönbrunn were peaceful and prosperous. In 1781 Matthew Elliott, leading 300 whites and Hurons, appeared at Gnadenhütten and urged the missionaries and Indians to depart to Sandusky. They did so, but returned the next year. Another troop of soldiers, frontiersmen and savages, under Colonel Williamson, and without civil or military authority, appeared, and brutally butchered the entire tribe, destroying their thriving village.

Godkin, Edwin L., born in England in 1831, came to America in 1856. In 1865 he established the *Nation*, and since 1881 has been an editor of the *Evening Post*.

"God-Speed," a vessel sent in 1602 with the "Discovery" by the East India Company on a voyage of exploration toward Greenland. She was afterward sent with the "Susan Constant" and the "Discovery" with colonists to Virginia in 1606 by the Virginia Company.

Godwin, Parke, born in 1816, was connected with the *New York Evening Post* from 1837 to 1853, contributed largely to the *Democratic Review*, and published political, biographical and historical works, especially a history of France to 843 A. D.

Goff, Nathan, born in 1843, was promoted major during the Civil War, and was elected to the West Virginia Legislature in 1867. He was State District Attorney from 1868 to 1881, Secretary of the Navy in 1881 and a U. S. Congressman from 1884 to 1890.

Goffe, William (1605–1679), regicide, was born in England. He became a major-general in the English army, was one of the judges who sentenced Charles I. to death, and was prominent in political affairs during the Protectorate. Upon the return of Charles II., he fled to America in 1660, landing at Boston. He was concealed in New Haven from 1661 to 1664, when he went to Hadley, Mass., where he remained until just before his death.

Gold. The first law affecting the coinage of gold into lawful money was enacted April 2, 1792. By this law any person could have gold bullion converted into coin eleven parts pure to one part alloy. Its ratio to silver was fifteen to one, and gold coins were legal tender to any amount. In March, 1795, a charge of four cents per ounce was made for coining gold bullion below the standard. Under the law of April 21, 1800, a sum was retained for coining gold below the standard. January 18, 1837, the standard gold coin was made nine-tenths pure and one-tenth alloy. February 21, 1853, it was enacted that gold coins were to be exchanged for silver coins at par in sums not exceeding $100, and a charge of one-half per cent was made for refining. February 12, 1873, it was enacted that one-fifth of one per cent was to be charged for coining standard gold. By the law of January 14, 1875, no charge was to be made for converting standard gold bullion into coin. For the history of the individual coins, see Double Eagle, Eagle, Half Eagle, Three-Dollar Piece, Quarter Eagle and Dollar.

Gold, Production of. Up to 1830 the amount of gold produced in the United States was exceedingly small. In the next two decades an annual average of $700,000 was obtained from the mines in the Southern States. The discovery of gold in California raised the annual product to $10,000,000 in 1848, to $40,000,000 in 1849, and to $50,000,000 in 1850. In 1853 it reached its maximum, $65,000,000. In the decade 1861–70 it averaged $47-000,000; in the decade 1871–80, $40,000,000; in the decade 1881–90, about $34,000,000. In 1892–93 it was $33,000,000.

Golden Circle, Knights of the, an organization formed among the "Copperheads" during the Civil War to rescue Confederate prisoners held by the United States.

"Golden Hind," the vessel which accompanied Sir Humphrey Gilbert's "Squirrel" in the colonization expedition of 1583. Gilbert was lost, and Captain Edward Haies returned with the "Golden Hind" to England bearing the news.

Goldsborough, Louis M. (1805–1877), entered the navy at the age of seven, served in the Mediterranean in 1827, was promoted commander in 1841, and aided in the bombardment of Vera Cruz in 1847. In 1861 he was in command of the North Atlantic squadron, and planned the capture of Roanoke Island in 1862. He retired in 1873, as rear-admiral, having been longer in the service than any other officer.

Gooch, Sir William (1681–1751), was Governor of Virginia from 1727 to 1747, when he returned to England. He was created a baronet in 1746, and was appointed major-general.

Goodhue, Benjamin (1748–1814), a Massachusetts member of the Continental Congress from 1784 to 1789, was a U. S. Congressman from 1789 to 1795, and a (Federalist) Senator from 1796 to 1800. He drafted many of the present revenue laws, and served on the Committee on Commerce in the Senate.

Goodrich, Samuel G. (1793–1860), served in the Massachusetts Senate in 1838 and 1839, and was U. S. Consul at Paris from 1851 to 1855. He published many juvenile and educational works, usually under the name of Peter Parley, famous among which was a popular history of the United States.

Goodyear, Charles (1800–1860), was born in Connecticut. By persistent experiment he discovered the vulcanizing process by which he rendered india-rubber useful.

Gordon, John B., born in 1832, was promoted lieutenant-general in the Confederate service, represented Georgia in the U. S. Senate from 1873 to 1880, and was elected Governor of Georgia in 1886.

Gordon, William (1730–1807), an Englishman, emigrated to Massachusetts in 1770, and was active in Massachusetts politics. He returned to England in 1786, and published a valuable "History of the Rise, Progress and Establishment of the Independence of the United States."

Gorgeana, a town incorporated in 1642 under the grant of the charter of Maine to Sir Ferdinando Gorges and others. The grant was made December 2, 1631, of 24,000 acres on both sides of the Acomenticus River. Gorgeana was founded in 1641 as Acomenticus.

Gorges, Sir Ferdinando (1565?–1647), was one of the founders of the original Plymouth Company, and sent out a number of unsuccessful expeditions to the New England coast. In 1620 he became a member of the Council for New England. In 1622 he, with Mason, obtained a grant of

Northern New England; in 1629, of Western Maine, separately. Under a fuller proprietary grant of 1639, he established a government at Saco, Acomenticus and Gorgeana.

Gorman, Arthur P., born in 1839, was a page in the U. S. Senate from 1852 to 1866, served in the Maryland Legislature from 1869 to 1879, and has been a U. S. Senator from 1881 to 1894. He is one of the chief Democratic political managers.

Gorton, Samuel (1600?–1677), emigrated to America from England in 1636, was banished from Massachusetts for religious reasons, and finally settled in Rhode Island, where he founded a religious sect. He afterward named the place Warwick, in honor of the earl from whom he obtained redress for his grievances, when in 1644–1647 he was persecuted by Massachusetts.

Gosnold, Bartholomew, died in 1607, an English navigator appointed by Lord Southampton to found a colony in New England. He landed on the coast of Maine, sailed around Cape Cod, and planted an unsuccessful colony in Buzzard's Bay on the island of Cuttyhunk. He sailed on another expedition with Newport in 1606, and assisted in founding Jamestown.

Gough, John B. (1817–1886), came to America from England in 1829. He led a dissipated life until 1842, when he reformed and devoted his efforts to temperance reform. He relied entirely on moral influences and disregarded organized or legislative efforts. He was famous as an orator.

Gould, Hannah F. (1789–1865), born in Massachusetts, was an extensive contributor of verse to various periodicals, and published several popular poetical works.

Gould, Jay (1836–1893), first engaged in surveying, but entered the brokerage business in 1857 and amassed an immense fortune through railroad speculations. He was said to control nearly one-eighth of the railroad mileage in the United States.

Gourgues, Dominique de (1537–1593), a French soldier, set sail in 1567, with three vessels and about 230 men, to punish the Spaniards led by Menendez, for killing French explorers in Florida. He enlisted the services of the Indians and attacked Fort San Mateo on the St. John's River, Florida, completely annihilated the garrison, and likewise destroyed the fortifications at the mouth of the river.

Governor. When the American colonies were founded, "Governor" was used in two senses in England,—to denote the commander of a fortified post, like Hull or Tangier, and to denote the head of a great trading corporation, like the East India Company or the Massachusetts Company. The Governor of an American colony got his name by derivation from both these sources, probably. When the Revolution broke out and the royal Governors fled, the new State Constitutions usually made provision for a single executive, called the Governor. At first he was chosen by the Legislatures in most States south of New York, but now by the people. In the colonial period, the

Governors of Rhode Island, of Connecticut, and of Massachusetts down to 1691, were chosen by the people; those of proprietary colonies by the proprietors; those of royal colonies by the crown.

Governor's Island, N. Y., called Nutten Island by its original settlers, the Dutch, received its present name from having been the property of Governor Wouter van Twiller. It was fortified and occupied by the colonial troops during the Revolution.

Graduation Act, an act passed by Congress in 1854 to cheapen, for the benefit of actual settlers and for adjoining farms, the price of lands which had been long on the market.

Grady, Henry W. (1851–1889), journalist and orator, became associated with the *Atlanta Constitution* in 1880. He made himself the spokesman of the "New South," and delivered a famous speech on "The New South" in 1886, and one upon "The Future of the Negro" in 1889.

Grafton, Augustus Henry Fitzroy, Duke of (1736–1811), English statesman, opposed Townsend's policy of taxing the American colonies in 1766. He sought to prevent the war with the colonies, and opposed the measures of Lord North.

Graham, George (1772?–1830), commanded in the War of 1812, was acting Secretary of War from 1815 to 1817, and was U. S. Land Commissioner from 1823 to 1830.

Graham, William A. (1804–1875), represented North Carolina in the U. S. Senate from 1840 to 1843, was Governor of the State from 1845 to 1849, Secretary of the Navy in Fillmore's Cabinet from 1850 to 1853, and Whig candidate for Vice-President in 1852.

Grahame, James (1790–1842), born in Scotland, published a "History of the Rise and Progress of the United States of North America till the British Revolution of 1688," which was recognized as a thorough and authoritative work.

Granby Token, a private or unauthorized coinage issued in Connecticut in 1737 by John Higley, of Granby. It was made of copper. Obverse, a deer and legend, Value Me as You Please; Roman numerals III. and crescent. Reverse, three hammers upon a triangular field, each bearing a crown. Legend: I Am Good Copper.

Grand Army of the Republic, organized during the winter of 1865–66 at Springfield, Ill., chiefly through the activity of Dr. B. F. Stephenson, late surgeon of the Fourteenth Illinois Infantry. The first post was established at Decatur, Ill., in 1866. The ritual is secret. All soldiers and sailors of the U. S. army, navy and marine corps between April 12, 1861, and April 9, 1865, are eligible for membership, provided they have had an honorable discharge. The membership in 1893 was 407,781. National conventions have been held each year. The first commander-in-chief was Stephen A. Hurlbut, of Illinois. Grand army posts have been established in nearly every city in the North and West.

Grand Gulf, Miss., assaulted, during Grant's expedition along the Mississippi, by that general and Admiral Porter, who commanded eight Federal gunboats, April 29, 1863. Wade held the place with a small Confederate force. The position was bombarded for some hours without avail.

Granger, Francis (1792–1868), son of Gideon, a New York Assemblyman from 1826 to 1831, was National Republican candidate for Vice-President in 1836, a U. S. Congressman from 1835 to 1837 and from 1839 to 1843, and was Whig Postmaster-General in 1841.

Granger, Gideon (1767–1822), served in the Connecticut Legislature, and was one of the originators of the school fund. He was Postmaster-General of the United States from 1801 to 1814 in the Cabinets of Jefferson and Madison, and was a member of the New York Senate from 1819 to 1821, where he advocated an extensive system of internal improvements.

Granger, Gordon (1821–1876), active in the Mexican War at Vera Cruz, Chapultepec and city of Mexico, fought on the Federal side during the Civil War at Island No. 10, Chattanooga, Missionary Ridge and Mobile, and was brevetted major-general.

Granger, Robert S., general, born in 1816, promoted captain in the Mexican War, had commands in the Civil War at Lebanon, Lawrenceburg, in Nashville and Middle Tennessee in 1863, and Alabama in 1864. He retired in 1873.

Grangers. The popular name for the "Patrons of Husbandry," a secret association devoted to the promotion of agricultural interests, organized in Washington, December 4, 1867. By the end of 1875 it numbered 1,500,000 members in every section of the United States. Its organization was somewhat similar to that of the Freemasons, but both men and women were admitted to membership. Though fundamentally non-political, it exerted considerable political influence in its contests with railroad corporations for cheaper rates.

Grant, James (1720–1806), met with a severe defeat in command of an expedition against Fort Duquesne in 1758. He commanded two brigades of British troops at Long Island, and was in command of New Jersey during the battles of Trenton and Princeton. He served as a major-general in the battles of Brandywine and Germantown in 1777, and defeated Lee at Monmouth in 1778.

Grant, Julia Dent, born in 1826, married General Grant in 1848, was with him, when practicable, during the Civil War, and accompanied him in his travels.

Grant, Ulysses S. (1822–1885), the greatest Federal general in the Civil War, was born at Point Pleasant, O., and was graduated from West Point in 1843. He was commissioned a lieutenant, fought in the battles of Palo Alto and Resaca de la Palma, and was brevetted captain in 1847 for conduct at Chapultepec. In 1854 he resigned his commission and engaged in business until 1861. Soon after the outbreak of the war he was given command of the forces at Cairo, Ill., and in 1861 seized Paducah. In 1862 he gained possession of Fort Henry and Fort Donelson, strongly contested points, the surrender of which was the first brilliant victory of the national arms. For this success he was commissioned major-general. In conjunction with the forces of General Buell he defeated the Confederates at Pittsburg Landing and soon afterward was assigned to command in Tennessee. He defeated General Price (1863) and succeeded in taking Vicksburg from Pendleton after repeated attacks. Having thus secured the Mississippi, he was appointed major-general in the regular army and placed in command of the Western army. He gained brilliant victories about Chattanooga and was appointed by President Lincoln to the newly revived rank of lieutenant-general. Leaving Sherman to conduct the chief Western army from Tennessee to the sea, he assumed control of the movements against the Confederates defending Richmond, commanded by General Lee. With dogged persistence and at great sacrifice of life he fought the battles of the Wilderness, Spottsylvania and Cold Harbor, destroying the railroads which brought supplies to the Confederates, taking Petersburg in 1865 and compelling the entire command to surrender on April 9 at Appomattox Court House, thereby ending the war. In the period of reconstruction which followed he played a most honorable part, often being placed in difficult positions by the animosity between President Johnson and Congress. In 1868 he was unanimously nominated for President by the Republicans, was elected and served two terms, from 1868 to 1876. During his administration occurred the passage of the Fifteenth Amendment, the funding of the national debt, civil service reform was inaugurated, the Treaty of Washington was negotiated with Great Britain, and specie payment was resumed in 1875. His administration as President was not wholly successful, some of his advisers proving most unworthy. He possessed an unassuming manner, yet was self-reliant and prompt in his decisions, calm and patient in all circumstances, and won the admiration of all by his moral and physical courage. He published "Personal Memoirs."

Grasse, François J. P., Count de (1723–1788), born in France, was appointed commander of a French fleet of twenty-nine vessels and 3000 men to aid the American colonists against Great Britain in 1781. He aided in the siege of Yorktown, blockading the York and James Rivers, and sent troops to aid in the decisive engagement by which Cornwallis was compelled to surrender.

Gray, Asa (1810–1888), born in New York, was recognized both in this country and in Europe as one of the most eminent botanists of his time. He published a large number of valuable botanical works.

Gray, Elisha, born in 1835, is a successful inventor of various electrical appliances, chiefly for the telegraph and telephone, among them being his speaking telephone and multiplex telegraph.

Gray, George, born in 1840, Attorney-General of Delaware from 1879 to 1885, was a delegate to the National Democratic Conventions of 1876, 1880 and 1884, and was a U. S. Senator from 1885 to 1893.

Gray, Horace, born in 1828, reporter of the Massachusetts Supreme Court from 1854 to 1861, was Associate Justice of it from 1864 to 1873, when he became Chief Justice. He was appointed a Justice of the U. S. Supreme Court in 1882.

Gray, Isaac P., born in 1828, was a captain in the Civil War, and served in the Indiana Senate from 1868 to 1872, when he was elected Lieutenant-Governor. He was Governor from 1885 to 1889, as a Democrat.

Gray, Robert (1755–1806), born in Rhode Island, traded with the Indians on the northwest coast, and returned in 1790 via China, being the first to carry the American flag around the world. He sailed into the Columbia River in 1792, from which arose the American claim to Oregon.

"**Great Awakening**," a religious revival between 1734 and 1744, through Massachusetts and Connecticut, induced by the eloquence of Jonathan Edwards and George Whitefield. Edwards had a parish at Northampton, Whitefield was an Englishman. Their preaching aroused the greatest religious enthusiasm, and made hundreds of converts. The awakening was looked upon with disfavor in England.

Great Bridge, Va., an engagement of the Revolution, occurring December 9, 1775, near the Dismal Swamp, between Lord Dunmore, commanding a band of British and Tories, and Colonel Woodford leading 300 colonial soldiers. Dunmore attacked Woodford's camp, and was defeated with the loss of 100 men, Woodford sustaining no loss.

Great Britain. (See also Revolution.) The definitive treaty of peace which ended the Revolutionary War between the United States and Great Britain was concluded September 3, 1783. Failure to fulfill some of the provisions of this treaty—notably the evacuation of the northern frontier posts—led to the negotiation of the Jay Treaty. This concession (of evacuation) with some doubtful commercial privileges was almost the only advantage secured by the new treaty, which gave more than it gained, and proved very unpopular, though it was ratified. British orders in council, damaging to American commerce, and the arbitrary impressment of American seamen, resulted in the War of 1812–15 (see next art.), which was ended by the treaty of peace known as the Treaty of Ghent, which provided for commissions to settle the northern boundary. A commercial convention was concluded in 1815. The Convention of 1818 reaffirmed the right of the United States to the enjoyment of the northeastern fisheries subject to certain renunciations. It referred to arbitration the question of the return of the slaves captured during the War of 1812, which was finally decided in favor of the United States, and an indemnity paid. It attempted to settle the northwest boundary. The Ashburton Treaty of 1842 determined the long-disputed northeast boundary and provided for the mutual suppression of the slave trade. The acquisition of California and the question of its approaches across the Isthmus led to new difficulties with Great Britain. The Clayton-Bulwer Treaty of 1850 was concluded to settle all difficulties as to Central American rights, but a difficulty of interpretation led to the conclusion of the Dallas-Clarendon Treaty of 1854, which failed of ratification, and the matter was not satisfactorily adjusted for several years. In 1853 a claims convention was concluded, a reciprocity treaty in 1854, and a treaty for the suppression of the slave trade in 1862—afterward modified. A naturalization convention was concluded in 1870. A treaty (Treaty of Washington) was concluded May 8, 1871, to settle questions arising from the American Civil War. It provided for a commission of arbitration which awarded $15,500,000 to the United States, and settled important questions of international law. (See "Alabama" Claims and Geneva Arbitration.) This treaty further adjusted differences relating to the northeastern fisheries, and $5,500,000 were awarded to Great Britain. Also the northwestern boundary dispute (or San Juan question) was referred to the Emperor of Germany, who decided in favor of the United States. An extradition treaty was concluded in 1890. The latest difficulty between the two nations has been the Behring Sea dispute. This arose over the right to take seals in certain waters claimed by the United States as under its exclusive jurisdiction. A treaty of arbitration was signed February 29, 1892, which provided for a tribunal of arbitration. It met in Paris, and on August 15, 1893, signed an agreement which denies exclusive American jurisdiction beyond the three-mile limit, and grants damages for seizures by the United States, but establishes protective regulations binding upon both nations. In 1892 a reciprocity treaty was concluded respecting the British West Indies.

Great Britain, Second War with. The war between England and France, resumed in 1803, resulted in innumerable aggressions upon the commerce of neutrals. The Berlin and Milan Decrees and the orders in council, issued by the two combatants in the effort to destroy each other's resources, subjected to capture on the one hand all vessels trading with England, and on the other hand all vessels trading with France or regions subject to France—practically nearly the whole continent of Europe. England, moreover, insisted on the impressment of seamen and the exercise of the right of search. The Non-Importation Act, the embargo and the Non-Intercourse Act brought neither belligerent to terms, and negotiations with England failed to check British aggressions. The result was the growth, especially in the West, of a resolute war party, led by Clay, Calhoun, Crawford, Grundy, Cheves, Lowndes and others, who succeeded in forcing President Madison's hand, and in June, 1812, brought on a declaration of war with England. The military and naval forces of the United States were exceedingly small in comparison with those of Great Britain, the country disunited and the executive weak. The theatre of land operations was at first the Canadian frontier. In 1812 the Americans lost Detroit and Chicago, and were checked in attempts to invade Canada by way of Niagara. In 1813 Perry's victory on Lake Erie secured that lake and Detroit, but in the regions of Ontario and the St. Lawrence an American occupation of Upper Canada proved temporary, and no substantial gains were made. On the sea the little American navy won brilliant and encouraging victories in 1812. In 1813 it was on the whole unsuccessful, but privateers, to the end of the war, inflicted enormous damage on British shipping. In 1814 the army on the Canadian frontier, better commanded than heretofore, won victories at Lundy's Lane and Plattsburg. But the abdication of Napoleon left England free to employ more troops in America. A force which landed in Chesapeake Bay captured Washington, but was repulsed from Baltimore. Meanwhile

NAVAL COMMANDERS OF WAR 1812.

D. Porter. William Bainbridge. Stephen Decatur.

James Lawrence. Oliver H. Perry. Charles Stewart.

New England gave violent expression to its dissatisfaction with the war, especially through the Hartford Convention. As neither nation was making substantial gains, negotiations for peace were begun, and finally peace was concluded by the Treaty of Ghent (1814). The treaty said nothing of either the rights of neutrals or the impressment of seamen. Yet the effect of the war had been to increase the confidence of the Americans and their national feeling, and to withdraw the country's politics permanently from dependence on those of Europe. Before the news of peace arrived, Jackson won a brilliant victory at New Orleans over a formidable British force which had been sent to occupy the mouth of the Mississippi (1815).

Great Meadows. Toward the end of May, 1754, Washington encamped with 150 men on a meadow near the Youghiogeny River between the Alleghany and Laurel Ridges. His instructions were to advance upon Fort Duquesne, which had been seized by the French during the preceding year. When at Great Meadows he learned that a body of French were in his vicinity. Taking a portion of his force and an Indian guide he surprised the French who were hidden in a hollow in the forest, and at once opened fire. Several, among whom was their commander Jumonville, were killed, and over twenty taken prisoners. This was the beginning of the French and Indian War, and indeed was the first engagement of the Seven Years' War.

Greece. The United States sympathized with the efforts of the Greeks to throw off the Turkish yoke, but early attempts at Governmental action in their favor were frustrated. A commercial treaty was concluded in 1837.

Greeley, Horace (1811–1872), was born in New Hampshire. In 1833 he edited the *Evening Post*, the first daily penny paper ever issued, and in 1834 founded the *New Yorker*. He was editorially connected with the *Jeffersonian* and the *Log Cabin*, campaign journals of considerable popularity, and in 1841 issued the first number of the *Tribune*, which he continued to edit until his death. It was at first Whig, then Anti-Slavery Whig, then Republican, employed the most eminent men of the day on its staff, proclaimed the most popular and radical views, and was the most influential paper in America. From 1848 to 1849 he represented New York in the U. S. Congress, where he redressed abuses of the mileage system. He earnestly advocated the abolition of slavery during the war, and made most powerful appeals to the administration through the columns of his paper. During the period of reconstruction he advocated universal amnesty and impartial suffrage, and became one of the bondsmen of Jefferson Davis in 1867. In 1872 he was Presidential candidate for the Liberal Republican and Democratic parties, but was defeated by General Grant. Eccentric in habit and in thought, frank and open-minded, firm in his convictions, ever mindful of the welfare of society, he was called by John G. Whittier, "the later Franklin."

Greely, Adolphus W., born in Maine in 1844, was brevetted major for services in the Civil War, and soon afterward entered the Signal Service. In 1881 he commanded an expedition of twenty-five men which established an observation station at the farthest point north yet attained. When rescued in 1884, only seven men had survived. He was chief of the Signal Service from 1887 to 1892. In 1887 he became a brigadier-general.

Green, Duff (1780–1875), an influential politician who edited an opposition organ during John Quincy Adams' administration, and the *U. S. Telegraph* (an "official" organ) during Jackson's first term. He supported Clay in 1832, and Calhoun in 1836.

Green Bay, Wis., the location of Jesuit missions for the conversion of the Indian tribes along the Great Lakes during the latter part of the seventeenth century. Chief among these was the mission of St. Francis Xavier, founded by Father Marquette in 1669.

"Green Bay Intelligencer," first newspaper published in Wisconsin. It was founded December 11, 1833, by Suydam and Ellis at Green Bay. In August, 1836, it was united with the *Spectator* and called the *Wisconsin Democrat.* In 1840 it was removed to Southport (Kenosha).

Green Briar Creek, Va., an encampment of Confederate forces under Lee. Reynolds, the Federal commander in that quarter, left his camp at Elkwater, October 2, 1861, with 5000 men and a large artillery force and advanced against the Confederates. Kimball attacked the Confederates' front and right, while Milroy cleared the Green Briar bridge. The fighting continued fiercely for some time, but there was no decisive victory, for Reynolds, having gained the bridge, sounded the recall.

Green Mountain Boys, a band of Vermont mountaineers who, led by Ethan Allen and Benedict Arnold, captured Fort Ticonderoga May 10, 1776, securing fifty British prisoners and 200 cannon. They rendered effective service throughout the Revolution.

Greenback Party, organized in a Greenback Convention at Indianapolis, November 25, 1874, which assembled to adopt resolutions opposing the specie resumption bill proposed at that time in Congress and passed January 14, 1875. The Greenback party platform advocated the withdrawal of all national and State bank currency, and the substitution therefor of paper currency issued by the Government, and that coin should only be used in payment of interest on the national debt. The Greenback Presidential candidate in 1876, Peter Cooper, of New York, received 81,740 votes, chiefly from the Western States.

Greenback Labor Party, an outgrowth of the Greenback party, formed in Ohio in 1875. In 1878 a union of the Labor Reform and the remnants of the old Greenback party was effected and was made national by the Convention of February 22 of that year, at Toledo, O. The platform adopted was similar to that of the Greenback party. It advocated the withdrawal of currency from all national and State banks and corporations, a paper currency issued by the Government, and that coin should only be paid for interest on the national debt when so specified. They also demanded an eight-hour law, the prohibition of Chinese immigration, of land grants to railroads and of special grants to corporations and bondholders. In 1878 they elected fourteen Congressmen. Their national convention was held at Chicago, June 9, 1880,

James B. Weaver, of Iowa, and B. J. Chambers, of Texas, being the Presidential nominees. Their popular vote reached 308,578. In 1884 the Presidential candidate of the party was B. F. Butler, who received 175,370 votes. In 1887 the Union Labor party was organized.

Greenbacks. The popular name for the legal-tender Treasury notes which the U. S. Government issued during the war. Although the right of the Government to issue "bills of credit," legal-tender notes, was disputed by many, the necessities of the Government caused the passage of an act of that effect on February 25, 1862. This authorized the issue of $150,000,000 of such notes. Acts authorizing further issues of the same amount were passed on June 11, 1862, and March 3, 1863. The legal-tender notes rapidly depreciated, the price of gold averaging 220 throughout 1864, and even on one day rising to 285. By Act of 1866 the total amount outstanding was reduced to $356,000,000 within two years. Since 1878 it has been $346,681,016.

Greenbriar Company, a land company organized October 29, 1757, in opposition to the Ohio and Loyal Companies. The Greenbriar Company obtained a grant of 100,000 acres, chiefly along the Ohio River.

Greene, Christopher (1737–1781), served in the Rhode Island Legislature from 1772 to 1774, was appointed commander in Arnold's expedition to Quebec and in 1777 made a brilliant defence of Fort Mercer against the Hessians.

Greene, George W. (1811–1883), U. S. Consul at Rome in 1837, served in the Rhode Island Legislature from 1867 to 1869 and wrote a history of the Revolution and a life of General Nathanael Greene.

Greene, Nathanael (1742–1786), general, born in Warwick, R. I., served in the Rhode Island Assembly in 1770. He joined a military company in 1774 and was commissioned brigadier-general in 1775. He was active in the engagement at Dorchester Heights, and was made major-general in 1776. He fought at Trenton and at Princeton and saved the American forces from defeat at Brandywine by a rapid march and skillful management. He commanded the left wing at Germantown, skillfully covering the retreat, and in 1778 was appointed quartermaster-general while retaining his rank in the field. He presided at the trial of Major André. In 1780 he succeeded Gates in command of the Southern forces. One of his detachments, under General Morgan, having gained a decisive victory at Cowpens, Greene joined him with reinforcements and attacked Cornwallis at Guilford Court House. He then began a brilliant campaign in South Carolina, engaging Lord Rawdon at Camden, capturing Forts Watson, Motte and Granby, regaining Orangeburg, Augusta and Fort Ninety-six, and winning a decisive victory at Eutaw Springs. Soon afterward a detachment under General Wayne took possession of Savannah and Greene occupied Charleston. He disbanded his troops in 1783. By his skill in military manœuvres he proved himself one of the most brilliant generals of that period, second only to Washington, among those of the Revolution.

Greenough, Horatio (1805–1852), designed a model from which Bunker Hill Monument was made; constructed the "Rescue," and a statue of Washington, and became one of the most eminent of American sculptors.

Greenway Court, the home of Lord Fairfax in a valley of the Virginia Mountains. It was built in 1745, in Frederick County.

Grenville, George (1712–1770), became a member of the English Parliament in 1741, was a lord of the Admiralty in 1744, a lord of the Treasury in 1747, treasurer of the navy and privy councillor in 1754, leader of the House of Commons in 1761, secretary of state and first lord of the Admiralty in 1762, and was first lord of the Treasury (Prime Minister) and chancellor of the exchequer, from 1763 to 1765. In 1765 he secured the passage of the act imposing stamp duties on America, and strenuously opposed the repeal of the Stamp Act in 1766. He was an able statesman, but possessed a very imperious nature.

Grenville, Sir Richard (1540–1591), an English navigator, set out with seven vessels and 108 colonists for Carolina on a colonizing expedition for Sir Walter Raleigh in 1585. He landed the colonists at Roanoke Island, but they soon afterward returned to England on account of troubles with the Indians. In 1586 he renewed the attempt. In 1591, with only one ship, he attacked a Spanish fleet of fifty vessels and sunk four of them, but was mortally wounded.

Grenville Act, so called after the British Minister, George Grenville; an act extending the navigation acts, placing imposts on foreign molasses, an increased duty on sugar, regulating English manufactures, and prohibiting trade between America and St. Pierre and Miquelon, two small French islands off Newfoundland.

Gresham, Walter Q., born in 1832, was a member of the Indiana Legislature from 1860 to 1861, served during the Civil War, and was promoted major-general in 1865. He was U. S. District Judge in Indiana from 1869 to 1883, when he was appointed Postmaster-General in Arthur's Cabinet, and in 1884 was for a short time Secretary of the Treasury. From 1884 to 1893 he was a Judge of the U. S. Circuit Court. In 1893 he became Secretary of State in Mr. Cleveland's Cabinet, though till 1892 a Republican.

Grey, Charles (1729–1807), major-general, accompanied Howe from England in 1775, surprised and defeated General Wayne's force near the Schuylkill on September 20, 1777, had a command at Germantown and Tappan, and destroyed the shipping and stores at New Bedford in 1778.

Greytown, a town on the Mosquito Coast of Nicaragua, bombarded and destroyed in 1854 by the U. S. ship "Cyane." A negro had been shot by a steamship captain in May, and the mayor of Greytown ordered the captain's arrest. The passengers resisted, among them Borland, the U. S. Minister. The next day Borland was assaulted on the street. In July the "Cyane" was despatched to the town. Commander Hollins sent to the mayor demanding immediate payment of the extortionate demands of a transit company, with which the town authorities had quarreled. This was refused. Hollins opened fire and destroyed the town.

Grier, Robert C. (1794–1870), admitted to the bar in 1817, was District Judge of Alleghany from 1838 to 1846, when he became a Justice of the U. S. Supreme Court and served until 1870.

Grierson, Benjamin H., born in 1826, conducted a successful cavalry raid from La Grange to Baton Rouge in 1863, and was successively promoted for dashing cavalry exploits until appointed a major-general of the U. S. army in 1866.

Griffin, Charles (1826–1867), fought at Bull Run, had commands at Malvern Hill, Antietam, Fredericksburg and Gettysburg, took a prominent part in Grant's Peninsular campaign, and was made major-general in the U. S. army in 1865.

Griffin, Simon G., general, born in 1824, in 1862 fought at Camden, Antietam and Fredericksburg, and assisted in taking Vicksburg. He fought also at the Wilderness, Spottsylvania and Petersburg, and aided in the defeat of General Lee at Appomattox.

Grimes, James W. (1816–1872), Governor of Iowa from 1854 to 1858, was a U. S. Senator from 1859 to 1871, and chairman of the Committee on Naval Affairs from 1864 to 1871. He was one of the Republicans who voted "Not guilty" at President Johnson's trial.

Grinnell, Henry (1800–1874), a successful merchant, devoted the later years of his life to the extension of geographical knowledge, and sent out two expeditions to the polar seas.

"**Gripen**," a sloop furnished for emigrants in the Swedish colonization expedition of 1637. It reached Delaware Bay in March, 1638, and the emigrants formed settlements along the Delaware River.

Griswold, Roger (1762–1812), represented Connecticut in the U. S. Congress from 1795 to 1805, was appointed Judge of the Connecticut Supreme Court in 1807, and chosen Governor in 1811.

Griswold, Rufus W. (1815–1857), associate editor of numerous periodicals including *Graham's Magazine* and the *International Magazine*, was the author of "Poets and Poetry of America" and "Prose Writers of America."

Griswold, Fort, Capture of, September 6, 1781. In view of the siege of Cornwallis in Yorktown, Clinton attempted a diversion upon Connecticut. Benedict Arnold commanded. The only spirited resistance was offered by the garrison of Fort Griswold, 157 in number. After losing 192 of his 600 regulars Arnold carried the fort. No quarter was given. Only twenty-six escaped. New London was laid in ashes, and before sunset the enemy returned up the Sound. The descent was wanton and useless.

Groesbeck, William S., born in 1815, represented Ohio in the U. S. Congress from 1857 to 1859, was a State Senator in 1862 and of counsel for President Johnson in the impeachment trial.

Gros Ventres, a name applied to two Indian tribes of different origin: the Gros Ventres of the Missouri and the Gros Ventres of the prairie. The latter tribe, after wandering east and joining various tribes temporarily, finally settled about 1824 near Milk River with the Blackfeet. Treaties were made with them in 1851, 1853 and 1865, and the Indians have since continued friendly. They have suffered considerably from hostilities with other tribes. They now occupy a reservation in Montana.

Grover, Cuvier (1829–1885), a lieutenant-colonel at Williamsburg and Fair Oaks, commanded a division in the Shenandoah campaign and was brevetted major-general for services at Fisher's Hill in 1864.

Grover, Lafayette, born in 1823, chairman of the Oregon Democratic Committee from 1866 to 1870, was Governor of Oregon from 1870 to 1878. He decided for the Democratic elector in the disputed Presidential election of 1876, and was a U. S. Congressman from 1877 to 1883.

Grow, Galusha A., born in 1824, represented the "Wilmot district" in Pennsylvania in the U. S. Congress as a Whig and Republican from 1851 to 1863 and was Speaker of the House from 1861 to 1863. He served on the Committees on Indian Affairs, Agriculture and Territories, being chairman of this committee for four years. He was a delegate to the Republican National Conventions of 1864 and 1868. In 1894 he was elected Congressman-at-large by an enormous majority (188,000).

Grundy, Felix (1777–1840), born in Virginia, was a member of the Kentucky Constitutional Convention of 1799, and a member of the State House of Representatives from 1800 to 1806. He represented Tennessee in the U. S. Congress from 1811 to 1814 and was a member of the Tennessee House of Representatives from 1815 to 1819. He was a U. S. Senator from 1820 to 1838, and was Attorney-General in Van Buren's Cabinet from 1838 to 1839, when he again became a U. S. Senator and served until his death.

Guadalupe Hidalgo, Treaty of, was negotiated with Mexico by Nicholas P. Trist for the United States in 1848, at the conclusion of the Mexican War. By this treaty Mexico ceded to the United States the territory of Texas, New Mexico and Upper California, and agreed upon the Rio Grande River as the boundary between herself and Texas. The United States agreed to pay Mexico $15,000,000 and to assume all claims of its citizens against Mexico arising before the treaty. It reserved to Mexicans in the ceded territory the option to remove or remain and assured protection of their rights of property.

Guatemala. One treaty has been concluded between the United States and Guatemala—a treaty of peace, amity, commerce and navigation, concluded March 3, 1849. Requisite notice having been given this treaty ceased to operate November 4, 1874. A reciprocity treaty was concluded in 1892.

"**Guerriére,**" frigate. (See "Constitution.")

Guess, George, or Sequoyah (1770–1843), an Indian half-breed who devised the alphabet used by the Cherokees. It consists of eighty-five characters, mostly borrowed from the English, each representing a single sound.

Guilford Court House, Battle of, March 15, 1781. After the battle of Cowpens Morgan turned north and Cornwallis pursued. Greene resolved to crush Cornwallis, thus separated from his base of supplies. In person he joined Morgan in the Catawba Valley, and finally his main force effected a conjunction with Morgan at Guilford Court House, N. C. Cornwallis was anxious for an engagement, but Greene crossed into Virginia, hoping to get reinforcements. Not succeeding, and fearing that the people of North Carolina might think their cause deserted, he marched south again. By a number of marches and countermarches he eluded Cornwallis until he found himself in a position to fight at Guilford Court House. His force was 4404. Cornwallis had 2213, all veterans. Greene placed in front his North Carolina militia, in his second line his Virginia militia, and in his third line his Maryland and Virginia regulars. The first line soon broke, but the second was pushed back only after a desperate struggle. In the third line the right wing was victorious, but the left was beaten for a while, until Colonel Washington's cavalry restored it. Cornwallis was now reduced to the defensive. He retired in good order and took position on a hill near Guilford Court House. All attempts to dislodge him were vain. At evening Greene retired with a loss of 400. The British had fought bravely, losing 600. They were too crippled to act, and Cornwallis could only retreat. He had been outgeneraled. It was a strategic victory for the Americans and Cornwallis was forced to abandon the Carolinas.

Gunboats. The "gunboat system" was inaugurated during Jefferson's administration, $50,000 being appropriated at his suggestion, February 28, 1803, to build gunboats. In 1806, $60,000 more were appropriated for the building of 240 gunboats for the defence of fifteen principal harbors. The seamen of the towns were to be trained to man them, and they were to be drawn up under sheds when not in use. The gunboat question speedily became a political issue, the Federalists opposing it and favoring a strong navy, the Republicans favoring it. The last appropriation was made in 1813. The gunboats were used to some extent during the War of 1812.

Gunston Hall, Fairfax County, Va., the home of George Mason, of Revolutionary fame. This old mansion continued in the possession of the Mason family until after the Civil War.

Guntown, Miss. Here, June 10, 1864, while the Confederate cavalryman Forrest was raiding through Mississippi, Kentucky and Tennessee, he was met by Sturgis leading a force of 8000 Federals. Forrest had 1000 men. He attacked Grierson, who led the Federal van, speedily routing him. Sturgis hurried up, but his troops were wearied out and not prepared for battle. They were put to flight and 200 baggage wagons were captured by the Confederates.

Gustavus Adolphus (1594–1632), King of Sweden from 1611 to 1632, in 1624 granted a charter to the Swedish West India Company founded by William Usselinx, and pledged himself to subscribe 400,000 daler of the royal treasury to the company's stock.

Guthrie, James (1792–1869), was a member of the Kentucky Senate from 1831 to 1840, Secretary of the Treasury in Pierce's Cabinet from 1853 to 1857, and a U. S. Senator from 1865 to 1868.

Guyot, Arnold (1807–1884), came to America from Switzerland in 1848, was a professor at Princeton from 1854 to 1884, and became eminent as a promoter of geographical and meteorological science.

Gwin, William W. (1805–1885), represented Mississippi in the U. S. Congress from 1841 to 1843, and was a U. S. Senator from California from

1850 to 1861, during which time he served on the Finance and Naval Committees. He was a pro-slavery Democrat.

Gwinnett, Button (1732–1777), came to America from England in 1770, represented Georgia in the Continental Congress from 1775 to 1776, and signed the Declaration of Independence.

Gwynn's Island, Va. Here in 1776 Lord Dunmore was entrenched with his British and Tory troops. December 8 the colonial troops, under Lewis and Stephen, attacked and dislodged him, forcing him to take to his ships, which were shelled as they sailed away. Dunmore was wounded.

H.

Habeas Corpus, Suspension of. On July 5, 1861, Attorney-General Bates gave an opinion in favor of the President's power to declare martial law and suspend the writ of *habeas corpus*. A special session of Congress approved this opinion. Thereafter many arbitrary arrests were made, arousing much indignation. September 24, 1862, the suspension was made general by the President so far as it might affect persons arrested by military authority for disloyal practices. An act of Congress, March 3, 1863, again authorized the suspension of the writ by the President in cases of prisoners of war, deserters, those resisting drafts and offenders against the military or naval service. The arrest of Vallandigham, in Ohio, and of Milligan, in Indiana, caused great excitement. The case of the latter being brought before the Supreme Court of the Union, that body decided that Congress could not give to military commissions the power of trial and conviction, and that the suspension of the privilege of *habeas corpus* did not suspend the writ itself. In the case of the Ku-Klux rebellions there was a brief suspension of *habeas corpus* in 1871.

Habersham, Joseph (1751–1815), was a prominent patriot in Georgia during the Revolution. He was Postmaster-General in the administrations of Washington, Adams and Jefferson from 1795 to 1801.

Hadley, Mass., settled in 1659, became the refuge of the two English regicides, Goffe and Whalley, in 1664. The town was attacked by Indians during King Philip's War. The savages were repulsed by the townspeople under the leadership of Colonel Goffe, one of the regicides, who suddenly came from his hiding-place for that purpose.

"**Hail Columbia**," a stirring national song. The music was composed in 1798 by Pfyles, leader of the orchestra at the John Street Theatre, New York, and was for a time known as the "President's March." The words were composed the same year by Judge Hopkinson, after which the air became immensely popular, it having been produced in a period of great political excitement.

Hakluyt, Richard (1553–1616), English author, in 1582 published "Divers Voyages Touching the Discovery of America," and as a result of further investigations in France wrote "A Particular Discourse covering Western

Discoveries." In 1587 he produced the "History of Four Voyages made by French Captains into Florida," and in 1589 published "The Principal Navigations, Voyages and Discoveries made by the English Nation." In 1606 he appealed to the king for a charter for the colonization of Virginia, and was one of the members of the South Virginia Company.

Hale, Edward Everett, born in Massachusetts in 1822, has been pastor of the South Congregational Church since 1856. He is a popular orator and author, and has done considerable historical work, being an authority on Spanish-American affairs, has contributed to histories of the United States, and published "Franklin in France."

Hale, Eugene, born in 1836, was a member of the Maine Legislature in 1867 and 1868, a U. S. Congressman from 1869 to 1879, and has been a Republican Senator from 1861 to the present time (1894).

Hale, John P. (1806–1873), born in Rochester, N. H., was admitted to the bar in 1830. He was a member of the New Hampshire House of Representatives in 1832, and was appointed U. S. Attorney for the district of New Hampshire from 1834 to 1840. He represented New Hampshire in the U. S. Congress from 1843 to 1845. He was a U. S. Senator from 1847 to 1853, being the first zealous opponent of slavery in that body, and was nominated in 1852 as the Presidential candidate of the Free-Soil party. He was again a U. S. Senator from 1855 to 1865, and was appointed Minister to Spain by President Lincoln, serving from 1865 to 1869.

Hale, Nathan (1755–1776), born in Connecticut, joined a volunteer company at the first news of the Revolutionary War, participated in the siege of Boston, and was made captain in 1776. He captured the British supply ship "Asia," and volunteered to reconnoitre the position of the British forces. He was apprehended and hanged as a spy, his last words being, "I only regret that I have but one life to lose for my country."

Hale, Nathan (1784–1863), editor of the *Boston Daily Advertiser* from 1814 to 1863, was one of the founders of the *North American Review*, and was active in promoting industrial improvement.

Half-breeds, a term applied in New York State, especially about 1880–1884, to those members of the Republican party who would not fully support, first, General Grant's candidacy for a third term, and second, the system of the spoilsmen and machine politicians of their own party. (See "Stalwarts.")

Half Cent, a copper coin, the coinage and issue of which were authorized by Congress in 1792. The weight of this coin was 132 grains, but this was changed to 104 grains when, in 1793, its coinage was again authorized. This coin was not issued during the years 1798, 1799, 1801, 1812 to 1824 inclusive, 1827, 1830, 1837 to 1848 inclusive, and 1852. It was discontinued in 1857.

Half Dollar, silver coin. Its coinage was authorized (at weight 208 grains) in April, 1792, and begun in 1794. Its weight was reduced in 1853 to 192 grains. This coin is a legal tender to the amount of ten dollars. There were no issues during the years 1798, 1799, 1800, 1816.

Half Eagle, a gold coin of the value of five dollars, stamped upon the reverse with a figure of the national bird, and hence the name. Its coinage was authorized in 1792, and begun in 1795. The first return of gold coins was made July 31, 1795, 744 half eagles. Authorized a second time in 1837; legal tender to an unlimited amount. No coinage 1816–17.

Half-King, the name by which the English called a chieftain of Indians on the Ohio, friendly to the English, who assisted Washington on his expedition of 1753 and took part with him in the affair of the Great Meadows in 1754.

"**Half Moon,**" the vessel in which Henry Hudson, under the auspices of the East India Company, discovered and explored in 1609 the river which bears his name.

Half-Pay Question. At the close of the Revolution it was the first care of Congress to cut down the expenses. April 26, 1778, by a majority of one State, half-pay had been voted for life to the officers as a means of keeping the army together. In the four years following five different votes were passed, each annulling the former one. In 1782 it was proposed to remit the whole matter to the States. Finally in 1783, after the appearance of the Newburgh addresses, it was decided to commute the half-pay for life into five years' full pay in one gross sum, certificates to be issued therefor at six per cent. This measure was unpopular.

Half-way Covenant, a concession made on the part of the Church by the New England Synod convened at Northampton in 1657, mainly in order to secure a more facile working in relation to the State. The requirements for church membership were relaxed in order that certain civil privileges might be obtained by those who had neither the ability nor willingness to make profession of religious experience. Such persons were admitted on grounds of baptism, but were still denied the Lord's Supper. This half-way covenant aroused much controversy, and was later opposed by Jonathan Edwards and his followers.

Halifax Commission. Under the provisions of the fisheries treaty of 1871 between Great Britain and the United States, the fishermen of the latter country were allowed to take fish along the shores of Canada and Newfoundland. The inhabitants of these States complained, and accordingly a commission of representatives from each country met at Halifax, Nova Scotia, in 1877, to determine the amount of compensation to be paid by the United States for the fishing privileges accorded them. The sum of $5,500,000 was awarded Great Britain.

Hall, Asaph, born in 1829, has been connected with all the astronomical observations of the U. S. Government since 1863. In 1877 he discovered the satellites of Mars, and has made important observations of double stars.

Hall, Charles F. (1821–1871), made Arctic expeditions fitted out by Henry Grinnell in 1860 and 1864, and commanded a U. S. Government expedition to the polar region in 1871, making many valuable scientific observations.

Hall, James, born in 1811, was given charge of the New York Geological Surveys from 1836 to 1841, was State Paleontologist from 1843 to 1879 and has made many valuable contributions to science.

Hall, Lyman (1725–1790), a member of the Savannah Conventions of 1774 and 1775, represented Georgia in the Continental Congress from 1775 to 1780 and signed the Declaration of Independence.

Hall, Nathan K. (1810–1874), represented New York in the U. S. Congress from 1847 to 1849 and was appointed Postmaster-General in Fillmore's Cabinet, serving from 1850 to 1853, when he became a U. S. District Judge, serving till 1874.

Halleck, Fitz-Greene (1790–1867), writer, born in Connecticut, was a counting-room clerk from 1811 to 1849. In partnership with J. R. Drake he published the "Croakers" in 1819. He wrote "Twilight," "Fanny," "Marco Bozzaris" and "Young America." He was a fluent writer with a brilliant and polished style.

Halleck, Henry W. (1815–1872), born in New York, graduated at the U. S. Military Academy in 1839. He published "Elements of Military Art and Science" in 1846, which was a classic work at that time, and a treatise on "International Law." He was prominent in the military and political movements in California from 1846 to 1854, and in 1861 was appointed major-general of the U. S. army and assigned to the Department of Missouri, and successfully organized that district. In 1862 he received command of the Mississippi Department, and was soon after appointed commander-in-chief of the army, which position he retained until Grant was made lieutenant-general. After the war he commanded the Pacific Division until 1869, and the Division of the South from 1869 to 1872.

Halpine, Charles G. (1829–1868), connected with the *New York Herald*, *Tribune* and other periodicals from 1852, entered the army in 1861, became a major and composed the humorous work of "Miles O'Reilly."

Halstead, Murat, born in 1829, was associated with numerous Ohio periodicals from 1851 to 1883, when he became editor of the *Commercial Gazette*, a combination of his *Commercial* and the *Cincinnati Gazette*. Subsequently he removed to New York.

Hamilton, Alexander (January 11, 1757–July 12, 1804), Secretary of the Treasury, was born at Nevis in the West Indies. He was on the one side of Scottish, on the other of French birth. Deprived of parental care at an early age, he developed an astonishing precocity, and was in 1772 sent to New York City. There, after a short period of preparation, he entered King's (now Columbia) College. While the Revolutionary fever was at its height Hamilton, in July, 1774, made a public speech on the patriotic side, marvelous for a boy of seventeen. He followed up this success by a vigorous war of pamphlets. When hostilities began Hamilton organized a cavalry company and served at Long Island and White Plains. As a member of Washington's staff he rendered valuable aid; resigning from membership in the staff in 1781 he ended a brilliant military career at Yorktown, studied law, and married the daughter of General Schuyler. For a short time,

1782–1783, he was in the Continental Congress. He had risen to eminence at the New York bar, when he took part in the Annapolis Convention of 1786. There followed two years of contests and triumphs of the greatest renown to himself and moment to his country. Hamilton was one of the chief members of the Constitutional Convention of 1787. He advocated a very strong central government, but accepted the results of that assembly, and returned to New York to further by pen and voice the ratification of our National Constitution. It is little exaggeration to say that Hamilton was practically the Federal party in New York. Of the eighty-five papers in the *Federalist* fifty-one are undisputedly his, and he had a part in the production of others. At the State ratifying Convention in 1788 at Poughkeepsie he contended almost single-handed against a two-thirds majority, which he converted into a minority. He entered Washington's Cabinet as Secretary of the Treasury in 1789. His report on the public credit, reports on revenue, the mint, the bank, manufactures, etc., were of the utmost value in placing the finances on a sound footing. Meanwhile within the Cabinet he was confronted with Jefferson, advocate of radically different ideas; the two great leaders quarreled almost incessantly, and Hamilton resigned in 1795. He had previously accompanied the army for the suppression of the Whiskey Insurrection. He defended Jay's Treaty with Great Britain in the able "Camillus" letters, and was concerned in the preparation of Washington's Farewell Address. He was in 1798 appointed inspector-general in view of the imminent war with France. But he quarreled with President Adams and intrigued against the latter and in favor of Pinckney. Hamilton and Burr had been political enemies; the latter, while Vice-President, brought on a duel at Weehawken, N. J., July 11, 1804, in which Hamilton was mortally wounded. He wrote, besides the papers mentioned above, the "Pacificus" letters, report on the public debt in 1789, etc. Hamilton was perhaps the most brilliant of American statesmen; his state papers were models of luminous and convincing argumentation; and he had an extraordinary genius for administrative organization. His weaknesses were, an imperious self-confidence, and want of popular sympathies. His works were edited by H. C. Lodge in 1885, who has also written Hamilton's biography. Other lives are by J. C. Hamilton and J. T. Morse, Jr.

Hamilton, Andrew (1676–1741), emigrated from Scotland in 1697, was Attorney-General of Pennsylvania from 1717 to 1724, an Assemblyman from 1729 to 1739, and in the "Zenger" libel suit first advanced the doctrine that in such cases evidence of the truth of the libel might be presented in defence.

Hamilton, Paul (1762–1816), active in the Revolution, was Comptroller of South Carolina from 1799 to 1804, Governor from 1804 to 1806, and Secretary of the Navy in Madison's Cabinet from 1809 to 1813.

Hamilton College, Clinton, N. Y., was founded by Presbyterians in 1793 as Hamilton Oneida Academy, chartered as a college in 1812. Its law school was founded in 1854.

Hamlet Case (1850), was the first recorded action under the Fugitive Slave Act of 1850. Hamlet, a free negro with a family, was arrested in New

York by a Deputy U. S. Marshal as a fugitive slave of Mary Brown, of Baltimore, and after a hasty examination surrendered in accordance with the law. Indignation was aroused and he was finally redeemed.

Hamlin, Hannibal (1809–1893), was admitted to the bar in 1833. He was a member of the Maine Legislature from 1836 to 1840 and in 1847, being chosen Speaker in 1837, 1839 and 1840. He was a Democratic Representative in Congress from 1842 to 1846, was elected a U. S. Senator in 1848 and served till 1857. He changed his party affiliation on account of anti-slavery sentiments, and was chosen Governor by the Republicans in 1857. He resigned and served in the U. S. Senate from 1857 to 1861, when he was elected Vice-President of the United States on the ticket with Abraham Lincoln, and was a member of the Senate from 1869 to 1881, when he was appointed Minister to Spain and served one year.

Hammond, James H. (1807–1864), editor of the *Southern Times*, a nullification paper, represented South Carolina in Congress from 1835 to 1836, was Governor of the State from 1842 to 1844, and a U. S. Senator from 1857 to 1861, when he delivered the pro-slavery speech which won for him the name of "Mudsill Hammond." He published "The Pro-Slavery Argument" and "Sketch of the Life of Calhoun."

Hampden-Sidney College, in Prince Edward County, Va., was founded as Prince Edward Academy, in 1776, by Presbyterians, and chartered as a college eight years later. Near by is the Presbyterian Union Theological Seminary, which was chartered in 1866. From 1837 to 1850 it had a medical school.

Hampton, Wade (1754–1835), represented South Carolina in Congress from 1795 to 1797 and from 1803 to 1805, and commanded on the Northern frontier from 1813 to 1814. He owned 3000 slaves.

Hampton, Wade, born in 1818, was in his early life successively a member of the South Carolina House of Representatives and Senate. At the beginning of the Civil War he enlisted in the Confederate service and afterward commanded a force known as Hampton's Legion of Cavalry, which distinguished itself at Bull Run, Seven Pines, Gettysburg and Trevillion's Station. He was very successful in raids and in detachment service. In 1876 he was the Democratic candidate for Governor of South Carolina against D. H. Chamberlain and gained the disputed office. He was elected to the U. S. Senate in 1879 and served until 1891.

Hampton, Va., was attacked out of revenge by Admiral Warren, after his defeat at Craney Island. A battery and 500 Virginia militia defended the village. Some 2500 British were landed, and soon drove the militia in defeat. The Americans lost thirty men, the British fifty. The village was then pillaged and several women outraged. Deep indignation was aroused on both sides of the sea, and an investigation was made by a British commission.

Hampton Roads, Va., or the "Monitor" and "Merrimac" fight, the most famous naval battle of the Civil War, occurring March 8–9, 1862. March 8 the Confederate iron-clad "Merrimac," commanded by Franklin Buchanan, was sent to raise the blockade of James and Elizabeth rivers by destroying the Union war-vessels. The Union frigate "Cumberland" was utterly destroyed and sunk by the "Merrimac," which next, aided by three wooden Confederate steamers, attacked and burned the "Congress." March 9 the "Monitor," a Union iron-clad of a new type, appeared, and a fight of four hours followed. Captain Worden, of the "Monitor," was temporarily blinded and Lieutenant Greene took command. The "Merrimac" was finally compelled to withdraw.

Hancock, John (1737–1793), born in Massachusetts, was a member of the Massachusetts Legislature from 1766 to 1772. It was his ship, the "Liberty," which caused a riot when seized by the royal customs officials for an alleged evasion of the laws, and he was one of the commissioners who demanded the removal of the British troops after the Boston massacre. In 1774 he was elected to the Provincial Congress at Concord, Mass., and together with Samuel Adams, was exempted from pardon in Governor Gage's proclamation of 1775. He represented Massachusetts in the Continental Congress from 1775 to 1780 and from 1785 to 1786, being chosen president from 1775 to 1777, and was a signer of the Declaration of Independence, his name standing first upon that document. In 1776 he was commissioned major-general of the Massachusetts militia, and in 1780 commanded the State troops in the expedition against Rhode Island. He was a delegate to the Massachusetts Constitutional Convention of 1780, and was Governor of the State from 1780 to 1785 and from 1787 to 1792, and in the Presidential election of 1789 received four electoral votes. He was a man of strong and popular character, of courtly and pleasing manner and liberally used his large fortune for benevolent purposes.

Hancock, Winfield S. (1824–1886), born in Pennsylvania, graduated from the U. S. Military Academy in 1844. He was brevetted first lieutenant for gallantry at Contreras and Churubusco during the Mexican War. He was appointed brigadier-general of volunteers in 1861, and joined the Army of the Potomac. He served under General McClellan in the Peninsular campaign, commanding at Yorktown, Williamsburg and Savage's Station, and was promoted colonel U. S. army for his meritorious service. He led his brigade at South Mountain and Antietam, commanded as major-general at Fredericksburg, Chancellorsville and Gettysburg, and was prominent at the Wilderness, Spottsylvania, Cold Harbor and Petersburg. In 1865 he received command of the Army of the Shenandoah, and in 1866 was made a major-general in the regular army. He was the Presidential candidate of the Democratic party in 1880, but was defeated by James A. Garfield. General Grant said of him, "Hancock stands the most conspicuous figure of all the general officers who did not exercise a separate command. He commanded a corps longer than any other one, and his name was never mentioned as having committed in battle a blunder for which he was responsible."

Hanging Rock, Battle of, August 6, 1780. At this place General Sumter surprised the British post. The Tory regiment fled, and its panic was communicated to the British regulars. At the outset no American had more than ten bullets, but before the close of the engagement they armed themselves from the dead and wounded. Among those engaged was Andrew Jackson. This success strengthened the patriot cause in all parts of South Carolina.

Hanover. Commercial treaties were concluded between the United States and Hanover in 1840, 1846 and 1861, and an extradition treaty January 18, 1855. All are now obsolete.

Hanover Court House, Va., an engagement, May 27, 1862, between the rear ranks of Porter's column of McClellan's army and a Confederate brigade commanded by Branch. The latter attacked Morell's division with considerable success, but Porter, hearing the firing, immediately wheeled and came to the rescue. The Confederates retreated rapidly, leaving a large number of prisoners and small arms.

Hanseatic Republics. A convention of friendship, commerce and navigation was concluded between the United States and the Free Hanseatic Republics of Lübeck, Bremen and Hamburg in 1827, and a consular convention in 1852. (See Bremen.)

Hard Cider. (See Log Cabin.)

Hardee, William J. (1817–1873), born in Georgia, was brevetted major and lieutenant-colonel for gallant conduct in the Mexican War. In 1856 he produced a work for the Government on the tactics of infantry, known as "Hardee's Tactics." In 1861 he enlisted in the Confederate service as a colonel at Fort Morgan, and was soon afterward made brigadier-general. He gained a success at Shiloh, was prominent in the campaign about Murfreesboro, and fought at Chattanooga. He surrendered with General Johnston's army at Durham Station in 1865.

Hards, in the political history of New York, a faction of the Democratic party, existent from 1852 to 1860, which inclined to alliance with the pro-slavery Democracy elsewhere, as distinguished from the "softs." In part the "hards" or "hardshells" were identical with the "hunkers" of preceding years.

Harlan, James, born in 1820, represented Iowa in the U. S. Senate from 1855 to 1865, when he became Secretary of the Interior in Lincoln's Cabinet, serving until 1866. He was again a U. S. Senator from 1866 to 1873.

Harlan, John M., born in 1833, served in the Union army from 1861 to 1867, was Attorney-General of Kentucky from 1863 to 1867, was a member of the Louisiana Commission appointed by Hayes, and became a Justice of the U. S. Supreme Court in 1877. In 1893 he was a member of the Court of Arbitration on the Behring Sea dispute.

Harlem Plains, a battle in the Revolutionary War, on September 16, 1776. Just after Howe's occupation of New York his advanced guard of English and Highland troops, under Colonel Leslie, came into conflict with some troops of Virginia under Major Leitch, and of Connecticut under Knowlton. Both sides were reinforced. Knowlton, attempting to flank the British, was killed. The Americans retreated, under orders from Washington, with a loss of sixty killed and wounded.

Harmar, Josiah (1753–1813), born in Philadelphia, served during the Revolutionary War, attaining the rank of lieutenant-colonel, and was commander-in-chief of the U. S. army from 1789 to 1792.

Harmonists, a socialistic community founded upon a religious basis by George Rapp, of Württemberg, in the Connoquenessing Valley, twenty-five miles from Pittsburgh, in 1803. There they built houses, churches, mills and manufactories, and by 1805 there were 750 persons settled there who formed the Harmony Society. After two years they decided to adopt celibacy, and prohibited the use of tobacco. This caused the withdrawal of certain of their people. In 1814 the Harmonists purchased 30,000 acres of land in Posey County, Indiana, settling there in 1815. There they remained until 1824, calling their settlement "Harmony." In 1824 they removed to their present location, on the Ohio River, not far from Pittsburgh. In 1831, a German adventurer, Bernhard Müller, settling among them, caused dissensions and a split in the society. Their numbers have decreased to less than 200.

Harnett, Cornelius (1723–1781), was prominent in the North Carolina Provincial Assembly from 1770 to 1771, aided in drafting a State Constitution in the Provincial Congress at Halifax in 1776 and served in Congress from 1777 to 1780.

Harney, William S. (1800–1889), joined the U. S. army in 1818, was brevetted major-general in 1865 for long and faithful service, and at the time of his death was the oldest officer in the U. S. army.

Harper, Robert Goodloe (1765–1825), born in Virginia, was admitted to the bar in 1786. He represented South Carolina in the U. S. Congress from 1795 to 1801, was promoted major-general for services in the War of 1812, and was elected a U. S. Senator from Maryland in 1816. He published various pamphlets upon diplomatic subjects of the day which won great popularity.

Harper, William R., born in 1856, and editor of *Hebraica* and the *Old Testament Student*, was professor of Semitic languages at Yale from 1886 to 1891, when he was chosen president of Chicago University.

Harper's Ferry, Va. In July, 1859, John Brown settled near Harper's Ferry and began, with the aid of some Kansas associates, the forcible liberation of slaves. October 17 he seized, with seventeen whites and five negroes, the United States arsenal at Harper's Ferry, and spent the next eighteen hours in freeing slaves, cutting telegraph wires, preparing defences and making prisoners of fifty white men. October 18, 1500 militia and marines arrived. They surrounded the armory engine house, burst open the door and captured Brown, three other whites and half a dozen negroes. Eight of the insurgents were killed. Brown was taken to Charlestown, Va., and there hanged, December 2, 1859.

Harper's Ferry, Va. (1862), was in possession of the Union troops, and captured by Stonewall Jackson September 15. The Union leaders, Miles and White, held the town with 11,000 men. Miles had posted a few regiments upon the heights commanding the town, but these were easily driven away by McLaws, while Jackson approached and bombarded the town, which surrendered as he was about to attack it. Miles was mortally wounded. The garrison was captured.

" **Harper's Magazine**," founded in 1850 by the Harper Brothers. It was originally an eclectic magazine containing the choicest contributions to English periodicals. This purely eclectic character was soon abandoned, and nearly every contemporaneous American and English writer of note has contributed to its pages.

Harris, Isham G., born in Tennessee in 1818, devoted his evenings to the study of law, and was admitted to the bar in 1841. He was elected to the Legislature of Tennessee from 1849 to 1853, and served as Governor of the State from 1857 until the occupation of Tennessee by the national army. He was an aide on General Johnston's staff, and served in the West throughout the war. He was elected a U. S. Senator in 1877, and has served until the present time (1894).

Harris, Joel Chandler, born in Georgia in 1848, was admitted to the bar and is editor of the Atlanta (Ga.) *Constitution*. He is the author of "Uncle Remus, His Songs and Sayings," and other stories of Southern life.

Harris, William T., born in 1835, founder and editor of the *Journal of Speculative Philosophy*, is prominent in educational circles, and from 1889 to 1893 was chief of the U. S. Bureau of Education.

Harrisburg, Pa., capital of the State since 1812. The town was laid out in 1785 and called Louisbourg. In 1791 it was incorporated under its present name. It became a city in 1860.

Harrisburg Convention. In 1827 a high tariff bill, known as the "Woolen Bill," was introduced into Congress by Clay and his adherents. It passed the House, but was defeated in the Senate by the casting vote of the Vice-President. Accordingly the protectionist faction, in 1828, called a convention at Harrisburg. The delegates were chiefly from New England and the Middle States. The convention presented the cause of protection to the people, and decided to seek an increased duty, not only on woolens, but on other specified articles of manufacture. This resulted in the passage of the high tariff bill of 1828.

Harrison, Benjamin (1740–1791), born in Virginia, was a member of the House of Burgesses in 1764, a member of the Correspondence Committee in 1773, and a delegate to the Continental Congress from 1774 to 1778. From 1778 to 1782 he was Speaker of the Virginia House of Burgesses, and ardently advocated united opposition to Great Britain. He was Governor of the State from 1782 to 1784, and when a delegate to the State Convention of 1788 opposed the ratification of the Constitution as being a national and not a Federal document.

Harrison, Benjamin, born August 20, 1833, twenty-third President of the United States, was the grandson of President William Henry Harrison, and was born at North Bend, Ohio. He was graduated at Miami University in 1852, and settled as a lawyer in Indianapolis. He was elected reporter of the

Indiana Supreme Court in 1860, but his term was interrupted by the war. He volunteered in 1862 and was colonel of an Indiana regiment; in the battles of Resaca and Peach Tree Creek in 1864 he won distinction. Leaving the army with the brevet of brigadier-general, he resumed his position of Supreme Court reporter. General Harrison was a successful lawyer and campaign orator, and in 1876 he received the Republican nomination for Governor, being defeated by a small majority. His name was presented to the Republican National Convention of 1880. Elected to the U. S. Senate, he served from 1881 to 1887. At the National Convention of 1888 he was a leading candidate from the start, received the nomination, and was elected over President Cleveland in a campaign in which protection was the principal issue. In his Cabinet, Blaine in the State and Windom in the Treasury Department were national figures. Proctor, and later Elkins, was in the War Department, B. F. Tracy in the Navy, Noble in the Interior, Rusk Secretary of Agriculture, Miller Attorney-General, and Wanamaker Postmaster-General. The administration was marked politically by the McKinley Tariff Act in 1890, with the attendant feature of reciprocity; the foreign relations with Chili and Hawaii were matters of interest. In 1892 the President was a candidate for renomination, and received the gift over his powerful rival, Blaine, who resigned from the Cabinet during the contest. President Harrison was in the election again confronted with Cleveland. The Democratic reaction, very marked in 1890, proved to be still in force, and the President was defeated and retired from office in 1893.

Harrison, Caroline Lavinia (Scott), born in Ohio, became the wife of Benjamin Harrison in 1854, and was a worthy and willing helpmeet in the struggles and perplexities of his career. She died during his Presidency, in 1892.

Harrison, William Henry (February 9, 1773–April 4, 1841), ninth President of the United States, was born in Virginia, and was son of Benjamin Harrison, a signer of the Declaration of Independence. He was educated at Hampden Sidney College, entered the army, and fought at Wayne's victory of 1794. In 1798 he became Secretary of the Northwest Territory, and in 1799 delegate to Congress. In 1800 he was appointed Governor of the new Indiana Territory. He was still Governor when the Indian outbreak occurred, and his victory at Tippecanoe, November 7, 1811, gave to him a national reputation and an epithet for life. In the War of 1812 he was major-general, first of Kentucky militia, and then in the regular army. He defended Fort Meigs against the British in 1813, and on October 5 of the same year he achieved his second noted military exploit by defeating Proctor and Tecumseh at the battle of the Thames. General Harrison resigned from the army in 1814. From 1816 to 1819 he was Congressman, from 1825 to 1828 U. S. Senator, and U. S. Minister to the United States of Colombia 1828–1829. As the Whig candidate for President in 1836 he was defeated by Van Buren. In December, 1839, the Whig Convention put Harrison again before the country, and Van Buren was again his antagonist. The campaign of 1840 was without precedent or successor. The "log cabin and hard cider" charged by his opponents against his early record, became a tower of strength to him; a "campaign ball" was set rolling across the country; and "Tippecanoe and Tyler too" were fairly "sung into the White House." In his Cabinet Webster as Secretary of State was the ablest member. Fatigue and exposure and importunities of office-seekers caused his death after a month of service,—the first death of a President while in office. General Harrison, though by no means brilliant, was an able administrator, and a man of good sense.

Harrison, Fort, Ind., a small fort, commanded by Captain Zachary Taylor with fifty men, attacked September 5, 1812, by Indians and partly burned. The fort was saved by reinforcements with the loss of only three men.

Harrison, Fort, Va., wrested from the Confederates by a small detachment of Grant's Federal army, September 28, 1864, during the campaign in the vicinities of Richmond and Petersburg.

Harrodsburg, Ky., the oldest town in the State. The first cabin was built here in 1774 by Captain James Harrod.

Hart, John (1708–1780), known as "Honest John Hart," represented New York in the Continental Congress from 1774 to 1777, signed the Declaration of Independence, and in 1777–1778 was chairman of the New York Committee of Safety.

Harte, Francis Bret, born in New York in 1839, was associated with the San Francisco *Golden Era* in 1857, edited for a short time the *Californian*, and in 1868 established the *Overland Monthly*. He has mostly written sketches of American frontier life. From 1880 to 1885 he was U. S. Consul at Glasgow.

Hartford, Conn., was settled in 1635 by emigrants from eastern Massachusetts, under the lead of Thomas Hooker. The Constitution for the colony, the first framed in America, was written here in 1639. It became the capital of the colony. In 1687 Sir E. Andros demanded the charter from the assembly in session in the city, but it was concealed, it is said, in the "Charter Oak." Trinity College was founded in Hartford in 1823.

Hartford, Convention at. In November, 1780, a convention of delegates from all the Northern States was held at Hartford, which sought methods of furnishing men and supplies for continuing the War of Independence. They passed resolutions in favor of a better financial system and a stronger Federal government.

Hartford Convention met at Hartford, Conn., December 15, 1814, and adjourned January 5, 1815. It consisted of delegates from Massachusetts, Connecticut and Rhode Island and was the outgrowth of the opposition of the New England Federalists to the war with Great Britain which was then in progress and which was especially injurious to the commercial interests of New England. The New England States strongly denounced the policy of the Democratic administration in the conduct of the war, especially in respect to forcible drafts. The convention was held in secret and a report was falsely circulated that it looked toward a dissolution of the Union. The general aim of the convention seems to have been to propose certain reforms in the direction of States' rights. Its proceedings brought upon the New England Federalists great odium.

Hartranft, John F. (1830–1889), entered the army in 1861, had commands at Roanoke, Antietam and Fredericksburg, was brigadier-general at the Wilderness, Spottsylvania and Petersburg and brevetted major-general in 1865. He was Governor of Pennsylvania from 1872 to 1878.

Harvard, John (1607–1638), was born in London, England. He was ordained a clergyman, but, being a Puritan, emigrated to New England in 1637 and became a freeman of the Massachusetts colony. At his death he bequeathed half of his property or about 750 pounds, and his entire library of 320 volumes, to the college which bears his name.

Harvard University, the oldest college in the United States, at Cambridge, Mass. It was founded in 1636, and chartered in 1650 by the General Court. In 1638 it was named after Rev. John Harvard, who left it probably £750. Its first class, consisting of nine, was graduated in 1642. It received State aid, in addition to private benefactions, till 1814, but its official connection with the commonwealth continued till 1865, after which time the control of the university was vested in its alumni. Besides its academic department it has schools of theology, law, medicine, science and dental surgery, founded respectively in 1819, 1817, 1782, 1848 and 1868.

Hatcher's Run, Va., scene of two severe engagements during the Civil War, while Grant and Lee were manœuvring about Richmond and Petersburg. October 27, 1864, Grant endeavored to force a passage of Hatcher's Run and move against the South Side Railroad. Finding no assailable point in the Confederate lines he decided to withdraw, when suddenly the Confederates fell furiously upon Hancock's rear ranks. Hancock turned and drove them back to their fortifications. From February 5 to 7, 1865, there was also some severe fighting about Hatcher's Run between Hancock, who was endeavoring to push the Federal lines to that stream, and the Confederates under Gordon and Hill. Hancock was successful.

Hatteras Inlet, N. C., location of two Confederate forts commanded by Samuel Barron, and deemed a valuable passage for landing the ammunition and supplies of the Confederacy, and for sending cotton out of the country. General Butler and Commodore Stringham fitted out an expedition against these forts, Clark and Hatteras, and sailed from Hampton Roads August 26, 1861, with ten vessels carrying 158 guns and 900 men. Fort Clark, the weaker position, was speedily reduced, August 27, by the guns of the Federal ships "Minnesota," "Wabash" and "Susquehanna," and Hatteras was captured after protracted bombardment the next day. Barron and 700 Confederates were made prisoners.

Hatton, Frank, born in 1846, was Assistant Postmaster-General from 1881 to 1884, when he was made Postmaster-General in Arthur's Cabinet, being the youngest officer ever in a U. S. Cabinet except Alexander Hamilton.

Havemeyer, William F. (1804–1874), mayor of New York City from 1845 to 1851, and from 1872 to 1874, was president of the Bank of North America from 1851 to 1861, and very prominent in the overthrow of the Tweed ring.

Haverford College, Pa., was founded by the Friends in 1833.

Haw, Battle of the, February 25, 1781. About 400 loyalists had collected near the Haw. Henry Lee, by passing for Tarleton's force, got among them. The trick was discovered and a hot fight followed in which ninety loyalists were slain and many wounded. Lee's loss was light.

Hawaii. A treaty of commerce and for the extradition of criminals was concluded between the United States and Hawaii in 1849, and a reciprocity treaty in 1875, extended by the Convention of 1887. Treaty rights were further confirmed by Act of Congress in 1891. The *coup d'état* of January, 1893, deposed the queen and established a republic, which immediately asked for annexation by the United States. An annexation treaty was concluded February 14, 1893, providing for the cession to the United States of all rights of sovereignty in the Hawaiian Islands and their dependencies; for reference to the U. S. Congress of all questions of administration, the provisional government meanwhile to continue under United States guidance; for the assumption by the United States of the Hawaiian debt to the limit of $3,250,000; for the regulation of Chinese immigration; and for the support of deposed royalty. The close of the session of Congress prevented its ratification by that body, and the incoming administration proving hostile to the treaty it remains still unratified (May, 1894).

Hawkins, Sir John (1520–1595), an Elizabethan navigator who was engaged in the West India slave trade. His first voyage was made in 1562. In 1565 he captured a cargo of slaves in Guinea and traded along the coast of Florida. His last voyage was made in 1567 with Sir Francis Drake. He was knighted in 1588 for services against the Spanish Armada.

Hawks, Francis L. (1798–1866), of North Carolina, for a time a successful lawyer, entered the Episcopal ministry and became eminent in his profession. He is the author of numerous political and ecclesiastical works, and of a history of North Carolina.

Hawley, Joseph R., born in 1826, was admitted to the Connecticut bar in 1850. In 1857 he became editor of the *Hartford Evening Press*, which advanced the interests of the Republican party. He was the first Connecticut volunteer in the Civil War, enlisted as a captain, and was mustered out as brevet major-general in 1865. In 1866 he was elected Governor of Connecticut, and in 1868 was president of the National Republican Convention, in that of 1872 secretary of the Committee on Resolutions and its chairman in 1876. He was a U. S. Congressman from 1872 to 1881, when he was chosen Senator, serving until the present time (1894). He is a pleasing speaker and a strong Republican.

Hawthorne, Nathaniel (1804–1864), was born at Salem, Mass. He contributed his early productions to periodicals such as the *New England Magazine*, the *American Magazine*, the *Democratic Review* and the *Token*. In 1837 appeared his "Twice Told Tales," and in 1849 he published the "Scarlet Letter," which at once brought him into prominence. In 1853 he was appointed Consul at Liverpool by President Pierce, and served until 1857. He is the greatest romance-writer that America has produced.

Hay, John, born in 1838, was assistant secretary to President Lincoln in 1861. He served several months in the Civil War, and from 1865 to 1867 was secretary of legation to Paris, chargé d'affaires at Vienna until 1868, and secretary at Madrid until 1870. He became associated with the *New York Tribune*, and from 1879 to 1881 was First Assistant Secretary of State. He is widely known for his dialect sketches and poems, and for Nicolay and Hay's life of Lincoln.

Hayburn vs. State. Attorney-General Randolph in 1792 moved that the Supreme Court issue a mandamus to the Circuit Court of Pennsylvania to admit Hayburn of that State to the United States pension list. Randolph declared he made the motion *ex officio* with a view to seeing the provisions of the Act of Congress of March 23, 1792, relating to pensions, executed. The court would not allow this, so he next pleaded the merits of the case. Judgment was postponed and never given, since the Act of Congress of 1793 provided for pensioners in another way. Whether the Act of 1792 was constitutional was not decided by the court; but the judges were individually of that opinion, and this gives the case a certain importance, being a very early one, among those involving such considerations.

Hayden, Ferdinand V. (1829–1887), born in Massachusetts, was a surgeon in the Civil War. He has superintended geological and geographical surveys of the territories of the United States, and has published valuable and extensive reports.

Hayes, Isaac I. (1832–1881), made three voyages of exploration to the Arctic regions, served as surgeon during the Civil War, and was a member of the New York Assembly from 1865 to 1870.

Hayes, Lucy Ware (Webb), married President R. B. Hayes in 1852, was renowned for her sympathetic devotion to the soldiers wounded in the Civil War, and for her efforts, while occupying the White House, to promote the interests of temperance and other good causes.

Hayes, Rutherford Birchard (October 4, 1822–January 17, 1893), nineteenth President of the United States, was born at Delaware, O., and graduated at Kenyon College in 1842. He practiced law in Fremont, O., and became city solicitor in Cincinnati. On the outbreak of the war he volunteered, and rose from major of Ohio infantry to brigadier-general and brevet major-general. He was wounded at the battle of South Mountain, and distinguished himself in the Shenandoah campaign of 1864 at Winchester, Fisher's Hill and Cedar Creek. He entered Congress in 1865, and, having been elected Governor of his State, he occupied that position from 1868 to 1872. He was defeated for Congressman in 1872, but elected Governor in 1875 on the "honest money" issue, after a campaign which attracted national attention. It was this success which caused Governor Hayes' name to be presented to the Republican National Convention of 1876. The two leading candidates, Blaine and Bristow, were set aside, and Hayes was nominated on the seventh ballot. (For the doubtful result and final settlement of this extraordinary Hayes-Tilden campaign, see Electoral Commission.) Mr. Hayes was declared elected March 2, 1877, and inaugurated March 5. He

STATESMEN OF THE MIDDLE PERIOD.

Thomas H. Benton. Robert Winthrop.
Stephen A. Douglas. Edward Everett.
Silas Wright.
John C. Calhoun. Daniel Webster.
Henry Clay. W. L. Marcy.

selected Evarts for the State Department, Sherman for the Treasury, McCrary for War, R. W. Thompson for the Navy, Schurz for the Interior, Devens Attorney-General and D. M. Key Postmaster-General. During his administration occurred the great railroad strikes of 1877, and the resumption of specie payments in 1879. President Hayes favored civil service reform, a conciliatory policy in the South, vetoed the Bland bill and vetoed a Chinese restriction bill. After the close of his term, in 1881, he lived in retirement in Ohio.

Haymarket Massacre (Chicago), an Anarchist riot, originating in labor troubles which culminated in an open-air meeting in Haymarket Square May 4, 1886. Violent speeches were made by the Anarchists Spies, Parsons and Fielden. A bomb was thrown among the police, causing great loss of life. Spies, Parsons, Fischer, Engel, Schwab, Lingg and Neebe were arrested and tried. The first four were hanged November 11, 1887. Fielden and Schwab were imprisoned for life. Lingg committed suicide. Governor Altgeld, of Illinois, pardoned Fielden and Schwab in 1893.

Hayne, Isaac (1745–1781), born in South Carolina, entered the colonial army at the outbreak of the Revolution, and when the British took possession of Charleston in 1780 was paroled. In 1781 he made an incursion against the British, was pursued by a superior force and taken prisoner. He was sentenced to death by the British without a trial and hanged.

Hayne, Paul H. (1830–1886), "The Laureate of the South," editor of numerous periodicals, exerted a powerful influence upon the literary life of the South, and published a great number of poems.

Hayne, Robert Young (1791–1839), served during the War of 1812, and was a member of the South Carolina Legislature from 1814 to 1818, in which year he was Speaker. From 1818 to 1822 he was Attorney-General of the State, and in 1823 was sent to the U. S. Senate, where he strenuously opposed the protective system, denying its constitutionality. He asserted that under the Constitution a State had the right to arrest the operation of such Federal enactments as she considered unconstitutional. This led to the famous debate between Webster and Hayne in 1830, respecting State rights and nullification. He was chairman of the State Convention in 1832, which reported the celebrated ordinance of nullification, and was Governor of South Carolina from 1832 to 1834, when that State prepared to enforce the nullification ordinance and make armed resistance against the Federal authority; but the tariff bill of Henry Clay compromised the difficulties. Hayne was a brilliant speaker.

Hays, Alexander (1819–1864), enlisted in the Civil War as a colonel in the Maryland campaign, fought at Chancellorsville and Gettysburg, was brevetted colonel U. S. A., and was killed at the battle of the Wilderness.

Hayti. It was not until November 3, 1864, that a treaty of amity, commerce and navigation, and for the extradition of criminals, was concluded between the two nations. The attitude of the United States up to that time toward this negro republic was fixed by considerations growing out of the slavery question.

Hayward, a town officer appointed in the early New England colonies to look after hedges and boundaries of private property and prevent encroachment. Also his office was akin to that of the impounder and common driver.

Hazelwood, John (1726?–1800?), born in England, was a commodore in the Pennsylvania navy in 1776, and while commander of the State navy in 1777 and of the Continental vessels on the Delaware River, became prominent for skill and success.

Hazen, William B. (1830–1887), commanded in the Mexican War, led a brigade at Shiloh, Chickamauga and Missionary Ridge, was promoted major-general, and was afterward prominent in the Signal Service, of which he was chief from 1880 to 1887.

Headley, Joel T., born in 1813, became an assistant editor of the *New York Tribune* in 1846, and has written numerous popular works of history and biography, including a life of Washington.

Heath, William (1737–1814), was chosen captain of the Suffolk regiment before the Revolution, and commanded the Boston artillery in 1770. He was a Massachusetts Assemblyman in 1761 and from 1771 to 1774, and a member of the Committee of Safety and of the Provincial Congress from 1774 to 1775. He was made brigadier-general in 1774 for meritorious services, and was promoted major-general in 1775. He was a member of the convention which ratified the Constitution, was a State Senator from 1791 to 1792, and a probate judge from 1793.

Heintzelman, Samuel P. (1805–1880), graduated at West Point, served as a captain in the Mexican War, and was brevetted major for bravery. He was commissioned colonel in the Civil War, and afterward commanded as brigadier-general at Alexandria, Bull Run, Yorktown, Williamsburg and Fair Oaks, and in 1863 commanded the Northern Department. He was retired in 1869 with the full rank of major-general U. S. A.

Heister, Leopold Philip von (1707–1777), Hessian lieutenant-general and commander of all the Hessians in America, landed at Long Island in command of two Hessian brigades in 1776, and aided the British against the colonies at that place and at White Plains. In 1777 he was recalled, at the desire of Howe.

Helena, capital of Montana, was settled in 1864.

Helena, Mo., fortified and occupied by 4500 Federals under Prentiss in 1863. The Confederates, Holmes, Price and Marmaduke, assaulted this position July 4 with 8000 soldiers. Charge after charge was made, but all proved ineffectual. The National batteries inflicted terrible losses upon the assaulting troops. Holmes ordered a retreat about noon, having lost fully twenty per cent of his army.

Helper, Hinton R., born in 1829, author of "The Impending Crisis of the South," a book which, in the anti-slavery struggles just before the war, made a profound impression, as presenting the views of the non-slaveholding whites of the South. He was U. S. Consul at Buenos Ayres from 1861 to 1867.

Helps, Sir Arthur (1817–1875), is the English author of "Conquerors of the New World and Their Bondsmen," "The Spanish Conquest in America and its Relation to the History of Slavery," and lives of Columbus, Pizarro and Cortez.

Henderson, John B., born in 1826, was a member of the Missouri Legislature in 1848 and 1856, and while a U. S. Senator from 1863 to 1869 was one of the Republicans who opposed the impeachment of President Johnson.

Henderson, Richard (1734–1785), a Judge in the North Carolina Supreme Court in 1769, organized the "Transylvania Land Company" in 1775, and established a government over that Western region, but was declared guilty of an infringement of the rights of Virginia by the Legislature of that State.

Henderson, Thomas J., born in 1824, was a member of the Illinois Legislature from 1855 to 1860, was brevetted brigadier-general in 1865 for services in the Civil War, and was a U. S. Congressman from 1875 to the present time (1894).

Hendrick (1680?–1755), a Mohawk chief who represented the Six Nations at a treaty congress in 1754 at Albany, and who faithfully aided the British against the French.

Hendricks, Thomas A. (1819–1885), was admitted to the bar in 1843. He was elected to the Indiana House of Representatives in 1848, and became a State Senator in 1849. In 1850 he was chosen a member of the convention to revise the State Constitution, and represented Indiana in the Congress of the United States from 1851 to 1855. He was appointed by President Pierce Commissioner of the General Land Office, serving from 1855 to 1859, and from 1863 to 1869 was a U. S. Senator. He was Governor of Indiana from 1872 to 1877, and in 1876 was the Democratic candidate for Vice-President of the United States on the ticket with Samuel J. Tilden. He was the unanimous choice of the Democratic party for Vice-President in 1884, and was elected on the ticket with Grover Cleveland for President, but died during his first year of office.

Hening's Statutes, the first complete collection ever published of the laws of any colony and State, with inclusion of those obsolete and repealed. Hening's "Statutes at Large of Virginia" was published, beginning in 1809, by W. W. Hening, largely at the instance of President Jefferson. It is of great value as a source of history. (13 vols.)

Hennepin, Louis (1640?–1701), a missionary of the Order of Recollets of St. Francis, was born in Belgium. He came to Canada in 1673, and founded a convent at Fort Frontenac in 1676. He accompanied La Salle's expedition to the West and to the Niagara and the Upper Lakes in 1678, and constructed Fort Crèvecœur in Illinois. Hennepin and his followers proceeded down the Mississippi until captured by the Sioux in 1680. On his return to Europe he published his "Description de la Louisiane nouvellement découverte au sud-ouest de la Nouvelle France," and in 1697 his "Nouvelle découverte d'un très-grand pays situé dans l'Amérique, entre le Nouveau-Mexique et la mer Glaciale." He claimed to be the first to descend to the mouth of the Mississippi, but this is open to dispute.

Henry VII. (1457–1509), King of England from 1485 to 1509, granted on March 5, 1495, to John Cabot, his three sons, their heirs and assigns, a patent for the discovery of unknown lands in the Eastern, Western and Northern seas, with a right to occupy such territories and to have exclusive commerce with them, paying to the king one-fifth part of all the profits. The enterprise was to be "at their own proper cost and charge." In his book of private expenses for 1497 there is an item, "To him that found the new isle, £10," no doubt referring to Cabot.

Henry, John. In 1809 John Henry was sent by Sir John Craig, Governor of British North America, to report upon the state of affairs and political feeling in the New England States. Hoping for a reward, Henry painted the New England disaffection to the Union in very high colors in all his correspondence with Craig. Failing of his reward he returned to the United States and sold, in 1812, the whole correspondence to President Madison. The latter sent the documents to Congress in the belief that they proved an attempt on Great Britain's part to annex New England. Nothing of the sort was proved.

Henry, Joseph (1797–1878), physicist, made highly valuable contributions to science, particularly in the line of electricity, magnetism and meteorology. He was director of the Smithsonian Institute.

Henry, Patrick (May 29, 1736–June 6, 1799), was born in Hanover County, Va. He failed in farming and trading, and started his career as a lawyer, with somewhat slender equipment, in 1760. He attracted attention by a noted speech in 1763, and in 1765 he entered the House of Burgesses and uttered his famous arraignment of the Stamp Act. He was a leader in organizing the committees of correspondence, and was a delegate to the first Continental Congress. In 1775 occurred his "liberty or death" speech, and he was active in the beginning of hostilities as a colonel and commander of Virginia troops. He took the lead in organizing the Virginia State Government, and was its first Governor, being elected in 1776, 1777 and 1778, and in 1784 and 1785. His jealousy of State privileges and devotion to democracy led him to oppose the Federal Constitution of 1787. He was the Anti-Federalist leader in the State, and was prominent in the ratifying convention of 1788. For a short time, 1794–1795, he was U. S. Senator, was finally a Federalist, and was for many years a member of the Virginia Legislature. Patrick Henry was noted for eloquence, but did not in constructive statesmanship compare with some of the other great Virginians. His life has been recently written by William Wirt Henry. There are other lives by Wirt and M. C. Tyler.

Henry, Cape, Va., named in April, 1607, by Admiral Newport, in honor of Henry, Prince of Wales, son of James I. of England.

Henry, Fort, Tenn., captured February 6, 1862, by the Federals, Commodore Foote and General Grant, commanding seven Union gunboats and a land force of 17,000. Fort Henry and Fort Heiman, a neighboring Confederate stronghold, were held by General Tilghman with 2734 men. Heiman was early abandoned. Foote was to reduce Fort Henry and Grant to cut off the retreat of the garrison. The Union gunboats commenced firing at six thousand yards, gradually nearing the fort. Tilghman held out bravely, but the bursting of a twenty-four-pounder gun, wounding many of his men, forced him to surrender his staff and himself. By his orders Colonel Heiman had been directed to attempt a retreat with the main body of the garrison. This move was accomplished through Grant's late arrival, owing to recent floods.

Henshaw, David (1791–1852), a Massachusetts Senator in 1826, and a Representative in 1839, was appointed Secretary of the Navy by President Tyler, but, being soon afterward rejected by the Senate, served only from 1843 to 1844.

Henson, Josiah (1787–1881), whose life furnished the basis for "Uncle Tom's Cabin," was a negro slave in Maryland, but gained his freedom by flight to Canada, and became pastor of a church.

Hepburn vs. Griswold, one of the "legal-tender cases" in the U. S. Supreme Court, decided 1864. In 1860 Mrs. Hepburn promised to pay Griswold on February 20, 1862, $11,250, legal tender at that time (1860) being gold and silver only. In 1862, during the Civil War, the United States issued $150,000,000 of its own notes to be received as lawful money in payment of public and private debts within the United States. Mrs. Hepburn's note being overdue, suit was brought by Griswold in the Court of Chancery of Kentucky in 1864. Mrs. Hepburn tendered United States notes in payment, which were refused, though the court declared the debt absolved. The Court of Appeals reversed this judgment, and, it being brought to the U. S. Supreme Court, that body confirmed the judgment of the Court of Appeals of Kentucky, on the ground that the Act of 1862 was not intended to impair contracts made prior to its passage. This decision was reversed in Knox *vs.* Lee and Julliard *vs.* Greenman.

"Herald of Freedom." The first issue of this newspaper was made October 21, 1854, in Wakarusa, Kansas, but it was really printed in Pennsylvania. It was the first newspaper of Kansas. It was afterward established at Lawrence, January 6, 1855. After this the office was destroyed and the paper suspended for a time. It was soon renewed, however, and continued until 1859, when it was finally suspended.

Herbert, Hilary A., was born in South Carolina in 1834, and was admitted to the bar. He enlisted in the Confederate army as a captain, and was promoted colonel. He was wounded in the battle of the Wilderness in 1864. He represented Alabama in the Congress of the United States from 1877 to 1893, when he became Secretary of the Navy in the Cabinet of President Cleveland.

Herkimer, Nicholas (1715–1777), was appointed a colonel of militia in 1758, and commanded at Fort Herkimer against the French and Indians. He was appointed brigadier-general of militia by the State Convention in 1776, and marched against Sir John Johnson's force of Tories and Indians. He was mortally wounded at Oriskany in an expedition for the relief of Fort Stanwix, which was besieged by St. Leger in 1777.

Hermitage, the home of Andrew Jackson, at Nashville, Tenn., to which he moved from Hunter's Hill about 1804. The house in which he lived during the last twenty-five years of his life was not built until 1819.

Herndon, William L. (1813–1857), entered the navy in 1828, explored the Amazon for the U. S. Government in 1851 and 1852, and bravely died while aiding passengers on the sinking mail steamer, "Central America."

Herrera, José Joaquin (1792–1854), became president of Mexico in 1845; but was deposed for favoring the independence of Texas. He was second in command during the war with the United States. He was again president from 1848 to 1851.

Herrman, Augustine (1605?–1686), established the Virginia tobacco trade about 1629. He was prominent in the affairs of New Netherlands. He was created Lord of Bohemia Manor, a large tract of land southwest of the Delaware, in 1662.

Hesse. A convention for the abolition of *droit d'aubaine* and taxes on emigration was concluded between the United States and Hesse in 1844.

Hessians. Early in 1776, the British Government made treaties with various German petty princes, by which it obtained mercenaries for the war in America. Under these treaties, the Landgrave of Hesse-Cassel sent 17,000 troops, the Duke of Brunswick 6000, the Count of Hesse-Hanau 2400, the Margrave of Anspach 2400, the Prince of Waldeck and the Prince of Anhalt-Zerbst about 1000 each. In all, England paid the princes about £1,800,000. The Hessians on the whole fought well. Some of them settled in this country and Nova Scotia. About 17,000 returned to Germany.

Hewes, George R. T. (1751–1840), was one of the foremost among the patriots in the "Boston Tea Party" in 1773. He afterward joined the army and was stationed at West Point.

Hewes, Joseph (1730–1779), served in the North Carolina Senate in 1763. He was a prominent member of the Continental Congress in 1774, and signed the Declaration of Independence.

Hewitt, Abram S., born in 1822, represented New York in the U. S. Congress from 1874 to 1886, except one term, and advocated a moderate tariff and honest money. He was one of the scientific commissioners sent by the United States to the French Exposition of 1867. He was chairman of the Democratic National Committee in 1876. He was chosen mayor of New York City in 1886, and served one term.

Heyward, Thomas, Jr. (1746–1809), a member of the first South Carolina Committee of Safety, was a delegate to Congress from 1775 to 1778, and signed the Declaration of Independence. In 1780, he commanded a battalion in the siege of Charleston.

Hickey Plot, a conspiracy in 1776 to assassinate General Washington at New York. Thomas Hickey, one of the general's life guards, was the ringleader. He was hanged in June, 1776. David Matthews, mayor of New York, was implicated, and Governor Tryon was suspected. Matthews was imprisoned.

Hickory, Old, a nickname given to General Jackson, on account of his toughness and powers of resistance.

Hicks, Elias (1748–1830), a celebrated preacher of the Society of Friends, denied the divinity of Christ and a vicarious atonement, thereby causing a division of the Society into Orthodox and "Hicksite" Quakers.

Hicksites, a body that seceded from the Society of Friends in the year 1827 under the leadership of Elias Hicks, of Jericho, L. I. They still retain the name of "Friends," but hold Socinian views in regard to the Trinity and the atonement. Number of members in 1890, 22,000.

Higginson, Francis (1588–1630), came as pastor to Massachusetts from England in 1629, settled at Salem, and wrote "New England's Plantations, or a Short and True Description of the Commodities and Discommodities of the Country."

Higginson, Thomas Wentworth, was born in 1823. He was early identified with the anti-slavery cause. He left the ministry in 1858, and has since devoted himself to literature. He enlisted in the Civil War in 1862, was made colonel of the first regiment of colored troops, and captured Jacksonville. He was a Massachusetts Congressman in 1880 and 1881. He is an earnest advocate of woman suffrage. He has contributed largely to current literature, and has published two histories of the United States.

"**Higher Law.**" During the controversy in Congress, in 1850, over the admission of California as a free or slave State, Senator Seward, of New York, representing the Free-Soil Whigs, declared the common domain devoted to justice and liberty, not only by the Constitution, but by a "higher law than the Constitution," and that California must be admitted with no compromise.

Highlanders. After the troubles of 1715 and 1745 bodies of Highlanders came to the colonies and settled in the back districts of South Carolina as Indian traders and farmers. When Oglethorpe came over in 1733 with his letters patent for the district afterward called Georgia, he found numerous settlements of Highlanders occupying portions of his territory. They gave him invaluable aid in his difficulties with the Spaniards and the unfriendly Indians. The Highlanders were opposed to the introduction of negroes.

High-minded Federalists, a name given in ridicule to a set of New York Federalists, supporters of DeWitt Clinton, because of their overfrequent use of that adjective.

Higley Token (see Granby Token), a private or unauthorized coinage issued in Connecticut by John Higley, of Granby, in 1737. It was made of copper. The obverse bore a deer and a legend, Value Me As You Please, the Roman numerals III. and a crescent; the reverse, three hammers on a triangular field, each bearing a crown; legend, I Am Good Copper.

Hildreth, Richard (1807–1865), in 1832 became associate editor of the *Boston Atlas*, which attained considerable eminence as a daily Whig journal. In 1837 he published articles opposing the annexation of Texas, and while residing in the South published the anti-slavery novel, "Archy Moore," republished as "The White Slave." In 1840 he published "Despotism in America," in 1843 a "Theory of Politics," and in 1854 "The Legal Basis of Slavery." He is most prominent as author of a history of the United States in six volumes, which is brought down to the close of Monroe's first term, and is of excellent quality, though of warm Federalist sympathies.

Hill, Ambrose P. (1825–1865), graduated from the U. S. Military Academy in 1847 and served during the Mexican War. At the outbreak of the Civil War he was appointed a colonel in the Virginia volunteers and fought at Bull Run. He was promoted brigadier-general for bravery and commanded at Williamsburg, and was afterward promoted major-general. He took a prominent and aggressive part in the battles around Richmond, had important commands at Antietam, Fredericksburg and Chancellorsville, and was brevetted lieutenant-general. He led a corps at Gettysburg, and met his death in defence of Petersburg.

Hill, Benjamin Harvey (1823–1882), born in Georgia, was admitted to the bar in 1845. He was elected to the Georgia House of Representatives in 1851, 1859 and 1860. He was a Unionist member of the State secession convention and strenuously opposed the ordinance of secession, but after its passage supported the Confederacy. He was a delegate from Georgia to the Confederate provisional Congress, and was a member of the Confederate Senate till 1865. He published "Notes on the Situation," ably opposing the reconstruction measures. He earnestly supported Horace Greeley for the Presidency in 1872. He served in the U. S. Congress from 1875 to 1877, and on the Electoral Commission, and was a member of the U. S. Senate from 1877 to 1882.

Hill, David B., politician, born in 1843, was a member of the New York Assembly in 1871 and 1872. He was president of the Democratic State Conventions of 1877 and 1881. He was Lieutenant-Governor of New York in 1882, and Governor from 1885 to 1891. He was in 1891 elected U. S. Senator for the term expiring in 1897.

Hill, David H. (1821–1889), general, was born in South Carolina. He was graduated from West Point in 1842. He was brevetted major for gallant service at Chapultepec during the Mexican War. He enlisted in the Confederate service in 1861, gained a victory at Big Bethel, and was promoted major-general in 1862. He gained distinction in the "Seven Days'" battles about Richmond and at Boonesboro and Fredericksburg. He commanded in North Carolina and at Richmond and Petersburg. He was engaged at Chickamauga, and surrendered in 1865.

Hill, Nathaniel P., born in 1832, has been prominent in the development of mining industries in the West. He was a U. S. Senator from Colorado from 1879 to 1885, and was the leading advocate of bimetallism.

Hill, Thomas (1818–1891), president of Harvard from 1862 to 1868, accompanied Agassiz on the exploring expedition to South America. He published numerous mathematical works.

Hillard, George S. (1808–1879), scholar and lawyer, was a delegate to the Massachusetts Constitutional Convention of 1853. He was a U. S. District

Attorney from 1866 to 1870. He was the author of "Six Months in Italy" and numerous biographies.

Hillhouse, James (1754–1832), Senator, was a captain in the Revolutionary War. He was a Representative in the Connecticut Legislature from 1786 to 1789. He represented Connecticut in the U. S. Congress as a Federalist from 1791 to 1795, and from 1796 to 1810 was a U. S. Senator. From 1810 to 1825 he was commissioner of the Connecticut School Fund. He was a member of the Hartford Convention.

Hilliard, Henry W., born in 1808, author of the "Junius Brutus" papers, represented Alabama in the U. S. Congress from 1845 to 1851. He was a brigadier-general in the Confederate army. He was Minister to Brazil from 1877 to 1881.

Hillsboro, N. C., an encampment of Sherman's Federal army of 85,000 men in 1865, during his pursuit of Johnston's Confederate troops 45,000 strong. April 14 Sherman ordered his army to move from Hillsboro, which is near Raleigh, to cut off Johnston's retreat toward Charlotte. As this movement was about to be begun Johnston sent to negotiate a surrender by conditional treaty for all Confederates under arms. This treaty was drawn up April 18.

Hindman, Thomas C. (1818–1868), was a lieutenant in the Mexican War. He represented Mississippi in Congress as a Democrat from 1858 to 1861. He was a brigadier-general in the Western Confederate army, and became major-general. He was assassinated for having exacted too severe discipline.

Hindoos, a nickname applied to the Know-Nothing party in consequence of their candidate for the Presidency, Daniel Ullman, who was alleged to have been a native of Calcutta.

Hiscock, Frank, Senator, born in 1834, was a New York District Attorney from 1860 to 1863. He was a U. S. Congressman from 1877 to 1886, when he became a U. S. Senator for the term ending in 1893.

"Historical Magazine," an important periodical, devoted to American history, and edited by Henry B. Dawson. The full title was "The Historical Magazine and Notes and Queries Concerning the Antiquities, History and Biography of America." Eighteen volumes were published, from 1857 to 1873.

Historical Societies. The first such in the United States was the Massachusetts Historical Society, founded in 1791. The New York Historical Society was established in 1809, the American Antiquarian Society in 1812, the American Historical Association in 1884.

Hitchcock, Edward (1793–1864), an eminent American geologist, published "Report on the Geology of Massachusetts" and "The Religion of Geology." He was prominent for his labors on the fossils of the Connecticut Valley.

Hoar, Ebenezer R., born in 1816, was a Judge of the Court of Common Pleas of Massachusetts from 1849 to 1855 and of the Massachusetts Supreme Court from 1859 to 1869. He was Attorney-General of the United States from 1869 to 1870 in Grant's Cabinet. He was a member of the commission which negotiated the Treaty of Washington. He represented Massachusetts as a Republican in the U. S. Congress from 1873 to 1875.

Hoar, George F., born in 1826, was a member of the Massachusetts Legislature in 1852 and 1857. He represented Massachusetts in the U. S. Congress as a Republican from 1869 to 1877, and in the Senate from 1877 to the present time (1894). He was a delegate to the Republican National Conventions of 1876, 1880, 1884 and 1888. He was a member of the Electoral Commission in 1877.

Hobart, Augustus C. (**Hobart Pasha**) (1822–1886), entered the British navy in 1836. During the Civil War he commanded the "Don," a successful blockade runner off the coast of North Carolina. He was placed in command of the Turkish fleet in the war of Turkey against Russia in 1877.

Hobart College, Geneva, N. Y., was chartered in 1825 by Episcopalians.

Hobkirk's Hill, Battle of, April 25, 1781. Greene, being unable to assault or invest Camden, S. C., took his position ten miles north at Hobkirk's Hill. Here Lord Rawdon attacked him. Greene had nearly won when victory slipped from his grasp. The famous Maryland brigade fell into disorder through misunderstanding of orders and deranged Greene's plan. He was driven from his post and forced to retire. His general scheme, however, was so good that Rawdon gained nothing from his victory, being forced to evacuate Camden by the capture of Fort Watson.

Hodge, Charles (1797–1878), professor of theology at Princeton from 1822 to 1878, founded the *Princeton Review*, which he edited until it was combined with the *Presbyterian Quarterly* in 1871. He was author of a "Systematic Theology," and of great influence upon Presbyterian theological thought.

Hoe, Richard M. (1812–1886), born in New York, invented a rotary press known as "Hoe's lightning press," which in one minute will print, cut and fold a sheet of paper 800 feet long.

Hoffman, Charles Fenno (1806–1884), of New York, was editorially connected with the *Knickerbocker Magazine*, the *American Monthly Magazine* and the *Literary World*. He was an author of poems and popular songs, and wrote "The Administration of Jacob Leisler" and "The Pioneers of New York."

Hoffman, John T., born in New York in 1828, became a member of Tammany in 1858. He was mayor of New York City from 1865 to 1869, and Governor of New York State from 1869 to 1873.

Holden, Edward S., born in 1846, was connected with the U. S. Naval Observatory from 1873 to 1886, when he became director of the Lick Observatory. He is the author of a life of Sir William Herschel and "Monograph of the Central Parts of the Nebula of Orion," an exhaustive treatise.

Holden, William W., born in 1818, edited the *Raleigh Standard* from 1843 to 1868. He signed the ordinance of secession in 1861. While Governor of North Carolina in 1868 he was prominent in suppressing the Ku Klux outrages.

Holland, Josiah G. (1819–1881), an editor of the *Massachusetts Republican* from 1849 to 1866, published a "History of Western Massachusetts" and a "Life of Abraham Lincoln." In 1870 he established *Scribner's Monthly*.

Holland. (See Netherlands.)

Holland Land Company, an association of Dutch capitalists to whom Robert Morris sold in 1792–93 the greater part of a valuable tract of land, west of the Genesee River, which he had purchased the year before from the State of Massachusetts.

Holland Patent, the first land-grant in the present county of Orange, New York. It was made to six Dutch patentees by Governor Dongan, of New York, in 1686. The land was to be held in free and common socage of King James II.

Holley, Myron (1779–1841), while in the New York Assembly from 1816 to 1824, advocated the construction of the Erie Canal. He was prominent among the Anti-Masons, and afterward labored in behalf of the Liberty party.

Hollins, George N. (1799–1878), naval officer, served in the Algerian War in 1815. By his unauthorized bombardment of Nicaragua in 1855 he nearly involved the United States in difficulties with Great Britain. A Confederate naval officer during the Civil War, he commanded the naval forces below New Orleans which Farragut defeated in April, 1863.

Holly Springs, Miss., held by the Federals under Colonel Murphy as General Grant's hospital and depot of supplies. It was captured by the Confederate leader, Van Dorn, December 20, 1862, and the entire store of ordnance and medical supplies, besides 100 barrels of gunpowder, was destroyed. Grant had telegraphed Murphy to fortify his position and hold out until he could send reinforcements, but the latter was forced to yield.

Holman, William S., of Indiana, born in 1822, was a judge of probate from 1843 to 1846 and prosecuting attorney from 1847 to 1849. He was a member of the Indiana Constitutional Convention in 1850, and served in the State Legislature from 1851 to 1852. He represented Indiana in the U. S. Congress as a Democrat from 1859 to 1865, from 1867 to 1877 and from 1879 to the present time (1894), obtaining the name of the "Great Objector" by his opposition to many expenditures.

Holmes, Abiel (1763–1837), a Massachusetts clergyman, was the author of a life of Ezra Stiles and "Annals of America," brought down to 1820, which is a standard authority; father of Dr. O. W. Holmes.

Holmes, Isaac E. (1796–1867), served in the South Carolina Legislature in 1826 and 1832, where he proposed the nullification acts. He was a Democratic U. S. Congressman from 1838 to 1851.

Holmes, John (1773–1843), was a member of the Massachusetts Legislature from 1802 to 1803 and from 1813 to 1817. He was a Democratic U. S. Congressman from 1817 to 1827 and from 1829 to 1833

Holmes, Oliver Wendell, born in Massachusetts in 1809, is an eminent physician, but is famed chiefly in literature. He was one of the founders of the *Atlantic Monthly* in 1857. In this periodical appeared his "Autocrat of the Breakfast Table," "Professor at the Breakfast Table," "Elsie Venner," etc. He has written many most popular poems, and is author of memoirs of John Lothrop Motley and Ralph Waldo Emerson. Died October 7, 1894.

Holmes, Theophilus H. (1804–1880), was brevetted major for services in the Mexican War. He organized the North Carolina troops in 1861, and commanded in the Confederate army in Northern Virginia and in the Trans-Mississippi Department.

Holmes vs. Walton, New Jersey. This seems to have been the first instance of an American court's assuming the authority to pronounce upon the constitutionality of an act of the Legislature. The Legislature of New Jersey had, in 1779, passed an act making lawful a trial before a jury of six men. In the case of Holmes *vs.* Walton the constitutionality of this act was questioned, and upon its being decided unconstitutional by the Court of Appeals, the act was repealed and a constitutional jury of twelve men substituted.

Holst, Hermann E. von, historian, was born in Livonia in 1841. From 1867 to 1872 he was engaged in literary work in America. He is the author of a standard work on "The Constitutional History of the United States, 1750–1861." Also has written a life of John C. Calhoun and "The Constitutional Law of the United States." In 1872 he became a professor at Strasburg, in 1874 at Freiburg, whence he was called to the University of Chicago in 1891.

Holt, Joseph, born in Kentucky in 1807, was appointed by President Buchanan Commissioner of Patents in 1857, and Postmaster-General in 1859, and succeeded John B. Floyd as Secretary of War in 1860. Although previously a Democrat he supported the administration of President Lincoln, who appointed him judge advocate of the army. In 1865 he was brevetted major-general U. S. A. for services in bureau of military justice. Died 1894.

Homestead Law, securing to any citizen the right to enter upon 160 acres of unappropriated lands at $1.25 an acre, and after five years' actual residence to own it, was passed May 20, 1862. It has proved of immense value in stimulating the settlement of the West.

Homestead Riots. On the final refusal of the workingmen's association to accept certain changes in the wage scale, the proprietors of the Carnegie Steel Mills, at Homestead, Pa., closed the works July 1, 1892. The employes declared a strike about the same time. A mob prevented the sheriff from placing pickets in the mills. July 6 a body of 300 Pinkerton detectives arrived. A bloody fight between these men and the strikers immediately took place, resulting in considerable loss on both sides. The Pinkertons surrendered. The Pennsylvania militia was then ordered out and remained at Homestead until September to protect the mills. Many of the strikers were arrested and indictments were found against them.

Honduras. A commercial treaty was concluded between the United States and Honduras in 1864. By Art. XIV. the United States guaranteed the neutrality of an interoceanic railway in return for concessions by Honduras. A reciprocity treaty was concluded in 1892.

Honey Springs, Ind. Terr. Here, July 17, 1863, General Blunt with 3000 Federal troops destroyed Cooper's command of 6000 Confederates. This force was lying in wait for Blunt, and the latter learning this, charged upon them.

Hood, John Bell (1831–1879), born in Kentucky, graduated at the U. S. Military Academy in 1853. He enlisted in the Confederate service in 1861, and soon after was appointed brigadier-general of the Texas brigade. He was brevetted major-general for gallant service at Gaines' Mill. He served in the Maryland campaign and fought at Bull Run, Boonesboro, Fredericksburg, Antietam and Gettysburg. He reinforced General Bragg at Chickamauga, and in 1864 commanded a corps under General Johnston. He succeeded Johnston in command and attempted to crush Sherman in his march to the sea, but was unsuccessful. He was soon afterward defeated by General Thomas at Franklin and at Nashville. He was succeeded by General Richard Taylor.

Hooker, Charles E., born in 1825, was a Mississippi Congressman from 1859 to 1861. He was a colonel in the Confederate service. He served in the U. S. Congress as a Democrat from 1875 to 1883 and from 1887 to the present time (1894).

Hooker, Joseph (1814–1879), born in Massachusetts, was graduated from West Point in 1837. He was brevetted lieutenant-colonel for his very gallant service during the Mexican War from 1846 to 1848. He was appointed a brigadier-general of the National forces in 1861, and commanded a division in 1862 in the Army of the Potomac. He was brevetted major-general for services at Yorktown, Williamsburg and Malvern Hill. He had important commands at South Mountain, Antietam and Fredericksburg. In 1863 he succeeded Burnside in command of the Army of the Potomac, and conducted the battle of Chancellorsville, but, being unsuccessful, was soon after succeeded by General Meade. He was assigned command in the Army of the Cumberland, and fought at Lookout Mountain and Missionary Ridge. He accompanied Sherman in his march through Georgia until after the siege of Atlanta. He was brevetted major-general in the regular army in 1865, and retired in 1868. He was a brave and skillful tactician, but had not the abilities requisite for commander-in-chief.

Hooker, Thomas (1586–1647), fled from England to Holland in 1630 on a charge of non-conformity. He escaped to New England in 1633, and was chosen pastor at Newtown (now Cambridge) of the eighth church established in the Massachusetts colony. With one hundred members of the community he emigrated to Connecticut in 1636, and founded the town of Hartford. He was chosen pastor of the church at that place and was very prominent in all the affairs of the colony. He was author of "Survey of the Summe of Church Discipline."

Hooper, Samuel (1808–1875), was a member of the Massachusetts Legislature from 1851 to 1854, and of the U. S. Congress as a Republican from 1861 to 1875. He served on the Committees of Ways and Means, Banking and Currency, and War Debts.

Hooper, William (1742–1790), was a member of the North Carolina Legislature in 1773, and of the Continental Congress from 1774 to 1777. He signed the Declaration of Independence. He was author of the "Hampden" essays in 1773.

Hopkins, Edward (1600–1657), came to America from England in 1637. He was Governor of Connecticut in the even years from 1640 to 1654. He aided in forming the union of the New England colonies in 1643.

Hopkins, Esek (1718–1802), of Rhode Island, was appointed commander-in-chief of the navy by the Continental Congress in 1775. In 1767, in command of the first colonial fleet, he captured the British ships "Hawke" and "Bolton." He was retired in 1777 for neglect to appear before the Naval Committee on a charge of unnecessary delays. He afterward was prominent in Rhode Island politics.

Hopkins, Johns (1795–1873), was the founder of Johns Hopkins University at Baltimore, which he endowed with about $3,500,000. He also gave an equal sum for the foundation of a hospital at Baltimore.

Hopkins, Lemuel (1750–1801), aided by Trumbull, Humphreys, Barstow and others, called the "Hartford Wits," published "The Anarchiad," which advocated an efficient Federal constitution. He wrote satirical poems entitled the "Echo," "The Political Greenhouse," and "The Hypocrite's Hope."

Hopkins, Mark (1802–1887), born in Massachusetts, was professor of moral philosophy from 1836 to 1887 at Williams College, and its president from 1836 to 1872. He was author of the "Law of Love" and an "Outline Study of Man."

Hopkins, Samuel (1721–1803), theologian, was born in Connecticut. He was ordained in 1743, and became a pastor at Newport, R. I., in 1770. He was prominent in the Rhode Island anti-slavery movements in 1774. His religious views exerted a powerful influence. He wrote "A System of Doctrines."

Hopkins, Stephen (1707–1785), was a member of the Rhode Island Assembly during most of the years from 1732 to 1752, and was Speaker at various sessions, 1738–1749. He was one of the committee, at the Albany Convention of 1754, which drafted a plan of colonial union. He was Governor of Rhode Island from 1755 to 1757, from 1758 to 1762, from 1763 to 1765 and from 1767 to 1768. He was a Rhode Island delegate to the Continental Congress from 1774 to 1780, and signed the Declaration of Independence. In 1765 he published "The Grievances of the American Colonies Candidly Examined." He was the most eminent Rhode Island statesman of the last century.

Hopkinsianism, the doctrine advocated by Samuel Hopkins, minister at Newport from 1770, as an addition to Calvinism, that holiness consisted in pure, disinterested benevolence, and that all self-seeking was necessarily sinful. It exerted a liberalizing influence on the theology of the day.

Hopkinson, Francis (1737–1791), was admitted to the bar in 1761. He was a New York Councilman from 1774 to 1776. He was a delegate to the Continental Congress from 1776 to 1777, serving on the committee to draft articles of confederation and advocating and signing the Declaration of Independence. He was appointed head of the Navy Department in 1775. He aided the cause of liberty by witty satires and popular poems and songs. He was Judge of Admiralty for Pennsylvania from 1779 to 1789, and a U. S. District Judge from 1790 to 1791.

Hopkinson, Joseph (1770–1842), was one of the counsel in the Pennsylvania insurgents' trials, and defended Judge Chase in his impeachment trials. He represented Pennsylvania in the U. S. Congress as a Federalist from 1815 to 1819. He was a U. S. District Judge from 1828 to 1842, and a member of the Pennsylvania Constitutional Convention of 1837. He composed "Hail Columbia."

"**Hornet**," eighteen guns, Captain Lawrence, off Brazil on February 24, 1813, attacked the "Peacock," a British brig, eighteen guns. Within fifteen minutes the "Peacock" was sinking, and struck her colors. Before all the wounded could be moved she sank, carrying nine British and three American seamen with her. On March 23, 1815, in the South Atlantic, the British brig "Penguin," of eighteen guns, challenged the "Hornet." The battle lasted twenty-three minutes. The "Penguin" was boarded and captured, losing among others her commander. After scuttling the prize the "Hornet" returned to the United States. In the latter part of April, 1815, the "Hornet" was chased by the "Cornwallis," seventy-four guns, and only escaped capture by throwing overboard all its guns save one, its anchors, boats and heavy stores.

Horry, Peter, a brigadier-general under General Francis Marion during the Revolutionary War, wrote a "Life of Marion" in conjunction with Rev. Mason L. Weems.

Horse-Shoe Bend, Ala., a battle, March 29, 1814, between General Andrew Jackson's army of 3000 whites, chiefly Tennessee militia, and friendly Cherokee Indians, and 700 or 800 Creek warriors. The Creeks had fortified themselves in the horse-shoe of the Tallapoosa River. Jackson advanced his cannon to within 200 yards of the barricade and began firing, while the Cherokee allies swam the river and attacked the Creeks in the rear. An assault was then ordered and the fort carried, about 500 Creeks being killed, and an equal number of women and children being captured.

Horsford, Eben N. (1818–1893), chemist, was one of the originators of the Lawrence Scientific School, at Cambridge, Mass. He made liberal endowments to Wellesley College, and wrote extensively upon the Norse and other early voyages to America.

Hosmer, Harriet, born in Massachusetts in 1830, is a prominent American sculptor. Her best works are "The Sleeping Fawn," "Puck," "Zenobia in Chains" and "Beatrice Cenci."

Hotchkiss, Benjamin B. (1830–1885), was considered at the time of his death the first artillery engineer in the world. He invented among others, a machine gun and a magazine rifle.

Houdon, Jean Antoine (1740–1828), French sculptor, visited the United States in 1785, and modeled the statue of Washington which is in the capitol at Richmond and is regarded as the best likeness of Washington.

House of Representatives, a term first employed in colonial and State Legislatures to denote the lower or popular branch. In the Randolph plan, brought before the Convention of 1787, the lower branch of the Federal Legislature is called simply the "first branch." The name House of Representatives first appears in the report of the committee of detail. (See arts. Apportionment, Slave Representation, Previous Question, Mace, etc.) The House has twice chosen the President, in 1801 (Jefferson), and in 1825 (J. Q. Adams). The chief law regulating elections of Representatives was passed in 1875.

Houston, Samuel (1793–1863), enlisted in the U. S. army in 1813, and was promoted lieutenant for bravery in the Creek War, 1813–1814. He represented Tennessee in the U. S. Congress as a Democrat from 1823 to 1827, and was Governor of Tennessee from 1827 to 1829. He was a member of the Texas Constitutional Convention in 1833. As commander-in-chief of the Texan army he secured the independence of Texas. He was president of Texas from 1836 to 1838 and from 1841 to 1844, secured the annexation of Texas to the United States and represented it in Congress from 1845 to 1859. He was again chosen Governor of Texas in 1859 and served until he refused to espouse the Confederate cause in 1861.

Howard, Jacob M. (1805–1871), was a member of the Michigan Legislature in 1838 and represented that State in the U. S. Congress from 1841 to 1843. He drafted the first Republican platform in 1854 and gave the party its name. He was a U. S. Senator from 1862 to 1871.

Howard, John Eager (1752–1827), colonel, joined the Revolutionary army at the outbreak of the war, and was a captain under General Mercer at White Plains in 1776. He commanded as major at Germantown and Monmouth, fought at Camden in 1780 with the rank of lieutenant-colonel, and won great fame at Cowpens in 1781. He was Governor of Maryland from 1789 to 1792. In 1796 he declined the portfolio of Secretary of War in Washington's Cabinet. He was a U. S. Senator from 1796 to 1803.

Howard of Effingham, Lord, Governor of Virginia from 1683 to 1688. He succeeded Lord Culpepper, and was very unpopular for his extortions, usurpations, dissolving of the assembly, multiplication of fees and arbitrary imprisonments. Colonel Ludwell was sent to England to make complaints against him.

Howard, Oliver Otis, born in 1830, was graduated from the U. S. Military Academy in 1854. He was appointed colonel of a Maine regiment in

1861. He commanded a brigade at Bull Run, and for his gallant service was promoted brigadier-general. In 1862 he fought at Fair Oaks and Antietam, and was promoted major-general. He served at Fredericksburg, Gettysburg, Lookout Mountain and Missionary Ridge. In 1863 he was assigned command in the Army of the Cumberland, and later in the Army of the Tennessee. He accompanied Sherman in his march to the sea, and was present at Johnston's surrender in 1865. He was Commissioner of the Freedmen's Bureau from 1865 to 1874. In 1886 he was commissioned major-general, and assigned to the Pacific Division; in 1888 he was transferred to the Atlantic Division.

Howard's Reports, twenty-four volumes of law reports by Benjamin C. Howard, containing cases from the U. S. Supreme Court of the years 1843–1860.

Howe, Elias (1819–1867), born in Massachusetts, was the inventor of the first successful sewing-machine, in 1846. He served in a Connecticut regiment during the Civil War, and aided the Government by large loans.

Howe, George A., Viscount (1724–1758), came to America from England in command of a regiment in 1757. He was promoted brigadier-general and in 1758 served under Commander-in-chief Abercrombie at Fort Ticonderoga, where he met his death. He was a very able and popular officer and exerted a powerful influence over his subordinates.

Howe, Henry, born in Connecticut in 1816, was author of "Our Whole Country" and "Historical Collections" of New York, New Jersey, Ohio and Virginia, in which much material was preserved.

Howe, Julia Ward, born in 1819, composed the "Battle Hymn of the Republic" in 1861. She is an earnest advocate of woman suffrage and has been prominent in many reform movements.

Howe, Richard (Earl Howe) (1725–1799), a British rear-admiral, was appointed commander-in-chief of the naval forces in North America in 1776. In conjunction with his brother, Sir William Howe, he was commissioned to conciliate the colonies, but found this impossible. He then took possession of Long Island and New York in 1776 and of Philadelphia in 1777. In 1778 he encountered the French fleet, under Count d'Estaing, off the coast of Rhode Island; both fleets were badly shattered by a storm which prevented a decisive engagement. He resigned his charge to Admiral Byron soon afterward and returned to England. He published "Narrative of the Transactions of the Fleet" in 1780, vindicating his conduct during his command in America. He afterward became an admiral, and won the great victory of June 1, 1794, over the French.

Howe, Robert (1732–1785), was a member of the North Carolina Assembly from 1772 to 1773. He was a delegate to the Colonial Congress in 1774. He was appointed colonel, and aided in expelling Governor Dunmore from Virginia. He was excepted in Sir William Howe's proclamation of royal clemency. He commanded the North Carolina troops in the defence of Charleston, and fought at Savannah. He commanded at West Point in 1780.

Howe, Samuel G. (1801–1876), founded a school for the blind in 1832, subsequently called the Perkins Institution, of which he was superintendent till 1876, and at which Laura Bridgman was educated. From 1851 to 1853 he edited the *Commonwealth*. When commissioner to Santo Domingo in 1871 he advocated annexation to the United States. He was author of an "Historical Sketch of the Greek Revolution," in which he had participated.

Howe, Timothy O. (1816–1883), was a member of the Maine Legislature in 1845. From 1850 to 1855 he was a Judge of the Circuit and Supreme Courts of Wisconsin. He represented Wisconsin in the U. S. Senate as a Republican from 1861 to 1879, and served on the Committees of Finance, Commerce, Pensions and Claims. He advocated the right of the National Government to establish territorial governments in the seceded States. He was a delegate to the International Monetary Conference in 1881. He was appointed Postmaster-General in Arthur's Cabinet in 1881 and served until his death.

Howe, Sir William (1729–1814), served under General Wolfe at Quebec in 1759. In 1775 he succeeded General Gage as commander-in-chief of the British forces in America. He commanded the British troops at Bunker Hill. In conjunction with his brother, Richard, he defeated the colonial armies at Long Island and at White Plains in 1776, and captured Forts Washington and Lee. He defeated Washington at Brandywine in 1777, and entered Philadelphia. After repulsing the American attack at Germantown he went into winter quarters in Philadelphia, and was accused of spending his time in the pursuit of pleasure. He was removed from command in 1778, and superseded by Sir Henry Clinton. He was a well-educated general and a favorite with his officers, but unsuccessful in strategy and incapable of managing a large army. He is described by General Henry Lee as "the most indolent of mortals, who never took pains to examine the merits or demerits of a cause in which he was engaged."

Howells, William Dean, born in Ohio in 1837, was Consul to Venice from 1861 to 1865. He became an editor of the *Atlantic Monthly* in 1866, and was editor-in-chief from 1872 to 1881. He is perhaps the most prominent of American novelists. He is an advocate of the modern "realistic fiction" which portrays life as it actually is. He has written lives of Abraham Lincoln and Rutherford B. Hayes.

Hoxie, Vinnie R., sculptor, born in 1846, designed the marble statue of Abraham Lincoln in the Capitol at Washington, and modeled the bronze statue of Admiral Farragut in Washington.

Huamantla, Mexico. Here, October 9, 1847, General Santa Anna endeavored to cut off and destroy a convoy commanded by General Lane, of the American army, *en route* from El Pinal to Puebla. The attempt was unsuccessful.

Hubbard, Lucius F., born in 1836, fought at Vicksburg and Nashville during the Civil War, and was brevetted brigadier-general. He was elected to the Minnesota Legislature by the Republicans in 1872 and 1874, and was Governor of Minnesota from 1882 to 1887.

Hubbard, Samuel D. (1799–1855), represented Connecticut in the U. S. Congress as a Whig from 1845 to 1849. He was Postmaster-General in Fillmore's Cabinet from 1852 to 1853.

Hubbard, William (1621–1704), came to America from England in 1630. He was a pastor at Ipswich, Mass., from 1665 to 1703. He was author of a "History of New England" and "A Narrative of Troubles with the Indians."

Hubbardton, Battle of, July 7, 1777. The fugitive garrison from Ticonderoga was overtaken by Fraser with 900 men at Hubbardton, Vt. He was checked until Riedesel, with 1000 men, came up and put the Americans to flight. This was an episode in Burgoyne's invasion.

Hubbell, Jay A., born in 1829, of Michigan, served in the U. S. Congress as a Republican from 1873 to 1883. As chairman of the Republican Congressional Committee in the campaign of 1880, he was noted for his pursuit of assessments from office-holders.

Hudde, Andreas (1600?–1663), came to America from Holland in 1629, and was employed in New Netherlands by the Dutch West India Company. He was Governor of the Dutch colony on the Delaware from 1645 to 1655.

Hudson, Henry, was born in the latter part of the sixteenth century. He made two voyages under the direction of the Muscovy Company in search of a northwest passage. In the first expedition made in 1607 he explored the coast of Greenland, and was the first to suggest the existence of an open polar sea. His second voyage in 1608 was unsuccessful. In 1609 he commanded an expedition for the Dutch East India Company. After coasting along Labrador he sailed southward, touching at Newfoundland, Penobscot Bay, Cape Cod and the Chesapeake. He sailed up the Hudson as far as the present site of Albany. On his last voyage in 1610 he entered the strait and bay which bear his name. His crew became mutinous because of severe hardships and set Hudson adrift in a small boat. Nothing was ever heard from him or his seven companions. He wrote "Divers Voyages and Northern Discoveries" and "A Second Voyage."

Hudson Bay Company, chartered by Charles II. May 16, 1670, for the "discovery of a new passage to the South Sea, and for the finding of some trade for furs, minerals and other considerable commodities." Adopting the suggestion of Sir Alexander Mackenzie, it combined with the Northwest Company in 1821, and obtained a more extensive charter. It was ever the most formidable rival of the United States as a claimant of the northwest regions. Despite the treaty of 1783, which granted that territory to the United States, the company persisted in making settlements, and, being on the disputed ground, it had the advantage of our Government. Every possible means was employed, and for a long time successfully, to prevent immigration from the States. The Selkirk settlement in Oregon was made in 1811–12, and later it was decided to seize and hold Oregon by force, turning over the Indians to the Jesuits and furnishing troops to protect the priests and repel intruders. The boundary settlement of 1846 finally excluded the company.

Huger, Isaac (1742–1797), was appointed lieutenant-colonel of the first South Carolina regiment in the Revolution. He was commissioned brigadier-general in the U. S. army in 1779, and engaged in all the important battles of the Southern army. He fought at Stono, Savannah, Charleston, Guilford Court House and Hobkirk's Hill.

Hughes, John (1797–1864), prelate, born in Ireland, came to America in 1817. He was ordained a priest in 1826. He was made Bishop of New York in 1842. He is the founder of St. John's College. In 1850 he was made Archbishop of New York. He was prominent in the Catholic controversies regarding the public-school system of New York and the tenure of church property.

Huguenots. The first Huguenots to settle in this country were a small band who had been induced to emigrate under the charter of the Carolinas granted to Sir Robert Heath in 1630. Upon reaching Virginia means of transportation failed, so they remained in that colony. The revocation of the Edict of Nantes in 1685 drove multitudes from France. Other parties came to Virginia about 1700 under Claude Philippe de Richebourg. In Massachusetts they made a settlement at Oxford in 1686, but were massacred and driven away by the Indians. By 1737, they had become an important element in South Carolina, where they founded at Charleston the "South Carolina Society," a benevolent organization. They also made early settlements in the Middle States, notably in New York. Jay, Revere and Laurens were of this stock.

Hull, Isaac (1773–1843), born in Connecticut, entered the merchant marine in 1784. In 1798, he was commissioned a lieutenant in the American navy. He commanded the "Argus" in 1804, and engaged in the Barbary Wars. In 1806, he was commissioned captain, and in 1807 assigned to the command of the "Constitution." He was highly honored for successfully evading an attack of a superior British force in 1812. Soon afterward he captured the British ship "Guerrière" with a loss of fourteen men killed and wounded, while the enemy lost seventy-nine. This was the first and most famous naval victory during the war. He afterward commanded the Pacific and Mediterranean squadrons, and served on the Board of Naval Commissioners.

Hull, William (1753–1825), was chosen captain in a Connecticut regiment in 1775. He fought at White Plains, Trenton, Princeton, Saratoga, Fort Stanwix and Stony Point. He attained the rank of major. From 1805 to 1812 he was Governor of Michigan. In 1812 he was placed in command of the Army of the Northwest, with headquarters at Detroit. He regarded himself as compelled by superior forces and by lack of proper facilities to surrender Detroit to the British. He was tried by court-martial and sentenced to death, but was reprieved by Madison.

Humphreys, Andrew A. (1810–1883), was assigned to the corps of topographical engineers in 1838 and engaged in the coast survey. He served on the staff of General McClellan in 1862. He commanded a division at Fredericksburg and Chancellorsville and a corps at Gettysburg. In 1863 he became chief of staff to General Meade. He was chief of engineers from 1866 to 1879, when he retired.

Hundred, a territorial and political division of a county, borrowed from England, and instituted in some of the colonies, notably in Maryland and Virginia. It was also to be found in Maine and Delaware, and was based upon the old Hundred system of the English counties. In Virginia the "Hundred" was in some instances synonymous with the parish or the plantation, and again it was subdivided into parishes. The chief officer of the Hundred was usually the constable.

Hunkers. A name applied originally to conservative Democrats in New York, but also used in other States. Though the name was not in use until 1844 the faction to which it applied existed as early as 1835. The Hunkers, in New York, opposed the "loco-foco" faction, the barn-burners and radicals; and finally divided into the "hards" and the "softs." They represented the inertia of the State Democratic party. From 1835 to 1840 they opposed the loco-foco war on bank charters. Later they opposed a revision of the Constitution and the radicals, and were disinclined to oppose slavery. The faction ceased to exist about 1860.

Hunt, Henry J. (1819–1889), was prominent during the Mexican War. He served on McClellan's staff in 1861, and was chief of artillery in the Army of the Potomac from 1862 to 1865, engaging in all its battles.

Hunt, Thomas Sterry (1826–1892), scientist, made valuable original contributions to the advancement of chemical and geological science. He invented the ink with which "greenbacks" were printed.

Hunt, Ward (1810–1886), was a New York Congressman in 1839. In 1865 he became a Judge of the New York Court of Appeals, and from 1872 to 1882 was an Associate Justice of the U. S. Supreme Court.

Hunt, William H. (1824–1884), of Louisiana, was appointed Judge of the U. S. Court of Claims in 1878. He was Secretary of the Navy in Garfield's Cabinet from 1881 to 1882, when he was appointed Minister to Russia.

Hunter, David (1802–1886), commanded the main column of McDowell's army in the Manassas campaign in 1861 and commanded a division at Bull Run. He succeeded General Frémont in command of the Western Department. He commanded the Department of Kansas from 1861 to 1862, when he was transferred to the Southern Department. He organized the first regiment of colored troops. In 1864 he commanded the Department of West Virginia. He was president of the commission which tried the assassins of President Lincoln. He was brevetted major-general in 1865 and retired from service in 1866.

Hunter, Joseph (1783–1861), was assistant keeper of the public records in London from 1833 till his death. He made valuable researches and discoveries in relation to the early settlements in New England. He secured for the Massachusetts Historical Society a transcript of the "History of the Plymouth Plantation." by Governor Bradford, from the original in the Fulham Library.

Hunter, Robert M. T. (1809–1887), served in the Virginia Legislature in 1833. He represented Virginia in the Congress of the United States as a Whig from 1837 to 1843 and from 1845 to 1847, and was Speaker from 1839 to 1841. He was a U. S. Senator from 1847 to 1861, and ardently advocated all pro-slavery legislation. He was a member of the provisional Congress at Richmond in 1861. From 1861 to 1862 he was Secretary of State in the Confederate Government. From 1862 to 1865 he served in the Confederate Senate in opposition to the administration of Mr. Davis. He was one of the peace commissioners to confer with President Lincoln in 1865. He was treasurer of Virginia from 1877 to 1880.

Huntington, Frederick D., born in 1826, was chosen Protestant Episcopal Bishop of Central New York in 1869. He has been a frequent contributor to periodicals, and has published "Lectures on Human Society" and sermons.

Huntington, Samuel (1732–1796), of Connecticut, signed the Declaration of Independence in 1776, was President of the Continental Congress from 1779 to 1781, and Governor of Connecticut from 1786 to 1796.

Hunton, Eppa, born in 1823, was commonwealth attorney in Virginia from 1849 to 1862. He was made a brigadier-general in the Confederate service. While a U. S. Congressman from 1873 to 1881 he served on the Electoral Commission as a Democrat.

Hurd, Frank H., born in 1841, was a member of the Ohio Senate in 1866. He was elected to the U. S. Congress as a Democrat in 1874, 1878 and 1882. He is an ardent and able advocate of free trade.

Hurlburt, Stephen A. (1815–1882), served in the National army during the Civil War. He was Minister to Colombia from 1869 to 1872. He represented Illinois in the U. S. Congress as a Republican from 1873 to 1877.

Hurons, a tribe of Indians formerly occupying territory near Lake Huron. Among them the French began the famous Huron mission in 1632. They allied themselves with the Algonquins against the Iroquois, which latter nation destroyed several of their villages, finally dispersing them in 1649. Many found their way to Canada.

Hutchinson, Anne (Marbury) (1600?–1643), came to America from England in 1634. She was expelled from the Massachusetts colony for preaching Antinomian doctrines and accusing the authorities of being under a "covenant of works." She had won a large following. She founded Portsmouth, R. I., on the island of Aquidneck, which she purchased from the Indians. She was afterward murdered by the Indians near Manhattan, where she settled.

Hutchinson, Thomas (1711–1780), Governor, was a member of the General Court of Massachusetts from 1737 to 1739, 1740, and 1741 to 1749. He was Speaker from 1746 to 1748. He restored a healthy condition of trade by redeeming the depreciated paper currency. In 1754 he was one of the commissioners at the Albany Convention, and aided in drafting a plan of colonial union. He was appointed Lieutenant-Governor of Massachusetts in 1756. In 1760 he was appointed Chief Justice. In 1765 his house was sacked by a mob infuriated by the notion that he was a party to the obnoxious stamp acts, and his valuable library of historical pamphlets and documents was destroyed. In 1770 he was appointed Governor of the province. The report was circulated that he was largely responsible for the oppressive acts of the ministry, and this was intensified by Dr. Franklin's publication of some of Hutchinson's letters to England which had fallen into his hands. In 1774 he sailed to England, where he spent the remainder of his life. He was a conscientious and high-minded Tory. He wrote a valuable history of Massachusetts.

Hylton vs. United States. In 1795 Hylton, of Virginia, was presented by the District Attorney before the Circuit Court for refusing to pay duty upon certain carriages, which, he averred, were kept for his own private use. The decree was against the defendant, and the case was transferred to the Supreme Court of the United States. The argument turned entirely upon the question of the tax being direct or indirect. The court decided it to be indirect since it must be incapable of apportionment and could not be uniform. Accordingly judgment was affirmed for the defendant.

I.

Iberville, Pierre le Moyne d' (1661–1706), engaged in the Canadian expedition against the English forts on the Hudson, fought at Fort Mousipi and Fort Quitchilchouen, and in 1688 captured two English vessels. In 1690 he was one of the leaders against Schenectady. In 1694 he took Fort Nelson, and, in command of a frigate, captured three English ships, including the "Newport." He destroyed Fort Pemaquid, and reduced nearly all Newfoundland. In command of the "Pelican," in 1697, he destroyed several British ships, and captured Fort Bourbon. In 1698 he ascended the Mississippi and built Fort Biloxi, the first port on the river. In 1701 he transferred the colony to Mobile. In 1706 he captured Nevis Island.

Icaria, a communistic settlement founded in 1856, in Iowa, by the followers of the Frenchman, Étienne Cabet. The latter, in 1848, had persuaded a number of persons to settle with him in the Red River country of Texas. This colony failed because of Cabet's extravagant ideas. In 1850 the colony moved to Nauvoo in Illinois, a deserted village of the Mormons. Thence they moved again in 1856 (Cabet dying that same year at New Orleans), to their present settlement near Corning, Iowa, calling it the Icaria Commune, in reminiscence of Cabet's book, "Icarie." Most of the people, less than 100 in all, are French, though there are a few Germans.

Idaho, a State, was formed from the Louisiana cession. It was organized as a part of Oregon for a time, and later was joined to Washington. It was given a territorial government of its own in 1863, and was admitted as a State July 3, 1890. The population in 1890 was 84,385. Suffrage is denied to Mormons. The Republicans control the State. In 1892 the Cœur d'Alène riots, caused by a strike of the miners, were suppressed by U. S. troops. History by Bancroft.

Illinois, a State of the American Republic, was formed from the Northwest Territory, which was organized in 1787. The State was originally a possession of France, who surrendered her claims to England in 1763. The first settlement was a mission at Kaskaskia, founded by Marquette in 1675. In 1679 La Salle built Fort Crèvecœur, and in 1682 established a colony at Cahokia, and in 1700 Kaskaskia was founded. George Rogers Clark, with a Virginia force, seized Cahokia and Kaskaskia in 1778, and Illinois was made a county of Virginia. March 1, 1784, Virginia surrendered her claim over Illinois to the United States. In 1809 it was erected into a territory comprising the present States of Illinois, Wisconsin and part of Michigan. December 3, 1818, Illinois with its present boundaries became a State. The Black Hawk War broke out in 1832. Rev. Elijah P. Lovejoy was murdered by a mob at Alton because of his attempt to publish an anti-slavery newspaper in 1837. From 1840 to 1844 the Mormons caused excitement which led to the death at the hands of a mob of two of their leaders and the emigration of the sect from the State. The southern part of the State has usually been Democratic, the northern part Anti-Democratic. Down to 1860 the vote of Illinois was invariably Democratic in Presidential elections. Including and since that time it has been Republican until 1892, when it was Democratic. In 1858 Lincoln and Douglas canvassed the State together for election to the U. S. Senate. Douglas won. In 1877 David Davis, an Independent, was elected to the Senate by Democrats and Independents. The present Constitution was made in 1870. The population of Illinois in 1818 was 34,620, in 1890 it was 3,826,351. History by Ford.

"**Illinois Intelligencer,**" the first newspaper published in Illinois. It was established in 1815, at Kaskaskia, by Mathew Duncan, and was removed to Fayette County in 1820. It was afterward called the *Vandalia Whig and Illinois Intelligencer* and was suspended in 1839.

Impeachments. There have been seven impeachments made by the Congress of the United States. During the session of 1797–98, William Blount, U. S. Senator from Tennessee, was impeached by the House and tried by the Senate for treasonable negotiations with Great Britain for the transfer of New Orleans. He was acquitted for want of jurisdiction. March 3, 1803, Judge John Pickering, of the Federal Court of New Hampshire, was impeached and removed from the bench for drunkenness and profanity. November 30, 1804, Judge Samuel Chase, of the U. S. Supreme Court, was impeached for arbitrary conduct and the introduction of political disquisitions in his charges to grand juries. He was not removed. December 13, 1804, Judge James Peck, of the Federal Court of Missouri, was impeached for punishing as contempt of court a criticism of his opinions. He was acquitted. December 29, 1860, Judge West H. Humphreys, of the Federal District Court of Tennessee, was impeached and removed from the bench for aiding the Rebellion. November 25, 1867, the House impeached President Andrew Johnson, charging him with having removed Stanton, Secretary of War, in violation of the Tenure of Office Act, with having appointed General L. Thomas contrary to the same act, with conspiracy with Thomas and others for the intimidation of Stanton and the unlawful disbursement of the War Department's moneys, and with inducing General Emory, commanding the Department of Washington, to disobey orders. The House adopted the resolution of impeachment by a vote of 126 to 42. After the trial before the Senate, the vote stood 35 to 19. The necessary two-thirds were not secured. But the Senate adjourned *sine die*, without voting upon some of the articles of charge. Hence the Chief Justice entered a verdict of acquittal on the record. March 2, 1876, William W. Belknap, Secretary of War, was impeached on the charge of bribery for appointments. He was acquitted.

"Impending Crisis," a book by H. R. Helper, of North Carolina, appearing in 1857. It earnestly opposed slavery on economical grounds. The book was used as a campaign document by the Republican party in 1860, and 140,000 copies were sold between 1857 and 1861. Helper purported to represent the sentiments of Southern non-slaveholding whites.

Imports. The specie value of the imports from foreign countries in 1791 was $29,200,000. In 1807, just before the embargo, it was $138,500,000. By 1814 it had sunk to only $13,000,000, but rose to $147,000,000 in 1816. Reduced by the tariff act of that year, it again rose to $190,000,000 in 1836, just before the crash of 1837. In 1857 it was $361,000,000; in 1867, $418,-000,000; in 1877, $492,000,000; in 1887, $752,000,000; in 1892, $897,000,000.

Impost Amendment. (See Revenue Scheme.)

Impressment. For many years prior to the breaking out of the War of 1812 the British Government claimed the right of stopping and searching American vessels, and impressing into the British service British seamen who happened to be serving under the American flag. Great Britain refused to allow the right of expatriation and change of allegiance by naturalization. She was then engaged in war with France and accordingly claimed the services of all her maritime citizens, no matter what ceremonies of naturalization they might have undergone abroad. Hence many American sailors were wilfully impressed. This grievance aided in a large measure in bringing about the embargo system and the War of 1812.

Income Tax. But one income tax has been imposed by the Federal Government, and it arose from the necessities of the Government incident to the Rebellion. August 5, 1861, Congress authorized a tax of three per cent on all incomes over $800 per annum. In July, 1862, an act was passed taxing all incomes under $5000 five per cent, with an exemption of $600 and house-rent actually paid. Incomes in excess of $5000 and under $10,000 were taxed two and one-half per cent additional, and incomes over $10,000 five per cent additional with no exemptions. Further taxes of five per cent on incomes of Americans living abroad and of one and one-half per cent on incomes from United States securities were laid, these expiring in 1865. In 1864 a special tax of five per cent was imposed on incomes above $600. A readjustment the same year imposed a five per cent tax on incomes between $600 and $5000; ten per cent on incomes above $5000.

Independence Hall, Philadelphia, scene of the Declaration of Independence, July 4, 1776. The hall was begun in 1732 and completed in 1741. J. Kearsely was the architect, and E. Wooley the builder. It was first occupied as the Pennsylvania State House in October, 1735. The tower was built in 1750. The Constitutional Convention of 1787 also met here.

Independent Treasury. Until 1840 the United States Government had never ventured to assume entire control of its own funds, depending in a great measure upon the two successive banks of the United States, and various State banks selected by the Secretary of the Treasury for depositories. The creation of an independent or sub-treasury system was an outcome of the panic of 1837. President Van Buren's message to Congress that year strongly recommended such a system. Silas Wright, of New York, submitted a sub-treasury bill, which prohibited Government agents from receiving anything but gold and silver. Finally, in 1840, the bill became a law, and sub-treasuries were created at New York, Boston, Charleston and St. Louis, the mint at Philadelphia and the branch mint at New Orleans being also made places of deposit. The Whigs and some Democrats were violently opposed to this system, and effected its repeal in 1841 in favor of the national banking system. It again became a law in 1846 under Polk, and has continued since.

Independents, the name given in England to those who favored that form of church government which in America is called Congregational; so called from the independence of one church from all others, which prevails under their system. The English Independents of the Commonwealth period were in close relations with the Puritan colonists of New England.

Independents, in recent politics, men independent of both the Republican and the Democratic parties; more especially applied in 1884 to those Republicans who "bolted" the nomination of Blaine.

Indian Affairs, Commissioner of. In 1832 Congress authorized the President to appoint a commissioner who, under the direction of the Secretary of War, should have general superintendence of all Indian affairs. These affairs had formerly been managed by War Department clerks. Since 1849 this commissioner has been under the direction of the Secretary of the Interior.

Indian Bible. In 1661 John Eliot, an English missionary among the Massachusetts Indians, published through the Cambridge press the first edition of the New Testament, which he had translated into the Indian dialect. The whole Bible appeared three years later, and second editions of both were published, the former in 1680, the latter in 1685. Eliot was assisted in the publication of the second edition by John Cotton, of Plymouth, son of the Boston minister. Eliot drew from the Scriptures a frame of government for the commonwealth and for the Indians, but these were suppressed as reflecting on the kingly government. Eliot's "Indian Bible" is now one of the most valued of rarities.

Indian Territory is a portion of the public land of the United States which has been set apart for various tribes of Indians who have been moved thither from various portions of the United States. Jefferson first suggested such a territory, and on June 30, 1834, an Act of Congress set apart for the use of the Indians all the country west of the Mississippi which was not included within Missouri, Louisiana and Arkansas. This has been diminished by the organization of various States and Territories, so that at present (1894) the area is only about 25,000 square miles. The principal tribes are the Cherokees, Choctaws, Creeks and Chickasaws. During the Civil War many of the tribes made treaties with the Confederate States. In 1870, an attempt was made to organize a State. In 1866, the Indians agreed to grant the right of way through their land to railroads. Agents of the United States live among the Indians and protect them from encroachments from the whites. The United States has jurisdiction over all cases in which a white man is a party. Sale of intoxicating liquors is prohibited. In 1881–82 attempts were made by "boomers" from Kansas to force their way into the Territory. An Act of Congress of May 2, 1890, erected the unoccupied portion of the Territory into a separate Territory to be called Oklahoma. The population of the Territory is about 75,000.

Indiana, a State of the Union, often called the Hoosier State, was formed from the Northwest Territory. The first settlement was made at Vincennes in 1702, by the French. This place was captured by Clark during the American Revolution. After the erection of Ohio as a separate Territory, the Northwest was called Indiana, with Vincennes its capital. In 1805 and 1809, the Territories of Michigan and Illinois were organized as separate Territories. November 7, 1811, General Harrison defeated the Indians at Tippecanoe. December 11, 1816, Indiana became a State. Slavery was forbidden by the Ordinance of 1787, by which the Northwest was organized. Except in 1836 and 1840, the electoral votes were cast for Democratic candidates until 1860, when Lincoln carried the State, since which date the Republicans have failed in but one Presidential election, that of 1876, until 1884. The Democrats have carried the State in the elections of 1874, 1876, 1878, 1882, 1884, 1890, 1892. The present Constitution was made in 1851. The population of the State in 1816 was 63,805; in 1890 it was 2,192,404. History by Dunn.

Indiana, Historical Society of, founded in 1831. Its publications have been few.

"Indiana Gazette," first newspaper of Indiana, published in 1804 at Vincennes, Knox County, by Elihu Stout. Its office was burned in 1806.

Indianapolis, Ind., settled in 1819. It became the capital of the State in 1828, and received a city charter in 1847.

Indians. The Indians were so called from the original supposition made that their land was India. When Englishmen came to this country there were probably about as many Indians in it as now,—from two hundred to three hundred thousand. They were divided into tribes. In the Northern part of the United States these tribes were either of the Algonquin or of the Iroquois race; in the South, either of that which is called Mobilian or of the Natchez. Their tribal government was loose and weak. They had chieftains, but these had little real power. Confederacies of tribes were sometimes formed, but did not usually last beyond a single war. The Indian was in general in the hunting and fishing stage of civilization. His relations with the settlers were more frequently hostile than friendly, which caused settlement to be more compact than in Spanish-American regions, where the aborigines were less warlike. There was also much trade with the Indian, especially in furs. Likewise there was some effort to convert the Indians to Christianity, though these efforts on the part of the English and Protestant colonies were lamentably small when compared with the work of the French Jesuits. (See Praying Indians.) On their part the Indians learned something of civilization, especially in the articles of fire-arms and fire-water. For individual wars and tribes, see articles under their names.

Ingalls, John J., born in 1833, was admitted to the bar in 1857. He was a member of the Wyandotte Constitutional Convention in 1859. He was Secretary of the Kansas Council in 1860, Secretary of the State Senate in 1861 and a member in 1862. He served in the U. S. Senate as a Republican from 1873 to 1891. He was an able debater.

Ingersoll, Charles J. (1782–1862), represented Pennsylvania in the U. S. Congress as a Democrat from 1813 to 1815 and from 1841 to 1847. He was District Attorney from 1815 to 1829. He wrote a history of the War of 1812.

Ingersoll, Jared (1749–1822), was a delegate from Pennsylvania to the Continental Congress from 1780 to 1781. He was a member of the convention which framed the Federal Constitution in 1787. He was twice chosen Attorney-General of Pennsylvania and was U. S. District Attorney for Eastern Pennsylvania. He was defeated as Federal candidate for Vice-President of the United States in 1812.

Ingersoll, Joseph R. (1786–1868), was a Whig Representative to Congress from Pennsylvania from 1835 to 1837 and from 1843 to 1849. He was Minister to England from 1852 to 1857.

Ingersoll, Ralph I. (1788–1872), was a prominent member of the Connecticut Legislature from 1819 to 1825, a Democratic Representative to Congress from 1825 to 1833, and Minister to Russia from 1846 to 1848.

Ingersoll, Robert G., was born in 1833. He served in the Civil War as a colonel. In 1866 he was appointed Attorney-General of Illinois. He was counsel for the defence for the "Star route" conspirators, who were acquitted in 1883. He is a popular Republican campaign orator. He is well known for his attacks upon the Christian religion.

Ingham, Samuel D. (1779–1860), represented Pennsylvania in the U. S. Congress as a Democrat from 1813 to 1818, and from 1822 to 1829. He was Secretary of the Treasury from 1829 to 1831 in Jackson's Cabinet.

Ingle, Richard, born early in the seventeenth century, usurped the government of Maryland in 1645, in revenge for the seizure of his ship by the royalist Governor in 1642.

Ingraham, Duncan N. (1802–1891), entered the U. S. navy in 1812. While commander of the "St. Louis" in the Mediterranean, in 1853, he secured the liberation of Martin Koszta, a prospective American citizen, who had been seized by Greeks at Smyrna at the instigation of Austrian officials. In 1861 he was appointed chief of ordnance, construction and repair in the Confederate navy.

Inman, Henry (1801–1846), of New York, achieved his greatest success as an American artist in portrait painting. Among his portraits are those of William Wirt, De Witt Clinton, Halleck, Van Buren, Seward and William Penn.

Interior Department, created by law in 1849, and called in the title of the act the Home Department. Its functions were formerly distributed among the departments of State, Treasury, War and Navy. These functions are the regulation of patents, copyrights, the census, public documents, public lands, mines, mining, judicial accounts, Indian affairs, bureau of education, etc.

Internal Improvements, at Federal Expense. The Constitution did not provide for internal improvements, hence they have become a party question. Since 1789 money has been steadily appropriated by Congress for improvements lying strictly within Federal jurisdiction, as for light-houses, buoys, beacons and public piers. The first actual appropriation for other internal improvement was in 1806, when a sum was appropriated for the construction of the Cumberland Road, which should penetrate the Western States and be the means of transmitting emigrants and mails in time of peace, and troops in time of war. About the same time a road was begun through Georgia on the route to New Orleans. Congress passed a resolution in 1818, declaring its power to appropriate money for the construction of roads and canals, and for the improvement of water-courses. March 3, 1823, the first act for harbor improvement passed Congress. April 13, 1824, $30,000 was appropriated for the survey of such roads and canals as the President should deem of national importance, and $300,000 was subscribed to the stock of the Chesapeake and Delaware Canal. In May, 1822, President Monroe vetoed the Cumberland Road Bill, declaring that Congress had no power under the Constitution to carry out a system of internal improvements at Federal expense. This, and Jackson's veto of the Maysville Turnpike Road Bill in 1830, threw the matter into the hands of the States. But see River and Harbor Acts.

Internal Revenue. The receipts from internal revenue steadily rose during the period from 1791 to 1801, reaching $1,000,000 in the latter year. They then declined to almost nothing. In the War of 1812 they rose again, reaching $5,000,000 in 1816; and again declined to nothing in 1849 and the subsequent years to 1862. Under the new system then inaugurated they rose to $309,000,000 in 1866, and have been above $100,000,000 in every year since ($154,000,000 in 1892).

Interstate Commerce Commission, a commission appointed by Act of Congress February 4, 1887. It has jurisdiction of rates on interstate traffic, and can inquire into the management of the business of all common carriers subject to the provisions of "An act to regulate commerce."

Interstate Commerce Law. In 1884 Representative Reagan, of Texas, submitted a bill to the House for the regulation of interstate commerce, and about the same time a similar bill was proposed in the Senate. Both bills failed. Thereafter yearly debates took place concerning these and similar bills, until, February 4, 1887, the Reagan bill was finally passed and approved. It provides for the appointment of a commission, consisting of five persons, who shall see to it that railroad and other such companies establish and preserve a just and uniform rate of transportation. This particularly affects such corporations as control continuous lines from one State to another, either by land or by water, or both. The law has been very effective in preventing gross discriminations in charges for freight and issuing of passes.

Inventions. The American gift for invention is remarkable, and has been much stimulated by our patent system. On the whole, the most important inventions may be said to have been: Whitney's invention of the cotton gin in 1793; McCormick's reaper, patented in 1834; the steam hammer in 1838; Goodyear's method of vulcanizing rubber (1839); the telegraph, brought into use in 1844; the sewing machine (1846); the power loom (1846); the surgical use of anæsthetics (1846); the rotary printing press (1847); the telephone about 1876 and more recently the phonograph.

Iowa, one of the United States, was formed from the territory obtained from France by the purchase of Louisiana. Its name, signifying the beautiful country, is derived from the river of the same name. The first settlement in the State was made by Dubuque, a Frenchman from Canada, in 1788, on the site of the city which now bears his name. After the organization of Missouri, in 1820, the territory to the north was neglected by Congress until 1834, when it was made a part of Michigan. In 1836 it was added to the Wisconsin Territory, and in 1838 the Territory of Iowa was created. Application for admission as a State was refused by Congress until December 28, 1846, when Iowa became a State. From 1846 to 1854 the State was solidly Democratic. Since 1854 the Republicans have controlled the State until the election of Boies as Governor in 1889. In 1882 an amendment to the State Constitution prohibiting the manufacture and sale of intoxicating liquors was adopted by a large popular majority, but was declared void because of informalities in its passage. The present Constitution was made in 1857. The population of Iowa in 1846 was 81,920, in 1890 it was 1,911,896.

Iowa, Historical Society of, founded in 1857. It published "Annals" from 1862 to 1875 and from 1882 to 1884, and the "Iowa Historical Record" since 1885.

Iredell, James (1750–1799), came to America from England in 1767. He was a Judge of the North Carolina Supreme Court from 1777 to 1778. He was a commissioner to revise the laws of the State from 1787 to 1791. He was a leader of the Federalists in the North Carolina Convention of 1788, and was appointed a Justice of the U. S. Supreme Court in 1790. Life by McRee.

Ireland, John, born in 1827, was a member of the Texas Secession Convention of 1861. He was a Judge of the Texas Supreme Court from 1875 to 1882, and was elected Governor of the State in 1882 and 1884.

Iron. The first iron manufactured in the United States was forged at the bloomery of the Virginia Company, on the James River, in 1622. This foundry was burned by the Indians. The Massachusetts Bay colonists erected a foundry at Lynn in 1631. John Winthrop, Jr., built a blast furnace at Hammersmith in 1644, and works at Braintree two years later. In 1702 a successful furnace was established at Plymouth, pig-iron being obtained chiefly from Pennsylvania. In 1732 there were four furnaces in successful operation in Virginia between the Potomac and Rappahannock Rivers. The iron manufactured there was exported to England, but the Massachusetts trade in iron was almost wholly domestic. The Ancram Works, built in New York in 1740, to use Salisbury ore, made, between 1750 and 1756, 3318 tons of pig-iron and 1302 tons of bar iron. It was here that the great chain, weighing 186 tons, which was stretched across the Hudson in 1778, was forged in six weeks. The first iron works of Pennsylvania were established on the Schuylkill in 1717. The Revolution gave a great impetus to the iron trade. Rolling mills for the manufacture of steel rails were first used in 1840 at the Mount Savage Works and at the Great Western Works. Since then the manufacture of iron and particularly of steel has made wonderful progress. The Bessemer steel made in this country is considered most excellent. The Carnegie system, consisting of the enormous works at Homestead, Pa., and a number of minor plants, the Bethlehem Steel and Iron Company, of Bethlehem, Pa., have been unusually successful in the manufacture of steel rails and platings, the latter plant having received the contracts for the steel plates of many of the United States war-ships. Many flourishing iron and steel works are now in operation in most of the Northern and Middle States, notably Pennsylvania, and in some Southern States. The annual output is enormous. In 1890 the United States produced 18,000,000 tons of iron ore, 9,202,703 tons of pig-iron and 4,277,071 tons of steel.

"Ironsides, Old," the popular name for the frigate "Constitution," a name made additionally famous by Dr. Holmes' poem.

Iroquois, or Six Nations, an Indian confederation occupying Central New York, and consisting when first known, of the Mohawks, Oneidas, Onondagas, Cayugas and Senecas. Later the Tuscaroras were added. In the seventeenth century they carried on extensive hostilities against the French and suffered severe losses. They allied themselves with the Dutch and subsequently with the English, though they afterward joined Pontiac. Peace was restored, but in 1774 a part of the western bands took up arms against the whites. During the Revolution the Iroquois, with the exception of those in Canada, favored England. They fought against the colonists and committed extensive ravages. At the close of the war nearly all emigrated to Canada, except the Oneidas and Tuscaroras, with whom the Government made a treaty in 1784. In 1785 and 1788, the Indians began to cede lands. In the War of 1812, the English and American Iroquois were arrayed against each other, but peace was soon restored. The tribes became scattered, some going west and still others seeking their relatives in Canada.

Irrepressible Conflict, an expression first used by William H. Seward in an address at Rochester, New York, October 28, 1858, in reference to the inevitable clash between freedom and slavery.

Irving, Washington (1783–1859), born in New York, spent a large part of his life abroad. In 1807, in copartnership with his brother, he established the *Salmagundi*. In 1808 he published his "Knickerbocker History of New York." In 1819 appeared the "Sketch Book," which proved a great success. This was followed by "Tales of a Traveler," "Life of Columbus," which is his best historical work, "The Conquest of Granada," and "The Alhambra." From 1829 to 1832 he was Secretary of Legation in London. He served as Minister to Spain from 1842 to 1846. His greatest work is a "Life of Washington" in five volumes (1855). He is one of the most popular of American authors. His productions are marked by ease and grace rather than by originality.

Irwinsville, Ga., scene of the capture, May 11, 1865, of Jefferson Davis, President of the Confederacy, by Colonels Harnden and Pritchard, who had been dispatched in pursuit of the fleeing President after the surrender of Lee's and Johnston's army. There was no bloodshed, except the accidental killing of two Federal soldiers by their comrades.

Isaac Case (1839), a fugitive slave case, in which the Governor of New York refused to arrest three colored men charged by the Governor of Virginia with abetting a slave's escape. He maintained that this was not a crime in New York.

Island No. 10, Mississippi River, had been fortified by General Polk, Confederate, and was commanded by General Mackall with about 8000 troops of Beauregard's army. It was bombarded three weeks by Commodore Foote, commanding seven Federal gunboats, and surrendered April 8, 1862. The evacuation was forced by Pope with a large land force. He, under cover of a vigorous fire from two gunboats, which had run past the island by night, brought his men across the river in transports. The defenders of the batteries fled, and were pursued into the swamps. Nearly 7000 prisoners were taken, together with an immense quantity of ammunition and supplies.

Italy. The United States was prompt to recognize the new kingdom of Italy, and in 1868 a consular convention was concluded, and another in 1878, which were both superseded by that of 1881. A commercial convention was concluded in 1871. Extradition conventions were concluded in 1868 and 1884. The murder of Italian citizens in New Orleans in 1890 and the refusal of the U. S. Government to interfere with the course of State judicial procedure led to the temporary withdrawal of the Italian Minister, but though none were brought to justice, diplomatic relations were soon restored.

"Itata." During the struggle between the President and Congress of Chili, in 1891, the "Itata," Congressional cruiser, put in at San Diego, Cal., for supplies of ammunition. Violation of United States neutrality was alleged and an officer seized the vessel. The "Itata" put him ashore and escaped. Pursued by the "Charleston" it surrendered. But a United States court has since decided that its arrest was unwarranted.

Iuka, Miss., an encampment of several thousand Confederate troops under General Price. Grant sent Rosecrans with 9000 men to destroy Price's army and prevent his co-operation with Bragg. Rosecrans, after some delay, attacked the Confederates and a fierce battle followed, September 19–20, 1862, both sides losing heavily. At night the Federals lay down on their arms, expecting to renew the fight next day, but the Confederates moved during the night. Rosecrans pursued, but did not overtake them.

Iverson, Alfred (1798–1873), represented Georgia in the U. S. Congress as a Democrat from 1847 to 1849 and from 1855 to 1861. He was also a brigadier-general in the Confederate army.

Izard, George (1777–1828), was commissioned major-general in 1814 for services in the War of 1812. He was Governor of Arkansas Territory from 1825 to 1828.

Izard, Ralph (1742–1804), was a commissioner to Tuscany from 1776 to 1779, and resided at Paris. He pledged his estate as security for a Governmental debt during the Revolutionary War. He represented South Carolina in the Continental Congress from 1781 to 1783. He was a U. S. Senator from 1789 to 1795. He was able and eloquent, but possessed an uncontrollable temper.

J.

Jackson, Andrew (March 15, 1767–June 8, 1845), seventh President of the United States, was born on the border of North and South Carolina. He began his military career at the early age of thirteen at the battle of Hanging Rock; occupations of a miscellaneous nature followed, and in 1788 he was public prosecutor in the western district of North Carolina, now Tennessee. He was in 1796–1797 the first Congressman from the State of Tennessee, and in 1797–1798 was U. S. Senator. From 1798 to 1804 he was a Judge of the State Supreme Court. His life as a planter, not infrequently chequered with disputes and duels, was broken by the War of 1812. Jackson, "Old Hickory," as he was called, commanded the Southwestern troops against the Creeks, whom he overwhelmed at the Horse-Shoe Bend of the Tallapoosa, March 27, 1814. He was made a major-general, stormed Pensacola, and held New Orleans against Pakenham's invasion. The sweeping victory, January 8, 1815, of his riflemen over the flower of the Peninsular army, made Jackson for all time an American hero of the country in general and of the Democratic party in particular. General Jackson's actions in Florida, capture of St. Marks in 1818, and summary execution of two British subjects, led to considerable discussion. He was appointed Governor of Florida in 1821, and became U. S. Senator in 1823. In 1824 he received ninety-nine electoral votes for President, but was beaten in the House of Representatives. (See Adams, J. Q.) Elected in 1828 over the President, he entered office in 1829, the first Representative of the new West and of the "masses." In his Cabinet, outside of Van Buren, there were few names of note; Jackson's real advisers were a coterie of practical politicians, Lewis, Kendall and others of the so-called "Kitchen Cabinet." In 1831 he reorganized his Cabinet, and the next year was re-elected over Clay. The chief features of his eight years, 1829–1837, were his vigorous opposition to nullification and to the United States Bank, his censure by the Senate, his introduction of the "Spoils System," his settlement of the French spoliation dispute, and his "Specie Circular" of 1836. After his retirement he continued to be regarded as the leader of the party, and died at the "Hermitage," near Nashville. Jackson was of heroic character, but headstrong, arbitrary, vindictive and subject to the influence of politicians. Lives by Parton and W. G. Sumner.

Jackson, Francis J. (1770–1814), known as "Copenhagen Jackson," succeeded Erskine as Minister Plenipotentiary to the United States, when the conflict between the British ship "Leopard" and the U. S. "Chesapeake" was in dispute. He returned in 1811, his character not having been such as to promote mutual accommodation of differences.

Jackson, Helen (Maria Fiske) Hunt (1831–1885), authoress, after the death of her husband, Edwin B. Hunt, in 1863, began writing prose and poetry for periodicals under the pen-name of H. H. In 1876 she married William S. Jackson. She was appointed special commissioner to the Mission Indians of California by President Arthur in 1883, as a consequence of her special interest in them, as shown by her writings, *e. g.*, "Ramona" and "A Century of Dishonor."

Jackson, Howell E., was born in 1832. He served in the Tennessee Legislature in 1880. He represented Tennessee in the U. S. Senate as a Democrat from 1881 to 1886, when he was appointed a U. S. Circuit Judge. In 1893 he was appointed by President Harrison a Justice of the Supreme Court.

Jackson, Thomas Jonathan (1824–1863), a native of Virginia, was graduated at West Point in 1846, in time to see service in the Mexican War. He taught in the Virginia Military Institute, and was, like so many other West Pointers, lifted by the Rebellion from obscurity. Having sided with the Confederacy he was intrusted with a brigade, whose firm stand at the first battle of Bull Run led to its commander's epithet, "Stonewall Jackson." His military fame was well grounded by the extraordinary rapidity of his movements in the Shenandoah campaign of 1862, where he outgeneraled the Federals Frémont, Banks and others, gained the battles of Front Royal, May 23, Winchester, May 25, Cross Keys, June 8, and Port Republic, June 9. Hastily joining Lee before Richmond, he decided the victory at Gaines' Mills, June 27. On August 9 he defeated the Federals at Cedar Creek. His bold march ended in the victory over Pope at the second battle of Bull Run. In the invasion he seized Harper's Ferry September 15, and commanded the left wing at Antietam. At Fredericksburg he led the right wing of Lee's army, and at Chancellorsville May 2, 1863, his flanking movement around Hooker's right resulted in success. But "Stonewall" Jackson was by mistake shot by his own men in this battle and died a few days later.

Jackson, William (1759–1828), major, entered a South Carolina regiment in 1775. He fought at Stono, Savannah and Charleston. He was secretary to the convention which framed the Federal Constitution in 1787, his notes of which are preserved.

Jackson, Fort, La., a Confederate stronghold on the south of the bend in the Mississippi River. It was garrisoned by a small force under the command of General Duncan, and was bombarded during Farragut's expedition against New Orleans, finally surrendering to General Butler, April 27, 1862.

Jackson City, Miss., scene of a battle and sack during the Civil War. The battle took place May 14, 1863, between McPherson's division of Grant's army then operating along the Mississippi River, and a South Carolina brigade of Johnston's army, commanded by Walker. Crocker's troop bore the brunt of this fight, defeating the Confederates by their impetuous and untiring charges. The latter fled to their defences in the town, but were shelled out of these by Sherman. July 10–17, after the fall of Vicksburg, Johnston had again retreated to his intrenchments. There he was invested by Sherman's troops, who partially surrounded the town and opened fire upon it. Ammunition gave out, however, and Johnston, taking advantage of a lull, destroyed as much of the town as he could and retreated under cover of a dense fog, July 17.

Jacobin Clubs. (See Democratic Societies.)

James I. (1566–1625), King of Great Britain from 1603 to 1625, granted, April 10, 1606, to a company of London merchants, a patent for the colonization of America. Of this company were formed the Virginia and Plymouth Companies, the efforts of the latter failing totally. The Virginia Company was granted a charter to establish a plantation between 41° and 34° north latitude, the Plymouth between 45° and 38°. The first settlement made by the Virginia Company was at Jamestown in 1607. The persecutions of the Separatists in England caused a body of that sect to obtain a grant of land from the Virginia Company. These Pilgrims intended to settle between the Hudson and the Delaware, but storms drove them to the north, and they established the Plymouth colony in 1620. The king permitted this, but would not give a special charter. He became hostile to the Virginia Company, and in 1624 brought it to an end by *quo warranto* proceedings.

James II. (1633–1701), King of Great Britain from 1685 to 1688, had in 1664, as Duke of York, received from his brother, Charles II., a proprietary grant of New Netherland, then recently conquered from the Dutch. Under his authority was promulgated the code called the "Duke's Laws." His grant included all the territory between the Connecticut and the Delaware, Long Island, Eastern Maine, Nantucket and Martha's Vineyard. As king, he adopted a policy for annulling the colony charters and solidifying the English possessions in America. Sir Edmund Andros was sent over in 1686 with orders to ignore all colonial political machinery and to govern the country through a council. The charters of Connecticut and Rhode Island were immediately demanded for annullment, the latter colony only complying. In 1688 Andros was made Governor of New York and New Jersey, as well as New England, his jurisdiction extending from Delaware Bay to the confines of New France.

James, Henry, novelist, born in 1843, son of Henry James, theologian, was educated in Europe, and has lived there during many of the years since. He is noted as a writer of cosmopolitan spirit, graceful style, subtle insight and realistic tendency. His novels mostly have to do with the life of Americans in Europe.

James, Thomas L., born in New York in 1831, edited the *Democratic Republican* from 1856 to 1866. While postmaster of New York, from 1873 to 1881, he inaugurated many reforms. He was appointed Postmaster-General in Garfield's Cabinet in 1881, and served until Arthur's administration in 1882. He introduced thorough reform in the postal service.

James Island, S. C., scene of two brief engagements during the Civil War. In the first, which occurred June 10, 1862, during the advance of the Federals under Hunter against Charleston, Lamar, holding the island with 25,000 Confederates, easily defeated, at Secessionville, and drove from the island, Benham, leading 6000 Federals. In the second, July 16, 1863, Terry, who had made a lodgment upon the island with a small force, was expelled by the Confederates under Hagood. Terry's movement was a feint to draw the Confederates' attention from Fort Wagner, on Morris Island, in an assault upon which he intended to join General Gillmore.

Jameson, John A. (1824–1890), publicist, was Judge of the Chicago Superior Court from 1865 to 1883. He was author of "The Constitutional Convention: its History, Powers and Modes of Proceeding," a standard work.

Jamestown, Va., first English settlement in the United States, was founded in 1607 by 105 colonists under Christopher Newport. During the first season the colony was saved from destruction by the efforts of Captain John Smith. On July 30, 1619, the first colonial assembly in America was held here. On March 22, 1622, several hundred colonists were massacred by the natives. The town was burned in 1676 during Bacon's rebellion. In 1699 it ceased to be the capital.

Japan. The United States was among the first of foreign powers to obtain rights of intercourse with Japan. Commodore Perry concluded a treaty of friendship and commerce March 31, 1854. The rights of Americans in Japan were further extended by the Convention of 1857, and a still more extensive treaty was concluded in 1858, by which the former treaties were partially or wholly abrogated. In 1860 a Japanese embassy was sent to the United States. By the Convention of October 22, 1864, Japan agreed to pay an indemnity of $3,000,000 to the United States, Great Britain, France and the Netherlands for damages. (See "Shimonoseki.") The share of the United States was returned to Japan in 1883. Commercial treaties were concluded in 1866 and 1878, the latter not now binding. An extradition treaty was signed April 29, 1886.

Jasper, William (1750–1779), enlisted in a South Carolina regiment in 1776. In the attack of Fort Moultrie he exposed himself to the fire of the enemy in order to recover the State flag, which had been shot from the parapet. He was very successful in detachment service. He was mortally wounded in the assault on Savannah.

"Java," frigate. (See "Constitution.")

Jay, John (December 12, 1745–May 17, 1829), Chief Justice of the Supreme Court, was born in New York City, of Huguenot descent. He graduated at King's (Columbia) College in 1766, and in the Revolutionary period was prominent on the patriotic side as a member of the Committee of Correspondence. As delegate to the first Continental Congress of 1774 he was an author of the "Address to the People of Great Britain." He was a member of the

Second Congress, and as delegate to the New York Convention he helped in drafting the State Constitution. In 1777 he was Chief Justice of the State. In 1780 he became Minister to Spain, and was soon associated with Adams and Franklin in negotiating the peace; Jay's services in this treaty were conspicuous. During the years 1784–1789 he was Secretary of Foreign Affairs. With Hamilton and Madison he wrote the *Federalist*, of which five essays are indisputably by Jay. He was a member of the New York Convention of 1788 which ratified the Constitution, and in 1789 Washington appointed him first Chief Justice of the Supreme Court. In 1792 he was the unsuccessful Federalist candidate for Governor of New York. In 1794 Jay was sent as special envoy to England to negotiate the treaty which, under the name of the "Jay Treaty," became an object of such fierce abuse. His last public service was as Governor of New York, 1795–1801. Life by William Jay.

Jay, John, (1817–1894), was Minister to Austria from 1869 to 1875. From 1883 to 1887 he was a member of the New York Civil Service Commission. He has published many influential anti-slavery, legal, political and historical pamphlets.

Jay, William (1789–1858), son of John Jay, was a Judge of the Westchester County Court, N. Y., from 1818 to 1843. He devoted his efforts to the abolition of slavery and war. He published a "Life of John Jay," a "View of the Action of the Federal Government in Behalf of Slavery," "War and Peace" and "Causes and Consequences of the Mexican War."

Jay Treaty, a treaty concluded in 1794 by John Jay and Lord Grenville, representing the United States and Great Britain respectively. The treaty provided for peace and friendship between the two countries; an evacuation of the British posts in the United States by June, 1796; free commercial and Indian intercourse on the American continent; unrestricted navigation of the Mississippi; indemnity by England to American citizens for recent unlawful captures; corresponding indemnity by America for certain Genêt captures of 1793, by privateers fitted out in our ports; and a limited trade between the United States and the British West Indies, by which our carrying trade was sadly curtailed. The treaty was generally unpopular in this country.

Jay-hawkers, guerrilla bands which carried on an irregular warfare in and around Eastern Kansas during the early part of the Civil War and before that time.

Jefferson, Joseph, actor, born in 1829, was employed in strolling theatre companies from 1832 to 1850. He made his first success as "Asa Trenchard" in "Our American Cousin." He has won his greatest fame as an actor by his rendering of Rip Van Winkle. His acting is marked by variety, vivacity and naturalness.

Jefferson, Martha Wayles (1748–1782), born in Virginia, widow of Bathurst Skelton, became the wife of Thomas Jefferson in 1772. She was carefully educated, beautiful and accomplished, and a devoted wife.

Jefferson, Thomas (April 2, 1743–July 4, 1826), third President of the United States, was born at Shadwell, Albemarle County, Va. He was graduated at William and Mary College, studied law, and entered upon its practice and the care of his estate. In 1769 he entered the House of Burgesses, and became active in the Revolutionary agitation; but his activity then and later was as a writer rather than as a speaker. He drafted the instructions to the Virginia delegates to the first Continental Congress, and was in consequence proscribed in Great Britain. As a delegate to the second Continental Congress he is of course chiefly remembered for his draft of the Declaration of Independence. Soon after signing that document he left Congress to re-enter the Virginia Legislature, where he labored strenuously for democratic reforms in the laws respecting the church and the descent of landed property. While Governor of Virginia, 1779–1781, he was called upon to resist the British invasion of the State. He was again in the Legislature, and for a short time in Congress. In 1784 he went to France as Plenipotentiary, and there wrote his "Notes on Virginia," and observed the outbreak of the Revolution. At the end of 1789 Jefferson returned to America, and entered upon his duties as Secretary of State in Washington's first Cabinet. In the ensuing years he became the central figure in the Democratic-Republican party which was forming in opposition to the Federalists. Hamilton, ablest of the Federalist leaders, was also in the Cabinet, and between the two divergence of views developed into continual disputes. Jefferson finally resigned in 1794. The great party of which he was the head gave him, in 1796, almost as many electoral votes as were given to Adams. He became accordingly Vice-President. At this epoch he prepared a "Manual of Parliamentary Practice," was president of the Philosophical Society, and drafted the Kentucky Resolutions of 1798. In the election of 1800–1801 Jefferson's party defeated Adams and the Federalists, but the defective provisions of the Constitution gave to Jefferson and Burr seventy-three electoral votes each, and there was no election; the House of Representatives accordingly took up the matter, and a bitter struggle ended in the choice of Jefferson for first place. In his Cabinet Madison was Secretary of State, Gallatin of the Treasury, Dearborn of War, Robert Smith of the Navy, and Lincoln Attorney-General. His administration was marked by the abolition of some usages of an aristocratic nature, by the Tripolitan War, the Louisiana Purchase (which see), the Lewis and Clark expedition, the "Chesapeake" incident, and the Embargo. (See Embargo.) President Jefferson was re-elected in 1804, and retired from office in 1809, but continued to be regarded as the adviser of the party. He was interested in later life in plans for education in Virginia, and superintended the planting of the University of Virginia. He died at Monticello in his native State. His political theories have had more influence upon the public life of America than those of any other one man. There are biographies by H. S. Randall, Tucker, Parton, and a more recent life by Schouler.

Jenkins Ferry, Ark. Here, April 30, 1864, while Steele, with a small Federal force, was attempting to cross the Saline River, Kirby Smith fell upon him. Steele turned and, ordering a counter charge, succeeded in dispersing the Confederates.

Jenkins, Thornton A., born in 1811, served during the Mexican War. He commanded in Farragut's fleet from 1862 to 1865. He was chief of the Bureau of Navigation from 1865 to 1869.

Jersey, East and West. (See New Jersey.)

Jersey Prison Ship, an unseaworthy sixty-four-gun ship, lying off the Brooklyn shore of New York harbor from 1776 to 1783, and used by the British as a prison for captured American sailors. Their treatment was most inhuman. Eleven thousand are said to have died of cold and starvation.

Jesuits. The efforts of the Jesuits to convert the Indians belong in general rather to the history of New France and Canada than to that of the United States. But their expeditions extended into the West, where they had missionary establishments at Green Bay, Wisconsin, and elsewhere. In the two English colonies in which Catholics were tolerated, Pennsylvania and Maryland, all the priests seem to have been Jesuits down to the suppression of that order by the Pope in 1773.

Jesup, Thomas S. (1788–1860), born in Virginia, was brevetted colonel for services at Chippewa and Niagara in 1814. He was promoted major in 1818. He commanded the army in Florida in 1836.

Jewell, Marshall (1825–1883), was elected Governor of Connecticut in 1869, 1871 and 1872. He was Minister to Prussia from 1873 to 1874. In 1874 he was appointed Postmaster-General; after introducing numerous reforms, he resigned in 1876. He was a member of the Republican National Convention in 1880, and was elected chairman of the National Republican Committee.

Jews. Settlements began to be made by these people early in the eighteenth century in South Carolina and Georgia. About 1734 they began to come in considerable numbers to Georgia, but the trustees of the Oglethorpe grant objected to them, and promptly checked their immigration on religious grounds. In 1749 they had established a flourishing body at Charleston, and had built a meeting-house. By 1765 a small number had also established themselves at New York. Others settled at Newport.

Jogues, Isaac (1607–1646), came to Canada from France in 1630, and spent his life among the Indians as a Jesuit missionary. He was twice taken captive by the Mohawk Indians, terribly tortured, and finally killed by them.

Johns Hopkins University, Baltimore, Md., was chartered in 1867, and named in honor of its principal benefactor, who bequeathed a fund of $3,000,000. It was intended especially for post-graduate work, and has done much for research.

Johnson, Andrew (December 29, 1808–July 31, 1875), seventeenth President of the United States, was born at Raleigh, N. C. He had no advantages of education, and was in early life a tailor; his energy triumphed over drawbacks, and in Tennessee, where he had settled, he became a member of the Legislature, and represented the State in Congress in 1843–1853. In 1853–57 he was Democratic Governor of the State, and immediately thereafter was U. S. Senator, serving until 1862. He was a strong Unionist, and was by President Lincoln appointed military Governor of Tennessee in 1862. In 1864 he was selected by the Republicans for the second place on the ticket, was elected, and by the startling death of Lincoln he was lifted into national prominence. President Johnson took the oath of office April 15, 1865. Though elected as a Republican he had never ceased to hold many Democratic principles; Congress was heavily Republican; their divergence of views, accented by Johnson's peculiarities of temper, caused a bitter quarrel between executive and Congress. The veto of the Freedmen's Bureau Bill and of the Civil Rights Bill in 1866, the veto of the Congressional plan of reconstruction and the Tenure of Office Bill in 1867 mark the stages of the controversy. In 1867 President Johnson suspended and then removed Secretary Stanton, and was forthwith impeached by the House of Representatives. The trial before the Senate, March–May, 1868, resulted in his acquittal, as the President's enemies mustered one less than the necessary two-thirds vote. Johnson lived in retirement after 1869, except for a short term as U. S. Senator in 1875.

Johnson, Cave (1793–1866), represented Tennessee in the U. S. Congress as a Democrat from 1829 to 1837, and from 1839 to 1845. He was Postmaster-General in Polk's Cabinet from 1845 to 1849.

Johnson, Edward (1599–1672), captain, came to America from England about 1630. He served in the Massachusetts General Court from 1643 to 1671, except 1648. He wrote a narrative of New England history from 1628 to 1652, called "The Wonder-working Providence of Sion's Saviour in New England."

Johnson, Eliza McCardle (1810–1876), born in Tennessee, married Andrew Johnson in 1826, and devoted herself to his advancement. Ill-health prevented her from accompanying him in his public life.

Johnson, Sir Henry (1748–1835), came to America from England in 1775, and commanded a battalion of British troops from 1776 to 1778. From 1778 to 1781, he commanded a regiment in the Jerseys, Virginia and Carolina.

Johnson, Herschel V. (1812–1880), represented Georgia in the U. S. Senate as a Democrat from 1848 to 1849. He was Judge of the Georgia Supreme Court from 1849 to 1853. He was Governor of the State from 1853 to 1857. He was defeated as Democratic candidate for Vice-President of the United States in 1860, on the Douglas ticket. He served in the Confederate Senate.

Johnson, Sir John (1742–1830), was knighted in 1765 and succeeded to the baronetcy of Sir William Johnson, his father, in 1774. He fled from New York to Canada in 1776 on account of his loyalist principles. In 1777 he invested Fort Stanwix and fought at Oriskany. In 1780 he superintended the atrocious depredations in the Cherry Valley and conducted the raids in the Mohawk Valley. He was afterward Governor of Upper Canada.

Johnson, Reverdy (1796–1876), lawyer and diplomatist, reached a high rank at the Maryland bar, and was U. S. Senator 1845–1849, and Attorney-General in President Taylor's administration, 1849–50. He was a member of the Peace Conference, and in 1863 re-entered the Senate as a Republican. He held a prominent position among the leaders, and in 1868 was sent to represent this country at London. Besides achieving great popularity in

England, he negotiated the so-called Johnson-Clarendon Treaty, which, however, failed of ratification by the U. S. Senate. Mr. Johnson returned in 1869.

Johnson, Richard M. (1781–1850), served in the Kentucky Legislature in 1804. He represented Kentucky in the U. S. Congress as a Republican from 1807 to 1819. In 1812 he commanded a regiment in the war. In 1813 he fought at Chatham and in the battle of the Thames, where he is said to have killed Tecumtha. He served in the U. S. Senate from 1819 to 1829, and in the U. S. House of Representatives from 1829 to 1837. He was elected Vice-President of the United States by the Senate in 1837, and served from 1837 to 1841, with Martin Van Buren as President.

Johnson, Richard W., born in 1827, fought at Pittsburg Landing in 1861, commanded a division in 1862 at Chickamauga and Missionary Ridge. He published a life of General Thomas.

Johnson, Samuel (1696–1772), was an eminent Episcopal clergyman in the Connecticut colony from 1725 to 1754. He was influential in the endowment of Yale, and was president of King's College (Columbia) from 1754 to 1763.

Johnson, Thomas (1732–1819), represented Maryland in the Continental Congress from 1774 to 1777. He was Governor of Maryland from 1777 to 1779. He was a Justice of the U. S. Supreme Court from 1791 to 1793.

Johnson, Sir William (1715–1774), was born in Ireland, and, having emigrated to America, settled in the Mohawk Valley. In this region, then mainly an Indian wilderness, Johnson's tact, ability and knowledge of the Indian character, made him the central personage. He was colonel of the Six Nations, commissary of Indian affairs, and member of the Governor's council. His headquarters was Fort Johnson, near Amsterdam. The influence of the Johnson family held the Six Nations to the English alliance in the French and Revolutionary wars. Johnson attended the Albany Congress in 1754, and the next year was appointed to command in the north. For the victory at the head of Lake George, September 8, 1755, really won by General Lyman, Johnson received the credit together with a baronetcy and a sum of money. In 1759, after the fall of Prideaux, he succeeded to the command in the attack on Fort Niagara.

Johnson, William (1771–1834), was a member of the South Carolina Legislature from 1794 to 1798. In 1804 he was appointed a Justice of the U. S. Supreme Court and served till his death. His principles were opposed to the nullification movements of 1831–1833. He published a "Life of Nathanael Greene."

Johnson, William S. (1727–1819), was a Connecticut delegate to the Stamp-Act Congress in 1765. He was London agent of the colony from 1766 to 1771. He was Judge of the Connecticut Supreme Court from 1772 to 1774, served in the Continental Congress from 1784 to 1787, and aided in drafting the Constitution. He was a U. S. Senator from 1789 to 1791, then president of Columbia College till 1800.

Johnston, Albert Sidney (1803–1862), a distinguished Confederate general, was born in Kentucky, and graduated at West Point in 1826. He served in the Black Hawk War, entered soon after the army of Texas, and became Secretary of War for that republic. He passed through the Mexican War, was for a short time a planter, and again in the U. S. army rose to be paymaster and colonel. He commanded skillfully the expedition to Utah, and was in charge of the Department of the Pacific when the war broke out. Having espoused the Confederate cause he was appointed a general and entrusted with command in the West. He fortified the strategic point of Bowling Green, but his forces were driven back, and he was compelled to concentrate at Corinth. From this point he planned a surprise on Grant's army lying at Pittsburg Landing. The attack was executed in one of the fiercest battles of the war, but General Johnston was killed in the afternoon of the first day while leading a charge. Life by W. P. Johnston.

Johnston, Alexander (1849–1889), was admitted to the bar in 1876. He was professor of jurisprudence and political economy at Princeton from 1883 to 1889. He was an enthusiastic student of American history. He published a "History of American Politics," "Representative American Orations," "History of the United States for Schools," and a history of Connecticut.

Johnston, Joseph Eggleston (February 3, 1807–March 21, 1891), a celebrated Confederate general, was born in Virginia, and graduated at West Point in 1829. He had a long career of service in the old army in the wars with Black Hawk, the Seminoles, as engineer in Scott's campaign in Mexico, where he distinguished himself at Chapultepec, and finally as quartermaster-general. The Confederate Government appointed him a major-general, and he commanded at the first battle of Bull Run. He had charge of the operations in Virginia down to the middle of McClellan's Peninsula campaign, when he was severely wounded at the battle of Fair Oaks, and was replaced by General Lee. He had meanwhile been raised to the full rank of general, and in 1863 he was sent to relieve Pemberton before Vicksburg, but failed. In the following December he succeeded to the command of Bragg's defeated army; with this force he was the next year opposed to Sherman in the mountains of northern Georgia, and the skillful manœuvring of these two great masters of strategy has elicited warm praise. President Davis, displeased with Johnston, put Hood in his place; but the next winter the two old antagonists were again pitted against each other in North Carolina, where Johnston surrendered April 26, 1865. Subsequently he was a railroad president and a Congressman from Virginia. He wrote a "Narrative of Military Operations." Life by Hughes.

Johnstone, George, born in Scotland, died in 1787. He became Governor of West Florida in 1763. He was a British Commissioner to the United States in 1778. He published "Thoughts on Our Acquisitions in the East."

Joint High Commission. (See "Alabama" Claims.)

Joliet, Louis (1645–1700), a noted French explorer, was born in Quebec and educated at a Jesuit college. The scope of his explorations was the

COMMANDERS IN THE MEXICAN WAR.

R. F. Stockton. Philip Kearney.

Winfield Scott.
Santa Anna.

John C. Fremont. Zachary Taylor.

same as Marquette's and La Salle's, the linking together of the great systems of the St. Lawrence lakes and the Mississippi. With Marquette he started from Mackinaw, ascended Lake Michigan and descended the Illinois River in 1673 to its mouth in the "Father of Waters;" thence he descended the great river to the present State of Arkansas, and returned to Canada. The chief credit of the exploration of the Mississippi, whether due to Joliet, his distinguished associate, or to La Salle, is a controverted question.

Jonathan, or Brother Jonathan. The use of this expression, to denote the Yankee or American, is said to have sprung from General Washington's habitual use of it to designate Governor Jonathan Trumbull, of Connecticut, a valued helper in the conduct of the war.

Jones, Anson (1798–1858), was prominent in gaining the independence of Texas. He was Minister from Texas to the United States from 1837 to 1839. He was Secretary of State in Texas from 1841 to 1844 and President in 1845, at the time of the annexation.

Jones, Jacob (1768–1850), entered the U. S. navy in 1799. He was a lieutenant of the "Philadelphia" from 1801 to 1803. In command of the "Wasp" he captured the British brig "Frolic" in 1812. This was one of the first important naval victories of the war. In 1813 he commanded the "Macedonian" in Decatur's squadron.

Jones, James C. (1809–1859), was a member of the Tennessee Legislature in 1837 and 1839. He was Governor of Tennessee from 1841 to 1845, and was a Whig Senator of the United States from 1851 to 1857.

Jones, John P., born in England in 1830, a rich mine-owner, has been a Republican member of the U. S. Senate from Nevada from 1873 to the present time (1894) and has been prominent as an advocate of the free coinage of silver. He was a member of the Brussels Monetary Conference of 1892.

Jones, John Paul (July 6, 1747–July 18, 1792), a naval hero, was born in Scotland and had been engaged in the merchant marine previous to his settlement in Virginia, shortly before the beginning of the Revolutionary War. On the opening of hostilities he volunteered with enthusiasm in the service of his adopted country, was appointed first lieutenant, and made a number of successful cruises. In 1777 he sailed to France. From Brest as headquarters he conducted in his ship, the "Ranger," a remarkable expedition to the British coasts, for which his old acquaintance with the localities had well fitted him. In St. George's Channel he took prizes, landed at Whitehaven and terrorized the seaboard for a short time. He captured the British "Drake," and his success led him in 1779 to start in command of a small fleet against the eastern shore of the island; his own vessel was the "Bon Homme Richard." With this fleet he encountered off Scarborough a British convoy and ships of war. One of the fiercest naval fights on record followed between Jones' vessel and the British "Serapis" on the evening of September 23, 1779. The "Serapis" finally struck, but the American ship was completely disabled, and the losses in the close-range struggle were great. Jones received the thanks of Congress and a gold sword from Louis XVI. After the war he was a rear-admiral in the Russian navy, and died in Paris.

Jones, John W. (1791–1848), represented Virginia in the U. S. Congress as a Whig from 1835 to 1845, when he declined re-election. He was Speaker of the House from 1843 to 1845.

Jones, William (1760–1831), served in the battles of Trenton and Princeton during the Revolution. He represented Pennsylvania as a Democrat in the U. S. Congress from 1801 to 1803. He was Secretary of the Navy in 1813 and 1814. Subsequently he was president of the U. S. Bank.

Jones Case, a fugitive slave case. George Jones, a respectable colored man, was arrested in New York in 1836, on a fictitious charge of assault and battery. He was taken before Recorder Riker and was released to his kidnappers as their property, their word being taken as sufficient evidence. This was a favorite method of kidnapping.

Jonesboro, Ga. A series of short, but sharp engagements during Sherman's investment of Atlanta in 1864, the town being then held by Hood with some 60,000 Confederates. Sherman's force was nearly 100,000 strong. There was some fighting between Atlanta and Jonesboro August 19 and 20, Kilpatrick having been dispatched to destroy the Macon railroad and encountering a cavalry troop under Ross, whom he defeated. Kilpatrick was in his turn defeated the next day by a Confederate infantry force. Meantime Hardee had been sent from Atlanta to Jonesboro by Hood to guard his communications. On August 31 Hardee fell upon the Federal right under Howard and a desperate battle took place, in which Hardee was decidedly worsted. Hardee retreated that same night.

Jouett, James E., born in 1828, served during the Mexican War. In command of the "Santee" in 1861, he captured the "Royal Jacket," and was active at Mobile under Commodore Farragut. In 1886 he became a rear-admiral.

Journals of Congress. "The Journals of Congress" from 1774 to 1788 were first published at Philadelphia in thirteen volumes, octavo, 1777–1788, but they were reprinted at Washington in four volumes, octavo, 1823. The proceedings of the Constitutional Convention were published at Boston in 1819, entitled "Journal, Acts and Proceedings of the Convention Assembled at Philadelphia which Framed the Constitution of the United States." There was also published at Boston, in 1821, a work in four volumes, entitled "Secret Journals of the Acts and Proceedings of Congress from the First Meeting thereof to the Dissolution of the Confederation by the Adoption of the Constitution of the United States." The Journals of the Congress under the Constitution have been printed each session, according to the requirement of the Constitution.

Joutel, Henri, French explorer, came to America in 1684. He published authentic accounts of the last expedition of La Salle, and his own explorations in the Mississippi Valley.

Juarez, Benito P. (1806–1872), was Governor of Mexico from 1847 to 1852, including part of the war with the United States. He was Minister of Justice and Religion from 1855 to 1857. He was Secretary of the Interior from 1857 to 1858. In 1858 he assumed the control of the executive, and was recognized by the U. S. Government in 1859. He maintained his government against the clerical party with difficulty throughout the revolutionary troubles, but from the withdrawal of the French and the death of Maximilian until his own death he ruled the republic.

Judd, Sylvester (1789–1860), edited the *New Hampshire Gazette* from 1822 to 1834. He carefully studied the history of Massachusetts and Connecticut, and published "Thomas Judd and his Descendants," and "A History of Hadley."

Judiciary. Except in the earliest days of the Puritan colonies, the judiciary in the colonies was modeled on that of England. In each, the Governor (in the general case) constituted the court of admiralty, the court of equity, and the ecclesiastical and highest probate court. There was a supreme or superior common-law court, from which appeals lay to the Governor and council, and ultimately to the King in Council. County courts were commonly held after the forms of the justices' courts of quarter session in England; and there was a similar system of lowest courts, held by individual justices. When, at the beginning of the Revolution, the States made their new Constitutions, they either abolished those courts which were not common-law courts or reorganized them, or gave their functions to the common-law courts. Otherwise little change was made in the system. Under the Continental Congress the beginnings of a Federal judiciary are seen in the operations of the commissions which decided land cases between States, and in those of the commissioners of appeal in prize causes, which in 1781, under the Articles of Confederation, was erected into a more regular court. The Constitution of 1787 provided for a supreme court, and such inferior courts as Congress might establish. By the Judiciary Act of 1789, Congress established circuit and district courts. (See arts. Supreme Court, Circuit Courts and District Courts.) These constituted the Federal system until 1891, when the Circuit Courts of Appeal were added. Colonial judges were mostly appointed by the Governors. In some States this feature was retained; in most, it has now become the rule that judges are elected by the people. Beside the strictly Federal courts provided by the Constitution, Congress has established a system of Territorial courts, and the Court of Claims (see art.).

Judson, Adoniram (1788–1850), was a successful American missionary to Burmah from 1813 to 1850. He thoroughly mastered the Burmese language and translated a number of books, including the entire Bible.

Juilliard vs. Greenman, a case involving a question of legal tender, brought by plaintiff on writ of error from the Circuit Court of New York to the Supreme Court of the United States in 1884. Juilliard having contracted a sale to Greenman, the latter offered payment in United States notes, which the plaintiff refused, demanding payment in gold or silver. The Circuit Court found a verdict for the defendant, on the ground that notes issued by the United States are legal tender for payment of any debt. The Supreme Court confirmed this judgment, thus affirming the constitutionality of the Legal Tender Act of 1862.

Julian, George W., born in 1817, was a Free-Soil Representative to Congress from Indiana from 1849 to 1851. He was the Free-Soil candidate for Vice-President of the United States in 1852. He was vice-president of the first Republican convention in 1856 and chairman of the organization committee. He was a Republican member of the U. S. Congress from 1861 to 1871.

Jumonville, N. Coulon de (1725?–1754), was sent by the French in 1754 to summon Washington to surrender the fort at Great Meadows. He was killed in an attack which was represented as a violation of international law by the French, but probably was not.

Justice, Department of. This department was not created until June 22, 1870, though the office of Attorney-General, who is at its head, was created September 24, 1789. The earlier Attorneys-General had leisure to practice as attorneys. An assistant was first given the Attorney-General in 1859, a second in 1868, a third in 1871. In 1861 the Attorney-General was given supervision of all U. S. district attorneys and marshals.

K.

Kalakaua, David (1836–1891), was made king of Hawaii in 1874 and established his government with the aid of American and English ships. He died in San Francisco while negotiating a treaty of reciprocity with the United States.

Kalb, Johann, self-styled **Baron de Kalb** (1721–1780), visited America as a secret agent of the French Government in 1768. He was encouraged by Franklin and Silas Deane to join the Continental army, and accompanied Lafayette to the United States in 1777. He was appointed major-general and served under Washington in New Jersey and Maryland. In 1780 he was despatched to South Carolina in command of the Delaware and Maryland troops. At Camden his troops defeated the opposing British force, but were subsequently surrounded and DeKalb was mortally wounded.

"**Kalmar Nyckel**" ("Key of Kalmar"), a Swedish man-of-war furnished as an emigrant ship in the Swedish colonization expedition of 1637. The ship entered Delaware Bay in March, 1638, and its passengers settled along the Delaware River.

Kamper vs. Hawkins, a case adjourned from the District Court of Dumfries, Va., to the General Court in November, 1793. It involved the constitutionality of an act of the State Legislature of 1792, which authorized a district court in term time, or a judge thereof in vacation, to exercise the same power of granting injunctions to stay proceedings on any judgment obtained in a district court, and of proceeding to the dissolution or final hearing of such cases, as was prescribed for the High Court of Chancery. The court decided that this law was not wholly in accordance with the Constitution, but that there was no alternative for a decision between the Legislature and the judiciary except an appeal to the people.

Kane, Elisha K. (1820–1857), served in the navy as a surgeon from 1843 to 1850. He accompanied E. J. DeHaven in 1850 on his Arctic expedition. In 1853–55 he commanded the "Advance" in an Arctic exploring expedition. He reached latitude 80° 35′, and made valuable and accurate scientific observations, which he published in his reports.

Kansas. The territory of the State of Kansas formed a part of the Louisiana and Texas cessions. The greater part was acquired by the United States in 1803. The portion lying south of the Arkansas River and west of longitude 100° W. was ceded to the United States by Texas in 1850. The region was explored in 1541 by Coronado, a Spaniard. In 1819–1820 it was partly explored by Major Long, of the United States army. In 1854 Stephen A. Douglas introduced a bill into Congress providing for the organization of the Kansas and Nebraska territories, and the repeal of the Missouri Compromise of 1820, whereby slavery was prohibited north of 36° 30′. The existence of slavery was left to the decision of the people of the State when admitted. The introduction and passage, May 30, 1854, of this bill caused intense political excitement. Emigrants from Arkansas and Missouri immediately began to move into Kansas to hold the State for the pro-slavery party. On the other hand the Massachusetts Emigrant Aid Society sent out colonies to keep slavery out of the State. The "Kansas struggle" then began. The pro-slavery men, aided by bands from Missouri, elected the Territorial delegate to Congress, November 29, 1854. March 30, 1855, an election took place for a Territorial Legislature, in which the pro-slavery men were again successful. At this election 5427 votes were cast for their candidates, and 791 for their opponents, and yet there were but 2905 legal voters in the country. This Legislature met at Pawnee in July, and immediately proceeded to vote Kansas a slave Territory. On the other hand the anti-slavery men met in convention at Topeka, and adopted a State Constitution which prohibited slavery, October–November, 1855. This Constitution was ratified by popular vote, December 15. An election for a Legislature was held under this Constitution in January. May 21 Lawrence was pillaged. In the same year a party under John Brown murdered five men. A bill for the admission of the State was defeated in the Senate, and the State Legislature was dispersed by Federal troops in 1856. A pro-slavery convention adopted the Lecompton Constitution, which was submitted to a popular vote with or without slavery. The anti-slavery men refused to vote, and the Constitution was adopted. At a second election, January 4, 1858, it was defeated, and again on August 3 at another election ordered by Congress. In 1859 a constitutional convention at Wyandotte adopted a Constitution prohibiting slavery, which was ratified October 4. January 29, 1861, Kansas was admitted into the Union. The State was steadily Republican until 1882, when the Democrats carried the election. In 1892 the electoral votes of the State were cast for the candidate of the People's party. The population of the State in 1890 was 1,427,096; in 1860 it was 107,206. History by Spring.

Kansas Aid Society, a Congressional association formed in 1854 for the purpose of aiding free immigration into Kansas to prevent the establishment of slavery, which had been made possible by the passage of the Kansas-Nebraska Act then recently adopted. Slavery advocates from Missouri were at that time active in endeavoring to bring about the establishment of slavery.

Kansas City, Mo., was laid out in 1830, but its growth dates from 1860.

Kansas-Nebraska Bill. Under the provisions of this bill, which was passed by Congress May 22, 1854, Kansas and Nebraska were separated and organized into Territories. The importance of this bill lay in the fact that it practically repealed the Missouri Compromise. In the bill as reported by Stephen A. Douglas, the question of slavery in the two Territories was to be settled within the Territories, and if adopted the fugitive slave law was to apply. The status of Nebraska was easily settled as a free Territory, but the question caused much trouble in Kansas. The passage of the act had much to do with bringing on the Civil War.

Kapp, Friedrich (1824–1884), came to America from Germany in 1850. He wrote lives of Generals Kalb and Steuben, and numerous works relating to slavery and the relations between Germany and the United States.

Kaskaskia, Ill., a French settlement, settled in the latter part of the seventeenth century, garrisoned in 1778 by British soldiers. Colonel George Rogers Clark captured it with three companies of Kentucky recruits on the night of July 4, after a short struggle and with but little bloodshed.

Kasson, John A., born in 1822, was chairman of the Iowa Republican Committee from 1858 to 1860. He was appointed Assistant Postmaster-General in 1861 and served till 1862. He represented Iowa in the U. S. Congress as a Republican from 1863 to 1867, from 1873 to 1877 and from 1881 to 1884. He was Minister to Austria from 1877 to 1881 and to Germany from 1884 to 1885.

Kautz, August V., born in Germany in 1828, was brevetted colonel U. S. army for services during the Civil War. He engaged in the Peninsular campaign in 1862, at South Mountain, Petersburg and Richmond, and was noted for his cavalry raids in southern Virginia in 1864.

Kearny, Lawrence (1789–1868), served in the navy during the War of 1812. He was successful in destroying piracy and smuggling. He was influential in negotiating the Treaty of 1845 with China.

Kearny, Philip (1815–1862), entered the army in 1837. He was sent by the U. S. Government in 1839 and 1840 to report upon the cavalry tactics of the French. During the Mexican War he was brevetted major for gallantry at Contreras and Churubusco. In 1861 he was assigned command of a brigade in the Army of the Potomac. He engaged at Williamsburg and served with the Army of Virginia. In 1862 he was assigned command of a division and fought at Bull Run. He was killed in the battle of Chantilly.

Kearny, Stephen W. (1794–1848), served throughout the War of 1812. He was promoted brigadier-general in 1846, with command in the West. During the Mexican War he established a provisional government in Santa Fé and fought the battle of San Pasqual, after which he was made major-general. In 1847 he was Governor of California. He wrote a "Manual of the Exercise and Manœuvring of U. S. Dragoons."

"Kearsarge," the U. S. man-of-war which destroyed and sunk the Confederate cruiser "Alabama" off Cherbourg harbor, in France, June 19, 1864. In 1894 it was wrecked on a reef in the Caribbean Sea.

"Kearsarge" and "Alabama," a famous naval battle of the Civil War occurring June 19, 1864, just off the harbor of Cherbourg, France. The Confederate war-ship "Alabama" was at that time engaged in destroying Union vessels in European waters. She was commanded by Semmes; had eight guns and sixty men. Winslow commanded the "Kearsarge," the National ship having been dispatched in search of the "Alabama." The "Kearsarge" had seven guns and sixty-two men. The "Kearsarge" lay waiting for the Confederate ship outside the harbor. The battle took place some seven miles out at sea. The "Alabama" began the firing without much effect upon her opponent. When the "Kearsarge" opened fire, her superiority in point of management and gunnery was at once evinced. One of her shells cut off the "Alabama's" mizzenmast and another exploded, killing half her crew. She was speedily disabled and sunk. Semmes escaped.

Keifer, Joseph Warren, born in 1836, represented Ohio in the U. S. House of Representatives as a Republican from 1877 to 1885. He was Speaker of the House from 1881 to 1883.

Keith, Sir William (1680–1749), was commissioned Lieutenant-Governor of Pennsylvania and Delaware from 1717 to 1726. He served in the Pennsylvania Assembly in 1727 and 1728. He published a "History of Virginia."

Kelley, Benjamin F. (1807–1891), during the Civil War fought at Philippi, Romney and Blue Gap. In 1863 he commanded the Department of West Virginia. He was brevetted major-general in 1864 for services at Cumberland, New Creek and Morefield.

Kelley, William D. (1814–1890), was admitted to the bar in 1841. He was Judge of the Philadelphia Court of Common Pleas from 1846 to 1856. He was a member of the Republican National Convention of 1860, and represented Pennsylvania in the U. S. Congress as a Republican from 1861 to 1890. He published "The New South" and many influential political writings, and was noted as a strong protectionist.

Kellogg, William P., born in 1831, represented Louisiana in the U. S. Senate as a Republican from 1868 to 1871. Kellogg was recognized by the U. S. Government as Governor of Louisiana in 1872 in opposition to the rival government led by McEnery. (See art. Louisiana.) He served until 1877. He again served in the U. S. Senate from 1877 to 1883, and in the House of Representatives from 1883 to 1885.

Kelly's Ford. (See Rappahannock Station.)

Kemble, Frances Anne, born in London in 1809, has won distinction both in Europe and in the United States as an actress in historical plays. She has also been successful as a reader of Shakespeare.

Kendall, Amos (1789–1869), of Kentucky, born in Massachusetts, earnestly supported Jackson in 1824. In 1829 he was appointed an auditor in the

Treasury Department. He was one of the chief men in Jackson's administration, guiding the anti-bank policy, and advising and directing the President in all his duties. He was Postmaster-General of the United States from 1835 to 1840 in the Cabinets of Jackson and Van Buren. He was an ardent anti-slavery advocate; and, though a Jackson Democrat, earnestly supported the administration during the Civil War. He wrote a "Life of Andrew Jackson, Private, Military and Civil" (uncompleted).

Kendall vs. United States. In 1835, Barry, then Postmaster-General, made certain contracts with Stokes and others of the District of Columbia, for carrying the mail of the United States. Kendall, Barry's successor, refused to pay to Stokes certain sums of money mentioned in the contract. Stokes applied to the Circuit Court of the District of Columbia for a mandamus to compel Kendall to pay. This was granted. Kendall brought the case before the Supreme Court of the United States, and the decree of the Circuit Court was confirmed on the ground that the mandamus did not seek to control the Postmaster-General in his official duty, but to enforce the performance of a mere ministerial act.

Kenesaw Mountain, Ga. To this strong position General Johnston had retreated about June 11, 1864, with about 60,000 Confederates, Sherman following him closely with 100,000 Federal troops. Johnston succeeded in fortifying himself quite strongly. A smart skirmish took place June 14, and General Polk, of Confederate fame, was killed. On the 17th an assault was ordered by Sherman, which caused Johnston to contract his line. After this, during ten days, Johnston's cannon kept booming away from the heights, while Sherman's army lay in the valley below, almost untouched. On the 22d an ineffectual attack was made by Hooker and Schofield, in which the Nationals lost heavily. This is known as the affair of "Kulp's House." Again on the 27th Sherman caused two attacks to be made simultaneously and from different quarters. So Hooker and McPherson advanced against the Confederates' left and centre. Both assaults failed disastrously. Nearly 3000 Federals were missing in killed and wounded. July 1, however, McPherson made a more successful attack and Johnston was compelled to retire.

Kennan, George, born in Ohio in 1845, has made in Siberia a thorough investigation of the Russian exile system, the results of which he has published in a book entitled "Siberia and the Exile System." He had earlier published "Tent-Life in Siberia."

Kennebec Expedition, an expedition along the Kennebec River, sent out by Washington under Benedict Arnold, in 1775, to co-operate with Montgomery's Canada expedition. Arnold was assisted in this campaign by a number of Indians. With 1100 men Arnold reached Fort Augusta, Maine, and thence proceeded through the wilderness along the Kennebec toward Quebec. Upon reaching that place, which was garrisoned by a small force, he made the ascent at Wolfe's Cove and demanded a surrender. The garrison refused and Arnold, becoming frightened, drew off. He despatched Burr to Montreal, which had been captured by Montgomery. The latter joined Arnold at Quebec and together they assaulted the town. Montgomery was killed and his force drew off under Campbell. Arnold kept Carleton, the

English commander, shut up in Quebec for three months, till he was driven away by Burgoyne.

Kennebec Purchase. In 1628, William Bradford and others, of the Plymouth colonists, obtained a grant of territory for fishing purposes along the Kennebec and Cobbiseecontee Rivers. This was sold, in 1661, to Tyng and others, and was called the "Kennebec Purchase." This grant was made by the Council for New England.

Kennedy, John P. (1795–1870), was a member of the Maryland House of Delegates from 1820 to 1823. He represented Maryland in the U. S. Congress as a Whig from 1838 to 1839, and from 1841 to 1845. He was Secretary of the Navy in Fillmore's Cabinet from 1852 to 1853. He wrote a life of William Wirt and one of George Calvert.

Kent, Edward (1802–1877), was a member of the Maine Legislature from 1829 to 1833. He was Governor of Maine in 1838 and 1840, being chosen by the Whigs. From 1849 to 1853 he was U. S. Consul at Rio Janeiro. From 1859 to 1873 he was a Justice of the Maine Supreme Court.

Kent, James (1763–1847), jurist, was a member of the New York Legislature in 1790 and 1792. He was a Judge of the New York Supreme Court from 1798 to 1804, and Chief Justice from 1804 to 1814. He was Chancellor of New York from 1814 to 1823. He published "Commentaries on American Law," which is the standard general treatise on American law.

Kenton, Simon (1755–1836), a Kentucky pioneer, served as a scout in the colonial army till 1778. He commanded a Kentucky battalion from 1793 to 1794. He was engaged in the battle of the Thames in 1813.

"Kentucke Gazette." This journal was established at Lexington, Ky., August 18, 1787, the first important newspaper of Kentucky, and continued to be published for seventy-five years.

Kentucky was originally a part of Virginia. The first settlements were made by James Harrod and others at Harrodsburg in 1774; and by Daniel Boone at Boonesborough in 1775. A land company in 1775 attempted to organize a separate government under the name of Transylvania. In 1776 Kentucky became Kentucky County of Virginia. The refusal of Virginia and the National Government to allow a separate government and the indignation over the provision concerning the navigation of the Mississippi led to efforts being made to form an independent republic with alliance with Spain or Canada. June 1, 1792, the State was admitted into the Union. The close union of political feeling with Virginia was shown by the passage of the "Kentucky and Virginia Resolutions" of 1798 and 1799, which protested against the passage of the Alien and Sedition Acts by the Federalists. The Democrats controlled the State until 1830, except in 1824, when the electoral votes were cast for Clay. Kentucky became a Whig State, and so remained until 1856, when the Democrats carried the State. In 1860 the electoral votes were cast for Bell. In 1861 the Governor sympathized with the South, but the Legislature refused to call a convention, and elected delegates to the Peace Congress at Washington. For a time the State attempted to remain neutral, but the State Legislature in September, 1861, pronounced emphatically in favor of the Union. Since the war the State has been uniformly Democratic. A new Constitution was made in 1890–91. The population of the State in 1792 was 73,077; in 1890, 1,858,635. History by Shaler.

Kentucky Resolutions. These resolutions were the outgrowth, together with the Virginia Resolutions, of a feeling that the Federal party was making a strained and illegitimate use of the powers granted to the Federal Government by the Constitution. The resolutions were directly due to the passage of the Alien and Sedition laws. The Kentucky Resolutions were framed by Thomas Jefferson, and introduced, in 1798, into the Kentucky Legislature by John Breckenridge. They were passed for the purpose of defining the strict-construction view of the relative powers of State and Government. They were nine in number. They declared that the Union was not based on the "principle of unlimited submission to the General Government;" that the Constitution was a compact, to which each State was a party as over against its fellow States; and that, in all cases not specified in the compact, each party had a right to judge for itself, as well of infractions as of the mode and measure of redress. They proceeded to set forth the unconstitutionality of the Alien and Sedition Acts, and invited other States to join in declaring them void. No favorable response was evoked. In 1799 the Kentucky Legislature went further, and declared a nullification of a Federal law by a State to be the rightful remedy in cases of Federal usurpation. Upon these resolutions the doctrines of nullification and secession were later founded.

Kenyon College, Gambier, O., was chartered in 1824 by Episcopalians as a theological seminary, but a collegiate and a preparatory department were afterward added. In 1840 the seminary was constituted into a separate school.

Keokuk (1780?–1848), chief of the Sacs and Foxes tribes of Indians, possessed extraordinary courage and powers of oratory. He used his influence to prevent the Black Hawk War in 1832. In 1837 he made a tour through the principal cities in the East and attracted great attention by his eloquent speeches. He always maintained friendship for the whites.

Kernan, Francis (1816–1892), was reporter of the New York Court of Appeals from 1854 to 1857. He represented New York in the U. S. Congress as a Democrat from 1863 to 1865, and in the Senate from 1875 to 1881.

Kerr, Michael C. (1827–1876), was a member of the Indiana Legislature in 1856 and 1857. He was reporter of the Indiana Supreme Court from 1862 to 1865. He represented Indiana in the Congress of the United States as a Democrat from 1865 to 1873, and was Speaker from 1875 to 1876. He served on the Committees on Elections, Civil Service and Ways and Means.

Kersaint, Gui Pierre de P. (1742–1793), French naval commander, served in Canada in 1762, and aided the colonists from 1777 to 1783. He captured two British ships in 1777. He commanded a fleet in Chesapeake Bay in 1783.

Key, David M., born in 1824, served in the Confederate army throughout the war. He represented Tennessee in the U. S. Senate as a Democrat from 1875 to 1877. He was Postmaster-General in Hayes' Cabinet from 1877 to 1880. From 1880 to the present time (1894) he has been a U. S. District Judge in Tennessee.

Key, Francis Scott (1780–1843), wrote "The Star-Spangled Banner" after watching the bombarding of Fort McHenry by the British in 1814. (See art. McHenry, Fort.) The song became immensely popular.

Keyes, Erasmus D., general, was born in Massachusetts in 1810. He served under General Scott from 1860 to 1861. He fought at Bull Run and commanded a corps at Fair Oaks and Richmond. He retired in 1864.

Kickapoos, a tribe of Algonquin Indians who early centred around the Illinois. In 1779 they joined Colonel Clark against the English, but soon manifested hostility toward the new government. Peace was not fully made until after Wayne's victory in 1795. They then ceded a part of their lands, as they did also in 1802, 1803 and 1804. They joined Tecumseh and fought at Tippecanoe in 1811. In the War of 1812 they allied themselves with the English, but suffered disastrous defeats. In 1815, 1816 and 1819 they ceded more territory, and in 1822 the majority removed from the Illinois to the Osage. Some became roving bands. In 1854 they were removed to Kansas, and in 1863 a party migrated to Mexico, whence 400 returned to Indian Territory in 1873.

Kidd, William, born in Scotland, died in 1701. He early proved himself a bold and skillful navigator. He received a reward from the New York Council in 1691 for his services to the colonies. In 1696 he was placed in command of the "Adventure," of thirty guns and 154 men, to destroy piracy. He was led to engage in the traffic he was commissioned to destroy, and became one of the most noted of pirates. In 1699 he returned to New England, was arrested and sent to England, where he was hanged.

Kieft, Wilhelm (1600?–1647), the fifth Dutch Governor of New Netherlands, ruled from 1638 to 1647. He concentrated the government in himself. He improved the condition and appearance of New Amsterdam, repaired the forts, prohibited illegal traffic, enforced obedience to the police ordinances of the town, erected public houses and improved the system of land tenure. His rule was nevertheless tyrannical and despotic, and he was detested by the people. He organized the first representative assembly in New Netherlands in 1641, but dissolved it in 1643. He was recalled in 1647 at the request of the colonists.

Kilbourn vs. Thompson, an important case decided by the U. S. Supreme Court in 1880. Kilbourn was summoned as a witness before the House of Representatives of the United States in 1876, and required to answer questions and produce certain papers. This he refused to do, and accordingly Thompson, sergeant-at-arms of the House, was ordered to arrest and imprison him for forty-five days in the common jail of the District of Columbia. He was released on a writ of *habeas corpus*, and brought suit before the Supreme Court against Thompson and certain Congressmen on the plea of illegal imprisonment. The court decided that the House might punish its own members for disorderly conduct, but that the Constitution did not invest either House with a general power of punishment for contempt.

Kilpatrick, Hugh Judson (1836–1881), cavalry officer, engaged at Big Bethel, Falmouth and Bull Run. He commanded a cavalry brigade at Leesburg in 1862, and at Richmond, and a division at Gettysburg, Boonesborough and Resaca. He took part in Sherman's march to the sea. He was Minister to Chili from 1865 to 1868, and in 1881. He was a popular Republican campaign orator.

Kilpatrick's Raid, a cavalry expedition, February 25 to March 4, 1864, led by the Federal general of that name, who with 5000 horsemen swept around Lee's army, then lying near Richmond. The object of this raid was to relieve the Union troopers imprisoned in Libby prison. This purpose was not accomplished, but Kilpatrick succeeded in inflicting considerable loss upon the Confederates by destroying railroads and bridges and cutting up several of their regiments.

Kimball, Herbert C. (1801–1868), was chosen one of the twelve Mormon apostles in 1835. He aided in establishing the Mormons in the valley of the Great Salt Lake. In 1847 he became a counsellor of Brigham Young.

Kinderhook, N. Y., noted for a time as the place of residence of Martin Van Buren.

King, Horatio, born in 1811, was a clerk in the U. S. Postal Department from 1839 to 1854. He was First Assistant Postmaster-General from 1854 to 1861. In 1861 he was Postmaster-General in Buchanan's Cabinet.

King, Preston (1806–1865), was a New York Assemblyman from 1834 to 1837. He was a Democratic U. S. Congressman from 1843 to 1847 and from 1849 to 1853. He was a Republican U. S. Senator from 1857 to 1863.

King, Rufus (1755–1827), was born in Maine and graduated at Harvard. He came prominently forward as a member of the Massachusetts Legislature and a delegate to the Continental Congress. In the latter body he moved in 1785 the provision against slavery in the Northwest Territory, afterward adopted in 1787. He was a leading member of the Constitutional Convention of 1787, and went home to work zealously for the ratification of the Constitution by Massachusetts. Having removed to New York he was a Federalist U. S. Senator from that State in 1789–1796, and wrote some of the "Camillus" papers. He was Minister to London, 1796–1803, and again in the Senate 1813–1825. In 1816 he was an unsuccessful candidate for Governor, and the same year received thirty-four electoral votes for President, having been the Federalist candidate for Vice-President in 1804 and 1808. His last service was again at the Court of London in 1825–1826. Life and works by King (1894).

King, Thomas Starr (1824–1863), a famous Unitarian clergyman who won distinction as a lecturer in the East and in California. At the outbreak of the Civil War he was an earnest advocate of the Union cause.

King, William R. (1786–1853), represented Alabama in the U. S. Congress as a War Democrat from 1811 to 1816. He was Secretary of Legation to Russia from 1816 to 1818. He was a U. S. Senator from 1819 to 1844, and Minister to France from 1844 to 1846. He was a U. S. Senator from 1846 to 1853, when he was elected Vice-President of the United States, but soon died.

King George's War. Immediately upon the breaking out in Europe of the war of the Austrian succession, 1744, there began between the English and French colonies a frontier war known as King George's. The French made an attack in 1744 upon the northeastern settlements, and privateers from Louisbourg, in Cape Breton, harassed the New England coast. In 1745 the General Court of Massachusetts proposed a colonial expedition against Louisbourg, the strongest French fort north of the Gulf of Mexico. Massachusetts voted 3250 men and the other colonies a proportionate number. William Pepperell, of Maine, commanded the expedition. After a siege of two months Louisbourg capitulated, June 17, 1745. Another expedition was contemplated against Quebec, but the Treaty of Aix-la-Chapelle terminated the war (1748).

King William's War. In 1689, upon the accession of William and Mary, war was declared between England and France, and at once spread to the colonies. During 1690 Governor Frontenac, of Canada, sent three Indian expeditions against the English frontiers. Many settlers were killed and scalped. A colonial Congress, the first ever held, assembled at New York in 1690, and the next summer Sir William Phipps was sent with a fleet and 1800 New England men against Acadia and Port Royal, both of which he captured. Acadia was retaken by the French the next year. In 1696 the French took Newfoundland, and massacred the inhabitants of Andover, Mass. The trouble ended with the Treaty of Ryswick in 1697.

King's Mountain, Battle of, October 7, 1780. Colonel Ferguson, with 1200 men, had been despatched by Cornwallis to scour the highlands of South Carolina and enlist the Tories. Ferguson soon found the backwoodsmen rising against him, and was closely beset by 3000 militia. He took a position at King's Mountain on the border between the Carolinas. In his rear was a precipice, and in front woods and broken ground. One division of the Americans lured him from his position, and the other two then attacked his flanks. Ferguson himself fell, and 389 of his men were killed, 716 were taken prisoners. The Americans lost their brilliant leader, Colonel James Williams. Of their troops twenty-eight were killed and sixty wounded. History by Draper.

King's Province. In 1664 a royal commission was sent to the colonies with the power to regulate all the New England colonies. This commission in 1665 took the whole Narragansett country away from all the provinces and converted it into the "King's Province," under Rhode Island management. In 1729 it became King's County, Rhode Island.

Kingsborough, Edward K., Viscount (1795–1837), published a famous work of nine volumes on "The Antiquities of Mexico," which reproduces in *fac simile* the Mexican records and paintings then existing.

Kingston, N. C. Here, December 14, 1862, General Foster, *en route* with 11,000 Federals to destroy the important railroad junction at Goldsboro, fell in with the Confederate General Evans, commanding 6000 troops. An engagement was immediately begun. Evans was posted between a dense swamp and the bridge over the Neuse River. This was speedily captured and the Confederates dispersed.—Again, March 8 and 10, 1865, there was some sharp fighting between the Federals under Cox, of Schofield's army, and the Confederates under Bragg and D. H. Hill. Bragg was in full retreat from Wilmington when he was overtaken by Cox. Bragg was compelled to retire to Goldsboro March 10. There were about 12,000 men engaged on either side.

Kirk, John Foster, born in 1824, came to the United States from Canada in 1842. From 1847 to 1859 he was assistant to William H. Prescott. He edited *Lippincott's Magazine* from 1870 to 1886. He published a "History of Charles the Bold."

Kirkwood, Samuel J., born in 1813, was prosecuting attorney of Richland County, Ohio, from 1845 to 1849. He was Governor of Iowa from 1859 to 1863. He represented Iowa in the U. S. Senate as a Republican from 1866 to 1867. He was Governor of Iowa from 1875 to 1877, and a U. S. Senator from 1877 to 1881, when he became Secretary of the Interior in Garfield's Cabinet, serving till 1882.

Kitchen Cabinet, a coterie of intimate friends of President Jackson, who were supposed to have more influence over his actions than his official advisers. They were: General Duff Green, editor of the *United States Telegraph* at Washington, the confidential organ of the administration; Major William B. Lewis, of Nashville, Tenn., Second Auditor of the Treasury; Isaac Hill, editor of the *New Hampshire Patriot*, and Amos Kendall, of Kentucky, Fourth Auditor of the Treasury.

Kittanning, Burning of, September, 1756. During the French and Indian War, an attack was made in early September, 1756, by Colonel Armstrong upon Kittanning, a nest of Delaware Indians. The place was completely surprised, the houses burned, the chief killed, and much ammunition furnished by the French destroyed. The English loss was about twenty.

Klamaths, a name given to several Indian tribes living in Oregon and California. The influx of whites into California led to troubles in 1851, but a treaty soon restored peace. In 1864 they ceded large tracts of land and went on a reservation.

Knights of Labor, an order founded in Philadelphia in 1869 by Uriah S. Stevens and formally organized in 1871 for the protection of working people and the development of educated labor. It was secret until the name was made public in 1881. By that time nearly all trades were represented. It is governed by a national executive board and local assemblies which have power to order "strikes" and "boycotts." The membership is over 500,000. The chief strike so ordered was that on the Missouri Pacific system in 1886. It failed.

Knott, James Proctor, born in 1830, was chairman of the Judiciary Committee in the Missouri Legislature from 1857 to 1859, when he became State Attorney-General, and served till 1862. He represented Kentucky in the U. S. Congress as a Democrat from 1867 to 1871 and 1875 to 1883. He was chairman of the Judiciary Committee from 1875 to 1883. He was elected Governor of Kentucky in 1883, and served till 1887.

Know-Nothings, Know-Nothing Party, a name given to the members of the American party, because, being members of a secret order, when they were asked anything about its organization or concerns, they professed to know nothing about the matter.

Knox, Henry (1750–1806), an American cabinet officer, was born in Boston and was a bookseller before the Revolution. He exchanged this occupation for that of an artillery officer, fought at Bunker Hill, and obtained much credit for his transfer of ordnance in the winter of 1775–1776 from the Canadian frontier and the Lake George region to the army around Boston. He was made a brigadier-general of artillery, fought with distinction at Trenton, Brandywine, Monmouth and Yorktown, and received the grade of a major-general. He was active in the Cincinnati Society, and became Secretary of War under the old Congress in 1785. Washington reappointed him to this position, which he filled until 1795.

Knox, John Jay (1828–1892), was Deputy Comptroller of the Currency from 1867 to 1872 and Comptroller from 1872 to 1884. He drafted and prepared the Coinage Act of 1873. He wrote a "History of Banking in the United States."

Knox vs. Lee, a legal-tender case brought before the Supreme Court of the United States in 1870 by writ of error from the Circuit Court of Texas. A flock of sheep, belonging to Mrs. Lee, of Pennsylvania, had been seized by the Confederate authorities and sold to Knox for Confederate money. Mrs. Lee brought suit for recovery and demanded payment in gold or silver, though at the time of the sale greenbacks were deemed legal tender. The defendant objected and the court sustained the objection, saying there was no difference in value in law between the two. Judgment was found for the plaintiff and was confirmed by the Supreme Court of the United States. This decision overruled in part that given in the case of Hepburn *vs.* Griswold.

Knoxville, Tenn., occupied by Burnside with a strong Federal force, 12,000 men, in 1863, and beleagured and assaulted without success, November 17 and 29, by Longstreet, who had pursued the Federal general thither. The first assault proving a failure, Longstreet decided to reduce Burnside by siege, but fearing Grant might come up and destroy him, he attempted another assault on the 29th. The Confederates made a desperate charge, pushing each other up the parapet and many forcing their way through the embrasures. They were hurled back each time with heavy loss, and at last drew off to bury their dead. The siege continued, however, for some days. Grant had ordered Sherman to go to Burnside's assistance. Sherman started to do so, but meantime the battle of Chattanooga took place, and Sherman did not arrive until December 4. Then, after a short battle, Longstreet was compelled to raise the siege and retire.

"Knoxville Gazette," earliest newspaper in Tennessee. It was established at Knoxville in 1793, by R. Roulstone, the same year that printing was introduced into the State.

Knyphausen, Baron Wilhelm von (1716–1800), came to the United States as second in command of the Hessians in 1776. In 1777 he was placed in command of the German auxiliaries. He fought at Long Island, White Plains, Fort Washington, Brandywine and Monmouth. During the absence of Sir Henry Clinton in 1780, he was in command of New York. He returned to Europe in 1782.

Kohl, John G. (1808–1878), visited America from Germany from 1854 to 1858. He published many valuable works relating to the United States, including a series of maps and "History of the Discovery of the U. S. Coast," "History of the Two Oldest Charts of the New World," "History of the Discovery of the Northeastern Coast of America," "History of the Discovery of America," "History of the Discovery and Voyage through the Straits of Magellan," and "Travels in the United States."

Kosciuszko, Tadeusz (1746–1817), came to America from Poland in 1775. He was commissioned colonel under General Gates in 1776, and distinguished himself by his engineering skill. He superintended the fortification at West Point. He was brevetted brigadier-general in 1783. He was afterward prominent in the defence of Poland in 1794.

Kossuth, Louis (1802–1894,) was provisional Governor of Hungary during the Hungarian war for independence in 1848 and 1849. Exiled, he visited the United States from 1851 to 1852, and attempted to arouse the American people to support the cause of Hungary. The U. S. Government refused to interfere in the affairs of European powers. His eloquence aroused great enthusiasm.

Koszta, Martin. In 1853 Koszta, an Hungarian refugee, was captured in the harbor of Smyrna and confined on an Austrian brig. The U. S. agent demanded his release, on the ground that he had taken the preliminary steps for becoming an American citizen. Captain Ingraham, commanding an American war-sloop, threatened to fire on the brig unless Koszta was released. He was therefore turned over to the French Consul until the matter could be arranged, and was afterward released. Ingraham's action was approved by both Houses of Congress the next year, May 7.

Ku-Klux Klan, also called the "White League," the "Invisible Empire," the "Knights of the White Camelia," a society founded at Pulaski, Tenn., in 1866, during the reconstruction period. It was originally organized for purposes of amusement, but spread rapidly and terrorized the whole South by its mysterious movements. It opposed such organizations as the "Loyal Union League" and "Lincoln Brotherhood," formed among the newly freed negroes by the more disreputable class of whites through the South. The negroes were in some cases persecuted and frightened nearly to death and prevented from voting. The Klan was disbanded in 1869 by the order of the Government. Some members were arrested, but not convicted of misdemeanor.

L.

Labor. (See Progressive Labor party, Union Labor party, United Labor party.)

Labor Department, at first a bureau connected with the Department of the Interior. It was established as a department June 27, 1884. The chief officer is the Commissioner of Labor, whose duty it is to diffuse useful information among the people on labor questions, and to report the effect of customs laws upon the currency and agricultural interests.

Labor Statistics, Bureaus of. (See Bureaus.)

Laboulaye, Édouard R. L. (1811–1883), was a prominent French student of law and political institutions. He was an admirer of American institutions, and advocated the cause of the Union during the war. He wrote "Political History of the United States," "The United States and France," "Paris in America," "The State and its Limits" and translated Channing's works.

La Colle Mill, Canada, March 30, 1814, War of 1812. To clear the way to Montreal, General Wilkinson, with 4000 Americans, pushed on against the British entrenched at La Colle Mill. The place was defended at first by 200 men, but this number was increased to almost 1000 men during the battle by reinforcements. The British position was so well fortified that the assaults were easily repulsed; counter-charges were likewise unsuccessful. After two hours of desperate fighting the Americans withdrew with a loss of thirteen killed and 128 wounded; the British lost eleven killed and forty-six wounded. The military career of General Wilkinson ended with this battle; he was relieved from command, tried by court-martial, but acquitted.

Laconia, now the State of New Hampshire. August 10, 1622, a grant was made to Sir Ferdinando Gorges of the land between the Merrimac and Sagadahock (Kennebec) Rivers. November 7, 1629, a grant was made to George Mason between the Merrimac and the Piscataqua. In 1631 Mason and Gorges formed the Laconia Company and obtained an additional grant between Naumkeag and the Piscataqua.

La Corne, Pierre, a French-Canadian soldier who defeated the Indians at Lachine Rapids in 1747, and commanded at Grand Pré. He was an emissary to the Acadians in 1749. He fought at Quebec.

Lafayette, Marquis de [Marie Jean Paul Joseph Roche Yves Gilbert du Motier] (September 6, 1757–May 20, 1834), a French general, was born in Auvergne of a noble family distinguished in the service of the State. As a boy he was a page to the queen. He was still a mere youth when the outbreak of the American Revolution excited the sympathy of many high-spirited young Frenchmen, Lafayette among others. Having equipped a ship at his own expense he sailed from Bordeaux, with the nominal disapproval of the French Government, in April, 1777. Landing in South Carolina he proceeded northward, was in July appointed a major-general, and soon became a fast friend of Washington. He was wounded at Brandywine, served at Monmouth and in the Rhode Island campaign, and sailed for France in 1779, returning in time to sit on the board of judges against André. In 1781 he commanded in Virginia against Arnold and then against Cornwallis, and earned distinction by his conduct of affairs against the able British general. After the war he returned to France, paid in 1784 a short visit to America, and on the breaking out of the French Revolution he was for a time one of the foremost figures. He commanded the National Guard, but by 1792 the Jacobins removed him, as a moderate, from the eastern department; escaping to Belgium he fell into the hands of the Prussians and Austrians and was imprisoned, chiefly at Olmütz, until 1797. He did not accept office during the Napoleonic régime, but was a member of the Chamber of Deputies in the Restoration period. In 1824–25 he visited the United States and was received with the utmost enthusiasm. His last conspicuous service was as commander of the National Guard in the revolutionary days of 1830.

Lafayette College, Easton, Pa., was chartered by Presbyterians in 1826, and fully organized four years later as a college preparatory to the professions. In 1866 a scientific department was added through the gift of half a million dollars from Mr. Pardee. A law department was opened in 1875.

Lafitte, Jean (1780?–1826), pirate, came to New Orleans from France about 1809. With his brother Pierre he engaged in smuggling and piracy. Attempts to destroy their traffic were unsuccessful and they made a settlement at Barataria, on the island of Grand Terre. In 1814 the British made tempting offers to engage against the United States during the war, but they were refused, and the documents containing the proposals were sent to the Legislature. Believing them forgeries the Government sent an expedition against the buccaneers and destroyed their settlement. They afterward joined the forces of General Jackson and served during the war, on promise of pardon. From 1817 to 1821 Lafitte occupied Galveston, nominally as Mexican Governor.

Lake Borgne, Naval Battle on. Here Admiral Cochrane, with his fleet to attack New Orleans, had his passage disputed by some small war-vessels, carrying in all 182 men and twenty-three guns, Lieutenant Jones commander. He at once sent, December 14, 1812, sixty barges with 1200 men under Captain Lockyer to capture the American fleet. The engagement was long and desperate, but resulted in a victory for the British at an expense of 300 killed and wounded. The American loss was six killed and thirty-five wounded.

Lake Erie, Battle on, a celebrated naval battle of the War of 1812. The American fleet, hastily built and equipped for the occasion, consisted of eight small vessels, two of twenty guns each, the rest only fourteen guns in all. The "Lawrence," Commodore Perry, was the flagship. The British squadron, Commodore Barclay, consisted of six vessels of seventy guns in all. The battle for the mastery of the lake began September 10, 1813. Perry's ship was flying the motto, "Don't give up the ship." The "Lawrence" for two hours bore the brunt of the battle till it was almost a total wreck. In a small rowboat, amid the fire of the British fleet, Perry now crossed over to the "Niagara," which was almost untouched. On reaching this, he at once hoisted his pennant and dashed through the British line. Within ten minutes the flagship and three other British ships had surrendered. The other two were pursued and captured. Perry at once sent his famous despatch: "We have met the enemy, and they are ours." The American loss was twenty-seven killed and ninety-six wounded; the British, 200 killed and 600 made prisoners.

Lake George, Battle at. In the French and Indian War, on August 26, 1755, William Johnson, with about 2000 men, appeared at Lake George. His purpose was to advance upon Ticonderoga. Dieskau, the French commander, advanced with 1500 men to cut off Johnson's communications. A division sent out to prevent this was cut to pieces. The French followed the retreating force to Fort William Henry, but were repulsed. Johnson did not follow up his victory. The English loss was 242, the French 228.

Lake of the Woods. By the Treaty of 1782–83 the boundary line between the British and American possessions ran along the forty-ninth parallel on a line with the source of the Mississippi. The Louisiana Purchase in 1803 broke up conclusions as to the fairness of this line. Much dispute and negotiation followed. Finally by the Webster-Ashburton Treaty of 1842, the line was agreed upon which ran across Lake Superior, then up a waterway agreed upon, thence down a stream to the Lake of the Woods and across that lake to a point at the northwest corner (49° 23′ 55″ north latitude), and then south to the 49° parallel and along it westerly to the Rocky Mountains.

Lamar, Lucius Q. C. (1825–1893), represented Mississippi in the U. S. Congress as a Democrat from 1857 to 1861. He became a colonel in the Confederate service. In 1863 he was sent as a commissioner to Russia. He was a member of the U. S. House of Representatives from 1872 to 1877, and a Senator from 1877 to 1885. He was an effective speaker and an opponent of the "inflation policy." He was Secretary of the Interior in Cleveland's Cabinet from 1885 to 1888, when he became a Justice of the U. S. Supreme Court.

Lamar, Mirabeau B. (1798–1859), was commissioned major in the Texan revolution. He was vice-president of Texas from 1836 to 1838, and president from 1838 to 1841. He was prominent at Monterey during the Mexican War.

Lamb, Martha J. R. N. (1829–1893), was born in Massachusetts. She was the author of a "History of the City of New York," and many historical essays for periodicals. From 1883 to 1892 she was editor of the *Magazine of American History*.

Lamont, Daniel S., of New York, was born in 1851. He was private secretary to President Cleveland during his first administration. He became Secretary of War in Cleveland's Cabinet in 1893.

Lancaster, Joseph (1778–1838), came to America from England in 1818. He was one of the inventors of the "monitorial" system of instruction and gave a great stimulus to popular education.

Lancaster, Pa., was founded in 1718, and was called Hickory Town until 1730. In 1777 Congress sat here for a few days, and from 1799 to 1812 it was the capital of the State. It became a city in 1818.

Land Bank. In 1714, during Governor Dudley's rule of Massachusetts, the downfall of credit and general scarcity of circulating medium induced certain merchants to suggest the erection of a Bank of Credit in Boston, founded on land security, and to promote subscription promised £200 annually to Harvard College. Dudley was greatly opposed to this measure and his son wrote an able paper setting forth the objections to such a scheme. To forestall the action of the bank, the province, by law, issued £50,000 to be let out on mortgages of real estate, and these bills were in circulation during thirty years. The Land Bank scheme was thus prevented.

Land Office. This office is charged with the surveying and disposal of the public lands of the United States. Until 1812, no such office existed, the Secretary of the Treasury acting as the agent in the sale or disposal of the public lands. When the office of the Commissioner of the General Land Office was created, it remained a bureau of the Treasury Department, though reorganized in 1836, until 1849, when, on the creation of the Interior Department, the Land Office became a part of it.

Lander, Frederick W. (1822–1862), conducted several trans-continental explorations for the United States. He was appointed brigadier-general during the Civil War, and won distinction at Philippi, Hancock and Blooming Gap.

Lands, Public. After the Revolution the Federal Government found great difficulty in regulating the enormous tracts of public lands, which had been acquired through purchase and conquest from the Indians and by the cessions of the various States of their outlying territories. In 1787 the price of public land was 66⅔ cents per acre, and large tracts north of the Ohio were disposed of. Unauthorized entries were frequently made, however, and force had to be used for dislodgment. In 1790 Hamilton proposed that the public lands should be set apart in townships ten miles square, and disposed of to suit different classes of purchasers on a credit basis. The rectangular system was in fact adopted in 1796. Up to the year 1800 all sales had been made from the territory now included in Ohio and amounted to 1,484,047 acres. In 1800 local registers were established. The credit basis of sale caused numerous purchases, but payment was slow and in discouragingly small amounts, while the debtors constantly cried for relief. The States, too, claimed a share in the profits. Upon the question of ceding public lands to new States, Henry Clay prepared for the land committee a report reviewing the history of the public lands and concluding that it was inexpedient either to reduce the price of the lands or to cede them to the new States. In 1835 speculation in public lands became popular, owing to the inflated condition of the currency, which proved injurious to the public interests. In 1836 Jackson issued his "specie circular." (See art.) It was not until in 1840 that the right of pre-emption was accorded to settlers. By 1850 it became common to make grants of lands to States, corporations and individuals for public improvements, such as railroads and canals. In 1862 the homestead laws, granting free settlement on public lands, tended greatly to simplify matters and to promote real settlement.

Lane, Henry Smith (1811–1881), was a Republican member of the Indiana Legislature from 1838 to 1843. He was a lieutenant-colonel during the Mexican War. He served in the U. S. Senate from 1861 to 1867.

Lane, James Henry (1814–1866), commanded a brigade at Buena Vista in the Mexican War. He represented Indiana in the U. S. Congress as a Democrat from 1853 to 1855. He was a leader of the Free-Soil party and prominent in the Kansas disturbances from 1855 to 1859. He represented Kansas in the U. S. Senate as a Republican from 1861 to 1866.

Lane, Joseph (1801–1881), served in the Indiana Legislature from 1822 to 1846. He was brevetted major during the Mexican War. He was engaged at Buena Vista, Huamantla and Matamoras and commanded at Atlixco. He was a delegate from Oregon to the U. S. Congress as a Democrat from 1851 to 1857. He was a U. S. Senator from 1859 to 1861. He was defeated as candidate for Vice-President of the United States on the Breckinridge ticket in 1860.

Lane, Sir Ralph (1530?–1604), assumed charge of Sir Walter Raleigh's Virginia colony sent out in 1585. The colony was established on Roanoke Island, but was abandoned in 1585, and Lane returned to England.

Langdon, John (1741–1819), was a delegate from New Hampshire to the Continental Congress from 1775 to 1776 and in 1783. He devoted his estate to the cause of the Revolution, and fought at Bennington and Saratoga. He was a delegate to the Constitutional Convention of 1787. He was a Democratic U. S. Senator from 1789 to 1801. He was Governor of New Hampshire from 1805 to 1809, and from 1810 to 1811.

Langlade, Charles M. de (1729–1800), led the Ottawas in the defeat of General Braddock in 1755. He aided Montcalm during the siege of Quebec, and was active in the battle on the Plains of Abraham. In 1777 he led a band of Indians in aid of the English under Burgoyne. From 1780 to 1800 he was commander-in-chief of the Canadian militia.

Lanier, Sidney (1842–1881), poet, served in the Confederate army during the Civil War. He composed the ode for the opening of the Centennial Exhibition in 1876.

Lansing, John (1754–1829), was a delegate from New York to the Continental Congress from 1784 to 1788. He was a delegate to the Constitutional Convention of 1787 which framed the Constitution, but refused to sign it, and opposed its ratification. In 1790 he was appointed a Justice of the New York Supreme Court, and in 1798 became Chief Justice. From 1801 to 1814 he was Chancellor of the State.

Lansing, Mich., was settled about 1847, when it became the capital of the State. It received a city charter in 1859.

La Pérouse, Jean T. de G. (1741–1788), commanded "L'Amazone" in D'Estaing's flotilla in the Revolutionary War. In 1780 he destroyed five

English vessels, and in 1782 destroyed the British posts on Hudson Bay. From 1786 to 1788 he explored the Pacific.

Larkin, Thomas O., born in 1803, U. S. Consul at Monterey, Cal., was prominent in all the movements which led to the separation of California from Mexico, and in the organization of its government.

La Salle, Sieur de [Robert Cavelier] (1643–1687), a distinguished French explorer, was born at Rouen. In 1669 he emigrated to Canada, and began the series of his remarkable journeys in the West. He visited Lake Michigan and the Illinois River, but whether he at this early stage saw the Mississippi is a disputed problem. In 1673 he received a grant of the station at Fort Frontenac (now Kingston). He was again in France in 1677, but the next year was back in Canada and had reached Niagara. He ascended the chain of lakes to Mackinaw, thence up Lake Michigan and down the Illinois River to Peoria. Disappointments followed; but he was able to renew the canoe voyage, descend the Illinois and Mississippi to its mouth, which he reached in April, 1682, and to claim the entire region for Louis XIV. Returning to France, he organized an expedition which, in 1684, sailed directly for the mouth of the great river. But the explorers landed by mistake at Matagorda Bay, and after harassing wanderings La Salle was murdered by his followers within the limits of Texas.

Latimer Case (1842), the first of a series of famous fugitive slave trials which took place in Boston. George Latimer was seized without a warrant. A writ of *habeas corpus* was denied, and the defendant was kept in the custody of the city jailer pending the securing of evidence against him. A writ of personal replevin, under the Act of 1837, securing trial by jury, was denied, the act being held illegal under the Prigg decision. Great indignation was aroused in Boston, and Latimer was finally released by his jailer on the payment of $400. The State Act of 1843 followed, forbidding officers to aid in the capture of fugitive slaves, or to permit the use of State jails for their imprisonment.

La Tour, Charles A. de St. E., died in 1665. He was lieutenant-general of Acadia from 1631 to 1644. He was Governor and lieutenant-general of Acadia from 1650 to 1654.

Laud, William (1573–1644), Archbishop of Canterbury from 1633 to 1641, sought to establish uniformity of worship by enforcing conformity to the Church of England. He increased the power of the clergy and punished all dissenters. His persecutions of the Puritans, who maintained liberty of conscience, caused them to seek refuge in other lands and many came to America. He was impeached in 1642 and executed in 1644.

Laudonnière, René de (d. after 1586), founded a Huguenot colony in 1564 at Fort Caroline, Florida (Port Royal, S. C.), which was destroyed by the Spaniards under Menendez in 1565. He published a history of Florida in 1586.

Laurens, Henry (1724–1792), was a member of the first South Carolina Provincial Congress in 1775. He was a delegate from South Carolina to the Continental Congress from 1777 to 1780, and was its president from 1777 to

1778. He was appointed Minister to Holland in 1779; was captured during the voyage by the British, and confined in prison for fifteen months. In 1781 he was appointed one of the commissioners to negotiate a treaty of peace with Great Britain. In 1782 he signed the preliminary Treaty of Paris. Impaired health forced him to retire from public life.

Laurens, John (1756–1782), became an aide to Washington at the outbreak of the Revolution, and is said to have engaged in all of Washington's battles. He fought at Brandywine, Monmouth, Germantown, Charleston and Savannah. In 1781 he was appointed a commissioner to France, and obtained aid in money and supplies. He fought at Yorktown, and while serving under General Greene, was killed in a skirmish.

Law, John (1671–1729), established a private bank in Paris in 1716. In 1718 his plan of a National Bank and an issue of paper money was adopted by the French regent. In 1719 depreciated national currency was received at its par value in payment for shares in Law's scheme for colonizing the Mississippi Valley. Speculation and the inflated currency caused a panic in 1720.

Lawrence, Abbott (1792–1855), represented Massachusetts in the U. S. Congress as a Whig from 1835 to 1837. He was Minister to Great Britain from 1847 to 1852. He founded the Lawrence Scientific School at Harvard College.

Lawrence, James (1781–1813), was engaged in naval warfare on the Barbary coast from 1804 to 1809, commanding the "Argus," "Vixen" and "Wasp." In 1813 while commanding the "Hornet" he captured the British brig "Peacock" after an engagement of fifteen minutes with a loss of only one killed and two wounded. When placed in command of the "Chesapeake" he accepted a challenge from Captain Broke of the "Shannon." His defeat was caused by the imperfect discipline of the newly shipped crew. Lawrence was mortally wounded. His last injunction was, "Don't give up the ship."

Lawrence, William B. (1800–1881), was acting Governor of Rhode Island in 1851. He was one of the chief American authorities upon international law, and edited an edition of Wheaton published in 1855.

Lawrence, Kan., was founded in 1854, and became the headquarters of the anti-slavery settlers during the struggle which followed. On August 25, 1863, the town was burned by Confederate guerrillas under Quantrell, and 145 of the inhabitants massacred.

Lea, Henry C., born in 1825, of Philadelphia, organized the system of municipal bounties during the Civil War. He wrote "Superstition and Force," a "History of the Inquisition of the Middle Ages," and other scholarly works on mediæval history.

"Leander." April 25, 1806, while the feeling in this country was intensely bitter toward Great Britain, a shot from the British war-ship "Leander," then lying off Sandy Hook, killed John Pierce, helmsman on an American coaster. The citizens of New York denounced the outrage in a mass meeting, and called upon the National Government for better protection of the harbor. A proclamation of the President interdicted British supplies and ordered the arrest of the "Leander's" captain, if found within our jurisdiction.

Lear, Tobias (1762–1816), became private secretary to Washington in 1785, and for several years superintended his domestic affairs. He was a commissioner to conclude peace with Tripoli in 1805.

Leavenworth, Kan., was settled in 1854. Fort Leavenworth was established near the site of the city in 1827.

Leavitt, Joshua (1794–1873), was an ardent temperance reformer and anti-slavery advocate. He was chairman of the national committee of the Liberty party from 1844 to 1847. He was connected with the New York *Independent* from 1848 to 1873.

Lechford, Thomas (1590?–1644), came to America from England in 1638, but returned in 1641. He wrote "Plaine Dealing or Newes from New England," which contains much valuable information.

Lecky, William E. H., born in 1838, English historian, wrote a "History of the Rise and Influence of the Spirit of Rationalism in Europe," and a "History of European Morals from Augustus to Charlemagne," but is of especial interest to Americans as the author of a "History of England in the Eighteenth Century," publication of which began in 1878, which gives an admirable account of the American Revolution from the modern English point of view.

Lecompton Constitution, a Constitution adopted by the pro-slavery party of Kansas in a convention held at Lecompton September 5, 1857. The Constitution sanctioned slavery, and prohibited the passage of emancipation laws by the Legislature. It was provided that the Constitution should not, as a whole, be submitted to the people of the territory; they were only to vote for "the Constitution with slavery" or "the Constitution without slavery." Free-State settlers abstaining, the former alternative prevailed by a large majority. Later, without authorization from the convention, the Territorial Legislature ordered a vote on the Constitution as a whole. It was voted down by a large majority, slave-State settlers now abstaining.

Ledyard, John (1751–1789), of Connecticut, traveler, accompanied Captain James Cook on his last voyage, and published an account of it. He afterward traveled through Russia and Siberia.

Ledyard, William (1750–1781), defended Fort Griswold, Conn., with 157 untrained men against the British in 1781. After the surrender the British, commanded by Major Bromfield, massacred the entire garrison.

Lee, Ann (1736–1784), founded the "Shakers" in 1771. She declared herself the "second appearing of Christ." She emigrated from England to the United States in 1774 and established her colony at Watervliet, N. Y.

Lee, Arthur (1740–1792), of Virginia, brother of R. H. Lee and Francis Lightfoot Lee, was prominent as author of the "Monitor's Letters," "An Appeal to the English Nation" and "Junius Americanus." In 1770 he was appointed London agent of the Massachusetts colony. In 1776 he was appointed with Franklin and Deane to secure a treaty of alliance with

France. In 1777 and 1778 he was commissioner to Spain and Prussia. From 1782 to 1785 he was a member of the Continental Congress. From 1784 to 1789 he was a member of the Board of Treasury of the Confederation. He opposed the adoption of the Constitution. He was a man of learning and talents, but vain and captious. Life by R. H. Lee.

Lee, Charles (1731–1782), was born in England, and served in the army at Braddock's defeat and through the French and Indian War. Some years of miscellaneous experiences in the Portuguese service and on the Polish staff, interspersed with pamphleteering, left him a lieutenant-colonel on half-pay. Removing to America in 1773 he contrived to pose as a great military light, and was in 1775 appointed the second in rank of the major-generals. He was at the siege of Boston, commenced the fortifications of New York, and received the credit of the victory at Charleston in 1776. In the autumn campaign of that year he disregarded Washington's orders to leave Northcastle, and was soon afterward captured at Baskingridge in New Jersey. He had intrigued against Washington, and it has recently been proved that in captivity he negotiated with the Howes. He was exchanged in time to receive command of the van at Monmouth; his disgraceful retreat there is well known. After the battle he was suspended for disobedience, misbehavior and disrespect, and was eventually dismissed from the army. He died in obscurity at Philadelphia.

Lee, Charles (1758–1815), was a delegate from Virginia to the Continental Congress. He was naval officer of the Potomac till 1795. He was U. S. Attorney-General from 1795 to 1801.

Lee, Fitzhugh, born in 1835, was promoted major-general in the Confederate army, and served as a cavalry commander in all the campaigns of the Army of Northern Virginia. He was elected Governor of Virginia in 1885. He was a nephew of Gen. R. E. Lee.

Lee, Francis Lightfoot (1734–1797), brother of R. H. Lee and A. Lee, was a member of the Virginia House of Burgesses from 1765 to 1772. He was a delegate to the Continental Congress from 1775 to 1779. He signed the Declaration of Independence, and aided in drafting the Articles of Confederation.

Lee, Henry (1756–1818), a Revolutionary partisan hero, was a member of the Virginia family of Lees, and graduated at Princeton. He attained distinction in the latter half of the war as major of a partisan corps called "Lee's Legion," whence he derived his epithet of "Light-Horse Harry." He performed a brilliant exploit in 1779, in the capture of Paulus Hook, and received a gold medal. In 1781 he ably covered the retreat of Greene's army, took a distinguished part at Guilford, Eutaw Springs, and the operations in the Carolinas and Georgia. He was a member of the Continental Congress, of the ratifying convention of 1788, was a Federalist, and Governor of Virginia in 1792–1795. In 1794 he led the expedition to suppress the Whiskey Rebellion. As Congressman, 1799–1801, it was his lot to pronounce the eulogy on Washington, containing the famous characterization, "First in war," etc. His death was caused by injuries inflicted by a Baltimore mob in 1814.

Lee, Richard Henry (1732–1794), a member of a noted Virginia family, was educated in England. For many years, 1761–1788, he was a leader in the Virginia House of Burgesses and Legislature. He earnestly opposed the slave trade, the Stamp Act, and was one of the first among the patriot chiefs to suggest the employment of the famous committees of correspondence. As a delegate to the first Continental Congress he was on the committee to draft the address, and in the Second Congress he drew up the address to the people of Great Britain. On June 7, 1776, he moved the resolutions of independence. Meanwhile as the war proceeded, Lee was active in strictly Virginian as well as in national matters, and opposed vigorously the paper-money policy in his State. He was president of Congress, and in 1788 he was an Anti-Federalist champion for the rejection of the Federal Constitution. From 1789 to 1792 he was U. S. Senator. Life by R. H. Lee.

Lee, Robert Edward (January 19, 1807–October 12, 1870), the great general of the Confederacy, was the son of Henry Lee (" Light-Horse Harry ") and was born at Stratford, Va. He was graduated with high standing at West Point in 1829. In the Mexican War he served as chief engineer on the staff of General Wool, and was distinguished in the advance on the capital, especially at Chapultepec. From 1852 to 1855 he was commandant at West Point. In 1859 he was sent against John Brown's raid on Harper's Ferry, and he had reached the rank of lieutenant-colonel by 1861. When his State seceded, Lee resigned, April 20, from the U. S. army, accepted the command of the State forces, and in May was appointed a general in the Confederate army. For a year he was inconspicuously employed in Virginia and South Carolina. The wounding of General J. E. Johnston at Fair Oaks, May 31, 1862, called Lee to supreme command. Henceforth his history is that of the Army of Northern Virginia. He commanded in the Seven Days' battles, beat Pope at the second battle of Bull Run, and immediately began his first invasion of the North. Chance revealed his plans to McClellan. His prestige was not impaired by the drawn battle of Antietam, and the army and its general gained new honors by the victories of Fredericksburg and Chancellorsville. His second invasion of the North resulted disastrously at Gettysburg. In the next year, 1864, he was pitted against Grant, whom he opposed stubbornly at the Wilderness, Spottsylvania and Cold Harbor. The long siege of Petersburg and Richmond followed. Lee's efforts to ward off the break-up of the Confederacy were unavailing. Compelled to evacuate Richmond on April 2, 1865, he sought to effect a junction with Johnston, but was hemmed in by Grant's army and forced to surrender at Appomattox April 9. Soon afterward he became president of Washington College in Lexington, Va. (now Washington and Lee University), and remained there until his death. Lee was a man of singularly noble character, and much revered and beloved. Life by J. E. Cooke.

Legal-Tender Cases. After the breaking out of the Civil War Congress was compelled in 1862 to issue $150,000,000 in Treasury notes, and made them legal tender for payment of private debts and all public dues except duties on imports and interest on the public debt. These notes became the circulating medium to a large extent. The constitutional validity of these

Legal-Tender Acts was strongly contested, especially in their application to debts contracted prior to their passage. Their constitutionality was generally maintained by the State courts, however. In 1869, this question came before the Supreme Court of the United States in the case of Hepburn *vs.* Griswold. The validity of the acts was in this instance maintained only in so far as it did not affect the obligations of contracts made prior to their passage. A year later, in the case of Knox *vs.* Lee, this decision was overruled, and the constitutionality of the act was upheld in its applicability to pre-existing debts, though by a majority of the court only. The composition of the court had meantime been altered, two new judges having been appointed. See Hepburn *vs.* Griswold, Knox *vs.* Lee, and Juilliard *vs.* Greenman.

Legaré, Hugh S. (1789–1843), was an anti-nullification member of the South Carolina Legislature from 1820 to 1822 and 1824 to 1830. He was State Attorney-General from 1830 to 1832. He was chargé d'affaires at Brussels from 1832 to 1836. Was a member of the U. S. Congress as a Union Democrat from 1837 to 1839, and was Attorney-General of the United States in Tyler's Cabinet from 1841 to 1843, and Secretary of State in 1843.

Legislature. The first elected representative legislature in America was that which met at Jamestown, Va., in 1619. The colonies of Southern New England started with primary assemblies, from which representative assemblies were soon developed. In New York the first true legislature was assembled in 1683. In general the colonial legislatures were modeled on the British Parliament, the procedure of which they followed closely. To king, lords and commons corresponded the governor, the council appointed by him, and the representatives of the people, variously called house of burgesses, house of delegates, assembly, or house of representatives. These last were elected by voters having a property qualification, two members or more for each county in the Middle and Southern States, one or two from each town in New England. The Revolution broke up the upper houses or councils, and the new constitutions substituted what in Virginia (1776) and then in the other States was called a senate. Pennsylvania and Georgia had at first legislatures of but one house. The legislatures of the Southern States were generally given the power to choose the governor. The Constitution of 1787 gave the State Legislatures the right to choose U. S. Senators. All the amendments to the Federal Constitution have been ratified by them. In general it has been felt that State Legislatures have been declining in excellence during the last two generations. State constitutions have imposed more and more restrictions upon their action.

Leisler, Jacob (born in Germany, died 1691), came to America in the service of the Dutch West India Company. From 1683 to 1688 he was one of the commissioners of the New York Court of Admiralty. In 1689 he headed a revolution against the Jacobite office-holders. He was placed at the head of the provisional Government, and continued in office until 1691. He was succeeded by Henry Sloughter, and soon afterward executed on a charge of treason. In 1695 Parliament reversed the charge.

Leland Stanford Jr. University, Palo Alto, Cal., was founded by means of the gifts of Senator Stanford in memory of his son. These gifts in land and money are estimated at twenty million dollars. The university opened in October, 1891.

Le Moine, Sauvolle (1671?–1701), was educated in France, where he was eminent for his attainments. He was appointed first colonial Governor of Louisiana by Louis XIV., serving from 1699 to 1701.

Lenox, James (1800–1880), was founder of the Lenox Library, New York, which in many respects surpasses in value any other library of Americana. The collection of rare books and manuscripts is valued at nearly a million dollars.

Lenox Library, a library in New York City, especially noted for its richness in rare Americana. It was collected by James Lenox, who at his death in 1880 left it, with funds for increase, to trustees for the benefit of American scholarship.

Letcher, John (1813–1874), represented Virginia in the U. S. Congress as a Democrat from 1851 to 1859. He was Governor of the State from 1860 to 1864, and aided the Confederate cause.

"**Levant**," ship. (See "Constitution.")

Leverett, Sir John (1616–1679), came to America from England in 1632. He was a delegate to the Massachusetts General Court from 1651 to 1653, and in 1663. He was major-general from 1663 to 1673, Governor from 1673 to 1679.

Lévis, François G., duc de (1720–1787), was second in command at Quebec when it was captured by the British in 1759, and succeeded Montcalm in command of the French forces. In 1760 he was forced to capitulate to the English.

Lew Chew. The United States concluded with Lew Chew a treaty of friendship and commerce in 1854.

Lewis, Andrew (1720–1781), came to America (Virginia) from Ireland in 1732. He commanded at the battle of Point Pleasant in 1774 and served in the Continental army from 1775 to 1777.

Lewis, Francis (1713–1803), came to America from England in 1735. He was a member of the New York delegation in the first Colonial Congress at New York City in 1765. He was a member of the Continental Congress from 1776 to 1779. He signed the Declaration of Independence and in 1779 was a commissioner of the Board of Admiralty.

Lewis, Meriwether (1774–1809), explorer, was secretary to President Jefferson from 1801 to 1803. He commanded an expedition with William Clark across the continent from 1803 to 1806. They ascended the Missouri River, named three of its tributaries the Jefferson, Madison and Gallatin Rivers, and descended the Columbia River to its mouth. From 1807 to 1809 he was Governor of Missouri Territory.

Lewis, Morgan (1754–1844), served in the Continental army from 1776 to 1783, commanding at Stone Arabia and Crown Point. He was Chief

Justice of New York from 1801 to 1804 and Governor from 1804 to 1807. He was a major-general in the Niagara campaign and commanded at Sackett's Harbor and French Creek.

Lewis and Clark Expedition. In 1804–06, Meriwether Lewis and William Clark, under orders from President Jefferson, ascended the Missouri to its sources, crossed the Rocky Mountains, struck the head waters of the Columbia River, floated down that river to its mouth and explored a great deal of the Oregon country. Their explorations covered nearly all the country south of the 49° parallel. Their company was composed of nine Kentuckians and fourteen soldiers. They started for the East March 23, 1806, having explored nearly the whole of the Northwest regions. History, edited by Coues.

Lewisites, in New York political history, the followers of Morgan Lewis, who was related by marriage to the Livingstons, and was Governor of New York from 1804 to 1807. In the latter year the Lewisites and Burrites united and became known as "Martling men," later Bucktails.

Lexington, Ky., was settled in 1775 by Colonel Robert Patterson. The town was incorporated in 1782, and the first Legislature of the State met here. The State University was removed here in 1865.

Lexington, Mass., Battle of, April 19, 1775. On the night of April 18, 1775, 8000 British regulars were secretly despatched from Boston to arrest Samuel Adams and John Hancock at Lexington, and to seize the military stores collected at Concord. News of their approach was spread through the intervening towns by Paul Revere, and at daybreak, when the British arrived at Lexington, they found fifty minute-men drawn up on the village green. The advance guard, under Major Pitcairn, fired upon them, but they held their ground until the main body of the British, under Lieutenant-Colonel Smith, appeared. They then gave way, and the regulars pushed forward to Concord. Here they were unable to discover any military stores, and while they were committing some depredations affairs took a sudden turn. 200 regulars, who guarded Concord bridge, were routed by some 400 minute-men who had hastily collected from neighboring towns. The position of the British thus became perilous. About noon they started for Boston, subjected to a galling fire from all sides. Exhausted by their march of eighteen miles and their fast of fourteen hours, they fell into a disorderly flight, and were saved only by the timely assistance of Lord Percy, who came from Boston with 1200 reinforcements and two cannon. Seven miles from Boston their passage was for a while disputed by a force of militia. The whole countryside was out against them; once more their retreat became a rout, and at sunset they entered Charlestown under the welcome protection of the fleet, on the full run, just in time to avoid an encounter with Colonel Pickering and 700 Essex militia. The loss of the British was 273, that of the Americans ninety-three. In the first place the battle showed that the colonists could not be frightened into submission. It also showed the efficiency and promptness of the town militia. Twenty-three towns were represented among the wounded and slain, and by the end of the week 16,000 men were besieging Gage in Boston.

Lexington, Mo., assaulted and captured August 20, 1861, by 28,000 Confederates, led by McCulloch. Mulligan, with a National force of 3000, held the town. Repeated attacks were made and thirteen pieces of artillery were brought to bear upon the besieged, but the latter held out bravely for a long time. Finally the Confederates constructed movable breastworks of hemp bales and, rolling these before them, they compelled Colonel Mulligan to surrender unconditionally, the water supply of the town having given out and he being severely wounded.

Leyden, an inland city of Holland, where the Pilgrims, after leaving England and living for a time in Amsterdam, settled in May, 1609. They were about 100 English men, women and children. A church was organized in 1611 and for a time things went well. But controversies arose and they could not accommodate themselves to the conditions of life in Leyden. In 1617 Carver and Cushman were dispatched to London to negotiate with the Virginia Company for settlement on their territory. An agreement was speedily concluded. In July, 1620, a small ship, the "Speedwell," was bought and fitted out in Holland, and the Pilgrims left Leyden for Delfthaven, thence to embark for Southampton, where the "Mayflower" awaited them.

Libby Prison, a large building in Richmond, Va., named for its owner, who used it as a ship-chandlery before the Civil War. During the war it became famous as a Confederate military prison, in which many Federal soldiers were confined.

Liberal Republican Party, an abortive offshoot from the regular Republican party in 1870–72. Its origin was a reaction from the coercive measures to maintain the newly-granted rights of the negroes and suppress the Ku-Klux organizations. A union of the Liberal Republicans and the Democrats was first formed with considerable success in Missouri in 1870–71. They advocated universal suffrage, universal amnesty, a reform of the tariff and a "cessation of the unconstitutional laws to cure Ku-Klux disorders." A general convention assembled at Cincinnati in May, 1872, and nominated Horace Greeley for President, whom the Democrats also nominated. He was defeated because many Democrats refused to vote for him. B. Gratz Brown, of Missouri, was the candidate for Vice-President.

Liberia, a negro republic on the west coast of Africa. It was at first a colony of free negroes founded by the American Colonization Society in 1816 for the betterment of the negroes in the United States. It was at first governed by the whites, but became independent in 1847. After the Civil War many of the freed slaves in the United States were permitted and, indeed, encouraged to migrate to Liberia, and financial aid was afforded them to do so. A treaty of commerce was concluded in 1862.

"**Liberty**," a sloop belonging to John Hancock, which was seized in 1768 in Massachusetts on the ground of having evaded the customs. Considerable excitement arose, and the royal revenue officers, in pretended fear of their lives, took refuge on the man-of-war "Romney."

Liberty Bell, cast in London and received at Philadelphia in August, 1732, when it was hung in the Pennsylvania State House, afterward known as Independence Hall. The bell was broken up and recast in April, and again in June, 1753. It announced the Declaration of Independence, July 4, 1776. It was cracked July 8, 1835, while being tolled in memory of Chief Justice Marshall. The bell was exhibited in the Pennsylvania State Building at the World's Columbian Exhibition at Chicago in 1893.

Liberty Tree, the tree on which a Boston mob hanged the effigy of Andrew Oliver, of Boston, in August, 1765. Oliver had agreed to become distributor of stamps under the famous Stamp Act passed that year.

Libraries. The first library established in the United States was that of Harvard College, founded in 1638. In 1700 a public library was founded in New York City. It was afterward converted, in 1754, into a subscription library. Dr. Franklin and his associates, in 1731, started in Philadelphia a library company and the first subscription library. The Library of Congress was begun in 1800, on the establishment of the seat of government at Washington. The Public Library of Boston, founded in 1848, stands next to the Library of Congress in point of the number and value of its collections. It contains over 500,000 volumes and has eleven subsidiary branches. The school-district library system originated in New York State in 1838 and has been adopted by a large number of the other States. From 1820 to 1870 twenty-nine subscription or mercantile libraries were established in various cities. There are now in the United States nearly 4000 libraries of 1000 volumes or more, which are more or less free and public. Their increase and success throughout the Union has been enormous.

Library of Congress. Founded by Act of Congress April 24, 1800, and permanently organized on the basis of a report made by John Randolph December 21, 1801, $5000 being appropriated for the purchase of books. It was and is now located in the Capitol Building. When the British held Washington for a single day, August 25, 1814, the Capitol was burned and with it the library. The same Congress bought 6700 volumes from Thomas Jefferson for $23,950. In 1824 an Act of Congress provided for an annual appropriation of $5000 for purchasing books, and the library was placed in the central Capitol Building. In 1851 a second fire destroyed about 30,000 volumes. In 1852 $75,000 were appropriated for the reconstruction of the rooms and $75,000 for the immediate purchase of books. The library numbered 75,000 books in 1860. A new and separate library building is now (1894) being constructed. The library now numbers more than 675,000 volumes.

Lick, James (1796–1876), bequeathed his immense fortune to philanthropic enterprises. He founded the famous Lick Observatory at Mount Hamilton, Cal.

Lieber, Francis (1800–1872), born and educated in Germany, came to America in 1827. He published the Encyclopædia Americana in 1832. He ardently upheld the Union during the Civil War, and was often consulted by the executive. He wrote many important political works, among them a "Manual of Political Ethics," "Legal and Political Hermeneutics" and "Civil Liberty and Self-Government." He was professor in the South

Carolina College from 1838 to 1856 and in Columbia College from 1857 to 1872.

Lieutenant, in colonial Virginia the leading officer of a county, corresponding to the lord-lieutenant of an English county. His duties were to enroll and lead the militia, and also to supervise the administration of the tobacco laws and hold a court for minor offences.

Lieutenant-General. This office was first created in 1798, General Washington being chosen to fill it. It was abolished in 1799, and was not revived until 1855, being then filled by General Winfield Scott. In 1864 General Grant was appointed to this grade, and on his appointment to the generalship, William T. Sherman was chosen lieutenant-general in 1866. General Philip H. Sheridan was made lieutenant-general in 1883. With his death in 1888 the office became extinct.

Ligonia. (See Lygonia.)

Liliuokalani, born in 1838, succeeded to the throne of Hawaii in 1891. She was deposed and a provisional government established in 1893. She charged the U. S. Minister with complicity in the revolution, and attempted in vain to secure restoration.

Lincoln, Abraham (February 12, 1809–April 15, 1865), the sixteenth President of the United States, was born in Hardin County, Ky. Both there and in Indiana, to which in 1816 the family removed, as well as in Illinois, whither they went in 1830, Lincoln had the privations and also the training of a backwoodsman's life. His later epithet of the "rail-splitter" is a reminiscence of this early period, and he also about this time made a flat-boat voyage to New Orleans. In the Black Hawk War of 1832 he served as captain and private. He tried keeping store and failed, studied law, was postmaster of New Salem in Illinois, and deputy surveyor of the county. As a politician he had better success, and after one defeat served in the Legislature from 1834 to 1842. Meanwhile he removed to Springfield and built up a law practice. From 1847 to 1849 he was a Whig Congressman, but was not notably prominent. His importance dates from the Kansas-Nebraska controversy. In its progress he became the Republican State leader, and in 1858 he took part with Stephen A. Douglas in a series of joint debates in canvassing for the U. S. Senatorship. Lincoln was defeated, but the discussion had aroused great interest, and his utterances, *e. g.*, "a house divided against itself cannot stand," brought him into national prominence. In February, 1860, he delivered a remarkable political speech at Cooper Institute, New York. He was pressed for the Presidency by many Western Republicans in the Chicago Convention in May, though Seward was in the lead at the outset. Amid great excitement Lincoln was nominated on the third ballot, and elected, by 180 electoral votes, over Douglas, Breckenridge and Bell. This first victory of the Republicans decided the Secessionists, and when the new President delivered his conciliatory inaugural address the country was drifting toward civil war. In the Cabinet Seward had the Department of State, Chase the Treasury, Cameron, and soon afterward Stanton, War, Welles the Navy, Caleb B. Smith the Interior,

ANTI-SLAVERY MEN.

Joshua R. Giddings. John Brown. Wm. Lloyd Garrison.
Wendell Phillips. Charles Sumner.

Edward Bates was Attorney-General, and Montgomery Blair Postmaster-General. Immediately on the fall of Fort Sumter the President, April 15, 1861, called for 75,000 volunteers to put down the Rebellion. He soon issued a call for additional troops, instituted a blockade, and summoned Congress to meet in extra session July 4. As the "War President" Lincoln is identified with a great part of the history of the struggle. Foreign complications, military and naval movements, domestic politics, as well as routine administrative duties, all claimed his attention; to the people and the armies he was endeared as "Father Abraham;" innumerable anecdotes are related bearing on his humor, strong common sense and sympathy. On September 22, 1862, profiting by the partial success of Antietam, he issued a preliminary proclamation fixing the coming January 1 as the date for freeing slaves in insurgent States. The Emancipation Proclamation to that effect accordingly appeared at the opening of 1863. On the nineteenth of November, 1863, he pronounced on the battlefield of Gettysburg his short but famous eulogy. He was renominated by the Republicans June 8, 1864, and elected over McClellan, receiving 212 electoral votes. "Malice toward none, charity for all" was the burden of his second inaugural. He had visited Richmond after its fall, and was pondering the questions of reconstruction, when on the night of April 14 he was shot by Wilkes Booth in Ford's Theatre at the capital, and died the next morning. Among the many lives may be mentioned those by Raymond, Morse, Herndon and the extended one by Nicolay and Hay.

Lincoln, Benjamin (1733–1810), was major-general of the Massachusetts militia from 1774 to 1775 and commanded them at White Plains in 1776. In 1777 he was second in command under General Gates at Bemis Heights. He commanded the Southern army from 1778 to 1780, when he was besieged by the British at Charleston and forced to capitulate. He received the sword of Cornwallis at Yorktown in 1781. He was Secretary of War from 1781 to 1784. He was a member of the Massachusetts Convention that ratified the Constitution.

Lincoln, Levi (1749–1820), served in the Massachusetts Constitutional Convention of 1780. From 1801 to 1805 he was Attorney-General of the United States. He was Lieutenant-Governor of Massachusetts from 1807 to 1808 and acting Governor in 1809.

Lincoln, Levi (1782–1868), was a member of the Massachusetts House of Representatives from 1814 to 1822. He was Governor of Massachusetts from 1825 to 1834. He was a Whig member of the U. S. Congress from 1835 to 1841.

Lincoln, Mary Todd (1818–1882), married Abraham Lincoln in 1842. Her family sympathized with the Confederate cause, and this, together with the death of her husband and of three sons, unsettled her reason.

Lincoln, Robert T., born in 1843, is the son of Abraham Lincoln. He served in the Federal army from 1864 to 1865. He was admitted to the Illinois bar and practiced until 1881. He was Secretary of War in the Cabinets of Garfield and Arthur from 1881 to 1885. He was appointed U. S. Minister to Great Britain in 1889, serving till 1893.

Lincoln, Neb., was laid out in July, 1867, and shortly after became the capital of the State.

Linn, Lewis F. (1795–1843), served during the War of 1812 as a surgeon. He was a member of the Kentucky Legislature in 1827. He represented Kentucky in the U. S. Senate as a Democrat from 1833 to 1843.

"**L'Insurgente.**" (See "Constellation.")

"**Little Belt.**" (See "President.")

Little Crow, chief of the Sioux tribe of Indians, led an outbreak of the Indians on the Upper Minnesota in 1862, but was defeated at Wood Lake. He was shot while making a raid in 1863.

Little Giant, a nickname for Stephen A. Douglas, of Illinois, because of his small stature and great abilities.

"**Little James,**" a small vessel, which, in company with the "Ann," brought reinforcements to the Pilgrims at Plymouth in August, 1623.

Little Magician, a nickname given to Martin Van Buren on account of his dexterity in political manipulations.

Little Rock, Ark., founded in 1820, became the capital of the then Territory the same year. During the Civil War it was held by the Confederates until it was captured by General Steele (September 10, 1863).

"**Little Sarah,**" a privateer fitted out in 1793, at Philadelphia, by Citizen Genêt, the newly arrived French Minister. She sailed under French colors and was manned by American seamen, and cruised for British vessels. This was done against the prohibition of the American Executive.

Little Turtle, chief of the Miami Indians, died in 1812. He commanded at the defeat of General Harmar on the Miami in 1790, and of General St. Clair at St. Mary's in 1791. He was one of the signers of the Greenville treaty in 1795.

Little Van, a nickname for Martin Van Buren, eighth President of the United States.

Livermore, Mary A., born in 1821, distinguished herself during the Civil War by her labors in the Sanitary Commission. She is one of the foremost lecturers upon woman suffrage and temperance reform.

Livingston, Brockholst (1757–1823), served at Ticonderoga, and with Benedict Arnold at the surrender of Burgoyne in 1777. In 1807 he was appointed an Associate Justice of the U. S. Supreme Court, and served till his death.

Livingston, Edward (1764–1836), a brother of Robert R. Livingston, graduated at Princeton, and reached early in life a commanding position at the New York bar. From 1795 to 1801, he was a Democratic Congressman. While district attorney in the following years he became entangled in business, was deeply indebted to the Government, and removed to Louisiana to retrieve his fortunes. He was Congressman from that State in 1822–1829, U. S. Senator 1829–1831, Secretary of State 1831–1833, and Minister to

France 1833–1835. His rank as a lawyer was very high, and his influence, by his codes and legal writings, was profound upon law here and in Europe. (See Batture Cases.)

Livingston, Philip (1716–1778), was a member of the New York Assembly from 1758 to 1769. He was a delegate to the Stamp-Act Congress of 1765, and a member of the Continental Congress from 1774 to 1778. He was one of the committee to prepare an address to the people of Great Britain, and a signer of the Declaration of Independence.

Livingston, Robert R. (1746–1813), graduated at King's (now Columbia) College and became a lawyer, member of the New York Assembly, and delegate to the Continental Congress. He served on the committee of five which drafted the Declaration of Independence. He was Secretary for Foreign Affairs in 1781–1783, and was a prominent Federalist in the ratifying convention at Poughkeepsie in 1788. Meanwhile from 1777 to 1801 he was Chancellor of the State of New York, and in this position he administered the oath of office to Washington in 1789. While U. S. Minister to France in 1801–1805 he helped to negotiate the Louisiana Purchase. He is remembered also for his connection with many societies in New York City, and his association with Fulton in the beginnings of steamboat navigation.

Livingston, William (1723–1790), was a delegate from New Jersey to the Continental Congress from 1774 to 1776. He was Governor of New Jersey from 1776 to 1790. In 1787 he was a delegate to the convention that framed the Constitution and signed that instrument.

Livingston Manor, in New York, adjoining that of Rensselaerswyck, was granted by Governor Dongan in 1686 to Robert Livingston, an immigrant from Scotland.

Livingston vs. Jefferson. (See Batture Cases.)

Local Government. England, at the time when the first settlements were made in the United States, had well-developed local institutions, the country being subdivided into counties, the counties into hundreds, the hundreds into parishes or townships. In the Southern colonies, where the plantation system prevailed and the settlers were scattered over a large area, it was natural that, of the institutions to which the settlers were accustomed, they should keep in use rather those of the county. In the New England colonies, where population was more compact, it was rather the township's set of officers and institutions that were employed. Hence there grew up in the United States two types of local government,—in New England the township system, in the South the county system. In the Middle colonies a form of local government was instituted which kept in active existence both sets of institutions, and this is the type now most common in the West. History by Howard.

Local Option, the determination by the people of a town or other minor political community as to whether or not any licenses to sell intoxicating liquors shall be granted. This principle is established in many sections of the various States.

Locke, David R. (1833–1888), was author of a series of patriotic satires known as the "Nasby" letters. They exerted great influence during the Civil War in crushing the rebellion.

Locke, John (1632–1704), English philosopher and statesman, drew up a constitution for the government of Carolina, at the request of the proprietaries. (See "Fundamental Constitutions.")

Lockwood, Belva A. B., born in 1820, was admitted to practice before the Supreme Court and the Court of Claims in 1879. She was the candidate of the Women's National Rights party in California for President of the United States in 1884.

Lockwood, James B. (1852–1884), accompanied the Lady Franklin Bay expedition with A. W. Greely in 1882, and attained the most northerly point of land ever reached, at 83° 24′ N.

Loco-foco, the radical faction, 1835–1837, of the Democratic party, properly of New York, though the name was afterward made national. During the Federalist control of the Government, the method of granting bank charters and controlling banks was charged by the opposing faction with favoritism and corruption. Upon their gaining control, things did not, in the opinion of many, improve; and in 1835 there was formed in New York the "Equal Rights party," opposed to special privileges in granting bank charters to corporations. At a meeting in Tammany Hall, October 29, 1835, the regular Tammany Democrats tried to gain control. Finding themselves outnumbered, they turned out the lights and retired. The Equal Rights men produced candles and "loco-foco" matches, and continued the meeting. Hence the name. This party was beaten at the elections, but nevertheless exercised considerable influence.

Locust Grove, Va., a battle of the Civil War during Meade's operations in Northern Virginia. This battle was desultory and lasted during two days, November 27–29, 1863. Meade's army had crossed the Rapidan, and at Payne's Farm, near Locust Grove, French's division had encountered the Confederate troops of Lee under Edward Johnson and Lee. That night Sedgwick and Warren were ordered to meet at Locust Grove for a co-operative attack on the Confederates. They intended to mass their forces and assault the Confederate flank, but the move failed. On the twenty-eighth there was a sharp battle of batteries, which accomplished little. The Federals were then ordered to retire.

Lodge, Henry Cabot, born in 1850, was assistant professor of history at Harvard College, and in 1880 and 1881 a member of the Massachusetts Legislature. He was elected as a Republican to the Congress of the United States from Massachusetts in 1886 and served till 1893, when he entered the Senate. He has published a "Short History of the English Colonies in America," "Studies in History" and lives of George Cabot, Alexander Hamilton and Daniel Webster.

Log Cabin and Hard Cider. In the campaign of 1840 the Whig candidate, Harrison, was a military man of plain manners. One of the Democratic papers, scoffing at the Whigs for taking a candidate not of the first calibre, advised that Harrison be given a log cabin and a barrel of hard cider, and he would stay contentedly in Ohio. This was taken up by the Whigs, and really helped to make their candidate popular with the masses. Log cabins were erected in great numbers in the cities, and were carried in processions, accompanied with barrels of cider. Horace Greeley edited a highly successful campaign paper called the *Log Cabin*. This appeal to the popular imagination has caused this to be called the "log cabin and hard cider campaign."

Logan, Benjamin (1752–1802), a Kentucky pioneer, renowned for his great courage and endurance. He distinguished himself at Fort Logan, Chillicothe and Bryan's Station during Indian troubles.

Logan, John (1725?–1780), chief of the Mingo tribe of Indians, lived peacefully among the whites until 1774. In 1774 his family were massacred by Ohio settlers, and Logan instigated a war. The terrible barbarities were terminated by the defeat of the Indians at the Great Kanawha. He sent a famous pathetic message to Lord Dunmore, Governor of Virginia, reviewing his wrongs.

Logan, John Alexander (1826–1886), volunteered in the Mexican War, and became thereafter a lawyer and politician in Illinois. He was a Democratic Congressman in 1859–1861, but left Congress for the army, fought at Bull Run, and was made a colonel of Illinois volunteers. At Belmont, Fort Henry, Fort Donelson, and in the Western army generally he was prominent, was appointed major-general, commanded a division in the Vicksburg campaign and a corps under Sherman in 1864, and on the battlefield of Atlanta succeeded McPherson in the Army of the Tennessee. "Black Jack" Logan was, in fact, one of the most noted non-West-Pointers of the war. He was Republican Congressman 1867–1871, and Senator 1871–1877 and 1879–1886. He received some votes at the Convention of 1884, and was nominated for second place on the ticket with Blaine, but not elected. He wrote "The Great Conspiracy."

Logstown, a small settlement on the Ohio River in colonial times, notable from the fact that it was the place in which the Virginia government, by a treaty with Indians, June 13, 1752, secured permission to erect a fort at the forks of the Ohio. The undertaking was delayed, and the French anticipated it by building Fort Duquesne.

London Company, the Virginia Company proper, as distinguished from the Plymouth or North Virginia Company. It was chartered in 1606, obtaining permission to colonize the territory between Cape Fear and Long Island. The first settlement was at Jamestown, Va., in 1607. The charter was taken away by James I. in 1624, and the company dissolved.

Long Island, N. Y., was settled about 1636 by the Dutch. The English settled the eastern portion of the island in 1640. Long Island passed into the hands of the Duke of York in 1664, and again came under Dutch control in 1673. In 1674, the island was again acquired by the British. At the beginning of the Revolution Washington made efforts to defend it against the English. It was taken by Howe in 1776, and was held by Great Britain until the close of the war.

Long Island, Battle of, August 27, 1776. The British plan of campaign was now to crush Washington in New York, seize the Hudson and thus divide the colonial forces. As Washington was inferior in numbers and efficiency he occupied Brooklyn Heights with 9000 men. Howe's only course was to dislodge him. He landed his men at Gravesend, L. I., and after four days' reconnoitring advanced in three divisions, 20,000 strong. Two divisions met the American outposts, 5000 in number, under Stirling and Sullivan. On the arrival of the third division in their rear they utterly routed the Americans and captured Stirling and Sullivan and 1000 of their men. The British now appeared before the American position, but refrained from an assault, preferring a siege. Clearly perceiving the danger of such a course Washington conveyed his army over to New York under cover of night, thus brilliantly snatching from the enemy the fruits of his victory; for although New York had been taken, the colonial army was still unsubdued.

Longfellow, Henry W. (1807–1882), became a popular poet by the production of "The Psalm of Life" in 1838. This was followed by "Hyperion," "Hiawatha," "Tales of a Wayside Inn," "The Courtship of Miles Standish," etc., and a translation of Dante. The historical Craigie House was his home. He was a poet of genial temperament, beloved by all.

Longstreet, James, born in 1821, a Confederate general, graduated at West Point in 1842. He fought in the Mexican War, and had reached the rank of paymaster when he entered the service of the Confederacy. He distinguished himself at Bull Run, Williamsburg, the Seven Days' battles, led a corps at the second battle of Bull Run, and was renowned as a hard fighter. He commanded the Confederate left at Fredericksburg, the right at Gettysburg, and the left at Chickamauga. Soon after he was sent against Knoxville, but failed to take it. Returning to the Army of Northern Virginia he fought at the Wilderness and almost constantly down to Appomattox. After the war he held various offices in the customs and revenue service, was postmaster and marshal, and under President Hayes was U. S. Minister to Turkey.

Longwoods, Canada. Here Captain Holmes, while on the way to attack Fort Talbot, was attacked by the British March 3, 1814. The British lost more men, but the Americans were forced to return empty-handed.

Lookout Mountain. (See Chattanooga.)

Lopez, Narcisso, a military adventurer and refugee from Havana, who in 1849, 1850 and 1851, planned, with the aid of Governor Quitman, of Mississippi, and other Southerners, the capture and annexation of Cuba. The first expedition was frustrated by President Tyler. The second, 300 strong, landed at Cardenas and captured the town, but was quickly expelled. Lopez was arrested in Savannah, Ga., but released for want of evidence. The third expedition landed at Las Pazas in 1851. The inhabitants fled instead of giving their aid. The invaders were set upon by the Government troops and quickly dispersed. Lopez fled to the mountains, but was captured and executed at Havana, September 1, 1851.

Loring, William W. (1818–1886), was brevetted lieutenant-colonel for services in the Mexican War. He served in the Confederate Army of Northern Virginia, and commanded a division at Vicksburg and Chattanooga.

Los Angeles, Cal., was settled by the Spaniards in 1781. Gold discovered here in 1842 was the first authentic finding of the precious metal in California. The city was occupied by Stockton in 1846, but was retaken by the Californians. It was again captured in 1847.

Losantiville, Ohio, the name originally given to the settlement which is now the city of Cincinnati, by its founders, Patterson, Denman and Filson, of New Jersey, who had purchased land from the Scioto Company in 1788. The name is compounded of "os," Latin for mouth; "anti," Greek for opposite; "ville," French for city; and "L," the initial of the Licking River. The name was changed in 1790.

Lossing, Benson J. (1813–1891), of New York, author and wood-engraver, published "Pictorial Field-Book of the Revolution," and others of the Civil War and War of 1812, a "National History of the United States," the "Statesman's Manual," lives of Zachary Taylor, Winfield Scott, Washington, etc., a history of New York, and "Biographies of Eminent Americans."

Lotteries. The history of American lotteries begins with that which the charter of 1612 authorized the Virginia Company to hold for the benefit of its colonizing schemes. In the eighteenth century they were extraordinarily popular in America. Legislatures authorized lotteries for every species of public improvement, for the building of churches and colleges, for the repair of losses to individuals by fire and otherwise; *e.g.*, Faneuil Hall, after the fire of 1761, was rebuilt by lottery. The Continental Congress tried to raise money by lottery in 1777. The sums annually employed by Americans in lottery speculations probably amounted to hundreds of thousands. The last lottery supported by governmental encouragement was the Louisiana State Lottery. An act of Congress passed in 1890 attemped to crush it by forbidding it the use of the U. S. mails.

Loudon, Forts. There were two fortifications of this name during the colonial period. Both were erected for the purpose of defence against the Indians. One was erected in Loudon County, Tenn., on the Tennessee River, about 1750, and was the scene of an Indian massacre a few years later. The other was built in 1752 near Winchester, Va., for the protection of the town. It was a square with four bastions, mounting twenty-four guns and large enough to contain 450 men.

Loudoun, John C., Earl of (1705–1782), succeeded William Shirley as commander-in-chief of the British forces in North America in 1756. He proved incapable and irresolute in the campaign against the French at Louisbourg. He laid an embargo on commerce in 1757, which was very unpopular. In 1757 he was succeeded by General Amherst.

Louis XVI. (1754–1793), succeeded to the throne of France in 1774. He gave the American colonies very considerable aid during the Revolution, and burdened France with a debt in their behalf. His war with Great Britain lasted from 1778 to 1782. He was executed in 1793. (See French Revolution.)

Louisbourg, Cape Breton, Canada, a fort erected by the French in 1720. Upon the breaking out of King George's War in 1744, privateers were sent out from Louisbourg to harass the New England coast. Governor Shirley, of Massachusetts, succeeded in raising, in 1745, a strong force of men and ships, to which all the New England States, New York and Pennsylvania contributed, either in money or supplies. An army of 3250 men was dispatched against the fort under the command of William Pepperell, of Maine. This force began the siege April 30. Five unsuccessful attacks were made. Finally, the French garrison becoming mutinous, the commander of Louisbourg surrendered, June 17. The fort was restored to the French by the Treaty of Aix-la-Chapelle in 1748. It was again captured by Shirley in 1758, during the French and Indian War. On June 2, 1758, the British appeared before this fortress with 10,000 men under Amherst, and forty-one sail under Boscawen. The fort was defended by 3080 regulars, five ships and seven frigates. On June 8, in spite of surf and a spirited resistance, the British gained a foothold on the island. The outposts were soon captured and lines drawn around the citadel. The French ships were burned or captured. The garrison attempted a sortie, but was repulsed. Half the men were in hospitals. On July 27 the fort capitulated, and the strongest point in America, and great stores, fell into the hands of the English.

Louisiana, the Creole State, was acquired by purchase from France in 1803. It was first visited by the Spaniard De Soto in 1541, who was buried in the Mississippi. In 1682 La Salle descended the river and took formal possession of the region in the name of Louis XIV., in whose honor it was named. In 1706 New Orleans was founded by Bienville. John Law secured control of the colony as a part of his Mississippi scheme in 1717. In 1762 France transferred her title to Spain, who restored the country again to France in 1800. Napoleon, following the plan of La Salle, proposed to found a new France in America, but was finally induced to sell the entire territory to the United States for $15,000,000 (1803). The following year the Territory of Orleans was formed from the portion of this vast purchase south of 33° north latitude. The northern portion was organized as the Louisiana Territory, the name of which was afterward changed to Missouri. In April, 1812, the Territory of Orleans became the State of Louisiana. The final battle of the War of 1812 was fought at New Orleans after peace had been made at Ghent, but before the news had reached America. General Jackson repulsed with great slaughter the attack of the British under Sir Edward Pakenham upon New Orleans. From 1812 until 1830 the State was Democratic. After 1830 until 1850 the Whigs were usually in the majority. The State was carried for Polk in 1844 by fraud. The sugar planters wished for protection against foreign sugar. An ordinance of secession was passed in convention January 26, 1861. New Orleans was captured by United States forces April 25, 1862. The State was restored to its place in the Union June 25, 1868. The present Constitution was made in that year. In July, 1871, the Republican party became divided into two factions, led by Warmoth and Kellogg. In January, 1872, there were two rival Legislatures; open conflict had been prevented by troops. Two candidates, McEnery and Kellogg, were nominated for Governor, and on January 14, 1873, both were inaugurated as Governor. Two rival U. S. Senators were elected. The Kellogg government was supported by the President at Washington. In 1876 the vote of the State was claimed by both parties, but was finally given to the Republicans by the Electoral Commission. Since 1876 the State has been Democratic in all elections. The population in 1812 was 76,556; in 1890, 1,118,587. History by Gayarré.

Louisiana, District of. In 1804, when that southern part of the Louisiana Purchase which is now called the State of Louisiana was organized as the Territory of Orleans, all that was north of this was organized as the "District of Louisiana," under the Governor of Indiana Territory. In 1805 it was given a separate government as the Territory of Louisiana. In 1812 its name was changed to Missouri Territory.

Louisiana Historical Society, founded at New Orleans in 1860 and recently reorganized. It is now in a flourishing condition, and has collected over 1000 manuscripts and volumes.

Louisiana vs. Jumel, an important case before the U. S. Supreme Court, decided in 1882. The plaintiffs, holding bonds issued under the act of the Louisiana Legislature of 1874, known as Act No. 3, demanded payment of these bonds in 1880. Payment was refused in obedience to Article 3 of the Louisiana State Debt Act of 1880, carrying out provisions contained in the new Constitution of that State. This article recited that coupons of consolidated bonds falling due in January, 1880, were remitted. Suit was brought against officers of the State. The Circuit Court of Louisiana decided for the defendant, and its decision was confirmed by the Supreme Court of the United States on the ground that relief could not be awarded against officers obeying the supreme power of the State; that the money is the State's property, not held in trust by the officers, except in the capacity of her servants.

Louisville, Ky., founded in 1778 by a company of settlers under Colonel George Rogers Clark. It became a city in 1828. The introduction of steam navigation on the Ohio in 1812 gave it importance as a centre of river trade.

"**Louisville Courier-Journal**," probably the most influential newspaper in Kentucky. In 1868 there existed in Louisville three newspapers, the *Journal*, *Courier* and *Democrat*. These journals were consolidated that same year, and called the *Louisville Courier-Journal*. It is now published daily by the *Courier-Journal* Company.

Lovejoy, Elijah P. (1802–1837), established the St. Louis *Observer* in 1833, in which he ardently attacked slavery. He was compelled by violent pro-slavery sentiment to remove his paper to Alton, Ill., in 1836, where his establishment was sacked three times by a mob. At the fourth attack one of the mob was killed, whereupon he was shot by his assailants.

Lovejoy, Owen (1811–1864), was very prominent in the anti-slavery cause in Illinois from 1836 to 1856. He represented Illinois in the U. S. Congress as a Republican from 1857 to 1864.

Lovelace, Francis (1618?–1675?), became Governor of New York in 1668. He established an arbitrary rule, and so oppressed the people that New York surrendered to a Dutch fleet in 1673 without opposition. He returned to England in 1673.

Lovell, Mansfield (1822–1884), fought at Chapultepec and Monterey in the Mexican War. He surrendered New Orleans to Admiral Farragut in 1862, commanded at Coffeeville and fought against Sherman at Kenesaw.

Low, Seth, born in 1850, while mayor of Brooklyn from 1881 to 1885, introduced many reforms and carefully guarded public interests. He became president of Columbia College in 1890.

Lowell, Edward J., born in 1845, published "The Hessians and the other German Auxiliaries of Great Britain in the Revolutionary War," 1884, and "The Eve of the French Revolution," 1893.

Lowell, James Russell (1819–1891), was born at Cambridge, graduated at Harvard, and devoted himself to belles-lettres, becoming eventually professor of that department and of modern languages at his university. Aside from his work as editor of the *Atlantic* and of the *North American Review*, his essays, "Among My Books," etc., his poems, "Fable for Critics," "Cathedral," "Commemoration Ode," etc., his political activity is to be noted. His "Biglow Papers," 1846–1848, helped powerfully the anti-slavery cause; a second series appeared in the period of the war. Lowell won general esteem as U. S. Minister to Spain 1877–1880, and to England 1880–1885. The volume, "Democracy and Other Essays," contains some of his contributions to political philosophy.

Lowell, John (1743–1802), secured the insertion of the clause "all men are born free and equal" in the Massachusetts bill of rights. He was a member of the Continental Congress from 1782 to 1783. He was a Judge of the U. S. Court of Appeals from 1782 to 1789, and U. S. District Judge from 1789.

Lowell, John (1769–1840), was a supporter of the Federalist party and a zealous opponent of the War of 1812. He published many political pamphlets, among them an "Inquiry into the Subject of the 'Chesapeake'" and "Mr. Madison's War."

Lowell, Mass., was made a town in 1826 and incorporated as a city ten years later. The first cotton mill was started in 1823, and this industry has since grown to mammoth proportions.

Lowndes, Rawlins (1722–1800), was appointed a Judge in South Carolina by the crown, and affirmed the validity of unstamped public papers. He was president of the province from 1778 to 1780. He opposed the adoption of the Constitution as fatal to liberty.

Lowndes, William J. (1782–1822), was a member of the South Carolina Legislature from 1806 to 1810. He represented South Carolina in the U. S. House of Representatives from 1810 to 1822. He served on the Committee of Ways and Means from 1818 to 1822. He earnestly supported the War of 1812. He was a brilliant debater, and called by Henry Clay "the wisest man he had ever known in Congress."

Loyal Company, a land company chartered June 12, 1749, in opposition to the Ohio Company. Its patentees obtained a grant of 800,000 acres in the Northwest Territory, chiefly along the Ohio River.

Loyalists. From 1688 on, there was in every colony a party favorable to the crown. When the Revolutionary movements began, this party became more active. In no colony was there an overwhelming majority in favor of revolution. In some the majority was unfavorable. The loyalists in New England and the Middle States comprised a large part of the most respectable and eminent men. It is now recognized that a large number of them were patriotic in their resistance to the efforts to overturn the existing government. As the Revolution progressed they were treated with increasing harshness. Tories were ostracized, and in some cases tarred and feathered. Acts banishing them and confiscating their property were passed by most of the colonial conventions and legislatures. During the British occupation of New York, Philadelphia and the Southern States, loyalist regiments and more irregular organizations were formed and took part in the war, often with great bitterness. Exasperation against them was so great that at the end of the war most of them felt obliged to go into exile when the British troops withdrew. Thousands from the North went to New Brunswick, Nova Scotia and Canada. From the South many went to the Bahamas and West Indies. In the Treaty of 1783 the British endeavored to have articles inserted which should provide compensation for the dispossessed loyalists, but no more was secured than a promise to recommend the matter to the States. The States refused to do anything in the matter, though subsequently some ameliorations of their hardships were secured.

Luce, Stephen B., rear-admiral, born in 1827, was engaged in the battle of Port Royal, on the "Wabash," in 1862. He commanded the monitor "Nantucket" in 1863, and the "Pontiac" from 1864 to 1865. He was rear-admiral U. S. N. from 1885 to 1890.

Ludlow, Roger (1590–1665 ?), removed from Massachusetts to Connecticut in 1635. He is supposed to have drafted the Connecticut Constitution. In 1639 he founded the town of Fairfield. In 1654 he went to Virginia.

Lundy, Benjamin (1789–1839), originated an anti-slavery association in Ohio called the "Union Humane Society" in 1815. He contributed anti-slavery articles to periodicals, and from 1812 to 1836 edited *The Genius of Universal Emancipation*, published at Baltimore after 1824. He advocated negro colonization. He was one of the first to deliver anti-slavery lectures and the first to found societies for the encouragement of free labor. Garrison was an assistant to him at first. Lundy was a Quaker.

Lundy's Lane, Canada, a battle in the War of 1812. After the defeat of the British at Chippewa, General Drummond advanced to meet the victorious American army led by General Jacob Brown. The latter sent forward General Scott to menace the forts on the Niagara River. Near the Falls, July 24, 1814, he fell in with General Riall with 1800 men, who were posted on a hill near Lundy's Lane. Scott sent forward Major Jesup, who by a flank movement gained the British rear and kept back reinforcements. Meantime Scott was hotly engaged against a much larger force. The American main army soon arrived, and Colonel Miller stormed a battery which was the key to the British position. The British, with the reinforcements that now had arrived, attempted in vain to recapture this position. At midnight, after six hours of fighting, the battle ceased. The British next day took possession of the battlefield and four of the cannon captured. Both parties claimed the victory. The Americans lost about 850 men, the British nearly 900 in all.

Lunt, George (1803–1885), served several terms in the Massachusetts Legislature. He was a U. S. District Attorney from 1849 to 1853. While editor of the *Boston Daily Courier* from 1857 to 1865 he exerted a powerful influence on the Democratic politics of the period. He wrote "Three Eras of New England" and "Origin of the Late War."

Luther vs. Borden, a celebrated case in the U. S. Supreme Court. In 1842 Luther, of Massachusetts, brought action of trespass in the Circuit Court of Rhode Island against Borden for entering his house by force. In 1841 a portion of the people of Rhode Island had framed a new Constitution and elected Thomas W. Dorr Governor in opposition to the charter government. (See Dorr War.) That government, King being the executive, declared the State under martial law, and Luther's house was searched, he being implicated in the armed conspiracy against the constitutional government. Luther pleaded the constitutionality of the new government, but the Circuit Court found judgment against him and this the Supreme Court of the United States confirmed, 1842. But it was decided that the question of the constitutionality of a State government lay rather with Congress than the judicial courts. Also it was decided that under martial law suspected persons might be legally arrested by State authority.

Lutherans in America. Dr. H. M. Mühlenberg is generally regarded as the founder of this church in America. Lutherans had settled in the country as early as 1621, and sent out probably the first missionaries to the Indians, but they remained unorganized till 1742 when Dr. Mühlenberg was induced to leave Halle, in order to organize the churches scattered throughout the colonies. The first synod was held in 1748, and others were held annually thereafter. The church grew rapidly under the care of its organizer. Schools were established, churches built, ministers ordained, and its numbers steadily increased till his death in 1787. The Civil War broke the church into Northern and Southern Synods, and doctrinal questions divided the former into two sects, but there is now a movement on foot to unite all bodies into one General Conference. Membership in 1890, 1,231,000.

Luxemburg. The United States concluded an extradition treaty with Luxemburg in 1883.

Luzerne, Anne César de la (1741–1791), French diplomatist, was minister to the United States from 1779 to 1783.

Lygonia, a plantation in what is now the State of Maine, purchased April 7, 1643, by George Cleves, of Casco, and Alexander Rigby, of England. Cleves immediately set up his authority, claiming jurisdiction as deputy-president of the province of Lygonia, over a large portion of the territory granted to Ferdinando Gorges in 1639. The Massachusetts Bay government was called in as arbitrator, and decided in favor of Cleves and Rigby in 1646, after much dispute.

Lyman, Phineas (1716–1774), of Connecticut, in 1755 was commander-in-chief of the Connecticut forces at Crown Point, and erected Fort Edward. He succeeded Sir William Johnson in command at Lake George in 1755. He commanded the Connecticut troops at Ticonderoga and Crown Point in 1759, and at Oswego and Montreal. He commanded in the Havana expedition in 1762.

Lynch, William F. (1801–1865), planned and carried out the exploration of the Jordan and the Dead Sea in 1848. He entered the Confederate navy, commanding at Roanoke Island, at Albemarle Sound and at Smithville.

Lynch-law, the law administered during the Revolutionary period by Charles Lynch, a Virginia planter, and his associates, to Tories and other British sympathizers. The victims were hung up by their thumbs until they shouted: "Liberty forever!" but were never killed. In later years and at the present time the term is applied to summary executions without trial and usually by mob violence. It is practiced largely in the West and South, lynch-law executions being, in the United States at large, about twice as numerous as legal ones.

Lyon, Mary (1797–1849), founded Mount Holyoke Seminary at South Hadley, Mass., in 1837, and was its principal until 1849. She was thus a pioneer in the higher education of women in America.

Lyon, Matthew (1746–1822), came to America from Ireland in 1759. He represented Vermont in the U. S. Congress as an Anti-Federalist and Democrat from 1797 to 1801. He was a U. S. Congressman from Kentucky from 1803 to 1811. A strong Democrat, he was prosecuted under the Sedition Act of 1798.

Lyon, Nathaniel (1818–1861), served with distinction at Contreras, Churubusco and the city of Mexico during the Mexican War. He served in Kansas during the political struggles and supported the cause of the Free-Soil party. In 1861 he was placed in command of the U. S. arsenal at St. Louis, and soon afterward succeeded General Harney in command of the department. He defeated the Confederates at Booneville and at Dug Spring under McCulloch. He was defeated at Wilson's Creek by a superior force, and during the battle he was killed.

Lyons, Richard B. P., Viscount, (Lord Lyons) (1817–1887), was British Minister at Washington from 1858 to 1865. During the trying times of the Civil War he successfully conducted intricate negotiations and laudably discharged the duties of his position.

Lyon's Creek, Canada. An American force sent to destroy some supplies was here attacked October 19, 1814, by the British under Colonel Murray. The latter was defeated with the loss of 150 men, the Americans lost sixty-seven in all.

M.

McArthur, Duncan (1772–1839), served during the War of 1812, commanding the Army of the West in 1814. He was a Democratic U. S. Congressman from Ohio from 1823 to 1825. He was Governor of Ohio from 1830 to 1832.

McClellan, George Brinton (December 3, 1826–October 29, 1885), a noted American general, was born at Philadelphia, educated at the University of Pennsylvania and at West Point, where he was graduated in 1846. His service in the Mexican War was followed by duty as instructor in the Military Academy. He was sent to Europe as an expert to follow the course of the Crimean War, and published as a result, "The Armies of Europe." For a few years he was engineer for the Illinois Central Railroad, and a railroad president. Appointed major-general, and entrusted with command in West Virginia at the beginning of the Civil War he broke up Garnett's army, and was summoned to Washington after the Bull Run catastrophe. In August, 1861, he became commander of the Army of the Potomac, and in November he succeeded General Scott as commander-in-chief. McClellan's services in organizing the army were invaluable. Excess of caution and friction between the Washington authorities and himself led to disappointments in his achievements against the enemy. He commanded through the Peninsula campaign, executing his famous "change of base," was relieved of the command, reappointed September 7, 1862, after Pope's disasters, and commanded in the Antietam campaign. On November 7 he was removed and placed on waiting orders. He resigned from the army in 1864, and was the same year the Democratic candidate for President, receiving twenty-one electoral votes. He was Governor of New Jersey 1878–1881. "Little Mac" was phenomenally popular with the soldiers of the Army of the Potomac in spite of outside criticism. See "McClellan's Own Story" for his defence.

McClelland, Robert (1807–1880), represented Michigan in the U. S. Congress as a Democrat from 1843 to 1849. He was Governor of Michigan from 1852 to 1853. He was Secretary of the Interior in Pierce's Cabinet from 1853 to 1857.

McClernand, John A., born in 1812, represented Illinois in the U. S. Congress as a Democrat from 1843 to 1851 and from 1859 to 1861. He organized a brigade in 1861, and commanded it at Belmont and Fort Donelson. He commanded a division at Shiloh, Vicksburg, Arkansas Post and on the Big Black River. He retired in 1864.

McCloskey, John (1810–1885), cardinal, was Bishop of Albany from 1847 to 1864. He was Archbishop of New York from 1864. In 1875 he was made a cardinal.

McClure, Alexander K., born in 1828, was elected as a Republican to the Pennsylvania Legislature in 1857 and 1858, and to the Senate in 1859. He founded the *Philadelphia Times* in 1875, which met with unusual success.

McCook, Alexander McD., general, born in 1831, commanded a regiment at Bull Run, and a division at Shiloh and in the Tennessee and Mississippi campaigns. He commanded a corps at Perryville, Stone River and Chickamauga.

McCormick, Cyrus H. (1809–1884), born in Virginia, invented the reaping-machine in 1831.

McCosh, James, born in 1811, came to America from Scotland in 1868 to assume the presidency of the College of New Jersey (Princeton), and held that position till 1888. He wrote "The Methods of the Divine Government," and "An Examination of Mill's Philosophy." Died 1894.

McCrary, George W. (1835–1890), represented Iowa in the U. S. Congress as a Republican from 1869 to 1877. He was Secretary of War in Hayes' Cabinet from 1877 to 1879. He was a U. S. Circuit Judge from 1879 to 1884.

McCrea, Jane (1753–1777), was taken prisoner by Indians led by Le Loup, a Wyandotte chief, in 1777. On the way to the English camp they were met by other Indians led by Duluth, sent by David Jones, Miss McCrea's lover, to escort her to the English camp, where they were to be married. During the ensuing quarrel Le Loup shot Miss McCrea. The versions of this event are many.

McCulloch, Benjamin (1811–1862), commanded a company during the Mexican War at Monterey, Buena Vista and the city of Mexico. He was a U. S. Marshal from 1853 to 1857. He was commissioned brigadier-general in the Confederate service in 1861 and fought with distinction at Wilson's Creek and Pea Ridge, where he met his death.

McCulloch, Hugh, born in 1808, was cashier and manager of a bank at Fort Wayne, Ind., from 1835 to 1856, and president of the Indiana State Bank from 1856 to 1863. While Comptroller of the Currency (a new office) from 1863 to 1865 he organized the bureau and inaugurated the national banking system. He was Secretary of the Treasury in the Cabinets of Lincoln and Johnson from 1865 to 1869. He successfully accomplished the funding of the national debt. He was again Secretary of the Treasury from 1884 to 1885.

McCulloch vs. Maryland, a famous case in the U. S. Supreme Court, brought by writ of error from the Court of Appeals of Maryland to the Supreme Court in 1819. McCulloch was cashier of a branch established in Baltimore by the Bank of the United States, of Philadelphia, which had been incorporated by an act of Congress in 1816. The action was one of debt brought by the State of Maryland against McCulloch, who, it was averred, had refused to comply with an act of the Maryland General Assembly of 1818, which imposed a "tax upon all banks or branches thereof in the State of Maryland, *not chartered by the Legislature.*" The decision of the Court of Appeals of Maryland had been against the plaintiff. The Supreme

Court reversed this decision, declaring that the Bank Act of 1816 was constitutional, and that therefore the act of the Maryland Legislature of 1818 was contrary to the Constitution of the United States, and therefore void, because States have no power, by taxation or otherwise, to impede or control the operations of constitutional laws enacted by Congress to carry into execution any of the powers of the Federal Government.

McDonald, Joseph E. (1819–1891), was a county prosecuting attorney from 1843 to 1847. He represented Indiana in the U. S. Congress as a Democrat from 1849 to 1851. He was Attorney-General of Indiana from 1856 to 1860. He was a U. S. Senator from 1875 to 1881, and was in favor of hard money and a protective tariff.

Macdonough, Thomas (1783–1825), commodore, served in the Tripoli expedition under Decatur from 1803 to 1804. He gained a celebrated victory over a superior British squadron under Commodore Downie at Plattsburg on Lake Champlain in 1814. The British fleet consisted of sixteen vessels with ninety-five guns and 1000 men, and lost about 200, besides prisoners. The American force consisted of fourteen vessels, carrying eighty-six guns and 850 men, and lost 112 men.

McDowell, Irvin (1818–1885), graduated at West Point in 1838 and served, like so many other West-Pointers, in the Mexican War. In 1861 he was appointed brigadier-general, and placed in charge of the Army of the Potomac. His plans for the first battle of Bull Run were admittedly excellent, but nothing could check the demoralization of the green troops. His reputation as a general was unjustly involved in the collapse of the army, and he was never again intrusted with high command. He was a corps commander in Virginia in 1862, fought at the battles of Cedar Mountain and second Bull Run; after the war he was a commander of various military departments, was promoted major-general in 1872, and retired in 1882.

McDuffie, George (1788–1851), represented South Carolina as a Democrat in the U. S. House of Representatives from 1821 to 1834. While chairman of the Ways and Means Committee he favored the maintenance of a U. S. bank. He drafted the address of South Carolina to the people of the United States in 1832. He was Governor of South Carolina from 1834 to 1836, and was a U. S. Senator from 1842 to 1846.

Mace. The mace used in the House of Representatives from 1789 on (ebony fasces surmounted by a silver eagle upon a silver globe) was destroyed when the British burned the Capitol in 1814. The present one was made in 1842.

"**Macedonian,**" frigate. (See "United States.")

"**McFingal,**" the most famous political satire of the Revolutionary period, was written by John Trumbull, of Connecticut (1750–1831), and was published in 1782. It is an imitation of Butler's "Hudibras."

McGillivray, Alexander (1740–1793), chief of the Creek Indians, aided the British during the Revolution. He afterward conducted atrocious raids along the Cumberland River. He had a strong mind, but was treacherous and cruel.

McGlynn, Edward, Roman Catholic priest, born in 1837, aided in founding the Anti-Poverty Society in 1887. He was removed from the pastorate of St. Stephen's Church, New York, on account of discountenancing parochial schools and advocating in public the land theories of Henry George, but was restored to favor in 1892.

McHenry, James (1753–1816), came to Philadelphia from Ireland about 1771. He served during the Revolution as surgeon and aide. He was a member of the Maryland Senate from 1781 to 1786, a delegate from Maryland to the Continental Congress from 1783 to 1786, and a member of the Constitutional Convention in 1787. He was Secretary of War from 1796 to 1801 in the Cabinets of Washington and Adams.

McHenry, Fort, Baltimore, garrisoned by 1000 men under Major Armistead during the War of 1812, guarded Baltimore against an attack by sea. September 13, 1814, Admiral Cochrane with sixteen heavy war-vessels opened bombardment upon the fort. Its guns failed to reach the fleet till some of the British vessels approached nearer. They met so warm a reception that they withdrew, badly damaged. A force of 1000 men, landed to surprise the fort in the rear, was repulsed. At midnight the firing ceased; next day the British withdrew and Baltimore was safe. The only damage was on the American side, four killed and twenty-four wounded. During the bombardment Francis S. Key, a prisoner on board the British fleet, wrote the "Star-Spangled Banner."

McHenry Case (1851). One McHenry, a respectable colored resident of Syracuse, N. Y., was arrested in October as a fugitive slave. He escaped the officers, but was recaptured. A convention of the Liberty party was then in session, and fully 2000 people hastened to the court house and rescued McHenry, who escaped to Canada. The U. S. Marshal was tried for kidnapping, but acquitted.

McKean, Thomas (1734–1817), Governor, was prominent in the Stamp-Act Congress of 1765 as a delegate from Delaware, and aided in drafting the memorial to the lords and commons. He was a member of the Continental Congress from Delaware from 1774 to 1783, and its president in 1781. He aided in drafting the Articles of Confederation, and was prominent in securing the Declaration of Independence, of which he was one of the signers. He was Chief Justice of Pennsylvania from 1777 to 1799, and Governor from 1799 to 1808.

Mackinaw (originally Michillimackinac), was from the middle of the seventeenth century a centre of the Northwestern fur-trade. In the War of 1812 the first move of the British was to send a body of two hundred regulars and Canadians, with Indian allies, who, on July 17, 1812, captured this American post. An attempt to recapture it in 1814 was unsuccessful.

McKinley, John (1780–1852), represented Alabama in the U. S. Senate as a Democrat from 1826 to 1831. He was a U. S. Congressman from 1833 to 1835. From 1837 to 1852 he was a Justice of the U. S. Supreme Court.

McKinley, Wm., Jr., Congressman and Governor of Ohio, was born at Niles, O., in 1844, and served as a volunteer in the Civil War. He was a member of the House of Representatives from 1877 to 1891, and as chairman of the Committee of Ways and Means had the chief hand in framing the Tariff Act of October 1, 1890, commonly called the McKinley Act. From January, 1892, to January, 1894, he was Governor of Ohio, and was re-elected for the term next ensuing.

McKinley Act, a bill submitted in Congress by Representative McKinley, of Ohio, and which became law October 1, 1890. It provided for a high rate of duty on a large number of articles imported from foreign countries, but made sugar free. This act was designed to reduce the national revenue and increase protection.

McLane, Louis (1786–1857), of Delaware, was Representative in Congress from 1817 to 1827, Senator from 1827 to 1829, Minister to England from 1829 to 1831, and Secretary of the Treasury in Jackson's Cabinet from 1831 to 1833, when he resigned rather than order the removal of the deposits (see art. Deposits). He was then Secretary of State for a year. In 1845–46 he was again Minister to England.

McLane, Robert M., born in 1815, was a Democratic U. S. Congressman from Maryland from 1847 to 1851. He was Minister to China from 1854 to 1856, to Mexico from 1859 to 1860 and to France from 1885 to 1889.

McLaws, Lafayette, born in 1821, was graduated at West Point, resigned from the U. S. army in 1861, and became a major-general in the Confederate service. He distinguished himself as a division commander at Harper's Ferry, Antietam, Fredericksburg, Chancellorsville and Gettysburg.

McLean, John (1785–1861), born in New Jersey, but brought up in Ohio, was a Representative from Ohio from 1813 to 1817, and Postmaster-General from 1823 to 1829, in the administrations of Monroe and John Quincy Adams. From 1830 to 1861 he was an Associate Justice of the Supreme Court of the United States. In the Dred Scott case he dissented from the opinion of Chief Justice Taney.

McLeod, Alexander, a Canadian temporarily in New York State in 1841, was arrested and indicted for participation in the "Caroline" affair (see art.). The British Minister demanded his release, alleging that, the case being international, jurisdiction over it belonged to the U. S. Government, not to the State courts. Such was also the view of the U. S. Government. But the courts of New York held, on the contrary, that the burning of the "Caroline" was not an act of magistracy on the part of the Canadian Government, that McLeod was therefore individually responsible and amenable to the New York courts. He proved an alibi.

McMaster, John Bach, born in 1852, is the author of a "History of the People of the United States from the Revolution to the Civil War," of which three volumes have appeared, and a "Life of Benjamin Franklin."

McMillin, Benton, born in Kentucky in 1845, was a Representative in Congress from Tennessee from 1879 to the present time (1894), and of late one of the most prominent Democratic leaders.

Macomb, Alexander (1782–1841), entered the U. S. army in 1799, and at the outbreak of the War of 1812 was adjutant-general of the army. Taking service in the field he, in September, 1814, won the victory of Plattsburg over Sir George Provost, and was made major-general. From 1835 to 1841 he was commander-in-chief of the army.

Macon, Nathaniel (1757–1837), of North Carolina, Representative from 1791 to 1815, was Speaker of the House of Representatives from 1801 to 1807. From 1815 to 1828 he was a Senator from North Carolina. A Democratic-Republican of the strictest type, he was noted for his political uprightness and purity. He was a principal member of the faction called "Quids."

Macon, Fort, N. C., captured from the Confederates by General Parke, commanding 35,000 troops from Burnside's army, April 23, 1862. The fort was garrisoned by 500 Confederates under Colonel White.

"**Macon Bill No. 2**," a bill so called from its author, Nathaniel Macon, was passed by Congress on May 1, 1810, as a means of extricating the United States from the difficulties caused by the aggressions of England and France. It provided that commerce should be free, but that if either England should withdraw her Orders in Council or France her Berlin and Milan Decrees, intercourse should be prohibited with the nation which retained them.

Macon Road, Ga., a battle during Sherman's investment of Atlanta, July 26, 1864. McCook, commanding 4000 Federals, was defeated and captured by 6000 Confederates of Hood's army under Ransom.

McPherson, James B. (1828–1864), a brilliant young general of the Civil War, was graduated from West Point in 1853. In 1862 and 1863 he was with Grant in the Tennessee and Vicksburg campaigns, commanding a corps with distinguished success. In the spring of 1864 he was put in command of the Army of the Tennessee, and assisted Sherman in his advance into Georgia. He had a most important part in the fighting against Johnston at Resaca, New Hope Church, Dallas and Kenesaw Mountain. He was killed in the battle against Hood at Atlanta, July 22, 1864.

McPherson, John R., born in 1833, was a member of the New Jersey Senate from 1870 to 1873. He was elected to the U. S. Senate from New Jersey as a Democrat in 1876, 1883 and 1889.

MacVeagh, Wayne, lawyer, born in Pennsylvania in 1833, was U. S. Minister to Turkey from 1870 to 1871, headed a commission of investigation in Louisiana appointed by President Hayes in 1877, was Attorney-General of the United States under Garfield in 1881, and in 1893 was appointed Minister to Italy.

Madagascar. The United States concluded a commercial treaty with Madagascar in 1867, which was modified and enlarged in 1881.

Madison, Dorothy Paine (1772–1849), wife of President Madison, was a beautiful and accomplished Quakeress. Her first husband was John Todd, a Philadelphia lawyer. She married Mr. Madison in 1794, and was unusually successful as a President's wife.

Madison, James (1751–1836), fourth President of the United States, was born in King George County, Va. He was well educated, graduated at Princeton in 1772, and was early distinguished for sound judgment, discretion, acquirements, industry and patriotism. In 1774 he was a member of the Committee of Public Safety of Orange County, and in 1776 became a member of the Virginia Convention. From 1780 to 1784 he was a member of the Continental Congress, and, in spite of his youth and modesty, had a leading share in its deliberations, and especially its committee-work, for which his sensible and methodical mind was peculiarly apt. In the Virginia Assembly (1784–87) he did great service in securing religious liberty and in promoting the movement toward a better union of the States. Probably no one else contributed more to this end in all America. He was a member of the Alexandria-Mount-Vernon Conference of 1785, of the Annapolis Convention of 1786, and of the Constitutional Convention of 1787, in which he had the most influential part, through his own talents for constructive statesmanship and also through his persuasive and conciliatory spirit. In 1788 he wrote a portion of the *Federalist*, and did more than any one else to secure the ratification of the Constitution by Virginia. From 1789 to 1797 he was a leading member of Congress, inclining more and more to the doctrines and party of Jefferson. He wrote the Virginia resolutions of 1798. From 1801 to 1809 he was Secretary of State in Jefferson's Cabinet, and from 1809 to 1817 he was President of the United States, being elected over C. C. Pinckney in 1808, and over DeWitt Clinton in 1812. The chief event in his administration was the War of 1812, which he managed feebly. His Cabinet consisted of Robert Smith (1811–17 James Monroe), Secretary of State; Albert Gallatin (1814 G. W. Campbell, 1814 A. J. Dallas, 1816 W. H. Crawford), Secretary of the Treasury; William Eustis (1813 John Armstrong, 1814 J. Monroe, 1815 W. H. Crawford), Secretary of War; Paul Hamilton (1813 William Jones, 1814 B. W. Crowninshield), Secretary of the Navy; Cæsar A. Rodney (1811 William Pinckney, 1814 Richard Rush), Attorney-General. The Vice-Presidents were George Clinton, 1809–1813; Elbridge Gerry, 1813–1814. From 1817 to his death Madison lived in retirement at Montpelier, Va. Life by Rives.

Madison, Fort (near St. Louis). Attacked September 5, 1812, by a party of Winnebagoes. After three days' fighting the Indians withdrew. The American loss was one man.

Madison, Wis., was chosen as the State capital in 1836, while yet a wilderness.

Madoc, or Madog, a Welsh prince, son of Owain Gwynedd, is said, in accordance with a tradition first published in the sixteenth century, to have sailed west about 1171 and discovered America. The first mention of this Madog is in a Welsh poem of the fourteenth century. He is not known to have existed, and the story of his discovery is not now believed by the most competent authorities.

Magazines. The first American literary periodical was the "General Magazine and Historical Chronicle," issued by Franklin at Philadelphia in 1741. In the same year and place appeared the "American Magazine," but neither lived a year. In 1743 an "American Magazine and Historical Chronicle" began to be published in Boston. The first which appeared in New York was the "Independent Reflector," weekly, 1752. Other important magazines of the eighteenth century were the "Pennsylvania Magazine" of 1775, the "American Museum," 1787–1797; the "Massachusetts Magazine," 1789–1796, and the "New York Magazine," 1790–1797. Of much more value were the "Portfolio," Philadelphia, 1801–1825, and the "Monthly Anthology," Boston, 1803–1811. The first important review was the "North American Review," founded in 1815 at Boston. The chief predecessor of the modern literary and miscellaneous magazines of America was the "Knickerbocker," 1832–1860. Of the leading magazines of the present time, Harper's was founded in 1850, Scribner's (later the "Century Magazine") in 1870, the "Atlantic Monthly" in 1857.

Magoffin, Beriah (1815–1885), a prominent member of the Democratic party, was Governor of Kentucky from 1859 to 1862. His sympathies inclined toward the Confederates, but he maintained a policy of neutrality.

Magruder, John B. (1810–1871), Confederate major-general, commanded the forces in the Peninsula in 1862, the Department of Texas during the remainder of the war, after which he served under Maximilian in Mexico.

Maguaga, Mich., about fourteen miles from Detroit, scene of a minor engagement in the War of 1812, August 9, 1812. Colonel Miller, attempting to clear the road to Detroit, attacked the British and Indians, under General Proctor and Tecumseh. Though successful. he was obliged to give up his advance movement.

Mahon, Philip H. Stanhope, Lord (afterward Earl Stanhope) (1805–1875), an English statesman, wrote a "History of England from the Peace of Utrecht to the Peace of Versailles (1713–1783)," which is recognized as a standard work, and presents a moderate English view of the Revolution.

Mahone, William, born in 1826, Confederate major-general, and noted for hard fighting in several battles, especially at Petersburg, about 1878 organized and became the leader of the party called Readjusters, advocating repudiation of the State debt of Virginia. From 1881 to 1887 he was a Senator from Virginia.

Maine, name probably meaning main-land, as distinguished from the islands off its coast. It was first settled by a party led by George Popham in 1607, but this was temporary. By grants of 1622, 1629 and 1639, Sir Ferdinando Gorges obtained the territory between the Piscataqua and the Kennebec. In 1652 and again in 1668, Massachusetts obtained possession of this part of Maine. Eastern Maine, held by the Duke of York from 1664, fell to Massachusetts in 1691. The "District of Maine" remained a part of Massachusetts till 1820, when it was admitted to the Union as a separate State on April 15. Its Constitution, framed in that year, is still in operation. In 1842 the Ashburton Treaty settled the long-standing dispute regarding its northeast boundary. Its boundary with New Hampshire had been settled in 1737. The "Maine law," prohibiting the manufacture and sale of intoxicating liquors, was passed in 1851 and permanently in 1858. Maine was almost constantly Democratic from 1820 to 1854; almost constantly Republican from 1856 to the present time (1894). In 1880 a Democratic Governor and council "counted in" a Democratic-Greenback Legislature, and for a brief period there were two bodies claiming to be Legislatures. In 1790 the population of Maine was 97,000, in 1820 298,000, in 1890 661,000.

Maine Historical Society, founded in 1822, has published several volumes.

Maine Law, a law prohibiting the sale of intoxicating liquors as a beverage, first adopted in Maine in 1851.

Malbone, Edward G. (1777–1807), born in Newport, R. I., was the most eminent painter of miniatures who has ever appeared in America. He pursued his art in Providence, Boston, New York and Philadelphia, and from 1800 in Charleston, S. C.

Malden, Upper Canada, was during the earlier part of the War of 1812 the centre of British operations against Detroit and the Northwest. After Harrison's victory on the Thames it was evacuated, October, 1813.

Mallory, Stephen R. (1813–1873), of Florida (though of New England parentage), was a Senator from Florida from 1851 to 1861. During most of this time he was chairman of the Committee on Naval Affairs. On the formation of the Confederate Government he was appointed by President Davis Secretary of the Navy, which office he held during the continuance of the Confederacy.

Malvern Hill, a battle in the Civil War, the last of the "Seven Days'" battles, July 1, 1862, by which McClellan completed his change of base to the James River. After the battle of Frayser's Farm, McClellan had retreated with his 85,000 Federal troops to Malvern Hill, a strong position on an elevated plateau shaped like an amphitheatre. His lines were securely posted behind fences, ditches and hedges, their batteries and infantry commanding the slope which the Confederates must ascend to attack them. Lee ordered an attack, which was meant to be made simultaneously by all parts of his line at a given signal, the "Confederate yell." But his lieutenants were so separated that the signal could not be heard, and the attacks were therefore feeble and disorganized. D. H. Hill and Magruder bore the brunt of the fight. Time after time they charged the impregnable Federal position, but in vain. They were always driven back with fearful slaughter. The battle lasted until nightfall. During the night McClellan retired under cover of a violent storm.

Manassas, Va., the field of two engagements during the Civil War. July 21, 1861, Johnston and Beauregard, with 31,000 Confederates, defeated 28,000 Federals under McDowell. August 29–30, Pope, Federal, with 40,000 troops, was defeated by Lee and Jackson. (See Bull Run, two battles of.)

"Mandamus Councillors," a name opprobriously applied by the revolutionary party in Massachusetts to those members of the council of the province who, in August, 1774, accepted appointment by writ of mandamus at the hands of Governor Gage. By the charter of 1691 councillors had been elected by the House of Representatives. The Massachusetts Charter Act of 1774, to punish Massachusetts, gave the Governor power to appoint them.

Mandans, a small tribe of Indians, numbering about 500, now dwelling on a reservation in Dakota. They are first heard of about 1772. They then lived on the Missouri, about 1500 miles up from its mouth. They are of light complexion, hence many vain attempts to trace their descent from the supposed Welsh colony of Prince Madoc.

Manderson, Charles F., born in 1837, was appointed colonel during the Civil War. He was elected to the U. S. Senate as a Republican from Nebraska in 1883 and 1887, serving till 1893.

Mangoaks, a tribe of Indians in North Carolina, into whose country Ralph Lane, commander of Raleigh's colony, in 1586 attempted an expedition, on information of a pearl fishery among them.

Mangum, Willie P. (1792–1861), of North Carolina, was a Representative from that State from 1823 to 1826, and Senator from 1831 to 1836 and from 1840 to 1853, serving as a Whig. In 1836 he received the electoral votes of South Carolina for the Presidency.

Manhattan, the original, apparently Indian, name of the island on which New York is now situated. In 1613 the first settlement was made, of the nature of a trading-post. In 1626 Peter Minuit, director for the Dutch West India Company, bought the island of the Indians for sixty guilders ($24).

"**Manifest Destiny,**" a cant phrase enjoying much vogue in the forties, signifying the manifest destiny of the United States to acquire complete supremacy upon the American continent. The notion, though in some aspects a patriotic and noble one, was made a cover for unscrupulous aggressions upon weaker powers, as in the case of the Mexican War.

Manley, John (1733–1793), born in England, but settled in Marblehead, Mass., was commissioned by Washington to cruise off Boston and intercept Gage's supplies, October 24, 1775. He opened the naval operations of the Revolution by capturing the "Nancy," laden with military supplies, on November 29. In 1776 he was made the second captain in the U. S. navy, and commanded the "Hancock" in 1776 and 1777, and privateers subsequently. He was twice made a prisoner. In 1782 he commanded the "Hague."

Mann, Horace (1796–1859), of Massachusetts, educator, was graduated at Brown University in 1819. From 1837 to 1848 he was secretary of the Massachusetts State Board of Education. He reformed the educational system of the State, introducing normal schools and teachers' conventions, and exerted a wide influence throughout the country in regard to educational matters. From 1848 to 1853 he was an anti-slavery Whig Congressman, and from 1853 to his death was president of Antioch College.

Manning, Daniel (1831–1887), of New York, chairman of its Democratic State Committee from 1881 to 1884, was appointed Secretary of the Treasury by President Cleveland in 1885, and served as such till 1887.

Manors, in the United States. Manors of the English type, *i. e.*, landed estates granted on such terms that the right of property carried with it rights of jurisdiction, were created in several of the colonies. In 1636 the Proprietor of Maryland ordained that every grant of 2000 acres to any man should be erected into a manor. Bohemia Manor, My Lady's Manor and Doughoregan Manor are celebrated, as also Penn Manor in Pennsylvania. Under the Duke of York Martha's Vineyard was the Manor of Tisbury. In New Netherland the Dutch West India Company erected manors for the patroons. (See Patroons, Anti-renters.)

Mansfield, J. K. F. (1803–1862), general, was commander of the Department of Washington during the earlier part of the Civil War, and was killed at Antietam.

Mansfield, William Murray, Lord (1704–1793), the most eminent of English judges, was Chief Justice of the King's Bench from 1756 to 1788. He maintained the right of Great Britain to tax the American colonies and was one of the most zealous opponents of the repeal of the Stamp Act. (See also Sommersett's Case.)

Manteo, a friendly Indian of the Roanoke region, was helpful to Raleigh's colony of 1585–86. He had visited England with Amidas and Barlow just before.

Manufactory Bank, a short-lived scheme in Massachusetts in 1740 to establish a bank by securing its issues by a mortgage on the real estate of each subscriber to the amount of his subscription. It was supported by traders and people in the rural districts and by the House of Representatives, but was opposed by a strong party. It issued £50,000 of notes and then failed.

Manufactures. American manufactures began with the making of glass at the Jamestown colony. At first the chief manufactures in the colonies were of ships, lumber and iron. Domestic manufactures continued till long after the Revolution to be an important portion, especially in the article of cloth. Soon the amount of American exports of manufactured articles was so great that English manufacturers complained. In 1699 Parliament enacted that no woolen manufactures should be shipped from the colonies. The iron manufacture was repressed by a series of laws beginning in 1719. Export of hats was forbidden in 1731, and several other similar prohibitions were enacted. The Revolution stimulated manufactures and States tried to foster them by bounties. Yet in 1789 they were still in their infancy. The country was mainly agricultural, though there were some important manufactures of heavy iron goods, paper, glass, gunpowder, rum, leather and textiles, and excellent ships were built. The slightly protective tariff of 1789 increased manufactures, the War of 1812 still more so, insomuch that in 1815 the amount of capital in the cotton and woolen industries was probably $50,000,000. After the war a great development of American manufactures began, those created by the war demanding increased protection, and receiving it in the tariffs of 1824 and 1828. Manufacturing towns arose, and American life ceased to be exclusively agricultural and rural. This development, however, was almost entirely in the North.

When the Civil War broke out, the South was almost without manufactures, while the industrial life of the North was becoming more and more varied. Since the war the manufactures of the United States have developed to such an extent that they are the leading manufacturing country of the world, and make one-fourth of its entire total of manufacturing. The amount of manufacturing done in the United States seems to have about doubled from 1880 to 1890. The history of some of the leading industries is treated in separate articles.

Marble, Manton, born in 1835, was proprietor and editor of the *New York World*, a free-trade Democratic journal, from 1862 to 1876. He has published an account of the election of 1876.

Marbois, François de Barbe-, Marquis de (1745–1837), was sent from France to the United States as secretary of legation in 1779, and remained until 1785. When appointed to cede Louisiana to the United States in 1803, he secured 30,000,000 francs more than the French administration had demanded. He wrote "Complot d'Arnold et Sir Henry Clinton contre les États-Unis d'Amérique," and "L'Histoire de la Louisiane et de la Cession."

Marbury vs. Madison. William Marbury and others, having been appointed justices of the peace in the District of Columbia by President Adams, with the consent of the Senate, and having, on President Jefferson's accession, failed to receive their respective commissions of appointment, moved the Supreme Court to issue a mandamus to James Madison, Secretary of State, commanding him to deliver their several commissions. The court decided that Marbury was legally entitled to his commission, but that the Constitution did not invest it with the authority to issue a mandamus in such a case. The rule was discharged February, 1803. Thus the court declared unconstitutional a portion of an Act of Congress, the Judiciary Act of 1789, which purported to grant such authority. This was the first important case in which the Court set aside an act of Congress because of conflict with the Constitution.

March Fourth, the day chosen for the Presidential inauguration. Its choice dates from the year 1788, that day being designated, after the ratification of the Constitution by the States, as inauguration day, by the Congress of the old Confederation. They fixed on the first Wednesday in January, 1789, for the choice of the electors; the first Wednesday in February for the voting by the electors; the first Wednesday in March (March 4 that year) for the inauguration. The Twelfth Amendment makes this the constitutional day.

March to the Sea, General Sherman's celebrated march from Atlanta to Savannah with a Union army of over 60,000 men, November 15 to December 21, 1864. Burning the Confederate shops, depots and storehouses, and leaving Thomas with two corps to look after Hood, Sherman set out with the Fifteenth, Seventeenth, Fourteenth and Twentieth corps of infantry, 5063 cavalry under Kilpatrick, 1812 artillerymen, and enormous trains of wagons and ambulances. The line of march extended nearly sixty miles through the very heart of the Confederacy, passing through Rough and Ready, Jonesboro, Covington, McDonough, Macon, Milledgeville, Gibson,

Louisville, Millen, Springfield and many smaller towns. The march was 300 miles in length. The soldiers were allowed to pillage freely, discriminating between the rich and poor. The Georgia Central Railroad was wholly destroyed, besides thousands of dollars' worth of other property. Foraging parties preceded the army, and scouts were kept constantly on the lookout for Confederate attacks. Sherman lost 764 men on the march. Savannah was captured, after some days of siege, December 21, Sherman presenting the city to Lincoln as a "Christmas present."

Marcy, Randolph B. (1812–1887), served in the Mexican War, and was brevetted major-general for services during the Civil War. From 1869 to 1881 he was inspector-general. He published "Exploration of the Red River" in 1852.

Marcy, William Larned (1786–1857), an American Cabinet officer, graduated at Brown, became a lawyer, took part in the War of 1812, and became a Democratic editor in Troy. He was one of the leaders in the "Albany Regency," and a master in political management. In 1823–1829 he was Comptroller of New York, Associate Justice of the State Supreme Court 1829–1831, and in 1831–1833 member of the U. S. Senate, where he made his famous "to the victors belong the spoils" speech. He was Governor of New York 1833–1839, Secretary of War 1845–1849, and Secretary of State 1853–1857. In the latter office he has won general regard for his able treatment of difficult international questions.

Margry, Pierre, born in 1818, made extensive investigations and valuable discoveries while archivist of the marine and colonies in Paris, concerning La Salle and explorations in the Mississippi Valley.

Mariana, a tract of country, which included a large portion of the present State of New Hampshire, granted to John Mason in 1629, by the council for New England. It extended from the Salem River to the Merrimac.

Marine, Secretary of, an office created by act of the Continental Congress, February 7, 1781, to supersede the Board of Admiralty in the supervision of naval affairs. The duties corresponded to those of the present Secretary of the Navy, with certain restrictions, but before the end of the year its duties were given to the Treasury Department.

Marine Hospital Service. In 1798 an act was passed in accordance with which twenty cents per month might be detained from the wages of all seamen, to be paid over to the collector of the ports where ships might enter on their return voyages, toward a fund for the erection of hospitals for merchant seamen. This service has been placed under the charge of the Department of the Treasury.

Marines. The United States Marine Corps was first established by Act of Congress November 10, 1775, authorizing the enlistment of two battalions to be called the "first and second battalions of marines." The Marine Corps was re-established by Act of Congress July 11, 1798. By this act the marines are at any time liable to do duty in the forts and garrisons of the United States. While enlisted they are exempt from arrest for debt or contract.

There is no regimental organization, but the corps may be formed into companies as the President directs. The marines are at all times subject to the laws and regulations of the navy. By the Act of 1874, the commander-in-chief of marines is entitled to the rank and pay of a colonel.

Marion, Francis (1732–1795), a Revolutionary general, was a South Carolinian planter, of Huguenot descent. He fought in the Cherokee War and sat in the Provincial Congress. Enlisting at the opening of the Revolution he was present at the British repulse off Charleston 1776, and took part in the unfortunate Savannah expedition of 1779. His noted period is the last three years of the war. He organized in 1780 a celebrated partisan corps, "Marion's brigade," famous for the activity of its movements, telling blows and simplicity of fare. Marion, surnamed the "Swamp-Fox," operated in the neighborhood of the Pedee River and other parts of the Carolinas. He was engaged in the capture of Fort Watson, took Georgetown, commanded the right at Eutaw Springs, and continued his harassing of the British through 1782. He was subsequently a State Senator.

Mark, a silver coin weighing eleven pennyweights six grains, offered by Morris to the Continental Congress in 1783 for consideration as a national coin, but not accepted. It was equivalent to ten of his "cents," seventy of ours. Obverse: An eye, the centre of a glory, thirteen-points cross, equidistant a circle of as many stars. Legend: Nova Constellatio. Reverse: U. S. 1.000, a wreath surrounding. Legend: Libertas. Justitia. 1783. This, with the quint, were known as the Nova Constellatio patterns.

Markham, William (1635?–1704), came from England in 1681, and was Deputy-Governor of Pennsylvania and Delaware until 1682. He was Deputy-Governor of Delaware from 1691 to 1693 and Lieutenant-Governor of Pennsylvania from 1694 to 1699.

Marmaduke, John S. (1833–1887), was promoted major-general in the Confederate service, and fought at Shiloh, Little Rock and Fort Scott. He was elected Governor of Missouri in 1884, and served till his death.

"Marmion," Case of the. Under an act of the South Carolina Legislature passed in 1822, any free negroes entering the ports of the State on ships could be imprisoned until the ship departed. This was done in the case of the "Marmion." In 1824 the Attorney-General and in 1823 the District Court of the United States rendered opinions that this law was incompatible with the Constitution and the international obligations of the United States.

Marquette, Jacques (1637–1675), one of the most noted of the "pioneers of France in the New World," was born at Laon in France, and entered the Jesuit order. In 1666 he emigrated to Canada. In the course of his missionary work among the Indians in the Great Lake region he made various explorations. He founded a mission at Sault Sainte Marie and one at Mackinaw. Marquette and Joliet, in 1673, made a long journey by canoes by way of the Illinois River to the Mississippi and down that stream to Arkansas; of this voyage Marquette has left an account in his journal. The next year he built a log hut on the site of Chicago, and thence pushed on to Kaskaskia. While laboring among the Illinois Indians his health gave way, and he died on his return to the North.

Marsh, George P. (1801–1882), represented Vermont in the U. S. Congress as a Whig from 1843 to 1849. He was Minister to Turkey from 1849 to 1853, and to Italy from 1861 to 1882, and was a distinguished scholar.

Marshall, Humphrey (1812–1872), represented Kentucky in the U. S. Congress as a Whig from 1849 to 1852, and from 1855 to 1859. He was a brigadier-general in the Confederate army and a Confederate Senator.

Marshall, James W. (1812–1885), discovered the first gold in California while superintending the construction of a mill-race in Coloma.

Marshall, John (September 24, 1755–July 6, 1835), the greatest of American jurists, was born at Germantown, Fauquier County, Va. He was deprived of a collegiate education, and was a youth when the Revolutionary War began. Young Marshall served as a regimental officer through the struggle, and fought at Brandywine, Monmouth, etc. He then applied himself to the law, entered the Virginia House of Burgesses and the council. As a member of the convention for ratifying the Federal Constitution in 1788, he contended on the Federalist side ably and successfully against the eloquence of Patrick Henry and his colleagues. With Gerry and C. C. Pinckney he was Envoy to France in 1797 at the time of Talleyrand's attempted bribery of the United States. Returning the next year he served as Congressman in 1799–1800, and as Secretary of State 1800–1801. President Adams in 1801 appointed Marshall Chief Justice of the Supreme Court, which position he held until his death. He is famous in the national annals for his great opinions defining and interpreting the Federal Constitution, and aiding to consolidate the Union. He presided over the Burr trial, and in 1829 was a member of the Virginia convention for revising the State Constitution. Marshall wrote a life of Washington in five volumes, afterward revised and condensed in two volumes. His writings were edited by Story.

Marshals. The Judiciary Act of 1789 provided for officers called marshals, whose functions with respect to the Federal courts were to be like those of sheriffs with respect to the State courts. In 1790 they were entrusted with the census enumeration, and so frequently with respect to later censuses.

Marshfield, Mass., noted as the home of Daniel Webster. He died and was buried there.

Martha's Vineyard, discovered in 1602 by Bartholomew Gosnold, who gave the name to a smaller island now called No Man's Land, whence it was transferred. Martha's Vineyard was at first called Capawak. It was settled in 1642 by Thomas Mayhew, an English merchant, who purchased the island from Lord Stirling, to whom it had been granted with other territory. Mayhew established a missionary post and made many converts among the Indians. In 1644, the island was placed under the jurisdiction of Massachusetts by the Federal Commissioners of New England. It was later transferred to New York, but was restored to Massachusetts in 1692.

Martin, François X. (1762–1846), born in France, became a printer in North Carolina, then moved to New Orleans. He was for thirty years a Judge of the Supreme Court of Louisiana, and Chief-Justice from 1837 to 1845. He wrote histories of North Carolina and Louisiana.

Martin, Luther (1744–1826), Attorney-General of Maryland, was a member of the Annapolis Convention. He was a delegate from Maryland to the Continental Congress from 1784 to 1785. He was a member of the Constitutional Convention of 1787, but opposed the adoption of the Constitution. He was counsel for defence in the trials of Judge Chase and Aaron Burr, having in his later years become a Federalist.

Martin vs. Hunter's Lessee, Virginia. In 1791 Martin brought a suit of ejectment against the defendant in the District Court of Virginia for the recovery of certain lands. This court decided for the defendant. The Court of Appeals of Virginia reversed this decision, and their judgment was in turn reversed by the Supreme Court of the United States in 1816. This judgment the Court of Appeals of Virginia refused to execute, being of the "unanimous opinion that the appellate power of the Supreme Court of the United States does not extend to this court under a sound construction of the Constitution of the United States," and "that the Act of Congress to that effect is not in pursuance of the said Constitution." The Supreme Court overruled this decision and established its prerogative upon such points.

Martling Men, in New York political history, the members of a union of Burrites and Lewisites (followers of Morgan Lewis), mostly Democrats, formed in 1807. So called because their usual place of meeting was "Martling's long room." They were connected with the Tammany Society, and were later known as Bucktails.

Maryland, one of the original thirteen States. Maryland was founded by Cecil Calvert, Lord Baltimore, a Roman Catholic, in 1634. His father, George Calvert, was a member of the London Company and Secretary of State under James I. from 1618 to 1625. He had made an unsuccessful attempt to found a colony on Newfoundland in 1621 (see Avalon) and in 1629 he had landed in Virginia with forty Catholic colonists, but they were not welcomed by the Protestants of Virginia and soon returned home. Charles I. then gave to Baltimore a charter for the land north of the Potomac River as far as the forty-first degree of latitude and to the source of the Potomac River on the west. This territory lay within the grant to Virginia. The name Maryland was given in honor of the queen, Henrietta Maria. The government of the colony was to be in the hands of the proprietor. St. Mary's, the first settlement, was founded in 1634 by two hundred colonists, many of whom were Protestants. Baltimore maintained toleration for all. But from 1691 until the Revolution the Protestants were strong enough to disfranchise the Catholics. In 1635 Clayborne, a Virginian who had a trading post on Kent Island, within the grant to Maryland, and who had been ejected by Calvert, invaded Maryland at the head of a party of rangers and obtained temporary control of the colony.—Maryland refused to ratify the Articles of Confederation which had been adopted by Congress in 1777 until March 1, 1781. The State had no western territory herself and demanded that Virginia, New York and other States should surrender their claims to lands beyond the Alleghanies to the General Government. When their intention to do this was signified by those States, Maryland ratified the articles and they became at once binding on all the States. The Constitution was adopted April 28, 1788, by a vote of sixty-three to eleven. The Federalists controlled the State until 1802. In 1812 the Hanson riots in Baltimore, caused by an attack on a Federalist newspaper office, resulted in the restoration of the State to the Federalist party. From 1820 to 1850 the State was Anti-Democratic (Whig). The American party controlled the State from 1854 to 1859. In 1860–61 the people generally were opposed to secession. The Civil War began with the Baltimore riots in 1861. From 1868 to the present time (1894) the State has been Democratic. The population of the State in 1790 was 319,728; in 1890, 1,042,390. History by Scharf.

"Maryland Gazette," earliest newspaper published in Maryland. It was established at Annapolis in 1727 by William Parks, and continued irregularly as a weekly until about 1736, when it was suspended. In 1745 another *Gazette* appeared, which, with the exception of a short suspension in 1765 on account of the Stamp Act, was published regularly during the Revolution, and still exists as a weekly journal, there being but one newspaper in the United States of prior origin. Maryland was the fourth colony in which a newspaper was established.

Maryland Historical Society was founded in 1844, and has issued many separate publications, and also the printed archives of the colony.

Maryland in Liberia, a negro colony, composed largely of Maryland free negroes, founded in Liberia in February, 1834, by the Maryland State Colonization Society, which had been organized three years before. Expeditions had been sent out and landed at Monrovia in 1831 and 1832, but these had proved unsuccessful, and the colonists were removed to Cape Palmas, where the "Maryland" settlement was finally made. This settlement was an entire success. John Russworm, a citizen of Monrovia, was chosen as the first Governor in 1836.

"Maryland Journal and Baltimore Advertiser," the third newspaper established in Maryland. It appeared in Baltimore in 1773, and together with the *Maryland Gazette* constituted the entire Revolutionary press of the State. This paper was edited and published by William Goddard. Its publication was finally suspended in 1797.

Mason, Charles (1730–1787), an English surveyor, was commissioned with Jeremiah Dixon from 1763 to 1767 to survey the boundary line between Pennsylvania and Maryland, famous as marking the boundary between the free and the slave States.

Mason, George (1725–1792), an American Revolutionary leader, was one of the great Virginians of that epoch. He drafted in 1769 the "non-importation" resolutions in the Virginia Assembly, and was one of the chief members of that body. In 1776 he drafted the Bill of Rights and the new State Constitution. He had an active part in the debates of the Federal

Convention of 1787, but refused to sign the Constitution, and went home to throw the weight of his great influence on the Anti-Federalist side in the ratifying Convention of 1788. Life by Miss K. M. Rowland.

Mason, James M. (1798–1871), Senator, was a member of the Virginia House of Delegates from 1826 to 1832. He represented Virginia in the U. S. Congress as a Jackson Democrat from 1837 to 1839. He was a U. S. Senator from 1847 to 1861. He was author of the Fugitive Slave Law of 1850. He was appointed Confederate Commissioner to England in 1861, serving till 1865. (See art. "Trent Affair.")

Mason, Jeremiah (1768–1848), was Attorney-General of New Hampshire in 1802. He was a Federalist U. S. Senator from New Hampshire from 1813 to 1817. His reappointment as president of the Portsmouth branch of the U. S. Bank caused dissatisfaction in Jackson's administration, and led to the destruction of the U. S. Bank. He was one of the most vigorous, acute and powerful advocates America has produced.

Mason, John, born in England, died in 1635. He came to Newfoundland as Governor in 1616. In 1622 he, with Sir Ferdinando Gorges, obtained a grant of the territory from the Merrimac to the Kennebec. In 1629 he secured New Hampshire (Laconia) as a separate grant.

Mason, John (1600–1672), came to America from England in 1630. He was one of the founders of Windsor, Conn., in 1635. He successfully conducted the Pequot War in 1637. He was major of the Connecticut forces from 1637 to 1672, and Deputy-Governor of Connecticut from 1660 to 1670. He published "Relation of Trouble by the Indians."

Mason, John Y. (1799–1859), represented Virginia in Congress as a Democrat from 1831 to 1837. He was Secretary of the Navy in Tyler's Cabinet from 1844 to 1845, Attorney-General in Polk's from 1845 to 1846, and Secretary of the Navy from 1846 to 1849. He was Minister to France from 1854 to 1859, and joined with Buchanan and Soulé in the Ostend Manifesto.

Mason and Dixon's Line, the boundary line between Pennsylvania and Maryland, so called from the names of the two English surveyors, Charles Mason and Jeremiah Dixon, who were employed by William Penn and Lord Baltimore to mark it off in 1766, after the settlement of the case of Penn *vs.* Baltimore. Mason and Dixon marked the line with boundary posts, having on one side the arms of Penn and on the other those of Baltimore. The line was famous as the line between free States and slave States.

Massachusetts derives its name from an Indian word meaning the "great hills," *i. e.*, the Blue Hills near Boston. The first settlement made by Gosnold on Cuttyhunk, in 1602, was a failure. The first permanent settlement was made (1620) at Plymouth, by 120 English Independents from Leyden. The colonists who came over in the "Mayflower" intended to found a settlement in Northern Virginia, and had obtained a charter from the London Company for that purpose. When forced to land in Massachusetts they signed the famous compact on board the "Mayflower," in which they agreed to abide by such laws as should be passed for the welfare of the colony. Their leaders were John Carver and William Bradford. For four years they struggled under the disadvantage of a system of communism. In 1627, the colonists purchased the financial interest of the London merchants who had advanced money for the enterprise. The colony was never able to obtain a charter from the king because of its avowed opposition to the Church of England, and in 1691 it was incorporated with Massachusetts Bay colony. The foundation of the latter colony was laid by some Dorchester merchants, who in 1623 made a settlement on Cape Ann for trading purposes. In 1626 this settlement was moved to Salem by Conant. Two years later certain leading Puritans of England obtained a grant from the Plymouth Company for the land from three miles south of the Charles River to three miles north of the Merrimac, and westward to the "South Sea." Organizing ostensibly as a trading company, they obtained a charter from Charles I. In 1630 the government of the company was moved to America, and one thousand conforming Puritans came over under Winthrop, Dudley, Higginson and Skelton, and founded Charlestown, Cambridge, Watertown, Roxbury and Boston. None but church members were allowed to vote. In 1631, upon the refusal of Watertown to pay a tax, because of no representation, the House of Representatives was formed of two members from each town. In 1644, the General Court became bicameral. Massachusetts prepared to resist by force an attack from England on her charter in 1634. Harvard College was founded (1636), and Roger Williams banished from the colony for preaching against the connection of church and State. In 1637 occurred the trouble with Anne Hutchinson and the Antinomians. In the same year the Pequods of Connecticut were crushed. In 1641 the first body of statutes, called the "Body of Liberties," was adopted. Massachusetts joined the New England confederation in 1643. In 1648 the Cambridge platform was formulated, and four years later a colonial mint was established. The first Quakers arrived in Boston in 1656, and a law was soon passed against "Quakers and Ranters." In 1674 King Philip's War broke out. The charter was revoked in 1684, and two years later Andros was sent over as royal Governor. A new charter was obtained in 1691, by which the religious qualification was abolished and the colony made a royal province, its Governor to be appointed by the crown. Witchcraft appeared at Salem and twenty persons were executed as witches in 1692. Massachusetts aided England in the French and Indian Wars, by capturing Port Royal in 1690, and Louisbourg in 1745. The boundary line with New Hampshire was settled in 1737. From 1765 to 1776, the history of the State is the history of the American Revolution. 1765: Stamp Act passed and Massachusetts issued a call for the "Stamp-Act Congress" to meet in New York. 1768: English troops were sent to Boston. 1770: "Boston Massacre." 1773: "Boston Tea-Party," when $100,000 worth of tea was destroyed. 1774: Boston port was closed by the English. The colony, being virtually deprived of her charter, organized a government of her own. 1775: April 19, battles of Lexington and Concord. June 17, battle of Bunker Hill. Massachusetts furnished, all years together, 92,563 men to the army. In 1780 a new State Constitution was adopted, which was drawn up largely by John Adams. By a judicial interpretation of the preamble of this Constitution, the institution of slavery was destroyed. In 1786 occurred Shay's Rebellion at Worcester and Springfield. A severe struggle took place over the adoption of the Federal Constitution, which was finally adopted February 6, 1788, by a vote of 187 to 168. The opponents of the Constitution were led by S. Adams, Hancock and Gerry. Its advocates were Rufus King, Theophilus Parsons and Fisher Ames. The State was usually kept Federalist until 1823 by the ability of the Federalist leaders and her large commercial interests, injured by the foreign policy of the Democrats. The Embargo Act caused great indignation in the State. It was opposed to the War of 1812, and in 1814 sent representatives to the Hartford Convention. In 1820 Maine became a separate State. In 1823 the Democrats came into power permanently, and the Federalists became extinct. From this time Massachusetts allied herself with Pennsylvania, Kentucky, Louisiana and other States in the support of a protective tariff. This change was caused by the growth of her manufacturing industries. In 1833 the Congregationalist church was dis-established. Davis, a Whig, was elected Governor in 1834. In 1839 Morton was elected Governor by the Democrats by a majority of two. The State cast a large vote for the candidates of the Liberty party in 1844 and 1845, and for those of the Free-Soil party in 1848 and 1849. In 1850, by a coalition of Democrats and Free-Soilers, the latter secured the election of Charles Sumner as U. S. Senator. The Republicans controlled the State from 1856 to 1874. In 1878 B. F. Butler was elected Governor by the discontented Democrats and the Greenback party. The Democrats elected the Governor in the years 1882, 1890, 1891 and 1892. The State is uniformly Republican in Presidential elections. The population of Massachusetts in 1790 was 378,787; in 1840, 737,699; in 1890, 2,238,943. History by Barry.

Massachusetts Company. On March 19, 1628, there was granted to six patentees, of whom John Humphrey and John Endicott were destined to be most prominent, territory extending from the Atlantic to the Western Ocean, and in width from a line running three miles north of the Merrimac to one running three miles south of the Charles. This was the Massachusetts Bay Company. Endicott was sent over the same year and effected a settlement at Naumkeag, or Salem, September 6. March 4, 1629, a charter was granted to the Governor and Company of Massachusetts Bay, and under this instrument Massachusetts conducted her affairs for fifty-five years. The colony was ruled by the Governor and thirteen councillors. The charter was transferred from England to America with Winthrop.

Massachusetts Historical Society, the first historical association established in the United States. It was organized at Boston in 1791 "to collect, preserve and communicate materials for a complete history of the country." It has published fifty-six volumes of "Collections" and twenty-one of "Proceedings," upon a great variety of historical subjects. Since the establishment of this association, students of history in many of the other States have founded similar societies.

Massachusetts Indians, at the time of the English settlement of the State, were composed of five Algonquin tribes, recently decimated by pestilence. The Nipmucks occupied central Massachusetts, the Pennacooks what is now New Hampshire, the Massachusetts the lands around Massachusetts

Bay, the Nausets Cape Cod, while the Pokanokets lived in the south-eastern portion of the State. All except the Nausets were friendly to the settlers, and this tribe entered into a peace with the Plymouth colonists. Missions were begun on Martha's Vineyard in 1644, and in 1651 Indian converts under John Eliot were gathered at Natick. The converts were termed Praying Indians. At length discontent arose which in 1675 led to King Philip's War.

"**Massachusetts Spy**," founded at Boston, August 1, 1770. This newspaper was established to support the Whig element in the New England colonies in opposition to the *Boston Chronicle*, which favored the British Government. It was edited by Isaiah Thomas, and was suspended in six months for a time, but was begun again and removed to Worcester. Contributions were at first made by members of both political parties, but its sympathies were so evidently revolutionary that the royalist writers withdrew. Notable among the contributions concerning political questions were those signed "Centinel," "Leonidas" and "Mucius Scævola." It is still published daily and weekly.

Massasoit (1580?–1660), chief of the Wampanoag Indians, made a treaty of peace and mutual protection with the Plymouth colony in 1621, which was kept for over fifty years. He resided in what is now the town of Warren, R. I. He was always friendly to the colonists, and warned them of intended Indian attacks. He was father of King Philip.

Mather, Cotton (1663–1728), graduated from Harvard before he was sixteen years old. He was active in urging on the witchcraft persecutions. He wrote much against intemperance, and in every way aimed at being useful to society, but was exceedingly meddlesome, pedantic and conceited. He was probably the most learned man in America at the time in which he lived, having a wide acquaintance with books and foreign languages. His works number 382. The chief is his "Magnalia Christi Americana," a church history of New England, published in 1702.

Mather, Increase (1639–1723), was pastor of the North Church, Boston, from 1664 till his death. He was prominent both in church and State. He was opposed to the "half-way covenant," and secured the summoning of the synods of 1679 and 1680. He zealously opposed the surrender of the Massachusetts charter to Charles II. in 1683, and secured a new charter for the colony in 1688. He was president of Harvard College from 1685 to 1701. He wrote a life of Reverend Richard Mather, "A History of the War with the Indians," and many other works.

Mather, Richard (1596–1669), came to Massachusetts from England in 1635. He was pastor of the church in Dorchester from 1636 till his death. He drew up the celebrated "Cambridge Platform" of church discipline, aided in making the New England version of the Psalms, and published an elaborate defence of the New England churches. He was an able and a powerful preacher.

Matthews, Stanley (1824–1889), commanded a brigade at Murfreesboro, Chickamauga and Lookout Mountain in the Civil War. He represented

Ohio in the U. S. Senate as a Republican from 1877 to 1879. He was a Justice of the U. S. Supreme Court from 1881 to 1889.

Maurepas, Jean F. P., Comte de (1701–1781), was French Minister of State from 1738 to 1749 and from 1774 to 1781. He aided in negotiating the treaty of alliance with the United States in 1778.

Maury, Matthew F. (1806–1873), naval officer, wrote a famous "Physical Geography of the Seas." In 1861 he commanded in the Confederate navy, and afterward was Confederate Commissioner in Europe.

Maxey, Samuel B., born in 1825, served during the Mexican War, and was made major-general in the Confederate service. He represented Texas in the U. S. Senate as a Democrat, from 1875 to 1887.

Maximilian, (Ferdinand Max. Joseph) (1832–1867), Archduke of Austria, became prominent for his enlightened administration of the Lombardo-Venetian kingdom. In 1863 France called an assembly of notables in Mexico, which approved a monarchical form of government and offered the crown of Mexico to Maximilian. He became emperor in 1864, but his reign was disturbed by a powerful republican faction. He was able to maintain his position only by aid of French troops, which were withdrawn at the solicitation of the United States. Maximilian was soon afterward deposed and shot.

"Mayflower" Compact, the compact made by the Pilgrim Fathers in the cabin of the "Mayflower," in Provincetown harbor, November 11, 1620, whereby, before landing, they bound themselves into a "civil body politic," and promised obedience to the laws they should make as such.

Maynard, Horace (1814–1882), represented Tennessee in the U. S. Congress as an American and Republican from 1857 to 1863 and from 1866 to 1875. He was Minister to Russia from 1875 to 1880. He was Postmaster-General in Hayes' Cabinet from 1880 to 1881.

Mazzei Letter, a private business letter written by Thomas Jefferson to an Italian named Mazzei in 1796. The paragraph therein contained, to the effect that "an Anglican monarchical aristocratical party" had sprung up in America, whose avowed object was "to draw over us the substance, as they had already done the forms, of the British Government," did much toward arousing animosity against Jefferson, when the letter became public property in 1797. It had been translated into Italian, then into French, and finally appeared in an English paper. An allusion in it to men who had been "Samsons in the field and Solomons in the council" was construed as an attack on Washington.

Meade, George Gordon (1815–1872), a Federal general in the Civil War, graduated at West Point in 1835, fought in the Mexican War and against the Seminoles, and was busy in the surveying department. Soon after the Rebellion had commenced, he was assigned to a brigade in the Army of the Potomac, was wounded in the Seven Days' battles, and fought at the second battle of Bull Run. At Antietam and Fredericksburg he commanded a division, and at Chancellorsville a corps. At the end of June, 1863, Meade was appointed to supersede Hooker in command of the Army of the Potomac; Lee's great invasion of the North was in progress, and Meade was near Frederick. Almost immediately afterward occurred the battle of Gettysburg (which see). The chief credit for this decisive Union victory is variously claimed for the commander-in-chief, for Hancock, Howard, Reynolds and other corps commanders; Meade arrived on the battlefield about noon of the second day. He was made brigadier-general in the regular army, and the next year major-general. Under Grant in 1864–65 he was in immediate charge of the Army of the Potomac, and after the war held command of different departments.

Meagher, Thomas F. (1823–1867), was banished from Ireland in 1849 for political reasons, and came to the United States in 1852. He commanded a New York brigade at Manassas, Antietam and Fredericksburg.

Mechanicsville, Va., a battle of the Civil War occurring June 26, 1862, during McClellan's attempted approach to Richmond. Lee crossed the Chickahominy with 35,000 Confederates, intending to join Jackson's 25,000 troops and demolish Porter's command of 20,000 of McClellan's troops and cut off the latter's communications with his base. Jackson was for once late in arriving, and Richmond was for a time in considerable danger. A. P. Hill's division advanced first and encountered at Mechanicsville a small force of Confederates, who were dispersed. Just beyond the town McCall was drawn up with a strong force on Beaver Dam Creek. The Confederates attempted to turn McCall's flanks, but were repulsed with great loss each time.

Mecklenburg Declaration. It has been vigorously affirmed and vigorously denied that, on May 20, 1775, a convention of the inhabitants of Mecklenburg County, North Carolina, passed resolutions in favor of independence from Great Britain, and actually declaring the independence of Mecklenburg County. The declaration first became generally known in 1818. It was alleged, however, that the original documents were destroyed by fire in 1800. The probability is that the story arises from action taken on May 31, 1775, when resolutions were passed importing resistance to the royal governor, but not independence.

Mecklenburg-Schwerin. Mecklenburg-Schwerin acceded to the commercial treaty between the United States and Hanover in 1846 and to the German extradition treaty in 1853.

Mecklenburg-Strelitz. Mecklenburg-Strelitz acceded to the extradition treaty between Germany and the United States in 1853.

Medary, Samuel (1801–1864), founded the *Ohio Statesman*, a powerful Democratic paper, and edited it until 1858. He is said to have originated the campaign cry, "Fifty-four forty or fight."

Mediterranean Fund. In 1801–02 the wars with the Barbary pirates necessitated a slight increase in import duties, and the money thus accruing was termed the "Mediterranean Fund." This was made a basis for the increase of protection in the tariff levied in 1816.

STATESMEN OF THE CIVIL WAR PERIOD.

Horace Greeley.
Thaddeus Stevens.
Henry Wilson.
Edwin M. Stanton.
Horatio Seymour.
Thurlow Weed.
B. F. Wade.
Wm. H. Seward.

Meigs, Montgomery C., born in 1816, was superintending engineer in the construction of Forts Wayne, Porter, Niagara, Ontario and Montgomery. He was quartermaster-general of the U. S. army from 1861 to 1882, when he retired.

Meigs, Return Jonathan (1734–1823), was a major in Arnold's expedition to Quebec in 1775. At Sag Harbor in 1777 he took ninety prisoners, destroyed twelve ships and much forage without the loss of a man. He commanded a regiment at Stony Point.

Meigs, Return Jonathan, Jr. (1765–1825), represented Ohio in the U. S. Senate as a Democrat from 1809 to 1810. He was Governor of Ohio from 1810 to 1814. He was Postmaster-General from 1814 to 1823 in the Cabinets of Madison and Monroe.

Meigs, Fort (War of 1812). After the massacre at the River Raisin, the main body of Americans entrenched themselves on the Maumee, building the fort. Here they were besieged, April 26, 1813, by more than 2000 British and Indians, commanded by General Procter and the chief Tecumtha. On May 5 General Clay arrived with reinforcements for the Americans. Of these 800 attacked the British batteries, and the rest tried to cut their way through the enemy. The batteries were taken, but recaptured by the British, the Americans losing all of the 800 but 170 who escaped to Fort Meigs. The other detachment, aided by timely sorties from the fort, defeated the force opposed to them and thus broke up the siege. The Indian allies deserted the British, who returned to Canada.

Melville, George W., born in 1841, became chief engineer of the De Long Arctic expedition in 1879, and commanded the only party which survived the expedition. He was made a chief engineer in the U. S. navy in 1881.

Melville, Herman (1819–1891), deserted from a whaling vessel in the Marquesas Islands, and spent several months among the Typees. His novels and accounts of his adventures were very popular.

Memminger, Charles G. (1803–1888), born in Germany, settled in South Carolina. He was Secretary of the Treasury in the government of the Confederate States.

Memphis, Tenn., was laid out as a village in 1820 and incorporated in 1831. During the Civil War it was early held by the Confederates with a fleet of eight vessels under Commodore Montgomery. It was rendered defenceless and captured by the Federals June 6, 1862. Commodore Davis left Fort Pillow June 4, with nine Union vessels, and proceeded at once to Memphis, before which the Confederate fleet lay. An attack upon these ships was immediately begun. Four ram-boats under the Union commander, Ellet, joined Davis and did much toward destroying the Confederate fleet. Several of the Confederate ships had their boilers shot through and their crews scalded to death. Their fleet was utterly demolished. During 1870–80 the city was ravaged by yellow fever.

Menendez de Avilés, Pedro (d. 1574), Spanish commander, in 1565 founded St. Augustine, Fla., and destroyed the French Huguenot settlement at Port Royal.

Mennonites, a sect that sprang up in Holland and Germany about the time of the Reformation, through the influence of Simon Menno. In doctrine they are allied to the Baptists. Members of this body came to this country as early as 1683, and by invitation of William Penn settled in Pennsylvania. In 1727 they published a Confession of Faith. In this country there are several varieties of Mennonites, differing mainly in externals, and numbering in all about 60,000 members.

Menomonees, a tribe of Algonquin Indians, were unfriendly to the English, but took sides against the colonists during the Revolution. In 1812 also they allied themselves with the British, taking part in several engagements. Treaties were made in 1817, 1825, and 1827. In 1831 they began to cede their lands around Green Bay and Lake Michigan. They aided the Government in the Sac and Fox War and in the Rebellion.

Mercer, Hugh (1720?–1777), came to America from Scotland in 1747. He served in the French and Indian War. He was chosen brigadier-general in 1776, with command of the flying camp. He commanded a column at Trenton and led the advance at Princeton, where he was surrounded by the British and fought to the death rather than surrender.

Mercer, John F. (1759–1821), served during the Revolution. He represented Virginia in the Continental Congress from 1782 to 1785. He was a U. S. Congressman from Maryland from 1792 to 1794, and Governor of Maryland from 1801 to 1803.

Mercer, Fort, Capture of, November, 1777. Fort Mercer, on the Jersey shore of the Delaware, below Philadelphia, with Fort Mifflin opposite, commanded the stream. To ensure his supplies, Howe attempted to carry the forts October 22. He lost 400 Hessian troops and their commander, Donop; American loss, thirty-seven. After a month's hard work, assisted by 6000 men from New York, he carried the works and wrested control of the Delaware from the Americans.

Merchant Marine. In early colonial times American shipbuilders and merchants became such dangerous commercial competitors, from the superiority of their ships and the greater efficiency of their sailors, that the British Government, by the Navigation Acts, beginning in 1645, prohibited importation into the colonies except in English or colonial-built vessels. While the Navigation Acts restricted trade, they fostered shipbuilding. The merchant marine continued to thrive after the Revolution. Between 1789 and 1797 the registered tonnage increased 384 per cent, owing chiefly to the general state of war in Europe and the consequent increase in carrying trade. From 1837 to 1847 the tonnage rose from 810,000 to 1,241,000, to 2,268,000 in 1857, and culminated with 2,496,000 tons in 1861. The maximum tonnage of the United States at any one time registered and enrolled (or engaged in foreign and domestic trade), and in the fisheries, was in 1861, reaching 5,539,813 tons. It thus nearly equaled the tonnage of the whole of the rest of the maritime world, excepting Great Britain, whose tonnage was slightly greater. But since this time, from various causes, the American merchant marine service has declined until it is now wholly insignificant. This is due largely to the fact that, when iron and steam vessels began to be used, the facilities for constructing them were limited, and the navigation laws prohibited merchants from taking advantage of British superiority in construction. Income taxes and heavy taxes on gross receipts, especially since the Civil War, have greatly handicapped shipowners. The coastwise trade, too, has fallen largely into the hands of foreigners.

Meredith, William M. (1799–1873), was Secretary of the Treasury in Taylor's Cabinet from 1849 to 1850. He was Attorney-General of Pennsylvania from 1861 to 1867, and president of the Pennsylvania Constitutional Convention of 1873.

Merry Mount, a settlement on Massachusetts Bay instituted by Thomas Morton and a band of unruly followers shortly after the landing of the Pilgrims (1625). In 1628 John Endicott, one of the six patentees of the Bay colony, visited the Merry Mount settlement and broke it up by force, "caused their May-pole to be cut down, rebuked them for their profaneness, admonished them to look there should be better walking." Morton was in England at that time.

Merryman's Case, a case before the U. S. Supreme Court. The petitioner was arrested at his home in Maryland, in 1861, for treason, by order of a major-general of the National army. He was imprisoned at Fort McHenry, Baltimore. Chief Justice Taney, of the Supreme Court of the United States, granted a writ of *habeas corpus*, which the officer in charge at Fort McHenry refused to execute, on the ground that the President had suspended the writ of *habeas corpus*. The majority of the court decided that no such power was vested in the President, Congress alone having such privilege; that a military officer has no right to arrest a person not subject to the rules and articles of war, except in the aid of judicial authority.

Message, a written communication to Congress by the President. Regular messages are sent at the opening of each session of Congress; special messages, whenever an occasion for them arises. During the administrations of Washington and John Adams the messages were delivered orally by the President to the two Houses assembled together. From Jefferson's time they have been delivered in writing through the President's private secretary, and then printed for distribution.

Methodist Episcopal Church. This denomination first assumed its present name at the conference held 1784. Previous to that time the scattered followers of this belief had met in *societies*, like those established in Great Britain by Rev. John Wesley. At the same conference the church was organized for missionary and pioneer work under charge of bishops sent to this country by Mr. Wesley, who was recognized as the spiritual father of the denomination. Its success during the next few years was remarkable. The zeal and energy of its preachers and the work of the lay members brought about within sixteen years an increase of membership and preachers almost fourfold. This church was the first officially to acknowledge the U. S. Constitution, and was very active in every anti-slavery movement. The first session of its general conference was held in 1812, at which time the membership was about 195,000. In 1843 the anti-slavery party in the church withdrew in dissatisfaction and founded the Wesleyan Methodist connection. Two years later the Southern Methodists, dissatisfied in their turn, seceded and formed the Methodist Episcopal Church South. The Northern church, however, maintained its power and now has one and a half million members. In literature, education and mission work it has always displayed great energy. In 1890 it numbered 2,240,000 members.

Methodist Episcopal Church South. This body was identified with the main Methodist body till the slavery question caused a secession. The rules of the church forbade any preacher to own slaves. This especially irritated the South, and when in 1844 Bishop Andrews, of Georgia, came into possession of slaves by marriage, the question was so bitterly discussed that the year following the Southern churches seceded with nearly a half million members. The war greatly hindered the progress of the new church, but since that time it has made rapid progress, and has greatly aided in missionary work in the border States and destitute parts of the South. Number of members in 1890, 1,210,000.

Methodist Protestant Church is the name assumed by a body that seceded from the Methodist Episcopal Church in 1830. The sect differs from its parent church mainly in ecclesiastical government. They abolish the episcopal office and admit the laity to an equal participation with the clergy in administration and government. The slavery question divided this denomination, and both wings are growing slowly, but now are practically one in work and aims. Number of members in 1890, 142,000.

Metric System. This system was legalized by Act of Congress in July, 1866; and in 1873 and 1876 appropriations were made for procuring metric standards for the States and for the construction and verification of standard weights and measures for the custom house and the several States.

Mexican War, April, 1846, to September, 1847. The cause of the war was the revolt of Texas from Mexico and the subsequent annexation of that State to the Union in 1845. Not only had Texas revolted, but she claimed and carried into the Union with her a far more extended territory than had been accorded in the original Mexican arrangements. In November of 1845, President Polk sent Slidell, a member of Congress from the South, to Mexico to treat with President Herrera concerning some indemnity for Texas and also to negotiate for California. Slidell was not received, for Paredes, the soldier, had succeeded Herrera. Polk at once ordered General Zachary Taylor, then commanding the army, to advance through the disputed territory and take a position on the left bank of the Rio Grande River. Here, near Matamoras, April 23, 1846, he was attacked by the Mexicans under Arista, and a portion of his forces were captured. While Taylor struck Mexico General Kearney marched into New Mexico, conquered the whole country, raised the United States flag, and, sending Doniphan to join Wool at Chihuahua, he proceeded to California, which was speedily conquered, chiefly through the efforts of Lieutenant Frémont. Scott now assumed command of the army in Mexico, but Taylor continued to command in the North. Taylor fortified himself at Corpus Christi for a time in the defence of Texas, but later advanced into the heart of Mexico, leaving a garrison at Fort Brown opposite Matamoras. This place was afterward bravely defended by Major Brown. The battle of Palo Alto was the first great battle of the war, occurring May 8, 1846. The Mexicans under Ampudia and Arista were defeated. Then followed in quick succession the battles of Resaca de la Palma, Buena Vista and a number of lesser fights, all disastrous to the Mexican cause. Thus Taylor penetrated into northern Mexico. Then Scott landed at Vera Cruz and marched on the Mexican capital. Santa Anna, the Mexican general, was badly defeated at the battles of Cerro Gordo, Contreras and Churubusco. Finally, General Scott, after a series of brilliant victories, marched on the city of Mexico, arriving in August, 1847. After detailed operations of siege and bombardment, which terminated in the Mexican defeat at Molino del Rey, September 7 and 8, and a final scathing bombardment, the capital surrendered September 14, thus terminating the war. The war was plainly one of unjust aggression on a minor power, with the object of winning more territory for new slave States.

Mexico. The independence of Mexico was recognized by the United States in March, 1822. A treaty of limits was signed in 1828, with additional articles in 1831 and 1835 and a commercial treaty in 1831. The war of 1846 was caused by Mexico's resentment over the annexation of Texas by the United States. After a succession of victories the United States obtained in February, 1848, the treaty of Guadalupe Hidalgo, by which Mexico ceded California, Utah, Arizona and New Mexico to the United States in consideration of a payment of $15,000,000 by the United States and the assumption of $3,000,000 of unsettled claims against Mexico which were paid by the U. S. Government in 1851. By the Gadsden Treaty of 1853 a half million of square miles of territory were added to the United States, and rights of transit over the Isthmus of Tehuantepec. In 1861 an extradition treaty was concluded, and in 1868 a naturalization convention and a convention for the establishment of a claims commission. Claims against Mexico were finally allowed to the amount of about $4,000,000, and against the United States to the amount of about $150,000. A reciprocity convention was concluded in 1883, but is not in operation owing to a failure of the necessary legislation. The boundary between Mexico and the United States was fixed by the Convention of 1884.

Mexico, City of. By the fights of Contreras, Churubusco, Molino del Rey and Chapultepec, Scott's forces approached closer and closer to the capital. As a sequel of the last-named fight, he was in possession of two of the gates on the evening of September 13, 1847. Next morning, the officials of the republic having fled, the authorities of the city surrendered unconditionally. Scott made a triumphal entry into the city, unopposed by any organized resistance.

Miantonomo, sachem of the Narragansett Indians, died in 1643. He concluded an alliance with Massachusetts in 1636 and aided in the Pequot War. He deeded the present site of Providence to Roger Williams.

Michigan, a State of the American Union, was formed from the Northwest Territory. It was first explored and settled by the French. Marquette in 1668 established a mission at Sault Ste. Marie. In 1701 Detroit was founded. In 1763 the French surrendered their claims to the English, who in 1783 surrendered it to the United States, although actual possession was not given until 1796. In 1787 Michigan was included in the Northwest Territory which was organized by the ordinance of that year. In 1805 it was created a separate territory. During the War of 1812 the inhabitants suffered from the English. A boundary dispute with Ohio was settled in favor of that State by the Act of Congress of 1836, which provided for the admission of Michigan. The inhabitants accepted the conditions, and Michigan became a State January 26, 1837. Except in the year 1840 the State was Democratic until 1856, since which time it has been Republican in Presidential elections. The "Maine Liquor Law" was passed in 1855 and repealed in 1875. In 1840 Michigan had a population of 212,267, in 1890 2,093,889. The present Constitution was made in 1850. History by Cooley.

Michigan, Historical Society of, founded in 1874. It published three volumes of "Pioneer Collections," between 1877 and 1880.

Michigan, University of, Ann Arbor. Its founding is due to grants of land made by Congress. First opened to students 1842. It was the first State university to attain high distinction. Its school of medicine was established in 1850, its law school in 1859, its school of homœopathy in 1875.

Middlebury College, Middlebury, Vt., was chartered in 1800, by Congregationalists.

Middleton, Arthur (1742–1787), aided in framing the South Carolina Constitution in 1776. He represented South Carolina in the Continental Congress from 1776 to 1778, and signed the Declaration of Independence. He served during the Revolutionary War, and was a member of the Continental Congress from 1781 to 1783. He was author of several influential political essays signed "Andrew Marvell."

Midnight Appointments, official appointments of sixteen circuit judges and other inferior officers made by John Adams during the last three weeks of his Presidential term, many of the papers being signed just before midnight of March 3, 1801. These appointments were made in a spirit of pique at Jefferson's success, and the officers chosen were in every instance Federalists, bitterly opposed to Jefferson's principles.

Mifflin, Thomas (1744–1800), had served in the Pennsylvania Legislature before he entered the first Continental Congress. In the war he was at first aide-de-camp to Washington, and then quartermaster-general. He covered the retreat of the army in the evacuation of Brooklyn in 1776, and soon afterward was appointed major-general and a member of the Board of War. With Conway and Gates he was associated in the intrigues against Washington, and in 1778 he was retired from the office of quartermaster-general. He was president of Congress in 1783, member of the Federal Convention of 1787, and a signer of the Constitution. He was Governor of Pennsylvania from 1790 to 1799.

Mifflin, Fort. Fort Mifflin, on an island in the Delaware and, with Fort Mercer, commanding the stream, was captured by the British in the latter part of November, 1777. (See Mercer, Fort.)

Milan Decree, a decree issued by Napoleon December 7, 1807, in which he declared to be "denationalized," whether found in Continental ports or on the high seas, any vessel which should submit to search by a British vessel, or should touch or set sail for or from Great Britain or her colonies. This was in retort to the British Orders in Council of November 11, 1807, which declared, among their provisions, any vessel and cargo good prize if it carried a French consular certificate of the origin of the cargo.

Mileage. The First Congress provided that each member should receive, beside his pay, six dollars for each twenty miles traveled in going and returning. In 1818 this was raised to eight dollars. An act of 1856 limited this to two sessions. In 1866, the railroad having long since come in, the mileage was reduced to twenty cents a mile.

Miles, Nelson A., born in 1839, was distinguished at Fair Oaks and Malvern, commanded a brigade at the Wilderness, Spottsylvania and Fredericksburg. He has since been successful in the Western Indian campaigns, and in 1890 became a major-general in the U. S. army.

Military Academy. This academy was established at West Point, in New York State, in 1802, and is connected with and under the supervision of the National War Department. At first provision was made for only ten cadets, but in 1812 Congress authorized provision for 250. The present corps of cadets consists of one from each Congressional district, one from each territory, one from the District of Columbia and ten from the United States at large. Most of the leading generals of the Civil War, on both sides, were graduates of West Point.

Militia. The Constitution empowers Congress to "provide for calling forth the militia to execute the laws of the Union, suppress insurrections and repel invasions." In 1792 an act was passed "to provide for the national defence by establishing a uniform militia throughout the United States," by the enrollment of "every free able-bodied white male citizen," between the ages of eighteen and forty-five. The Act of March 2, 1867, permitted the enrolling of negroes. In 1862, the length of time for which the militia might be called out was fixed at nine months. The militia has been called out three times: in 1794, at the time of the Whisky Insurrection in Pennsylvania; during the War of 1812, and in 1861 during the Civil War.

Mill at Newport, an ancient stone structure at Newport, R. I. When and by whom it was constructed is still a disputed question. Former antiquarians have proclaimed it the work of Northmen of the eleventh century. But more recent investigations have quite satisfactorily proved it to have been a windmill erected by Governor Arnold, of Rhode Island, some time between 1670 and 1680. The design corresponds to that of a mill in Chesterton, England.

Mill Springs, or Fishing Creek, Ky. Here General Crittenden, commanding 5000 Confederates, was defeated by General Thomas and a Union army of 8000, January 19, 1862. Crittenden planned a night attack, which miscarried, owing to Thomas' strong position. The Confederates made a desperate charge, but were repulsed by an Ohio regiment and took refuge in an intrenched camp. General Zollicoffer, Confederate, was killed.

Mill-boy of the Slashes, a designation applied to Henry Clay, who was born in humble circumstances in the portion of Hanover County, Virginia, known as the "Slashes," and, like other farm-boys, used to ride to mill.

Miller, Cincinnatus H. (**Joaquin**), born in 1841, was a Western adventurer until 1866, when he became judge of Grant County, Ore., and served till 1870. He has published several poetical and prose works, among them "Songs of the Sierras."

Miller, James (1776–1851), entered the army as major in 1810. He commanded at Brownstown in 1812, and fought at Fort George, Chippewa and Lundy's Lane. He was Governor of Arkansas from 1819 to 1825.

Miller, Samuel F. (1816–1890), was an ardent anti-slavery advocate and a Republican leader in Iowa. He was a Justice of the U. S. Supreme Court from 1862 to 1890, and was regarded by many as its leading member.

Miller, Warner, born in 1838, was a member of the New York Legislature from 1874 to 1878. He represented New York in the U. S. Congress as a Republican from 1878 to 1881, and in the Senate from 1881 to 1887.

Miller, William (1782–1849), born in Massachusetts, served on the Canadian frontier in 1812. He proclaimed that the coming of Christ would occur in 1843, and founded the sect of "Millerites," or "Adventists."

Miller, William H. H., born in 1841, became a law-partner with General B. Harrison in 1874. He was Attorney-General in Harrison's Cabinet from 1889 to 1893.

Milligan's Case, a case decided by the U. S. Supreme Court in 1866. This case involved the right of a citizen to demand a writ of *habeas corpus* under particular circumstances. In October, 1864, during the Civil War, Milligan was brought before a military commission convened at Indianapolis by General Hovey. He was tried and sentenced to death for participation in rebellious schemes. By the Habeas Corpus Act of Congress, 1863, lists were to be furnished in each State of persons suspected of violating national laws. But any such persons, arrested and no indictment found against them by the Circuit Court, should be freed on petition verified by oath. Milligan was not indicted by the Circuit Court. He objected to the authority of the military commission and sued for a writ of *habeas corpus* in the Circuit Court. There was a division of opinion and the case came before the Supreme Court in 1866. That body decided that the writ should be issued and the prisoner discharged. Regarding the military commission, it was maintained that such power of erecting military jurisdictions remote from the seat of war was not vested in Congress, and that it could not be exercised in this particular case; that the prisoner, a civilian, was exempt from the laws of war and could only be tried by a jury; and finally, that the writ of *habeas corpus* could not be suspended constitutionally, though the privilege of that writ might be.

Milliken's Bend, La. In this engagement of the Civil War, a colored regiment which lay in intrenchments commanded by the Union General Dennis, was destroyed, June 6 and 7, 1863, by 2500 Confederates led by Henry McCulloch.

Mills, Robert (1781–1855), of South Carolina, was architect of the General Post-Office, Treasury and Patent-Office buildings at Washington. He made the original design of the Washington Monument.

Mills, Roger Q., born in 1832, was a member of the Texas Legislature in 1859 and 1860. He represented Texas in the U. S. Congress as a Democrat from 1873 to 1892, when he was elected to the U. S. Senate. When chairman of the Ways and Means Committee from 1887 to 1889, he drafted the Mills bill, making marked reductions in the tariff.

Milwaukee, Wis., dates its development from 1833, before which time it was known only as an Indian trading post, occupied by Solomon Juneau, who is generally regarded as the founder of the city. He settled there in 1818.

Mims, Fort, Ala., thirty-five miles above Mobile, on the Alabama River. August 21, 1813, this fort, then held by some 500 men, women and children, whites, half-breeds, Indians and negroes, and commanded by two half-breeds, Beasley and Bailey, was attacked by 800 Creek warriors, led by McQueen and Weathersford, two half-breeds. The fort was completely taken by surprise and could offer little resistance. Beasley and Bailey and over 200 others were scalped, but the negroes were saved for slaves.

Mining. The early land grants to corporations and individuals reserved a certain per cent of all minerals which might be discovered therein, to the crown. The Congress of the Confederation also passed a law to a somewhat similar effect. By an Act of 1807 the President was authorized to lease lands containing minerals, but this method was found ineffectual because of the immense number of illegal entries. This was especially noticeable in the Lake Superior copper district. The Acts of 1846 and 1847 authorized the sale of mineral lands in Arkansas, Illinois, Iowa, Wisconsin and Michigan and granted the right of pre-emption, though not on the same basis as in the case of non-mineral public lands. In 1847–48 the discovery of gold in California caused great excitement. Thousands of miners entered upon the public lands and took the Government so by surprise that during twenty years they remained in undisturbed possession. Gold mining began in Arizona in 1850, in Oregon in 1852, in Colorado in 1859, in Idaho and Montana in 1860. The first mining was the "gulch" and "placer," and these "placer" miners adopted regulations of their own which afterward were recognized by the Government as ruling the distribution of claims, so long as they did not interfere with the Government requirements. A great many laws have been passed to govern the distribution of mines and mining lands. This distribution is now ruled by the ordinary common-law right to the surface and all beneath it, *plus* a certain addition and *minus* a certain deduction, the addition being the right of the locator to follow veins of which his land contains the apex, downward, between the end planes of his location, into his neighbor's land; and the deduction being a similar right possessed by the adjoining neighbor.

Mining District. In 1849 the great rush for the mineral belts of the Sierra Nevada and the Rocky Mountains occurred. In 1866 there were 500 organized districts in California, 200 in Nevada, 100 each in Arizona, Idaho and Oregon. These districts were created and organized by "all the free-men of the camp," who elected officers and clothed them with authority to enforce the laws they ordained. These laws were, as a rule, obeyed in the strictest sense.

Minisink, N. Y. During 1779 constant raids were made by the British and Indians along the border settlements of New York. On the night of July 19, 1779, Brant, an Indian chief, commanding a force of 160 miscellaneous troops, descended upon Minisink, a village in Ulster County. The citizens of Goshen, 120 strong, under Colonel Hathorn, went in pursuit. They were completely cut to pieces and Minisink was raided, though Sullivan's army of 2312 men was not far away.

Minneapolis, Minn., was incorporated as a city in 1867. In 1872 the city of St. Anthony, incorporated in 1860, was united to Minneapolis.

Minnesota, a State of the Union, was formed partly from the Northwest Territory and partly from the Louisiana Purchase. In 1678 Duluth visited the territory, and in 1680 Hennepin discovered and named the Falls of St. Anthony. In 1763 France ceded the eastern part to England, by whom it was ceded to the United States in 1783; the rest was acquired in 1803. Settlements were made near St. Paul by 1830, and at Stillwater in 1843. Minnesota was organized as a territory in 1849, and included the modern territory of the Dakotas. It had been a part of the territory of Missouri, and later of Iowa. May 11, 1858, Minnesota became a State. In 1862 serious attacks were made by the Sioux Indians. The State has always been Republican. Its present Constitution was made in 1857. The population of the State in 1860 was 172,023; in 1890 it was 1,301,826. History by Neill.

Minnesota, Historical Society of, founded in 1849. It published a volume of "Annals" in 1856. A considerable portion of its collections was lost by fire in 1881.

"**Minnesota Register**," the first newspaper of any importance issued in Minnesota. It was printed at Cincinnati and dated St. Paul. McLean and Owens edited and published this journal. In August, 1849, it was consolidated with the *Chronicle*, and was then called the *Chronicle and Register*. Its publication was continued until 1851, and since that time has been suspended.

Mints. The first U. S. mint was established at Philadelphia for the purpose of national coinage by the Act of Congress of April 2, 1792. The machinery and first metal used were imported. In 1792–93, coppers were coined, in 1794 silver dollars, and in 1795 gold eagles. Steam power was introduced in 1816. In 1835 branch mints were established at New Orleans, at Charlotte, N. C., at Dahlonega, Ga., in 1852 at San Francisco, in 1864 at Dallas City, Ore., and in 1870 at Carson City, Nev. Assay offices were established at New York in 1854, at Denver, Colo., in 1864, and at Boise City, Idaho, in 1872. These were considered branches of the Philadelphia mint until 1873, when the coinage act of that year made them separate mints and assay offices. These mints are bureaus of the Treasury Department and are all under the general supervision of the chief officer of that department. The mints at Charlotte and Dahlonega were suspended in 1861, that of New Orleans from 1860 to 1879, that of Dallas in 1875, that of Carson in 1885. In 1652 Massachusetts had established a colonial mint at Boston for the purpose of coining shillings and minor pieces, but this soon became inoperative.

Minuit or Minnewit, Peter (1580?–1641), born in Wesel, Germany, was made Governor of New Netherlands by the Dutch West India Company in 1625. He purchased Manhattan Island from the Indians, built Fort Amsterdam, and held office till 1631. Under the auspices of the Swedish West India Company, he planted a Swedish settlement on the Delaware, and built Fort Christiana in 1638.

Minute-men, members of a military force authorized by the Provincial Congress of Massachusetts in 1774. They were to hold themselves ready to take the field at a minute's notice.

Miranda's Plot, a scheme devised by some of the Federalist leaders of 1798, notably King and Hamilton, to join Great Britain in obtaining possession of the French and Spanish lands in America. One Miranda, of Caracas, undertook to secure the disaffection of the Spanish provinces. By this joint enterprise Great Britain was to obtain the West Indies, and the United States Florida and Louisiana east of the Mississippi. The plot fell through because President Adams refused to favor it.

Mischianza, an elaborate spectacular entertainment given to General Howe by his officers on his departure from Philadelphia in 1778. It was devised by André.

Missionary Ridge. (See Chattanooga.)

Missiones, Spanish religious establishments conducted by Franciscan friars for the civilization and conversion of the Indians in Mexico and California. The first mission founded in California was at San Diego, in 1769; a second was established at Monterey a few months later. Before many years had elapsed there was a line of twenty-one prosperous missiones between San Diego and Point Reyes. In 1834 there were 30,650 Indians connected with the missiones. The property of the missiones was very extensive. Their decline began in the attempt at secularization by the Spanish Government. The priests had absolute control over the Indians, treating them more like slaves than free men, yet they taught them much both of religious and practical matters.

Mississippi was admitted as a State December 10, 1817. It was explored by De Soto, a Spaniard, in 1539, and by the Frenchmen, Joliet and Marquette, who came down the Mississippi in 1673. In 1682 La Salle took formal possession of the territory for the King of France. Biloxi was settled by the French under Iberville in 1699. After the Louisiana bubble the colonies in Mississippi grew slowly. The French ceded the territory to England in 1763, and it was included within the State of Georgia until 1798, when it was organized as a territory by the U. S. Government under provisions like those of the Ordinance of 1787, with the exception of the article relative to slavery. The State has cast its electoral votes for Democratic candidates except in the years 1840, 1848 and 1872. In 1842 the State repudiated its bonds to the amount of $5,000,000. In 1850 Jefferson Davis and Henry S. Foote were candidates for U. S. Senator, and canvassed the State on the issue of the advisability of secession. Davis, the leader of the pronounced Secessionists, was beaten by a small majority. An ordinance of secession was passed by a State Convention January 7, 1861, but was not submitted to a popular vote. The State furnished the President, Jefferson Davis, of the Confederacy. Mississippi was readmitted February 23, 1870. In 1875 the white Democracy resorted to intimidation to keep the blacks from the polls, and succeeded in securing possession of the State, which has been Democratic since that date. The population of the State in 1817 was 75,512; in 1890 it had increased to 1,289,600. The present Constitution was made in 1891.

Mississippi Company. This land company was started in 1769 by some wealthy and prominent Virginians as a rival to the Walpole Company, which, in 1766, had obtained a grant of 500,000 acres along the Scioto River.

Mississippi Company. (See Compagnie de l'Occident.)

Missouri was formed originally from the Louisiana cession. The country was first settled by the French. In 1805 the southern portion of the Louisiana country was organized as a territory under the name of Orleans, and the northern portion under that of Louisiana. When Louisiana was admitted as a State, in 1812, the northern portion was called Missouri Territory. In 1817 Missouri asked leave of Congress to frame a State Constitution. This was the cause of a fierce contest in Congress over the question of the existence of slavery in Missouri, which was settled by the famous compromise (1820) of Henry Clay. (See Missouri Compromise.) This provided for the admission of Missouri as a slave State, but that in future slavery should be prohibited in all territory forming part of the Louisiana cession north of 36° 30′. Missouri adopted a State Constitution July, 1820, which established slavery and forbade the immigration into the State of free negroes. This negro clause led to another contest in Congress, and another compromise, whereby Missouri was admitted August 10, 1821. The electoral vote of the State was cast for Clay in 1824, since which time the State has been Democratic except during the period from 1862 to 1870, when the Republicans were in control. In 1849 the Democratic party in the State split into the "hards," or Benton men, and the "softs," or pro-slavery party. A State Convention met in 1861, which proved to be of Union sentiment. An unsuccessful attempt was made by the State officers to make an armed rebellion against the Union, and they were forced to flee from the State. The powers of government were then assumed by the convention, which, in 1863, passed an ordinance of gradual abolition of slavery. In 1864 Lincoln carried the

State. The Republicans divided in 1870 over the disfranchising clauses of the Constitution. The "Liberal" Republicans, headed by Carl Schurz and B. G. Brown, elected Brown Governor of the State. In 1872 the State elected Greeley electors, and in 1874 the Republican party disappeared. Since then the State has been Democratic. The population of the State in 1821 was 66,586; in 1890, 2,679,184. The present Constitution of the State was made in 1875. History by Carr.

Missouri Compromise, a compromise effected by the Act of Congress of March 3, 1820, between those who desired the extension of slavery into the regions beyond the Mississippi and those who desired its restriction. Missouri having applied for admission as a State, Tallmadge, of New York, in February, 1819, proposed an amendment which would ultimately destroy slavery in the new State. The House passed the bill with this amendment; the Senate refused to concur. Next year the bill, in the same form, passed the House again. The Senate voted to admit Maine, provided Missouri was admitted as a slave State. The House rejected the proposal. Thomas, of Illinois, proposed as a compromise the arrangement mentioned in the preceding article. When Missouri's Constitution was laid before Congress, however, it appeared that she had introduced clauses excluding free negroes from the State. The House then refused to admit Missouri. Clay effected a further compromise, whereby Missouri agreed not to deprive of his rights any citizen of another State.

"**Missouri Gazette.**" This newspaper was established at St. Louis in 1808 by Joseph Charles. The name was changed in 1822 to the *Missouri Republican*, under which title it is published at the present time, daily, tri-weekly and weekly.

Mitchel, Ormsby M. (1809–1862), secured the establishment of the observatory at Cincinnati, O., in 1843. He invented numerous astronomical instruments. He made extensive observations of stars, nebulæ and sun-spots. He served in the Army of the Ohio from 1861 to 1862, engaging at Bowling Green, Nashville and Bridgeport. He commanded the Department of the South in 1862, but died of yellow fever.

Mitchell, Donald G., born in 1822, a graceful and pleasant American author, has published "Reveries of a Bachelor," "Dream Life" and the "Edgewood" books.

Mitchell, John H., born in 1835, represented Oregon in the U. S. Senate as a Republican from 1873 to 1879. He was again elected in 1885 and 1891; his present term will expire in 1897.

Mobile, Ala., was founded as a fort by Lemoyne d'Iberville in 1711. In 1763, by the Treaty of Paris, Mobile was ceded to Great Britain, but was recovered for the United States in 1813, having previously passed into the possession of the Spanish in 1780. In 1819 it was incorporated as a city. Mobile was besieged and bombarded March 27 to April 9, 1865, by 45,000 Federal troops led by General Canby. Maury held the city with 9000 Confederates. His defences consisted of a system of irregular earthworks called Spanish Fort. This was invested April 4 by Smith and

Granger, and was bombarded without much success. On the eighth, however, 300 yards of the Confederate defences were captured, together with 500 prisoners and fifty guns. The works were then evacuated. On the morning of the ninth a general assault was made upon the city, and nearly all the works were carried, 3423 men and forty guns being captured. Mobile was evacuated two days later and surrendered by its mayor April 12.

Mobile Bay, Ala., scene of a naval engagement between the Federal and Confederate fleets, August 5 to 23, 1864. Farragut commanded the National fleet of eighteen vessels, fourteen of these being of wood and four ironclads, the "Tecumseh," "Winnebago," "Manhattan" and "Chickasaw." The Confederate Admiral Buchanan had far fewer vessels, three gunboats, the "Morgan," "Gaines" and "Selma" and the ram "Tennessee." Still he was defended by three strongly garrisoned forts, Gaines, Morgan and Powell, at the harbor's entrance, and the "Tennessee" was deemed a host in itself. Farragut entered the harbor with the gunboat "Brooklyn" leading and the entire fleet firing upon Fort Morgan, whence a lively reply was begun. The "Tecumseh" immediately struck a torpedo and was sunk. The fleet became confused and for some moments was in great danger. But Farragut forged ahead with the flag-ship "Hartford" and was attacked by the "Tennessee." The other Federal vessels quickly destroyed the "Selma" and chased away the "Morgan" and the "Gaines." The "Monongahela" and the "Lackawanna" were struck by the "Tennessee," but the latter was disabled by a broadside at close range from the "Hartford." The other boats closed around her. Her smokestack and steering chains were gone, her crew panic-stricken and she soon became unmanageable. She therefore surrendered. The Confederate forts were shelled for several days. Fort Powell was blown up and abandoned. Forts Gaines and Morgan surrendered.

Modoc Indians originally occupied lands on Klamath Lake, Cal. They began attacks against the whites as early as 1847. Hostilities continued until 1864, when they ceded their lands and agreed to go on a reservation which was not set apart until 1871. In the meantime they were placed on the Klamath reservation, and later on the Yainax reservation. A band under Captain Jack left the reservation and settled on Lost River, whence they refused to depart (1872). Hostilities followed, Captain Jack retreated to the Lava Beds and was not finally conquered until June, 1873.

Mohawks or Agmegue, one of the Five Nations of the Iroquois. The English early secured their friendship, and during the French and Indian Wars they proved valuable allies of the colonists. In the Revolutionary War the tribe under Brant carried on hostilities against the Americans. In 1784 the Mohawks retired to Upper Canada.

Mohicans, an Algonquin tribe of Indians, early settled around the Hudson. In 1628 they were driven to the Connecticut River by the Mohawks, but a part subsequently returned to their old home. Others who had previously gone eastward became known as the Pequots. The Mohicans were continually friendly to the English colonists during the struggle with the French, and also served the Americans in the Revolution. The tribe finally became divided. Some were assigned a reservation at Red Springs, and many became citizens.

Molasses Act, an act passed by the British Parliament in 1733 to protect the molasses and sugar of the British West Indies. By this act a heavy duty was laid on all sugar and molasses imported into the American colonies from the French islands.

Molino del Rey (King's Mill), Mexico, a range of massive stone buildings situated a short distance from the city of Mexico. Here General Worth, September 8, 1847, defeated the Mexican leaders, Leon, Perez and Alvarez. Scott sent Worth to attack this fortress by night, but this being found impracticable, Worth drew up his lines during the night and commenced battle at dawn, Wright leading the storming party, Garland cutting off support from Chapultepec, McIntosh facing the Mexican right and Cadwalader the centre. The Mexicans fought bravely, but were overcome with much loss. Number engaged: Americans, 3500; Mexicans, 10,000.

"**Moniteur,**" first newspaper issued in Louisiana. Printing was introduced into the State in 1804, and the *Moniteur* was established the same year by a Frenchman named Fontaine.

"**Monitor,**" the National iron-clad constructed in 1862 by John Ericsson, after a new type, under contract with the Union Government. She engaged in battle and partially disabled the enormous Confederate ram "Merrimac," March 9, 1862, after a fight of four hours, during which repeated charges were made by both vessels. She was commanded by Captain Worden. (See Hampton Roads.) The "Monitor" foundered and was sunk in a gale off Cape Hatteras in December, 1862.

Monmouth, Battle of, June 28, 1778. On June 18 the British evacuated Philadelphia and started for New York. Washington determined to strike a sudden and crippling blow upon the British army. He set out along a parallel road, and by June 27 was in a position at Allentown, N. J., to command the British flank. The British then turned east. Washington's purpose was now to crush the British left wing, which was moving in the rear. General Charles Lee was sent to accomplish this manœuvre. He was treacherous, and instead of acting in the offensive, as ordered, he threw away his advantage, and with 6000 men began a retreat without striking a blow. His men were nearly exhausted by the heat, and were falling into disorder when Washington suddenly appeared. Word had been sent him of Lee's strange action. Severely rebuking Lee, Washington at once set about restoring order among the demoralized troops. Owing to his energy a disgraceful flight was changed into a drawn battle. The American loss was 362, that of the British 416. Lee was court-martialed, and Clinton made good his escape to New York.

Monocacy, Md. In this engagement of the Civil War, which took place July 9, 1864, during the Confederate advance upon Washington, the Union General Wallace, commanding 8000 men, was defeated by Early, who led nearly 19,000 Confederates. Wallace's dispositions for battle were as follows: Tyler held the Baltimore pike on the right, Ricketts the Washington pike on the left, and Wallace the centre. The Confederates first attacked Brown, who was holding the Monocacy bridge. Then, forcing a passage of the river, they charged upon Ricketts and Tyler. These leaders defended themselves bravely, though nearly surrounded. The battle continued all day, and Wallace retreated in the evening.

Monroe, Elizabeth Kortright (1768–1830), married President James Monroe in 1786. She is described as "an elegant and accomplished woman with a dignity of manner that peculiarly fitted her for her station."

Monroe, James (April 28, 1758–July 4, 1831), fifth President of the United States, was born in Westmoreland County, Va. He entered William and Mary College, but left it in 1776 to enter the army. He was present at Trenton, Brandywine, Monmouth, etc., and in 1782 was already a member of the Virginia Assembly. He was soon a member of the State Council, and a delegate to the Continental Congress. In the Ratifying Convention of 1788, he ardently upheld the Anti-Federalist side. As U. S. Senator 1790–1794, envoy to France 1794–1796, and Governor of Virginia 1799–1802, he was naturally a Republican and an exponent of Jefferson's views. President Jefferson sent him in 1802 as additional envoy to France, where he helped Livingston to negotiate the Louisiana Purchase of 1803. Thence he was sent as Minister to London, where he remained until 1807. He had just commenced another term as Governor in 1811, when he was appointed Secretary of State. This office he held until 1817, combining with it in 1814–1815 the War portfolio. As Republican candidate for President in 1816, Monroe received 183 electoral votes, and in 1820 he had almost no opposition; the eight years of his administrations are in fact embalmed in American history as the so-called "era of good feeling." His Cabinet included J. Q. Adams in the State Department, Crawford Treasury, Calhoun War, and Wirt Attorney-General. The period is marked by the acquisition of Florida, Seminole War, Missouri Compromise, seaboard defence policy, the visit of Lafayette, and the Monroe Doctrine (which see). There is a short life by President D. C. Gilman.

Monroe Doctrine. After the overthrow of the empire of the first Napoleon, France, Russia, Prussia and Austria formed an alliance for preserving the balance of power and suppressing revolutions within each other's dominions. The Spanish colonies in America having revolted, it was rumored that this alliance contemplated their reduction, although the United States recognized their independence. George Canning, the English Secretary of State, proposed that the United States join England in the prevention of such suppression. After consulting with Jefferson, Madison, John Quincy Adams and Calhoun, President Monroe embodied in his annual message to Congress in 1823 a clause which has since become celebrated as the "Monroe Doctrine." Referring to the proposed intervention of the allied powers the message stated that we "should consider any attempt on their part to extend their system to any portion of this hemisphere as dangerous to our peace and safety;" and again, "that the American continents, by the free and independent condition which they have assumed and maintain, are henceforth not to be considered as subjects for future colonization by any European powers." The doctrine thus set forth has been maintained by the United States on many subsequent occasions, notably in matters relating to the Isthmus of Panama and in the case of the French intervention in Mexico under Maximilian.

Montana was admitted as a State November 8, 1889. It was organized as a territory in 1864. It formed a part of the Louisiana cession. In 1890 and 1891 a deadlock in the Legislature was caused by a disputed election in Silver Bow County. Since its admission as a State Montana has been Republican. The population in 1890 was 132,159.

Montauks, an Indian tribe which, at the time of the settlement of Long Island by whites, occupied the east end of the island. In 1659 they were nearly exterminated by the Block Island Indians. In 1660, 1662, 1670 and 1687 they conveyed their lands to certain bodies of settlers at Easthampton, reserving the right to live on them or parts of them. They are now nearly extinct again.

Montcalm, Louis Joseph, Marquis de (1712–1759), the ablest French general in America, was born near Nîmes, and entered the army at the age of fifteen years. He had experience in the War of the Austrian Succession, and in 1756 was sent by the Government to take command in the New World. The jealousy of the Canadian Governor, Vaudreuil, hampered Montcalm, but the first years of his command mark the high-water point of French success. In 1756 he took Oswego, and the next year besieged and received the surrender of Fort William Henry at the head of Lake George; this surrender was followed by a massacre of the captives on the part of Montcalm's Indian allies. On July 8, 1758, he repulsed Abercromby's overwhelming force at Ticonderoga. The next year Wolfe made his formidable attack on Quebec. For weeks the French commander's skillful precautions foiled the British. On the thirteenth of September Wolfe's army scaled the Heights of Abraham, and in the defeat Montcalm was mortally wounded, and died the following day. The great account of the period is Parkman's "Montcalm and Wolfe."

Monterey, Mexico, scene of a six days' battle and siege during the Mexican War, September 20–25, 1846. General Taylor commanded the American army and General Ampudia held the town with 10,000 Mexicans. Taylor began operations by cutting off communications and attempting to storm the western heights, later disposing his troops so as to attack all points at once. During two days his efforts were unsuccessful. Finally Captain Backus, of the First Infantry, by firing into Fort Tenería from a captured tannery, won that stronghold. La Federacion heights, Forts Obispado and Diablo and the Saltillo road were captured in succession. In unsuccessful attacks on Fort Diablo, 394 officers and men were lost. By September 23 Taylor practically held the town. On September 25 Ampudia was allowed to evacuate, carrying one field battery and his small arms. This ended the campaign on the Rio Grande. Number engaged: Americans, 6600; Mexicans, 10,000.

Monterey, Pa. Here, July 5, 1863, just after the battle of Gettysburg, while Lee was in full retreat from that battlefield, one brigade of his army was overtaken by Kilpatrick, commanding two National brigades. The Confederates were under Jones, and were on board a railroad train. The fight took place about midday, and the Confederates were defeated. Kilpatrick burned their train, captured their guards and resumed his march.

Montgomery, Richard (1736–1775), came to America as a British soldier in 1757. He was engaged at Louisbourg in 1758 and at Montreal in 1760. He retired from the British army in 1772. He was a delegate to the Provincial Congress in New York City in 1775. He was appointed brigadier-general in the Continental army. The disability of General Schuyler placed him in command of the expedition to Canada in 1775, and he captured Fort Chambly, St. John's and Montreal. He led the assault on Quebec, and was killed at the first discharge of the British artillery.

Montgomery, Ala., founded in 1817, became the capital of the State in 1847. From February, 1861, to May, 1862, it was the capital of the Confederate Government, and was captured by the Union troops in 1865.

"**Monthly Anthology,**" a magazine established at Boston in 1803 by an association of literary men. It was continued until 1811. It contained articles by such writers as Tudor, Buckminster, Thatcher, Kirkland, J. S. J. Gardiner, J. Q. Adams and G. Ticknor.

Monticello, the birthplace and home of Thomas Jefferson, near Charlottesville, Va. The mansion was built by Jefferson's father in 1735, but was remodeled and enlarged in later years. It is now owned by a New York merchant.

Montmorenci (July 31, 1759). In the French and Indian War the leading final act was Wolfe's expedition. After waiting a month before Quebec Wolfe determined to make an assault. The point chosen was the Heights of Montmorenci. He landed his troops on the muddy shore at low tide. They carried the shore battery, but were overwhelmed by the fire from above. Under the protection of a shower they managed to retreat with a loss of 50c men.

Montpelier, the home of James Madison, in Orange County, Va. It was here that Madison died in 1833. The Montpelier mansion was erected by him shortly after his return from Congress, though his father had owned the estate.

Montpelier, Vt., was made capital of the State in 1805.

Montreal. After the loss of Quebec in 1759, the centre of the French force was Montreal. Upon this the English forces advanced from Quebec under Murray, from Lake Champlain under Haviland and from Lake Ontario under Amherst. The various outposts were driven in, and by September 6 the English with 17,000 invested the town. The French were reduced to 2200 by desertion, and Vaudreuil, feeling resistance to be useless, surrendered, September 8, 1759. The whole colony passed to the English, and the French army and officers were sent back to France. On the twelfth of November, 1775, General Montgomery captured the city of Montreal. It was a part of a scheme of the Revolutionary Americans to conquer Canada, which threatened their strategic centre, New York.

Moore, Alfred (1755–1810), fought at Charleston and Fort Moultrie during the Revolution. He was Attorney-General of North Carolina from 1792 to 1798. He was a Justice of the U. S. Supreme Court from 1799 to 1805.

Moorefield, Va., a sharp skirmish August 7, 1864, between small bodies of Confederate and Union troops under B. Johnson and Averill respectively. The Confederates were defeated and Averill captured 500 prisoners.

Moore's Creek, Battle of, February 27, 1776. At Moore's Creek, N. C., Colonel Caswell, with 1000 militia, defeated 1600 loyalists, took 900 prisoners, 2000 stand of arms and £15,000 in gold. This victory was as inspiring in the South as Lexington had been in New England.

Moquis, an Indian tribe in Arizona on the Little Colorado and San Juan Rivers. They killed or expelled the early missionaries who visited them, but of late years have been peaceable. They have suffered greatly from the attacks of Apaches and Navajos.

Moravian Brethren. These form an evangelical church which flourished in Bohemia before the Reformation, was stamped out about 1627 and revived during the first half of the eighteenth century. They first settled in Georgia in 1735, but soon moved to Pennsylvania. They instituted a communism of labor; the lands were owned by the church, and its members worked them, receiving in return the necessities of life. This plan existed till 1762, and greatly aided the church in sending out its itinerant ministers and missionaries. They also for a long time excluded from their communities all outsiders, but this system gradually died out and has now altogether disappeared. The American church still maintains its connection with the parent churches in Europe and is growing rapidly, owing largely to its active missionary spirit. Number of members in 1890, 12,000.

Morey Letter, a letter published in a New York newspaper in 1880, near the end of the Garfield campaign, purporting to have been written by Garfield to "H. L. Morey, Employers' Union, Lynn, Mass." It expressed sympathy with capital rather than labor. It was proved to be a forgery.

Morfontaine, Treaty of, a name sometimes given to the convention negotiated September 30, 1800, between the United States and the French Republic, which had then recently come under the rule of the first consul, Bonaparte. It was negotiated by Ellsworth, Murray and Davie for the United States, and Joseph Bonaparte for France. It provided for restoration of captured ships and property, and more liberal rules respecting neutrals, but postponed the French spoliation claims.

Morgan, Daniel (born about 1736, died 1802), was born of Welsh parentage in New Jersey. He fought from the battle of the Monongahela through the French and Indian War, and Pontiac's War, and settled as a farmer in Virginia. In the Revolution he led a company of Virginian riflemen to Washington's army before Boston. Joining Arnold's romantic expedition to Canada, he showed great valor in the assault on Quebec, where he was captured. Released, he won distinction under Washington in 1777, and was sent with his rifle corps to reinforce Gates. In the two battles of Stillwater Morgan played a leading part. He resigned in 1779, but rejoined the army in 1780 as brigadier-general. At the opening of 1781 he gained at Cowpens one of the most brilliant victories of the war. Thereupon he conducted a famous retreat over the Catawba, and effected a junction with Greene. General Morgan was a Congressman from Virginia in 1797.

Morgan, Edwin D. (1811–1883), was a member of the New York Senate from 1850 to 1863. He was chairman of the Republican National Committee from 1856 to 1864. He was Governor of New York from 1858 to 1862, and commanded the Department of New York during the Civil War. He was a U. S. Senator from 1863 to 1869.

Morgan, John (1725–1789), established the University of Pennsylvania Medical School in 1765, and was physician-in-chief of the American army from 1775 to 1777.

Morgan, John H. (1826–1864), commanded a Confederate cavalry force from 1862 to 1863. He annoyed the National forces by successful and destructive raids in Ohio, Indiana, Kentucky and Tennessee, during one of which he was shot.

Morgan, John T., born in 1824, was promoted brigadier-general in the Confederate service. He has represented Alabama in the U. S. Senate as a Democrat since 1877. His term expires in 1895.

Morgan, Lewis H. (1818–1881), the "Father of American Anthropology," made extensive investigations concerning the kinships of the races. He published "Systems of Consanguinity and Affinity of the Human Family" and "Ancient Society."

Morgan, William, of Batavia, N. Y., born about 1775, proposed in 1826 to expose the secrets of the Order of Freemasons, of which he had been a member. His sudden disappearance soon afterward, and apparent abduction by the Masons, caused great excitement. An Anti-Masonic party was formed in most free States, and William Wirt was nominated for president in 1831. Morgan, it is now known, was taken from Batavia to Niagara and killed, his body being sent over the falls.

Mormons, a sect mainly located in Utah and the Territories and States in its neighborhood, to the number of 150,000, but having also about 60,000 converts in other parts of the United States and foreign countries. The sect was founded by Joseph Smith, of Sharon, Vt., and Palmyra, N. Y., the first organized conference being held June 1, 1830, at Fayette, N. Y. The distinguishing features of their belief are polygamy, materialism and baptism for the remission of sins. The Mormons first settled in Missouri, but were expelled thence, probably because of their anti-slavery sentiments. In 1839 they settled at Nauvoo, Ill. In 1844 an Illinois mob killed the leader Smith. Emigrating again, by 1848 they were settled at Salt Lake City. Brigham Young, the president, was appointed Governor of Utah Territory in 1850 by President Fillmore, but he turned out to be wholly in sympathy with the Mormons, and resisted the Federal troops in 1857. Since that time the Government has experienced many difficulties in regulating the relations of the Mormons and Christians in Salt Lake City. In 1882 the Edmunds Act disfranchised polygamists.

"**Morning Post,**" first penny paper established in this country, founded in New York City January 1, 1833, by Horatio David Shepard, with Horace Greeley and Francis V. Story as partners, printers and publishers. It was suspended after one month.

Morocco. A treaty of peace and friendship was concluded between the United States and Morocco in 1787 for fifty years. This was renewed in 1836. In 1865 the United States joined with the European powers in a convention with Morocco concerning the administration and maintenance of the lighthouse at Cape Spartel; and similarly in 1880 in a convention for the establishment of the right of protection in Morocco.

Morrill, Anson P. (1803–1887), was elected Governor of Maine by the Legislature in 1855. He represented Maine in the U. S. Congress as a Republican from 1861 to 1863.

Morrill, Justin S., born in 1810, represented Vermont in the U. S. Congress as a Republican from 1855 to 1867. He was many times Chairman of the Ways and Means Committee. He is author of the famous Morrill Tariff of 1861 and is a strong advocate of protection. He has been a member of the U. S. Senate from 1867 to the present time (1894).

Morrill, Lot M. (1813–1883), was president of the Maine Senate in 1856. He was Governor of Maine from 1858 to 1861. He represented Maine in the U. S. Senate as a Republican from 1861 to 1876. He was a faithful worker and familiar with financial, naval and Indian affairs. He was Secretary of the Treasury in Grant's Cabinet from 1876 to 1877.

Morrill Tariff, so called after its framer, Justin S. Morrill, of Vermont. This tariff became law just before the war, March 2, 1861. It restored the protective rates of 1846 and substituted specific for *ad-valorem* duties. The Tariff Act of 1864, also under the management of Morrill, was distinctly a war tariff used to advance the protectionist notions of its framers. It taxed every possible article indiscriminately and at the highest rates.

Morris, Charles (1784–1856), Commodore, served in the war with Tripoli from 1801 to 1805. He was lieutenant of the "Constitution" in the engagement with the "Guerrière." He was Chief of the Ordnance Bureau from 1851 to 1856.

Morris, George P. (1802–1864), journalist, was famous as a song-writer, composing "Woodman, Spare That Tree," "My Mother's Bible" and "Long Time Ago." He published "Prose and Poetry of Europe and America."

Morris, Gouverneur (1752–1816), an American Statesman, was half-brother of Lewis Morris, a signer of the Declaration of Independence. He was graduated at King's (Columbia) College in 1768, and was admitted to the bar of New York. He was a delegate to the New York Provincial Congress and to the Continental Congress, and was an influential adviser in financial matters. He was assistant to Robert Morris when the latter was Superintendent of Finance; he attended the Federal Convention of 1787 and revised the final draft of the Constitution. After passing some time in France, he went as a diplomatic agent to England in 1791, and was Minister to France 1791–1794. For some years he traveled in Europe. Returning he was U. S. Senator 1800–1803. He was a champion of canals, and chairman of the canal commissioners. Morris was a noted writer of satires and addresses and a prominent Federalist. Lives by Sparks and by Roosevelt.

Morris, Lewis (1726–1798), was a delegate from New York to the Continental Congress from 1775 to 1777. He was a commissioner to the Western Indians in 1775 to induce them to join the colonists against the British. He signed the Declaration of Independence. He was major-general of the New York State Militia.

Morris, Robert (1734–1806), the financier of the Revolution, was born in Liverpool. Having settled in Philadelphia he built up a flourishing business there. He opposed the Stamp Act, and signed the Declaration of Independence. In Congress he gave valuable services to the Committee of Ways and Means, and in February, 1781, he was elected Superintendent of Finance. Among his acts was the organization of the Bank of North America at the end of 1781. In 1784 he retired, but served in the Pennsylvania Legislature, as delegate to the Constitutional Convention of 1787, and U. S. Senator 1789–1795. He had previously declined the office of Secretary of the Treasury. In his later years he was unsuccessful in business, and was at one time imprisoned for debt. There is a biography by Gould and one by W. G. Sumner.

Morrison, William R., born in 1825, served during the Mexican War. He commanded a regiment in the Civil War. He represented Illinois in the U. S. Congress as a Democrat from 1863 to 1865 and from 1873 to 1887, and was chairman of the Ways and Means Committee from 1873 to 1875. He has been a member of the Interstate Commerce Commission from its origin in 1887 to the present time (1894).

Morse, Jedediah (1761–1826), minister at Charlestown, Mass., from 1789 to 1820, was noted as a compiler of early American geographical works.

Morse, John T., born in 1840, has published "Law of Arbitration and Award," "Famous Trials" and "Life of Alexander Hamilton." He has edited the "American Statesmen" series, contributing the volumes on "John Quincy Adams," "Thomas Jefferson," "John Adams" and "Abraham Lincoln."

Morse, Samuel F. B. (1791–1872), was engaged in painting in his early life and gained considerable prominence as an artist. He conceived the idea of an electro-magnetic telegraph in a conversation with Charles T. Jackson in 1832. He immediately applied himself to the task, and in 1837 exhibited his invention. After repeated appeals Congress appropriated $30,000 in 1843 for a telegraph line between Washington and Baltimore, which was successfully tested in 1844. The number and character of the honors he received was seldom equalled. His system is almost universally employed.

Morton or Mourt, George (1585–1628?), brought emigrants and supplies from England to the Pilgrims in 1623. He edited in England in 1622

"Mourt's Relation of the Beginning and Proceeding of the English Plantation at Plymouth," an important original source.

Morton, John (1724–1777), signer of the Declaration of Independence, had previously been a delegate to the Stamp Act Congress of 1765, and speaker of the Pennsylvania Assembly from 1772 to 1775.

Morton, J. Sterling, of Nebraska, was born in 1832. He conceived the idea of Arbor Day for tree planting. He became Secretary of Agriculture in Cleveland's Cabinet in 1893.

Morton, Levi P., born in 1824, founded the banking house of Morton, Rose & Co. in 1869, which was the fiscal agent of the U. S. Government from 1873 to 1884. He represented New York in the U. S. Congress as a Republican from 1878 to 1881. He was Minister to France from 1881 to 1885 and was Vice-President of the United States from 1889 to 1893.

Morton, Marcus (1784–1864), represented Massachusetts in the U. S. Congress as a Democrat from 1817 to 1821. He was Governor of Massachusetts from 1840 to 1841 and from 1843 to 1844.

Morton, Nathaniel (1613–1685), came to America from England in 1623. He was secretary of the Massachusetts colony from 1647 to 1685. He wrote "New England's Memorial," a carefully prepared history of early colonial days.

Morton, Oliver Perry (1823–1877), was a leading lawyer in Indiana, a judge, and a founder of the Republican party. As the party candidate for Governor he was defeated, but in 1860 was elected Lieutenant-Governor. As Lane, the Governor, was chosen to the U. S. Senate, Morton became Governor. His term included the Civil War period, and his vigor in equipping and forwarding troops and suppressing disaffection made him foremost among the "War Governors." Since the Indiana Legislature in 1863–1865 refused its co-operation, he declined to summon it during those years. He was re-elected Governor in 1864. From 1867 to 1877 he was U. S. Senator, and one of the most energetic and extreme of the Republican leaders. He was chairman of the Committee on Privileges and Elections, and a member of the Electoral Commission. He was a prominent candidate before the National Convention in 1876.

Morton, Thomas (1575?–1646), emigrated to Plymouth from England in 1622. He made a settlement at Mount Wollaston or "Merry Mount," (now Braintree) where he made himself obnoxious to the Puritans by his revels. He was twice seized and transported to England, where he published "The New England Canaan" in 1632. For this satire he was imprisoned on his return in 1643.

Mosby, John S., born in 1833, enlisted in the Confederate cavalry in 1861, and served under General Johnston in the Shenandoah campaign. In 1862 he became a scout and made raids upon McClellan's army. In 1863 he led a band of guerillas in Northern Virginia, being successful at Chantilly, Dranesville and Warrenton Junction. He was consul at Hong Kong from 1876 to 1882.

"**Mother Ann.**" (See Lee, Ann.)

Motley, John Lothrop (1814–1877), historian, studied at Harvard and Göttingen, and was secretary of the U. S. legation at St. Petersburg in 1841. In 1856, he published "The Rise of the Dutch Republic," which was immediately recognized as a brilliant and scholarly production. During the Civil War he zealously upheld the national cause in Europe. From 1861 to 1868, he produced "The History of the United Netherlands." He was Minister to Austria from 1861 to 1867, and to England from 1869 to 1870. In 1874 he published the "Life of John of Barneveld." He wrote an address entitled "Historic Progress and American Democracy." Life by Dr. O. W. Holmes.

Mott, Lucretia (1793–1880), entered the ministry of the Friends in Philadelphia in 1818. She adhered to the Hicksite branch. She was one of the original founders of the American Anti-Slavery Society. In 1840 she was sent as a delegate to the World's Anti-Slavery Convention at London. Her exclusion from it increased the woman-suffrage agitation, in which she became a leader.

Mott, Valentine (1785–1865), of New York, was one of the most successful surgical operators of his time. He held professorships in medical colleges almost continuously from 1809 to 1860.

Moultrie, Fort, Battle of, June 28, 1776. When the British attempted to capture Charleston, S. C., they found the city defended by a palmetto fort on Sullivan's Island, under command of Colonel Moultrie. After a ten hours' engagement the fleet withdrew. The American loss had been only thirty-seven, that of the British, 205, and only one of their ten sail remained seaworthy. After refitting, Clinton and Parker sailed to New York. For more than two years there was no further invasion of the South.

Moultrie, William (1731–1805), represented South Carolina in the Continental Congress in 1775. He successfully defended Sullivan's Island in Charleston Harbor against a British fleet in 1776. The fort there was named in his honor. He defeated the British at Beaufort and successfully defended Charleston in 1779. He was Governor of South Carolina in 1785 and 1794. He wrote "Memoirs of the Revolution."

Moundbuilders, a name given to a prehistoric race the principal remains of which are extensive earthworks found in the Mississippi Valley extending from the lakes southward to the gulf. Many of these are clearly defensive works or places of sepulture. Fort Hill, Ohio, has a line of circumvallation about four miles in extent. These defensive works also include structures used for religious purposes. Many mounds are of regular outline assuming the form of various geometrical figures. In Newark, Ohio, works of this character cover an area of more than two square miles. A mound near St. Louis is 700 feet long by 500 broad at the base and ninety feet high. Some mounds of this character contain skeletons. Mounds, such as those near Wheeling, W. Va., and Miamisburg, Ohio, are evidently the graves of distinguished personages. In Wisconsin and Iowa are earthworks which assume the outline of men and animals. One in Adams County, Ohio, has the form of a serpent. It is over 1000 feet in length and its mouth is partially closed around an egg of perfectly regular dimensions. The figure reaches a height of about five feet. Various theories prevail as to the question what race built the mounds. It is now frequently thought to have been a race related to the Indians.

Mount Crawford, Va. At this place 4500 Confederates under Jones were defeated disastrously by a somewhat stronger force of Federals commanded by Hunter. The fight took place June 5, 1864. Jones was killed.

Mount Holyoke Seminary and College, South Hadley, Mass., was first chartered (1836) as a seminary, but rechartered (1888) as a college for the higher education of women. The founder was Miss Mary Lyon.

Mount Vernon, the home and burial-place of George Washington, on the western bank of the Potomac in Fairfax County, Va. Mount Vernon mansion was built by Lawrence Washington in 1743, and was named in honor of Admiral Vernon. In 1858 it was purchased from John A. Washington by the Ladies' Mount Vernon Association for $200,000, and is now a place of public resort.

Mountain Meadow Massacre. In the autumn of 1857, a body of thirty-six Arkansas and Missouri emigrants en route to California, were brutally murdered at Mountain Meadow, Utah, by a band of Indians, who were incited thereto by Lee, a Mormon fanatic. It was the period of the first troubles between the United States Government and the Mormons. Brigham Young had made threats of turning the Indians loose upon west-bound emigrants, but the Mormons, as a body, were innocent of the massacre. The emigrant party was encamped at Mountain Meadow when the attack began, September 7. They threw up earthworks and defended themselves for four days. Lee, under pretence of friendship, succeeded in drawing them out and murdering the whole party.

Mugwump, a word of the Massachusetts Indians, meaning a great personage (mugquomp). After long use in localities, and occasional use in politics, it came into prominence in 1884, being then applied to those independent members of the Republican party, who openly refused to vote for the party's candidate, Blaine. Thus the name came to be applied to all Independent Republicans.

Muhlenberg, Frederick A. C. (1750–1801), represented Pennsylvania in the Continental Congress in 1779 and 1780. He was president of the State convention that ratified the Constitution. He was a U. S. Congressman from 1789 to 1795 and was twice Speaker, 1789–1791, 1793–1795.

Muhlenberg, John P. G. (1746–1807), was a pastor at Woodstock, Va., from 1772 to 1775. He enlisted in the National army as a colonel in 1775. He won distinction at Charleston, Brandywine, Germantown, Monmouth, Stony Point and Yorktown. He represented Pennsylvania in the U. S. Congress from 1789 to 1791, 1793 to 1795 and from 1799 to 1801.

Mulligan Letters, letters which James Mulligan, bookkeeper for Warren Fisher, of Boston, testified before a Congressional committee in 1876, had been written by James G. Blaine to Mr. Fisher. The importance of these letters during the campaign of 1884 was due to the discussion as to whether they were or were not discreditable to Blaine.

Mumfordsville, Ky., scene of an encounter between Chalmers, leading the advance guard of Bragg's army of 25,000 Confederates, and 21,000 Federals under Wilder and Dunham. The Confederates began the fight and were repulsed in their first attack. But Bragg gradually drew his forces about Wilder until there was no chance of escape for that leader, who accordingly surrendered, September 17, 1862.

Munn vs. Illinois, one of the "elevator cases" decided by the Supreme Court of the U. S. In 1872, Munn and Scott, lessees of a grain elevator and warehouse in Chicago, were found guilty in the Criminal Court of Cook County, Ill., of violating Article thirteen of the State Constitution relating to the storage of grain. They had neglected to take out a license and give bond, and were charging rates higher than prescribed in the above-mentioned act. They were fined, and the decision was confirmed by the Supreme Court of Illinois, whence the case was transferred to the Supreme Court of the United States. That body confirmed the judgment on the ground that the Act of the Illinois Legislature was not repugnant to the national Constitution, and that a State could lawfully determine how a man might use his own property, when the good of other citizens was involved.

Murcheson Letter, a letter received in October, 1888, by Lord Sackville-West, British Minister at Washington, from one Charles Murcheson, representing himself to be a naturalized citizen of English birth, and asking the Minister how he should vote in the impending Presidential election. Lord Sackville openly advised, as favorable to British interests, Cleveland. This caused great indignation. Sackville's recall was requested and his passports sent him.

Murfree, Mary N., born in Tennessee about 1850, has published articles on Tennessee life under the pen-name of Charles Egbert Craddock. She is author of "In the Tennessee Mountains," "Where the Battle Was Fought," and "The Despot of Broomsedge Cove."

Murfreesboro, Tenn., was occupied by an encampment of 1400 national troops under Crittenden and Duffield in 1862. These troops were defeated and expelled July 13 by the Confederate cavalryman Forrest, who came upon them unexpectedly and routed them after a sharp fight. Forrest captured a quantity of valuable stores. The second and great battle of Murfreesboro took place December 31, 1862, and January 1, 1863, Bragg, commanding 62,000 Confederates, being opposed to 43,000 Federals led by Rosecrans. Bragg was about to go into winter quarters and was not expecting an engagement, when suddenly Rosecrans moved against him, forcing him to concentrate his troops. This he did, marching his army between Rosecrans and the town and drawing it up with Breckenridge on the right, Polk in the centre and Hardee on the left. Opposing these were the Federal leaders, Crittenden, Thomas and McCook. The Confederates were on the west side of Stone River. Rosecrans had planned to strike first, but Bragg anticipated him. Both had massed their forces on the left, and on December

31, as Rosecrans' left was hurriedly crossing Stone River, Bragg's left fell upon it so furiously as completely to sweep away Johnson's division and rushed forward upon Sheridan, having demolished Davis in the charge. Sheridan held out firmly, raking the Confederates with his batteries and forcing them back. He was finally driven from his position, but he saved the day. Rosecrans now massed his batteries on a knoll and withstood the Confederate charges until night. Storms on January 2 and 3 prevented battle, and on the fourth Bragg had retired after slight skirmishing. Again in 1863, in a seven days' irregular skirmish and battle, June 23–30, during Rosecrans' campaign in Tennessee, that general defeated and drove the Confederate, Bragg, from the intrenchments he had thrown up during several months at Tullahoma, near Murfreesboro, after which place the battle is sometimes called. Rosecrans had 60,000 men, Bragg 40,000. Bragg's army was posted in a long line from Murfreesboro, past Tullahoma and along the Duck River. June 24 Rosecrans sent McCook and Wilder to capture Booker's Gap and Liberty Gap, two important mountain passes. This move was successful. Granger had in the meantime dislodged the Confederates from Guy's Gap, capturing three guns and a large body of prisoners. By the twenty-seventh Rosecrans was prepared for a flank movement against the Confederates. This was so well planned and executed that Bragg vacated his intrenchments and fled across Elk River on the night of the twenty-ninth.

Murphy, Henry C. (1810–1882), represented New York in the U. S. Congress as a Democrat from 1843 to 1845 and from 1847 to 1849. He was Minister to the Netherlands from 1857 to 1861. He was a student and writer on the Dutch history of New York.

Muscat. The United States concluded a treaty of amity and commerce with Muscat in 1833.

Museum, National. (See National Museum.)

Museum, Philadelphia, the earliest public establishment of this sort in the United States. It was founded by Charles Wilson Peale in 1785, and had as a nucleus a stuffed paddle-fish and the bones of a mammoth.

Myer, Albert J. (1827–1880), author of a "Manual of Signals for the U. S. Army and Navy," was chief of the signal service from 1863 to 1864 and from 1866 to 1870. He inaugurated the present system of meteorological observations.

N.

Nantucket, Mass., was settled in 1659. It was annexed to New York in 1664 and in 1693 ceded to Massachusetts. The town was incorporated as Sherburne in 1673, but in 1795 was given its present name. The year 1712 marked the beginning of Nantucket's history as a whaling port.

Napoleon (I.) Bonaparte (August 15, 1769–May 5, 1821), general of the French Army of Italy 1796–1798, commander in Egypt 1798–1799, First

Consul 1799–1804, Emperor of the French 1804–1814, and (after the captivity in Elba) again during the "Hundred Days" in 1815, and an exile in the island of St. Helena 1815–1821. He enters into American history through the fact that he was head of the government at the time of the Louisiana Purchase of 1803, and that his "Continental" commercial policy and attempts to cripple Great Britain are largely bound up with the American commercial and naval troubles of Jefferson's and Madison's administrations, which ended in the War of 1812.

Napoleon III. (1808–1873), of France, was the son of Louis Bonaparte, King of Holland. He was elected President of the French Republic in 1848, and in 1852 established an imperial government. From 1862 to 1867 he attempted to establish Archduke Maximilian on the Mexican throne. The demand of U. S. Secretary of State Seward for the withdrawal of French troops from Mexico in 1866 was conceded by Napoleon. During the Civil War he inclined toward recognition of the independence of the Confederate States, but did not take that step.

Nares, Sir George S., born in England in 1831, commanded an Arctic expedition in the "Alert" and "Discovery" from 1875 to 1876. He attained latitude 83° 10′ 26″ N., and made valuable scientific observations.

Narragansett Country, the lands occupied by the Narragansett Indians at the coming of the English, but especially applied to that territory along the west shore of Narragansett Bay from Wickford to Point Judith. It was long a scene of rivalry between two land companies, John Hull, of Pine Tree Shilling fame, purchasing lands about Pettaquamscut Rock in 1660, and Atherton's company making similar purchases the same year near Wickford. This territory was also a bone of contention between Rhode Island and Connecticut during fifty years. It was detached from Rhode Island and became the King's Province in 1665, but was afterward restored and was called King's County till the Revolution, when its name became Washington County.

Narragansetts, a tribe of Rhode Island Indians, formerly inhabiting the western shores of the bay bearing their name. Though they at first engaged in no open war against the settlers, yet they were held in distrust. In 1636 Roger Williams gained their friendship, and in 1644 they ceded their lands to the king. Troubles arose in 1645, and an expedition was sent against them. The Indians, however, hastened to make a treaty. At the outbreak of Philip's War they were suspected and were attacked by the whites. Hostilities followed which was terminated by a bloody encounter in a swamp at South Kingstown. The Indians were almost annihilated; the remnant, however, settled at Charlestown, R. I.

Narváez, Panfilo de (1470–1528), was active in conquering the West Indies for Spain. In 1520 he was sent by Velasquez, Governor-General of Cuba, to conquer Mexico, but was defeated by Cortés at Cempoala. He was made Governor of Florida by Spain in 1528, and led an expedition of 400 men into the interior of Florida. They suffered severe hardships and were shipwrecked at the mouth of the Mississippi.

Nashville, Tenn., was settled in 1780 and became the capital of the State in 1843. In December, 1864, it was the scene of the "Battle of Nashville," which practically ended Hood's campaign in Tennessee. His army numbered about 40,000 men, while Thomas opposed him with 56,000 Federals. After the battle of Franklin, Thomas, though victorious, fell back December 1, 1864, to Nashville and occupied a strong position protected by Forts Negley, Morton, Confiscation, Houston and Gillem. Hood arrived December 2, and formed his line with his salient resting on Montgomery Hill, 600 yards from Thomas' centre. Storms prevented fighting until the fifteenth. Then Steedman attacked the Confederates on the right, and Smith and Wilson advanced against their left. Two redoubts were carried and many prisoners captured, after which an attack was made on Montgomery Hill with considerable success. On the sixteenth a combined attack was inaugurated against the Confederate line, its chief force being concentrated upon the centre. Both sides lost heavily. Another assault by Smith and Schofield won the day. The Confederates broke and fled in all directions.

Nashville Convention, a convention of delegates from the Southern States at Nashville, Tenn., June, 1850, suggested by the Mississippi State Convention of the previous year. The convention was called to consider the slavery question and the encroachments of Northern abolitionists. It did not meet with universal approval. The Wilmot proviso and the Missouri Compromise were disapproved of, but resolutions of open resistance advanced by Texas, South Carolina and Mississippi were voted down. The convention met again in November, and again moderate resolutions were adopted.

Nassau. The United States concluded a convention for the abolition of the droit d'aubaine and taxes on emigration with Nassau in 1846.

Nassau, Fort, erected on the site of the present town of Gloucester, N. J., by Captain Cornelius Jacobsen Mey, representing the Dutch West India Company in 1623. It was abandoned and rebuilt a number of times, and finally abandoned in 1651.

Nast, Thomas, born in 1840, came to America from England in 1846. He is one of the foremost pictorial satirists of the day. He is a Republican and has been prominent in political movements, such as the overthrow of the Tweed ring.

Natchez, Miss., was settled by the French in 1716. In 1729 the Natchez Indians burnt the settlement and massacred the inhabitants. The French soon recaptured the town and held it until 1763, when it passed to Great Britain. From 1779 to 1798 it was occupied by the Spaniards. In 1798 it was occupied by the United States and became the capital of the Territory of Mississippi and so remained until 1820. In 1862 Natchez was captured by a portion of Farragut's fleet.

Natchitoches, La., a brief engagement, followed by desultory skirmishing, March 31, 1864, between detachments of Franklin's division of Banks' Army under Mower, and several regiments of Confederates led by Dick Taylor. This was during Banks' campaign in the Southwest. The Confederates were defeated, but there was no great loss on either side. The Confederates retreated, Franklin pursuing them.

Natick, Mass., was incorporated in 1781. In 1651 a band of John Eliot's Indian converts came here from Newton, and in 1660 the first Indian church in New England was erected. The settlement numbered several hundred Indians, and had a simple government of its own.

National Banks. The free banking system of the State of New York (1838) gave all parties freedom to establish banks, and required securities to be deposited with the State for bank issues. In December, 1861, Secretary Chase recommended to Congress a similar system of national banks. He repeated this recommendation in 1862. The Act of February 25, 1863, authorized the free formation of banks, entitled to issue notes to the amount of ninety per cent of the par value of the United States bonds which each bank deposited with the Treasury Department. The system was to be supervised by an official called the comptroller of the currency. $300,000,000 of bank notes in all might be issued. A revised act was passed June 3, 1864. The Act of 1865 taxing State bank notes forced most of these to become national banks. The Act of 1870 increased the total amount of issue to $354,000,000. The system greatly benefited the Government in the placing of its bonds, and gave the country a superior system of banking, the Government guaranteeing the notes. There are now nearly 4000 national banks, with capital amounting to nearly $700,000,000, and deposits aggregating nearly $1,800,000,000.

National Board of Health, instituted by Act of Congress, March 3, 1879, to consist of eleven members, seven civilian physicians, one army surgeon, one navy surgeon, one medical officer of the marine hospital service and one officer of the Department of Justice.

National Cemeteries, for soldiers and sailors, originated in 1850. The army appropriation bill for that year appropriated $10,000 for purchasing a lot near the city of Mexico for the interment of United States soldiers who fell near that place during the Mexican War. The remains of Federal soldiers who fell in the Civil War have been interred in seventy-eight national cemeteries.

"**National Intelligencer**," a tri-weekly newspaper established in Washington by Samuel H. Smith, in 1800, as the organ of Jefferson's administration. This journal was in reality an offshoot of a publication begun at Philadelphia in 1793 by Joseph Gales, the elder. Gales was an English immigrant, whose republican principles had forced him to leave England. In 1810 Joseph Gales, Jr., became one of the editors of the *National Intelligencer* and was joined in 1812 by William Seaton, also an English immigrant. This paper wielded considerable influence in political circles. Its publication was suspended in 1866.

National Republican Party, the name assumed by those who broke away from the old Democratic-Republican party after the defeat of Adams by Jackson in 1828. Jackson's drift against the bank, protective tariff and other features of Adams' policy brought about their open organization. In

1831 they nominated Clay and indorsed a protective tariff, a system of internal improvements, and a cessation of removals from office for political reasons. Clay was defeated. In 1835 the party, reinforced by other elements, took the name of Whig.

National Road. March 29, 1806, Congress authorized the President to appoint three commissioners to lay out a road from Cumberland on the Potomac, to the Ohio River, and $30,000 were appropriated for the expenses. The road was built as far as Illinois in 1838, the last act in its favor being of May 25 of that year. The total amount appropriated was $6,821,246. Bills appropriating money for this were often opposed in Congress on grounds of the unconstitutionality of appropriations for internal improvements.

National University. The establishment of a National University in the central part of the United States was first conceived by George Washington about 1790, when the shares he received from the Potomac Company had proved so valuable. He wished to appropriate this stock toward the founding of such an institution. This stock, and that accruing from the James River Company, left by his will for such purposes, were, however, divided between two charity schools, one on the James (see Washington and Lee University), and one on the Potomac. Washington strongly disapproved of foreign education for the American youth.

Nationality is determined in the United States by the Federal law and not by the State. Members of the nation are, of course, also members of the State in which they reside. The Constitution established no rules regarding the acquisition or loss of American nationality, which is therefore governed by the subsidiary or common law of the land. All persons born within the United States are considered to have acquired nationality. The Naturalization Act of 1790 endowed children born of American parents beyond the sea with American nationality. The act of 1855 restricted this to the children of citizen fathers. The Civil Rights Act of 1866 declared "all persons born in the United States and not subject to any foreign power" to be citizens of the United States. The Fourteenth Amendment (1868) defines them as "all persons born or naturalized in the United States, and subject to the jurisdiction thereof."

Naturalization. Section eight of article one of the Constitution empowered Congress "to establish an uniform rule of naturalization." This power was first exerted in the Act of March 26, 1790, providing that, under certain conditions, any free white alien might be admitted to citizenship by any court of record of the State in which he resided. These conditions were: Previous residence of two years in the United States and of one year in the State; good character; and an oath to support the Constitution. These conditions have undergone changes. An act of 1795 required five, an act of 1798 fourteen years' residence. The act now in force, of April 14, 1802, provides for proof of five years' residence in the United States and of one in the State; good character; an oath of allegiance, and a renunciation of titles and of prior allegiance. No alien may be naturalized if his country be at war with the United States.

Navajos, a tribe of Apache Indians, occupying the northern part of New Mexico and Arizona. The Mexicans continually attempted to reduce them, but failed. After long-continued hostilities against the whites, Colonel Carson compelled them in 1863 to leave their country and remove to Bosque Redondo as prisoners of the Government. In 1868 they were removed to Fort Wingate, and in 1869 were again placed in their old country.

Naval Academy. This institution was not founded by formal legislation, but was begun by the Navy Department when George Bancroft was Secretary of the Navy. The first act of Congress regarding it was that of August 10, 1846, providing $28,200 for repairs, improvements and instruction under the direction of the Navy Department at Fort Severn, Annapolis, Md. In March, 1847, a like sum was appropriated for the same purpose. During the Civil War the Academy was for a time located at Newport, R. I.

Naval Militia. On March 2, 1891, at the suggestion of Secretary Tracy, regarding the importance of a trained naval militia, Congress appropriated $25,000 to purchase arms for the militia, to be expended under the direction of the Secretary of the Navy.

Naval Observatory. This bureau was established in 1842 under the name of the "Depot for Naval Charts and Instruments." It is under the supervision of the Bureau of Navigation.

Naval Officer, in colonial times, an officer, not of the navy, but of the treasury, charged with the execution of the navigation acts. Similarly, from the beginning of the present Government in 1789, an official of the Treasury Department has, under this name, watched over the execution of the American navigation laws at the larger ports, while at the smaller the duties have been performed by the collector of the port.

Naval War College, a course of lectures on and instruction in the manipulation of torpedoes. This course was established by the Government at Coaster's Harbor Island in Newport in 1889. The course continues during three months each year. The members of the class are chiefly officers and men in the torpedo service, though the topics of the lectures are designed to correspond with all branches of naval improvement and advancement.

Navigation Act, a famous marine law first promulgated by the British Government in 1651 (or even, in a sense, in 1645) for the protection of British commerce and the carrying trade. Its renewal with a few changes was made in 1660, soon after the accession of Charles II. The act related to five subjects: Coasting trade; fisheries; commerce with the colonies; commerce with European countries; commerce with Asia, Africa and America, and was chiefly a move in England's struggle with the Dutch for the possession of the carrying trade of the world. The parts important to American history were those providing that all colonial trade should be carried on in ships built and owned in England and the colonies, (a provision which powerfully stimulated colonial ship-building) and that, in the case of many specified goods, trade should be with England only. The act was largely rendered inoperative by colonial smuggling. The efforts at last made to enforce it were among the chief causes of the Revolution.

Navigation Laws of the United States. In the Convention of 1787 a compromise was effected between the New England members, who desired that the Federal Government might have the power to regulate commerce, and the Southern members, who desired the slave-trade to be kept open for a time. Thus the Constitution gave Congress power to pass navigation laws. By Act of 1789 a tonnage tax of six cents per ton was levied on all American vessels, and one of fifty cents a ton on all vessels built and owned in foreign countries and entering American ports. In 1792 the act requiring American registration was passed. In 1793 the coasting trade was closed to foreign vessels. In 1816, 1817 and 1820 the American navigation laws were made still more closely like those of Great Britain. Tonnage taxes were renewed at the time of the outbreak of the Civil War, and were raised to thirty cents a ton.

Navy. In 1775 the States began the creation of State naval establishments. At the end of the year Congress began the organization of a Continental navy. Thirteen frigates were ordered to be constructed. With these, some exploits were performed. But most of the naval achievements of the Revolutionary War were accomplished by the privateers, and by 1781 all thirteen of the Federal vessels had been either captured or destroyed. The one ship of the line completed was presented to the King of France. A new navy was created by Congress in 1797 and 1798, when the "Constitution," "United States" and "Constellation" were built, and the purchase of other vessels, to the number of twenty-four, was authorized. Adams and the Federalists favored increase of the navy; Jefferson and the Republicans disliked it. Jefferson's gunboat system was tried instead, and the American navy was allowed to dwindle, until at the outbreak of the War of 1812 the United States had about twenty vessels, as against England's 830. The victories won secured larger appropriations that year, and a larger navy resulted, which, after the conclusion of this war, was used against Algiers. By a resolution of 1819, ships-of-the-line were to be named after the States, frigates after the rivers of the United States, and sloops-of-war after the chief cities and towns. At the outbreak of the Civil War there were but forty-two vessels in commission, and these had been scattered over the globe by Secretary Toucey. A new navy had to be constructed, in order to maintain the blockade of Southern ports, and to assist the operations of land forces on the Atlantic coast, on the Gulf and in inland waters. Steam and armor-plate and the invention of the turreted "Monitor" revolutionized naval architecture during the war. By January 1, 1864, the National Government had 588 vessels (seventy-five of them ironclads), with 4443 guns, and 35,000 men. After the war the navy was reduced. Great sums continued to be expended upon it, but with so little effect that, in 1882, in a nominal navy of 140 vessels, there were but thirty-eight that were capable of sea-going service. At that time a new policy regarding the navy was inaugurated, and now, after great expenditures, the navy consists, including vessels in process of construction, of six battleships, twenty-one cruisers, and a dozen or so other vessels. The principal achievements of the navy are to be found under the names of the vessels.

Navy, Department of the, one of the eight executive departments at Washington, was created by an Act of Congress April 30, 1798, and has been largely developed in later days. In 1862 the hydrographic office was established. An assistant secretary was added in 1890.

Neal, John (1793–1876), first came into prominence by his articles upon American politics and customs. He was one of the most brilliant journalists of his time, dealing with literature, history and biography, and wrote novels of some prominence in their day.

Nebraska originally constituted a portion of the Louisiana cession of 1803. The first white men to visit the Nebraska country were Lewis and Clark in 1804–05. The territory was organized in 1854, May 30, and included, besides Nebraska, Montana, Wyoming, the Dakotas and part of Colorado. The bill for the organization of the territory was introduced by Stephen A. Douglas, and provided that any States which should be formed from the territory should exercise their own choice in regard to the existence of slavery. This set aside the famous Missouri Compromise of 1820, and aroused the utmost indignation at the North. In 1863 the territory was reduced to its present limits, and in 1867 it became a State. The State has been Republican, except in the year 1890, when a Democratic Governor was elected. The population in 1867 was 60,000; in 1890 it was 1,058,910.

Necessity, Fort (July 3, 1754). From Great Meadows Washington had advanced toward Fort Duquesne, but hearing that a large detachment of French were on foot he fell back to his former position. Here he hastily erected a rude entrenchment which he called Fort Necessity. On July 1st his garrison amounted to about 300 men. The French numbered nearly 500, including Indians. On July 3d they approached the fort in a pouring rain. The French had a superior position, and the fight raged intermittently for nine hours. At length a parley sounded, and after little delay the garrison capitulated with honors of war, surrendering prisoners taken at Great Meadows and being assured of unmolested retreat.

Negro Plot. March 18, 1741, a fire occurred in the chapel and barracks at Fort George on the Battery in New York. It was generally believed to be accidental, but charges were set afloat that it arose from a plot by the negroes to burn the town. Eight other fires of a mysterious nature within a month strengthened this belief. Mary Burton, a servant of one John Hughson, furnished testimony implicating a number of sailors and negroes. Twenty whites and over 160 slaves were seized and imprisoned. Finally Mary Burton's accusations inculpated persons of such character that danger from that direction checked the fury. It was charged that the Spanish were inciting plots among the negroes through Roman Catholic priests. Four whites were hanged, eighteen negroes hanged and thirteen burned at the stake.

Negro Troops were employed to a slight extent in the Revolutionary War. Though a few generals made use of them in the first two years of the Civil War, and Congress authorized their employment at the Sea Islands, the first general provision for their enlistment was made in July, 1863. After that they were employed in considerable numbers, and at times with great success.

Negroes. In 1790 there were 757,000 colored people in the United States; in 1800 there were 1,002,000; in 1810, 1,378,000; in 1820, 1,772,000; in 1830, 2,329,000; in 1840, 2,874,000; in 1850, 3,639,000; in 1860, 4,442,000; in 1870, 4,880,000; in 1880, 6,581,000; in 1890, 7,470,000. (See also Slavery.)

Neill, Edward D. (1823–1893), of Minnesota, was a chaplain during the Civil War. He has written "English Colonization in America," "Concise History of Minnesota," and extensive works upon the histories of Virginia and Maryland, the chief being "The Virginia Company of London" and "Terra Mariæ."

Nelson, Samuel (1792–1873), of New York, was a Circuit Judge from 1823 to 1831. He was a Justice of the New York Supreme Court from 1831 to 1837 and its Chief Justice from 1837 to 1845. He was a Justice of the U. S. Supreme Court from 1845 to 1872. He was a member of the Joint High Commission, which in 1871 negotiated the Treaty of Washington.

Nelson, Thomas (1738–1789), was a member of the Virginia Conventions of 1774, 1775 and 1776. He represented Virginia in the Continental Congress from 1776 to 1777 and in 1779. He signed the Declaration of Independence. He was Governor of Virginia in 1781. He expended his vast estate for the colonial cause.

Nelson, William (1825–1862), of Kentucky, organized several regiments in 1861. He commanded a division at Shiloh and Richmond. He commanded Louisville when threatened by General Bragg in 1862. He was shot in an altercation with General J. C. Davis.

Nelson's Farm. (See Glendale.)

Netherlands. The republic of the United Netherlands was one of the first to welcome the United States into the sisterhood of nations. Her willingness to establish commercial relations led to a rupture with Great Britain. In 1782 a treaty of amity and commerce was concluded, which became abrogated by the republic of the United Netherlands losing its independence. At the Congress of Vienna the kingdom of the Netherlands was established, from which Belgium revolted in 1830. A commercial treaty was signed in 1839, and consular conventions in 1855 and 1878. A convention relative to extradition was concluded in 1880. (See Belgium.)

Neutrality, Armed. (See Armed Neutrality.)

Neutrality, Proclamation of. Upon the declaration of war between France and Great Britain in 1793 it was decided unanimously by President Washington and his Cabinet that a proclamation of neutrality should issue and that a French minister should be received. Jay was appointed to draft the proclamation. It declared the intention of the United States to pursue a line of conduct friendly to both nations, and enjoined upon the citizens to avoid a contravention of this disposition under pain of prosecution. Curiously enough the word "neutrality" was omitted in the proclamation, though enforced with fairness by the President. It was probably purposely omitted.

Neuville, Jean G., Baron Hyde de (1776–1847), was exiled to the United States from France from 1806 to 1814. He was French Minister to the United States from 1816 to 1822, and negotiated the French treaty of 1822.

Nevada was formed from the Mexican cession of 1848. Prior to that date no settlement had been made in the State. In that year settlements were made by Mormons in the Carson and Washoe Valleys. In 1859 silver was discovered. In 1861 Nevada was organized as a territory, and October 31, 1864, it was admitted as a State. In 1866 its territory was increased by portions of Arizona and Utah. Until 1870 the Republicans controlled the State. In that year the Democrats elected the Governor, who was re-elected in 1874. In 1880 the Presidential electors were Democratic, in 1892 they were of the People's party. The population of the State in 1864 was 40,000; in 1890 it was 45,761.

New Albion. The name given to what is now Upper California and Oregon by Sir Francis Drake in 1579. In that year Drake took possession of this territory in the Queen's name, but it was not claimed by the British till three centuries later.—June 21, 1634, Sir Edmund Plowden obtained a grant of territory, called in the letters patent "New Albion." The boundaries of this New Albion were so defined as to include all of New Jersey, Maryland, Delaware and Pennsylvania embraced in a square, the eastern side, forty leagues in length, extending from Sandy Hook to Cape May, together with Long Island and all other "isles and islands within ten leagues of the shore." The province was made a county palatine with Plowden as earl. Little effort at settlement was made, and nothing come of the grant.

New Amsterdam. (See New York City.)

New Archangel. (See Sitka.)

New Bedford, Mass., was set off from Dartmouth, of which it was originally a part, in 1787. It received a city charter in 1847. Its history as a great whaling port began as early as 1755.

New Berne, or Newbern, at one time capital of the province of North Carolina, was founded about 1693 by Christopher de Grafenried, a Swiss baron. During the Civil War, Newbern was an important seaport in the possession of the Confederates. It was captured and partially burned by the Union leader, Burnside, March 14, 1862. The gunboats shelled the woods as Burnside advanced, thereby clearing the way. An insignificant fortification was destroyed near the town. Burnside captured forty-six guns, three light batteries and a large amount of stores. Later, in 1864, Newbern was occupied by the Federal General, Foster, with a small force. Pickett commanded the Confederates in that section then. February 1 and 2, he attacked Foster's outposts and captured them, inflicting slight losses. Then he assaulted the main encampment, sending at the same time a regiment to attack the Federal gunboat, "Underwriter," then lying at the Newbern dock. Little was accomplished by these attacks, and Pickett retired.

New England. The name was first given to the region by Captain John Smith, in his map of 1616. Though formed into separate colonies and

States, the region has always had a certain degree of unity, as a region of Puritan colonies, of similar religious and political predilections and similar industries and economic life. In 1643 most of its colonies were united in the New England Confederation. See United Colonies of New England.

New England, Council for, a "Council established at Plymouth, in the county of Devon, for the planting, ordering, ruling and governing of New England in America." It was incorporated November 3, 1620, and was little else than the reorganization of the Plymouth, or North Virginia Company of 1606. Ferdinando Gorges was the moving spirit of the new corporation. Bradford obtained from this company a patent permitting the settlement of the Pilgrim Fathers. In 1621 Gorges obtained an additional grant of territory called Laconia, which comprised parts of the present States of Maine and New Hampshire. The lands of the new company, which now extended from Long Island to the Bay of Fundy, were distributed among twenty noblemen.

"New England Courant," the fourth newspaper published in the colonies. It was established in 1721 at Boston, by James Franklin, who had been deprived of the printing of the *Boston News Letter*. Franklin's friends were much opposed to the publication of a new journal, for they thought one quite sufficient for the entire continent. But Franklin inaugurated a new departure in journalism by attacking the Government officials and lampooning the clergy. On this account the suppression of his paper was threatened, whereupon Benjamin Franklin assumed the editorship, and continued the publication with the same freedom. It was finally suppressed in 1727.

New England Emigrant Company, a corporation formed at Boston in 1855 to control emigration to the newly formed Territory of Kansas in the interest of the anti-slavery party. Slavery in Kansas had been made possible by the adoption of the Kansas-Nebraska bill, and slavery advocates in Missouri were actively at work for its establishment. The Emigrant Company aided immeasurably in making Kansas a free State.

New England Shilling, the name given to the first coins issued in 1652 by the mint established in that year at Boston. They were of the value of "12d, 6d and 3d peeces," stamped N E on the face and XII, VI or III on the reverse to denote the value. The value of the first named equaled eighteen and one-fourth cents.

New France was founded by Champlain's settlement of Quebec in 1608. Cultivating friendly relations with the Indians, fur-traders soon explored the St. Lawrence basin, the Great Lakes and the Mississippi, while Jesuit missions still further extended French influence. But the province was over-governed by Louis XIV., and though some of the governors were able men, the creation of a strong empire was prevented by paternalism, crushing out all individual initiative, by excessive centralization, by official corruption and by religious bigotry. In 1690 the English colonies had eight times as large a population, in 1754 twenty times as great. But New France proved herself strong in a military sense. See the wars,—King William's War, Queen Anne's War, King George's War, French and Indian War, and the chief officials, Frontenac and Montcalm. The final struggle was for the possession of the Ohio and Mississippi Valleys, and was a part of the Seven Years' War. Its result was, to prevent the French scheme of connecting Canada and Louisiana in one great empire, and entirely to destroy New France. The Treaty of Paris (1763) gave it all to England. Histories by Parkman.

New Granada. (See Colombia.)

New Hampshire was one of the original thirteen States. In 1622 Sir Ferdinando Gorges and John Mason obtained a grant of the land lying between the Merrimac and the Kennebec rivers. Rye, Dover and Portsmouth were settled by Churchmen and royalists. In 1629 Mason obtained a separate grant for the territory between the Merrimac and the Piscataqua. Upon the death of Mason the colony was left to itself until 1641, when it was annexed to Massachusetts. In 1679 New Hampshire was made a royal province; in 1685 it was again annexed to Massachusetts, and in 1749 it again became a royal province. At the outbreak of the Revolution, in 1775, New Hampshire was advised by the general government to form a temporary government. Constitutions were adopted in 1776, 1784 and 1792, which last has been twice amended in 1852 and 1877. The National Constitution was ratified with difficulty, June 21, 1788, by a vote of 57 to 46. At first New Hampshire was Federalist. In 1805 the Democrats secured control of the State, which they held until 1855, except in the years 1809–1810, 1813–1816. The Democrats attacked the charter of Dartmouth College in 1816, and the case was argued successfully in favor of the royal charter before the U. S. Supreme Court by Daniel Webster. Complaints were made in 1829 by Hill and Woodbury, the Jackson leaders in the State, that Mason, the president of the Portsmouth branch of the U. S. Bank, was guilty of partiality in his loans. This led to the bank troubles of Jackson's administration. From 1856 to 1894 the State was usually Republican. The population in 1790 was 141,885; in 1890 it was 376,530. History by Belknap.

"**New Hampshire Gazette**," a newspaper established in 1756 at Portsmouth, N. H., by D. Fowle. This was the first newspaper in the State. In 1772 it was called the *New Hampshire Gazette and Historical Chronicle;* in 1776 the *Freeman's Journal or New Hampshire Gazette;* in 1788 the *New Hampshire Gazette and General Advertiser;* in 1796 the *New Hampshire Gazette* again. It is now published as the weekly edition of the *Daily Chronicle*, established in 1852.

New Hampshire Grants. (See Vermont.)

New Hampshire Historical Society, founded in 1823, has issued nine volumes of "Collections" and a volume of its proceedings.

New Haven Colony. In 1638 a body of immigrants under Theophilus Eaton and John Davenport settled at Quinnipiack, on the Sound, where they lived for a year without government other than religious unity. Then they formed a government and established the New Haven colony. This colony entered the New England Confederacy, formed in 1643 for protection against the Canada settlers, the Dutch and Indians. In 1662 the younger Winthrop obtained from Charles II. a charter for the Connecticut colony, which charter included the New Haven colony. The latter resisted obstinately for many months, and was supported by Massachusetts and Plymouth. On the arrival of the royal commission, she was forced to give way and become absorbed in Connecticut (1664).

New Ireland. In 1779, a British force and fleet under McNeill and Mowatt held possession of what is now known as the Castine peninsula, in Maine. An expedition was sent from Boston to dislodge them. This failed. The British, as a result of their success, endeavored the next year to erect Maine into a province under the name of New Ireland.

New Jersey was one of the original thirteen States. The Dutch made a small settlement in the south, and in 1655, under Governor Stuyvesant, erected Fort Nassau on the Delaware River, and forced the Swedes, who had made a settlement in 1638, to acknowledge their rule. When the Duke of York secured the country, in 1664, he granted the territory between the Delaware and the Hudson to Lord Berkeley and Sir George Carteret, and gave it its present name in honor of Carteret, who had held the island of Jersey for Charles II. during the Great Rebellion. In 1665 some English emigrants settled Elizabethtown. New Englanders founded Middletown and Newark in 1666. Berkeley finally sold his share to certain Quakers, who sold it to a party headed by William Penn (1676). A boundary line was agreed upon, running from Little Egg Harbor northwest to the Delaware at 41° 40′ north latitude. 400 Quakers settled in West New Jersey in 1677. William Penn and his associates purchased East New Jersey in 1682. In 1686 writs of *quo warranto* were issued against the governments of both Jerseys, but the proprietary rights were undisturbed. The two colonies were united in a royal colony in 1702. New Jersey was a principal theatre of fights in 1777 and 1778. First Constitution, 1776 (present, 1844). New Jersey ratified the National Constitution December 18, 1787. A property qualification of £50 for voting existed until 1820. The political parties have always been nearly equal, and have experienced few changes in strength. During the war the State was strongly Democratic. Since the war the State has cast its votes for Democratic Presidential candidates with the exception of 1872. The State Legislature has usually been in the hands of the Republicans. The population of the State in 1790 was 184,139; in 1890 it was 1,444,933. History by Scott.

New Jersey Historical Society, founded in 1845, has issued eight volumes of "Collections" and twenty volumes of its proceedings.

New Jersey Plan, a scheme of a Federal Constitution suggested in the Convention of 1787 by William Paterson, of New Jersey, June 15. It proposed: The enlargement and correction of the Articles of Confederation; that Congress should remain a single body, and should regulate taxation and commerce, and should choose the executive; that requisitions from States should be continued; that a judiciary should be established; that naturalization should be uniform; that the executive should coerce refractory States or individuals, and other provisions of less importance. This plan was unfavorably reported, the Randolph plan being preferred, as creating a stronger government and doing more to remedy the defects of the Confederation.

New Jerseymen Foreigners. The saying that New Jersey is a foreign State comes down from the time when Joseph Bonaparte, ex-king of Spain and Naples, after the downfall of Napoleon, sought an asylum in the United States. As an alien he was obliged to obtain a special act of legislature to enable him to hold real estate. Pennsylvania refused, but New Jersey consented, and he established himself in princely magnificence at Bordentown. Hence men of other States used humorously to declare that the Jerseymen, with their foreign prince, were foreigners, and their State not a part of the Union.

"New Lights," religious revivalists in Massachusetts and Connecticut in 1734 and for some years later, during the period known as the "Great Awakening." The movement was started by Jonathan Edwards and became a wild passion under the ministrations of George Whitefield. The "New Lights" were so called in contradistinction to the "Old Lights," or more conservative churchmen.

New London, Conn. In 1781 New London was a resort of privateers and a favorite depot for the West India trade. September 7, the traitor, Benedict Arnold, was sent by Clinton against this town. He succeeded in plundering and destroying a large amount of property. Fort Griswold, on the opposite side of the Thames, was carried, and its commander, Colonel Ledyard, and sixty soldiers mercilessly killed. Arnold retired when the militia began to assemble. (See also Blue Lights.)

New Madrid, Mo., a strong Confederate position, fortified by General Leonidas Polk and garrisoned by troops from Beauregard's command. It was captured by the Federals under General Pope, March 14, 1862. Pope had been dispatched by Halleck for this purpose and, moving down the Mississippi River, had encamped two miles from New Madrid. Siege guns having been brought from Cairo, General Plummer was sent by night to sink trenches and place sharp-shooters. This having been accomplished, firing began early March 13. Three of the six Confederate gunboats were speedily disabled, and the next night, in the midst of a storm, New Madrid was evacuated. Many valuable supplies were captured.

New Mexico was organized as a Territory September 9, 1850, from territory acquired from Mexico. The Spaniard Nuñez visited the country in 1537, and Coronado in 1540. In 1581 Bonillo explored the region and named it New Mexico. Santa Fe was founded about 1609. The Spaniards had great difficulty with the Pueblo Indians. General Kearny captured Santa Fe in 1846, and two years later, by the treaty of Guadalupe Hidalgo, the United States came into possession of New Mexico. The Territory of New Mexico was organized by Act of Congress September 9, 1850. In 1853 a portion of the "Gadsden Purchase" was annexed. In 1866 the Territory was finally reduced to its present boundaries. The fear that a State church would be established by the Mexicans in the State has prevented its admission into the Union. The population of the Territory in 1890 was 153,593. History by Bancroft.

New Netherland. (See New York.)

New Netherlands Company. This company was formed in 1615 after the ascent of Hudson River by the Englishman who gave that river his name. Hudson was at that time in the employ of Holland. The company was founded by Amsterdam merchants, who obtained a monopoly of the trade for three years, and established a settlement at Manhattan and trading posts on the Delaware River. The company was succeeded by the Dutch West India Company.

New Orange, the name given to the city of New York in 1673, when the colony of New Netherland was retaken from England by the States General of Holland. It was so called in honor of the Prince of Orange.

New Orleans, La., was founded in 1718 by Jean Baptiste Lemoyne de Bienville, and a few years later (1722) was made the capital of the vast territory known as Louisiana. In 1765 the town received the exiles from Acadia, and in 1768 rose in arms against the cession of Louisiana to Spain. The following year the people were compelled to submit by a large Spanish force. In 1788 and 1794 the town was almost totally destroyed by fire. In 1803 the city, with the rest of Louisiana, was turned over to France, and by France to the United States. In 1807, Burr's conspiracy was here foiled, and on January 8, 1815, occurred the battle of New Orleans. In December, 1814, 7000 British troops, under General Pakenham, were transported from Jamaica to Lake Borgne for an attack on New Orleans. General Jackson made every possible preparation to resist them. On December 23, December 28 and January 1, he had gained minor successes over them. But Pakenham was reinforced to 10,000 men. The decisive battle occurred on January 8, 1815. General Jackson with 5000 men drew up his first line in three detachments, two on the left bank and one of 800 men under General Morgan on the right bank. The line was defended by numerous batteries and redoubts, and by an armed vessel, the "Louisiana." General Pakenham, with 10,000 veteran troops, planned an attack in three divisions. On the night before the battle Colonel Thornton was ordered to cross the river and attack General Morgan. At dawn, the British second division, under General Gibbs, attacked Jackson's left, and soon after, the third division, under General Keane, attacked the right. This last movement was at first successful and captured part of Jackson's works, but the battery and musketry fire was so deadly that they fell back in disorder. Meantime from this division General Keane had detached half to assist the second division under General Gibbs. This had attacked Jackson's strongest position. As they advanced to the charge they were killed by the hundreds, yet did not falter. When within 200 yards of the American line, the Kentucky and Tennessee riflemen, deadly shots, four ranks deep, fired line by line. The slaughter was terrible, but the British, now reinforced by General Keane's troops, pressed on up to the very parapets. But Generals Pakenham and Gibbs were both mortally wounded. General Keane and Major Wilkinson, the next in command, were so severely wounded that they were carried from the field and the British fell back in disorder. Colonel Thornton's division had meantime captured General Morgan's position on the right bank of the river, but was recalled in view of the defeat on the other side. The British lost in this battle 700 killed, 1400 wounded, and 500 prisoners. The American loss was eight killed and thirteen wounded. Occurring after the conclusion of peace at Ghent, the battle had no lasting results, but was famous as the one great success won by American land forces in the War of 1812. In the Civil War New Orleans was captured and occupied, May 1, 1862, by Captain Farragut and General Butler, after four days, April 24 to 27, inclusive, spent in bombarding Forts Jackson and St. Philip, the Confederate strongholds below the city, and in defeating the Confederate fleet. The Union armament consisted of four sloops of war, seventeen gunboats, twenty-one bomb-schooners, these latter in charge of Commander Porter, and two sailing vessels. Lovell, for the Confederates, commanded thirteen armed steamers, the steam battery "Louisiana," of sixteen guns, and the ram "Manassas," besides a flotilla of five ships and rafts. There was in addition a land force of some 3000 men. Crossing the bar April 8, Farragut spent several days in preparing for a bombardment of Forts Jackson and St. Philip. April 27 the bombardment began, 1400 shells being thrown in one day. The Union fleet was then arranged in two columns and prepared to pass the forts, Farragut's column firing upon Fort Jackson, Bailey's upon Fort St. Philip. A chain had been placed across the river, but this was broken; the "Hartford," Farragut's ship, got safely through under cover of Porter's mortar-boats, and the others followed. The forts were silenced, and the Confederate flotilla attacked and almost entirely destroyed. Lovell fled and Farragut demanded the surrender of New Orleans from the mayor. This was finally granted and Butler took charge. In 1890, great excitement against murderous Italians led to lynchings by a mob.

New Plymouth. (See Plymouth Colony.)

New Somersetshire, a grant of territory extended to William Gorges in 1636, and comprising those settlements along the coast of Maine, which had not been included in the Ferdinando Gorges patent of 1631. William Gorges was appointed Deputy-Governor.

New Sweden, the name given to the colony which the Swedes in 1638 established on the Delaware River and Bay. (See Delaware.)

New York was one of the original thirteen colonies. Henry Hudson, in the employ of the Dutch East India Company, discovered the Hudson River (1609) while seeking for a passage to India. The Dutch carried on fur trade with the Indians with no serious attempt at colonization until (1621) the formation of the Dutch West India Company, when the patroon system was introduced (which gave rise to the anti-rent difficulties of 1839–46). Settlements were made at Fort Nassau (Albany) 1614, and New Amsterdam (New York) 1623. The four Dutch Governors were Minuit, Van Twiller, Kieft and Stuyvesant. In 1664 Nicolls captured the colony for the English and introduced the mixed system of local government. At this time the population was very heterogeneous, eighteen languages being spokon. Andros was made Governor of New England and New York in 1688. His deputy, Nicholson, was overthrown in New York by Leisler. In 1690 the first colonial congress met at Albany to consider Indian troubles. About 1700 Captain Kidd, the pirate, was captured. The "negro plot" of 1741 caused terrible excitement. During the Revolution the State contained many

Tories. In 1777 the first State Constitution was adopted (others, 1821 and 1846). The National Constitution was with difficulty adopted July 26, 1788. The political history of New York until 1807 was a struggle of the great families for control. In 1798 Burr introduced the "machine" into the politics of New York City. The Livingstons and Clintons introduced the spoils system in 1801. From 1823 to 1850 New York was for the most part under the control of the Albany Regency. When Van Buren entered Jackson's Cabinet he carried the practical methods used by the Regency into national politics. The Erie Canal was opened in 1825, and the following year the first railroad, the Hudson and Mohawk, was chartered. In 1826 William Morgan, who had divulged some of the secrets of the Masonic Order, disappeared, and the Masons were charged with his murder. The Anti-Masonic party was formed and nominated William Wirt, of Virginia, for President in 1831. The "loco focos" opposed the grant of special banking privileges. The "hunkers" desired the extension of the canal system, the "barn-burners" its restriction. In 1850 the Regency disappeared. In 1855 the "know-nothing" party elected State officers below the Governor. After this the State was Republican until 1862, when the Democrats elected the Governor. During the Civil War the State furnished 467,047 troops to the Union army. In 1873 the Democratic party was thoroughly organized by Samuel J. Tilden. In 1871–72 William M. Tweed was convicted of peculation in New York City. The failure of Jay Cooke & Co. caused a financial panic in 1873. John Kelly led a revolt of Tammany against the regular Democratic candidate, Robinson, in 1879, and caused the election of a Republican Governor. Garfield refused to grant the control of the patronage in New York to the Senators, Conkling and Platt, whereupon they resigned their seats and appealed to the Legislature for re-election, but were defeated in July, 1881. A division of Republicans into "stalwarts" and "half breeds" followed. In recent years the Republicans have carried the elections of the years 1872, 1879, 1881, 1883, 1888 and 1893. In 1882 Cleveland was elected Governor by a majority of 192,854. A constitutional convention sits in 1894. The population of New York, which in 1790 was 340,120, in 1890 was 5,997,853. The fifth State in 1790, it became the most populous in 1820, and has remained such ever since. History by Roberts.

New York City, formerly called New Amsterdam, was settled by the Dutch in 1623. In August, 1664, the city surrendered to the British under the Duke of York, and the name was changed to New York, an English form of government being established. In July, 1673, the Dutch recaptured the city and named it New Orange. It was restored to the British crown, however, on November 10 of the following year. The English government granted liberal charters to the city in 1686 and 1732. In 1688 occurred Leisler's revolt. In 1741 a supposed plot of negro slaves to burn the city and murder the whites was discovered, and a number of negroes were hanged or burned at the stake. In 1765 a congress of colonial delegates, called the Stamp Act Congress, met in this city and drew up a declaration of rights against Great Britain's arbitrary taxation. In 1774 a ship laden with tea was sent back to England, and chests on another vessel were thrown overboard. After the battle of Long Island the city fell into the hands of the

British who occupied it until the close of the Revolution. From 1784 to 1797 New York was the State capital and from 1785 to 1790 the seat of the United States Government. Washington was inaugurated here April 30, 1789. The completion of the Erie Canal in 1825 made New York the outlet of the surplus produce of the West. In July, 1863, a serious draft riot occurred. In 1872 the "Tweed Ring," which had been plundering the city through the possession of the municipal offices, was broken up. The era of elevated railroads began in 1878. Columbia College was incorporated here in 1754 as King's College. The population of the city was in 1790, 33,131; 1810, 96,373; 1820, 123,706; 1840, 312,710; 1860, 805,658; 1870, 942,292; 1880, 1,206,299; 1890, 1,515,301.

"**New York Gazette,**" established as first news journal of New York by William Bradford in New York City, 1725. It was discontinued about 1742, but was begun again the same year by James Parker as the *Gazette and Weekly Post Boy*. Parker formed a partnership with Holt. The latter published the paper alone for some years, but then relinquished it to Parker, when he started his *Journal*. Parker died in 1770, and the *Gazette* survived him only two years, most of its subscribers having followed Holt and the *Journal*. It was finally suspended in 1772. This newspaper was the organ of the New York government and steadily supported the latter through a period of bitter controversy.

"**New York Herald,**" established May 6, 1835, by James Gordon Bennett. The price was one penny, and the first numbers were printed on a four page paper 30 x 24. The *Herald* was a lively competitor with the *Sun* for the support of the masses. From its beginning a specialty was made of shipping news. The editor proposed that the *Herald* should be an independent journal. The price was afterward raised to three cents.

New York Historical Society was founded in 1804 and incorporated in 1809. It has published twenty-five volumes of "Collections," and four volumes of its proceedings.

"**New York Packet and American Advertiser.**" This newspaper was founded in New York City, in 1776, by Samuel Loudon and was at first issued as a weekly. It was afterward removed to Fishkill, but brought back to New York after the Revolution and published there during several years as a daily. It was then suspended.

"**New York Sun,**" first successful penny paper established in the United States. It was founded in September, 1833, by Benjamin H. Day, a printer, who promised in his prospectus to publish all the news of the day for one penny. The success of the paper was due rather to the demand of the people for such a journal than to its able management. The first number was a folio of twelve columns, ten inches to the column. The price was raised to two cents per copy after the Civil War.

"**New York Times,**" established in 1850 by Henry J. Raymond, who had been associated with Horace Greeley in the editorship of the *Tribune*. The *Times* had a strong financial backing and gained an immediate success. It became a member of the Associated Press in the year of its initial appearance, and remained one of the most important of American papers.

"**New York Tribune,**" established April 10, 1841, by Horace Greeley, as a penny paper. Its success was assured from the start, although the *Sun* endeavored to hinder its circulation. Greeley's assistants were Henry J. Raymond, and Charles A. Dana, present editor of the New York *Sun*. George William Curtis, Bayard Taylor, Albert Brisbane and other distinguished writers contributed to its columns.

"**New York Weekly Journal,**" the second newspaper issued in the colony of New York. It is considered a prototype of the modern American political journal. John Peter Zenger established this paper in New York City in 1733, the first issue appearing November 3. It was founded avowedly for the purpose of opposing the administration of Governor Cosby. The columns were filled with sharp criticisms and poetical fusillades, contributed by opponents of the Government. Its publication was suspended in 1752, but revived by John Holt in 1766, with new types and printing apparatus.

Newark, N. J., was founded in 1666 by a company of Puritans from Connecticut. It was at first governed mainly according to Mosaic law. During the Revolution the town was several times ravaged.

Newberry, John S. (1822–1892), geologist, has made extensive exploration in the Western United States, which revealed the vast resources of the West. He conducted the Mississippi Valley Sanitary Department from 1861 to 1866.

Newburg, N. Y., founded in 1708 by a band of Germans under a grant from Queen Anne. The town was afterward settled chiefly by the Scotch and English, who gave it the name of Newburg in 1743. A new patent was obtained in 1752, and the town was systematically laid out. In 1782, after the defeat of Cornwallis, Washington encamped his army at Newburg. Here the army was disbanded April 19, 1783.

Newburg Addresses, two anonymous appeals issued in 1783 to the officers of Washington's army, then encamped at Newburg, to hold a meeting for the consideration of the question of the money then due them by Congress. The addresses were written by Captain Armstrong, of Pennsylvania, and were supposed to have been instigated by the Gates faction. Washington immediately denounced the meeting as subversive of discipline, and called a regular meeting of the officers for March 16. Gates was placed in the chair, and Washington's friends carried motions declaring "their unshaken confidence in Congress," and denouncing the "infamous proposals" of the anonymous addresses.

Newburyport, Mass., was settled in 1635. It was distinguished for its patriotism during the Revolution and in the War of 1812, and was down to that time an important shipping port.

Newcomb, Simon, born in 1835, came to the United States from Canada in 1853. Since 1884 he has been professor of mathematics in the Johns Hopkins University. For his astronomical work he has received the highest honors at home and abroad.

Newgate Prison. (See Simsbury.)

Newmarket, in the southwestern part of Virginia. Near this place, May 15, 1864, Sigel, with 10,000 Federal troops, was defeated by Breckinridge, commanding about an equal force of Confederates. The Federals were aiming at the Confederate resources near Staunton and Lynchburg, and Breckinridge moved to meet them. There was some skirmishing and then Breckinridge ordered a charge which decided the day. In this fight 225 cadets from the Virginia Military Institute took part.

Newport, Christopher, born in England about 1565, was one of the founders of Jamestown, Va., in 1606. In 1608 he brought settlers and supplies to the colonists from England and returned with a cargo of yellow mica, thinking it was gold. He again came over in 1610 with Lord Delaware. He returned to England in 1612. He wrote "Discoveries in America."

Newport, R. I., was settled in 1638 by a party of colonists from Massachusetts under William Coddington. Newport was in the last century an important seat of commerce. It early resisted the overbearing policy of the British Government, and her citizens burned the English sloop "Liberty," stationed in the harbor to exact an unpopular tax. During the Revolution 8,000 British and Hessian troops held the town and committed ravages on all sides. On their retirement many prominent Loyalist citizens emigrated with them. Newport contains the "Old Stone Mill," supposed by some to have been built by the Northmen. It was permanently incorporated as a city in 1853.

"Newport Mercury," the second newspaper published in Rhode Island. It was founded and edited by James Franklin, and the first numbers appeared at Newport in September, 1758. This journal attained considerable success, becoming at once self-supporting. It has never been suspended since the first publication, and continues at the present time under the original title.

Newspapers. The first genuine newspaper established in the United States was the *Boston News Letter*, founded at Boston in 1704 by Postmaster John Campbell, and continued until 1776. Previous to this there had been issued at Boston three publications of one number each. Of these the first, called a *Newspaper Extraordinary*, consisted wholly of extracts from a letter of Dr. Increase Mather, who was then in London endeavoring to obtain a new charter for Massachusetts. This letter was published by Samuel Green in 1689. On September 25, 1690, appeared the first and only number of *Publick Occurrences Foreign and Domestic*, issued by Benjamin Harris. The authorities promptly seized and suppressed the paper as "a pamphlet published contrary to law and containing reflections of a very high nature." In 1697 B. Green and J. Allen republished a news letter, bearing no title, which had been issued in London the same year. It was printed on a single page, and contained small news items from the continent. After the *Boston News Letter*, there appeared in 1719 the *Boston Gazette*, Andrew Bradford issuing the *American Weekly Mercury* at Philadelphia the same year. James Franklin established the *New England Courant* at Boston two years later. This was suppressed for its attacks upon the Government and clergy, but was revived by Benjamin Franklin. William Bradford began the *Gazette* at New York in 1725, and John Peter Zenger the *New York Weekly Journal* in 1733, in the cause of the people against the Colonial Government. Zenger's paper may be regarded as a prototype of the modern news journal. Newspapers were founded in the other colonies in the following order: In Maryland, at Annapolis, in 1727; in South Carolina, at Charleston, in 1731; in Rhode Island, at Newport, in 1731; in Virginia, at Williamsburg, in 1736; in North Carolina, at New Berne, in 1755; in Connecticut, at New Haven, in 1755; in New Hampshire, at Portsmouth, in 1756; in Georgia, at Savannah, in 1763; in Vermont, at Westminster, in 1781. Between 1704 and 1775 seventy-eight different newspapers had been printed with varied success in the colonies. Of these, thirty-nine were in actual process of publication at the outbreak of the Revolution. The papers most influential in advancing the revolutionary cause were the *Boston Gazette* and the *Massachusetts Spy*. On the British occupation of Boston, New York and Philadelphia, most of the Whig journals were suspended. It has been estimated that the thirty-nine newspapers of 1775 circulated about 1,200,000 copies annually. After the Federal Constitution was adopted the newspapers fell largely into the hands of English immigrants, men of versatility and talent. Violent partisan controversies arose. The most influential papers of this period were the *Columbian Centinel*, published at Boston during forty years, commencing in 1784, by Benjamin Russell; the *New York Minerva*, established at New York in 1793 by Noah Webster; the *New York Evening Post*, established as the central organ of the Federalists in 1801; the *Philadelphia Aurora*, founded by Benjamin Franklin Bache in 1790, and afterward edited with vindictive partisanship by William Duane, an Englishman; the *Philadelphia National Gazette*, established in 1791 by Philip Freneau; and the *National Intelligencer*, established at Washington by Samuel H. Smith in 1800. The first daily newspaper was the *American Daily Advertiser*, appearing in Philadelphia in 1784. In 1810 there were twenty-seven daily newspapers in existence. They were published in New York, Boston, Philadelphia, Baltimore, New Orleans, Charleston, Alexandria, Va., and Georgetown, D. C. By 1880 they had increased to 968. The first penny paper was the New York *Sun*, established in 1833 by Benjamin Day. The first Sunday paper was the *Sunday Courier*, appearing in New York in 1825, with but little success. The chief period of the political influence of editors in the United States was that beginning in 1830 and ending after the war. Before that date the editor was often of little account, but from 1830 to 1870 the paper was often known chiefly as the organ of the individual editor's opinions.

Newton, John, born in 1823, commanded a brigade at South Mountain and Antietam. He commanded a division at Fredericksburg and Chancellorsville and a corps at Gettysburg. He superintended the removal of obstructions in Hell Gate, N. Y., in 1885.

Nez Percés, an Indian tribe in Idaho. They have remained friendly to the whites, covering Colonel Steptoe's retreat in the Oregon War. In 1854 they disposed of a part of their land, and a part went on a reservation.

Niagara, Fort. During the French War, in the summer of 1759, the English under Prideaux laid siege to Fort Niagara, which was defended by a garrison of 600. Prideaux was reinforced by Johnson with 2300, partly Indians. After a few weeks an attempt was made to succor the French. This party was beaten off and no alternative was left but to surrender. This the garrison did with honors of war on July 24. By the capture of Niagara, the English cut off the French from all their posts in the interior.—In the War of 1812, on November 21, 1812, a severe bombardment was opened against this fort from the British fortifications on the Canadian side. The artillery duel lasted all day, resulting in slight damage to the fort and the loss of four killed and five wounded. Later, in retaliation for the burning of Newark by the Americans, Colonel Murray, with about 1000 British and Indians, crossed over from Canada, December 19, 1813, and made a night attack upon the fort. The main gate, through gross negligence, was found wide open, the commander was away and the men asleep! The fort was captured without much difficulty, but some slight resistance aroused the passions of the British and a number of Americans were massacred. From this point as a centre the whole Niagara frontier was ravaged and made desolate. With the fort were captured 344 men and immense stores of arms, ammunition and military supplies.

Niagara Falls, so called from an Iroquois Indian word meaning the "thunder of water." It was first visited and described in 1678 by a French missionary, Father Hennepin. In 1751 Kalm, a Swedish naturalist, published a description of the Falls in the *Gentleman's Magazine*. Professor James Hall made a trigonometrical survey and a map of the Falls for the United States Coast Survey in 1842.

Nicaragua. (See also Walker, William.) A commercial treaty was concluded between the United States and Nicaragua in 1867 by which Nicaragua grants free transit to the United States in consideration of the guarantee of the neutrality of routes of communication between the Atlantic and Pacific. An extradition convention was concluded in 1870 and a reciprocity treaty in 1892.

Nicaragua Canal. The Maritime Canal Company of Nicaragua, capital $100,000,000, was incorporated under a charter granted by Congress in 1889, permission having been previously obtained from the Nicaragua Government for the exclusive right of constructing and operating an inter-oceanic ship canal. Excavations were begun October 8, 1891, at San Juan del Norte, or Greytown. The total length of the proposed waterway is 169⅔ miles. The reservoirs of Lakes Nicaragua and Managua furnish an adequate high water level supply. In 1892 the canal had been opened one mile from Greytown. The sum then expended in plant and work amounted to $600,000. A bill reported unanimously by the Senate Foreign Committee, recommending a government guarantee of $100,000,000, has been withdrawn.

Nichola, Lewis (1717–1807), came to America from Ireland in 1766. He was of great service to the colonies during the Revolution by his military knowledge and suggestions. He was brevetted brigadier-general in 1783.

Nicholas, Wilson C. (1757–1820), became an officer in the colonial army and commanded Washington's life-guard until 1783. He was a member of the Virginia Convention that ratified the Federal Constitution. He represented Virginia in the U. S. Senate as a Democrat from 1800 to 1804 and in the House from 1807 to 1809. He was Governor of Virginia from 1814 to 1817.

Nicholson, Alfred O. P. (1808–1876), represented Tennessee in the U. S. Senate as a Democrat from 1841 to 1843 and from 1859 to 1861. He wrote the famous "Nicholson Letter" to aspirants for the Presidential nomination in 1848.

Nicholson, Sir Francis, colonial Governor, died in 1728. He was Lieutenant-Governor of New York in 1688, Governor of Virginia from 1690 to 1692 and from 1699 to 1705, and of Maryland from 1694 to 1699. He commanded at Port Royal in 1710. He was Governor of Nova Scotia from 1712 to 1717 and of South Carolina from 1721 to 1725.

Nicholson, James W. A. (1821–1887), commanded the "Isaac Smith" at Port Royal in 1861. From 1863 to 1864 he commanded the "Shamrock" and in 1864 the monitor "Manhattan" at Fort Gaines and Fort Morgan.

Nicolay, John G., born in 1832, came to America from Bavaria in 1838. He was secretary to President Lincoln from 1860 to 1865. He was U. S. Consul at Paris from 1865 to 1869. He wrote "The Outbreak of the Rebellion," and, with Colonel John Hay, a voluminous work called "Abraham Lincoln: a History."

Nicolet, Jean, a French trader and explorer, who traveled as far west as Wisconsin about 1634. His reports of the Mississippi led the Jesuits to believe it a passage to India.

Nicollet, Jean N. (1786–1843), came to America from France in 1832. He carefully explored the Mississippi Valley, making scientific observations and collecting valuable ethnological information. He prepared a map of the West for the Government.

Nicolls, Sir Richard (1624–1672), came to America with a fleet from England in 1664. New Netherlands surrendered to him without resistance, and he remained Governor till his resignation in 1667. He changed the name to New York, published the first code of English law in America, established English municipal government in the city, and managed the affairs of the colony most creditably.

Niles, Hezekiah (1777–1839), was the founder of *Niles' Register*, a weekly journal, which he edited from 1811 to 1836, and published "The Principles and Acts of the American Revolution."

Niles, John M. (1787–1856), represented Connecticut in the U. S. Senate as a Democrat from 1835 to 1839, and from 1843 to 1849. He was Postmaster-General in Van Buren's Cabinet from 1840 to 1841.

"Niles's Register," a weekly journal established at Baltimore by Hezekiah Niles in 1811, and discontinued by his son in 1849. It was a weekly repository of the documentary and political history of the country, reported with impartiality and fidelity. These reports were made with a fullness not attempted by the local newspapers. *Niles's Register* had a large circulation for many years. It is frequently quoted by historical writers.

Ninety-Six, Fort, Evacuation of, June 29, 1781. One by one the British had evacuated the strongholds in the interior of South Carolina. Fort Ninety-Six alone remained in their possession. This was strongly garrisoned and held out against Greene for twenty-eight days. Rawdon then appeared with 2000 men and Greene prudently retired. The British General, however, could not hold the fort and keep his army so far from the sea-board. Accordingly he evacuated it and retired upon Charleston.

Nipmucks, a tribe of New England Indians, situated in southern-central Massachusetts. The majority of the Nipmucks did not at first join with Philip in his war against the colonists, but were active against the English during the struggle in Connecticut (1675). In January, 1676, the remnant of Philip's tribe, with the Narragansetts, the Quaboag and River Indians, effected a junction with the Nipmucks. On the overthrow of Philip the Nipmucks fled north and west.

Nixon, John (1733–1808), of Massachusetts, was prominent in the pre-revolutionary movements. He commanded at Fort Island in 1776, and led a battalion at Princeton. He was president of the Bank of North America from 1792 to 1808.

No Man's Land. In 1845 Texas, on being admitted into the Union, ceded to the United States that strip of her land which lay north of 36° 30′ North latitude. This piece, 167 miles by 35, was without government until 1890, when it became a part of Oklahoma.

Noah, Mordecai M. (1785–1851), was Consul-General at Tunis from 1813 to 1816. He edited the Democratic *National Advocate* from 1816 to 1826. He attempted to organize an establishment of the Jews at Grand Island in Niagara River.

Noble, John W., born in 1831, served during the Civil War. He was Secretary of the Interior in Harrison's Cabinet from 1889 to 1893.

Nominations. In the earlier stages of American political development, nominations to elective offices were made by private, informal agreements among active politicians, or by the more organized caucus; or else the candidate announced his candidacy publicly, and ran for the office without other nomination. Next came the legislative caucus. From 1796 to 1816 candidates for the Presidency, for one party or the other, were selected by caucuses of the members of Congress belonging to that party. The practice fell into dislike by 1824 (see Caucus). Nominations of State officers to be elected by the people were similarly made by party caucuses in the Legislature. But this gave, in the case of a given party, no representation of those districts whose legislative delegates were not of that party. Hence arose a modification of the caucus, the caucus being supplemented by the addition of delegates specially sent up from those unrepresented districts. From this developed the nominating convention pure and simple (see art. Convention, Nominating) and this institution, developed in the States, was soon transferred to the Federal arena.—In the case of most U. S. officers of importance, not elected by the people, the President nominates, subject to confirmation by the Senate, as provided by the Constitution of 1787. See arts. Removals, and Tenure of Office Act.

Non-Importation Agreement, a compact entered into by the merchants of New York and Boston in 1765, unanimously binding themselves to order no new merchandise from England and to countermand old orders. This was in retaliation for the Stamp Act. The agreement was rendered in 1767 in consequence of the Townshend Acts and was strictly observed until 1770, when tea only was prohibited.

Non-intercourse Act, an Act of Congress passed March 1, 1809, to be substituted for the Non-importation Act and the embargo. It was to continue until the next session of Congress, but was revived by the Acts of June 28, 1809, May 1, 1810, and March 2, 1811. It forbade the entrance to American ports of public or private British or French vessels, all commercial intercourse with France or Great Britain, and the importation, after May 20, 1809, of goods grown or manufactured in France or Great Britain or their colonies.

Nootka Sound. In 1789 the Spaniards seized a number of British vessels in Nootka Sound, in what was then called California, on the ground that they were intruding on Spanish possessions. War nearly resulted. But by the provisions of the so-called Nootka Convention, October 28, 1790, England and Spain agreed to trade along the coast side by side, respecting each other's settlements.

Nordhoff, Charles, born in 1830, came to America from Prussia in 1843. He has been Washington correspondent of the *New York Herald* since 1871. He wrote "Secession in Rebellion," "The Freedmen of South Carolina," "The Communistic Societies of the United States" and "Politics for Young Americans."

Norfolk, Va., was founded in 1705 and became a city in 1845. At the beginning of the Revolution, December 9, 1775, a skirmish took place at Norfolk between Virginia sharpshooters and Governor Dunmore, who had erected a fort to guard the southern approach to Norfolk against any chance rebels. After a hot fire of fifteen minutes, in which the Governor's force lost sixty-seven men, the loyalists retired. The Governor sought the fleet and in revenge fired the town with red-hot shot. Norfolk was scourged by the yellow fever in 1855. During the early part of the Civil War Norfolk was the principal naval depot of the Confederacy. The Union troops obtained possession of the city May 19, 1862, and held it for the remainder of the war.

Normand, Jacques E. (1809–1867), came as an exile to the United States from France in 1848. He established the communistic colony of La Réunion in Texas in 1851, which was afterward expelled by the Government. He has published numerous works on communism.

Norsemen. The vikings of Norway and Iceland are represented in the Icelandic sagas as having voyaged to America about the year 1000. The most famous of these accounts is that respecting Leif Ericsson (see art.). The sagas speak of settlements made on this coast, which maintained their connection with Greenland and the other Norse countries for several centuries. Attempts have been made to locate these settlements at given points on the American coast, as in Rhode Island, but with little success, it is believed by the most scientific authorities. The name of their chief settlement was Vinland. Columbus is supposed by many to have obtained knowledge of their voyages. The idea of connecting the Old Mill at Newport with the Norsemen is now abandoned.

North, Frederick, Earl of Guilford (1733–1792), known as Lord North until 1790, became a Lord of the Treasury in 1763. In 1765 he advocated the Stamp Act and maintained the right of England to tax the colonies. He was Chancellor of the Exchequer and leader of the House of Commons in 1767. From 1770 to 1782 he was First Lord of the Treasury and Prime Minister of England. He followed the policy of George III. in the coercion of the colonies and proposed the enforcement of the tea duty in 1773 and the Boston port bill in 1774. As head of the government he managed the war against America. After Yorktown, the failure of the king's efforts being manifest, he resigned.

"**North American Review,**" a review founded in 1815 by William Tudor, at Boston, and originally published every two months, though now a monthly. Among its contents were found, beside reviews, a variety of miscellaneous and poetical articles. It soon passed into the control of an association of literary men, who met regularly in their editorial capacity. Many changes were made in the magazine and an uniform high standard was maintained throughout. Its earlier files contain the best collection of American literary, political, critical and scientific thought during the first sixty or seventy years from its foundation.

North Anna River, Va., a two days' conflict during the Civil War. Grant commanding 127,000 Federals was endeavoring to push on to Richmond, while Lee opposed him with 110,000 Confederates. The fight occurred May 23 and 25, 1864. When Grant arrived at the North Anna River he found Lee's lines drawn up in a strong position on the other side of the stream. Warren was dispatched across the Jericho Ford by Grant to attack Lee's left, it being his weak point. It was soon strengthened, but Warren managed to repulse Hill's assault and finally drove the Confederates back and entrenched himself near their position, after capturing 1000 prisoners. Hancock meantime had driven McLaws from an ugly fortification at the Chesterfield bridge. Grant thought that his passage of the river was assured on the 24th, but Lee had chosen an impregnable position along the North Anna and Little rivers and some marshes. When Burnside attempted to cross on the 25th, his advance division under Crittenden was driven back with fearful slaughter. Grant therefore decided to retire, June 26th.

North Bend, Ohio, noted for a time as the place of residence of William Henry Harrison.

North Carolina was one of the original thirteen colonies. The first attempts to make a settlement were made by Raleigh. His failures caused

GENERALS OF CIVIL WAR.

George Gordon Meade. D. C. Buell. James B. McPherson. Joseph Hooker.
A. E. Burnside. George B. McClellan. Nathaniel P. Banks. W. S. Rosecranz.
Philip H. Sheridan. Ulysses S. Grant. William T. Sherman.
Benjamin F. Butler. Irvin McDowell. John A. Logan. Winfield S. Hancock.
David Hunter. Henry W. Halleck. George H. Thomas. John Pope.

a prejudice against the region. Soon after the settlement of Virginia, 1607, the territory was explored and small settlements made by hunters and adventurers from Virginia. Charles I. gave the territory to his attorney-general, Sir Robert Heath, in 1629. In 1653, Roger Greene with Virginian dissenters founded the first permanent settlement in North Carolina, at Albemarle. A party of New Englanders made a settlement on the Cape Fear River, 1660, but soon left the country in disgust and were followed by a company from Barbadoes who, in 1665, established the colony of Clarendon, on the Cape Fear River. In 1663, Charles II. gave both Carolinas to eight of his favorites. The territory extended to the parallel 36° 30′ on the north, to 29° on the south, and west to the South Sea. The king gave a charter to the proprietors in 1665, and in 1669 the colonial Legislature attempted to attract immigrants by a law which prevented the collection of all debts incurred by settlers before moving to the Carolinas. In the same year Locke's Fundamental Constitutions attempted to institute the feudal system, but without success, and in 1693 the attempt was abandoned. In 1700 the two colonies were separated, and in 1729 North Carolina became a royal colony. In May, 1775, the "Mecklenburg Declaration of Independence" is said to have been issued by the inhabitants of Mecklenburg County (see art). The first State Constitution was made in 1776 (the present in 1868). The population of the State was large but ill-organized at the time of the Revolution. The State refused to ratify the national Constitution until 1789, and was thus next to the last of the thirteen States to accept that document. The State was Democratic until 1840, when it was controlled by the Whigs until 1852, since which date it has been Democratic. In 1860–61, the sentiment was at first decidedly opposed to secession on the ground that it would be impolitic; but upon Lincoln's call for troops, the Legislature in special session called a State Convention, which on May 20, 1861, passed a secession ordinance. North Carolina was dissatisfied with the Confederate Government, and it was even proposed to secede from the Confederacy. North Carolina was restored to her place in the Union July 11, 1868. In 1869 the Ku Klux Klan appeared in Alamance and Caswell Counties, and Federal aid was solicited by Governor Holden. In 1868 and 1872, Grant carried the State for the Republicans. Since that time the State has been Democratic. The population of the State in 1790 was 393,-751; in 1890 it was 1,617,947. History by Moore.

North Carolina, University of, at Chapel Hill, was chartered in 1787 and organized eight years later.

"**North Carolina Gazette,**" the first newspaper issued in North Carolina. It was established at New Berne in 1749 by James Davis. Its publication was suspended in 1761, but it was revived in 1768. Publication was finally suspended at the outbreak of the Revolutionary War.

North Carolina Historical Society, founded in 1840, but not chartered until 1875. Its headquarters are at Chapel Hill.

North Dakota was originally a part of the Louisiana cession. Before the settlement of the boundary between the United States and Canada it was under British rule. A settlement was made at Pembina in 1812 by

Lord Selkirk, who supposed that the region belonged to the English. With South Dakota it was organized as the Territory of Dakota in 1861. In 1889, November 2, North Dakota became a State. A prohibitory law went into effect July, 1890. Prior to the appearance of the Farmers' Alliance the State was Republican. The population in 1890 was 182,719.

North German Union. The United States concluded a naturalization convention with the North German Union in 1868. (See Germany.)

North Point (near Baltimore). Here the British force while pushing forward to attack Baltimore on September 12, 1814, came upon the American army and immediately joined battle. After two hours' hard fighting, the British right put to flight the American left, which in its retreat threw the rest of the line into confusion and forced a general retreat. The Americans fell back toward Baltimore, leaving behind their wounded and two field pieces.

Northeast Boundary. The Treaty of 1783 defined the Northeast boundary of the United States, toward Canada, as extending from the source of the St. Croix due north to the highlands or watershed between the Atlantic and St. Lawrence systems, thence along those highlands to the northwesternmost head of the Connecticut River. Disputes over this definition lasted from that time to 1842. In 1831 the king of the Netherlands, as arbitrator, made an award which neither party was willing to accept. Finally, by the Webster-Ashburton Treaty of 1842, the present line was agreed upon, not greatly differing from that suggested by the Dutch king, and giving about seven-twelfths of the disputed territory to the United States and about five-twelfths to Great Britain.

Northup Case. Solomon Northup, the son of a freedman, was enticed from his home in Saratoga where he had a family and earned a comfortable livelihood. He was drugged and carried to Washington where he was placed in a slave pen. He was then conveyed South and sold to a hard master with whom he remained for twelve years. He was at length rescued from his servitude through the efforts of Northern friends.

Northwest Boundary Question. The territory bounded north by latitude 54° 40′, east by the Rocky Mountains, south by latitude 42°, and west by the Pacific Ocean has been claimed at various times and to various extents by Russia, Spain, Great Britain and the United States. The Russian claim, which rested mainly upon occupation by fur traders, was settled by a treaty January 11, 1825. Under this treaty the United States were to make no settlements north of latitude 54° 40′, and Russia none south of that latitude. England and Russia agreed upon the same terms. The Spanish claims were confined south of latitude 42° by the treaty which ceded Florida in 1819. Great Britain had little or no claim by discovery. The United States' claim rested upon the voyage of Gray up the Columbia River in 1792, and the explorations of Lewis and Clark through the Rocky Mountains and through the Oregon country in 1805–06, under the orders of Jefferson. By the treaty of October 20, 1818, the whole territory west of the Rocky Mountains was to be opened to both countries for ten years, and, in 1827, the joint occupation for an indefinite period was agreed upon. Later this produced dissatisfaction, and after considerable negotiation, Great Britain was induced in 1846 to accept latitude 49° as the boundary from the Rocky Mountains to the channel between Vancouver's Island and the mainland.

Northwest Territory, and the Ordinance of 1787 for its government. The Northwest Territory, consisting of the area west of Pennsylvania, north of the Ohio River, and east of the Mississippi, came under the control of the Continental Congress by reason of the cessions made by Virginia (1784), New York (1782), Massachusetts (1785) and Connecticut (1786). In 1784 Jefferson brought forward an ordinance for the government of this territory. Its leading features were that it provided for its erection into States, and their entrance into the Union on equal terms with the rest. A clause which would have prohibited slavery after 1800 was voted down. In 1787 a new ordinance was framed upon this and passed on September 13. The credit of its final form, including the forbidding of slavery, has been attributed to Nathan Dane, member of the Continental Congress from Massachusetts, and, more largely of late, to Dr. Manasseh Cutler, of the same State, agent of the Ohio Company. The ordinance provided that no land was to be taken up until it had been purchased from the Indians and offered for sale by the United States; no property qualification was required of electors or elected; a temporary government, consisting of an appointed governor and law-making judges, might be established until the adult male population of the territory increased to 5000; then a permanent and representative government would be permitted, with the right of sending a representative to Congress, who should debate, but not vote. When the number of inhabitants in any of the five divisions of the territory equalled 60,000, it should be admitted as a new State; the new States should remain forever a part of the United States; should bear the same relation to the Government as the original States; should pay their apportionment of the Federal debts; should in their governments uphold republican forms, and slavery should exist in none of them. It also provided for equal division of the property of intestates, and for the surrender of fugitive slaves from the States. Under this government Arthur St. Clair was Governor of the territory from 1788 to 1802, when Ohio became a State. The western portions were then organized as the Territory of Indiana, the northern as the Territory of Michigan, in 1805.

Northwestern University, Evanston, Ill., was founded by the Methodists in 1851.

Norton, Charles Eliot, born in 1827, was associate editor of the *North American Review* from 1864 to 1868. He has written "Considerations on Some Recent Social Theories" and "Historical Studies of Church Building in the Middle Ages;" has translated Dante, and edited the correspondence of Carlyle with Emerson and that of Lowell. He is professor of the fine arts in Harvard University.

Norton, John (1606–1663), came to the Massachusetts colony from England in 1635. He aided in framing the "Cambridge Platform" in 1648. He went to England in 1662 with Governor Bradstreet to confer with Charles II.

Norumbega, the name given by early explorers to various parts of the Eastern coast. In 1539 it was applied to the whole coast from Cape Breton to Florida; in 1556, to that country lying between Cape Breton and the Jersey coast, and after that time till the seventeenth century to New England. In 1605 Champlain applied it to the territory now comprised in the State of Maine, the Norumbega River being identical with the Penobscot. David Ingram, who was put ashore in the Gulf of Mexico by Hawkins in 1568, traveled afoot to the St. John's River, passing through Massachusetts and Maine. He described Norumbega as a splendid Indian city. Humphrey Gilbert, Walker and Rut were the earliest English explorers of Norumbega.

Norway. (See Sweden and Norway.)

Nott, Eliphalet (1773–1866), was president of Union College, New York, from 1804 to 1866 and one of the most distinguished of American educators. His address on the death of Alexander Hamilton became famous.

Nova Cæsarea, the Latin name for New Jersey. The island of Jersey derives its name from the Latin name Cæsarea, given to it in Roman times.

Nova Constellatio Coinage, two silver coins invented by Robert Morris in 1783 for national coinage, but not accepted by the Continental Congress. They were called the Mark and the Quint. Their values were respectively about seventy and thirty-five cents, their weights eleven pennyweights six grains, and five pennyweights fifteen grains. There were only a few pattern pieces struck off. For description of this coinage (see Mark, and Quint.)

Nova Suecia, the Latin name for New Sweden.

Novum Belgium, a name used in the seventeenth century as the Latin equivalent of New Netherland.

Novum Eboracum, the Latin name for New York, York in England having originally been called Eboracum by the Romans, whence Eoforwic, whence York.

Noyes, John H. (1811–1886), founded a colony of Perfectionists at Putney, Vt., in 1838. He removed to Oneida, N. Y., in 1848 and established there a socialistic community. He wrote a "History of American Socialism."

Nullification, the formal suspension by a State government of the operation of a law of the United States within the territory under the jurisdiction of the State, was first suggested as the rightful remedy in the case of illegal stretches of Federal legislative authority, in the Kentucky Resolutions of 1799. Practical exemplifications of its operation were afforded by Pennsylvania in the Olmstead case in 1809, by Georgia in the matter of the Cherokees (1825–30), etc. But the theory was most completely developed by John C. Calhoun, and its most important application was in South Carolina in 1832, in her protest against the tariff of that year, which was exceedingly distasteful to the Southern States. Calhoun's nullification contemplated a suspension of the objectionable law by an aggrieved State, until three-fourths of the States in national convention should overrule the nullification. The question turned upon the dogma of State sovereignty. The State Legislature of 1832, made up of nullifiers, put the State in a position for war and passed various acts resuming powers expressly prohibited to the States by the Constitution. December 11, President Jackson issued the "nullification proclamation," declaring nullification to be incompatible with the existence of the Union and contrary to the Constitution. February 1, 1833, a bill called the "bloody bill," was passed by Congress, authorizing the enforcement of the tariff. February 26, Clay submitted a compromise tariff bill, which was enacted. In consequence of this the South Carolina Convention repealed the nullification ordinance on March 16, 1833.

Nye, James W. (1814–1876), was a New York county judge from 1840 to 1848. He was appointed Governor of Nevada in 1861, and represented Nevada in the U. S. Senate as a Republican from 1865 to 1873.

O.

Oak Grove, Va., a point much coveted by McClellan during the Peninsular campaign, just previous to the siege of Richmond. Heintzelman's corps, with a portion of Sumner's and Keyes', was dispatched to capture this place. From here it was McClellan's intention to strike the Old Tavern. On June 25, 1862, Heintzelman, moving along the Williamsburg road, encountered a small detachment of Lee's army. An engagement at once took place, Sickles and Grover, of Hooker's division, bearing the brunt of the attack. The position was won after a Federal loss of over 500 men.

Oak Hill, the residence of James Monroe, during the latter part of his life, in Loudoun County, Va. The Oak Hill mansion was planned by Monroe himself.

Oath. The Constitution provides that before the President "enter on the execution of his office he shall take the following oath or affirmation:" "I do solemnly swear (or affirm) that I will faithfully execute the office of President of the United States, and will, to the best of my ability, preserve, protect and defend the Constitution of the United States." This oath is administered by the Chief Justice of the Supreme Court. A similar oath is required of all officers National and State, and belonging to the executive, legislative and judicial departments. The first Act of Congress provided for oaths of office.

Oberlin College, Oberlin, Ohio, was opened in 1833 as the "Collegiate Institute," but changed its name in 1850. It was founded by Congregationalists. Its theological department was opened in 1835.

Oberlin-Wellington Case (1858). A negro named John Rice was captured near Wellington, O., by Kentucky kidnappers. An Oberlin College student gave the alarm, and the kidnappers were pursued by a large crowd, who rescued the negro. For this infraction of the law thirty-seven citizens of Oberlin and Wellington were indicted. During the progress of the case the greatest excitement prevailed over the entire country. No severe penalties were imposed upon the offenders.

O'Brien, Fitz-James (1828–1862), came to America from Ireland in 1850. He served on the staff of General Lander in 1862, and died of wounds received in battle. He was a brilliant writer of prose and verse.

Observatories. The first telescope used in the United States for astronomical purposes was set up at Yale College in 1830. The first observatory building was erected at Williams College, in 1836, by Professor Hopkins. In 1838, the Hudson Observatory was organized in connection with the Western Reserve University, in 1839 that of Harvard. The West Point Observatory soon followed. A Government Observatory was erected at Georgetown, D. C., in 1847, but has since been removed to Mount Lookout, near Washington. The Ann Arbor Observatory, Mich., founded in 1854, has accomplished valuable work, as has also the United States Naval Observatory at Washington. Many of the colleges have now more or less efficiently equipped observatories. In 1874 James Lick, of San Francisco, gave $750,000 for a telescope and other apparatus for an observatory. Accordingly the Lick Observatory was erected on Mount Hamilton, Cal., being completed in 1888. The Lick telescope is one of the most powerful in the world, and with it numerous interesting and valuable discoveries have been made.

Ocala Platform, of the Farmers' Alliance congress, December 8, 1890. It demanded the abolition of national banks; the establishment of sub-treasuries which should lend money directly to the people at low rates of interest; free coinage of silver; low tariff; the prohibition of alien ownership of land, and a graduated income tax. So called from the place of meeting, Ocala, Fla.

O'Callaghan, Edmund B. (1797–1880), came to New York from Canada in 1837. He was author of a "History of New Netherland," and editor of "Documentary History of New York," "Documents Relating to the History of New York" (11 vols.), "Remonstrance of New Netherlands," etc.

O'Conor, Charles (1804–1884), of New York, was admitted to the bar at the age of twenty. He sympathized with the Confederates during the Civil War. He was nominated for President of the United States by the "Labor Reform" branch of the Democratic party in 1872. He was counsel for Jefferson Davis when he was indicted for treason. He was largely the means of destroying the "Tweed Ring," and was noted as a lawyer.

Oconostota (before 1730–after 1809), head king of the Cherokee Indians. He captured Fort Prince George and Fort Loudon, and massacred the garrisons in revenge for an attack by English settlers in 1756. He aided the English in the Revolutionary War by harassing the frontiers of Virginia and the Carolinas, but was soon afterward dethroned.

Odd Fellows. The first lodge of the Independent Order of Odd Fellows in the United States was organized at Baltimore in April 1819, by Thomas Wildey and four others. Lodges were established in Boston in 1820, and in Philadelphia in 1821, receiving charters from the Grand Lodge at Baltimore. Since then the order has been established in every State and Territory of the Union.

Odell Town (Canada, near Lake Champlain). Here Lieutenant-Colonel Forsyth had two small skirmishes with the British, June 22, 1814, in which the former was successful, but lost his own life. The British loss was seventeen killed.

Ogden vs. Saunders, an important case in the U. S. Supreme Court, decided in 1827. Ogden, of Louisiana, declared upon certain bills of exchange drawn upon the defendant Saunders, a citizen of Kentucky, but then living in New York. Saunders pleaded a certificate of discharge under the Act of the New York Legislature of 1801 for the relief of insolvent debtors. The District Court of Louisiana found judgment for the plaintiff. On a writ of error the case was brought before the Supreme Court, which decided in 1827 that the power to pass bankruptcy laws did not belong exclusively to the United States, and that the fair exercise of that power by the States need not involve a violation of the obligation of contracts; but that the State law could not discharge a debt due to a citizen of another State.

Ogdensburg, N. Y. February 22, 1813, Colonel McDonell, with 800 British soldiers, attacked the village and also Fort Presentation, commanded by Colonel Forsyth. The attack upon the fort was repulsed, but that on the village was successful. The British now reformed and moved against the fort which, however, had meanwhile been evacuated, the Americans retreating to Black Lake, nine miles away. Two armed sloops and the barracks were burned, the village plundered, and fifty-two prisoners made. The American loss was five killed and fifteen wounded; the British, six killed and forty-eight wounded.

Oglesby, Richard J., born in 1824, engaged in the Mexican War. In the Civil War he commanded a brigade at Fort Henry and Fort Donelson. From 1863 to 1864 he commanded the Sixteenth Army Corps. He was Governor of Illinois from 1864 to 1869 and in 1872. He was a Republican U. S. Senator from 1873 to 1879, and was again Governor from 1884 to 1888.

Oglethorpe, James Edward (1698–1785), the founder of Georgia, was an officer in the British army and a member of Parliament, whose sympathies had become directed toward the misfortunes of debtors. In 1732 he received from the king a grant of land for the purpose of founding a colony for this class, and in 1733 founded Savannah. The settlement prospered fairly. Oglethorpe, who had twice returned to England, commanded an unsuccessful expedition against St. Augustine in 1741 in the war with Spain. The next year he repelled a Spanish attack on the colony, and returned finally to England in 1743. Subsequently, for the conduct of a force against the Young Pretender he received severe criticism. In 1752 he resigned the charter of Georgia to the crown.

O'Hara, Charles (1730?–1802), came to Virginia from England in command of a regiment in 1780. He served at Cowpens, led the left wing of Cornwallis' army at Guilford, and surrendered at Yorktown.

Ohio, a State of the Union, was formed from the Northwest Territory. It was originally explored by the French, and at the time of the French and Indian War was claimed by both English and French. The former's claim was made good by the treaty of 1763. In 1774 the "Quebec Act" joined Ohio and the whole Northwest to Canada, but this act was nullified by the treaty of 1783. South of 41° north latitude Ohio formed a part of the cession of Virginia to the general government in 1783. The territory north of that line was claimed by Connecticut by virtue of the charter of Charles II., which extended her territory to the South Sea. The jurisdiction over this part was ceded to the United States by Connecticut in 1786, but the ownership of the lands was retained by that State, which gave rise to the name, "The Connecticut Reservation," or "Western Reserve." In 1786 the Ohio Company, composed of Massachusetts people, obtained control of 1,500,000 acres through the agency of Manasseh Cutler. The following year Congress passed the Ordinance of 1787 for the government of the Northwest Territory. This provided for not more than five nor less than three States, forbade slavery and provided for the support of education. In 1788 Marietta was founded by settlers under General Putnam. In 1791 St. Clair's army was surprised and cut to pieces by the Indians, who were finally defeated by General Wayne in 1794. In 1800 Ohio was set off from the Northwest under a separate government, and in 1803 was admitted as a State. A boundary dispute with Michigan, called the "Toledo War," was settled in favor of Ohio by the act of Congress which provided for the admission of Michigan in 1836. The Democrats held control of the State until 1824, when Clay obtained its electoral votes. From 1824 until 1838 the Whigs usually controlled the State because of their policy of internal improvements and protective tariff. From 1838 until 1855 the Democrats were successful, except in the years 1840 and 1844. In 1848 a deadlock occurred in the organization of the Legislature, which resulted in favor of the Democrats and in the election of Salmon P. Chase, a Free-Soil Democrat, to the U. S. Senate. In 1855 the Republicans elected a Governor, and in 1856 Republican electors were chosen as in all subsequent Presidential elections. In State elections the State has been usually Republican, as at present (1894). The "Pond Law," for the taxation of liquor selling, was declared unconstitutional in 1882, and was followed by the "Scott Law," which was upheld by the courts. Ohio furnished 319,659 troops to the Union army. In 1863 General Morgan, who had invaded Ohio, was captured at New Lisbon. The State furnished some of the most successful generals of the Union army. The population of the State in 1802 was 41,915; in 1890 it was 3,672,316. The present Constitution was made in 1851. History by Howe.

Ohio Company. In 1749 George II. granted to a band of wealthy Virginians, calling themselves the Ohio Company, a tract of land containing 500,000 acres, and lying mostly to the west of the mountains and south of the Ohio River. Thomas Lee was the projector of this company, but it was later conducted by Lawrence Washington. The conditions of the grant were that 100 families should be established upon it, a fort should be built and a garrison maintained. Numerous store houses were also established.

Ohio Company (the second), formed March 1, 1786, on the suggestion and in the house of Rufus Putnam, of Rutland, Mass. March 3, Putnam, Cutler, Brooks, Sargent and Cushing reported an association of 1000 shares, each of $1000 in Continental certificates, or $125 in gold. A year was allowed for subscription. Land was to be purchased from Congress, in tracts lying between the Ohio and Lake Erie. May 9, 1787, Parsons, agent for the company, appeared before Congress and was well received. Congress granted certain lots free of charge, and an enormous tract was bought at about eight or nine cents per acre in specie. Colonization was immediately begun, and slavery was prohibited. The company had much influence in shaping the Ordinance for the Government of the Northwest Territory.

Ohio Historical Society, founded in 1831, and reorganized in 1867. This, together with the Firelands Historical Society and the Licking County Pioneer Historical Society, organized respectively in 1857 and 1867, have furnished much valuable information regarding early settlements in Ohio.

Ojibways, or Chippewas, a tribe of Algonquin Indians living on the shores of Lake Huron and Lake Superior. Early wars with neighboring tribes greatly reduced their numbers. They joined Pontiac. During the Revolution they were allies of England, but made peace by treaties in 1785 and 1789. They joined in the Miamis' uprising, but, reduced by Wayne, made peace in 1795. They ceded most of their lands on Lake Erie in 1805. They renewed hostilities in 1812, but joined in the peace of 1816, and relinquished all their lands in Ohio. Other treaties ceding territory followed, and by 1851 nearly the entire tribe had moved west of the Mississippi.

Oklahoma, a Territory of the United States, was organized May 2, 1890. It was formed from Indian Territory and the Public Land. The Territory was first opened to settlers April 22, 1889, and in 1890 the population was 61,834, including that of Green County, which is claimed by Texas. The population now (1894) is more than double what it was in 1890.

"Old Bullion," a nickname of Senator Benton. (See art.)

Old Colony, a name given in Massachusetts history to the territory formerly occupied by the Plymouth colony, and absorbed into that of Massachusetts Bay in 1691, now Plymouth and Bristol counties.

Old Dominion, a name commonly given to Virginia, which in colonial documents is frequently called "His Majesty's Dominion" of Virginia.

"Old Lights," the name applied to the orthodox conservative churchmen to distinguish them from the "New Lights," or revivalists, followers of Jonathan Edwards and George Whitefield during the period of the "Great Awakening" in 1734, and later in Massachusetts and Connecticut.

Old Man Eloquent, the nickname for John Quincy Adams, sixth President of the United States, used during his latter years in the House of Representatives, with allusion to a line in Milton's sonnet to the Lady Margaret Ley in which Milton thus refers to Isocrates.

Old Public Functionary, a nickname of President James Buchanan, he having alluded to himself under that designation in a message to Congress in 1859.

Old South Church, a church built in Boston in 1730, and famous during the period just preceding the Revolution as a place for public meetings held by the Revolutionary party. During the siege of Boston the British used it as a riding-school, and the New England Library which the Rev. Thomas Prince had gathered in its belfry was scattered. It is now used as a museum of historical relics, and as a hall for lectures on American history, known as the "Old South Lectures," of patriotic object.

Old State House. In 1658 a "Town House" was erected, on what is now State Street, Boston, with money left by Captain Keayne, of Boston, for that purpose. This Town House was in use as the capitol of the colony until 1711, when it was destroyed by fire. In the next year there was erected on the same site the building which is standing to-day and is called the Old State House. It has long been used as an office building, but was formally rededicated in 1882, when the whole history of the old building was rehearsed in addresses by prominent citizens.

Oldenburg. In 1846 Oldenburg acceded to the commercial treaty between the United States and Hanover, and in 1852 to the German extradition treaty of that year.

Oldham, John (1600?–1636), came to Plymouth from England in 1623. His murder by Indians on Block Island in 1636 was a chief incident leading to the Pequot War.

Oliver, Andrew (1706–1774), loyalist, was a member of the Massachusetts Council from 1746 to 1765, provincial secretary from 1756 to 1770 and Lieutenant-Governor from 1771 to 1774. Mob violence compelled him to resign the appointment as stamp officer in 1765.

Olmstead et als. vs. Rittenhouse's Executrixes, a celebrated case of capture involving questions of prerogative regarding which the decisions of the Federal commissioners were set at naught by a State Court of Admiralty, and which aided in establishing the Supreme Court. Olmstead and others, of Connecticut, being pressed into British service aboard the sloop "Active" in 1777, took possession of the sloop, and were in turn captured by Houston, commanding the Pennsylvania armed brig "Convention." The State Court of Admiralty of Pennsylvania adjudged a large share of the prize money to the State, the officers and crew of the "Convention," and the owners, officers and crew of a privateer which assisted in the capture. Olmstead and others appealed to the Federal Commissioners of Appeals and received a favorable verdict. This the State Court set aside and deposited the moneys with David Rittenhouse, State Treasurer. His executrixes were sued in 1802 before the Supreme Court, and judgment was executed in favor of Olmstead and others, in 1809, against violent opposition from Pennsylvania. (See Peters, U. S. *vs.*)

Olmsted, Frederick Law, born in 1822, landscape architect, wrote the works condensed in "The Cotton Kingdom," so prominent during the Rebellion. He superintended the construction of Central Park, New York, Jackson Park, Chicago, and many others.

Olney, Jesse (1798–1872), published a "Geography and Atlas" in 1828, which revolutionized geographical methods. It reversed the ancient system of beginning with astronomy and the solar system and concluding with the earth.

Olney, Richard, of Massachusetts, was born in 1835. He is considered one of the highest authorities on corporation law and on general probate law. He became Attorney-General in Cleveland's Cabinet in 1893.

Olustee, Fla. At this place, February 20, 1864, Seymour, commanding 6000 of Gillmore's Federal army then operating in the Department of the

South, fell in with a Confederate ambush of nearly 13,000 men under Finnegan. Gillmore had ordered Seymour to give up his contemplated expedition to the Suwanee River, but the order came too late. Seymour was wholly defeated in less than half an hour, and had to retreat with great haste, leaving 1400 killed and wounded.

Olympia, capital of Washington State, was settled in 1846, and laid out as a town in 1851. It became a city in 1859.

Omahas, a tribe of Dakota Indians, lived on the Quicoure at the beginning of the century. Treaties in 1815 and 1820 ceded lands at Council Bluffs, and other treaties of a similar nature were made in 1825 and 1830. In 1854 they gave up more of their lands. Their reservation lies in the northeastern part of Nebraska. They have suffered much from the hostility of the Sioux.

O'Mahony, John F. (1816–1877), born in Ireland, came to the United States in 1854. He organized the Fenian brotherhood in 1860, whose object was the freeing of Ireland. He translated the "History of Ireland" by Geoffrey Keating.

Omnibus Bill, a bill submitted to Congress by Henry Clay, January 29, 1850, at the time of the application of California for admission to the Union. The bill provided for the admission of California with her free constitution; territorial governments in New Mexico and Utah without express restriction upon slavery; a territorial boundary line between Texas and New Mexico in favor of the former; a more effective fugitive slave law; and denial to Congress of power to interfere with the slave trade between slave States. After much cutting and amendment the bill was passed in July, 1850, as a series of acts.

Oneida Community, a communistic settlement at Oneida, N. Y., founded in 1848 by John Humphrey Noyes, of Vermont. They call themselves Perfectionists. They possess property in common, believe in the faith cure, and permit freedom of sexual intercourse within the limits of the community, which practice they deem less conducive to selfishness than the ordinary relationship of man and wife.

Oneidas, a tribe of American Indians formerly of the Iroquois confederacy, from an early period lived in New York State. They were generally favorable to the English, but in the Revolution supported the colonists. For this their villages were ravaged and their property destroyed. By a treaty in 1794, the Government made compensation for their losses. In 1785 and 1788, they ceded lands to the State of New York. Later, some went to Canada, and in 1821, a large number acquired lands on Green Bay.

O'Neill, John (1834–1878), served in the National army from 1861 to 1864. He commanded the Fenian expedition to Canada in 1867 and captured Fort Erie. Further operations were prevented by United States authorities.

O'Neill, Peggy. (See Eaton, Margaret L.)

Onis, Nuis de (1769–1830), while minister from Spain to the United States from 1815 to 1819, negotiated the treaty by which Spain ceded Florida to the United States (1819).

Onondagas, a tribe of Iroquois in New York State, and head of the "five nations." They were early won over to the English and often served against the French. During the Revolution they joined the English. In September, 1788, they ceded all their territory to the State of New York, with the exception of a small tract which they have since continued to hold.

Ontario, Fort, erected in 1756 during the French and Indian wars by the English troops under Shirley at Oswego, N. Y. It was attacked the same year, while commanded by Colonel Mercer, by Montcalm. Both Oswego and Ontario were captured, and the latter was burned to the ground.

Opequon. (See Winchester.)

Opera. In the autumn of 1825 the first Italian opera ever introduced into the United States was given at the Park Theatre in New York. Garcia's daughter, afterward famous as Malibran, appeared in Rossini's "Barber of Seville."

Orange, Fort, erected in 1623, near the present site of Albany, by Captain Cornelius Jacobsen Mey, representing the Dutch West India Company.

Orange River Free State. A treaty of commerce and extradition was concluded between the United States and the Orange River Free State in 1871.

Ord, Edward O. C. (1818–1883), commanded the national forces at Dranesville in 1861. He led the left wing of Grant's army at Iuka and Hatchie in 1862. He led a corps at Vicksburg, Jackson, Richmond and Fort Harrison. In 1865 he commanded the Department of Virginia and the Army of the James at Petersburg and in the subsequent battles ending at Appomattox Court House.

Orders in Council. Decrees issued by the king of Great Britain and his Privy Council, of which the most famous were those prohibiting commercial intercourse by neutral countries with States with whom he was at war. A proclamation of June 8, 1793, had prohibited trade with France and directed the seizure of neutral ships engaged in such traffic. Similar orders were issued in 1794. November 11, 1807, the famous Orders in Council prohibited direct trade from the United States to any European country under Napoleon's power.

Ordinance of 1787. (See Northwest Territory.)

Ordinary was in England the title of a bishop or his deputy acting as an ecclesiastical judge. In the United States, in the colonial period, the colonial governor was ex-officio ordinary, or head of the ecclesiastical courts of the colony, which then had jurisdiction of matrimonial and testamentary causes. In New Jersey the probate judge is still called an ordinary.

Oregon, a State of the American Union, was acquired by treaty with England in 1846. It was visited by Drake in 1558 and, it is said, by Juan de Fuca in 1592. In 1792 Vancouver, an English officer, surveyed the coast from 30° to 60° north latitude. Robert Gray, of Boston, had previously discovered the Columbia River. It was claimed by the United States that the "Oregon country," included between 42° and 54° 40′, formed a part of the Louisiana cession, but England refused to recognize the claim. Lewis and Clark surveyed the country in 1804–1806. In 1818 the United States and England agreed upon a treaty of joint occupancy, which was renewed in 1827. Russia had claims to the Oregon country south of 54° 40′, which she finally withdrew. Emigration from the United States into the region was stimulated by the reports of Dr. Whitman, a missionary, who made a perilous journey on horseback to Washington in the winter of 1842–43, and urged the Government at Washington to assert the claims of the United States to that region. The people of Oregon formed a provisional government in 1843. In the Presidential campaign of 1844 the Democratic platform demanded the reoccupation of Oregon. The cry "fifty-four-forty or fight" threatened war with England, which was averted by the treaty of 1846, whereby the northern boundary of the United States at 49° north latitude was extended to the Fuca Strait. In 1848 the territory of Oregon was organized and made to include the present States of Washington and Idaho. A State constitution was adopted in 1857, which forbade slavery and the immigration of negroes. The "anti-negro" provision prevented the admission of Oregon until 1859, February 14. In politics the State was at first Democratic, but in 1860 the Republicans secured the electoral vote of the State for Lincoln by a plurality. From 1860 to 1868 the State was Republican in all elections. In 1868 the Democrats carried the State, and again in 1870, 1874, 1878. At other elections the Republicans have been successful, except in 1892, when the electoral votes were cast for the fusion candidate. The population of Oregon in 1860 was 52,465; in 1890, 313,767. Histories by Bancroft and Barrows.

"Oregon Spectator." This was the first newspaper printed in Oregon. It was established at Oregon City, and the first issues appeared during February 1846.

O'Reilly, John B. (1844–1890), born in Ireland, transported for treason in 1866, escaped from Australia to the United States in 1869. He was editor of the "Pilot" from 1874 to 1890, and was noted as a poet.

Original Package. In 1890 the Supreme Court of the United States, in the case of Leisy & Co. *vs.* Hardin, held that the plaintiffs, brewers in Illinois, had the right to bring beer into Iowa and sell it in the original packages, regardless of the Iowa prohibitory law. Their decision rested on the right of Congress to have exclusive control of interstate commerce. Congress immediately passed an act giving the State control of the liquors so imported, though in the original packages.

Oriskany, Battle of. On August 6, 1777, General Herkimer with 800 men started to relieve Fort Stanwix, now besieged by St. Leger and his Indians. At Oriskany, ten miles away, he halted and attempted to concert an attack and a sortie. The plan miscarried. Herkimer advanced and was attacked by the Indians and Tories in a deep ravine. The battle raged furiously for hours, despite a terrific thunder-storm, and was one of the most cruel and bloody of the war. Each side lost a third of its number. The Americans remained masters of the field, although badly disabled. The sortie from the fort was a success, and badly crippled the enemy.

Orkney, Earl of. In 1704 the Earl of Orkney was made titular Governor of Virginia, a sinecure which he held for forty years, with an annual emolument of £1200.

Orleans, Territory of. In March, 1804, the region purchased from France under the name of Louisiana was divided by Congress into two territories—the District of Louisiana and the Territory of Orleans, the latter being the present area of the State of Louisiana. In February, 1811, an act was passed "to enable the people of the Territory of Orleans to form a constitution and State Government." April 12, 1812, an act was passed for the admission of the State of Louisiana into the Union.

Orr, James L. (1822–1873), represented South Carolina in the U. S. Congress as a Democrat from 1849 to 1859, and was Speaker from 1857 to 1859. He was a Confederate senator from 1861 to 1865, and Governor of South Carolina from 1865 to 1868.

Orth, Godlove S. (1817–1882), was a member of the Indiana Senate from 1842 to 1848. He was prominent in the Peace Conference of 1861. He represented Indiana in the U. S. Congress as a Republican from 1863 to 1871 and from 1873 to 1875. He was active in securing the recognition of the right of expatriation by European governments. He framed the "Orth bill," which reorganized the diplomatic and consular system. He was Minister to Austria from 1875 to 1877, and again a Congressman from 1879 to 1882.

Orton, James (1830–1877), professor in Vassar College, was recognized as an authority on the subject of the geology and physical geography of the west coast of South America and the Amazon Valley, which he had carefully explored.

Osage Indians, were early driven to the Arkansas. They allied themselves with the French against England. In 1808 they ceded lands to the Government; and made further cessions in 1815, 1818, 1822, 1825 and 1839. At the beginning of the Civil War 1000 went South; treaties in September, 1865, and May, 1868, prepared for the removal of the whole. In 1870 the tribe conveyed their lands to the Government and agreed to remove to Indian Territory.

Osborn vs. U. S. Bank, Ohio, an important case in the U. S. Supreme Court. Ralph Osborn, auditor of the State of Ohio, per J. L. Harper, his deputy, took by force from the U. S. Bank at Chillicothe, $100,000 and delivered it to the State Treasurer as just payment to the State under the law which was passed by the State's Legislature levying taxes upon banks doing business in the State with the consent of the law. The Circuit Court of Ohio decided that a restitution be made with interest. The Supreme Court, the case being appealed thereto, confirmed the decision of the Circuit Court, omitting the interest (1824). (See McCulloch vs. Maryland.)

Osceola (1804–1838), chief of the Seminole Indians, inaugurated the second Seminole War in 1836 by killing General Thompson in revenge for the enslavement of his wife. He conducted the war for over a year, fighting at the Withlacoochee River, Micanopy and Fort Drane. He was seized while negotiating a treaty under a flag of truce with General Jesup near St. Augustine in 1837.

Osgood, Samuel (1748–1813), was a delegate from Massachusetts to the Continental Congress from 1780 to 1784, Commissioner of the Treasury from 1785 to 1789, and Postmaster-General from 1789 to 1791.

Ostend Manifesto. In 1852 France and Great Britain, fearful of the filibustering expeditions against Cuba and the possible future favor of the United States toward such expeditions, suggested a tripartite convention in which each should disclaim all intention to obtain possession of Cuba and should discountenance such intention by another power. October 9, 1854, the American Ministers to Great Britain, France and Spain, James Buchanan, John Y. Mason and Pierre Soulé, met at Ostend and drew up the "Ostend Manifesto." This declared that a sale of Cuba to the United States would be advantageous to both governments; but that if Spain refused to sell, it was incumbent upon the Union to "wrest it from her," rather than see it Africanized like San Domingo.

Oswald, Richard (1705–1784), was appointed by Great Britain diplomatic agent in 1782 to negotiate the treaty of peace with the United States which was signed at Paris in 1783.

Oswego, Capture of. In the French and Indian War, in July, 1756, Montcalm hastened from Ticonderoga to Oswego. It was hoped to divert the English from Ticonderoga. The expedition was conducted with secrecy, and by August 10 Montcalm was near the fort. On the thirteenth he forced the abandonment of Fort Ontario, opposite Oswego. On the fourteenth Oswego, subject to bombardment and assault, surrendered. The English force was about 1000, of whom fifty were killed. The attacking party numbered 3000. Both forts were burned.—In the War of 1812, May 5, 1814, Sir James Yeo with about 3000 land troops and marines attacked Oswego, defended by a fort garrisoned by 300 men under Colonel Mitchell. The first attack was repulsed by a heavy cannon placed near the shore. The second attack, the next day, was successful, and the garrison retreated up the river. The British withdrew after burning the barracks and seizing the stores and a war schooner. The American loss was sixty-nine men; the British, nineteen killed and seventy-five wounded.

Otis, Harrison Gray (1765–1848), represented Massachusetts in the U. S. Congress as a Federalist from 1797 to 1801. He was Speaker of the Massachusetts Legislature from 1803 to 1805, and president of the Senate from 1805 to 1806 and from 1808 to 1811. He was prominent at the Hartford Convention in 1814. He was a U. S. Senator from 1817 to 1822.

Otis, James (1725–1783), patriot and orator, was graduated at Harvard in 1743, and rose to the first place at the Boston bar. When the British Government adopted a stronger coercive policy with its Writs of Assistance in 1761, Otis opposed the measure in a celebrated speech. He was a member of the Massachusetts Legislature, and published in 1764 an influential pamphlet entitled "Rights of the Colonies Vindicated." He moved the appointment of a Stamp Act Congress, and was one of the delegates, and he made a spirited opposition to Townshend's acts. In 1769 he was severely beaten by some British officers and became insane for the remainder of his life. Otis ranks as one of the eloquent orators of the pre-Revolution period.

Ottawas, a tribe of Algonquin Indians, aided the French against England. During the Revolution they were under British influence. They joined in treaties made in 1785 and 1789, but took up arms with the Miamis soon after, again making peace in 1795. Numerous treaties ceding territory around Lake Michigan to the United States followed. A part went south of the Missouri in 1833, where they lost their identity. A band of Ottawas in Ohio removed to the Osage in 1836. Those remaining became scattered. The emigrants again removed to Indian Territory in 1870. In 1836 the Michigan Ottawas ceded all their lands except reservations.

Ottendorfer, Oswald, born in Moravia in 1826, fled to America in 1850. He became an editor of the *Staats-Zeitung*, and afterward its proprietor and manager, making it an independent reform journal.

Ottoman Porte. The United States concluded a commercial treaty with the Ottoman Porte in 1830. The translation of an article of this treaty relating to extra-territorial jurisdiction caused an extended dispute. In 1862 another commercial treaty was concluded, which has ceased to be in operation, though the most favorable commercial relations continue.

Otto's Reports, more often cited as United States Reports (Otto), are law reports of cases from the United States Supreme Court 1875–1881, and are contained in fifteen volumes.

Owen, Robert (1771–1858), came to the United States from Scotland in 1824 and founded an unsuccessful communistic society at New Harmony, Ind.

Owen, Robert Dale (1800–1877), came to the United States from Scotland in 1824 with the communistic colony established at New Harmony, Ind., by his father. He was a member of the Indiana Legislature from 1835 to 1838, and represented Indiana in the U. S. Congress as a Democrat from 1843 to 1847. He was chargé d'affaires at Naples from 1853 to 1855 and Minister from 1855 to 1858, and was of some note as a writer.

Oxenstjerna, Axel (1583–1654), Chancellor of Sweden, subscribed, in 1624, to the stock of the Swedish West India Company, and later was personally interested in the Swedish settlements along the Delaware.

P.

Paca, William (1740–1799), opposed all taxation of the colonies by England. He was a member of the Maryland Legislature from 1771 to 1774. He represented Maryland in the Continental Congress from 1774 to 1779 and signed the Declaration of Independence. He was a State Senator from 1777 to 1779, Judge of the Federal Court of Appeals 1780–1782, and Governor of Maryland from 1782 to 1786. He was U. S. Judge for the District of Maryland from 1789 to 1799.

Pacific Railroads. The outbreak of the Civil War and the feeling of necessity of a better connection with the Pacific coast, induced the Government to make large grants in favor of the Central Pacific, Union Pacific and Kansas Pacific Railroads, by an act of July 1, 1862. Later, 47,000,000 acres were granted to the Northern Pacific. The Central Pacific and Union Pacific were completed in 1869. The construction and finance of the Union Pacific were managed by the Crédit Mobilier (see art.) and involved in legislative scandals. In 1878 the office of Commissioner of Railroads was instituted, to supervise the accounts of the Pacific railways.

Packard, Alpheus S. (1798–1884), was a professor at Bowdoin College, chiefly of Greek, from 1824 to 1884, and was librarian of the Maine Historical Society for forty-eight years.

Packard, Alpheus S., born in 1839, has made valuable contributions to entomology and paleontology. He arranged the generally accepted classification of insects. He published a great number of scientific monographs, and a popular "Zoology." Since 1878 he has been a professor in Brown University.

Paddock, Algernon S., born in 1830, was secretary of Nebraska Territory from 1861 to 1867. He represented Nebraska in the U. S. Senate as a Republican from 1875 to 1881, and from 1887 to 1893.

Paducah, Ky., scene of the first disaster encountered by the Confederate leader Forrest during his great raid through Kentucky, Tennessee and northern Mississippi in 1864. Forrest had 5000 men, while Hicks lay fortified in Paducah with 800 National troops. March 25 Forrest demanded a surrender. Hicks refused peremptorily. Forrest then charged the earthworks again and again, but with signal failures each time. He was obliged to retreat, having suffered severe losses.

Page, John (1744–1808), represented Virginia in the U. S. Congress as a Democrat from 1789 to 1797. He was Governor of Virginia from 1802 to 1805. He published "Political Addresses," and was an early friend of Jefferson.

Page, Thomas J., born in 1808, made an extensive exploration of La Plata River. He became a commander in the U. S. navy in 1855. He was active in the construction of the Confederate navy.

Page, Thomas Nelson, born in 1853, is a popular writer of stories and poems in the negro dialect. Some of his chief stories have been published under the title of "In Ole Virginia," etc.

Page, William (1811–1885), of Albany, was one of the most famous American artists. He won great distinction for his portrait-painting. He was famous as a colorist, and was an accurate draughtsman.

Paine, Robert Treat (1731–1814), was a member of the Massachusetts Assembly from 1773 to 1774, and of the Provincial Congress from 1774 to 1775. He was a delegate from Massachusetts to the Continental Congress from 1774 to 1778 and signed the Declaration of Independence. He was Attorney-General of Massachusetts from 1780 to 1790, and a Judge of the Massachusetts Supreme Court from 1790 to 1804, when he resigned. He was an able lawyer and an impartial judge.

Paine, Robert Treat (1773–1811), is eminent as the author of several remarkable poems, among them being "The Invention of Letters," "The Ruling Passion," and the song "Adams and Liberty."

Paine, Thomas, generally styled Tom Paine (1737–1809), a native of England, passed his early years there as an exciseman, political writer, and ardent republican. He came to America in 1774 and edited the *Pennsylvania Magazine*. In 1776 he published a pamphlet, "Common Sense," advocating independence, which was widely circulated and created a profound impression. At intervals through the war he published the "Crisis," and was secretary to the Congressional Committee on Foreign Affairs. His services in the Revolution were of undoubted value. Subsequently he was clerk to the Pennsylvania Legislature. He was in France at the opening of the French Revolution, and in England where he published in 1791 his "Rights of Man," and was outlawed in consequence. Escaping to France he was elected to the Convention, was imprisoned by the Jacobins, and wrote his "Age of Reason." He returned to the United States, and died in New York. Life by Conway.

Pakenham, Sir Edward M. (1778–1815), served in the Peninsular War and in the South of France under the Duke of Wellington. He succeeded General Ross in command of a British force employed against New Orleans in 1814. His troops were defeated by General Jackson on January 8, 1815, and he was killed during the battle.

Palatinate. Palatinates were in Europe districts the ruler of which received from the king almost royal rights of ruling in his province. Maryland was by its charter erected into a palatinate after the model of the palatinate of Durham in England, and so continued as long as it was under proprietary government. The proprietors of Carolina were at first given their province as a palatinate.

Palfrey, John G. (1796–1881), was editor of the *North American Review* from 1835 to 1843. He was Secretary of State in Massachusetts from 1844 to 1848, and represented Massachusetts in the U. S. Congress as a Whig from 1847 to 1849. He wrote a valuable "History of New England," a "Life of Colonel William Palfrey" and "The Progress of the Slave Power."

Palmer, James S. (1810–1867), commanded the "Flirt" during the Mexican War. He commanded the "Iroquois" at Vicksburg, and was Farragut's flag-captain at New Orleans and Mobile.

Palmer, John M., born in 1817, Senator, was a member of the Illinois Senate from 1852 to 1854. He commanded a brigade at New Madrid, Island No. 10, Farmington and Stone River, and a corps in Sherman's Georgia campaign in 1864. He was Governor of Illinois from 1869 to 1873. He was elected to the U. S. Senate as a Democrat in 1891.

Palmer, Thomas W., born in 1830, was a member of the Michigan Senate from 1879 to 1880. He represented Michigan in the U. S. Senate as a

Republican from 1883 to 1889, and from 1889 to 1890 was Minister to Spain.

Palmetto Ranche, Tex., last engagement of the Civil War, occurring May 11, 1865. Colonel Barrett with 450 Federal soldiers endeavored to surprise General Slaughter, commanding 600 Confederates. Barrett was defeated with a loss of eighty men.

Palo Alto, Texas, first important battle of the Mexican War, May 8, 1846. General Taylor commanded the United States forces, Generals Arista and Ampudia the Mexican. Arista opposed Taylor's march from Point Isabel to Matamoras to relieve Major Brown, firing upon his advancing columns. Ringgold's battery replied, while Taylor ordered the main portion of his troops to deploy into line. Taylor acted on the defensive, depending upon his batteries. The battle lasted one afternoon, at the close of which Arista began to retire, defeated, but in fairly good order. The Americans numbered 2300, the Mexicans 6000.

Panama Canal. The Panama Canal Company (French) was organized by Count de Lesseps, March 3, 1880, and under the concession obtained from the Colombian Government, was to construct and open the canal by March 3, 1892. The face value of the shares issued was approximately $500,000,000, but after $266,000,000 had been expended, the company in 1889 became bankrupt. The total length of the proposed waterway is forty-five and one-half miles, and the work actually done is variously estimated at one-third, one-fifth and one-tenth of the whole. In 1891 Lieutenant Wyse obtained an extension of the concession for ten years, provided a company be formed for its completion; otherwise the Colombian Government will seize the property. In November, 1892, the French Government instituted criminal proceedings against the leading officials of the Canal Company.

Panama Congress, was called by the Spanish-American Republics in 1826. The United States sent delegates too late for the preliminary meeting and the adjourned congress for 1827 never occurred. Among the objects of the proposed congress interesting to the United States were: The establishment of liberal doctrines of commercial intercourse; assent to the doctrine that free ships make free goods, and an agreement that "each will guard against the establishment of any future European colony within its borders." The failure of the Congress showed that an alliance between the United States and the petty Republics was inadvisable. President John Quincy Adams was warmly in favor of the proposed meeting, but Congress did not favor it.

Pan-American Congress, an international conference of representatives from the United States and from seventeen States of Central and South America, which assembled at Washington, October 2, 1889, on the invitation of the United States. Its purpose was to adopt some plan of arbitration for the settlement of disputes, and plans for the improvement of business intercourse and means of communication between the countries. San Domingo was the only State to refuse the invitation. The delegates were taken on a tour of inspection through the Union, prior to assembling for the business convention. Nothing very definite was arrived at in the convention, which was of value chiefly through its exposition of the commercial status and resources of the various countries. The Bureau of American Republics was established at the suggestion of this convention.

Panics, or commercial crises in United States history, begin with that of 1819, due to speculation and disorder following upon the War of 1812. The next followed in 1837. The years preceding had been years of extraordinary speculation, carried on with a most unsound banking system. Jackson gave the final impetus to the panic by his "specie circular," which struck a great blow at credit, and forced many banks to suspend specie payments. The country gradually righted itself without the aid of governmental interference, which Van Buren refused to give. In 1857 another period of inflation was followed by another crisis. After the war came another period of inflation, and, as a result, the panic of 1873. The crisis of 1893 seems to have been rather due to financial legislation than to an unsound condition of the business of the country at large.

Paoli, Pa. Here the British, under Major-General Grey, made a night attack upon Wayne's encampment, September 20, 1776. Wayne was utterly surprised and could make no effective resistance. He lost 150 men.

Paper. The first attempt at the manufacture of paper in the United States was made in 1690 by William Rittinghuysen and William Bradford, who established a paper mill at Roxbury near Philadelphia. The paper was made wholly of linen rags. In 1710 William de Wers erected a second mill in Germantown, and the third, erected in 1714, on the Chester Creek in Delaware, furnished Benjamin Franklin with paper. By 1810 the number of paper mills in the United States was estimated at 185, nearly every State possessing one or more. In 1870 there were nearly 700 of these establishments, manufacturing printing, writing and wrapping paper, with a capital of $34,365,000.

Paraguay. A commercial treaty was concluded between the United States and Paraguay in 1853, but Paraguay failed to ratify. Differences arose which led to the manifestation of force by the United States, and treaties of indemnity, commerce and navigation were concluded in 1859.

Paris, Louis Philippe d'Orleans, Comte de, eldest grandson of Louis Philippe, king of the French, born in Paris in 1838, became an aide-de-camp to General McClellan in 1861. He returned to England in 1862. He has published several volumes of a "Histoire de la Guerre Civile en Amérique," which is to be completed in eight volumes. He has since been noted because of his claims to the French throne.

Paris, Declaration of. At the Peace of Paris, in 1856, the following declaration with regard to the conduct of war was subscribed to by all the parties to the treaty, and has since been accepted by nearly all civilized nations, except the United States. (1) Privateering is and remains abolished. (2) Neutral goods in enemies' ships and enemies' goods in neutral ships, except contraband of war, are not liable to capture. (3) Paper blockades are unlawful. The United States refused to agree to the abolition of privateering. This cost them heavily in the Civil War.

Paris, Monetary Conferences at. There have been three International Monetary Conferences held in Paris. The first was assembled June 17, 1867, at the solicitation of France, "to consider the question of uniformity of coinage and seek for the basis of ulterior negotiations." The United States and nearly every nation of Europe were represented. No definite decision could be reached, the convention adjourning July 6. On August 16, 1878, the second International Monetary Convention assembled at Paris, at the suggestion of the United States, "to adopt a common ratio between gold and silver for the purpose of establishing internationally the use of bimetallic money and securing fixity of relative value between those metals." The collective decision of the European delegates was that this would be impossible, monetary questions being necessarily governed by the special situation of each state or group of states. Adjournment took place August 29. The Conference of April 8, 1881, assembled at the call of France and the United States, to adopt a settled relative and international value between gold and silver. The Conference adjourned July 8, having arrived at no agreement. (See Brussels.)

Paris, Treaty of (1763), was a treaty concluded between Great Britain, France, Spain and Portugal. France ceded to Great Britain Canada, Cape Breton and the islands and coasts of the St. Lawrence. The Mississippi River from its source to the Iberville and a line thence through Lakes Maurepas and Pontchartrain to the Gulf of Mexico were to bound the Spanish and British possessions. Spain ceded Florida to Great Britain. England renounced her pretensions to Cuba in favor of Spain and surrendered her forts in Spanish America.

Paris, Treaty of (1782–83). See Versailles, by which name that treaty is more familiarly known, though in reality the treaty between the United States and Great Britain was signed at Paris and not, like the treaty between Great Britain and France, at Versailles.

Parish. In England the parish was, at the time of the settlement of America, the unit of local government. Its leading institutions were apparently adopted in the town government of the New England colonies, but in the Southern colonies were imitated exactly, with the same name. The Virginia parish, for instance, was usually a sub-division of the county. Besides its religious duties, the vestry of the parish had to choose church-wardens and with them to take charge of the poor, of public processioning of bounds, of the counting of tobacco, and of other administrative matters. They chose the clergyman and provided for his salary. In New England the word parish had only an ecclesiastical significance. In South Carolina the parish was the chief subdivision of the colony, there being no counties. In Louisiana the same is still true.

Parke, John G., born in 1827, was first in command at Fort Macon. He fought at South Mountain and Antietam, and was chief of staff to General Burnside at Fredericksburg and Vicksburg. He was promoted major-general of volunteers.

Parker, Amasa J. (1807–1890), represented New York in the U. S. Congress as a Democrat from 1837 to 1839. He was a Judge of the New York Supreme Court from 1847 to 1855.

Parker, Foxhall A. (1821–1879), commanded the "Mahaska" from 1862 to 1863. From 1863 to 1866 he commanded the Potomac flotilla. He was chief signal officer of the navy from 1873 to 1876.

Parker, Sir Hyde (1739–1807), British naval officer, served on the "Phœnix" on the American station, and in 1776 engaged in the attack on New York. He conveyed the troops which captured Savannah in 1778.

Parker, Joel (1816–1888), was a member of the New Jersey Assembly from 1847 to 1850, and prosecuting attorney from 1852 to 1857. He was Governor of New Jersey from 1862 to 1866 and in 1870. The National Labor Convention in 1872 nominated him for Vice-President of the United States. He was a Judge of the New Jersey Supreme Court from 1880 to 1888.

Parker, Sir Peter (1721–1811), left England in 1775 as post-captain in the "Bristol" to co-operate with Sir Henry Clinton in an attack on Charleston, S. C. He made a gallant but unsuccessful assault on Fort Moultrie in 1776. He aided Lord Howe in the capture of New York, and commanded the squadron that took possession of Rhode Island. In 1782 he took De Grasse prisoner.

Parker, Sir Peter (1786–1814), was sent in command of the "Menelaus" to patrol Chesapeake Bay and blockade Baltimore harbor in 1814. He wantonly destroyed and plundered public and private property, and completely destroyed all domestic commerce during the month of his blockade. His conduct was exceedingly exasperating to the Americans. He was killed during one of his skirmishing "frolics."

Parker, Theodore (1810–1860), was pastor of a Unitarian church at West Roxbury, Mass., from 1837 to 1845. In 1845 he established the "Twenty-Eighth Congregational Society" in Boston. He was an ardent opponent of all pro-slavery sentiments, and exerted a powerful anti-slavery influence. He was the leader of a new and more practical phase of the Unitarian movement.

Parkman, Francis (1823–1893), attained high rank as a historian and writer by a series of works relating to the rise and fall of the French dominion in America. During his later years he was regarded as the foremost of American historians. In the preparation of his series he frequently visited Europe to consult the French archives. It is a work of great candor and fairness, and is notable for its brilliant and graphic style and evidences of careful research. It includes "The Conspiracy of Pontiac," "Pioneers of France in the New World," "The Discovery of the Great West," "The Jesuits in North America," "The Old Régime in Canada," "Count Frontenac and New France under Louis XIV.," "A Half-Century of Conflict," and "Montcalm and Wolfe."

Parliament. The right of Parliament to legislate for the colonies was not seriously questioned during the earlier portions of colonial history. In

1761 James Otis denied the right of Parliament to tax the colonists, since they were not represented in Parliament. The Stamp Act of 1765, and other measures of taxation caused by the Seven Years' War, caused the same protest to be made generally. From this the revolutionary party advanced to the position that Parliament had also no right to legislate for the colonies. The Declaratory Act of 1766 and the Townshend Acts of 1767 aimed to perpetuate the system. The Parliament of 1768–1774, noted for aversion to popular rights in England, as well as in America, abetted the king in all his American policy. Chief among their measures of this purport were the Boston Port Act, the Massachusetts Charter Act, the Quebec Act and the Quartering Act.

Parris, Samuel (1653–1720), born in England, was a clergyman in Salem, Mass., from 1689 to 1696. In 1692 his daughter and niece accused Tituba, a slave, of bewitching them. Mr. Parris beat Tituba until she confessed. The delusion spread, and during the horrors of the "Salem witchcraft," here inaugurated, nineteen persons were hanged. He afterward acknowledged his error.

Parrott, Robert P. (1804–1877), invented the system of rifled cannon and projectiles which bears his name. The Parrott guns exhibit great endurance, one at Charleston having been fired 4606 times before bursting, and were of great service in the Civil War.

Parsons, Samuel H. (1737–1789), was a member of the Connecticut Assembly from 1762 to 1780. He planned the capture of Ticonderoga in 1775. He fought at Long Island in 1776, and commanded a brigade at White Plains and the troops at New York Highlands from 1778 to 1779. He succeeded General Israel Putnam in command of the Connecticut line in 1780. He had an important part in the forming of the Ohio Company, the securing of the Ordinance for the Government of the Northwest Territory and the early settlement of Ohio.

Parsons, Theophilus (1750–1813), was graduated at Harvard, and rose to the leading position among the lawyers of Massachusetts. He was a member of the famous Essex Junto. He was foremost among the Federalists in the Ratifying Convention of 1788. Aside from service in the State Legislature he held no further political office. He was Chief Justice of the Massachusetts Supreme Court from 1806 until his death.

Parsons' Case, a celebrated law case won by Patrick Henry in November session of the Court of Hanover County, Va., in 1763. This case involved the constitutionality of the "option law" or "two penny act," passed by the Virginia Legislature in 1758. The operation of this act affected each parish minister, compelling him to receive the value of the 16,000 pounds of tobacco, due for his year's services, in paper money of the colony, amounting to £133 instead of £400 sterling, the selling value of the tobacco. The clergy appealed to the crown. The crown disallowed (vetoed) the law. Under this disallowance the Rev. James Maury having sued for damages, the court squarely "adjudged the act to be no law," and decided for the plaintiff. A new trial was allowed on a demurrer, and Henry was retained as counsel for the defendant. His eloquence induced the jury, a picked jury, to return one penny damages for the plaintiff. Success in this famous case made Henry's reputation at once.

Parton, James (1822–1891), came to the United States from England in 1827. He published lives of Horace Greeley, Aaron Burr, Andrew Jackson, Benjamin Franklin and Thomas Jefferson, "General Butler in New Orleans," "Noted Women in Europe and America," "How New York is Governed" and "Captains of Industry." Of these his Jackson is the most important.

Pastorius, Francis D. (1651–1719), came to America from Germany in 1683 and founded a colony of Germans and Dutch at Germantown, Pa. He signed the first protest made in America against slavery in 1688.

Patent Office. This office, or bureau, was created in 1836 in the Department of State, the chief officer being the Commissioner of Patents. The Patent Office was transferred to the Department of the Interior in 1849, when this latter department was created. Originally patents were signed by the President, then by the Secretary of State and the Commissioner of Patents; now by the Secretary of the Interior and the Commissioner.

Patents. The Constitution confers upon Congress the power to issue patents for useful inventions. A few patents had been issued by the States. The first patent law, passed in 1790, granted letters patent upon any new invention, for fourteen years, to both citizens and foreigners. Application had to be made to the Secretaries of War, the State and the Navy. The Act of 1793 permitted the issue of patents to citizens only and required a fee of $30. States were not permitted to issue patents. This was decided in the case of Gibbons *vs.* Ogden in New York. In 1836, the year of the establishment of the patent office, a law was passed requiring a preliminary examination of the novelty and patentability of inventions. Under the Law of 1842 patents were granted for seven years. This term was afterward extended to its present length of seventeen years. Finally by the Act of 1870 patents are to be granted to any person who can prove the newness and desirability of his invention, on payment of the required fee. The number of patents, annually issued, which in 1844 was 502, is now (1894) about 25,000.

Paterson, William (1745–1806), was a New Jersey Delegate to the Continental Congress from 1780 to 1781. He was a member of the Federal Convention of 1787, and proposed the preservation of State sovereignty, in what was called the "New Jersey Plan." He was a U. S. Senator from 1789 to 1790, Governor of New Jersey from 1791 to 1793, and a Justice of the U. S. Supreme Court from 1793 to 1806.

Pathfinder, the nickname of General John C. Frémont, given him because of his valuable western explorations from 1837 to 1853.

Patrol, a military system adopted by the parishes of most of the Southern colonies, notably South Carolina. The patrol was a sort of police for the parish, and was designed especially to prevent and subdue insurrections among the slaves. In South Carolina the patrol was established by law in 1704. The patrollers furnished their own pistols and horses. They rode from plantation to plantation and arrested all slaves who could not show passes from their owners. This system soon became general through the South, and continued under various forms for many years.

Patrons of Husbandry, or "Grangers," a secret association formed at Washington, December 4, 1867, for the promotion of agricultural interests. It somewhat resembles the order of the Masons. By 1875, it numbered 1,500,000 members in every section of the country. Though not intended for political purposes, its aim to cheapen transportation involved it in a *quasi*-political warfare with railroad corporations.

Patroons. In 1629 the Dutch West India Company, in order to effect a permanent agricultural colonization of New Netherland, granted a charter of "Privileges and Exemptions" to any members of the company who would within four years plant a colony of fifty anywhere in New Netherland, except on Manhattan Island. These wealthy grantees were called Patroons, and were privileged to rule their colonies in absolute feudal style, the colonists being bound to them for a certain number of years. This system was soon found to be disadvantageous, since it tended to debar the less wealthy class of individual colonists. In 1640 the charter was modified and extended to any good citizen of the Netherlands. In later years there were frequent quarrels between the Patroons and the provincial government.

Patterson, Daniel T. (1786–1839), commanded the naval forces at New Orleans in 1814, co-operating with General Jackson. He commanded the flotilla that destroyed the stronghold of Jean Lafitte at Barataria.

Patterson, Robert (1743–1824), came to Pennsylvania from Ireland in 1768. He served in the Colonial army, was appointed Director of the Mint by President Jefferson in 1805 and served till 1824.

Pattison, Robert E., born in 1850, was comptroller of Philadelphia from 1877 to 1882. He was Governor of Pennsylvania from 1883 to 1887, and was again elected in 1890, to serve from 1891 to 1895.

Patton, Jacob H., born in 1812, has published "A Concise History of the American People," "The Democratic Party, Its History and Influences," "A Brief History of the Presbyterian Church in the United States," and "The Natural Resources of the United States."

Paul vs. Virginia, an important case before the U. S. Supreme Court. In 1866 Samuel Paul, of Virginia, was indicted by the Circuit Court of Petersburg and sentenced to pay a fine of fifty dollars for refusing, in his capacity of insurance agent for a New York company, to comply with that statute of the State of Virginia which required the deposit in the State Treasury of certain moneys in State bonds by insurance companies not incorporated under the State laws, or the agents of such companies, in return for a license. The Court of Appeals of Virginia confirmed the decree of the Circuit Court, and the Supreme Court of the United States confirmed that of the Court of Appeals on the ground that the State statute in question did not conflict with the clause of the National Constitution, which declares that "the citizens of each State shall be entitled to all the privileges and immunities of citizens in several States," nor with the power of Congress to "regulate commerce with foreign nations and among the several States."

Paulding, James K. (1779–1860), was associated with Washington Irving in the publication of the "Salmagundi" in 1807. He was Secretary of the U. S. Navy from 1838 to 1841. He was a facile essayist and humorist. He wrote "Life of Washington," "The Backwoodsman," "Slavery in the United States," "Old Continental, or the Price of Liberty," and "The Dutchman's Fireside," a novel.

Paulding, John (1758–1818), was one of the three captors of Major André, and it was largely due to his influence that André was delivered to the authorities. He served throughout the Revolution.

Paulus Hook, Capture of, August 18, 1779. Paulus Hook was a sandy isthmus on the site of Jersey City. This place was captured from the British by Major Lee with 300 men. A mistake of the British favored their surprise. One hundred and fifty-nine prisoners were taken.

Pawnee Indians, for a long time inhabitants of Nebraska on the Platte, have always been friendly to the Americans. By a treaty in 1833 they sold lands south of the Nebraska. They were afterward attacked by the Sioux and their lands devastated. In 1857 they sold more of their lands, but the Government did not protect them from further ravages of the Sioux.

Payne, Henry B., born in 1810, represented Ohio in the U. S. Congress as a Democrat from 1875 to 1877. He was a member of the Electoral Commission in 1877, and a U. S. Senator from 1885 to 1891.

Payne, John Howard (1792–1852), was an author and actor of considerable merit and fame at home and abroad. He is eminent as the author of "Home, Sweet Home," which he composed for his drama, "Clari, or the Maid of Milan." His renown as a song-poet was unsurpassed. He was U. S. Minister to Tunis from 1841 to 1845 and from 1851 till his death.

Pea Ridge, Ark., a hot engagement, March 7, 1862, between 10,500 Union soldiers under General Curtis and 20,000 Confederate troops, including some 6000 Cherokee Indians, commanded by General Van Dorn, who had superseded Price and McCulloch. The Confederates began the fight, advancing toward Sugar Creek, along which Curtis had deployed his forces, Davis occupying the centre, Carr the right and Sigel the left. McCulloch first attacked the Union left, and then, moving to the east, endeavored to join Van Dorn and Price against Curtis' left and centre. This movement was prevented by Sigel. At the close of the first day the National army had been defeated on their right, and the Confederates on their right. The following day the Confederates were compelled to retreat through the defiles of Cross Timber Hollow, being unable to withstand the cross firing of Davis and Sigel. The loss on both sides was quite heavy, the Confederates faring the worst.

Peabody, Andrew P. (1811–1893), was editor of the *North American Review* from 1854 to 1863, and professor of Christian morals at Harvard from 1860 to 1881. He won esteem as a profound thinker, facile writer and lovable teacher.

Peabody, George (1795–1869), born in Danvers, Mass., was a most liberal philanthropist. From 1814 to 1837 he was in mercantile business in

CONFEDERATE GENERALS.

Braxton Bragg.
P. G. T. Beauregard.
James Longstreet.
Joseph E. Johnston.

David H. Hill.
J. E. B. Stuart.
Robert E. Lee.
Leonidas Polk.
John B. Hood.

Thomas Jonathan Jackson.
A S. Johnston.
A. P. Hill.
Jubal A. Early.

Baltimore. In 1838 he established the famous banking firm of George Peabody and Company in London. He founded the Peabody Institute at Baltimore in 1857 with $1,000,000, gave $2,500,000 for constructing lodging-houses for the poor in London, and $3,500,000 for the promotion of education in the South. His public charities exceeded $10,000,000.

Peabody Museum, instituted as part of Harvard University in 1866 by George Peabody, an American banker, living in England. The best organized work in archæology and ethnology accomplished in the United States has been done under the auspices of this institution.

Peace Commission. In May, 1778, a Peace Commission was sent to the colonies by Lord North. The Commission offered all manner of conciliatory terms: an extension of the privileges of trade, an abolition of the quartering act, a representation of the colonies in Parliament, an arrangement for sustaining Continental bills of credit, and an almost independent colonial administration. The terms were refused and a treaty with France concluded.

Peace Conference. In January, 1861, the Legislature of Virginia passed a resolution inviting the various States to appoint delegates to meet at Washington to consider an adjustment of the national difficulties then pending. This Conference met February 4 and adjourned February 27. Twenty-one States were represented. As a result of the deliberations of the Conference a constitutional amendment was proposed which prohibited slavery north of the parallel of 36° 30′ northern latitude; south of this line it was to exist without restraint. It denied the right of passing laws giving freedom to slaves temporarily in the free States or to fugitive slaves, and forbade Congress from controlling slavery in the Southern States, but prohibited the slave trade. The amendment was brought up in the Senate, but failed of introduction in the House.

Peach Tree Creek, Ga., a battle, July 20, 1864, during Sherman's celebrated march through Georgia. Sherman was then advancing on Atlanta, and Johnston proposed to attack him as he crossed Peach Tree Creek, or else allow him to attack the Georgia State troops at the Decatur and Marietta roads and then fall upon his flank. Sherman advanced with Thomas on the right, Schofield in the centre and McPherson on the left. June 20 Hood advanced to the attack and endeavored to cut Thomas off from Schofield and McPherson. Stewart's corps attacked Sherman's right centre under Newton, who, though surprised, held his ground. Hooker's whole corps was left uncovered and suffered severely, but managed to drive the Confederates back. Thus the attack failed. Sherman had 30,000, Hood 50,000.

"**Peacock,**" eighteen guns, Captain Warrington. April 29, 1814, this sloop attacked, off Florida, the British brig, "Épervier," eighteen guns. The battle lasted forty minutes, resulting in the capture of the "Épervier" and the killing and wounding of twenty-two of its men. It had aboard $118,000 in specie, and proved a very valuable prize. On June 30, 1815, the "Peacock" attacked and captured the "Nautilus," fourteen guns. This took place after the treaty of peace. Next day, on ascertaining this fact, Captain Warrington gave up the "Nautilus" and returned home.

" Peacock," brig. (See " Hornet.")

Peale, Charles Wilson (1741–1827), of Pennsylvania, was prominent as a portrait painter. He was a member of the Pennsylvania Legislature in 1779. He painted likenesses of nearly all the prominent officers in the Continental army. He painted the first portrait of Washington in 1772. His versatility was marked.

Peale, Rembrandt (1778–1860), of Pennsylvania, attained prominence as a portrait painter. One of his most famous pictures is a likeness of Washington. He painted the famous "Court of Death" and "The Roman Daughter."

Pearce, James A. (1805–1862), represented Maryland in the U. S. Congress as a Democrat from 1835 to 1839 and from 1841 to 1843. He was a U. S. Senator from 1843 to 1862.

Peary Expedition. In 1891 Lieutenant R. E. Peary conducted a scientific Arctic exploration to Greenland under the auspices of the Academy of Natural Sciences of Philadelphia. He sailed in June and reached McCormick Bay the following month. From this place Peary and his wife and party made a number of exploring tours, reaching as far north as 82°. A journey of 1300 miles was accomplished in sleds, and much valuable geographical and geological research was made. A relief party was dispatched to McCormick Bay in 1892.

Peck, John J. (1821–1878), of New York, served in every battle except one during the Mexican War. He commanded a brigade at Williamsburg and Fair Oaks and was in command at Suffolk against Longstreet in 1863.

Peculiar Institution, a phrase applied to negro slavery about 1852 by the *South Carolina Gazette* and afterward in general use.

Pedro II. (1825–1891), was Emperor of Brazil from 1841 to 1889. He opened the Amazon to the commerce of all nations in 1867. He visited the United States in 1876 and aided President Grant in opening the Centennial Exhibition. He was deposed in 1889.

Pegram, Robert B., of Virginia, born in 1811, resigned from the U. S. navy in 1861 and entered the Confederate service. He commanded the "Nashville" in 1861 and the "Virginia" ("Merrimac"). Died 1894.

Peirce, Benjamin (1809–1880), won distinction for his original and extensive work in pure and in applied mathematics. He was a professor at Harvard from 1833 to 1867. He published many mathematical works.

" Pelican," the ship in which Sir Francis Drake made his famous voyage around the world, leaving England November 15, 1577, and returning to that country September 26, 1580.

" Pelican," sloop. (See " Argus.")

Pemaquid, the first permanent settlement made in Maine. It was established by John Brown, of New Harbor, who bought lands from the Indians July 15, 1625. It was also the name originally given to the Kennebec River, near which the settlement was located.

Pemberton, John C. (1814–1881), was graduated from the U. S. Military Academy in 1837. He served against the Seminoles in Florida from 1837 to 1839. He was an aide on General Worth's staff during the Mexican War, and was promoted major for services at Monterey and Molino del Rey. He joined the Confederates in 1861 as staff officer to General Johnston. In 1862 he was assigned command of South Carolina, Georgia and Florida and constructed Fort Wagner and Battery B. He received command in Mississippi, and in 1863 was defeated at Champion Hills and Vicksburg by General Grant, after commanding Vicksburg during its siege.

Pendergrast, Garrett J. (1802–1862), in command of the "Cumberland" protected Hampton Roads at the beginning of the Civil War and prevented the U. S. vessels from falling into the hands of the Confederates.

Pendleton, Edmund (1721–1803), one of the principal Virginian patriots and orators, served in the House of Burgesses and as a member of a Committee of Correspondence, and was a delegate to the first Continental Congress. As president of the Virginia Convention, he was the head of the State Government 1775–1776, and afterward president of the Committee of Safety. He drew up the resolutions instructing the State representatives in Congress to agitate for independence. He was also Speaker of the Legislature and President of the Court of Appeals. His most important service was in 1788, when he was one of the leaders of the Federalist phalanx in the convention called to ratify the Federal Constitution.

Pendleton, George Hunt (1825–1889), was a member of the Ohio Senate, and from 1857 to 1865 was a Democratic Congressman and sat in important committees. When McClellan was nominated for President in 1864, Pendleton received the second place on the ticket. In 1869 he was defeated for Governor of Ohio. While U. S. Senator, 1879–1885, he was chairman of the Committee on Civil Service Reform, and his name is attached to an act in furtherance of that measure. President Cleveland in 1885 appointed Senator Pendleton Minister to Germany, where he remained until 1889.

Pendleton Act, an act for the reformation of the national civil service, introduced into the Senate by Pendleton, of Ohio in 1880, but which did not become a law until January 6, 1883. It provides for open competitive examinations for admission to the public service in Washington, and in all custom-houses and post-offices where the official force is of as many as fifty; for the appointment of a Civil Service Commission of three persons and for the apportionment of appointments according to the population of States.

Pends d'Oreilles, or Kalispels, a tribe of Selish Indians, inhabiting Montana, Idaho, Washington and British America. They have always been friendly to the whites.

"**Penguin**," brig. (See "Hornet.")

Peninsular Campaign. July 21, 1861, McClellan was appointed to command all the Federal troops about Washington. The popular cry was at that time: "On to Richmond!" McClellan, after months of delay, finally landed his forces at Fort Monroe, April 2, 1862, and marched up between the York and James Rivers toward Richmond, where Johnston lay encamped.

A month was spent besieging Yorktown, and after all the Confederates escaped. At the battle of Williamsburg, May 4, McClellan was successful, and again at the battle of Fair Oaks, May 31. Then followed the fights at Mechanicsville, Gaines' Mills, White Oak Swamp, Frayser's Farm and Malvern Hill, on the whole disastrous to the national cause. By the end of July the Peninsular Campaign was ended and Richmond had not been reached, though probably at one time it might have been. McClellan retreated through the Chickahominy swamp to a base on James River.

Penitentiary. The first penitentiary was founded, by the influence of the Friends of Pennsylvania, at Philadelphia in 1786. This was followed soon after by the New York prisons at Sing Sing and Auburn. In the Philadelphia Penitentiary the system of solitary confinement prevailed, but the New York methods imposed silence rather than solitude, and upon this latter plan were based the penitentiaries of other States, which soon began to be established. The prison system throughout the country became so noted for its perfect and humane discipline that in 1831 De Tocqueville and Beaumont came to the United States on their noted tour of inspection.

Penn, John (1741–1788), represented North Carolina in the Continental Congress from 1775 to 1776 and from 1778 to 1780. He signed the Declaration of Independence. During the invasion of North Carolina by Lord Cornwallis he was placed at the head of public affairs in the State with almost dictatorial powers.

Penn, John (1729–1795), born in England, was Proprietary Governor of Pennsylvania from 1763 to 1771 and from 1773 to 1775. He attempted to be neutral during the Revolution.

Penn, Richard (1735–1811), came to America from England in 1763. He was Lieutenant-Governor of Pennsylvania from 1771 to 1773. His rule was marked by unprecedented prosperity.

Penn, William (October 14, 1644–July 30, 1718), the founder of Pennsylvania, was born in London, the son of Admiral Penn. While at Oxford he joined the new sect of Quakers, and was expelled from the university. For a few years he traveled in France and Italy, and became a court favorite in England. From this life he turned to become a minister of the Friends. This step led to a break with his father, to imprisonment in the Tower, in Newgate and to other persecutions. He was aided, however, by his friendship with the Duke of York. Penn wrote numerous tracts and theological works, "No Cross, no Crown," among others. He had already sent many emigrants to America, when Charles II. gave him in 1681 an extensive grant. He sailed to his new possession in 1682, laid out the city of Philadelphia and negotiated the famous treaty with the Indians under the elm tree. He returned to England in 1684, and had considerable influence at court after his friend came to the throne as James II. He was deprived of his government in 1692, but it was restored two years later. A visit to his colony in 1699 resulted in improving the condition of affairs. The new commonwealth had from the first a more tolerant basis than its neighbors. Penn returned to England after a few years. In the latter part of his life he became involved in difficulties and passed some time in the Fleet Prison. Life by Ellis, by Janney, and by W. H. Dixon. Macaulay's insinuations in his history have been refuted.

Penn vs. Baltimore, a case involving the boundaries between Penn's and Lord Baltimore's land grants from the crown. Charles Calvert, the third Lord Baltimore, met Penn's deputy in 1682, Penn in 1683, but nothing was decided, though Penn obtained a new grant from the Duke of York reaching into Delaware and even into Maryland; also a letter from the king requesting Baltimore to hasten the adjustment of the boundary. The case was taken to London and decided in Penn's favor. A compromise was arranged in 1732, and enforced by the Court of Chancery in 1760, in accordance with which a line was run by Mason and Dixon, fixing the boundary in 1767 as now. (See art. Mason and Dixon's Line.)

Pennamite War, a name sometimes employed to designate the Wyoming controversy between Pennsylvania and Connecticut. (See Wyoming Controversy.)

Pennington, William (1796–1862), was Governor of New Jersey from 1837 to 1842. In 1839 occurred the Broad Seal War, arising from his issuing commissions under the great seal of the State to five Democratic Congressmen whose election was contested by the Whigs and whose votes would determine the Speakership of the U. S. Congress. He was a Republican U. S. Congressman from 1859 to 1861 and Speaker.

Pennsbury Manor, the name of William Penn's country house in Bucks County, four miles above Bristol, on the Delaware, built during Penn's first visit on land purchased from the Indians in 1681.

Pennsylvania, commonly called the "Keystone State," was one of the original thirteen colonies. William Penn obtained (1681) a grant of land of 40,000 square miles from Charles II. as payment of a debt of £16,000 due to Penn's father, an admiral in the English navy. Penn proposed to found a colony for the benefit of the Quakers. The king gave it its name in honor of Penn. To encourage emigration Penn offered a popular government, with toleration for all religious beliefs. His penal code was reformatory. The Dutch and Swedes already had settlements within his grant, but they were incorporated in the new colony. In 1682 Philadelphia was founded from plans drawn in England. Penn established a proprietary government and his wise administration and humane treatment of the Indians caused the colony to flourish. His rights passed to his heirs, of whom they were purchased in 1776 by the State. Pennsylvania had difficulty with Connecticut over the territory north of latitude 41°, which by previous grant had been given to the latter State. In 1776 this region was organized as the county of Westmoreland and was represented in the Connecticut Legislature. This quarrel at one time threatened to cause war between the two States, but in 1782 the territory in dispute was given to Pennsylvania by the decision of a Federal court sitting at Trenton. Indian massacres occurred in this region in the years 1755, 1763 and 1778. The southern boundary line was surveyed by two English surveyors, Mason and Dixon (1763–67). Delaware, which was included in Penn's grant, was erected into a colony by itself (1703) with a legislature of its own, but under the same governor as Pennsylvania. In 1756 stage coaches were established between Philadelphia and New York. The first Continental Congress met in Philadelphia September 5, 1774. The Declaration of Independence (1776), the Battle of Germantown (October 4, 1777) and Valley Forge (1777–1778) identify the State with the Revolution. The State included many Tories. A constitution for the State was made in 1776. The Federal Constitutional Convention of 1787 met in Philadelphia. The constitution was ratified by a State Convention (December 12, 1787). A new State constitution was made in 1790, another in 1838, the present in 1873. The "Whiskey" Rebellion (1794) was a protest against an Act of Congress of 1790 which increased the tax on distilled spirits, largely manufactured in Western Pennsylvania. In national politics the State was for many years the Keystone State. From 1825 to 1884 the electoral votes were never cast for an unsuccessful candidate. Before 1825 the State was divided by the difference in the occupations and nationality of the people of the eastern and western sections. The discovery of coal and the use of anthracite in the production of iron (1839) led Pennsylvania to support a protective tariff. In 1835 the Anti-Masons elected a Governor. Since the formation of the Republican party, Pennsylvania has been a steadily Republican State. From 1856 to 1887 the machinery of the party was under the control of Simon Cameron. In 1882 and 1890 the Democrats elected the Governor. Pennsylvania was loyal in the support of the Union cause and furnished 362,284 men for the army. The greatest battle of the war, Gettysburg, was fought on her soil (July 1–3, 1863). The population of the State in 1790 was 434,373; in 1890 it had increased to 5,258,014. History by Proud.

Pennsylvania, The Historical Society of, founded in 1824, has issued fourteen volumes of "Memoirs," and supported the "Pennsylvania Magazine of History and Biography."

Pennsylvania, University of, Philadelphia. This institution was founded as an academy in 1749, and incorporated in 1755. In 1779 it became a university, finally completing its organization in 1791. The medical department was founded in 1765, and the law department in 1789. Marked progress has been made in recent years since the removal of the university to its present site. The college was at the first befriended by Franklin.

"Pennsylvania Gazette," a semi-weekly newspaper established at Philadelphia December 24, 1728, by Samuel Keimer. The full title was *The Universal Instructor in all Arts and Sciences and Pennsylvania Gazette.* Keimer soon turned it over to the management of his apprentice, Benjamin Franklin, who quickly made it the most valuable newspaper property in this country. The semi-weekly publication was, however, changed to a weekly, owing to lack of subscription. Franklin retired from the management of the *Gazette* in 1766. The *Gazette* did good service to the Revolutionary cause until the British occupation of Philadelphia. Publication was suspended until after evacuation. It was then renewed and survived another brief suspension in 1815. The first part of the title was dropped when Franklin assumed the management. In 1845 the *Gazette* was merged in the *Daily North American*, which is still published.

"**Pennsylvania Journal and Weekly Advertiser,**" founded in Philadelphia December 2, 1742, by William Bradford 3d. This journal divided the field with the *Pennsylvania Gazette* until the British occupation of Philadelphia, when it was suspended for a period, but was afterward revived. The *Journal* made a successful venture as a semi-weekly in 1788. It was discontinued in 1797, and gave place to the *Daily American*, a daily newspaper.

"**Pennsylvania Packet, or the General Advertiser,**" was founded in November, 1771, by John Dunlap at Philadelphia. During the British occupation of Philadelphia it was removed to Lancaster. After the evacuation it was brought back and published tri-weekly. It was afterward changed to a daily, and appeared under the title *Pennsylvania Packet and Daily Advertiser* in 1784.

Penny (Maryland), a copper coin of the value of two cents, coined in England by Lord Baltimore in 1659, and issued in Maryland the same year. The obverse or face of this penny was stamped with a profile bust of Lord Baltimore. The reverse contained a ducal coronet upon which were erected two masts, each bearing a flying pennant with the legend Denarium: Terræ-Mariæ. This coin was issued simultaneously with the Maryland shilling.

Penobscot Expedition, 1779. About 900 men were sent out from Boston against a British post on the Penobscot. A combined land and naval attack was planned. The land force debarked and gallantly assaulted the fort. Owing to disagreement between the commanders, the marines did not support them, and a British fleet now appearing on the scene forced all assailants to retire. It was an unfortunate affair. The commander, Saltonstall, and the generals, Lowell and Wadsworth, were publicly censured.

Pensacola, Fla., was first settled by French colonists about 1696 and came into the possession of the Spaniards in 1699. It fell alternately into the hands of the French, Spaniards and British until finally captured by the Spaniards in 1781. This Spanish post, though neutral, allowed the British to enlist there Indians against the United States in the War of 1812 and to make the town a rendezvous for British forces. General Jackson with 4000 men advanced from Fort Montgomery, and on November 6, 1814, demanded from the Spanish Governor possession of the forts. This was refused and early next day Jackson stormed the town. The forts were at once surrendered and the British driven from the harbor. This prompt action on Jackson's part prevented another Indian war, drove the British from an important point, and punished the Spanish for their violation of the laws of neutrality. Jackson again took possession of the town in 1818. In 1819 it became a part of the United States. At the beginning of the Civil War the navy yard and adjacent forts were seized by the Confederates, and later several engagements occurred with the Federal forces.

Pensions. The germ of the United States pension system lay in the provision by Congress near the beginning of the Revolutionary War that officers who should continue in the service till the end of the war should receive half pay during seven years thereafter. In 1785 Congress recommended to the States that they should make provision for invalid pensioners, and in 1808 the United States assumed the pension obligations of the States.

These were only for persons disabled in the service. In 1818 an act was passed granting pensions to all who had served nine months or more in the Revolutionary army, and were in indigent circumstances. More claimants applied than could possibly have survived from Washington's army, and the amount required to be paid during the first year was eleven times what had been estimated, and in the second year seventeen times. Subsequent acts provided for wars subsequent to the Revolution. Acts of 1836, 1848 and 1853 provided pensions for all widows of Revolutionary soldiers whenever married. A curious result has been that in 1868, when all Revolutionary pensioners were dead, there remained 888 widows of such soldiers. In 1893 thirteen remained. Acts of July 14, 1862, and subsequent dates, provided pensions for soldiers and sailors disabled in the Civil War, and for the dependent relatives of those who had died. Under these acts expenditures for pensions reached a maximum ($34,443,895) in 1871, and then declined until, on January 25, 1879, the Arrears Act was passed, allowing "back-pay" on all pensions to which claim was then successfully laid. This act doubled the total annual sum in two years. Meanwhile an act of 1871 had pensioned all who had served a certain time in the War of 1812, and their widows, if married before the Treaty of Ghent. (In 1893 there were 86 such, but 5425 widows). In 1887, a service pension act for the Mexican War was passed. Finally, the Act of June 27, 1890, called the Dependent Pension Act, pensioned all who served ninety days in the War of the Rebellion and were honorably discharged, and who are incapacitated for manual labor, and the widows, children and dependent parents of such. The effect has been nearly to double the number of pensioners, and to raise the annual charge for pensions above $160,000,000, nearly twice the ordinary annual expenditure for the German army. Thirty years from the war, there are now nearly a million pensioners, though probably only two million individuals served in the Union army and navy. The total expenditure for pensions since 1861, has been about $1,700,000,000. In 1869, pensions were provided for retiring U. S. Judges, and widows of Presidents have been pensioned by special act.

Pensions, Bureau of. Down to 1849, the pension system of the United States was administered by the War and Navy Departments. In that year it was given over to the Department of the Interior, then created.

People's Party. Organized during the National Union Conference at Cincinnati, May 19, 1891, and formed chiefly from the various Farmers' Alliances. A national committee was appointed to look after the interests of the new organization, and the platform of the Farmers' Alliance was indorsed advocating free silver; the sub-treasury plan; equal taxation; revenues limited to the necessity of the Government; a graduated income tax; the election of President, Vice-President and Senate by a direct vote of the people; and prohibition of alien ownership of land. The National Convention at Omaha, Neb., July 2, 1892, nominated James B. Weaver, of Iowa, for President, and James G. Field, of Virginia, for Vice-President. Weaver obtained a popular vote of 1,030,128 and an electoral vote of twenty-three.

Pepperrell, Sir William (1696–1759), was a member of the Massachusetts Legislature in 1726, and in 1727 became a member of the council. He was Chief Justice of the Court of Common Pleas from 1730 to 1759. In 1745 he was active in procuring men and supplies for an expedition against the French in Canada. He commanded the force that captured Louisbourg and was made a baronet. He was active in raising and equipping troops during the French War of 1755, and commanded the forces on the frontier of Maine and New Hampshire.

Pequots, a tribe of New England Indians, entered into a treaty with the colonists at Boston in 1634, but soon became hostile. Expeditions were sent against them and they in turn attacked Wethersfield and killed many settlers. In 1637, an expedition under Mason surprised the Indians at a fort near the present Groton, Conn. A desperate struggle followed in which the Indians were overcome with great loss. The remnant was nearly annihilated in a subsequent battle at Fairfield swamp. Many of the Pequots were sold as slaves, and the remainder of the tribe separated and later became widely scattered.

Percival, James G. (1795–1856), of Connecticut, was a popular poet, and composed several remarkable lyrics. He was a man of varied and extensive knowledge and a fluent writer.

Percy, George (1586–1632), came to Virginia from England about 1607. He succeeded Lord Delaware as Governor, temporarily, in 1611. He wrote "A Discourse of the Plantations of the Southerne Colonie in Virginia."

Percy, Hugh, Duke of Northumberland (1742–1817), in 1775 (being then known as Earl Percy) led a brigade to reinforce the British at Lexington, and allowed wanton plundering by his troops during the retreat. Several citizens were murdered. In 1776 he led a column at the reduction of Fort Washington and was the first to enter the American lines. He returned to England in 1776.

Perfectionists. (See Oneida Community.)

Perry, Arthur L., born in 1830, has been professor of history and political economy at Williams College since 1853. He is an ardent advocate of free trade. He has written "Foes of the Farmers" and two books on "Political Economy."

Perry, Matthew Calbraith (1794–1858), brother of the victor of Lake Erie, served as a boy in the War of 1812, and later against the pirates. He rendered important services while in command of the Brooklyn Navy Yard, and was promoted to be commodore in 1841. His aid in the capture of Vera Cruz in 1847 was valuable, as was his blockade of the coast. Commodore Perry is best remembered for his connection with Japan. He organized and commanded the expedition to that country—then outside the list of friendly nations—in 1853, and signed a treaty with its government in 1854, thus opening the "Mikado's Empire" to western influences.

Perry, Oliver Hazard (1785–1819), an American naval hero, was a native of Rhode Island, and entered the navy as midshipman in 1799. He was in the Tripolitan War, and afterward devoted his attention to ordnance. In

1813 he was appointed to command on Lake Erie. With great efforts and extraordinary rapidity he built a fleet on the lake and drilled his men. His preparations being completed, he sailed from Put-in Bay in command of a squadron of nine vessels, of which the "Lawrence" and "Niagara" were the chief. The British commander, Barclay, had six. Their battle of September 15, 1813, in which Perry showed great ability, resulted in the capture of the entire British squadron, and was immortalized in the laconic dispatch, "We have met the enemy and they are ours." Perry co-operated in the victory of the Thames, was made captain, and served in the defence of Baltimore.

Perryville, Tenn., the chief battle in Bragg's invasion of Kentucky. On October 8, 1862, General Bragg, leading 40,000 Confederate troops, was retreating from Kentucky into East Tennessee, when at Perryville he was overtaken by General Buell, with 58,000 Federals. Bragg was forced to turn and give battle. The fight lasted nearly all day, and was at times hand to hand. The National left, being composed of raw recruits, was destroyed, but the rest of the line, under General Philip H. Sheridan, held out bravely and repelled every attack of the Confederates, following them up with counter attacks. Buell's loss was 4300, including Generals James S. Jackson and William T. Terrill. Bragg's casualties were even heavier. Bragg was compelled to retire. Buell did not follow him.

Persia. The United States concluded a treaty of friendship and commerce with Persia in 1856.

Personal Liberty Laws, statutes passed by the Northern States to protect the negroes within their borders. The first acts were passed about 1840, though Indiana and Connecticut had previously provided that fugitives might have a trial by jury. After the Prigg decision, many of the States passed Acts prohibiting the use of State jails in fugitive slave cases. The Fugitive Slave Law of 1850 aroused the most violent opposition in the North, and before 1856 many of the States had passed personal liberty acts. Beside prohibiting the use of State jails, these laws forbade State judges and officers to assist claimants or issue writs. Trial was to be given all alleged fugitives. Heavy penalties were provided for the violation of these laws. Such acts were passed in Vermont, Connecticut, Rhode Island, Massachusetts, Michigan, Maine, Wisconsin, Kansas, Ohio and Pennsylvania. Of the Northern States, New Jersey and California alone sanctioned the rendition of fugitives.

Peru. The United States concluded a treaty of peace and commerce with the Peru–Bolivian Confederation in 1836. A claims convention was concluded in 1841 with Peru, by which Peru agreed to pay $300,000 indemnity to United States citizens. A commercial treaty was concluded in 1851. A convention relative to the rights of neutrals at sea was concluded in 1856. Claims conventions were concluded in 1862, 1863 and 1868. A commercial treaty was concluded in 1870, and an extradition treaty the same year. A commercial treaty was concluded in 1887.

Pet Banks, the name applied to certain State banks selected by the Treasury Department as places of deposit for Federal funds withdrawn from the Bank of the United States. This practice was in vogue during the period between 1833 and 1836. The banks were chosen, it was said, not because of fitness, but on the principle of the accepted system of granting bank charters, namely, of party fidelity. This gave rise to competition among the Democratic banks and a wholesale granting of charters, which was followed by speculation and inflation of the currency.

Peters, Hugh (1599–1660), came to America from England in 1635. In 1636, he succeeded Roger Williams as pastor of the first church in Salem, and excommunicated Williams' adherents. He took an active part in public affairs. In 1638, he was appointed to collect and revise the Massachusetts Colonial Laws. In 1641, he was a commissioner to England and influenced the removal of imposts on New England commerce. He afterward played an important part in the English Civil War.

Peters, Richard (1744–1828), was secretary of the Continental Board of War from 1776 to 1781, represented Pennsylvania in the Continental Congress from 1782 to 1783, and was a U. S. district judge from 1789 to 1828.

Peters, Samuel (1735–1826), became a Church-of-England minister in the churches of Hartford and Hebron, Conn., in 1762. He was suspected of being a Tory, and in 1774 was required to make a written declaration that he had not communicated with England concerning the controversies with the colonies and would not do so. Soon afterward he fled to England. He wrote a satirical "History of Connecticut" of little historical value.

Peters, United States vs., a Supreme Court case of the year 1809. Judge Peters, of the U. S. District Court for Pennsylvania, decided for the plaintiffs in the case of Olmstead and others *vs.* Rittenhouse's Executrixes, but refrained from carrying his judgment into execution because of a statute passed by Pennsylvania forbidding this. A mandamus was then asked for against Peters. The Supreme Court (Judge Marshall), declaring that the Legislature of a State cannot annul the judgment or determine the jurisdiction of a U. S. Court, granted the mandamus, and the decree was executed, against the opposition of the Pennsylvania authorities and even of the Pennsylvania militia. (See Olmstead et als. *vs* Rittenhouse's Executrixes.)

Peters' Reports, sixteen volumes of law reports by Richard Peters, Jr., containing cases from the United States Supreme Courts, 1828–1842.

Petersburg, Va. About this town and Richmond, from June, 1864, to April, 1865, there was the most celebrated campaign of the Civil War. Gradually Grant had forced Lee's Army of Northern Virginia southward until the Confederates lay posted about Petersburg and Richmond. Grant's army, including drivers, camp followers, etc., numbered nearly 120,000 men, while Lee was at the head of about 70,000. By June 10, 1864, the Confederates were strongly posted, Lee, with the main command, at Petersburg, and Longstreet on the left at Chapin's Bluff, the line extending along the Boydton Road and Hatcher's Run eastward. The campaign was opened by Butler, then commanding the Army of the James at Bermuda Hundred. June 10, a Federal force was sent by him under Gillmore and Kautz to destroy the Appomattox bridges and attempt the capture of Petersburg.

This expedition failed signally. June 14, Grant sent Smith with a large force upon a similar expedition. Smith delayed, thus giving the Confederates time to assault and defeat him. Grant lost 9000 men in these two expeditions. The siege of Petersburg practically commenced June 18. Butler had affected a valuable lodgment at Deep Bottom, and, on the twenty-first, forces under Hancock and Wright endeavored to destroy the Weldon Road, but this was frustrated by Hill, who attacked and defeated the Federals disastrously. Then followed Sheridan's victory at Yellow Tavern and Wilson's and Kautz's raid. June 25, Burnside proposed and began the construction of a mine to blow up the Confederate lines about Petersburg. This mine was in process of construction until July 23, and was sprung July 30. It consisted of a shaft 520 feet long with lateral terminations forty feet in each direction and was charged with 8000 pounds of powder. Burnside was to rush into the breach and seize Cemetery Hill, commanding the town. A crater 200 feet long by sixty wide was formed by the explosion, and one Confederate regiment was blown up, but the rest poured such a murderous fire upon the advancing Federals that 4000 men were lost, and the attempt failed. After this things remained comparatively quiet around Petersburg until February, 1865. Then Lee, having been appointed commander-in-chief of the entire Confederate force, perceiving that his situation was becoming desperate, determined to evacuate Richmond and Petersburg and join Johnston in the south. To cover his retreat, he sent a strong force on the night of March 24, 1865, to assault Fort Steedman. The fort was carried at the first assault, but reinforcements failed to come, and the Federals under Parke quickly repelled the assault. Of 5000 Confederates, 3000 were killed, and Lee's retreat was prevented. The National line then extended without a break from the Appomattox to Dinwiddie Court House. April 1, the fatal battle of Five Forks occurred, Sheridan defeating the Confederates after a desperate fight. They were also defeated at Quaker and Boydton Roads. April 2, Grant ordered a united attack along the Confederate line from Appomattox to Hatcher's Run. Everywhere the Confederates met defeat after fearful losses. On April 3, Lee evacuated Richmond and Petersburg simultaneously.

Petigru, James L. (1789–1863), was Attorney-General of South Carolina from 1822 to 1830. He ardently opposed the nullification and secession movements. He codified the Laws of South Carolina.

Petition. The Constitution prohibits Congress from making any law to abridge "the right of the people peaceably to assemble and to petition the Government for a redress of grievances." February 11, 1790, a petition signed by Franklin was offered to Congress praying the abolition of slavery, but it was unnoticed. Between 1830 and 1844 numerous petitions from abolitionists poured in. February 8, 1835, Henry L. Pinckney, of South Carolina, suggested that resolutions be adopted to the effect that Congress cannot constitutionally interfere with slavery in any of the States. The committee on these resolutions reported favorably and suggested that thereafter abolition petitions be laid on the table. These were adopted. John Quincy Adams opposed these "gag rules" during ten years, finally accomplishing their abolition in 1844.

Petroleum. Its existence was known to the Indians of Western New York, and it was collected in small quantities by them and by the early settlers of New York and Pennsylvania, amounting sometimes to as much as twenty barrels in a year. The first organized and successful effort to bore for petroleum was made in 1854 by a New York company along Oil Creek, N. Y. Oil was struck at seventy-one feet, and as much as a thousand barrels per day was obtained. Oil fields were quickly located elsewhere in New York and in Pennsylvania, Ohio and West Virginia, those of Pennsylvania proving the richest. The latter yielded 3,000,000 barrels in 1862. Gasolene, naphtha, kerosene, paraffine and other products soon began to be manufactured from the petroleum.

Pettaquamscut Purchasers, a company formed by John Hull, of Pine Tree Shilling fame, in 1660, which bought lands from the Indians about Pettaquamscut Rock, in the Narragansett country. This company was in constant collision with Atherton's company at Wickford. (See Narragansett Country.)

Pettit, Charles (1736–1806), was secretary of New Jersey from 1772 to 1778. He was assistant quartermaster-general of the Continental army from 1778 to 1783. He represented Pennsylvania in the Continental Congress from 1785 to 1787.

Pewter Muggers, a New York faction of the Democratic party which was opposed to the Tammany candidates in 1828. Their meetings being held in a Frankfort Street resort over *pewter mugs*, the name was affixed by their opponents.

"**Phebe**," brig. (See "Essex.")

Phelps, Edward J., born in 1822, was second comptroller of the Treasury from 1851 to 1853. After the breaking up of the Whig party he became a Democrat. He became professor of law at Yale in 1881. He was Minister Plenipotentiary to England from 1885 to 1889.

Phelps, Elizabeth Stuart, born in Massachusetts in 1844, has been prominent in temperance reform and efforts for the advancement of woman. She wrote "The Gates Ajar," "Hedged In," and many stories.

Phelps, John W. (1813–1885), of Vermont, served during the Mexican War. In the Civil War he commanded a brigade at Newport News, reduced Ship Island, and fought at New Orleans. He was candidate of the American party for President in 1880.

Phelps, Samuel S. (1793–1855), was a Judge of the Vermont Supreme Court from 1831 to 1838. He represented Vermont in the U. S. Senate from 1839 to 1851, and from 1853 to 1854. He was a pro-slavery Democrat.

Phelps, William Walter, born in 1839, represented New Jersey in the U. S. Congress as a Republican from 1873 to 1875. He was Minister to Austria from 1881 to 1882. He was a U. S. Congressman from 1883 to 1889, when he became Minister to Germany and served until 1893. He is known as a staunch supporter of a protective tariff. Died June 17, 1894.

Philadelphia, Pa., was founded by commissioners appointed by William Penn in 1681. The site of the present city was originally settled by Swedes. In 1683 Philadelphia was chosen as the capital of the colony, and continued to be such for 117 years. During the earlier part of the Revolution the city was the virtual capital of the colonies. Here the first Continental Congress convened in 1774; on July 4, 1776, the Declaration of Independence was adopted; on July 9, 1778, the Articles of Confederation were signed; and in 1787 the Constitution of the United States prepared. Here also, in 1786, the "Protestant Episcopal Church of North America" was organized. In December, 1790, Congress convened here, and continued to hold its sessions in the city for ten years. The first American bank was established here in 1781, and the first United States Mint in 1792. In 1876 the centennial celebration of the independence of the colonies was held in Philadelphia, and in 1882 the bi-centennial of the landing of William Penn was observed. The University of Pennsylvania was incorporated here in 1779. The city was from the first noted for philanthropic institutions.

Philip, King, chief of the Wampanoags, died in 1676. He was the son of Massasoit, and succeeded to the chieftainship in 1662. He was for many years friendly to the whites, but realized the decline of the Indian race, and was led to hostilities by the encroachments of the colonists, which rendered his tribe restless and discontented. In 1675 he inaugurated "King Philip's War," and enlisted in his service nearly all the New England tribes. Thirteen towns were destroyed, and 600 colonists lost their lives. He was killed at Mount Hope, R. I., and his tribe was almost annihilated.

Philippa, or Philippi, W. Va., the first engagement during McClellan's West Virginia campaign. Here Colonel Porterfield, commanding 1000 Confederate troops, was surprised and routed June 3, 1861, by Colonels Kelly and Dumont, with two regiments of McClellan's army. This occurred subsequently to West Virginia's rejection of the secession ordinance. Porterfield was engaged in burning bridges along the Baltimore and Ohio Railroad.

Philipse, Frederick (1626–1702), came to New Amsterdam from Holland about 1640. In 1693 part of his vast estate was erected by royal charter into the "Manor of Philipseborough." For over fifty years he was very prominent in colonial affairs.

Phillipps, Adelaide (1833–1882), came to America from England in 1840. She was for many years the leading contraltò singer in America. Her voice had a compass of two and a half octaves.

Phillips, John (1719–1795), with his brother Samuel, founded Phillips Andover Academy in 1780, and in 1781 founded Phillips Exeter Academy with an endowment of $134,000.

Phillips, Wendell (1811–1884), one of the greatest platform orators of the country, was born in Boston and graduated at Harvard in 1831. He became a lawyer, but from 1837 onward gave his chief energies to the abolitionist movement. He was the lecturer of the cause, as Garrison was the writer. For many years he labored against a hostile sentiment. He succeeded Garrison as president of the anti-slavery society. He was, moreover, an ardent advocate of the temperance and woman suffrage reforms, a champion of the greenback party, and an eloquent and acceptable lecturer on various topics, such as the "Lost Arts," etc.

Phillips, William (1731–1781), was appointed a major-general in the British army in America in 1776. He commanded at St. John till 1777, when he became second in command to Burgoyne at Montreal. By his skill and energy as an artilleryman he forced the evacuation of Ticonderoga by General St. Clair. He was prominent in the two Saratoga battles, and succeeded Burgoyne in the command of the surrendered troops. He was promoted lieutenant-general in 1780. In 1781 he joined General Benedict Arnold with 2000 men and assumed command. He died of typhoid fever soon afterward.

Phips, Sir William (1651–1695), engaged in trade and in 1687 recovered £300,000 from a wrecked Spanish vessel. In 1690 he commanded the expedition which captured Port Royal and made an unsuccessful attempt to reduce Quebec with a naval force of thirty-four vessels and about 2000 men. While in England in 1692 he was appointed Governor of Massachusetts. He was prominent in the suppression of witchcraft. He was a man of great industry and integrity. He died while visiting England to answer charges against him.

Piatt, Donn (1819–1891), was Secretary of Legation at Paris from 1853 to 1857, and for nine months was Chargé d'Affaires. He served on the staff of General Schenck during the Civil War.

Pickens, Andrew (1739–1817), served in the Cherokee War in 1761. In 1779 he defeated the British under Colonel Boyd at Kettle Creek and was active at the battle of Stono. He commanded the militia at Cowpens, captured Augusta and led the Carolina militia at Eutaw Springs. He served in the South Carolina Legislature from 1783 to 1794, and was a U. S. Congressman from 1793 to 1795. He was again in the South Carolina Legislature from 1801 to 1812. He negotiated numerous treaties with the Southern Indians.

Pickens, Francis W. (1805–1869), represented South Carolina in the U. S. Congress as a Nullifier from 1834 to 1843. He was Governor of South Carolina from 1860 to 1862. He demanded the surrender of Fort Sumter and gave the order to fire upon the "Star of the West."

Pickering, John (1777–1846), of Massachusetts, was celebrated for his philological studies, and was one of the founders of American Comparative Philology. He published "A Vocabulary of Americanisms" and "Remarks on the Indian Languages of North America."

Pickering, Timothy (1745–1829), was a Harvard graduate and militia officer in Massachusetts, who entered actively into the civil and military life of the Revolution. He was made adjutant-general of the army in 1776, and member of the board of war, and in 1780 he became quartermaster-general, materially aiding Washington's final movements. He held this position until 1785, and then settled in Pennsylvania. In 1791 he negotiated a treaty with the Six Nations, and the same year he was called to the office of Postmaster-

General. This position he, in 1795, exchanged for that of Secretary of War, and a few months later he took charge of the State Department, which he held until 1800. Becoming again identified with Massachusetts Pickering represented that State in the U. S. Senate 1805–1811 and the House 1813–1817. He was a radical Federalist and a member of the Essex Junto. As a vigorous opponent of the Embargo he was at one time extremely unpopular. Life by Pickering and Upham.

Pickett, George E. (1825–1875), served with distinction during the Mexican War at Vera Cruz, Contreras and Chapultepec. He joined the Confederates and in 1862 commanded a brigade under General Johnston. He was active at Richmond and Gaines' Mills, and commanded a division at Fredericksburg, Gettysburg and Petersburg. His command was routed at Five Forks, and he surrendered with General Lee. He was famous for a cavalry charge at Gettysburg.

Pierce, Franklin (November 23, 1804–October 8, 1869), fourteenth President of the United States, was born at Hillsborough, N. H., graduated at Bowdoin (where he was associated with Hawthorne and Longfellow), and became a lawyer in his native State. While very young he was Speaker in the Legislature, and Democratic Congressman from 1833 to 1837. He was U. S. Senator 1839–1842, declined a Cabinet offer from President Polk, and volunteered in the Mexican War. Appointed to a brigade he showed bravery in the battles of Contreras and Churubusco. This "war record" made him President. He was President of the State Constitutional Convention in 1850, and attained high rank at the bar. At the Democratic National Convention of 1852 Pierce was nominated on the forty-ninth ballot, triumphing over the more prominent competitors, Marcy, Cass, Buchanan and Douglas. In the election the Whig party collapsed and Pierce received 254 electoral votes. The noted names in his Cabinet were Marcy in the State Department, Jefferson Davis Secretary of War, and Caleb Cushing Attorney-General. His administration was marked at home by the Kansas-Nebraska question and the development of the slavery controversy, and abroad by the Koszta incident, the Japan treaty and the Nicaraguan affairs. President Pierce was defeated for renomination in 1856, and after 1857 lived in retirement.

Pierce, Henry L., born in 1825, was a member of the Massachusetts Legislature from 1860 to 1866. He represented Massachusetts in the U. S. Congress as a Republican from 1873 to 1877.

Pierce, William (1740?–1806), served with distinction during the Revolution. He represented Georgia in the Continental Congress from 1786 to 1787. A member of the Constitutional Convention of 1787, he opposed the plan adopted.

Pierpont, John (1785–1866), was an ardent reformer, in Massachusetts, and earnestly supported the temperance and anti-slavery movements. He wrote many poems, one of the most famous being "Warren's Address at the Battle of Bunker Hill."

Pierre, capital of South Dakota, was founded in 1829 near the site of old Fort Pierre.

Pierrepont, Edwards (1817–1892), was a member of the Union Defence Committee in New York. In 1864 he was active in organizing the War Democrats. He was appointed prosecutor of John H. Surratt, one of the conspirators against President Lincoln. He was active in destroying the Tweed ring. He was Attorney-General in Grant's Cabinet from 1875 to 1876, and Minister to England from 1876 to 1878.

Pietas et Gratulatio, a somewhat famous series of adulatory poems in Latin emanating from Harvard College in 1762 on the accession of George III.

Pigot, Sir Robert (1720–1796), commanded the left wing of the British force at Bunker Hill, where he displayed great skill and bravery. He commanded in Rhode Island in 1778.

Pike, Albert (1809–1891), attained high reputation as a lawyer. He edited the Arkansas Revised Statutes in 1836. He fought in the Mexican War and organized a force of Cherokees for the Confederates, engaging at Pea Ridge and Elkhorn.

Pike, Zebulon M. (1779–1813), U. S. army, explored the Mississippi to its source in 1805. From 1806 to 1807 he was engaged in geographical explorations in Louisiana territory and discovered Pike's Peak in the Rocky Mountains. He was seized by the Spanish Government for trespassing on Spanish territory, but was soon afterward released. In 1813 he was assigned to the principal army as adjutant and inspector general. He commanded the expedition against York, Upper Canada, and was killed by the explosion of a magazine of a captured fortification.

Pilgrim Fathers, the first settlers in Massachusetts. In 1608, a party of Puritans, chiefly from the north of England, weary of the constant religious persecutions, left England and settled at Amsterdam, whence they later moved to Leyden. But they could not conform to the customs of Holland. Accordingly in 1617, Robert Cushman and John Carver were sent to England to treat with the Virginia Company for a grant of settlement in its territory in America. This was readily obtained. Early in 1620, the Pilgrims embarked from Delfthaven in the "Speedwell," a vessel chartered in Holland. Arriving at Southampton, they found the "Mayflower," which Cushman had brought from London, awaiting them. August 5, 1620, the "Mayflower" and the "Speedwell" left Southampton for the New World. Twice the "Speedwell" put back for repairs, and the second time she was left, the "Mayflower" sailing alone from Plymouth with 102 passengers, September 6. Their destination was to a point near the Hudson River, but the wind drove them to the north. Skirting along Cape Cod, November 11 (O. S.), the "Mayflower" dropped anchor off what is now Provincetown. Later the Pilgrims landed on Plymouth Rock, and thus the colony of Plymouth was begun. The leaders of the Pilgrims were Bradford, Brewster, Cushman, Miles Standish, and Carver. The name comes from a passage in the journal of William Bradford.

Pilgrim Society, a society founded at Plymouth in 1820. It erected Pilgrim Hall in 1824, and has a valuable collection of portraits and memorials of the early settlers.

Pilgrims, Landing of. Tradition has not entirely determined who landed on Plymouth Rock; whether the exploring party of ten men who landed December 11 (old style), or the whole company. It is generally conceded that the first landing occurred at that place, that being the most convenient within sight. Elder Thomas Faunce, in 1741, then ninety-one years old, declared he had heard of it from the oldest planters.

Pillow, Gideon J. (1806–1878), commanded the right wing of the American army at Cerro Gordo and led a division at Churubusco, Molino del Rey and Chapultepec. In 1861 he was appointed brigadier-general in the provisional Confederate army. He commanded under General Polk at Belmont. When the command devolved upon him at Fort Donelson, he gave it over to General Buckner and escaped.

Pillow, Fort, Tenn., held by the Confederates with 6000 troops and protected by eight ironclads under Commander Hollins. This place was captured by the Union flag officer, Davis, who assailed it with a fleet of gunboats, and captured it June 4, 1862. The Confederate flotilla was utterly destroyed in less than an hour. Some ships had their boilers shot through and some were butted and sunk. The fire was then directed against the fort itself, which was speedily reduced, and evacuated by the garrison. The Union troops did not hold it long, however, abandoning it in consequence of operations on the Tennessee River. In 1864, the fort was held by 550 Federals under Major Booth, 260 of these soldiers being negroes. The fort was assaulted April 13 and captured by the Confederate cavalryman, Forrest, leading 4000 soldiers. The first assault was unsuccessful, but Booth was killed and Bradford, leader of the colored troops, took command. The Federals were assisted by their gunboat "New Era," but this aid availed little, because of the high banks of the river. Forrest sent in a flag of truce demanding a surrender, which was refused. Another assault was ordered and this time an entrance was gained. Nearly the whole garrison were killed.

Pinchback, Pinckney B. S., born in 1837, of African descent, was a member of the Louisiana Senate in 1868. He was Governor during the impeachment of Governor Warmoth. He was elected to the U. S. Senate in 1873, but was disallowed his seat.

Pinckney, Charles (1758–1824), was a member of the South Carolina Legislature from 1779 to 1780. He was a delegate to the Continental Congress from 1777 to 1778 and from 1784 to 1787. He was a member of the Constitutional Convention of 1787, and drafted one of the constitutions proposed. He was Governor of South Carolina from 1789 to 1792 and from 1796 to 1798, a U. S. Senator from 1797 to 1801, Minister to Spain from 1803 to 1805, Governor from 1806 to 1808. He was a Democratic U. S. Congressman from 1819 to 1821. C. C. Pinckney and Thomas Pinckney were his cousins.

Pinckney, Charles Cotesworth (1746–1825), an American statesman, was Attorney-General of his colony, South Carolina, and member of its Provincial Congress in 1775. He held the rank of major in the war, fought at Charleston, Brandywine and Germantown, and surrendered at Charleston in 1780. He was a member of the Federal Convention in 1787, and the Federalist leader in his State's ratifying convention in 1788. Pinckney declined a Cabinet position, but accepted in 1796 the mission to France; the Directory, however, refused to acknowledge him. The French proposals to bribe the American envoys called from him the well-known phrase: "Millions for defence, but not a cent for tribute!" He was appointed major-general for the expected war with France. Pinckney was the Federalist candidate for Vice-President in 1800, and for President in 1804 and 1808.

Pinckney, Henry L. (1794–1863), was a member of the South Carolina Legislature from 1816 to 1832, and represented South Carolina in the U. S. Congress as a Democrat from 1833 to 1837.

Pinckney, Thomas (1750–1828), brother of C. C. Pinckney, was an aide to General Lincoln and Count d'Estaing in the Revolution. He fought at Stono and was taken prisoner at Camden. He was Governor of South Carolina from 1787 to 1789, and Minister to Great Britain from 1792 to 1796. He negotiated the treaty with Spain securing free navigation of the Mississippi. In 1796 he was a Federalist candidate with Adams. He was a U. S. Congressman from 1797 to 1801.

Pinckney Plan, a plan for a Federal Constitution, proposed May 29, in the Convention of 1787, by Charles Pinckney, of South Carolina. It resembled the Randolph Plan, but no copy of it has been preserved. Many years afterward Pinckney produced a document which he declared to be this, but it was not.

Pine, Robert E. (1730?–1788), came to Philadelphia from England in 1783. He was prominent as an artist and painted portraits of many of the heroes of the Revolution, including Washington and Robert Morris.

Pine Tree Shilling, the name given to the largest of the coins issued in 1652 by the first mint established in Boston. These coins had the value of "12d., 6d. and 3d. pieces," that value being denoted by the figure XII, VI or III stamped upon the reverse. The obverse contained the representation of a pine tree encircled by a grained ring, with the legend "Mathosets In." Weight, 72 grains; value, 18¼ cents.

Pinkerton, Allan (1819–1884), fled from Scotland as a Chartist to America in 1842. He established Pinkerton's Detective Agency in Chicago in 1850, and organized the secret service of the National army in 1861.

Pinkerton Law. The Sundry Civil Appropriation Act of August 5, 1892, provides "that no employé of the Pinkerton Detective Agency, or similar agency, shall be employed in any Government service, or by any officer of the District of Columbia."

Pinkney, William (1764–1822), orator, was a member of the Maryland House of Delegates from 1788 to 1792 and of the Executive Council from

1792 to 1795. He was a commissioner to London under Jay's treaty from 1796 to 1804, Attorney-General of Maryland in 1805, commissioner in England (jointly with James Monroe) from 1806 to 1807, and Minister from 1807 to 1811. He was Attorney-General in Madison's Cabinet from 1811 to 1814, Minister to Russia from 1816 to 1818, and represented Maryland in the U. S. Senate from 1820 to 1822. He was a most eloquent advocate. Life by Wheaton.

Pinzon, Martin A. (1441–1493), is reported by some to have visited the New World in 1488 and by others to have seen charts of Norman explorers. He aided Columbus in fitting out his expedition, and was given command of "La Pinta." He parted from Columbus in the West Indies and attempted to usurp the honors of the discovery by arriving first at the Court, but was prevented by storms.

Pinzon, Vicente Y. (1460?–1524?), commanded "La Niña" in the expedition of Columbus in 1492. In 1499, he discovered Brazil and the Amazon. He made two subsequent voyages to South America in 1506 and 1508.

Piracy. Many of the colonies were infested by pirates during the latter years of the seventeenth and the earlier portion of the eighteenth centuries. In North Carolina and South Carolina and in the ports of the Spanish colonies to the south, the pirate Teach, called "Black Beard," made frequent ravages and was gladly received by the inhabitants of Charleston in the matter of trade. Teach's headquarters were in North Carolina. From thence he preyed upon the Spanish possessions in the south and traded as far north as Philadelphia, where prominent citizens were in league with him and with Evans, another pirate. He was finally driven away by Governor Johnson, of North Carolina. In New York and along the Eastern coast the celebrated Captain Kidd terrorized the coast settlers for a number of years. Piracy was made a capital offence in the New England colonies. During the middle of the nineteenth century the American Government contended for an international declaration that the slave-trade should be treated as piracy.

Pitcairn, John (1740?–1775), born in Scotland, was for several years a British officer (major) in Boston. He led the advance in the expedition to Lexington and Concord, and is said to have given the order to fire upon the militia at Lexington, although he denied the charge. He was killed at Bunker Hill while leading the final assault.

Pitcher, Moll, wife of a Revolutionary soldier, who distinguished herself by her bravery at the battle of Monmouth in 1778. Her husband was killed while discharging a cannon. Moll promptly took his place, vowing to avenge his death. General Washington commended her bravery and gave her a commission as a sergeant.

Pitkin, Timothy (1766–1847), was Speaker of the Connecticut Legislature for five consecutive sessions. He represented Connecticut in the U. S. Congress as a Federalist from 1805 to 1819. He was regarded as an authority on U. S. political history. He wrote "Statistical View of the Commerce of the United States of America" and "A Political and Civil History of the United States from 1763 to 1797."

Pitt, William (1759–1806), second son of the Earl of Chatham, became Prime Minister of England in 1783. He inforced the English navigation acts against the United States with great severity, yet his policy was liberal in the main. He resigned office in 1801.

Pitt, Fort, a large fortification erected in 1759 by the British upon the site of Fort Duquesne at the junction of the Monongahela and Allegheny Rivers. Duquesne had been destroyed and abandoned by the French the previous year. Fort Pitt was so called in honor of the British minister. Its site is now in Pittsburgh, Pa. See Duquesne, Fort, and Pittsburgh.

Pittsburgh, Pa., dates its history as a town from 1764, when its first streets were laid out. Previous to this time it had been a military station under the name of Fort Pitt, and still earlier (1755–1758) was the scene of a struggle between England and France for its possession, the French having founded Fort Duquesne here in 1754. Pittsburgh was incorporated as a city in 1816. In 1845 it was visited by a disastrous conflagration in which $5,000,000 worth of property was consumed.

Pittsburgh Landing. (See Shiloh.)

Plaisted, Harris M., born in 1828, commanded a brigade at Charleston and served in Grant's Richmond campaign. He represented Maine in the U. S. Congress as a Republican from 1875 to 1877, and was Governor of Maine from 1881 to 1883.

Plater, George (1736–1792), represented Maryland in the Continental Congress from 1778 to 1781. He was president of the Maryland Convention that ratified the Federal Constitution, and was Governor of Maryland in 1792.

Platforms. The "first platform ever adopted by a national convention" was that of a "national assembly of young men," held at Washington in May, 1832, to indorse the nomination of Clay by the National Republican party. In 1844 both the Whigs and the Democrats drew up a "platform," but in 1848 the Whigs refused to commit themselves by a platform. After this the adoption of party platforms by national conventions became general.

Platt, Orville H., born in 1827, was a member of the Connecticut Senate from 1861 to 1862, and of the Legislature from 1864 to 1869. He was elected to the U. S. Senate as a Republican, and served from 1879 to the present time (1894).

Platt, Thomas C., born in 1833, represented New York in the Congress of the United States as a Republican from 1873 to 1877. He was chosen a member of the U. S. Senate in 1881, but resigned soon afterward with Roscoe Conkling on account of a disagreement with President Garfield concerning the appointment to the collectorship of the port of New York. He has since been a prominent Republican manager.

Platte Country, the name, previous to 1854, given to that territory stretching west from Missouri to the Rocky Mountains, and which now comprises the States of Kansas and Nebraska. A bill was introduced into Congress in 1854 by Douglas, of Illinois, for the organization of the territory, the slavery question to be determined by the inhabitants, in direct violation of the Missouri Compromise. (See Kansas-Nebraska Bill.)

Plattsburgh (Lake Champlain). In August, 1814, General Prevost with 14,000 men and a flotilla of sixteen vessels advanced from the St. Lawrence to attack the American land force entrenched at Plattsburgh and the fleet on Lake Champlain. The American land force consisted of 3500 troops and about 4000 militia, under General Macomb. The naval force was made up of fourteen vessels, commanded by Captain Macdonough. The British army on September 5 was eight miles away. The next day it advanced in two columns, but was held partly in check by the American militia. On reaching the north bank of the Saranac General Prevost constructed works and on the eleventh tried to force his way across in two places. At the same time the two fleets fought desperately for over two hours in Plattsburgh Bay. This ended with the defeat of the British, who lost about 200 men and the commodore of the fleet. The news of this victory came to the fighting armies at the critical part of the battle and turned the tide in favor of the Americans. The British fled to Champlain, leaving behind the sick and wounded and a vast amount of stores. On September 24 they returned to Canada, having lost in all, killed, wounded, missing and deserters, nearly 2000 men. The American loss in the land battle was 150.

Pleasant Hill, La., a brief but fierce engagement of the Civil War, April 9, 1864. After the battle of Sabine Cross Roads, in which Banks had been defeated, he fell back to Pleasant Hill with his army, now reduced to about 8000 men. Kirby Smith, leading nearly 20,000 Confederates, followed in hot pursuit. During the morning there was some sharp skirmishing, and about five o'clock a fierce fight took place. Banks' troops, greatly outnumbered and in a woful condition, nevertheless fought valiantly. Smith was finally obliged to leave the field, having lost several guns he had captured the day before. Banks marched on to Grand Ecore.

Pleasonton, Alfred, born in 1824, served with distinction in the Mexican War. He served throughout the Virginia peninsular campaign, and commanded a brigade at Boonesborough, South Mountain, Antietam, Fredericksburg and Chancellorsville, where his brilliant action saved the national army from serious disaster. He was commander-in-chief of cavalry at Gettysburg. He retired in 1888 with the rank of colonel in the regular army.

Plowden, Sir Edmund, was a patentee of a grant by Charles I. in 1634, embracing New Jersey, Maryland, Delaware and Pennsylvania. A county palatinate was erected, called "New Albion," of which he was Governor. He visited the colony in 1641, but remained mostly in Virginia till his return in 1648. The Swedes disputed his jurisdiction, and the colony prospered only in the alluring accounts published in its interests.

Plowden, Francis, son and heir of Sir Edmund Plowden, succeeded in 1634, with his brothers George and Thomas Plowden, to the shares of four patentees of New Albion, but obtained no profit therefrom.

Plumb, Preston B. (1837–1891), attained the rank of lieutenant-colonel during the Civil War. He represented Kansas in the U. S. Senate as a Republican from 1877 to 1891.

Plumed Knights, certain Republican campaign clubs formed during the Presidential campaign of 1884 in honor of Mr. Blaine. The name is derived from a speech of Colonel Robert Ingersoll, in which he gave that designation to Blaine.

Plymouth, N. C., wrested from the Federals, April 17, 20, 1864, while occupied by Wessells, commanding a garrison of 2400 men, by Hoke leading 7000 Confederates. Hoke came upon the town in the night, thus surprising Wessells. The Confederate ram "Albemarle" took part in the fight, driving away the Union gunboats "Southfield," "Miami" and "Bombshell," while Hoke took the town. Forts Wessells and Warren were also taken by Hoke. Fort Warren was valiantly defended against numerous assaults, but it was lightly garrisoned, and was finally forced to surrender. Fort Wessells also held out bravely, but having lost the protection of the gunboats, it too succumbed.

Plymouth Brethren. This sect was formed in England and Ireland about 1830 with John Darby as its principal founder. They reject organizations and creeds, but retain the ordinances. Their number in the United States is small.

Plymouth Colony, the first settlement in Massachusetts, founded by a party of Puritans from the north of England, November 11, 1620 (O. S.). These first settlers, called the Pilgrim Fathers, after having spent a number of years at Amsterdam and Leyden in search of religious liberty, secured a grant from the Virginia Company and embarked from Plymouth, England, September 6, 1620, on the "Mayflower." They were 108 in number. (See art. "Pilgrim Fathers.") During the first winter they endured great suffering and many died. John Carver was chosen as the first Governor of the colony. No royal charter was ever granted, though the colony was in existence nearly seventy years. The colonists bound themselves to obey certain laws, which they should frame themselves on principles of justice and moderation. In 1622–23, the number of the colonists was increased by new arrivals in the "Fortune," "Ann" and "Little James." Plymouth colony became a member of the New England Confederation (see United Colonies of New Egland) in 1643. By the Massachusetts charter of 1691, it was united with the colony of Massachusetts Bay.

Plymouth Company, a company formed of Plymouth and Bristol merchants, and also called the North Virginia Company. It was incorporated in 1606, and obtained a charter from James I., with grant of land between Long Island and Passamaquoddy Bay. This company was the rival of the London company. In May, 1607, two ships were despatched to America bearing a company of colonists commanded by George Popham. An abortive attempt at permanent settlement was made on the Kennebec River, but Popham died and the remaining colonists returned home. The company still continued to exist till its reorganization in 1620 as the New England Company, or Council for New England.

Plymouth Rock, in Plymouth harbor, the landing place of the "Mayflower's" Pilgrims on December 11, 1620 (O. S.). John Alden and Mary Chilton were supposed to have been the first persons to step upon the famous rock. (See Pilgrims, Landing of.)

Pocahontas (1597?–1616), daughter of Powhatan, was reported by Captain John Smith to have saved his life in 1607, when he was about to be slain by her father's tribe. In 1609 she informed the colonists of an intended Indian attack. She was baptized in 1613 and christened Rebecca. In 1614 she married John Rolfe, and in 1616 went to England. She was presented at the Court of King James as "Lady Rebecca." She was graciously received, and was an object of much interest. She died in England. From her descended many of the illustrious families of Virginia.

Pocket Veto. (See Veto.)

Pocotaligo, S. C. At this place on October 22, 1862, General Brannan, who had been assigned to destroy railroad connection between Charleston and Savannah, commanding 4448 Federal troops, encountered some 5000 Confederates under Walker. A brisk fight followed. Brannan's supply of cartridges gave out, and he was getting decidedly the worst of the fight. He therefore retreated precipitately. On January 14, 1865, just previous to Sherman's march from Savannah through the Carolinas, Howard was ordered to seize this place and establish there a depot of supplies for the Federal army. The seizure was effected after a sharp engagement with 5000 Confederates under Beauregard.

Poe, Edgar A. (1809–1849), was one of the most remarkable of American poets and writers of stories. He was connected with numerous periodicals in which appeared some of his best works. He led a very varied life and developed a gloomy and weird style and a sarcastic criticism which were peculiarly his own. Among his works are "The Raven," "The Gold Bug" and "Eureka."

Poindexter, George (1779–1853), represented Mississippi in the U. S. Congress as a Democrat from 1807 to 1813. He served on General Jackson's staff in the War of 1812, was again a delegate in Congress from 1817 to 1819, and was Governor of Mississippi from 1819 to 1821. He prepared a revised code of the laws of Mississippi in 1822. He was a U. S. Senator from 1830 to 1835.

Poinsett, Joel R. (1779–1851), was sent to South America in 1809 by Madison to ascertain the prospects of the revolutionists. He represented South Carolina in the U. S. Congress as a Republican from 1821 to 1825. He was sent to Mexico as Commissioner in 1822, and was Minister there from 1825 to 1829. He was an ardent opponent of nullification. He was Secretary of War in Van Buren's Cabinet from 1837 to 1841.

Point Pleasant, Va. Here occurred October 10, 1774, a fierce battle between the Virginia troops of Lord Dunmore, under General Andrew Lewis, and a strong Indian army led by the Shawnee chief, Cornstalk. The Indians crossed the Ohio River at night and fell upon Lewis' encampment about sunrise. Colonel Charles Lewis and Colonel Fleming were killed, besides many others. But General Lewis managed to save his camp and rout the savages with heavy losses.

Poland, Luke P. (1815–1887), was a Judge of the Vermont Supreme Court from 1848 to 1860 and Chief Justice from 1860 to 1865. He represented Vermont in the U. S. Senate as a Republican from 1865 to 1867 and in the House from 1867 to 1875. He was chairman of the committees to investigate the Ku-Klux Klan outrages and the Crédit Mobilier transactions.

Polk, James Knox (November 2, 1795–June 15, 1849), eleventh President of the United States, was born in Mecklenburg County, N. C. Having graduated at the University of North Carolina, he became a lawyer in Tennessee, and represented that State as a Democratic Congressman, 1825–1839. He became chairman of the Ways and Means Committee, and in 1835–1839 he was Speaker of the House. From 1839 to 1841 he was Governor of Tennessee, and failed of re-election in 1841 and 1843. The Democratic National Convention selected Polk in 1844 as a "safe" compromise candidate. He was elected over Clay after a hard struggle, having 175 electoral votes. Being inaugurated March 4, 1845, he selected Buchanan for the State Department, R. J. Walker for the Treasury, Marcy for War, and the historian Bancroft for the Navy. The Mexican War, which President Polk favored, was prosecuted successfully during his administration, and the Oregon controversy with England was peacefully settled in 1846. The revenue "Walker Tariff" received his approval. He vetoed river and harbor bills in 1846 and 1847. The California gold discoveries occurred near the end of his term. He died in Nashville a few months after his retirement from office.

Polk, Leonidas (1806–1864), was engaged in the service of the Episcopal Church after 1831, and was Bishop of Louisiana from 1841 to 1861. He strongly sympathized with the secession movement, and, being a West-Pointer, was appointed major-general, and superintended the construction of fortifications at New Madrid, Fort Pillow, Island No. 10 and Memphis. He commanded at Belmont, and led a corps at Shiloh and Corinth. He commanded the right wing at Chickamauga, where it was asserted that his disobedience of orders saved the National army from annihilation. He served with General Johnston in opposing General Sherman at Atlanta, and was killed near Kenesaw Mountain in June, 1864.

Polk, Sarah C. (1803–1891), of Tennessee, married James K. Polk in 1824. She was a great favorite in Washington society, and although she introduced numerous reforms and innovations in the White House, maintained her popularity.

Polk, William (1758–1834), served as major of a North Carolina regiment at Brandywine and Germantown, and fought at Camden and Eutaw Springs. He was a Tennessee Congressman from 1787 to 1794.

Poll Tax, a tax levied upon each poll or head of population. The Federal Government has the power to levy such a tax in proportion to the enumeration or census, but has never exercised the power. In 1641 a poll tax was levied in Maryland, each person being made to pay forty pounds of tobacco yearly for the support of the parish minister and the building of churches. Similar laws were passed in other colonies at various times. In 1860, according to a report made to the New York Legislature, twenty-seven States and Territories employed the poll tax. Some States, as South Carolina, have constitutional provisions for levying the poll tax. In others, as in Massachusetts, its payment is made a qualification for voting.

Pollard, Edward A. (1828–1872), edited the *Richmond Examiner* from 1861 to 1867. He ardently advocated the Confederate cause and severely criticised Jefferson Davis. From 1867 to 1869 he published "Southern Opinion." He wrote a "Southern History of the War," "The Lost Cause," "Lee and His Lieutenants," "The Lost Cause Regained" and "Life of Jefferson Davis with the Secret History of the Southern Confederacy."

Pollock, James (1810–1890), represented Pennsylvania in the U. S. Congress as a Whig from 1844. He was Governor of Pennsylvania from 1855 to 1858. He was director of the U. S. mint from 1861 to 1866 and from 1869 to 1879.

Polygamy, instituted and practiced by the Mormons under the leadership of Joseph Smith in 1830, in New York. In 1838, the Mormons emigrated to Missouri, and in 1839 to Illinois. Their polygamous institutions could not be tolerated in either of these, so they gradually emigrated to Utah, where, from 1848 to 1882, they practiced polygamy unrestricted. Polygamists controlled and held all local offices, with a few exceptions. In 1882, Senator Edmunds submitted a bill to restrict and eventually abolish polygamy. Under its provisions polygamists have been excluded as officeholders. A great number of persons have been convicted and sentenced for polygamy, and the Supreme Court has upheld the law.

Pomeroy, Samuel C. (1816–1891), was an organizer of the New England Emigrant Aid Society, and founded a colony at Lawrence, Kan., in 1854. He represented Kansas in the U. S. Senate as a Republican from 1861 to 1873.

Pomeroy, Seth (1706–1777), engaged in the capture of Louisbourg in 1745. He served in the Massachusetts Legislature in 1774 and 1775. He fought at Bunker Hill, and was appointed brigadier-general, but declined.

Poncas, a tribe of Dakota Indians, have suffered greatly from the attacks of the Sioux, who drove them beyond the Missouri. In 1858 they sold lands to the Government and went on a reservation near the Yanktons. In 1865 they were assigned a reservation on the Missouri.

Ponce de Leon, Juan (1460–1521), a Spanish explorer, was according to some accounts an associate of Columbus on his second voyage. He became Governor of the eastern part of the island of Hayti, was led to attempt the colonization of Porto Rico, and effected the conquest of that island. It was in 1512 that, searching for a fountain of perpetual youth, he discovered the coast of Florida near St. Augustine. He returned to Spain, and in 1521 sailed to the Florida coast; landing not far from his former point of discovery, he lost the greater part of his force, returned disappointed to Cuba, and soon died. The Spanish claims to the regions were based on his voyages.

Pond Law. After 1875 the regulation of the liquor traffic in Ohio became a leading question in State politics. In 1882 the Republicans adopted the so-called "Pond Law" for the taxation of liquor selling. It was declared unconstitutional by the Supreme Court of the State. It required of dealers to take out a high license and also to give a bond.

Pontiac (born about 1720, died 1769), one of the Indian chiefs most dangerous to the English, was a leader of the Ojibways, Ottawas and Pottawatomies. He acquired great influence, and is said to have contributed to Braddock's defeat. Though he consented to the surrender of Detroit to the British at the end of the French and Indian War, he forthwith organized a wide-spread conspiracy in 1762. Assembling a large force near Detroit, he fired the warriors in a remarkable oration, but the plot was disclosed, and Pontiac's siege from May to October, 1763, was fruitless. He fought during the siege the battle of the Bloody Bridge. Although Detroit was saved, many other English posts, Sandusky, Mackinaw, Presque Isle, etc., fell before Pontiac's allies. The great chief signed a treaty in 1766, and three years later was murdered. See Parkman's "Conspiracy of Pontiac."

Pontiac War, a war in 1763 between the English and American settlers along the Pennsylvania and Virginia frontier, and a confederacy of Delaware, Shawanese and Seneca Indians, led by Pontiac, a Shawanese chief. These Indians had been dishonorably treated by the settlers arriving after the capture of Fort Duquesne. They were, besides, incited to the attack by the French fur traders. In June of 1763 a simultaneous attack was made along the whole frontier; the trading posts between the Ohio and Lake Erie were taken and the settlers and English traders were scalped. The settlers retaliated by slaughtering the inhabitants of Conestoga, a body of Christianized Indians on the Susquehanna. General Bouquet invaded the Indian country by way of Pittsburgh, Bradstreet along the lakes. The war was thus brought to an end (1764). It was an afterpiece to the French and Indian War.

Poole, William F. (1821-1894), librarian, devoted much attention to American history. He published "Cotton Mather and Salem Witchcraft," "The Popham Colony," "The Ordinance of 1787" and "Anti-Slavery Opinions Before 1800."

Poor, Enoch (1736–1780), accompanied Schuyler's expedition to Canada in 1776. He commanded a brigade at Stillwater and led the attack at Saratoga. He served under Lafayette at Monmouth, and led a brigade against the Six Nations in 1779.

"Poor Richard," a fictitious name assumed by Benjamin Franklin, in connection with the almanac, commonly called "Poor Richard's Almanac," which he began to publish in 1732, under the name of Richard Saunders, or Poor Richard.

Poore, Benjamin Perley (1820–1887), newspaper correspondent, made a valuable collection of French historical documents for Massachusetts from 1844 to 1848. He wrote "Life of General Taylor," "The Conspiracy Trials in 1865," "Life of Burnside" and "Reminiscences."

Pope, John (1770–1845), represented Kentucky in the U. S. Senate as a Democrat from 1807 to 1813. He was Territorial Governor of Arkansas from 1829 to 1835. He represented Kentucky in the U. S. Congress from 1837 to 1843.

Pope, John (1823–1892), an American general, was graduated at West Point in 1842, and fought at Monterey and Buena Vista. He was engaged in the exploration of Minnesota and the survey of the Pacific Railroad, and in 1861 received a command in Missouri. He captured a Confederate force at Blackwater in December, 1861, New Madrid and Island No. 10 in the Mississippi in the spring of the following year. These successes led to his promotion to be major-general of volunteers, brigadier-general in the regular army, and to his appointment to the Army of Virginia, formed in the summer by the union of various corps. Pope took command, with "headquarters in the saddle," and conducted an unfortunate and much criticized campaign against Lee, culminating in the reverses of Second Bull Run and Chantilly at the end of August and first of September, 1862. He was relieved of the command in Virginia, and was employed in bringing the Minnesota Indians to terms. After the war Pope was a department commander until his retirement in 1886. He attained the grade of major-general in 1882.

Popham, George (1550–1608), came to America from England in 1607 with two ships and 100 men, and founded the first New England settlement at Fort George, Me.

Popham Colony. In 1607 two ships, the "Mary and John," commanded by George Popham, and the "Gift of God," commanded by Raleigh Gilbert, were sent out by Sir Ferdinando Gorges. They reached the mouth of the Kennebec River in Maine on August 19. Popham was left to establish a colony at Sabino, and Gilbert returned. Popham died during the winter, and when a ship arrived the next year the colony was broken up.

Poplar Spring, Va., wrested from the Confederates and occupied by Grant October 1, 1864, during the campaign in the vicinities of Richmond and Petersburg.

Popular Sovereignty. This term originated about the time of the acquisition of additional territory from Mexico in 1848. A suggestion was made of a middle course between the Wilmot Proviso, which prohibited the introduction of slavery into newly acquired or organized territories, and the positive permission of slavery under federal legislative enactment; namely, the question was to be settled by the inhabitants of the territories. The Kansas-Nebraska bill of 1854 purported to enforce the popular sovereignty idea. The Dred Scott decision of 1857 decided against it. The Democratic National Convention of 1856 approved of non-interference by Congress with slavery in the Territories. Douglas, of Illinois, was an ardent advocate of this policy, and he vainly defended it against the Dred Scott decision. The popular sovereignty idea disappeared with the outbreak of the rebellion. It was called in derision "squatter sovereignty."

Population. Careful estimates place the population of New Hampshire in 1700 at about 5000; Massachusetts and Maine, 70,000; Rhode Island, 6000; Connecticut, 25,000; New York, 25,000; New Jersey, 14,000; Pennsylvania and Delaware, 20,000; Maryland, 30,000; Virginia, 80,000, and the Carolinas, perhaps 15,000. Population grew very fast in the colonial period. In 1754 the total population of the thirteen colonies is supposed to have been 1,425,000, of whom Virginia contained 284,000 (three-fifths white); Massachusetts and Maine, 211,000; Pennsylvania and Delaware, 206,000; Maryland, 148,000; Connecticut, 137,000; New York, 96,000. In 1775 the colonies probably contained fewer than 3,000,000. The population of New England was almost purely English, that of New York largely Dutch, tha of Pennsylvania largely German and Scotch-Irish, while colonies to the southward contained many of these last two races and some Huguenots. The first census was taken in 1790. The following tables show the results of the successive censuses (exclusive of Alaska and Indian Territory):

The following table gives the total population of the United States at each census, and the number of inhabitants per square mile of settled area:

Census.	Total.	Settled area.	Census.	Total.	Settled area.
1790	3,929,214	16.4	1850	23,191,876	23.7
1800	5,308,483	17.4	1860	31,443,321	26.3
1810	7,239,881	17.7	1870	38,558,371	30.3
1820	9,633,822	18.9	1880	50,155,783	32.0
1830	12,866,020	20.3	1890	62,622,250	....
1840	17,069,453	21.1			

The following table exhibits the population of each State and Territory at each census:

	1790	1800	1810	1820	1830	1840	1850	1860	1870	1880	1890
Alabama				127,901	309,527	590,756	771,623	964,201	996,992	1,262,505	1,513,017
Arizona									9,658	40,440	59,620
Arkansas				14,255	30,388	97,574	209,897	435,450	484,471	802,525	1,128,179
California							92,597	379,994	560,247	864,694	1,208,130
Colorado								34,277	39,864	194,327	419,198
Connecticut	237,946	251,002	261,942	275,148	297,675	309,978	370,792	460,147	537,454	622,700	746,258
Dakota								4,837	14,181	135,177	N. D. 182,719 S. D. 328,808
Delaware	59,096	64,273	72,674	72,749	76,748	78,085	91,532	112,216	125,015	146,608	168,493
District of Columbia		14,093	24,023	33,039	39,834	43,712	51,687	75,080	131,700	177,624	230,392
Florida					34,730	54,477	87,445	140,424	187,748	269,493	391,422
Georgia	82,548	162,686	252,433	340,985	516,823	691,392	906,185	1,057,286	1,184,109	1,542,180	1,837,353
Idaho									14,999	32,610	84,385
Illinois			12,282	55,162	157,445	476,183	851,470	1,711,951	2,539,891	3,077,871	3,826,351
Indiana		5,641	24,520	147,178	343,631	685,806	988,416	1,350,428	1,680,637	1,978,301	2,192,404
Iowa						43,112	192,214	674,913	1,194,020	1,624,615	1,911,896
Kansas								107,206	364,399	996,096	1,427,096
Kentucky	73,677	220,955	406,511	564,135	687,917	779,828	982,405	1,155,684	1,321,011	1,648,690	1,858,635
Louisiana			76,556	152,923	215,739	352,411	517,762	708,002	726,915	939,946	1,118,587
Maine	96,540	151,719	228,705	298,269	399,455	501,793	583,169	628,279	626,915	648,936	661,086
Maryland	319,728	341,548	380,546	407,350	447,040	470,019	583,034	687,049	780,894	934,943	1,042,390
Massachusetts	378,787	422,845	472,040	523,159	610,408	737,699	994,514	1,231,066	1,457,351	1,783,085	2,238,943
Michigan			4,762	8,765	31,639	212,267	397,654	749,113	1,184,059	1,636,937	2,093,889
Minnesota							6,077	172,023	439,706	780,773	1,301,826
Mississippi		8,850	40,352	75,448	136,621	375,651	606,527	791,305	827,922	1,131,597	1,289,600
Missouri			20,845	66,557	140,455	383,702	682,044	1,182,012	1,721,295	2,168,380	2,679,184
Montana									20,595	39,159	132,159
Nebraska								28,841	122,993	452,402	1,058,910
Nevada								6,857	42,491	62,266	45,761
New Hampshire	141,835	183,858	214,460	244,022	269,328	284,574	317,976	326,073	318,300	346,991	376,530
New Jersey	184,139	211,149	245,562	277,426	320,823	373,306	489,555	672,035	906,096	1,131,116	1,444,933
New Mexico							61,547	93,516	91,874	119,565	153,593
New York	340,120	589,051	959,049	1,372,111	1,918,608	2,428,921	3,097,394	3,880,735	4,382,759	5,082,871	5,997,853
North Carolina	393,751	478,103	555,500	638,829	737,987	753,419	869,039	992,622	1,071,361	1,399,750	1,617,947
Ohio		45,365	230,760	581,295	937,903	1,519,467	1,980,329	2,339,511	2,665,260	3,198,062	3,672,316
Oklahoma											61,834
Oregon							13,294	52,465	90,923	174,768	313,767
Pennsylvania	434,373	602,365	810,091	1,047,507	1,348,233	1,724,033	2,311,786	2,906,215	3,529,951	4,282,891	5,258,014
Rhode Island	68,825	69,122	76,931	83,015	97,199	108,830	147,545	174,620	217,353	276,531	345,506
South Carolina	249,073	345,591	415,115	502,741	581,185	594,398	668,507	703,708	705,606	995,577	1,151,149
Tennessee	35,691	105,602	261,727	422,771	681,904	829,210	1,002,717	1,109,801	1,258,520	1,542,359	1,767,518
Texas							212,592	604,215	818,579	1,591,749	2,235,523
Utah							11,380	40,273	86,786	143,963	207,905
Vermont	85,425	154,465	217,895	235,966	280,652	291,948	314,120	315,098	330,551	332,286	332,422
Virginia	747,610	880,200	974,600	1,065,116	1,211,405	1,239,797	1,421,661	1,596,318	1,225,163	1,512,565	1,655,980
Washington								11,594	23,955	75,116	349,390
West Virginia									442,014	618,457	762,794
Wisconsin						30,945	305,391	775,881	1,054,670	1,315,497	1,686,880
Wyoming									9,118	20,789	60,705

Population, Centre of. The centre of the population of the United States at the time of the census of 1790, lay some twenty-three miles to the east of Baltimore. In 1800, it was about the same distance west of Baltimore; in 1810, about forty miles west-northwest of Washington; in 1820, sixteen miles north of Woodstock, Va.; in 1830, nineteen miles west-southwest of Moorefield, W. Va.; in 1840, sixteen miles south of Clarksburg, W. Va.; in 1850, twenty-three miles southeast of Parkersburg, W. Va.; in 1860, twenty miles south of Chillicothe, O.; in 1870, forty-eight miles east by north of Cincinnati; in 1880, in Kentucky, eight miles west by south of Cincinnati; in 1890, in Southern Indiana.

"Porcupine, Peter," pseudonym of William Cobbett. (See art.)

Port Gibson, Miss., a battle of the Civil War, taking place May 1, 1863, during Grant's campaign along the Mississippi River. Grant was pursuing with some 25,000 Federals the Confederate Pemberton, who was retreating toward Vicksburg with a large army. Near Port Gibson, Grant's advance, under that general himself, overtook Pemberton's rear, about 12,000 men under Bowen. A battle immediately took place. Bowen, though greatly outnumbered, defended himself stoutly. Bowen held a strong position along both branches of the Port Gibson road, and consequently divided the forces of the Federals as he slowly fell back. He was defeated, but managed to retire in good order.

Port Hudson, La., in possession of Confederate troops, 6000 strong, under Gardner in 1863. It was assailed on three separate occasions by the Federals, as being a desirable position from which to command the Mississippi from New Orleans to Vicksburg. The fort surrendered to General Banks after the fall of Vicksburg. The first attempt to reduce it was made March 8, by Banks and Farragut, the Federal admiral. Farragut essayed to pass the batteries of the fort with his fleet, while Banks, with a land force of 12,000, diverted the attention of the garrison. Farragut's fleet consisted of the "Hartford," the "Mississippi," the gunboats "Albatross," "Essex" and "Sabine," and several mortar-boats. This attempt was an utter failure. Farragut's fleet had to return to Prophet's Island badly disabled by the fort's batteries. On May 23 of the same year, Banks again invested the fort with 15,000 men, Augur coming to his aid with 3500 more. May 24, Augur defeated a body of Confederates under Miles, driving them back within their works. Being informed on May 24 that the Confederates were endeavoring to escape, Banks determined on a general assault, the Federal naval force under Farragut having come to his assistance. The struggle was a severe one, but the Confederates resisted every attack. So the siege went on. Each day Farragut's guns riddled the Confederate works, and many Federals were killed by the Confederate sharpshooters. Gardner held out gallantly until he heard that Vicksburg had been captured. Then he surrendered July 9, 1863.

Port Republic, Va. Here, June 13, 1862, Jackson, with 8000 Confederates, defeated and pursued 3000 Federals under Carroll and Tyler, of Shields' command. The latter had attempted to capture a cattle train which they supposed to be guarded only by some 300 cavalry. Instead they found

Jackson with two strong brigades and three batteries. The Federals fought with spirit, Colonel Candy recapturing by an impetuous charge a Federal battery which had been taken by the enemy. However, on Taylor's appearance with a fresh brigade the Unionists retired. Jackson pursued them five miles, capturing 450 prisoners and 800 muskets.

Port Royal in Acadia, now Annapolis, Nova Scotia, was founded in 1605 by the Sieur De Monts, and in 1607 more permanently by Poutrincourt. In 1614 the settlement was ravaged by Samuel Argall, from Virginia. In 1628 it was captured by the English, but restored in 1632; again captured in 1690, but retaken in 1691; finally taken in 1710, and named Annapolis.

Port Royal, S. C., was first settled in 1562 by a band of Huguenots under Jean Ribault. The colony was soon reinforced by René Laudonnière, but it was not wholly successful, even at the first. Then Pedro de Menendez, appointed Spanish Governor of Florida, after founding St. Augustine in 1565, marched along the coast and destroyed the French settlement, while Ribault was sailing unsuccessfully against St. Augustine. In revenge for this a French gentleman, Dominic de Gourgues, in 1567 destroyed the Spanish settlement at St. Augustine by a private expedition.—During the late Civil War, to complete the Federal blockade of the Southern coast, Commodore Dupont, commanding the Federal frigate, "Wabash," fourteen gunboats, thirty-four steamers and twenty-six sailing vessels, attacked the fort, November 7, 1861. The works were garrisoned by 1700 South Carolina troops under Generals Drayton and Ripley and were protected by Commodore Tattnall with six Confederate gunboats. The expedition started from Fort Monroe late in October. The fleet entered the harbor between the two forts, firing upon them simultaneously. Then sailing in an elliptical track the ships concentrated their fire upon Fort Walker, which surrendered after three hours. Fort Beauregard was also speedily reduced. The Confederate fleet had been prevented from rendering assistance by a few gunboats.

Port Royal Island, Battle of, February 3, 1779. During the Southern campaign of the Revolution General Prevost sent Major Gardiner with 200 men to seize Port Royal Island. General Moultrie with about an equal number attacked and defeated Gardiner. The American loss was trifling. The British lost most of their officers and many privates.

Porter, Albert G., born in 1824, represented Indiana in the U. S. Congress as a Republican from 1859 to 1863. He was first Comptroller of the U. S. Treasury from 1878 to 1880, Governor of Indiana from 1880 to 1884, and Minister to Italy from 1889 to 1892.

Porter, Andrew (1743–1813), fought in the battles of Trenton, Princeton, Brandywine and Germantown, and received the personal commendation of Washington. He accompanied General Sullivan in the expedition against the Six Nations in 1779.

Porter, David (1780–1843), an American naval hero, came of a seafaring family, and fought in the wars with France and Tripoli. In 1812 he was appointed a captain, and with the "Essex" captured a number of British prizes and the man-of-war "Alert." In 1813 he started on a cruise in the

Pacific with the "Essex," in the course of which he nearly destroyed the British whale-fishery in that ocean. In the harbor of Valparaiso on March 28, 1814, the "Essex" and the "Phœbe" fought a desperate battle, in which the former, completely disabled, was compelled to surrender. Porter fought against the West India pirates in 1824, and from 1826 to 1829 directed the Mexican navy. He was then U. S. Consul to the Barbary States, and from 1831 until his death he was U. S. Minister resident to Turkey.

Porter, David Dixon (June 8, 1813–February 13, 1891), son of David Porter, and one of the most distinguished American naval officers, accompanied his father in his voyages, and became a midshipman in 1829. He had served in the Mexican War, and had commanded California mail steamers, when the Civil War called out his powers. With the control of the mortar fleet he, in April, 1862, bombarded Forts Jackson and St. Philip, aiding Farragut in the great feat of taking New Orleans. He was continuously active in the operations near Vicksburg that year, commanded the Mississippi squadron, and captured Arkansas Post in January, 1863. Promoted to be rear-admiral Porter, in May, 1863, took Grand Gulf near Vicksburg and coöperated with Grant in the reduction of that stronghold. The following year he aided Banks in the Red River expedition. Transferred the same year to the North Atlantic squadron Admiral Porter commanded the powerful naval contingents in the two assaults on Fort Fisher, December, 1864, and January, 1865; in the latter, Porter and General Terry succeeded in reducing this last of the important sea fortresses left to the Confederates. He was promoted to be vice-admiral in 1866 and admiral in 1870. Until 1869 he was superintendent of the naval academy. Besides writing a life of his father and other naval works Admiral Porter was also a successful novelist.

Porter, Fitz-John, born in 1822, was graduated at West Point in 1845, and almost immediately took part in the Mexican War. Assigned to the Army of the Potomac in the Rebellion, he was soon in command of a corps, and distinguished himself in the Seven Days' battles, especially at Gaines' Mill and Malvern Hill. He was now promoted to be major-general of volunteers. Shortly afterward part of the Army of the Potomac was transferred to Pope's command. Porter and his corps were present at the second battle of Bull Run, August 29 and 30, 1862, and his conduct became the subject of warm controversy. He remained inactive on the first day, and took a leading part on the day following; for this he was deprived of command, but restored, and served in the Antietam campaign. In November, however, he was court-martialed, and cashiered in January. Many efforts to reverse the decision were unavailing until 1886, when an act of Congress restored him to the army with the rank of colonel. He has held several commissionerships in New York City.

Porter, Horace, born in 1837, was chief of artillery at the capture of Fort Pulaski, in 1861. He fought at Antietam, was chief of ordnance at Chickamauga, and was an aide to General Grant from 1864 to 1865.

Porter, James M. (1793–1862), was appointed Secretary of War in 1843 by President Tyler, and served till 1844. He was a prominent Pennsylvania jurist.

Porter, Noah (1811–1892), was president of Yale College from 1871 to 1886. He was principal editor of revised editions of "Webster's Unabridged Dictionary," and was one of the most scholarly metaphysicians in America.

Porter, Peter B. (1773–1844), represented New York in the U. S. Congress as a Democrat from 1809 to 1813. He served on the Canadian frontier. He was Secretary of War in J. Q. Adams' Cabinet from 1828 to 1829.

"**Portfolio,**" the first American periodical which reached an age of over ten years. It was established in Philadelphia by Dennie in 1801, and was published monthly until 1825. Its pages contained contributions from the pens of many distinguished writers of that period, and upon a variety of subjects.

Portland, Me., settled in 1632, was bombarded by the British in 1775, rebuilt in 1783 and incorporated in 1786. From 1820 to 1832 it was the capital of the State. A city charter was obtained in 1832. It was the scene of a disastrous fire in 1866.

Portsmouth, N. H., was settled in 1623, incorporated as a town in 1633, and as a city in 1849. It was the State capital until 1807. In 1694 the town was attacked by Indians, and several persons killed. In 1774 the inhabitants refused to receive a cargo of British tea.

Portsmouth, R. I., one of the original settlements in Rhode Island, was founded in 1637 by William Coddington and other followers of Anne Hutchinson, from Massachusetts. At first an independent community, it was united with Newport in 1640 to form the colony of Rhode Island. Providence was joined with them in 1644.

Portugal. A commercial treaty was concluded between the United States and Portugal in 1840. By the treaty of 1851 provision was made for the payment of certain claims of American citizens against Portugal.

Post Office. In the colonies, especially the more thickly-settled colonies of the North, some slight arrangements for postal communication were made before 1692. On February 17 of that year King William and Queen Mary granted to Thomas Neale a patent making him postmaster-general for the colonies. At once several colonies passed acts establishing and regulating a postal system. In 1710, under Queen Anne, an act of Parliament established a uniform system for all the colonies. Of the postmasters-general for America in the colonial period the most famous was Franklin, who in 1774 was deprived of his office for his attitude in the American conflict. William Goddard thereupon planned a "Constitutional Post Office," upon a plan which Congress adopted July 26, 1775, on that date establishing a system, with Franklin as postmaster-general. The Articles of Confederation and the Constitution gave Congress power over the matter. Congress, in 1790, continued the post office with little substantial change. The plan to conduct the post office system simply on an expense-paying basis originated about 1840. At the International Postal Conference held at Berne in 1874 the Universal Postal Union was formed with rates of five cents per half-ounce on all letters passing between the countries composing the Union. In 1790 there were seventy-five post offices in the United States; in 1820, 4500; in 1860, 28,000; in 1894, 70,000.

Post Office Department. This department existed already before 1789. (See art. Post Office.) Congress continued it by several temporary enactments, and on May 8, 1794, gave it a permanent establishment. The postmaster-general was not a member of the President's Cabinet until General Jackson's administration (1829), the exigencies of the spoils system then requiring it. In 1820 a four years' term for postmasters was instituted. (See art. Star-route Frauds.)

Postage. Letter postage is now two cents for any distance in the United States. From 1792 to 1845 letter postage ranged from six to twenty-five cents, according to the distance. In 1845 the rate was reduced to five cents for 300 miles and under, and ten cents for greater distances. In 1851 it was made three cents for 3000 miles, prepaid, otherwise five cents, and was doubled for greater distances. In 1863 there was established a uniform rate of three cents, which was changed to two cents per ounce in 1883. Mailable matter is now divided into four classes: first, letters; second, regular publications; third, books; fourth, merchandise. Until 1845 letters were single or double according as there was one piece of paper or two. Stamps were introduced in 1847, but did not become general till 1855, when letters were required to be prepaid. Registration was established in 1855; postal money orders in 1864; the free-delivery system in 1865 in places containing a population of 50,000. In 1892 the free-delivery system was extended.

Postage Stamps were introduced in 1847, but did not come into general use until 1855, when letters were required to be prepaid. Stamped envelopes were first furnished in 1852 and postal cards in 1872.

Postal Currency, a substitute for fractional currency during the Civil War, owing to the scarcity of silver. This was invented by General Spinner, United States Treasurer under Lincoln. Postage stamps were pasted upon the paper used for government securities and representing different sums. These bits of paper were circulated among the clerks of the department, and became for a while the medium of small exchange.

Potomac Company, was chartered in 1784, with General Washington as president, for the purpose of connecting the Potomac valley with the West by means of a canal, and for general land improvement. The Chesapeake and Ohio Canal Company succeeded it in 1828.

Pottawatomies, a tribe of Algonquin Indians, early occupied what is now lower Michigan and upper Illinois and Indiana. Joining Pontiac, they surprised Fort St. Joseph in 1763. During the Revolution they were hostile to the Americans, but joined in the treaty of 1795. The tribe was then composed of settled bands and the wandering Prairie band. In 1812 they aided England, but by treaties in 1815 and subsequently, ceded nearly all their territory. A large tract was assigned to them on the Missouri. In 1867, 1400 became citizens, but the Prairie band continued under the Indian Department.

Potter, Alonzo (1800–1865), became Episcopal Bishop of Pennsylvania in 1845. He founded the Episcopal Hospital and the Divinity School at Philadelphia. He possessed remarkable executive ability.

Potter, Clarkson N. (1825–1882), represented New York in the U. S. Congress as a Democrat from 1869 to 1875 and from 1877 to 1881. He was prominent in the election controversies of 1876.

Potter, Henry C., born in 1835, son of Bishop Alonzo Potter, was rector of Grace Church, New York, from 1858 to 1883. In 1883 he became assistant bishop to his uncle, Horatio Potter. In 1887, on the latter's death, he became Bishop of New York.

Potter, Horatio (1802–1887), became rector of St. Peter's, Albany, N. Y., in 1833, provisional bishop in 1854, and Bishop of New York in 1861. His able administration brought great prosperity to his diocese.

Potter, James (1729–1789), came to Pennsylvania from Ireland in 1741. He was made brigadier-general of Pennsylvania troops in 1777 and served with distinction throughout the war under General Washington.

Potter, Robert B. (1829–1887), led the assault at Roanoke Island, commanded a regiment at Cedar Mountain and Chantilly, and carried the bridge at Antietam. He led a division at Vicksburg, the Wilderness and Petersburg.

Pourré, Don Eugenio, leader of the Spanish expedition from St. Louis against Fort St. Joseph, an English stronghold within the limits of the present State of Michigan in 1781. The fort was captured the same year.

Powell, John W., born in 1824, was a lieutenant-colonel of Illinois artillery during the Civil War. He secured the establishment of the U. S. Geological Survey and the Bureau of Ethnography at the Smithsonian Institution, and is director of the former.

Powers, Hiram (1805–1873), sculptor, went from Ohio to Florence, Italy, in 1837, where he afterward resided. Among his most popular statues are "Eve Tempted," "The Greek Slave" and "The Fisher-Boy." He is eminent for his busts of distinguished men, including Adams, Jackson, Webster, Marshall, Longfellow and Sheridan. He executed statues of Washington, Webster, Calhoun, Franklin and Jefferson.

Powhatan (1550?–1618), was the chief of thirty tribes of Indians, numbering about 8000, occupying territory between the James and York rivers in Virginia. He was visited by Captain John Smith in 1609, who made negotiations for provisions. A gilded crown was brought from England and Powhatan was declared "emperor of the Indies." He never trusted the whites and was in constant collision with them. In retaliation for an attempt of Captain Smith to capture him, he planned the destruction of the Jamestown settlement, but was prevented, the colonists being warned by his daughter, Pocahontas.

Powhatan Indians, a confederation of thirty Indian tribes south of the Potomac, in existence at the time of the settlement of Jamestown. It was conjectured that the entire federation numbered eight thousand souls.

Pownall, Thomas (1720–1805), came to America from England in 1753. He immediately sympathized with American political tendencies. He was Governor of Massachusetts from 1756 to 1760. While a member of the

British Parliament from 1767 to 1781 he ardently opposed oppressive measures toward the colonies. He wrote "Colonial Constitutions," "The Administration of the Colonies" and "Description of the Middle States of America."

Prairie Grove, Ark. At this place the Union leaders Blunt and Herron with 12,000 troops defeated nearly twice as many Confederates under Hindman and Marmaduke, December 7, 1862. Hindman attacked Herron while that general was separated from the main command. Herron returned the attack, pushing his batteries across Illinois Creek and effectually silencing the Confederates for a time. Meanwhile Blunt arrived and attacked the Confederate flank, as it was about to execute a flank movement against Herron. This resulted in defeat for the Confederates though they occupied a strong position.

Pratt, Orson (1811–1881), became one of the twelve Mormon apostles in 1835. He was for many years a member and seven times was Speaker of the Utah Legislature. He wrote "The Great First Cause" and "Patriarchal Order."

Praying Indians, a name given to those New England Indians who were early won to the Christian faith. During Philip's War they remained friendly to the colonists, a company of them enlisting under Major Gookin in July, 1675. They acted as scouts and spies and rendered valuable service against Philip. (See Eliot, John, and Natick.)

Preble, Edward (1761–1807), commodore, joined a privateer in 1777. In 1779 he engaged in the attacks of the "Protector" on the British privateer, "Admiral Duff." He served on the "Winthrop" when that vessel captured an armed brig. He was commissioned lieutenant in 1798, and in 1799 commanded the "Essex." In 1803 he commanded the "Constitution" and the squadron against the Barbary States. His operations resulted in the treaty of 1805, by which tribute by the United States and the slavery of Christian captives was abolished.

Preble, George H. (1816–1885), rear-admiral, served in the Mexican War. He commanded the "Macedonian" against Chinese pirates in 1854. He commanded the "Katahdin" and the "St. Louis" during the Rebellion, and wrote a "History of the United States Flag."

Pre-emption Law. The first pre-emption act was passed March 3, 1801. It was a special act affecting the Symmes colonization scheme on the Miami River. Between that time and 1841 about eighteen pre-emption acts were passed, all of a more or less special nature. The first general law was passed in 1830. That of 1841, which is now in force, grants, upon considerations of residence and improvement, freedom of entry upon 160 acres of public lands to any person over twenty-one years of age. Twelve to thirty-three months are allowed for payment, and the amount varies with the value and situation of the tract pre-empted.

Prentice, George D. (1802–1870), edited the Louisville, Ky., *Journal* from 1831 to 1870. He was the principal advocate of the Whig party in Kentucky, and vigorously opposed secession. He wrote a "Life of Henry Clay."

Prentiss, Benjamin M., born in 1819, was a captain during the Mexican War. In 1861 he was made colonel of Illinois volunteers, and placed in command at Cairo. He defeated the Confederates at Mount Zion, served under General Grant at Shiloh and was taken prisoner. He was made major-general, and defeated Generals Holmes and Price at Helena, Ark.

Prentiss, Sergeant S. (1808–1850), orator, was a member of the Mississippi Legislature in 1835. He represented Mississippi in the U. S. Congress as a Whig from 1838 to 1839. He made eloquent speeches against the repudiation of the Mississippi State debts.

Presbyterian Church in the United States. This sect owes its origin to the numerous members of the Presbyterian Churches of Scotland and Ireland who moved to the American colonies for greater freedom. The first Presbytery was formed at Philadelphia about the year 1705, largely through the labors of Francis Makemie. In 1716 the first Synod was held, with about twenty-five churches represented. In 1729 the Westminster Confession and Catechisms were formally adopted. In 1741 a schism on educational questions took place, but was healed in 1758. The first General Assembly met in 1789, and the Confession and Catechisms were again adopted, with some slight changes. In 1811 the Cumberland Presbyterian Church was formed by members who had seceded from the parent church. A still greater schism arose in 1838 between the conservative and the progressive wings of the denomination. These reunited in 1871, at which time the total membership was about 435,000. From both these bodies the Southern members withdrew, and formed separate organizations, which, however, united in 1864. The parent church, since the reunion of 1871, has made rapid progress, and by its devotion to education and missions has raised a high standard for its clergy and membership. In recent years much controversy has been aroused by the trial of Dr. Briggs for heresy. Number of members in 1890, 788,000.

Presbyterian Church South. This body was organized December 4, 1861, when the Southern Presbyterians seceded and organized a new General Assembly. The power and educational institutions of this body were greatly weakened by the losses of the war. In 1890 there were 180,000 members.

Prescott, Richard (1725–1788), British soldier, came to Canada from England in 1773. He surrendered in 1775 on the reduction of Montreal by the Americans. He commanded in Rhode Island from 1776 to 1777.

Prescott, William (1726–1795), served as a captain in the Provincial army under General Winslow in the expedition against Nova Scotia in 1755. In 1774 he commanded a regiment of minute-men. In 1775 with a brigade of 1000 men he constructed entrenchments at Bunker Hill. In the ensuing battle he displayed great skill and bravery, and was one of the last to leave the entrenchments when it was found necessary to retreat. In 1777 he served under General Gates at Saratoga. He afterward served several years in the Massachusetts Legislature.

Prescott, William Hickling (1796–1859), grandson of the commander at Bunker Hill, was graduated at Harvard in 1814. Abundant means enabled him to carry out his purposes of prolonged historical research, though his partial blindness was a great hindrance. Prescott's works nearly cover the period of Spanish greatness. They appeared in this order: "Ferdinand and Isabella" (1838), "Conquest of Mexico" (1843), "Conquest of Peru" (1847), "Philip the Second" (1855–58), to which should be added the continuation of Robertson's "Charles V." Prescott had access to many valuable original sources, including the Spanish archives at Simancas, and his histories are permanently attractive for their charm of style. Life by Ticknor.

President. Penn, in 1696, in his scheme for a general government for the colonies, gave its executive the title of president; the Albany Convention proposed that of president-general. The Continental Congress had its president. In the Convention of 1787, it was decided on June 4 that there should be a single executive, to whom on August 6 the style of President was given. Beside executive functions, he was invested with the veto power. The First Congress debated titles for him, but without finding any better than Mr. President. The first two Presidents read their speeches to Congress, Jefferson began the practice of sending messages instead. Up to the ratification of the Twelfth Amendment (1804) the President and Vice-President were not separately voted for. He who obtained the largest number of electoral votes was President, he who stood next Vice-President. Jefferson and J. Q. Adams were elected by the House of Representatives. Tyler, Fillmore, Johnson and Arthur were originally elected Vice-Presidents. The following have been the Presidents of the United States:

Name.	State.	Political party.	Qualified.
George Washington	Virginia	Federalist	April 30, 1789
George Washington	Virginia	Federalist	March 4, 1793
John Adams	Massachusetts	Federalist	March 4, 1797
Thomas Jefferson	Virginia	Dem.-Republican	March 4, 1801
Thomas Jefferson	Virginia	Dem.-Republican	March 4, 1805
James Madison	Virginia	Dem.-Republican	March 4, 1809
James Madison	Virginia	Dem.-Republican	March 4, 1813
James Monroe	Virginia	Dem.-Republican	March 4, 1817
James Monroe	Virginia	Dem.-Republican	March 5, 1821
John Quincy Adams	Massachusetts	National Republican	March 4, 1825
Andrew Jackson	Tennessee	Democratic	March 4, 1829
Andrew Jackson	Tennessee	Democratic	March 4, 1833
Martin Van Buren	New York	Democratic	March 4, 1837
William H. Harrison	Ohio	Whig	March 4, 1841
John Tyler	Virginia	Elected by Whigs	April 6, 1841
James K. Polk	Tennessee	Democratic	March 4, 1845
Zachary Taylor	Louisiana	Whig	March 5, 1849
Millard Fillmore	New York	Whig	July 9, 1850
Franklin Pierce	New Hampshire	Democratic	March 4, 1853
James Buchanan	Pennsylvania	Democratic	March 4, 1857
Abraham Lincoln	Illinois	Republican	March 4, 1861
Abraham Lincoln	Illinois	Republican	March 4, 1865
Andrew Johnson	Tennessee	Republican	April 15, 1865
Ulysses S. Grant	Illinois	Republican	March 4, 1869
Ulysses S. Grant	Illinois	Republican	March 4, 1873
Rutherford B. Hayes	Ohio	Republican	March 5, 1877
James A. Garfield	Ohio	Republican	March 4, 1881
Chester A. Arthur	New York	Republican	September 20, 1881
Grover Cleveland	New York	Democratic	March 4, 1885
Benjamin Harrison	Indiana	Republican	March 4, 1889
Grover Cleveland	New York	Democratic	March 4, 1893

President (of a State). The first constitutions of Pennsylvania and New Hampshire (1776) provided, not for a single executive head, but for an executive council, of which one member was president. Delaware, South Carolina, and the New Hampshire Constitution of 1784 provided for a single head, but called him president. South Carolina in 1778, Pennsylvania in 1790, Delaware and New Hampshire in 1792, altered the title to Governor.

"President" and "Little Belt." During 1811, and for some time previous, British cruisers hovering about our coast had captured many American vessels bound for France, and had made a number of impressments. In May, 1811, Commodore John Rodgers, commanding the American frigate "President," was ordered to put to sea from Chesapeake Bay and protect our commerce. When thirty miles off Cape Charles, May 16, Rodgers descried a vessel, which he supposed to be the British man-of-war "Guerrière." He decided to approach her and make inquiries regarding impressment. This vessel was the "Little Belt," a small British frigate. She showed no colors and sailed away, the "President" pursuing. Overhauling her about eight o'clock, Rodgers declared she ran up colors which could not be recognized for the darkness, and fired upon the "President." The fire was immediately returned and the "Little Belt" was disabled in about eighteen minutes. The dispute as to which was in fault was never settled. When Foster, the British Minister arrived, however, it was mutually agreed to drop the affair of the "Little Belt" and the "Constitution" outrage.—In September, 1814, the "President," under Decatur, was captured by the "Endymion" and other British vessels.

Presidential Succession. The Constitution provides for the succession of the Vice-President in case of the death, removal, resignation or disability of the President, and gives Congress power to provide what officer shall succeed in case of the death, removal, etc., of the Vice-President. In 1793, Congress provided that in such case the president of the Senate should succeed, and then the Speaker of the House of Representatives. This was of doubtful constitutionality, and attended with some inconveniences and dangers. Hence Congress in 1886 provided that in such case the succession should next pass to the Secretary of State, then to the Secretary of the Treasury, then successively to the Secretary of War, the Secretary of the Navy, the Postmaster-General, the Secretary of the Interior, and the Attorney-General.

"President's March," a popular national air composed in 1789 by Pfyles, leader of the orchestra at the John Street Theatre, New York. It was played for the first time on Trenton Bridge as Washington rode over on his way to be inaugurated. Later Judge Hopkinson set the words of "Hail Columbia" to the air, and it became immensely popular under that name.

Presidio, the military settlements made by the Spanish in California. They were massive forts, the chief being at Los Angeles, Santa Barbara, Monterey and San Diego. That of Los Angeles was the first established, it being begun some time before 1795, but the later forts were of more importance. Regular armed forces were placed in these fortresses, and villages grew up around them. They were primarily intended to protect the religious missions, but the soldiers and friars were in constant collision. The commander of a presidio exercised no little influence in the management of the province.

Press, Freedom of the. In the original Constitution of the United States there was no provision regarding the freedom of the press, it being left to be regulated by the States in accordance with the established opinion of the people. But the first Congress passed an amendment to the Constitution securing the freedom of the press against the Federal Government. Previous to this the States had nearly all inserted in their constitutions clauses permitting freedom of speech and publication to every citizen. Citizens were of course held responsible for abuses of this liberty. In States, as New York and New Jersey, where no such provision was made in the original Constitution, the freedom of the press was considered as established under the common law, but provisions to that effect were embodied in later constitutions. During British rule of the colonies this freedom was much restricted by the Star Chamber Press-censorship regulation of 1637, which was confirmed by Parliament in 1643.

Preston, John S. (1809–1881), was an able orator, and when Commissioner from South Carolina to Virginia in 1861, made a most elaborate plea in favor of secession. He served on the staff of General Beauregard from 1861 to 1862.

Preston, William B. (1805–1862), represented Virginia in the U. S. Congress as a Whig from 1847 to 1849. He was Secretary of the Navy in Taylor's Cabinet from 1849 to 1850, and was a Confederate Senator in 1862.

Preston, William C. (1794–1860), was a member of the South Carolina Legislature from 1828 to 1832, and a leader of the nullification party. He was a Democratic member of the U. S. Senate from 1833 to 1842.

Previous Question. The previous question, said to have been invented in the House of Commons by Sir Harry Vane, was not used in the practice of the House of Representatives in its first twenty-two years, to prevent further debate. Its use in its present manner originated on February 28, 1811, in a decision by the House upon appeal taken on a point of order.

Prevost, Augustine (1725–1786), British soldier, was captain of the Royal Americans under Wolfe at Quebec. He was brevetted major-general for the capture of the fort at Sunbury, Georgia, in 1778. He defeated General John Ashe at Brier Creek in 1779, and made an unsuccessful attack upon Charleston. He successfully defended Savannah against the Americans in 1779.

Price, Sterling (1809–1867), a Confederate general, was Speaker of the Missouri Lower House, and Congressman from that State in 1845–1846. In the Mexican War he commanded a regiment under Kearny and gained success in New Mexico and Chihuahua. He was Governor of Missouri in 1853–1857. He was one of the commanders in the defeat of Lyon at Wilson's Creek in 1861. The same year he captured Lexington in Missouri. He was defeated at Iuka the next year, fought at Corinth, made in 1863 an unsuccessful attempt on Helena, and in 1864 resisted General Steele's advance on the Red River region.

Prideaux, John (1718–1759), served in the British army against the French in America. In 1759 he commanded an expedition against Fort Niagara which was successful.

Priestley, Joseph (1733–1804), an English Unitarian clergyman, made many discoveries in chemistry and discovered oxygen in 1774. His theological views were obnoxious, and in 1791 his church and property were destroyed by a mob. In 1794 he came to the United States from London and continued his investigations in science and philosophy at Northumberland, Pa.

Prigg vs. Pennsylvania. In 1837 Edward Prigg caused a fugitive Maryland slave-woman to be returned to her mistress, in violation of a Pennsylvania statute forbidding the carrying of any negro out of the State in order to enslave him. The case was finally brought before the Supreme Court of the United States, where it was contended that the statute was unconstitutional since it conflicted with the National Fugitive Slave Act of 1793. The opinion was handed down that the national law must be carried out by national authorities alone.

Prime, Benjamin Y. (1733–1791), of New York, composed many popular songs and ballads during the Revolution. He was an able physician and a celebrated linguist. He wrote "Columbia's Glory," a poem, and "The Patriotic Muse."

Prince, Thomas (1687–1758), was connected with the Old South Church in Boston, from 1718 to 1758. He collected many valuable manuscripts and documents relating to New England history, many of which were destroyed by the British in 1776. He wrote an accurate and scholarly "Chronological History of New England."

Prince Society, an organization established in Boston for publishing only. It has issued a series of valuable annotated volumes relating to the early history of Massachusetts.

"Princeton." February 28, 1844, President Tyler and a large party sailed down the Potomac on the man-of-war "Princeton," to see Commodore Stockton's "Peacemaker" throw its 200-pound balls. The "Peacemaker" exploded and many people were killed, among them two members of the Cabinet, Abel P. Upshur, Secretary of State, and Thomas W. Gilmer, Secretary of the Navy. The President narrowly escaped.

Princeton, Battle of, January 3, 1777. After his bold stroke at Trenton, Washington found himself confronted by Cornwallis. Being unable to cope with his superior force, he resorted to strategy. Leaving his camp-fires burning and a few men working in the trenches, he passed around the British left and encountered their reinforcements at Princeton. These he routed, thus cutting the British line, forcing Cornwallis to retreat upon New York, and making himself master of communication between New York and Philadelphia. The British lost 200 killed and 300 taken prisoners, besides a number of cannon. The American loss was 100.

Princeton College (properly the College of New Jersey), was founded under the auspices of the Presbyterian Synod of New York and chartered in 1746 and again in 1748. It suffered greatly during the Revolution and its main building was used as a hospital and as barracks. The college continued weak till the presidency of Dr. Jas. McCosh, who assumed charge in 1868. His administration was marked by great energy and activity. New buildings were erected, the endowment largely increased and the curriculum improved and enlarged. Its theological seminary was founded in 1812 and is now well endowed and equipped. James Madison was graduated here in 1771.

Printing, First. The first printing press in the American colonies was established by Stephen Day at Cambridge, Mass., in 1638. Its first productions were the Freeman's Oath, a calendar, and the Bay Psalm-book. In 1685, William Bradford established his printing press in Philadelphia. Its first issue was the *Kalendarium Pennsilvaniense.*

Printing Presses. Previous to the Revolution all presses were built on the same plan—a flat platen, impressing against type arranged on a flat bed. Impressions were obtained with a screw, and fifty an hour was the maximum capacity. In 1810, Kœnig substituted the revolving cylinder for the platen, and obtained 1000 per hour in the *London Times* office. Steam printing presses were first used by the *New York Sun* in 1835. Hoe's press inventions of 1828 and 1847 made possible 20,000 per hour, and Craske's discoveries in 1861 in *papier maché* stereotyping increased the rapidity of the presses. Improvements were continually made in the Hoe, Walter and Bullock presses, and the first perfecting Hoe press was erected for the *New York Commercial Advertiser* in 1880; capacity 20,000 per hour.

Printz, Johan (1600–1663), came to America from Sweden, and was Governor of the Swedish colony on the Delaware from 1641 to 1654. His rule was marked by great military and commercial advancement.

Prisons. The prisons of the United States down to the year 1786, and in most States later, shared the evil arrangements common in the prisons of Europe. (For an instance, see Simsbury.) In 1786 the first penitentiary was established, that of Philadelphia, and before long the Pennsylvania system became famous as the best in the world.

Privateers. In the colonial wars Great Britain derived great advantage from the colonial privateers. Upward of 400 privateers, which were fitted out in the ports of the British colonies, did great damage to French property, ravaging the West India Islands belonging to France, and making numerous captures along the coast of France herself. After the breaking out of the Revolution, the Continental Congress decided in March, 1776, that permission be accorded to citizens to fit out privateers against the British. Privateers were therefore fitted out at Salem, Cape Ann, Newburyport, Bristol and other seaport towns, and greatly aided by their ravagings the revolutionary cause. During the year 1776 American privateers captured 342 British vessels, and these privateer adventures became so lucrative that the sailors could scarcely be induced to enter the national service. January 28, 1778, an American privateer assailed in the night the British fort of New Providence, in the Bahamas, capturing the fort and a sixteen-gun man-of-war. Hardly had the War of 1812 been declared when privateers began to be fitted out, small vessels most of them, which chiefly infested the West Indies, capturing British craft of every description. The privateers were usually schooners or brigs of 200 or 300 tons, carrying from 80 to 100 men. Twenty-six were fitted out in New York in the summer of 1812. The list of all private armed vessels during the entire War of 1812 numbers more than 500. In 1813, of 400 British vessels captured, four-fifths were taken by privateers. The "Reindeer," "Avon" and "Blakeley," built near Boston in 1814 in an incredibly short time, were fair samples of the privateers of the later years of the war. They were larger and better equipped than the earlier privateers. They did not confine their captures to merchant vessels, but boldly attacked and often defeated British war ships. They hung about the coasts of the West Indies and the Canary Islands and even of Great Britain and Ireland, doing immense damage to the British cause.

Privy Council. This body, the constitutional advisers of the British king, was from 1700 superseded for the most important business by the cabinet. But it still retained one important function with respect to the colonies. One of its four committees had cognizance, as a judicial court, of appeals from the highest colonial courts. It is not known that appeals to the King in Council were taken from colonial courts before 1675. Some of the colonies refused to concede such appeals until after this. But later statutes granted such appeal in all cases involving more than a certain sum, usually two hundred or three hundred pounds.

Prize Causes, Court of Appeal in. (See Court of Appeal in Cases of Capture.)

Prize Courts. During the colonial wars, cases of prize were adjudged by the admiralty courts held by the colonial governors as vice-admirals, or by judges whom they appointed, with appeal to commissioners in England. On the beginning of naval warfare and privateering in the Revolution, the States erected admiralty courts to deal with this class of cases. The Continental Congress established a court of appeal for such causes when in dispute between States. Under the Judiciary Act of 1789, the U. S. District Courts were made prize courts, with appeal to the Supreme Court.

Proctor, Henry A. (1787–1859), came to America in 1812 as colonel in the British army. He repulsed General Hull at Amherstburg, and gained victories at Brownstown and at the River Raisin. He was repulsed from Fort Meigs by General Harrison and by Major Croghan from Fort Stephenson in 1813, and totally defeated by General Harrison at the battle of the Thames.

Proctor, Redfield, born in 1831, was Governor of Vermont in 1878. He was Secretary of War in Harrison's Cabinet from 1889 to 1891, when he became a U. S. Senator.

Progressive Labor Party, the radical, or socialistic element that withdrew from the United Labor Party at Syracuse, N. Y., August 19, 1886. They advocated a common inheritance of land and wealth and industries, and upheld all the tenets of extreme socialism.

Prohibition appeared first as an issue in purely State politics in the Maine Legislature in 1837, a prohibitory bill being introduced, but defeated. Later, in 1846 (permanently in 1851), a prohibitory law was passed in Maine. Following the lead of Maine, prohibitory laws were enacted between 1850 and 1856, in Rhode Island, Massachusetts, Vermont, Michigan, New York, Iowa and Connecticut. Other States have tried the experiment and local option has been established in some of the towns and counties of these and many other States. Prohibition first appeared as a national issue during the session of the Right Worthy Grand Lodge of Good Templars, held in Oswego, N. Y., May 25, 1869. A committee was appointed to issue a call for a convention. This convention assembled at Chicago, September 1, 1869, and formed the National Prohibition Reform party. The first nominating convention of this party was held at Columbus, O., February 22, 1872. James Black, of Pennsylvania, was nominated for President and polled 5608 votes. Prohibition has largely entered into both national and State politics since that time, but is most influential in the States. In 1876 Henry W. Blair, of New Hampshire, introduced into the House a joint resolution to amend the Federal Constitution by prohibiting from and after 1900 the manufacture and sale of distilled alcoholic intoxicating liquors. It was not adopted. In national politics the Prohibition vote has steadily increased. In 1876 its Presidential candidate, Green Clay Smith, received 9522 votes; in 1880 Neal Dow received 10,305; in 1884 John P. St. John, 150,369; in 1888 Clinton B. Fiske, 250,-290; in 1892 John Bidwell, 268,361.

"Propagation of the Gospel," Societies for. The first of these societies was organized July 27, 1649, under the title of "Corporation for Promoting and Propagating the Gospel among the Indians of New England." It was dissolved in 1661. Its chief publications were what are known as the "Eliot Tracts," John Eliot being one of the moving spirits in American mission work among the Indians at that time. The second society of this kind was organized April 7, 1662, and was called "Corporation for the Propagation of the Gospel in New England and Parts Adjacent in America." It still exists. Its work was broken up for a time by the American Revolution, but was continued in New Brunswick. The third, the "Society for the Propagation of the Gospel in Foreign Parts," was chartered June 16, 1701, and long maintained a useful missionary activity in the American colonies. The fourth and last society of this sort was incorporated by the State of Massachusetts in 1778, and was known as the "Society for Propagating the Gospel among the Indians and Others in North America." The influence of these societies was widely felt and tended to promote missionary movements in the different colonies.

Proprietaries. Many proprietary governments were instituted in America by the crown, as in New York, New Jersey and the Carolinas, but only Pennsylvania, Delaware and Maryland remained such until the time of the Revolution. In proprietary governments, the proprietor appointed the Governor, and in general performed all those acts of government which in royal governments were performed by the crown. The laws of Pennsylvania and Delaware were subject to the supervision and control of the crown; those of Maryland were not.

Protection. The American Government has maintained the policy of protection during all its history, except during the years from the establishment of the Walker tariff of 1846 to that of the Morrill tariff of 1861. The first tariff, that of 1789, was one in which, though the amount of protection was moderate, the principle of protection was distinctly recognized. From 1824 to 1846 tariffs were arranged in accordance with the American system, *i. e.*, the combination of protection with the policy of internal improvements at national expense. (See art. Tariff.)

Protestant Episcopal Church. This is the name of what may be called the Church of England in America. Its history begins with the settlement at Jamestown (1607), among whose settlers was a clergyman, Rev. R. Hunt, who labored zealously in the colony throughout his life. The clergy were supported by grants from the Legislature, and afterward by tithes, and the interests of the church were carefully fostered by the Virginia Company and by the successive royal governors. William and Mary College was chartered in 1692 in order to educate the clergy for the colonial churches. By 1701 Maryland for the most part had become Episcopal and attempts were soon made to establish the church in the more southern colonies, but with poor success. In New York City Trinity Church was founded 1696, and generally throughout the Middle States the church was spread through the agency of the "Society for Propagating the Gospel," chartered 1701. By the time of the Revolution there had been established in New England thirty-six churches. This war greatly lessened the influence of the church, which naturally was English in sympathy, but in 1785 the first general convention was held and remodeled the organization to suit the new political condition. Two years later American bishops were consecrated in London (Seabury in Scotland in 1784), and thus the formal organization of the American church was completed. During the next twenty years the church lost almost all its power through dissension and the withdrawal of State aid, but from that time on a steady growth has been manifest, and the church in 1890 numbered 532,000 communicants.

Providence, R. I., was settled in 1636 by Roger Williams and his company, who were forced to leave Massachusetts because of their religious opinions. The town was nearly destroyed by the Indians in 1676. Providence was incorporated as a city in 1832. Brown University was removed hither in 1770.

Providence Plantations. March 14, 1644, Roger Williams obtained from the Parliamentary Commissioners a patent which associated the towns of Providence, Portsmouth and Newport in one community, though it prescribed no criterion of citizenship, and no form of organization. Massachusetts claimed these settlements in the Narragansett Country, but failed to make good her claim. Plymouth also threatened trouble concerning the ownership of the territory. Williams endeavored to institute a system of government, but the scheme proved a failure at first. The Providence Plantations remained distinct from the Rhode Island colony until they were united under the charter of 1663.

Provoost, Samuel (1742–1815), was rector of Trinity Church, New York, from 1784 to 1800. He was Bishop of New York from 1787 to 1801, one of the first bishops consecrated for America.

Prox, or Proxy. In old Rhode Island usage, a list of candidates at an election, a ticket, or ballot; in Connecticut, an election, or election-day.

Prussia. The United States concluded with Prussia treaties of amity and commerce in 1785 and 1799, and a treaty of commerce and navigation in 1828. Prussia joined with the other German States in an extradition convention in 1852.

Pruyn, Robert H. (1815–1882), served in the New York Assembly from 1848 to 1850 and in 1854. He was Minister to Japan from 1861 to 1865, and greatly increased American power in the East.

Pryor, Roger A., born in 1828, was a special commissioner to Greece in 1855. He represented Virginia in the U. S. Congress as a Democrat from 1859 to 1861. He became a brigadier-general in the Confederate service, and since the war has been a prominent lawyer in New York.

Public Land. (See No Man's Land.)

"Publick Occurrences, both Foreign and Domestick," the first newspaper published in America, though it can hardly be called a newspaper, as no second number appeared. It was issued at Boston in 1690 by Benjamin Harris and printed by Richard Pierce. A year earlier there had been published at Boston, by Samuel Green, extracts from a letter of Dr. Increase Mather, who was then endeavoring to secure a new charter for Massachusetts. *Publick Occurrences*, four days after its appearance, was spoken of in the General Court of Massachusetts as a pamphlet published "contrary to law and containing reflections of a very high nature." It was accordingly suppressed, though the contents were innocent enough, and the court forbade "anything in print without license obtained from those appointed by the Government to grant the same." *Publick Occurrences* was printed on three pages of a folded sheet, one page being blank, two columns to a page, 7 x 11. It was designed for a monthly issue.

Puebla, Mexico, occupied at the close of the Mexican War by 500 American soldiers under Colonel Childs. General Santa Anna, after evacuating the city of Mexico, besieged this place from September 24 to October 1, 1847, hoping to take it and thus cut off Scott's communications with Vera Cruz. The siege was ineffectual.

Pueblo Indians, early inhabited what is now New Mexico. They have always been in a state of semi-civilization and by a decision of the Supreme Court in 1857 were declared citizens of the United States. They have invariably been peaceful and friendly to the whites.

Pueblos, the purely civic colonies established in California by the Spanish. They were so called to distinguish them from the missiones and presidios. Pueblo lands were vested, either by proprietary right in the individual, or in companies of individuals, reserving to them certain rights as citizens and colonists. The first settlers were also allowed money and supplies to start on. The first pueblo settlement in Alta California was made in 1771. The inhabitants of pueblos were permitted by a decree of Philip II., of Spain, to elect their own magistrates, of whom the alcalde was the chief. Lands outside the pueblo grants were reserved to the king, but might be used as a common pasturage.

Pugh, George E. (1822–1876), was an aide to General Lane in the Mexican War. He represented Ohio in the U. S. Senate as a Democrat from 1855 to 1861.

Pugh, James L., born in 1820, represented Alabama in the U. S. Congress as a Democrat from 1859 to 1861. He served in the Confederate Senate from 1862 to 1865. He has been a member of the U. S. Senate from 1879 to the present time (1894).

Pulaski, Kazimierz (1748–1779), was outlawed for leading the insurgents in Poland, and came to America in 1777. He was placed on Washington's staff and rendered valuable assistance at Brandywine and Germantown. From 1777 to 1778 he served under General Wayne as a brigadier-general. He was given command of a body of foreigners, deserters and prisoners of war, which became famous as "Pulaski's legion." He made a vigorous but unsuccessful attack on the British at Charleston in 1779. He commanded the French and American cavalry in the siege of Savannah and was mortally wounded.

Pulaski, Fort, opposite Savannah, Ga., captured after a bombardment of fifteen hours by the Union commander Gillmore, April 10, 1862. Savannah was thus cut off from the outside world and remained in possession of the Federals.

Puritans. The name Puritans was first used in England to designate those Protestant members of the Church of England who, while not desiring to separate from or to destroy the existing establishment, desired to see it infused with a spirit of greater earnestness and purged of many still-remaining Catholic ceremonies. The settlers of Massachusetts Bay came from this set, which is not to be confounded with the Separatists or Independents, from whom the Pilgrim Fathers came. The Separatists were the extreme wing of the Puritan party, we may say, so extreme that they preferred to abandon the Established Church, and would gladly have seen it abolished. As the contest in England went on, and deepened into civil war, the Puritans mostly became either Presbyterians or Independents. Similarly in America circumstances made of the settlers at the Bay a body of Independents whose ecclesiastical polity did not differ from that of the Plymouth Pilgrims. The Puritan spirit was one of severe moral earnestness, united with a Calvinistic theology. Their opposition to amusements grew more and more severe, and the persecuting spirit prevailed among them. Toward the end of the century, Puritanism in Massachusetts began to relax. In New Haven it was more rigid than in Massachusetts; in Connecticut somewhat less so. Rhode Island was partly Puritan in sentiment (using Puritan in the general, or English sense), but never under control of the Puritans. In the other colonies there were some Puritan settlements, as at Newark in New Jersey, at Providence (Annapolis) in Maryland, and at Dorchester in South Carolina.

Putnam, Israel (1718–1790), a Revolutionary general, was born at Danvers, Mass., and settled as a farmer in northeastern Connecticut, near Pomfret.

Putnam's early life is associated with many romantic episodes, the wolf hunt, his service in the French and Indian War with Rogers' Rangers, his rescue of Fort Edward, and his narrow escape from death by burning while a prisoner of the Indians. He was in command of a regiment with General Amherst in the Canadian campaign of 1760. In the stirring times following he was one of the chief "Sons of Liberty." How at the news of Lexington he dropped his plough and rode in a day to Cambridge is a fireside story. Putnam was made commander of the Connecticut troops and a brigadier. He commanded at Bunker Hill conjointly with Colonel Prescott. Forthwith he was appointed one of the major-generals, and had charge of the centre in the siege of Boston. In the defence of Long Island he was entrusted with the works on Brooklyn Heights, and in the retreat from New York his name is often mentioned. For a short time he was Governor of Philadelphia, and was then in 1777 placed in command of the defences in the Highlands of the Hudson. He was engaged in the repulse of Tryon's troops in the south-west of Connecticut, in connection with which is related the somewhat apocryphal story of Putnam's escape on horseback down a flight of stone steps.

Putnam, Rufus (1738–1824), of Massachusetts, was appointed lieutenant-colonel in 1775. He superintended the construction of defences about New York and at West Point. He fought at Stillwater and served under General Wayne. Afterward he was prominent in the settlement of Ohio.

Pynchon, John (1621–1703), came to America from England in 1630 and became chief magistrate at Springfield in 1652. He rendered great assistance during the Indian Wars. He was an assistant under the Massachusetts charter from 1665 to 1686.

Pynchon, William (1590–1662), came to New England from England in 1630. He founded a settlement at Springfield, Mass., in 1636. He was given the government of the settlement in 1640, and managed affairs very successfully. While in England in 1650, he published "The Meritorious Price of Our Redemption," which caused great excitement as being heretical.

Q.

Quackenbush, Stephen P. (1823–1890), U. S. Navy, had charge of the "Delaware," the "Unadilla," the "Pequot," the "Patapsco" and the "Mingo." He fought at Roanoke Island, Winton, Malvern Hill and Harrison's Landing, and captured the "Princess Royal."

Quaker Hill, Battle of, August 29, 1778. On the night of August 28, the Americans on Rhode Island fell back toward Butts Hill at the northern end of the island. Contrary to Greene's advice the enemy were allowed to occupy Quaker and Turkey Hills. From these hills the British assailed the Americans, but were repulsed and driven back to Turkey Hill. The hottest of the battle took place on the low ground between the hills. The American loss in killed and wounded was 206; that of the British 222.

Quaker Road, Va., among the last of the battles of the celebrated campaign of the Civil War about Richmond and Petersburg. It occurred March 29, 1865, Grant having ordered a general advance of his left against the Confederate lines in order to intercept Lee's meditated withdrawal to North Carolina. Warren's corps, while pushing along the Quaker Road to strike the Boydton Road, fell in with a body of Confederates. The latter were defeated and 100 prisoners taken.

Quakers. (See Friends.)

Quarantine. In the United States quarantine enactments were passed by the colonial legislatures and afterward for many years by the States. The first national quarantine act was passed February 23, 1799, requiring Federal officers to aid in the execution of State or municipal quarantine regulations. April 29, 1878, a national quarantine act was passed. March 3, 1883, $100,000 were appropriated for maintaining quarantine points along the coast. On September 1, 1892, owing to the presence of cholera, President Harrison proclaimed a twenty-days' quarantine of New York.

Quarter Dollar. Its issue was authorized (weight 104 grains) by Congress in 1792, and its coinage was begun in 1796. It was reduced to 93 grains in 1853. This coin is legal tender to the amount of ten dollars. There were no issues of the quarter dollar during the years 1798 to 1803 inclusive, 1808 to 1815 inclusive, 1817, 1824, 1826 and 1830.

Quarter Eagle, a gold coin of the value of two and a half dollars, authorized in 1792, coinage begun 1796. The weight was slightly reduced in 1834. The reverse of this coin contains a figure of the national bird, and hence the name of the coin. As a legal tender the value of this coin is unlimited. No coinage 1800, 1801, 1809 to 1821.

Quartering Acts. In 1765 Parliament passed an act compelling the colonies to provide the garrisons in America with fire, candles, vinegar, salt, bedding, cooking utensils and liquors. It was the first act requiring the colonies to tax themselves for imperial objects. In 1774 an act was passed legalizing the quartering of troops in the town of Boston. Both acts were most distasteful to the colonists.

Quay, Matthew S., born in 1833, attained the rank of colonel during the Civil War. He was a member of the Pennsylvania Legislature from 1864 to 1866, Secretary of the State from 1873 to 1878 and from 1879 to 1882, and State Treasurer in 1885. He was elected to the U. S. Senate as a Republican in 1887 and re-elected in 1893.

Quebec. In June, 1759, Wolfe appeared before Quebec with 4000 men and a fleet. The French under Montcalm, numbering 16,000, held all the heights on the north bank of the river. Wolfe seized the heights on the south, thus commanding the basin and getting his artillery trained on the town. The French plan was the defensive. Wolfe got his ships past the city, making the line of defence longer. He also entrenched himself on the French left and made a furious assault at Montmorenci (q. v.) As the season wore on he was obliged to strike a blow before winter. This he did on September 13, and gained a decisive advantage on the Plains of Abraham (q. v.) The

French were disorganized. Vaudreuil proved incompetent and ordered the garrison to capitulate when provision gave out. This the gallant Ramesay was forced to do just as aid came from Montreal. The citadel capitulated September 17, 1759. The English garrisoned the place. The French made an attempt to regain it the following spring, but were driven back. The fall of the citadel was the death-blow to French power in North America. At the beginning of the Revolution, as a part of the scheme for the conquest of Canada, a force was sent against Quebec under Benedict Arnold. After numberless privations, he arrived at Quebec on November 13, 1775, and drew up for battle the 700 men who remained of his force. December 3 Montgomery came with 500 men, and on December 31 a furious attack was made upon the town from opposite sides. The repulse was due mainly to the unfortunate death of General Montgomery. Arnold also was severely wounded. The expedition was a blank failure.

Quebec Act, an act of the British parliament in 1774, designed to prevent that newly acquired province from joining for freedom with the other colonies. The property of the Catholic church was guaranteed to it, and the boundaries of Quebec were extended to the Mississippi River on the west, and to the Ohio on the south, beside the present Canada. This was the territory now included in the five States northwest of the Ohio.

Queen Anne's War. In 1702 there broke out in Europe the war of the Spanish succession, which was known in this country as Queen Anne's War. It was chiefly a series of bushranging skirmishes between the frontiersmen of the English and French settlements. In 1704 and 1705 James Moore, of South Carolina, with 50 whites and 1000 Creek Indians, attacked and destroyed several Spanish settlements in Florida. The French retaliated by a water attack on Charleston in 1706, but they were easily defeated and driven away. In 1704 a body of 350 Canadians and Indians massacred the inhabitants of Deerfield, Mass. Three attempts were made by New England troops, 1704, 1707 and 1710, to capture Acadia, the last proving successful. The war was ended by the Treaty of Utrecht in 1713.

Queenstown, Ontario. General Van Rensselaer, in command of the American troops on the Niagara frontier, mustered nearly 6000 men at or near Lewiston. On the night of October 12, 1812, he sent over about 1000 men to attack Queenstown preparatory to a further invasion of Canada. General Brock, the capturer of Detroit, in person commanded the British forces, but was killed early in the action. The rest of the American troops refused to cross the river, and the attacking party, overpowered by numbers, was compelled to surrender. The American loss in killed and wounded was 190, in prisoners 900; the British lost about 130 killed, wounded and prisoners.

Quids. The name applied to a faction of the Republican party, led by John Randolph from 1805 to 1811. They were opposed to the nomination of Madison, Jefferson's choice for the succession. They declared war on the administration party in 1806, as governing Congress by backstairs influence. From that time they were called "quids," or the *tertium quid*, as distinguished from the two great parties. They opposed the restrictive system, and nominated Monroe in 1808. Their leading ground of divergence from the administration was that it had moved away from the ground occupied by the party when in opposition, and in the direction of centralization and federal encroachment.

Quincy, Josiah (1744–1775), of Boston, attained high rank as a lawyer. He denounced the Stamp Act and other oppressive measures of Parliament in a series of articles in the Boston *Gazette*, signed "Hyperion." In 1770 he defended Captain Preston and the British soldiers implicated in the Boston Massacre. In 1774 he published an able work entitled "Observations on the Boston Port Bill," which clearly indicated war and American independence as the final result of the controversies. In 1774 he went to England as a confidential agent of the colonial patriots, and was active in strengthening the American cause, but died on his return.

Quincy, Josiah (1772–1864), was the son of the Revolutionary patriot of the same name, and graduated at Harvard. Very early in life he began a political career, was a member of the Massachusetts Legislature, and after a defeat entered Congress in 1805. He was a Federalist and in sympathy with the Essex Junto. During his Congressional service, which lasted until 1813, he made many notable speeches, particularly against the Embargo, on the Louisiana question, and in support of the navy. From 1823 to 1828, Mr. Quincy was mayor of Boston, and from 1829 to 1845, president of Harvard College, where he favored the elective system, introduced marking regulations, and acquired the great telescope. He wrote histories of Harvard College and of Boston.

Quint, a silver coin equal to about thirty-five cents and weighing five pennyweights, fifteen grains, presented to the Continental Congress in 1783, by Robert Morris for consideration as a national coin, but not accepted. Obverse: an eye, thirteen points cross, equidistant, a circle of as many stars. Legend: Nova Constellatio. Reverse: U. S. 500., a wreath surrounding. Legend: Libertas, Justitia. This coin, with the mark, formed the Nova Constellatio coinage.

Quitman, John A. (1799–1858), was chancellor of the Mississippi Superior Court from 1828 to 1831, and from 1832 to 1835. He was a member of the Mississippi Senate in 1835, and ex-officio Governor for a time. He commanded a brigade at Monterey, led the assault at Vera Cruz, commanded at Alvarado, and stormed Chapultepec. He was appointed by General Scott Governor of the City of Mexico. He was Governor of Mississippi from 1850 to 1851, and served in the U. S. Congress as a Democrat from 1855 to 1858. He early maintained the right of secession, and suggested a Southern Confederacy.

Quivira, an Indian town of the sixteenth century, presumably situated in what is now the State of Kansas, and reputed to contain fabulous wealth. It was visited by twenty-nine Spaniards under Coronado, a Spanish leader, in 1541. The exploring band traveled northward through Mexico over the plains for several months, led by wandering Indian tribes. Quivira, when finally reached, was found to be an ordinary Indian village.

Quorum. During the first fifty Congresses the rule requiring the presence of a quorum, in order to invalidate the proceedings, had been interpreted to mean that the constitutional quorum (one-half), was shown to be present by the count of votes. In September, 1890, the Speaker (T. B. Reed, of Maine), ruled that he might decide a quorum to be present when enough members were visibly present, though some did not vote.

R.

Rafn, Karl C. (1795–1864), Danish archæologist, made a careful study of the ancient Norwegian and Icelandic sagas, especially those concerning expeditions to North America. He held that the Scandinavians discovered America in the tenth century, that the coast as far as Massachusetts and Rhode Island had been partially colonized, and that the Vikings reached Florida. His best known work is "Antiquitates Americanæ."

Raguet, Condy (1784–1842), of Philadelphia, was U. S. Consul at Rio Janeiro from 1822 to 1825, and chargé d' affaires from 1825 to 1827. He negotiated a treaty with Brazil. He was a prominent writer on free trade.

Railroads. The first railroad constructed in America was projected by Gridley Bryant in 1825, and extended from Quincy, Mass., to the nearest tide-water. It was four miles long. The second railroad extended from mines near Mauch Chunk, Pa., to the Lehigh River. It was begun in 1827. Stephenson's locomotive came into use in 1829, and by 1830 there were twenty-three miles of railroad completed in the United States. The New York Central road was projected in 1825; the Boston and Albany in 1827; the Baltimore and Ohio in 1828; the Pennsylvania in 1827; the Maryland and South Carolina in 1828. In 1840 there were 2200 miles completed; in 1850, 7500; in 1860, 29,000; in 1870, 49,000; in 1880, 93,671, and in 1893, 171,805 miles, showing total assets of $11,482,000,000. The consolidation of railway companies began in 1853, forming a germ of the grand trunk system. Government aid was first extended to railroads in 1850, in the case of the Illinois Central, by a large land grant. In 1862 the Union Pacific Company was granted both land and pecuniary aid. To the Northern Pacific were granted 47,000,000 acres; to the Atlantic and Pacific 42,000,000 acres. These roads were begun in 1864 and 1866 respectively. In 1869 Vanderbilt consolidated the Hudson River and New York Central roads, forming a trunk line to the West. The United States now contains about one-half of the railway mileage of the world.

Rail-Splitter, a nickname for Abraham Lincoln, who in his youth earned money to educate himself by splitting rails for a neighbor.

Rains, Gabriel J. (1803–1881), served during the Mexican War. He joined the Confederates in 1861, led a division at Wilson's Creek, and served at Shiloh, Perryville and Seven Pines.

Rale. (See Rasle.)

Raleigh, Sir Walter (1552–1618), one of the celebrated Elizabethan navigators, was a native of Devonshire. He served with the French Huguenots under Coligny, in the Netherlands, and in Ireland. His first scheme to colonize America failed in 1579. He encouraged the ill-fated expedition of his half-brother, Gilbert, and soon after, in 1584, despatched Amidas and Barlow to make a settlement. This attempt, as well as the subsequent one of Grenville and Lane in 1585, and that of White in 1587, all under Raleigh's auspices, miscarried, and the introduction of tobacco and potatoes into Europe were the chief material results. Raleigh led an expedition up the Orinoco, served at Cadiz and against the Armada, and was a friend of Spenser, and himself an author. In 1603 he was disgraced and put in the Tower, where he wrote a "History of the World." Released after many years, he made an unfortunate voyage to Guiana, was re-arrested on his return and executed.

Raleigh, N. C., became the State capital in 1792. It was founded at that time for that purpose. It was occupied by Sherman's army of 85,000 Federals, during his pursuit of Johnston commanding 45,000 Confederate troops. Sherman passed through this town April 13, 1865, and encamped a few miles beyond. This took place without bloodshed, as Johnston's army was in full retreat toward Charlotte. Kilpatrick's cavalry was hurried forward in pursuit of the retreating Confederates.

Rall, Johann G. (1720?–1776), was one of the Hessians hired by George III. to serve in America. He fought at White Plains and Fort Washington, and was surprised and killed at the battle of Trenton.

Rambouillet Decree, a decree issued by Napoleon, March 23, 1810, ordering the immediate seizure and sale of American vessels, whether in French ports or those of territories occupied by French armies. This decree was not known in the United States until July. The decree was issued in retaliation for the repeal of our non-intercourse act, Napoleon avowing his determination to prohibit any commercial intercourse with the allies of France which was not enjoyed by that country also.

Ramsay, David (1749–1815), a physician, was a member of the South Carolina Legislature from 1776 to 1783. He was taken prisoner at Charleston in 1780, and confined eleven months as a hostage. He represented South Carolina in the Continental Congress from 1782 to 1786. He wrote a "History of the American Revolution," "Life of George Washington," "History of South Carolina" and "History of the United States."

Ramsey, Alexander, born in 1815, represented Pennsylvania in the U. S. Congress as a Whig from 1843 to 1847. He was territorial Governor of Minnesota from 1849 to 1853, and Governor of that State from 1859 to 1863. He was a Republican member of the U. S. Senate from 1863 to 1875, and Secretary of War in Hayes' Cabinet from 1879 to 1881.

Randall, Alexander W. (1819–1872), was a member of the Wisconsin Assembly in 1855. He was a district judge in 1856. He was Governor of Wisconsin from 1857 to 1861, and was energetic in raising troops for the

Civil War. He was Minister to Italy from 1861 to 1862, Assistant Postmaster-General in Johnson's Cabinet from 1866 to 1869.

Randall, James R., born in 1839, wrote many popular songs in support of the Southern cause, among them "Maryland, My Maryland" and "The Battle-Cry of the South." He became editor of the *Constitutionalist* in 1866.

Randall, Samuel J. (1828–1890), represented Pennsylvania in the U. S. Congress as a Democrat from 1863 to 1890. He distinguished himself by speeches against the "Force Bill" in 1875. While chairman of the Committee on Appropriations, from 1875 to 1876, he curtailed expenditures by a systematic reduction in appropriations. He was Speaker from 1876 to 1881. He was prominent as a leader in opposition to the Morrison tariff bill in 1884. He served on Committees of Banking, Rules and Elections. He was prominent in tariff debates as a leader of the protectionist wing of the Democratic party.

Randolph, Edmund Jennings (1753–1813), was a member of one of the most noted Virginian families. Soon after leaving William and Mary College he became prominent as a patriotic leader, and was active in the Virginia Constitutional Convention of 1776. He was Attorney-General of the State, delegate to the Continental Congress, and member of the Annapolis Convention of 1786. While Governor of Virginia, 1786–1788, he sat in the Federal Convention of 1787, introduced the "Virginia Plan," and was a leading debater. He refused to sign the Constitution, yet defended it the next year in the State Ratifying Convention. He was in Washington's Cabinet as Attorney-General, 1789–1794, and Secretary of State 1794–1795. In the latter position he was involved in some charges made in connection with the French minister, and resigned. Life by Conway.

Randolph, Edward (1620?–after 1694), came to New England in 1675 as a commissioner of the British Government. He returned exaggerated accounts of the population and wealth of the colonies, and urged measures of taxation and oppression. By his efforts the charter of Massachusetts was conditionally forfeited. He was secretary of New England and a member of the Governor's council from 1686 to 1689.

Randolph, John, of Roanoke (June 2, 1773–June 24, 1833), was a near relative of Edmund Randolph. He was educated at Princeton and Columbia, and in 1799 entered the National House of Representatives from Virginia. Though very young, he soon became a leader on the Democratic side. His strict constructionism, however, was of the most thorough-going stamp, and he was frequently at variance with Jefferson and other party chiefs. Randolph was renowned for an eloquent satire of a peculiarly bitter kind, whose effect was enhanced by his personal eccentricities. He was foremost in the conflict against the Yazoo frauds and the Embargo. He also opposed Madison and the War of 1812. His career in the House lasted until 1825, with a break from 1813 to 1815. From 1825 to 1827 he was U. S. Senator. He invented the epithet "dough-faces" for Northern sympathizers with slavery, and styled the union of Adams and Clay a "coalition between the blackleg and the Puritan," which remark led to a duel with Clay. President

Jackson sent him in 1830 as U. S. Minister to Russia, but his stay abroad was brief. There are lives of Randolph by Garland and by Henry Adams.

Randolph, Peyton (1721–1775), was appointed king's attorney in Virginia in 1748, and held office till 1766. He was elected to the Virginia House of Burgesses in 1748, and was chairman of a committee to revise the colonial laws. He drew up the remonstrance against the Stamp Act in 1765, but opposed Patrick Henry's resolutions. He was elected president of the first Continental Congress in 1774, but soon afterward resigned on account of ill health. He presided over the Virginia conventions of 1774 and 1775. He was again a member of the Continental Congress in 1775.

Randolph, Theodore F. (1816–1883), was a New Jersey Senator from 1861 to 1865, Governor of New Jersey from 1868 to 1872, and a Democratic U. S. Congressman from 1875 to 1881.

Randolph Plan, the scheme of a Federal constitution proposed in the Convention of 1787 by Edmund Randolph of Virginia. It was the first plan submitted, being presented May 29. It was composed of fifteen resolutions and proposed a correction of the Articles of Confederation; representation by population in two branches of Congress, the first chosen by the people, the second by State Legislatures; congressional control of taxation and commerce; congressional veto of State enactments; that Congress should choose the executive; that the executive with part of the judiciary should have a limited veto on Acts of Congress, and other less important provisions. The plan was favorably reported and many of its suggestions were used in the drafting of the Constitution as it now exists.

Ransom, Matt W., born in 1826, was Attorney-General of North Carolina from 1852 to 1855, and a member of the State Legislature from 1858 to 1860. He attained the rank of brigadier-general in the Confederate service and was engaged in all the important battles of the Army of Northern Virginia. Since 1872 he has served in the U. S. Senate as a Democrat. His present term expires in 1895.

Ransom, Thomas E. G. (1834–1864), fought at Charleston, Fort Henry, Fort Donelson and Shiloh, and served on General Grant's staff at Vicksburg. He commanded a division at Sabine Cross-roads and a corps in operations about Atlanta. He died in Georgia.

Rantoul, Robert (1805–1852), was a member of the Massachusetts Legislature from 1833 to 1837. He made a powerful and famous appeal for the abolition of capital punishment. He was counsel for Thomas Sims in his celebrated fugitive slave case. He was U. S. District Attorney for Massachusetts from 1845 to 1849, and served in the U. S. Senate as a Democrat from 1851 to 1852. He was an eloquent speaker on moral, political and educational reforms.

Rapp, George (1770–1847), founded the Harmonists, a socialistic religious sect. They emigrated to Pennsylvania from Germany in 1803. Their community is prosperous, and noteworthy for its morality and the promotion of education.

Rappahannock Station and Kelly's Ford, Va. This battle of the Civil War took place November 7, 1863, during Meade's and Lee's operations in Northern Virginia. Sedgwick, advancing toward the Rappahannock River, came upon about 2000 Confederates of Ewell's column of Lee's army under Godwin. Russell's division of the famous sixth corps was ordered to charge. This they did so successfully that Godwin was routed and 1600 prisoners were taken. An engagement took place the same day at Kelly's Ford near the station.

Rasin River (Frenchtown, now Monroe, Mich.) General James Winchester with about 1000 Kentuckians, under orders of General Harrison, erected fortifications at the rapids of the Maumee. After this was done he sent ahead two-thirds of his men to drive the British from Frenchtown and, on the success of this movement, himself followed with the rest of his forces. Here he was attacked by General Proctor with 1500 British and Indians on January 22, 1813. Taken by surprise the Americans, after a brief defence, fled to the woods. A surrender was effected with full assurance of safety. The captives were hurried to Malden, leaving the sick and wounded Americans behind. These were at once massacred by the Indians, save a few who were taken to Detroit for ransom. The Americans lost 197 killed and missing, and 737 prisoners. The British loss was 24 killed and 158 wounded. "Remember the River Rasin" was long a war cry of Kentuckian soldiers.

Rasle, Sebastien (1658–1724), came to America as a Catholic missionary from France in 1689. He assumed charge of the mission of Norridgewock, on the Kennebec, about 1695. The Indians were induced by him to support the French. He was wrongfully charged with causing Indian depredations, and a price was put on his head. His church was three times destroyed, and he was finally surprised and shot by the English colonists.

Ratification of the Constitution. The Constitution was by its own terms to become binding on the States ratifying when it had been ratified by conventions of nine States. Signed September 17, 1787, it was at once transmitted to Congress, and by Congress to the States. It was ratified by the convention of Delaware on December 7; by Pennsylvania on December 12; by New Jersey on December 18; by Georgia on January 2, 1788; by Connecticut January 9; by Massachusetts on February 6, with recommendations of amendment; by Maryland on April 28; by South Carolina on May 23, and by New Hampshire on June 21, 1788, making nine. Virginia ratified June 25, 1788; New York, July 26, 1788; North Carolina, November 21, 1789; Rhode Island, May 29, 1790. In the last four the debate was especially warm, and in general, ratification was secured with difficulty. Hamilton and Madison had a leading part in bringing it about. The well-to-do and commercial classes generally supported it. For the ratification of amendments, see art. Amendments.

Raum, Green B., born in 1829, served with distinction during the Civil War. He represented Illinois in the U. S. Congress as a Republican from 1867 to 1869, was Commissioner of Internal Revenue from 1876 to 1883, and Commissioner of Pensions from 1889 to 1893.

Rawdon, Francis (1754–1826), Lord Rawdon, came to America as a British soldier in 1773. He was a captain at Bunker Hill. As aide to Sir

Henry Clinton he fought at Long Island, White Plains, Fort Washington, Fort Clinton; also at Monmouth. He led a corps at the battle of Camden in 1780, and defeated General Nathanael Greene at Hobkirk's Hill, relieved Fort Ninety-Six and fortified Orangeburg. He incurred much obloquy for the execution of Colonel Isaac Hayne. Afterward he was made Earl of Moira, Marquis of Hastings, and Governor-General of India.

Rawlins, John A. (1831–1869), became a successful lawyer in Illinois. He ably defended the Union cause. He became an aide to Grant when commissioned brigadier-general in 1861, and served with him throughout the War. Although he knew nothing of military affairs at the beginning of the War, yet he showed remarkable executive ability and became General Grant's chief of staff in 1865. He exerted great influence over General Grant, and rendered valuable advice in many of the important manœuvres. He was Secretary of War in Grant's Cabinet in 1869.

Raymond, Henry J. (1820–1869), became assistant editor of the New York *Tribune* on its foundation in 1841. He was connected with the *Courier* and *Enquirer* from 1843 to 1851. In 1851 he established the New York *Times*, and was of great influence as its editor. He represented New York in the U. S. Congress as a Republican from 1865 to 1867. He wrote a "Life of Daniel Webster" and "The Life and Public Services of Abraham Lincoln."

Raymond, Miss. In this battle, May 12, 1863, during Grant's Mississippi campaign of the Civil War, 6000 Federals under McPherson defeated Gregg leading 7000 Confederates. Grant was moving his army along the Big Black River in two columns. McPherson commanded the corps on the extreme left, eight miles from the main line. Early on the twelfth of May Gregg fell upon Logan's division of McPherson's troops. The fight lasted three hours and was very severe. The Confederates were pursued.

Raynal, Guillaume T. F., called Abbé (1713–1793), published a philosophical history of the discovery and conquest of the American colonies which contained attacks on the Roman Catholic Church and was condemned by it, but was widely popular.

Read, George (1733–1798), a signer of the Declaration of Independence, was before the war Attorney-General of Delaware and member of the Legislature. He wrote the noted address to George III., and was a leading member of Congress. He was a delegate to the Annapolis Convention of 1786, and to the Federal Constitutional Convention of the following year. From 1789 to 1793 he was U. S. Senator from Delaware, and Chief Justice of the State from 1793 until his death. (Life by Read.)

Read, John Meredith (1797–1874), was a U. S. District Attorney from 1837 to 1844. He was Judge of the Pennsylvania Supreme Court from 1860 to 1872. His legal opinions had a wide reputation.

Read, Thomas (1740–1788), was the first to obtain the rank of commodore in the American navy. He rendered valuable assistance at the battle of Trenton. He commanded the frigate "George Washington."

CONFEDERATE STATESMEN.

Robert Toombs.
Judah P. Benjamin.
Jefferson Davis.
Alexander H. Stephens.

Read, Thomas Buchanan (1822–1872), poet and artist, was born in Pennsylvania. Among his poems "Sheridan's Ride" is the most popular, and one of his chief artistic productions was a painting illustrating that poem.

Readjusters, a political faction formed from the Democratic party of Virginia in 1878. Its formation was due to a bill which passed the State Legislature in March of that year for refunding the State debt. The party was led by William Mahone and was violently opposed to the payment of the debt. In 1879 and 1881, by a fusion with the Republicans they gained control of the State government, and sent William Mahone to the United States Senate.

Reagan, John H., born in 1818, was a member of the Texas Legislature from 1847 to 1849. He represented Texas in the U. S. Congress as a Democrat from 1857 to 1861. He was Postmaster-General of the Confederacy from 1861 to 1865. He again served in the U. S. Congress from 1875 to 1887, and was a Senator from 1887 to 1891.

Rear-Admiral. This rank was created by Act of Congress in 1862, along with that of commodore, it being at the time the highest naval grade. Those of admiral and vice-admiral, outranking it, were created several years later.

Rebellion. (See Civil War.)

Reciprocity. A reciprocity agreement between the United States and Canada was concluded in 1854, and terminated in 1866. A similar one was made with Hawaii in 1875. Various others, of an equally special sort, were from time to time made by the United States. The matter was brought into a new phase by the tariff act of 1890 (McKinley Act), which provided that the duties on sugar, molasses, coffee, tea and hides, which had been removed, might be reimposed by the President in case of any countries which levied what he thought unjust or unreasonable duties on the agricultural products of the United States. With this resource in hand, the President entered on negotiations which resulted in the conclusion of reciprocity treaties with Brazil, Spain (for Cuba and Porto Rico) and San Domingo (1891), and Salvador, Germany, Great Britain (for the West Indies), Nicaragua, Honduras, Guatemala and Austria-Hungary (1892).

Reconstruction. One of the leading problems remaining after the Civil War was how to reconstruct the governments of the States which had seceded. Mr. Lincoln had proceeded upon the theory that nothing more was necessary than that a sufficient number of the citizens should form a State Government, of which the officials were loyally desirous of maintaining constitutional relations with the Government of the Union. The separation of West Virginia from Virginia had been accomplished by a Virginian Legislature so constituted. President Johnson proceeded upon the same theory. In Congress other theories were broached, some even going so far as to hold that the seceding States had ceased to exist as States, and constituted a territory respecting which Congress was at liberty to make such arrangements as it chose. The view generally upheld by Congress was that the Southern States could be re-admitted only on such terms as Congress should impose. Its maintenance of this view was largely owing to its belief that the substantial results of the war in respect to the enfranchisement and civil rights of the negro could not be secured in any other way, because of the reluctance of some Southern Legislatures to accept these results. Before Congress met in December, 1865, Johnson had recognized provisional governments in all the Southern States but one, on their accepting the Thirteenth Amendment. But Congress proposed the Fourteenth Amendment, and insisted on its acceptance as a pre-requisite to re-admission of any State. In 1867 it passed the Reconstruction Act, which divided the South into five military districts, under the command of generals of the army, who were to effect a registration of voters, including negroes, and excluding those disqualified by the Fourteenth Amendment. These voters should elect a convention, which should make a constitution, ratified by them. It should then be submitted to Congress, and if it was acceptable to Congress, the State should be reinstated whenever its Legislature had ratified the Fourteenth Amendment. The result was the notorious black or "carpet-bag" governments. Under this act Alabama, Arkansas, Florida, Louisiana and the Carolinas were re-admitted. Tennessee had already been re-admitted by Congress in 1866. Georgia, Mississippi, Texas and Virginia were required also to ratify the Fifteenth Amendment, and were not re-admitted until 1870. In 1868 the Supreme Court, in the case of Texas *vs.* White, sustained the Congressional, as over against the Presidential, theory of reconstruction.

Record, Congressional, successor to the *Congressional Globe*. It contains a complete report of Congressional debates, proceedings and enactments from 1872 down to the present time.

Red Bank. (See Mifflin, Fort.)

Red-Cross Society. The American (National) Association of the Red-Cross, for the relief of the wounded in war and of sufferers by floods and other similar catastrophes, was founded at Washington, May 21, 1881.

Red-Jacket (1751–1830), chief of the Wolf tribe of the Senecas, served with the Six Nations against the Americans during the Revolution. In the War of 1812 he assisted the United States. He made an eloquent speech against the treaty of Fort Stanwix in 1784. He lacked courage, and was an inverate opponent of Christianity, schools and missionaries, but was a sagacious statesman and an eloquent orator.

Red Line Map, a map made by the Frenchman D'Anville in 1746. It had been sent to Vergennes, the French Minister, by Franklin in 1782, and was discovered among the Paris archives by Jared Sparks. A strong red line drawn near the ridge, in which the Kennebec and Penobscot Rivers rise, more than favored the English claims, respecting the northeast boundary of the United States. Sparks sent it to Webster, who was anxious lest the English should hear of it. It was used in a secret session of the Senate, and with the Maine commissioners to induce a ratification of the treaty, and was afterward made a ground of reproach against Webster by opponents of the treaty.

Red Stone Old Fort, Pa., built as a store-house by the Ohio Company, was the scene of important movements during the French and Indian War. Here General Dinwiddie ordered the English forces to assemble until they could advance against the French (1754). The fort was burned by the French after the English defeat at Fort Necessity. During the Whisky Rebellion a committee of insurrectionists held a meeting here August 28, 1794.

Redemptioners, or indented servants. From the earliest settlement of the American colonies, particularly the middle colonies, indented servants formed a large part of the population. Many came over from England under bond for their passage to serve a number of years. Many also were kidnapped and placed in enforced slavery for a term of years. They served four, five, or seven years, according to contract. At the end of these terms they were released, awarded fifty acres of land and became free citizens. Hence the term "Redemptioners." This system was introduced in Virginia in 1607 with the first colony; in Massachusetts in 1631. It also existed in Maryland, New York, Connecticut and Pennsylvania. The practice was not discontinued in the middle colonies until 1750.

Redpath, James (1833–1891), came to America from Scotland in 1848. He was an ardent abolitionist. He founded the Haytian Bureau of Emigration. He assisted Jefferson Davis in preparing his "History of the Southern Confederacy," and engaged in the Irish Home Rule movement.

Reed, John (1781–1860) represented Massachusetts in the U. S. Congress as a Federalist from 1813 to 1817 and as a Whig from 1821 to 1841. He was Lieutenant-Governor of Massachusetts from 1844 to 1851.

Reed, Joseph (1741–1785), was president of the Pennsylvania Convention of 1775. He became aide-de-camp, secretary and adjutant-general to General Washington, and was active in organizing the business of headquarters. He served in the Long Island campaign and at Brandywine, Germantown and Monmouth. He was elected to Congress in 1777 and signed the Articles of Confederation in 1778. He was president of the Pennsylvania Executive Council from 1778 to 1781. He was an earnest opponent of slavery and of the proprietary system of government in Pennsylvania. He wrote "An Address to the People of Pennsylvania." Life by Reed.

Reed, Thomas B., speaker, born in 1839, was a member of the Maine Legislature from 1868 to 1870, and State attorney-general from 1870 to 1873. He was then elected to the U. S. Congress as a Republican, and has served by re-election to the present time (1894.) He was speaker from 1889 to 1891 and introduced changes in parliamentary practice giving greater powers to the speaker, especially in the matter of deciding upon the presence of a quorum.

Reeder, Andrew H. (1807–1864), of Pennsylvania, was appointed Governor of Kansas in 1854, but was removed in 1855 for not exerting official influence against the Free-State movement. When chosen U. S. Senator under the Topeka constitution in 1856 he was not allowed his seat.

Reformed Church (Reformed Dutch Church). This denomination originated in Holland, and its first synod was held in Antwerp in 1563. Emigrants from Holland brought its teachings to this country and a church was organized as early as 1619 in New Amsterdam. The denomination grew slowly, owing partly to persecutions from the English, but about 1737 felt strong enough to ask for a separate organization from the parent church in Holland. This was finally effected in 1772 through the agency of Dr. John H. Livingston, and in 1792 the new organization was completed. At that time there were 136 churches and fifty ministers. The constitution then adopted was revised in 1842, and again in 1874. The denomination in 1890 numbered 310,000 communicants, living largely in the Middle States, and some parts of the West.

Reformed Episcopal. This church separated from the Protestant Episcopal in December, 1873, on the ground that the parent church was drifting from evangelism and the true principles of the church. The Rev. G. D. Cummins, D. D., assistant bishop of the diocese of Kentucky, was the leader of the movement. In 1890 this church had 8500 communicants.

Reformed Presbyterians. In 1743 members of the Scottish church of this name, who were settled in the American colonies, organized and subscribed to the Old Scottish Covenant. In 1798 the first Presbytery was formed, and two years later it ordained that no slave-holder should be admitted to membership. In 1833 a schism took place on the church's attitude toward the State. The main body now ruled that its members should not act as American citizens nor in any way identify themselves with the political system of the United States. This position is still maintained. Number of members in 1890, 17,000.

Refunding. On August 31, 1865, the debt of the United States consisted of $2,845,907,627, of which only $1,109,568,192 was funded debt. Partial enactments enabled the Secretary of the Treasury, by December, 1867, to convert floating debt, compound interest notes, 7–30's, and U. S. notes, into funded debt of the amount of nearly $700,000,000. The refunding act of 1870 authorized the issue of certain amounts of five per cent, four and one-half per cent, and four per cent bonds, to take the place of the existing bonds, mostly sixes. During the next ten years, this substitution had been carried on to an extent which lessened the annual interest charge by $20,000,000, (reducing it from $82,000,000 to $62,000,000). In 1881 the annual interest charge was reduced almost $20,000,000 again, by the Windom refunding scheme, which converted $460,000,000 of five and six per cent bonds into bonds bearing three and one-half per cent interest.

Regicides. In July, 1660, there arrived at Cambridge, Mass., Edward Whalley and his son-in-law, William Goffe, two of the judges who had condemned Charles I. For some months they appeared in public and joined in devotional meetings in Cambridge and Boston, where they were kindly received. Upon the news of the passage by Parliament of the Indemnity Act, marking Whalley and Goffe for vengeance as regicides, they fled to New Haven and were received and concealed by Davenport in the "Judges' Cave." They were concealed from pursuit at New Haven and Milford for nearly two years. After this they fled to a cave in New Hampshire, but were there discovered by some Indians, and returned to Hadley, Mass., where they were concealed until their death, Whalley dying in 1674, Goffe in 1679. When King Philip attacked Hadley in 1675, Goffe appeared and led the defence. Dixwell, another regicide, also escaped to New England.

Register of Debates, a record of Congressional proceedings from December, 1824, to October, 1837. It was published in twenty-nine volumes, and contains many valuable State papers and public documents, besides the debates and routine Congressional work. It is a continuation of the "Annals of Congress," and was succeeded by the *Congressional Globe*.

Regulators, the name given to a body of insurgents in North Carolina just before the Revolution. Heavy taxes and fees aroused the resistance of the back-country people against Governor Tryon in 1766. The rebellion spread, but Tryon signally defeated the armed bands at Alamance, on the Haw, in 1771. His successor, Martin, compromised with the "Regulators."

Reid, Samuel C. (1783–1861), commanded the privateer "General Armstrong," and fought one of the most remarkable battles on record at Fayal in 1814 with a British squadron. He designed the present form of the U. S. flag.

Reid, Whitelaw, journalist, born in 1837, was one of the leading war correspondents during the Civil War. He became an editor of the New York *Tribune* in 1869, and its proprietor in 1872. He was Minister to France from 1889 to 1892. He wrote "After the War," a description of the South, and "Ohio in the War," which is a valuable historical work. In 1892 he was the candidate of the Republicans for Vice-President, but was defeated, with Harrison.

"Reindeer," sloop. (See "Wasp.")

Relief Party, a political party existing in Kentucky between the years 1820 and 1826. This party advocated the relief of delinquent debtors. They elected the Governor, and passed a bill to this end in 1824. The bill was deemed unconstitutional. The Anti-Relief party regained control in 1826.

Remington, Philo, of New York, born in 1816, superintended the business of E. Remington and Sons, who produced the celebrated Remington rifles and developed the successful Remington type-writer.

Removals. The Constitution of 1787 gave the President power to appoint officers with the consent of the Senate, but did not state whether the power of removal was also to be exercised under this restraint. Debate on this arose in 1789, and it was concluded to allow the power of removal to rest with the President alone. This remained the policy of the Government until the passage of the Tenure-of-Office Act, (see Art.) in 1867.

Reno, Jesse L. (1823–1862), general, served at Contreras, Churubusco, Chapultepec and Vera Cruz during the Mexican War. He commanded a brigade in Burnside's North Carolina expedition at Roanoke Island, Fort Barton and New Berne. He commanded a corps under General Pope at

Manassas and at South Mountain, where he was killed while leading an assault.

Rensselaerswyck, a Dutch colony of New York, established in 1630 by Kilian van Rensselaer, a pearl merchant and member of the Amsterdam Chamber. He purchased territory from the Indians, which is now comprised in Albany and Rensselaer counties, and established the first settlement near Fort Orange, the present site of Albany. This long remained an independent manor. (See Anti-Renters.)

Representatives. (See House of Representatives.)

Republican Party. The name of Republicans was, in the earlier history of the Union, taken by the party formed by Jefferson, as distinguishing them from their Federalist opponents, stigmatized as monarchists. But this party has been treated in an article under the name of Democrats, by which they were also known. In 1854 the name was revived, to be applied to a new party, at first characterized primarily by opposition to the extension of slavery to the territories. The compromise of 1850 had resulted in the disruption and decay of the Whig party. There was a brief interval before parties could be re-formed upon the basis of the slavery question purely. The passage of the Kansas-Nebraska Act by the Democrats in 1854 caused a general coalition of Northern Free-Soilers, Whigs, Democrats, Know-Nothings and Abolitionists, united in opposition to that measure and the consequent repeal of the Missouri Compromise. At first known as "Anti-Nebraska Men," the coalitionists took in that same year the name of Republicans. They at once won a plurality of Congress, and in 1856 held their first national convention at Philadelphia, which nominated Fremont and Dayton. Defeated then, in 1859 they again controlled the House. In 1860 Democratic divisions enabled them to elect Lincoln. For the next fourteen years the party, reinforced for a time by "War Democrats," was supreme. It controlled the National Government, enlarged its powers by broad construction of the Constitution, carried on the war, abolished slavery, reconstructed the governments of the seceding States and controlled them, maintained the protective system and refunded the debt. It carried the election of Lincoln in 1864 and of Grant in 1868 and 1872. The Liberal Republican schism of 1872 indicated a reaction from the radical policy followed in regard to reconstruction, and was followed by extensive defeats in the "tidal wave" of 1874, due partly to official corruption in high places. Yet the party managed, though barely, to carry the election of Hayes in 1876, and elected Garfield in 1880. In 1884 the nomination of Blaine caused the "bolt" of the "mugwumps," and the election of a Democratic President. The party then became, more distinctly than in the years just preceding, the party of high protection. In 1888 it elected Harrison. Defeated in 1892, it was again successful in State elections in 1893. Its strength has always lain in the North. In addition to the principles already mentioned, it has of late advocated a more stirring foreign policy than that of the Democrats, and larger expenditures for pensions and other national objects.

Republican Party, in Pennsylvania, a party existing under the first constitution, that of 1776–1790, which desired the substitution of a stronger government for that set up in 1776. They formed the germ of the Federal party in Pennsylvania. Their opponents were styled Constitutionalists.

Repudiation. The Constitution provides that the States can make no laws which shall impair the obligation of contracts; yet the Eleventh Amendment provides that the jurisdiction of the National Supreme Court does not extend to suits brought against a State by a citizen of another State. Hence the States have been at liberty either to repudiate or to acknowledge debts. Repudiation has been adopted at various times and in various degrees by Georgia, Louisiana, Mississippi, Alabama, Florida, the Carolinas, Arkansas, Tennessee, Minnesota, Michigan and Virginia. The repudiation of the last mentioned State involved the largest sum, ($33,000,000), now partially liquidated. In some of the other States too, bills have been passed in the Legislature, since the repudiating acts, for refunding the debt.

Requisitions upon the States were the only means of raising money which the Articles of Confederation left to the Continental Congress. This proved entirely ineffectual. From 1782 to 1786 Congress made calls amounting in the aggregate to more than $6,000,000, but only a million of this had been paid in by the end of March, 1787.

Resaca de la Palma, Texas. On May 9, 1846, General Zachary Taylor utterly routed General Arista and drove him from this stronghold, to which the latter had retired after the battle of Palo Alto. The Mexican artillery, baggage, war material and Arista's private correspondence were captured. Captain May, of Taylor's dragoons, won the day by charging upon and silencing the Mexican guns. General Taylor's army numbered 2000 men; that of Arista 5000 men.

Resaca, Ga. Here was fought, May 14 and 15, 1864, one of the first battles of Sherman's celebrated campaign through Georgia. Marching toward Atlanta with his main command, Sherman sent McPherson to seize Resaca and cut off Johnston's supplies by the railroad. McPherson failed to gain this point, and Johnston immediately availed himself of the opportunity and posted his own army in this desirable position. Sherman turned back and marched against him. Sherman had 100,000 troops; Johnston about 55,000. May 14, Sherman was in position around Resaca on the north and west, and on that day there was continual skirmishing and artillery firing. Johnston refused to leave his entrenchments, and the Union leader would not attack them. Finally McPherson gained an elevated position, from which he could destroy the railroad bridge over the Oostenaula River. Johnston tried in vain to dislodge him. Meantime Hooker made a brilliant charge, and Sherman sent a detachment across the stream on pontoons to help destroy the bridge. Johnston, seeing his communications so seriously threatened, retreated on the night of the fifteenth.

Resumption. (See Specie Resumption.)

Returning Boards. Although in general it is a fixed principle in American constitutional law that judicial functions belong solely to the judiciary department, and the returning boards are allowed only ministerial functions, yet in Florida, South Carolina and Louisiana returning boards with judicial powers were constituted by the reconstructed State governments, by statute. This action, probably quite unconstitutional, led to the troubles of 1876, connected with the Presidential election. The returning boards used their judicial power to manipulate the returns to such a degree that the rights of the contest were practically indiscoverable.

Revels, Hiram R., born in 1822, represented Mississippi in the U. S. Senate as a Republican from 1870 to 1871. He was the first man of African descent to sit in the U. S. Senate.

Revenue. In 1793 the revenue of the Federal Government was $4,600,-000; in 1813, $14,300,000; in 1833, $33,500,000; in 1853, $61,600,000. During the war it rapidly rose until it attained its maximum in 1866, $520,-000,000. Thence it declined, until in 1878 it was $257,400,000. During the ensuing decade it averaged about $340,000,000. In the fiscal year ending June 30, 1893, it was $461,700,000. In every year the largest item in these receipts has been customs revenue. In war times and since the Civil War, internal revenue (see art.) has been large. Sales of public lands have been a large source of revenue at times, especially just before the panics of 1837 and 1857.

Revenue Flag, instituted by act of Congress, March 2, 1799, to consist of "sixteen perpendicular stripes, alternate red and white, the Union of the ensign bearing the arms of the United States in dark blue on a white field."

Revenue Scheme, a scheme proposed by the Continental Congress, in order to enable it to meet its money obligations. Requisitions upon the States, the only mode allowed to Congress by the Articles of Confederation, had proved a failure. In 1781 Congress proposed an amendment to the Articles, whereby it would be empowered to levy a five per cent duty on imports, to pay the Revolutionary debt. Rhode Island refused her assent. In 1783 Congress asked for this power for only twenty-five years. After many delays, New York refused in 1787, making impossible that unanimous consent which was necessary in order to validate an amendment to the Articles. Then the only plan was that of a Constitutional Convention.

Revere, Paul (1735–1818), was a copper plate engraver in Boston, Mass., and produced many caricatures illustrative of the pre-Revolutionary topics. He was one of the prime movers of the Boston tea party. On the night of April 18–19, 1775, he apprised the citizens of Lexington and Concord of the intended expedition of the British. This is the subject of Longfellow's poem, "Paul Revere's Ride." In 1775 he printed the provincial paper money of Massachusetts, and erected a mill for the manufacture of gunpowder. He engaged in the unsuccessful Penobscot expedition in 1779.

Revolution and Revolutionary War. The Revolution, by which the thirteen American colonies separated themselves from Great Britain, had several causes. Increase of population in America would naturally cause a desire for independence, especially after the French had been driven out (1763). Just at this time the government of George III., under Grenville, resolved to enforce more strictly the Navigation Act and other laws restricting

American trade in the interest of England, to station garrisons in America, and to pay a part of the expense by a stamp-tax. The Stamp Act aroused violent opposition, expressed through the Stamp-Act Congress of 1765. Taxation by Parliament without representation in Parliament was declared illegal and tyrannous. The British Government persisted in the principle, taxing various imports from 1767 to 1770, and tea thereafter. Boston Tea-party led Parliament to pass acts retaliating upon Boston and altering the charter of Massachusetts. The colonies, already brought into concert through their Committees of Correspondence, convened in Continental Congress at Philadelphia in September, 1774. They published a declaration of rights, protested to king and Parliament, and engaged in an association, or non-importation agreement. In April, 1775, Gage, the British commander at Boston, encountered resistance at Lexington and Concord, and war began. A local army, though defeated at Bunker Hill, besieged Boston. A second Continental Congress organized a regular or Continental army, appointed Washington commander-in-chief, and pursued the war. Boston was captured, and the British troops under Howe retired to New York. Acting from this centre, they gained considerable successes over Washington. Meanwhile Congress issued its Declaration of Independence (July 4, 1776), and provisionally governed the new republic, the United States of America. Under its advice, the colonies, now called States, made for themselves constitutions and organized new governments in place of the defunct royal governments. It also framed a new and more regular scheme of Federal government, called the Articles of Confederation; but unanimous consent to its adoption was not obtained until 1781. Congress had great difficulty in getting men and money. Many were disaffected or indifferent to the cause of revolution. The Continental paper money depreciated rapidly, and loans were hard to raise. In 1776 the war for the most part went against them. In 1777 Howe occupied Philadelphia, their capital, defeating the Americans at Brandywine and Germantown. But this prevented him from co-operating with Burgoyne, who was marching down from Canada to New York in the effort to cut off New England from the rest of the Union. In October Burgoyne surrendered at Saratoga. This success enabled the Americans to conclude, in February, 1778, a treaty of alliance with France, which brought them French aid in men and money. During the remainder of the war the efforts of the British commander, Clinton, were mainly directed against the southern end of the American line. Savannah was taken in 1778, Charleston in 1780, and Gates was badly defeated at Camden. The war in the South was managed with much severity, but successfully for the Americans after the appointment of Greene. Cornwallis, marching northward through the Carolinas, took up a position in Virginia, at Yorktown, where, in October, 1781, he was compelled to surrender to a French-American army which Washington had brought down from the North, the French fleet assisting. This virtually ended the war. England was obliged to consent to American independence. Preliminaries having been arranged in 1782, peace was made on these terms at Paris in 1783, the United States being conceded a territory extending from Canada to Florida and westward to the Mississippi. Histories by Bancroft and Fiske.

Reynolds, John F. (1820–1863), was brevetted major for gallantry at Monterey and Buena Vista during the Mexican War. He commanded a Pennsylvania brigade in the Peninsular campaign at Gaines' Mill and Glendale, and led a division at the second battle of Bull Run. In 1862 he commanded the Pennsylvania militia for the defence of the State. He was promoted major-general and commanded the First Corps at Fredericksburg. He led the left wing at the beginning of the battle of Gettysburg, where he was killed.

Reynolds, Joseph J., born in 1822, was brevetted major-general for services during the Civil War. He fought at Chickamauga, was chief-of-staff at Chattanooga and commanded the Department of Arkansas from 1864 to 1866.

Rhea Letter. On January 6, 1818, Andrew Jackson, then department commander in the Southwest, wrote to President Monroe regarding the Seminole troubles in Florida and advising the prompt seizure of East Florida, which he declared could be done "without implicating the Government." He offered to accomplish the seizure himself within sixty days, if it should be indicated to him that it were desirable. John Rhea, a Congressman from Tennessee, was the secret channel through which he hoped Monroe's assent might be signified. It was not. In 1831, during Jackson's administration, in the height of his quarrel with Calhoun, which turned in part upon the Seminole affair, Rhea wrote to Monroe, hoping to elicit from him something that would implicate him as approving Jackson's plan. Monroe, on his death-bed in New York, denounced Rhea's insinuations as utterly false.

Rhett, Robert B. (1800–1876), represented South Carolina in the U. S. Congress as a Democrat from 1837 to 1849, and in the U. S. Senate from 1851 to 1852. He was a radical States'-rights secessionist.

Rhind, Alexander C., born in 1821, commanded the "Crusader" in 1861. He was prominent in the attacks on Charleston in 1863, and fought at Fort Wagner and Fort Fisher. He was commissioned rear admiral and retired in 1883.

Rhode Island was one of the original thirteen States. Its dual origin is indicated by its official title, "The State of Rhode Island and Providence Plantations," and by its two capitals, Providence and Newport. Roger Williams, the patron saint of the State, was banished from Massachusetts Bay Colony because of his attacks on the theocratic government of that colony. He advocated complete separation of church and State, and entire toleration for all creeds. He founded Providence in 1636. Two years later the Antinomians or followers of Anne Hutchinson founded Portsmouth, and in 1639 Newport was settled. March 14, 1644, a charter was granted by which these settlements were united in one colony with a popular government. This charter was revoked, and in 1663 a new one was granted, which continued to be the fundamental law until 1842. This gave the entire power of government to the people. Rhode Island applied for admission to the New England Confederation, but her application was denied. In 1742, the western boundary line was finally settled with Connecticut; but not until 1862 was the eastern boundary with Massachusetts determined. Brown University was founded in 1764. The devotion of the colony to the American cause was shown in 1772, by the affair of the Gaspé. Rhode Island was not represented in the convention of 1787, and did not ratify the Constitution until May 29, 1790. This delay was due to the desire of the agricultural classes to retain the power to levy import taxes and to make paper money a legal tender. In presidential elections, save in 1804, the State was Federal until 1816, when the electoral votes were cast for Monroe. From 1824 to 1850, the State was Whig, with the exception of the year 1836. An unjust apportionment of representatives and a property qualification for voting led to Dorr's rebellion in 1842, when a new constitution was adopted which widened the suffrage, but the property restriction was not entirely removed until (1886–1888) the adoption of the Bourn amendment which retained the property qualification for election to city councils only. From 1856 until the present time (1894) the State has been Republican in Presidential elections. The Democrats elected the Governor in 1887, 1889, 1890 and 1891. The extension of the suffrage has strengthened the Democratic party. From 1886 to 1889 there was a prohibitory amendment against intoxicants. In 1893 an amendment to the constitution provided for plurality elections. The population of Rhode Island, which in 1790 was 68,825, in 1890 was 345,506. History by Arnold.

Rhode Island, Battle of, August 29, 1778. Newport, R. I., had been seized and garrisoned by the British with 6000 men under Pigott. Sullivan and Lafayette on land and Count d'Estaing on sea concerted an attack. Butts' Hill on Rhode Island was seized by Sullivan. Estaing was forced to meet Howe and the English fleet, but a terrible storm averted battle, and Estaing retired to Boston to refit. Pigott attempted to carry Butts' Hill, August 29. The British met with a bloody repulse. The Americans, however, were obliged to evacuate by the arrival of Clinton with 5000 reinforcements.

"**Rhode Island Gazette,**" established at Newport, September 27, 1732, by James Franklin, was the first newspaper of Rhode Island. Publication was suspended in May, 1733.

Rhode Island Historical Society was founded in 1822, and has published eight volumes of collections and begun the issue of a quarterly.

Riall, Sir Phineas (1769–1851), came to America as a British major-general in 1813. He commanded at Chippewa and Lundy's Lane in 1814. He was brave and energetic, but unskillful in military operations.

Ribaut, Jean (1520–1565), a Huguenot, sailed from France on a colonizing expedition in 1562. After exploring the Florida coast, he planted a colony at Port Royal, called Fort Charles, which was unsuccessful. In 1565 he was appointed Governor of this colony. He was driven off by a Spanish fleet, and when he surrendered later to Menendez, the entire party was massacred.

Rice. The production of rice was begun in 1695 in South Carolina, when the captain of a brigantine from Madagascar, which touched at Sullivan's Island, presented one of the colonists with a small bag of the vegetable. Its cultivation spread rapidly through the South and has long been one of the chief sources of revenue. In 1870, 72,635,021 pounds were produced in the United States, South Carolina leading with 32,304,825 pounds. This was a marked decrease from the production previous to the Civil War. (In 1850, 215,313,497 pounds.) The culture at present is much less successful than in former years.

Rice, Alexander H., born in 1818, represented Massachusetts in the U. S. Congress as a Republican from 1859 to 1867. He served on the naval committee. He was Governor of Massachusetts from 1876 to1879.

Rich Mountain, W. Va., occupied by Colonel Pegram, with a regiment of Confederates and six guns of General Garnet's command. July 11, 1861, McClellan ordered Rosecrans to attack this position. Climbing the mountain during a heavy storm, Rosecrans, with 1900 men, forced Pegram to retire after a fierce fight. Pegram and his entire force were captured the next day by McClellan.

Richardson, Henry H. (1838–1886), was the architect of Trinity Church, Boston, and many other noble structures. His architecture is noticeable for harmony and massiveness rather than for elaborate details. He was recognized as the leader of the new school of American architects.

Richardson, Israel B. (1815–1862), of Vermont, was brevetted major for services at Contreras, Churubusco and Chapultepec. He led a brigade at Bull Run, and commanded a division at Chickahominy, South Mountain and Antietam, where he was mortally wounded.

Richardson, William A., of Massachusetts, born in 1821, was Secretary of the U. S. Treasury in Grant's Cabinet from 1873 to 1874. He was a Justice of the U. S. Court of Claims from 1874 to 1885, when he became Chief Justice.

Richmond, Dean (1804–1866), gained an enviable reputation for his upright dealings in business. He was a leader of the Democratic party in New York. He secured the consolidation of the New York Central Railroad.

Richmond, Ky. Here, August 29–30, 1862, 16,000 Federals under Mason and Cruft were utterly routed by about an equal number of Confederates, led by Kirby Smith. August 29 a smart skirmish occurred, in which Mason had a slight advantage. The next day he encountered Smith's entire force and was wholly defeated, Cruft and himself escaping by flight. The Union loss was very heavy.

Richmond, Va., was founded in 1742 and made the capital of the State in 1779. In 1781 it was burned by Arnold. Richmond was the seat of government of the Confederate States during the Civil War. In April, 1865, on the capture of Petersburg by General Grant, it was evacuated and fired by the Confederate troops. The conflagration lasted for over twenty-four hours.

Richmond and Petersburg Railroad, Virginia, attacked by General Smith, May 6 and 7, 1864, with about 20,000 men of Butler's Army of the James during the occupation of Bermuda Hundred by that general. Smith commenced to destroy the railroad at Walthall Junction, but D. H. Hill came up with a strong Confederate force. Smith stopped and gave battle to the Confederates. Hill was driven away after some sharp fighting. Then Smith continued his destruction of the road, tearing it up for several miles. He was suddenly recalled by Butler, May 7, the latter having heard that Lee was advancing in full force.

"Richmond Enquirer." This newspaper was established at Richmond in 1804 by T. Ritchie. It continued for many years, and exercised great influence in the politics of Virginia.

Ricketts, James B. (1817–1887), of New York, served during the Mexican War. He commanded a Federal battery at Alexandria and Bull Run, led a division at Chantilly, South Mountain, Antietam, in the Richmond campaign, and at Cedar Creek.

Riders, objectionable party measures, likely to be vetoed on their own merits, which are added to important bills to secure their passage. The first use of the rider, of national importance, was the joining in 1820 of the bill for the admission of Maine to that permitting slavery in Missouri, so as to compel the acceptance of both or neither. These were afterward separated. The Army Appropriation Bill of 1856 had a rider attached prohibiting the employment of Federal troops for the enforcement of territorial law in Kansas. The President signed this measure, but protested against the rider. In 1879 the Democrats in Congress attempted by riders on appropriation bills to bring to an end the Federal interference in Southern politics. President Hayes, by firm use of the veto, dealt a severe blow at this objectionable practice. State Constitutions have frequently prevented it by allowing the Governor to veto separate items in appropriation bills.

Riding, a division of the provinces held by James, Duke of York, instituted by the "Duke's Laws." The riding was borrowed from Yorkshire, England.

Ridpath, John C., of Indiana, born in 1840, is author of a "Popular History of the United States," a "Monograph on Alexander Hamilton," "Life and Work of Garfield," "Life of James G. Blaine," "History of Texas," and a "Cyclopædia of Universal History."

Riedesel, Baron Friedrich A. (1738–1800), major-general, came to America in 1776 in command of 4000 troops from Brunswick employed by the British. He served in Burgoyne's expedition in 1777, and fought at Ticonderoga, Hubbardton and Saratoga. Captured there, he was afterward exchanged. He was placed in command of Long Island in 1780 and transferred to Canada in 1781. He returned to Germany in 1783. He was a skillful general.

Riedesel, Frederica C. L. (1746–1808), married Baron Riedesel in 1762, and came to America in 1777. She was with her husband in all his campaigns and captivity, ministered to the sick and wounded, and wrote interesting accounts of the Americans.

Rigdon, Sidney (1793–1876), was one of the propagators of the doctrine of the Mormons, and was one of the presidents of the church. He refused to recognize Brigham Young as leader of the church, and was excommunicated.

Rinehart, William H. (1825–1874), of Baltimore, one of the most prominent of American sculptors, produced, among his works of art, "Indian Girl," "The Woman of Samaria," "Love Reconciled with Death," "Clytie," and a statue of Chief-Justice Taney.

Ringgold, Ga., an engagement of the Civil War, November 27, 1863, during Bragg's precipitate flight from the battle-field of Chattanooga. Hooker, commanding a Federal brigade, was in hot pursuit, when at Ringgold, near a narrow mountain gap, he encountered a body of Confederates under Cleburne blocking his passage. These troops were immediately charged by Hooker, and the fight lasted all the afternoon. Hooker was defeated and driven back with great loss.

Ripley, Eleazar W. (1782–1839), major-general, was a member of the Massachusetts Legislature from 1810 to 1812. He served in the attack on York (now Toronto), Canada, and commanded a brigade under General Brown on the Niagara frontier, fighting at Chippewa and Niagara. He was prominent in defence of Fort Erie. He represented Louisiana in the U. S. Congress as a Jackson Democrat from 1835 to 1839.

Ripley, George (1802–1880), was the chief promoter of the Brook Farm experiment at Roxbury, Mass., from 1844 to 1846. He edited the *Harbinger*, a Fourierite organ, from 1844 to 1848, and was assistant editor of "The American Cyclopædia." He was literary editor of the New York *Tribune* from 1847 to 1880. He had an extensive literary knowledge, and was a severe critic.

Rising, Johan C., born about 1600, came to America from Sweden in 1654. He captured Fort Casimir from the Dutch and became Governor of New Sweden, but was expelled by Governor Stuyvesant, of New Amsterdam, in 1655.

Ritchie, Thomas (1778–1854), founded the *Enquirer* at Richmond, Va., in 1804, and edited it until 1845. His paper was a powerful organ of the States'-Rights Democrats. He edited the *Union* from 1845 to 1849.

Rittenhouse, David (1732–1796), a famous astronomer, was a member of the Pennsylvania Committee of Safety in 1776 and treasurer of Pennsylvania from 1777 to 1789. He was director of the U. S. mint from 1792 to 1795.

River and Harbor Acts. President Polk vetoed a river and harbor bill in 1846 and Pierce another in 1854. From this time to 1870 appropriations for the improvement of rivers and harbors were inserted not infrequently in appropriation bills. Since 1870 they have been separate. From $2,000,000 in 1870 the appropriations rose to $19,000,000 in 1882–83. Since then biennial appropriations have been the rule. That of 1891 was of $25,000,000.

River Brethren, a religious denomination which came into existence about the close of the Revolution, named probably from their baptizing only in rivers, or perhaps because they originated near the Susquehanna River; akin in doctrine to the Mennonite Baptists.

Rives, William C. (1793–1868), represented Virginia in the U. S. Congress as a Democrat from 1823 to 1829. While Minister to France from 1829 to 1832 he negotiated the Indemnity Treaty of 1831. He was a U. S. Senator from 1833 to 1834 and from 1836 to 1845, Minister to France from 1849 to 1853, and a Confederate Congressman from 1861 to 1864. He wrote an elaborate life of Madison.

Rivington, James (1724?–1802), came to America from England in 1760, and founded the *New York Gazetteer* in 1773, which became very obnoxious to the patriots. He furnished Washington with valuable information on the British movements.

"**Rivington's New York Gazetteer,**" or, the *Connecticut, New Jersey, Hudson's River and Quebec Weekly Advertiser.* This newspaper was established in New York City April 22, 1773. It was distinctly royalist in its sympathies, its circulation extended exclusively among the Tories, and it was issued under the protection of the king's army. Rivington was obliged to suspend publication in 1775, but renewed in 1777 under the title *Rivington's New York Loyal Gazette*, afterward changed to *Royal Gazette.* The publication was finally suspended in 1783, when the British withdrew from New York.

Roach, John (1815–1887), came to New York from Ireland in 1829. He established extensive ship-building works in Pennsylvania which built six monitors and many other vessels for the U. S. Government.

Roanoke Colony. In 1584 Sir Walter Raleigh, having obtained a large grant of land from Queen Elizabeth, sent out, April 9, seven vessels and 108 settlers under the command of Sir Richard Grenville. After skirting the West Indies and Hispaniola, they landed at Roanoke, in North Carolina, June 20. Ralph Lane was left in charge of the settlement and Grenville returned to England. During the following winter Lane made numerous exploring expeditions and suffered greatly from Indian attacks. In the spring he received some aid in men and supplies from Sir Francis Drake, but finally the settlers persuaded Drake to take them home. Soon after Grenville arrived with new settlers. These had been destroyed by the Indians when, in 1587, a new colony of Raleigh's, under White, came out. White himself returned to England. When he came back (1590) he found the colony vanished. It seems to have been destroyed by the savages, though there is a theory that descendants of the colonists are still to be found among North Carolina half-breeds.

Roanoke Island, N. C., a valuable stronghold of the Confederacy, being the key to their defences south of Norfolk, and a protection for the landing of supplies in that city. It was defended by three earthworks: Pork Point, Weir's Point and Fort Blanchard, and commanded by General Wise. Against this place the National Government dispatched Burnside and Goldsborough with thirty-one gunboats, fourteen transports and 11,500 troops.

With great difficulty a landing was effected February 7, 1862, the Confederate fleet was dispersed and destroyed at Elizabeth City, N. C., the earthworks were demolished and 2500 Confederates made prisoners.

Roanoke River, N. C., scene, on May 5, 1864, of a naval engagement between Captain Melancthon Smith, commanding the Federal double-enders "Sassacus," "Mattabesett," "Wyalusing" and "Miami" and some smaller vessels, and the Confederate ram "Albemarle," Captain Worley, and two gunboats. The Federal fleet was badly disabled, and the "Albemarle" too was damaged. After the battle she steamed up the river, and in October was destroyed by the Federal commander Cushing, a daring exploit.

Roberts, Benjamin S. (1811–1875), was brevetted lieutenant-colonel for services in the Mexican War. He served as chief of cavalry under General Pope in 1862, and fought at Cedar Mountain and Bull Run.

Roberts, Jonathan (1771–1854), represented Pennsylvania in the U. S. Congress as a Democrat from 1811 to 1814. He earnestly supported the War of 1812. He was a U. S. Senator from 1814 to 1821.

Robertson, George (1790–1874), represented Kentucky in the U. S. Congress as a Democrat from 1817 to 1821. He was Speaker of the Kentucky Legislature from 1823 to 1827, and Chief Justice of Kentucky from 1829 to 1843.

Robertson, James (1710–1788), came to America in 1756 as major of British troops. He commanded a brigade at the battle of Long Island. He was appointed royal Governor of New York in 1779.

Robertson, James (1742–1814), held the Cherokee Indians in check during the Revolution. He founded settlements on the Cumberland River in 1779. He defeated the designs of the half-breed McGillivray (q. v.) for twelve years.

Robertson, William (1721–1793), Scottish historian, published eight books of a "History of America," dealing with the settlement and history of the Spanish colonies. A "History of Virginia until 1688" was published from his manuscripts.

Roberval, Jean F. de la R. (1500?–1547), led a colonizing expedition to Canada from France in 1542. He was soon afterward recalled, and perished while conducting another expedition.

Robeson, George M., born in 1827, was Secretary of the Navy in Grant's Cabinet from 1869 to 1877. He represented New Jersey in the U. S. Congress as a Republican from 1879 to 1883.

Robinson, Beverly (1723–1792), of New York, commanded the Loyalist American regiment during the Revolution. He was concerned in the treasonable negotiations of Arnold, and was prominent in the trial of Major André. His immense estate was confiscated.

Robinson, Charles, born in 1818, had a prominent part in the early struggles of the Forty-niners in California. In 1856 he was elected Governor of Kansas by the Free-State party under the Topeka Constitution, and again under the Wyandotte Constitution in 1859.

Robinson, Edward (1794–1863), was a careful student of Biblical literature. He made extensive researches in the Holy Land and published many works relating to Biblical literature, history and geography.

Robinson, Ezekiel G., born in 1815, was president of Brown University from 1872 to 1889. He has a high reputation as a teacher, preacher and orator. He made a careful translation of Neander's "History of the Planting of the Church," and has written on philosophy and ethics.

Robinson, George D., born in 1834, represented Massachusetts in the U. S. Congress as a Republican from 1877 to 1883. He was Governor of Massachusetts from 1883 to 1886.

Robinson, John (1575?–1625), was suspended from the Church of England for nonconformity, and in 1608 fled to Holland. He ardently advocated the plan of emigrating to America and made arrangements with the Virginia Company for sending his congregation thither. In 1620 the Pilgrims sailed from Southampton, and Robinson took leave of them in a memorable sermon. He intended to follow them, but was prevented by illness before arrangements could be made. After his death many more of his followers came to America. He wrote "A Justification of Separation from the Church of England," and was a man of noble and tolerant spirit.

Robinson, John C., born in 1817, served in the Mexican War. He commanded a brigade at Richmond and a division at Fredericksburg, Chancellorsville and Gettysburg, and fought at the Wilderness and Spottsylvania.

Robinson, Lucius (1810–1891), joined the Republican party and was Comptroller of New York from 1861 to 1865. He returned to the Democratic party and was elected Governor in 1876, serving till 1880.

Robinson, William Erigena (1814–1892), came to America from Ireland in 1836. He was prominent as a correspondent of the *New York Tribune*, under the name of "Richelieu." He represented New York in the U. S. Congress as a Democrat from 1866 to 1868 and from 1880 to 1884. He secured the passage of a bill in 1868 asserting the rights of expatriation and naturalization.

Rochambeau, Comte de [Jean Baptiste Donatien de Vimeure] (1725–1807), the principal French military figure in the Revolutionary War, aside from Lafayette, served in the War of the Austrian Succession and the Seven Years' War. In 1780 he was sent to America in command of a considerable force, and fixed his headquarters at Newport. Having concerted his plans with Washington, he marched to the neighborhood of New York in the summer of 1781, effected a junction with his ally, and the two moved rapidly southward to Yorktown. Rochambeau conducted assaults on the town, and received a fair share of the credit for the feat. He returned to France in 1783. Later he was a field marshal, but was inconspicuous in the French Revolution.

Rochester, Nathaniel (1752–1831), served in North Carolina in the Revolution as commissary-general. He purchased large tracts near Rochester, N. Y., which was named for him. He served in the Legislatures of North Carolina, Maryland and New York.

Rockingham, Charles W. Wentworth, Marquis of (1730–1782), while Prime Minister of England from 1765 to 1766, secured the repeal of the Stamp Act. He became Premier again in 1782 and began the negotiation of the Treaty of Paris with the United States.

Rockingham Convention, the first State party convention held in New Hampshire. August 5, 1812, a mass meeting of 1500 voters assembled at Portsmouth, Rockingham County, adopted a platform, nominated a full ticket, State, Electoral and Congressional, and joined in a vigorous address to President Madison.

Rocky Face Ridge, Ga., a strong position from which Johnston, with an army of 55,000 Confederates during four days, May 5–9, 1864, opposed the advance of Sherman's army, 99,000 strong, on Atlanta. McPherson flanked the Confederate left and endeavored to carry Resaca, but without avail. He then fell back to Snake Creek Gap, and, on May 7, Sherman passed his troops through this defile, threatening Johnston's rear, while Howard's division menaced his front. Johnston, perceiving he was about to be hemmed in, fell back to Resaca to strengthen his position.

Rocky Mountain, Battle of, July 30, 1780. Rocky Mountain, one of the strategic points of South Carolina, was seized by the British in 1780. On the above date Sumter, with a small force, made a spirited but unsuccessful attack upon the post.

Rodgers, Christopher R. P. (1819–1892), commanded the "Wabash" at Port Royal. He was fleet captain at Fort Sumter in 1863. From 1863 to 1866 he commanded the "Iroquois." He retired, a rear admiral, in 1881.

Rodgers, John (1771–1838), a naval hero, served in 1799 in the war against France, and later in the Tripolitan War. He took command in the Mediterranean in 1805, and compelled Tripoli and Tunis to sign treaties. While in command of the "President" in 1811, Rodgers had an encounter with the British "Little Belt," an affair which increased the tension between the two nations. In the ensuing war he took many prizes; he was also present at the defence of Baltimore in 1814. After peace was restored he held for many years the office of naval commissioner.

Rodgers, John (1812–1882), rear-admiral, engaged in the Port-Royal expedition in 1861, and commanded the "Galena" in the battle of Drury's Bluff. In command of the monitor "Weehawken," he captured the Confederate iron-clad "Atlanta" in 1863. He commanded the "Dictator" from 1864 to 1865. He was distinguished for his courage and superior ability. He was superintendent of the U. S. Naval Observatory from 1877 to 1882.

Rodman, Thomas J. (1815–1871), invented the Rodman guns, which are cast about a hollow core through which a stream of cold water runs. He was an inspector of ordnance during the Civil War.

Rodney, Cæsar (1728–1784), was a delegate from Delaware to the Stamp Act Congress at New York in 1765. He was Speaker of the Delaware Assembly from 1769 to 1774, and of the Delaware popular Convention in 1774. He was a member of the Continental Congress from 1774 to 1776, was a member of the committee to draft a statement of rights and grievances, and signed the Declaration of Independence. He served under General Washington in the Delaware campaign from 1776 to 1777, and was president of Delaware from 1778 to 1782.

Rodney, Cæsar A. (1772–1824), represented Delaware in the U. S. Congress as a Democrat from 1803 to 1805. He was Attorney-General in Jefferson's and Madison's Cabinets from 1807 to 1811. As commissioner to South America in 1817 he advocated the recognition of the Spanish-American republics. He was a U. S. Congressman from 1821 to 1822 and a U. S. Senator from 1822 to 1823. He was appointed Minister to the Argentine provinces in 1823.

Rodriguez's Canal (near New Orleans). Just before the battle of New Orleans, General Jackson had made this his line of defence against the British, who on January 1, 1815, endeavored to storm the works. They were repulsed with heavy loss, abandoning five heavy cannon.

Roe, Francis A., born in 1823, commanded the "Pensacola" in passing Forts Jackson and St. Philip in Farragut's squadron. He commanded the "Katahdin" from 1862 to 1863. He commanded the "Sassacus," destroyed blockade runners and fought against the "Albemarle."

Roebling, John A. (1806–1869), came to Pennsylvania from Germany in 1831. He established a large wire manufactory in Trenton, N. J. He constructed the Niagara and Cincinnati suspension bridges, and began the construction of the Brooklyn Bridge in 1869.

Roebling, Washington A., born in 1837, was a colonel in the Civil War, serving at South Mountain, Antietam and Bull Run. He succeeded his father in the construction of Brooklyn Bridge, which was completed in 1883.

Rogerenes, a sect of Seventh-Day Baptists, followers of Jonathan Rogers, of New London, Conn. The sect originated about 1675. Beside keeping the Saturday as the holy day, they opposed the use of medicines and family prayers.

Rogers, John, of New York, born in 1829, came into prominence as a sculptor in 1860 for his group, "The Slave Auction." He has gained great celebrity for his statuettes illustrating war subjects and rural life.

Rogers, Robert (1727–1800), commanded "Rogers' Rangers" during the French War. In 1759 he destroyed the Indian village at St. Francis. In 1765 he was appointed Governor of Mackinaw, Mich., by the crown. He was paroled by Congress at the outbreak of the Revolution. He raised "The Queen's Rangers," a corps which was distinguished during the war. In 1777 he went to England, and in 1778 was banished from America.

Rogersville, Tenn., a brief fight, November 6, 1863, between detachments of Burnside's Federal troops and some Confederates from Longstreet's command. This took place during Longstreet's pursuit of Burnside toward Knoxville.

Roman Catholic. (See Catholic.)

Romero, Matias, born in 1837, was Mexican chargé d' affaires at Washington from 1860 to 1863, when complicated diplomatic questions were at issue. He was Minister to the United States from 1863 to 1868, and from 1882 to the present time (1894.)

Romney, W. Va. October 25, 1861, Colonel Kelly, who was then guarding the Allegheny section of the Baltimore and Ohio Railroad, surprised a Confederate battalion. Sixty prisoners were taken besides all the camp equipage, provisions and munitions. Colonel Wallace, of Indiana, also, June, 1861, routed a Confederate force from Romney.

Roorback, a general term for political forgery, originating in the publication for political purposes of alleged extracts from the "Travels of Baron Roorback," in 1844.

Roosevelt, Robert B., born in 1829, edited the *New York Citizen* from 1868. He represented New York in the U. S. Congress as a Democrat from 1871 to 1873, and was Minister to the Netherlands from 1888 to 1889.

Roosevelt, Theodore, born in 1858, was a Republican member of the New York Assembly from 1880 to 1884. He was an ardent advocate of political reform, and succeeded in abolishing many political abuses. He is author of a "History of the Naval War of 1812," of lives of Benton and Gouverneur Morris in the American Statesmen Series, and of "The Winning of the West." Since 1889 he has been a member of the U. S. Civil Service Commission.

Root, George Frederick, born in 1820, has composed many songs of national popularity, including "Battle Cry of Freedom," "Just Before the Battle, Mother," "Tramp, Tramp, the Boys are Marching," and "There's Music in the Air."

Ropes, John C., born in St. Petersburg in 1836, has contributed to the publications of the Military Historical Society of Massachusetts. He has written, "The Army under Pope," in "Campaigns of the Civil War," a book on Napoleon, and one on the Waterloo campaign.

Rosa Americana, a coinage issued in 1722 by Great Britain for America, of a mixed metal resembling brass, and called Rosa Americana or Wood's money, after its manufacturer William Wood. The royal letters patent described this money as two-pence, pence and half-pence. The obverse was stamped with a laureated head of George the First; the reverse with a double rose from which projected five barbed points. Legend: Rosa Americana, 1722 above, and below, Utile Dulci.

Rose, George (1744-1818), was British Minister to the United States from 1807 to 1808, to negotiate concerning the Chesapeake affair. As he made demands which the United States would not concede the embassy resulted only in delay.

Rose, Sir John (1820–1888), came to Canada from Scotland in 1836. He was British Commissioner to the United States in 1864 and 1869. In 1870, as confidential agent he made preliminary negotiations toward the Treaty of Washington.

Rosecrans, William Starke, born in 1819, an American general, was graduated at West Point in 1842. Previous to the war he was a professor at the academy, an engineer and a financier. Being appointed colonel of Ohio volunteers in 1861, he served in West Virginia, and won the battle of Rich Mountain, July, 1861. He next succeeded McClellan in the Department of the Ohio, and gained the victory of Carnifex Ferry in September. Appointed commander of the Army of the Mississippi, he conquered at Iuka, September, 1862, at Corinth, October, and succeeded Buell as commander of the Army of the Cumberland. He fought the great battle of Murfreesboro', showed skillful strategy in the next months, and was defeated at Chickamauga. After this Rosecrans was superseded, sent to the West, and put on waiting orders. He resigned in 1867. He was Minister to Mexico, 1868–1869, Democratic Congressman from California, 1881–1885, and Register of the U. S. Treasury from 1885 to 1893.

Rosewell, a famous old Virginia homestead on Carter's Creek, near the York River. It was begun in the seventeenth century by Mann Page, and finished by his son and widow.

Ross, George (1730–1779), was a member of the Pennsylvania Assembly from 1768 to 1770. He was appointed to prepare the Pennsylvania declaration of rights. He served in the Continental Congress from 1774 to 1777, and signed the Declaration of Independence. He was active in reorganizing the government of Pennsylvania, and in urging aggressive measures against British oppression. He was appointed judge of admiralty in 1779.

Ross, John (1790–1866), chief of the Cherokee Indians, successfully resisted the encroachments of the Georgia Legislature upon the Cherokee land titles in 1829. He opposed the treaty of New Echota in 1835, but was compelled by the United States to remove to a reservation.

Ross, Robert (1770?–1814), came to America in 1814 in command of a force of British soldiers. He defeated the Americans at Bladensburg, burned the capitol and other public buildings at Washington, and was killed at North Point.

Rosser, Thomas L., born in 1836, attained the rank of major-general in the Confederate service. He commanded the Virginia cavalry under General Early in 1863, fighting at Cedar Creek.

Rouarie, Armand T. (1756–1793), came to the United States from France in 1777. He served with Lafayette in New Jersey and under General Gates against Cornwallis. He fought at Warren Tavern, Camden and Yorktown.

Rough and Ready, a nickname of President Zachary Taylor, earned during his Mexican campaigns.

Roumania. The United States concluded a consular convention with Roumania in 1881.

Rousseau, Lovell H. (1818–1869), was a member of the Indiana Legislature in 1844 and 1845. He distinguished himself at the battle of Buena Vista in the Mexican War. He led a brigade at the battle of Shiloh and fought at Perryville. He commanded a division of the army of the Cumberland at Stone River, Chattanooga and Chickamauga. He represented Kentucky in the U. S. Congress as a Republican from 1865 to 1867. He was sent to receive Alaska from the Russian Government and assume control of the territory in 1867.

Rowan, Stephen C. (1808–1890), vice-admiral, came to America from Ireland. He entered the U. S. navy in 1826. He assisted in the capture of Monterey and San Diego in 1846 during the Mexican War, and commanded a naval brigade under Commodore Stockton at San Gabriel and La Mesa. In the Civil War he commanded the "Pawnee" at Acquia Creek and Hatteras. He commanded the fleet in the attack on Roanoke Island in 1862, fought at New Berne and captured Fort Macon. He commanded "The New Ironsides" off Charleston from 1862 to 1864. He became superintendent of the Naval Observatory in 1882.

Royal African Company, an English slave-trading corporation organized about 1720 for the especial purpose of transporting slaves to the colonies. In the Carolinas special care was enjoined upon the Government to encourage this trade.

Ruger, Thomas H., born in 1833, commanded a brigade in the Rappahannock campaign and a division at Gettysburg. He commanded a division against General Hood in 1864 and led a division in North Carolina in 1865. He became a brigadier-general in 1886.

Ruggles, Benjamin (1783–1857), represented Ohio in the U. S. Senate as a Democrat from 1815 to 1833. He was called the "wheel-horse of the Senate" on account of his industrious habits.

Ruggles, Timothy (1711–1795), served in the Massachusetts General Court twenty-three years between 1739 and 1770. He commanded a regiment at Crown Point in 1755, was second in command at Lake George, and led a brigade in General Amherst's Canadian expedition. When a delegate to the Stamp-Act Congress in New York in 1765, and its president, he refused to sign the addresses and petitions. He espoused the British cause during the Revolution.

Rule of 1756, a rule of international law laid down by the English Courts in the War of 1756, to the effect that where a European country has forbidden trade with its colonies in times of peace, it shall not open it to neutrals in time of war. In 1793 the English Prize Courts enforced this doctrine against American neutral carriers, the U. S. Government protesting.

"Rum, Romanism and Rebellion." At a meeting of clergy, in which all denominations were supposed to be represented, held in the Fifth Avenue Hotel, New York, during the Presidential campaign of 1884 in the interest of the Republicans, Rev. R. B. Burchard described the Democrats as the party of "Rum, Romanism and Rebellion." This remark was unfortunate for the Republicans, and aided in a great measure to win the election for the Democrats.

Rumford, Benjamin Thompson, Count (1753–1814), of Massachusetts, sympathized with the pre-Revolutionary movements, but the jealousy of his fellow-officers in the New Hampshire regiments alienated his patriotism. He carried dispatches from Howe to England in 1776. He raised the "King's American Dragoons" in New York in 1781 and was appointed lieutenant-colonel. He went to England in 1783. He entered the service of the Elector of Bavaria, acquired great influence, and was made prime minister and a count in 1790. He contributed valuable observations and discoveries to science, particularly on the nature and effects of heat and in chemistry, of which he was one of the founders.

Rumsey, James (1743–1792), of Maryland, invented a steamboat in 1786, but died in England before he could perfect his invention.

Rush, Benjamin (1745–1813), was prominent in the pre-Revolutionary movements. He was chairman of the committee of the Pennsylvania Conference which decided for independence. He was a member of the Continental Congress in 1776 and signed the Declaration of Independence. He was physician-general of the Middle Department from 1777 to 1778, and was a member of the Pennsylvania Convention of 1787. He was treasurer of the U. S. Mint from 1799 to 1813. His observations and discoveries in medical science were second to none, and he was noted for philanthropy.

Rush, Richard (1780–1859), was Attorney-General of Pennsylvania in 1811, Attorney-General of the United States in Madison's Cabinet from 1814 to 1817, temporary Secretary of State in 1817, Minister to England from 1817 to 1825, and Secretary of the Treasury in J. Q. Adams' Cabinet from 1825 to 1829. He was candidate for Vice-President of the United States on the ticket with Adams in 1828. He was Minister to France from 1847 to 1851. He published "Memorials of a Residence at the Court of St. James."

Rusk, Jeremiah M. (1830–1893), entered the National army in 1862, and served under General Sherman with the rank of lieutenant-colonel from the siege of Vicksburg till 1865. He represented Wisconsin in the U. S. Congress as a Republican from 1871 to 1877, and was Governor of Wisconsin from 1882 to 1888. He was Secretary of Agriculture in Harrison's Cabinet from 1889 to 1893.

Rusk, Thomas J. (1802–1856), was active in the struggle of Texas for independence. He represented Texas in the U. S. Senate as a Democrat from 1846 to 1856.

Russell, Benjamin (1761–1845), of Massachusetts, founded the *Columbian Centinel*, a Federalist organ of great influence, which he edited till 1828. He published the *Boston Gazette* from 1795 to 1830. He originated the phrase "era of good feeling," and the word "gerrymander."

Russell, William E., was born in 1857. He was mayor of Cambridge, Mass., from 1885 to 1889. He was Governor of Massachusetts from 1890 to 1893. He advocated tariff and industrial reforms, and was a prominent leader of the young democracy.

Russia. Russia has always been particularly friendly to the United States, recognizing its independence immediately upon the settlement of peace with Great Britain in 1783. By the Treaty of 1824 the navigation and fisheries of the Pacific were regulated, and a favorable commercial treaty was secured in 1832 by the United States. A convention relative to neutral rights at sea was concluded in 1854. By the Treaty of 1867 Russia ceded all its American possessions to the United States for $7,200,000. An extradition treaty long pending went into effect June 24, 1893.

Rutgers College, New Brunswick, N. J., was established by royal charter in 1770 under the name of Queen's College. It received its present name in 1825 in honor of a gift of $5000 from Colonel Henry Rutgers. Till 1865 it was controlled by the synod of the Protestant Reformed Church, which church must still furnish its president and three-fourths of its trustees. During the Revolution its exercises were suspended, and till 1863 the college suffered from financial embarrassments. Since then it has greatly increased in endowment and influence.

Rutgers vs. Waddington, a case tried before Mayor James Duane, of New York, in 1784. Under the provisions of the "Trespass Act," passed some time before by the New York State Legislature, Elizabeth Rutgers had sued Joshua Waddington, a wealthy Tory merchant, for unlawful trespass upon and possession of certain real estate. Alexander Hamilton appeared for the defendant. It was alleged that the Trespass Act was contrary to the provisions of the Treaty of 1783, by which protection was promised the Tories, and likewise violated principles of the law of nations. The court, however, refused to assume jurisdiction over acts of Assembly, to set them aside on any ground. It gave the case to the defendant by an equitable interpretation of the statute itself.

Rutledge, Edward (1749–1800), was a delegate from South Carolina to the Continental Congress from 1774 to 1777. He signed the Declaration of Independence. He was a member of the first Board of War in 1776, and a member of the committee to draw up Articles of Confederation. He was a commissioner to confer with Lord Howe in 1776. He commanded a company of artillery during the siege of Charleston. He was a member of the South Carolina Legislature from 1782 to 1798, and Governor of South Carolina from 1798 to 1800.

Rutledge, John (1739–1800), an eminent statesman of South Carolina, attended the Stamp Act Congress of 1765, and the First and Second Continental Congresses. He was in 1776 the president of the State Government, and served as Governor 1779–1782. He was also Chancellor of the State, and a member of the Federal Convention of 1787. Rutledge ranked among the Federalist leaders. President Washington appointed him in 1795 Chief Justice of the U. S. Supreme Court, but the nomination was rejected by the Senate.

Ryswick, Treaty of, in 1697, ended the war which, in Europe, was called the War of the Grand Alliance; in America, King William's War.

S.

Sabine Cross Roads, La. Here during Banks' Red River expedition of 1864 General Banks' advance-guard of 8000 Federals was defeated, as it marched toward Shreveport, by 20,000 Confederates led by Kirby Smith. Banks was totally unprepared for battle, his line of march extending over twenty miles. Suddenly, April 8, the Confederates emerged from the forest and bore down upon the disorganized line, and charged the Federals with great fury. Their line gave way almost immediately. The Confederates pursued them over three miles, until, at Pleasant Grove, Emory's division was met drawn up to receive them. A brief skirmish followed, and then the Confederates desisted. Banks lost heavily.

Sackett's Harbor, N. Y. The first attack upon this place in the War of 1812, was made on July 29, 1812, by a fleet of five British vessels that bombarded the fortifications. They were repulsed with the loss of thirty-two men killed and wounded; the Americans lost not a man. A second and last attempt was made May 29, 1813. Six British vessels and forty bateaux with 1000 troops aboard under command of Governor-General Sir George Prevost, attacked the militia and regulars under General Jacob Brown. The militia fled at the first fire; therefore, the officers in charge of the storehouses, thinking the Americans defeated, set fire to the storehouses, whereby half a million dollars' worth of supplies were destroyed. General Brown, however, succeeded in rallying the militia, and the British, believing them to be reinforcements, turned and fled, leaving their dead and wounded behind.

Sackville, Lord. (See West, Lionel Sackville-.)

Sacramento, Cal., was founded in 1841, and became the capital of California in 1845. It obtained a city charter in 1863.

Sacramento, N. M., a narrow pass where, February 23, 1847, the American Colonel Doniphan defeated a force of Chihuahuans four times superior in numbers to his own.

Sacs, an Algonquin tribe of Indians, formerly centred near the Detroit River, were driven beyond Lake Michigan by the Iroquois and settled near Green Bay, where they subsequently joined with the Foxes. They aided Pontiac, and during the Revolution supported the English. In 1812, the Rock River Sacs aided Great Britain. In 1804 and 1816 they ceded lands. Their later history is that of the Foxes.

Safety Fund, the beginning of reform in the banking system. The Safety Fund Act was passed by the New York Legislature in 1829, upon the suggestion of Governor Martin Van Buren. It required that banks chartered by the State should pay into the State Treasury a certain percentage of their capital stock to serve as a fund out of which the liabilities of any of them that might fail should be made good. But the deposit was eventually found too small, and a different system was adopted later.

Sage, Russell, born in 1816, represented New York in the U. S. Congress as a Whig from 1853 to 1857. He has had immense interests in railroads, for many of which he has been a director.

St. Augustine, Fla., the oldest town in the United States, was settled by the Spaniards under Menendez in 1565, when a fort was erected. It was several times attacked by the French, English and Indians. It came into the possession of the English by the Treaty of 1763, was ceded to Spain in 1783, and transferred to the United States in 1819.

St. Brandan's Isle, a legendary island supposed to have existed to the southwest of the Canary Islands and to have been discovered by the Irish Monk, St. Brandan, and seventy-five brother monks in the sixth century, after seven years spent in the search for the land of saints. This legend is traceable as far back as the eleventh century. Each of the various early geographers gives it a different location. The legend had some influence upon the discovery of America.

St. Charles, Ark., occupied in 1862 by the Confederates, 100 strong, under Williams and protected by Fry with a gunboat, the "Maurepas," and several batteries. The Federals under Commander Kilty and Colonel Graham stormed and took this place June 17. They had five gunboats and a regiment.

St. Clair, Arthur (1734–1818), came to America as a British soldier in 1758. He served under General Amherst at Louisbourg, and distinguished himself at Quebec. Joining the American cause, he accompanied General Sullivan in the expedition to Canada in 1776. He commanded a brigade at Trenton and Princeton. He was appointed major-general and succeeded General Gates at Ticonderoga, which he surrendered in 1777. He fought at Yorktown. He represented Pennsylvania in the Continental Congress from 1785 to 1787, and was Governor of the Northwest Territory from 1789 to 1802.

St. John, John P., born in 1833, served during the Civil War, attaining the rank of lieutenant-colonel. He served in the Kansas Senate from 1873 to 1874, and was Governor of Kansas from 1878 to 1882. He was the candidate of the Prohibition party for President of the United States in 1884.

St. John's College, Annapolis, Md., was chartered in 1784, opened five years later. It was closed during the Civil War.

St. Joseph, Fort, an English fort situated, in 1781, within the limits of the present State of Michigan. It was captured that same year by sixty-five Spanish militiamen and sixty Indians, under Don Eugenio Pourré, from the Spanish settlement at St. Louis on the Mississippi. The avowed intention of Spain in this expedition was hostility to England, but in reality it meant proposed encroachment on our possessions, a fact quickly perceived by John Jay and Benjamin Franklin, then ministers at Madrid and Paris, respectively.

Saint Leger, Barry (1737–1789), came to America as a British soldier in 1757. He commanded a company at Louisbourg in 1758 and served under Wolfe at Quebec in 1759. He commanded the British expedition against Fort Stanwix and distinguished himself by his strategy at Oriskany. From 1780 to 1781 he conducted a guerilla warfare, with headquarters at Montreal.

St. Louis, Mo., settled as a trading post in 1764, was occupied by Spanish troops in 1771 and was under Spanish rule for thirty years. In May, 1780, the town was attacked by Indians and thirty citizens killed. In 1803 it became American, and the seat of government of the "District of Louisiana;" in 1822 a city. In 1849 St. Louis was visited by an extensive conflagration which destroyed many of the business houses of the town. Population in 1810, 1600; in 1860, 160,773; in 1890, 450,245.

Saint Luc, La Corne de (1712–1784), was active against the British during the old French War. He led the Indians on the left column in Montcalm's expedition against Fort William Henry. He distinguished himself at Ticonderoga in 1758. He engaged in the contests about Quebec in 1760. He espoused the cause of the crown during the Revolutionary War and received the co-operation of the Indians.

St. Lusson, Simon F. D., Sieur de, was sent to explore the Lake Region in 1670. In 1675 he concluded a treaty with seventeen Indian tribes and took possession of the country for France.

St. Mary's, the first settlement made in Maryland. Governor Calvert, with his ship, the "Ark," effected a landing, March 27, 1634, and the emigrants took possession of their new home, calling it St. Mary's. The town afterward went to decay.

St. Paul, Minn., was settled as a trading post in 1838, and laid out in 1849–50. It was the capital of Minnesota from the origination of the territorial government in 1849.

St. Philip, Fort (Mississippi River, below New Orleans). This fort, considered the key to Louisiana, was garrisoned by about 400 men under Major Overton, when, January 9, 1815, an attack upon it was made by five British vessels. The bombardment lasted nine days and resulted in the killing of two Americans and the wounding of seven others. The British withdrew without capturing the fort. In the Civil War, this fort was garrisoned by a small Confederate force under General Duncan. It was on the north side of the bend in the Mississippi River. It was bombarded during Farragut's expedition against New Orleans and surrendered to General Butler, April 27, 1862.

St. Regis (on the boundary between Nova Scotia and Canada), an Indian village occupied by the British, and captured October 22, 1812, by Major Young. Forty prisoners, army supplies and a flag were among the spoils.

St. Simon, an island off the coast of Georgia, south of Savannah, ceded to James Oglethorpe by the Creek Indians under the treaty of 1733. In 1742 it was attacked by a Spanish fleet of fifty-one sail under Monteano, Governor of St. Augustine. Oglethorpe drove off the Spaniards with a small force.

Salaries, Congressional. Clause 1 of Art. I, Sect. 6, of the Constitution provides that "the Senators and Representatives shall receive a compensation for their services, to be ascertained by law, and paid out of the Treasury of the United States." Under the Articles of Confederation each State provided payment for its own members of Congress, but in the convention of

1787 it was thought best that they be made independent of their States in this respect. Pinckney suggested that the Senate, representing the wealth of the country, be allowed no salary, but the proposition was voted down. The First Congress voted that its members be paid $6.00 per day and $6.00 for each twenty miles of travel going and coming. The rates have been repeatedly changed. They were: From 1789 to 1815, $6.00 per day; from 1815 to 1817, $1500 per year; from 1817 to 1855, $8.00 per day; from 1855 to 1865, $3000 per year; from 1865 to 1871, $5000 per year; from 1871 to 1874, $7500 per year; and since 1874, $5000 per year. The Senators and Representatives have received the same compensation, except during 1795, when the Senators received $7.00 per day. The Speaker of the House and the president *pro tempore* of the Senate receive $8000 per year. A mileage of twenty cents is allowed. The change in 1816 from $6.00 per day to $1500 per year was received with great disfavor, as was that of 1873, to take effect from March 4, 1871, which is known as the "salary grab." All changes in Congressional salaries have been retroactive, covering from twelve to twenty-four months. Acts affecting salaries prior to 1866 were separate acts. Since then they have frequently been sections of an appropriation act.

Salaries, Executive. By the Act of Congress of September 24, 1789, and again February 18, 1793, the salary of the President was made $25,000, that of the Vice-President $5000. That of the President continued the same until March 3, 1873, when it was raised to $50,000. The salary of the Vice-President was raised to $8000 in 1853, to $10,000 March 3, 1873, and was reduced to $8000 again January 20, 1874. These salaries are paid monthly. A furnished house is provided for the President. The Constitution provides that a salary shall be voted for the President, which shall not be diminished during his term of office. Hence that part of the "salary grab" act of 1873 which affected his salary was not repealed. Of the Cabinet officers, the Secretary of State and the Secretary of the Treasury received in 1789 a salary of $3500, the Secretary of War $3000, the Attorney-General $1500. The Postmaster-General had $2000. In 1819, the salary of the four secretaries was made $6000, that of the Postmaster-General $4000, and that of the Attorney-General $3500. In 1853, all were made equal, $8000; in 1873, $10,000; in 1874, $8000 again.

Salaries, Judicial. The Constitution provides that the salaries of judges, voted by Congress, shall not be lessened during their term of office. When the courts were first organized in 1789, the Chief Justice of the Supreme Court was paid $4000, the Associate Justices $3500 each. The District Judges received from $1000 to $1800. These salaries have been raised from time to time. Since March, 1873, the Chief Justice of the Supreme Court has received $10,500; the Associate Justices $10,000; the Circuit Court Judges $6,000 each, and the District Judges from $3500 to $5000, until 1891, when the salary of all District Judges was fixed at $5000.

Salary Grab, the popular name for the general increase in Federal salaries in 1873. The Constitution provides for the compensation of the President, Senators, Representatives, Justices and Federal officers from the

Federal treasury. The Act of March 3, 1873, provided that the President's salary be increased from $25,000 to $50,000, that of the Chief Justice from $8500 to $10,500, those of the Vice-President, Cabinet officers, Associate Justices and Speaker of the House from $8000 to $10,000, and of Senators and Representatives from $5000 to $7500. Another Act, March 4, 1873, was retroactive as regarded the salaries of members of Congress during the previous two years. This, the essence of the "salary grab," excited so much indignation that the laws were repealed, except those affecting the salaries of the President and Justices.

Salem, Mass. The first house was built here in 1626 by Roger Conant, and the town was settled in 1628 by John Endicott. The next year eleven ships came from England bringing 406 immigrants who settled in the vicinity. In this year the first church organization in the Massachusetts colony was effected here. In 1692 the town was stirred up by the famous witchcraft delusion which resulted in the execution of nineteen alleged witches on Gallows Hill. The town was incorporated in 1630 and assumed a city government in 1836.

Salem, Oregon, was settled in 1834, incorporated in 1853, and became capital of the State in 1860.

Salisbury, N. C., a Confederate prison camp defended by Gardiner with 3000 soldiers. It was captured April 12, 1865, by 4000 Federal cavalry under Stoneman. All its guns and 1364 prisoners were taken, besides enormous quantities of ammunition and provisions.

Salt Lake City, capital of Utah, was settled by the Mormons under Brigham Young in 1847.

Saltonstall, Dudley (1738–1796), was commodore of the expedition against a British post on the Penobscot River in 1779, where the disastrous defeat by Sir George Collier was charged to him.

Saltonstall, Gurdon (1666–1724), was Governor of Connecticut from 1708 to 1724. He was prominent in the political affairs of the colony, and distinguished for his learning and eloquence.

Saltonstall, Sir Richard (1586–1658), came to Massachusetts from England in 1630 as Assistant to Winthrop. He began the settlement of Watertown, but returned to England in 1631. He was a patentee of Connecticut, and sent a vessel to take possession of the territory. He wrote letters of remonstrance to John Cotton and John Wilson in regard to the persecution of persons for their religious convictions.

Salvation Army. The United States branch of this organization, which originated in England in 1865, was established in 1880. There are now in this country 536 corps and outposts, about 1700 officers, with 15,000 adherents.

Salzburgers. Numerous immigrants from among these people, Protestants driven out by the oppressions of the Prince-Bishop of Salzburg, settled in what was afterward Georgia previous to the granting of Oglethorpe's patent in 1733. Their chief settlement was a mere hamlet called Ebenezer. They and the Highlanders aided Oglethorpe considerably in his troubles with the Spaniards and unfriendly Indians. They owned land on the communal system. They were chiefly farmers and Indian traders and were opposed to the introduction of negroes.

Sam, a nickname of the American or "Know-nothing" party, current from 1854 to 1860.

Samoa. The United States concluded a treaty of friendship and commerce with Samoa in 1878. German aggressions and native difficulties resulted in the establishment of a joint protectorate of the islands by the United States, Germany and Great Britain by the treaty of Berlin in 1889.

Samoset, born about 1590, was a chief of the Pemaquid Indians in Maine. He learned English from the colonists of Monhegan Island, sent out by Sir Ferdinando Gorges. Soon after the landing of the Pilgrims he entered Plymouth, saying, "Welcome, Englishmen." He brought Squanto, who had visited England, to act as interpreter, and manifested a friendly interest toward the colonists.

San Antonio, Tex., was founded in 1714 by the Spaniards. A fort and a mission were established. The city was an important centre during the Mexican and Texan Wars. It was incorporated in 1733.

San Diego, Cal. A settlement made near the site of the present city by Father Junipero in 1768 was the first in the State.

San Domingo. The revolt of the blacks of San Domingo, under Toussaint Louverture against the French had an important connection with the history of the United States. Bonaparte as First Consul conceived the idea of forming a great French colonial empire in the Mississippi Valley, to balance the influence of the Anglo-Saxon race in America. To this end he acquired Louisiana from Spain by the treaty of San Ildefonso. But San Domingo was to be his military base, and its reconquest was to be a first step. His failure in attempts to recover it, coming at the same time with the opportunity of renewing war with England, caused him, instantly abandoning the whole scheme, to sell Louisiana to the United States.

San Domingo. (See also Dominican Republic.)

San Domingo Question. In 1869 the desirability of San Domingo as a coaling station for U. S. vessels and other American interests there caused a movement toward the annexation of that republic to the United States. President Grant sent General Babcock to examine into the matter and, on his favorable report, a treaty was concluded November 29, 1869. The Senate rejected the treaty June 30, 1870, and the movement became generally unpopular. Grant still persisted and Congress concurred in sending a commission, consisting of Wade, White and Howe, to examine the matter in 1871. Their report was favorable, but Congress continued to disapprove of annexation. Grant abandoned the question in a special message in April, 1871.

San Francisco, Cal., was settled as a fortified town and Spanish mission in 1776. In 1846 an American man-of-war took possession of the place. The discovery of gold in 1849 caused the city to grow enormously. The city was granted a charter in 1850. Three disastrous fires occurred in that year amounting to about $8,000,000 in property destroyed.

San Ildefonso, Treaty of, a secret treaty between France and Spain, October 1, 1800, by which Louisiana was retroceded by Spain to France in consideration of an agreement advantageous to the royal family of Spain relative to Tuscany. This treaty was directly instrumental in bringing about the purchase of Louisiana by the United States in 1803.

San Jacinto, Battle of, fought in 1836, was the closing battle of the war for Texan independence. General Houston, at the head of about 700 Texans, defeated 1536 Mexicans under Santa Anna. Many of General Houston's troops had openly enlisted in New Orleans and the independence of Texas was looked upon with favor by the U. S. Government.

San Juan de Ulua, a fortified castle on an island in the harbor of Vera Cruz, Mexico. General Winfield Scott bombarded the city and fort from March 22 to 28, 1847. March 29, both city and fort were called upon to surrender and agreed to do so.

San Juan Question. In negotiating the treaty of 1846, by which the forty-ninth parallel, from the Rocky Mountains to the sea, was made the boundary between the American and British possessions, a controversy arose concerning the course of the line through the channel which divides Vancouver Island from the mainland. The Americans contended for the Canal de Haro, the British for the Rosario Strait. To avoid conflict, it was decided that both nations occupy the island of San Juan at opposite ends. In 1872 the German Emperor, acting as arbitrator, decided for America.

San Salvador. A treaty of amity, commerce and navigation was concluded between the United States and San Salvador in 1850. May 23, 1870, an extradition convention was signed, and on December 6 a treaty of amity, commerce and consular privileges was concluded. A reciprocity treaty was concluded in 1891.

Sanborn, Franklin B., born in 1831, has been prominent in the reform of caritative institutions. He aided in organizing the American Social Science Association and became its secretary in 1873. He wrote a "Life of Thoreau," and "Life and Letters of John Brown."

Sand-Lots. In 1879 the followers of Dennis Kearney, a labor agitator of San Francisco, were wont to assemble in the vacant lots of the city, called "the sand-lots," to listen to his inflammatory speeches. He was called the Sand-lot Orator.

"Sand-lot Constitution," the California constitution of 1879.

Sands, Benjamin F. (1811–1883), commanded the "Dacotah" at Fort Caswell in 1862. He was senior officer of the North Carolina Blockading Squadron from 1862 to 1865. He commanded the "Fort Jackson" in both attacks on Fort Fisher.

Sands, Joshua R. (1795–1883), fought in the engagement with the "Royal George" in 1812. He commanded the "Vixen" during the Mexican War, fighting at Alvarado, Tabasco, Laguna and Tuxpan.

Sands, Robert C. (1799–1832), of New York, was assistant editor of the *New York Review* from 1825 to 1827, and of the *Commercial Advertiser* from 1827 to 1832. He wrote with Bryant and Verplanck "The Talisman."

Sandy Creek. An American flotilla with supplies for the fleet at Sackett's Harbor was attacked here May 30, 1814, by two gunboats, but defeated and captured them. The British lost sixty-eight killed and wounded and 170 prisoners.

Sandys, Sir Edwin (1561–1629), was an active member of the first London Company for Virginia. He was made treasurer of the company in 1619. He established representative government in Virginia, and contributed largely to its prosperity. He aided the Pilgrims in securing a charter.

Sandys, George (1577–1644), was treasurer of Virginia from 1621 to 1624. He built the first water-mill, the first iron-works and the first ship in Virginia, and his translation of Ovid was English America's first literary production.

Sanford, Nathan (1777–1838), was a U. S. District-Attorney from 1803 to 1816. He represented New York in the U. S. Senate as a Democrat from 1815 to 1821 and from 1826 to 1831.

Santa Anna, Antonio Lopez de (1795–1876), a turbulent Mexican politician, entered the Spanish army in Mexico, sided finally with the patriots, opposed Iturbide, and became a politico-military leader of national prominence. He was President 1832–1835. The next year he marched against the Texan revolutionists, stormed the Alamo, and was defeated by Houston at San Jacinto and captured. He was head of the executive in 1839, and again President 1841–1844; overthrown, he was once more President in 1846, and in 1847 was beaten by Taylor at Buena Vista. After Scott's victories and conquest of the capital Santa Anna resigned, but reappeared as President and dictator in 1853–1855. He frequently attempted to regain power, and was a marshal under the empire, but died in obscurity.

Santa Barbara, Cal., occupies the site of a mission founded in 1786. It was visited by an earthquake in 1806. It was occupied by U. S. troops during Frémont's campaign.

Santa Fe, N. M., was first visited by the Spaniards in 1542 and settled in 1609, according to the latest authorities. It was captured by the Indians in 1680 and the settlement burned. It was recaptured in 1694. It has suffered several subsequent attacks from the natives, the most serious being in 1837. It was occupied August 18, 1846, by an American army under General Kearny after a march of sixteen days from Bent's Fort on the Arkansas River. The occupation was achieved without bloodshed. From captured parties of scouts it was learned that the Mexican General Armijo was lying in wait with a large army, but no engagement took place.

Santa Rosa Island, Fla., was attacked the night of October 9, 1861, by Confederate soldiers, who surprised and routed Wilson's New York Zouaves, but were themselves compelled to retire the next day.

Saratoga, Battle of, September 19, October 7, October 17, 1777. Baum's defeat at Bennington and St. Leger's failure at Fort Stanwix rendered Burgoyne's position perilous. The Continental armies were daily increasing, and there were no signs of help from Howe. Burgoyne determined to take the offensive and crossed the Hudson. The Americans, under Gates, held a strong position at Bemis' Heights. Burgoyne decided to storm their encampment and to try to turn their flank simultaneously. His plan was discovered and thwarted by Arnold, who made a furious opposition until he too was outflanked by Riedesel, who had been dispatched against the Heights. It was a drawn battle. Gates showed his incompetency by keeping his 11,000 men in camp, while Arnold with 3000 held the British in check. The battle was bloody, both British and Americans losing a fourth of the men engaged. For eighteen days nothing was done. Then news came to Burgoyne that his supplies were cut off, and he was forced to engage again, though he had but 4000 to oppose to 16,000. Again with 1500 picked men under Fraser he tried to turn the American flank and again Arnold thwarted him. Both Fraser and Arnold were disabled. The Americans gained the field. October 7, Gates with 20,000 men followed up the retreating army, who found their passage across the Hudson blocked. No word reached Burgoyne from Clinton, and he accordingly treated in regard to surrender. The terms agreed upon were that the British should march out with honors of war, lay down their arms, march to Boston, embark for England and not serve against Americans again. This was called the "Convention of Saratoga," to respect Burgoyne's feelings. Arms were laid down October 17. Thus failed the first attempt to cut in twain the American military line. The Convention was broken by Congress.

Sardinia. The United States concluded a commercial treaty with Sardinia in 1838.

Sargent, Aaron A. (1827–1887), represented California in the U. S. Congress as a Republican from 1861 to 1863, and from 1869 to 1873, and was a U. S. Senator from 1873 to 1879. He was Minister to Germany from 1882 to 1884.

Sassacus, (1560 ?–1637), chief of the Pequot Indians, led an attack on a fort at Saybrook and massacred its inmates. The English under John Mason destroyed the Pequot settlement in 1637.

Saulsbury, Eli (1817–1893) represented Delaware in the U. S. Senate as a Democrat from 1871 to 1889.

Saulsbury, Willard (1820–1892), was Attorney-General of Delaware from 1850 to 1855. He represented Delaware in the U. S. Senate as a Democrat from 1859 to 1871. He earnestly supported the Union and sought to prevent the Civil War. He formed the famous Saulsbury combination with his brothers Gove and Eli, which ruled Delaware politics for thirty years. He was Chancellor of Delaware from 1874 to 1892.

Sault Ste. Marie, Mich., was first settled in 1641 by Jesuits, and during the seventeenth century was famous as a centre for missionary expeditions and explorations.

Saunders, Alvin, born in 1817, was territorial Governor of Nebraska from 1861 to 1867. He represented Nebraska in the U. S. Senate as a Republican from 1877 to 1883.

Saunders, Romulus M. (1791–1867), represented North Carolina in the U. S. Congress as a Democrat from 1821 to 1827 and from 1841 to 1845. He was Minister to Spain from 1846 to 1849.

Savage's Station, Va., a battle during McClellan's Peninsular campaign, occurring June 29, 1862. Magruder, with a detachment of Lee's army, while moving along the Williamsburg road, came upon Sumner and Heintzelman retiring toward Savage's Station with a large number of McClellan's troops. An engagement immediately took place, the Confederates attacking Sumner's corps, which was endeavoring to bar the road into the White Oak Swamp. Sumner maintained his ground stoutly against repeated assaults, and in the evening the national army retired into the swamp.

Savannah, Ga., was settled in 1733 by Oglethorpe, as the first settlement in the colony. In the Revolution it was captured by the British. In December, 1778, 3000 British under Colonel Campbell attacked Savannah. Howe, the American commander, held out against a force three times his own until a negro guided the British to the American rear. The British lost but twenty-four, and secured the capital of Georgia and 400 prisoners. In September, 1779, the French under D'Estaing and the Americans under Lincoln undertook the siege of Savannah. The plan was to make two real and two feigned attacks before dawn. The plan miscarried. A brave but unavailing assault was made, in which Sergeant Jasper distinguished himself by rescuing his colors, though twice mortally wounded. After an obstinate struggle of fifty-five minutes the assailants were driven back. The British loss was trifling. The French and Americans lost about 800 men. Estaing sailed away and Georgia was left in the undisputed possession of the British.—In 1864 the city was occupied, after ten days' siege and fighting, December 10 to 21, by Sherman as the finale of his celebrated march to the sea. Sherman's army was 60,000 strong. Hardee held Savannah with 15,000 Confederates. After great difficulty experienced in approaching the town, Sherman began his investment December 10. On the 12th, Hazen was sent with his division of the Fifteenth Corps to capture Fort McAlister, since Sherman desired to communicate with the Federal fleet, which lay off Savannah under the command of Dahlgren. Hazen took the fort, which was manned by 200 Confederates and had twenty-three guns, after about fifteen minutes of desperate assault, and communication with the fleet was established. Thereupon Sherman summoned Hardee to surrender, but the latter refused. Sherman accordingly put his siege guns in position and prepared for assault. Hardee, seeing himself about to be surrounded, evacuated the city on the night of the 20th by means of a pontoon bridge.

Savings Banks. (See Banks, Savings.)

Sawyer, Philetus, born in 1816, represented Wisconsin in the U. S. Congress as a Republican from 1865 to 1875. He was a member of the U. S. Senate from 1881 to 1893.

Saxe, John G. (1816–1887), was prominent in journalism, but won distinction by his poems, mostly humorous.

Saxony. The droit d'aubaine and taxes on emigration were abolished by the Convention of 1845 between the United States and Saxony.

Saybrook, Conn., was founded in 1635 by a party sent out by John Winthrop, and was given its name in 1639 by George Fenwick, who conveyed the settlement to the jurisdiction of Connecticut in 1644. It was named for Lords Saye and Brooke.

Saybrook Platform. May 13, 1708, at the suggestion of the Colonial Legislature of Connecticut, a synod of four lay delegates and twelve ministers met at Saybrook to adopt some more energetic system of church government than then existed. They adopted the Confession of Faith of the Reforming Synod held at Boston in 1680 and provided for "one consociation or more" of churches in each county "for mutual affording to each other such assistance as may be requisite, upon all occasions ecclesiastical," and that a general association of church representatives should meet each year at election time.

Saye and Sele, William Fiennes, Lord (1582–1662), a Puritan lord, was prominent in colonization enterprises. In 1632 he and others obtained a grant for a colony on the Connecticut River, afterward called Saybrook, from his name and that of Lord Brooke. In 1633 he procured a grant in New Hampshire.

Schaff, Philip, born in Switzerland in 1819, died 1893, was president of the American Bible Revision Committee. He was president of the Society of Church History from 1888 till his death. He published an important "History of the Christian Church."

Schaumburg-Lippe. Schaumburg-Lippe acceded to the German extradition convention with the United States in 1854.

Schell, Augustus (1812–1884), was chairman of the New York Democratic Committee from 1853 to 1856, and of the National Committee in 1860 and 1872. After the overthrow of the Tweed ring he was active in reorganizing Tammany.

Schenectady, N. Y., was settled in 1661 by Arent Van Corlear, who erected a fort here. The Indians and French massacred nearly all the inhabitants on February 9, 1690, and in 1748 again a large number of people were killed. It was incorporated as a city in 1798. Union College was incorporated here in 1795.

Schenk, Robert C. (1809–1890), represented Ohio in the U. S. Congress as a Whig from 1843 to 1851. He was Minister to Brazil from 1851 to 1853, negotiating important commercial treaties. He commanded a brigade at Bull Run, and served under General Rosecrans in the Shenandoah Valley. He led a division at Cross Keys and was engaged in the second battle of Bull Run. He again served in the U. S. Congress as a Republican from

1863 to 1871. He served on the Joint High Commission which negotiated the Treaty of Washington, and was Minister to England from 1871 to 1876.

Schley, Winfield S., born in 1839, engaged in the capture of Port Hudson in 1862. He commanded the expedition which rescued A. W. Greely at Cape Sabine, in Grinnell Land, in 1884.

Schlosser, Fort, near Niagara, a fort held by Major Mallory which was captured and burned by the British, December, 1813, during the raid of Colonel Murray in retaliating for the burning of Newark.

Schofield, John M., born in 1831, was graduated at West Point in 1853. In the beginning of the war he served in Missouri. Afterward he held command of that department and later of the Department of the Ohio. In the Atlanta campaign he commanded a corps. He defeated Hood at the battle of Franklin, November 30, 1864, and fought at the following battle of Nashville. In the beginning of 1865 he commanded in North Carolina, and united his force with Sherman's army. He was then sent on a special mission to France. Since that time he has been a department commander, except in 1868–1869, when he was Secretary of War, and 1876–1881, when he was Superintendent at West Point. He was made major-general in 1869, and succeeded Sheridan as commander-in-chief in 1888.

Schoolcraft, Henry Rowe (1793–1864), an expert on Indian affairs and ethnologist, studied the natural sciences and passed many years as Indian agent for the Government in the region of the great lakes. Mackinaw was his headquarters. He led a Government expedition in 1832. At various times he was commissioned in regard to Indian matters. Besides poems, Schoolcraft wrote a number of books of travel, and works relating to American languages and antiquities.

Schools. There has been much controversy as to whether the public school, *i. e.*, the school supported by the public and free to the poor, was first established in New England (Massachusetts) or in New Netherland, with the weight of evidence inclining to the latter. The Boston Latin School seems to be the direct successor of one founded in 1635, the Roxbury Latin School was founded in 1657, the Penn Charter School at Philadelphia in 1698. Governor Berkeley's famous remark made in 1670, that he thanked God there were no free schools in Virginia, is often quoted. The South being thinly settled, efforts to maintain schools were seldom successful. Boys were sent abroad, or were educated by tutors or by the parish clergyman or by lettered servants. In New England a certain amount of education was general and compulsory. The Society for the Propagation of the Gospel in Foreign Parts did something for education in American colonies. The disorders of the Revolutionary period probably caused some falling off in elementary education. The Constitution left the matter to the States. The "Blair Bill," which passed the Senate in 1884 and 1886, proposing to give Federal money to States, in proportion to the number of their illiterates, for education, was defeated in the House.

Schouler, James, of Massachusetts, born in 1839, has published many valuable legal treatises and an excellent "History of the United States under the Constitution," in five volumes. Since 1889 he has lectured on American History at the Johns Hopkins University.

Schurman, Jacob G., born in 1854, Canadian educator, became professor of philosophy at Cornell University in 1884, and its president in 1892. He has published "Kantian Ethics and the Ethics of Evolution," and "The Ethical Import of Darwinism."

Schurz, Carl, was born in 1829 at Cologne, in Prussia. He took part in the revolutionary movements of 1849, escaped from Germany, and eventually settled in the United States. He soon attracted attention as an able political orator; President Lincoln appointed him Minister to Spain in 1861, but he resigned and entered the army. He commanded a division at the second battle of Bull Run and at Chancellorsville, and had charge of a corps at Gettysburg. After the war he was a journalist. In 1869–1875 he was Republican U. S. Senator from Missouri. He was active in the Liberal Republican movement of 1872. He was Secretary of the Interior in President Hayes' Cabinet 1877–1881; editor of the New York *Evening Post* 1881–1884, and has since been engaged in business. His life of Clay is in the Statesmen Series.

Schuyler, Eugene (1840–1890), was U. S. Consul at Moscow from 1866 to 1869, and at Reval from 1869 to 1870. He was secretary of the U. S. Legation at St. Petersburg from 1870 to 1876; was Consul-General at Constantinople from 1876 to 1878; Consul at Birmingham, England, from 1878 to 1879; Chargé d'Affaires and Consul-General at Bucharest from 1880 to 1882, and Minister Resident and Consul-General to Greece, Roumania and Servia from 1882 to 1884. He wrote a work on Turkestan, and "American Diplomacy and the Furtherance of Commerce."

Schuyler, Peter (1657–1724), enjoyed great influence with the Five Nations and negotiated many treaties. He commanded an expedition against the French on Lake Champlain in 1691. He was second in command in the expedition against Montreal in 1709. He went to England with five Indian chiefs in 1710 to solicit vigorous measures against the French. He was acting Governor of New York from 1719 to 1720.

Schuyler, Peter (1710–1762), of New York, commanded Oswego when captured by Montcalm in 1756. He led a regiment in 1759 under General Amherst during the conquest of Canada.

Schuyler, Philip John (November 22, 1733–November 18, 1804), an American general and statesman, was born at Albany. He fought in the French and Indian War, and was afterward a member of the New York Assembly and one of the leaders among the patriots. He was a delegate to the first Continental Congress in 1774, and was included in the first list of major-generals in the next year. Schuyler's familiarity with Northern New York fitted him for his assignment to the command in that region. There was soon unfortunately a divided authority in that department, as intrigues gave a command there also to General Gates. Schuyler was, in 1777, reinstated, and put in charge of the defence against Burgoyne's invasion. Before he could reap the results of his efforts he was superseded by Gates. General Schuyler resigned from the army in 1779, but continued to be a trusted adviser of Washington and Indian commissioner. He was frequently State Senator, and was a Federalist U. S. Senator in 1789–1791 and 1797–1798. He was a strong advocate of the canal system in the State. Life by Lossing.

Schuyler, Fort. After Herkimer's defeat at Oriskany there was danger of St. Leger's descending upon Albany. All depended upon the relief of Fort Schuyler. Contrary to the advice of his officers, General Schuyler sent a relief party of 800 volunteers. The fort was relieved and St. Leger's troops dispersed (August 16, 1777).

Schwatka, Frederick (1849–1892), commanded the Arctic expedition in 1878 which discovered traces of Sir John Franklin's party. In 1889 he made valuable discoveries relating to Aztec civilization.

Scioto Company, a land-speculating organization formed in 1787 for the purchase of territory along the Ohio and Scioto. John Cleves Symmes, Joel Barlow and William Duer, of New York, were largely interested. Barlow was sent to Europe in the company's interest as emigration agent. Symmes parcelled out the lands to other parties, the tract which now embraces the city of Cincinnati falling to the share of Matthias Denman, Robert Patterson and John Tilson, of New Jersey.

Scofield, Glenni W. (1817–1891), represented Pennsylvania in the U. S. Congress as a Republican from 1863 to 1875. He was Register of the U. S. Treasury from 1878 to 1881, and a Justice of the U. S. Court of Claims from 1881 to 1891.

Scotch-Irish, the name used in America to designate immigrants from the north of Ireland, mostly Presbyterians of Scotch descent. Scots had been settled in the north of Ireland during the "Plantation of Ulster" in the reign of James I. Thence some came to America early. But the large emigrations were just after the famous siege of Londonderry in 1689, and again in 1718 and the years immediately succeeding. The largest settlements of them were made in the hilly parts of Pennsylvania, in the valley of the Shenandoah, and in the Carolinas. In all these, they occupied the highland regions, back from the coast, and formed a sturdy, independent, Presbyterian population. Jackson, Calhoun, and many other eminent men were of this stock. In New England their chief settlements were at Londonderry, Antrim, etc., in New Hampshire, founded about 1719.

Scotch-Irish Congresses. The first was held at Columbia, Tenn., in May, 1889, at which time the Scotch-Irish Society was organized. The purpose of the society and the yearly conventions is the preservation of Scotch-Irish history and associations. The second Congress was convened at Pittsburgh, Pa., May 29–June 1, 1890; the third at Louisville, Ky., May, 1891;

the fourth at Atlanta, Ga., April 28, 1892; the fifth at Springfield, Ohio, in May, 1893; the sixth at Des Moines, Iowa, in June, 1894.

Scott, Dred (1810?–after 1857), a negro slave born in Missouri. His suit for freedom is known as the Dred Scott case (see art.). He was afterward owned by C. C. Chafee, of Massachusetts. In 1857 he was emancipated in St. Louis.

Scott, John M. (1730–1784), was one of the founders of the Sons of Liberty. He advocated extreme measures against England. He commanded a brigade at Long Island, and represented New York in the Continental Congress from 1780 to 1783.

Scott, Robert K., born in 1826, commanded a regiment at Fort Donelson and Shiloh. He led a brigade at Hatchie River and a division at Port Gibson and Champion Hills. He was Governor of South Carolina from 1868 to 1871.

Scott, Thomas A. (1824–1881), won distinction in the management of railroads. His energy and business qualifications contributed largely to the success of the Pennsylvania Railroad system.

Scott, Winfield (June 13, 1786–May 29, 1866), a distinguished American general, was born near Petersburg, Va. Educated at William and Mary College, he entered the army at the age of twenty-two. In the opening year of the War of 1812 he was taken prisoner at the battle of Queenstown Heights. Being released, he served in the campaign of 1813, was made a brigadier-general, and distinguished himself at the battles of Chippewa and Bridgewater in 1814. He was promoted to be major-general, and saw little more service for a generation. In the Nullification excitement he commanded at Charleston, and he served against the Seminoles and Creeks, succeeding Macomb as commander-in-chief of the U. S. army in 1841. In the second year of the Mexican War General Scott took command of the main army. He besieged and took Vera Cruz, stormed Cerro Gordo, and reached Puebla. Having rested his army, he pushed on to the plain of the capital, won the victories of Contreras, Churubusco, Molino del Rey and Chapultepec, and entered the city of Mexico, September 14, 1847. In 1852 he was the Whig candidate for President, and was overwhelmingly defeated by Pierce. Later he was engaged on a commission for rectifying the boundary line with Great Britain. The outbreak of the war found him still in command of the army, but he retired in October, 1861. Scott's imposing stature, strict discipline, and attachment to military etiquette won for him the epithet of "Old Fuss and Feathers."

Scott Law, a liquor law passed by the Legislature of Ohio in 1883. It forbids the selling of liquor on Sunday; levies a tax of $200 yearly on general liquor dealers, and $100 on sellers of malt liquors, the whole tax to go into the county and municipal treasuries.

"Scribner's Monthly," projected by James G. Holland and Roswell B. Smith in 1870 at New York. In 1881 this company sold out to a new company formed by Smith, which began the *Century Magazine* in the same year. The *Scribner's Magazine* was re-established in 1887.

Scrooby, a small hamlet in the northern part of Nottinghamshire, England, one of the strongholds of Puritanism in the latter part of the sixteenth century. Thence came a number of the Pilgrim Fathers.

Scrub Race. The Presidential campaign and election of 1824 was termed the "scrub race." The candidates were not nominated by Congressional caucus, as had been the custom. Crawford, of Georgia, was put forward by a quasi-caucus; New England's candidate was John Q. Adams; Clay was nominated by Kentucky, Louisiana, Missouri, Illinois and Ohio; and Andrew Jackson by Tennessee and other States. Jackson received the largest popular vote, but Adams was chosen by the House.

Scudder, Horace E., of Massachusetts, was born in 1838. He has published the series of "American Commonwealths," "Men and Manners in America," "Noah Webster," and a "History of the United States." He has lately been the editor of the *Atlantic Monthly*.

Seabury, Samuel (1729–1796), of New York, clergyman, was obnoxious to the colonists on account of the publication of pamphlets signed "A Westchester Farmer," entitled "Free Thoughts on the Proceedings of the Continental Congress," "The Congress Canvassed," and "A View of the Controversy between Great Britain and her Colonies." He was made Bishop of Connecticut in 1784, one of the first three Episcopal bishops. He was prominent in the organization of the Episcopal Church in America.

Seal, Confederate, adopted by the Confederate Congress, April 30, 1863, was designed by Thomas J. Semmes, of Louisiana. The device represents an equestrian portrait of Washington, surrounded by the principal agricultural products of the Confederacy.

Seal of the United States. July 4, 1776, Congress appointed Benjamin Franklin, John Adams and Thomas Jefferson a committee to prepare a device for the great seal of the United States. The committee reported various devices during several years. William Barton, of Philadelphia, was appointed to submit designs. Sir John Prestwich, an English antiquarian, suggested a design to John Adams in 1779. Combining the various designs of Barton and Prestwich, a seal was adopted June 20, 1782. Arms: Paleways of thirteen pieces argent and gules; a chief azure; the escutcheon on the breast of the American eagle displayed proper, holding in his dexter talon an olive branch and in his sinister a bundle of thirteen arrows; and in his beak a scroll with the motto: *E Pluribus Unum*. Crest: a glory breaking through a cloud proper and surrounding thirteen stars. Reverse: A pyramid unfinished. In the zenith an eye in a triangle, surrounded with a glory proper, over the eye the words, *Annuit Coeptis*. Beneath the pyramid, MDCCLXXVI, and words, *Novus Ordo Seculorum*.

Search. Great Britain, in the period before the War of 1812, claimed and exercised the right of search on two grounds. Search was made for deserting English sailors, and many American seamen were impressed as such, and search was made for such goods as were declared subject to confiscation in accordance with the paper blockade of the Continent and the Orders in Council. This was one of the grievances on account of which the War of 1812 was begun, but was not remedied by the Treaty of Ghent. The right of search for the purposes of suppression of the slave-trade was carefully regulated by several treaties between Great Britain and the United States.

Seaton, William W. (1785–1866), was joint editor with Joseph Gales of the *National Intelligencer* from 1812 to 1860, and sole editor from 1860 to 1866. With Mr. Gales he published "Annals of Congress from 1798 to 1824," "Register of Debates in Congress from 1824 to 1837," and "American State Papers."

Secession. After the adoption of the Constitution of 1787 the thought that the States were sovereign remained familiar to the minds of many, if not most, Americans. This led easily to the thought of secession by a State or States as a remedy for aggressive action on the part of the Federal Government. The Federalists of New England made threats of secession in 1811 and 1814. As the slavery agitation began to be foremost among political issues, secession was extensively suggested as the constitutional right of the Southern States if the system of slavery was attacked. South Carolina was ready to secede in 1850. In 1860, upon news of the election of Lincoln, she did so, December 20, by convention, which passed an ordinance purporting to repeal her adoption of the Constitution in 1788 and to revive her independence. Mississippi seceded January 9, 1861, Florida January 10, Alabama January 11, Georgia January 19, Louisiana January 26, Texas February 1,—all by conventions. These seven States formed the Confederate States of America, February 4, 1861. Buchanan's government could find no constitutional warrant for coercing a seceded State. After the firing on Fort Sumter and the decision of Mr. Lincoln and the North to suppress rebellion by armed force, four more States seceded—Arkansas May 6, North Carolina May 20, Virginia May 23, Tennessee June 8. In most of these States there had been strong opposition to secession, but on the ground that it was inexpedient. That a State had a right to secede was the nearly universal belief. The national Government never recognized this right, nor the validity of the ordinances. (See arts. Confederate States, Civil War.)

Secretaries. The first heads of executive departments bearing this title were instituted in 1781. (See art. Executive, and those on the several departments now represented in the Cabinet.)

Seddon, James A. (1815–1880), represented Virginia in the U. S. Congress as a Democrat from 1845 to 1847 and from 1849 to 1851. He was Confederate Secretary of War from 1862 to 1865.

Sedgwick, Catherine Maria (1789–1867), of Massachusetts, established and managed a private school from 1813 to 1863. She published many novels illustrative of American life and manners.

Sedgwick, John (1813–1864), graduated at West Point in 1837, and served in the Seminole and Mexican Wars. In the opening phase of the Rebellion he led a brigade in the Army of the Potomac, and commanded a division at Fair Oaks, the Seven Days' Battles, and Antietam. He was a corps general at Chancellorsville, and directed the left wing at Gettysburg. In November, 1863, he captured a Confederate division at the River Rapidan. In the terrible fighting of the Wilderness General Sedgwick was as usual foremost, and was killed at Spottsylvania.

Sedgwick, Robert (1590–1656), came to Massachusetts about 1635 from England. In 1652 he became commander of the Massachusetts militia. He engaged in the expedition against Penobscot in 1654 and against the Spanish West Indies in 1655.

Sedgwick, Theodore (1746–1813), represented Massachusetts in the Continental Congress from 1785 to 1786. He served in the U. S. Congress as a Federalist from 1789 to 1796 and in the U. S. Senate from 1796 to 1799. He was Speaker of the U. S. House of Representatives from 1799 to 1801. He was a Judge of the Massachusetts Supreme Court from 1802 to 1813.

Sedition Law. The Sedition law was an act passed by the Federal majority in Congress in 1798. It was passed in order to put an end to the scurrilous and abusive tone of the press, which was largely controlled by aliens, French, English, Irish and Scotch refugees. It was modelled on two English acts of 1795. It provided heavy fines and imprisonment for any who should combine or conspire against the operations of the Government, or should write, print or publish any "false, scandalous and malicious writings" against it, or either House of Congress, or the President, with intent to bring contempt upon them or to stir up sedition; truth of the libel could be offered in defence. The Alien and Sedition laws called out the Virginia and Kentucky resolutions, and by their severity occasioned the fall of the Federal party.

Seelye, Julius H., born in 1824, was professor of mental and moral philosophy at Amherst College from 1858 to 1875, and its president from 1877 to 1891. He represented Massachusetts in the U. S. Congress as a Republican from 1875 to 1877.

Selectmen, the chief officers of a New England town. English parishes had their vestries, which were of two sorts, common vestries, composed of all the rate-payers, and select vestries. In the latter, concerns were managed by select vestrymen. Hence the term selectmen, as used in New England, for the governing board of a town. The practice is found in Massachusetts as early as the issue of the "Body of Liberties." The selectmen acted under the orders of the town-meeting.

NAVAL COMMANDERS OF CIVIL WAR.

D. G. Farragut. S. F. Dupont. John L. Worden.
Raphael Semmes.
A. H. Foote. John A. Dahlgreen.
John A. Winslow. David D. Porter.

Selfridge, Thomas O., born in 1837, commanded a siege battery at Vicksburg. He commanded the "Osage" in the Red River Expedition, and the "Huron" at Fort Fisher. He was distinguished for courage and coolness.

Seminole War. The Seminoles were a nation of Florida Indians, composed chiefly of Creeks and remnants of other tribes. During the War of 1812, the British had been materially aided by the Seminoles. The combined British and Indian stronghold—the "Negro Fort," on the Appalachicola—was a constant menace to Georgia. During 1817, there were constant collisions and massacres of the whites. General Gaines accomplished little. Florida was then held by Spain. In January, 1818, Andrew Jackson was given command, and in less than six months completely reduced the Seminoles, burning their towns and defeating them day after day. Ambrister and Arbuthnot, English adventurers in league with the Spanish and Indians, were summarily hanged. Pensacola was captured and the whole of East Florida was taken possession of. After the acquisition of Florida, many slaves fled to the Seminoles. The Government endeavored to recover them, and to force the Seminoles to remove to the West. War with the Seminoles ensued and was carried on with severity on both sides. General Thompson, the U. S. agent, finding their chiefs opposed to migration, put Osceola in chains. War followed and Osceola killed Thompson and others at Fort King on December 28, 1835, and cut to pieces a body of troops under Major Dade. After a most disastrous struggle they were partially conquered, and in 1837 agreed to emigrate. Osceola, however, fled and renewed the war. He was finally taken by treachery and the conflict ended (1842). By treaty of 1845 the Seminoles were removed west of the Mississippi; in 1856 they were assigned lands west of the Creeks.

Semmes, Raphael (1809–1877), a Confederate naval commander, served for many years in the American navy, including the Mexican War, and in 1861 joined the Southern side. In the period just before the commencement of hostilities, he was very active in procuring supplies for the naval department of the new Confederacy. As commander of the "Sumter" he captured many American merchantmen until he was blockaded at Tangier. He then sold the "Sumter," and in 1863 assumed charge of the "Alabama." In this privateer he made sixty-two captures, but the "Alabama's" career was ended off Cherbourg, June 19, 1864, by the "Kearsage." (See "Alabama" and "Kearsarge.") Semmes escaped in a British vessel, made his way to the South, and was appointed rear-admiral. He was arrested in 1865 after the close of the war, but was released.

Senate. The name Senate was first applied to an American institution of government in the Virginia Constitution of 1776. Thence it was adopted into all those States whose legislatures were organized with two branches. The State Senates were in some cases elected by voters having a higher property qualification than the electors of the lower branch. In the deliberations of 1787 the Federal upper House was at first designated as the "second branch." The name Senate first appears in the report of the committee of detail, August 6. One of the chief compromises of the Constitution was that effected by Connecticut, which harmonized the conflicting interests of large and small States by arranging that, while Representatives should be apportioned to population, each State should have two Senators, chosen by the State Legislature. In 1789 the Senate was divided into three classes by lot, one-third retiring every two years. Down to 1795 the Senate sat with closed doors. Invested with the executive powers of concurrence in appointments and treaties, it has been, as a rule, stronger than the House, though the reverse is usually true of upper Houses. Elections of Senators were not governed by any Federal law until 1866, when an act was passed providing for the present mode of election.

Senecas, a tribe of Iroquois Indians, lived in Western New York. They allied themselves with Pontiac, destroying Venango, attacking Fort Niagara, and cutting off an army train near Devil's Hole in 1763. During the Revolution they favored the English. General Sullivan invaded their territory and devastated it. They made peace in 1784. They ceded a great part of their land, and in 1812 joined the American cause, though a part in Ohio joined the hostile tribes of the West, making peace in 1815. This band removed to Indian Territory in 1831, but the rest remained in New York.

Separatists, a sect which arose, chiefly in the North of England, about 1567, inspired by the exhortations of ministers who believed the gospel should be preached freely and "the sacraments administered without idolatrous gear," and who, like Robert Brown, called upon the people "to separate" from the Church of England. A number of them emigrated to Holland in 1608. Their chief strength was about Scrooby, in Nottinghamshire. A number of the Pilgrim Fathers belonged to this sect.

Separatists (of Zoar), the inhabitants of a communistic settlement in Ohio, called Zoar. They originated in Württemberg, whence, in 1817, a number of them emigrated to this country to secure religious freedom. They were dissenters from the Established Church. Arriving at Philadelphia, they procured a tract of 6500 acres of land in Ohio, and founded the village of Zoar, choosing Joseph Bäumeler as leader. It was not their original intention to form a communistic society, but necessity compelled them to do so later. At first marriage was prohibited, but in 1830 this rule was abolished.

Sergeant, John (1779–1852), represented Pennsylvania in the U. S. Congress as a Federalist from 1815 to 1823, from 1827 to 1829, and from 1837 to 1842. He was the Whig candidate for the Vice-Presidency in 1832, on the ticket with Clay.

Servia. The United States concluded commercial and consular conventions with Servia in 1881.

Sessions of Congress.

Cong.	Sess.	From	To
1	1	March 4, 1789	Sept. 29, 1789
	2	Jan. 4, 1790	Aug. 12, 1790
	3	Dec. 6, 1790	March 3, 1791
2	1	Oct. 24, 1791	May 8, 1792
	2	Nov. 5, 1792	March 2, 1793
3	1	Dec. 2, 1793	June 9, 1794
	2	Nov. 3, 1794	March 3, 1795
4	1	Dec. 7, 1795	June 1, 1796
	2	Dec. 5, 1796	March 3, 1797
5	1	May, 15, 1797	July 10, 1797
	2	Nov. 13, 1797	July 16, 1798
	3	Dec. 3, 1798	March 3, 1799
6	1	Dec. 2, 1799	May 14, 1800
	2	Nov. 17, 1800	March 3, 1801
7	1	Dec. 7, 1801	May 3, 1802
	2	Dec. 6, 1802	March 3, 1803
8	1	Oct. 17, 1803	March 27, 1804
	2	Nov. 5, 1804	March 3, 1805
9	1	Dec. 2, 1805	April 21, 1806
	2	Dec. 1, 1806	March 3, 1807
10	1	Oct. 26, 1807	April 25, 1808
	2	Nov. 7, 1808	March 3, 1809
11	1	May 22, 1809	June 28, 1809
	2	Nov. 27, 1809	May 1, 1810
	3	Dec. 3, 1810	March 3, 1811
12	1	Nov. 4, 1811	July 6, 1812
	2	Nov. 2, 1812	March 3, 1813
13	1	May 24, 1813	Aug. 2, 1813
	2	Dec. 6, 1813	April 18, 1814
	3	Sept. 19, 1814	March 3, 1815
14	1	Dec. 4, 1815	April 30, 1816
	2	Dec. 2, 1816	March 3, 1817
15	1	Dec. 1, 1817	April 30, 1818
	2	Nov. 16, 1818	March 3, 1819
16	1	Dec. 6, 1819	May 15, 1820
	2	Nov. 13, 1820	March 3, 1821
17	1	Dec. 3, 1821	May 8, 1822
	2	Dec. 2, 1822	March 3, 1823
18	1	Dec. 1, 1823	May 27, 1824
	2	Dec. 6, 1824	March 3, 1825
19	1	Dec. 5, 1825	May 22, 1826
	2	Dec. 4, 1826	March 3, 1827
20	1	Dec. 3, 1827	May 26, 1828
	2	Dec. 1, 1828	March 3, 1829
21	1	Dec. 7, 1829	May 31, 1830
	2	Dec. 6, 1830	March 3, 1831
22	1	Dec. 5, 1831	July 16, 1832
	2	Dec. 3, 1832	March 3, 1833
23	1	Dec. 2, 1833	June 30, 1834
	2	Dec. 1, 1834	March 3, 1835
24	1	Dec. 7, 1835	July 4, 1836
	2	Dec. 6, 1836	March 3, 1837
25	1	Sept. 4, 1837	Oct. 16, 1837
	2	Dec. 4, 1837	July 9, 1838
	3	Dec. 3, 1838	March 3, 1839
26	1	Dec. 2, 1839	July 21, 1840
	2	Dec. 7, 1840	March 3, 1841
27	1	May 31, 1841	Sept. 13, 1841
	2	Dec. 6, 1841	Aug. 31. 1842
	3	Dec. 5, 1842	March 3, 1843
28	1	Dec. 4, 1843	June 17, 1844
	2	Dec. 2, 1844	March 3, 1845
29	1	Dec. 1, 1845	Aug. 10, 1846
	2	Dec. 7, 1846	March 3, 1847
30	1	Dec. 6, 1847	Aug. 14, 1848
	2	Dec. 4, 1848	March 3, 1849
31	1	Dec. 3, 1849	Sept. 30, 1850
	2	Dec. 2, 1850	March 3, 1851
32	1	Dec. 1, 1851	Aug. 31, 1852
	2	Dec. 6, 1852	March 3, 1853
33	1	Dec. 5, 1853	Aug. 7, 1854
	2	Dec. 4, 1854	March 3, 1855
34	1	Dec. 3, 1855	Aug. 18, 1856
	2	Aug. 21, 1856	Aug. 30, 1856
	3	Dec. 1, 1856	March 3, 1857
35	1	Dec. 7, 1857	June 14, 1858
	2	Dec. 6, 1858	March 3, 1859
36	1	Dec. 5, 1859	June 25, 1860
	2	Dec. 4, 1860	March 2, 1861
37	1	July 4, 1861	Aug. 6, 1861
	2	Dec. 2, 1861	July 17, 1862
	3	Dec. 1, 1862	March 3, 1863
38	1	Dec. 7, 1863	July 2, 1864
	2	Dec. 5, 1864	March 3, 1865
39	1	Dec. 4, 1865	July 28, 1866
	2	Dec. 3, 1866	March 2, 1867
40	1	March 4, 1867	March 30, 1867
		July 3, 1867	July 20, 1867
		Nov. 21, 1867	Nov. 30, 1867
	2	Dec. 3, 1867	July 25, 1868
		Sept. 21, 1868	. . . .
		Nov. 1, 1868	Nov. 10, 1868
	3	Dec. 7. 1868	March 3, 1869
41	1	March 4, 1869	April 9, 1869
	2	Dec. 6, 1869	July 15, 1870
	3	Dec. 5, 1870	March 3, 1871
42	1	March 4, 1871	April 20, 1871
	2	Dec. 4, 1871	June 8, 1872
	3	Dec. 2, 1872	March 3, 1873
43	1	Dec. 1, 1873	June 23, 1874
	2	Dec. 7, 1874	March 3, 1875
44	1	Dec. 6, 1875	Aug. 15, 1876
	2	Dec. 4, 1876	March 3, 1877
45	1	Oct. 15, 1877	Dec. 1, 1877
	2	Dec. 3, 1877	June 19, 1878
	3	Dec. 2, 1878	March 3, 1879
46	1	March 18, 1879	July 1, 1879
	2	Dec. 1, 1879	June 16, 1880
	3	Dec. 6, 1880	March 3, 1881
47	1	Dec. 5, 1881	Aug. 8, 1882
	2	Dec. 4, 1882	March 3, 1883
48	1	Dec. 3, 1883	July 7, 1884
	2	Dec. 1, 1884	March 3, 1885
49	1	Dec. 7, 1885	Aug. 5, 1886
	2	Dec. 6, 1886	March 3, 1887
50	1	Dec. 5, 1887	Oct. 20, 1888
	2	Dec. 3, 1888	March 3, 1889
51	1	Dec. 2, 1889	Oct. 1, 1890
	2	Dec. 1, 1890	March 3, 1891
52	1	Dec. 7, 1891	Aug. 5, 1892
	2	Dec. 5, 1892	March 3, 1893
53	1	Aug. 7, 1893	Nov. 3, 1893
	2	Dec. 4, 1893	. . . .

Seven Cities. (See Cibola.)

Seven Days, an unbroken series of battles, between the Federal and Confederate troops, June 26 to July 2, 1862, known as the Seven Days' Fight around Richmond. McClellan's army was 92,500 strong, June 26; Lee's forces numbered 80,762. June 26, A. P. Hill, with 30,000 Confederates, defeated and drove the Nationals from Mechanicsville. June 27, Longstreet, Jackson and Hill, with 55,000 Confederates, attacked and routed 25,000 Federals under Porter at Gaines' Mills on the Chickahominy. Porter crossed the river to Savage's Station, where he defeated Magruder June 28. June 29 and 30, the Federals were again defeated at Frayser's Farm and White Oak Swamp. McClellan retreated to Malvern Hill, where a furious but indecisive battle occurred. After this McClellan retreated to the James. During the Seven Days' fight the Federals lost 15,249 men; the Confederates 19,000.

Seven Pines, or Fair Oaks, Va. May 31, 1862, McClellan's army had crossed the Chickahominy and advanced toward Richmond. Johnston, with a heavy force of Confederates, attacked Keyes' corps at Seven Pines. Keyes defended himself stoutly, but the rain had washed away the bridges over the Chickahominy and reinforcements came up slowly, so he held his line with difficulty. After protracted and fierce fighting, reinforcements came up under Sumner, and the Confederates were repulsed, Johnston himself receiving severe wounds.

Seven-thirties, treasury notes of the United States bearing interest at the rate of 7.30 per cent per annum (.02 per cent a day). They were first authorized in order to meet the expenses of the war by act of July 17, 1861. The total amount issued, before the war was concluded, amounted to $830,000,000.

Seven Years' War, a war between England and Prussia on the one hand, and France and Austria on the other, lasting from 1756 to 1763. A part of it went on in India, and a part in America. The latter phase of it is in American history called the French and Indian War. The war was concluded by the Treaty of Paris in 1763, France losing Canada and Louisiana. (See French and Indian War.)

Seventh of March Speech, Daniel Webster's celebrated speech "For the Union and Constitution" in the Senate, March 7, 1850. It essentially approved of the Clay Compromise and advocated yielding on the part of Northern abolitionists to Southern slavery principles in order to maintain the Union in harmony. Calhoun's doctrine of peaceable secession was denounced as impossible.

Sevier, John (1745–1815), one of the chief pioneers of the West, was born in Virginia, and was a hardy Indian fighter from his early years. He was present at the battle of Point Pleasant in 1774, and was one of the commanders at King's Mountain in 1780. When the Tennessee district of North Carolina in 1784 declared its independence as the State of Franklin, it chose Sevier for Governor. He assumed the office but the temporary State was soon taken back. Sevier became Congressman in 1790. When Tennessee finally entered the Union he was its first Governor, serving from 1796 to 1803. He was again Congressman from 1811 to 1815. There is a biography by Gilmore.

Sewall, Samuel (1652–1730), Chief Justice of Massachusetts, came to America from England in 1661. He was an "assistant" of Massachusetts from 1684 to 1688, a member of the Executive Council from 1692 to 1725, and judge of the probate court from 1692 to 1718. He was prominent in the Salem witchcraft trials and afterward publicly acknowledged his error. He was Chief Justice from 1718 to 1728. He published "The Selling of Joseph," one of the first tracts advocating the rights of slaves, and kept a diary, since published, which gives an interesting and amusing picture of life in Puritan Boston.

Seward, Frederick W., born in 1830, son of W. H. Seward, was Assistant U. S. Secretary of State from 1861 to 1869 and from 1877 to 1881. He published the "Life and Letters of William H. Seward."

Seward, George F., born in 1840, was Consul at Shanghai, China, from 1861 to 1863, Consul-General to China from 1863 to 1876, and Minister to China from 1876 to 1880.

Seward, William Henry (May 16, 1801–October 10, 1872), a distinguished American statesman, was born in Orange County, N. Y. He was graduated at Union College in 1820, and having studied law he entered on its practice at Auburn. The anti-Masonic excitement broke out soon afterward, and Seward was carried into the State Senate on a wave of this feeling in 1830. In 1834 he was defeated as the Whig candidate for Governor. About this time began the political partnership of Thurlow Weed, Horace Greeley and Seward, which was far-reaching in its influence on State and National affairs. Seward was Governor in 1839–1843. In 1849 he entered the U. S. Senate. He was in that body one of the leaders of the anti-slavery men, and when the Republican party was formed he was among its foremost orators. Among his numerous speeches were that in 1850, which spoke of the "higher law," and the "irrepressible conflict" oration of 1858. In 1860, at the Chicago Convention, Seward was at the start the leading candidate for the Presidential nomination. The many elements opposed to him proved too strong, and Lincoln was nominated. The new President called his chief rival to the Department of State. Secretary Seward's tenure of his office, 1861–1869, covers the highly important periods of the Civil War and of reconstruction. Many were the delicate questions, especially with England, as in the "Trent" affair and throughout the struggle, also with France in the Mexican episode. Seward's ability in the conduct of the foreign relations has been generally praised. On the night of Lincoln's assassination he was stabbed and dangerously injured. In 1867 he negotiated the purchase of Alaska, and he made various West Indian treaties which failed of confirmation. He traveled extensively after retiring from office, and the narratives of his travels, as well as his speeches, have been published. Life by Seward.

Seymour, Horatio (May 31, 1810–February 12, 1886), a prominent Democratic statesman, was in early life the military secretary of Governor Marcy of New York. With the politics of that State he was thereafter identified. As Assemblyman, Mayor of Utica, and Speaker of the Assembly, he had become noted as a leader of the Democratic party, and in 1850 he was defeated as its candidate for Governor. In 1853–1855 he was Governor, but the State was close, and the Republicans held control for a few years. Seymour's attitude in the Civil War is difficult to characterize. He supported the Union, but could hardly be reckoned as a "War Democrat." In 1862 he was elected Governor over the Republican candidate, and served 1863–1865. During his term occurred the Draft Riots in New York City, July, 1863. Governor Seymour's speech to the mob has been the subject of severe criticism. He was defeated for re-election in 1864. In 1868 he presided over the Democratic National Convention, and received against his will the nomination for President. In the election he was defeated by General Grant, receiving only eighty electoral votes.

Seymour, Truman (1824-1891), U. S. A., served in the Mexican War. He aided in the defence of Fort Sumter in 1861. He commanded the left wing at Mechanicsville in 1862, led a division at Malvern Hill, and was brevetted colonel for services at South Mountain and Antietam. He fought at Morris Island and Fort Wagner, and captured Jacksonville. He led a brigade at the Wilderness and Petersburg.

Shackamaxon, scene of William Penn's famous treaty with the Indians in 1682, near Chester, Pa. By this treaty the confidence and friendship of the Indians were secured, and their land was fairly purchased.

Shadrach Case (1851). In May, 1850, a fugitive slave from Virginia, named Frederic Wilkins, came to Boston, and secured employment under the alias of Shadrach. Subsequently he was arrested and jailed in the United States Court-house pending trial. Shadrach was rescued by a body of colored people and conveyed in safety to Canada. Intense excitement prevailed in Boston, and spread over the entire country upon Congress turning its attention to the infringement of the law. Mr. Clay introduced a resolution requesting the President to send to Congress information regarding the matter. President Pierce issued a proclamation announcing the facts, and calling upon the people to prevent future disturbances.

Shaftesbury, Anthony Ashley Cooper, Earl of (1621–1683), was one of the nine proprietors who received a grant of Carolina in 1663, extending from the Virginia frontier to the river St. Mathias in Florida. He was prominent in the management of the colony, and secured for it the constitution drafted by Locke in 1667. It established a territorial aristocracy with the proprietors at the head, granting religious toleration. Shaftesbury was a famous party-leader in England, and was Lord Chancellor from 1672 to 1673.

Shakers, a communistic association founded at New Lebanon, N. Y., in September, 1787, by a party of the followers of Ann Lee, of England, founder of the sect. James and Jane Wardley were at the head of this society. The formation of the society was due chiefly to the influence of a religious revival, and the name is derived from the peculiar dance with which they accompany their worship. Ann Lee was supposed to have had a special revelation from heaven. She died at Watervliet, N. Y., in 1784, after a number of years spent in preaching and making converts.

Shanley vs. Haney (1762), an English case in equity brought by an administrator to recover money given by his intestate to a negro brought to England as a slave. The suit was dismissed by Lord Northington, who held that a slave became free as soon as he set foot on English territory. (See Sommersett.)

"**Shannon**," frigate. (See "Chesapeake.")

Sharpless, James (1751–1811), came to America from England in 1794, and executed many portraits of distinguished Americans in pastel, the most noteworthy being that of Washington.

Sharswood, George (1810–1883), was President-Judge of a district court from 1851 to 1867 and a Judge of the Pennsylvania Supreme Court from 1867 to 1882. He published many valuable legal works.

Shaw, Lemuel (1781–1861), was Chief Justice of the Massachusetts Supreme Court from 1830 to 1860. He is regarded as one of the foremost of New England jurists.

Shawmut, the name of an Indian settlement, which once stood upon the site of Boston. The latter town was long known to the Indians by that name.

Shawnees, a tribe of Algonquin Indians, after wandering about the east were driven west by the Iroquois. They first aided the French in their final struggle until won over to the English. They joined Pontiac and from time to time continued hostilities until the peace of 1786. They took part in the Miami War, but, finally reduced by General Wayne, they submitted under the Treaty of 1795. In 1812 a part joined the English. The Missouri band ceded their lands in 1825, and the Ohio band in 1831. They became somewhat scattered, but the main band in Kansas ended tribal relations in 1854.

Shawomet, a place on the Pawtuxet River, R. I., where in 1643 the turbulent English adventurer, Gorton, and a few friends concluded a purchase of land from Miantonomo, a chief of the Narragansett Indians, and established the town of Warwick, one of the elements which combined to make Rhode Island.

Shays, Daniel (1747–1825), served as an ensign at the battle of Bunker Hill and attained the rank of captain during the Revolutionary War. In 1786 he was the chief leader of the insurrection known as "Shays' Rebellion" (q. v.) After the rebellion he lived for a year in Vermont. He received pardon from Governor Bowdoin of Massachusetts and settled in New York in 1788.

Shays' Rebellion. After the close of the Revolution, much discontent and indeed actual want prevailed through New England, especially in Western Massachusetts. The annual State tax amounted to $1,000,000. Riots and armed mobs were frequent, the especial grievances being the high salary of the Governor, the refusal to issue paper money, and the specific taxes to pay the interest on the State debt. December 5, 1786, 1000 armed men under Daniel Shays took possession of Worcester and prevented the session of the Supreme Court. Springfield was mobbed by the same men. General Lincoln, commanding 4000 militia, attacked Shays near Springfield, January 25, 1787, quickly routing his force. They fled to Amherst, where 150 were captured. The insurgents were pardoned on laying down their arms.

Shea, John D. Gilmary (1824–1892), published "The Discovery and Exploration of the Mississippi Valley," "Novum Belgium," "The Operations of the French Fleet under Count de Grasse" and an extensive and valuable "History of the Catholic Church in the United States."

Sheaffe, Sir Roger H. (1763–1851), served in the British army in Canada from 1802 to 1811. He defeated the American troops at Queenstown in 1813, and defended York (now Toronto) when attacked.

Shelburne, Wm. P. Fitz-Maurice, Earl of, (1737–1805), while President of the Board of Trade in Grenville's Cabinet in 1763, opposed the Stamp Act and other measures oppressive to the American colonies. He sought to moderate the arbitrary colonial policy of Grafton and Townsend, and ardently opposed the colonial administration of Lord North. He became Premier in 1782, and negotiated the preliminaries of peace with the United States. He resigned in 1783.

Shelby, Isaac (1750–1826), served in the battle of Point Pleasant in 1774. He distinguished himself at the battle of Long Island Flats, Tenn., with the Indians in 1776. In 1780 he defeated the British at Cedar Springs and Musgrove's Mill. He planned and engaged in the battle of King's Mountain. He was Governor of Kentucky from 1792 to 1796 and from 1812 to 1816. In 1812 he organized a body of 4,000 volunteers and joined General Harrison in Canada, taking part in the victory of the Thames.

"Shenandoah," a British-Confederate cruiser. She sailed from London as the "Sea King," October 8, 1864, commanded by Captain James J. Waddell, of the Confederate navy. Making for Madeira, her name was changed to the "Shenandoah." From Madeira she sailed for Melbourne, destroying a number of United States merchant ships on her way. Thence she went to Behring Sea and did great damage to the whaling vessels. At the close of the war the "Shenandoah" was surrendered to the British Government and afterward turned over to the United States.

Shepard, Thomas (1605–1649), was charged with non-conformity in England and came to America in 1635. He was pastor of the church at Cambridge, Mass., from 1635 to 1649. He was influential in the establishment of Harvard College at that place. He was one of the most influential men in New England and a writer on theological subjects.

Sheridan, Philip Henry (March 6, 1831–August 5, 1888), one of the great Unionist generals of the war, was born at Albany, and graduated at West Point in 1853. In the first stages of the Civil War he was quartermaster, but in 1862 he received a cavalry command. At the battle of Perryville he

STATESMEN OF RECENT TIMES.

George F. Edmunds. Allen G. Thurman.

John Sherman. Carl Schurz.

James G. Blaine.

William M. Evarts. Samuel J. Tilden.

George Wm. Curtis.

John G. Carlisle. Thomas F. Bayard.

led a division, and on the bloody field of Murfreesboro he especially distinguished himself. Appointed major-general of volunteers, he fought at Chickamauga, and at Missionary Ridge he shared with Hooker and others the honors of the day. The great period of his career was now approaching. Grant gave him, in 1864, the charge of the cavalry corps in the Army of the Potomac; he was present at the Wilderness, fought the battle of Todd's Tavern, conducted an extended raid in May and June, and was in August placed in charge of the Army of the Shenandoah. He defeated Early at Winchester and Fisher's Hill, and was absent at Winchester, when, on October 19, 1864, the enemy made a sudden attack on his army at Cedar Creek. "Little Phil's" ride from "Winchester, twenty miles away," to the battle-field, his reforming the army and turning defeat into a brilliant victory, is the theme of story and poetry. He was made a major-general in the regular army. In the operations of 1865 he took the leading part, won the battle of Five Forks, April 1, and helped materially in the dénouement at Appomattox. In 1869 he was promoted to be lieutenant-general and in 1888 general. In 1883 he succeeded General Sherman as commander-in-chief of the army. He wrote "Personal Memoirs."

Sheridan's Raid in Virginia. On the day of the battle of Spottsylvania Court House, May 8, 1864, Grant ordered Sheridan to ride with his cavalry entirely around the Confederate army, destroying bridges and depots, tearing up railroads and capturing trains. Sheridan followed his commands to the letter. He destroyed ten miles of railroad, captured several trains, cut all the telegraph wires and recaptured 400 prisoners, who had been taken by the Confederates in the Wilderness. The Confederate cavalry under J. E. B. Stuart was immediately dispatched to intercept him. They met at Yellow Tavern, and a hot engagement took place. The Confederates were finally defeated, and Stuart himself, the most famous cavalryman of the Southern army, was mortally wounded. Sheridan then rode on toward Richmond. The outer defences were at that time quite weak, and the Union leader found little difficulty in dashing through the Confederate lines and capturing a large number of prisoners. The inner works were too strong for him, so he retreated and rejoined Grant May 25.

Sherman, John, born May 10, 1823, American statesman, is the brother of General W. T. Sherman. Having been a surveyor, he settled to the practice of law at Mansfield, O. Since he entered the House of Representatives in 1855 his official career has been unbroken. He was the Republican candidate for Speaker in 1859, and was chairman of the Ways and Means Committee. In 1861 he entered the U. S. Senate. He was foremost in the financial and other measures, and personally recruited an Ohio brigade. For several years he was chairman of the important Finance Committee. He visited Louisiana at the time of the Tilden-Hayes excitement, and in 1877 left the Senate to enter President Hayes' Cabinet. During his administration of the Treasury Department occurred the Resumption of Specie Payments in 1879, for which Secretary Sherman had made careful preparation. In 1881 he re-entered the Senate. His name has been several times presented to Republican National Conventions. In 1880 Garfield headed the

Ohio delegation in Sherman's favor, and was himself nominated. In 1888 Sherman was at first in the lead, but Harrison finally won. Senator Sherman has been chairman of the Committee on Foreign Relations, and his name is attached to the Silver Purchase Act of 1890 (repealed in 1893.)

Sherman, Roger (1721–1793), a signer of the Declaration of Independence, was a shoemaker in early life, a surveyor, lawyer, Judge of the Superior Court of Connecticut, and member of the Legislature. He was a delegate to the first and second Continental Congresses, was one of the committee of five to draft the Declaration, and a member of the Connecticut committee of safety. He was an influential delegate to the Federal Constitutional Convention of 1787. He supported the Constitution in the ratifying convention of his State, and wrote the valuable "Citizen" letters. In the first Congress he was a member of the House of Representatives 1789–1791, and U. S. Senator 1791–1793. Few of his contemporaries have a more honorable record of usefulness through the entire revolutionary period.

Sherman, Thomas W. (1813–1879), was brevetted major for services at Buena Vista during the Mexican War. He commanded the land forces of the Port Royal Expedition in 1861. In 1862 he commanded a division in the Army of the Tennessee, engaging at Corinth. He was active in the engagements about New Orleans and led the left wing at Port Hudson in 1863.

Sherman, William Tecumseh (February 8, 1820–February 14, 1891), one of the most famous generals of recent times, was born at Lancaster, Ohio, and graduated at West Point in 1840. He was engaged in the Seminole War, and in the Mexican War took part in the expedition to California. In 1853 he resigned, and was in business in California, New York and Kansas. In 1860–1861 he was superintendent of a military college in Louisiana. When the Rebellion began he was appointed colonel. At the first battle of Bull Run he commanded a brigade. In October he was transferred to the department of the Cumberland, but was removed the next month. Sherman was one of the few who early in the war foresaw the severity of the contest. In 1862 he was assigned to the Army of the Tennessee, and with his division contributed materially to the victory of Shiloh. Made major-general of volunteers and corps commander, he had a signal share in the success of the Vicksburg campaign. He was now promoted to be brigadier-general in the regular army, and commanded the left wing at the battle of Chattanooga. Immediately afterward he was sent to relieve Burnside at Knoxville. When Grant in 1864 assumed command of all the Federal armies he intrusted Sherman with the task of crushing the Rebellion in the West. Accordingly in the spring General Sherman with a powerful force moved southward, opposed by General J. E. Johnston in the mountains of Northern Georgia. These great strategists contended at Dalton, Resaca, Kenesaw Mountain, etc. (See arts.) In the vicinity of Atlanta three severe battles were fought with Hood, and that city was taken. In November Sherman started on his famous "march to the sea," reaching Savannah at Christmas time. He was now a major-general in the regular army. Leaving Savannah in February, he entered Columbia, fought the battles of Averysboro and Bentonville, and after Lee's surrender, concluded a treaty with Johnston; as this was rejected by the Government, another treaty on September 26, 1865, was framed, and Johnston's army surrendered. General Sherman was promoted to be lieutenant-general in 1866, and succeeded Grant as general and commander-in-chief in 1869. He retired from the army in 1883. He is the author of "Memoirs." Sherman was of a firm, straightforward, soldierly character.

Sherman Act, a bill submitted by Senator Sherman, of Ohio, and passed by Congress July 14, 1890. This act provided that the Secretary of the Treasury purchase each month 4,500,000 ounces of silver bullion at market price, treasury notes of legal-tender character to be issued in payment therefor, and these notes to be redeemable on demand, in coin at the treasury. It also provided that 2,000,000 ounces be coined each month into standard silver dollars, and that the silver legislative act of February 28, 1878, be repealed. The purchasing clause of the Sherman act was repealed in 1893.

Shields, Charles W., born in 1825, has occupied at Princeton Theological Seminary a professorship of the harmony of science and revealed religion since 1865. He is the author of extensive philosophical works.

Shields, James (1810–1879), soldier, came to the United States from Ireland in 1826, and was a member of the Illinois Legislature in 1836. He was Commissioner of the General Land Office from 1845 to 1847. He commanded a brigade during the Mexican War, gaining distinction at Cerro Gordo and Chapultepec. He represented Illinois in the U. S. Senate as a Democrat from 1849 to 1855. He commanded a division in General Banks' army and gained a victory at Winchester in 1862, but was defeated at Port Republic by General Jackson.

Shilling. In America this coin was first issued from the mint at Boston. Its coins were of the value of "12d, 6d and 3d peeces," and "every shilling weighing the three-penny trojweight and lesser peeces proportionably." The first struck were mere planchets stamped near the border NE, and on the reverse the value indicated by XII, similarly impressed. The first struck were known as the "New England Shilling" and these were followed by the "Willow Tree," "Oak Tree" and "Pine Tree" coins. Their weight was 72 grains, and their value 18¼ cents. The tree coins all bore the same date, the "Pine Tree" being the most conspicuous. Maryland also, 1659, had shillings coined in London by Lord Baltimore; their weight was 66 grains, and their value 16.73 cents. They bore a profile bust of Lord Baltimore, an escutcheon with his arms and the figure XII denoting the value. There was also the Bermuda shilling or Hogge penny, one of the earliest coins used in America.—As a money of account the shilling, like the pound, varied much in value from colony to colony. In New England and Virginia the shilling equalled, in 1790, a sixth part of the Spanish or Mexican silver dollar; in New York and North Carolina an eighth; in New Jersey, Pennsylvania, Delaware and Maryland two-fifteenths; in South Carolina and Georgia three-fourteenths.

Shiloh or Pittsburg Landing, Tenn., the most important of the battles between the western armies during the Civil War, resulting in frightful loss of life on both sides. This fight lasted two days, April 6 and 7, 1862, the Confederates being forced to retreat on the afternoon of the second day. Grant commanded the Federals, numbering 40,000, and expected 7000 more under Buell to join him. His line extended two miles along Lick Creek, Prentiss holding the left, McClernand the centre and William T. Sherman the right. The Confederates, 45,000 strong, were led by Albert Sidney Johnston with Beauregard, Bragg and Hardee as his chief lieutenants. Johnston, confident of success, began the attack by falling heavily upon Sherman's and McClernand's divisions. These generals gave way, but the Confederates sustained great losses. In the afternoon Johnston was shot and Beauregard assumed command of the Confederates. An opening in Prentiss' ranks enabled the Confederates to gain a considerable advantage the first day. The next morning Grant, now joined by Buell, assumed the offensive. Throughout the day the advantage lay with the Federals. A charge led by Grant himself in the afternoon began the rout, but the roads were too rough to permit of pursuit. The Federal losses were about 13,500, the Confederate about 14,000.

Shimonoseki, a town of Japan commanding the straits leading from the inland sea to the Sea of Japan. June 25, 1863, the American steamer Pembroke was fired upon by the Japanese for attempting to enter the straits, which had been ordered closed by the Mikado. July 16, the United States ship "Wyoming" destroyed two vessels and attacked the batteries in retaliation. September 5, 1864, a combined squadron of American, British, French and Dutch ships attacked the forts and destroyed them. The Mikado was forced to pay an immense indemnity to each nation, the United States receiving $785,000. This sum, vastly beyond the real damage, was paid 1864–1874. In 1883 it was returned to Japan, but without the interest.

Shipbuilding. This was in the colonial period one of the foremost branches of manufacturing industry in the colonies, especially in New England. In Massachusetts the business began in the first years. In 1698 it was enacted that no vessel of more than thirty tons should be built save under the supervision of a competent shipwright. The first schooner, an American invention, was built at Gloucester, in 1713. The American ships competed powerfully with those of England, and were thought the best and cheapest in the world. They formed America's chief manufacture for export.

Shiras, George, of Pennsylvania, was born in 1832, and was appointed to succeed Justice Bradley in the U. S. Supreme Court in 1892.

Shires. In 1643 the General Court of Massachusetts Bay colony ordered that the whole colony, which then included the present State of New Hampshire, be divided into four "shires": Essex, Middlesex, Suffolk and Norfolk. In all the colonies the name was used for "county."

Shirley, William (1693–1771), Governor, came to Massachusetts from England in 1734. He was Royal Governor of Massachusetts from 1741 to 1749. He planned the successful expedition against Cape Breton in 1745. He was again Governor of Massachusetts from 1753 to 1756, and was commander of the forces in British North America at the outbreak of the French War in 1755.

Shogeoquady Creek (near Buffalo). A British force which had crossed the Niagara to capture American batteries and vessels was here defeated with heavy loss, August 3, 1814, by the Americans under Major Morgan.

Shoshones, or Snake Indians, consisted of various bands, chief among which were the Buffalo Eaters, on Wind River, and the Tookarika, on the Salmon. Some of the bands near Humboldt River and Great Salt Lake began hostilities in 1849. In 1862 California volunteers nearly exterminated the Hokandikah. Treaties with various bands followed in 1863, 1864 and 1865. Hostilities were afterward renewed for a period. The Government attempted to collect the whole nation, and they were assigned various reservations.

Shubrick, William B. (1790–1874), served on the "Constitution" in the defence of Norfolk and in the capture of the British ships "Cyane" and "Levant" in the War of 1812. He commanded the Pacific squadron during the Mexican War.

Shute, Samuel, (1653–1742) was colonial Governor of Massachusetts from 1716 to 1723. He was continuously engaged in controversy with the Legislature regarding the prerogative.

Siam. Treaties of amity and commerce were concluded between the United States and Siam in 1833 and 1856, the latter of which was modified in 1867. The liquor traffic was regulated by an agreement in 1884.

Sibley, Henry H. (1811–1891), was a delegate from Wisconsin Territory to Congress in 1849. He represented Minnesota in the U. S. Congress as a Democrat from 1849 to 1853, and was Governor in 1858.

Sibley, Henry H. (1816–1886) engaged in the important operations during the Mexican War. He commanded the Confederate forces which defeated Colonel Canby at Valverde, in New Mexico. He subsequently commanded a brigade under General Taylor and General Smith.

Sibley, John L. (1804–1885) was assistant librarian at Harvard from 1841 to 1856 and librarian from 1856 to 1877. He published "Biographical Sketches of Graduates of Harvard University," in three volumes.

Sickles, Daniel Edgar, born in 1823, was prior to the war a lawyer, Democratic member of the New York Legislature, Secretary of Legation at London, and Congressman from 1857 to 1861. He had command of a brigade in the Peninsula campaign and at Antietam, a division at Fredericksburg, and a corps at Chancellorsville and at Gettysburg, where his services were conspicuous. After the war he was sent abroad on a mission, and retired from the army with the rank of major-general in 1869. From 1869 to 1873 he was U. S. Minister to Spain. In 1893 he re-entered the House of Representatives as a Democrat from New York City.

Sigel, Franz, general, born in 1824, was prominent in the insurrection in Baden in 1848 and 1849. He came to the United States in 1852. He ardently upheld the National cause during the Civil War. He captured Camp Jackson in Missouri, fought the battle of Carthage, and was second in command at Wilson's Creek in 1861. He commanded the right wing at Pea Ridge in 1862, and led a corps at Cedar Creek and the second battle of Bull Run. He was defeated by General Breckinridge at New Market in 1864.

"Signers." (See Declaration of Independence, and Convention of 1787.)

Sigourney, Lydia H. (1791–1865), of Connecticut, was a writer of graceful prose and poetry of elevated moral tone. She wrote "Traits of the Aborigines of America" and "Pocahontas."

Silliman, Benjamin (1779–1864), "The Nestor of American Science," professor in Yale College from 1802 to 1853, founded the "American Journal of Science" in 1818, and was sole editor until 1838. He exerted his influence for the Union and the abolition of slavery.

Silver. Under the law of April 2, 1792, first of the coinage laws, the ratio between silver and gold was made one to fifteen. Silver bullion could be presented for coinage into lawful money, 1485 parts pure to 179 parts alloy, one-ninth being retained for coinage expense. The law of March 3, 1795, caused two cents per ounce to be charged for coining silver bullion below the standard. April 21, 1800, it was enacted that a sum equivalent to the expense of refining should be retained for coining silver below the standard. May 19, 1828, the law provided for coining silver below the standard a charge equal to expense of materials and a charge for wastage. June 28, 1834, a certain deduction (one-half per cent) was made for coining standard silver, if paid in coin five days after deposit. January 18, 1837, the standard silver coin was made nine-tenths pure and one-tenth alloy, and silver coins were to be legal tender for any amount. The dollar weighed 412⅓ grains. By the law of February 21, 1853, the weight of the half dollar was reduced from 206¼ to 192 grains, and it was made legal tender to the amount of only $5. No private deposits for such coinage were to be received, but the mint was to purchase bullion and turn out coins to be exchanged with gold at par value in sums not exceeding $100. February 12, 1873, the law made the weight of the trade dollar 420 grains, the half dollar 193.75 grains. Silver bullion could be deposited for coinage into trade dollars only, and the mint was to purchase bullion for the coinage of coins less than $1.00. By the law of July 22, 1877, the trade dollar ceased to be a legal tender. By the law of February 28, 1878, silver dollars of the weight of 412½ grains were made legal tender for all debts and the treasury was to purchase and coin not less than $2,000,000 worth of bullion per month and not more than $4,000,000. June 2, 1879, silver coins less than $1.00 were made legal tender to the amount of $10. By the law of July 14, 1890, the Secretary of the Treasury was directed to purchase at market price silver bullion to the amount of 4,500,000 ounces per month, issuing in payment treasury notes, to be a legal tender for debt. So much bullion was to be coined as might redeem these notes, and the Act of 1878 was repealed. In 1893 the silver-purchase clause of this act was repealed. (For the history of the individual silver coins see Dollar, Trade Dollar, Half Dollar, Quarter Dollar, Twenty-Cent Piece, Dime, Five-Cent Piece and Three-Cent Piece.)

Silver, Production of. The silver mines of the United States were discovered in 1859. The production rose to $2,000,000 in 1861; to $11,250,000 in 1865; to $16,000,000 in 1870; to $32,000,000 in 1875; to $38,500,000 in 1880; to $51,600,000 in 1885, and to $75,000,000 in 1892.

Silver Greys, a nickname applied to the conservative element of the Whig party, because many of them withdrew from a meeting owing to a disagreeable measure. Some one remarked: "There go the 'Silver Greys,'" (they were gray-haired respectabilities), and the expression became a sobriquet.

Simcoe, John G. (1752–1806), came to America as a British soldier and commanded a regiment at Brandywine. He organized the "Queen's Rangers," which were active in the South and surrendered with Cornwallis at Yorktown.

Simms, William Gilmore (1806–1870), of South Carolina, wrote a number of poems, the best of which is "Atlantis, a Tale of the Sea." He is best known for his romances, illustrative of Southern life, and founded on Revolutionary and border incidents in South Carolina. Life by Trent.

Sims Case (1851), a famous fugitive slave case, which illustrates a common method of the seizure of negroes under the law of 1850. Sims was arrested in Boston on a false charge, and immediately claimed as the property of a Mr. Potter, of Virginia. He was sent back to Virginia on a certificate signed by the United States Commissioner, despite the intense indignation of the people, which ran so high that the court house was surrounded with chains and guarded by a company of armed men called afterward "Sims Brigade."

Simsbury, Conn., worthy of note because of the old copper mine which was used as a prison for captured Tories by the colonial sympathizers during the Revolution. The prison was used until 1827.

Sinking Fund. A sinking fund was created by act of August 12, 1790, to apply the surplus of income from imports and tonnage to the reduction of the debt. An act of 1795 put the entire matter of the public debt and its extinction in the hands of the Commissioners of the Sinking Fund.

Sioux, or Dakota Indians, first dwelt near the head waters of the Mississippi. Later several bands wandered to the Missouri, and some remained near the St. Peter's. They aided the English in 1812, but soon after made peace with the Government. In 1837 they ceded to the United States all their lands east of the Mississippi, and in 1851 made further grants. Hostilities arose in 1854, but the Indians were defeated in 1855, and peace followed. In 1862 a general uprising took place, and a large number of whites and Indians were killed. They were finally conquered, and many bands fled to Dakota. In 1863 the Minnesota Sioux were removed to Crow Creek, and some bands fled to British territory. A few bands continued hostilities. An unsatisfactory treaty was made with the Sioux by General Sherman in 1868. Sitting Bull and other chieftains were unreconciled. May 15, 1876, General Custer and 1100 men were destroyed at Little Big Horn River by a force of 9000 Sioux.

Sitka, or New Archangel, capital of Alaska, was settled in 1799 by Baranoff, but dates its growth from the time of the transference of the territory to the United States (1867).

Sitting Bull (1837–1890), was chief of the Sioux Indians who massacred General Custer's party on Little Big Horn River in 1876. He escaped to Canada, but surrendered in 1880.

Six Nations. (See Iroquois.)

"**Skinners,**" bands of marauders, adherents of the American cause, who infested what was known as the neutral ground in New York State during the Revolution. They were continually skirmishing with the "Cowboys," the British camp followers and adherents.

Slater, John F. (1815–1884), of Norwich, Conn., gained a large fortune in cotton manufacturing. He contributed the Slater Fund of $1,000,000 for the education of freedmen in the South.

Slater, Samuel (1768–1835), came to America from England in 1789 to introduce cotton machinery in the American States. His machinery was constructed from memory, as communication of models of English machinery was forbidden. He started his new cotton-spinning machinery at Pawtucket, R. I., in 1790, which was the beginning of cotton manufacture in America. He established mills at Webster and Slaterville, Mass.

Slaughter House Cases, three in number (at first five, but two dismissed on compromise). These cases arose out of an act of the Louisiana Legislature of 1869 to protect the health of New Orleans and to incorporate the "Crescent City Live-stock, Landing and Slaughter House Company." The Butchers' Benevolent Association of New Orleans protested against this act as creating a monopoly. Suit was also brought against the State by Paul Esteben and others, on ground that their business was injured. It was claimed by the plaintiffs that the creation of a monopoly of this sort by a State's Legislature was directly opposed to that clause of the Fourteenth Amendment to the Constitution, which prohibits State Legislatures from enforcing laws "which shall abridge the privileges or immunities of the citizens of the United States." The Supreme Court of Louisiana decided that this act did not conflict with the Fourteenth Amendment, and the Supreme Court of the United States confirmed the decision, thus decidedly limiting the scope of that Amendment.

Slave Representation. One of the chief subjects of dispute in the Convention of 1787, as in the case of previous attempts to make a constitution, was that of representation of that part of the population of certain States which consisted of slaves. It was contended on the one hand that, being persons, they should be represented, and on the other hand that, being property, they should be made the object of taxation. The compromise which was reached, and which continued in force until the abolition of slavery, provided that, for purposes of reckoning alike a State's proportion of representatives and its proportion of direct taxes, its population should be computed by adding to the whole number of free persons, exclusive of untaxed Indians, "three-fifths of all other persons," *i. e.*, of slaves. This mode of counting population was first suggested in 1783, by the Continental Congress, as a basis for the apportionment of contributions from the States, to be agreed upon as an amendment to the Articles of Confederation.

Slave Trade. The importation of negro slaves into the American colonies began with the year 1619, when a Dutch vessel brought a cargo of slaves into James River. In 1713, by the Treaty of Utrecht, Great Britain obtained the contract for supplying slaves to the Spanish West Indies. This stimulated the general slave trade. Some colonies desired to prohibit the importation of slaves, but Great Britain forced it upon them. Virginia passed several such acts, but they were vetoed. Pennsylvania passed bills prohibiting slave trading in 1712, 1714 and 1717, but they were vetoed. Massachusetts passed a similar bill in 1774, which was vetoed. It was prohibited by Rhode Island in 1774, by Connecticut the same year and by the non-importation covenant of the colonies October 24, 1774. It was forbidden by nearly all the States during the Revolution. The slave trade question was an important one in the formation of the Constitution. The Southern States, except Virginia and Maryland, demanded it, hence it was compromised by allowing Congress to prohibit it after 1808. The act of March 22, 1794, prohibited the carrying of slaves by American citizens from one foreign country to another. That of May 10, 1800, allowed United States warships to seize vessels engaged in such traffic. That of February 28, 1803, prohibited the introduction of slaves into States which had forbidden slavery. In 1808 the importation of slaves into the United States was forbidden. The acts of April 20, 1818, and March 3, 1819, authorized the President to send cruisers to Africa to stop the slave trade. Various projects for renewing the trade arose in the fifties. It was in reality never given up until 1865. No restrictions were placed upon domestic slave trading.

Slave Trade Tribunals. By the treaty of 1862 with Great Britain respecting the slave trade, it was agreed that when vessels suspected of being engaged in that traffic were detained by public vessels of either government, they should be brought for trial before one of three mixed courts established for that purpose at Sierra Leone, the Cape of Good Hope and New York. That at New York was, as the treaty permitted, removed to Washington, where it was reckoned a branch of the Department of the Interior. By the treaty of 1870 the system was abolished.

Slavery. Slavery in the American colonies began with the importation of a cargo of slaves into Virginia by a Dutch ship in 1619. In the other colonies it was gradually introduced. The slave trade was favored by the British Government during the eighteenth century. Meantime a sentiment unfavorable to it began to develop in the colonies. The Germantown Quakers drew up a memorial against it in 1688, Boston town-meeting in 1701. Woolman and other Quakers preached against it. Slaves were few in the North, but numerous in the South, where their increase and the danger felt from them caused severe laws respecting them. The Revolution, as a movement for liberty, with its declaration proclaiming all men free and equal, joined with the humanitarian spirit of the close of the century to increase anti-slavery sentiment. The Northern States either abolished slavery or provided for gradual emancipation. All the States but the southernmost forbade the importation of slaves from abroad. But the sentiment soon declined. In the Constitution of 1787, States were given representation in the House of Representatives for three-fifths of their slaves, and Congress was forbidden to prohibit the slave trade until 1808. The invention of the cotton-gin made slave labor more profitable than ever before, and the South began to defend slavery as a positive good, in spite of its obvious economic disadvantages. Abolition societies, first formed about 1793, languished after 1808. The Missouri Compromise of 1820 arranged that the area west of the Mississippi and north of 36° 30′ should not be open to slavery, except in the case of Missouri. The Ordinance of 1787 had forbidden slavery in the region north of the Ohio. The American Colonization Society tried to palliate the evils of slavery by emancipation and deportation. About 1830 the agitation against slavery took on a more ardent phase, and henceforth for thirty years slavery was the most absorbing of political themes. Slave labor demanded more and more new land, and the Government was led to the annexation of Texas and the war with Mexico largely by this need. After bitter disputes, the territory so acquired was thrown open to slavery if the settlers desired it; this was done by the Compromise of 1850. The Kansas-Nebraska Act of 1854 extended the same permission to territory north of 36° 30′, repealing the Missouri Compromise; and the Supreme Court (case of Dred Scott) sustained such repeal. The question of slavery in the territories proved the crucial question. Many in the North who had no desire for the abolition of slavery in States where it was already existent and legal were unwilling to see it extended, while slave-owners claimed Constitutional right to protection of their property in slaves, as essential if they were to have any share in the common territories. The Fugitive Slave Law of 1850 and the unwillingness of Northern people to execute it assisted to precipitate conflict. Finally, in 1860, the election of Lincoln was taken by the South as proof that their claims were to be disregarded, and secession and Civil War resulted. As a means of crushing rebellion, President Lincoln, on January 1, 1863, issued his Emancipation Proclamation. The Thirteenth Amendment (1865) abolished slavery.—In 1790 there were 698,000 slaves in the United States (40,000 in the North, 293,000 in Virginia, 107,000 in South Carolina, 103,000 in Maryland, 101,000 in North Carolina); in 1800, 894,000; in 1810, 1,191,000; in 1820, 1,538,000; in 1830, 2,009,000; in 1840, 2,487,000; in 1850, 3,204,000; in 1860, 3,954,000, the last being about one-fourth of the total population of the Southern States.

Slidell, John (born about 1793, died 1871), a Louisiana lawyer, and Congressman from that State in 1843–45. He was sent as U. S. Minister to Mexico in 1845, but was not received. From 1853 to 1861 he was a prominent member of the U. S. Senate, on the State-rights side. Having joined the Confederacy, Slidell was despatched as commissioner to France. With the other Confederate commissioner, Mason, he was seized en route by the American naval commander, Wilkes. (See Trent Affair.) Having been released, he continued his voyage to France, but did not induce the Government to side openly with the South. He settled in England after the war.

Slocum, Henry Warner (1827–1894), graduated at West Point in 1852. He was a colonel in the first battle of Bull Run, and continued with the Army of the Potomac as brigade and division commander, serving in the Peninsula and Antietam campaigns. In the great contests of Fredericksburg, Chancellorsville and Gettysburg he had charge of a corps, and in the last-named struggle he directed the right wing. As commander of the left wing he made the march with Sherman to the sea and through the Carolinas. He was a Congressman from New York 1869–1873 and 1885–1887, and was at different times mentioned as Democratic candidate for President.

Smalley, George W., born in 1833, won distinction as a war correspondent of the *New York Tribune* during the Civil War, and has for some years past been its representative in England.

Small-Pox. This disease raged at Boston in 1722–24. Cotton Mather advised the Turkish method of inoculation, and asked Dr. Zabdiel Boylston to make a trial of it. It was generally opposed by government and people, and Mather had a grenade thrown through his window in consequence.

Smallwood, William (1732–1792), commanded the Maryland battalion at Brooklyn Heights, White Plains, Fort Washington and Germantown. He distinguished himself at Camden. He was Governor of Maryland from 1785 to 1788.

Smith, Andrew J., born in 1815, commanded a Federal brigade at Corinth, Vicksburg and Pleasant Hill. He commanded the force which captured Fort de Russy and a corps at Nashville and Mobile.

Smith, Buckingham (1810–1871), was U. S. Secretary of Legation in Mexico from 1850 to 1852, and at Madrid from 1855 to 1858. He made valuable researches concerning the colonial history of Florida and Louisiana.

Smith, Caleb B., (1808–1864), represented Indiana in the U. S. Congress as a Whig from 1843 to 1849. He was Secretary of the Interior in Lincoln's Cabinet from 1861 to 1862, when he became a U. S. District Judge.

Smith, Charles Emory, born in 1842, became editor of the *Albany Express* in 1865, and of the *Albany Journal* in 1870. Since 1880 he has conducted the *Philadelphia Press*. He was Minister to Russia from 1890 to 1892.

Smith, Charles F. (1807–1862), was brevetted colonel for gallant service during the Mexican War. He fought at Monterey, Vera Cruz, Cerro Gordo, San Antonio, Contreras, Churubusco and the City of Mexico. The four companies in his command were known as "Smith's Light Battalion." He was assigned command in Kentucky at the outbreak of the Civil War, and distinguished himself by his skill. He fought at Fort Henry and led a division at Fort Donelson, which stormed and captured the high ground which commanded the fort. He died while preparing to advance upon Shiloh.

Smith, Edmund Kirby (1824–1893), distinguished himself at Cerro Gordo and Contreras during the Mexican War. He was appointed brigadier-general in the Confederate army, fought at Bull Run in 1861, led the advance in General Bragg's Kentucky campaign, defeated the National forces at Richmond, Ky., and fought at Perryville and Murfreesboro. In 1863 he received command of the Trans-Mississippi Department, where he organized a government, established factories for supplying the troops with munitions of war, and rendered the district self-supporting. His forces were the last to surrender in the Civil War.

Smith, Erasmus P. (1814–1882), was adviser in international law to the Mikado of Japan from 1871 to 1876. He has published a "Political Economy," which is based on purely physical laws.

Smith, Francis (1720?–1791), colonel, came to America as a British soldier, and commanded the troops sent to Concord in 1775. He fought at Lexington and Concord, and commanded a brigade at Long Island, and at Quaker Hill in 1778.

Smith, Gerrit (1797–1874), was prominent for his philanthropy in every good cause. He represented New York in the U. S. Congress as an Ultra-Abolitionist from 1853 to 1854. He identified himself with the anti-slavery party, and did all in his power for emancipation. He contributed liberally to the national cause during the Rebellion. He signed the bail-bond of Jefferson Davis with Horace Greeley.

Smith, Goldwin, born in 1823, came to America from England in 1868, and settled in Canada in 1871. He had been a prominent champion of the U. S. Government during the Civil War. He has advocated the annexation of Canada to the United States. He has written "The Civil War in America," "Experience of the American Commonwealth," and "The United States, an Outline of Political History" (1893).

Smith, Green C., born in 1832, commanded a regiment at Lebanon, Tenn. He represented Kentucky in the U. S. Congress as a Unionist from 1863 to 1866, and was Governor of Montana from 1866 to 1869. In 1876 he was the Presidential candidate of the Prohibition party.

Smith, Hoke, born in 1855, organized and became president of the Atlanta, Ga., *Evening Journal* in 1887. He became Secretary of the Interior in Cleveland's Cabinet in 1893.

Smith, James (1720?–1806), came to America from Ireland in 1729. He raised the first Pennsylvania company in 1774 for resisting Great Britain. He aided the patriotic cause by "An Essay on the Constitutional Power of Great Britain over the Colonies in America." He represented Pennsylvania in the Continental Congress from 1776 to 1778, and signed the Declaration of Independence.

Smith, John (1579–1632), a noted explorer and historical writer, was of English birth, and led a most adventurous early life. He traveled extensively, though the narratives of his various exploits are somewhat apocryphal. He was in the Netherlands, fought against the Turks, and joined Newport's expedition, which founded Virginia in 1607. In the outward voyage Smith was imprisoned. He soon after his release became the practical head of the struggling colony. He explored the Chickahominy region and was taken prisoner by Powhatan (to which epoch belongs the famous Pocahontas legend). The next year he made a long exploration of the Chesapeake Bay and its tributaries. He was president of the colony, but in 1609 met with an accident and returned to England. In 1614 he was on the New England coast, engaged in discoveries. He wrote voluminously, but is suspected of romantic exaggeration and coloring. His chief works were: "A True Relation," "Generall Historie of Virginia," and a "Description of New England."

Smith, John (1735–1816), represented Ohio in the U. S. Senate as a Democrat from 1803 to 1808. He was charged with being connected with Burr and Blennerhasset, but it was not proved.

Smith, John Cotton (1765–1845), was a member of the Connecticut Legislature from 1796 to 1800, and represented Connecticut in the U. S. Congress as a Federalist from 1800 to 1806. He was Judge of the State Supreme Court in 1809, Lieutenant-Governor in 1810 and Governor from 1813 to 1818. He was president of the American Bible Society from 1831 to 1845.

Smith, John E., born in 1816, led a regiment at Forts Henry and Donelson, and at Shiloh and Corinth. He commanded a division in the Vicksburg campaign and fought also at Missionary Ridge.

Smith, Joseph (1805–1844), claimed to have visions of a new religious faith about 1823, and from the revelations he produced the Book of Mormon. A church was founded in 1830, and in 1831 they emigrated from New York to Kirtland, Ohio, thence to Missouri. They were driven away by the citizens in 1838 and settled Nauvoo, Ill. The colony increased rapidly, and a charter was obtained. Smith gained almost unlimited power, and in 1843 sought to establish polygamy as an essential feature of their religion. Dissensions occurred and Smith was arrested. A mob surrounded the jail, and he was shot.

Smith, Joshua Toulmin (1816–1869), of England, visited America from 1837 to 1842, and published his "Discovery of America by the Northmen in the Tenth Century," which is regarded as an important authority.

Smith, Melancthon (1724–1798), was a member of the first New York Provincial Congress in 1775. In 1777 he was a commissioner for detecting and defeating conspiracies in the State. He was a delegate from New York to the Continental Congress from 1785 to 1788. In the New York convention in 1788 to consider the ratification of the Constitution, he supported the Anti-Federal party.

Smith, Melancthon, born in 1810, commanded the "Massachusetts" at the capture of Biloxi. He destroyed the Confederate ram "Manassas" when commanding the "Mississippi" at New Orleans, and served at Port Hudson and Fort Fisher.

Smith, Meriwether (1730–1790), was a member of the Virginia House of Burgesses in 1770 and of the Revolutionary conventions of 1775 and 1776. He was a delegate to the Continental Congress from 1778 to 1782, and a member of the convention that ratified the Federal Constitution in 1788.

Smith, Morgan L. (1822–1874), fought at Forts Henry and Donelson, and led a brigade at Shiloh and Corinth. He commanded a division at Vicksburg, Missionary Ridge, Knoxville and Chattanooga.

Smith, Nathan (1762–1822), represented Connecticut in the U. S. Congress as a Federalist from 1795 to 1799. He was a Judge of the Connecticut Supreme Court from 1806 to 1819. He was a leader at the Hartford convention in 1814.

Smith, Persifer F. (1798–1858), served with distinction throughout the Mexican War, commanding a brigade at Monterey, Churubusco, Contreras, Chapultepec and the City of Mexico. He was commissioner of armistice with Mexico in 1847.

Smith, Richard, born in 1823, came to America from Ireland in 1841. He became an editor of the Cincinnati *Gazette* in 1854, and in 1880 vice-president of the consolidated *Gazette* and *Commercial*, and has had an important part in politics.

Smith, Robert (1757–1842), of Maryland, served as a volunteer at the battle of Brandywine. He was one of the Presidential electors in 1789, and was the last surviving member. He served in the Maryland Senate in 1793, and was a member of the House of Delegates from 1796 to 1800. He was Secretary of the Navy in Jefferson's Cabinet from 1802 to 1805, and though appointed Attorney-General in 1805, really served as Secretary of the Navy from 1805 to 1809. He was Secretary of State in Madison's Cabinet from 1809 to 1811, when he was succeeded by Monroe.

Smith, Samuel (1752–1839), of Maryland, fought at Long Island, Harlem and White Plains, and was distinguished at Brandywine and Fort Mifflin, which he commanded. He also fought at Monmouth. He represented Maryland in the U. S. Congress as a Democrat from 1793 to 1803, in the U. S. Senate from 1803 to 1815, and again in the House from 1816 to 1822. He was again U. S. Senator from 1833 to 1835. He attempted, with his brother Robert, to control Madison's administration.

Smith, Samuel F., of Massachusetts, born in 1808, is the author of the national hymn, "My Country, 'tis of Thee."

Smith, Thomas K. (1820–1887), commanded a Federal regiment at Pittsburgh Landing, Corinth and Vicksburg. He led a division in the Red River expedition in 1863.

Smith, Truman (1791-1884), represented Connecticut in the U. S. Congress as a Whig from 1839 to 1843 and from 1845 to 1849, and in the U. S. Senate from 1849 to 1854.

Smith, William (1762-1840), represented South Carolina in the U. S. Congress as a Democrat from 1797 to 1799. He was a circuit judge from 1799 to 1816. He served in the South Carolina Senate from 1806 to 1808. He was a U. S. Senator from 1817 to 1823 and from 1826 to 1831. He was a strict State-rights advocate, but opposed nullification.

Smith, William (1796-1887), represented Virginia in the U. S. Congress as a Democrat from 1841 to 1843. He was Governor of Virginia from 1845 to 1848, and again a Congressman from 1853 to 1861.

Smith, William F., born in 1824, was engaged at the battle of Bull Run on the staff of General McDowell. He commanded a division at Yorktown, Williamsburg, Fair Oaks, Savage Station and Malvern Hill in 1862. He led a division at South Mountain and Antietam. He commanded a corps at Fredericksburg. He engaged in the operations about Chattanooga in 1863, and fought at Missionary Ridge. He rendered valuable services by placing a bridge across the Tennessee at Brown's Ferry, which made possible the victories at Chattanooga. He commanded a corps at Cold Harbor and Petersburg in 1864, and has written extensively on the war.

Smith College, Northampton, Mass., a college for girls founded by Sophia Smith, was chartered in 1871, but opened first in 1875.

Smithson, James (1754-1829), of England, bequeathed his estate of $500,000 for founding the Smithsonian Institution which was erected at Washington in 1846 "for the increase and diffusion of knowledge among men."

Smithsonian Institution, a scientific establishment in Washington, was organized by Act of Congress August, 1846, under the provisions of the will of James Smithson, which bequeathed $515,169 to the United States Government.

Smuggling. The British navigation laws and laws protective to manufactures caused bold and extensive smuggling throughout the colonies during the latter part of the seventeenth and half of the eighteenth centuries. Respectable merchants and prominent public men felt no qualms of conscience in cheating the revenue officers by illicit trade with pirates and with West India merchants. New York was the principal port for smugglers, though Boston, Philadelphia and Charleston were also enriched by smuggled goods. Governor Bellomont, of New York, found in 1700, that a "lycencious trade with pyrats, Scotland and Curaçao" had sprung up and the province of New York "grew rich, but the customes, they decreased." All this led to the attempt of the British Government to enforce the Acts of Trade, which did much to precipitate the Revolution.

Smyth, Alexander (1765-1830), came to America from Ireland in 1775. He represented Virginia in the U. S. Congress as a Democrat from 1817 to 1825 and from 1827 to 1830. He wrote "Regulations for the Infantry."

Socialistic Labor Party, organized at Baltimore by a congress of socialists in 1883. A manifesto was issued setting forth their demands and principles, both being moderate. The party is composed of local sections in nearly every city, these sections being divided into branches.

Softs, or Softshells, the name given to a faction of the Democratic party in New York from 1852 to 1860, partly identical with the "barnburners" of the preceding period, and disinclined to alliance with the pro-slavery democracy of the South.

Sojourner Truth (1775–1883), was freed from slavery in New York in 1817. She was an effective lecturer upon politics, temperance, women's rights and slavery.

Soley, James Russell, born in 1850, professor at Annapolis, has superintended the governmental publication of the naval records of the Civil War since 1883. He has been Assistant Secretary of the Navy from 1890 to 1893. He published "The Boys of 1812," the "Autobiography of Commodore Morris," and several books of naval history.

Somers, Richard (1778–1804), was given command of the "Nautilus" in Preble's squadron during the Tripolitan War from 1803 to 1804. He commanded a division of gunboats, and was distinguished for gallantry. He attempted to destroy the Tripolitan fleet by exploding a bomb-vessel in their midst. All on board were killed by the premature explosion of the vessel.

Sommersett Case. Sommersett was a slave, brought to London from Boston in October, 1769. In October, 1771, he escaped from his master, but was soon secured and brought before Lord Mansfield. The negro was discharged on the ground that in England slavery could exist only by positive law, and in the absence of such law a person could not be deprived of liberty on the ground that he was a slave. This decision determined the future course of England in the delivery of fugitives.

Sonoma, a Californian stronghold, taken June 14, 1846, without an engagement, by Ezekiel Merritt and twenty American soldiers of Captain Frémont's command. It is to be remembered in connection with the Bear Flag revolt in California, partially incited by Frémont. The fort, at the time of its capture, was ungarrisoned, being inhabited only by Colonel Vallejo, an old Mexican officer.

Sons of the American Revolution, a society of the male descendants of soldiers, sailors and conspicuous patriots during the Revolution, originally organized in California July 4, 1876. It has now thirty State branches.

Sons of Liberty. The name was first assumed by a society organized in Connecticut, in 1755, to advance theological liberty. Barré, in his speech in Parliament February 6, 1765, applied the words to the whole body of American patriots. They advocated non-importation, aided in the hanging in effigy of the stamp distributor, Oliver, in 1765, and proposed, in 1774, the organization of a Continental Congress. They embraced mainly the younger and more ardent element.

Sons of the Revolution, an organization of the same nature as the Sons of the American Revolution, first established in New York in 1875. It has now seventeen State branches.

Soulé, Pierre (1802–1870), was driven from France on account of his extreme liberal ideas and his attacks on the ministry of Charles X. He came to the United States in 1826. After studying law at New Orleans, he represented Louisiana in the U. S. Senate as a Democrat in 1847 and from 1849 to 1853. He was Minister to Spain from 1853 to 1855, and was one of the ministers who framed the celebrated "Ostend Manifesto" in 1854. He was an able and eloquent defender of the Southern cause while in public life.

South, University of the, Sewanee, Tenn., was chartered by Episcopalians in 1858, but not opened for ten years on account of the war. The theological department was opened in 1876.

South American Republics, Recognition of. As early as 1817 Henry Clay had ardently advocated in Congress the appropriation of money for sending an accredited minister to the self-liberated State of Buenos Ayres. His motion was, however, rejected. By 1822, through the efforts of Bolivar and other patriotic South American liberators, Chili, Peru, New Grenada and Venezuela had been practically freed from Spanish dominion. In March, 1822, President Monroe, in a special message to Congress, recommended the recognition of these republics and the establishment of international relations with them. Congress passed an almost unanimous resolution to this effect in the same year, and by 1825 arrangements had been made for an exchange of ministers.

South Carolina was one of the original thirteen States of the American Union. It was partially explored by the Spaniards in 1525, who named it Chicora. French Huguenots under Ribaut attempted to plant a colony at Port Royal in 1562, but the colonists soon abandoned the undertaking and returned to France. In 1670 William Sayle and a party of Englishmen founded Charleston. Charles II. gave the territory between 29° north latitude and 36° 30′ north latitude to eight of his favorites (1663), and in 1665 he issued a charter to the proprietors by which the virtual control of the colony was placed in their hands. They employed Locke, the philosopher, to draw up a constitution which should provide an ideal government. Locke's Fundamental Constitutions, or the "Grand Model," attempted in vain to set up the feudal system and was formally abandoned by the proprietors in 1693. In 1700 the colony was separated from North Carolina, the boundary being fixed in 1732. South Carolina became a royal colony in 1729. The Southern boundary caused a dispute with Georgia which was settled in 1787 in favor of Georgia. South Carolina then ceded her western territory, consisting of a strip twelve miles wide, to the general government. During the Revolution the important battles of Fort Moultrie, Cowpens, King's Mountain, Camden and Eutaw Springs were fought in South Carolina. The first constitution was made in 1776, the present in 1868. The National Constitution was ratified May 23, 1788, by a vote of 149 to 73. For some years the Federalists retained control of the State because of the wealth and influence of their leaders. In 1800 Pinckney refused the offer of the Democrats in the Legislature to choose electors favorable to Jefferson and himself and stood by his colleague, Adams, in his defeat. From this time the State was solidly Democratic. By the famous compromise of 1808 the apportionment of representatives was made according to population and taxes. The State protested against the gross inequality of the tariff of 1828 by the "South Carolina Exposition," in which the doctrine of nullification was defended. In 1832 the tariff of 1828, the "tariff of abominations," was modified, but the principle of protection still retained, whereupon South Carolina in convention at Columbia on November 24, 1832, declared the tariff acts of 1828 and 1832 null and void and prohibited payment of duties after February 1, 1833. Henry Clay's compromise tariff was passed in 1833 and at the same time a force bill became law; on March 11, 1833, the nullification ordinance was repealed. South Carolina was the mother of secession and after 1850 she was ready to secede at any time when she could rely upon the aid of the other States. December 20, 1860, an ordinance of secession was passed, to sustain which the State furnished 60,000 troops out of a population including only 47,000 voters. April 12, 1861, Fort Sumter was fired on. South Carolina was re-admitted June 25, 1868. From 1868 to 1873 the ("carpet-bag") State government was exceedingly corrupt. In 1870 and 1871 the Ku Klux Klan aimed at the suppression of the negro vote by outrage. In 1876 the Republicans carried the State in a disorderly election. Since that time the State has been steadily Democratic. The population of South Carolina in 1790 was 249,033; in 1890 it was 1,151,149.

South Carolina, University of, at Columbia, was chartered as a college in 1801, organized as a university in 1865.

"South Carolina Gazette." There were four "gazettes" published in South Carolina during the early years of journalism. The first was established at Charleston, January 8, 1732, by Thomas Whitmarsh, it being the first newspaper of the colony. Publication was suspended within a year. In February, 1734, Lewis Timothy began in Charleston the second "gazette." This was suspended several times, and finally ceased to exist in 1800. Robert Wells founded, in 1758, the third, called the *South Carolina and American General Gazette.* Publication suspended 1780. The fourth, called the *South Carolina Gazette and Country Journal*, was published 1765, by Charles Crouch. Publication suspended at the Revolution.

South Carolina Historical Society, founded at Charleston in 1855. It has a small library, including some important manuscripts. It has published three volumes of collections and a part of a fourth.

South Company (Södre Compagnie, Compagnia Australis, Suyder Compagnie, General-Handels-Compagnie). See Swedish West India Company.

South Dakota was originally a part of the Louisiana cession. Before the settlement of the boundary between the United States and Canada the territory was under British rule. Dakota was organized as a territory in 1861, and in 1889, November 2, the two Dakotas were admitted as States. The manufacture or sale of intoxicating liquors was prohibited by an act of 1890. The State is Republican. Its population in 1890 was 328,808.

South Mountain, Md., an engagement, during Lee's expedition into Maryland, which continued throughout the day, September 14, 1862, between the main body of Lee's army and several divisions of Burnside's column of McClellan's army. Jackson had been dispatched by Lee to capture Harper's Ferry, he himself moving toward South Mountain, whither he was pursued by McClellan's troops. The engagement was opened by an attempt by the Confederates, under Hill, to oppose the Union troops' passage of Catoctin Creek. This was unsuccessful, and the Confederates retired farther up the mountain, guarding all passages with batteries. Cox, Reno, Hooker and Ricketts forced their way up the right and left country roads and succeeded in carrying the eminence, outflanking the Confederates on the right and left. The latter were forced to retreat in the night, leaving their dead.

South Sea. So near was the South Sea or Pacific Ocean thought to be to the Atlantic at the time of the granting of the colonial charters that several of them granted lands extending to the South Sea. Such were the charter of the Virginia Company, granted in 1609, and the charters of Massachusetts Bay, Connecticut and Carolina.

Southampton, Henry Wriothesley, Earl of (1573–1624), was active in the colonization of America, sending, among others, expeditions under Bartholomew Gosnold in 1602, and under Lord Arundel in 1605. He was treasurer (*i. e.*, president) of the Virginia Company from 1620.

Southampton Insurrection. (See Turner, Nat.)

Southard, Samuel L. (1787–1842), represented New Jersey in the U. S. Senate as a Democrat from 1821 to 1823. He was Secretary of the Navy in the Cabinets of Monroe and Adams from 1823 to 1829. He was acting Secretary of the Treasury from March to July in 1825, Governor of New Jersey in 1832, and a U. S. Senator from 1833 to 1842.

Southwest Territory, a territory of the United States, comprising all the region ceded by North Carolina (now Tennessee) and the narrow strip ceded by South Carolina. This was organized in 1790 as the Southwest Territory, with institutions resembling those of the Northwestern, except for the admission of slavery. With the admission of Tennessee in 1796 and the organization of the Mississippi Territory in 1798, this Territory went out of existence.

Spaight, Richard Dobbs (1758–1802), was a delegate from North Carolina to the Continental Congress from 1782 to 1784, and to the Convention of 1787, and was a signer of the Constitution. He was Governor of North Carolina in 1792, and served in the U. S. Congress as a Democrat from 1798 to 1801.

Spain. Spain was an ally of France and the United States from 1778 to 1782. From 1783 she possessed all to the south and west of the United States. By the treaty of October 27, 1795, between the United States and Spain, the southern boundary of the United States was defined, the navigation of the Mississippi was granted, and New Orleans made a port of deposit.

A claims convention was concluded in 1802, but Spain did not ratify it until 1818. The cession of Louisiana in 1803 and the occupation of West Florida in 1810 caused some trouble with Spain. By the treaty of 1819 the Floridas were ceded to the United States, and the Sabine agreed upon as the western boundary of Louisiana; the United States assumed claims of $5,000,000 due from Spain to United States citizens. Soon after, Mexico and the Central and South American States secured their independence of Spain. Claims conventions were concluded in 1834 and 1871. An extradition convention was concluded in 1877, which was amended by the convention of 1882. A reciprocity agreement was made February 13, 1884. A reciprocity treaty, relative to American trade with the islands of Cuba and Porto Rico, was concluded with Spain in 1891.

Sparks, Jared (1789–1866), an American historical writer, was graduated at Harvard in 1815, and after a short experience as a Unitarian clergyman, became the editor of the *North American Review* in 1824; this position he held until 1831. Afterward he was professor in Harvard, and president of that college in 1849–1853. His voluminous works include the edition of the "Diplomatic Correspondence of the American Revolution" in twelve volumes; the writings of Washington with a life, in twelve volumes; the "Library of American Biography" (of which Sparks himself wrote the lives of Arnold, Allen and others), an edition of Franklin's works, and a biography of Gouverneur Morris. His life and letters have been edited by H. B. Adams in 1893.

Speaker. After the model of the English House of Commons, the popular branch of each colonial legislature had its speaker. When, at the time of the Revolution, the State constitutions were formed, some States gave this same title to the presiding officers of their upper houses. The Constitution of 1787 provides for the office of speaker of the House of Representatives, in saying "The House of Representatives shall choose their Speaker and other officers;" but that the Speaker should be, as he now is, the most important and influential official of the Federal Government, next after the President, was not contemplated by the framers of the Constitution. This has come about gradually, as a consequence of the development of the system of standing committees (see art. Committees) and of the entrusting of their appointment to the Speaker. The first speaker of the modern kind, more a leader of the House than a mere presiding officer, was Speaker Clay.

AMERICAN HISTORIANS.

John Lothrop Motley. Washington Irving. John Fiske.
George Bancroft.
Wm. H. Prescott. Francis Parkman. Jared Sparks.

Speakers of the House of Representatives. The numbers at the left refer to the successive Congresses.

Congress.	Name.	State.	Term.
1	F. A. Muhlenberg	Pennsylvania	April 1, 1789, to March 4, 1791.
2	Jonathan Trumbull	Connecticut	October 24, 1791, to March 4, 1793.
3	F. A. Muhlenberg	Pennsylvania	December 2, 1793, to March 4, 1795.
4	Jonathan Dayton	New Jersey	December 7, 1795, to March 4, 1797.
5	Jonathan Dayton	New Jersey	May 15, 1797, to March 4, 1799.
6	Theodore Sedgwick	Massachusetts	December 2, 1799, to March 4, 1801.
7	Nathaniel Macon	North Carolina	December 7, 1801, to March 4, 1803.
8	Nathaniel Macon	North Carolina	October 17, 1803, to March 4, 1805.
9	Nathaniel Macon	North Carolina	December 2, 1805, to March 4, 1807.
10	Joseph B. Varnum	Massachusetts	October 26, 1807, to March 4, 1809.
11	Joseph B. Varnum	Massachusetts	May 22, 1809, to March 4, 1811.
12	Henry Clay	Kentucky	November 4, 1811, to March 4, 1813.
13*a*	Henry Clay	Kentucky	May 24, 1813, to January 19, 1814.
13*b*	Langdon Cheves	South Carolina	January 19, 1814, to March 4, 1815.
14	Henry Clay	Kentucky	December 4, 1815, to March 4, 1817.
15	Henry Clay	Kentucky	December 1, 1817, to March 4, 1819.
16*a*	Henry Clay	Kentucky	December 6, 1819, to May 15, 1820.
16*b*	John W. Taylor	New York	November 15, 1820, to March 4, 1821.
17	Philip P. Barbour	Virginia	December 4, 1821, to March 4, 1823.
18	Henry Clay	Kentucky	December 1, 1823, to March 4, 1825.
19	John W. Taylor	New York	December 5, 1825, to March 4, 1827.
20	Andrew Stevenson	Virginia	December 3, 1827, to March 4, 1829.
21	Andrew Stevenson	Virginia	December 7, 1829, to March 4, 1831.
22	Andrew Stevenson	Virginia	December 5, 1831, to March 4, 1833.
23*a*	Andrew Stevenson	Virginia	December 2, 1833, to June 2, 1834.
23*b*	John Bell	Tennessee	June 2, 1834, to March 4, 1835.
24	James K. Polk	Tennessee	December 7, 1835, to March 4, 1837.
25	James K. Polk	Tennessee	September 5, 1837, to March 4, 1839.
26	Robert M. T. Hunter	Virginia	December 16, 1839, to March 4, 1841.
27	John White	Kentucky	May 31, 1841, to March 4, 1843.
28	John W. Jones	Virginia	December 4, 1843, to March 4, 1845.
29	John W. Davis	Indiana	December 1, 1845, to March 4, 1847.
30	Robert C. Winthrop	Massachusetts	December 6, 1847, to March 4, 1849.
31	Howell Cobb	Georgia	December 22, 1849, to March 4, 1851.
32	Linn Boyd	Kentucky	December 1, 1851, to March 4, 1853.
33	Linn Boyd	Kentucky	December 5, 1853, to March 4, 1855.
34	Nathaniel P. Banks	Massachusetts	February 2, 1856, to March 4, 1857.
35	James L. Orr	South Carolina	December 7, 1857, to March 4, 1859.
36	William Pennington	New Jersey	February 1, 1860, to March 4, 1861.
37	Galusha A. Grow	Pennsylvania	July 4, 1861, to March 4, 1863.
38	Schuyler Colfax	Indiana	December 7, 1863, to March 4, 1865.
39	Schuyler Colfax	Indiana	December 4, 1865, to March 4, 1867.
40	Schuyler Colfax	Indiana	March 4, 1867, to March 4, 1869.
41	James G. Blaine	Maine	March 4, 1869, to March 4, 1871.
42	James G. Blaine	Maine	March 4, 1871, to March 4, 1873.
43	James G. Blaine	Maine	December 1, 1873, to March 4, 1875.
44*a*	Michael C. Kerr	Indiana	December 6, 1875, to August 20, 1876.
44*b*	Samuel J. Randall	Pennsylvania	December 4, 1876, to March 4, 1877.
45	Samuel J. Randall	Pennsylvania	October 15, 1877, to March 4, 1879.
46	Samuel J. Randall	Pennsylvania	March 18, 1879, to March 4, 1881.
47	J. Warren Keifer	Ohio	December 5, 1881, to March 4, 1883.
48	John G. Carlisle	Kentucky	December 3, 1883, to March 4, 1885.
49	John G. Carlisle	Kentucky	December 7, 1885, to March 4, 1887.
50	John G. Carlisle	Kentucky	December 5, 1887, to March 4, 1889.
51	Thomas B. Reed	Maine	December 2, 1889, to March 4, 1891.
52	Charles F. Crisp	Georgia	December 8, 1891, to March 4, 1893.
53	Charles F. Crisp	Georgia	August 7, 1893, to ———.

Specie Circular, a treasury circular drafted by Senator Benton and issued at President Jackson's orders, July 11, 1836, which directed that nothing but gold and silver should be received in payment for the public lands. This was Jackson's last financial exploit. The circular was issued quite in opposition to the sentiment or will of Congress. The next Congress passed a bill to rescind this specie circular, but Jackson killed it by a pocket veto. The circular created much indignation throughout the country, and contributed greatly to the financial crash of 1837.

Specie Resumption. In 1861, after the breaking out of the Civil War, the banks of New York suspended coin payments, and their example was followed by most of the banks through the country. Congress authorized the issue of large quantities of United States notes, to be a legal-tender. January 14, 1875, an act was passed by Congress ordering the resumption of specie payments of Government contracts to begin January 1, 1879. To this end the purchase of bullion and the manufacture of subsidiary coin was at once begun for the redemption of fractional notes. These notes were rapidly presented for redemption, compelling the Government to run its mints over business hours.

Speed, James (1812–1887), was prominent in urging Kentucky to refrain from disunion, and was active in the national cause. He was U. S. Attorney-General from 1864 to 1866 in the Cabinets of Lincoln and Johnson.

"**Speedwell,**" the ship which was to have sailed with the "Mayflower" in 1620, and which joined her at Southampton for that purpose, having brought the Pilgrims from Delfthaven thither. Twice she started and twice she put back, first to Dartmouth and then to Plymouth; finally the "Mayflower" sailed alone.

Spencer, John C. (1788–1855), represented New York in the U. S. Congress as a Democrat from 1817 to 1819. He served in Tyler's Cabinet as Secretary of War from 1841 to 1843 and as Secretary of the Treasury from 1843 to 1844.

Spencer, Joseph (1714–1789), was appointed brigadier-general in the Continental army in 1775. He served at Boston and New York and commanded the unsuccessful Rhode Island expedition. He represented Connecticut in the Continental Congress in 1779.

Spies, August V. T. (1855–1887), Anarchist, came to the United States from Germany in 1871. He was hanged as one of the instigators of the Haymarket massacre in Chicago in 1886, when sixty-two policemen were wounded.

Spinner, Francis E. (1802–1890), represented New York in the U. S. Congress as an anti-slavery Democrat from 1855 to 1861. He was U. S. Treasurer from 1861 to 1875, and ended his service without the discrepancy in his accounts of a penny.

Spiritualists, a name applied to the believers in the theory that spirits can and do act through sensitive organizations known as mediums. It first came into prominence in the United States through the manifestations of the Fox Sisters, at Hydeville, N. Y., 1848. The phenomena consist of the moving of physical objects, rappings, spirit-photographing, etc. The believers in these manifestations are not yet completely organized into a separate body, but issue periodicals aud books in great numbers.

Spofford, Ainsworth R., born in 1825, has been librarian of Congress since 1864. He has published "The American Almanac" (annual) and "A Practical Manual of Parliamentary Rules."

Spoils System. The system of partisan use of the offices, as a means of rewarding those who have worked for the election of the appointer and of punishment for those who have not, was earlier developed in New York and Pennsylvania than elsewhere, largely because of the existence in those States of a large body of apathetic non-English voters. In New York the ill-devised council of appointment had much to do with the growth of the system, and so had Aaron Burr. In the Federal Government, Jefferson carried out the system to a considerable extent. The Act of 1820 prescribing a four-years' term for many officers favored its growth. Finally, the politicians who surrounded Jackson brought it to its full development as an engine of party warfare. It has since been a regular reature of American politics in every administration, tempered of late by the provisions of the Civil Service Act of 1883. The phrase was derived from a statement of Senator W. L. Marcy, of New York, in a speech in the Senate in 1832. Speaking of the New York politicians, he said: "They see nothing wrong in the rule that to the victor belong the spoils of the enemy."

Spotswood, Alexander (1676–1740), was Governor of Virginia from 1710 to 1723, and greatly improved the condition of the colony by wise laws and careful administration. He was Deputy Postmaster-General of the colonies from 1730 to 1739.

Spottsylvania Court House, Va., an indecisive, but hard-fought and sanguinary engagement during the Civil War (1864). Grant led the Union army of about 135,000 men, while Lee's Confederates numbered a little over 100,000. After the battle of the Wilderness, Grant wished to cut off Lee's communications with Richmond, and with this intention he hurried forward toward Spottsylvania Court House. Lee hastened in the same direction and, by obstructing the Federal route with felled trees and skirmishers, managed to arrive first, Warren's advance corps of Grant's army being detained on the road. On May 7, 1864, there was some slight skirmishing. May 8, Grant sent Sheridan's cavalry corps to ride around the Confederate army, tearing up bridges and railroads and demolishing trains. This corps engaged J. E. B. Stuart's Confederate cavalry, defeating them and killing their leader. The National line was formed with Hancock holding the right, Warren and Sedgwick the centre, and Burnside the left. On the 9th and 10th, assaults were made upon a salient or weak point in the Confederate defences by Hancock, and then by Upton, but the Confederates remained firm. It rained on the 11th and there was no fighting. On the 12th a desperate charge by Hancock captured the coveted salient. The Confederate Edward Johnston and 4000 men were taken. This captured point the Confederates charged again and again, and there was frightful slaughter on both sides. From this "death angle," the Confederates retired at midnight.

Sprague, Charles (1791–1875), poet, was cashier of the Globe Bank, Boston, from 1824 to 1865. He won distinction by his poems. He wrote a "Shakespeare Ode," "The Brothers" and "The Family Meeting," etc.

Sprague, Peleg (1793–1880), represented Maine in the U. S. Congress as a National Republican from 1825 to 1829, and in the U. S. Senate from 1829 to 1835. He was U. S. Judge for the Massachusetts district from 1841 to 1865.

Sprague, William, born in 1830, was Governor of Rhode Island from 1860 to 1863. He represented Rhode Island in the U. S. Senate as a Republican from 1863 to 1875.

Spring Hill, Tenn., scene of a defeat of 2600 Federal troops, led by Colonel Coburn, by General Van Dorn, commanding 20,000 Confederates, March 5, 1863. Coburn had been sent thither by Rosecrans to co-operate with Sheridan, who was making demonstrations against Forrest toward the South. Van Dorn fell upon him when quite unprepared for battle. Coburn fought gallantly during one entire day, despite the fact that he was completely surrounded by Van Dorn's superior numbers. In the evening his ammunition had given out and his forces were greatly reduced, so he had to surrender 1300 of his infantry. Later, November 29, 1864, a brief battle was fought here during Hood's campaign in Tennessee, between a small detachment of Hood's army and a company of Federals from Thomas' force under Stanley. The latter was guarding a baggage-train when the Confederates came upon him. There was to decisive victory.

Springer, William M., born in 1836, was secretary of the Illinois Constitutional Convention in 1862. He has represented Illinois in the U. S. Congress as a Democrat since 1875. He was a member of the Potter committee on the Presidential election of 1876, and of the joint committee which reported the Electoral Commission Bill. He has been prominent in tariff legislation.

Springfield, Ill., became the State capital in 1837. It was laid out in 1822, and was incorporate as a city in 1840. It was the residence of Lincoln before he became President.

Springfield, Mass., was settled in 1635 by emigrants from Roxbury. In 1675 the settlement was burned by Indians. Springfield dates its importance from the opening of the Boston and Albany Railroad in 1838. It received a city charter in 1852.

Springfield, Mo., occupied by Brown with 2400 Federal militia in 1862–63. Marmaduke, commanding 4000 Confederates, appeared suddenly January 8, 1863, from Arkansas, and fell upon Brown's outposts. The latter's five earthworks were speedily destroyed. Brown fought gallantly from ten o'clock till dark. Marmaduke then withdrew, having lost over 200 men. Brown's loss was even more severe. He himself lost his right arm.

Springfield, N. J., Battle of, June 23, 1780. In June, 1780, General Clinton advanced to seize the American stores at Morristown, N. J. On the twenty-third his army of about 5000 men met the Americans at Springfield. The Americans were unable to resist and were driven back to the Short Hills. Here Greene formed them again and the British could not force their position. The British then fired the village and retreated. The loss of the Americans was estimated at about sixty, that of the British about 300.

"**Squatter Sovereignty.**" A term derisively used as a substitute for the phrase "popular sovereignty," which Douglas and others used to characterize their plan of leaving it to the inhabitants of each territory to decide, without Congressional interference, whether it should become a free State or a slave State.

Squier, Ephraim G. (1821–1888), was chargé d'affaires to the Central American States in 1849, and U. S. Commissioner to Peru in 1863. He made valuable historical and geographical investigations in Central and South America.

Stamp Act. In 1765 George Grenville, Chancellor of the English Excheqner, proposed a bill for taxing the colonies through a stamp duty. No serious opposition was expected. But the measure aroused great excitement in America as an attempt at taxation without representation.

Stamp Act Congress, a body of delegates from all the colonies except New Hampshire, Virginia, North Carolina and Georgia, which met at New York October 7, 1765, and adjourned October 25. The action of this Congress consisted of an address to the king, petitions to Parliament and a declaration of the rights and grievances of the colonies. It protested that the colonies could only be taxed by their own representatives in the colonial assemblies; claimed the inherent right of trial by jury, and declared the Stamp Act to have a manifest tendency to subvert the rights and liberties of the colonies. The House of Commons objected to the declaration as that of an unconstitutional gathering.

Stanbery, Henry (1803–1881), was Attorney-General in Johnson's Cabinet from 1866 to 1868, when he resigned to become leading counsel for the President in the impeachment trial.

Standish, Myles (1584?–1656), came to America with the Pilgrims in 1620. He led the exploring expeditions to discover a suitable place for settlement. He was appointed military captain in 1621, being the first commissioned military officer in New England. He rendered valuable service in repelling Indian hostilities. He visited England in 1625 as agent for the colony and returned with supplies in 1626. He founded Duxbury in 1632. He was a member of the executive council, and for many years treasurer of the colony. His courtship of Priscilla Mullens was commemorated by Longfellow, in his "Courtship of Miles Standish."

Stanford, Leland (1824–1893), became a successful merchant in California. He was Governor of California from 1861 to 1863. As president of the Central Pacific Railroad he superintended its construction over the mountains. He served in the U. S. Senate as a Republican from 1884 to 1893. He founded Leland Stanford, Jr., University in California with $20,000,000, which offers all branches of education.

Stanley, David S., born in 1828, led a division at Island No. 10 and Corinth in 1862. He was active in Sherman's Georgia invasion. He fought at Murfreesboro, Nashville and Franklin.

Stanley, Henry M., explorer, born in 1840, came to the United States from Wales in 1855. He has made exploring expeditions in Africa in 1870–72, 1874–77, 1879–82 and 1887–89, accounts of which he has published.

Stannard, George J. (1820–1886), fought at Bull Run and Harper's Ferry. He led a brigade at Gettysburg in 1863. He led the advance on Petersburg and Richmond, and captured Fort Harrison in 1864.

Stanton, Edwin McMasters (1814–1869), the great War Secretary of the Civil War, built up a large legal business in Ohio and Pennsylvania before the Rebellion, but held no offices except reporter to the Ohio Supreme Court. President Buchanan called him to his Cabinet as Attorney-General in 1860. In 1862 President Lincoln selected him to succeed Cameron as Secretary of War. His conduct of this department was very energetic; he was, however, embroiled at times with politicians and officers; especially notable were his controversies with McClellan and Sherman. Continuing in Johnson's Cabinet, he differed seriously with the President, and was suspended in August, 1867. This action brought to a head the quarrel between Congress and the President. Stanton was restored in January, 1868, removed in February. The President's impeachment followed. By President Grant Stanton was nominated as Justice of the Supreme Court, but he died soon afterward.

Stanton, Elizabeth Cady, born in 1815, has been prominent as an advocate of woman suffrage. She has addressed legislatures, committees and conventions. She was a candidate for Congress in New York in 1868.

Stanwix, John (1690–1765), came to America from England in 1756 as commander of a battalion and was assigned command in the Southern District. In 1758 he constructed the important fortress called Fort Stanwix at the Oneida carrying-place on the Mohawk River. In 1759 he repaired old Fort Du Quesne at Pittsburgh. He returned to England in 1760.

Stanwix, Fort, erected in 1758 on the Mohawk River, at what was called "the great carrying place," by Brigadier-General Stanwix. The name was afterward changed to Fort Schuyler. It was built to protect the country from the depredations of the Six Nations, and treaties were concluded there between those Indians and the English, determining the boundaries of the Indian Territory in 1768. In 1777 Peter Gansevoort was placed in command of the fort and was besieged for nearly a month by the English under St. Leger. He refused to capitulate, however, and St. Leger was compelled to withdraw. The fort was abandoned in 1781, being partially destroyed by the floods of that year.

"Star of the West," a steamer sent by the Federal Government from New York, January 5, 1861, laden with reinforcements and supplies for Fort Sumter. She appeared off the Charleston bar January 9, but was promptly fired upon by the batteries of Fort Moultrie and Morris Island, and being struck by a shell put back to New York. She was afterward, April 20, 1861, seized by the Confederates in the harbor of Indianola.

Star Routes, the name applied to postal lines over which the mail cannot be carried by railroad or steamboat. In 1881 the second assistant Postmaster

General, Thomas J. Brady, and others, including Senator S. W. Dorsey, of Arkansas, were accused of combining with certain mail contractors to defraud the Government. The combination had originally 134 routes, upon which the compensation for service under the contract amounted to $143,169. By increasing the number of trips per week, shortening the contract time for each trip and allowing therefor, the compensation was raised to $622,808. Dorsey was brought to trial in 1882. Dorsey denied all charges and the first jury failed to bring a decision. A second trial took place in 1883 and Dorsey was acquitted. Brady's trial was postponed, and no decision was found against him. But the corrupt combination was broken up.

"Star-Spangled Banner." This song was composed September 13, 1814, during the bombardment of Fort McHenry, by Francis S. Key, a young Baltimorean, who had gone down the harbor in a cartel vessel. It was published and sung at the theatres to the air of "Anacreon in Heaven," and immediately became popular.

Stark, John (1728–1822), a noted Revolutionary general, was a native of New Hampshire. He was a hero of the Indian border warfare, and was at one time captured. He fought in the French and Indian War, and was active in the Revolution, being one of the principal leaders at Bunker Hill. He served in Canada, at Trenton and Princeton, and resigned in 1777. But the danger of Burgoyne's invasion called out the New Hampshire militia, and they demanded Stark as a commander. At Bennington, August 16, 1777, Stark overthrew the Hessian detachment, and in this way powerfully contributed to the catastrophe of Saratoga. He was made a brigadier-general, and served until the close of the war. His life has been written by Everett.

Stars and Bars, the flag of the Confederacy. March 5, 1861, the Flag Committee appointed in the Provisional Senate of the Southern States recommended that "the flag of the Confederate States shall consist of a red field with a white space extending horizontally through the centre, and equal in width to one-third the width of the flag." It was first displayed March 4, 1861, simultaneously with the inauguration of Lincoln, being unfurled over the State House at Montgomery, Ala. In 1863 the Confederate Senate adopted a white flag with one blue star in the centre, the Stars and Bars bearing too close a resemblance to the Stars and Stripes. Johnston and Beauregard also adopted a "battle flag," a red ground with a blue diagonal cross and white stars.

"Starving Time." In 1609, after the departure of Captain John Smith for England, the settlers of Jamestown, Va., were, during many months, reduced to the last extremities, being obliged to eat rats, snakes, toads and even dead bodies to prevent starvation. This was known as the "starving time."

State, Department of. Under the Continental Congress, foreign affairs were at first managed by a committee. January 10, 1781, the office of Secretary for Foreign Affairs was instituted. Livingston held it till 1783, Jay from 1784 to 1789. In the First Congress a Department of Foreign Affairs and a Home Department were at first planned, but on July 27, 1789, the Department of State was formed, uniting the functions of the two.

Staten Island, N. Y., was bought from the Indians by Michael Pauw in 1631 and later transferred to the Dutch West India Company. It was settled by colonists under De Vries in 1637, and two years later burned and ravaged by the Raritan Indians. The West India Company acquired the patroon titles on the island, but in 1665 it was confiscated by the Duke of York.

States. The Declaration of Independence declared "that these united colonies are, and of right ought to be, free and independent States." Thirteen States thenceforth existed. Whether they were from the beginning independent and sovereign, or whether the primary allegiance of the citizen was from the first due to the United States, has been much debated. The fact is, that both views can find countenance in public and official expressions of that early time, and that the Union has come to be supreme in all men's minds only by historic processes. Ardent advocacy of "State-rights" was associated with the theory that the Constitution was a voluntary compact, and led to the doctrines of nullification and secession.—The States at once organized governments modeled on those of the colonial period, with strict severance of the legislative, executive and judiciary departments. It has been one of the chief causes of the success of the American Union that, from the beginning, its scheme provided for the admission of new States. On October 10, 1780, the Continental Congress resolved that the western territory to be ceded to the United States "shall be settled and formed into distinct, republican States, which shall become members of the Federal Union, and have the same rights of sovereignty, freedom and independence, as the other States." The first States so admitted were Vermont and Kentucky. The act admitting Kentucky was passed on February 4, 1791, to take effect June 1, 1792; that admitting Vermont was passed February 18, 1791, to take effect March 4, 1792. The date usually regarded as the date of admission of a State is that on which the act took effect. A list of the States, in order of accession, follows:

States, Admission of. (The date given is that when admission took effect.)

State			Date
Delaware	ratified the Constitution		December 7, 1787
Pennsylvania	do.	do.	December 12, 1787
New Jersey	do.	do.	December 18, 1787
Georgia	do.	do.	January 2, 1788
Connecticut	do.	do.	January 9, 1788
Massachusetts	do.	do.	February 6, 1788
Maryland	do.	do.	April 28, 1788
South Carolina	do.	do.	May 23, 1788
New Hampshire	do.	do.	June 21, 1788
Virginia	do.	do.	June 25, 1788
New York	do.	do.	July 26, 1788
North Carolina	do.	do.	November 21, 1789
Rhode Island	do.	do.	May 29, 1790
Vermont	was admitted to the Union		March 4, 1791
Kentucky	do.	do.	June 1, 1792

State			Date
Tennessee	was admitted to the Union		June 1, 1796
Ohio	do.	do.	November 29, 1802
Louisiana	do.	do.	April 30, 1812
Indiana	do.	do.	December 11, 1816
Mississippi	do.	do.	December 10, 1817
Illinois	do.	do.	December 3, 1818
Alabama	do.	do.	December 14, 1819
Maine	do.	do.	March 15, 1820
Missouri	do.	do.	August 10, 1821
Arkansas	do.	do.	June 15, 1836
Michigan	do.	do.	January 26, 1837
Florida	do.	do.	March 3, 1845
Texas	do.	do.	December 29, 1845
Iowa	do.	do.	December 28, 1846
Wisconsin	do.	do.	May 29, 1848
California	do.	do.	September 9, 1850
Minnesota	do.	do.	May 11, 1858
Oregon	do.	do.	February 14, 1859
Kansas	do.	do.	January 29, 1861
West Virginia	do.	do.	June 19, 1863
Nevada	do.	do.	October 31, 1864
Nebraska	do.	do.	March 1, 1867
Colorado	do.	do.	August 1, 1876
North Dakota	do.	do.	November 2, 1889
South Dakota	do.	do.	November 2, 1889
Montana	do.	do.	November 8, 1889
Washington	do.	do.	November 11, 1889
Idaho	do.	do.	July 3, 1890
Wyoming	do.	do.	July 10, 1890

States' Rights. All parties have, of course, professed to be friendly to all the rights of the States under the Constitution. But the term "States' rights" as a political watchword in U. S. history has meant the rights of the States as interpreted by those who have held the theory that the States are partners to a constitutional compact, that their rights include essential rights of sovereignty, and that the paramount allegiance of the citizen is due to his State rather than to the Federal Government. It was State rights conceived in this sense which were made the basis of the movements for nullification and secession.

Steamboat. Rumsey and Fitch invented the steamboat before Fulton, but he was the first to make a practical success of it. His boat, the "Clermont," made a successful trip up the Hudson in 1807. The "Clermont" was a paddle-wheel boat, of twenty horse-power. Fulton and R. R. Livingston obtained from the State of New York a monopoly of the use of this invention on New York waters during thirty years. (See Gibbons *vs.* Ogden.) In 1819 the steamboat "Savannah" sailed from America to Liverpool. Almost immediately steamboats began to be used on the Mississippi and other Western rivers, and contributed enormously to the development of population and agriculture in the great central valley. In 1818 the first steamer appeared on the Great Lakes,—the "Walk-in-the-Water." By 1830 there was a daily line from Buffalo to Detroit. Steam navigation across the Atlantic was established in 1838.

Stedman, Edmund Clarence, born in 1833, contributed many poems to the New York *Tribune* after 1859. He was war correspondent of the New York *World* from 1861 to 1863. Since 1865 he has been a stock-broker in New York. He wrote "The Diamond Wedding," "How Old John Brown took Harper's Ferry," "Alice of Monmouth," "Poets of America," "Gettysburg," and edited a "Library of American Literature."

Stedman, Fort, Va., garrisoned in 1865 by troops from Grant's army, then operating around Richmond and Petersburg. It was assailed on the night of March 25 by two divisions of Lee's army under Gordon. The assault was a surprise, and the fort was quickly captured. The assault was intended as a ruse, under cover of which Lee planned to retreat from Petersburg. The plan failed, however, for the Federals, quickly recovering themselves, retook the fort, March 27.

Steedman, Charles (1811–1890), in command of the "Bienville," led a column of vessels at Port Royal. He commanded the "Paul Jones" at Fort McAllister in 1862, and the "Ticonderoga" at Fort Fisher in 1864.

Steedman, James B. (1818–1883), commanded a regiment with distinction at Philippi and Perryville. He led a brigade at Chickamauga, and a division in the Atlanta campaign in 1864. He served at Nashville.

Steel. (See Iron.)

Steele, Frederick (1819–1868), served with distinction during the Mexican War at Contreras and Chapultepec. He commanded a brigade at Dug Spring and Wilson's Creek in 1861. He led a division at Round Hill and Helena, and a corps in the Yazoo Expedition, and captured Arkansas Post in 1863. He commanded a division at Vicksburg, and served at Little Rock and Mobile.

Stephens, Alexander Hamilton (February 11, 1812–March 4, 1883), Vice-President of the Southern Confederacy, was born in Georgia, and graduated at Franklin College in 1832. He practiced law, served in the Legislature of Georgia, and from 1843 to 1859 was a Whig member of the national House of Representatives. He supported Douglas in his slavery policy, but opposed secession strongly in 1860. Nevertheless, when the step had once been taken, he sided with the Confederacy, and was its Vice-President, 1861–1865. He differed with President Davis as the war progressed. In 1864, he favored peace, and in 1865 he took part in the Hampton Roads Conference. He was imprisoned in 1865, but was shortly afterward released. Having been elected U. S. Senator, he was refused a seat. From 1875 to 1882, Stephens was again a Congressman from Georgia. In the latter year he was elected Governor of his State, but died soon after entering upon the duties of the office. Of his works the most valuable is his "Constitutional View of the War Between the States," in two volumes. Life by Johnston and Browne.

Stephenson, Fort (Fremont, O.), garrisoned by 160 men under Major Croghan, was attacked August 1, 1813, by General Proctor and Tecumtha with 4000 men. After a heavy bombardment, a charge was made but gallantly repulsed. The British lost 121, the Americans only one killed.

Sterett, Andrew (1760?–1807), was executive officer of the "Constellation," which captured the French frigate "L'Insurgente" in 1799 and "La Vengeance" in 1800. In command of the "Enterprise," he captured "L'Amour de la Patrie" and a Tripolitan cruiser after a desperate encounter. The Tripolitan vessel three times renewed the conflict after surrendering, and was completely dismantled, while the "Enterprise" did not lose a man.

Sterne, Simon, born in 1839, has been prominent in political reform in New York. He has written "Representative Government and Personal Representation," and a "Constitutional and Political History of the United States."

Steuben, Friedrich Wilhelm August Heinrich Ferdinand von, called Baron Steuben (1730–1794), the disciplinarian of the American Revolutionary army, was born at Magdeburg. He fought in the war of the Austrian Succession and through the Seven Years' War. He was then an aide to Frederick the Great and held a lucrative position, which he exchanged in 1778 for service on the side of the Americans. Congress appointed him inspector-general, and his services in drilling the troops were invaluable. He commanded the left wing at the battle of Monmouth, and took part in the siege of Yorktown. He was a member of the board which decided the fate of André. He identified himself even more than Lafayette with the country to which he had given his aid, settling in New York and receiving from Congress in his last years a grant of land near Utica.

Stevens, Henry (1819–1886), of Vermont, was an authority on the early colonial history of America. In 1845 he went from Vermont to England in search of Americana, and remained there until his death. He was agent of the British Museum for procuring books of all kinds regarding America, and assisted in forming libraries in America. He wrote "Bibliotheca Americana," "Notes on the Earliest Discoveries in America," and other such books.

Stevens, Isaac I. (1818–1862), was Governor of Washington Territory from 1853 to 1857, when he became a delegate to the U. S. Congress, serving till 1861. He commanded a division at Newport News, and fought at Manassas and Chantilly, where he was killed.

Stevens, John (1749–1838), made valuable discoveries in steam navigation. He constructed a boat propelled by screws in 1804. He conceived the idea of a railroad system and devised the first locomotive in America.

Stevens, John Austin, of New York, born in 1827, was founder of the *Magazine of American History*. He wrote "Colonial Records of the New York Chamber of Commerce" and "Albert Gallatin" in the American Statesmen Series.

Stevens, John L., of Maine, was envoy extraordinary to Sweden and Norway from 1877 to 1883, and to Hawaii from 1889 to 1893. He was prominent in the deposition of Queen Liliuokalani, and in the negotiations for the annexation of Hawaii to the United States.

Stevens, Thaddeus (1792–1868), a Republican politician of influence, was graduated at Dartmouth, and settled to the practice of law in Pennsylvania. He was a Whig member of the Pennsylvania Legislature, and as Congressman in 1849–1853 he opposed the Compromise of 1850. He was again in Congress from 1859 to 1868 as a Republican, of the radical type, and advocated drastic measures. He urged emancipation and the Fourteenth Amendment, as well as acts of confiscation; he was chairman of the important Committees of Ways and Means and of Reconstruction, proposed the impeachment of President Johnson, and was chairman of the board of managers of the impeachment proceedings.

Stevens, Thomas H., born in 1819, fought at Port Royal and commanded the leading vessel at Fort Clinch. He captured many prizes, and was engaged at Petersburg, Charleston and Mobile.

Stevenson, Adlai Ewing, born in 1835, Vice-President of the United States, was a lawyer, practising at Bloomington, Ill. From 1875 to 1877 and 1879 to 1881 he was a Democratic Congressman from Illinois, and from 1885 to 1889 he was First Assistant Postmaster-General in President Cleveland's first administration. He received, in 1892, the Democratic nomination for the second place on the ticket with Cleveland, was elected, and entered office in 1893.

Stevenson, Andrew (1784–1857), was a member of the Virginia Legislature from 1804 to 1820. He represented Virginia in the U. S. Congress as a Democrat from 1823 to 1834, when he resigned. He served as Speaker of the House from 1827 to 1834. He was Minister to England from 1836 to 1841.

Stevenson, John W. (1812–1886), represented Kentucky in the U. S. Congress as a Democrat from 1857 to 1861. He was Governor of Kentucky from 1867 to 1871, and a U. S. Senator from 1871 to 1877.

Stewart, Alexander (1740 ?–1794), born in England, served in the Southern campaign during the Revolution. He was defeated by General Greene at Eutaw Springs in 1781, and retreated to Charleston.

Stewart, Alexander T. (1803–1876), came to America from Ireland in 1823. He conducted at New York the most extensive dry goods business in the world.

Stewart, Alvan (1790–1849), of New York, won distinction as an advocate of temperance and slavery reform. He was the first to earnestly advocate a political party to promote the abolition of slavery.

Stewart, Charles (1778–1869), entered the U. S. navy in 1798. He captured the French ships, "Deux Amis," "Diana" and "Louisa Bridger," while commanding the "Experiment" in 1800. During the Tripolitan War he was executive officer of the "Constitution," and commanded the "Siren" from 1803 to 1806. While commanding the "Constitution" he captured the "Pictou" and the British brigs "Catherine" and "Phœnix" in 1813. In 1814 he captured the "Lord Nelson" and the "Susan." In 1815 he took the British ships of war, "Cyane" and "Levant." He received the sobriquet of "Old Ironsides," and died a rear-admiral. He was the grandfather of Charles Stewart Parnell.

Stewart, Gideon T., born in 1824, was active in organizing the Prohibition party, and has been prominent in Ohio politics. He was the Prohibition candidate for the Vice-Presidency on the ticket with G. C. Smith in 1876.

Stewart, William M., born in 1827, discovered the celebrated Eureka diggings in California. He was chosen a member of the Nevada Territorial Council in 1861, and represented Nevada in the U. S. Senate as a Republican from 1864 to 1875. In 1887 he was again elected to the U. S. Senate. His present term expires in 1899. He has been prominent in coinage legislation.

Stiles, Ezra (1727–1795), was president of Yale College from 1778 to 1795. He was one of the most learned Americans of his time. He wrote an "Account of the Settlement of Bristol, R. I.," and a history of the regicides in America.

Stillé, Charles J., of Pennsylvania, born in 1819, has written "How a Free People Conduct a Long War," "Northern Interest and Southern Independence," "The Historical Development of American Civilization," a "History of the U. S. Sanitary Commission," and lives and letters of John Dickinson and General Anthony Wayne.

Stillwater. (See Saratoga.)

Stirling, Lord. (See Alexander, Sir William.)

Stockbridge, Mass., was formerly the home of the Stockbridge or Housatonic Indians, among whom an interesting mission was established, and who removed westward in 1788.

Stockbridge Indians, a band of Connecticut Mohegans, who were collected by Rev. Mr. Sargeant at Stockbridge in 1736. Like the rest of their tribe, they always continued in friendly relations with the English colonists. Between 1820 and 1830 they emigrated from New York to Wisconsin; here the majority soon became citizens.

Stockton, John P., born in 1826, was U. S. Minister to Rome from 1857 to 1861. He represented New Jersey in the U. S. Senate as a Democrat from 1865 to 1866 (when his election was declared illegal), and from 1869 to 1875.

Stockton, Richard (1730–1781), was admitted to the bar in 1754 and attained great reputation. He became a member of the New Jersey Executive Council in 1768 and a Judge of the Provincial Supreme Court in 1774. He hoped for a reconciliation between the colonies and England, and wrote "An Expedient for the Settlement of the American Disputes," in which he proposes a plan of colonial self-government. He was a delegate from New Jersey to the Continental Congress from 1776 to 1777, and signed the Declaration of Independence. He was appointed to inspect the Northern army, but was captured by Loyalists. He never recovered from the effects of the ill-usage he received.

Stockton, Robert Field (1795–1866), grandson of Richard Stockton, was in the navy in the War of 1812, and was distinguished in the ensuing Algerine War. He was engaged in the establishment of Liberia and in the capture of slavers and pirates. He was the chief promoter of the Delaware and Raritan Canal. As captain he commanded a squadron on the California coast in the Mexican War, and co-operated with Frémont in the conquest of that province. He captured Los Angeles, and organized a government. Commodore Stockton left the navy in 1850 and was U. S. Senator from New Jersey in 1851–1853. He was a delegate to the Peace Congress of 1861.

Stoddard, Richard H., of New York, was born in 1825. He has been a literary reviewer for periodicals since 1880. His reputation as a poet is considerable. He wrote "Abraham Lincoln," an ode; "Putnam the Brave," etc.

Stoddert, Benjamin (1751–1813), of Maryland, distinguished himself at the battle of Brandywine. He was Secretary of the Board of War from 1777 to 1781. He was Secretary of the Navy in Adams' Cabinet from 1798 to 1801, being thus the first Secretary of the Navy.

Stone, Charles P. (1824–1887), served with honor during the Mexican War. He led a brigade in General Patterson's Shenandoah campaign in 1861. While commanding the "corps of observation" in the Army of the Potomac from 1861 to 1862, he was defeated at Ball's Bluff. He served at Port Hudson in 1863, and was chief of staff to General Banks from 1863 to 1864.

Stone, David M., born in 1817, has been connected with the *New York Journal of Commerce* since 1849, and its editor-in-chief since 1866. He is regarded as an authority on commercial matters.

Stone, Lucy (1818–1893), was prominent as an ardent anti-slavery advocate. In 1869, she aided in forming the American Woman's Suffrage Association. She edited the *Womans' Journal* in Boston from 1872 on.

Stone, Thomas (1743–1787), was a delegate from Maryland to the Continental Congress from 1775 to 1779, and signed the Declaration of Independence. From 1779 to 1783 he was a prominent member of the Maryland Senate. He again served in the Continental Congress from 1784 to 1785. He was a member of the committee to draft a plan of confederation.

Stone, William (1603?–1695?), was appointed Governor of Maryland in 1649, and founded the settlement of Providence, now Annapolis. He was removed from office in 1653.

Stone, William L. (1792–1844), an editor of the *New York Commercial Advertiser* from 1821, wrote many tales of border life, a "History of the N. Y. Convention of 1821" and "Border Wars of the American Revolution."

Stone River. (See Murfreesboro.)

Stoneman, George, born in 1822, graduated at the U. S. Military Academy in 1846. He refused to surrender Fort Brown to the Secessionists in 1861 by order of his superior officer, General Twiggs. He commanded the cavalry of the Army of the Potomac from 1861 to 1862. He led a division at the second battle of Bull Run, and a corps at Fredericksburg. He commanded a cavalry raid toward Richmond in 1863; was engaged in the Atlanta campaign in 1864; and fought at Salisbury and Asheville. He was Governor of California from 1883 to 1887.

Stono Ferry, Attack upon, June 20, 1779. Lincoln's first attempt to dislodge the British at Charleston was made at Stono Ferry. Maitland's 800 men offered a stout resistance to Lincoln's 1200. The Americans retired, losing 301. The British loss was somewhat less. Three days later the fort was evacuated.

Stony Creek, Canada, War of 1812. A body of Americans under General Chandler, while pursuing General Vincent, encamped June 6, 1813, at Stony Creek. During the gloom of night they were surprised and attacked by Vincent. The British, after severe fighting, were repulsed with the loss of 178 killed, wounded and captured; the American loss was 154, including the capture of both General Chandler and General Winder.

Stony Point, Capture of, July 16, 1779. While the Americans were building a fort at Stony Point in May, 1779, Clinton ascended the Hudson, captured it and increased its strength. Washington detailed General Wayne to regain this position. With 1200 men he undertook the task. Not a gun was loaded. The troops depended solely upon a bayonet charge. They got so near the fort without being observed that with one rush they entered the fort and soon forced the garrison to surrender. The American loss was fifteen killed and eighty-three wounded. The British lost sixty-three killed and 553 taken prisoners. The humanity of the Americans contrasted favorably with the reckless brutality of the British in their surprises.

Storrs, Richard S., born in 1821, has been pastor of the Church of the Pilgrims at Brooklyn, N. Y., since 1846. He is one of the most eloquent pulpit orators in America. He wrote "Early American Spirit," "The Declaration of Independence and its Effects," and a life of St. Bernard.

Story, Joseph (1779–1845), jurist, was admitted to the bar at Salem, Mass., in 1801. He represented Massachusetts in the U. S. Congress as a Democrat from 1808 to 1809. In 1811 he was appointed an Associate Justice of the U. S. Supreme Court and continued in that office until his death. He was professor of law at Harvard from 1829 to 1845. His success as a teacher and his ability as a jurist place him among the foremost of Americans. He wrote valuable legal treatises including his famous "Commentaries on the Constitution of the United States," and "Commentaries on the Conflict of Laws." Life by W. W. Story.

Story, William W., born in 1819, has written several legal books. He is distinguished as an artist and poet. Among his best known works are statues of his father, Joseph Story, Chief-Justice Marshall, and George Peabody. He published "Life and Letters of Joseph Story."

Stoughton, William (1632–1701), was an agent of the Massachusetts colony in England from 1676 to 1679. He was Lieutenant-Governor and Chief Justice of Massachusetts from 1692 to 1701, and Acting Governor from

1694 to 1699. He was Chief Justice of the Supreme Court during the witch-craft trials.

Stowe, Calvin E. (1802–1886), was professor of Biblical literature at Lane Seminary from 1830 to 1850, and at Andover Seminary from 1852 to 1864. He was sent by Ohio to examine the European school system in 1836. He was the husband of Mrs. H. B. Stowe.

Stowe, Harriet Beecher, born in 1812, was the daughter of Lyman Beecher, a clergyman of intense intellectual activity and joyous disposition, whose influence upon Mrs. Stowe was very marked. In 1836 she married Calvin E. Stowe. During her residence in Ohio she acquired some knowledge of Southern life and of the condition of the slaves. The passage of the fugitive slave law, and the favor with which it was received, called forth her well-known work, "Uncle Tom's Cabin," in 1852. (See art.) She wrote "Dred," "The Minister's Wooing," and other novels.

Stratford, the old Lee mansion in Westmoreland County, Va. It was erected by Richard Lee, an Englishman, who came to Virginia as secretary to one of the king's council. It was the birth-place of Robert E. Lee.

Stringham, Silas H. (1798–1876), entered the U. S. navy in 1809. He served in the "President" during the engagements with the "Little Belt" and "Belvidere." He served in the Algerine War in 1815. He was executive officer of the "Hornet" from 1821 to 1824 and captured the pirate ship "Moscow." He commanded the "Ohio" at the bombardment of Vera Cruz in 1847, and the squadron which, assisted by the military force under General Butler, reduced Forts Hatteras and Clark in 1861.

Strong, Caleb (1745–1819), Governor, was a member of the Massachusetts Committee of Correspondence and Safety from 1774 to 1775, and of the Massachusetts general court from 1776 to 1778. He aided in drafting the State constitution in 1779. He was a member of the Massachusetts Senate from 1780 to 1789. In 1787 he was a member of the convention that framed the Constitution of the United States. He was a Federalist U. S. Senator from 1789 to 1796, and Governor of Massachusetts from 1800 to 1807 and from 1812 to 1816.

Strong, William, born in 1808, represented Pennsylvania in the U. S. Congress as a Democrat from 1847 to 1851. He was a Justice of the Supreme Court of Pennsylvania from 1857 to 1868, and a Justice of the U. S. Supreme Court from 1870 to 1880, when he retired. He was a member of the electoral commission in 1877.

Stuart, Alexander H. H. (1807–1891), represented Virginia in the U. S. Congress as a Whig from 1841 to 1843. He was Secretary of the Interior in Fillmore's Cabinet from 1850 to 1853. He was a member of the Virginia Senate from 1857 to 1861, and zealously opposed the policy of secession. He was a delegate to the National Union Convention at Philadelphia in 1866.

Stuart, Gilbert (1755–1828), born in Rhode Island, studied painting in Europe and painted portraits of many distinguished Europeans. He returned to America in 1793 and painted several portraits of Washington, the first of which was destroyed, and the second is in the Boston Athenæum. His pictures are very numerous and exhibit rare genius in portraying individual character.

Stuart, James E. B. (1833–1864), Confederate cavalry general, was graduated at the U. S. Military Academy in 1854. He commanded the Confederate cavalry at Bull Run in 1861. In 1862 he conducted a daring reconnaissance of McClellan's army on the Chickahominy. He fought at the second battle of Bull Run, and led the advance of Jackson's Maryland invasion. He fought at South Mountain and Antietam. His command formed the Confederate extreme right at Fredericksburg. He temporarily commanded Jackson's corps at Chancellorsville. He was mortally wounded at Yellow Tavern, where he attempted to check Sheridan's advance.

Stuart, Moses (1780–1852), was professor of sacred literature at Andover Seminary from 1810 to 1848. He was an enthusiastic Hebrew scholar, and has been called the father of Biblical science in America.

Sturgeon, Daniel (1789–1878), was treasurer of Pennsylvania in 1838 and 1839. He represented Pennsylvania in the U. S. Senate as a Democrat from 1839 to 1851, and was treasurer of the U. S. Mint from 1853 to 1858.

Sturges vs. Crowninshield, an action brought against the defendant, before the Circuit Court of Massachusetts, 1811, for payment of two promissory notes. Transferred to the Supreme Court of the United States in 1819. The defendant had pleaded a discharge by the insolvency law of New York before the Circuit Court, but judgment was found against him. This judgment was reversed by the Supreme Court, which recognized the insolvency law of New York as constitutional, but with certain limitations.

Sturgis, Samuel D. (1822–1889), served in the Mexican War. He commanded a division at South Mountain, Antietam and Fredericksburg, and was chief of cavalry of the Ohio Department from 1863 to 1864.

Stuyvesant, Peter (1612–1682), the last Dutch Governor or director-general of New Netherlands, arrived in 1647. Various controversies arose with the New England settlements, and with the patroons. He was intolerant in religious affairs, and raised a vigorous opposition on account of his contempt for popular rights. Trade, however, flourished during his administration. In 1655 he attacked the Swedish colony of Delaware, and annexed it to the Dutch possessions. When the English fleet came to New Amsterdam in 1664, Stuyvesant could make no effective resistance, and signed a treaty of surrender September 9. He continued to reside in New York, on his extensive farm of Great Bouwerie, and died there.

Subsidies. In early use the word denoted a special tax, then it signified the payment made to an ally for assisting in war. It is now the term applied to pecuniary aid rendered by the State to industrial enterprises of individuals. The granting of monopoly rights was the earliest form of subsidies in the United States. National aid has been in a number of instances tendered to railroad corporations, chiefly in land grants, many millions of acres being granted to the Northern Pacific, the Union Pacific, the Illinois Central, the Mobile and Ohio and the Kansas Pacific Railroads. In the case of the Union Pacific, in addition to a land grant of 33,000,000 acres, the

United States pledged itself to $25,000 per mile, half the cost. Subsidies have been granted for the encouragement of the United States steam marine at various times since 1850, the Pacific Mail Steamship Company being the chief of these contractors.

Sub-Treasury. (See Independent Treasury.)

Suffrage. Restricted suffrage was the rule in America till well into the present century. Massachusetts and New Haven colonies for a time gave the suffrage to none but church members. In most of the colonies a freehold qualification prevailed, sometimes the "forty-shilling freehold" of English law, sometimes a freehold of so many acres. The constitutions made in the Revolutionary period mostly provided for the former in the Northern States, for the latter in the Southern, while New Hampshire, Pennsylvania, Delaware and Georgia had simply a requirement of tax-paying. The Constitution of 1787 left this matter entirely to the States, allowing all to vote for Congressmen in a given State who could vote for the members of the State House of Representatives. After 1789, the influence of democratic principles led to the abolition of property qualifications in Georgia in 1798; in Maryland in 1801 and 1809; in Massachusetts in 1821; in New York in 1821; in Delaware in 1831; in New Jersey in 1844; in Connecticut in 1845; in Virginia in 1850; in North Carolina in 1854 and 1868; in South Carolina in 1865; in Rhode Island, except in some municipal elections, in 1888. The Fifteenth Amendment forbids any State, or the United States, to deny the suffrage to any citizen because of race, color or previous condition of servitude. The new States have mostly provided for manhood suffrage from the first, often even for the suffrage of aliens in process of naturalization. For the extension of the suffrage to women, (see art. Woman Suffrage.)

Sugar Act, an act passed by Parliament in 1733 and renewed in 1763, by which heavy duties were laid upon all sugar and molasses imported into the American colonies from foreign colonies. It was one of the direct causes of the Revolution.

Sullivan's Island, Battle of. (See Fort Moultrie.)

Sullivan, James (1744–1808), born in Maine, was a member of the Massachusetts Provincial Congress in 1775. He was a Judge of the Massachusetts Supreme Court from 1776 to 1782, a delegate to the Continental Congress from 1784 to 1785, and Attorney-General of Massachusetts from 1790 to 1807. He was Governor of Massachusetts from 1807 till his death. Life by Amory.

Sullivan, John (1740–1795), a Revolutionary general, was a native of Maine and a major of militia before the war. He was a New Hampshire delegate to the First Continental Congress, and was appointed brigadier-general in 1775. He was engaged in the siege of Boston and in Canada in the unsuccessful attack on Three Rivers. Sullivan became a major-general in 1776, was one of the principal commanders in the battle of Long Island and in the autumn campaign of 1776, fought at Trenton and Princeton, and made a raid on Staten Island. He led the right wing at Brandywine and Germantown, and won the battle of Butts Hill in Rhode Island in 1778. The next year he ravaged the country of the Six Nations. He served in Congress, and was a Federalist in New Hampshire in the contest of 1788. Life by Amory.

Sully, Thomas (1783–1872), came to America from England in 1792. He is famous for his paintings, "Washington Crossing the Delaware," Thomas Jefferson, Fanny Kemble, Queen Victoria, Lafayette and "The Capture of Major André."

Summit Point, Va., a battle of the Civil War during Sheridan's campaign in the Shenandoah Valley and Early's sortie against Washington. Sheridan was retreating toward Halltown with the intention of strengthening his position there, for he had heard that Early was expecting reinforcements under Anderson and that others might come. On the road through Summit Point, he fell in with several detachments of Early's troops. Rodes's and Ramseur's infantry were advanced to the attack, and a fierce skirmish occurred. The Federals lost quite heavily and were decidedly worsted. Getty's division of the Sixth Corps lost 250 killed and wounded.

Sumner, Charles (January 6, 1811–March 11, 1874), an American statesman and orator, was born at Boston, graduated in 1830 at Harvard, and studied law. On returning from an extended European tour, 1837–1840, he became profoundly interested in the anti-slavery question. Without entering into active politics, he became noted as an orator. Among his speeches at this period were those on the "True Grandeur of Nations" in 1846, and on the "Scholar, Jurist, etc.," in 1846. Sumner, who had been a moderate Whig, helped organize the Free-Soil party in 1848, and was defeated for Congress the same year. In 1851, after a prolonged struggle of three months in the Massachusetts Legislature, he was elected U. S. Senator by a coalition of Democrats and Free-Soilers. He speedily became the chief advocate in the Senate of the anti-slavery sentiment. His speech, "Freedom National, Slavery Sectional," gave the signal of his course. That on the "Crime against Kansas," in May, 1856, provoked a personal assault from a Southern Representative, Preston Brooks. Sumner was severely injured, and did not resume his seat until 1859. He was meanwhile re-elected Senator as a Republican, and re-elected twice, serving until his death. In 1861 he became chairman of the Committee of Foreign Affairs and was one of the chief friends and advisers of President Lincoln. He opposed Johnson, but supported the Alaska purchase. In 1871 he strongly opposed the San Domingo Treaty, broke with President Grant and the Republican Senators, and was removed from his chairmanship. He supported Greeley in 1872, and gave his closing efforts to the furtherance of the civil rights of colored citizens. Complete works in fifteen volumes. "Memoir and Letters," by E. L. Pierce.

Sumner, Edwin V. (1797–1863), general, led the cavalry charge at Cerro Gordo in 1847, commanded the reserves at Contreras and Churubusco and led the cavalry at Molino del Rey. He was Governor of New Mexico from 1851 to 1853. He succeeded General Johnston in command of the Pacific Department from 1861 to 1862. He commanded the left wing at the siege of Yorktown, led a corps at Fair Oaks, was twice wounded during the Seven Days' battles, and commanded a corps at Antietam. He led a division at Fredericksburg and retired in 1863.

Sumner, Increase (1746–1799), was a member of the Massachusetts Legislature from 1776 to 1780 and of the Senate from 1780 to 1782. He was a Justice of the Massachusetts Supreme Court from 1782 to 1797. He was a member of the convention that adopted the Federal Constitution in 1788, and was Governor of Massachusetts from 1797 to 1799.

Sumner, William G., born in 1840, became professor of political economy at Yale College in 1872. He has written a "History of American Currency," a "History of Protection in the United States," a life of Andrew Jackson, and "The Financier and Finances of the American Revolution."

Sumter, Thomas (1734–1832), soldier, conducted partisan warfare at the beginning of the Revolution. He defeated a force of British and Tories, made an unsuccessful attack on Rocky Mount and routed the British at Hanging Rock. He severed the communications of Cornwallis and captured his supply train. He was severely defeated by Colonel Tarleton at Fishing Creek. He defeated Major Wemyss at Broad River, and repelled Colonel Tarleton at Blackstock Hill. He represented South Carolina in the U. S. Congress as a Democrat from 1789 to 1793 and from 1797 to 1801, and in the Senate from 1801 to 1809. He was Minister to Brazil from 1809 to 1811.

Sumter, Fort, Charleston Harbor, opening engagement of the Civil War, April 12, 13, 1861, Major Anderson commanding the fort with 129 Union soldiers, General Beauregard the Confederate forces of about 6000 volunteers. During the early period of secessionist agitation Anderson had commanded the whole of Charleston harbor, including Forts Sumter, Moultrie, Johnson and Castle Pinckney. To obtain possession of these was the chief solicitude of South Carolina. Anderson, fearful of being surprised in unfortified Fort Moultrie, where he was stationed, moved his forces secretly to Sumter on the night of December 26, 1861. On that day a commission of three, deputed by the South Carolina Convention, arrived at Washington to treat with President Buchanan and make complaints against Anderson. Anderson's move caused a postponement of their accorded interview with Buchanan and, upon Governor Pickens' seizure of Fort Moultrie, Castle Pinckney, the Charleston Arsenal, Custom House and Post Office, the President refused their demand of the withdrawal of the Federal troops. Pickens immediately proceeded to assemble volunteers and strengthen the captured forts. Beauregard was chosen to command the Confederate troops. Meantime "The Star of the West," a merchant-steamer, was chartered and stocked with provisions for Anderson's relief. She sailed from New York January 5, 1861, with 250 recruits. On entering Charleston harbor and showing the United States flag she was fired upon from Fort Moultrie and compelled to put to sea again. Pickens demanded Anderson's surrender, which was refused. On April 8, 1861, President Lincoln notified Pickens and Beauregard that an attempt would be made to supply Anderson with provisions. This decided the Confederates for war, and on April 12, Anderson having again refused to evacuate on terms agreeable to Beauregard, the latter commenced to fire on Fort Sumter. The bombardment continued two days. April 14 Anderson surrendered because of lack of provisions and because portions of the fort were in flames. The firing upon Fort Sumter did more than any of the previous acts of the secessionists to rouse the North to resistance. Immense enthusiasm for the cause of the Union was immediately awakened.—Fort Sumter was assailed by Admiral Dahlgren's fleet on the night of September 8, 1863. This attack was led by Commodore Stephens and proved an utter failure, Beauregard's batteries easily driving off the attacking troops. In February, 1865, the Union flag was once more raised over Fort Sumter.

Sunbury. In the autumn of 1778, Sunbury, Ga., had resisted a force sent north from Florida by the British general Prevost. Early in January, 1779, Prevost marched to Savannah, and on his way captured Sunbury and its garrison.

Sunday Laws. In the New England colonies laws were early passed forbidding labor, travel or play on the "Sabbath." A Massachusetts Act of 1649 provided for the beginning of this prohibition on the evening of Saturday. In New York the "Duke's Laws" (1665) forbade the profanation of the Lord's Day by travel or labor. Pennsylvania in the first laws (those of 1682) forbade labor. South Carolina, in 1684, forbade profanation of the Sabbath. Virginia, in 1692, forbade travel or profanation. All the colonies, Puritan or not, seem to have had such laws, and these continued in existence after the Revolution.

Sunday Newspapers. The first started in this country was the *Sunday Courier*, which appeared in New York in 1825 and lived but a few months. Several other Sunday journals, however, followed the *Sunday Courier*. Of these the *Atlas*, started in 1837 by three journeymen printers, was the most successful. Prior to the Civil War about a dozen of these Sunday papers were begun and discontinued after a short time. They gradually became more successful, many of the dailies issuing a Sunday edition. The public sentiment was strongly against them at first. By 1880 there were 225 Sunday papers, half that number being Sunday editions of dailies.

Superintendent of Finance, an office established by Act of the Continental Congress, February 7, 1781, to supersede the Treasury Board, which was suspected of carelessness. Robert Morris filled this office. He was authorized to examine the state of the finances and report plans for improvement; to direct the execution of orders respecting revenue and expenditure and control the public accounts. In 1784 Morris resigned and the office was abolished.

Supreme Court. The Constitution of 1787 provided for a Supreme Court. The Judiciary Act of 1789 prescribed its times of session and its rules of procedure. Washington appointed Jay Chief Justice and the court began its sessions in 1790. For a dozen years it had little business. John Marshall, Chief Justice from 1801 to 1835, first made the court a great power in the Government. The influence of his decisions in strengthening and nationalizing the Government cannot be over-estimated. For the court's power to set aside State and Federal laws as unconstitutional see art. Unconstitutionality. The court continued to be composed of Federalists long after the Federalists lost control of Congress and the executive. At first it consisted of the Chief Justice and five Associate Justices. A sixth was added in 1807, two more in 1837, a ninth in 1863. From 1836 to 1864, under Chief Justice Taney, the court was Democratic, and more inclined to the support of State rights. In the important Dred-Scott case it gave a decision favorable to slavery. During the war the Supreme Court was made Republican. During the conflict between Congress and President Johnson, Congress, to prevent him from appointing any judges, enacted laws which reduced the number of Associate Justices to seven. In 1870 an eighth was added, by reason of which the court reversed its decision in the Legal Tender cases. The court has been throughout its history the most powerful tribunal of this century. The leading cases which have appeared before it are treated in separate articles. A list of the Justices follows. History by Carson. (For the reports see next art.)

Supreme Court, Chief Justices and Associate Justices.

Chief Justices.	Associate Justices.	State.	Term of Service.
John Jay		New York	1789 to 1795.
	John Rutledge	South Carolina	1789. Declined.
	William Cushing	Massachusetts	1789 to 1810.
	Robert H. Harrison	Maryland	1789 to 1790.
	James Wilson	Pennsylvania	1789 to 1798.
	John Blair	Virginia	1789 to 1796.
	James Iredell	North Carolina	1790 to 1799.
	Thomas Johnson	Maryland	1791 to 1793.
	William Paterson	New Jersey	1793 to 1806.
John Rutledge	(Not confirmed)	South Carolina	1795 to 1795.
William Cushing		Massachusetts	1796. Declined.
	Samuel Chase	Maryland	1796 to 1811.
Oliver Ellsworth		Connecticut	1796 to 1800.
	Bushrod Washington	Virginia	1798 to 1829.
	Alfred Moore	North Carolina	1799 to 1804.
John Jay		New York	1800. Declined.
John Marshall		Virginia	1801 to 1835.
	William Johnson	South Carolina	1804 to 1834.
	Brockholst Livingston	New York	1807 to 1823.
	Thomas Todd	Kentucky	1807 to 1826.
	Levi Lincoln	Massachusetts	1811. Declined.
	John Quincy Adams	Massachusetts	1811. Declined.
	Joseph Story	Massachusetts	1811 to 1845.
	Gabriel Duvall	Maryland	1811 to 1835.
	Smith Thompson	New York	1823 to 1843.
	Robert Trimble	Kentucky	1826 to 1828.
	John McLean	Ohio	1829 to 1861.
	Henry Baldwin	Pennsylvania	1830 to 1844.
	James M. Wayne	Georgia	1835 to 1867.
Roger B. Taney		Maryland	1836 to 1864.
	Philip P. Barbour	Virginia	1836 to 1841.
	William Smith	Alabama	1837. Declined.
	John Catron	Tennessee	1837 to 1865.
	John McKinley	Alabama	1837 to 1852.
	Peter V. Daniel	Virginia	1841 to 1860.
	Samuel Nelson	New York	1845 to 1872.
	Levi Woodbury	New Hampshire	1845 to 1851.
	Robert C. Grier	Pennsylvania	1846 to 1870.
	Benjamin R. Curtis	Massachusetts	1851 to 1857.
	John A. Campbell	Alabama	1853 to 1861.
	Nathan Clifford	Maine	1858 to 1881.
	Noah H. Swayne	Ohio	1862 to 1881.

CHIEF JUSTICES OF SUPREME COURT.

John Jay. Salmon P. Chase. Melville W. Fuller.
Oliver Ellsworth. M. R. Waite.
John Rutledge. J. Marshall. R. B. Taney.

Chief Justices.	Associate Justices.	State.	Term of Service.
	Samuel F. Miller	Iowa	1862 to 1890.
	David Davis	Illinois	1862 to 1877.
	Stephen J. Field	California	1863 to ——.
Salmon P. Chase		Ohio	1864 to 1873.
	Edwin M. Stanton	Pennsylvania	1869.*
	William Strong	Pennsylvania	1870 to 1880.
	Joseph P. Bradley	New Jersey	1870 to 1892.
	Ward Hunt	New York	1872 to 1886.
Morrison R. Waite		Ohio	1874 to 1887.
	John M. Harlan	Kentucky	1877 to ——.
	William B. Woods	Georgia	1880 to 1887.
	Stanley Matthews	Ohio	1881 to 1889.
	Horace Gray	Massachusetts	1881 to ——.
	Samuel Blatchford	New York	1882 to 1893.
	Lucius Q. C. Lamar	Mississippi	1888 to 1893.
Melville W. Fuller		Illinois	1888 to ——.
	David J. Brewer	Kansas	1889 to ——.
	Henry B. Brown	Michigan	1891 to ——.
	George Shiras, Jr.	Pennsylvania	1892 to ——.
	Howell E. Jackson	Tennessee	1893 to ——.
	Edward D. White	Louisiana	1894 to ——.

Supreme Court Reports begin with the volume numbered 2 Dallas, and consist of the following: Dallas, 3 vols., 1790–1800; Cranch, 9 vols., 1800–1815; Wheaton, 12 vols., 1816–1827; Peters, 16 vols., 1828–1842; Howard, 24 vols., 1843–1860; Black, 2 vols., 1861–1862; Wallace, 23 vols., 1863–1875; from this point they are numbered 90 U. S., 91 U. S., etc.

Surplus, Distribution of. The distribution of the treasury surplus among the States in preference to appropriating it to internal improvements was advocated by President Jackson in 1829, the debt having been paid, while the compromise of 1832 forbade the reduction of the tariff. In 1836 a bill to this effect was passed by Congress, and to it was joined a bill to regulate the public deposits. Afterward an attempt was made to separate the two bills, but this failed. The bill provided that all the money in the treasury, January 1, 1837, in excess of $5,000,000, was to be deposited with the States in the proportion of their membership in the electoral college, and in four installments. The States were to give certificates of deposits, payable to the Secretary of the Treasury on demand. Jackson defended this step on the ground that many of the States were "improvement States," with a growing money market and a large debt, and therefore in urgent need of funds. The States mostly misused the money. Only three of the four installments were paid, when the crash of 1837 came upon the Federal Government, and no more was paid. History by Bourne.

"**Susan Constant**," a vessel sent with colonists to Virginia in 1606 by the Virginia Company. She was commanded by Christopher Newport, and was accompanied by the "God-Speed" and the "Discovery." The colonists landed May 13, 1607.

Susquehannah Company, a land company formed in 1754, chiefly of Connecticut farmers, for the colonization of the Wyoming country. By

*Died before his commission took effect.

a treaty with the Five Nations, July 11, 1754, an enormous tract of country was purchased for £2000. It began at the southern boundary of Connecticut and followed in a northerly direction the course of the Susquehannah to northern Pennsylvania. In 1785–1786 many disputes arose between the Susquehannah Company and the Pennsylvania claimants of the territory. This was called the "Pennamite War." (See Wyoming Controversy.)

Susquehannas, or Conestogas, an extinct tribe of Indians, once inhabiting lands on the Susquehanna River. They waged fierce wars with neighboring tribes, and became so troublesome to Maryland that they were proclaimed public enemies in 1642. In 1652 they ceded lands to the colony. In 1675, after a bitter struggle with the Iroquois, they were overthrown. Some, retreating to Maryland, were attacked by the whites. The Indians then ravaged the frontier until completely cut off. A remnant of the tribe, during a period of excitement against the Indians, was butchered at Lancaster, Pa., 1763.

Sutter, John A. (1803–1880), came to America from Baden in 1834. In 1841 he founded a settlement on the present site of Sacramento. The first gold in California was found on his estate in 1848.

Swaanendael, a settlement established in 1632 on the Delaware River at the site of the present town of Lewiston, Del., by Godyn, Blommaert, De Vries and others. A fort was also built. Trouble soon arose with the Indians and the inhabitants were massacred.

Swamp Fight, a fight in the Narragansett country, in what is now South Kingstown, R. I., on December 19, 1675, during King Philip's War. Philip and his allies, entrenched in a strong palisade in the midst of a swamp, were attacked by the forces of Massachusetts, Plymouth and Connecticut, and defeated with great slaughter; the stockade was destroyed.

Swamp Lands. In 1849 Congress passed a resolution which led to the grant of enormous tracts of overflowed and swamp lands to the States for their disposal. These were in many instances regranted to railroad corporations.

Swann, Thomas (1805–1883), was president of the Baltimore and Ohio Railroad from 1847 to 1853, Governor of Maryland from 1865 to 1869, and a Democratic U. S. Congressman from 1869 to 1879.

Swansea, Mass., was attacked by the Indians on June 20, 23, 25, 1675, during King Philip's War. Many houses were burned and terrible atrocities committed.

Swayne, Noah H. (1804 1884), was U. S. District Attorney for Ohio from 1831 to 1841. He was a Justice of the U. S. Supreme Court from 1862 to 1881, when he resigned.

Sweden and Norway. Sweden was the first nation to offer voluntarily her friendship to the United States. A treaty of amity and commerce was concluded in 1783. With Sweden and Norway a commercial treaty was concluded in 1816, and another in 1827. An extradition convention was concluded in 1860, and a naturalization convention in 1869. A new extradition treaty was concluded January 14, 1893.

Swedenborgians (New Jerusalem Church). A sect named after its founder, Emanuel Swedenborg, and because they believe that his teachings superseded the old form of Christianity and brought in the "New Jerusalem." Swedenborg himself founded no church, but his followers organized bodies in sympathy with his teachings. The first church in the United States was founded at Baltimore, 1792, and since 1817 a general convention meets annually, which now represents some five thousand members.

Swedes. The Swedish element in U. S. history came originally in the settlement of New Sweden. (See Delaware.) The Swedish language was spoken there until after the Revolution, when the Swedish king ceased to send out a Swedish pastor, as he had hitherto done, because it seemed no longer necessary. Swedish immigration to the United States began to be important about 1846, and increased rapidly after 1876. Immigrants from Sweden and Norway have constituted six per cent of all immigrants since 1820.

Swedish West India Company, or the South Company, founded in October, 1624, by Willem Usselinx, of Antwerp, under a charter granted by Gustavus Adolphus, of special trading privileges with America. The king subscribed 400,000 daler, and stock was taken by other Swedes, among them Chancellor Oxenstjerna. Combining later with certain Dutch merchants, the company effected settlements along the Delaware River. The charter extended to 1646.

Sweeney, Thomas W. (1820–1892), came to the United States from Ireland in 1832. He served with distinction during the Mexican War. He served at Wilson's Creek and Fort Donelson, and led a brigade at Shiloh. He commanded a division in the Atlanta campaign, and fought at Snake Creek Gap, Resaca, Dallas, Kenesaw Mountain and Atlanta. He engaged in the Fenian invasion of Canada in 1866.

Sweet, Benjamin J. (1832–1874), was severely wounded at Perryville in 1861. In 1864 he took command of the prison at Camp Douglas, Chicago, where he defeated two well-planned attempts to liberate the prisoners and burn Chicago.

Swett, Samuel (1782–1866), of Massachusetts, served on the staff of General Izard during the War of 1812. He wrote "History of the Battle of Bunker Hill," "Who was Commander at Bunker Hill?" and "Defence of Timothy Pickering against Bancroft's History."

Swinton, William (1833–1892), became connected with the *New York Times* in 1858 and became a war correspondent in 1862. He traveled in the South in 1867 and collected material for a "History of the Civil War." He wrote the *Times*' "Review of McClellan," "Campaigns of the Army of the Potomac," "The Twelve Decisive Battles of the War," and an excellent series of school books.

Swiss. In 1711 a number of Swiss and Germans emigrated to South Carolina led by Jean Pierre Purry, and in 1732 an extensive tract was granted to a new body from Neufchatel, along the Savannah River.

Swiss Confederation. The United States concluded, in 1847, with the Swiss Confederation a convention for the mutual abolition of droit d'aubaine and taxes on emigration. In 1850 a convention of friendship, commerce and extradition was concluded.

Sykes, George (1822–1880), served with distinction during the Civil War. He commanded a battalion at Bull Run. He had charge of the infantry in the defence of Washington from 1861 to 1862. He led a division at Gaines' Mills and a corps at Fredericksburg and Gettysburg. He commanded a corps in the Army of the Potomac till 1864, when he was sent to Kansas.

Symmes Purchase. John Cleves Symmes and his associates bought in 1787 a tract of land along the Ohio and Miami Rivers. The tract originally contained 1,000,000 acres, but was reduced later to 248,540 acres, because of the partial failure of the colonization plans. The first pre-emption law was passed in 1801 for the furtherance of this scheme.

T.

Taft, Alphonso (1810–1891), of Ohio, was Secretary of War in Grant's Cabinet from March to May, 1876, when he was made Attorney-General and served till 1877. He was Minister to Austria from 1882 to 1884, and to Russia from 1884 to 1885.

Talbot, Silas (1751–1813), rendered brilliant service in the navy during the Revolution, capturing many British vessels. He represented New York in the U. S. Congress as a Federalist from 1793 to 1795.

Talcott, John (1630–1688), was treasurer of the Connecticut colony from 1660 to 1676. He was one of the patentees named in the charter of 1662. He commanded the colonial army during the Indian wars.

Taliaferro, William B., born in 1822, was prominent in the Confederate army of Northern Virginia from 1861 to 1863. He commanded at Morris and James Islands in 1863. In 1864 he commanded the district of South Carolina.

Talladega, a village of the Creek Indians of Alabama in 1813. November 7, Andrew Jackson, then conducting a campaign against the Creeks, received a message from Talladega, which was a friendly town, begging aid against the hostile tribes. Jackson replied by marching to Talladega and defeating the Creeks, November 8.

Tallahassee, Fla., was selected as the seat of the territorial government in 1822. It was laid out in 1824, and became a city in 1827. Tallahassee was occupied May 10, 1865, by General McCook and 500 Federal soldiers for the purpose of receiving the surrender of the Confederates in that section, who were commanded by Sam Jones. No fighting of consequence occurred.

Talleyrand-Périgord, Charles Maurice, Prince de (1754–1838), the famous French diplomatist, was minister of foreign affairs in France when

Pinckney, Marshall and Gerry were sent from the United States on a special mission in 1797. He demanded (1) a disavowal of President Adams' hostile expressions toward France; (2) a loan, and (3) douceurs, which the American envoys refused to concede. The unofficial French negotiators, Hottinguer, Bellamy and Hauteval, were designated as X, Y and Z in the reports sent to the United States. These X, Y, Z papers aroused great indignation against France. Later, Talleyrand made overtures for more favorable negotiations. He had visited the United States in 1794. He was still Minister at the time of the Louisiana cession of 1803.

Tallmadge, Benjamin (1754–1835), commanded detachments during the Revolution at Brandywine, Germantown, Monmouth, Lloyd's Neck and Fort George. He represented Connecticut in the U. S. Congress as a Federalist from 1801 to 1817.

Tallmadge, James (1778–1853), represented New York in the U. S. Congress as a Democrat from 1817 to 1819. He proposed the exclusion of slavery from Missouri as a condition of its admission to the Union as a State, and delivered a widely popular speech in opposition to slavery. He was Lieutenant-Governor of New York from 1826 to 1827. He was one of the founders of the American Institute at New York and its president from 1831 to 1850.

Talmage, Thomas DeWitt, born in 1832, has been pastor of the Central Presbyterian Church in Brooklyn since 1869. He is a popular preacher and lecturer.

Tammany (seventeenth century), was chief of the Delaware Indians. He was a brave and influential chieftain about whom there are many traditions. He is the patron of the Democratic organization called the Tammany Society.

Tammany. In 1789 William Mooney, an Irish-American politician, founded in New York City the Columbian Order, a secret society, which in 1805 was incorporated as the Tammany Society, named after the Indian Tammany, and wearing Indian insignia, especially a buck's tail. In 1800, by careful work under Aaron Burr, the order controlled New York City politics. Next, under Daniel D. Tompkins, it became the administration wing of the Democratic party in New York City, upholding Madison and opposing the Clintons. The Bucktails and the Albany Regency controlled the State for a long period. In 1822 the power over the society had gone into the hands of its general committee. Stricter and stricter organization followed, and Tammany developed into a machine for securing success in elections and power and plunder for its chieftains. Always indifferent to principles, it grew worse after the influx of foreigners into the city, till after the war its corruption culminated in the scandalous performances of the Tweed Ring. (See art.) Since the defeat of the Tweed Ring in 1871, Tammany, under the control of John Kelly, Richard Croker and others, has been famous for strict control over a large body of voters, strict devotion to the spoils system, looseness of allegiance to the Democratic party, and indifference to the welfare and interests of the great city which it has almost constantly ruled.

Taney, Roger Brooke (1777–1864), Chief Justice of the U. S. Supreme Court, was graduated at Dickinson College, became a member of the Maryland Legislature, and settled in Baltimore. Lawyer and politician, at first Federalist and later Jacksonian Democrat, he was Attorney-General 1831–1833, and was appointed by President Jackson as Secretary of the Treasury in 1833, to take the place of a less subservient official. Taney was not confirmed by the Senate, but in his few months of service he ordered the removal of the Government deposits from the bank. The President nominated him as Chief Justice of the U. S. Supreme Court in 1835, and he was confirmed in the following year. In his long service, until his death, various important questions were decided, chief of which in interest was the Dred Scott case in 1857. Life by Tyler.

Tappan Patent, a grant of land in what is now Orange County, N. Y., made in 1686 by Governor Dongan, of New York, to six Dutch patentees. The land was to be held in free and common socage of King James II.

Tariff. Before 1789 colonies and States occasionally levied tariffs on imports, sometimes of a protective nature. The diversity of these tariffs and the consequent hindrances to commerce formed one cause of the cementing of a stronger union in 1787. The new Constitution gave Congress power to regulate commerce. In 1789 the First Congress passed a tariff act which imposed on imports duties averaging about eight per cent ad valorem. In 1790, and again in 1792, the rates were slightly increased. They were in large part so adjusted as to give protection to American industries. This policy Hamilton and the Federalists constantly advocated, largely for political reasons. The War of 1812 gave artificial stimulus to American manufactures, which was accordingly continued by the tariff of 1816, which imposed duties of about twenty-five per cent on leading manufactures, the agricultural South and commercial New England protesting. In 1824 a new tariff act was passed, increasing duties on metals and agricultural products. Clay now made himself the leader in advocacy of the "American system," so-called, the combination of a higher protective tariff with Federal expenditures for internal improvements. A protectionist convention at Harrisburg urged higher duties. In 1828 a tariff called the "tariff of abominations" imposed duties on raw materials. It was passed by reason of political intrigues, rather than by reason of economic considerations. The South protested violently, urging not only the injustice of a high tariff from which exporting States received no benefit, but also its unconstitutionality. Calhoun and South Carolina took the lead in this remonstrance. Though the tariff of 1832 went back nearly to the rates of 1824, it retained the principle of protection. South Carolina then proceeded to nullify the act. Though Jackson met nullification with vigorous repression, Congress compromised in the tariff of 1833, which provided for a gradual reduction of duties to a uniform revenue rate, to be reached in 1842. In 1846 a new tariff was enacted, which, though not quite a tariff "for revenue only," was rather a revenue than a protective tariff. A still lower tariff came in in 1857. This remained until 1861, when the Morrill Tariff went into effect, in accordance with the policy of the Republicans, now in power, who favored high protective duties. The Civil War caused large increase of the rates to meet

Government expenses and stimulate manufactures. These continued long after the war. In 1882 a Tariff Commission was appointed to consider readjustments, and the Republicans made some slight reductions. Since then they have returned to advocacy of high protection, while the Democrats, since President Cleveland's message of 1887, have favored reduction of the rates. The McKinley Act of 1890 maintained and strengthened the protective system. A Democratic bill for moderate reduction was introduced into the House in December, 1893. History by Taussig.

Tariff Commission, a commission appointed by an Act of Congress of March 28, 1882, to consist of nine members appointed from civil life by the President. The duty of this commission was to investigate questions relating to the commercial, mercantile, agricultural, manufacturing and mining interests of the United States and make suggestions for the establishment of a judicious tariff, or a revision of the existing tariff and the internal revenue laws.

Tarleton, Sir Bannastre (1754–1833), colonel, came to America from England with Lord Cornwallis in 1776. He engaged in Colonel Harcourt's raid upon Baskingridge, N. J. In 1779 he organized the "British Legion," or "Tarleton's Legion," in South Carolina, with which he conducted partisan warfare. He slaughtered Colonel Buford's regiment at Waxhaw Creek and fought bravely at Camden and Fishing Creek. He was defeated at Blackstock Hill by General Sumter and his force was almost annihilated at Cowpens by General Morgan. He surrendered with Cornwallis at Yorktown. He wrote "A History of the Campaigns of 1780 and 1781 in the Southern Provinces of North America."

Tattnall, Josiah (1795–1871), served in a seamen's battery on Craney Island during the War of 1812. He served in Decatur's squadron during the Algerine War. He was given command of the "Spitfire" at the outbreak of the Mexican War and commanded the Mosquito division at the siege of Vera Cruz. In 1861 he entered the Confederate service and was given command of the naval defences of Georgia and South Carolina. He led an attack on Port Royal in 1861. In 1862 he commanded the "Merrimac." He was active in the defense of Savannah.

Taxables, in the Southern colonies, meant persons upon whom a poll-tax was paid (called tithables in Virginia). In Maryland, for instance, taxables included all males and all female slaves of sixteen years or more, excepting beneficed clergymen of the Church of England, paupers and disabled slaves.

Taxation. In the earlier days of the American colonies there was little need of taxation; quit rents satisfied the proprietary or company. Voluntary contributions, forfeitures, fines and payments for land defrayed the greater part of the colonial expenses. By the year 1653, however, we find the colonists complaining of the injustice of chimney and head money, tithes on grain, flax, hemp, tobacco, butter, cheese and excessive export duties. In 1796 most of the States passed laws to regulate taxation, adopting various methods of apportionment and collection, and varying often in the objects taxed. All levied a tax on land except Delaware, and there was a uniform poll tax in nine; other things taxed were horses and cattle and farm stock, stock in trade of merchants, money on hand or at interest, houses, slaves, carriages, billiard tables, processes of law and official papers. The period between 1796 and the Civil War was the transition period as regards taxation, the modern system of taxation being gradually developed. About 1851 a uniform rate of taxation began to be introduced in some States. The Federal Government has raised little money by direct taxes (see art. Direct Taxes), and has used the income tax only in the Civil War. It has raised its revenue through indirect taxation. (See Excise, Internal Revenue, Tariff.)

"**Taxation no Tyranny,**" a famous pamphlet against the cause of the American colonies, written by Dr. Samuel Johnson, and published in London in 1775.

Taylor, Bayard (1825–1878), author, came into prominence by his accounts of a pedestrian tour in Europe from 1844 to 1846. In 1847 he became an editor on the staff of the *Tribune*. He made extensive travels through Europe, Asia and Africa. He was Secretary of Legation at St. Petersburg from 1862 to 1863 and Minister to Berlin in 1878. He wrote an admirable translation of Goethe's Faust.

Taylor, George (1716–1781), came to America from Ireland in 1736. He served in the Pennsylvania Legislature from 1764 to 1769. He represented Pennsylvania in the Continental Congress from 1776 to 1777, and signed the Declaration of Independence.

Taylor, John (1750–1824), called John Taylor of Caroline, represented Virginia in the U. S. Senate as a Democrat from 1792 to 1794 and from 1822 to 1824. During the interval he served in the Virginia House of Delegates, where he moved the celebrated Virginia Resolutions of 1798. He wrote "Inquiry into the Principles and Policy of the Government of the United States," "Construction Construed and the Constitution Vindicated" and "New Views of the Constitution of the United States," leading works of the State-rights school.

Taylor, John (1770–1832), was admitted to the bar in 1793. He was a member of the South Carolina Legislature for a number of years, represented South Carolina in the U. S. Congress as a Democrat from 1807 to 1810, when he became a U. S. Senator and served until 1816. He was a U. S. Congressman from 1816 to 1817, and Governor of South Carolina from 1826 to 1828.

Taylor, John (1808–1887), came to Canada from England in 1832. He became a Mormon apostle in 1838, and succeeded to the presidency of the Mormon Church in 1877. He was indicted for polygamy in 1885.

Taylor, John W. (1784–1854), represented New York in the U. S. Congress as a Democrat from 1813 to 1833. He was Speaker of the House from 1820 to 1821, during the passage of the Missouri Compromise, and from 1825 to 1827. He delivered the first speech in Congress plainly opposing the extension of slavery. He aided in organizing the National Republican and the Whig parties.

Taylor, Richard (1826–1879), son of President Zachary Taylor, was a member of the Louisiana Legislature from 1856 to 1860. He was a member of the Louisiana Secessionist Convention. He commanded a Louisiana regiment at Bull Run, and a brigade in General Jackson's Virginia campaign. He distinguished himself at Middletown, Winchester, Cross Keys, Port Republic and the seven days' battles before Richmond. In 1863 and 1864 he commanded the department west of the Mississippi. He defeated General Banks at Sabine Cross-Roads in 1864. In 1864 he commanded the East Louisiana Department. He wrote "Destruction and Reconstruction."

Taylor, William R. (1811–1889), commanded the "St. Mary's" during the Mexican War and served at the siege of Vera Cruz. He commanded the "Housatonic" from 1861 to 1863, and the "Juniata" at Fort Fisher.

Taylor, Zachary (September 24, 1784–July 9, 1850), twelfth President of the United States, was born in Orange County, Va. He received an appointment to the U. S. army as first lieutenant in 1808. In 1812 he conducted a defence of Fort Harrison against the Indians. After the long period of comparative peace he served in the Black Hawk War, and becoming colonel, was appointed to command against the Seminoles in Florida. There, in December, 1837, he won the battle of Okeechobee. When war with Mexico was approaching, Taylor was ordered to the disputed Texan frontier. He gained the victory of Palo Alto, May 8, 1846, Resaca de la Palma, May 9, and occupied Matamoras. He was made major-general, and stormed Monterey in September. In the following campaign General Taylor, who had been compelled to detach some of his best troops, was attacked by vastly superior forces under Santa Anna, and gained a brilliant victory at Buena Vista, February 22–23, 1847. "Old Rough and Ready" was now the national hero. The following year the Whigs nominated him as candidate for President over such competitors as Clay and Webster, and he was elected and entered on his duties in 1849. The California question complicated with the absorbing slavery topic was the chief matter in President Taylor's administration; he died before the compromise was completed.

Taylor vs. Reading, a New Jersey case, memorable because one of the earliest cases in which a court took upon itself to pronounce upon the constitutionality of a legislative enactment. The Legislature of New Jersey passed an act in 1795, upon the petition of the defendants in the case of Taylor *vs.* Reading, declaring that in certain cases payments made in Continental money should be credited as specie. The Court of Appeals deemed this an *ex post facto* law, and as such unconstitutional and inoperative.

Tazewell, Littleton W. (1774–1860), was a member of the Virginia House of Delegates from 1796 to 1800, a Congressman from 1800 to 1801. He heartily supported the War of 1812. He was appointed a commissioner to Spain in 1819 under the treaty for the purchase of Florida. He represented Virginia in the U. S. Senate as a Democrat from 1825 to 1833. He was a prominent member of the convention to revise the Virginia constitution in 1829, and was Governor of Virginia from 1834 to 1836. In 1840 he received eleven electoral votes for Vice-President. Life by Grigsby.

Tea. June 29, 1767, at the instance of Lord North, Parliament passed an act levying a high duty on tea imported into the colonies. In 1769 the citizens of Boston sent vigorous resolutions to the King denouncing this act. It was partially repealed in 1770, but the East India Company was later assisted by the Government in shipping a surplus quantity of tea to Boston. December 1, 1773, the citizens of Boston held a meeting to consult concerning the most effectual method of preventing the landing of this tea. Another meeting was held December 10, and parties of citizens disguised as "Mohawks," made a raid upon the vessels and threw the tea overboard. In several of the other colonies the landing of tea was prohibited and the cargoes sent whence they came.

Tecumseh, or Tecumtha, (1768?–1813), chief of the Shawnee Indians, joined his brother Ellskwatawa, "the Prophet," in an attempt to organize the Western Indians in a confederacy against the whites. The scheme was defeated by the battle of Tippecanoe in 1811. He aided the British in the War of 1812, serving at Raisin River and Maguaga. He was joint commander at Fort Meigs, where he protected the American forces from massacre. He served at Lake Erie, and led the left wing at the battle of the Thames, where he was killed.

Telegraph. The telegraph was first brought into practical use in the United States by Professor S. F. B. Morse. He began his experiments in 1832, aided by L. D. Gale and George and Alfred Vail. In 1837 he filed a caveat in the Patent Office at Washington, and in 1840 obtained a patent covering the improvements he had made in the meantime. The first line established was between Baltimore and Washington, it being successfully operated May 27, 1844. In October, 1842, Morse had attempted to operate a line from Governor's Island to the Battery in New York, but this experiment failed. Samuel Colt, in 1843, laid a submarine cable from Coney Island and Fire Island, at the mouth of New York harbor, up to the city, and operated it successfully for a time. In 1860 it was estimated that there were over 50,000 miles of telegraph lines in operation in the United States, and at present the lines extend over 190,000 miles. In 1857 Cyrus W. Field attempted to connect Europe and America by means of an Atlantic cable. The first attempt failed, but the laying of the cable was finally accomplished August 5, 1858. (See Atlantic Cable.)

Telephone. The invention of the telephone is claimed by Gray, of Chicago; Bell, formerly of the Institute of Technology, of Boston, now of Washington, and several others. The possibility of such an instrument was discovered previous to 1873, but the first satisfactory results were not obtained until 1877, when Bell completed and put into practical use a telephone line between Salem and Boston, Gray achieving a like result the same year in a line set up between Chicago and Milwaukee, a distance of eighty-five miles. By 1880 there were in existence 148 telephone companies and private concerns, operating 34,305 miles of wire (1893, 308,000 miles). Conversation can now be carried on easily between New York and Chicago, and for even greater distances. The Bell Company is the most extensive. Two suits have been brought against the patent, but both have failed.

AMERICAN INVENTORS.

Peter Cooper.
Charles Goodyear.
Samuel F. B. Morse.
Eli Whitney.
Samuel Colt.
Richard M. Hoe.
Thomas A. Edison.
Cyrus W. Field.
Elias Howe.
E. B. Bigelow.
Oliver Evans.
Alexander Graham Bell.
Cyrus H. McCormick.
Robert Fulton.

Teller, Henry M., born in 1830, was major-general of Colorado militia from 1862 to 1864. He represented Colorado in the U. S. Senate as a Republican from 1876 to 1882. From 1877 to 1878, he was chairman of the special committee on election frauds. He was Secretary of the Interior in Arthur's Cabinet from 1882 to 1885. He was again elected to the U. S. Senate in 1885 and 1891.

Temperance. (See Prohibition.)

Ten-Forties, bonds bearing five per cent interest, redeemable at any time after ten years from the date of issue, and payable in full at the end of forty years, issued by the U. S. Government in 1864.

Ten-Hour Law. In the early years of manufactures the working day sometimes extended to thirteen or fourteen hours. After the passage of the ten-hour law in England in 1847, the working classes in this country demanded a similar law. In 1853, the manufacturing companies in Lowell, Lawrence and Fall River voluntarily reduced the working day to eleven hours. In 1874, Massachusetts enacted a law prescribing a ten-hour day for all females and all males under eighteen years of age employed in textile factories. Similar laws have been passed elsewhere.

Tennessee was originally a part of North Carolina. The first settlements were made by a company of hunters on the Watauga in the eastern part of the State in 1769. When North Carolina proposed to surrender the territory to the U. S. Government, these settlers protested, and formed a separate State Government under the name of Frankland or Franklin. They elected a Governor, John Sevier, and a legislature which requested admission to the Union as a State. In 1788 the State Government was overthrown by the inhabitants of the State who were favorable to North Carolina, an act of amnesty was passed by the Legislature of North Carolina, and Sevier was admitted as a Senator. In 1794 a Territorial Government was organized under provisions like those of the Ordinance of 1787, except that slavery should not be abolished. The State was admitted into the Union, June 1, 1796. Knoxville was the capital until 1802, when it was changed to Nashville. The vote of the State was cast for Democratic candidates until 1835. The legislature nominated Jackson for the Presidency in 1824 and the State supported him almost unanimously. In 1835 the Whigs elected Cannon Governor, and in 1836 cast the electoral votes for Hugh L. White, the candidate of the Southern States-Rights faction of the Whig party. The Whigs secured the electoral votes of the State at each election until 1856, when Buchanan carried the State. In January, 1861, a popular vote defeated a proposal for the State to secede from the Union. June 8, 1861, the Secessionists carried the State. During the war the State furnished 31,092 to the Union army. The State was the scene of some of the fiercest battles, as Island No. 10, Nashville, Chickamauga, Lookout Mountain and Missionary Ridge. July 24, 1866, the State was restored to the Union. The present constitution was made in 1870. Since 1874, State politics have been shaped by the problem of the State debt. In 1880 this resulted in the election of a Republican Governor. The population of the State in 1796 was 77,202; in 1890 this had increased to 1,767,518. History by Ramsey.

Tennessee Bond Cases, seventeen causes decided by the Supreme Court of the United States in 1885, wherein it was held that the statutory lien upon railroads created by an act of the Tennessee Legislature in 1852, was for the benefit of the State and not of the holders of State bonds issued under that act.

Tennessee Historical Societies. One was founded at Nashville in 1847. Another was organized at Knoxville more recently.

Tenure of Office Act. By the Constitution the Senate is associated with the President in the making of appointments to office. But it was concluded in 1789 that removals were entirely in the discretion of the President. This remained the rule until 1867, when Congress, in the course of its quarrel with President Johnson, passed over his veto the Tenure of Office Act. This act provided that, with certain exceptions, every officer appointed with the concurrence of the Senate should retain his office until a successor should be in like manner appointed. During the recess of the Senate the President might, for specified causes, suspend an officer until the Senate could act. If the Senate approved, the officer might then be removed, otherwise not. Johnson's ignoring of the act in the case of Secretary Stanton, in 1868, led to his impeachment. The act was repealed in 1887.

Terra Mariæ, the Latin equivalent of Maryland. The charter of Maryland, alone among the colonial charters, was written in Latin.

Territories. Several states had extensive claims to Western lands. They were also claimed for the United States, as won by all in common, through the Revolutionary War. New York ceded her claims in 1781, Virginia in 1784, Massachusetts in 1785, Connecticut in 1786 and in 1800, South Carolina in 1787, North Carolina in 1790, Georgia in 1802. Subsequent additions of territory have been made by annexation (see art.) Preparatory to their admission as States, the separate regions of this domain have been organized as Territories, the first organized being the Northwest Territory, by the Ordinance of 1787. The Southwest Territory was organized in 1790. The history of each Territory can be found under its name or that of the State of the same name. At first the form of government of a Territory was modeled on that in the Ordinance for the Government of the Northwest Territory. Afterward two types were developed. In those of the second class, the Governor, Secretary, Judges and Legislative Council of thirteen were all appointed by the President. In those of the first class, to which lately all organized Territories have belonged, there is a bicameral Legislature, the House of Representatives being elected by the people. Convening, the House nominates eighteen persons, from among whom the President chooses a Legislative Council of nine. A delegate represents each Territory in Congress, but without vote.

Terry, Alfred Howe (1827–1890), an American general, was one of the most successful of the civilian officers in the War of the Rebellion. Before the struggle he had been a lawyer, paying some attention to militia matters. During the first year he commanded a regiment at the capture of Port Royal and Fort Pulaski. Being made a brigadier-general, he served in 1862–1863 in the operations near Charleston. He commanded a corps in the Army of the James, and fought at Chester Station, Drewry's Bluff and the siege of Petersburg. He was intrusted with the military part of the second attempt on Fort Fisher, January, 1865, co-operating with the admiral. The successful storming of the fort on January 14 made Terry a brigadier-general in the regular army. He captured Wilmington, and was a departmental commander after the war. General Terry became major-general in 1886, and retired in 1888.

Texas, the largest State in the Union, popularly known as the "Lone Star State," formed originally a part of the Spanish possessions in America. The United States surrendered her claim that Texas was included in the Louisiana purchase, by the treaty of 1819–1821 with Spain, whereby the United States obtained possession of Florida and settled the eastern boundary of Texas. Meanwhile Mexico had declared her independence of Spain, and Texas with Coahuila formed a State of Mexico, and in 1827 adopted a State Constitution which forbade the importation of slaves and provided for the gradual abolition of slavery. Moses Austin, an American, obtained a large grant of land in Texas in 1820, and formed a settlement of Americans, which increased rapidly. A new State Constitution was formed in 1833 by a convention of the 20,000 settlers, but Mexico refused to recognize it. When Santa Anna, the President of Mexico, attempted to reduce the Mexican States to the condition of departments in 1835, Texas immediately seceded, March 2, 1836, and proclaimed her independence, which she maintained by the defeat of Santa Anna at the head of 1500 troops by General Sam Houston with only 700 or 800 Americans, in the battle of San Jacinto, April 21, 1836. A constitution was adopted favoring slavery. Houston was elected President. The United States, England, France and Belgium recognized the new government as independent (1837). From this time until December 29, 1845, when Texas was finally annexed to the United States, the question of its annexation was the Gordian knot of American politics. Treaty negotiations failing, annexation was accomplished by joint resolution of both Houses of Congress. The dispute over the western boundary of Texas led to the Mexican War (q. v.). March 25, 1850, Texas ceded all claims to territory outside of her present limits to the United States for $10,000,000. February 1, 1861, an ordinance of secession was passed. During the war there was a large influx of slaves from the other States. The State was restored to its place in the Union March 30, 1870. The State has been uniformly Democratic except for a brief period prior to 1873. The population of Texas in 1850 was 212,592; in 1890, 2,235,523. The present constitution was made in 1876. History by Yoakum.

"**Texas Gazette and Brazoria Advertiser,**" first newspaper of Texas. It was established at Brazoria in 1830. September 4, 1832, it was merged in the *Constitutional Advocate and Texas Public Advertiser*, which was suspended in 1833.

Texas vs. White et al. This case was tried before the Supreme Court of the United States on the original bill in 1868. In 1851 the United States issued to the State of Texas 5000 coupon bonds for $1000 each, payable to State of Texas or bearer, in arrangement of certain boundary claims. Part of these bonds were seized during the Civil War by the revolutionary government of Texas and sold to White & Chiles and others of New York and other States, though said bonds were only payable if endorsed by a recognized Governor. In 1866 a bill was filed for an injunction to recover these bonds. This was granted on the ground that the action of a revolutionary government did not affect the right of Texas as a State of the Union, having a government acknowledging her obligations to the National Constitution. The Court pronounced the Union an indestructible Union of indestructible States and the act of secession void.

Thames, Canada. At this river a final stand was made by General Procter and Tecumtha, when pursued by General Harrison in the War of 1812. The position chosen was poor and very favorable to the American advance. October 5, 1813, Harrison with 3000 men attacked and by a vigorous charge of cavalry under Colonel Johnson drove the British in great confusion from the field. Tecumtha was slain and General Procter himself barely escaped capture. This defeat ended his disgraceful career. The Americans lost forty-five and the British forty-eight, besides thirty-three Indians; 477 prisoners were captured. The results of the battle were: The Indian Northwestern Confederacy was destroyed; the British power in Upper Canada was broken, and practically all that had been lost by General Hull at Detroit was regained.

Thatcher, Henry K. (1806–1880), commanded the "Constellation" on the Mediterranean station from 1862 to 1863. In command of the "Colorado" he led the first division of Commodore Porter's fleet in both attacks on Fort Fisher. He succeeded Farragut in command of the Western Gulf squadron at Mobile, whose surrender he secured. He was promoted rear-admiral and retired in 1868.

Thayer, Eli, born in 1819, of Worcester, Mass., founded the Emigrant Aid Company which settled Lawrence, Topeka, Manhattan and Ossawatomie. These settlements in Kansas exerted a powerful influence for the anti-slavery cause. He represented Massachusetts in the U. S. Congress as a Republican from 1857 to 1861. He wrote "The Kansas Crusade."

Thayer, John M., born in 1820, led a brigade at Donelson and Shiloh and commanded a division at Vicksburg and a column at Chickasaw. He represented Nebraska in the U. S. Senate as a Republican from 1867 to 1871, and was Governor of Nebraska from 1886 to 1891.

Thayer, Sylvanus (1785–1872), was superintendent of the Military Academy at West Point from 1817 to 1833. During his administration the academy became one of the best in the world. From 1833 to 1863 he fortified Boston Harbor.

Theatre. The first theatre in the United States was opened at Williamsburg, Va., September 5, 1752. This was followed by others at Annapolis, Md., and at New York, in Nassau Street, in 1753. Theatres were opened at Albany in 1769, at Baltimore in 1773, at Charleston, S. C., in 1774, at Newbern, N. C., in 1788, and at Boston in 1792.

Thomas, George Henry (July 31, 1816–March 28, 1870), a distinguished American general, was born in Virginia, and graduated at West Point in 1840. He fought against the Seminoles, and in the Mexican War was distinguished at Monterey and Buena Vista. In the summer of 1861 he had charge of a brigade in Virginia, and later in the year was promoted to the command of a division in the Western army. At Mill Spring, in Kentucky, January 19, 1862, General Thomas gained the first marked Union success in the war. He led the right wing at Perryville, and the centre at Murfreesboro'. At the battle of Chickamauga, September 19–20, 1860, Thomas' ability prevented a serious disaster, and earned for him the title of the "Rock of Chickamauga." He fortified Chattanooga, received command of the Army of the Cumberland, and was made brigadier-general in the regular army. In command of his army he had a prominent share in the battle of Missionary Ridge and in the hard fighting of Sherman's campaign in 1864. In September, 1864, he was detached from Sherman's army, and was ordered to oppose General Hood. This service culminated in his decisive victory of Nashville, December 15, 16, 1864. General Thomas received the thanks of Congress, and was promoted to be major-general in the regular army. After the war he was a departmental commander. Life by Van Horne.

Thomas, Isaiah (1749–1831), edited the *Massachusetts Spy* from 1771 to 1801. He earnestly supported the Revolutionary movement by his paper. From 1775 to 1801 he published the celebrated *New England Almanac*. He founded the American Antiquarian Society, to which he gave valuable books, files of newspapers and estates. He wrote "A History of Printing in America."

Thomas, Jane (eighteenth century), was the wife of John Thomas, colonel of the Spartan regiment of South Carolina. She distinguished herself by aiding in repelling an attack upon her house by the Tories.

Thomas, Jesse B. (1777–1850), was territorial delegate to Congress from Indiana from 1808 to 1809. He represented Illinois in the U. S. Senate as a Democrat from 1818 to 1829. He introduced the Missouri Compromise in 1820.

Thomas, John (1725–1776), of Massachusetts, commanded a regiment under General Amherst at Crown Point in 1760, and aided in the capture of Montreal. He was appointed a brigadier-general by the Provincial Congress in 1775. He had charge of the fortification of Dorchester Heights, which led to the evacuation of Boston by the British. In 1776 he was given command in Canada, but died of small-pox.

Thomas, Lorenzo (1804–1875), was chief of staff of General Butler during the Mexican War. He was adjutant-general of the army from 1861 to 1863. He organized colored troops from 1863 to 1865. In 1868 President Johnson, in the course of his quarrel with Secretary Stanton, appointed Thomas Secretary of War. This led directly to the impeachment of Johnson.

Thomas, Philip F. (1810–1890), represented Maryland in the U. S. Congress as a Democrat from 1839 to 1841. He was Governor of Maryland from 1848 to 1851, and Comptroller of the State Treasury from 1851 to 1853. He was Secretary of the Treasury in Buchanan's Cabinet from December, 1860, to January, 1861. He was refused a seat in the Senate in 1868, as having given aid and comfort to the Rebellion. He was a U. S. Congressman from 1875 to 1877.

Thomas, Theodore, born in 1835, came to America from Germany in 1845. He has been influential in introducing a higher class of music in America. He has been leader of the Philharmonic Society, and for a time director of music at the World's Fair.

Thompson, George, the abolitionist (born in Liverpool, England, in 1804, died in Leeds, England, in 1878), was active in the anti-slavery agitations respecting the British colonies, and came to this country in 1834 at the request of William Lloyd Garrison and others, to speak in behalf of abolition. He spoke in different parts of the country and his efforts led to the formation of 150 anti-slavery societies. He was finally threatened by mobs in Boston and fled to England in 1835. He aided greatly in preventing the recognition of the Southern Confederacy by the British Government.

Thompson, Jacob (1810–1885), represented Mississippi in the U. S. Congress as a Democrat from 1839 to 1851. He was Secretary of the Interior in Buchanan's Cabinet from 1857 to 1861, and used that position to aid schemes of secession. He was Governor of Mississippi from 1862 to 1864. In 1864 he was sent as a Confederate commissioner to Canada, where he promoted the scheme to release the prisoners at Camp Douglas, Chicago, and burn the city.

Thompson, John R. (1823–1873), of Virginia, was editor of the *Southern Literary Messenger* from 1847 to 1859. He exerted a great influence upon Southern literary tastes. He wrote "The Burial of Latané," "The Death of Stuart," and other poems popular in the South.

Thompson, Richard W., born in 1809, served in the Indiana Legislature from 1834 to 1838, and represented Indiana in the U. S. Congress as a Whig from 1841 to 1843, and from 1847 to 1849. He was a Circuit Judge in Indiana from 1867 to 1869. He was Secretary of the Navy in Hayes' Cabinet from 1877 to 1881.

Thompson, Smith (1768–1843), was a Judge of the New York Supreme Court from 1802 to 1818. He was Secretary of the Navy in Monroe's Cabinet from 1818 to 1823, and a Justice of the U. S. Supreme Court from 1823 to 1843.

Thomson, Charles (1729–1824), came to America from Ireland in 1740. His influence during the Revolution was such that he was called "the Sam Adams of Philadelphia, the life of the cause of liberty." He was Secretary of the Continental Congress during its entire history, from 1774 to 1789. He made careful records of the proceedings and took valuable notes.

Thoreau, Henry D. (1817–1862), of Massachusetts, was a poet and author, of idealistic aspirations, a fine scholar, a transcendentalist and a lover of nature. He wrote "Walden, or Life in the Woods," "The Maine Woods" "A Yankee in Canada," etc.

Thorfinn, died after 1016. He went to Greenland from Norway in 1006. According to the Sagas, in 1007 he sailed for Vinland with three ships and 160 persons, sighted Newfoundland and Nova Scotia, sailed along the New England coast and landed upon some island, where they spent the winter. The next three years were spent in a bay which some have identified with Mount Hope Bay, where they traded with the Esquimaux. They returned in 1011.

Thornton, Sir Edward, born in 1817, was Minister from England to the United States from 1867 to 1881. He was a member of the commission on the Alabama claims in 1871, and an arbitrator of the American and Mexican Claims Commission in 1873.

Thornton, Matthew (1714–1803), came to America from Ireland about 1717. He was Judge of the New Hampshire Supreme Court from 1776 to 1782. He represented New Hampshire in the Continental Congress from 1776 to 1778 and signed the Declaration of Independence.

Thorvald Ericsson, died in 1004. He is said to have came to America (Rhode Island?) from Iceland with thirty men in 1002, in 1003 to have explored the southern coast of New England and in 1004 the northern coast.

Three-Cent Piece, a silver coin issued in 1851, having been authorized the same year. Its weight in grains was 12.375. In 1853 its weight was changed to 11.52. The coinage was discontinued by an Act of Congress of 1873. This coin was a legal tender to the amount of thirty cents. Nickel three-cent pieces began to be coined in 1865.

Three-Dollar Piece, a gold coin, authorized in 1853; coinage begun 1854. This coin has always been a legal tender to an unlimited amount.

Throckmorton, James W., born in 1825, was a member of the Texas Legislature from 1851 to 1861, and Governor of Texas from 1866 to 1867. He was a Democratic U. S. Congressman from 1875 to 1879 and from 1883 to 1887.

Throop, Enos T. (1784–1874), represented New York in the U. S. Congress as a Democrat from 1815 to 1816. He was Governor of New York from 1829 to 1832, Minister to Naples from 1838 to 1842.

Thurman, Allen Granbery, born in 1813, an American statesman, is an eminent lawyer, settled in Columbus, Ohio. He is a life-long Democrat; from 1845 to 1847 he was Congressman from Ohio; he was Justice of the State Supreme Court 1851–1854, and its Chief Justice 1854–1856. In 1867 he was defeated for Governor by General Hayes. From 1869 to 1881 he was a U. S. Senator. While his party was in the minority Senator Thurman was its leader, and afterward he had the chairmanship of the Judiciary Committee. He was at one time president *pro tem.* of the Senate. He was the sponsor for the Thurman Act, which compelled the Pacific railroads to fulfil their obligations to the Government. President Garfield appointed him a delegate to the Paris Monetary Convention of 1881. Thurman received votes in the Democratic National Conventions of 1876, 1880 and 1884. In 1888 he was nominated by acclamation for second place on the ticket with Cleveland, but was defeated in the election.

Thwaites, Reuben G., born in 1853, was an editor of the *Wisconsin State Journal* from 1877 to 1886. He has given much attention to Western history. He wrote "Historic Waterways," and a small history of the colonies.

Ticknor, George (1791–1871), of Massachusetts, was admitted to the bar in 1813. From 1815 to 1819 he was in Europe engaged in philological study and collecting a library which was unsurpassed in Spanish literature. He was professor of modern languages and literature at Harvard from 1819 to 1835. He wrote a "History of Spanish Literature," which is recognized as a masterly work. His letters have been published.

Ticonderoga. During the French and Indian War, in June, 1758, a British and Provincial force of 15,000 men advanced upon Ticonderoga, then occupied by the French. Montcalm had only 3600. After some indecision he retired to the site of the fort and threw up earthworks. During their advance the English lost Howe, and the command fell to the incompetent Abercromby. Without support of artillery he attempted to carry the fort by a bayonet charge. He was disastrously repulsed with a loss of 1944 to 277 on the side of the French. He retreated precipitately. On July 22, 1759, General Amherst appeared before Ticonderoga. He met little opposition and placed his artillery in position. On the night of the 23d, Bourlamaque retired from the fort with the best troops. The garrison kept up a brisk fire until the night of the 26th, when they abandoned the place and fired a train to the magazine. The fort was blown up and the place fell into English hands.—In the Revolutionary War also the strategic importance of Ticonderoga was recognized. A force under Ethan Allen arrived on the shore of Lake Champlain in the early morning of May 10, 1775. There were not enough boats to carry over all his forces, and so with only eighty-three men he descended upon the little garrison, who surrendered without a blow. Thus the colonists gained the key to the route to and from Canada, and captured a number of cannon and a considerable quantity of powder and ball, which they much needed. On July 1, 1777, Burgoyne in his march south appeared before Ticonderoga. The British seized a position which commands the fort and compelled the garrison, 3000 in number, to evacuate. These retired into the Green Mountains, the women and wounded to Fort Edward (July 5, 1777).

"Tidal Wave," the term applied to the unprecedented success of the Democratic party in elections, State and Congressional, from 1872 to 1876. This was due to the corruption of the Republican administration. The tidal wave resulted in the contested election of 1876–77.

Tiffin, Edward (1766–1829), came to America from England in 1784. He was Governor of Ohio from 1803 to 1807, and represented Ohio in the U. S. Senate as a Democrat from 1807 to 1809.

Tilden, Samuel Jones (February 9, 1814–August 4, 1886), an American statesman, was educated at Yale and the University of New York. He acquired a high position at the New York bar, became famous as a counsel for corporations, and amassed wealth. Though interested in New York politics and very influential in the counsels of the Democratic party, Mr. Tilden held no office for many years, except in 1845 in the Assembly, and the next year in the State Constitutional Convention. By about the close of the war he had become the recognized leader of the New York Democracy. He was one of the most expert party managers of modern times. In strenuously opposing the Tweed ring in 1871 and the following years, as well as in antagonizing other abuses, Tilden acquired such prestige that in 1874 as candidate for Governor he was elected over Dix by 50,000 majority. He served from 1875 to 1877. His success caused his nomination for President by the National Convention in 1876. In the remarkable election Tilden had a substantial popular majority, but the result of the electoral vote was in doubt. (See Electoral Commission.) The extra-constitutional Electoral Commission admitted 184 votes for Tilden and 185 for Hayes. Governor Tilden, the "sage of Gramercy Park," continued to be regarded as the party adviser, the "great defrauded." He wrote letters declining in advance the nomination in 1880 and 1884. By the provisions of his will a large sum was left for a free public library in New York.

Tilghman, Matthew (1718–1790), was a member of the Maryland General Assembly from 1751 to 1774. He was a delegate to the Continental Congress from 1774 to 1777. He was president of the Revolutionary Convention which directed the State Government from 1774 to 1777. To him was largely due the drafting and organizing of the government of Maryland.

Timber Culture. March 3, 1873, Congress passed the Timber Culture Act, granting to settlers 160 acres of treeless lands for the encouragement of tree culture. An act of June 3, 1878, authorized the sale at $2.50 per acre of forest lands on the Pacific Coast, and at the same time prohibited timber depredations on the public lands.

Timrod, Henry (1829–1867), of South Carolina, became popular in the South for his war lyrics written during the Civil War. He was a poet of genius and delicate imagination.

Tingey, Thomas (1750–1829), came to America from England and served in the Continental navy during the Revolution. He commanded the Washington Navy Yard from 1804 to 1829.

Tippecanoe, a nickname of President William Henry Harrison, originating in his victory over the Indians on the Tippecanoe River, in Indiana, in 1811.

Tithables, in Virginia, all persons liable to poll-tax, to wit, all males and all female slaves of more than sixteen years.

Tithingman, a sort of Sunday constable, who preserved order in meeting and discharged various police functions of a similar nature. The office was peculiarly a New England institution, though rare instances of tithingmen were to be found in Maryland and elsewhere. In towns where there were Indian inhabitants, it was the duty of the tithingman to preserve order among them.

Tobacco, introduced to the knowledge of civilized nations on the discovery of America, where it was found in use by the Indians on the islands and on the mainland as far north as Virginia. It was cultivated in Portugal and France early in the sixteenth century. Its cultivation was begun by the earliest settlers in Virginia and Maryland, to whom it was frequently the sole, yet lucrative, source of income. It was used as a legal tender in Maryland in 1733, during a period of depreciation in the colonial currency, and was widely used as a medium of barter and exchange and payment of debt. Virginia led in the production of tobacco during many years, her annual production frequently reaching 20,000,000 pounds. Kentucky now leads. Tobacco is at present widely cultivated in the Southern, Middle, Western and even the New England States, that of the Connecticut valley being deemed especially adapted for cigar wrappings. In 1889 there was a total production of 565,795,000 pounds in the United States, valued at $43,666,-665. During the years 1865–1892 the total internal revenue receipts from tobacco amounted to $896,512,367.

Tocqueville, Alexis Charles Henri Clerel de (1805–1859), a French publicist and politician, visited the United States in 1831–1832 on a mission to examine the penitentiary system. He published in 1835–40 "Democracy in America," the most important commentary on American affairs by a foreigner until the appearance of "Bryce's American Commonwealth." De Tocqueville was afterward member of the Chamber of Deputies and of the French Academy, and in 1849 was Minister of Foreign Affairs.

Tod, David (1805–1868), was Minister to Brazil from 1847 to 1852. He was a champion of the "peace policy" in 1861, but when Governor of Ohio from 1862 to 1864 was a firm supporter of the Government.

Todd, Thomas (1765–1826), a prominent Kentucky jurist, was an Associate Justice of the U. S. Supreme Court from 1807 to 1826.

Tohopeka. (See Horse-shoe Bend.)

"Toledo War," a boundary controversy between Ohio and Michigan, which came to a head in 1835, just previous to Michigan's application for admission to the Union. The controversy was over that territory which contained the city of Toledo, and its history may be traced back to the ordinance of 1787 respecting the division of the Northwest Territory. In 1835 Ohio proposed to assume control of the disputed tract. Michigan responded by making such action highly penal, and appealed to the Federal Government. An armed collision seemed imminent. Finally it was agreed that Michigan should be admitted to the Union and awarded certain territory in the north, provided she would give up her clearly rightful claim to the Toledo country.

Tom the Tinker, the popular watchword of the rebels of western Pennsylvania during the Whisky Rebellion of 1794, originating in the destruction of the house of an obnoxious official by a mob, which gave out that it was being tinkered.

Tompkins, Daniel D. (1774–1825), Vice-President of the United States, was graduated at Columbia, and became a leading lawyer and Democratic politician in the State of New York. He was a Judge in the Supreme Court of the State, and its Governor from 1807 until 1817. While holding this office he opposed the Bank and gave an efficient support to the War of 1812. Governor Tompkins was elected Vice-President in 1816 on the ticket with Monroe, and re-elected in 1820, serving from 1817 to 1825.

Tonga. The United States concluded a treaty of amity, commerce and navigation with Tonga in 1886.

Tonty, Chevalier Henri de (1650?–1704), accompanied La Salle to Canada in 1678 and explored with him the Mississippi. Later he twice descended to the mouth of the Mississippi in search of La Salle.

Toombs, Robert (1810–1885), one of the most influential Secessionists, was graduated at Union College and rose to distinction as a lawyer in Georgia. He served in the Creek War, in the legislature, and as a State-Rights Whig in Congress from 1845 to 1853. While in Congress he favored and took part in the compromise measures of 1850. He was U. S. Senator from Georgia 1853–1861. Senator Toombs was one of the most active champions of the slave power, and when the crisis occurred in 1860 he was second to none in energy as a disunionist. He aided powerfully in forcing his State to secede. During the war he was at different times Congressman, Secretary of State, and a brigadier-general. Afterward he practised law, and refused persistently to take the oath of allegiance to the Government. In his last years he devoted himself to a contest with the railroad power.

Topeka, Kan., was founded in 1854, received a city charter in 1857 and became the State capital in 1861.

Topeka Constitution. On October 23, 1855, a constitutional convention, representing the anti-slavery population of Kansas, met at Topeka. This convention adopted the boundaries set by the Kansas-Nebraska bill, prohibited slavery after July, 1857, and conferred the right of suffrage on "white male citizens" and on "every civilized male Indian who has adopted the habits of the white man." This free State convention was dispersed by Federal troops. The bill to admit Kansas to the Union under the provisions of the Topeka constitution passed the House, but failed in the Senate.

Torbert, Alfred T. A. (1833–1880), led a Federal brigade at Manassas, Crampton's Gap and Gettysburg in 1862. In 1864 he was placed in command of a division of cavalry in the Army of the Potomac. He fought at Cold Harbor, Trevillian Station, Winchester and Cedar Creek. He commanded at Tom's River, Liberty Mills and Gordonsville. He was Consul General at Paris from 1873 to 1878.

Tories. (See Loyalists.) The name Tory had been employed in England from 1679 to designate those who were desirous to increase the power of the king. The term had become odious by reason of the Jacobite conspiracies, and was revived in America as a term of reproach.

Totten, Joseph G. (1788–1864), was chief engineer of the army on the Canadian frontier during the war of 1812. During the Civil War he had charge of the engineering bureau at Washington.

Toucey, Isaac (1796–1869), represented Connecticut in the U. S. Congress as a Democrat from 1835 to 1839. He was chosen Governor of Connecticut by the Legislature in 1846. He was Attorney-General in Polk's Cabinet from 1848 to 1849, and a U. S. Senator from 1852 to 1857. He was Secretary of the Navy in Buchanan's Cabinet from 1857 to 1861, and was charged with favoring the seceding States by dispersing the navy.

Tourgee, Albion W., born in 1838, served in the national army during the Civil War. He prepared a report on the condition of the Southern States for the Loyalists' Convention in 1866. He published "The North Carolina Code," and "A Fool's Errand," and other books on the Reconstruction period.

Toussaint Louverture, leader of the revolted negroes of Hayti and President of the Haytian Republic, is connected with the history of the United States through Bonaparte's San Domingo expedition. The First Consul intended, after conquering the island, to make it the basis of an expedition which should create in Louisiana a French colonial empire. Toussaint's resistance and the destruction of French troops by yellow fever balked this plan, and Napoleon sold Louisiana to the United States.

Towle, George M. (1841–1893), was U. S. Consul at Nantes, France, from 1866 to 1868, and at Bradford, England, from 1868 to 1870. He wrote "Glimpses of History," "Heroes of History," and other popular historical books.

Town. In New England the word town has constantly been used in the sense of township, meaning the primary subdivision of the county, a large area, rural or urban. In the Middle colonies and the South it meant, as in England, an incorporated municipality of greater or less size. Thus in Massachusetts nearly all the territory of the colony was occupied with towns, while in the South there were a few towns here and there. As to the origin of the New England town various theories have been held. To some it has seemed an original creation of the early settlers, to others an imitation of the English parish.

Town-Meeting, the meeting of all freemen of a town in primary assembly for the discussion of local affairs and the election of local officers. This has been one of the most characteristic of New England institutions, and one of the most valuable, because of the education it has afforded in politics. Jefferson on this account wished that something similar might be introduced into Virginia. In the type of local government which has been instituted in the northernmost row of Western States, the township usually has a town-meeting. In the row of States west of the Middle States, this is not usual.

Townsend, Edward D., born in 1817, was the principal executive officer of the War Department, under Secretary Stanton, during the Civil War. He wrote "Anecdotes of the Civil War in the United States."

Townsend, George A., born in 1841, reported the Peninsular campaign for the New York *Herald* in 1862. He was war correspondent for the *World* in 1864 and 1865. He wrote "The Real Life of Abraham Lincoln" and various tales of Maryland life.

Townshend, Charles (1725–1767), English statesman, was made Commissioner of Trade and Plantations in 1749, and made a careful study of the American colonies. In 1763 he was made First Lord of Trade and Plantations. He ardently supported Grenville's Stamp Act in 1765 and was in favor of imposing upon the colonies heavy burdens. He advocated the annulling of the colonial charters and the establishment of a uniform system of Government. In 1766 he became Chancellor of the Exchequer. He secured the passage of an act in 1767 which levied burdensome duties on such articles as tea, paper and glass. He was a man of ready wit and brilliant oratory, but unwise.

Townshend Acts, two acts proposed in Parliament, April 16, 1767, at the instance of Charles Townshend, then Chancellor of the Exchequer. They were to go into effect November 20. They provided for the appointment of commissioners to enforce more effectually the laws of trade with the colonies; granted duties on glass, paper, colors and tea, and legalized writs of assistance. The revenue was to defray the charge of the administration of justice and support the civil government in the provinces. The people of Massachusetts opposed them by renewing their non-importation agreements.

Tracy, Benjamin F., lawyer, born in 1830, was elected a district attorney in New York in 1854 and 1856. He led a regiment at the battles of the Wilderness and Spottsylvania, and had charge of the prison camp at Elmira. He was a U. S. District Attorney from 1866 to 1873, and was Secretary of the Navy in Harrison's Cabinet from 1889 to 1893.

Trade Dollar, a silver coin issued in 1873–1874 for use in China, in competition with Spanish and Mexican dollars. It was not intended for circulation in the United States, though it was made a legal tender to the amount of five dollars at the time of its issue; this provision was repealed in 1876. Its actual value was less than that of the standard dollar.

Trades' Unions. These associations of workingmen, for concerted action upon questions of wages, hours of labor and for mutual relief, were begun in this country in 1852 by the formation of the International Typographical Union, followed in 1859 by the Machinists' and Blacksmiths' International Union, and the Iron Moulders' Union of North America. The Brotherhood of Locomotive Engineers was organized in 1863, the Journeymen Tailors' National Trades Union in 1865, the Coopers' International Union in 1870, the Cigarmakers' International Union about the same time, the Miners' National Union in 1873. There are beside numerous other lesser and local associations.

Transcendentalism. This movement derived its name from the German philosophy of Schelling, and signified the philosophy of those who deemed the objective realities of the world to be best studied by interrogating the subjective consciousness. The school of the transcendentalists prevailed in New England, especially at Concord, Mass., in and after 1830. Emerson was its leader, but many of his followers were unpractical and visionary men, whose philosophy was of little value to the actual world. The movement exercised great influence on Unitarian religion, on various reforms and especially on the anti-slavery cause.

Transylvania Company, a colonization company, organized in North Carolina in 1775. Its grants were obtained directly from the crown, no colonial government being permitted to issue land warrants.

Travis, William B. (1811–1836), while fighting for the independence of Texas was besieged at Fort Alamo by the Mexicans in 1836. After desperate fighting, when only six men were left, they surrendered on promise of protection, but were slaughtered by command of Santa Anna.

Treason against the United States is defined in the Constitution as consisting "only in levying war against them, or in adhering to their enemies, giving them aid and comfort." A motion to give Congress the sole power of defining the punishment of treason was lost in the convention of 1787. Most of the States have inserted in their constitutions a provision regarding treason similar to that of the National Constitution. There has been practically no instance of an indictment for treason against a State except that of Dorr in Rhode Island. At the end of the Civil War there were no prosecutions for treason, because the idea of State allegiance had in many States so long predominated over that of national allegiance. April 30, 1790, an act was passed making treason punishable by death. Burr's case was the principal one under this act. July 17, 1862, an act of Congress provided that treason should also be punishable by the liberation of the guilty person's slaves.

Treasury Board, established by the Continental Congress February 17, 1776, to consist of a standing committee of five Congressmen who should have control over minor officials and act as a Ways and Means Committee. The Committee of Claims and the Treasury Office of Accounts were the principal bureaus under the Board's supervision. September 26, 1778, an Act of Congress provided for securing a house for the various offices of the department, thus forming the germ of the present treasury system. Provision was also made for the annual appointment of a comptroller, auditor and treasurer, thus doing away with the Treasury Office of Accounts. The Treasury Board ceased to exist in September, 1781, when a Superintendent of Finance was instituted. After Robert Morris resigned this office, from 1785 to 1789 the Treasury was again under a board of commissioners.

Treasury Department. Under the Continental Congress financial matters were at first managed by a committee. The Treasury Office of Accounts was created in 1776. In 1778 the department was given an organization much like that of the present time. In 1781 the office of Superintendent of Finance was created, and the department put under a single head. In 1785 the Board was restored. The First Congress, by Act of September 2, 1789, established the present Treasury Department.

Treasury Notes. Treasury notes, receivable for all dues to the Government, but not made a legal tender, were first issued to meet the expenses of the War of 1812. In 1812 issues of five millions were authorized, in 1813 of five millions more, in 1814 of eighteen millions, in 1815 of eight millions more. The rate of interest was 5 2-5 per cent. The financial panic of 1837 caused further issues of sixteen millions in 1837 and 1838, $4,000,000 in 1839, $6,000,000 in 1840, $8,000,000 in 1841, $11,000,000 in 1842, and

$2,000,000 in 1844. The Mexican War caused issues of $26,000,000, under Act of 1846. The panic of 1857 was met by issues to the amount of $53,-000,000. These notes usually had but a short time to run. The Civil War required the issue of enormous quantities of treasury notes. Those which bore a legal tender character are treated of under Greenbacks. The Government also met temporary exigencies by the issue of demand notes and fractional and postal currency. The chief variety of notes resembling the treasury notes hitherto issued, receivable for dues to Government, but not legal tenders, was the 7.30's, of which $830,000,000 were issued. These were nearly all paid by the end of 1869. The Sherman Act of 1890 provided for the issue of treasury notes wherewith to make the monthly purchases of silver bullion required by that Act.

Treasury Office of Accounts, an office created in April, 1776, by the Continental Congress. It was under the supervision of the standing committee of the treasury, and was under the immediate direction of an auditor-general, assisted by clerks, whose business it was to audit accounts and report to Congress through the Treasury Board.

Treat, Robert (1622–1701), came to Connecticut from England early in the seventeenth century. He was a deputy from 1653 to 1659, and an assistant from 1659 to 1664. He opposed the union of New Haven and Connecticut. He commanded the Connecticut forces in King Philip's War. He was Deputy-Governor of Connecticut from 1676 to 1683, and Governor from 1683 to 1698, except two years under Sir Edmund Andros from 1687 to 1689. He was again Deputy-Governor from 1698 to 1708.

Treaties. The first treaty negotiated by the United States was the treaty of alliance with France, February, 1778. Other treaties negotiated under the Continental Congress were with the Netherlands (1782), with Great Britain, treaty of peace, (1783), with Sweden (1783), with Prussia (1785), and with Morocco (1787). The Constitution of 1787 gave the President the power of making treaties, with the consent of two-thirds of the Senate. In 1795, in the matter of the Jay Treaty, the House attempted to claim for itself a control over the treaty-making power, through the power of making appropriations. An account of individual treaties may be found under the name by which each is familiarly known, or the country with which it was concluded.

Trenchard, Stephen D. (1818–1883), commanded the "Rhode Island" during the Civil War and was active in both attacks on Fort Fisher. He was promoted rear-admiral and commanded the North Atlantic Squadron from 1876 to 1878.

Trent Affair. In 1861 the Confederate Government sent John Slidell and J. M. Mason as commissioners to France and Great Britain respectively. They ran the blockade to Havana and embarked thence in the British merchant ship "Trent." November 8 the "Trent" was stopped in the old Bahama channel by Captain Wilkes of the United States ship "San Jacinto." Mason and Slidell were seized and taken to Boston as prisoners. Wilkes' action was generally approved in the North; yet it involved a breach of international law, and Mason and Slidell were surrendered to Great Britain because its neutral rights had been transgressed, and to prevent the war which that country threatened.

Trenton, N. J., was first settled in 1680 and received its name in 1720 in honor of Colonel William Trent. It was chosen as the capital of the State in 1790 and became a city two years later.

Trenton, Battle of, December 26, 1776. After retreating across the Delaware, Washington received reinforcements and determined to strike a blow upon the British centre at Trenton. Neither his right wing nor centre was able to cross the river. However, with only 2500 men he crossed the stream filled with floating ice, marched nine miles in a blinding snowstorm and took Trenton by surprise. The commander, Rall, and seventeen of his men were slain. One thousand Hessians were taken prisoners. Only four Americans perished, two killed in action, and two frozen to death.

Trescot, William H., born in 1822, was Secretary of Legation to England from 1852 to 1853. He was assistant U. S. Secretary of State from 1857 to 1860. He served in the South Carolina Legislature from 1862 to 1868. He was U. S. counsel before the Fisheries Commission at Halifax in 1877. He was a Plenipotentiary to revise the treaties with China in 1880, and Special Envoy to the South American belligerents in 1881. He has written several books on diplomatic history.

Trevett vs. Weeden, among the earliest instances of a court's assuming authority to pronounce upon the constitutionality of an act of the legislature. By an Act of the Rhode Island Legislature of 1786, paper money issued by the State was made a legal tender. Weeden refused to receive this currency in payment of a debt. The Superior Court of the State summarily dismissed the case as not within the jurisdiction of the court. Though the record is imperfect, it is deemed virtually certain that the court pronounced the act of the legislature unconstitutional and void.

Trevillian Station, Va. Here during Grant's campaign against Richmond, Sheridan, while raiding along the Virginia Central Railroad, met and defeated a strong force of Confederate cavalry under Wade Hampton. Sheridan captured 500 prisoners, June 11 and 12, 1864.

Triangle, a reach of land toward Lake Erie purchased by Pennsylvania from the Government, September 4, 1788. It formerly was part of New York.

Trianon Decree, a secret decree issued at the palace of the Trianon, France, August 5, 1810, by Napoleon, ordering the immediate confiscation of all American vessels and merchandise brought in previous to May 1, 1810, and ordering that, until November 1, American vessels were to be allowed to enter French ports, but not to unload without his permission. At the same time he offered to revoke the Milan and Berlin decrees, November 1. This was a ruse to entrap American vessels, and it succeeded admirably.

Trimble, Isaac R. (1802–1888), commanded a Confederate brigade at Gaines' Mills and Slaughter Mountain, and captured Manassas Junction in 1862. He led a division at Chancellorsville and Gettysburg.

Trimble, Robert (1777–1828), was appointed Chief Justice of Kentucky in 1810. He became U. S. District Attorney in 1813, and was District Judge of Kentucky from 1816 to 1826. He was a Justice of the U. S. Supreme Court from 1826 to 1828.

Trinity College, Hartford, Conn., founded by Episcopalians, was chartered in 1823. Till 1845 its name was Washington College. Besides the usual college course it had a theological department till 1851, when this was merged into the Berkeley School at Middletown.

Tripoli. After several ineffectual attempts to come to an understanding with Tripoli the United States concluded a treaty of peace and friendship November 4, 1796. A threat by the Bashaw of further depredations led to a chastisement of Tripoli by the U. S. navy, which resulted in a peace without purchase and favorable commercial privileges by the treaty of June 4, 1805. (See next article.)

Tripolitan War. During the latter part of the eighteenth century the United States had followed the method employed by many European nations of protecting our commerce from the depredations of the Barbary States by the annual payment of tribute money. In 1801 the demands of the Bashaw of Tripoli being unusually exorbitant, President Jefferson determined to abolish this practice. Commodore Dale was despatched with a squadron to make demonstrations along the coast of Tripoli. He captured a large cruiser and for a time overawed the Bashaw. In 1803 Preble was sent to take command, Congress having recognized war with Tripoli. Several captures were made. Captain Bainbridge, of the "Philadelphia," however, ran his vessel on a rock, and she was taken by the Tripolitans with all on board. Decatur in the "Intrepid" ran up the harbor of Tripoli at night and burned the "Philadelphia" under the fire of the batteries on the shore. Tripoli was invested and bombarded during the summer. Finally June 4, 1805, a treaty of peace and friendship was concluded with the Bashaw, the United States agreeing to pay $60,000 for the ransom of the officers and crew of the "Philadelphia." (See Derne Expedition.)

Trollope, Frances M. (1780–1863), visited America from England from 1829 to 1831. She published "Domestic Manners of the Americans," "The Refugee in America," and "Adventures of Jonathan Jefferson Whitlaw," which depicted rude and ludicrous phases of American life in a manner much disliked at the time.

Trumbull, Benjamin (1735–1820), was pastor at New Haven from 1760 to 1820. He wrote a "General History of the United States," and an excellent "History of Connecticut from 1630 to 1713."

Trumbull, James Hammond, born in 1821, was Secretary of State for Connecticut from 1861 to 1865. He is one of the leading American philologists in respect to Indian languages. He has published the earlier volumes of the "Colonial Records of Connecticut" and "The Blue Laws of Connecticut."

Trumbull, John (1750–1831), passed the entrance examination at Yale College in 1757. He published in 1772 "The Progress of Dullness," a satire on the prevailing mode of education. In 1773 appeared his "Elegy on the Times," a poem on the Boston Port Bill and other colonial topics. In 1774 he published the first two cantos of "McFingal," in which he described the American character and customs and satirized their extravagances. The popularity of this poem was enormous. With Humphreys, Barlow and Hopkins he wrote "Anarchiad." He was Judge of the Connecticut Supreme Court from 1801 to 1819.

Trumbull, John (1756–1843), is noted for his historical paintings, such as "The Declaration of Independence," "The Battle of Bunker Hill," and "Death of Montgomery." He painted portraits of Washington and Jefferson.

Trumbull, Jonathan (1710–1785), was Chief Justice of the Connecticut Supreme Court from 1766 to 1769, and Governor of Connecticut from 1769 to 1783. He was the only one of the colonial Governors who espoused the people's cause. He aided the colonists with all his power, and was one of the principal advisers of Washington. (See "Jonathan, Brother.")

Trumbull, Jonathan (1740–1809), represented Connecticut in the U. S. Congress as a Federalist from 1789 to 1795, and in the U. S. Senate from 1795 to 1796. He was Governor of Connecticut from 1798 to 1809.

Trumbull, Lyman, born in 1813, was admitted to the bar in 1837. He was Secretary of State for Illinois from 1841 to 1842, and a Justice of the Illinois Supreme Court from 1848 to 1853. He represented Illinois in the U. S. Senate as a Democrat from 1855 to 1861 and as a Republican from 1861 to 1873.

Truxtun, Thomas (1755–1822), was made lieutenant of the privateer "Congress" in 1776. In 1777 he commanded the "Independence" and captured three large ships. In 1781 he commanded the "St. James," with which he disabled a superior British vessel. In 1798 he was placed in command of the "Constellation," and commanded a squadron to protect American commerce in the West Indies. In 1799 he captured the French frigate "L'Insurgente" after a severe engagement, and in 1800 he gained a victory over the French frigate "La Vengeance."

Tryon, William (1725–1788), born in Ireland, was appointed Lieutenant-Governor of North Carolina in 1764. He was Governor from 1765 to 1771. He suppressed the revolt of the "Regulators" with great cruelty. He became Governor of New York in 1771, and continued in office until 1778. He was detested by the patriots for his inhumanity and the destruction of Danbury, Fairfield and Norwalk, Conn.

Tucker, George (1775–1861), came to Virginia from Bermuda about 1787. He represented Virginia in the U. S. Congress as a Democrat from 1819 to 1825. He wrote an excellent "Political History of the United States," extending from 1789 to 1841.

Tucker, John Randolph, born in 1823, was Attorney-General of Virginia from 1857 to 1865. He represented Virginia in the U. S. Congress as a Democrat from 1875 to 1887. He is an able orator.

Tucker, Josiah (1711–1799), dean of Gloucester from 1758 to 1799, wrote numerous able works in politics and economics concerning the American Revolution. He strongly urged the recognition of the independence of the American colonies.

Tucker, St. George (1752–1828), jurist, came to Virginia from Bermuda in 1771. He was a lieutenant-colonel at Yorktown, a member of the Annapolis Convention in 1786, and a U. S. District Judge from 1813 to 1827. His edition of Blackstone contained important disquisitions on the Constitution from the point of view of the State-rights school.

Tucker, Samuel (1747–1833), of Massachusetts, while commander of the "Franklin" and the "Hancock" in 1776, captured more than thirty vessels. From 1777 to 1780 he commanded the "Boston," and captured many prizes, including the sloop-of-war "Thorn." He commanded the "Thorn" from 1780 to 1781, when he was captured by the British frigate "Hind." He was a member of the Massachusetts Legislature from 1814 to 1818.

Tullahoma. (See Murfreesboro.)

Tunis. Tunis, like the rest of the Barbary powers, was early a source of annoyance to the American commerce of the Mediterranean. A treaty was purchased in 1797 by the payment of $107,000. This treaty was altered by the convention of February 24, 1824.

Tunnel Hill, Ga., scene of sharp skirmishing, February 23 and 25, 1864, between Federal and Confederate troops of Grant's and J. E. Johnston's armies, and commanded respectively by Palmer, and Stewart and Anderson. The Confederates were on their way to reinforce Polk's army in Mississippi, and Grant sent Palmer to intercept them. There was no decisive victory for either side, for Palmer, hearing of Johnston's advance, fell back.

Turgot, Anne Robert J. (1727–1781), the famous French statesman, was influential in obtaining the French treaty of alliance with the United States in 1778. He wrote "Réflexions sur la situation des Américains des États-Unis."

Turkey. (See Ottoman Porte.)

Turnbull, Robert J. (1775–1833), of South Carolina, was a leader of the nullification party and published "The Crisis" and "The Tribunal of Dernier Ressort" in its interests.

Turner, Nat (1800?–1831), a negro slave, was the instigator of the Southampton insurrection in Virginia in 1831. He believed himself chosen by the Lord to free his people. At an appointed time he set out with his followers from house to house to kill all white persons. Fifty-five were killed before the insurgents were dispersed. After hiding for a time Turner was captured and hanged.

Turner, Thomas (1808–1883), served in the navy during the Mexican War. He captured two Spanish ships purchased for the secessionist party in 1860 at Vera Cruz. He commanded the "New Ironsides" with ability at Charleston in 1863.

Tuscaroras, originally one of the Six Nations of Iroquois, migrated toward North Carolina. In 1711 they attempted to massacre the whites, but were defeated in the battle of the Neuse January 28, 1712. Hostilities were resumed, but they were overthrown in 1713 and 800 taken prisoners. The tribe then fled to New York, except a small part, who had remained friendly. These subsequently removed. The Tuscaroras early favored the English, but joined with the colonists during the Revolution.

Tuttle, Herbert H., born in 1846, was engaged in journalism till 1880. In 1881 he became professor of history, politics and international law at Cornell, and has published an important history of Prussia.

Tweed, William M. (1823–1878), represented New York in the U. S. Congress as a Democrat from 1853 to 1855. When appointed street commissioner in 1863, he began the organization of the Tweed Ring (q. v.) His position as State Senator from 1867 to 1871, grand sachem of the Tammany society from 1869 to 1871, and commissioner of public works from 1863 to 1871, gave him immense political influence, and every officer in the State became under his sway. He was indicted in 1871 and sentenced in 1873 to twelve years' imprisonment for peculation.

Tweed Ring, a political ring, famous for its unscrupulous dishonesty, which governed New York, State and city, from 1860 to 1871. The ring was composed of William M. Tweed, A. Oakey Hall, Peter B. Sweeney and Richard B. Connolly. These men, through bribery and influence among the lower classes, particularly the foreign element, having first gained control of Tammany Hall, so manipulated the mayoralty election of 1865 as to secure the city government. In 1866, Hall was elected mayor; Sweeney was made city and county treasurer; Tweed, superintendent of the street department; and Connolly, city comptroller. They carried into effect a new city charter which gave them absolute control of fiscal appropriations. When the Ring was finally overthrown in 1871, through publications of its frauds on the taxpayers, and the untiring efforts of Samuel J. Tilden, a prominent Democrat, it was discovered that the city debt had increased from $20,000,000 to $101,000,000. Tweed died in prison; Sweeney and Connolly went into exile, and Hall also left the country.

Twenty-Cent Piece, a silver coin authorized in 1875, and issued chiefly for use in the Pacific States. Its coinage was discontinued in 1878. It was a legal tender to the amount of five dollars.

Twiggs, David E. (1790–1862), served during the War of 1812. He commanded the right wing at Palo Alto and Resaca de la Palma. He fought at Monterey, and led a brigade at Vera Cruz and a division at the capture of Mexico. He was in command of the Department of Texas in 1861 and surrendered his army and military stores to the Confederate General McCulloch. He was dishonorably dismissed from the U. S. army.

Two-Cent Piece was first issued in 1864. Weight in grains 96. Its issue was discontinued in 1873. Upon the issue of 1864 first appeared the motto "In God We Trust." It was legal tender to the value of twenty-five cents.

Two-Penny Act, an act passed by the Virginia Assembly in 1755, to endure ten months, permitting that all debts now payable in tobacco should, at the debtor's option, be payable in money, at the rate of sixteen shillings and eight pence for every hundred-weight of tobacco. This equals two-pence a pound; hence the name. (See Parsons' Cause.)

Two Sicilies. A claims convention was concluded in 1832, which provided for the payment of 2,115,000 Neapolitan ducats to the United States for Napoleonic (Muratist) commercial depredations. A commercial treaty was concluded in 1845, and a commercial and extradition treaty in 1855.

Tyler, John (March 29, 1790–January 17, 1862), tenth President of the United States, was a native of Virginia, and was graduated at William and Mary College in 1806. He early became a lawyer and member of the Legislature. From 1816 to 1821 he was Congressman, and from 1825 to 1827 Governor of Virginia. He represented his State and the Democratic party in the U. S. Senate 1827–1836. He opposed the Democrats in various points, and received some Whig electoral votes for President in 1836. He served as a Whig member of the Legislature, and received the second place on the ticket with Harrison. They were elected in the "Tippecanoe and Tyler too" hurrah campaign of 1840, and one month after the inauguration Tyler, by Harrison's death, succeeded to the office of President. He called an extra session of Congress, vetoed the Bank bills, and broke with the Whig leaders. All the members of his Cabinet, except Webster, resigned in the autumn of 1841. He finally reorganized the Cabinet with Whigs and Democrats both, of whom Calhoun was the most prominent. The tariff of 1842, the Oregon excitement, and the annexation of Texas mark President Tyler's administration. He was nominated by a Democratic Convention in 1844, but withdrew from the contest. After retiring in 1845, he was in retirement until 1861, when he acted as president of the Peace Convention. Soon afterward he was elected to the Confederate Congress. Life by Tyler.

Tyler, Letitia C. (1790–1842), married John Tyler in 1813. She was especially fitted for the social duties of the White House, but her health was delicate, and she died soon after coming to Washington. In 1844 President Tyler married Julia Gardiner, of New York (1820–1889).

Tyler, Moses Coit, born in 1835, became professor of American history in Cornell University in 1881. He wrote a "History of American Literature," and a life of Patrick Henry.

Tyler, Robert O. (1831–1874), commanded an artillery division at Fredericksburg. He was in command of the artillery reserve at Chancellorsville, Gettysburg and in the Rapidan campaign. He led a division at Spottsylvania and a brigade at Cold Harbor.

Tyndale, Hector (1821–1880), commanded a brigade at Chantilly, Bull Run and Antietam in 1862. In 1863 he led a division at Wauhatchie and Chattanooga.

Tyner, James N., born in 1826, represented Indiana in the U. S. Congress as a Republican from 1869 to 1875. He was Postmaster-General in Grant's Cabinet from 1876 to 1877, and Assistant Postmaster-General from 1877 to 1881.

U.

Uncas (1588?–1682) revolted from the Pequot Indians in 1635 and became chief of the Mohegans. He made treaties of peace with the colonists, and in 1637 greatly assisted Colonel Mason's expedition against the Pequots, for which he received part of their land. In 1643 he defeated Miantonomo, chief of the Narragansetts, and put him to death. He was always friendly to the whites and faithful to his treaties.

Uncle Sam. An explanation which has been offered for this phrase is that the "U. S." on some Government supplies in the War of 1812 was humorously declared to be the initials of one Uncle Sam Wilson, a contractor.

"Uncle Tom's Cabin," first published in the *National Era*, at Washington, from June, 1851, to April, 1852, and appearing in book form in Boston in 1852. Mrs. Stowe seems to have been at first disappointed as to its success, but during the next five years 500,000 copies were sold through the States. It served to stimulate abolitionists' sentiments in a remarkable degree, stirring to their profoundest depths thousands of minds in the North which could never have been reached by politicians. It played no small part in creating an anti-slavery party, though its delineations of outrages perpetrated upon the slaves were in a great measure misleading and the work of imagination.

Unconstitutionality. The judicial power of declaring laws unconstitutional is sometimes spoken of as if it were a peculiar power specially conferred upon the U. S. Supreme Court. On the contrary, it is a natural and necessary incident of the ordinary judicial function of deciding cases, as this must operate under a system which involves two sorts of laws, the one (called constitutions) superior to the other (called statutes). In case of conflict between the two in any case brought before a judge, he must decide in accordance with the former. This was pointed out as long ago as 1787, by James Iredell. Similarly, in the colonial period, in the case of chartered colonies, the Privy Council acting on appeals, or the colonial courts themselves, might set aside a colonial statute as repugnant to the charter. Soon after the enacting of the first written constitutions in America, courts began to exercise this function with respect to those constitutions. The first such case observed is the New Jersey case of Holmes *vs.* Walton, in 1779. In Commonwealth *vs.* Caton, in Virginia, in 1782, there was an approach to this. Similar cases followed in Rhode Island (Trevett *vs.* Weeden, 1786) and in North Carolina (Bayard *vs.* Singleton, 1787). The first case in which the U. S. Supreme Court set aside a Federal statute as contrary to the Constitution was that of United States *vs.* Yale Todd, (1794), but the first famous one was that of Marbury *vs.* Madison (1803.) The first case in which it set aside a State law was that of United States *vs.* Peters, (1809). For particulars, see these cases. History by Coxe.

Underground Railroad, a name given to a mysterious organization which made it its business to aid in the escape of fugitive slaves. The movement originated among the Quakers of Pennsylvania, and the system was gradually extended until a chain of stations was established a day's journey apart and leading from Kentucky and Virginia across Ohio, and from Maryland through Pennsylvania and New York to Canada. The stations were private houses, and the inmates were known to be pledged to the cause. The fugitives reached these stations after nightfall, were fed and clothed when it was necessary and given a night's rest. The sick were provided with a place in which to remain until they were restored to health. Levi Coffin, a Quaker, and the reputed president of the organization, assisted in the escape of about 100 slaves annually for many years. He always had a carriage in readiness to convey the fugitives to a place of safety and organized sewing circles to provide clothing for the destitute. Harriet Tubman, a colored woman, who had escaped North, made nineteen journeys to the South and brought back bands of fugitives always without detection. The greatest secrecy was observed in all of the movements of the organization. The Underground Railroad was formally organized in 1838, but did not reach its perfection until the passage of the Fugitive Slave Law in 1850 aroused the Abolitionists to still greater exertions. History by Still.

Underhill, John, died about 1672. He came to America from England in 1630. He commanded in the expedition against the Pequots in 1637, and was conspicuous in the Dutch and Indian Wars from 1643 to 1646.

Underwood, Francis H., born in 1825, greatly aided the Free-Soil movement. He was clerk of the Superior Court in Boston from 1859 to 1870, and U. S. Consul to Glasgow, Scotland, from 1885 to 1888. He has written novels and lives of Lowell, Longfellow and Whittier.

Underwood, Joseph R. (1791–1876), was Judge of the Kentucky Court of Appeals from 1828 to 1835. He represented Kentucky in the U. S. Congress as a Whig from 1835 to 1843, and in the U. S. Senate from 1847 to 1853.

Union College, Schenectady and Albany, N. Y., was incorporated in 1795 by the regents of the University of New York State. The Dudley Observatory at Albany is a department. The medical school was established in 1838, the law school in 1851.

Union Labor Party, a descendant of the Greenback party. It was organized at Cincinnati, February 23, 1887, and included in its platform some of the principles of the Knights of Labor.

Unitarians. The first Unitarian church in the United States, King's Chapel, of Boston, became such by secession from the Episcopal body under Rev. James Freeman. In 1801 the original church of Plymouth, the oldest Congregational church in America, joined the new movement. From 1815 to 1825 the controversy between the two parties among the Congregationalists was carried on with great bitterness, and resulted in the division of many churches. Harvard College about this time came under the influence of the Unitarians. Rev. W. E. Channing, of Newport, R. I., greatly aided the new movement by his tongue and pen. The body has been especially characterized by literary culture, refinement and social virtue, but remains small and confined mainly to New England.

Unitas Fratrum, or United Brethren. (See Moravians.)

United Brethren in Christ. This sect arose soon after 1752 at Lancaster, Pa., through the labors of Rev. C. W. Otterbein, and afterward of Rev. Martin Boehm. Their purpose was to spread pure and earnest evangelical religion. Conferences began to be held annually, beginning at Baltimore in 1789. In 1800 the societies were united into one body with the above name and elected their two leaders as bishops. At first there was no formulated system of doctrine, but in 1815 a creed was adopted at the annual conference, which still remains unchanged. The body has always favored radical reforms, an active missionary spirit and democracy in church government. Its membership lies principally in rural districts and numbered in 1890, 225,000.

United Colonies of New England. In May, 1643, at the solicitation of the Colonial Government of Connecticut, the colonies of Massachusetts Bay, Plymouth, Connecticut and New Haven met by delegates at Boston, and bound themselves together under a written constitution for mutual protection against the Indians, and the French and Dutch settlers of Canada and New York. This league existed forty years. Each colony had one vote in controlling the league. Each managed its own internal affairs, the general management of the confederation being intrusted to a board of eight commissioners. After 1664 the confederation languished, and in 1684 it expired.

United Empire Loyalists. After the close of the Revolution, of the expatriated Tory exiles, exceeding 30,000 in number, many fled to Canada, Nova Scotia and New Brunswick, where they formed societies called the United Empire Loyalists. These associations kept burning a bitter hatred toward the Americans, and border disturbances were kept up for a long time.

United Labor Party, organized in New York City in 1886. They ran Henry George as candidate for mayor that year. They proposed the formation of a national organization, and declared that values arising from the growth of society belonged to the community as a whole.

United States. Up to the Declaration of Independence the title employed had been United Colonies, after that it was United States of America. Their independence was first acknowledged by France, in the treaty of 1778. Great Britain acknowledged it by the treaty of 1783. The government at first consisted simply of the Continental Congress. From March 1, 1781, the constitution in force was the Articles of Confederation; from June 21, 1788, the present Constitution. The area was at first about 850,000 square miles; the population in 1790 less than four millions. (See Annexations, Population.)

"**United States,**" a frigate of forty-four guns built in 1798, met on October 25, 1812, near the island of Madeira, the British frigate "Macedonian," likewise of forty-four guns. The fight at first was at long range, in which the "Macedonian" was badly damaged; this vessel, in attempting to draw nearer, lost nearly all its masts and spars. Seeing further resistance to be useless it surrendered. Of its 300 men it lost thirty-six killed, sixty-eight wounded. The "United States" lost five killed and six wounded. The "United States" with its prize then returned home and anchored January 1, 1813, in New York harbor.

"United States Telegraph." The publication of this newspaper was begun in Washington in 1826 by Duff Green. Jackson was then President and the *U. S. Telegraph* was established as the organ of his administration. This journal was afterward suspended, having achieved but little success, and was superseded as official organ in 1830 by the *Globe*, edited by Francis P. Blair.

United States vs. Peters. (See Peters.)

United States vs. Todd. In 1794 Todd was by decree of the Circuit Court of Connecticut admitted to the U. S. pension list. It was afterward (in 1794) decided by the Supreme Court of the United States that the Circuit Court could not constitutionally make such decrees, nor could it act in the capacity of a commission not of judicial function. This related to the Act of Congress of 1792, relating to pensions, and formed the first instance in which the U. S. Supreme Court pronounced upon the constitutionality of an Act of Congress.

Universalists. The main tenet of their belief was held by some Christians in the third century, but as a modern teaching it owes its development to the founders of the denomination who advocated their views about the middle of the eighteenth century, almost simultaneously in England and the American colonies. The first convention of delegates met in Oxford, Mass., in 1785, and adopted the name of "Independent Christian Society, commonly called Universalists." In 1790 a general convention met in Philadelphia and drew up a platform of government and a confession of faith. Two years later the New England churches organized a convention for New England, and ten years later adopted the Profession of Belief which is still in vogue. This latter convention is now the General Convention. The body numbered about 49,000 members in 1890.

Universities. The first project of a university in America was made by the Virginia Company in 1619, when it made a grant of 10,000 acres of land for a university at Henrico. But the highest educational establishments of the colonial period were no more than colleges, and are more fitly treated under that title. Washington greatly desired the establishment of a national university, and left funds for that purpose, but his plan was never realized. The first true university, in the sense in which that term was used in Europe, was the University of Virginia, chartered in 1819 and opened in 1825. Since then several types of university have developed in the United States, viz., that which is a university in the sense of consisting of an aggregation of several schools, academic and professional, *e. g.*, Harvard; the State universities, of which the University of Michigan was the first to attain eminence; and that which is occupied with advanced or post-graduate instruction primarily, such as Johns Hopkins and Clark Universities.

University Extension. This movement was introduced into the United States in 1890 by the American Society for the Extension of University

Teaching, founded in Philadelphia by Provost William Pepper, of the University of Pennsylvania. During 1891–92 over sixty lecture centres were established in various towns. A seminary for training University Extension lecturers was opened at Philadelphia in October, 1892. More than 100 colleges now participate in the movement. The movement has spread widely and has flourishing lecture centres in New England and the West.

Upland, the original name of Chester, Pa. It was settled by the Swedes in 1645, and in 1682 possessed a mixed population of Swedes, Dutch and English.

Upshur, Abel P. (1790–1844), was a member of the Virginia Legislature from 1824 to 1826, a Judge of the General Court of Virginia from 1826 to 1841, and a member of the State Constitutional Convention in 1829. He was Secretary of the Navy in Tyler's Cabinet from 1841 to 1843, and Secretary of State from 1843 to 1844, when he was killed on board the "Princeton." He wrote an important exposition of the State-rights theory of the Constitution.

Upton, Emory (1839–1881), commanded a battery at Yorktown and Gaines' Mill and an artillery brigade at South Mountain and Antietam. He led a brigade at Fredericksburg, Gettysburg and in the Rapidan campaign. He fought in the "Wilderness," led a column at Spottsylvania and fought at Petersburg. He led a division at Opequan in 1864. He wrote a "System of Infantry Tactics."

Ursuline Convent, mobbed and burned by Protestant rioters of Boston August 12, 1834. Strange stories had been circulated about the cruel treatment of the inmates of the convent, and the straiter sect of native Americans became riotous in opposition to the unruly Irish and other foreign Roman Catholic element.

Usher, John P. (1816–1889), of Indiana, was First Assistant Secretary of the Interior from 1862 to 1863, when he became Secretary of the Interior in Lincoln's and Johnson's Cabinets, serving till May, 1865.

Usselinx, Willem (1567–1647), of Antwerp, merchant, planned the Dutch West India Company, which was chartered in 1621, but becoming dissatisfied, went over into the service of Gustavus Adolphus in 1624, and founded the Swedish West India Company, which was chartered in 1626. The remainder of his life was spent in efforts in behalf of that company in various countries of Europe. Life by Jameson.

Utah forms a part of the Mexican cession of 1848. When the Mormons were driven from Illinois and Missouri they migrated to the present territory of Utah, which was inhabited by the Ute or Utah Indians, whence the name of the territory. Salt Lake City was founded, and the following year (1849) a convention asked in vain for admission into the Union for the new State of "Deseret." A territorial government was organized in 1850, with Brigham Young as Governor. In 1857 Federal troops were sent into the territory to compel obedience. Admission into the Union was again demanded in 1862 and again refused. The "Edmunds Bill," passed in 1882, aimed at the suppression of polygamy and disfranchised all polygamists, but has not succeeded as yet (1894), because of the large number of monogamous Mormons who control the Legislature, and the difficulty of securing convictions under the law. The opening of mines has attracted many "Gentiles" into the territory. The population of Utah, which in 1890 was 207,905, would some time ago have warranted its erection into a State were it not for the existence of polygamy, which would fall under the protection of the State Legislature if Utah were admitted. December 13, 1893, a bill passed the House for its admission. History by Bancroft.

Utes, a tribe of Indians in New Mexico, Utah, Colorado and Nevada. They have generally been friendly to the whites, but the Utah bands have carried on hostilities with the Mormons. Subsequently disturbances occurred between them and miners at Pike's Peak and they defeated Major Ormsby on Truckee River. In 1865 large tracts of land were ceded to the United States. Later trouble arose with Black Hawk, a chief of the Pah Utes, and for several years bloody warfare followed.

Utrecht, Treaty of, concluded between France, Great Britain, Portugal, Prussia, Savoy and Holland in 1713, ended the war of the Spanish Succession, called in America "Queen Anne's War." France ceded to Great Britain Hudson's Bay and Straits, Nova Scotia, Newfoundland and the adjacent islands. Spain granted to a British company the exclusive right for thirty years of supplying Spanish America with negroes, and engaged not to transfer any land or lordship in America.

V.

Vail, Alfred (1807–1859), of New Jersey, was associated with Professor Morse in the invention of the telegraph. The alphabetical characters and many of the essential features of the telegraph are his invention.

Vallandigham, Clement Laird (1822–1871), a lawyer and active Democratic politician in Ohio, served in the Legislature of that State, and was Congressman 1857–1863. He bitterly opposed the Government as the war progressed, and became noted as the most extreme of Northern sympathizers with the Confederacy. General Burnside arrested him, and he was banished. From the Confederate States he went to Canada, and while there was nominated for Governor by the Ohio Democrats in 1863. He was defeated by Brough by a majority of 100,000. The following year he was a member of the Democratic National Convention.

Vallandigham's Case. In 1863 Clement L. Vallandigham, of Ohio, was tried, convicted and imprisoned for uttering opinions disloyal to the Union by a military commission appointed by General Burnside. Vallandigham applied to the Supreme Court to review by *certiorari* the proceedings of the military commission, claiming to have been unlawfully convicted. The Supreme Court maintained the decision of the commission on the ground that it had no power to review proceedings ordered by a general officer of the United States army.

Valley Forge, site of Washington's winter encampment, 1777–78, twenty miles from Philadelphia on the west side of the Schuylkill. His force at this encampment was 11,000 strong, but in miserable condition for lack of proper food and clothing. There was great suffering, borne with wonderful patience throughout the winter. The men had no shoes and were obliged to forage for supplies.

Valverde, N. M., an engagement, occurring February 21, 1861, between 1500 Unionists, chiefly volunteers, under Canby, and 2000 Texan rangers commanded by Sibley and Green. Colonel Roberts, Federal, first routed Major Pryon, but the latter, falling back, was supported by Green. The Texans made a spirited dash upon the Federal lines, heedless of the volley of grape and canister. The Federal troops fled in the utmost confusion.

Van Buren, John (1810–1866), son of Martin Van Buren, was Attorney-General of New York from 1845 to 1847. He was active in the political canvass of 1848, when his father was a candidate of the Free-Soil party for the Presidency.

Van Buren, Martin (December 5, 1782–July 24, 1862), eighth President of the United States, was born at Kinderhook, N. Y. He rose to eminence in his State both as a lawyer and as a Democratic politician. He is noted as an adroit party manager, and was styled in his time the "Little Magician." He was a State Senator, U. S. Senator 1821–1828, Governor 1828–1829, and Secretary of State under Jackson 1829–1831. President Jackson, in 1831, appointed him U. S. Minister to England, but the Senate refused to confirm the nomination. He was elected with Jackson for the latter's second term, serving as Vice-President 1833–1837, and was the chosen heir to the succession. Elected by 170 electoral votes over the Whig candidate, Harrison, in 1836, he inherited the results of Jackson's measures. The two foremost places in President Van Buren's Cabinet were held by Forsyth in the State and Woodbury in the Treasury Department. Among the features of public interest in his administration were the disastrous panic of 1837, the independent treasury system and the pre-emption law. In 1840 he was pitted against his former antagonist, but with the opposite result; he received only sixty electoral votes. In 1844 Ex-President Van Buren had a majority, but not a two-thirds majority of votes in the Democratic National Convention; he opposed the annexation of Texas, and was discarded for Polk. In 1848 he was the Free Soil candidate, and diverted enough Democratic votes to defeat Cass and elect Taylor. Life by E. M. Shepard.

Van Corlear, Arendt (1600?–1667), came to America from Holland in 1630. He became superintendent of a "colony" having jurisdiction from the Hudson to the Mohawk Rivers. He founded the settlement at Schenectady, and had great influence with the Indians.

Van Cortlandt, Oloff S. (1600–1684), came to New Netherlands from Holland in 1638 in the service of the West India Company. He was prominent in political affairs, and from 1655 to 1664 was a burgomaster of New Amsterdam.

Van Cortlandt, Pierre (1721–1814), was a member of the New York Assembly from 1768 to 1775. He was a member of the first Provincial Congress, and was Lieutenant-Governor of New York from 1777 to 1795.

Van Cortlandt, Stephanus (1643–1700), held every prominent office in the province of New York except the Governorship. He was Mayor of New York almost continuously from 1677 to 1700. His estate was erected into a lordship and manor in 1697.

Van Dorn, Earl (1820–1863), was promoted for gallant service at Cerro Gordo, Contreras and Churubusco, and aided in the capture of the City of Mexico. In 1856 he commanded an expedition against the Comanches. In 1861 he joined the Confederacy and succeeded Jefferson Davis as major-general of the Mississippi forces. He captured the steamer "Star of the West," and received the surrender of Major Sibley and Colonel Reeve. In 1862 he commanded the trans-Mississippi Department. He was defeated at Pea Ridge and Corinth. He captured valuable stores at Holly Springs in 1862.

Van Rensselaer, Kilian (1595–1644), was prominent in forming the Dutch West India Company. He sent an agent from Holland to the New Netherlands, who purchased a vast estate comprising the present counties of Albany, Columbia and Rensselaer. He named it Rensselaerswyck and colonized it with emigrants. Under his management through a director the colony became a powerful, almost independent, province.

Van Rensselaer, Solomon (1774–1852), led the attacking party at Queenstown Heights in 1812. He represented New York in the U. S. Congress as a Federalist from 1819 to 1822.

Van Rensselaer, Stephen (1765–1839), was a member of the New York Senate from 1791 to 1795, and Lieutenant-Governor from 1795 to 1801. He served in the New York Assembly from 1808 to 1810. He was appointed commander of the forces on the northern frontier in 1812, and fought the battle of Queenstown Heights. He was a canal commissioner from 1816 to 1839. He represented New York in the U. S. Congress as a supporter of Adams from 1822 to 1829. He founded the Rensselaer Polytechnic Institute at Troy.

Van Rensselaer Manor. (See Rensselaerswyck.)

Van Twiller, Wouter or Walter (1580 ?–after 1646), was chosen Governor of New Netherlands by the Dutch West India Company in 1633, and served until 1637. He ably maintained the commercial interests of the colony, but was an incompetent Governor, and was constantly involved in quarrels with the English in the Massachusetts and Connecticut colonies.

Van Wart, Isaac (1760–1828), was an active supporter of the patriot cause during the Revolution. With John Paulding and David Williams he intercepted Major André in 1780.

Van Wyck, Charles H., born in 1824, represented New York in the U. S. Congress as a Republican from 1859 to 1863 and from 1867 to 1871. He represented Nebraska in the U. S. Senate from 1881 to 1887.

Vance, Zebulon B. (1830–1894), represented North Carolina in the U. S. Congress as a State-Rights American from 1858 to 1861. He was colonel of a Confederate regiment from 1861 to 1862; Governor of North Carolina from 1862 to 1864, and greatly aided the Confederate cause. He was again Governor from 1876 to 1879, and was a U. S. Senator from 1879 to 1894.

Vancouver, George (1758–1798), British naval officer, took part in the second and third voyages of Captain Cook. In 1791 he was appointed by the British Government to survey the northwest coast of North America from 30° north latitude, northward. He returned to England in 1795. A report of his careful survey was published entitled "Voyage of Discovery to the North Pacific Ocean and Round the World." England's claim to Oregon was mainly founded on it.

Vanderbilt, Cornelius (1794–1877), amassed a large fortune by steamboat transportation. In 1851 he established a steamship line between New York and California via Nicaragua. In 1855 he established a line between New York and Havre. In 1857 he turned his attention to railroads, and became one of the foremost "railroad kings" in America. He founded Vanderbilt University at Nashville, Tenn.

Vanderbilt, William H. (1821–1885), son of Cornelius, became president of the New York Central and Hudson River and New York and Harlem Railroads in 1877, and at his death was probably the richest man in America.

Vane, Sir Henry (1612–1662), a noted Puritan statesman, came to Boston in 1635, and was Governor of the Massachusetts colony the next year. He sided with Mrs. Hutchinson in the celebrated Antinomian controversy. He was a member of the General Court, but soon returned to England. He was knighted, entered Parliament, became treasurer of the navy, and was prominent in the impeachment of Strafford, as commissioner to Scotland, and member of the Westminster Assembly. In the Commonwealth he sat in the Council of State, was a Republican leader, and frequently opposed to Cromwell. He presided over the State Council in 1659, and at the Restoration was excepted from the general pardon. Although not one of the Regicides, yet as a strong Republican he was executed by Charles II. on general charges of treason. He is supposed to have invented the "previous question" and the constitutional convention. Life by Hosmer.

Varick, Richard (1753–1831), was secretary to General Schuyler in the Northern Department from 1776 to 1780. He was Washington's recording secretary from 1781 to 1783, and was Mayor of New York from 1791 to 1801.

Varnum, James M. (1748–1789), commanded a regiment at White Plains, led the troops at Red Bank, and served under Lafayette in Rhode Island. He represented Rhode Island in the Continental Congress from 1780 to 1782 and from 1786 to 1787.

Varnum, Joseph B. (1750–1821), was a member of the Massachusetts Legislature from 1780 to 1787, of the Massachusetts Convention of 1788, and of the Governor's Council from 1787 to 1795. He represented Massachusetts in the U. S. Congress as a Democrat from 1795 to 1811, acting as Speaker from 1807 to 1811. He was a U. S. Senator from 1811 to 1817.

Vassar, Matthew (1792–1868), came to America from England in 1796. In 1861 he founded Vassar College at Poughkeepsie, N. Y., with an endowment of $778,000.

Vassar College, Poughkeepsie, N. Y., an institution for the higher education of women, was first chartered in 1861, but opened four years later. It was named after Matthew Vassar, its founder.

Vaudreuil, Louis P. de R. (1721–1802), entered the French navy in 1740 and became chef d'escadre in 1777. He participated in the capture of Grenada under Count d'Estaing. He assisted at the siege of Savannah in 1779, assuming command of the fleet during the assault. He commanded a division under Count de Grasse in the Chesapeake engagement with Admiral Graves and in the siege of Yorktown.

Vaudreuil, Philippe de R., Marquis de (1640–1725), came to Canada from France in 1687 as commander of the forces. He defended Quebec against the English in 1690 and in 1710. He became Governor of Montreal in 1702 and of Canada in 1703.

Vaudreuil, Pierre F. de R. (1698–1765), Marquis de Vaudreuil-Cavagnal, born in Canada, was made Governor of Three Rivers in 1733 and of Louisiana in 1742. He was appointed Governor of Canada in 1755. He was estranged from Montcalm, the commander of the Canadian troops, but did all in his power to avert the capture of Quebec. He capitulated for the surrender of Quebec in terms distasteful to the authorities, but an investigation exonerated him.

Vaudreuil, Pierre F. de R. (1704–1772), captured Fort Massachusetts and gained a victory on Lake St. Sacrament and took many prisoners. He organized the Canadian army that besieged the forts at Oswego and Ontario.

Vaughan, Benjamin (1751–1835), was prominent in the negotiations for peace between England and the United States in 1783. He was not officially connected with the transaction, but as a friend of Franklin and Lord Shelburne. He was a member of Parliament from 1792 to 1796. He came to America in 1796. He accumulated a large library and wrote many political articles.

Vaughan, Sir John (1738–1795), British soldier, came to America from England in 1775. He led the grenadiers at Long Island, and commanded a column at Forts Clinton and Montgomery. In 1779 he captured Stony Point.

Venezuela. The United States concluded a treaty of peace, friendship, navigation and commerce with Venezuela in 1836. By the Convention of 1859 Venezuela agreed to pay claims of $130,000. A commercial and extradition treaty was concluded in 1860.

Vera Cruz, Mexico, deemed the gateway to the heart of Mexico during the Mexican War, was besieged by General Scott with 12,000 men, March

23–29, 1847. General Morales commanded the town with 4390 men. Scott found no difficulty in landing his soldiers from the island of Lobos, his rendezvous, and in placing his batteries. The town was poorly fortified and Scott's bombardment effected great ruin. On March 25 Morales held a council of war. He was advised to surrender, but refused to do so, and resigned his command to General José Juan Landero. This general surrendered March 29. The Mexican officers were allowed to retain their arms and effects and the soldiers were permitted to retire to their homes. Scott then took possession.

Vergennes, Charles G., Count de (1717–1787), became Minister of Foreign Affairs in France in 1774. He gave efficient support to the American colonies during the Revolution. He counselled Louis XVI. to loan them money, to recognize their independence, and to sign the treaty of 1778, by which France aided them with forces, money and supplies. He was a negotiator of the treaty of Versailles in 1783. The American negotiators suspected him of intending to sacrifice their interests, and, disregarding their instructions, made a separate peace apart from France.

Vermont (the word means Green Mountains) was known during its early history as the New Hampshire grants. The district was claimed by both New York and New Hampshire, but refused to acknowledge the authority of either. New York obtained a decision of the king in her favor (1764), and endeavored to compel the settlers to pay for their land again. The people of Vermont resisted, organized militia, and remained independent. In 1777 Vermont declared her independence, and adopted as her constitution that of Pennsylvania, with some changes, one of which was the abolition of slavery. In 1789 New York agreed to recognize the separation of Vermont, and on March 4, 1791, the State was admitted into the Union. Until 1800 the State supported the Federalist party. After that date the State was Democratic until 1820. Vermont was represented in the Hartford Convention (1814) by one delegate. Since 1820 the State has been uniformly Anti-Democratic (Whig, then Republican). In 1832 the electors were Anti-Masonic. In 1882 the manufacture or sale of intoxicating liquors was prohibited. The population of Vermont in 1791 was 85,339; in 1890, 332,422. History by Robinson.

Vermont, University of, Burlington, was chartered in 1791, but opened in 1800. In 1865 the State added an agricultural department. The medical department was organized in 1809.

"Vermont Gazette." There were two gazettes established in Vermont. The first, called the *Vermont Gazette*, or *Green Mountain Post Boy*, was the first paper of the State, and was begun at Westminster by Spooner and Green, February 12, 1781, and was suspended two years later. In 1783, June 5, Haswell and Russell founded at Bennington the *Vermont Gazette*, or *Freemen's Depository*. With several changes of title, it survived till 1880.

Verona, Congress of (1822), a meeting of envoys of the great European powers to consult respecting the disturbances in Spain. Their project of interference for the sake of restoring Spanish power in the revolted colonies of South America was what led to the enunciation of the Monroe Doctrine in 1823.

Verplanck, Gulian C. (1786–1870), was a member of the New York Legislature from 1820 to 1822. He represented New York in the U. S. Congress as a Democrat from 1825 to 1833, and was a State Senator from 1838 to 1841. He wrote "The Bucktail Bards," a series of political pamphlets; "Discourses on American History, Arts and Literature;" "The American Scholar," and was joint editor of the *Talisman.*

Verrazano, Giovanni de (1470–1527), Florentine navigator, is said to have visited the north coast of North America in 1508. He engaged in plundering Spanish and Portuguese commerce, and became famous as a corsair. In 1522 he captured a treasure-ship sent from Mexico by Cortés. In 1524 he explored the coast of North America from 30° to 50°, and took possession for the king.

Versailles, Treaty of, a treaty of peace concluded at Versailles between commissions representing the United States and Great Britain. It was arranged in 1782, and was formally ratified September 3, 1783. Jay, Adams, Franklin and Laurens formed the American Commission. By this treaty the absolute independence of the United States was recognized. Florida was returned to Spain; the Americans relinquished their pretensions to the territory north of Lake Erie; the St. Lawrence river system, from the western end of Lake Superior to the forty-fifth parallel, was made the boundary; from the forty-fifth parallel to the sea, the boundary followed the highlands after an uncertain fashion, and was long a matter of bitter dispute; British right of navigation of the Mississippi was yielded, England according in return the American right of fishing on the Canadian and Newfoundland coasts; Loyalists and Tories were to be protected in America; English troops were to be withdrawn without destroying any property, or taking away any negro slaves belonging to Americans. This treaty was in reality signed in Paris, but is generally known by the above name, which properly belongs only to the treaty between England and France.

Vesey, Denmark (1767?–1822), a negro slave who purchased his freedom in 1800 and lived in Charleston. He maintained the right of slaves to strike for liberty, and organized a plot for a general insurrection around Charleston. Several thousand slaves were in the plot. The attempt was made in 1822, but was promptly suppressed, and U. S. troops guarded against a new attempt. The leaders were hanged.

Vespucius. (See Americus.)

Vest, George G., born in 1830, was a member of the Confederate Senate from 1863 to 1865. He was elected to the U. S. Senate as a Democrat from Missouri in 1879. His present term expires in 1897.

Vestries. In England every parish had its vestry. In America, wherever there were parishes of the Church of England, there were vestries. Wherever that church was the established church, the vestries had powers of civil government in local matters, as well as powers in ecclesiastical matters. In Virginia, for instance, the vestry, the members of which were self-elected, were the chief authority in local government in less matters than those of the county.

Vetch, Samuel (1668–1732), was adjutant-general of the Port Royal expedition in 1710, and after its capture was made Governor of Nova Scotia. He held office till 1713.

Veto. Except in Connecticut and Rhode Island, colonial Governors had the power of vetoing acts of the colonial Legislatures, and the crown had also a right of vetoing subsequently. None of the original State constitutions gave the executive of the State a veto till that of Massachusetts in 1780. In the Convention of 1787 various other plans for the veto were considered, such as a suspensory veto and one in which the Supreme Court should be associated with the President. The plan finally adopted resembled that of Massachusetts, Congress being given power to override the veto by a two-thirds vote of both houses. Since then all but four of the States have given their Governors the veto power. A Federal negative on State laws was also discussed, but wisely abandoned. The general feeling is that the veto power has been useful to good government. It was for a long time used but sparingly. Washington vetoed two bills, Adams and Jefferson (and also J. Q. Adams, Van Buren, Taylor and Fillmore) none, Madison six, Monroe one, Jackson twelve, Tyler nine, Polk three, Pierce nine, Buchanan seven, Lincoln three, Johnson twenty-one, Grant forty-three, Hayes twelve, Arthur four, Cleveland (first administration) 301, mostly private pension bills. Of acts passed over the veto, the numbers are: Tyler one, Pierce five, Johnson fifteen, Grant four, Hayes one, Arthur one, Cleveland two. The vetoes most important historically were those by which Madison, Monroe and Jackson checked the "internal improvement" policy, Tyler's bank and tariff vetoes, and those of Johnson upon the Freedmen's Bureau Acts, the Civil Rights Act, the Tenure of Office Act, and the Reconstruction Acts, all of which, save the first Freedmen's Bureau Bill, were passed over his veto. History by Mason.

Veto, Pocket. The Constitution provides that, if the President does not either sign or veto a bill within ten days, it shall become law without his signature, "unless the Congress by their adjournment prevent its return, in which case it shall not be a law." This gives the President opportunity to prevent a bill from becoming law, if it is passed in the last days of a session, by simply taking no action upon it. This is called the "pocket veto." It was first used by President Madison in 1812 in the case of a naturalization act. But the first conspicuous instances were those by General Jackson, seven of whose twelve vetoes were of this sort.

Vice-Admiral, a grade created by Act of Congress in 1864. It was at the time of creation the highest naval office, but was outranked by that of admiral, created two years later. By the Act of January 24, 1873, Congress provided that when the offices of admiral and vice-admiral became vacant the grades should cease to exist, that of rear-admiral to be then deemed the highest. On the death of Vice-Admiral Rowan in 1890 the grade became extinct. During the colonial period it was usual for the royal governor of a colony to be also appointed vice-admiral, which made him head of the colonial admiralty courts.

Vice-President. The office of Vice-President was provided by the Constitution of 1787, which provided that in case of the removal, death, resignation or disability of the President, his office should devolve on the Vice-President, whose only function meantime was to preside over the Senate. At first the electors did not vote for President and Vice-President separately, but he who received the second largest number of votes was made Vice-President. The modern practice was brought in by the Twelfth Amendment in 1804. The Vice-President has succeeded the President on four occasions, in each case by reason of the President's death: Tyler succeeded Harrison in 1841, Fillmore, Taylor, in 1850; Johnson, Lincoln, in 1865; Arthur, Garfield, in 1881. The attempt was made in 1841 to give Tyler only the title and rights of "Acting President," but he claimed the full office of President. A list of the Vice-Presidents follows:

Name.	State.	Political party.	Qualified.
John Adams	Massachusetts	Federalist	June 3, 1789
John Adams	Massachusetts	Federalist	December 2, 1793
Thomas Jefferson	Virginia	Dem.-Republican	March 4, 1797
Aaron Burr	New York	Dem.-Republican	March 4, 1801
George Clinton	New York	Dem.-Republican	March 4, 1805
George Clinton	New York	Dem.-Republican	March 4, 1809
Elbridge Gerry	Massachusetts	Dem.-Republican	March 4, 1813
Daniel D. Tompkins	New York	Dem.-Republican	March 4, 1817
Daniel D. Tompkins	New York	Dem.-Republican	March 5, 1821
John C. Calhoun	South Carolina	Dem.-Republican	March 4, 1825
John C. Calhoun	South Carolina	Dem.-Republican	March 4, 1829
Martin Van Buren	New York	Democratic	March 4, 1833
Richard M. Johnson	Kentucky	Democratic	March 4, 1837
John Tyler	Virginia	Elected by Whigs	March 4, 1841
George M. Dallas	Pennsylvania	Democratic	March 4, 1845
Millard Fillmore	New York	Whig	March 5, 1849
William R. King	Alabama	Democratic	March 4, 1853
John C. Breckinridge	Kentucky	Democratic	March 4, 1857
Hannibal Hamlin	Maine	Republican	March 4, 1861
Andrew Johnson	Tennessee	Republican	March 4, 1865
Schuyler Colfax	Indiana	Republican	March 4, 1869
Henry Wilson	Massachusstts	Republican	March 4, 1873
William A. Wheeler	New York	Republican	March 5, 1877
Chester A. Arthur	New York	Republican	March 4, 1881
Thomas A. Hendricks	Indiana	Democratic	March 4, 1885
Levi P. Morton	New York	Republican	March 4, 1889
Adlai E. Stevenson	Illinois	Democratic	March 4, 1893

Of these Clinton, Gerry, King, Wilson and Hendricks died in office; Clinton in 1812, Gerry in 1814, King in 1853, Wilson in 1875, Hendricks in 1885. Calhoun resigned in 1832.

Vicksburg, Miss., scene of an important battle and siege during the Civil War. The battle occurred December 28 and 29, 1862, while Grant and Sherman were forcing their way down the Mississippi with the Army of the West. The Confederate leader Johnston lay posted along the Yazoo River, holding the hills between Vicksburg and Haines' Bluff. Sherman caused a feint to be made upon the right of the enemy, while his main force attacked the centre, crossing the intervening bayou for that purpose. The fight was begun with a heavy play of artillery from both armies, and Sherman's troops were made to face a scathing fire of musketry during their attempt to reach the hills upon which the Confederates were posted. The Federal soldiers were obliged to scoop holes in the sand banks for steps. Every assault was repelled, and Sherman lost heavily. A heavy rain the next day made another attack impossible. By May, 1863, Grant and Sherman had so far been successful in their operations along the Mississippi that after having defeated the Confederates at Champion Hills and Big Black River, they had compelled Pemberton, the Confederate leader, to retreat into Vicksburg. By May 19 Grant had begun a siege of that town with an army of 30,000 men. Pemberton commanded over 25,000 Confederates. Grant's army was reinforced during the siege until it numbered 70,000. Johnston had telegraphed Pemberton to surrender the town and escape with his army if possible, but it was then too late. Porter held the Federal base of supplies along the Yazoo River. Before the city Grant occupied the centre, with Sherman on his right and McClernand on his left. On the Confederate side, Stevenson occupied five miles from the Warrenton Road to the railroad, with Bowen in reserve. The fortifications were bastioned earthworks, and there were provisions for two months. After some skirmishing, Grant ordered a grand assault May 22. But this proved a signal failure and cost him 2500 men; so he settled down to take the city by regular approaches. There was mining and counter-mining and a constant bombardment from Grant's batteries and the Federal gunboats and bomb-rafts, of which there were a number, both above and below the city. Pemberton held out bravely, for he had a great deal to contend with, both from lack of supplies and from discontent among his men. Finally, July 3, after forty-seven days of siege, perceiving that Grant contemplated a final assault, Pemberton asked for an armistice, and on July 4 he surrendered. The garrison was paroled and allowed to go free.

Vilas, William F., born in 1840, commanded a regiment at Vicksburg in 1863. He was Postmaster General in Cleveland's Cabinet from 1885 to 1887 and Secretary of the Interior from 1887 to 1888.

Villeré's Plantation (near New Orleans). The British, when moving upon New Orleans, encamped here. December 23, 1814, General Jackson made a night attack by land and river. After severe fighting the Americans withdrew. Their loss in all was 213 men; the British lost about 400.

Vincennes, Jean B. B. (1688–1736), Canadian explorer, attained great influence over the Miami Indians, among whom he resided for some time. He rendered valuable services against the Foxes near Detroit in 1712. In 1725 he built a fort and trading post on the present site of Vincennes, Ind. He joined the expedition of D'Artaguette against the Chickasaws, by whom they were finally defeated and burned at the stake.

Vincennes, Ind., oldest town in the State, was settled by the French in 1702. It came into the possession of England on the surrender of Canada in 1763, but was taken from them by the American army under General

George Rogers Clark in 1779. It became the capital of Indiana in 1800 and remained the seat of the Government until 1814.

Vinland. (See Norsemen.)

Vinton, Samuel F. (1792–1862), represented Ohio in the U. S. Congress as a Whig from 1823 to 1827 and from 1843 to 1851.

Vioménil, Antoine C. du H., Baron de (1728–1792), was appointed second in command of the French force under Count Rochambeau to aid the American colonists. He distinguished himself at Yorktown where he led the assault on the redoubt.

Virginia, the "Old Dominion," was one of the original thirteen States. Its shores were perhaps explored by Sebastian Cabot (1498) and Verrazano (1524), and certainly by Sir Walter Raleigh, who attempted to colonize the territory which he named Virginia in honor of Queen Elizabeth. In 1606, the London Company was chartered and obtained a grant of the land between the thirty-fourth and forty-first degrees of latitude. Three years later new boundaries were given to Virginia. Starting from Old Point Comfort it was to extend two hundred miles north and south, and "west and northwest" to the South Sea or Pacific Ocean. The London Company were to have the profits of the colony for twenty-one years, after which they were to pass to the crown. The government of the colony was placed in the hands of the two councils, one of which was resident in the colony. All settlers were guaranteed all rights as if living in England. One hundred and forty-three colonists set sail for Virginia and in 1607 founded Jamestown, the first permanent English settlement in America. For the first years the colonists were too largely "gentlemen," who were totally unfit to endure the hardships of pioneer life, and the colony was saved only by the exertions of John Smith. In accordance with royal instructions the colonists were burdened by the communal system until 1612. Samuel Argall as Governor in 1617 exercised all the tyranny of martial law until recalled the following year. Under his successor, Yeardley, the first representative assembly in the history of America convened (1619) at Jamestown. This encouraged immigration, and in the same year some women appeared in Virginia. Slavery was introduced (1619) by the sale of twenty African slaves from a Dutch man-of-war. Factions having appeared in the London Company a writ of *quo warranto* was issued against the charter, and in 1624 Virginia became a royal colony. Virginia remained loyal to Charles I. during his struggle with Parliament, and became the home of many royalist fugitives who were the ancestors of many of the most famous men in the history of the State. Charles II. repaid the loyalty of the people by granting the entire territory to Lords Arlington and Culpepper, and by the enforcement of the Navigation Act, which compelled the colonists to sell all their products in English markets. The discontent was increased by the tyranny of Governor Berkeley and an uprising of the Indians, and Bacon's Rebellion followed in 1676. Upon the death of Bacon his followers were defeated and many hanged. From this time until the Revolution the colony increased in population, wealth and influence, and was recognized as the leading power in the struggle against England. Her militia, under Washington, did good service in Braddock's campaign in the French and Indian War. The assembly was dissolved in 1774 by Governor Dunmore, when a protest was being drawn up against the Boston Port Bill, but the members immediately reassembled in convention. In May, 1776, another convention adopted the first constitution of the State. The delegates in Congress from Virginia proposed the declaration of the independence of the colonies. Virginia took a prominent part in the struggles of the Revolution which closed on her soil by the capture of Yorktown and Cornwallis, October 19, 1781. Much opposition was made to the Federal Constitution, which threatened to prevent its adoption, but it was finally ratified by a State convention on January 25, 1788. The boundaries have caused much dispute because of the extensive claims made by Virginia. Her western territory was surrendered to the general Government because of the reluctance of Maryland to ratify the Articles of Confederation until that should be done. Kentucky became a separate State in 1792. Virginia has been jealous of all encroachments by the national Government and has uniformly supported the Democratic party. Until 1825, the influence of Virginia in national politics was pre-eminent. In 1798, a protest was made to the centralizing policy of Hamilton and the Federalist party by the famous Kentucky and Virginia Resolutions. From 1806 to 1808, the "Quids," under John Randolph, strenuously opposed the nomination of Madison to the Presidency. The more rapid growth of the western part of the State caused injustice from the old apportionment of representation. A convention assembled in 1829, and a readjustment was accomplished in the constitution of 1830. In 1831, a negro insurrection broke out under Nat Turner, which taught the danger of all agitation of the slavery question. (John Brown and other abolitionists attempted to free the slaves at Harper's Ferry, 1859.) Virginia did her utmost to avoid war in 1860 and 1861, and called a peace convention of all the States. The people of Virginia knew that in case of war their State would be the battle-ground. An ordinance of secession was passed by a State convention April 17, 1861, and ratified by a popular vote May 23, 1861. During the war Richmond was the capital of the Confederacy, and Virginia the scene of many of the greatest battles. The State was readmitted January 26, 1870. The State was Democratic until the union of the Republicans and Readjusters under Mahone, who was elected U. S. Senator in 1879. There have been long-continued agitations respecting the payment of the State debt of $30,000,000, contracted before the war. In 1891 a settlement was made, the debt being scaled down to $19,000,000, to bear two and subsequently three per cent interest. The population of the State in 1790 was 747,610; in 1890, 1,655,-980. History by Cooke and by Howison.

Virginia, University of, Charlottesville, Va., was chartered in 1819 and opened in 1824. Its organization, plan of government and system of instruction are due to Thomas Jefferson, who planned it after the model of European universities, and by the original ideas upon which he founded it made it for a time the most influential school in America. It early developed the elective system. The department of medicine was founded in 1827, that of law in 1851. The university has prospered since the Civil War.

Virginia Company. On April 10, 1606, James I. set apart by charter the territory between Cape Fear and Passamaquoddy Bay to be settled by two rival companies, the Virginia Company of London, and the North Virginia or Plymouth Company. To the London, or Virginia Company proper, was granted the land between parallels 34° and 41° north, or between Cape Fear and Long Island. This company was composed of London merchants and adventurers. In 1606 an expedition consisting of three vessels and 143 men, commanded by Christopher Newport, was fitted out, and succeeded in founding, May 13, 1607, the first permanent English settlement in America at Jamestown, Va. In 1609 a new charter was granted and the company reincorporated under the name of the London Company of Virginia; still another in 1612. Other colonizing parties arrived in 1609, 1611 and 1619, and by 1620 the colony of Virginia was firmly established. The majority in the company was of the political party in England opposed to the court. It fell into difficulties with the king, who in 1624 caused its charter to be annulled. The company then dissolved.

Virginia Coupon Cases. There were eight of these cases. All related to the legislation of the State of Virginia in 1871, authorizing the receipt of coupons of the State's funded debt, in payment of taxes and debts due the State. These cases came before the Supreme Court of the United States in 1884. The act of the Virginia General Assembly of 1882 required payment of tax dues in "gold, silver, United States treasury notes, national bank currency, and nothing else." Hence the tax collectors refused to receive coupons in payment of taxes as authorized by the Act of 1871. The Supreme Court of the United States decided the Act of 1882 void as impairing the obligation of the contract of the Act of 1871, and judgment was found for the plaintiffs, the tax-payers.

"**Virginia Gazette.**" There were four "gazettes" published in Virginia in the last century and all at Williamsburg. William Parks established the first, August, 1736, it being the first newspaper published in the province. Publication suspended 1750. William Hunter founded the second, February, 1751. Publication was suspended after the Revolution. The third was begun by William Rind, May, 1766. Publication was suspended 1774. Davis and Clarkson published the fourth "gazette," beginning April, 1775, and continuing several years. There was also a *Virginia Gazette* published in Richmond for a very short period about 1804 by A. Davis, a semi-weekly.

Virginia Historical Society, organized in 1831 and chartered in 1834 under the title of "The Virginia Historical and Philosophical Society;" but its researches have been mainly devoted to history. John Marshall was one of the early presidents. The society has recently published a series of volumes of historical material.

Virginia Judges, case of the Superior Court Judges of Virginia. An act of the Virginia Legislature of 1779 constituted a Court of Appeals to consist of the Judges of the High Court of Chancery, General Court and Court of Admiralty. Afterward from time to time various acts were passed by the legislature affecting the privileges of the Court of Appeals. In 1788 this court declared that the legislature could not control the prerogatives of the court under the provisions of the State constitution; that the judges of this court could not be required to act as district judges; that the legislature could not reduce the salaries of the judges, their duties remaining the same, and that the existing judges could not be removed during good behavior. This is one of the earliest instances of a court's pronouncing upon the constitutionality of an act of the legislature.

Virginia Resolutions, resolutions passed by the Virginia Legislature in 1798, in antagonism to the loose construction view of the Federalists. The passage of the Alien and Sedition laws was the direct cause of their adoption. They were framed by James Madison and sent to the legislatures of the other States, by which they were not approved. They declared the Union to be a compact, each party to which had a right to "interpose" in order to protect and defend itself against infringements of the compact. They regretted the introduction of a broad construction of the constitution, as tending toward a monarchy. They protested against the Alien and Sedition laws as unconstitutional. With the Kentucky Resolutions of 1798 and 1799, these were the foundations of the later doctrines of nullification and secession.

"**Virginius**," an American merchant vessel, captured on the high seas near Jamaica by the Spanish man-of-war "Tornado," October 31, 1873, on the ground that it intended landing men to assist in the Cuban insurrection then in progress. Four Cubans found among the passengers, and Captain Fry, with a number of others, were executed. This caused considerable excitement in the United States. Spain, however, made immediate and ample reparation. The incident served to foment the filibustering spirit against Cuba, still rife among a certain class of statesmen in this country.

Volney, Constantin F. C. B., Count de (1757–1820), traveled in the United States from 1795 to 1799. He conducted a controversy regarding John Adams' work on the U. S. Constitution. He wrote "La loi naturelle" and "Tableau du climat et du sol des Etats Unis d'Amérique."

Volunteers. On April 15, 1861, after the news of the firing upon Fort Sumter reached Washington, President Lincoln promptly called for 75,000 volunteers. The Northern States eagerly responded. April 19, a Massachusetts regiment, *en route* to Washington, was attacked by a Baltimore mob. Jefferson Davis also called for volunteers, and the Southern States obeyed his call with alacrity. Later in 1861 Congress provided for the calling out of 500,000 volunteers, and throughout the war they continued a chief variety of fighting material.

Voorhees, Daniel W., born in 1827, was U. S. District Attorney for Indiana from 1858 to 1861. He represented Indiana in the U. S. Congress as a Democrat from 1861 to 1866 and from 1869 to 1873. In 1877 he became a U. S. Senator, and has served on the Finance Committee until the present time (1893). He has been prominent as an advocate of free silver coinage, but in 1893 led the opposition thereto. His present term expires in 1897.

W.

Waddell, James I. (1824–1886), entered the U. S. navy in 1841. He served during the Mexican War. He was made a lieutenant of the "Louisiana" in the Confederate service in 1862. In 1863 he took command of the "Shenandoah," with which he preyed upon the U. S. merchant marine, and made thirty-eight captures. He did not learn of the fall of the Confederacy until three months after its occurrence.

Wade, Benjamin Franklin (1800–1878), an American statesman, was a lawyer and Whig politician in Ohio; he had been in the State Senate and served as State Judge before his entrance into the U. S. Senate. His term in that body covers the long period of 1851–1869. He rapidly became known as one of the most outspoken anti-slavery and later Republican leaders. He strongly opposed the Kansas-Nebraska measure, and during the Rebellion he was chairman of the Joint Congressional Committee on the Conduct of the War. Senator Wade opposed President Lincoln to some degree on the Reconstruction problem, and was naturally in the opposition to President Johnson. He was chairman of the Committee on Territories, and was chosen President *pro tem.* of the Senate in 1867. President Grant appointed him to the San Domingo commission in 1871. Wade was a leading candidate for the vice-presidency in 1868, and chairman of the Ohio delegation in the convention that nominated Hayes.

Wadsworth, James S. (1807–1864), was a prominent supporter of the Free-Soil party in New York. In 1861 he was a delegate to the Peace Convention in Washington. He was volunteer aide to General McDowell at Bull Run in 1861. He was in command of a brigade before Washington, and was military governor of the District of Columbia in 1862. He commanded a division at Fredericksburg and at Gettysburg, where he lost over half his men. He was killed while leading his division at the Wilderness.

Wadsworth, Peleg (1748–1829), fought at Long Island in 1776, and was second in command of the Penobscot expedition in 1779. He represented Maine in the U. S. Congress from 1793 to 1807.

Wagner, Fort, S. C., in possession of a strong body of Confederates under Beauregard in 1863 and assaulted without success by General Strong with 11,500 Federals of Gillmore's command. Strong was assisted by Dahlgren with the Federal frigate, "Ironsides," and six monitors. The Federals desired to hold Fort Wagner in order to render the destruction of Fort Sumter easier. The Federal troops were secretly landed upon the south end of Morris Island and the Confederate works in that vicinity easily captured. July 17 a brief assault was made, which was quickly repulsed by the Confederates. July 18 the assault was resumed. Strong was mortally wounded and 1200 men were lost. Putnam, and Shaw, who led a colored regiment, were also killed. The assaults were continued upon Sumter, however, though that upon Wagner ceased. Sumter was practically destroyed by July 23, though Beauregard's force nearly twice outnumbered Gillmore's.

Waite, Morrison R. (1816–1888), Chief Justice, was admitted to the bar in 1839 and soon was acknowledged as a leader. He was a member of the Ohio Legislature in 1849. He won distinction as a counsel for the United States in the Alabama claims before the tribunal of arbitration at Geneva, Switzerland, from 1871 to 1872. He was elected President of the Ohio Constitutional Convention in 1874. He became Chief Justice of the U. S. Supreme Court in 1874 and served until his death.

Waldo Patent. In 1630, Beauchamp and others of Massachusetts obtained from the Council for New England a grant of thirty square miles on the Penobscot Bay and river. This was afterward called the "Waldo Patent," and is still in part held by the heirs or assigns of the grantees.

Waldseemüller, Martin (1470?–after 1522), German geographer, published an "Introduction to Cosmography, with the Four Voyages of Americus Vespucius." He advocated the name "America" for the New World, and seems to have been the author of its success.

Walke, Henry, born in 1808, commanded the gunboats at Belmont and the "Carondelet" at Forts Fisher, Donelson and Pillow in 1862. He commanded the "Lafayette" at Grand Gulf in 1863.

Walker, Amasa (1799–1875), was a member of the Massachusetts Senate in 1849. He was Secretary of the State from 1851 to 1853. He represented Massachusetts in the U. S. Congress as a Republican from 1862 to 1863. He was prominent in advocating new and reformatory measures, and was an authority on questions of finance. He published "Nature and Uses of Money and Mixed Currency" and "Science of Wealth, a Manual of Political Economy."

Walker, Francis A., born in 1840, was adjutant-general of the Second Army Corps during the Civil War. He was commissioner of Indian affairs from 1871 to 1872. He was professor of history and political economy at the Yale Scientific School from 1873 to 1881, when he became president of the Massachusetts Institute of Technology. He compiled the ninth and tenth censuses, and published "Money, Trade and Industry," several works on political economy and a history of the Second Army Corps.

Walker, Robert James (1801–1869), an American Cabinet officer, was educated in the University of Pennsylvania, studied law, and removed to Mississippi. He was Democratic U. S. Senator from that State from 1836 to 1845. He favored the annexation of Texas, and the same year refused the nomination for Vice-President. In 1845 President Polk called him to the Treasury Department which he conducted until 1849. He is identified with the "Walker revenue tariff" of 1846. He favored the warehouse system and the creation of the Interior Department. He was Governor of Kansas in 1857–1858, and during the war was U. S. financial agent in Europe.

Walker, William (1824–1860), organized an unsuccessful expedition in 1853 for the conquest of the State of Sonora, Mexico. In 1855 he was induced to aid the "Liberal" party in the Nicaragua troubles. He gained a victory at La Virgen, and took possession of Granada. He became Secretary of War and commander-in-chief. He gained undisputed control of Nicaragua and caused himself to be elected President in 1856. His government was recognized by the United States. He was defeated in an insurrection in 1857. He made two subsequent attempts to overthrow governments in Central America, in one of which he was captured and shot.

Walker vs. Jennison, a case, the decision in which in 1783 was the death-blow to slavery in Massachusetts. A negro servant had been beaten and imprisoned by a citizen who claimed him as his slave. The public would not overlook the offence. The Supreme Court held in Worcester County judged the defendant guilty of assault and fined him forty shillings. The Court held that the State Constitution of 1780, in declaring all men free and equal, had abolished slavery in Massachusetts.

Wallace, Lewis, born in 1827, a lawyer and politician in Indiana, volunteered in the war, and commanded a division at the battle of Fort Donelson. He was made major-general of volunteers. Previous to the battle of Shiloh General Wallace's division was stationed at Crump's Landing near the main army; his force could not reach the scene for the first day's fighting, but took part in the second day's work. He commanded the defences of Cincinnati in anticipation of Kirby Smith's attack; in July, 1864, in the battle of the Monocacy, Wallace, though defeated by Early, gained time to save the capital. He was Governor of Utah 1878–1881, and Minister to Turkey 1881–1885. Besides a life of President Harrison, General Wallace has written three successful novels: "A Fair God," "Ben-Hur" and "The Prince of India."

Wallace, William A., born in 1827, was a member of the Pennsylvania Senate from 1862 to 1867. He represented Pennsylvania in the U. S. Senate as a Democrat from 1875 to 1881.

Wallace, William H. L. (1821–1862), served during the Mexican War. He commanded a brigade at Fort Donelson and at Shiloh, where he was mortally wounded after a gallant stand against the enemy.

Wallace's Reports, law reports by John W. Wallace, in twenty-three volumes, of cases in the U. S. Supreme Court, 1863–1875.

Wallack, James W. (1794–1864), first came to the United States from England in 1818. He was a favorite actor in refined comedy. He established Wallack's Theatre in New York in 1861.

Wallack, John Lester (1820–1888), was proprietor of Wallack's Theatre, New York, from 1864 to 1888. He was a popular actor of refined comedy. He wrote "The Veteran" and "Rosedale" for the stage.

Walpole Grant. The Walpole Company was formed in 1766. In 1769 the company petitioned for a grant of 2,500,000 acres between 38° and 42° north latitude and east of the Scioto River. August 14, 1772, the grant was finally made by the crown. The Walpole Company was opposed by the Mississippi Company, formed some years later by a body of wealthy Virginia planters.

Walthall, Edward C., born in 1831, commanded a Confederate regiment at Fishing Creek, and a brigade at Missionary Ridge and Nashville. He was elected a U. S. Senator from Mississippi as a Democrat in 1885. His present term expires in 1895.

Walton, George (1740–1804), was prominent in the pre-Revolutionary movements in Georgia. He represented Georgia in the Continental Congress from 1776 to 1781, and signed the Declaration of Independence. He commanded a battalion at Savannah in 1778. He was Governor of Georgia in 1779 and 1789. He represented Georgia in the U. S. Senate from 1795 to 1796.

Walworth, Reuben H. (1788–1867), represented New York in the U. S. Congress as a Democrat from 1821 to 1823. He was Chancellor of New York from 1828 to 1848. He was pronounced by Joseph Story "the greatest equity jurist living."

Wampanoags, a tribe of Massachusetts Indians who at first showed great friendliness toward the whites. In 1621 they entered into an amicable compact with the Plymouth settlers, and continued in peaceable trade relations with them. Later Massasoit, the chief of the tribe, was on terms of friendship with Roger Williams. They, however, resisted all attempts to convert them to Christianity. Their last chief, Philip, resided at Mount Hope, and under him a disastrous war was waged with the whites, which in 1676 resulted in the overthrow of the tribe. Their power was broken, and they were rapidly dispersed.

Wampum, or Wompan, an Indian word meaning "strings of white beads." Wampum was used as money, according to tradition, first by the Narragansett Indians and was afterward generally adopted by the Indians along the eastern coast as a medium of exchange. It was also used as money by the colonists of New England and the Middle States, being deemed a legal tender from 1627 to 1661. Wampum was manufactured from beads made from the stems of periwinkle shells, common along the coast. These shells were both white and black, and the value of the latter as a medium of exchange was twice that of the former. The beads were strung together and sewn upon belts, and were also worn as necklaces and wristlets. The black beads were called "Suckanhock." Wampum was also known under the Dutch name "Sewon," or "Zeewand." Payments were made by stripping off individual beads, or by cutting off portions of the embroidered belts.

Wanamaker, John, born in 1838, of Philadelphia, established a system of co-operation among employees in his store, which is one of the largest in the United States. He was Postmaster-General in Harrison's Cabinet from 1889 to 1893.

War, Secretary of, an office created by Act of Continental Congress, February 7, 1781. This office was designed to supersede the Board of War. Benjamin Lincoln was the first Secretary (1781–83), Henry Knox the second (1785–89). Under Knox the department was developed and well conducted until the establishment of the present War Department in 1789.

War Democrats, members of the Democratic party who supported the administration during the Civil War, in spite of previous party connections with the secessionists.

War Department. The Continental Congress at first managed military affairs through a committee. In 1776 the Board of War and Ordnance was created, and in 1777 a new Board of War, not composed of members of Congress. In 1781 a Secretary of War was provided for. August 7, 1789, the First Congress established the War Department. Henry Knox, who had been "Secretary of War" since 1785, was continued in the new office.

War of 1812. (See Great Britain, Second War with.)

Ward, Artemus (1727–1800), became a major in 1755, and served under General Abercrombie against the French and Indians. He was a prominent member of the Massachusetts Legislature. He was made commander-in-chief of the Massachusetts forces in 1775. He was in nominal command at the battle of Bunker Hill, but was not in the field. He commanded the forces besieging Boston until the arrival of Washington, when he became second in command. He represented Massachusetts in the U. S. Congress as a Federalist from 1791 to 1795.

Ward, Frederick T. (1831–1862), attained high rank as a soldier in the service of the Chinese Emperor. At the time of the "Trent" affair between England and the United States he prepared to seize British vessels in Chinese waters.

Ward, John Q. A., born in 1830, won distinction as a sculptor by his statues, "The Freedman," "The Indian Hunter," "The Pilgrim," and "The Good Samaritan." He has executed statues of Washington, Putnam and Garfield.

Ward, Nancy (eighteenth century), prophetess of the Cherokee Indians, sympathized with the white settlers and saved many from the stake. She gave warnings of every raid of the Cherokees upon the whites.

Ward, Nathaniel (1578?–1652), was charged with non-conformity in England and came to Massachusetts in 1634. He compiled the "Body of Liberties" for the Massachusetts colony which was adopted by the general court in 1641. It was the first code of laws established in New England. He returned to England in 1646. He wrote "The Simple Cobbler of Aggawam in America," a political satire.

Ward, Samuel (1725–1776), was Governor of Rhode Island from 1762 to 1763 and from 1765 to 1767. He was a delegate to the Continental Congress from 1774 to 1775. He was a zealous patriot.

Ware, Henry (1764–1845), was Hollis professor of divinity in Harvard College from 1805 to 1840. His acceptance caused the separation of the Unitarians, of whom he became a leader, from the Orthodox Congregationalists.

Ware, William (1797–1852), was pastor of the First Congregational Church in New York from 1821 to 1836. He wrote "American Unitarian Biography," "The Works and Genius of Washington Allston" and "Life of Nathaniel Bacon," and also several historical novels, "Zenobia," "Aurelian," etc.

Ware vs. Hylton, a Supreme Court case of importance. In 1796 Ware, a citizen of Great Britain, brought suit against Hylton, of Virginia, for the recovery of a debt. Hylton refused payment on the plea that the act of the Virginia Legislature of 1777 enabled debtors of British subjects to pay such debts to the State loan office. Hylton claimed to have done this. The U. S. Circuit Court in Virginia decreed for the defendant, but the Supreme Court of the United States reversed this decision on the ground that the legislature had not the power to extinguish the debt, when payment of such debts had been stipulated in the Treaty of 1783.

Warner, Adoniram J., born in 1834, served in the Civil War. He represented Ohio in the U. S. Congress as a Democrat from 1878 to 1880, and from 1882 to 1886. He has published works upon economic questions.

Warner, Charles Dudley, born in 1829, has been an editor of the Hartford *Press* and *Courant* since 1860, and of *Harper's Magazine* since 1884. He has written "Studies in the South," "Mexican Papers" and "Studies in the Great West," which depict the political and social condition of those territories; "Washington Irving" in the "Men of Letters" series, of which he is editor, and "Backlog Studies."

Warner, Seth (1743–1784), of Vermont, was a leader of the inhabitants of the "New Hampshire Grants" in the conflicts of jurisdiction with New York authorities, by whom he was outlawed. He was second in command at Ticonderoga. He captured Crown Point. He participated in Montgomery's campaign in Canada. He commanded at Hubbardston and was active at Bennington. He retired in 1782 on account of ill health.

Warner, Susan (1819–1885), wrote "The Wide, Wide World," the most popular novel by an American except "Uncle Tom's Cabin." She also published "Queechy," and other novels.

Warren, Gouverneur Kemble (1830–1882), graduated at West Point in 1850. In the Civil War he was continuously in the Army of the Potomac. He was a colonel at Big Bethel, commanded a brigade in the Peninsula campaign, Second Bull Run, Antietam and Fredericksburg, was chief engineer of the army at Chancellorsville and Gettysburg; in the latter struggle he seized the important position of Little Round Top. He was distinguished as commander of a corps at Centreville, October, 1863, and led a corps through the Wilderness, North Anna, Cold Harbor and Petersburg campaign, until at the battle of Five Forks, April 1, 1865, he was removed by Sheridan. In 1879 he reached the grade of lieutenant-colonel in the regular army.

Warren, Joseph (1741–1775), an American patriot, was a graduate of Harvard and a physician of Boston. In the years immediately preceding the outbreak of the Revolution Dr. Warren was foremost among the Massachusetts patriots. He was a noted orator, a member of the Committees of Correspondence, president of the Provincial Congress of 1774, and chairman of the Committee of Public Safety. He was actively engaged in organizing the volunteers in the spring of 1775. The Massachusetts Provincial Congress made him a major-general. Waiving his rank, he fought at the battle of

Bunker Hill as a private soldier, and was the chief victim. His life has been written by A. H. Everett and by R. Frothingham.

Warren, Mercy (1728–1814), sister of James Otis, married James Warren in 1754. She wrote a "History of the American Revolution," which is valuable because of her personal acquaintance with many of the characters.

Warren, Sir Peter (1703–1752), was commodore of the fleet which conveyed Sir William Pepperrell's expedition against Louisbourg in 1745. He was promoted rear-admiral for his service.

Warrington, Lewis (1782–1851), entered the U. S. navy in 1800. He served with distinction on the "Vixen," of Preble's squadron, during the Tripolitan War. He served on the "Essex" and the "Congress" from 1811 to 1813. He commanded the sloop "Peacock," and captured the "Epervier" and fourteen merchantmen during 1814. He was chief of the Bureau of Ordnance from 1842 to 1851.

Warwick, R. I., early known as Shawomet, was settled in 1643 by a party under Samuel Gorton, who purchased the land from Miantonomo. It was one of the four towns which, in 1644, united to form the colony of Rhode Island. In 1648 the name of Warwick was given the colony. It was attacked by the Indians during King Philip's War and the town destroyed by fire.

Washburn, Cadwallader Colden (1818–1882), was the brother of E. B. Washburne. He settled in Wisconsin as a lawyer and financier. From 1855 to 1861 he was Congressman from Wisconsin. He was a delegate to the Peace Conference of 1861. In the war he commanded a corps, was major-general of volunteers, and served in the West. He was again a Republican Congressman 1867–1871, and Governor of Wisconsin 1872–1874.

Washburn, Emory (1800–1877), was Governor of Massachusetts in 1853 and 1854. He wrote a "Judicial History of Massachusetts, 1630 to 1675" and "Treatise on the American Law of Real Property."

Washburn, Israel (1813–1883), was admitted to the bar in 1834. He was a member of the Maine Legislature from 1842 to 1843. He represented Maine in the U. S. Congress as a Whig from 1851 to 1861. He was Governor of Maine from 1861 to 1863, and Collector of Customs at Portland from 1863 to 1877.

Washburn, William B. (1820–1887), represented Massachusetts in the U. S. Congress as a Republican from 1862 to 1872. He was Governor of Massachusetts from 1872 to 1874, and a U. S. Senator from 1874 to 1875.

Washburn, William D., born in 1831, was Surveyor-General of Minnesota from 1861 to 1865. He represented Minnesota in the U. S. Congress as a Republican from 1879 to 1885. He was elected to the U. S. Senate for the term ending in 1895.

Washburne, Elihu Benjamin (1816–1887), was a lawyer in Illinois, Whig Congressman, and afterward Republican Congressman from 1853 to 1869. He was chairman of the Committee of Commerce and of the Impeachment

Committee of 1868. His long service and care of public expenditures earned for him the epithets of "father of the house" and "watch-dog of the Treasury." President Grant appointed him Secretary of State, but he held office for a few days only. From 1869 to 1877 Mr. Washburne was U. S. Minister to France. He stayed in Paris through the siege of 1870–1871 and the days of the Commune, and was by the Germans intrusted with the charge of German interests also. His memoirs are published under the title "Recollections of a Minister to France."

Washington, Bushrod (1762–1829), jurist, a nephew of General Washington, was a member of the Virginia Convention in 1788 that ratified the Federal Constitution. He was a Justice of the U. S. Supreme Court from 1798 to 1829.

Washington, George (February 22, 1732–December 14, 1799), the first President of the United States, was born in Westmoreland County, Va. Some of the familiar anecdotes of his early life rest on the more than doubtful authority of Weems, one of his first chroniclers. At the age of sixteen he was compelled to leave school, and he became a surveyor. His appointment as adjutant-general and major at the early age of nineteen was preparatory to his selection for the first striking public event of his life, his service as messenger from the Virginian to the French Governor in 1753–1754. How he traversed the pathless forests of Western Pennsylvania is familiar; the following summer a battle at Great Meadows fought by his small force ushered in the long French and Indian War. Washington was obliged to surrender Fort Necessity. He resigned, but the next year served on Braddock's staff at the defeat of the Monongahela, and had a miraculous escape. Colonel Washington continued in the army until 1759, and had a part in the taking of Fort Duquesne in 1758. He married in 1759, and the same year entered the Virginia House of Burgesses. For several years he now led the life of a Virginia planter, at Mount Vernon. He was a delegate to the first and second Continental Congresses; by the latter body he was appointed commander-in-chief, June 17, 1775, and took command of the army under the historic elm at Cambridge, July 3. It was his task to put into the form of an organized force the raw and ill-equipped soldiers. His first enterprise succeeded; Boston was evacuated by the British, March 17, 1776, and the army was transferred to New York. After the Declaration of Independence, a disheartening series of reverses marked the half year: the battle of Brooklyn, the withdrawal from New York, White Plains, the fall of Fort Washington, and the melancholy retreat of the diminishing army across New Jersey. The *morale* of the troops and of the country was suddenly raised by Washington's brilliant surprise of Trenton and victory of Princeton. In the autumn of 1777 his army, though defeated at Brandywine and Germantown, kept a large British force occupied, and so contributed to the *dénouement* of the year, at Saratoga. Then came the gloomy winter at Valley Forge, and the cabal of Conway and Gates. The battle of Monmouth was won in the summer, but thereafter Washington's part was for some years in other phases of the war than in battles, and active hostilities drifted away principally to the south. The treason of Arnold in 1780 was a severe blow. In the following summer Washington showed the qualities of a great general

LADIES OF THE WHITE HOUSE.

Mrs. James K. Polk. Angelica Van Buren. (*Daughter-in-law of Martin Van Buren.*) Rose Elizabeth Cleveland. (*Sister of Grover Cleveland.*) Mrs. Martin Van Buren.
Mrs. Grover Cleveland.
Mrs. John Adams. Mrs. James A. Garfield. Mrs. John Quincy Adams.
Mrs. Benjamin Harrison. Martha Washington. Mary Ball Washington. (*Mother of George Washington.*) Mrs. Abraham Lincoln.
Harriet Lane Johnston. (*Niece of James Buchanan.*) Martha Jefferson. (*Daughter of Thomas Jefferson.*) Mrs. Ulysses S. Grant. Mrs. R. B. Hayes. Mrs. Andrew Johnson.
Mrs. Andrew Jackson. Mrs. James Madison. Mrs. Millard Fillmore. Mrs. John Tyler.

by his secret and rapid march from the Hudson to Chesapeake Bay, a march which resulted in the fall of Yorktown. His significance in the war was largely moral; there was a widespread confidence in his thorough devotion to the cause. He replied severely to the Newburg address of 1782 (which had hinted at monarchy). After a letter to the State Governors he took leave of the army and officers, and, December 23, 1783, resigned to Congress at Annapolis his commission. Deeply impressed with the need of a more efficient government, he presided over the Federal Convention of 1787. He was the unanimous choice for President, and was inaugurated at New York April 30, 1789. Elected again without opposition, he served until 1797. Of his Cabinet, Jefferson was Secretary of State, Hamilton of the Treasury, Knox of War, and Randolph Attorney-General. Washington made tours to the North and South. In 1793 he issued a neutrality proclamation. His part in Jay's treaty of 1795 caused a temporary loss of his popularity. On September 19, 1796, he issued his Farewell Address. Perhaps his greatness was even better shown by his conduct as President than by his generalship. When war with France seemed imminent in 1798, he was appointed lieutenant-general, but he died soon after at Mount Vernon. He has been universally deemed the greatest of Americans, and one of the noblest public characters of all time. His writings and life were edited by Sparks, twelve volumes, and more recently by Ford. Of other biographies there are: by Marshall, five volumes; Irving, five volumes; Everett, Hale, H. C. Lodge.

Washington, Martha (1732–1802), born Martha Dandridge, of Virginia, married Daniel Parke Custis in 1749, by whom she had four children. She inherited his vast estates and was one of the wealthiest women in Virginia. In 1759 she married George Washington. She was a competent housekeeper and her wealth enabled them to entertain in magnificent style. She fully sympathized with Washington's patriotic feelings and suffered many privations for the cause of independence.

Washington, Mary Ball (1707–1789), mother of General George Washington, was the second wife of Augustine Washington, whom she married in 1730. George was her oldest son. Left a widow in 1743, she managed her affairs with prudence and discretion, and brought up her six children well. She was an excellent mother to Washington, and was regarded by him with great veneration and affection. She lived many years at Fredericksburg, Va., in great simplicity, and died during the first year of her son's presidency.

Washington, William Augustine (1752–1810), distinguished himself at Long Island, Trenton and Princeton. In 1778 he was lieutenant in Colonel Baylor's dragoons. In 1779 he joined the army of General Lincoln in the South. He defeated Colonel Tarleton at Rantowles. He captured the post at Rudgely's in 1780. He commanded a light corps at Cowpens, Guilford Court House, Hobkirk's Hill and Eutaw Springs. He was a relative of General Washington.

Washington was formed from the Oregon country, which was claimed by England and the United States, and was recognized as belonging to the latter by the treaty of 1846. It was organized as a territory by an Act of Congress of March 2, 1853. Washington became a State, November 11, 1889. The State is usually Republican, but in 1884 and 1886 the Democrats carried the State. The population of the State in 1890 was 349,330. History by Bancroft.

Washington, D. C., capital of the United States, was selected as the seat of the Government in 1790. In 1800 it became the capital. In 1814 it was captured by the British troops and the Capitol and other public buildings burned. In 1871 Congress abolished the charter of the city and instituted a form of territorial government which resulted in a great number of improvements for the city. In 1874 the territorial government was in turn abolished and the city's affairs placed in the hands of three commissioners. (See art. District of Columbia.)

Washington, Fort, Battle of, November 16, 1776. The retreat of the Continental army had made Fort Washington untenable. Greene had orders to withdraw men and stores, but Congress interfered. He accordingly increased the garrison. Howe soon appeared before the fort but gained it only after a severe struggle, which cost him 500 men. One hundred and fifty Americans fell, 3000 were made prisoners, and great stores of artillery and small arms fell to the enemy.

Washington, Treaty of, ratified in 1871 and proclaimed in force, July 4, of that year, after thirty-four meetings of commissioners, representing England and the United States, and assembled at Washington. It provided for arbitration as to the Alabama Claims; as to claims of British subjects against the United States; as to fisheries, and as to the settlement of the Northwest boundary question. The arbitrators upon the Alabama Claims were to be five in number and were to be appointed by the President of the United States, the Queen of England, the King of Italy, the President of the Swiss Confederation, and the Emperor of Brazil. Their sessions were to be held at Geneva.

Washington and Jefferson College, Washington, Pa., Presbyterian, was formed in 1865 by the union of Jefferson College, chartered 1802, and Washington College, chartered 1806.

Washington and Lee University, Lexington, Va. An academy founded about 1773, and called Liberty Hall, was chartered in 1782, and named in 1796 Washington College in honor of a gift received from George Washington. In 1870 at the death of General R. E. Lee, its president, the name was changed to its present form. A law school was founded in 1867.

Washington College, Chestertown, Md., was founded in 1782.

Washington Elm, a tree at Cambridge, Mass., beneath which General Washington took command of the Continental army, July 3, 1775. The army then numbered 15,000 men fit for duty. The Washington Elm still stands.

"**Washington Gazette,**" the earliest news publication of the District of Columbia. The paper was established at Washington by Benjamin Moore, January 11, 1796. It was published semi-weekly, but has been discontinued.

Washington Monument, at Washington, D. C., an obelisk 555 feet high, was begun in 1848 by the Washington National Monument Society, and finished in 1884 by the U. S. Government.

"Wasp," sloop-of-war, eighteen guns, Captain Jones, left the Delaware October 13, 1812, for the West Indies. Five days later it attacked the "Frolic," twenty guns, convoying a fleet of merchantmen. The "Frolic" was soon disabled, boarded and captured, losing ninety of its 108 men. Within two hours after the capture the "Wasp" and its prize were captured by the British frigate the "Poictiers," seventy-four guns, and the Americans taken to Bermuda as prisoners.

"Wasp" (No. 2), eighteen guns, Captain Blakeley. In the British Channel he harassed British merchant-ships, and on June 28, 1814, fought with the "Reindeer." Both vessels were badly damaged, but finally the "Reindeer" was boarded and captured, losing twenty-five killed and forty-two wounded. The Americans lost twenty-seven in all. On September 1 it conquered the "Avon," eighteen guns, but was driven off by the arrival of several warships. September 21, near the Azores, it captured and sent home a valuable prize, the "Atlanta." On October 9 the "Wasp" was spoken by a Swedish bark, but was never heard of afterward.

Watauga Association, an organization formed in 1769 for the settlement of that territory now comprised in the State of Tennessee. The colonies thus established continued to be known as the settlements of the Watauga Association until 1777.

Waterbury, David (1722–1801), served in the French and Indian War. In 1776 he was second in command at Valcour Bay and was defeated. He commanded a brigade under Washington from 1781 to 1783.

Waterman, Robert W., born in 1826, was prominent in the political campaign in Illinois in 1856 and 1858. He was Lieutenant-Governor of California from 1886 to 1887, when he became Governor and served till 1891.

Watertown, Mass., was settled in 1630 by colonists under Sir Richard Saltonstall. In 1631 the townspeople declined to pay a tax of £60 levied by the "assistants," thus protesting against their autocratic rule, which bore fruit in the establishment of a more popular governmental plan in 1632. In 1775 the Provincial Congress met at Watertown.

Watson, Elkanah (1758–1842), was a zealous promoter of internal improvements, and conceived the project of the canals of New York. He founded the first agricultural society in New York.

Watson, James C. (1838 1880), was professor of astronomy at the University of Wisconsin from 1859 to 1869. His discoveries in astronomy have been numerous, and he has made valuable contributions to the science.

Watson, Fort, Capture of, April 23, 1781. This post commanded the road between Camden and Charleston, S. C. It was captured by Marion's men who erected a tower of pine logs so as to command the fort. As the fort had no artillery it was soon forced to surrender.

Watterson, Henry, born in 1840, was a staff officer in the Confederate service from 1861 to 1863 and chief of scouts in General Johnston's army in 1864. He has edited the Louisville *Courier-Journal* since 1868. He represented Kentucky in the U. S. Congress as a Democrat from 1876 to 1877. He is an aggressive advocate of free-trade and revenue reform. He wrote "Oddities of Southern Life and Character."

Waxhaw, Battle of, May 29, 1780. After the capture of Charleston, S. C., detachments of British troops set out to seize strategic points in the interior. One of these, 700 cavalry under Tarleton, pursued a Virginian regiment under Colonel Buford and overtook it at Waxhaw, S. C. Buford and 100 infantry saved themselves by flight. Though the rest sued for quarter, 113 of them were killed on the spot and 150 more were too badly hacked to be moved. Only 53 were taken prisoners.

Wayland, Francis (1796–1865), was pastor of the First Baptist Church, Boston, from 1821 to 1826. He was president of Brown University from 1827 to 1855. He was celebrated as an instructor, preacher and author. He possessed a strong personality which was stimulating to his pupils. He wrote "Elements of Moral Science," "Elements of Political Economy," "The Limitations of Human Responsibility," and "Slavery and Religion."

Wayne, Anthony (1745–1796), a noted general of the Revolution, was a native of Pennsylvania. A surveyor in early life, he became a member of the Legislature and Committee of Public Safety, and commanded a regiment in the Canadian invasion of 1775–1776. Later he had charge of the Ticonderoga forts. Being appointed brigadier-general he was in charge of a division at Brandywine and conducted a successful retreat. He was surprised at Paoli, commanded the right wing at Germantown, and was distinguished at Monmouth. His famous exploit was the storm of Stony Point, July 15, 1779. General Wayne suppressed the mutiny of the troops at Morristown, in January, 1781, had an honorable part in Virginia the same year and in Georgia in 1782. He was a member of the Pennsylvania ratifying convention of 1787. When the Indian affairs required a decisive policy, "Mad Anthony" was made major-general, and inflicted an overwhelming blow at the battle of Fallen Timbers, 1794, which led to an Indian treaty the following year. Life by Stillé.

Wayne, James M. (1790–1867), was Judge of the Georgia Supreme Court from 1824 to 1829. He represented Georgia in the U. S. Congress as a Democrat from 1829 to 1835. He was a Justice of the U. S. Supreme Court from 1835 to 1867.

Waynesboro, Va., scene of a victory in March, 1865, for 10,000 Federals under Sheridan, then commanding in the Shenandoah Valley, over Early who was intrenched at Waynesboro with 2500 Confederates. Early was completely routed, losing 1600 men, eleven guns, seventeen flags and 200 loaded wagons.

Ways and Means, a standing committee first created in the House of Representatives in 1795 (December 21). It has charge of the methods and provisions for collecting the government revenues, including the tariff system, internal taxation, financial measures and the public debt.

Weather Bureau, first suggested in 1817 by Josiah Meigs, then Commissioner of the Land Office, who established a system of meteorological registers in connection with the office. In 1819 a co-operative movement was begun by Surgeon-General Lovell, of the Army, who had weather reports made each month by the officers of different military posts. Some twenty years later the lake system of meteorological observations was established by the Engineer Department. In 1836 predictions of meteorological phenomena began to be made by the Smithsonian Institution, and the results of these, together with those of the Land Office and War Department, being published in 1839, formed the basis for a scientific meteorological bureau. In 1869 the "Weather Bulletin of the Cincinnati Bureau" appeared. In 1870 Congress made a money appropriation for the establishment of a Weather Bureau at Washington and ordered arrangements to be made for telegraphic communications between posts of observation all over the country. Until 1891 the Bureau was a bureau of the War Department; in that year it was transferred to the Department of Agriculture.

Weathersford, William (1770?–1824), Indian chief, led the Creeks against the U. S. forces during the War of 1812. In 1814 he voluntarily surrendered to General Jackson.

Weaver, James B., born in 1833, attained the rank of brigadier-general during the Civil War. He was a district attorney of Iowa in 1866. He became an editor of the *Iowa Tribune*. He was elected to Congress from Iowa as a Nationalist in 1879. In 1880 he was the candidate of the National party for the Presidency. He was again elected to Congress in 1884 and 1886. In 1892 he was the Presidential candidate of the People's party.

Webb, Alexander S., born in 1835, fought at Bull Run and commanded a brigade at Gettysburg, the Wilderness and Spottsylvania. He was chief of staff at Petersburg. He wrote "McClellan's Campaign of 1862."

Webb, James W. (1802–1884), edited the New York *Courier and Enquirer* from 1829 to 1861, which was the chief organ of the Whig party. He was Minister to Brazil from 1861 to 1869.

Webster, Daniel (January 18, 1782–October 24, 1852), a distinguished American orator and statesman, was born at Salisbury, N. H., was educated at Phillips (Exeter) Academy and at Dartmouth, where he was graduated in 1801. He taught school at Fryeburg, in Maine, studied law, was admitted to the bar in 1805, and began the practice of law in Boscawen, N. H. In 1807 he removed to Portsmouth. He was soon a leader of the bar, and from 1813 to 1817 was Congressman. In views he was then a moderate Federalist. He now settled in Boston, and in 1818 rose to the front rank of lawyers by his plea before the U. S. Supreme Court in the famous "Dartmouth College case," which involved the obligation of contracts and the powers of the Government. From 1823 to 1827 he was Congressman from Massachusetts, was chairman of the Judiciary Committee, and had attracted attention by his speeches on Greece and on free trade. He had become widely known as an orator. Among his great speeches were: at Plymouth, 1820, on the bi-centennial; at the laying of the corner-stone of Bunker Hill Monument, 1825; the eulogy on Adams and Jefferson, 1826. In 1827 Webster entered the U. S. Senate, and ranked chief among the orators, of the "giants" in Congress; Clay, Calhoun, Benton, to mention no others, were his contemporaries. He favored the protective tariff of 1828. Two years later he reached his highest point, in the debate on the "Foote resolution," where his reply to Hayne won for him the title of "Expounder of the Constitution." Webster opposed Nullification, was often pitted against Calhoun, took an active part in the Bank controversy, and was, with Clay, highest in the Whig party. He came within reach of the nomination for President. In 1836 he received the electoral vote of Massachusetts. President Harrison chose him for Secretary of State in 1841, and he—alone of the members of Tyler's Cabinet—refused to resign in September, 1841. He negotiated the Ashburton Treaty with Great Britain in 1842, and resigned in 1843. In 1845 he re-entered the Senate. He spoke on the Oregon question, gave a lame support to Taylor in 1848, and in 1850 in the Compromise excitement he alienated many former friends by his famous "seventh of March speech." He was again Secretary of State in 1850–1852. He received a few votes in the Convention of 1852, refused to support Scott, and died soon after at his home in Marshfield, Mass. Works and life in six volumes, edited by Everett. Life by G. T. Curtis and by H. C. Lodge.

Webster, Joseph D. (1811–1876), served during the Mexican War. He was chief of staff to General Grant in 1862 and during the Vicksburg campaign and to General Sherman from 1864 to 1865.

Webster, Noah (1758–1843), born in Connecticut, first came to prominence by the publication of a spelling book, of which 62,000,000 copies have been issued. In 1784 he published "Sketches of American Policy," which had influence upon the movement toward a national constitution. In 1787 he published "The Leading Principles of the Federal Constitution." In 1795 he wrote articles signed "Curtius," which were influential in behalf of the Jay treaty. In 1828 his first "Dictionary of the English Language" was published. He served in the legislatures of Connecticut and Massachusetts. Life by Scudder.

Webster, Pelatiah (1725–1795), was an ardent patriot during the Revolution. He was well versed in politics and finance. He wrote "Essays on Free Trade and Finance" and "The Union and Constitution of the Thirteen United States."

Wedderburn, Alexander (1733–1805), Attorney-General of England, was one of the greatest foes of the colonists in the Cabinet of Lord North and violently opposed their claims and advocated unlimited subjection.

Weed, Thurlow (1797–1882), one of the most influential journalists and politicians that the country has ever produced. He was early employed in a printing establishment and as a country journalist. He became connected with the *Rochester Telegraph* and with the *Anti-Masonic Enquirer*. In 1825 he was in the New York Legislature, but afterward avoided office.

Already influential in State and national politics, Weed, in 1830, founded the *Albany Evening Journal*, which he conducted until 1856 as a Whig, and later as a Republican organ. His influence was felt in nearly every nomination of the Whigs and Republicans from 1836 to 1876. For years he was a political partner of Seward, whom he favored for President in 1860. During the Civil War he was in Europe acting as an agent in behalf of the Union cause. Life by Barnes.

Weems, Mason L. (1760–1825), a wandering Virginian parson, wrote lives of Washington, Francis Marion, Benjamin Franklin and William Penn. They are unreliable. With him originated many anecdotes about Washington, including the story of the cherry-tree.

Weights and Measures, International Bureau of. To secure international uniformity and precision in standards of weight and measure an international bureau was established at Paris by a convention concluded May 20, 1875, between the United States, Germany, Austro-Hungary, Belgium, Brazil, the Argentine Confederation, Denmark, Spain, France, Italy, Peru, Portugal, Russia, Sweden and Norway, Switzerland, Turkey and Venezuela.

Weitzel, Godfrey (1835–1884), planned the capture of New Orleans in 1862. He commanded a division at Port Hudson and in the Lafourche campaign. He superintended the construction of defenses at Bermuda Hundred, James River and Deep Bottom. He commanded a corps at Fort Harrison in 1864, and was second in command at Fort Fisher. He commanded all the forces north of the Potomac after March, 1865.

Weldon Road, Va. General Grant, during his memorable operations about Richmond and Petersburg, attempted to capture this road from the Confederates under Lee, June 22 and 23, 1864. Hancock's and Wright's corps were detailed to effect this capture. A gap occurred between the two corps during the necessary movements, and into this the Confederate Hill threw a strong column. Both corps were struck upon the flank and thrown into confusion. The attack was finally repelled. On the twenty-third, Wright again made the attempt to seize the road and cut the telegraph wires. Hill drove him off, inflicting severe loss upon his troops. Grant lost 4000 men in these ineffectual attempts. Again, August 18, 1864, during the campaign about Petersburg, Grant seized the opportunity, while the main body of Lee's army was massed toward Richmond, of attacking the Weldon Railroad. Warren moved with the eighteenth and fifth corps and struck the road four miles from Petersburg. A gap occurring between the two corps, Lee thrust Mahone's division into the opening and captured 2000 prisoners, but was eventually driven back to his lines. Warren spent the next day in fortifying himself, and Lee, having attempted to dislodge him, was severely defeated. On the twenty-fifth, Gregg's cavalry were defeated while destroying the road.

Welles, Gideon (1802–1878), was from 1826 to 1854 an editor of the *Hartford Times* which became the chief organ of the Democratic party in Connecticut. He was a member of the Connecticut Legislature from 1827 to 1835, and State Comptroller in 1835, 1842 and 1843. He was an ardent opponent of slavery, and identified himself with the Republican party when it was organized. He was Secretary of the Navy in the Cabinets of Lincoln and Johnson from 1861 to 1869. He was an unsparing critic of official conduct. He wrote "Lincoln and Seward."

Wellesley College, Wellesley, Mass., founded by Henry F. Durant, for the higher education of women, was chartered in 1870, but first opened five years later.

Welling, James C., born in 1825, was an editor of the *National Intelligencer* from 1850 to 1865. This journal exerted great influence during the war. He became president of Columbian University in 1871. Died 1894.

Wells, David A., born in 1828, suggested the idea of folding newspapers and books by machinery. In 1864 he published "Our Burden and Our Strength," a political essay of great originality. He served on several U. S. commissions of revenue. He has written many pamphlets on economic subjects and "Our Merchant Marine," "A Primer of Tariff Reform" and "The Relation of the Tariff to Wages," and "Recent Economic Changes."

Wells College, Aurora, N. Y., for girls, was chartered in 1867.

Welsh. The Welsh early began to settle in Pennsylvania and seem to have been a valuable addition to the population. By 1765 several flourishing Welsh colonies had been established.

Welsh Barony, a tract of 40,000 acres granted by William Penn to a Welsh colony. The colonists were granted the right of local self-government. The Barony was conducted after the methods of the English manor.

Wentworth, Benning (1696–1770), was Governor of New Hampshire from 1741 to 1767. His grants of land in what is now southern Vermont, which was claimed by New York, are known in history as the "New Hampshire Grants."

Wentworth, Sir John (1737–1820), went to England as an agent of the New Hampshire colony in 1765 and was appointed Governor, serving till 1775. He was an able Governor and did much to increase the importance and prosperity of the colony. He became unpopular by complying with a request for aid by the British in Boston and went to England in 1775. He was Governor of Nova Scotia from 1792 to 1808.

Wentworth, John (1815–1888), was, from 1837 to 1861, editor and proprietor of the Chicago *Democrat*, which was the chief daily paper of the Northwest. He represented Illinois in the U. S. Congress as a Democrat from 1843 to 1851, and from 1853 to 1855. He was one of the founders of the Republican party and served as a Republican in the U. S. Congress from 1865 to 1867.

Wesley, Charles (1708–1788), was one of the founders of the society which was the beginning of Arminian Methodism. He wrote 7000 hymns, some of great merit, many of which are now in use. From 1735 to 1736 he was in Georgia, secretary to Governor Oglethorpe.

Wesley, John (1703–1791), of England, was the founder of the society called in derision the "Methodists," because of their methodical habits. From 1735 to 1738 he labored in Georgia. He formed a Methodist society in London. In 1769 some of his followers introduced Methodism in America.

Wesleyan University, Middletown, Conn., was chartered in 1831. It was founded by the Methodists, especially Wilbur Fisk.

West, Benjamin (1738–1820), born in Pennsylvania, went to Italy in 1760 and settled in England in 1763. He was one of the most famous painters of the day. He was one of the founders of the Royal Academy and was its president from 1792 to 1802 and from 1803 to 1815. He painted many famous religious pieces and "The Death of Wolfe" and "The Treaty of Penn."

West, Lionel Sackville Sackville-, born in 1827, was British Minister to the United States from 1881 to 1888, when he was recalled for publishing a letter giving advice in regard to voting in the United States. In 1888 he became Lord Sackville. (See Murcheson Letter.)

West India Company, Dutch, or Chartered West India Company (Geoctroyeerde Westindische Compagnie). This company was chartered by the States-General of the United Netherlands in 1621, at the instance of Willem Usselinx. It was given a monopoly of trade with America for twenty-four years, with the right to colonize and to make wars and alliances. It colonized and governed New Netherland (till 1664) and also certain West India islands and a part of Brazil. It was rechartered for twenty-five years in 1647. Its preoccupation with military efforts in Brazil prevented its doing much for New Netherland. (For the Swedish company of similar name see Swedish West India Company.)

West Jersey. (See New Jersey.)

West Point, N. Y., the chief of the Continental fortifications in the Hudson River Valley during the Revolution. In August, 1780, Benedict Arnold, already contemplating treason, obtained command of the post from Washington, and immediately entered into communication with Clinton, the British general. Major André was sent to arrange with Arnold for the surprise and surrender of the post. He was captured by three "Skinners," Continental marauders, while returning to New York after his interview with Arnold, having settled upon September 25 as the night for the surprise. When Arnold heard of his capture he immediately fled to the "Vulture," a British warship lying in the river, and Washington was quickly informed of his treason.—The Military Academy of the United States was established here in 1802. (See art. Military Academy.)

West Point, Va. Here, May 7, 1862, several strong detachments of Federals were landed from gunboats, and, under the command of Franklin and Sedgewick, attacked some Confederates led by Whiting and Wade Hampton. These latter, charging on the Federals from the woods, easily routed them, but were themselves compelled to retreat before the firing from the vessels. The losses were trifling on both sides.

West Virginia. The western and northwestern parts of Virginia refused to be bound by the ordinance of secession of April 17, 1861. A convention was called at Wheeling in May, 1861, which summoned a State convention. This convention refused to recognize the State officers who were in opposition to the National Government, elected Frank Pierpont Governor of Virginia, and called a State Legislature to meet at Wheeling. The convention voted to erect a new State to be called Kanawha, and the State Legislature, which had been called by this convention and which claimed to be the Legislature of the State of Virginia, gave its consent to the division of the State. West Virginia became a State of the Union June 19, 1863. An amendment to the State constitution of date 1866 disfranchised all persons who had aided the Rebellion. Until 1870 the State was controlled by the Republicans. The "Flick Amendment," 1871, extended the suffrage to negroes and removed the disfranchising clause of 1866. In 1872 Grant carried the State by a small majority, since which time the State has been steadily Democratic. The population of West Virginia in 1870 was 442,014; in 1890 it was 762,794.

Western Company. (See Compagnie de l'Occident.)

Western Reserve, or Connecticut Western Reserve. When Connecticut, in 1786, ceded her western lands to the United States, she reserved a large tract adjoining Pennsylvania, now forming the northeastern corner of Ohio. Hence this name. Complete cession of jurisdiction was made in 1800.

Westminster, Treaty of, negotiated in 1674, concluding a war between England and the Netherlands, is memorable in America from the fact that New Netherland, which had been taken from England by the Dutch, was restored under its provisions.

Weston, Thomas (1575–1624), formed a joint stock company for fitting out the expedition of the Pilgrims to America in 1620, but soon afterward withdrew from it as unprofitable. He organized a company of his own and sent an advance party in 1622 which founded a settlement at Wessagussett under a grant by the king to Sir Ferdinando Gorges. The settlers were improvident and soon returned to England.

Westover, a Virginia parish formed in 1720 of land along both sides of the James River, beginning at the Chickahominy. The famous old Westover mansion, still in existence, was the home of Colonel William Byrd.

Wethersfield, Conn., first settled in 1634, was one of the earliest settlements in the State, and one of the three towns which united in 1639 in framing the "Fundamental Orders" of the colony.

Whale-fishery began in the New England colonies as early as 1690, where it was prosecuted during nearly fifty years in small boats, since the whale frequented the northern coast during that period. In 1740 the Arctic and Antarctic coasts began to be explored in search of whales. In 1758 Massachusetts alone employed 304 vessels in the whale-fishery. The right whale was at first the object of capture, but after 1812 sperm-whales became equally desirable. In 1815 there were only 164 ships engaged in it. In 1830 the products of the fishery were 106,800 barrels of sperm, 115,000 barrels of whale oil, 120,000 pounds of whalebone, and 2,500,000 pounds of sperm candles. Since 1840 the whale-fishery has decreased, chiefly because of the scarcity of whale.

Whalley, Edward (1620–1676), regicide, joined the Parliamentary party in 1642. He led the horse at Bristol, Banbury, Worcester and elsewhere, and was entrusted with the custody of the king at Hampton Court. He sat in the high court of justice that condemned King Charles and signed the death warrant. He was a member of Cromwell's second and third Parliaments and the House of Lords. He fled to America with Goffe (q. v.) in 1660. (See Regicides.)

Wharton, Francis (1820–1889), was professor of international law at Boston University from 1866 to 1885, and from 1885 to 1889 was examiner of claims in the Department of State. He wrote "The State Trials of the United States during the Administrations of Washington and Adams," and "Digest of International Law," and edited "The Revolutionary Diplomatic Correspondence of the United States."

Wharton, Thomas (1735–1778), was a zealous opponent of the oppressive measures of England toward the colonies. He was chosen a member of the Philadelphia Committee of Correspondence in 1774. He became one of the Committee of Safety in 1775, and in 1776 became president of the Council of Safety, in which the executive authority temporarily resided. He was president of Pennsylvania from 1777 to 1778.

Wheatley, Phillis (1753–1784), was brought from Africa to America in 1761, and purchased in the slave market by John Wheatley. She showed remarkable ability, and learned easily. She acquired prominence by her poems.

Wheaton, Frank, born in 1833, of Rhode Island, commanded a brigade at Antietam, Fredericksburg, the Wilderness and Spottsylvania. He led a division at Cedar Creek and Petersburg, and is now (1894) a brigadier-general in the U. S. army.

Wheaton, Henry (1785–1848), of Rhode Island, edited the New York *National Advocate* from 1812 to 1815, in which the question of neutral rights was ably discussed during the war. From 1816 to 1827 he was reporter for the U. S. Supreme Court. His reports are exceedingly valuable, containing carefully prepared notes and citation of authorities on all difficult points. He was Chargé d'Affaires in Denmark from 1827 to 1835, Minister Resident to Prussia from 1835 to 1837, and Minister Plenipotentiary from 1837 to 1846. He wrote "Elements of International Law" which is acknowledged a standard authority, a "History of the Law of Nations," and a "History of the Northmen."

Wheaton's Reports, twelve volumes of law reports by Henry Wheaton, containing cases from the U. S. Supreme Courts from 1816 to 1827, with appendices containing discussions of the "Principles and Practice of Prize Courts," many of them written by Judge Story.

Wheeler, Joseph, born in 1836, entered the Confederate service and commanded a brigade at Shiloh. He commanded General Bragg's cavalry at

Green River and Perryville. He led the cavalry at Murfreesboro and at Chickamauga. In a raid in 1863 in Tennessee he destroyed national stores valued at $3,000,000. He engaged at Knoxville, Missionary Ridge and Lookout Mountain. He harassed General Sherman in his march to Atlanta, and fought at Atlanta and Aiken. He was elected to Congress from Alabama as a Democrat in 1880 and has served continuously since 1885.

Wheeler, William A. (1819–1887), was a U. S. District Attorney in New York from 1845 to 1849. He represented New York in the U. S. Congress as a Republican from 1861 to 1863 and from 1867 to 1877. He was author of the compromise in settlement of the political disturbances in Louisiana in 1876. He was elected Vice-President of the United States in 1877 on the ticket with President Hayes and served till 1881.

Wheeling Bridge Case, a case of original jurisdiction in the Supreme Court of the United States in 1855. The Wheeling and Belmont Bridge Company prepared to rebuild a bridge over the Ohio River, according to the plan of the original bridge, which an Act of Congress had declared not obstructive to commerce. The State of Pennsylvania declared it to be obstructive to commerce and applied to Justice Grier for an injunction to prevent its erection. This was granted, but the bridge was erected in defiance thereof. A majority of the Supreme Court refused to pass judgment against the Bridge Company for contempt, though acknowledging the right of Grier to issue the injunction. Judgment was given for the defendant on the ground that it was within the jurisdiction of Congress to determine what was and what was not an obstruction to commerce.

Wheelock, Eleazar (1711–1779), established an Indian missionary school at Lebanon, Conn., in 1754, which was removed to Dresden (now Hanover) N. H., in 1770, and became Dartmouth College.

Wheelock, John (1754–1817), was a lieutenant-colonel in the Continental army. He became president of Dartmouth College in 1779, succeeding his father. His quarrel with the trustees, culminating in 1815, led to the celebrated "Dartmouth College case."

Wheelwright, John (1592–1679), came from England as a Puritan to the United States in 1636. He was banished from Massachusetts in 1637 for sympathizing with Anne Hutchinson, and founded Exeter, N. H., in 1638.

Whigs. The name of Whigs was taken by the party in the colonies which furthered the Revolution, because their principles were but the application to America of those principles which the Whigs of England had advocated, and had secured through the Revolution of 1688. In 1834 the name was revived. The Federal party had virtually come to an end about 1817. Henceforth all American politicians were simply Republicans. But, as will usually happen in such cases, a divergence of views developed itself within the party. Adams and Clay and their followers, on the one hand, advocated a policy of protection and federal internal improvements and a broad or loose construction of the Constitution. Others, on the other hand, construing the Constitution strictly, opposed these things; these found a leader in Jackson. The former took the name of "National Republicans." Adams was their candidate in 1828. After his defeat their chief leader was Clay, whom they nominated for President in 1831. Their opposition to Jackson drew to them various elements and, as opponents of executive usurpation, the coalition took the old name of Whigs (1834). The Whig body always formed rather a coalition than a party. They were united in opposition to Jackson, but the Northern Whigs favored the U. S. Bank, a protective tariff, etc., while the Southern Whigs were strict constructionists. In the election of 1836 these various elements supported various candidates. In that of 1840 they united upon the "available" Harrison, and triumphantly elected him and Tyler in a campaign of unthinking enthusiasm. Harrison died, and the Whigs quarreled violently with Tyler. In 1844 they nominated their real leader, Clay, who narrowly missed election. The annexation of Texas and the Mexican War and the Wilmot proviso now brought slavery to the front as the leading issue of politics. This was fatal to the Whigs, for it was sure to divide the Northern and the Southern Whigs. In 1848 they preserved themselves temporarily by passing over Clay and Webster and nominating a military candidate, Taylor. He was elected. But when similar tactics were tried in 1852 (with Scott), the party was decisively defeated. It was disintegrating because of its inability to maintain any opinion on slavery. The Northern Whigs became Free-soilers, and by 1856, Republicans; the Southern, Democrats. Many Whigs went temporarily into the American party. A small portion of them formed the Constitutional Union Party, which nominated Bell and Everett in 1860. Parties became sectional, and the Whig party ceased to exist. Its chief leaders were, beside those mentioned, in the North, Winthrop, Choate, Seward, Weed and Greeley; in the South, Mangum, Berrien, Forsyth, Stephens, Toombs, Prentiss and Crittenden; in the West, McLean, Giddings, Ewing and Corwin.

Whipple, Abraham (1733–1819), of Rhode Island, commanded the privateer "Gamecock" during the French War from 1759 to 1760. He headed the expedition which burned the "Gaspé" in Narragansett Bay in 1772. In 1775 he was placed in command of two Rhode Island vessels and fought one of the first naval engagements of the Revolution. In 1776 he commanded the "Providence," which captured more prizes than any other American vessel.

Whipple, Edwin P. (1819–1886), was a frequent contributor to periodicals. He was famous as a lecturer, and his portraitures of eminent men were keen and critical. He was superintendent of the Merchants' Exchange in Boston from 1837 to 1860. He wrote "Recollections of Rufus Choate," "Character and Characteristic Men," "Washington and the Principles of the Revolution," and "Outlooks on Society, Literature and Politics."

Whipple, Henry B., born in 1822, became Episcopal Bishop of Minnesota in 1859. He has attained great influence with the Indians of the Northwest and is often consulted by Government authorities concerning the "Indian problem."

Whipple, William (1730–1785), was a delegate from New Hampshire to the Continental Congress in 1775, 1776 and 1778, and signed the Declaration of Independence. In 1777 he commanded a brigade at Saratoga and Stillwater, and he participated in General Sullivan's Rhode Island campaign in

1778. He was a member of the State Assembly from 1780 to 1784, and Judge of its Supreme Court from 1782 to 1785.

Whisky Insurrection, a revolt against the execution of a Federal excise law, which came to a head in western Pennsylvania in August, 1794, and was suppressed the same year. Scarcity of cash in the wild districts of North Carolina, Virginia and Pennsylvania, had made distillation the chief means of support among the mountaineers, whisky being used as a medium of exchange. The excise law was passed March 3, 1791. During the next three years there were constant protests and insurrectionary mass meetings headed by one Bradford. William Findley, John Smilie and Albert Gallatin were the quieter leaders. Revenue officers were tarred and feathered by Bradford and his followers, and there was a general state of lawless opposition despite the efforts of Findley and Gallatin. In October, 1794, 15,000 militia were ordered out by President Washington, and under General Henry Lee marched into western Pennsylvania, and the revolt was promptly suppressed. Bradford fled the country, but a number of the ring-leaders were arrested and imprisoned. The affair was important as exhibiting the power of the new Federal Government.

Whisky Ring, the name applied to an association of revenue officers and distillers, formed in St. Louis in 1872 to defraud the Government of the internal revenue tax on distilled liquors. By 1874 it had spread into national proportions. Distillers were often forced to enter the ring or expect ruin in their business. There were branches of the ring at Chicago, Milwaukee, Peoria, Cincinnati and New Orleans, and an agent at Washington to corrupt the Treasury agents. In 1874 about $1,200,000 of taxes were unpaid. In 1875, at the suggestion of Mr. George Fishback, editor of the *St. Louis Democrat*, the Secretary of the Treasury appointed Mr. Myron Colony, of the Cotton Exchange, to make a secret investigation of the frauds. Through his efforts indictments were brought against 238 persons, and the Government was shown to have been defrauded of $1,650,000 in ten months. Among those concerned was General Babcock, President Grant's private secretary, and many other Government officials.

Whitcomb, James (1795–1852), was Commissioner of the General Land Office from 1836 to 1841. He was Governor of Indiana from 1843 to 1848, and represented Indiana in the U. S. Senate as a Democrat from 1849 to 1852.

White, Andrew D., born in 1832, was a member of the New York Senate from 1863 to 1866. He was active in legislation for educational improvements and the incorporation of Cornell University. He was president of Cornell from 1867 to 1885. He was one of the commissioners to San Domingo in 1871. He was Minister to Germany from 1879 to 1881 and to Russia from 1892 to 1894.

White, Hugh L. (1773–1840), was a Justice of the Supreme Court of Tennessee from 1801 to 1807, when he became a U. S. District Attorney. He was again a Judge of the State Supreme Court from 1809 to 1817. He was a commissioner to adjust the claims of American citizens against Spain from 1820 to 1824. He represented Tennessee in the U. S. Senate as a

Democrat from 1825 to 1835 and from 1836 to 1839. He received the electoral votes of Tennessee and Georgia for President of the United States in 1836, as a Whig.

White, John (1575–1648), English clergyman, was one of the promoters of the Massachusetts colony. He established a colony of Puritans at Dorchester in 1630.

White, John (1805–1845), represented Kentucky in the U. S. Congress as a Whig from 1835 to 1845, when he became a district judge. He was Speaker of the House from 1841 to 1843.

White, Peregrine (1620–1704), son of one of the Pilgrims, was the first white child born in New England. He became a citizen of Marshfield, Mass., and filled several minor civil and military offices.

White, Richard Grant (1821–1885), critic, was connected with the *New York Courier and Enquirer* from 1845 to 1859. He wrote patriotic articles for periodicals during the Rebellion. He published "Poetry, Lyrical, Narrative and Satirical, of the Civil War," various literary essays and an edition of Shakespeare.

White, William (1748–1836), presided at the first American Episcopal Convention in 1785, and drafted the church constitution then adopted. He was made bishop of Pennsylvania in 1786, one of the first three American bishops. He was chaplain to Congress from 1787 to 1801.

White House, the President's house or executive mansion at Washington, called the "White House" because it is painted white. The cornerstone was laid in 1792, and President Adams was the first President who occupied the mansion. It was completed in 1800. When the British held Washington for a single day in 1814, the White House was burned together with the Capitol and other buildings. Congress authorized its restoration in 1815, and it was again ready for occupation in 1818 and has been occupied by each successive President since that time. Its model was the house of the Duke of Leinster at Dublin.

White House, Va. (near Mount Vernon). In the War of 1812 batteries were erected at this point September 1, 1814, to prevent the British fleet from descending the Potomac. This was successful for several days, but at last the fleet by a heavy bombardment forced the Americans to retire.

White House (on the Pamunkey), Va., a battle of the Civil War during Grant's expedition against Richmond. It occurred June 21, 1864, and the Confederates were defeated. A small Federal force held White House, and upon this Wade Hampton had contemplated an attack with a strong company of Confederates, chiefly cavalry. Just as the assault was about to be begun, Sheridan, who had been absent on an expedition against the West Virginia Central Railroad, came up with 6000 men. He immediately attacked Hampton's troops. These were utterly defeated and had to retreat with all possible haste. Sheridan captured a considerable number of prisoners.

White League, an organization formed in the South in 1874 to check the growth of political power among the negroes.

White Oak Swamp, Va., a battle occurring immediately subsequent to the battle of Savage's Station, June 30, 1862. Jackson, leading his own command and the brigades of A. P. Hill and Longstreet, had been ordered to sweep around the Chickahominy River and destroy the retreating Federals as they emerged from the swamp. Finding the bridge over this stream destroyed, he changed his course and pursued them through the swamp. Upon arriving at the White Oak Swamp bridge he found that demolished also. There he was met by Smith, Richardson and Naglee, and Ayres and Hazard of Franklin's Federal brigade. These troops immediately offered battle. Hazard was mortally wounded and his force literally cut to pieces. Ayres and the others held out for some time, but retired during the night leaving 305 sick and wounded.

White Plains, Battle of, October 28, 1776. After his occupation of New York, Howe attempted unsuccessfully to break the blockade by getting in the rear of the American position. Washington at length concentrated at White Plains and Howe tried an attack in front. He succeeded in gaining an unimportant position, losing 229 men to the enemies' 140. He was discouraged and fell back on Dobbs Ferry, making a feint upon Fort Washington and Philadelphia.

Whitefield, George (1714–1770), was influenced by Charles Wesley to join the Methodists, and in 1738 made his first voyage to America. He returned to England after a few months to obtain funds for building an orphanage in Savannah, Ga. The orthodox churches were closed to him, and he addressed vast assemblages in the open air. His eloquence and graceful delivery exerted a powerful influence over his hearers. A considerable sum was collected for his project. In 1740 he made a tour through the colonies. He made seven visits to America, and had immense revivalist success.

Whiting, William H. C. (1825–1865), commanded the Confederate brigade whose arrival won the battle of Bull Run. He constructed Fort Fisher and took command in 1864, defending it until 1865.

Whitman, Marcus (1802–1847), was sent to Oregon as a missionary physician in 1836. He reported to the U. S. Government the value of the then disputed territory. His colonization efforts did much to secure that region for the United States.

Whitman, Walt (1819–1892), was noted for the originality of his poetical writings, both as to thought and style. He wrote "Leaves of Grass," dealing with nineteenth century American life, "Democratic Vistas," etc.

Whitney, Eli (1765–1825), of Connecticut, was the inventor of the cotton-gin, which so facilitated the preparation of cotton that it increased its exportation from 189,500 pounds in 1791 to 41,000,000 pounds in 1803. In 1798 he established an arms-factory near New Haven, Conn., which was the first one in America. He supplied the Government with arms of a superior quality.

AMERICAN POETS.

William Cullen Bryant. Henry W. Longfellow. James Russell Lowell.

John G. Whittier. Oliver Wendell Holmes. Ralph Waldo Emerson.

Edgar A. Poe.

Whitney, Josiah D., born in 1819, has made valuable geological surveys of Ohio, the Lake Superior region, Mississippi and California. He became professor of geology at Harvard in 1865.

Whitney, William C., born in 1839, was prominent in the overthrow of the Tweed ring in 1871. He was corporation counsel for New York City in 1875, 1876 and from 1880 to 1882. He has been active in the organization of the Democracy of New York. He was Secretary of the Navy in Cleveland's Cabinet from 1885 to 1889.

Whitney, William D., (1827–1894), became professor of Sanskrit in Yale College in 1854 and of comparative philology in 1870. He was president of the American Oriental Society from 1884 to 1894. He was editor-in-chief of the "Century Dictionary."

Whittier, John G. (1807–1892), poet, was a member of the Massachusetts Legislature from 1835 to 1836. He was appointed secretary of the American Anti-Slavery Society in 1836. He edited the *Pennsylvania Freeman* from 1838 to 1839. He contributed editorials to the *National Era*, a Washington anti-slavery paper, from 1847 to 1859. With the exception of Longfellow he was the most popular American poet. He was a Quaker, and a man of philanthropic spirit. Prominent among his works are "Legends of New England" and "Snowbound."

Wicker, Lambert (1735–1778), was one of the first naval officers appointed in the Revolution. He conveyed Franklin to France in 1776 in the "Reprisal." He captured fourteen British vessels in five days.

Wickliffe, Charles A. (1788–1869), represented Kentucky in the U. S. Congress as a Democrat from 1823 to 1833. He was Postmaster-General in Tyler's Cabinet from 1841 to 1845.

Wide-Awakes, a political division of the Republican party, organized in 1860 to promote the election of Lincoln; one of the first organizations of uniformed torchlight-parade enthusiasts in American politics.

Wigglesworth, Michael (1631–1705), came to America from England in 1638. He was a pastor in Malden, Mass., from 1657 to 1705. He wrote "The Day of Doom," a famous Puritan poem which passed through ten editions.

Wilde, Richard H. (1789–1847), represented Georgia in the U. S. Congress as a Democrat from 1815 to 1817 and from 1827 to 1835. He composed the popular song, "My Life is Like the Summer Rose."

Wilderness, The, Va., a bloody and irregular fight during the Civil War between the Army of the Potomac, 116,000 strong, under Grant, and the Army of Northern Virginia, numbering about 80,000 Confederates, under Lee. The battle occurred March 6 and 7, 1864. Grant's lieutenants were Meade, Burnside and Hancock; Lee's were Ewell, A. P. Hill, Stuart and Longstreet. The Wilderness is an almost impenetrable waste of forest and underbrush, and in this the Confederates were posted. Grant's army crossed the Rapidan River on pontoons the night of March 5. Grant had planned to attack the Confederates, but Lee anticipated him, beginning the fight early March 6. Hancock's and Burnside's corps were hurried to the front. All day the fight continued. Artillery and cavalry were useless in the dense brush, so the fighting was confined to musketry at close range. The night was spent by both armies in constructing intrenchments. Early the next morning Lee feigned an attack upon the Union left, not wishing to make the battle general until Longstreet should come up. Hancock was ordered to assault Lee's right, which was weakest. About midday Longstreet arrived, but was soon wounded by his own men by mistake. At night the battle was undecided. Both sides lost heavily. Grant withdrew, and the Confederates retired to their intrenchments.

Wilkes, Charles (1798–1877), an American naval officer, was lieutenant and commander of the squadron which in 1838–1842 sailed on an exploring expedition through the Pacific, along its American coasts and in the Antarctic regions. He became captain in 1855. While in command of the "San Jacinto," November 8, 1861, he stopped the British ship "Trent," and took the Confederate commissioners, Mason and Slidell. This celebrated "Trent Affair," which nearly involved the United States in war with Great Britain, brought to Wilkes the thanks of the Navy Department, approval of Congress and popular praise, but was disavowed by the Government. He commanded the James River squadron, was commodore in 1862, was retired in 1864, and made a rear-admiral on the retired list.

Wilkins, William (1779–1865), represented Pennsylvania in the U. S. Senate as a Democrat from 1831 to 1834 and in the U. S. Congress from 1842 to 1844. He was Secretary of War in Tyler's Cabinet from 1844 to 1845.

Wilkinson, James (1757–1825), served in the Revolutionary War as adjutant-general and brigadier-general and Secretary of the Board of War. In 1794 he commanded the right wing under Wayne in his victory over the Indians. Made general of the army in 1796, he was stationed in the West, and was Governor of Louisiana Territory 1805–1806. For intrigues with Burr and Spain he was court-martialled in 1811, but acquitted, though not innocent. In the War of 1812 he was a major-general, but his efforts on the northern frontier ended in a fiasco. He was discharged from the army in 1815. His memoirs were published.

Wilkinson, John, born in 1821, commanded the Confederate ram "Louisiana" at New Orleans in 1862. He ran a regular blockade runner from Wilmington to Bermuda in 1863. In 1864 he destroyed merchant vessels with the "Chickamauga."

Willard, Emma (1787–1870), founded the Troy Female Seminary in 1821, which she conducted till 1838. She is considered the pioneer in the higher education of women in America. She wrote many popular school books.

Willard, Frances E., born in 1839, has been prominent in reform movements. She has been president of the Women's Christian Temperance Union since 1879. She became editor of the *Chicago Evening Post* in 1879.

Willcox, Orlando B., born in 1823, commanded a brigade at Bull Run. He led a division at Antietam and South Mountain and a corps at Fredericksburg. He commanded a division during the Richmond campaign from 1864 to 1865.

Willett, Marinus (1740–1830), of New York, served in the expeditions against Fort Ticonderoga and Fort Frontenac. He defended Fort Stanwix against the Tories and Indians in 1777. He commanded the forces in the Mohawk Valley from 1780 to 1783.

William III. (1650–1702), King of Great Britain from 1689 to 1702 (William and Mary king and queen 1689–1694), attempted in October, 1692, a union of the American colonies for the purpose of carrying on his war with the French. To this end a requisition was made on each colony north of the Carolinas for a fixed quota of men and money for the defence of New York, "the outguard of his Majesty's neighboring plantations in America." This is memorable as the first form of British regulation of the colonies after the revolution of 1688. William proposed to follow the policy of James II. for consolidating the colonies. In May, 1696, William appointed a board of commissioners for trade and plantations, which had a general supervision of the colonies till 1768. (See King William's War.)

William and Mary, College of, was founded at Williamsburg, Va., in 1693, upon the basis of a charter granted by King William and Queen Mary. Next to Harvard it is the oldest of American colleges. In colonial times it was of great importance. Jefferson, Monroe and Marshall studied here. The Revolution, the removal of the capital to Richmond, the foundation of the University of Virginia, and finally, in 1862, the destruction of the college buildings by Union soldiers, destroyed its prosperity. It has lately taken a new lease of life.

William Henry, Fort, erected on the shores of Lake George in 1755, during the French and Indian Wars by General Johnson, who then commanded the English and Continental troops in New York. During two years expeditions were sent out against the Canadian border. In 1757 a French expedition against it, under Vaudreuil and Rigaud, failed. The garrison, however, was in a wretched disorganized condition. The fort was again attacked in 1757 by a strong French and Indian force under General Montcalm. The latter besieged and bombarded it for several days, but Colonel Munro, the commanding officer, refused to surrender. Finally the fortifications were carried by storm, the fort was captured, many of the garrison murdered by the Indians, and the rest pursued to Fort Edward, on the Hudson.

Williams, Alpheus S. (1810–1878), commanded a corps at South Mountain, Antietam and Gettysburg and during Sherman's march to the sea. He represented Michigan in the U. S. Congress as a Democrat from 1875 to 1878.

Williams, David (1754–1831), served under Montgomery in the Canadian campaign from 1775 to 1776. He was one of the captors of Major André, with John Paulding and Isaac Van Wart.

Williams, Ephraim (1715–1755), of Massachusetts, Colonel, served in Canada in the French War from 1740 to 1748. He erected Fort Massachusetts in 1751. He bequeathed funds for founding Williams College, which was chartered in 1793.

Williams, George H., born in 1823, was a District Judge in Iowa from 1847 to 1852. He was Chief Justice of Oregon Territory from 1853 to 1857, and represented Oregon in the U. S. Senate as a Republican from 1865 to 1871. He was a member of the joint commission that arranged the Treaty of Washington in 1871. He was Attorney-General in Grant's Cabinet from 1872 to 1875.

Williams, James D. (1808–1880), was almost continuously a member of the Indiana Legislature from 1843 to 1874. He represented Indiana in the U. S. Congress as a Democrat from 1875 to 1876, and was Governor of Indiana from 1876 to 1880. He was a member of the State Board of Agriculture for seventeen years, and its president four years. He greatly improved educational facilities.

Williams, John (1644–1729), became pastor at Deerfield, Mass., in 1686. He was carried away captive to Montreal by Indians with his family in 1704. He wrote "The Redeemed Captive," a very popular account of his experiences.

Williams, Jonathan (1750–1815), was secretary to Benjamin Franklin in France from 1777 to 1785. He was chief engineer of the U. S. army from 1805 to 1812, and planned and constructed Forts Columbus, Clinton and Williams in New York harbor.

Williams, Roger (born about 1599, died 1683), founder of Rhode Island, was graduated at Pembroke College, Cambridge, England. He took orders, but soon became a Nonconformist. In 1631 he came to Massachusetts, and was an assistant pastor in Plymouth and Salem. In 1634 he became pastor in Salem. His opinions on civil and ecclesiastical matters did not meet with approval. He withdrew from the church in 1635; was summoned before the General Court and expelled from the colony. In January, 1636, he left Salem and founded Providence the same year, establishing friendly relations with the Indians. He formed a Baptist church in 1639, but soon withdrew from it. Visiting England he obtained a charter for the colony in 1644. He was at one time president of the colony, was engaged in various religious controversies and exerted his influence generally in favor of toleration and peace with the Indians. Rhode Island's religious freedom was due to him.

Williams, Samuel Wells (1812–1884), went to China as printer to the American Mission in 1833. He was U. S. Secretary of Legation and interpreter in China from 1855 to 1876, and Chargé d'Affaires nine times. He wrote "The Middle Kingdom," a standard book on China, and became professor of Chinese at Yale College.

Williams, William (1731–1811), accompanied Colonel Williams' expedition to Lake George in 1755. He was a member of the Connecticut Assembly for more than fifty years and a judge of probate for forty years. He represented Connecticut in the Continental Congress from 1776 to 1777 and from 1783 to 1784, and signed the Declaration of Independence.

Williams College, Williamstown, Mass., was first started as a free school in 1791, and incorporated as a college two years later. Dr. Mark Hopkins was its most famous president. At different times it has received aid from the State, the last being a gift of $75,000, given in 1868.

Williamsburg, Va., formerly capital of the colony, was built under an act of the Colonial Legislature of 1699. The city received a charter in 1722. In 1780 the seat of government was removed to Richmond. A battle between the Union and Confederate forces occurred here May 6, 1862. It was a nine hours' engagement between the rear columns of Magruder's army, retreating from Yorktown, and Hooker's division of McClellan's army, at the opening of the Peninsular campaign. Magruder had been reinforced from Johnston's army. Hooker had been sent in pursuit of the retreating Confederates, and he overtook them at Williamsburg. Longstreet's division had already passed the town, but returned. Hooker held his ground bravely, but was compelled to retreat before such odds.

Williamson, Hugh (1735–1819), while in London in 1774 was examined before the Privy Council regarding the Boston tea party. He was a delegate from North Carolina to the Continental Congress in 1784, 1785 and 1786. He was a member of the convention that framed the Federal Constitution in 1787. He represented North Carolina in the U. S. Congress as a Federalist from 1790 to 1793. He wrote a "History of North Carolina."

Willich, August (1810–1878), came to America from Germany in 1853. He commanded a German regiment from 1861 to 1862. He led a brigade at Chickamauga, in the Atlanta campaign and in Sherman's march to the sea.

Willing, Thomas (1731–1821), was head of the firm of Willing and Morris [Robert Morris] from 1754 to 1793, which was an agent of Congress during the Revolution. He represented Pennsylvania in the Continental Congress from 1775 to 1776. He was the first president of the U. S. Bank in 1791.

Willis, Nathaniel P. (1806–1867), poet, was connected with the New York *Mirror* from 1823 to 1842, and the *Home Journal* from 1848 to 1867. He wrote "Scenery of the United States and Canada," etc.

Wilmington, Del., was originally settled by Swedes, who at Christiana Creek, now a part of the city of Wilmington, established the first Swedish colony in America, April, 1638. The town, *i. e.*, its central portion, was founded in 1732, and incorporated as a borough in 1740. It became a city in 1832.

Wilmington, N. C., was founded in 1733. This town was wrested from the Confederates and occupied by the Federal troops 20,000 strong, under Schofield, February 22, 1865. The actual capture of the town itself was accomplished without bloodshed. Its protecting fortifications, Forts Fisher and Anderson, had been captured January 15 and February 18 respectively. After the Confederates Bragg and Hoke, who had held Fort Anderson with 6000 men, abandoned that stronghold, they retreated, February 20, through Wilmington, burning the steamers, cotton, naval and military stores, to prevent their falling into the hands of the Federals. On February 22, therefore, the town was occupied by Schofield without opposition.

Wilmot, David (1814–1868), represented Pennsylvania in the U. S. Congress as a Democrat from 1845 to 1851. He was author of the "Wilmot proviso," providing that slavery be excluded from territory to be purchased from Mexico in 1846. He was president judge of the Thirteenth District of Pennsylvania from 1853 to 1861. He presided over the Republican Convention of 1860, and served in the U. S. Senate as a Republican from 1861 to 1863, when he became Judge of the U. S. Court of Claims.

Wilmot Proviso. August 8, 1846, President Polk, in a special message to Congress, requested "money for the adjustment of a boundary with Mexico," that is, for the purchase of Mexican territory outside of Texas. A bill appropriating $2,000,000 was at once introduced into the House. David Wilmot, a Democrat, of Pennsylvania, proposed as an amendment the since famous "Wilmot Proviso," which "provided that neither slavery nor involuntary servitude shall ever exist in any part of said territory, except for crime, whereof the party shall first be duly convicted." The bill thus amended passed the House, but failed in the Senate. January 4, 1847, a bill appropriating $3,000,000 instead of $2,000,000 was proposed by Preston King. It passed the House with the proviso attached, but the latter was dropped in the Senate. For a number of years the Wilmot Proviso was brought up and debated whenever new territories were to be organized. It was discussed in the case of Oregon, California, Utah and New Mexico, but was not finally established until June 9, 1861, when Congress passed an act prohibiting "slavery in any territories of the United States now existing, or which may be hereafter formed or acquired."

Wilson, Alexander (1766–1813), naturalist, came to America from Scotland in 1794. He made a valuable collection of American birds and published nine volumes of an "American Ornithology." He enjoyed considerable reputation as a poet.

Wilson, Henry (February 16, 1812–November 22, 1875), Vice-President of the United States, was born in New Hampshire. He was in his early life a farmer, and a shoemaker in Natick, Mass. He was a Whig member of the Massachusetts Legislature, but renounced the Whig policy at the convention of 1848, and aided in forming the Free-Soil party. In 1853 he was the defeated Free-Soil candidate for Governor. A coalition of parties sent him to the U. S. Senate in 1855, and he was continued there by Republican votes until 1873. Senator Wilson was one of the principal opponents of slavery. During the war he was chairman of the Committee on Military Affairs. When President Grant was re-nominated in 1872, Senator Wilson received the second place on the ticket. They carried the country, and Wilson was Vice-President 1873–1875. He wrote various historical works, chief of which is "Rise and Fall of the Slave Power," in three volumes. Life by Nason.

Wilson, James (1742–1798), an American statesman, was born in Scotland, received a university education, and emigrated to Pennsylvania in 1766. He became an able lawyer, and was a delegate to the Continental Congress. He signed the Declaration of Independence, and was one of the signers who also sat in the Federal Convention of 1787. Of this body he was one of the foremost members, and was on the Committee which drafted the Constitution. On him fell the burden of its defence in the ensuing ratifying convention of Pennsylvania. In 1789 he was appointed by Washington an Associate Justice of the U. S. Supreme Court.

Wilson, James F., born in 1828, represented Iowa in the U. S. Congress as a Republican from 1861 to 1869. He was chairman of the Judiciary Committee from 1863 to 1869. He became a U. S. Senator in 1883. His present term expires in 1895.

Wilson, James H., born in 1837, served at Fort Pulaski in 1862 He led a divison at the Wilderness and Petersburg. He captured Selma, Montgomery, Columbus and Macon. He took Jefferson Davis prisoner in 1865.

Wilson, John (1588–1667), clergyman, came to America from England with the Puritans in 1630, and organized the first church in Boston, of which he was pastor till 1667.

Wilson, William L., born in 1843, has represented West Virginia in the U. S. Congress as a Democrat since 1883. He was a prominent member of the Ways and Means Committee that prepared the tariff bill of 1888, and, as chairman of that committee in 1893, prepared the new tariff bill of that year.

Wilson, Woodrow, born in 1856, professor at Princeton College, has become prominent for his writings upon political science. He wrote "Congressional Government, a Study in American Politics," and "The State;" also a historical book, "Division and Reunion, 1830–1880."

Wilson's and Kautz's Raid, Va., an expedition against the Confederate railroads and storehouses south of Richmond during Grant's campaign against that city, June 22–30, 1864. Wilson and Kautz, commanding 7000 cavalry troops from the Army of the Potomac and the Army of the James, succeeded in destroying several miles of the Weldon Railroad, a number of depots on the South Side Road and twenty-five miles of the Danville Road. They also attempted to dislodge Fitzhugh Lee from Roanoke Bridge, but failed.

Wilson's Creek, Mo. The Federal leaders, Lyon and Sigel, were here defeated with great loss by McCulloch and his Missouri and Arkansas volunteers, August 10, 1861. Lyon was killed and Sigel was compelled to retreat to Springfield. Lyon had come upon the Confederates by night, hoping to surprise them. The plan was well executed, but the disparity of force was too great, his army numbering only some 5000 men, while that of McCulloch was considerably over 12,000. In this fight the Federals lost over 1200 men, and the Confederates, though victorious, likewise sustained heavy casualties.

Wilson's Landing, Va., an outpost of General Butler's Army of the James in 1864. It was held by Wild with two colored regiments. May 24 Fitzhugh Lee's cavalry charged the post, but were defeated and driven back.

Winchell, Alexander (1824–1891), was professor of geology, zoölogy and botany at the University of Michigan from 1855 to 1873. He made valuable geological investigations in Michigan and Minnesota.

Winchester, James (1752–1826), served in the Revolutionary army. He was made commander of Fort Wayne in 1812. He fortified Maumee Rapids in 1813. He was defeated by a superior force of British and Indians under Colonel Proctor at Rasin River in 1813. (See Rasin River.)

Winchester, Va. Here occurred, during the Civil War, three sharp battles. March 11, 1862, Jackson, having evacuated Winchester, where he had been stationed, marched up the valley to be in easy communication with Johnston's army. Learning that Shields, weakened by the withdrawal of part of his force, was pursuing him, Jackson determined to engage that general. He commanded 10,000 Confederates, while Shields had 7000 Federals. However, the latter concealed his true strength by feigning retreat. The battle took place just outside of Winchester, Shields holding a strong position. The Confederates suffered a severe defeat.—Again, June 15, 1863, the Federal leader, Milroy, lay encamped near Winchester with about 7000 troops. Hooker was following Lee, who was then supposed to be marching on Washington. Ewell and Longstreet, leading 18,000 Confederates, came upon Milroy as they were hastening to join Lee. Milroy, ignorant of their superiority in numbers, held his post until it was too late to retreat. Then he defended himself as best he could, but in vain. The Confederate lines closed around him, defeating him utterly. Part of his army escaped to Harper's Ferry and part fled into Pennsylvania. Twenty-nine guns and 4000 prisoners were captured.—Also during Early's raid through the Shenandoah Valley part of his army encountered near Winchester, July 12, 1864, a small force of Federals under General Averell. The battle did not last long for Averell was greatly outnumbered. He was easily defeated, losing three guns and about 400 men. Early then marched on Chambersburg, Pa.—In 1864, while Sheridan, commanding 40,000 Federals, and Early with nearly as large an army of Confederates, were manœuvring around Winchester, an engagement occurred near that town, in which the Confederates were defeated, Sheridan capturing nearly 25,000 prisoners. The battle occurred September 19, and is sometimes called the battle of Opequon, from Early's position along the banks of that creek. The Federals opened the fight by charging upon and breaking Early's first line. This attack was repelled, but, being struck upon the flank, the Confederates gave way and fled in confusion to Winchester.

Winder, John H. (1800–1865), served with distinction at Contreras, Churubusco, Chapultepec and the City of Mexico. He entered the Confederate service and was commandant at Libby Prison, Belle Isle and Andersonville. He is charged with extreme cruelty.

Winder, William H. (1775–1824), led a successful expedition into Canada below Fort Erie in 1812. His brigade repelled the British attack at Stony Creek in 1813. He was in command at Bladensburg in 1814, and was disastrously defeated.

Windom, William (1827–1891), represented Minnesota in the U. S. Congress as a Republican from 1859 to 1869. He served in the U. S. Senate from 1870 to 1881. He was Secretary of the Treasury in Garfield's Cabinet in 1881, again a U. S. Senator from 1881 to 1883, and Secretary of the Treasury in Harrison's Cabinet from 1889 to 1891.

Windsor, Conn., was permanently settled in 1636 by Massachusetts settlers. A "trading house" was erected here by William Holmes and several associates for the Plymouth Colony in 1633. Windsor was one of the three towns which, in 1639, united in framing the "Fundamental Orders" of Connecticut.

Winebrenner, John (1797–1860), seceded from the German Reformed Church in Pennsylvania and founded a sect called the "Winebrennerians" in 1830. Their distinctive ordinances are baptism by immersion, washing of feet, and the Lord's Supper.

Winebrennerians (Church of God), a denomination organized in 1830 by Rev. John Winebrenner, of Harrisburg, Pa., in order to advocate a more intense Christian life. They have a church government like that of the Presbyterians and hold views like those, partly of the Baptists, partly of the Methodists.

Wines, Enoch C. (1806–1879), was prominent in the reform of penal institutions throughout the world. He secured the assembling of the first National Prison Congress in 1870, and was its secretary from 1870 to 1879.

Wingfield, Edward Maria, was active in colonizing Virginia under the patent of 1606. He came to Virginia from England in 1607. He was named first president of the colony, but was deposed in 1608. He wrote a "Discourse of Virginia."

Winnebagoes, a tribe of Dakota Indians, migrated east early, but were forced back to Green Bay. Early in the seventeenth century an alliance of tribes attacked and greatly reduced them. Later they were nearly exterminated by the Illinois. They joined with the French, and in the Revolution favored the English. They were also active in the Indian War of 1793–4, being reduced by Wayne. In 1812 they were friendly to the English. In 1816 they made a treaty of peace. Treaties in 1826 and 1827 fixed their boundaries. In 1829 they ceded large tracts of land. They made subsequent treaties and were removed from place to place until in 1866 they were given lands at Winnebago, Neb.

Winslow, Edward (1595–1655), one of the Pilgrim leaders, joined Robinson's congregation at Leyden in 1617, and was one of the prominent members of the "Mayflower" band. He was the diplomatist and commercial head of the colony. The first year he negotiated a lasting treaty with Massasoit, whose life he saved two years later. He conducted an exploring expedition into the interior, and visited England several times in the interests of the settlement. Winslow was often chosen assistant, and was three times Governor. In 1633 he dispatched a vessel up the Connecticut whose crew built a house on the site of Hartford, in rivalry with the Dutch claims. He represented his colony in the New England Confederation, and by Cromwell was appointed head commissioner of an expedition against the Spanish West Indies, which was, however, unsuccessful; Winslow died during its course. He wrote a historical work, the "Relation" or "Good Newes from New England," and several religious works, "Hypocrisie Unmasked," etc.

Winslow, John (1702–1774), of Massachusetts, was a member of the unsuccessful British expedition against Cuba in 1740. He executed the order for removing the Acadians from their homes in 1755. He commanded 8000 men against the French in 1756 and took command of Fort William Henry. He was a major-general in the Kennebec expedition against the French from 1758 to 1759. He became Chief Justice of the Court of Common Pleas in Plymouth County in 1762. He was prominent in the Stamp-Act troubles. He founded the town of Winslow, Maine, in 1766.

Winslow, John A. (1811–1873), of Massachusetts, entered the U. S. navy in 1827. He served with distinction during the Mexican War. While commanding the "Kearsarge" of seven guns and 163 men, he won a brilliant victory over the "Alabama," Captain Semmes, of eight guns and 149 men. The engagement lasted about an hour, at the end of which the "Alabama" sank. The "Alabama" lost forty killed, seventy taken prisoners, and thirty-nine escaped on the British yacht "Deerhound." The "Kearsarge" lost three men wounded, of whom one died. This was the most noted engagement between two vessels during the war.

Winslow, Josiah (1629–1680), was an "assistant" in the Plymouth colony from 1657 to 1673. He was one of the commissioners of the United Colonies from 1658 to 1672. He became commander of the Plymouth forces in 1659. He was Governor of the Plymouth colony from 1673 to 1680. He was elected general-in-chief of all the forces of the United Colonies in 1675.

Winsor, Justin, born in 1831, was superintendent of the Boston Public Library from 1868 to 1878, when he became librarian of Harvard University. He has written much upon American history, and has edited the co-operative works, "Memorial History of Boston" and "Narrative and Critical History of America." He wrote a "Reader's Handbook of the American Revolution" and numerous bibliographies; also, "Christopher Columbus" and "From Cartier to Frontenac."

Winthrop, John (January 22, 1588–March 26, 1649), one of the chief founders and historians of New England, was born near Groton, in England. He was educated at Trinity College, Cambridge, and became a justice of the peace and attorney. His sympathies were with the Parliamentary opposition to the Stuart policy, and in 1629 he was chosen Governor of Massachusetts. He arrived in Salem in the summer of 1630, and soon proceeded to the site of Boston. He continued as the chief magistrate until 1634. In the short following period, when Vane was Governor, and the Anne Hutchinson controversy was the burning question, Winthrop opposed Vane. He was Governor again from 1637 to 1640 and from 1646 until his death. No name stands higher among the colonists in respect to ability and character combined. Governor Winthrop wrote a valuable journal of events in the colony, published by Savage under the title "History of New England." His "Life and Letters" were edited by R. C. Winthrop.

Winthrop, John (1606–1676), son of the preceding, came to Massachusetts from England in 1631. He was an assistant of the Massachusetts colony from 1631 to 1649. He went to England in 1634 and obtained a commission to build a fort at the mouth of the Connecticut River. In 1646 he founded what is now New London, and became a Connecticut magistrate in 1650. He was elected Governor of Connecticut in 1657, and held office till his death, except one year. In 1663 he obtained a charter from Charles II. uniting the colonies of Connecticut and New Haven.

Winthrop, John (Fitz-John) (1639–1707), son of John Winthrop the younger, was a highly efficient agent of the Connecticut colony in London from 1693 to 1697. He was Governor of Connecticut from 1698 to 1707.

Winthrop, Robert C., born in 1809, a descendant of Governor Winthrop, was graduated at Harvard in 1828. He was a Whig in politics, and was Speaker of the Massachusetts House of Representatives. From 1841 to 1850 he represented his State in the lower House of Congress, where he acquired a reputation as a debater and orator. He was Speaker of the House in 1847–1849, and was defeated in 1849 for re-election to the chair. In 1850–1851 he was U. S. Senator, but a coalition of Democrats and Free-Soilers defeated him. The same year he failed as the Whig candidate for Governor. Winthrop received a plurality of votes, but as the law then required a majority the choice went to the legislature, where he was beaten. Mr. Winthrop has long been noted as a classic orator, particularly on historical themes. His addresses on anniversary occasions, as at the Yorktown Centennial in 1881, were greatly admired. He died November 17, 1894.

Winthrop, Theodore (1828–1861), was military secretary to General Butler at Fort Monroe. He aided in planning the attack on Little and Great Bethel, where he was killed. His posthumous novels attracted wide attention.

Wirt, William (1772–1834), a cabinet officer, and one of the ablest and most eloquent lawyers in the country. He was a Virginian and sat at one time in the State House of Delegates, but aside from that office he was not active in political life. One of his most celebrated speeches was that delivered in 1807 in the prosecution of Aaron Burr. From 1817 until 1829 Wirt was Attorney-General of the United States. In 1832 he was the Anti-Masonic candidate for President, and received seven electoral votes. Even better known than his addresses and essays were his "Letters of the British Spy," and his "Life of Patrick Henry." Life by Kennedy.

Wisconsin, a State of the Union, was the last State to be formed from the "Old Northwest." It was early explored by Nicolet, La Salle and French traders, who made the first settlement at Green Bay in 1639. In 1763 the treaty of Paris gave the territory to the English, under whose jurisdiction it remained until 1796, when it was ceded to the United States. In 1836 it was formed into a separate territory, and included besides its present area the present territory of Iowa and Minnesota and parts of the Dakotas. May 29, 1848, the State was finally admitted into the Union. The State was Democratic in national politics until 1856, when it was carried by the Republicans as at every subsequent Presidential election until 1892. In 1872 the Graham liquor law was passed requiring a license for the sale of liquor and a bond for payment of any damages from its sale. In 1874 the Potter law fixed the railroad rates for passengers and freight. In 1890 the Democrats elected the Governor, and in 1892 the Presidential electors. The present constitution dates from 1848. The population of the State in 1850, was 305,391; in 1890, 1,686,880.

Wisconsin, Historical Society of, founded in 1849 and reorganized in 1854. It has published several volumes of collections, and has formed a large library.

Wisconsin, University of, at Madison, was incorporated in 1838, but not organized till 1848. Grants of land from the nation and State aid have placed it upon a firm foundation. Besides its college course it has a department of law, founded in 1863, and colleges of mechanics and agriculture.

Wise, Henry A. (1806–1876), represented Virginia in the U. S. Congress as a Democrat from 1833 to 1843, but supported the Whig party in opposition to Jackson's bank policy. He was Minister to Brazil from 1844 to 1847. He was elected Governor of Virginia in 1856, after a severe struggle with the Know-nothings, whom he denounced as abolitionists in disguise. He served till 1859. During his administration occurred John Brown's raid. As a member of the Virginia Convention in 1861 he labored for conciliation. He led a Confederate brigade in the Kanawha Valley and defended Roanoke Island. He wrote a book of political history called "Seven Decades of the Union."

Wisner, Henry (1725–1790), was a delegate from New York to the Continental Congress from 1774 to 1776. He rendered valuable service to the patriot cause in the manufacture of munitions. He opposed the adoption of the Constitution as creating too centralized a government.

Witchcraft. The early New Englanders believed that human beings could, by compact with evil spirits, obtain power to suspend the laws of nature and thus injure their fellows. In 1671 Samuel Willard, a minister of Massachusetts, proclaimed that a woman of his congregation, Knapp by name, was bewitched, though her insanity was clearly proven. Between 1684 and 1693 more than 100 persons were tried and convicted of witchcraft and many of them were hanged. Special courts were appointed by Governor Phipps for the trial of witches. Witnesses were frequently guilty of open perjury, for the charge of witchcraft soon came to be used as a means of striking a private enemy. The witchcraft epidemic was especially prevalent at Salem, where a number of persons professed themselves bewitched and singled out those who had bewitched them. Educated men like Increase Mather firmly believed in it. In 1693 the superstition began to weaken chiefly through the writings and protests of Thomas Brattle and Robert Calef, of Boston. The same belief prevailed elsewhere at that time.

Witherspoon, John (1722–1794), came to America from Scotland in 1768 to accept the presidency of Princeton College, N. J. He was a prominent patriot at the beginning of the Revolution, and did much to influence the Scotch and Scotch-Irish to defend the patriot cause. He was a member of the Continental Congress from 1776 to 1779 and from 1780 to 1783. He signed and strongly advocated the Declaration of Independence, and signed the Articles of Confederation. He wrote "Considerations on the Nature and Extent of the Legislative Authority of the British Parliament."

Wolcott, Oliver (1726–1797), was a member of the Connecticut executive council from 1774 to 1786. He was Commissioner of Indian Affairs for the Northern Department in 1775. He was a delegate from Connecticut to the Continental Congress from 1776 to 1778, and signed the Declaration of Independence. He was placed in command of fourteen Connecticut regiments which he organized for the defence of New York. He led a brigade under General Gates at Saratoga. He served in Congress from 1780 to 1784. He was Lieutenant-Governor of Connecticut from 1786 to 1796, when he became Governor.

Wolcott, Oliver (1760–1833), was comptroller of public accounts of the United States from 1788 to 1789, auditor of the U. S. Treasury from 1789 to 1791, and Comptroller from 1791 to 1795. He was Secretary of the Treasury in the Cabinets of Washington and Adams from 1795 to 1801, but opposed Adams' policy, being guided by Hamilton. He was a U. S. Circuit Judge from 1801 to 1802, and Governor of Connecticut from 1817 to 1827.

Wolfe, James (1727–1759), one of the chief heroes in the "expansion of England," entered the army at an early age and fought in the war of the Austrian Succession and against the rising of the Young Pretender in 1745. He was a brigadier-general and commander of a division under General Amherst in the siege and taking of Louisbourg in 1758, and displayed great gallantry. He was promoted to be major-general and selected by Pitt for the great stroke of 1759, the capture of Quebec. In June with eight thousand troops Wolfe appeared near the city. Strongly fortified by nature and art, and under command of the ablest French general of the time, Montcalm, the Gibraltar of the New World resisted all attempts, direct and otherwise. Wolfe and the English became discouraged. A steep but practicable path from the river gave Wolfe his opportunity to surprise his enemy. On the heights of Abraham the French were completely defeated, September 13, 1759, and the surrender of Quebec soon followed. But Wolfe was killed in the moment of victory. See Parkman's "Montcalm and Wolfe."

Woman Suffrage. Twenty-eight States, a large majority of the Union, have given women some form of suffrage. In Arizona, Delaware, Idaho, Illinois, Indiana, Kansas, Kentucky, Massachusetts, Michigan, Minnesota, Montana, Nebraska, New Hampshire, New Jersey, North Dakota, Oklahoma, Oregon, South Dakota, Texas, Vermont, Washington and Wisconsin, women have various forms of school suffrage. In Wyoming women have had the same vote with men since 1869. This right was confirmed by the Constitutional Convention of 1889, and Wyoming was admitted to the Union in 1890. They have generally voted the Republican ticket, that party having been mainly instrumental in enfranchising them. In Utah women voted from 1870 until disfranchised by Congress in the "Edmunds Law" of 1882. A law was passed by the New York Assembly in 1891 enabling women to vote. This bill had been proposed in 1880. No vote was taken in the Senate. In Kansas they have equal suffrage with men at municipal elections. In Arkansas and Missouri they vote, by signing or refusing to sign petitions, on liquor license in many cases. In Louisiana they vote on allowing railroads to run through their parish. In Mississippi they were admitted in 1892, to vote on fence questions by the stock law. In Montana they vote on local taxation. In Delaware suffrage is granted them in several municipalities. In Colorado they have recently been allowed the same rights of suffrage with men.

Woman's Rights. The first woman's rights convention in the United States met at Rochester in 1848. (See Woman Suffrage, Equal Rights Party.)

Women's Christian Temperance Union, organized in 1874 for reforming the drinking class and securing the abolition of the liquor traffic. An organization, called the "Non-Partisan W. C. T. U.," was formed at Cleveland in January, 1890, as a protest against the attitude of the W. C. T. U. in politics.

Wood, Fernando (1812–1881), represented New York in the U. S. Congress as a Democrat from 1841 to 1843. He was elected mayor of New York City from 1855 to 1858 and from 1861 to 1863. At the outbreak of the Rebellion he recommended that New York secede and become a free city. He again served in the U. S. Congress from 1863 to 1865. He was a great power in the politics of the city.

Wood, Thomas J., born in 1823, served during the Mexican War. He commanded a division at Shiloh, Corinth, Stone River, Murfreesboro and Chickamauga. He engaged in Sherman's invasion of Georgia, and led a corps at Nashville in 1864.

Woodbridge, William (1780–1861), was Judge of the Michigan Supreme Court from 1828 to 1832, and Governor of Michigan from 1840 to 1841. He was a Democratic U. S. Congressman from 1841 to 1847.

Woodbury, Levi (1789–1851), was an earnest supporter of the War of 1812. He was appointed a Judge of the New Hampshire Supreme Court in 1817, and was Governor of New Hampshire from 1823 to 1824. He represented New Hampshire in the U. S. Senate as a Democrat from 1825 to 1831. He was Secretary of the Navy in Jackson's Cabinet from 1831 to 1834, when he was transferred to the Treasury Department, and continued in Van Buren's Cabinet till 1841. He again served in the U. S. Senate from 1841 to 1845, and was of great influence in the Democratic party. He was a Justice of the U. S. Supreme Court from 1845 to 1851.

Woods, Charles R. (1827–1885), commanded a regiment at Fort Donelson and Shiloh, a brigade at Corinth and a regiment at Vicksburg. He led a division in Sherman's Georgia campaign.

Woods, Leonard (1807–1878), was president of Bowdoin College from 1839 to 1866, when he visited Europe to gather materials for his "Discovery of Maine."

Woods, William B. (1824–1887), was a member of the Ohio Legislature from 1857 to 1860, serving as Speaker of the House in 1858. He was commissioned a lieutenant-colonel of Ohio volunteers, and fought at Shiloh, Arkansas Post, Resaca, Dallas, Atlanta, Lovejoy Station and Bentonville. He led a division in Sherman's march to the sea. He was a U. S. Circuit Judge from 1869 to 1880, when he became a Justice of the U. S. Supreme Court.

Wood's Coins (see Rosa Americana), coins issued by Great Britain for use in America in 1722 and made by William Wood after whom they were called Wood's coins, or Rosa Americana. They were of a mixed metal resembling brass, and the royal letters patent denominated them two pence, pence and half pence. Obversed stamped with laureated head of George the First; reverse with a double rose from which issued five barbed points. Legend, Rosa Americana 1722, Utile Dulci.

Woodworth, Samuel (1785–1842), was engaged in numerous journalistic ventures. He is chiefly memorable for his poems, of which the "Old Oaken Bucket" is the most popular.

Wool, John E. (1784–1869), served with great distinction at Queenstown Heights in 1812 and at Plattsburgh in 1814. He was inspector-general of the army from 1816 to 1841. He was active in organizing troops for the Mexican War. He was second in command to General Taylor at Buena Vista, where he selected the ground and arranged the forces. He commanded the Eastern Department from 1857 to 1860, Fort Monroe from 1861 to 1862, the Middle Military Department from 1862 to 1863, and the Department of the East in 1863.

Woollens Bill, the term applied to a celebrated tariff measure of 1827, because its most important provision was the advancement of the sliding scale, so carefully adjusted in 1824, from 33⅓ to 40 and 45 per cent on all woollen imports. The bill was introduced in the House in February, 1827, but failed in the Senate.

Woolsey, Melancthon T. (1782–1838), defeated the British at Sackett's Harbor in 1812. He was second in command on Lake Ontario in 1813, and captured several prizes with the "Sylph." He again defeated the British at Sackett's Harbor in 1814.

Woolsey, Theodore D. (1801–1889), was professor of Greek at Yale from 1831 to 1846, and president from 1846 to 1871. His opinions in international law were of great weight. He wrote "Introduction to the Study of International Law," "Political Science," "Communism and Socialism in their History and Theory," a "Manual of Political Ethics," and annotated editions of Lieber's "Civil Liberty and Self Government."

Wooster, David (1710–1777), general, commanded a sloop-of-war in the expedition against Louisbourg in 1745. He was a brigadier-general in the French War from 1756 to 1763. He was one of the originators of Arnold's expedition for the capture of Quebec in 1775. He was appointed one of the eight brigadier-generals of the Continental army and stationed in Canada, where he succeeded Montgomery in command for a short time. He was in command of Danbury when attacked by Governor Tryon's troops in 1777. He was killed in an assault on the enemy near Ridgefield, Conn.

Worcester, Joseph E. (1784–1865), edited the "American Almanac" from 1831 to 1843. He published valuable textbooks on history and geography, and his "Dictionary of the English Language," which attempted to represent the English language as it was, while Noah Webster's, in the original editions, represented it as Webster thought it ought to be.

Worcester vs. Georgia, an important case decided by the Supreme Court. Samuel Worcester, a missionary among the Cherokee Indians, was in 1831 seized by the authorities of Gwinnett County, Ga., indicted and sentenced to four years' imprisonment for residing among the Indians in defiance of an act of the Georgia Legislature of 1830. This act recites that any white person found living among the Indians without license from the Governor of Georgia is liable to imprisonment. Worcester pleaded the unconstitutionality of the act, and by writ of error the case was brought before the Supreme Court, 1832. That body confirmed Worcester's plea and found judgment in his favor, on the ground that the Georgia Act, being repugnant to the treaties made between the United States and the Cherokee nation, was unconstitutional and void.

Worden, John Lorimer, born in 1818, an American naval officer, entered the navy at the age of seventeen. The great deed with which his name is principally associated is the battle of the "Monitor" and "Merrimac" in Hampton Roads, March 9, 1862. Worden commanded the "Monitor" with great skill, in an action which must be ranked among the decisive struggles of the war. He received a vote of thanks from Congress and was promoted to be commander. He was engaged in the blockade, destroyed the privateer "Nashville," and took part in the attack on the Charleston forts in 1863. From 1870 to 1874 he was superintendent of the Naval Academy. Worden became commodore in 1868, rear-admiral in 1872, and was retired in 1886.

World's Fair. The World's Columbian Exposition was created by Act of Congress April 25, 1890. President Harrison, on December 24, 1890, proclaimed the Exposition to the world and invited foreign nations to participate. On October 21, 1892, the Exposition grounds and buildings at Chicago were formally opened and dedicated with appropriate ceremonies by Levi P. Morton, Vice-President of the United States, and presented by President Higinbotham, of the World's Columbian Exposition, to President Palmer, of the World's Columbian Commission. The Exposition opened May 1, 1893, and closed October 30, of the same year. The Exposition Act provided for a naval review, which took place in New York Harbor in April, 1893, many foreign nations participating. There were about 22,000,000 paid admissions to the Fair, and the receipts exceeded the expenditures by nearly $2,000,000. See Exhibitions and Centennial.

Worth, William J. (1794–1849), entered the army in 1812. He served as an aide to General Winfield Scott in the campaigns of 1813 and 1814. He distinguished himself at the battles of Chippewa and Niagara. He was in command of the Department of Florida from 1841 to 1846 and was active in subduing the Seminole Indians. He was second in command to General Taylor at the outbreak of the Mexican War. He conducted an assault at Monterey and led his brigade in the battles from Vera Cruz to the City of Mexico.

Wright, Carroll D., born in 1840, was chief of the Massachusetts Bureau of Labor Statistics from 1873 to 1888, of the U. S. Bureau of Labor from its organization in 1884, and of the Department of Labor since 1888. He is prominent as a statistician and investigator of social problems.

Wright, Elizur (1804–1885), became secretary of the American Anti-Slavery Society in 1833. He was an editor of numerous anti-slavery publications including the "Emancipator," "Human Rights," "The Massachusetts Abolitionist," the "Chronotype" and the "Commonwealth." He was prominent in insurance improvements, and was Insurance Commissioner of Massachusetts from 1858 to 1866. He aided in organizing the National Liberal League and was its president for three years.

Wright, Horatio G., born in 1820, fought at Bull Run and was chief engineer of the Port Royal expedition. He led a division at Secessionville and commanded the Department of the Ohio till 1863. He led a division at Gettysburg and a corps at Rappahannock Station, the Wilderness and Spottsylvania. He repulsed General Early's threatened invasion of Washington in 1864. He commanded at Cedar Creek and led a corps at Petersburg.

Wright, Sir James (1714?–1785), was appointed Chief Justice and Lieutenant-Governor of South Carolina in 1760. He became royal Governor of Georgia in 1764, but was compelled to retire in 1776.

Wright, Silas (1795–1847), was graduated at Middlebury College, and became a lawyer and influential politician in the State of New York. He was a member of the State Senate, and Congressman from 1827 to 1829. For the next four years he was Comptroller of New York. Then, 1833–1844, he was U. S. Senator, and one of the Democratic leaders in the Senate. From 1845 to 1847 he was Governor of the State. One of his acts was the calling out the militia to suppress the Anti-Renters. The local Democracy was at that time engaged in bitter factional fights, and Governor Wright was defeated for re-election in 1846. Life by Hammond.

Wright, William (1794–1866), represented New Jersey in the U. S. Congress as a Whig from 1843 to 1847, and in the U. S. Senate as a Democrat from 1853 to 1859 and from 1863 to 1866.

Writs of Assistance. In 1754 Parliament, at the petition of Shirley, then Governor of Massachusetts, passed an act providing for a more thorough enforcement of the navigation and revenue laws. General warrants were to be issued by the courts to revenue officers to continue for an indefinite period, and not returnable into the court, for the seizure and examination of goods imported by illicit traders. These were called writs of assistance. They were legalized by the Townshend Acts of 1767. The colonists vehemently objected to them, because their vague and general terms left the way open to great abuses against the liberty of the subjects, in the search of premises. In February, 1761, arguing against an application for such writs before the Superior Court of Massachusetts, James Otis declared the navigation laws illegal, and denied the claim of Parliament to legislate for the colonies.

Württemberg. The abolition of droit d'aubaine and taxes on emigration was agreed to by the Convention of 1844 between the United States and Württemberg. A naturalization and extradition convention was concluded in 1868.

Wyandotte Constitution, the final constitution of Kansas, adopted October 4, 1859, by a convention appointed by the Territorial Legislature of

Kansas, and under the provisions of which Kansas was admitted to the Union. The Constitution prohibited slavery; the Governor was to be elected for two years; suffrage was limited to whites, and Topeka was made the capital.

Wyatt, Sir Francis (1575 ?–1644), was appointed Governor of Virginia in 1621. He brought from England a constitution upon which subsequent forms of government in the colonies were modeled. Trial by jury, an annual assembly convoked by the Governor, an executive veto power, and the concurrence of the Virginia Company and the Colonial Assembly in all acts, were features. He governed from 1621 to 1626 and from 1639 to 1642.

Wyoming was organized as a territory in 1868. It was admitted as a State by Act of Congress approved July 10, 1890. Both male and female citizens are allowed the suffrage. The State has been Republican. The population in 1890 was 60,705.

Wyoming Controversy, a controversy which arose between Pennsylvania and Connecticut in 1782 regarding the jurisdiction of certain lands within the limits of the former State, but which had been settled by Connecticut adventurers. In 1784 the Pennsylvanians attempted to dispossess the Connecticut claimants. This led to bloodshed and to a revival of the Susquehanna Company in Connecticut for the establishment of the latter's claims. John Franklin, the moving spirit of the Susquehanna Company, was seized and imprisoned by Timothy Pickering, clerk and commissioner of the new county of Luzerne, formed by Pennsylvania from the Connecticut claims in 1787. The question was finally settled in favor of Pennsylvania's jurisdiction in 1790.

Wyoming Massacre, Pa. In 1776 two Continental companies had been placed in the Wyoming Valley for the protection of the settlers, chiefly Connecticut emigrants. Two years later Major John Butler, commanding a force 800 strong, of Indians, British and Tories, descended upon the valley. July 3, 230 Americans, in six companies, led by Colonel Zebulon Butler, attempted to oppose the British raids. Their unorganized lines fell upon the enemy about four o'clock in the afternoon. The Continentals were utterly routed and a brutal massacre followed. Butler could not restrain his Indians, who took 227 scalps. Women and children were, however, spared.

Wythe, George (1726–1806), jurist, became a member of the Virginia House of Burgesses in 1758 and served until the beginning of the Revolution. He drafted a remonstrance to Parliament against the Stamp Act in 1764. He was a delegate to the Continental Congress from 1775 to 1776 and signed the Declaration of Independence. He became Judge of the High Court of Chancery in 1777, and was sole chancellor of that court from 1786 to 1806. He was an ardent supporter of the Federal Constitution in the Virginia Convention of 1788, and was of great note as a lawyer.

X.

X Y Z Mission. In October, 1797, Marshall, Pinckney and Gerry were dispatched to France to treat with Talleyrand and endeavor to restore harmony and a good understanding, and commercial and friendly intercourse between the two republics. They had great difficulty in obtaining an interview with Talleyrand, being met instead by the latter's special agents, Hottinguer, Bellamy and Hauteval. In dispatches to the home Government the United States Commissioners designated these agents respectively as "X," "Y" and "Z," and hence the name. The special agents suggested that the Americans propose to Talleyrand the loan of a large sum of money by the United States, or that the latter Government accept the assignment from France of an extorted Dutch loan, and that one of the envoys return to America to arrange matters. The Commission indignantly refused these proposals, and broke up in 1798, having accomplished nothing definite. The envoys' report of their negotiations aroused intense feeling against France in the United States.

Y.

Yale, Elihu (1649–1721), Governor of Madras, went to England from New England in 1652. He gave various gifts amounting to about £900 to Yale College in a time of need, for which the college was named in his honor.

Yale University, New Haven, Conn., was chartered in 1701. During its first year it had only one student. Established first at Saybrook, it was moved in 1716 to New Haven. The college received its name from Elihu Yale, who gave gifts amounting to £900. The Medical School was opened in 1813, the Theological School in 1822, the Law School in 1824, the Sheffield Scientific School in 1847.

Yancey, William L. (1814–1863), served in both branches of the Alabama Legislature. He represented Alabama in the U. S. Congress as a Democrat from 1844 to 1847. He was a leader of the extreme party in the South. He proposed the formation of committees of safety in the Southern States "to fire the Southern heart." He made a tour through the North and West during the campaign of 1860, urging the rejection of the Republican candidate. He was a Confederate Commissioner to Europe from 1861 to 1862, when he became a member of the Confederate Senate. Life by Du Bose.

Yankee. The most probable explanation of this designation is that it is a corruption by the Massachusetts Indians of the word English, or perhaps of the French word Anglais.

Yankee Doodle. The history of the song is uncertain, but the air existed in England as far back as the middle of the last century.

Yates, Richard (1818–1873), was a member of the Illinois Legislature from 1842 to 1849. He represented Illinois in the U. S. Congress as a Whig from 1850 to 1854. He was Governor of the State from 1860 to 1864, and was active in the support of the Union. He represented Illinois in the U. S. Senate from 1865 to 1871.

Yates, Robert (1738–1801), of New York, was the author of numerous essays signed "The Rough Hewer," which advocated the patriot cause. He was a member of the New York Provincial Congress from 1775 to 1778.

He became one of the Committee of Safety in 1776. He became a Judge of the New York Supreme Court in 1776, and was Chief Justice from 1790 to 1798. He was a member of the convention that framed the Federal Constitution, but left the convention and opposed the ratification of the Constitution.

Yazoo City, Miss., wrested from the Confederates of Johnston's command by Herron and 5000 Union troops, July 13, 1863. Herron had been sent by Grant for this purpose. Chrisman commanded the garrison of 800. Herron was assisted by DeKalb with a gunboat, but the latter was sunk by a torpedo. Herron captured 300 prisoners, 800 horses, 200 bales of cotton and 250 small arms, besides a Confederate steamboat.

Yazoo Frauds. Georgia began her existence as a State with doubtful claims to the territory west of her present area, but she did not hesitate to pass laws regulating their disposal. In 1795 four land companies were formed and combined, in their operations in bribing the Georgia Legislature, under the name of the Yazoo Companies. By successfully bribing every member of the Legislature, except one, Robert Watkins, they induced that body to grant the companies, for a nominal consideration of $500,000, a tract of land containing 35,000,000 acres. These frauds aroused great indignation through the State. The act was declared unconstitutional and void by the grand jury of every county except two. February 13, 1796, the Anti-Yazoo party, having the majority in the Legislature, revoked the sale as a violation of the State Constitution. Immediately numerous claims sprang up, which had to be decided by Congress. Madison, Gallatin and Lincoln were appointed commissioners to investigate the claims. In 1802 Georgia ceded her western claims to the United States. The claims arising from the Yazoo Frauds were not decided until 1814. (See art. on the case of Fletcher *vs.* Peck.)

Yeamans, Sir John (1605?–1676?), born in England, was Governor of an unsuccessful colony called "Clarendon," founded in 1665 on Cape Fear River. He was Governor of South Carolina from 1671 to 1674, and introduced the first slaves into that colony in 1671.

Yeardley, Sir George (1580?–1627), was an early immigrant to Virginia from England, and was appointed Deputy-Governor in 1616. He was displaced by Samuel Argall, but was appointed Governor in 1619, and convened the first representative assembly in the Western Hemisphere. He was succeeded by Sir Francis Wyatt in 1621, but again held office from 1626 till his death.

Yellow Bayou, La., a brief skirmish, May 18, 1864, during Banks' Red River campaign, between the rear-guard of Bailey's troops under Mower and a small body of Confederates led by Polignac. The Confederates were worsted.

Yellow Fever. This disease first appeared in North America in 1780, ravaging Boston during the summer of that year. It subsequently visited New York and Philadelphia, especially in 1793 and 1797, the latter city having suffered later than 1822. More recent and malignant appearances of the epidemic have occurred in the Southern and Gulf States, the worst being that of 1878.

Yellow Tavern. (See Sheridan's Raid.)

Yellowstone Park. This tract was set apart by Congress in 1872 as a national park.

Yeo, Sir James L. (1782–1819), commanded the British forces on Lake Ontario during the War of 1812. He captured Oswego in 1814. He was defeated in York Bay by Captain Chauncey.

York, Me., second town settled in the State. The place was chartered by Sir F. Gorges in 1641 as a borough, and in 1642 as a city by the name of Gorgeana. On February 5, 1692, it was attacked by Indians, over 160 inhabitants massacred and the town burned.

York (now Toronto), Ontario. An attack was planned by the Americans preparatory to an invasion of Canada. April 27, 1813, General Pike with 1700 men and thirteen armed vessels effected a landing, and against a determined resistance fought his way to the town. The British, despairing of longer holding the place, blew up their powder-magazine. By this fifty-two Americans were killed, 180 wounded, and the rest thrown into confusion. During the dismay caused by the explosion General Sheaffe, in command of the British, withdrew with the larger part of his army, after having destroyed some vessels on the stocks and a large amount of stores. The town was then surrendered by the civil authorities together with 290 regulars and militia, a war-vessel and a large quantity of naval and military stores. The Americans lost in killed and wounded 286 including General Pike himself, the British 149. The provincial government buildings were burned.

Young, Brigham (1801–1877), the chief exponent of Mormonism and polygamy, was a Vermonter by birth, and a mechanic in New York. He was converted to Mormonism in 1831, and became an intimate associate of Smith. Commencing to preach the next year, he soon removed to Kirtland, Ohio, was chosen elder in 1832 and apostle in 1835. Brigham Young was one of the founders of the Nauvoo settlement in 1840, and in 1844 he succeeded Smith. Owing to persecution he conducted an emigration in 1846, and passed the following winter among the Indians of Nebraska. Having in 1847 explored the Salt Lake valley, he returned and led his band to the new home in 1848. He became Governor of Deseret in 1849, and was appointed Governor of the Territory of Utah in 1851. The next year he announced the dogma of polygamy, and systematically defied the National Government. He submitted, however, to Johnston's expedition of 1857. He remained president of the Mormon Church until his death.

Young, John (1802?–1852), represented New York in the U. S. Congress as a Whig from 1836 to 1837 and from 1841 to 1843. He was Governor of New York from 1847 to 1849, when he became Assistant U. S. Treasurer in New York City.

Young, John R., born in 1841, became connected with the Philadelphia *Press* in 1857, and was its war correspondent. He has since been an editor of the New York *Tribune* and *Herald*. He was Minister to China from 1882 to 1884.

Young Men's Christian Association. This organization was first established in the United States at Boston in 1851, having originated in London in 1844. The present (1894) aggregate membership of the 1438 American Associations is 245,809, and the net value of their property $14,208,043.

Yorktown (October 19, 1781). On his arrival in Virginia in May, 1781, Cornwallis found himself in command of 5000 veterans. Opposed to him was Lafayette with 3000 men, mostly raw militia. Cornwallis burnt and harried southern Virginia, but was unable to bring Lafayette to battle. Lafayette was continually reinforced and finding he could not catch him, on June 15 Cornwallis retreated to Richmond, and thence on the 20th toward the sea. In the first week of August, Cornwallis took his position at Yorktown with a garrison of 7000 men. Lafayette watched him from Malvern Hill. Washington now conceived the bold scheme of leaving Clinton unguarded in New York and of striking at Cornwallis in the South. The French fleet of thirty-four sail and 20,000 men under De Grasse was expected daily, and on August 17 news came that it was headed for the Chesapeake. Without giving Clinton any clue to his movements, Washington shifted a body of 2000 Continentals and 4000 French from West Point to Yorktown. The march was one of 400 miles and was accomplished between August 19 and September 18. The French fleet had already arrived, and kept the enemy's fleet at bay. Cornwallis was completely hemmed in by 16,000 men and the fleet. Each day the lines grew closer and no help came from Clinton. On October 14, two British redoubts were taken by storm. Next day the British made a fruitless sortie, and on the 17th a white flag was displayed. The British became prisoners of war. Cornwallis was directed to give his sword to General Lincoln. He sent it by General O'Hara. The number of the British who surrendered was 7247 soldiers and 840 seamen. This disaster utterly crippled the British forces in America and was considered by all parties the end of the war.

Z.

Zalinski, Edmund L. G., born in 1849, came to America from Poland in 1853. He served with distinction on the staff of General Miles from 1864 to 1865. He perfected the pneumatic dynamite torpedo gun.

Zanzibar. A treaty relative to import duty and consuls was concluded between the United States and Zanzibar in 1886.

Zenger's Case, first real struggle of the colonial press for freedom of speech against the Government. This case laid the foundation of the liberty of the press in America. In 1735 John Peter Zenger, at that time editor and publisher of the *New York Weekly Journal*, which had been established as an organ of the popular cause against the colonial government, was brought to trial for the publication of "false, scandalous, malicious, seditious libels" against the royal government of the colony of New York. Every possible means was employed to secure Zenger's condemnation, but no jury could be found or compelled to return a verdict of guilty.

Zeno Brothers, Nicolo (1340 ?–1391 ?) and **Antonio,** were Venetian navigators who visited Greenland and Newfoundland about 1380 or 1390, and are said to have navigated the coast of North America as far south as Virginia. The accounts written by Zeno were partially destroyed and their authenticity was doubted. Subsequent researches have strengthened belief in their authenticity. Zeno's map of Greenland and the northern coast of North America shows considerable accuracy.

Zinzendorf, Nicholas L., Count (1700–1760), visited America from Saxony (1741–1743), and organized the Moravian Church in America. He conducted seven conventions, preached in the Lutheran and Reformed Churches, and organized churches.

Zoar. (See Separatists.)

Zollicoffer, Felix K. (1812–1862), was an editor of the Columbia, Tenn., *Observer* from 1834 to 1841. He became an editor of the *Nashville Banner* in 1841. He was Comptroller of Tennessee from 1844 to 1849, represented Tennessee in the U. S. Congress as a Whig from 1853 to 1859, and was an advocate of extreme Southern views. He entered the Confederate service as a brigadier-general, and was killed in the battle of Mill Spring.

C.O.P.